D0593192

EX LIBRIS

PUBLIC LIBRARY

CHESTER C. CORBIN
PUBLIC LIBRARY

The Cambridge Edition of the Poets

POPE

EDITED BY

HENRY W. BOYNTON

The Cambridge Poets

edited by

BROWNING	Horace E. Scudder
ELIZABETH BARRETT BROWNING	Harriet Waters Preston
BURNS	W. E. Henley
BYRON	Paul E. More
CHAUCER	F. N. Robinson
DRYDEN	George R. Noyes
ENGLISH AND SCOTTISH POPULAR BALLADS	Helen Child Sargent, George L. Kittredge
HOLMES	Horace E. Scudder
KEATS	Horace E. Scudder
LONGFELLOW	Horace E. Scudder
AMY LOWELL	
JAMES RUSSELL LOWELL	Horace E. Scudder
MILTON	Harris Francis Fletcher
POPE	Henry W. Boynton
SCOTT	Horace E. Scudder
SHAKESPEARE	William Allan Neilson
SHELLEY	George E. Woodberry
SPENSER	R. E. Neil Dodge
TENNYSON	William J. Rolfe
THOREAU	Henry Seidel Canby
WHITTIER	Horace E. Scudder
WORDSWORTH	A. J. George

The
Complete Poetical Works
of
POPE

Pope's Villa, Twickenham

HOUGHTON MIFFLIN COMPANY BOSTON

Cambridge Edition

The Riverside Press Cambridge

821

Huntting 4 26 66   cop. 1.

EDITOR'S NOTE

AN attempt has been here made for the first time to include all of Pope's poetical work within the limits of a single volume; and to print the poems in an approximately chronological order. It has been often difficult, and sometimes impossible, to determine the exact date of a given poem; and the known order of composition has been modified so far as to permit a method of grouping the shorter poems which has been followed in other volumes of this series. Only the twelve books of the *Odyssey* which were Pope's own work are here included, and all of the notes to Homer are omitted. Most of Pope's own notes to the poems have been retained, except in the case of certain notes on *The Dunciad*, which are so voluminous or so trivial as to find no proper place within the necessary limits of this edition.

The allusions to Pope's contemporaries are so numerous, particularly in the *Satires*, the *Moral Essays*, and *The Dunciad*, that it has seemed advisable to rid the main body of notes of such names as are of especial importance, or are frequently mentioned. The Glossary of Names will, it is hoped, prove useful in obviating the necessity of cross-reference.

The text is the result of collation, but is based upon that of the standard Croker-Elwin-Courthope edition. As to the details of capitalization and abbreviation, a uniform though necessarily somewhat arbitrary usage has been adopted. The study of facsimiles has shown that the poet himself employed capitals quite without method. They are here used only in cases of personification or of especially important substantives. As a result of his religious preservation of the decasyllabic form of pentameter, Pope employed marks of abbreviation so profusely as often to produce a page distressing to the modern eye, and not really helpful to the modern ear. Many editors have therefore abandoned these marks altogether; in this edition they have been retained wherever they did not appear likely to prove a stumbling-block to the present generation.

The usual indexes have been furnished, and a brief bibliographical note, which, while it does not pretend to exhaustiveness, may be of aid to the general reader.

H. W. B.

ANDOVER, *March*, 1903.

TABLE OF CONTENTS

BIOGRAPHICAL SKETCH

ALEXANDER POPE was born in London, May 21, 1688. We cannot be sure of any-thing better than respectability in his ancestry, though late in life he himself claimed kinship with the Earls of Downe. His paternal grandfather is supposed to have been a clergyman of the Church of England. His mother, Edith Turner, came of a family of small gentry and landowners in Yorkshire. Alexander Pope, senior, was a successful linen merchant in London; so successful that he found it possible to retire early from business, and to buy a small estate at Binfield, on the edge of Windsor forest. To this estate, in Pope's twelfth year, the family removed from Kensington, and here they lived for sixteen years. In 1716 they removed to Chiswick, where a year later the father died. Soon afterwards Pope, then a man of note, leased the estate at Twickenham, on which he was to live till his death, in 1744.

The circumstances of Pope's early life were in many ways peculiar. One of the main reasons for the choice of Binfield was that a number of Roman Catholic families lived in that neighborhood. They formed a little set sufficiently agreeable for social purposes, though not offering much intellectual stimulus to such a mind as Pope's very early showed itself to be. But if to be a Roman Catholic in England then meant to move in a narrow social circle, it carried with it also more serious limitations. It debarred from public school and university; so that beyond the inferior instruction afforded by the small Cath-olic schools which he attended till his twelfth year, Pope had no formal education. Two or three facts recorded of this school experience are worthy of mention : that he was taught the rudiments of Latin and Greek together, according to the Jesuit method; that he left one school in consequence of a flogging which he had earned by satirizing the head master; and that at about the age of ten he built a tragedy on the basis of Ogilvy's translation of Homer. At twelve he had at least learned the rudiments of Greek, and could read Latin fluently, if not correctly. So far as his failings in scholar-ship are concerned, Pope's lack of formal education has probably been made too much of. He had no bent for accurate scholarship, nor was breadth and accuracy of scholarship an accomplishment of that age. Addison, whose literary career was preceded by a long period of university residence, knew very little of Greek literature, and had a by no means wide acquaintance with the literature of Rome. Yet scholarship in those days meant classical learning.

Pope might no doubt have profited by the discipline of a regular academic career. He needed, as Mr. Courthope says, ' training in thought rather than in taste, which he had by nature.' But such a mind as his is not likely to submit itself readily to rigid pro-cesses of thought. It is impossible not to see, at least, that the boy Pope knew how to read, if not how to study; and that what Latin and Greek he read was approached as lit-erature, — a method more common then than now, it is probable. ' When I had done with my priests,' he wrote to Spence, ' I took to reading by myself, for which I had a very great eagerness and enthusiasm, especially for poetry; and in a very few years I had dipped into a great number of English, French, Italian, Latin, and Greek poets. This I did without any design but that of pleasing myself, and got the language by hunting after the stories in the several authors I read : rather than read the books to get the language.' Virgil and Statius were his favorite Latin poets at this time, as is attested not only by the *Pastorals* and the early translations of the *Thebais*, but by the innumerable reminiscences, or 'imitations,' as Pope called them, which may be traced in his later work. In the meantime, as a more important result of his having to rely so much upon his own resources, his creative power was beginning to manifest itself with singular maturity. At twelve he wrote couplets which were long afterwards inserted without change in the *Essay on Criticism*, and even in *The Dunciad*. The *Pastorals*, composed at sixteen, though conventional in conception and not seldom mechanical in execution, contain passages in the poet's ripest manner. With the *Essay on Criticism*, published five years later, Pope reached his full power. Such development as is to be found in his later work is the result of an increase in mental breadth and satirical force. His style was already formed.

Whatever may have been the importance, for good and ill, of Pope's early method of education, a far more potent factor in determining the conduct of his life and the nature of his work lay in his bodily limitations. The tradition that in his childhood he was physically normal is made dubious by the reported fact that his father was also small and crooked, though organically sound. At all events, the Pope whom the world knew was anything but normal, — stunted to dwarfishness, thin to emaciation, crooked and feeble, so that he had to wear stays and padding, and all his life subject to severe bodily pain. Pope's relations with other men were seriously affected by this condition. Masculine society in eighteenth-century England had little place for weaklings. The late hours and heavy drinking of London were as little possible for the delicate constitution of Pope as the hard riding and heavy drinking of the country gentlemen with whom he was thrown at Binfield. In a letter from Binfield in 1710 Pope writes : 'I assure you I am looked upon in the neighborhood for a very sober and well-disposed person, no great hunter, indeed, but a great esteemer of the noble sport, and only unhappy in my want of constitution for that and drinking.' It is a misconception of Pope's character to suppose him lacking in a natural robustness of temper to which only his physical limitations denied outlet. Before reaching manhood he had been given more than one rude lesson in discretion. At one time over-confinement to his books had so much reduced his vitality as to convince him that he had not long to live. A fortunate chance put his case into the hands of a famous London physician, who prescribed a strict diet, little study, and much horseback riding. Pope followed the advice, recovered, and thereafter, for the most part, took excellent care of himself; it was the price which he had to pay for living. One unfortunate result was that he was thrown back upon the companionship of women, always petted, always deferred to, always nursed. Such conditions naturally developed the acid cleverness, the nervous brilliancy of the poet Pope ; and it is matter of great wonder that from such conditions anything stronger should survive; that there is, when all is said, so much virility and restraint in the best of his work.

The *Pastorals*, Pope's first considerable poetical achievement, were according to the poet written in 1704, at the age of sixteen. They were, like all modern pastorals, conventional; but they contain some genuine poetry, and are wonderful exercises in versification. Their diction is often artificial to the point of absurdity, but now and then possesses a stately grace, as in the famous lines : —

> ' Where'er you walk, cool gales shall fan the glade;
> Trees, where you sit, shall crowd into a shade;
> Where'er you tread, the blushing flowers shall rise,
> And all things flourish where you turn your eyes.'

Pope had probably been encouraged to write the *Pastorals* by Sir William Trumbull, to whom the first of them is inscribed. Trumbull was a man of Oxford training, who after a distinguished diplomatic career had come to end his life upon his estate near Binfield, and who had been drawn to the deformed boy by the discovery of their common taste for the classics. For some time before the publication of the *Pastorals* the manuscript was being circulated privately among such men of established literary reputation as Garth, Walsh, Congreve, and Wycherley, and such patrons of letters as George Granville, Halifax, and Somers. To Walsh in particular Pope afterward expressed his obligation. 'He used to encourage me much,' we read in a letter to Spence, written long after, 'and used to tell me there was one way left of excelling : for though we had several great poets, we never had any one great poet that was *correct;* and he desired me to make that my study and aim.' The dictum has become famous, but though Walsh probably meant, by 'correctness,' justice of taste as well as measured accuracy of poetic style, his over-praise of the *Pastorals* leads us to think that form was the main thing in his mind. If Pope's statement of the date at which the *Pastorals* were written is reliable, however (and we must keep in mind from the outset the fact that, as Mr. Courthope says, Pope in mature life 'systematically antedated his compositions in order to obtain credit for precocity'), he did not become acquainted with Walsh until some time after they were written. The critic's advice, therefore, amounted simply to an encouragement in pursuing the method which Pope had already adopted : in employing a more rigid metrical scheme than any previous poet, even Sandys or Dryden, had attempted. The bookseller Jacob Tonson was shown the manuscript, and offered to publish it ; and in 1709 it appeared in Tonson's *Sixth Miscellany.*

Through Walsh Pope became acquainted with Wycherley, who introduced the young poet to literary society in London ; that is, to the society of the London coffee-houses. The character of the older resorts had already begun to change. Even Will's had ceased to be the purely literary club of Dryden's day. It was natural that the age of Anne, in which increasing public honors were paid to literary men, should have been also an age in which literary men took an increasing interest in politics. At about the time wher Pope first came up to London, Whig and Tory were beginning to edge away from each other; and though Will's for a time remained a sort of neutral ground, the old hearty interchange of thought and companionship was no longer possible. Part-political, part-literary clubs, like the Kitcat, the October Club, and the Scriblerus Club, sapped the strength of the older and freer institution; and its doom was sealed when in 1712 Addison established at Button's a resort for literary Whigs.

During his first years of London experience, Pope probably knew Richard Steele more intimately than any one else. They had met at Will's, and through Steele Pope had been presented to Addison, and had later become a frequenter of Button's. It was Steele who urged Pope to write the *Ode on St. Cecilia's Day*, who got his *Messiah* published in *The Spectator* and printed various short papers of his in *The Guardian*. Another Whig friend was Jervas the painter, a pupil of Kneller, but an artist of no very considerable achievement. The poet at one time had some lessons in painting from him, and always held him in esteem. So far Pope allowed himself to associate with the Whigs; but he had no intention of taking rank as a Whig partisan. If he wrote prose for Whig journals, it was in honor of the Tory government that the conclusion was added to *Windsor Forest* in 1713. To Swift's admiration for this poem, Pope owed the beginning of his life-long friendship with the Dean; but it was a friendship which committed him no more to Toryism than Addison's had to Whiggery. 'As old Dryden said before me,' he wrote in 1713, 'it is not the violent I desire to please; and in very truth, I believe they will all find me, at long run, a mere Papist.' One amusing fact about Pope's early experience at Button's is that he is known to have commended the verses of Addison's satellites, Budgell and Tickell and Philips, whom later he was to attack so bitterly. The first cause of offence was not long in coming; and an offence sown in the mind of Pope was certain to grow very fast and to live very long. The story of Pope's falling out with Addison and his friends is the story of the first of a long series of personal enmities which embittered Pope's life, and, it is too clear, impoverished his work.

The *Pastorals* were published by Tonson at the end of a volume which opened with some exercises in the same kind of verse by Ambrose Philips. Pope was disposed to commend the work of Philips, even going so far as to say that 'there were no better eclogues in the language.' His ardor was somewhat cooled when *The Spectator*, in a paper which was unmistakably Addison's, printed an extended comparison of his work and Philips's, considerably to the advantage of the latter; and was converted into a cold rage by the fact that presently the position taken by *The Spectator* was expanded in five papers in *The Guardian*. The subtlety and ingenuity of Pope's method of retort was an interesting indication of the disingenuousness which became a settled quality of his prose writing. Whatever his poetry may not have been, it was certainly downright; but his method of getting it before the public, of annotating it, and of reinforcing its thought, was habitually circuitous and not seldom dishonest. Pope promptly wrote a sixth paper to *The Guardian*, ostensibly keeping to Tickell's argument, but really speaking in irony from beginning to end, picking out the weakest points in Philips's style and matter, and damning them by fulsome praise. Steele, it is said, was so far deceived as to print the paper in good faith. Pope's revenge among the wits was complete; but he never forgot a score by paying it. In the *Satires* and *The Dunciad*, poor namby-pamby Philips comes up again and again for a punishment to which, in recompense, he now owes his fame.

Pope's attitude toward Addison is a more serious matter to the critic. Up to the year 1714 Pope, whatever irritation he may have felt toward Addison, had chosen to 'take it out of' the followers of the great man rather than out of the great man himself. The insertion of the Tory passage in *Windsor Forest* might have been taken as a direct challenge to the Whig champion, whose famous celebration of the Whig victory at Blenheim had been so popular. That his relations with Addison were not affected by it is shown by his supplying a prologue for *Cato*, which was produced within a month of the publication of *Windsor Forest*. *Cato* itself was to supply the real bone of contention. It was attacked by the veteran critic John Dennis, against whose strictures Pope undertook to take up the cudgels, in an anonymous *Narrative of Dr. Robert Norris on the Frenzy of J. D.* It is uncertain whether Addison suspected that Pope was its author, and that his championship was inspired by the desire for personal revenge for Dennis's treatment of the *Essay on Criticism ;* but he disclaimed responsibility for the rejoinder in a letter written for him to the publisher by Steele. The result was a resentment which bore its final fruit in the lines on Atticus in the *Epistle to Dr. Arbuthnot.* Addison, it must be noticed, had warmly praised the *Essay on Criticism* (1711), and the simpler version of *The Rape of the Lock*, published a year later ; but the publication of Tickell's version of the first book of the *Iliad* simultaneously with Pope's first volume, and Addison's preference of the weaker version, does not leave the latter quite free from suspicion of *parti pris*.

Whatever may have been the rights of the difficulty between Addison and Pope, there is no doubt that in one point, evidently a mere point of judgment, Addison was wrong. After pronouncing the first version of *The Rape of the Lock*, published in 1712, 'a delicious little thing, and *merum sal*,' he advised against Pope's plan for expanding it. Without the additions which the author made, in spite of this advice, it would hardly stand, as it now does, an acknowledged masterpiece in its kind. Despite the apparently local and temporary nature of its theme, the poem attracted much greater attention when, in 1714, it appeared in the new form. The poem affords the purest expression of Pope's genius: his imagination applied without strain to a theme with which it was exactly fitted to cope, his satirical power exercised without the goad of personal rancor, and his light and elegant versification unhampered by the fancied necessity for weightiness. Nothing more just has been said about the poem than this by Hazlitt (*On Dryden and Pope*) : ' It is the most exquisite specimen of *filigree* work ever invented. It is as admirable in proportion as it is made of nothing : —

> " More subtle web Arachne cannot spin,
> Nor the fine nets, which oft we woven see
> Of scorched dew, do not in th' air more lightly flee."

It is made of gauze and silver spangles. The most glittering appearance is given to everything, — to paste, pomatum, billet-doux, and patches. Airs, languid airs, breathe around ; the atmosphere is perfumed with affectation. A toilette is described with the solemnity of an altar raised to the Goddess of Vanity, and the history of a silver bodkin is given with all the pomp of heraldry. No pains are spared, no profusion of ornaments, no splendor of poetic diction, to set off the meanest things. The balance between the concealed irony and the assumed gravity is as nicely trimmed as the balance of power in Europe. The little is made great, and the great little. You hardly know whether to laugh or weep. It is the triumph of insignificance, the apotheosis of foppery and folly. It is the perfection of the mock-heroic.'

If *The Rape of the Lock* was Pope's masterpiece in the field of impersonal satire, the *Essay on Criticism*, which belongs to the same period of the poet's life, was his masterpiece in the realm of poetic generalization. It was, according to the account of the poet, composed in 1709 and published in 1711. The present editor is inclined to think that justice has never been done to this extraordinary work, either as a product of precocity, or in its own right. It is, in his opinion, not only a manual of criticism, to which the practitioner may apply for sound guidance upon almost any given point, but an exhaustive satire upon false methods of criticism. It is a compendious rule of criticism which works both ways ; hardly less rigorous than Aristotle, hardly less catholic than Sainte-Beuve. It does not, as has been alleged, constitute a mere helter-skelter summary of critical platitudes: there is hardly a predicament in modern criticism from which it does not suggest an adequate means of extrication. At all events, it represented, as Mr. Courthope says, the ' first attempt to trace for English readers the just boundaries of taste.'

The *Essay on Criticism* was not, like *The Rape of the Lock*, devoid of the note of personal enmity which was to mark so much of the poet's later work. John Dennis had probably employed his slashing method in reviewing the *Pastorals*, and in the *Essay* Pope took occasion for revenge in the lines on Appius, which unmistakably applied to the author of *Appius and Virginia ;* and which after Dennis's rejoinder were to be followed up by the attacks in the *Satires* and *The Dunciad*.

With the accession of the house of Hanover in 1714 the literary situation in London was considerably modified. The common ground upon which Whigs and Tories had, with diminishing success, continued to associate, was taken from under their feet. Politics became the first issue, and literature was relegated to a subordinate position. Fortunately the list of subscribers to Pope's translation of the *Iliad* had been made up before the death of Anne. During the few years in which the process of public readjustment absorbed the attention of London, Pope was hard at work upon the most exacting task he had yet undertaken.

The removal of the family from Binfield to Chiswick was made by Pope's desire. He was now not only a famous author, but a man of fashion ; and on both accounts he wished to be nearer London. In leaving the coffee-house society — of which, in truth, he had never been a full member — he had found entrance into 'aristocratic circles;' and we hear much in his letters from this time on of the noblemen whose hospitality he accepted, while standing clear of their direct patronage. At Chiswick he found more society and less leisure. Many times during the next few years he accuses himself of laziness, but it does not appear that his mild junketings with the nobilities gave him more relaxation from the toil of his Homer translation than he needed. The first books of the *Iliad* were published in 1715, and the last books of the *Odyssey* in 1723. The cripple and man of the world who could do that in the intervals of his house parties and his sieges of physical pain was certainly producing his full share of work.

The *Iliad* was hailed with applause on all sides, and handsomely paid for. It was in one way a task for which the translator would appear to have been quite unfitted. *The Rape of the Lock* had proved him the mouthpiece of a conventional and sophisticated age; and conventionality and sophistication are not qualities to go naturally with Homer. The elegance of Pope's verse becomes at times a mincing neatness, and his fashionable poetic diction in the mouths of Hector and Achilles rings thin and metallic. But though Pope inevitably missed the simplicity and the hearty surge and swing of Homer, he did manage to retain something of his vigor; and his *Iliad* is still the classic English version. Only half of the *Odyssey* translation which followed was really the work of Pope, and even his own part was deficient in the spirit which had marked the first translation. It had indeed been undertaken from a very different motive: he could not hope to add greatly to the credit which his *Iliad* had gained for him, but the cash might readily be increased. The translator actually received nearly £9000 for both translations — a small fortune in those days. Pope's relations with his collaborators in the affair of the *Odyssey* are to be noticed, though they have perhaps been too much dwelt upon by the commentators. The facts are briefly these: Fenton translated four books and Broome eight. Both were Cambridge men of parts, Fenton the more brilliant and Broome the more thorough. The latter furnished also all the notes. Pope paid them a very small price for their labor, though not less than they had bargained for, and gave them very little credit for it. Moreover, when he found that there was some stir against him for advertising an *Odyssey* which was to be his only in part, he induced Broome to write a postscript note claiming only three books for his own share and two for Fenton's, and insisting that whatever merit they might have was due to Pope's minute revision.

Before attempting the *Odyssey*, Pope was unfortunately led to prepare an edition of Shakespeare, which showed some ingenuity in textual emendation. Phrases were, however, too frequently altered as 'vulgar,' and metres as 'incorrect.' The work was on the whole so mediocre as fairly to lay itself open to the strictures of Theobald, who was consequently made the original hero of *The Dunciad*. In 1718 the poet leased the estate at Twickenham, and set to work upon the improvements which became a hobby. He had planned to build a town house, but was fortunately dissuaded. The laying out of the tiny five acres of grounds is now a matter of history: the paths, the wilderness, the quincunx, the obelisk to his mother's memory, above all the grotto, — they are more like actors than stage properties in the quiet drama of Pope's later years.

His work after the completion of the Homer translation was almost entirely restricted to satire. Even the *Moral Essays* are largely satirical, for Pope's didacticism was always tinged with laughter. It was too seldom a kindly laughter. His capacity for personal hatred was suffered not only to remain, but to grow upon him; until it became at length one of the ruling motives of his literary life. His first conception of *The Dunciad* was formed as early as 1720. Sometime within the five years following he seems to have broached his project for wholesale revenge to Swift, who, oddly enough, dissuaded him : 'Take care the bad poets do not outwit you,' he wrote, 'as they have the good ones in every age, whom they have provoked to transmit their names to posterity. Mævius is as well known as Virgil, and Gildon will be as well known as you if his name gets into your verses.' Thereto Pope dutifully assents: 'I am much happier for finding our judgments jump in the notion that all scribblers should be passed by in silence. . . . So let Gildon and Philips rest in peace.' It is not many years later that we find Swift encouraging Pope to go on with *The Dunciad*, and Pope accepting the advice with an even better grace than in the former instance. The first judgment of both authors was of course the right one. *The Dunciad*, with all its cleverness, remains the record of a strife between persons whom we do not now care about. It has no determinable significance beyond that; it lacks the didactic soundness of his *Essay on Criticism*, and the graceful lightness of *The Rape of the Lock*. Only in a few detached passages in the *Moral Essays* and *Satires*, indeed, did he ever succeed in approaching either of these qualities.

'Pope's writings,' says Mr. Courthope, 'fall naturally into two classes: those which were inspired by fancy or reflection, and those which grew from personal feeling or circumstance.' The *Moral Essays* belonged to the former of these classes, the *Satires* to the latter. The *Moral Essays*, and more particularly the *Essay on Man*, are the product of a materialism which marked the age, and which was set before Pope in something like systematic form by Bolingbroke. As Bolingbroke was primarily a politician, and dabbled in philosophy only because the favorite game was for a great part of his life denied him, it could not be expected that much more than shallow generalization would come out of him. At all events, his system of sophistry was all that Pope needed for a thread upon which to string his couplets. Whatever we may think of the *Essay on Man* now, we need not forget that so keen a critic as Voltaire once called it 'the most beautiful, the most awful, the most sublime didactic poem that has ever been written in any language.' Even in our day a conservative critic can say of it : 'Form and art triumph even in the midst of error ; a framework of fallacious generalization gives coherence to the epigrammatic statement of a multitude of individual truths.'

Some of the difficulty that we have found in *The Dunciad* is present in the *Satires*. They are full of personalities. As a rule, however, the persons hit off are of some account, both in themselves and as types, rather than as mere objects of private rancor. Altogether these poems contain, besides the famous portraits of contemporaries, many passages of universal application to the virtues and the shortcomings of any practical age.

With the completion of the *Satires* in 1738, Pope's work was practically done. His remaining years were to be spent mainly in revising his works and correspondence; the final additions and alterations to *The Dunciad* being the only task of special importance which in his weakening health, and decreasing creative impulse, he was able to undertake. The range of the poet's possible achievement was never very great; and he had now lost most of the living motives of his work. He had numbered among his acquaintances all the prominent men of the time ; and not a few of them had been friends upon whom he depended for encouragement and companionship. Gay had died in 1732, Pope's mother a year later, and Arbuthnot in 1735. Swift was meantime rapidly breaking up in mind and body, and by 1740 Pope was separated from him by a chasm as impassable as that of death. Bolingbroke remained to him, and he was to have one other friend, Warburton, upon whom he relied for advice and aid during his last years, and who became his literary executor. These, however, were friendships of the mind rather than of the heart ; and there is something a little pathetic in the spectacle of the still brilliant poet's dependence upon the chill and disappointed politician Bolingbroke and the worthy and adoring Bishop Warburton, who can hardly have been a lively companion.

Critics are now fairly well agreed as to Pope's service to English poetry. Intellectually he was clever rather than profound, and, in consequence, though so much of his work was of the didactic type, he made few original contributions to poetic thought. A poem of Pope's is a collection of brilliant fragments. He kept a note-book full of clever distiches set down at random; presently so many couplets are taken and classified, others are added, a title is found, and the world applauds. If we except *The Rape of the Lock*, and possibly the *Epistle to Arbuthnot*, none of his poems can be called organic in structure. The patching is neatly done, but the result is patchwork. The *Essay on Man*, therefore, which most of his contemporaries considered his greatest work, appears to us a mosaic of cleverly phrased platitudes and epigrams. Many of the couplets have become proverbial ; the work as a whole cannot be taken seriously. ' But the supposition is,' says Lowell, ' that in the *Essay on Man* Pope did not himself know what he was writing. He was only the condenser and epigrammatizer of Bolingbroke — a very fitting St. John for such a gospel.' It is to another and less pretentious sort of work that we must turn to find the great versifier at his best.

The *Rape of the Lock* affords exactly the field in which Pope was fitted to excel. The very qualities of artificiality and sophistication which mar the Homer translations make the story of Belinda and her Baron a perfect thing of its kind. Here is the conventional society which Pope knew, and with which — however he might sneer at it — he really sympathized. The polished trivialities, the shallow gallantry, the hardly veiled coarseness of the London which Pope understood, are here to the life. Depth of emotion, of imagination, of thought, are absent, and properly so; but here are present in their purest forms the flashing wit, the ingenious fancy, the malicious innuendo, of which Pope was undoubtedly master.

In versification his merit is to have done one thing incomparably well. Not only is his latest work marked by the same wit, conciseness, and brilliancy of finish which gained the attention of his earliest critics, but it employs the same metrical form which in boyhood he had brought to a singular perfection. The heroic couplet is now pretty much out of fashion: ' correctness ' is no longer the first quality which we demand of poetry. No doubt we are fortunate to have escaped the trammels of the rigid mode which so long restrained the flight of English verse. But however tedious and wooden Pope's instrument may have become in later hands, however mistaken he himself may have been in emphasizing its limitations, there is no doubt that it was the instrument best suited to his hand, and that he secured by means of it a surprising variety of effect.

We have chronicled thus far a few of the facts of Pope's life and work. Something — it cannot be very much — remains to be said of his private character. It was a character of marked contradictions, the nether side of which — the weaknesses and positive faults — has, as is common in such cases, been laid bare with sufficient pitilessness. He was, we are told, malicious, penurious, secretive, unchivalrous, underhanded, implacable. He could address Lady Mary Wortley one day with fulsome adulation, and the next — and ever after — with foul abuse. He could deliberately goad his dunces to self-betrayal by his *Treatise on the Bathos*, and presently flay them in *The Dunciad* by way of revenge. He could by circuitous means cause his letters — letters carefully edited by him — to be published, and prosecute the publisher for outraging his sensibilities. He could stoop to compassing the most minute ends of private malice by the most elaborate and leisurely methods. He played life as a game composed of a series of petty moves, and, as one of his friends said, 'could hardly drink a cup of tea without a stratagem.'

But let us see what we might be fairly saying on the other side. If he was capable of malice, he was incapable of flattery; if he was dishonest in the little matters, he was honest in the great ones; if he held mediocrity in contempt, he had an ungrudging welcome for excellence. In later life he had encouragement for the younger generation of writers, — Johnson, Young, Thomson, and poor Savage. If he allowed a fancied injury to separate him from Addison, he had still to boast of the friendship of men like Gay, Arbuthnot, and Swift; and they had to boast of his. He nursed his mother in extreme old age with anxious devotion, and mourned her death with unaffected grief. In his best satirical mood, the best in English verse, he did not hesitate to arraign the highest as well as the lowest; not even Swift could be so fearless. Such things are to be remembered of this correct versifier and merciless satirist Pope: that with only half the body, and hardly more than half the bodily experience, of a man, he had his full share of a man's failings and a man's virtues; and that the failings were on the whole upon a less significant plane than the virtues.

Much has been written of Pope's attitude toward women, and much has been written of his acrid habit of mind. The relation between these facts has been, perhaps, insufficiently grasped. Pope was not by nature a celibate or a hater of women. He was, on the contrary, fond of their society, and anxious to make himself agreeable to them. His failure with Lady Mary Wortley Montagu was deserved; the relation was a mere affair of gallantry, which she took good care to snuff out when the adorer's protestations began to weary her. She was not a womanly person, and forestalled much public indignation at Pope's subsequent abuse by adopting an equally brutal system of retort.

His failure with Martha Blount was of a very different sort, and of far greater significance. She was the younger of two daughters belonging to one of the Roman Catholic families in Pope's Windsor Forest circle of acquaintance. With her and with her sister Teresa, Pope was for many years upon terms of the closest intimacy. They were not much alike; and though Pope made a habit of addressing them with guarded impartiality in his correspondence, it is to be seen almost from the first that his feeling for the more practical and worldly older sister was less warm than his feeling for the amiable and feminine " Patty." Eventually, after years of friendship, the poet made a few indirect overtures to Martha in the direction of marriage; and at last ventured to express himself plainly to Teresa. To his unspeakable humiliation and grief, she treated his honest declaration as an affront to her sister, and upon precisely the painful ground of his deformity, which had for so many years kept him from speaking. Pope could not help feeling that however Martha might, if left to herself, have received his advances, it was now out of the question to pursue them. His behavior under the circumstances was full of dignity. It was impossible for the friendship to be renewed upon the old footing, but his only revenge beyond that of the necessary withdrawal from familiar intercourse was to settle a pension upon Teresa at the time, and to leave most of his property by will to Martha. We can hardly imagine Pope madly in love, but that he had a calm and steadfast affection for Martha Blount we cannot doubt. He was disposed to marry, and he would have liked to marry her. She represented the ideal of womanhood in his mind; and to her, in the heat of his most savage bouts of idol-breaking, he pauses to raise a white shaft of love and faith.

If the present editor, after a careful and well-rewarded study of the poet and the man, has any mite of interpretation to offer, it is not that Pope was a greater poet, but that he was a better man, than he is commonly painted; an unamiable man, yet not for that reason altogether unworthy of regard; a man with little meannesses carried upon his sleeve for all the world to mock at, and with the large magnanimity which could face the world alone, without advantages of birth or wealth or education or even health, and win a great victory. Such a man cannot conceivably be supposed to have stumbled upon success. Not only inspired cleverness of hand, but force of character and sanity of mind must be responsible for his work. After the lapse of nearly two centuries it should perhaps be right to indulge ourselves somewhat more sparingly in condemnation of his foibles, and to recall more willingly the sound kernel of character which is the basis of his personality. Whatever slander he may have retailed about the camp-fire, whatever foolish vanity he may have had in his uniform, Pope fought the good fight. 'After all,' he wrote to Bishop Atterbury, who was trying to make a Protestant of him, 'I verily believe your Lordship and I are both of the same religion, if we were thoroughly understood by one another, and that all honest and reasonable Christians would be so, if they did but talk together every day; and had nothing to do together but to serve God and live in peace with their neighbors.'

H. W. B.

ANDOVER, *March*, 1903.

EARLY POEMS

ODE ON SOLITUDE

'This was a very early production of our Author, written at about twelve years old,' says Pope in one of his unsigned and unreliable notes. If the statement is true, it was probably written during the year 1700. It is apparently the earliest poem of Pope's which remains to us, though according to Roscoe, 'Dodsley, who was honoured with his intimacy, had seen several pieces of an earlier date.'

HAPPY the man whose wish and care
   A few paternal acres bound,
Content to breathe his native air
     In his own ground.

Whose herds with milk, whose fields with
    bread,
   Whose flocks supply him with attire,
Whose trees in summer yield him shade,
     In winter fire.

Bless'd who can unconcern'dly find
   Hours, days, and years slide soft away,
In health of body, peace of mind,
     Quiet by day;

Sound sleep by night: study and ease
   Together mix'd; sweet recreation;
And innocence, which most does please,
     With meditation.

Thus let me live, unseen, unknown,
   Thus unlamented let me die;
Steal from the world, and not a stone
     Tell where I lie.

A PARAPHRASE (ON THOMAS À KEMPIS, L. III. C. 2)

Supposed to have been written in 1700; first published from the Caryll Papers in the *Athenæum*, July 15, 1854.

SPEAK, Gracious Lord, oh, speak; thy servant hears:
   For I 'm thy servant and I 'll still be so:
Speak words of comfort in my willing ears;
   And since my tongue is in thy praises slow,
And since that thine all Rhetoric exceeds:
Speak thou in words, but let me speak in deeds!

Nor speak alone, but give me grace to hear
   What thy celestial Sweetness does impart;
Let it not stop when enter'd at the ear,
   But sink, and take deep rooting in my heart.
As the parch'd Earth drinks rain (but grace afford)
With such a gust will I receive thy word.

Nor with the Israelites shall I desire
   Thy heav'nly word by Moses to receive,
Lest I should die : but Thou who didst inspire
   Moses himself, speak Thou, that I may live.
Rather with Samuel I beseech with tears,
Speak, gracious Lord, oh, speak, thy servant hears.

Moses, indeed, may say the words, but Thou
   Must give the Spirit, and the Life inspire;
Our Love to thee his fervent breath may blow,
   But 't is thyself alone can give the fire:
Thou without them may'st speak and profit too;
But without thee what could the Prophets do?

They preach the Doctrine, but thou mak'st
    us do 't ;
They teach the myst'ries thou dost open
    lay ;
The trees they water, but thou giv'st the
    fruit ;
They to Salvation show the arduous way,
But none but you can give us strength to
    walk ;
You give the Practice, they but give the
    Talk.

Let them be silent then ; and thou alone,
    My God ! speak comfort to my ravish'd
    ears ;
Light of my eyes, my Consolation,
    Speak when thou wilt, for still thy ser-
    vant hears.
Whate'er thou speak'st, let this be under-
    stood :
Thy greater Glory, and my greater Good !

TO THE AUTHOR OF A POEM ENTITLED SUCCESSIO

Elkanah Settle, celebrated as Doeg in Dryden's *Absalom and Achitophel*, wrote *Successio* in honor of the incoming Brunswick dy-
nasty. Warburton (or possibly Pope) in a note
on *Dunciad*, I. 181, says that the poem was
' written at fourteen years old, and soon after
printed.' A good instance of Pope's economy
of material will be found in the passage upon
which that note bears : an adaptation of lines
4, 17 and 18 of this early poem. It was first
published in Lintot's *Miscellanies*, 1712.

BEGONE, ye Critics, and restrain your spite,
Codrus writes on, and will forever write.
The heaviest Muse the swiftest course has
    gone,
As clocks run fastest when most lead is on;
What tho' no bees around your cradle flew,
Nor on your lips distill'd their golden dew;
Yet have we oft discover'd in their stead
A swarm of drones that buzz'd about your
    head.
When you, like Orpheus, strike the war-
    bling lyre,
Attentive blocks stand round you and ad-
    mire.
Wit pass'd thro' thee no longer is the
    same,
As meat digested takes a diff'rent name;
But sense must sure thy safest plunder be,

Since no reprisals can be made on thee.
Thus thou may'st rise, and in thy daring
    flight
(Tho' ne'er so weighty) reach a wondrous
    height.
So, forc'd from engines, lead itself can
    fly,
And pond'rous slugs move nimbly thro' the
    sky.
Sure *Bavius* copied *Mœvius* to the full,
And *Chœrilus* taught *Codrus* to be dull;
Therefore, dear friend, at my advice give
    o'er
This needless labour ; and contend no more
To prove a *dull succession* to be true,
Since 't is enough we find it so in you.

THE FIRST BOOK OF STATIUS'S THEBAIS

TRANSLATED IN THE YEAR 1703

Though Pope ascribes this translation to
1703, there is evidence that part of it was done
as early as 1699. It was finally revised and published in 1712, but Courthope asserts that ' it
is fair to assume that the body of the composition is preserved in its original form.'

ARGUMENT

Œdipus, King of Thebes, having, by mistake, slain his father Laius, and married his
mother Jocasta, put out his own eyes, and resign'd the realm to his sons Eteocles and Polynices. Being neglected by them, he makes his
prayer to the Fury Tisiphone, to sow debate
betwixt the brothers. They agree at last to
reign singly, each a year by turns, and the
first lot is obtain'd by Eteocles. Jupiter, in a
council of the gods, declares his resolution of
punishing the Thebans, and Argives also, by
means of a marriage betwixt Polynices and
one of the daughters of Adrastus King of Argos. Juno opposes, but to no effect ; and
Mercury is sent on a message to the shades, to
the ghost of Laius, who is to appear to Eteocles, and provoke him to break the agreement.
Polynices, in the mean time, departs from
Thebes by night, is overtaken by a storm, and
arrives at Argos ; where he meets with Tideus,
who had fled from Calidon, having kill'd his
brother. Adrastus entertains them, having
receiv'd an oracle from Apollo that his daughters should be married to a boar and a lion,
which he understands to be meant of these
strangers, by whom the hides of those beasts
were worn, and who arrived at the time when

he kept an annual feast in honour of that god. The rise of this solemnity. He relates to his guests the loves of Phœbus and Psamathe, and the story of Chorœbus : he inquires, and is made acquainted, with their descent and quality. The sacrifice is renew'd, and the book concludes with a hymn to Apollo.

FRATERNAL rage, the guilty Thebes'
    alarms,
Th' alternate reign destroy'd by impious
    arms
Demand our song ; a sacred fury fires
My ravish'd breast, and all the Muse in-
    spires.
O Goddess ! say, shall I deduce my rhymes
From the dire nation in its early times,
Europa's rape, Agenor's stern decree,
And Cadmus searching round the spacious
    sea ?
How with the serpent's teeth he sow'd the
    soil,
And reap'd an iron harvest of his toil ; 10
Or how from joining stones the city sprung,
While to his harp divine Amphion sung ?
Or shall I Juno's hate to Thebes resound,
Whose fatal rage th' unhappy monarch
    found ?
The sire against the son his arrows drew,
O'er the wide fields the furious mother
    flew,
And while her arms a second hope contain,
Sprung from the rocks, and plunged into
    the main.
    But waive whate'er to Cadmus may
    belong,
And fix, O Muse ! the barrier of thy song
At Œdipus — from his disasters trace 21
The long confusions of his guilty race :
Nor yet attempt to stretch thy bolder
    wing,
And mighty Cæsar's conquering eagles
    sing ;
How twice he tamed proud Ister's rapid
    flood,
While Dacian mountains stream'd with
    barb'rous blood :
Twice taught the Rhine beneath his laws
    to roll,
And stretch'd his empire to the frozen
    pole ;
Or, long before, with early valour strove
In youthful arms t' assert the cause of
    Jove. 30
And thou, great heir of all thy father's
    fame,

Increase of glory to the Latian name,
O ! bless thy Rome with an eternal reign,
Nor let desiring worlds entreat in vain !
What tho' the stars contract their heav'nly
    space,
And crowd their shining ranks to yield
    thee place ;
Tho' all the skies, ambitious of thy sway,
Conspire to court thee from our world
    away ;
Tho' Phœbus longs to mix his rays with
    thine,
And in thy glories more serenely shine ; 40
Tho' Jove himself no less content would
    be
To part his throne, and share his Heav'n
    with thee ?
Yet stay, great Cæsar ! and vouchsafe to
    reign
O'er the wide earth, and o'er the wat'ry
    main ;
Resign to Jove his empire of the skies,
And people Heav'n with Roman deities.
    The time will come when a diviner flame
Shall warm my breast to sing of Cæsar's
    fame ;
Meanwhile permit that my preluding
    Muse
In Theban wars an humbler theme may
    choose. 50
Of furious hate surviving death she sings,
A fatal throne to two contending kings,
And funeral flames that, parting wide in
    air,
Express the discord of the souls they bear:
Of towns dispeopled, and the wand'ring
    ghosts
Of kings unburied in the wasted coasts ;
When Dirce's fountain blush'd with Gre-
    cian blood,
And Thetis, near Ismenos' swelling flood,
With dread beheld the rolling surges
    sweep
In heaps his slaughter'd sons into the
    deep. 60
    What hero, Clio! wilt thou first relate ?
The rage of Tydeus, or the prophet's
    fate ?
Or how, with hills of slain on every side,
Hippomedon repell'd the hostile tide ?
Or how the youth, with ev'ry grace
    adorn'd,
Untimely fell, to be forever mourn'd ?
Then to fierce Capaneus thy verse extend,
And sing with horror his prodigious end.

Now wretched Œdipus, deprived of
     sight,
Led a long death in everlasting night ;   70
But while he dwells where not a cheerful
     ray
Can pierce the darkness, and abhors the
     day,
The clear reflecting mind presents his sin
In frightful views, and makes it day within;
Returning thoughts in endless circles roll,
And thousand furies haunt his guilty soul:
The wretch then lifted to th' unpitying
     skies
Those empty orbs from whence he tore his
     eyes,
Whose wounds, yet fresh, with bloody
     hands he strook,
While from his breast these dreadful ac-
     cents broke : —   80
'Ye Gods ! that o'er the gloomy regions
     reign,
Where guilty spirits feel eternal pain ;
Thou, sable Styx ! whose livid streams are
     roll'd
Through dreary coasts, which I tho' blind
     behold ;
Tisiphone ! that oft has heard my prayer,
Assist, if Œdipus deserve thy care.
If you receiv'd me from Jocasta's womb,
And nurs'd the hope of mischiefs yet to
     come ;
If, leaving Polybus, I took my way
To Cyrrha's temple, on that fatal day   90
When by the son the trembling father died,
Where the three roads the Phocian fields
     divide ;
If I the Sphynx's riddles durst explain,
Taught by thyself to win the promis'd
     reign ;
If wretched I, by baleful furies led,
With monstrous mixture stain'd my mo-
     ther's bed,
For Hell and thee begot an impious brood,
And with full lust those horrid joys re-
     new'd,
Then, self condemn'd, to shades of endless
     night,
Forc'd from these orbs the bleeding balls
     of sight,   100
Oh hear ! and aid the vengeance I require,
If worthy thee, and what thou might'st in-
     spire.
My sons their old unhappy sire despise,
Spoil'd of his kingdom, and deprived of
     eyes ;

Guideless I wander, unregarded mourn,
Whilst these exalt their sceptres o'er my
     urn ;
These sons, ye Gods ! who with flagitious
     pride
Insult my darkness and my groans deride.
Art thou a father, unregarding Jove !
And sleeps thy thunder in the realms
     above ?   110
Thou Fury ! then some lasting curse entail,
Which o'er their children's children shall
     prevail ;
Place on their heads that crown distain'd
     with gore,
Which these dire hands from my slain
     father tore ;
Go ! and a parent's heavy curses bear;
Break all the bonds of Nature, and pre-
     pare
Their kindred souls to mutual hate and
     war.
Give them to dare, what I might wish to see,
Blind as I am, some glorious villany !
Soon shalt thou find, if thou but arm their
     hands,   120
Their ready guilt preventing thy com-
     mands :
Couldst thou some great proportion'd mis-
     chief frame,
They'd prove the father from whose loins
     they came.'
    The Fury heard, while on Cocytus' brink
Her snakes, untied, sulphureous waters
     drink ;
But at the summons roll'd her eyes around,
And snatch'd the starting serpents from
     the ground.
Not half so swiftly shoots along in air
The gliding lightning or descending star.
Thro' crowds of airy shades she wing'd her
     flight,   130
And dark dominions of the silent night ;
Swift as she pass'd the flitting ghosts with-
     drew,
And the pale spectres trembled at her
     view :
To th' iron gates of Tenarus she flies,
There spreads her dusky pinions to the
     skies.
The Day beheld, and, sick'ning at the sight,
Veil'd her fair glories in the shades of
     night.
Affrighted Atlas on the distant shore
Trembled, and shook the heav'ns and Gods
     he bore.

Now from beneath Malea's airy height 140
Aloft she sprung, and steer'd to Thebes
   her flight;
With eager speed the well known journey
   took,
Nor here regrets the Hell she late forsook.
A hundred snakes her gloomy visage shade,
A hundred serpents guard her horrid head;
In her sunk eyeballs dreadful meteors
   glow:
Such rays from Phœbe's bloody circle flow,
When, lab'ring with strong charms, she
   shoots from high
A fiery gleam, and reddens all the sky.
Blood stain'd her cheeks, and from her
   mouth there came 150
Blue steaming poisons, and a length of
   flame.
From every blast of her contagious breath
Famine and Drought proceed, and Plagues
   and Death.
A robe obscene was o'er her shoulders
   thrown,
A dress by Fates and Furies worn alone.
She toss'd her meagre arms ; her better
   hand
In waving circles whirl'd a funeral brand ;
A serpent from her left was seen to rear
His flaming crest, and lash the yielding
   air. 159
But when the Fury took her stand on high,
Where vast Cithæron's top salutes the sky,
A hiss from all the snaky tire went round:⎫
The dreadful signal all the rocks rebound, ⎬
And thro' th' Achaian cities send the ⎭
   sound.
Œte, with high Parnassus, heard the voice;
Eurotas' banks remurmur'd to the noise ;
Again Leucothea shook at these alarms,
And press'd Palæmon closer in her arms.
Headlong from thence the glowing Fury
   springs,
And o'er the Theban palace spreads her
   wings, 170
Once more invades the guilty dome, and
   shrouds
Its bright pavilions in a veil of clouds.
Straight with the rage of all their race ⎫
   possest, ⎪
Stung to the soul, the brothers start ⎬
   from rest, ⎪
And all their furies wake within their ⎭
   breast:
Their tortured minds repining Envy tears,
And Hate, engender'd by suspicious Fears;

And sacred thirst of Sway, and all the ties
Of Nature broke, and royal Perjuries ;
And impotent desire to reign alone, 180
That scorns the dull reversion of a throne :
Each would the sweets of sov'reign Rule
   devour,
While Discord waits upon divided power.
   As stubborn steers, by brawny plough-
   men broke,
And join'd reluctant to the galling yoke,
Alike disdain with servile necks to bear
Th' unwonted weight, or drag the crooked
   share,
But rend the reins, and bound a diff'rent
   way,
And all the furrows in confusion lay :
Such was the discord of the royal pair 190
Whom fury drove precipitate to war.
In vain the chiefs contrived a specious way
To govern Thebes by their alternate sway:
Unjust decree ! while this enjoys the state,
That mourns in exile his unequal fate,
And the short monarch of a hasty year
Foresees with anguish his returning heir.
Thus did the league their impious arms re-
   strain,
But scarce subsisted to the second reign.
   Yet then no proud aspiring piles were
   rais'd, 200
No fretted roofs with polish'd metals
   blazed ;
No labour'd columns in long order placed,
No Grecian stone the pompous arches
   graced ;
No nightly bands in glitt'ring armour wait
Before the sleepless tyrant's guarded gate;
No charges then were wrought in burnish'd
   gold,
Nor silver vases took the forming mould ;
Nor gems on bowls emboss'd were seen to
   shine,
Blaze on the brims, and sparkle in the
   wine.
Say, wretched rivals ! what provokes your
   rage ? 210
Say to what end your impious arms en-
   gage ?
Not all bright Phœbus views in early morn,
Or when his ev'ning beams the west adorn,
When the South glows with his meridian
   ray,
And the cold North receives a fainter
   day —
For crimes like these not all those realms
   suffice,

Were all those realms the guilty victor's
  prize !
But Fortune now (the lots of empire
  thrown)
Decrees to proud Eteocles the crown.
What joys, O Tyrant ! swell'd thy soul that
  day,   220
When all were slaves thou could'st around
  survey,
Pleas'd to behold unbounded power thy
  own,
And singly fill a fear'd and envied throne !
  But the vile vulgar, ever discontent,
Their growing fears in secret murmurs
  vent ;
Still prone to change, tho' still the slaves of
  state,
And sure the monarch whom they have to
  hate ;
New lords they madly make, then tamely
  bear,
And softly curse the tyrants whom they
  fear.
And one of those who groan beneath the
  sway   230
Of kings imposed, and grudgingly obey,
(Whom Envy to the great, and vulgar
  Spite,
With Scandal arm'd, th' ignoble mind's de-
  light)
Exclaim'd — " O Thebes ! for thee what
  fates remain,
What woes attend this unauspicious reign ?
Must we, alas ! our doubtful necks prepare
Each haughty master's yoke by turns to
  bear,
And still to change whom changed we
  still must fear ?
These now control a wretched people's fate,
These can divide, and these reverse the
  state :   240
Ev'n Fortune rules no more — O servile
  land,
Where exiled tyrants still by turns com-
  mand !
Thou Sire of Gods and men, imperial Jove!
Is this th' eternal doom decreed above ?
On thy own offspring hast thou fix'd this
  fate
From the first birth of our unhappy state,
When banish'd Cadmus, wand'ring o'er the
  main,
For lost Europa search'd the world in vain,
And fated in Bœotian fields to found
A rising empire on a foreign ground,   250

First rais'd our walls on that ill-omen'd
  plain
Where earth-born brothers were by bro-
  thers slain ?
What lofty looks th' unrivall'd monarch
  bears !
How all the Tyrant in his face appears !
What sullen fury clouds his scornful brow !
Gods ! how his eyes with threat'ning ar-
  dour glow !
Can this imperious lord forget to reign,
Quit all his state, descend, and serve again ?
Yet who before more popularly bow'd ?
Who more propitious to the suppliant
  crowd ?   260
Patient of right, familiar in the throne,
What wonder then ? he was not then alone.
Oh wretched we ! a vile submissive train,
Fortune's tame fools, and slaves in every
  reign !
' As when two winds with rival force
  contend,
This way and that the wavering sails they
  bend,
While freezing Boreas and black Eurus
  blow,
Now here, now there the reeling vessel
  throw ;
Thus on each side, alas ! our tott'ring state
Feels all the fury of resistless Fate,   270
And doubtful still, and still distracted
  stands,
While that prince threatens, and while this
  commands.'
  And now th' almighty Father of the Gods
Convenes a council in the bless'd abodes.
Far in the bright recesses of the skies,
High o'er the rolling heav'ns, a mansion lies,
Whence, far below, the Gods at once
  survey
The realms of rising and declining day,
And all th' extended space of earth,
  and air, and sea.   279
Full in the midst, and on a starry throne,
The Majesty of Heav'n superior shone :
Serene he look'd, and gave an awful nod,
And all the trembling spheres confess'd the
  God.
At Jove's assent the deities around
In solemn state the consistory crown'd.
Next a long order of inferior powers
Ascend from hills, and plains, and shady
  bowers ;
Those from whose urns the rolling rivers
  flow,

And those that give the wand'ring winds to
  blow :
Here all their rage and ev'n their murmurs
  cease,   290
And sacred Silence reigns, and universal
  Peace.
A shining synod of majestic Gods
Gilds with new lustre the divine abodes :
Heav'n seems improv'd with a superior ray,
And the bright arch reflects a double day.
The Monarch then his solemn silence broke,
The still creation listen'd while he spoke ;
Each sacred accent bears eternal weight,
And each irrevocable word is Fate.
  'How long shall man the wrath of
    Heav'n defy,   300
And force unwilling vengeance from the
  sky ?
O race confed'rate into crimes, that prove
Triumphant o'er th' eluded rage of Jove !
This wearied arm can scarce the bolt sus-
  tain,
And unregarded thunder rolls in vain :
Th' o'erlabour'd Cyclop from his task re-
  tires,
Th' Æolian forge exhausted of its fires.
For this I suffer'd Phœbus' steeds to stray,
And the mad ruler to misguide the day,
When the wide earth to heaps of ashes
  turn'd,   310
And Heav'n itself the wand'ring chariot
  burn'd ;
For this my brother of the wat'ry reign ⎫
Releas'd th' impetuous sluices of the main; ⎪
But flames consumed, and billows raged ⎬
  in vain.   ⎭
Two races now, allied to Jove, offend ;
To punish these, see Jove himself descend.
The Theban kings their line from Cadmus
  trace,
From godlike Perseus those of Argive race.
Unhappy Cadmus' fate who does not know,
And the long series of succeeding woe ? 320
How oft the Furies from the deeps of night
Arose, and mix'd with men in mortal fight;
Th' exulting mother stain'd with filial
  blood,
The savage hunter and the haunted wood ?
The direful banquet why should I pro-
  claim,
And crimes that grieve the trembling Gods
  to name ?
Ere I recount the sins of these profane, ⎫
The sun would sink into the western main, ⎬
And, rising, gild the radiant east again. ⎭

Have we not seen (the blood of Laius
  shed)   330
The murd'ring son ascend his parent's bed,
Thro' violated Nature force his way,
And stain the sacred womb where once he
  lay ?
Yet now in darkness and despair he groans,
And for the crimes of guilty Fate atones;
His sons with scorn their eyeless father
  view,
Insult his wounds, and make them bleed
  anew.   337
Thy curse, O Œdipus ! just Heav'n alarms,
And sets th' avenging Thunderer in arms.
I from the root thy guilty race will tear,
And give the nations to the waste of war.
Adrastus soon, with Gods averse, shall join
In dire alliance with the Theban line ;
Hence strife shall rise, and mortal war suc-
  ceed ;
The guilty realms of Tantalus shall bleed :
Fix'd is their doom. This all-rememb'ring
  breast
Yet harbours vengeance for the tyrant's
  feast.'
  He said ; and thus the Queen of Heav'n
    return'd
(With sudden grief her lab'ring bosom
  burn'd) :
'Must I, whose cares Phoroneus' towers
  defend,   350
Must I, O Jove ! in bloody wars contend ?
Thou know'st those regions my protection
  claim,
Glorious in Arms, in Riches, and in Fame :
Tho' there the fair Egyptian heifer fed,
And there deluded Argus slept and bled ;
Tho' there the brazen tower was storm'd of
  old,
When Jove descended in almighty gold !
Yet I can pardon those obscurer rapes,
Those bashful crimes disguis'd in borrow'd
  shapes ;
But Thebes, where, shining in celestial
  charms,   360
Thou camest triumphant to a mortal's
  arms,
When all my glories o'er her limbs were
  spread,
And blazing lightnings danced around her
  bed ;
Curs'd Thebes the vengeance it deserves
  may prove —
Ah ! why should Argos feel the rage of
  Jove?

Yet since thou wilt thy sister-queen control,
Since still the lust of Discord fires thy soul,
Go, raze my Samos, let Mycene fall,
And level with the dust the Spartan wall ;
No more let mortals Juno's power invoke,
Her fanes no more with eastern incense
   smoke, 371
Nor victims sink beneath the sacred
   stroke;
But to your Isis all my rights transfer,
Let altars blaze and temples smoke for her !
For her, thro' Egypt's fruitful clime re-
   nown'd,
Let weeping Nilus hear the timbrel sound.
But if thou must reform the stubborn
   times,
Avenging on the sons the fathers' crimes,
And from the long records of distant age
Derive incitements to renew thy rage ; 380
Say, from what period then has Jove de-
   sign'd
To date his vengeance ? to what bounds
   confin'd ?
Begin from thence, where first Alpheus
   hides
His wand'ring stream, and thro' the briny
   tides
Unmix'd to his Sicilian river glides.
Thy own Arcadians there the thunder
   claim,
Whose impious rites disgrace thy mighty
   name ;
Who raise thy temples where the chariot
   stood
Of fierce Œnomaüs, defil'd with blood ;
Where once his steeds their savage ban-
   quet found, 390
And human bones yet whiten all the
   ground.
Say, can those honours please ? and canst
   thou love
Presumptuous Crete, that boasts the tomb
   of Jove ?
And shall not Tantalus's kingdoms share
Thy wife and sister's tutelary care ?
Reverse, O Jove ! thy too severe decree,
Nor doom to war a race derived from thee ;
On impious realms and barb'rous kings
   impose
Thy plagues, and curse them with such
   sons as those.'
  Thus in reproach and prayer the Queen
   exprest 400
The rage and grief contending in her
   breast ;

Unmov'd remain'd the Ruler of the Sky,
And from his throne return'd this stern
   reply :
'T was thus I deem'd thy haughty soul
   would bear
The dire tho' just revenge which I prepare
Against a nation thy peculiar care :
No less Dione might for Thebes contend,
Nor Bacchus less his native town defend ;
Yet these in silence see the Fates fulfil
Their work, and rev'rence our superior
   will : 410
For by the black infernal Styx I swear
(That dreadful oath which binds the Thun-
   derer)
'T is fix'd, th' irrevocable doom of Jove ;
No Force can bend me, no Persuasion
   move.
Haste then, Cyllenius, thro' the liquid air ;
Go, mount the winds, and to the shades re-
   pair ;
Bid Hell's black monarch my commands
   obey, 417
And give up Laius to the realms of day,
Whose ghost yet shiv'ring on Cocytus' sand
Expects its passage to the further strand :
Let the pale sire revisit Thebes, and bear
These pleasing orders to the tyrant's ear ;
That from his exiled brother, swell'd with
   pride
Of foreign forces and his Argive bride,
Almighty Jove commands him to detain
The promis'd empire, and alternate reign :
Be this the cause of more than mortal hate;
The rest succeeding times shall ripen into
   Fate.'
  The God obeys, and to his feet applies
Those golden wings that cut the yielding
   skies ; 430
His ample hat his beamy locks o'erspread,
And veil'd the starry glories of his head.
He seiz'd the wand that causes sleep to fly,
Or in soft slumbers seals the wakeful eye ;
That drives the dead to dark Tartarean
   coasts,
Or back to life compels the wand'ring
   ghosts.
Thus thro' the parting clouds the son of
   May
Wings on the whistling winds his rapid
   way;
Now smoothly steers thro' air his equal
   flight,
Now springs aloft, and towers th' ethereal
   height ; 440

Then wheeling down the steep of heav'n
  he flies,
And draws a radiant circle o'er the skies.
  Meantime the banish'd Polynices roves
(His Thebes abandon'd) thro' th' Aonian
  groves,
While future realms his wand'ring thoughts
  delight,
His daily vision, and his dream by night.
Forbidden Thebes appears before his eye,
From whence he sees his absent brother fly,
With transport views the airy rule his own,
And swells on an imaginary throne.   450
Fain would he cast a tedious age away,
And live out all in one triumphant day :
He chides the lazy progress of the sun,
And bids the year with swifter motion
  run :
With anxious hopes his craving mind is tost,
And all his joys in length of wishes lost.
  The hero then resolves his course to ⎤
  bend |
Where ancient Danaus' fruitful fields ex- ⎬
  tend, |
And famed Mycene's lofty towers ascend ⎦
(Where late the sun did Atreus' crimes
  detest,   460
And disappear'd in horror of the feast) ;
And now by Chance, by Fate, or Furies led,
From Bacchus' consecrated caves he fled,
Where the shrill cries of frantic matrons
  sound,
And Pentheus' blood enrich'd the rising
  ground ;
Then sees Cithæron towering o'er the plain,
And thence declining gently to the main ;
Next to the bounds of Nisus' realm re-
  pairs,
Where treach'rous Scylla cut the purple
  hairs ;
The hanging cliffs of Scyron's rock ex-
  plores,   470
And hears the murmurs of the diff'rent
  shores ;
Passes the strait that parts the foaming
  seas,
And stately Corinth's pleasing site surveys.
'T was now the time when Phœbus yields
  to night,
And rising Cynthia sheds her silver light ;
Wide o'er the world in solemn pomp she
  drew
Her airy chariot, hung with pearly dew :
All birds and beasts lie hush'd : sleep steals
  away

The wild desires of men, and toils of day,
And brings, descending thro' the silent air,
A sweet forgetfulness of human care.   481
Yet no red clouds, with golden borders gay,
Promise the skies the bright return of day ;
No faint reflections of the distant light.
Streak with long gleams the scatt'ring
  shades of night ;
From the damp earth impervious vapours
  rise,
Increase the darkness, and involve the skies.
At once the rushing winds with roaring
  sound
Burst from th' Æolian caves, and rend the
  ground ;
With equal rage their airy quarrel try,   490
And win by turns the kingdom of the sky.
But with a thicker night black Auster
  shrouds
The heav'ns, and drives on heaps the roll-
  ing clouds
From whose dark womb a rattling tempest
  pours,
Which the cold north congeals to haily
  showers :
From pole to pole the thunder roars aloud,
And broken lightnings flash from every
  cloud.
Now smokes with showers the misty moun-
  tain-ground,
And floated fields lie undistinguish'd
  round ;
Th' Inachian streams with headlong fury
  run,   500
And Erasinus rolls a deluge on ;
The foaming Lerna swells above its bounds,
And spreads its ancient poisons o'er the
  grounds ;
Where late was dust, now rapid torrents
  play,
Rush thro' the mounds, and bear the dams
  away ;
Old limbs of trees, from crackling forests
  torn,
Are whirl'd in air, and on the winds are
  borne ;
The storm the dark Lycæan groves dis-
  play'd,
And first to light exposed the sacred shade.
Th' intrepid Theban hears the bursting sky,
Sees yawning rocks in massy fragments
  fly,   511
And views astonish'd, from the hills afar,
The floods descending, and the wat'ry
  war,

That, driv'n by storms and pouring o'er
  the plain,
Swept herds, and hinds, and houses to the
  main.
Thro' the brown horrors of the night he fled,
Nor knows, amaz'd, what doubtful path to
  tread ;
His brother's image to his mind appears,
Inflames his heart with rage, and wings his
  feet with fears.   519
So fares the sailor on the stormy main,
When clouds conceal Boötes' golden wain,
When not a star its friendly lustre keeps,
Nor trembling Cynthia glimmers on the
  deeps ;
He dreads the rocks, and shoals, and seas,
  and skies,
While thunder roars, and lightning round
  him flies.
Thus strove the chief, on ev'ry side dis-
  tress'd;
Thus still his courage with his toils in-
  creas'd.
With his broad shield opposed, he forced
  his way
Thro' thickest woods, and rous'd the beasts
  of prey,   529
Till he beheld where from Larissa's height
The shelving walls reflect a glancing light.
Thither with haste the Theban hero flies;⎫
On this side Lerna's pois'nous water lies, ⎬
On that Prosymna's grove and temple rise.⎭
He pass'd the gates which then unguarded
  lay,
And to the regal palace bent his way ;
On the cold marble, spent with toil, he lies,
And waits till pleasing slumbers seal his
  eyes.
Adrastus here his happy people sways,
Bless'd with calm peace in his declining
  days ;   540
By both his parents of descent divine,
Great Jove and Phœbus graced his noble
  line :
Heav'n had not crown'd his wishes with a
  son,
But two fair daughters heir'd his state and
  throne.
To him Apollo (wondrous to relate !
But who can pierce into the depths of fate ?)
Had sung — ' Expect thy sons on Argos'
  shore,
A yellow lion and a bristly boar.'
This long revolv'd in his paternal breast,
Sat heavy on his heart, and broke his rest ;

This, great Amphiaraus ! lay hid from
  thee,   551
Tho' skill'd in fate and dark futurity.
The father's care and prophet's art were
  vain,
For thus did the predicting God ordain.
Lo, hapless Tydeus ! whose ill-fated hand
Had slain his brother, leaves his native land,
And, seiz'd with horror in the shades of
  night,
Thro' the thick deserts headlong urged his
  flight :
Now by the fury of the tempest driv'n,
He seeks a shelter from th' inclement
  heav'n,   560
Till, led by fate, the Theban's steps he
  treads,
And to fair Argos' open courts succeeds.
When thus the chiefs from diff'rent lands
  resort
T' Adrastus' realms and hospitable court,
The King surveys his guests with curious
  eyes,
And views their arms and habit with sur-
  prise.
A lion's yellow skin the Theban wears,
Horrid his mane, and rough with curling
  hairs ;
Such once employ'd Alcides' youthful toils,
Ere yet adorn'd with Nemea's dreadful
  spoils.   570
A boar's stiff hide, of Calydonian breed,
Oenides' manly shoulders overspread ;
Oblique his tusks, erect his bristles stood,
Alive the pride and terror of the wood.
Struck with the sight, and fix'd in deep
  amaze,
The King th' accomplish'd oracle surveys,
Reveres Apollo's vocal caves, and owns
The guiding godhead and his future sons.
O'er all his bosom secret transports reign,
And a glad horror shoots thro' ev'ry vein :
To Heav'n he lifts his hands, erects his
  sight,   581
And thus invokes the silent Queen of
  Night : —
' Goddess of shades ! beneath whose
  gloomy reign
Yon spangled arch glows with the starry
  train ;
You who the cares of Heav'n and Earth ⎫
  allay,   ⎪
Till Nature, quicken'd by th' inspiring ⎬
  ray,   ⎪
Wakes to new vigour with the rising day;⎭

O thou who freest me from my doubtful
state,
Long lost and wilder'd in the maze of Fate,
Be present still, O Goddess! in our aid;
Proceed, and 'firm those omens thou hast
made.   591
We to thy name our annual rites will pay,
And on thy altars sacrifices lay ;
The sable flock shall fall beneath the
stroke,
And fill thy temples with a grateful
smoke.
Hail, faithful Tripos ! hail, ye dark abodes
Of awful Phœbus ; I confess the Gods ! '
  Thus, seiz'd with sacred fear, the Mon-
arch pray'd ;
Then to his inner court the guests convey'd,
Where yet thin fumes from dying sparks ⎫
arise,   600   ⎪
And dust yet white upon each altar lies, ⎬
The relics of a former sacrifice.   ⎭
The King once more the solemn rites re-
quires,
And bids renew the feasts and wake the
fires.
His train obey ; while all the courts around
With noisy care and various tumult sound.
Embroider'd purple clothes the golden
beds ;
This slave the floor, and that the table
spreads ;
A third dispels the darkness of the night,
And fills depending lamps with beams of
light ;   610
Here loaves in canisters are piled on high,
And there in flames the slaughter'd victims
fly.
Sublime in regal state Adrastus shone,
Stretch'd on rich carpets on his ivory
throne ;
A lofty couch receives each princely guest ;
Around, at awful distance, wait the rest.
  And now the King, his royal feast to
grace,
Acestis calls, the guardian of his race,
Who first their youth in arts of Virtue
train'd,
And their ripe years in modest Grace main-
tain'd ;   620
Then softly whisper'd in her faithful ear,
And bade his daughters at the rites appear.
When from the close apartments of the
night
The royal nymphs approach divinely
bright,

Such was Diana's, such Minerva's face,
Nor shine their beauties with superior grace,
But that in these a milder charm endears,
And less of terror in their looks appears.
As on the heroes first they cast their eyes,
O'er their fair cheeks the glowing blushes
rise ;   630
Their downcast looks a decent shame con-
fest,
Then on their father's rev'rend features
rest.
  The banquet done, the Monarch gives
the sign
To fill the goblet high with sparkling wine,
Which Danaus used in sacred rites of old,
With sculpture graced, and rough with ris-
ing gold.
Here to the clouds victorious Perseus flies, ⎫
Medusa seems to move her languid eyes, ⎬
And ev'n in gold, turns paler as she dies: ⎭
There from the chase Jove's towering
eagle bears,   640
On golden wings, the Phrygian to the
stars ;
Still as he rises in th' ethereal height,
His native mountains lessen to his sight,
While all his sad companions upward gaze,
Fix'd on the glorious scene in wild amaze,
And the swift hounds, affrighted as he
flies,
Run to the shade, and bark against the
skies.
  This golden bowl with gen'rous juice
was crown'd,
The first libation sprinkled on the ground ;
By turns on each celestial Power they call;
With Phœbus' name resounds the vaulted
hall.   651
The courtly train, the strangers, and the
rest,
Crown'd with chaste laurel, and with gar-
lands drest,
While with rich gums the fuming altars
blaze,
Salute the God in numerous hymns of
praise.
  Then thus the King: ' Perhaps, my noble
guests,
These honour'd altars, and these annual
feasts
To bright Apollo's awful name design'd,
Unknown, with wonder may perplex your
mind.   659
Great was the cause : our old solemnities
From no blind zeal or fond tradition rise ˙

But saved from death, our Argives yearly
pay
These grateful honours to the God of
Day.
' When by a thousand darts the Python
slain
With orbs unroll'd lay cov'ring all the
plain,
(Transfix'd as o'er Castalia's streams he
hung,
And suck'd new poisons with his triple
tongue)
To Argos' realms the victor God resorts,
And enters old Crotopus' humble courts.
This rural prince one only daughter
bless'd,   670
That all the charms of blooming youth
possess'd ;
Fair was her face, and spotless was her
mind,
Where filial love with virgin sweetness
join'd.
Happy ! and happy still she might have
prov'd,
Were she less beautiful, or less belov'd !
But Phœbus lov'd, and on the flowery side
Of Nemea's stream the yielding Fair en-
joy'd.
Now ere ten moons their orb with light
adorn,
Th' illustrious offspring of the God was
born ;   679
The nymph, her father's anger to evade,
Retires from Argos to the sylvan shade ;
To woods and wilds the pleasing burden
bears,
And trusts her infant to a shepherd's cares.
' How mean a fate, unhappy child, is
thine !
Ah ! how unworthy those of race divine !
On flow'ry herbs in some green covert
laid,
His bed the ground, his canopy the shade,
He mixes with the bleating lambs his cries, ⎫
While the rude swain his rural music tries, ⎬
To call soft slumbers on his infant eyes. ⎭
Yet ev'n in those obscure abodes to live 691
Was more, alas ! than cruel Fate would
give ;
For on the grassy verdure as he lay,
And breathed the freshness of the early
day,
Devouring dogs the helpless infant tore,
Fed on his trembling limbs, and lapp'd the
gore.

Th' astonish'd mother, when the rumour
came,
Forgets her father, and neglects her fame ;
With loud complaints she fills the yielding
air,
And beats her breast, and rends her flow-
ing hair ;   700
Then wild with anguish to her sire she
flies,
Demands the sentence, and contented dies.
' But touch'd with sorrow for the dead
too late,
The raging God prepares t' avenge her
fate.
He sends a monster horrible and fell,
Begot by furies in the depths of Hell.
The pest a virgin's face and bosom bears; ⎫
High on her crown a rising snake appears, ⎬
Guards her black front, and hisses in her ⎱
hairs.   ⎭
About the realm she walks her dreadful
round,   710
When night with sable wings o'erspreads
the ground,
Devours young babes before their parents'
eyes,
And feeds and thrives on public miseries.
' But gen'rous rage the bold Chorœbus
warms,
Chorœbus ! famed for virtue as for arms ;
Some few like him, inspired with martial
flame,
Thought a short life well lost for endless
fame.
These, where two ways in equal parts ⎫
divide,   ⎬
The direful monster from afar descried, ⎭
Two bleeding babes depending at her side;
Whose panting vitals, warm with life, she
draws,   721
And in their hearts imbrues her cruel
claws.
The youths surround her with extended
spears ;
But brave Chorœbus in the front appears ;
Deep in her breast he plunged his shining
sword,
And Hell's dire monster back to Hell re-
stor'd.
Th' Inachians view the slain with vast sur-
prise,
Her twisting volumes and her rolling eyes,
Her spotted breast and gaping womb im-
brued   729
With livid poison and our children's blood.

The crowd in stupid wonder fix'd appear,
Pale ev'n in joy, nor yet forget to fear.
Some with vast beams the squalid corse
    engage,
And weary all the wild efforts of rage.
The birds obscene, that nightly flock'd to
    taste,
With hollow screeches fled the dire re-
    past ;
And rav'nous dogs, allured by scented
    blood,
And starving wolves, ran howling to the
    wood.
    'But fired with rage, from cleft Par-
        nassus' brow   739
Avenging Phœbus bent his deadly bow,
And hissing flew the feather'd fates below.
A night of sultry clouds involv'd around
The towers, the fields, and the devoted
    ground:
And now a thousand lives together fled,
Death with his scythe cut off the fatal
    thread,
And a whole province in his triumph led.
    'But Phœbus, ask'd why noxious fires
        appear
And raging Sirius blasts the sickly year,
Demands their lives by whom his monster
    fell,
And dooms a dreadful sacrifice to Hell.
    'Bless'd be thy dust, and let eternal
        fame   751
Attend thy Manes, and preserve thy
    Name,
Undaunted Hero ! who, divinely brave,
In such a cause disdain'd thy life to save,
But view'd the shrine with a superior look,
And its upbraided godhead thus bespoke :
"With Piety, the soul's securest guard,
And conscious Virtue, still its own reward,
Willing I come, unknowing how to fear,
Nor shalt thou, Phœbus, find a suppliant
    here :   760
Thy monster's death to me was owed
    alone,
And 't is a deed too glorious to disown.
Behold him here, for whom, so many days,
Impervious clouds conceal'd thy sullen
    rays ;
For whom, as man no longer claim'd thy
    care,
Such numbers fell by pestilential air !
But if th' abandon'd race of human kind
From Gods above no more compassion
    find ;

If such inclemency in Heav'n can dwell,
Yet why must unoffending Argos feel 770
The vengeance due to this unlucky steel?
On me, on me, let all thy fury fall,
Nor err from me, since I deserve it all :
Unless our desert cities please thy sight,
Or funeral flames reflect a grateful light.
Discharge thy shafts, this ready bosom
    rend,
And to the shades a ghost triumphant
    send :
But for my country let my fate atone ;
Be mine the vengeance, as the crime my
    own."
    'Merit distress'd impartial Heav'n re-
        lieves :   780
Unwelcome life relenting Phœbus gives;
For not the vengeful Power, that glow'd
    with rage,
With such amazing virtue durst engage.
The clouds dispers'd, Apollo's wrath ex-
    pired,
And from the wond'ring God th' unwilling
    youth retired.
Thence we these altars in his temple raise,
And offer annual honours, feasts, and
    praise ;
These solemn feasts propitious Phœbus
    please ;
These honours, still renew'd, his ancient
    wrath appease.
    'But say, illustrious guest ! (adjoin'd
        the King)   790
What name you bear, from what high race
    you spring ?
The noble Tydeus stands confess'd, and
    known
Our neighbour prince, and heir of Calydon:
Relate your fortunes, while the friendly
    night
And silent hours to various talk invite.'
    The Theban bends on earth his gloomy
        eyes,
Confused, and sadly thus at length re-
    plies : —
'Before these altars how shall I proclaim,
O gen'rous Prince ! my nation or my
    name,
Or thro' what veins our ancient blood has
    roll'd ?   800
Let the sad tale for ever rest untold !
Yet if, propitious to a wretch unknown,
You seek to share in sorrows not your own,
Know then from Cadmus I derive my
    race,

Jocasta's son, and Thebes my native
    place.'
To whom the King (who felt his gen'rous
    breast
Touch'd with concern for his unhappy
    guest)
Replies — 'Ah ! why forbears the son to
    name
His wretched father, known too well by
    Fame ?
Fame, that delights around the world to
    stray,   810
Scorns not to take our Argos in her way.
Ev'n those who dwell where suns at dis-
    tance roll,
In northern wilds, and freeze beneath the
    pole,
And those who tread the burning Libyan
    lands,
The faithless Syrtes, and the moving
    sands ;
Who view the western sea's extremest
    bounds,
Or drink of Ganges in their eastern
    grounds ;
All these the woes of Œdipus have known,
Your fates, your furies, and your haunted
    town.
If on the sons the parents' crimes descend,
What prince from those his lineage can
    defend ?   821
Be this thy comfort, that 't is thine t' ef-
    face,
With virtuous acts, thy ancestors' dis-
    grace,
And be thyself the honour of thy race.
But see ! the stars begin to steal away,
And shine more faintly at approaching
    day;
Now pour the wine ; and in your tuneful
    lays
Once more resound the great Apollo's
    praise.'
    'O father Phœbus ! whether Lycia's
    coast
And snowy mountains thy bright presence
    boast ;   830
Whether to sweet Castalia thou repair,
And bathe in silver dews thy yellow hair ;
Or pleas'd to find fair Delos float no
    more,
Delight in Cynthus and the shady shore ;
Or choose thy seat in Ilion's proud abodes,
The shining structures rais'd by lab'ring
    Gods :

By thee the bow and mortal shafts are
    borne ;
Eternal charms thy blooming youth adorn;
Skill'd in the laws of secret Fate above,
And the dark counsels of almighty Jove.
'T is thine the seeds of future war to
    know,   841
The change of sceptres and impending woe,
When direful meteors spread thro' glowing
    air
Long trails of light, and shake their blazing
    hair.
Thy rage the Phrygian felt, who durst
    aspire
T' excel the music of thy heav'nly lyre ;
Thy shafts avenged lewd Tityus' guilty
    flame,
Th' immortal victim of thy mother's fame;
Thy hand slew Python, and the dame who
    lost
Her numerous offspring for a fatal boast.
In Phlegyas' doom thy just revenge ap-
    pears,   851
Condemn'd to furies and eternal fears ;
He views his food, but dreads, with lifted
    eye,
The mould'ring rock that trembles from on
    high.
    Propitious hear our prayer, O Power
    divine !
And on thy hospitable Argos shine ;
Whether the style of Titan please thee
    more,
Whose purple rays th' Achæmenes adore;
Or great Osiris, who first taught the swain
In Pharian fields to sow the golden grain;
Or Mitra, to whose beams the Persian
    bows,   861
And pays, in hollow rocks, his awful vows;
Mitra ! whose head the blaze of light
    adorns,
Who grasps the struggling heifer's lunar
    horns.'

IMITATIONS OF ENGLISH POETS

These imitations, with the exception of
Silence (Lintot, 1712), were not published till
1727. Pope says, however, that they were
'done as early as the translations, some of
them at fourteen and fifteen years old.' *The
Happy Life of a Country Parson* must have
been written later than the rest, as Pope did
not know Swift till 1713.

CHAUCER

WOMEN ben full of ragerie,
Yet swinken not sans secresie.
Thilke Moral shall ye understond,
From schoole-boy's Tale of fayre Irelond ;
Which to the Fennes hath him betake,
To filche the grey Ducke fro the Lake.
Right then there passen by the way
His Aunt, and eke her Daughters tway.
Ducke in his trowses hath he hent,
Not to be spied of ladies gent.   10
' But ho ! our Nephew,' crieth one ;
' Ho !' quoth another, ' Cozen John ;'
And stoppen, and lough, and callen out —
This sely Clerke full low doth lout :
They asken that, and talken this,
' Lo, here is Coz, and here is Miss.'
But, as he glozeth with speeches soote,
The Ducke sore tickleth his Erse-roote :
Fore-piece and buttons all-to-brest,
Forth thrust a white neck and red crest. 20
' Te-hee,' cried ladies ; clerke nought
    spake ;
Miss stared, and grey Ducke crieth
    ' quaake.'
' O Moder, Moder !' quoth the Daughter,
' Be thilke same thing Maids longen a'ter ?
Bette is to pine on coals and chalke,
Then trust on Mon whose yerde can talke.'

SPENSER

THE ALLEY

IN ev'ry Town where Thamis rolls his
    tyde,
A narrow pass there is, with houses low,
Where ever and anon the stream is eyed,
And many a boat soft sliding to and fro :
There oft are heard the notes of Infant
    Woe,
The short thick Sob, loud Scream, and
    shriller Squall :
How can ye, Mothers, vex your children
    so ?
Some play, some eat, some cack against
    the wall,
And as they crouchen low, for bread and
    butter call.

And on the broken pavement, here and
    there,
Doth many a stinking sprat and herring lie ;

A brandy and tobacco shop is neare,
And hens, and dogs, and hogs, are feeding
    by ;
And here a sailor's jacket hangs to dry.
At ev'ry door are sunburnt matrons seen,
Mending old nets to catch the scaly fry ;
Now singing shrill, and scolding eft be-
    tween ;
Scolds answer foul-mouth'd Scolds ; bad
    neighbourhood I ween.

The snappish cur (the passengers' annoy)
Close at my heel with yelping treble flies ;
The whimp'ring Girl, and hoarser scream
    ing Boy,
Join to the yelping treble shrilling cries ;
The scolding Quean to louder notes doth rise,
And her full pipes those shrilling cries
    confound ;
To her full pipes the grunting hog replies ;
The grunting hogs alarm the neighbours
    round,
And Curs, Girls, Boys, and Scolds, in the
    deep bass are drown'd.

Hard by a sty, beneath a roof of thatch,
Dwelt Obloquy, who in her early days
Baskets of fish at Billingsgate did watch,
Cod, whiting, oyster, mackrel, sprat, or
    plaice :
There learn'd she speech from tongues
    that never cease.
Slander beside her like a magpie chatters,
With Envy (spitting cat), dread foe to
    peace ;
Like a curs'd cur, Malice before her clat-
    ters,
And vexing ev'ry wight, tears clothes and
    all to tatters.

Her dugs were mark'd by ev'ry Collier's
    hand,
Her mouth was black as bull-dogs at the
    stall :
She scratchëd, bit, and spared ne lace ne
    band,
And bitch and rogue her answer was to all.
Nay, ev'n the parts of shame by name
    would call :
Yea, when she passëd by or lane or nook,
Would greet the man who turn'd him to
    the wall,
And by his hand obscene the porter took,
Nor ever did askance like modest virgin
    look.

Such place hath Deptford, navy-building
  town,
Woolwich and Wapping, smelling strong of
  pitch ;
Such Lambeth, envy of each band and
  gown,
And Twick'nam such, which fairer scenes
  enrich,
Grots, statues, urns, and Jo—n's dog and
  bitch.
Ne village is without, on either side,
All up the silver Thames, or all adown ;
Ne Richmond's self, from whose tall front
  are eyed
Vales, spires, meand'ring streams, and
  Windsor's tow'ry pride.

WALLER

ON A LADY SINGING TO HER LUTE

Fair Charmer, cease ! nor make your
  Voice's prize
A heart resign'd the conquest of your
  Eyes :
Well might, alas ! that threaten'd vessel
  fail,
Which winds and lightning both at once
  assail.
We were too bless'd with these enchanting
  lays,
Which must be heav'nly when an Angel
  plays :
But killing charms your lover's death con-
  trive,
Lest heav'nly music should be heard alive.
Orpheus could charm the trees ; but thus a
  tree,
Taught by your hand, can charm no less
  than he ;
A poet made the silent wood pursue ;
This vocal wood had drawn the poet too.

ON A FAN OF THE AUTHOR'S DESIGN

IN WHICH WAS PAINTED THE STORY OF CEPHALUS
AND PROCRIS, WITH THE MOTTO ' AURA VENI '

Come, gentle air ! th' Æolian shepherd
  said,
While Procris panted in the secret shade ;
Come, gentle air ! the fairer Delia cries,
While at her feet her swain expiring
  lies.

Lo, the glad gales o'er all her beauties
  stray,
Breathe on her lips, and in her bosom play ;
In Delia's hand this toy is fatal found,
Nor could that fabled dart more surely
  wound :
Both gifts destructive to the givers prove ;
Alike both lovers fall by those they love.
Yet guiltless too this bright destroyer lives,
At random wounds, nor knows the wounds
  she gives ;
She views the story with attentive eyes,
And pities Procris while her lover dies.

COWLEY

THE GARDEN

Fain would my Muse the flow'ry treasures
  sing,
And humble glories of the youthful
  Spring ;
Where op'ning roses breathing sweets dif-
  fuse,
And soft carnations shower their balmy
  dews ;
Where lilies smile in virgin robes of white,
The thin undress of superficial light ;
And varied tulips show so dazzling gay,
Blushing in bright diversities of day.
Each painted flow'ret in the lake below
Surveys its beauties, whence its beauties
  grow ;   10
And pale Narcissus, on the bank in vain
Transformèd, gazes on himself again.
Here aged trees cathedral walks compose,
And mount the hill in venerable rows ;
There the green infants in their beds are
  laid,
The garden's hope, and its expected shade.
Here orange trees with blooms and pen-
  dants shine,
And Vernal honours to their Autumn join;
Exceed their promise in the ripen'd store,
Yet in the rising blossom promise more.   20
There in bright drops the crystal fountains
  play,
By laurels shielded from the piercing day;
Where Daphne, now a tree as once a maid,
Still from Apollo vindicates her shade;
Still turns her beauties from th' invading
  beam,
Nor seeks in vain for succour to the
  stream.

The stream at once preserves her virgin
  leaves,
At once a shelter from her boughs receives,
Where summer's beauty midst of winter
  stays,
And winter's coolness spite of summer's
  rays.   30

WEEPING

While Celia's tears make sorrow bright,
  Proud grief sits swelling in her eyes ;
The sun, next those the fairest light,
  Thus from the ocean first did rise :
And thus thro' mists we see the sun,
Which else we durst not gaze upon.

These silver drops, like morning dew,
  Foretell the fervor of the day :
So from one cloud soft showers we view,
  And blasting lightnings burst away.
The stars that fall from Celia's eye
Declare our doom is drawing nigh.

The baby in that sunny sphere
  So like a Phaëton appears,
That Heav'n, the threaten'd world to spare,
  Thought fit to drown him in her tears ;
Else might th' ambitious nymph aspire
To set, like him, Heav'n too on fire.

EARL OF ROCHESTER

ON SILENCE

Silence ! coeval with Eternity,
Thou wert ere Nature's self began to be,
'T was one vast nothing all, and all slept
    fast in thee.

Thine was the sway ere Heav'n was
    form'd, or earth,
Ere fruitful thought conceiv'd Creation's
    birth,
Or midwife word gave aid, and spoke the
    infant forth.

Then various elements against thee join'd,
In one more various animal combin'd,
And framed the clam'rous race of busy
    humankind.

The tongue mov'd gently first, and speech
    was low,
Till wrangling Science taught its noise and
    show,
And wicked Wit arose, thy most abusive
    foe.

But rebel Wit deserts thee oft in vain ;
Lost in the maze of words he turns again,
And seeks a surer state, and courts thy
    gentle reign.

Afflicted Sense thou kindly dost set free,
Oppress'd with argumental tyranny,
And routed Reason finds a safe retreat in
    thee.

With thee in private modest Dulness lies,
And in thy bosom lurks in thought's dis-
    guise ;
Thou varnisher of fools, and cheat of all
    the wise !

Yet thy indulgence is by both confest ;
Folly by thee lies sleeping in the breast,
And 't is in thee at last that Wisdom seeks
    for rest.

Silence, the knave's repute, the whore's
    good name,
The only honour of the wishing dame ;
The very want of tongue makes thee a
    kind of Fame.

But couldst thou seize some tongues that
    now are free,
How Church and State should be obliged
    to thee !
At Senate and at Bar how welcome wouldst
    thou be !

Yet speech, ev'n there, submissively with-
    draws
From rights of subjects, and the poor
    man's cause ;
Then pompous Silence reigns, and stills the
    noisy Laws.

Past services of friends, good deeds of
    foes,
What fav'rites gain, and what the nation
    owes,
Fly the forgetful world, and in thy arms
    repose.

The country wit, religion of the town,
The courtier's learning, policy o' th' gown,
Are best by thee express'd, and shine in
    thee alone.

The parson's cant, the lawyer's sophistry,
Lord's quibble, critic's jest, all end in thee;
All rest in peace at last, and sleep eternally.

EARL OF DORSET

ARTEMISIA

Tho' Artemisia talks by fits
Of councils, classics, fathers, wits,
    Reads Malbranche, Boyle, and Locke,
Yet in some things methinks she fails :
'T were well if she would pare her nails,
    And wear a cleaner smock.

Haughty and huge as High Dutch bride,
Such nastiness and so much pride
    Are oddly join'd by fate :
On her large squab you find her spread,
Like a fat corpse upon a bed,
    That lies and stinks in state.

She wears no colours (sign of grace)
On any part except her face ;
    All white and black beside :
Dauntless her look, her gesture proud,
Her voice theatrically loud,
    And masculine her stride.

So have I seen, in black and white,
A prating thing, a magpie hight,
    Majestically stalk ;
A stately worthless animal,
That plies the tongue, and wags the tail,
    All flutter, pride, and talk.

PHRYNE

Phryne had talents for mankind ;
Open she was and unconfin'd,
    Like some free port of trade :
Merchants unloaded here their freight,
And agents from each foreign state
    Here first their entry made.

Her learning and good breeding such,
Whether th' Italian or the Dutch,
    Spaniards or French, came to her,
To all obliging she 'd appear ;
'T was *Si Signior*, 't was *Yaw Mynheer*,
'T was *S'il vous plait, Monsieur*.

Obscure by birth, renown'd by crimes,
Still changing names, religions, climes,
    At length she turns a bride :
In diamonds, pearls, and rich brocades,
She shines the first of batter'd jades,
    And flutters in her pride.

So have I known those insects fair
(Which curious Germans hold so rare)
    Still vary shapes and dyes ;
Still gain new titles with new forms ;
First grubs obscene, then wriggling worms,
    Then painted butterflies.

DR. SWIFT

THE HAPPY LIFE OF A COUNTRY PARSON

Parson, these things in thy possessing
Are better than the bishop's blessing :
A wife that makes conserves ; a steed
That carries double when there 's need ;
October store, and best Virginia,
Tythe pig, and mortuary guinea ;
Gazettes sent gratis down and frank'd,
For which thy patron 's weekly thank'd ;
A large Concordance, bound long since ;
Sermons to Charles the First, when prince ;
A Chronicle of ancient standing ;
A Chrysostom to smooth thy band in ;
The Polyglott — three parts — my text,
Howbeit — likewise — now to my next ;
Lo here the Septuagint — and Paul,
To sum the whole — the close of all.
    He that has these may pass his life,
Drink with the 'Squire, and kiss his wife ;
On Sundays preach, and eat his fill,
And fast on Fridays — if he will ;
Toast Church and Queen, explain the news,
Talk with Churchwardens about pews,
Pray heartily for some new gift,
And shake his head at Doctor S——t.

PASTORALS

Rura mihi et rigui placeant in vallibus amnes,
Flumina amem, sylvasque, inglorius!
VIRG.

The Pastorals, by Pope's account, were written at sixteen, in 1704. ' Beyond the fact that he systematically antedated his compositions in order to obtain credit for precocity,' says Courthope, ' there is nothing improbable in the statement.' They were first published in 1709, in Tonson's Sixth *Miscellany*. The *Discourse on Pastoral Poetry* did not appear till the edition of 1717, but is here given the place which he desired for it at the head of the *Pastorals:* and the original footnotes, referring to critical authorities, are retained.

DISCOURSE ON PASTORAL POETRY

There are not, I believe, a greater number of any sort of verses than of those which are called Pastorals; nor a smaller than of those which are truly so. It therefore seems necessary to give some account of this kind of poem; and it is my design to comprise in this short paper the substance of those numerous dissertations that critics have made on the subject, without omitting any of their rules in my own favour. You will also find some points reconciled, about which they seem to differ, and a few remarks which, I think, have escaped their observation.

The origin of Poetry is ascribed to that age which succeeded the creation of the world: and as the keeping of flocks seems to have been the first employment of mankind, the most ancient sort of poetry was probably pastoral.[1] It is natural to imagine, that the leisure of those ancient shepherds admitting and inviting some diversion, none was so proper to that solitary and sedentary life as singing; and that in their songs they took occasion to celebrate their own felicity. From hence a poem was invented, and afterwards improved to a perfect image of that happy time; which, by giving us an esteem for the virtues of a former age, might recommend them to the present. And since the life of shepherds was attended with more tranquillity than any other rural employment, the poets chose to introduce their persons, from whom it received the name of Pastoral.

A Pastoral is an imitation of the action of a shepherd, or one considered under that character. The form of this imitation is dramatic, or narrative, or mixed of both:[2] the fable simple, the manners not too polite nor too rustic: the thoughts are plain, yet admit a little quickness and passion, but that short and flowing: the expression humble, yet as pure as the language will afford; neat, but not florid; easy, and yet lively. In short, the fable, manners, thoughts, and expressions are full of the greatest simplicity in nature.

The complete character of this poem consists in simplicity,[3] brevity, and delicacy; the two first of which render an eclogue natural. and the last delightful.

If we would copy nature, it may be useful to take this idea along with us, that Pastoral is an image of what they call the golden age: so that we are not to describe our shepherds as shepherds at this day really are, but as they may be conceived then to have been, when the best of men followed the employment. To carry this resemblance yet further, it would not be amiss to give these shepherds some skill in astronomy, as far as it may be useful to that sort of life; and an air of piety to the gods should shine through the poem, which so visibly appears in all the works of antiquity; and it ought to preserve some relish of the old way of writing: the connection should be loose, the narrations and descriptions short,[4] and the periods concise. Yet it is not sufficient that the sentences only be brief; the whole eclogue should be so too: for we cannot suppose poetry in those days to have been the business of men, but their recreation at vacant hours.

But, with respect to the present age, nothing more conduces to make these composures natural, than when some knowledge in rural affairs is discovered.[5] This may be made to appear rather done by chance than on design, and sometimes is best shown by inference; lest, by too much study to seem natural, we destroy that easy simplicity from whence arises the delight. For what is inviting in this sort of poetry proceeds not so much from the idea of that business, as of the tranquillity of a country life.

---

[1] Fontenelle's *Discourse on Pastorals.*
[2] Heinsius *in Theocr.*
[3] Rapin *de Carm. Past.* p. 2.

[4] Rapin, *Réflex. sur l'Art Poét. d'Arist.* part ii. réfl. xxvii.
[5] Pref. to Virg. *Past.* in Dryd. Virg.

We must therefore use some illusion to render a pastoral delightful; and this consists in exposing the best side only of a shepherd's life, and in concealing its miseries.[1] Nor is it enough to introduce shepherds discoursing together in a natural way; but a regard must be had to the subject; that it contain some particular beauty in itself, and that it be different in every eclogue. Besides, in each of them a designed scene or prospect is to be presented to our view, which should likewise have its variety. This variety is obtained, in a great degree, by frequent comparisons, drawn from the most agreeable objects of the country; by interrogations to things inanimate; by beautiful digressions, but those short; sometimes by insisting a little on circumstances; and, lastly, by elegant turns on the words, which render the numbers extremely sweet and pleasing. As for the numbers themselves, though they are properly of the heroic measure, they should be the smoothest, the most easy and flowing imaginable.

It is by rules like these that we ought to judge of Pastoral. And since the instructions given for any art are to be delivered as that art is in perfection, they must of necessity be derived from those in whom it is acknowledged so to be. It is therefore from the practice of Theocritus and Virgil (the only undisputed authors of Pastoral) that the critics have drawn the foregoing notions concerning it.

Theocritus excels all others in nature and simplicity. The subjects of his Idyllia are purely pastoral; but he is not so exact in his persons, having introduced reapers [2] and fishermen as well as shepherds. He is apt to be too long in his descriptions, of which that of the cup in the first pastoral is a remarkable instance. In the manners he seems a little defective, for his swains are sometimes abusive and immodest, and perhaps too much inclining to rusticity; for instance, in his fourth and fifth Idyllia. But it is enough that all others learned their excellences from him, and that his dialect alone has a secret charm in it, which no other could ever attain.

Virgil, who copies Theocritus, refines upon his original; and, in all points where judgment is principally concerned, he is much superior to his master. Though some of his subjects are not pastoral in themselves, but only seem to be such, they have a wonderful variety in them, which the Greek was a stranger to.[3] He exceeds him in regularity and brevity, and falls short of him in nothing but simplicity and propriety of style; the first of which, perhaps,

was the fault of his age, and the last of his language.

Among the moderns their success has been greatest who have most endeavoured to make these ancients their pattern. The most considerable genius appears in the famous Tasso, and our Spenser. Tasso, in his Aminta, has as far excelled all the pastoral writers, as in his Gierusalemme he has outdone the epic poets of his country. But as this piece seems to have been the original of a new sort of poem, the pastoral comedy, in Italy, it cannot so well be considered as a copy of the ancients. Spenser's Calendar, in Mr. Dryden's opinion, is the most complete work of this kind which any nation has produced ever since the time of Virgil.[4] Not but that he may be thought imperfect in some few points: his eclogues are somewhat too long, if we compare them with the ancients; he is sometimes too allegorical, and treats of matters of religion in a pastoral style, as the Mantuan had done before him; he has employed the lyric measure, which is contrary to the practice of the old poets; his stanza is not still the same, nor always well chosen. This last may be the reason his expression is sometimes not concise enough; for the tetrastic has obliged him to extend his sense to the length of four lines, which would have been more closely confined in the couplet.

In the manners, thoughts, and characters, he comes near to Theocritus himself; though, notwithstanding all the care he has taken, he is certainly inferior in his dialect: for the Doric had its beauty and propriety in the time of Theocritus; it was used in part of Greece, and frequent in the mouths of many of the greatest persons: whereas the old English and country phrases of Spenser were either entirely obsolete, or spoken only by people of the lowest condition. As there is a difference betwixt simplicity and rusticity, so the expression of simple thoughts should be plain, but not clownish. The addition he has made of a calendar to his eclogues is very beautiful; since by this, besides the general moral of innocence and simplicity, which is common to other authors of Pastoral, he has one peculiar to himself; he compares human life to the several seasons, and at once exposes to his readers a view of the great and little worlds, in their various changes and aspects. Yet the scrupulous division of his pastorals into months has obliged him either to repeat the same description, in other words, for three months together, or, when it was exhausted before, entirely to omit it; whence it comes to pass that some of

---

[1] Fontenelle's *Discourse on Pastorals.*
[2] Θερίσται, Idyl. x. and Ἁλιεῖς, Idyl. xxi.

[3] Rapin, *Refl. on Arist.* part ii. refl. xxvii. — Pref. to the *Ecl.* in Dryden's Virg.
[4] Dedication to Virg. *Ecl.*

his eclogues (as the sixth, eighth, and tenth for example) have nothing but their titles to distinguish them. The reason is evident, because the year has not that variety in it to furnish every month with a particular description, as it may every season.

Of the following eclogues I shall only say, that these four comprehend all the subjects which the critics upon Theocritus and Virgil will allow to be fit for Pastoral; that they have as much variety of description, in respect of the several seasons, as Spenser's ; that, in order to add to this variety, the several times of the day are observed, the rural employments in each season or time of day, and the rural scenes or places proper to such employments, not without some regard to the several ages of man, and the different passions proper to each age.

But after all, if they have any merit, it is to be attributed to some good old authors ; whose works, as I had leisure to study, so, I hope, I have not wanted care to imitate.

I

SPRING ; OR, DAMON

TO SIR WILLIAM TRUMBULL

FIRST in these fields I try the sylvan
    strains,
Nor blush to sport on Windsor's blissful
    plains :
Fair Thames, flow gently from thy sacred
    spring,
While on thy banks Sicilian Muses sing ;
Let vernal airs thro' trembling osiers play,
And Albion's cliffs resound the rural lay.
You, that too wise for pride, too good
    for power,
Enjoy the glory to be great no more,
And carrying with you all the world can
    boast,
To all the world illustriously are lost !   10
O let my Muse her slender reed inspire,
Till in your native shades you tune the lyre :
So when the nightingale to rest removes,
The thrush may chant to the forsaken
    groves ;
But charm'd to silence, listens while she
    sings,
And all th' aërial audience clap their wings.
   Soon as the flocks shook off the nightly
    dews,
Two swains, whom love kept wakeful, and
    the Muse,

Pour'd o'er the whitening vale their fleecy
    care,
Fresh as the morn, and as the season
    fair :   20
The dawn now blushing on the mountain's
    side,
Thus Daphnis spoke, and Strephon thus
    replied :

DAPHNIS.

Hear how the birds on ev'ry blooming
    spray
With joyous music wake the dawning
    day !
Why sit we mute, when early linnets
    sing,
When warbling Philomel salutes the
    spring ?
Why sit we sad, when Phosphor shines so
    clear,
And lavish Nature paints the purple year ?

STREPHON.

Sing, then, and Damon shall attend the
    strain,
While yon slow oxen turn the furrow'd
    plain.   30
Here the bright crocus and blue violet
    glow ;
Here western winds on breathing roses
    blow.
I 'll stake yon lamb, that near the fountain
    plays,
And from the brink his dancing shade
    surveys.

DAPHNIS.

And I this bowl, where wanton ivy twines,
And swelling clusters bend the curling
    vines :
Four figures rising from the work appear,
The various seasons of the rolling year ;
And what is that, which binds the radiant
    sky,
Where twelve fair signs in beauteous order
    lie ?   40

DAMON.

Then sing by turns, by turns the Muses
    sing ;
Now hawthorns blossom, now the daisies
    spring ;
Now leaves the trees, and flowers adorn
    the ground :
Begin, the vales shall every note rebound.

STREPHON.

Inspire me, Phœbus, in my Delia's praise,
With Waller's strains, or Granville's moving lays!
A milk-white bull shall at your altars
stand,
That threats a fight, and spurns the rising
sand.

DAPHNIS.

O Love! for Sylvia let me gain the prize,
And make my tongue victorious as her
eyes: 50
No lambs or sheep for victims I 'll impart,
Thy victim, Love, shall be the shepherd's
heart.

STREPHON.

Me gentle Delia beckons from the plain,
Then, hid in shades, eludes her eager
swain;
But feigns a laugh to see me search
around,
And by that laugh the willing Fair is
found.

DAPHNIS.

The sprightly Sylvia trips along the green;
She runs, but hopes she does not run un-
seen.
While a kind glance at her pursuer flies,
How much at variance are her feet and
eyes! 60

STREPHON.

O'er golden sands let rich Pactolus flow,
And trees weep amber on the banks of
Po;
Blest Thames's shores the brightest beau-
ties yield:
Feed here, my lambs, I 'll seek no distant
field.

DAPHNIS.

Celestial Venus haunts Idalia's groves;
Diana Cynthus, Ceres Hybla loves:
If Windsor shades delight the matchless
maid,
Cynthus and Hybla yield to Windsor
shade.

STREPHON.

All nature mourns, the skies relent in
showers,
Hush'd are the birds, and closed the drooping flowers; 70

If Delia smile, the flowers begin to spring,
The skies to brighten, and the birds to
sing.

DAPHNIS.

All Nature laughs, the groves are fresh
and fair,
The sun's mild lustre warms the vital air;
If Sylvia smiles, new glories gild the shore,
And vanquish'd Nature seems to charm no
more.

STREPHON.

In spring the fields, in autumn hills I love,
At morn the plains, at noon the shady
grove,
But Delia always; absent from her sight,
Nor plains at morn, nor groves at noon
delight. 80

DAPHNIS.

Sylvia 's like autumn ripe, yet mild as May,
More bright than noon, yet fresh as early
day:
Ev'n spring displeases, when she shines not
here,
But bless'd with her, 't is spring throughout
the year.

STREPHON.

Say, Daphnis, say, in what glad soil appears
A wondrous tree, that sacred monarchs
bears?
Tell me but this, and I 'll disclaim the
prize,
And give the conquest to thy Sylvia's
eyes.

DAPHNIS.

Nay, tell me first, in what more happy fields
The thistle springs, to which the lily yields:
And then a nobler prize I will resign; 91
For Sylvia, charming Sylvia, shall be thine.

DAMON.

Cease to contend; for, Daphnis, I decree
The bowl to Strephon, and the lamb to
thee.
Blest swains, whose nymphs in ev'ry grace
excel;
Blest nymphs, whose swains those graces
sing so well!
Now rise, and haste to yonder woodbine
bowers,
A soft retreat from sudden vernal showers.

The turf with rural dainties shall be
    crown'd,
While opening blooms diffuse their sweets
    around.   100
For see ! the gath'ring flocks to shelter
    tend,
And from the Pleiads fruitful showers de-
    scend.

II

SUMMER; OR, ALEXIS

TO DR. GARTH

A SHEPHERD'S boy (he seeks no better
    name)
Led forth his flocks along the silver
    Thame,
Where dancing sunbeams on the waters
    play'd
And verdant alders form'd a quiv'ring
    shade.
Soft as he mourn'd, the streams forgot to
    flow,
The flocks around a dumb compassion
    show,
The Naïads wept in ev'ry wat'ry bower,
And Jove consented in a silent shower.
    Accept, O *Garth !* the Muse's early lays,
That adds this wreath of ivy to thy bays;
Hear what from love unpractis'd hearts
    endure,   11
From love, the sole disease thou canst not
    cure.
    Ye shady beeches, and ye cooling
        streams,
Defence from Phœbus', not from Cupid's
    beams,
To you I mourn ; nor to the deaf I sing :
The woods shall answer, and their echo
    ring.
The hills and rocks attend my doleful
    lay,
Why art thou prouder and more hard than
    they ?
The bleating sheep with my complaints
    agree,
They parch'd with heat, and I inflamed by
    thee.   20
The sultry Sirius burns the thirsty plains,
While in thy heart eternal Winter reigns.
    Where stray ye, Muses ! in what lawn or
        grove,
While your Alexis pines in hopeless love ?

In those fair fields where sacred Isis
    glides,
Or else where Cam his winding vales di-
    vides ?
As in the crystal spring I view my face,
Fresh rising blushes paint the wat'ry glass;
But since those graces please thy eyes no
    more,
I shun the fountains which I sought be-
    fore.   30
Once I was skill'd in ev'ry herb that grew,
And ev'ry plant that drinks the morning
    dew;
Ah, wretched shepherd, what avails thy art,
To cure thy lambs, but not to heal thy
    heart !
    Let other swains attend the rural care,
Feed fairer flocks, or richer fleeces shear :
But nigh yon mountain let me tune my
    lays,
Embrace my love, and bind my brows with
    bays.
That flute is mine which Colin's tuneful
    breath
Inspired when living, and bequeath'd in
    death :   40
He said, ' Alexis, take this pipe, the same
That taught the groves my Rosalinda's
    name.'
But now the reeds shall hang on yonder
    tree,
Forever silent, since despised by thee.
Oh ! were I made by some transforming
    power
The captive bird that sings within thy
    bower !
Then might my voice thy list'ning ears
    employ,
And I those kisses he receives enjoy.
    And yet my numbers please the rural
        throng,
Rough satyrs dance, and Pan applauds the
    song ;   50
The nymphs, forsaking ev'ry cave and
    spring,
Their early fruit and milk-white turtles
    bring ;
Each am'rous nymph prefers her gifts in
    vain,
On you their gifts are all bestow'd again.
For you the swains the fairest flowers de-
    sign,
And in one garland all their beauties join ;
Accept the wreath which you deserve alone,
In whom all beauties are comprised in one.

See what delights in sylvan scenes ap-
pear ! 59
Descending Gods have found Elysium here.
In woods bright Venus with Adonis stray'd,
And chaste Diana haunts the forest-shade.
Come, lovely nymph, and bless the silent
hours,
When swains from shearing seek their
nightly bowers ;
When weary reapers quit the sultry field,
And, crown'd with corn, their thanks to
Ceres yield.
This harmless grove no lurking viper hides,
But in my breast the serpent Love abides.
Here bees from blossoms sip the rosy dew,
But your Alexis knows no sweets but you.
O deign to visit our forsaken seats, 71
The mossy fountains, and the green re-
treats !
Where'er you walk, cool gales shall fan the
glade ;
Trees, where you sit, shall crowd into a
shade ;
Where'er you tread, the blushing flowers
shall rise,
And all things flourish where you turn
your eyes.
O ! how I long with you to pass my days,
Invoke the Muses, and resound your
praise !
Your praise the birds shall chant in ev'ry
grove,
And winds shall waft it to the powers
above. 80
But would you sing, and rival Orpheus'
strain,
The wond'ring forests soon should dance
again ;
The moving mountains hear the powerful
call,
And headlong streams hang list'ning in their
fall !
But see, the shepherds shun the noonday
heat,
The lowing herds to murmuring brooks
retreat,
To closer shades the panting flocks re-
move :
Ye Gods ! and is there no relief for love ?
But soon the sun with milder rays de-
scends
To the cool ocean, where his journey
ends. 90
On me Love's fiercer flames forever prey,
By night he scorches, as he burns by day.

III

AUTUMN; OR, HYLAS AND
ÆGON

TO MR. WYCHERLEY

BENEATH the shade a spreading beech dis-
plays,
Hylas and Ægon sung their rural lays ;
This mourn'd a faithless, that an absent
love,
And Delia's name and Doris' fill'd the
grove.
Ye Mantuan Nymphs, your sacred succour
bring,
Hylas and Ægon's rural lays I sing.
Thou, whom the Nine with Plautus' wit
inspire,
The art of Terence, and Menander's fire ;
Whose sense instructs us, and whose hu-
mour charms,
Whose judgment sways us, and whose
spirit warms ! 10
O, skill'd in Nature ! see the hearts of
swains,
Their artless passions, and their tender
pains.
Now setting Phœbus shone serenely
bright,
And fleecy clouds were streak'd with purple
light ;
When tuneful Hylas, with melodious moan,
Taught rocks to weep, and made the moun-
tains groan.
Go, gentle gales, and bear my sighs
away !
To Delia's ear the tender notes convey.
As some sad turtle his lost love deplores,
And with deep murmurs fills the sounding
shores ; 20
Thus, far from Delia, to the winds I
mourn,
Alike unheard, unpitied, and forlorn.
Go, gentle gales, and bear my sighs
along !
For her, the feather'd quires neglect their
song ;
For her, the limes their pleasing shades
deny ;
For her, the lilies hang their heads and die.
Ye flowers that droop, forsaken by the
spring,
Ye birds that, left by Summer, cease to
sing,

Ye trees, that fade when Autumn-heats re-
  move,
Say, is not absence death to those who
  love ?   30
Go, gentle gales, and bear my sighs
  away !
Curs'd be the fields that cause my Delia's
  stay !
Fade ev'ry blossom, wither ev'ry tree,
Die ev'ry flower, and perish all but she !
What have I said ? Where'er my Delia
  flies,
Let Spring attend, and sudden flowers
  arise !
Let op'ning roses knotted oaks adorn,
And liquid amber drop from ev'ry thorn !
Go, gentle gales, and bear my sighs
  along !
The birds shall cease to tune their ev'ning
  song,   40
The winds to breathe, the waving woods
  to move,
And streams to murmur, ere I cease to
  love.
Not bubbling fountains to the thirsty swain,
Not balmy sleep to lab'rers faint with pain,
Not showers to larks, nor sunshine to the
  bee,
Are half so charming as thy sight to me.
Go, gentle gales, and bear my sighs
  away !
Come, Delia, come ; ah, why this long de-
  lay ?
Thro' rocks and caves the name of Delia
  sounds,
Delia, each cave and echoing rock re-
  bounds.   50
Ye Powers, what pleasing frenzy soothes
  my mind !
Do lovers dream, or is my Delia kind ?
She comes, my Delia comes ! — Now cease,
  my lay,
And cease, ye gales, to bear my sighs
  away !
  Next Ægon sung, while Windsor groves
  admired :
Rehearse, ye Muses, what yourselves in-
  spired.
Resound, ye hills, resound my mournful
  strain !
Of perjur'd Doris dying I complain :
Here where the mountains, less'ning as
  they rise,
Lose the low vales, and steal into the
  skies :   60

While lab'ring oxen, spent with toil and
  heat,
In their loose traces from the field retreat:
While curling smokes from village-tops
  are seen,
And the fleet shades glide o'er the dusky
  green.
Resound, ye hills, resound my mournful
  lay !
Beneath yon poplar oft we pass'd the day :
Oft on the rind I carv'd her am'rous
  vows,
While she with garlands hung the bending
  boughs :
The garlands fade, the vows are worn
  away ;
So dies her love, and so my hopes decay.
Resound, ye hills, resound my mournful
  strain !   71
Now bright Arcturus glads the teeming
  grain,
Now golden fruits on loaded branches
  shine,
And grateful clusters swell with floods of
  wine ;
Now blushing berries paint the yellow
  grove :
Just Gods ! shall all things yield returns
  but love ?
Resound, ye hills, resound my mournful
  lay !
The shepherds cry, 'Thy flocks are left a
  prey ' —
Ah ! what avails it me the flocks to keep,
Who lost my heart while I preserv'd my
  sheep !   80
Pan came, and ask'd, ' What magic caus'd
  my smart,
Or what ill eyes malignant glances dart ?'
What eyes but hers, alas, have power to
  move !
And is there magic but what dwells in
  love ?
Resound, ye hills, resound my mournful
  strains !
I 'll fly from shepherds, flocks, and flow'ry
  plains ;
From shepherds, flocks, and plains, I may
  remove,
Forsake mankind, and all the world — but
  Love !
I know thee, Love ! on foreign mountains
  bred,
Wolves gave thee suck, and savage tigers
  fed.   90

Thou wert from Ætna's burning entrails
   torn,
Got by fierce whirlwinds, and in thunder
   born !
   Resound, ye hills, resound my mournful
      lay !
Farewell, ye woods ; adieu the light of
   day !
One leap from yonder cliff shall end my
   pains,
No more, ye hills, no more resound my
   strains !
   Thus sung the shepherds till th' approach
      of night,
The skies yet blushing with departing
   light,
When fallen dews with spangles deck'd the
   glade,
And the low sun had lengthen'd ev'ry
   shade.   100

IV

WINTER ; OR, DAPHNE

TO THE MEMORY OF MRS. TEMPEST

LYCIDAS.

THYRSIS ! the music of that murm'ring
   spring
Is not so mournful as the strains you sing ;
Nor rivers winding thro' the vales below
So sweetly warble, or so smoothly flow.
Now sleeping flocks on their soft fleeces
   lie,
The moon, serene in glory, mounts the
   sky ;
While silent birds forget their tuneful
   lays,
O sing of Daphne's fate, and Daphne's
   praise !

THYRSIS.

Behold the groves that shine with silver
   frost,
Their beauty wither'd, and their verdure
   lost.   10
Here shall I try the sweet Alexis' strain,
That call'd the list'ning Dryads to the
   plain ?
Thames heard the numbers as he flow'd
   along,
And bade his willows learn the moving
   song.

LYCIDAS.

So may kind rains their vital moisture
   yield,
And swell the future harvest of the field.
Begin : this charge the dying Daphne gave,
And said, ' Ye shepherds, sing around my
   grave ! '
Sing, while beside the shaded tomb I
   mourn,
And with fresh bays her rural shrine
   adorn.   20

THYRSIS.

Ye gentle Muses, leave your crystal spring,
Let Nymphs and Sylvans cypress garlands
   bring :
Ye weeping Loves, the stream with myrtles
   hide,
And break your bows, as when Adonis
   died !
And with your golden darts, now useless
   grown,
Inscribe a verse on this relenting stone :
' Let Nature change, let Heav'n and Earth
   deplore,
Fair Daphne's dead, and Love is now no
   more ! '
   'T is done ; and Nature's various charms
      decay,
See gloomy clouds obscure the cheerful
   day !   30
Now hung with pearls the dropping trees
   appear,
Their faded honours scatter'd on her bier.
See, where on earth the flow'ry glories lie,
With her they flourish'd, and with her they
   die.
Ah, what avail the beauties Nature wore ?
Fair Daphne's dead, and Beauty is no
   more !
   For her the flocks refuse their verdant
      food,
The thirsty heifers shun the gliding flood;
The silver swans her hapless fate bemoan,
In notes more sad than when they sing
   their own ;   40
In hollow caves sweet Echo silent lies,
Silent, or only to her name replies ;
Her name with pleasure once she taught
   the shore ;
Now Daphne's dead, and Pleasure is no
   more !
   No grateful dews descend from ev'ning
      skies,
Nor morning odours from the flowers arise;

No rich perfumes refresh the fruitful field,
Nor fragrant herbs their native incense
  yield.
The balmy zephyrs, silent since her death,
Lament the ceasing of a sweeter breath ; 50
Th' industrious bees neglect their golden
  store :
Fair Daphne 's dead, and sweetness is no
  more !
  No more the mountain larks, while
    Daphne sings,
Shall, list'ning in mid-air, suspend their
  wings ;
No more the birds shall imitate her lays,
Or, hush'd with wonder, hearken from the
  sprays ;
No more the streams their murmurs shall
  forbear,
A sweeter music than their own to hear ;
But tell the reeds, and tell the vocal shore,
Fair Daphne 's dead, and music is no
  more !   60
Her fate is whisper'd by the gentle breeze,
And told in sighs to all the trembling
  trees ;
The trembling trees, in every plain and
  wood,
Her fate remurmur to the silver flood ;
The silver flood, so lately calm, appears
Swell'd with new passion, and o'erflows
  with tears ;
The winds and trees and floods her death
  deplore,
Daphne, our Grief, our Glory now no more !
  But see ! where Daphne wond'ring
    mounts on high
Above the clouds, above the starry sky ! 70
Eternal beauties grace the shining scene,

Fields ever fresh, and groves for ever
  green !
There while you rest in amaranthine bowers,
Or from those meads select unfading
  flowers,
Behold us kindly, who your name implore,
Daphne, our Goddess, and our Grief no
  more !

LYCIDAS.

How all things listen, while thy Muse com-
  plains !
Such silence waits on Philomela's strains,
In some still ev'ning, when the whisp'ring
  breeze
Pants on the leaves, and dies upon the
  trees.   80
To thee, bright Goddess, oft a lamb shall
  bleed,
If teeming ewes increase my fleecy breed.
While plants their shade, or flowers their
  odours give,
Thy name, thy honour, and thy praise shall
  live !

THYRSIS.

But see, Orion sheds unwholesome dews ;
Arise, the pines a noxious shade diffuse ;
Sharp Boreas blows, and Nature feels de-
  cay,
Time conquers all, and we must Time obey.
Adieu, ye vales, ye mountains, streams, and
  groves ;
Adieu, ye shepherds' rural lays and loves ;
Adieu, my flocks ; farewell, ye sylvan
  crew ;   91
Daphne, farewell ; and all the world adieu !

WINDSOR FOREST

TO THE

RIGHT HON. GEORGE LORD LANSDOWN

Non injussa cano : —— te nostræ, *Vare*, myricæ,
Te Nemus omne canet : nec Phœbo gratior ulla est,
Quam sibi quæ *Vari* præscripsit pagina nomen.
VIRG. *Ecl.* vi. 10–12.

'This poem,' says Pope, 'was written at two different times: the first part of it, which relates to the country, in 1704, at the same time with the *Pastorals;* the latter part was not added till the year 1713, in which it was published.' The first 289 lines belong to the earlier date. The rest of the poem, with its celebration of the Peace of Utrecht, was added at the instance of Lord Lansdown, the Gran-

ville of the opening lines. The aim was obviously that Pope should do for the peaceful triumph of Utrecht what Addison had done for Marlborough's victory at Blenheim in 1704. It is printed here because the conclusion was an afterthought, and in spite of it the poem as a whole ' substantially belongs,' as Courthope remarks, ' to the Pastoral period.' Pope ranked it among his ' juvenile poems.'

THY forest, Windsor ! and thy green retreats,
At once the Monarch's and the Muse's seats,
Invite my lays. Be present, Sylvan Maids !
Unlock your springs, and open all your shades.
Granville commands : your aid, O Muses, bring !
What muse for *Granville* can refuse to sing ?
The groves of Eden, vanish'd now so long,
Live in description, and look green in song :
These, were my breast inspired with equal flame,
Like them in Beauty, should be like in Fame.   10
Here hills and vales, the woodland and the plain,
Here earth and water seem to strive again;
Not chaos - like together crush'd and bruis'd,
But, as the world, harmoniously confused:
Where order in variety we see,
And where, tho' all things differ, all agree.
Here waving groves a chequer'd scene display,
And part admit, and part exclude the day;
As some coy nymph her lover's warm address
Nor quite indulges, nor can quite repress.
There, interspers'd in lawns and opening glades,   21
Thin trees arise that shun each other's shades.

Here in full light the russet plains extend :
There wrapt in clouds the bluish hills ascend.
Ev'n the wild heath displays her purple dyes,
And 'midst the desert fruitful fields arise,
That crown'd with tufted trees and springing corn,
Like verdant isles, the sable waste adorn.
Let India boast her plants, nor envy we
The weeping amber or the balmy tree,   30
While by our oaks the precious loads are borne,
And realms commanded which those trees adorn.
Not proud Olympus yields a nobler sight,
Tho' Gods assembled grace his tow'ring height,
Than what more humble mountains offer here,
Where, in their blessings, all those Gods appear.
See Pan with flocks, with fruits Pomona crown'd,
Here blushing Flora paints th' enamell'd ground,
Here Ceres' gifts in waving prospect stand,
And nodding tempt the joyful reaper's hand ;   40
Rich Industry sits smiling on the plains,
And peace and plenty tell, a Stuart reigns.
Not thus the land appear'd in ages past,
A dreary desert, and a gloomy waste,
To savage beasts and savage laws a prey,
And Kings more furious and severe than they;

Who claim'd the skies, dispeopled air and
floods,
The lonely lords of empty wilds and woods:
Cities laid waste, they storm'd the dens
and caves
(For wiser brutes were backward to be
slaves); 50
What could be free, when lawless beasts
obey'd,
And ev'n the elements a Tyrant sway'd ?
In vain kind seasons swell'd the teeming
grain,
Soft showers distill'd, and suns grew warm
in vain :
The swain with tears his frustrate labour
yields,
And famish'd dies amidst his ripen'd fields.
What wonder then, a beast or subject slain
Were equal crimes in a despotic reign ?
Both doom'd alike, for sportive tyrants
bled,
But while the subject starv'd, the beast
was fed. 60
Proud Nimrod first the bloody chase began,
A mighty hunter, and his prey was man :
Our haughty Norman boasts that barb'rous
name,
And makes his trembling slaves the royal
game.
The fields are ravish'd from th' industrious
swains,
From men their cities, and from Gods their
fanes ;
The levell'd towns with weeds lie cover'd
o'er ;
The hollow winds thro' naked temples
roar ; 68
Round broken columns clasping ivy twin'd;
O'er heaps of ruin stalk'd the stately hind ;
The fox obscene to gaping tombs retires,
And savage howlings fill the sacred quires.
Aw'd by his nobles, by his commons curst,
Th' Oppressor ruled tyrannic where he durst,
Stretch'd o'er the poor and church his iron
rod,
And serv'd alike his vassals and his God.
Whom ev'n the Saxon spar'd, and bloody
Dane,
The wanton victims of his sport remain.
But see, the man who spacious regions gave
A waste for beasts, himself denied a
grave ! 80
Stretch'd on the lawn his second hope sur-
vey,
At once the chaser, and at once the prey !

Lo Rufus, tugging at the deadly dart,
Bleeds in the forest like a wounded hart !
Succeeding monarchs heard the subjects'
cries,
Nor saw displeas'd the peaceful cottage
rise :
Then gath'ring flocks on unknown moun-
tains fed,
O'er sandy wilds were yellow harvests
spread,
The forest wonder'd at th' unusual grain,
And secret transports touch'd the conscious
swain. 90
Fair Liberty, Britannia's Goddess, rears
Her cheerful head, and leads the golden
years.
Ye vig'rous Swains ! while youth fer-
ments your blood,
And purer spirits swell the sprightly flood,
Now range the hills, the gameful woods
beset,
Wind the shrill horn, or spread the waving
net.
When milder Autumn Summer's heat suc-
ceeds,
And in the new-shorn field the partridge
feeds,
Before his lord the ready spaniel bounds,
Panting with hope, he tries the furrow'd
grounds ; 100
But when the tainted gales the game be-
tray,
Couch'd close he lies, and meditates the
prey ;
Secure they trust th' unfaithful field beset,
Till hov'ring o'er them sweeps the swelling
net.
Thus (if small things we may with great
compare)
When Albion sends her eager sons to war,
Some thoughtless town, with ease and
plenty blest,
Near, and more near, the closing lines in-
vest ;
Sudden they seize th' amaz'd, defenceless
prize,
And high in air Britannia's standard flies.
See ! from the brake the whirring pheas-
ant springs, 111
And mounts exulting on triumphant wings :
Short is his joy ; he feels the fiery wound,
Flutters in blood, and panting beats the
ground.
Ah ! what avail his glossy, varying dyes,
His purple crest, and scarlet-circled eyes,

The vivid green his shining plumes un-
fold,
His painted wings, and breast that flames
with gold ?
Nor yet, when moist Arcturus clouds the
sky,
The woods and fields their pleasing toils
deny.   120
To plains with well-breathed beagles we
repair,
And trace the mazes of the circling hare
(Beasts, urged by us, their fellow beasts
pursue,
And learn of man each other to undo).
With slaught'ring guns th' unwearied
fowler roves,
When frosts have whiten'd all the naked
groves,
Where doves in flocks the leafless trees o'er-
shade,
And lonely woodcocks haunt the wat'ry
glade.
He lifts the tube, and levels with his eye ;
Straight a short thunder breaks the frozen
sky :   130
Oft, as in airy rings they skim the heath,
The clam'rous lapwings feel the leaden
death ;
Oft, as the mounting larks their notes pre-
pare,
They fall, and leave their little lives in
air.
In genial Spring, beneath the quiv'ring
shade,
Where cooling vapours breathe along the
mead,
The patient fisher takes his silent stand,
Intent, his angle trembling in his hand:
With looks unmov'd, he hopes the scaly
breed,
And eyes the dancing cork and bending
reed.   140
Our plenteous streams a various race sup-
ply,
The bright-eyed perch with fins of Tyrian
dye,
The silver eel, in shining volumes roll'd,
The yellow carp, in scales bedropp'd with
gold,
Swift trouts, diversified with crimson
stains,
And pikes, the tyrants of the wat'ry plains.
Now Cancer glows with Phœbus' fiery
car :
The youth rush eager to the sylvan war,

Swarm o'er the lawns, the forest walks
surround,
Rouse the fleet hart, and cheer the opening
hound.   150
Th' impatient courser pants in every vein,
And, pawing, seems to beat the distant
plain :
Hills, vales, and floods appear already
cross'd,
And ere he starts, a thousand steps are
lost.
See the bold youth strain up the threat-
'ning steep,
Rush thro' the thickets, down the valleys
sweep,
Hang o'er their coursers' heads with eager
speed,
And earth rolls back beneath the flying
steed.
Let old Arcadia boast her ample plain,
Th' immortal huntress, and her virgin
train ;   160
Nor envy, Windsor ! since thy shades have
seen
As bright a Goddess, and as chaste a
Queen ;
Whose care, like hers, protects the sylvan
reign,
The earth's fair light, and Empress of the
Main.
Here too, 't is sung, of old Diana stray'd,
And Cynthus' top forsook for Windsor
shade ;
Here was she seen o'er airy wastes to rove,
Seek the clear spring, or haunt the path-
less grove ;
Here arm'd with silver bows, in early
dawn,
Her buskin'd virgins traced the dewy
lawn.   170
Above the rest a rural nymph was famed,
Thy offspring, Thames ! the fair Lodona
named
(Lodona's fate, in long oblivion cast,
The Muse shall sing, and what she sings
shall last).
Scarce could the Goddess from her nymph
be known
But by the crescent and the golden zone.
She scorn'd the praise of beauty, and the
care ;
A belt her waist, a fillet binds her hair ;
A painted quiver on her shoulder sounds,
And with her dart the flying deer she
wounds.   a

It chanced as, eager of the chase, the maid
Beyond the forest's verdant limits stray'd,
Pan saw and lov'd, and, burning with de-
    sire,
Pursued her flight ; her flight increas'd his
    fire.
Not half so swift the trembling doves can
    fly,
When the fierce eagle cleaves the liquid
    sky ;
Not half so swiftly the fierce eagle moves,
When thro' the clouds he drives the trem-
    bling doves :
As from the God she flew with furious
    pace,
Or as the God, more furious, urged the
    chase.   190
Now fainting, sinking, pale, the Nymph
    appears ;
Now close behind, his sounding steps she
    hears ;
And now his shadow reach'd her as she
    run,
His shadow lengthen'd by the setting sun ;
And now his shorter breath, with sultry air,
Pants on her neck, and fans her parting
    hair.
In vain on Father Thames she calls for aid,
Nor could Diana help her injur'd maid.
Faint, breathless, thus she pray'd, nor
    pray'd in vain:
' Ah, Cynthia ! ah — tho' banish'd from thy
    train,   200
Let me, O let me, to the shades repair,
My native shades — there weep, and mur-
    mur there ! '
She said, and melting as in tears she lay,
In a soft silver stream dissolv'd away.
The silver stream her virgin coldness
    keeps,
For ever murmurs, and for ever weeps;
Still bears the name the hapless virgin
    bore,
And bathes the forest where she ranged
    before.
In her chaste current oft the Goddess
    laves,
And with celestial tears augments the
    waves.   210
Oft in her glass the musing shepherd spies
The headlong mountains and the downward
    skies ;
The wat'ry landscape of the pendent
    woods,
And absent trees that tremble in the floods :

In the clear azure gleam the flocks are
    seen,
And floating forests paint the waves with
    green ;
Thro' the fair scene roll slow the ling'ring
    streams,
Then foaming pour along, and rush into
    the Thames.
    Thou, too, great Father of the British
    Floods !
With joyful pride survey'st our lofty
    woods ;   220
Where tow'ring oaks their growing hon-
    ours rear,
And future navies on thy shores appear.
Not Neptune's self from all his streams re-
    ceives
A wealthier tribute than to thine he gives.
No seas so rich, so gay no banks appear,
No lake so gentle, and no spring so clear.
Nor Po so swells the fabling poet's lays,
While led along the skies his current
    strays,
As thine, which visits Windsor's famed
    abodes,
To grace the mansion of our earthly Gods :
Nor all his stars above a lustre show,   231
Like the bright beauties on thy banks be-
    low;
Where Jove, subdued by mortal passion
    still,
Might change Olympus for a nobler hill.
    Happy the man whom this bright court
    approves,
His Sov'reign favours, and his Country
    loves:
Happy next him, who to these shades re-
    tires,
Whom Nature charms, and whom the Muse
    inspires:
Whom humbler joys of home-felt quiet
    please,
Successive study, exercise, and ease.   240
He gathers health from herbs the forest
    yields,
And of their fragrant physic spoils the
    fields:
With chemic art exalts the mineral powers,
And draws the aromatic souls of flowers:
Now marks the course of rolling orbs on
    high;
O'er figured worlds now travels with his
    eye;
Of ancient writ unlocks the learned store,
Consults the dead, and lives past ages o'er:

Or wand'ring thoughtful in the silent wood,
Attends the duties of the wise and good, 250
T' observe a mean, be to himself a friend,
To follow Nature, and regard his end;
Or looks on Heav'n with more than mortal
      eyes,
Bids his free soul expatiate in the skies,
Amid her kindred stars familiar roam,
Survey the region, and confess her home!
Such was the life great Scipio once ad-
      mired: —
Thus Atticus, and *Trumbull* thus retired.
  Ye sacred Nine! that all my soul possess,
Whose raptures fire me, and whose visions
      bless,   260
Bear me, O bear me to sequester'd scenes,
The bowery mazes, and surrounding greens;
To Thames's banks, which fragrant breezes
      fill,
Or where ye Muses sport on Cooper's hill.
(On Cooper's hill eternal wreaths shall
      grow,
While lasts the mountain, or while Thames
      shall flow.)
I seem thro' consecrated walks to rove;
I hear soft music die along the grove:
Led by the sound, I roam from shade to
      shade,
By godlike Poets venerable made: 270
Here his first lays majestic Denham sung;
There the last numbers flow'd from Cow-
      ley's tongue.
Oh early lost! what tears the river shed,
When the sad pomp along his banks was
      led!
His drooping swans on every note expire,
And on his willows hung each Muse's lyre.
  Since Fate relentless stopp'd their heav-
      'nly voice,
No more the forests ring, or groves rejoice;
Who now shall charm the shades where
      Cowley strung
His living harp, and lofty Denham sung?
But hark! the groves rejoice, the forest
      rings!   281
Are these revived, or is it *Granville* sings?
'T is yours, my Lord, to bless our soft re-
      treats,
And call the Muses to their ancient seats;
To paint anew the flowery sylvan scenes,
To crown the forests with immortal greens,
Make Windsor-hills in lofty numbers rise,
And lift her turrets nearer to the skies;
To sing those honours you deserve to wear,
And add new lustre to her silver star! 290

  Here noble Surrey felt the sacred rage,
Surrey, the Granville of a former age:
Matchless his pen, victorious was his lance,
Bold in the lists, and graceful in the
      dance:
In the same shades the Cupids tuned his
      lyre,
To the same notes of love and soft desire;
Fair Geraldine, bright object of his vow,
Then fill'd the groves, as heav'nly *Mira*
      now.
  Oh wouldst thou sing what heroes Wind-
      sor bore,
What Kings first breathed upon her winding
      shore,   300
Or raise old warriors, whose ador'd remains
In weeping vaults her hallow'd earth con-
      tains!
With Edward's acts adorn the shining page,
Stretch his long triumphs down thro' every
      age,
Draw Monarchs chain'd, and Cressi's glori-
      ous field,
The lilies blazing on the regal shield:
Then, from her roofs when Verrio's colours
      fall,
And leave inanimate the naked wall,
Still in thy song should vanquish'd France
      appear,
And bleed for ever under Britain's spear. 310
Let softer strains ill-fated Henry mourn,
And palms eternal flourish round his urn.
Here o'er the martyr-king the marble
      weeps,
And, fast beside him, once-fear'd Edward
      sleeps,
Whom not th' extended Albion could con-
      tain,
From old Bellerium to the northern main;
The grave unites; where ev'n the great
      find rest,
And blended lie th' oppressor and th' op-
      prest!
  Make sacred Charles's tomb for ever
      known
(Obscure the place, and uninscribed the
      stone);   320
Oh fact accurs'd ! what tears has Albion
      shed,
Heav'ns! what new wounds! and how her
      old have bled!
She saw her sons with purple death expire,
Her sacred domes involv'd in rolling fire,
A dreadful series of intestine wars,
Inglorious triumphs, and dishonest scars.

At length great ANNA said, 'Let discord
    cease!'
She said! the world obey'd, and all was
    peace!
In that blest moment from his oozy bed
Old father Thames advanced his rev'rend
    head;   330
His tresses dropp'd with dews, and o'er the
    stream
His shining horns diffused a golden gleam:
Graved on his urn appear'd the moon, that
    guides
His swelling waters and alternate tides;
The figured streams in waves of silver
    roll'd,
And on her banks Augusta rose in gold.
Around his throne the sea-born brothers
    stood,
Who swell with tributary urns his flood: 338
First the famed authors of his ancient name;
The winding Isis, and the fruitful Thame;
The Kennet swift, for silver eels renown'd;
The Lodden slow, with verdant alders
    crown'd;
Cole, whose dark streams his flowery islands
    lave;
And chalky Wey, that rolls a milky wave:
The blue, transparent Vandalis appears;
The gulfy Lee his sedgy tresses rears;
And sullen Mole, that hides his diving
    flood;
And silent Darent, stain'd with Danish
    blood.
    High in the midst, upon his urn re-
    clin'd
(His sea-green mantle waving with the
    wind),   350
The God appear'd: he turn'd his azure
    eyes
Where Windsor-domes and pompous tur-
    rets rise;
Then bow'd and spoke; the winds forget to
    roar,
And the hush'd waves glide softly to the
    shore.
    'Hail, sacred Peace! hail, long-expected
    days,
That Thames's glory to the stars shall
    raise!
Tho' Tiber's streams immortal Rome be-
    hold,
Tho' foaming Hermus swells with tides of
    gold,
From Heav'n itself tho' sev'nfold Nilus
    flows,

And harvests on a hundred realms be-
    stows;
These now no more shall be the Muse's
    themes,   361
Lost in my fame, as in the sea their
    streams.
Let Volga's banks with iron squadrons
    shine,
And groves of lances glitter on the Rhine;
Let barb'rous Ganges arm a servile train,
Be mine the blessings of a peaceful reign.
No more my sons shall dye with British
    blood
Red Iber's sands, or Ister's foaming flood:
Safe on my shore each unmolested swain
Shall tend the flocks, or reap the bearded
    grain;   370
The shady empire shall retain no trace
Of war or blood, but in the sylvan chase;
The trumpet sleep, while cheerful horns are
    blown,
And arms employ'd on birds and beasts
    alone.
Behold! th' ascending villas on my side
Project long shadows o'er the crystal tide;
Behold! Augusta's glitt'ring spires in-
    crease,
And temples rise, the beauteous works of
    Peace.
I see, I see, where two fair cities bend
Their ample bow, a new Whitehall as-
    cend!
There mighty nations shall inquire their
    doom,   381
The world's great oracle in times to come;
There Kings shall sue, and suppliant states
    be seen
Once more to bend before a British Queen.
    'Thy trees, fair Windsor! now shall
    leave their woods,
And half thy forests rush into my floods,
Bear Britain's thunder, and her cross dis-
    play
To the bright regions of the rising day;
Tempt icy seas, where scarce the waters
    roll,
Where clearer flames glow round the
    frozen pole;   390
Or under southern skies exalt their sails,
Led by new stars, and borne by spicy
    gales!
For me the balm shall bleed, and amber
    flow,
The coral redden, and the ruby glow,
The pearly shell its lucid globe infold,

And Phœbus warm the ripening ore to
    gold.
The time shall come, when, free as seas or
    wind,
Unbounded Thames shall flow for all man-
    kind,
Whole nations enter with each swelling
    tide,
And seas but join the regions they divide;
Earth's distant ends our glory shall be-
    hold,   401
And the new world launch forth to seek the
    old.
Then ships of uncouth form shall stem the
    tide,
And feather'd people crowd my wealthy
    side;
And naked youths and painted chiefs ad-
    mire
Our speech, our colour, and our strange at-
    tire!
O stretch thy reign, fair Peace! from shore
    to shore,
Till conquest cease, and slavery be no
    more;
Till the freed Indians in their native groves
Reap their own fruits, and woo their sable
    loves;   410
Peru once more a race of kings behold,
And other Mexicos be roof'd with gold.
Exiled by thee from earth to deepest
    Hell,
In brazen bonds shall barb'rous Discord
    dwell:

Gigantic Pride, pale Terror, gloomy Care,
And mad Ambition shall attend her there:
There purple Vengeance, bathed in gore,
    retires,
Her weapons blunted, and extinct her fires:
There hated Envy her own snakes shall
    feel,
And Persecution mourn her broken wheel:
There Faction roar, Rebellion bite her
    chain,   421
And gasping Furies thirst for blood in
    vain.'
    Here cease thy flight, nor with unhal-
    low'd lays
Touch the fair fame of Albion's golden
    days:
The thoughts of Gods let *Granville's* verse
    recite,
And bring the scenes of opening fate to
    light.
My humble Muse, in unambitious strains,
Paints the green forests and the flowery
    plains,
Where Peace descending bids her olives
    spring,
And scatters blessings from her dovelike
    wing.   430
Ev'n I more sweetly pass my careless
    days,
Pleas'd in the silent shade with empty
    praise;
Enough for me that to the list'ning swains
First in these fields I sung the sylvan
    strains.

PARAPHRASES FROM CHAUCER

JANUARY AND MAY: OR, THE MERCHANT'S TALE

Pope says that this 'translation' was done at sixteen or seventeen years of age. It was first published, with the *Pastorals*, in 1709, in Tonson's sixth *Miscellany*. Eventually Pope grouped the Chaucer imitations with *Eloisa to Abelard*, the translations from Ovid and Statius and the brief *Imitations* of *English Poets*. To this collection be prefixed this Advertisement: —

'The following Translations were selected from many others done by the Author in his youth; for the most part indeed but a sort of Exercises, while he was improving himself in the Languages, and carried by his early bent to Poetry to perform them rather in Verse than Prose. Mr. Dryden's *Fables* came out about that time, which occasioned the Translations from *Chaucer*. They were first separately printed in Miscellanies by J. Tonson and B. Lintot, and afterwards collected in the Quarto Edition of 1717. The *Imitations of English Authors*, which are added at the end, were done as early, some of them at fourteen or fifteen years old; but having also got into Miscellanies, we have put them here together to complete this Juvenile Volume.'

Warburton asserts that Pope did not intend to include this group of poems in the final edition of his works.

THERE liv'd in Lombardy, as authors write,
In days of old, a wise and worthy Knight;
Of gentle manners, as of gen'rous race,
Blest with much sense, more riches, and some grace :
Yet, led astray by Venus' soft delights,
He scarce could rule some idle appetites:
For long ago, let priests say what they could,
Weak sinful laymen were but flesh and blood.
But in due time, when sixty years were o'er, 9
He vow'd to lead this vicious life no more ;
Whether pure holiness inspired his mind,
Or dotage turn'd his brain, is hard to find ;
But his high courage prick'd him forth to wed,
And try the pleasures of a lawful bed.

This was his nightly dream, his daily care
And to the heav'nly Powers his constan prayer,
Once, ere he died, to taste the blissful life
Of a kind husband and a loving wife.
These thoughts he fortified with reason still
(For none want reasons to confirm their will). 20
Grave authors say, and witty poets sing,
That honest wedlock is a glorious thing :
But depth of judgment most in him appears
Who wisely weds in his maturer years.
Then let him choose a damsel young and fair,
To bless his age, and bring a worthy heir;
To soothe his cares, and, free from noise and strife,
Conduct him gently to the verge of life.
Let sinful bachelors their woes deplore,
Full well they merit all they feel, ant more : 3
Unaw'd by precepts, human or divine,
Like birds and beasts, promiscuously they join ;
Nor know to make the present blessing last,
To hope the future, or esteem the past;
But vainly boast the joys they never tried,
And find divulged the secrets they would hide.
The married man may bear his yoke with ease,
Secure at once himself and Heav'n to please ;
And pass his inoffensive hours away,
In bliss all night, and innocence all day: 4
Tho' fortune change, his constant spouse remains,
Augments his joys, or mitigates his pains.
But what so pure which envious tongues will spare ?
Some wicked Wits have libell'd all the Fair.
With matchless impudence they style a wife
The dear-bought curse and lawful plague of life,
A bosom serpent, a domestic evil,
A night-invasion, and a midday-devil.

Let not the wise these sland'rous words re-
  gard,
But curse the bones of ev'ry lying bard.   50
All other goods by Fortune's hand are
  giv'n,
A wife is the peculiar gift of Heav'n.
Vain Fortune's favours, never at a stay,
Like empty shadows pass and glide away;
One solid comfort, our eternal wife,
Abundantly supplies us all our life:
This blessing lasts (if those who try say
  true)
As long as heart can wish — and longer
  too.
    Our grandsire Adam, ere of Eve pos-
  sess'd,
Alone, and ev'n in Paradise unbless'd,   60
With mournful looks the blissful scene
  survey'd,
And wander'd in the solitary shade.
The Maker saw, took pity, and bestow'd
Woman, the last, the best reserv'd of
  God.
A Wife ! ah gentle Deities ! can he
That has a wife e'er feel adversity ?
Would men but follow what the sex ad-
  vise,
All things would prosper, all the world
  grow wise.
'T was by Rebecca's aid that Jacob won
His father's blessing from an elder son: 70
Abusive Nabal ow'd his forfeit life
To the wise conduct of a prudent wife:
Heroic Judith, as old Hebrews show,
Preserv'd the Jews, and slew th' Assyrian
  foe:
At Hester's suit the persecuting sword
Was sheath'd, and Israel liv'd to bless the
  Lord.
    These weighty motives January the sage
Maturely ponder'd in his riper age ;
And charm'd with virtuous joys, and sober
  life,
Would try that Christian comfort call'd a
  wife.   80
His friends were summon'd on a point so
  nice
To pass their judgment, and to give ad-
  vice;
But fix'd before, and well resolv'd was he
(As men that ask advice are wont to be).
  'My friends,' he cried (and cast a
  mournful look
Around the room, and sigh'd before he
  spoke),

'Beneath the weight of threescore years I
  bend,
And, worn with cares, am hastening to my
  end.
How I have liv'd, alas ! you know too
  well —
In worldly follies which I blush to tell;   90
But gracious Heav'n has oped my eyes at
  last,
With due regret I view my vices past,
And, as the precept of the church decrees,
Will take a wife, and live in holy ease.
But since by counsel all things should be
  done,
And many heads are wiser still than one;
Choose you for me, who best shall be con-
  tent
When my desire 's approv'd by your con-
  sent.
  'One caution yet is needful to be told,
To guide your choice ; this wife must not
  be old :   100
There goes a saying, and 't was shrewdly
  said,
Old fish at table, but young flesh in bed.
My soul abhors the tasteless dry embrace
Of a stale virgin with a winter face :
In that cold season Love but treats his
  guest
With bean-straw, and tough forage at the
  best.
No crafty widows shall approach my bed;
Those are too wise for bachelors to wed.
As subtle clerks by many schools are made,
Twice married dames are mistresses o' th'
  trade: 110
But young and tender virgins, ruled with
  ease,
We form like wax, and mould them as we
  please.
  'Conceive me, Sirs, nor take my sense
  amiss;
'T is what concerns my soul's eternal bliss;
Since if I found no pleasure in my spouse,
As flesh is frail, and who (God help me)
  knows ?
Then should I live in lewd adultery,
And sink downright to Satan when I die:
Or were I curs'd with an unfruitful bed,
The righteous end were lost for which I
  wed;   120
To raise up seed to bless the Powers above,
And not for pleasure only, or for love.
Think not I dote ; 't is time to take a wife,
When vig'rous blood forbids a chaster life:

Those that are blest with store of grace
    divine,
May live like saints by Heav'n's consent
    and mine.
'And since I speak of wedlock, let me
    say,
(As, thank my stars, in modest truth I
    may)
My limbs are active, still I 'm sound at
    heart,
And a new vigour springs in ev'ry part. 130
Think not my virtue lost, tho' time has
    shed
These rev'rend honours on my hoary head:
Thus trees are crown'd with blossoms
    white as snow,
The vital sap then rising from below.
Old as I am, my lusty limbs appear
Like winter-greens, that flourish all the
    year.
Now, Sirs, you know to what I stand in-
    clin'd,
Let ev'ry friend with freedom speak his
    mind.'
    He said; the rest in diff'rent parts di-
    vide;
The knotty point was urged on either
    side: 140
Marriage, the theme on which they all
    declaim'd,
Some prais'd with wit, and some with rea-
    son blamed.
Till, what with proofs, objections, and re-
    plies,
Each wondrous positive and wondrous wise,
There fell between his brothers a debate:
Placebo this was call'd, and Justin that.
    First to the knight Placebo thus begun,
(Mild were his looks, and pleasing was his
    tone)
'Such prudence, Sir, in all your words ap-
    pears,
As plainly proves Experience dwells with
    years ! 150
Yet you pursue sage Solomon's advice,
To work by counsel when affairs are nice :
But, with the wise man's leave, I must
    protest,
So may my soul arrive at ease and rest,
As still I hold your own advice the best.
    'Sir, I have liv'd a courtier all my days,
And studied men, their manners, and their
    ways ;
And have observ'd this useful maxim still,
To let my betters always have their will.

'Nay, if my lord affirm'd that black was
    white, 160
My word was this, "Your Honour's in the
    right."
Th' assuming Wit, who deems himself so
    wise
As his mistaken patron to advise,
Let him not dare to vent his dangerous
    thought ;
A noble fool was never in a fault.
This, Sir, affects not you, whose ev'ry word
Is weigh'd with judgment, and befits a
    Lord :
Your will is mine ; and is (I will maintain)
Pleasing to God, and should be so to Man ;
At least your courage all the world must
    praise, 170
Who dare to wed in your declining days.
Indulge the vigour of your mounting
    blood,
And let gray fools be indolently good,
Who, past all pleasure, damn the joys of
    sense,
With rev'rend Dulness and grave Impo-
    tence.'
    Justin, who silent sate, and heard the
    man,
Thus with a philosophic frown began :
'A heathen author, of the first degree,
(Who, tho' not Faith, had Sense as well as
    we) 179
Bids us be certain our concerns to trust
To those of gen'rous principles and just.
The venture 's greater, I 'll presume to
    say,
To give your person, than your goods
    away :
And therefore, Sir, as you regard your
    rest,
First learn your lady's qualities at least :
Whether she 's chaste or rampant, proud or
    civil,
Meek as a saint, or haughty as the devil ;
Whether an easy, fond, familiar Fool,
Or such a Wit as no man e'er can rule.
'T is true, perfection none must hope to
    find 190
In all this world, much less in woman-
    kind;
But if her virtue prove the larger share,
Bless the kind Fates and think your fortune
    rare.
Ah, gentle Sir, take warning of a friend,
Who knows too well the state you thus
    commend :

And spite of all his praises must declare,
All he can find is bondage, cost, and care.
Heav'n knows I shed full many a private
    tear,
And sigh in silence lest the world should
    hear ;
While all my friends applaud my blissful
    life, 200
And swear no mortal 's happier in a wife :
Demure and chaste as any vestal nun,
The meekest creature that beholds the
    sun !
But by th' immortal Powers I feel the pain,
And he that smarts has reason to complain.
Do what you list, for me ; you must be
    sage,
And cautious sure ; for wisdom is in age :
But at these years to venture on the Fair !
By him who made the ocean, earth, and
    air, 209
To please a wife, when her occasions call,
Would busy the most vig'rous of us all.
And trust me, sir, the chastest you can
    choose,
Will ask observance, and exact her dues.
If what I speak my noble lord offend,
My tedious sermon here is at an end.'
   ' 'T is well, 't is wondrous well,' the
    Knight replies,
' Most worthy kinsman, faith, you 're
    mighty wise !
We, Sirs, are fools ; and must resign the
    cause
To heath'nish authors, proverbs, and old
    saws.'
He spoke with scorn, and turn'd another
    way : 220
   ' What does my friend, my dear Placebo,
    say ? '
' I say,' quoth he, ' by Heav'n the man 's
    to blame,
To slander wives, and wedlock's holy
    name.'
   At this the council rose without delay;
Each, in his own opinion, went his way;
With full consent, that, all disputes ap-
    peas'd,
The Knight should marry when and where
    he pleas'd.
   Who now but January exults with joy ?
The charms of wedlock all his soul employ :
Each nymph by turns his wavering mind
    possess'd, 230
And reign'd the short-lived tyrant of his
    breast :

Whilst fancy pictured ev'ry lively part,
And each bright image wander'd o'er his
    heart.
Thus, in some public forum fix'd on high,
A mirror shows the figures moving by;
Still one by one, in swift succession, pass
The gliding shadows o'er the polish'd
    glass.
This lady's charms the nicest could not
    blame,
But vile suspicions had aspers'd her fame;
That was with Sense, but not with Virtue
    blest ; 240
And one had Grace that wanted all the
    rest.
Thus doubting long what nymph he should
    obey,
He fix'd at last upon the youthful May.
Her faults he knew not (Love is always
    blind),
But every charm revolv'd within his mind:
Her tender age, her form divinely fair,
Her easy motion, her attractive air,
Her sweet behaviour, her enchanting face,
Her moving softness, and majestic grace.
   Much in his prudence did our Knight re-
    joice, 250
And thought no mortal could dispute his
    choice :
Once more in haste he summon'd ev'ry
    friend,
And told them all their pains were at an
    end.
' Heav'n, that (said he) inspired me first to
    wed,
Provides a consort worthy of my bed:
Let none oppose th' election, since on
    this
Depends my quiet and my future bliss.
   ' A dame there is, the darling of my
    eyes,
Young, beauteous, artless, innocent, and
    wise ;
Chaste, tho' not rich ; and, tho' not nobly
    born, 260
Of honest parents, and may serve my turn.
Her will I wed, if gracious Heav'n so
    please,
To pass my age in sanctity and ease ;
And thank the Powers, I may possess
    alone
The lovely prize, and share my bliss with
    none !
If you, my friends, this virgin can procure,
My joys are full, my happiness is sure.

'One only doubt remains : full oft, I've
  heard,
By casuists grave and deep divines averr'd,
That 't is too much for human race to know
The bliss of Heav'n above and earth be-
  low :   271
Now should the nuptial pleasures prove so
  great,
To match the blessings of the future state,
Those endless joys were ill exchanged for
  • these :
Then clear this doubt, and set my mind at
  ease.'
  This Justin heard, nor could his spleen
  control,
Touch'd to the quick, and tickled at the
  soul.
'Sir Knight,' he cried, 'if this be all you
  dread,
Heav'n put it past a doubt whene'er you
  wed;
And to my fervent prayers so far consent,
That, ere the rites are o'er, you may re-
  pent !   281
Good Heav'n, no doubt, the nuptial state
  approves,
Since it chastises still what best it loves.
  'Then be not, Sir, abandon'd to de- ⎫
  spair;   ⎪
Seek, and perhaps you 'll find among the ⎬
  Fair   ⎪
One that may do your business to a hair ; ⎭
Not ev'n in wish your happiness delay,
But prove the scourge to lash you on your
  way:
Then to the skies your mounting soul shall
  go,
Swift as an arrow soaring from the bow !
Provided still, you moderate your joy, 291
Nor in your pleasures all your might em-
  ploy :
Let Reason's rule your strong desires abate,
Nor please too lavishly your gentle mate.
Old wives there are, of judgment most
  acute,
Who solve these questions beyond all dis-
  pute ;
Consult with those, and be of better cheer ;
Marry, do penance, and dismiss your fear.'
  So said, they rose, nor more the work
  delay'd :
The match was offer'd, the proposals made.
The parents, you may think, would soon
  comply ;   301
The old have int'rest ever in their eye.

Nor was it hard to move the lady's mind ;
When Fortune favours, still the Fair are
  kind.
I pass each previous settlement and
  deed,
Too long for me to write, or you to read ;
Nor will with quaint impertinence display
The pomp, the pageantry, the proud array.
The time approach'd ; to church the par-
  ties went,
At once with carnal and devout intent :
Forth came the priest, and bade th' obedi-
  ent wife   311
Like Sarah or Rebecca lead her life ;
Then pray'd the Powers the fruitful bed to
  bless,
And make all sure enough with holiness.
  And now the palace gates are open'd ⎫
  wide,   ⎪
The guests appear in order, side by side, ⎬
And, placed in state, the bridegroom and ⎪
  the bride.   ⎭
The breathing flute's soft notes are heard
  around,
And the shrill trumpets mix their silver
  sound ;
The vaulted roofs with echoing music ring,
These touch the vocal stops, and those the
  trembling string.   321
Not thus Amphion tuned the warbling lyre,
Nor Joab the sounding clarion could in-
  spire,
Nor fierce Theodamas, whose sprightly
  strain
Could swell the soul to rage, and fire the
  martial train.
  Bacchus himself, the nuptial feast to
  grace,
(So poets sing) was present on the place :
And lovely Venus, Goddess of Delight, ⎫
Shook high her flaming torch in open ⎪
  sight,   ⎬
And danced around, and smiled on ev'ry ⎪
  Knight: 330 ⎭
Pleas'd her best servant would his courage
  try,
No less in wedlock than in liberty.
Full many an age old Hymen had not
  spied
So kind a bridegroom, or so bright a bride.
Ye Bards ! renown'd among the tuneful
  throng
For gentle lays, and joyous nuptial song,
Think not your softest numbers can display
The matchless glories of this blissful day ;

The joys are such as far transcend your
rage,
When tender youth has wedded stooping
age. 340
The beauteous dame sat smiling at the
board,
And darted am'rous glances at her lord.
Not Hester's self, whose charms the He-
brews sing,
E'er look'd so lovely on her Persian King :
Bright as the rising sun in summer's day,
And fresh and blooming as the month of
May!
The joyful knight survey'd her by his side,
Nor envied Paris with his Spartan bride:
Still as his mind revolv'd with vast delight
Th' entrancing raptures of th' approaching
night, 350
Restless he sat, invoking every Power
To speed his bliss, and haste the happy
hour.
Meantime the vig'rous dancers beat the
ground,
And songs were sung, and flowing bowls
went round.
With od'rous spices they perfumed the
place,
And mirth and pleasure shone in ev'ry face.
Damian alone, of all the menial train,
Sad in the midst of triumphs, sigh'd for
pain,
Damian alone, the Knight's obsequious
Squire, 359
Consumed at heart, and fed a secret fire.
His lovely mistress all his soul possess'd;
He look'd, he languish'd, and could take no
rest:
His task perform'd, he sadly went his way,
Fell on his bed, and loath'd the light of day:
There let him lie; till his relenting dame
Weep in her turn, and waste in equal
flame.
The weary sun, as learned poets write,
Forsook th' horizon, and roll'd down the
light;
While glitt'ring stars his absent beams
supply,
And night's dark mantle overspread the
sky. 370
Then rose the guests, and as the time re-
quired,
Each paid his thanks, and decently retired.
The foe once gone, our Knight prepared
t 'undress,
So keen he was, and eager to possess:

But first thought fit th' assistance to receive,
Which grave physicians scruple not to give:
Satyrion near, with hot eringoes stood,
Cantharides, to fire the lazy blood,
Whose use old Bards describe in luscious
rhymes,
And Critics learn'd explain to modern
times. 380
By this the sheets were spread, the bride
undress'd,
The room was sprinkled, and the bed was
bless'd.
What next ensued beseems not me to say;
'T is sung, he labour'd till the dawning day;
Then briskly sprung from bed, with heart ⎫
so light,   ⎪
As all were nothing he had done by night, ⎬
And sipp'd his cordial as he sat upright. ⎭
He kiss'd his balmy spouse with wanton
play,
And feebly sung a lusty roundelay: 389
Then on the couch his weary limbs he cast;
For ev'ry labour must have rest at last.
But anxious cares the pensive Squire op-
prest,
Sleep fled his eyes, and Peace forsook his
breast;
The raging flames that in his bosom dwell,
He wanted art to hide, and means to tell:
Yet hoping time th' occasion might betray,
Composed a sonnet to the lovely May;
Which, writ and folded with the nicest art,
He wrapt in silk, and laid upon his heart.
When now the fourth revolving day was
run, 400
('T was June, and Cancer had receiv'd the
sun)
Forth from her chamber came the beaute-
ous bride;
The good old Knight mov'd slowly by her
side.
High mass was sung; they feasted in the
hall;
The servants round stood ready at their
call.
The Squire alone was absent from the
board,
And much his sickness griev'd his worthy
lord,
Who pray'd his spouse, attended with her
train,
To visit Damian, and divert his pain.
Th' obliging dames obey'd with one con-
sent: 410
They left the hall, and to his lodging went.

The female tribe surround him as he lay,
And close beside him sat the gentle May:
Where, as she tried his pulse, he softly
   drew
A heaving sigh, and cast a mournful view!
Then gave his bill, and bribed the Powers
   divine,
With secret vows to favour his design.
  Who studies now but discontented May?
On her soft couch uneasily she lay:
The lumpish husband snored away the
   night,   420
Till coughs awaked him near the morning
   light.
What then he did, I 'll not presume to tell,
Nor if she thought herself in Heav'n or Hell:
Honest and dull in nuptial bed they lay,
Till the bell toll'd, and all arose to pray.
  Were it by forceful Destiny decreed,
Or did from Chance, or Nature's power
   proceed;
Or that some star, with aspect kind to love,
Shed its selectest influence from above; 429
Whatever was the cause, the tender dame
Felt the first motions of an infant flame;
Receiv'd th' impressions of the lovesick
   Squire,
And wasted in the soft infectious fire.
  Ye Fair, draw near, let May's example
   move
Your gentle minds to pity those who love!
Had some fierce tyrant in her stead been
   found,
The poor adorer sure had hang'd or
   drown'd:
But she, your sex's mirror, free from pride,
Was much too meek to prove a homicide.
  But to my tale: — Some sages have de-
   fin'd   440
Pleasure the sov'reign bliss of humankind:
Our Knight (who studied much, we may
   suppose)
Derived his high philosophy from those;
For, like a prince, he bore the vast expense
Of lavish pomp, and proud magnificence:
His house was stately, his retinue gay.
Large was his train, and gorgeous his array.
His spacious garden, made to yield to none,
Was compass'd round with walls of solid
   stone;
Priapus could not half describe the grace
(Tho' God of gardens) of this charming
   place: 451
A place to tire the rambling wits of France
In long descriptions, and exceed Romance:

Enough to shame the gentlest bard that
   sings
Of painted meadows, and of purling
   springs.
  Full in the centre of the flowery ground
A crystal fountain spread its streams
   around,
The fruitful banks with verdant laurels
   crown'd:
About this spring (if ancient Fame say
   true)
The dapper Elves their moonlight sports
   pursue: 460
Their pygmy King, and little fairy Queen,
In circling dances gambol'd on the green,
While tuneful sprites a merry concert
   made,
And airy music warbled thro' the shade.
  Hither the noble Knight would oft repair
(His scene of pleasure, and peculiar care);
For this he held it dear, and always bore
The silver key that lock'd the garden door.
To this sweet place in summer's sultry heat
He used from noise and bus'ness to re-
   treat;   470
And here in dalliance spend the livelong
   day,
Solus cum sola, with his sprightly May:
For whate'er work was undischarg'd abed,
The duteous Knight in this fair garden sped.
  But ah! what mortal lives of bliss se-
   cure?
How short a space our worldly joys endure!
O Fortune, fair, like all thy treach'rous
   kind,
But faithless still, and wav'ring as the
   wind!
O painted monster, form'd mankind to
   cheat,   479
With pleasing poison, and with soft deceit!
This rich, this am'rous, venerable Knight,
Amidst his ease, his solace, and delight,
Struck blind by thee, resigns his days to
   grief,
And calls on death, the wretch's last relief.
  The rage of jealousy then seiz'd his
   mind,
For much he fear'd the faith of woman-
   kind.
His wife, not suffer'd from his side to
   stray,
Was captive kept; he watch'd her night
   and day,
Abridg'd her pleasures, and confin'd her
   sway.   489

Full oft in tears did hapless May complain,
And sigh'd full oft; but sigh'd and wept in
vain;
She look'd on Damian with a lover's eye;
For oh, 't was fix'd; she must possess or
die:
Nor less impatience vex'd her am'rous
Squire,
Wild with delay, and burning with desire.
Watch'd as she was, yet could he not re-
frain
By secret writing to disclose his pain:
The dame by signs reveal'd her kind in-
tent,
Till both were conscious what each other
meant,
Ah! gentle Knight, what would thy eyes
avail, 500
Tho' they could see as far as ships can
sail?
'T is better, sure, when blind, deceiv'd to
be,
Than be deluded when a man can see!
Argus himself, so cautious and so wise,
Was overwatch'd, for all his hundred eyes:
So many an honest husband may, 't is
known,
Who, wisely, never thinks the case his own.
The dame at last, by diligence and care,
Procured the key her Knight was wont to
bear; 509
She took the wards in wax before the fire,
And gave th' impression to the trusty
Squire.
By means of this some wonder shall appear,
Which, in due place and season, you may
hear.
Well sung sweet Ovid, in the days of
yore,
What sleight is that which love will not
explore!
And Pyramus and Thisbe plainly show
The feats true lovers, when they list, can
do:
Tho' watch'd and captive, yet in spite of
all,
They found the art of kissing thro' a wall.
But now no longer from our tale to ⎤
stray, 520 ⎥
It happ'd, that once upon a summer's day ⎬
Our rev'rend Knight was urged to am'- ⎥
rous play: ⎦
He rais'd his spouse ere matin-bell was
rung,
And thus his morning canticle he sung:

'Awake, my love, disclose thy radiant
eyes;
Arise, my wife, my beauteous lady, rise!
Hear how the doves with pensive notes
complain,
And in soft murmurs tell the trees their
pain:
The winter's past; the clouds and tempests
fly;
The sun adorns the fields, and brightens all
the sky. 530
Fair without spot, whose ev'ry charming
part
My bosom wounds, and captivates my
heart!
Come, and in mutual pleasures let's en-
gage,
Joy of my life, and comfort of my age.'
This heard, to Damian straight a sign
she made
To haste before; the gentle Squire obey'd:
Secret and undescried he took his way,
And ambush'd close behind an arbour lay.
It was not long ere January came,
And hand in hand with him his lovely
dame; 540
Blind as he was, not doubting all was
sure,
He turn'd the key, and made the gate se-
cure.
'Here let us walk,' he said, 'observ'd
by none,
Conscious of pleasures to the world un-
known:
So may my soul have joy, as thou, my
wife,
Art far the dearest solace of my life;
And rather would I choose, by Heav'n
above,
To die this instant, than to lose thy love.
Reflect what truth was in my passion ⎤
shown, ⎥
When, unendow'd, I took thee for my ⎬
own, 550 ⎥
And sought no treasure but thy heart ⎦
alone.
Old as I am, and now deprived of sight, ⎤
Whilst thou art faithful to thy own true ⎥
Knight, ⎬
Nor age, nor blindness, robs me of de- ⎥
light. ⎦
Each other loss with patience I can bear,
The loss of thee is what I only fear.
'Consider then, my lady and my wife,
The solid comforts of a virtuous life.

As first, the love of Christ himself you
 gain;   559
Next, your own honour undefiled maintain;
And, lastly, that which sure your mind
 must move,
My whole estate shall gratify your love:
Make your own terms, and ere to-morrow's
 sun
Displays his light, by Heav'n it shall be done
I seal the contract with a holy kiss,
And will perform — by this, my dear, and
 this.
Have comfort, Spouse, nor think thy lord
 unkind ;
'T is love, not jealousy, that fires my mind:
For when thy charms my sober thoughts
 engage,   569
And join'd to them my own unequal age,
From thy dear side I have no power to
 part,
Such secret transports warm my melting
 heart.
For who that once possess'd those heav'nly
 charms,
Could live one moment absent from thy
 arms ? '
 He ceas'd, and May with modest grace
 replied
(Weak was her voice, as while she spoke
 she cried):
' Heav'n knows (with that a tender sigh
 she drew)
I have a soul to save as well as you;
And, what no less you to my charge com-
 mend,   579
My dearest honour, will to death defend.
To you in holy church I gave my hand,
And join'd my heart in wedlock's sacred
 band:
Yet after this, if you distrust my care,
Then hear, my lord, and witness what I
 swear:
 First may the yawning earth her bosom
 rend,
And let me hence to Hell alive descend;
Or die the death I dread no less than Hell,
Sew'd in a sack, and plunged into a well;
Ere I my fame by one lewd act disgrace,
Or once renounce the honour of my race.
For know, Sir Knight, of gentle blood I
 came;   591
I loathe a whore, and startle at the name.
But jealous men on their own crimes reflect,
And learn from thence their ladies to sus-
 pect :

Else why these needless cautions, Sir, to me ?
These doubts and fears of female con-
 stancy ?
This chime still rings in every lady's ear,
The only strain a wife must hope to hear.'
 Thus while she spoke a sidelong glance
 she cast,
Where Damain kneeling worship'd as she
 past.   600
She saw him watch the motions of her eye,
And singled out a pear tree planted nigh:
'T was charged with fruit that made a
 goodly show,
And hung with dangling pears was every
 bough.
Thither th' obsequious Squire address'd his
 pace,
And climbing, in the summit took his
 place;
The Knight and Lady walk'd beneath in
 view,
Where let us leave them, and our tale
 pursue.
 'T was now the season when the glorious
 sun
His heav'nly progress through the Twins
 had run;   610
And Jove, exalted, his mild influence
 yields,
To glad the glebe, and paint the flowery
 fields:
Clear was the day, and Phœbus, rising
 bright,
Had streak'd the azure firmament with
 light;
He pierc'd the glitt'ring clouds with golden
 streams,
And warm'd the womb of earth with genial
 beams.
 It so befell, in that fair morning tide
The fairies sported on the garden side,
And in the midst their monarch and his
 bride.
So featly tripp'd the light-foot Ladies
 round,   620
The Knights so nimbly o'er the green-
 sward bound,
That scarce they bent the flowers, or
 touch'd the ground.
The dances ended, all the fairy train
For pinks and daisies search'd the flowery
 plain,
While on a bank reclin'd of rising green,
Thus, with a frown, the King bespoke his
 Queen.

' 'T is too apparent, argue what you can,
The treachery you women use to man :
A thousand authors have this truth made
    out,
And sad experience leaves no room for
    doubt.   630
' Heav'n rest thy spirit, noble Solomon,
A wiser Monarch never saw the sun:
All wealth, all honours, the supreme de-
    gree
Of earthly bliss, was well bestow'd on thee !
For sagely hast thou said, " Of all mankind,
One only just, and righteous, hope to find :
But shouldst thou search the spacious
    world around,
Yet one good woman is not to be found."
  ' Thus says the King who knew your
    wickedness ;
The son of Sirach testifies no less.   640
So may some wildfire on your bodies fall,
Or some devouring plague consume you
    all;
As well you view the lecher in the tree,
And well this honourable Knight you see:
But since he 's blind and old (a helpless
    case),
His Squire shall cuckold him before your
    face.
  ' Now by my own dread Majesty I swear,
And by this awful sceptre which I bear,
No impious wretch shall 'scape unpunish'd
    long,   649
That in my presence offers such a wrong.
I will this instant undeceive the Knight,
And in the very act restore his sight:
And set the strumpet here in open view, ⎫
A warning to the ladies, and to you,   ⎬
And all the faithless sex, for ever to be ⎭
    true."
  ' And will you so,' replied the Queen, ⎫
    ' indeed ?   ⎬
Now, by my mother's soul, it is decreed, ⎮
She shall not want an answer at her need. ⎭
For her, and for her daughters, I 'll en-
    gage,
And all the sex in each succeeding age; 660
Art shall be theirs to varnish an offence,
And fortify their crimes with confidence.
Nay, were they taken in a strict embrace,
Seen with both eyes, and pinion'd on the
    place;
All they shall need is to protest and
    swear,
Breathe a soft sigh, and drop a tender
    tear:

Till their wise husbands, gull'd by arts like
    these,
Grow gentle, tractable, and tame as geese.
  ' What tho' this sland'rous Jew, this
    Solomon,
Call'd women fools, and knew full many a
    one ?   670
The wiser Wits of later times declare
How constant, chaste, and virtuous women
    are:
Witness the Martyrs, who resign'd their
    breath,
Serene in torments, unconcern'd in death;
And witness next what Roman authors tell,
How Arria, Portia, and Lucretia fell.
  ' But since the sacred leaves to all are
    free,
And men interpret texts, why should not
    we ?
By this no more was meant than to have ⎫
    shown   ⎬
That sov'reign goodness dwells in him ⎮
    alone,   680 ⎭
Who only Is, and is but only One.
But grant the worst ; shall women then be
    weigh'd
By every word that Solomon hath said ?
What tho' this king (as ancient story boasts)
Built a fair temple to the Lord of Hosts;
He ceas'd at last his Maker to adore,
And did as much for idol Gods, or more.
Beware what lavish praises you confer
On a rank lecher and idolater;
Whose reign indulgent God, says Holy
    Writ,   690
Did but for David's righteous sake permit;
David, the monarch after Heav'n's own
    mind,
Who lov'd our sex, and honour'd all our
    kind.
  ' Well, I 'm a woman, and as such must
    speak;
Silence would swell me, and my heart would
    break.
Know, then, I scorn your dull authorities,
Your idle Wits, and all their learned lies:
By Heav'n, those authors are our sex's foes,
Whom, in our right, I must and will op-
    pose.'
  ' Nay (quoth the King) dear madam, be
    not wroth: 700
I yield it up; but since I gave my oath,
That this much injur'd Knight again should
    see,
It must be done — I am a King,' said he,

'And one whose faith has ever sacred
  been —'
'And so has mine (she said) — I am a
  Queen:
Her answer she shall have, I undertake;
And thus an end of all dispute I make.
Try when you list; and you shall find, my
  lord,
It is not in our sex to break our word.' 709
  We leave them here in this heroic strain,
And to the Knight our story turns again;
Who in the garden, with his lovely May,
Sung merrier than the cuckoo or the jay:
This was his song, 'O kind and constant
  be,
Constant and kind I 'll ever prove to thee.'
  Thus singing as he went, at last he drew
By easy steps to where the pear-tree grew:
The longing dame look'd up, and spied her
  love
Full fairly perch'd among the boughs
  above.
She stopp'd, and sighing, 'O good Gods!'
  she cried, 720
'What pangs, what sudden shoots distend
  my side?
O for that tempting fruit, so fresh, so
  green!
Help, for the love of Heav'n's immortal
  Queen!
Help, dearest lord, and save at once the life
Of thy poor infant, and thy longing wife!'
  Sore sigh'd the Knight to hear his lady's
  cry,
But could not climb, and had no servant
  nigh:
Old as he was, and void of eyesight too,
What could, alas! a helpless husband do?
'And must I languish then (she said), and
  die, 730
Yet view the lovely fruit before my eye?
At least, kind Sir, for charity's sweet sake,
Vouchsafe the trunk between your arms to
  take,
Then from your back I might ascend the
  tree;
Do you but stoop, and leave the rest to
  me.'
  'With all my soul,' he thus replied
  again,
'I 'd spend my dearest blood to ease thy
  pain.'
With that his back against the trunk he
  bent;
She seiz'd a twig, and up the tree she went.

  Now prove your patience, gentle ladies
  all! 740
Nor let on me your heavy anger fall:
'T is truth I tell, tho' not in phrase re-
  fin'd;
Tho' blunt my tale, yet honest is my
  mind.
What feats the lady in the tree might do,
I pass, as gambols never known to you;
But sure it was a merrier fit, she swore,
Than in her life she ever felt before.
  In that nice moment, lo! the wond'ring
  Knight
Look'd out, and stood restor'd to sudden
  sight. 749
Straight on the tree his eager eyes he bent,
As one whose thoughts were on his spouse
  intent:
But when he saw his bosom-wife so dress'd,
His rage was such as cannot be express'd.
Not frantic mothers when their infants die
With louder clamours rend the vaulted sky:
He cried, he roar'd, he storm'd, he tore his
  hair;
'Death! Hell! and Furies! what dost thou
  do there?'
  'What ails my lord?' the trembling
  dame replied,
'I thought your patience had been better
  tried: 759
Is this your love, ungrateful and unkind,
This my reward for having cured the blind?
Why was I taught to make my husband
  see,
By struggling with a man upon a tree?
Did I for this the power of magic prove?
Unhappy wife, whose crime was too much
  love!'
  'If this be struggling, by this holy light,
'T is struggling with a vengeance (quoth
  the Knight):
So Heav'n preserve the sight it has re-
  stored,
As with these eyes I plainly saw thee
  whored;
Whored by my slave — perfidious wretch!
  may Hell 770
As surely seize thee, as I saw too well.'
  'Guard me, good Angels!' cried the
  gentle May,
'Pray Heav'n this magic work the proper
  way!
Alas, my love! 't is certain, could you see,
You ne'er had used these killing words to
  me:

So help me, Fates! as 't is no perfect sight,
But some faint glimm'ring of a doubtful
    light.'
'What I have said (quoth he) I must
    maintain,
For by th' immortal Powers it *seem'd* too
    plain — '
'By all those Powers, some frenzy
    seiz'd your mind   780
(Replied the dame): are these the thanks
    I find ?
Wretch that I am, that e'er I was so
    kind!'
She said; a rising sigh express'd her woe,
The ready tears apace began to flow,
And as they fell she wiped from either eye
The drops (for women, when they list, can
    cry).
    The Knight was touch'd; and in his looks
    appear'd
Signs of remorse, while thus his spouse he
    cheer'd;
'Madam, 't is past, and my short anger
    o'er!
Come down, and vex your tender heart no
    more.   790
Excuse me, dear, if aught amiss was said,
For, on my soul, amends shall soon be
    made:
Let my repentance your forgiveness draw;
By Heav'n, I swore but what I *thought* I
    saw.'
'Ah, my lov'd lord! 't was much unkind
    (she cried)
On bare suspicion thus to treat your bride.
But till your sight 's establish'd, for a while
Imperfect objects may your sense beguile.
Thus, when from sleep we first our eyes
    display,
The balls are wounded with the piercing
    ray,   800
And dusky vapours rise, and intercept the
    day;
So just recov'ring from the shades of
    night
Your swimming eyes are drunk with sud-
    den light,
Strange phantoms dance around, and
    skim before your sight.
Then, Sir, be cautious, nor too rashly deem;
Heav'n knows how seldom things are what
    they seem!
Consult your reason, and you soon shall find
'T was you were jealous, not your wife un-
    kind:

Jove ne'er spoke oracle more true than
    this,
None judge so wrong as those who think
    amiss.'   810
With that she leap'd into her lord's em-
    brace,
With well dissembled virtue in her face.
He hugg'd her close, and kiss'd her o'er
    and o'er,
Disturb'd with doubts and jealousies no
    more:
Both pleas'd and bless'd, renew'd their
    mutual vows:
A fruitful wife, and a believing spouse.
Thus ends our tale; whose moral next to
    make,
Let all wise husbands hence example take;
And pray, to crown the pleasure of their
    lives,
To be so well deluded by their wives.   820

THE WIFE OF BATH

HER PROLOGUE

Not published until 1714, but naturally
classified with January and May, and not im-
probably the product of the same period.

BEHOLD the woes of matrimonial life,
And hear with rev'rence an experienced
    wife;
To dear-bought wisdom give the credit due,
And think for once a woman tells you true.
In all these trials I have borne a part:
I was myself the scourge that caus'd the
    smart;
For since fifteen in triumph have I led
Five captive husbands from the church to
    bed.
Christ saw a wedding once, the Scripture
    says,
And saw but one, 't was thought, in all his
    days;   10
Whence some infer, whose conscience is too
    nice,
No pious Christian ought to marry twice.
But let them read, and solve me if they
    can,
The words address'd to the Samaritan:
Five times in lawful wedlock she was
    join'd,
And sure the certain stint was ne'er de-
    fin'd.

'Increase and multiply' was Heav'n's
command,
And that's a text I clearly understand:
This too, ' Let men their sires and mothers
leave,   19
And to their dearer wives for ever cleave.'
More wives than one by Solomon were
tried,
Or else the wisest of mankind's belied.
I've had myself full many a merry fit,
And trust in Heav'n I may have many yet;
For when my transitory spouse, unkind, ⎫
Shall die and leave his woful wife behind, ⎬
I'll take the next good Christian I can   ⎭
find.
    Paul, knowing one could never serve our
turn,
Declared 't was better far to wed than burn.
There's danger in assembling fire and tow;
I grant 'em that; and what it means you
know.   31
The same apostle, too, has elsewhere
own'd
No precept for virginity he found:
'T is but a counsel — and we women still
Take which we like, the counsel or our will.
    I envy not their bliss, if he or she
Think fit to live in perfect chastity:
Pure let them be, and free from taint or
vice;
I for a few slight spots am not so nice.
Heav'n calls us diff'rent ways; on these
bestows   40
One proper gift, another grants to those;
Not every man's obliged to sell his store,
And give up all his substance to the poor:
Such as are perfect may, I can't deny;
But by your leaves, Divines! so am not I.
    Full many a saint, since first the world
began,
Liv'd an unspotted maid in spite of man:
Let such (a God's name) with fine wheat
be fed,
And let us honest wives eat barley bread.
For me, I'll keep the post assign'd by
Heav'n,   50
And use the copious talent it has giv'n:
Let my good spouse pay tribute, do me
right,
And keep an equal reck'ning every night;
His proper body is not his, but mine;
For so said Paul, and Paul's a sound divine.
Know then, of those five husbands I have
had,
Three were just tolerable, two were bad.

The three were old, but rich and fond be-
side,
And toil'd most piteously to please their
bride;
But since their wealth (the best they had)
was mine,   60
The rest without much loss I could resign:
Sure to be lov'd, I took no pains to please,
Yet had more pleasure far than they had
ease.
    Presents flow'd in apace: with showers of
gold
They made their court, like Jupiter of old:
If I but smiled, a sudden youth they found,
And a new palsy seiz'd them when I
frown'd.
    Ye sov'reign Wives! give ear, and under-
stand:
Thus shall ye speak, and exercise command;
For never was it giv'n to mortal man   70
To lie so boldly as we women can:
Forswear the fact, tho' seen with both his
eyes,
And call your maids to witness how he lies.
    Hark, old Sir Paul! ('t was thus I used
to say)
Whence is our neighbour's wife so rich and
gay ?
Treated, caress'd, where'er she's pleas'd to
roam —
I sit in tatters, and immured at home.
Why to her house dost thou so oft repair ?
Art thou so am'rous ? and is she so fair ?
If I but see a cousin or a friend,   80
Lord! how you swell and rage like any
fiend!
But you reel home, a drunken beastly bear,
Then preach till midnight in your easy
chair;
Cry, wives are false, and every woman evil,
And give up all that's female to the devil.
    If poor (you say), she drains her hus-
band's purse;
If rich, she keeps her priest, or something
worse;
If highly born, intolerably vain,
Vapours and pride by turns possess her
brain;
Now gaily mad, now sourly splenetic,   90
Freakish when well, and fretful when she's
sick.
If fair, then chaste she-cannot long abide,
By pressing youth attack'd on every side;
If foul, her wealth the lusty lover lures,
Or else her wit some fool-gallant procures,

Or else she dances with becoming grace,
Or shape excuses the defects of face.
There swims no goose so gray, but soon or
late
She finds some honest gander for her mate.
Horses (thou say'st) and asses men may
try, 100
And ring suspected vessels ere they buy;
But wives, a random choice, untried they
take,
They dream in courtship, but in wedlock
wake;
Then, not till then, the veil's remov'd away,
And all the woman glares in open day.
You tell me, to preserve your wife's good
grace,
Your eyes must always languish on my
face,
Your tongue with constant flatt'ries feed
my ear,
And tag each sentence with 'My life! my
dear!'
If by strange chance a modest blush be
rais'd, 110
Be sure my fine complexion must be prais'd.
My garments always must be new and gay,
And feasts still kept upon my wedding day.
Then must my nurse be pleas'd, and fa-
v'rite maid;
And endless treats and endless visits paid
To a long train of kindred, friends, allies:
All this thou say'st, and all thou say'st are
lies.
On Jenkin, too, you cast a squinting eye:
What! can your 'prentice raise your jeal-
ousy?
Fresh are his ruddy cheeks, his forehead
fair, 120
And like the burnish'd gold his curling hair.
But clear thy wrinkled brow, and quit thy
sorrow;
I'd scorn your 'prentice should you die to-
morrow.
Why are thy chests all lock'd? on what
design?
Are not thy worldly goods and treasure
mine?
Sir, I'm no fool; nor shall you, by St. John,
Have goods and body to yourself alone.
One you shall quit, in spite of both your
eyes —
I heed not, I, the bolts, the locks, the spies.
If you had wit, you'd say, 'Go where you
will, 130
Dear spouse! I credit not the tales they tell:

Take all the freedoms of a married life;
I know thee for a virtuous, faithful wife.'
Lord! when you have enough, what need
you care
How merrily soever others fare?
Tho' all the day I give and take delight,
Doubt not sufficient will be left at night.
'T is but a just and rational desire
To light a taper at a neighbour's fire.
There's danger too, you think, in rich ar-
ray, 140
And none can long be modest that are gay.
The cat, if you but singe her tabby skin,
The chimney keeps, and sits content within:
But once grown sleek, will from her corner
run,
Sport with her tail, and wanton in the sun:
She licks her fair round face, and frisks
abroad
To show her fur, and to be catterwaw'd.
Lo thus, my friends, I wrought to my de-
sires
These three right ancient venerable sires.
I told them, Thus you say, and thus you
do; 150
And told them false, but Jenkin swore
't was true.
I, like a dog, could bite as well as whine,
And first complain'd whene'er the guilt was
mine.
I tax'd them oft with wenching and amours,
When their weak legs scarce dragg'd them
out of doors;
And swore the rambles that I took by night
Were all to spy what damsels they bedight:
That colour brought me many hours of
mirth;
For all this wit is giv'n us from our birth.
Heav'n gave to woman the peculiar grace
To spin, to weep, and cully human race. 161
By this nice conduct and this prudent
course,
By murm'ring, wheedling, stratagem, and
force,
I still prevail'd, and would be in the right;
Or curtain lectures made a restless night.
If once my husband's arm was o'er my side,
'What! so familiar with your spouse?' I
cried:
I levied first a tax upon his need;
Then let him — 't was a nicety indeed!
Let all mankind this certain maxim hold;
Marry who will, our sex is to be sold. 171
With empty hands no tassels you can lure,
But fulsome love for gain we can endure;

For gold we love the impotent and old,
And heave, and pant, and kiss, and cling,
   for gold.
Yet with embraces curses oft I mixt,
Then kiss'd again, and chid, and rail'd be-
   twixt.
Well, I may make my will in peace, and
   die,
For not one word in man's arrears am I.
To drop a dear dispute I was unable,   180
Ev'n though the Pope himself had sat at
   table;
But when my point was gain'd, then thus I
   spoke:
'Billy, my dear, how sheepishly you look!
Approach, my spouse, and let me kiss thy
   cheek;
Thou shouldst be always thus resign'd and
   meek!
Of Job's great patience since so oft you
   preach,
Well should you practise who so well can
   teach.
'T is difficult to do, I must allow,
But I, my dearest! will instruct you how.
Great is the blessing of a prudent wife,   190
Who puts a period to domestic strife.
One of us two must rule, and one obey;
And since in man right Reason bears the
   sway,
Let that frail thing, weak woman, have
   her way.
The wives of all my family have ruled
Their tender husbands, and their passions
   cool'd.
Fie! 't is unmanly thus to sigh and groan:
What! would you have me to yourself
   alone?
Why, take me, love! take all and every
   part!
Here's your revenge! you love it at your
   heart.   200
Would I vouchsafe to sell what Nature
   gave,
You little think what custom I could have.
But see! I'm all your own — nay hold —
   for shame!
What means my dear? — indeed — you
   are to blame.'
   Thus with my first three lords I pass'd
   my life,
A very woman and a very wife.
What sums from these old spouses I could
   raise
Procur'd young husbands in my riper days.

Tho' past my bloom, not yet decay'd
   was I,   209
Wanton and wild, and chatter'd like a pie.
In country dances still I bore the bell,
And sung as sweet as ev'ning Philomel.
To clear my quail-pipe, and refresh my
   soul,
Full oft I drain'd the spicy nut-brown
   bowl;
Rich luscious wines, that youthful blood
   improve,
And warm the swelling veins to feats of
   love:
For 't is as sure as cold engenders hail,
A liquorish mouth must have a lech'rous
   tail:
Wine lets no lover unrewarded go,   219
As all true gamesters by experience know.
   But oh, good Gods! whene'er a thought
   I cast
On all the joys of youth and beauty past,
To find in pleasures I have had my part
Still warms me to the bottom of my heart.
This wicked world was once my dear de-
   light;
Now all my conquests, all my charms,
   good night!
The flour consumed, the best that now I
   can
Is ev'n to make my market of the bran.
   My fourth dear spouse was not exceed-
   ing true;
He kept, 't was thought, a private miss or
   two;   230
But all that score I paid — As how?
   you 'll say:
Not with my body, in a filthy way;
But I so dress'd, and danc'd, and drank,
   and din'd
And view'd a friend with eyes so very kind,
As stung his heart, and made his marrow
   fry,
With burning rage and frantic jealousy.
His soul, I hope, enjoys eternal glory,
For here on earth I was his purgatory.
Oft, when his shoe the most severely
   wrung,   239
He put on careless airs, and sat and sung.
How sore I gall'd him only Heav'n could
   know,
And he that felt, and I that caus'd the woe.
He died when last from pilgrimage I came,
With other gossips, from Jerusalem;
And now lies buried underneath a rood,
Fair to be seen, and rear'd of honest wood:

A tomb, indeed, with fewer sculptures graced
Than that Mausolus' pious widow placed,
Or where enshrin'd the great Darius lay;
But cost on graves is merely thrown away.
The pit fill'd up, with turf we cover'd o'er;
So bless the good man's soul! I say no more. 252
　Now for my fifth lov'd lord, the last and best;
(Kind Heav'n afford him everlasting rest!)
Full hearty was his love, and I can show
The tokens on my ribs in black and blue;
Yet with a knack my heart he could have won,
While yet the smart was shooting in the bone.
How quaint an appetite in women reigns!
Free gifts we scorn, and love what costs us pains. 260
Let men avoid us, and on them we leap;
A glutted market makes provision cheap.
In pure good will I took this jovial spark,
Of Oxford he, a most egregious clerk.
He boarded with a widow in the town,
A trusty gossip, one dame Alison;
Full well the secrets of my soul she knew,
Better than e'er our parish priest could do.
To her I told whatever could befall: 269
Had but my husband piss'd against a wall,
Or done a thing that might have cost his life,
She — and my niece — and one more worthy wife,
Had known it all: what most he would conceal,
To these I made no scruple to reveal.
Oft has he blush'd from ear to ear for shame
That e'er he told a secret to his dame.
It so befell, in holy time of Lent,
That oft a day I to this gossip went;
(My husband, thank my stars, was out of town)
From house to house we rambled up and down, 280
This clerk, myself, and my good neighbour Alse,
To see, be seen, to tell, and gather tales.
Visits to every church we daily paid,
And march'd in every holy masquerade;
The stations duly and the vigils kept;
Not much we fasted, but scarce ever slept.

At sermons, too, I shone in scarlet gay: ⎫
The wasting moth ne'er spoil'd my best ⎪
　array; ⎬
The cause was this, I wore it every day. ⎭
'Twas when fresh May her early blossoms yields, 290
This clerk and I were walking in the fields.
We grew so intimate, I can't tell how,
I pawn'd my honour, and engaged my vow,
If e'er I laid my husband in his urn,
That he, and only he, should serve my turn.
We straight struck hands, the bargain was agreed;
I still have shifts against a time of need.
The mouse that always trusts to one poor hole
Can never be a mouse of any soul.
　I vow'd I scarce could sleep since first I knew him, 300
And durst be sworn he had bewitch'd me to him;
If e'er I slept I dream'd of him alone, ⎫
And dreams foretell, as learned men have ⎪
　shown. ⎬
All this I said; but dreams, Sirs, I had ⎪
　none: ⎭
I follow'd but my crafty crony's lore,
Who bid me tell this lie — and twenty more.
　Thus day by day, and month by month we past;
It pleas'd the Lord to take my spouse at last.
I tore my gown, I soil'd my locks with dust,
And beat my breasts, as wretched widows — must. 310
Before my face my handkerchief I spread,
To hide the flood of tears I — did not shed.
The good man's coffin to the church was borne;
Around the neighbours and my clerk too mourn.
But as he march'd, good Gods! he show'd a pair
Of legs and feet so clean, so strong, so fair!
Of twenty winters' age he seem'd to be;
I (to say truth) was twenty more than he;
But vig'rous still, a lively buxom dame, 310
And had a wondrous gift to quench a flame.
A conjurer once, that deeply could divine,
Assur'd me Mars in Taurus was my sign.
As the stars order'd, such my life has been:
Alas, alas! that ever love was sin!
Fair Venus gave me fire and sprightly grace,
And Mars assurance and a dauntless face.

By virtue of this powerful constellation,
I follow'd always my own inclination.
But to my tale: — A month scarce pass'd
    away,
With dance and song we kept the nuptial
    day.   330
All I possess'd I gave to his command,
My goods and chattels, money, house, and
    land;
But oft repented, and repent it still;
He prov'd a rebel to my sov'reign will;
Nay, once, by Heav'n! he struck me on the
    face:
Hear but the fact, and judge yourselves
    the case.
Stubborn as any lioness was I,
And knew full well to raise my voice on
    high;
As true a rambler as I was before,
And would be so in spite of all he swore. 340
He against this right sagely would advise,
And old examples set before my eyes;
Tell how the Roman matrons led their life,
Of Gracchus' mother, and Duilius' wife;
And close the sermon, as beseem'd his wit,
With some grave sentence out of Holy Writ.
Oft would he say, 'Who builds his house
    on sands,
Pricks his blind horse across the fallow
    lands,
Or lets his wife abroad with pilgrims roam,
Deserves a fool's-cap and long ears at
    home.'   350
All this avail'd not, for whoe'er he be
That tells my faults, I hate him mortally!
And so do numbers more, I 'll boldly say,
Men, women, clergy, regular and lay.
My spouse (who was, you know, to learn-
    ing bred)
A certain treatise oft at evening read,
Where divers authors (whom the devil con-
    found
For all their lies) were in one volume
    bound:
Valerius whole, and of St. Jerome part;
Chrysippus and Tertullian, Ovid's Art, 360
Solomon's Proverbs, Eloisa's loves,
And many more than sure the church ap-
    proves.
More legends were there here of wicked
    wives
Than good in all the Bible and saints' lives.
Who drew the lion vanquish'd ? 'T was a
    man:
But could we women write as scholars can.

Men should stand mark'd with far more
    wickedness
Than all the sons of Adam could redress.
Love seldom haunts the breast where learn-
    ing lies,
And Venus sets ere Mercury can rise. 370
Those play the scholars who can't play the
    men,
And use that weapon which they have, their
    pen;
When old, and past the relish of delight,
Then down they sit, and in their dotage
    write
That not one woman keeps her marriage-
    vow.
(This by the way, but to my purpose now.)
It chanc'd my husband, on a winter's
    night,
Read in this book aloud with strange de-
    light,
How the first female (as the Scriptures
    show)
Brought her own spouse and all his race to
    woe;   380
How Samson fell; and he whom Dejanire
Wrapp'd in th' envenom'd shirt, and set on
    fire;
How curs'd Eriphyle her lord betray'd,
And the dire ambush Clytemnestra laid;
But what most pleas'd him was the Cretan
    dame
And husband-bull — Oh, monstrous! fie, for
    shame!
He had by heart the whole detail of woe
Xantippe made her good man undergo;
How oft she scolded in a day he knew, 389
How many pisspots on the sage she threw —
Who took it patiently, and wiped his head:
'Rain follows thunder,' that was all he said.
He read how Arius to his friend com-
    plain'd
A fatal tree was growing in his land,
On which three wives successively had
    twin'd
A sliding noose, and waver'd in the wind.
'Where grows this plant,' replied the
    friend, 'oh where ?
For better fruit did never orchard bear :
Give me some slip of this most blissful
    tree,
And in my garden planted it shall be.' 400
Then how two wives their lords' destruc-
    tion prove,
Thro' hatred one, and one thro' too much
    love :

That for her husband mix'd a pois'nous
    draught,
And this for lust an am'rous philtre
    bought ;
The nimble juice soon seiz'd his giddy
    head,
Frantic at night, and in the morning dead.
How some with swords their sleeping
    lords have slain,
And some have hammer'd nails into their
    brain,
And some have drench'd them with a
    deadly potion :
All this he read, and read with great de-
    votion.   410
Long time I heard, and swell'd, and
    blush'd, and frown'd ;
But when no end of these vile tales I
    found,
When still he read, and laugh'd, and read
    again,
And half the night was thus consumed in
    vain,
Provoked to vengeance, three large leaves
    I tore,
And with one buffet fell'd him on the floor.
With that my husband in a fury rose,
And down he settled me with hearty
    blows.
I groan'd, and lay extended on my side ;
' Oh ! thou hast slain me for my wealth,' I
    cried !   420
' Yet I forgive thee — take my last em-
    brace ' —
He wept, kind soul ! and stoop'd to kiss
    my face :
I took him such a box as turn'd him blue,
Then sigh'd and cried, ' Adieu, my dear,
    adieu ! '
But after many a hearty struggle past,
I condescended to be pleas'd at last.
Soon as he said, ' My mistress and my
    wife !
Do what you list the term of all your life ; '
I took to heart the merits of the cause,
And stood content to rule by wholesome
    laws ;   430
Receiv'd the reins of absolute command,⎫
With all the government of house and ⎪
    land,   ⎬
And empire o'er his tongue and o'er his ⎪
    hand.   ⎭
As for the volume that revil'd the dames,
'T was torn to fragments, and condemn'd to
    flames.

Now Heav'n on all my husbands gone
    bestow
Pleasures above for tortures felt below :
That rest they wish'd for grant them in
    the grave,
And bless those souls my conduct help'd
    to save !

THE TEMPLE OF FAME

Pope asserted that this poem was composed in
1711. Its date of publication is indicated by a
letter from Pope to Martha Blount, written in
1714, in which he speaks of it as ' just out.'
Eventually it was classed by the poet as a
' juvenile poem ' among the earlier translations and imitations. This *Advertisement* was
prefixed : —

The hint of the following piece was taken
from Chaucer's House of Fame. The design is
in a manner entirely altered ; the descriptions
and most of the particular thoughts my own :
yet I could not suffer it to be printed without
this acknowledgment. The reader who would
compare this with Chaucer, may begin with
his third Book of Fame, there being nothing
in the two first books that answers to their
title.

IN that soft season, when descending
    showers
Call forth the greens, and wake the rising
    flowers,
When opening buds salute the welcome
    day,
And earth relenting feels the genial ray;
As balmy sleep had charm'd my cares to
    rest,
And love itself was banish'd from my
    breast,
(What time the morn mysterious visions
    brings,
While purer slumbers spread their golden
    wings)
A train of phantoms in wild order rose,   9
And join'd, this intellectual scene compose.
I stood, methought, betwixt earth, seas,
    and skies,
The whole Creation open to my eyes ;
In air self-balanced hung the globe below.
Where mountains rise and circling oceans
    flow ;
Here naked rocks and empty wastes were
    seen,
There towery cities, and the forests green ;

Here sailing ships delight the wand'ring
   eyes,
There trees and intermingled temples rise :
Now a clear sun the shining scene displays,
The transient landscape now in clouds
   decays.   20
  O'er the wide prospect as I gazed around,
Sudden I heard a wild promiscuous sound,
Like broken thunders that at distance roar,
Or billows murm'ring on the hollow shore:
Then gazing up, a glorious Pile beheld,
Whose tow'ring summit ambient clouds
   conceal'd;
High on a rock of ice the structure lay,
Steep its ascent, and slipp'ry was the way;
The wondrous rock like Parian marble
   shone,   29
And seem'd, to distant sight, of solid stone.
Inscriptions here of various names I view'd,
The greater part by hostile time subdued;
Yet wide was spread their fame in ages past,
And poets once had promis'd they should
   last.
Some fresh engraved appear'd of wits re-
   nown'd;
I look'd again, nor could their trace be
   found.
Critics I saw, that other names deface,
And fix their own with labour, in their
   place:
Their own, like others, soon their place
   resign'd,
Or disappear'd and left the first behind. 40
Nor was the work impair'd by storms alone,
But felt th' approaches of too warm a sun;
For Fame, impatient of extremes, decays
Not more by envy than excess of praise.
Yet part no injuries of Heav'n could feel,
Like crystal faithful to the graving steel:
The rock's high summit, in the temple's
   shade,
Nor heat could melt, nor beating storm
   invade.
Their names inscribed unnumber'd ages past
From Time's first birth, with Time itself
   shall last: 50
These ever new, nor subject to decays,
Spread, and grow brighter with the length
   of days.
  So Zembla's rocks (the beauteous work
   of frost)
Rise white in air, and glitter o'er the coast;
Pale suns, unfelt, at distance roll away,
And on th' impassive ice the lightnings
   play;

Eternal snows the growing mass supply,
Till the bright mountains prop th' incum-
   bent sky:
As Atlas fix'd, each hoary pile appears, 59
The gather'd winter of a thousand years.
  On this foundation Fame's high temple
   stands;
Stupendous pile! not rear'd by mortal hands.
Whate'er proud Rome or artful Greece
   beheld,
Or elder Babylon, its frame excell'd.
Four faces had the dome, and ev'ry face
Of various structure, but of equal grace:
Four brazen gates, on columns lifted high,
Salute the diff'rent quarters of the sky.
Here fabled Chiefs in darker ages born,
Or Worthies old whom Arms or Arts
   adorn,   70
Who cities raised or tamed a monstrous
   race,
The walls in venerable order grace:
Heroes in animated marble frown,
And Legislators seem to think in stone.
  Westward, a sumptuous frontispiece
   appear'd,
On Doric pillars of white marble rear'd,
Crown'd with an architrave of antique
   mould,
And sculpture rising on the roughen'd gold.
In shaggy spoils here Theseus was beheld,
And Perseus dreadful with Minerva's
   shield: 80
There great Alcides, stooping with his toil,
Rests on his club, and holds th' Hesperian
   spoil:
Here Orpheus sings; trees moving to the
   sound
Start from their roots, and form a shade
   around:
Amphion there the loud creating lyre
Strikes, and beholds a sudden Thebes as-
   pire;
Cithæron's echoes answer to his call,
And half the mountain rolls into a wall:
There might you see the length'ning spires
   ascend,
The domes swell up, and widening arches
   bend,   90
The growing towers, like exhalations, rise,
And the huge columns heave into the skies.
  The eastern front was glorious to behold,
With diamond flaming, and barbaric gold.
There Ninus shone, who spread th' Assyrian
   fame,
And the great founder of the Persian name··

There in long robes the royal Magi stand,
Grave Zoroaster waves the circling wand;
The sage Chaldeans robed in white ap-
pear'd,
And Brahmans, deep in desert woods
revered. 100
These stopp'd the moon, and call' th' un-
bodied shades
To midnight banquets in the glimm'ring
glades;
Made visionary fabrics round them rise,
And airy spectres skim before their eyes;
Of talismans and sigils knew the power,
And careful watch'd the planetary hour.
Superior, and alone, Confucius stood,
Who taught that useful science, — to be
good.
But on the south, a long majestic race 109
Of Egypt's priests the gilded niches grace,
Who measured earth, described the starry
spheres,
And traced the long records of Lunar
Years.
High on his car Sesostris struck my view,
Whom sceptred slaves in golden harness
drew:
His hands a bow and pointed jav'lin hold ;
His giant limbs are arm'd in scales of gold.
Between the statues obelisks were placed,
And the learn'd walls with hieroglyphics
graced.
Of Gothic structure was the northern
side,
O'erwrought with ornaments of barb'rous
pride. 120
There huge Colosses rose, with trophies
crown'd,
And Runic characters were graved around ;
There sat Zamolxis with erected eyes,
And Odin here in mimic trances dies.
There on rude iron columns, smear'd with
blood,
The horrid forms of Scythian Heroes stood,
Druids and Bards (their once loud harps
unstrung)
And youths that died to be by poets sung.
These and a thousand more of doubtful
fame,
To whom old fables gave a lasting name, 130
In ranks adorn'd the temple's outward face;
The wall in lustre and effect like glass,
Which o'er each object casting various dyes,
Enlarges some, and others multiplies ;
Nor void of emblem was the mystic wall,
For thus romantic Fame increases all.

The temple shakes, the sounding gates
unfold,
Wide vaults appear, and roofs of fretted
gold,
Rais'd on a thousand pillars, wreath'd
around
With laurel foliage, and with eagles
crown'd. 140
Of bright transparent beryl were the walls,
The friezes gold, and gold the capitals;
As Heav'n with stars, the roof with jewels
glows,
And ever-living lamps depend in rows.
Full in the passage of each spacious gate
The sage Historians in white garments
wait;
Graved o'er their seats the form of Time
was found,
His scythe revers'd, and both his pinions
bound.
Within stood Heroes, who thro' loud alarms
In bloody fields pursued renown in arms.
High on a throne, with trophies charged, I
view'd 151
The youth that all things but himself sub-
dued;
His feet on sceptres and tiaras trod,
And his horn'd head belied the Libyan
God,
There Cæsar, graced with both Minervas,
shone;
Cæsar, the world's great master, and his
own;
Unmov'd, superior still in ev'ry state,
And scarce detested in his country's fate.
But chief were those who not for empire
fought,
But with their toils their people's safety
bought: 160
High o'er the rest Epaminondas stood;
Timoleon, glorious in his brother's blood;
Bold Scipio, saviour of the Roman state,
Great in his triumphs, in retirement great;
And wise Aurelius, in whose well-taught ⎤
mind
With boundless power unbounded virtue ⎬
join'd,
His own strict judge, and patron of man- ⎦
kind.
Much-suff'ring heroes next their hon-
ours claim.
Those of less noisy, and less guilty fame,
Fair Virtue's silent train: supreme of
these 171
Here ever shines the godlike Socrates:

He whom ungrateful Athens could expel,
At all times just, but when he sign'd the
  shell :
Here his abode the martyr'd Phocion
  claims,
With Agis, not the last of Spartan names:
Unconquer'd Cato shows the wound he
  tore,
And Brutus his ill genius meets no more.
  But in the centre of the hallow'd choir
Six pompous columns o'er the rest aspire:
Around the shrine itself of Fame they
  stand,   180
Hold the chief honours and the fame com-
  mand.
High on the first the mighty Homer
  shone ;
Eternal adamant composed his throne;
Father of verse ! in holy fillets drest,
His silver beard waved gently o'er his
  breast ;
Tho' blind, a boldness in his looks ap-
  pears ;
In years he seem'd, but not impair'd by
  years.
The wars of Troy were round the pillar
  seen;
Here fierce Tydides wounds the Cyprian
  Queen;   189
Here Hector, glorious from Patroclus' fall,
Here, dragg'd in triumph round the Tro-
  jan wall.
Motion and life did ev'ry part inspire,
Bold was the work, and prov'd the mas-
  ter's fire:
A strong expression most he seem'd t'
  affect,
And here and there disclosed a brave neg-
  lect.
  A golden column next in rank appear'd,
On which a shrine of purest gold was
  rear'd;
Finish'd the whole, and labour'd ev'ry
  part,
With patient touches of unwearied art. 199
The Mantuan there in sober triumph sate,
Composed his posture, and his look se-
  date;
On Homer still he fix'd a rev'rend eye,
Great without pride, in modest majesty.
In living sculpture on the sides were
  spread
The Latian wars, and haughty Turnus dead;
Eliza stretch'd upon the funeral pyre;
Æneas bending with his aged sire:

Troy flamed in burning gold, and o'er the
  throne
' Arms and the man' in golden ciphers
  shone.
Four swans sustain a car of silver
  bright,   210
With heads advanced, and pinions stretch'd
  for flight:
Here, like some furious prophet, Pindar
  rode,
And seem'd to labour with th' inspiring
  God.
Across the harp a careless hand he flings,
And boldly sinks into the sounding strings.
The figured games of Greece the column
  grace:
Neptune and Jove survey the rapid race;
The youths hang o'er the chariots as they
  run;
The fiery steeds seem starting from the
  stone;
The champions in distorted postures
  threat;   220
And all appear'd irregularly great.
  Here happy Horace tuned th' Ausonian
  lyre
To sweeter sounds, and temper'd Pindar's
  fire:
Pleas'd with Alcæus' manly rage t' infuse
The softer spirit of the Sapphic Muse.
The polish'd pillar diff'rent sculptures
  grace;
A work outlasting monumental brass.
Here smiling loves and bacchanals appear,
The Julian star, and great Augustus here;
The doves, that round the infant poet
  spread   230
Myrtles and bays, hung hov'ring o'er his
  head.
  Here, in a shrine that cast a dazzling
  light,
Sate fix'd in thought the mighty Stagy-
  rite;
His sacred head a radiant Zodiac crown'd,
And various animals his sides surround:
His piercing eyes, erect, appear to view
Superior worlds, and look all Nature
  thro'.
  With equal rays immortal Tully shone;
The Roman rostra deck'd the consul's
  throne;
Gath'ring his flowing robe, he seem'd to
  stand   240
In act to speak, and graceful stretch'd his
  hand:

Behind, Rome's Genius waits with civic
crowns,
And the great father of his country owns.
These massy columns in a circle rise,
O'er which a pompous dome invades the
skies;
Scarce to the top I stretch'd my aching
sight,
So large it spread, and swell'd to such a
height.
Full in the midst proud Fame's imperial
seat
With jewels blazed, magnificently great;
The vivid em'ralds there revive the eye, 250
The flaming rubies show their sanguine dye,
Bright azure rays from lively sapphires
stream,
And lucid amber casts a golden gleam.
With various-colour'd light the pavement
shone,
And all on fire appear'd the glowing throne;
The dome's high arch reflects the mingled
blaze,
And forms a rainbow of alternate rays.
When on the Goddess first I cast my sight,
Scarce seem'd her stature of a cubit's
height; 259
But swell'd to larger size, the more I gazed,
Till to the roof her tow'ring front she
rais'd.
With her, the temple ev'ry moment grew,
And ampler vistas open'd to my view :
Upward the columns shoot, the roofs as-
cend,
And arches widen, and long aisles extend.
Such was her form, as ancient bards have
told;
Wings raise her arms, and wings her feet
infold;
A thousand busy tongues the Goddess
bears,
A thousand open eyes, and thousand lis-
t'ning ears. 269
Beneath, in order ranged, the tuneful Nine
(Her virgin handmaids) still attend the
shrine ;
With eyes on Fame for ever fix'd, they sing;
For Fame they raise the voice, and tune
the string;
With Time's first birth began the heav'nly
lays,
And last, eternal, thro' the length of days.
Around these wonders as I cast a look,
The trumpet sounded, and the temple
shook,

And all the nations summon'd at the call,
From diff'rent quarters fill the crowded
hall.
Of various tongues the mingled sounds
were heard; 280
In various garbs promiscuous throngs ap-
pear'd :
Thick as the bees, that with the spring re-
new
Their flowery toils, and sip the fragrant
dew,
When the wing'd colonies first tempt the
sky,
O'er dusky fields and shaded waters fly,
Or, settling, seize the sweets the blossoms
yield,
And a low murmur runs along the field.
Millions of suppliant crowds the shrine at-
tend, 288
And all degrees before the Goddess bend;
The poor, the rich, the valiant, and the sage,
And boasting youth, and narrative old age.
Their pleas were diff'rent, their request
the same ;
For good and bad alike are fond of Fame.
Some she disgraced and some with honours
crown'd ;
Unlike successes equal merits found.
Thus her blind sister, fickle Fortune, reigns,
And, undiscerning, scatters crowns and
chains.
First at the shrine the learned world
appear,
And to the Goddess thus prefer their
prayer :
'Long have we sought t' instruct and please
mankind, 300
With studies pale, with midnight - vigils
blind ;
But thank'd by few, rewarded yet by none,
We here appeal to thy superior throne :
On Wit and Learning the just prize bestow,
For Fame is all we must expect below.'
The Goddess heard, and bade the Muses
raise
The golden trumpet of eternal praise :
From pole to pole the winds diffuse the
sound,
That fills the circuit of the world around ;
Not all at once, as thunder breaks the
cloud, 310
The notes at first were rather sweet than
loud ;
By just degrees they every moment rise,
Fill the wide earth, and gain upon the skies.

At every breath were balmy odours shed,
Which still grew sweeter as they wider
spread ;
Less fragrant scents th' unfolding rose ex-
hales,
Or spices breathing in Arabian gales.
Next these the good and just, an awful
train,
Thus on their knees address the sacred
fane :   319
' Since living virtue is with envy curs'd,
And the best men are treated like the
worst,
Do thou, just Goddess, call our merits
forth,
And give each deed th' exact intrinsic
worth.'
' Not with bare justice shall your act be
crown'd
(Said Fame), but high above desert re-
nown'd :
Let fuller notes th' applauding world amaze,
And the loud clarion labour in your praise.'
This band dismiss'd, behold another
crowd
Preferr'd the same request, and lowly
bow'd ;
The constant tenor of whose well-spent
days   330
No less deserv'd a just return of praise.
But straight the direful trump of Slander
sounds ;
Thro' the big dome the doubling thunder
bounds ;
Loud as the burst of cannon rends the
skies,
The dire report thro' every region flies,
In every ear incessant rumours rung,
And gath'ring scandals grew on every
tongue.
From the black trumpet's rusty concave
broke
Sulphureous flames, and clouds of rolling
smoke :
The pois'nous vapour blots the purple
skies,   340
And withers all before it as it flies.
A troop came next, who crowns and
armour wore,
And proud defiance in their looks they
bore :
' For thee (they cried) amidst alarms and
strife,
We sail'd in tempests down the stream of
life;

For thee whole nations fill'd with flames
and blood,
And swam to Empire thro' the purple
flood :
Those ills we dared, thy inspiration own ;
What virtue seem'd, was done for thee
alone.'
' Ambitious fools!' (the Queen replied,
and frown'd)   350
' Be all your acts in dark oblivion drown'd;
There sleep forgot, with mighty tyrants
gone,
Your statues moulder'd, and your names
unknown!'
A sudden cloud straight snatch'd them
from my sight,
And each majestic phantom sunk in night.
Then came the smallest tribe I yet had
seen;
Plain was their dress, and modest was their
mien:
' Great Idol of mankind ! we neither claim
The praise of Merit, nor aspire to Fame !
But safe in deserts from th' applause of
men,   360
Would die unheard of, as we liv'd unseen;
'T is all we beg thee, to conceal from sight
Those acts of goodness which themselves
requite.
O let us still the secret joy partake,
To follow Virtue ev'n for Virtue's sake.'
' And live there men who slight im-
mortal fame ?
Who then with incense shall adore our
name ?
But, mortals ! know, 't is still our greatest
pride
To blaze those virtues which the good
would hide.
Rise! Muses, rise ! add all your tuneful
breath;   370
These must not sleep in darkness and in
death.'
She said: in air the trembling music floats,
And on the winds triumphant swell the
notes;
So soft, tho' high, so loud, and yet so clear,
Ev'n list'ning angels lean'd from Heav'n to
hear:
To farthest shores th' ambrosial spirit flies,
Sweet to the world, and grateful to the skies.
Next these a youthful train their vows
express'd,
With feathers crown'd, with gay embroid'ry
dress'd:

'Hither' they cried 'direct your eyes, and
 see   380
The men of pleasure, dress, and gallan-
 try.
Ours is the place at banquets, balls, and
 plays,
Sprightly our nights, polite are all our days;
Courts we frequent, where 'tis our pleasing
 care
To pay due visits, and address the Fair;
In fact, 'tis true, no nymph we could per-
 suade,
But still in fancy vanquish'd ev'ry maid;
Of unknown Duchesses lewd tales we tell,
Yet, would the world believe us, all were
 well;   389
The joy let others have, and we the name,
And what we want in pleasure, grant in
 fame.'
 The Queen assents: the trumpet rends
 the skies,
And at each blast a lady's honour dies.
 Pleas'd with the strange success, vast
 numbers prest
Around the shrine, and made the same re-
 quest:
'What you' she cried, 'unlearn'd in arts
 to please,
Slaves to yourselves, and ev'n fatigued with
 ease,
Who lose a length of undeserving days,
Would you usurp the lover's dear-bought
 praise ?
To just contempt, ye vain pretenders, fall,
The people's fable, and the scorn of all.' 401
Straight the black clarion sends a horrid
 sound,
Loud laughs burst out, and bitter scoffs fly
 round;
Whispers are heard, with taunts reviling
 loud,
And scornful hisses run thro' all the crowd.
 Last, those who boast of mighty mis-
 chiefs done,
Enslave their country, or usurp a throne;
Or who their glory's dire foundation laid
On sov'reigns ruin'd, or on friends be-
 tray'd;
Calm, thinking villains, whom no faith could
 fix,   410
Of crooked counsels and dark politics;
Of these a gloomy tribe surround the
 throne,
And beg to make th' immortal treasons
 known.

The trumpet roars, long flaky flames expire,
With sparks that seem'd to set the world
 on fire.
At the dread sound pale mortals stood
 aghast,
And startled Nature trembled with the
 blast.
 This having heard and seen, some Power
 unknown
Straight changed the scene, and snatch'd
 me from the throne.
Before my view appear'd a structure
 fair,   420
Its site uncertain, if in earth or air;
With rapid motion turn'd the mansion
 round;
With ceaseless noise the ringing walls re-
 sound:
Not less in number were the spacious doors
Than leaves on trees, or sands upon the
 shores;
Which still unfolded stand, by night, by
 day,
Pervious to winds, and open every way.
As flames by nature to the skies ascend,
As weighty bodies to the centre tend,
As to the sea returning rivers roll, 430
And the touch'd needle trembles to the
 pole,
Hither, as to their proper place, arise
All various sounds from earth, and seas,
 and skies,
Or spoke aloud, or whisper'd in the ear;
Nor ever silence, rest, or peace is here.
As on the smooth expanse of crystal lakes
The sinking stone at first a circle makes;
The trembling surface by the motion
 stirr'd,
Spreads in a second circle, then a third;
Wide, and more wide, the floating rings
 advance,   440
Fill all the wat'ry plain, and to the margin
 dance:
Thus every voice and sound, when first they
 break,
On neighb'ring air a soft impression
 make;
Another ambient circle then they move;
That in its turn, impels the next above;
Thro' undulating air the sounds are sent,
And spread o'er all the fluid element.
 There various news I heard of love and
 strife,
Of peace and war. health, sickness, death,
 and life.   448

Of loss and gain, of famine, and of store,
Of storms at sea, and travels on the shore,
Of prodigies, and portents seen in air,
Of fires and plagues, and stars with blazing hair,
Of turns of fortune, changes in the state,
The fall of fav'rites, projects of the great,
Of old mismanagements, taxations new;
All neither wholly false, nor wholly true.
Above, below, without, within, around,
Confused, unnumber'd multitudes are found,
Who pass, repass, advance, and glide away, 460
Hosts rais'd by fear, and phantoms of a day :
Astrologers, that future fates foreshew,
Projectors, quacks, and lawyers not a few;
And priests, and party zealots, numerous bands,
With home-born lies or tales from foreign lands;
Each talk'd aloud, or in some secret place,
And wild impatience stared in ev'ry face.
The flying rumours gather'd as they roll'd,
Scarce any tale was sooner heard than told;
And all who told it added something new, ⎤
And all who heard it made enlargements │
too; 471 ⎬
In ev'ry ear it spread, on ev'ry tongue it │
grew. ⎦
Thus flying east and west, and north and south,
News travel'd with increase from mouth to mouth.
So from a spark that, kindled first by chance,
With gath'ring force the quick'ning flames advance;
Till to the clouds their curling heads aspire,
And towers and temples sink in floods of fire.
When thus ripe lies are to perfection sprung,
Full grown, and fit to grace a mortal tongue, 480
Thro' thousand vents, impatient, forth they flow,
And rush in millions on the world below.
Fame sits aloft, and points them out their course,
Their date determines, and prescribes their force;
Some to remain, and some to perish soon,
Or wane and wax alternate like the moon.

Around, a thousand winged wonders fly,
Borne by the trumpet's blast, and scatter'd thro' the sky.
There, at one passage, oft you might survey
A lie and truth contending for the way ; 490
And long 't was doubtful, both so closely pent,
Which first should issue thro' the narrow vent:
At last agreed, together out they fly,
Inseparable now the truth and lie;
The strict companions are for ever join'd,
And this or that unmix'd, no mortal e'er shall find,
While thus I stood, intent to see and hear,
One came, methought, and whisper'd in my ear:
' What could thus high thy rash ambition raise ?
Art thou, fond youth, a candidate for praise ? ' 500
' 'T is true,' said I, ' not void of hopes I came,
For who so fond as youthful bards of Fame ?
But few, alas! the casual blessing boast,
So hard to gain, so easy to be lost.
How vain that second life in others' breath,
Th' estate which wits inherit after death!
Ease, health, and life for this they must resign,
(Unsure the tenure, but how vast the fine!)
The great man's curse, without the gains, endure,
Be envied, wretched; and be flatter'd, poor;
All luckless wits their enemies profest, 511
And all successful, jealous friends at best.
Nor Fame I slight, nor for her favours call,
She comes unlook'd for, if she comes at all.
But if the purchase costs so dear a price
As soothing Folly, or exalting Vice;
Oh! if the Muse must flatter lawless sway,
And follow still where Fortune leads the way;
Or if no basis bear my rising name,
But the fall'n ruins of another's fame; 520
Then teach me, Heav'n! to scorn the guilty bays;
Drive from my breast that wretched lust of praise;
Unblemish'd let me live or die unknown;
Oh, grant an honest fame, or grant me none!'

TRANSLATIONS FROM OVID

SAPPHO TO PHAON

FROM THE FIFTEENTH OF OVID'S EPISTLES

Written, according to Pope, in 1707. First published in Tonson's *Ovid*, 1712.

SAY, lovely Youth, that dost my heart com-
    mand,
Can Phaon's eyes forget his Sappho's hand ?
Must then her name the wretched writer
    prove,
To thy remembrance lost, as to thy love ?
Ask not the cause that I new numbers
    choose,
The lute neglected and the lyric Muse ;
Love taught my tears in sadder notes to
    flow,
And tuned my heart to elegies of woe.
I burn, I burn, as when thro' ripen'd corn
By driving winds the spreading flames are
    borne !   10
Phaon to Ætna's scorching fields retires,
While I consume with more than Ætna's
    fires !
No more my soul a charm in music finds ;
Music has charms alone for peaceful minds.
Soft scenes of solitude no more can please ;
Love enters there, and I'm my own dis-
    ease.
No more the Lesbian dames my passion
    move,
Once the dear objects of my guilty love ;
All other loves are lost in only thine,
O youth, ungrateful to a flame like mine !
Whom would not all those blooming charms
    surprise,   21
Those heav'nly looks, and dear deluding
    eyes ?
The harp and bow would you like Phœbus
    bear,
A brighter Phœbus Phaon might appear ;
Would you with ivy wreathe your flowing
    hair,
Not Bacchus' self with Phaon could com-
    pare :
Yet Phœbus lov'd, and Bacchus felt the
    flame,
One Daphne warm'd, and one the Cretan
    dame ;

Nymphs that in verse no more could rival
    me,
Than ev'n those Gods contend in charms
    with thee.   30
The Muses teach me all their softest lays,
And the wide world resounds with Sappho's
    praise.
Tho' great Alcæus more sublimely sings,
And strikes with bolder rage the sounding
    strings,
No less renown attends the moving lyre,
Which Venus tunes, and all her loves in-
    spire ;
To me what Nature has in charms denied,
Is well by Wit's more lasting flames sup-
    plied.
Tho' short my stature, yet my name ex-
    tends
To Heav'n itself, and earth's remotest
    ends.   40
Brown as I am, an Ethiopian dame
Inspired young Perseus with a gen'rous
    flame ;
Turtles and doves of diff'rent hues unite,
And glossy jet is pair'd with shining white.
If to no charms thou wilt thy heart resign,
But such as merit, such as equal thine,
By none, alas ! by none thou canst be
    mov'd,
Phaon alone by Phaon must be lov'd !
Yet once thy Sappho could thy cares em-
    ploy,
Once in her arms you centred all your joy :
No time the dear remembrance can re-
    move,   51
For oh ! how vast a memory has Love !
My music, then, you could for ever hear,
And all my words were music to your
    ear.
You stopp'd with kisses my enchanting
    tongue,
And found my kisses sweeter than my
    song.
In all I pleas'd, but most in what was
    best;
And the last joy was dearer than the rest.
Then with each word, each glance, each
    motion fired,
You still enjoy'd, and yet you still desired,
Till, all dissolving, in the trance we lay,   61
And in tumultuous raptures died away.

The fair Sicilians now thy soul inflame;
Why was I born, ye Gods, a Lesbian
    dame ?
But ah, beware, Sicilian nymphs ! nor
    boast
That wand'ring heart which I so lately
    lost;
Nor be with all those tempting words
    abused,
Those tempting words were all to Sappho
    used.
And you that rule Sicilia's happy plains,
Have pity, Venus, on your poet's pains ! 70
Shall fortune still in one sad tenor run,
And still increase the woes so soon begun ?
Inured to sorrow from my tender years,
My parents' ashes drank my early tears:
My brother next, neglecting wealth and
    fame,
Ignobly burn'd in a destructive flame :
An infant daughter late my griefs in-
    creas'd,
And all a mother's cares distract my
    breast.
Alas ! what more could Fate itself impose,
But thee, the last, and greatest of my
    woes ?   80
No more my robes in waving purple flow,
Nor on my hand the sparkling diamonds
    glow ;
No more my locks in ringlets curl'd diffuse
The costly sweetness of Arabian dews,
Nor braids of gold the varied tresses bind,
That fly disorder'd with the wanton wind:
For whom should Sappho use such arts as
    these ?
He 's gone, whom only she desired to
    please !
Cupid's light darts my tender bosom move;
Still is there cause for Sappho still to
    love :   90
So from my birth the sisters fix'd my
    doom,
And gave to Venus all my life to come;
Or, while my Muse in melting notes com-
    plains,
My yielding heart keeps measure to my
    strains.
By charms like thine which all my soul
    have won,
Who might not — ah ! who would not be
    undone ?
For those Aurora Cephalus might scorn,
And with fresh blushes paint the conscious
    morn.

For those might Cynthia lengthen Phaon's
    sleep,   99
And bid Endymion nightly tend his sheep.
Venus for those had rapt thee to the skies;
But Mars on thee might look with Venus'
    eyes.
O scarce a youth, yet scarce a tender boy!
O useful time for lovers to employ!
Pride of thy age, and glory of thy race,
Come to these arms, and melt in this em-
    brace!
The vows you never will return, receive;
And take, at least, the love you will not
    give.
See, while I write, my words are lost in
    tears!
The less my sense, the more my love ap-
    pears.   110
Sure 't was not much to bid one kind adieu
(At least to feign was never hard to you):
'Farewell, my Lesbian love,' you might
    have said ;
Or coldly thus, 'Farewell, O Lesbian
    maid ! '
No tear did you, no parting kiss receive,
Nor knew I then how much I was to
    grieve.
No lover's gift your Sappho could confer,
And wrongs and woes were all you left
    with her.
No charge I gave you, and no charge could
    give,
But this, 'Be mindful of our loves, and
    live.'   120
Now by the Nine, those powers ador'd by
    me,
And Love, the God that ever waits on
    thee,
When first I heard (from whom I hardly
    knew)
That you were fled, and all my joys with
    you,
Like some sad statue, speechless, pale, I
    stood,
Grief chill'd my breast, and stopt my freez-
    ing blood;
No sigh to rise, no tear had power to flow,
Fix'd in a stupid lethargy of woe:
But when its way th' impetuous passion
    found,
I rend my tresses, and my breast I wound;
I rave, then weep; I curse, and then com-
    plain;   131
Now swell to rage, now melt in tears
    again.

Not fiercer pangs distract the mournful dame,
Whose first-born infant feeds the funeral flame.
My scornful brother with a smile appears,
Insults my woes, and triumphs in my tears;
His hated image ever haunts my eyes;
' And why this grief ? thy daughter lives,' he cries,
Stung with my love, and furious with despair,
All torn my garments, and my bosom bare,
My woes, thy crimes, I to the world proclaim,   141
Such inconsistent things are Love and Shame!
'T is thou art all my care and my delight,
My daily longing, and my dream by night:
O night more pleasing than the brightest day,
When fancy gives what absence takes away,
And. dress'd in all its visionary charms,
Restores my fair deserter to my arms!
Then round your neck in wanton wreaths I twine;
Then you, methinks, as fondly circle mine:
A thousand tender words I hear and speak;   151
A thousand melting kisses give and take:
Then fiercer joys — I blush to mention these,
Yet, while I blush, confess how much they please.
But when, with day, the sweet delusions fly,
And all things wake to life and joy but I,
As if once more forsaken, I complain,
And close my eyes to dream of you again:
Then frantic rise, and like some fury rove
Thro' lonely plains, and thro' the silent grove;   160
As if the silent grove, and lonely plains,
That knew my pleasures, could relieve my pains.
I view the grotto, once the scene of love,
The rocks around, the hanging roofs above,
That charm'd me more, with native moss o'ergrown,
Than Phrygian marble, or the Parian stone:
I find the shades that veil'd our joys before;
But, Phaon gone, those shades delight no more.

Here the press'd herbs with bending tops betray
Where oft entwin'd in am'rous folds we lay;   170
I kiss that earth which once was press'd by you,
And all with tears the with'ring herbs bedew.
For thee the fading trees appear to mourn,
And birds defer their songs till thy return:
Night shades the groves, and all in silence lie,
All but the mournful Philomel and I:
With mournful Philomel I join my strain,
Of Tereus she, of Phaon I complain.
A spring there is, whose silver waters show,
Clear as a glass, the shining sands below:
A flowery lotos spreads its arms above,   181
Shades all the banks, and seems itself a grove;
Eternal greens the mossy margin grace,
Watch'd by the sylvan genius of the place.
Here as I lay, and swell'd with tears the flood,
Before my sight a wat'ry virgin stood:
She stood and cried, ' O you that love in vain!
Fly hence, and seek the fair Leucadian main.
There stands a rock, from whose impending steep
Apollo's fane surveys the rolling deep;   190
There injur'd lovers, leaping from above,
Their flames extinguish, and forget to love.
Deucalion once with hopeless fury burn'd;
In vain he lov'd, relentless Pyrrha scorn'd;
But when from hence he plunged into the main,
Deucalion scorn'd, and Pyrrha lov'd in vain.
Haste, Sappho, haste, from high Leucadia throw
Thy wretched weight, nor dread the deeps below!'
She spoke, and vanish'd with the voice — I rise,
And silent tears fall trickling from my eyes.   200
I go, ye Nymphs! those rocks and seas to prove;
How much I fear, but ah, how much I love!
I go, ye Nymphs! where furious love inspires,
Let female fears submit to female fires.

To rocks and seas I fly from Phaon's hate,
And hope from seas and rocks a milder
fate.
Ye gentle gales, beneath my body blow,
And softly lay me on the waves below!
And thou, kind Love, my sinking limbs
sustain,
Spread thy soft wings, and waft me o'er
the main, 210
Nor let a lover's death the guiltless flood
profane;
On Phœbus' shrine my harp I 'll then be-
stow,
And this inscription shall be placed below:
' Here she who sung, to him that did in-
spire,
Sappho to Phœbus consecrates her lyre;
What suits with Sappho, Phœbus, suits with
thee;
The Gift, the Giver, and the God agree.'
But why, alas! relentless youth, ah why
To distant seas must tender Sappho fly ?
Thy charms than those may far more
powerful be, 220
And Phœbus' self is less a God to me.
Ah! canst thou doom me to the rocks and
sea,
Oh! far more faithless and more hard than
they ?
Ah! canst thou rather see this tender
breast
Dash'd on these rocks than to thy bosom
press'd ?
This breast which once, in vain! you liked
so well
Where the Loves play'd, and where the
Muses dwell.
Alas! the Muses now no more inspire;
Untuned my lute, and silent is my lyre. 229
My languid numbers have forgot to flow,
And fancy sinks beneath a weight of woe.
Ye Lesbian virgins, and ye Lesbian dames,
Themes of my verse, and objects of my
flames,
No more your groves with my glad songs
shall ring,
No more these hands shall touch the trem-
bling string:
My Phaon 's fled, and I those arts resign;
(Wretch that I am, to call that Phaon
mine!)
Return, fair youth, return, and bring along
Joy to my soul, and vigour to my song: 239
Absent from thee, the poet's flame expires;
But ah! how fiercely burn the lover's fires!

Gods! can no prayers, no sighs, no numbers
move
One savage heart, or teach it how to love ?
The winds my prayers, my sighs, my num-
bers bear,
The flying winds have lost them all in air!
Oh when, alas! shall more auspicious gales
To these fond eyes restore thy welcome
sails!
If you return — ah, why these long delays ?
Poor Sappho dies while careless Phaon
stays.
O launch thy bark, nor fear the wat'ry
plain; 250
Venus for thee shall smooth her native
main.
O launch thy bark, secure of prosp'rous
gales;
Cupid for thee shall spread the swelling
sails.
If you will fly — (yet ah ! what cause can be,
Too cruel youth, that you should fly from
me ?)
If not from Phaon I must hope for ease,
Ah let me seek it from the raging seas:
To raging seas unpitied I 'll remove,
And either cease to live or cease to love !

THE FABLE OF DRYOPE

FROM THE NINTH BOOK OF OVID'S
METAMORPHOSES

SHE said, and for her lost Galanthis sighs ;
When the fair consort of her son replies :
' Since you a servant's ravish'd form be-
moan,
And kindly sigh for sorrows not your own,
Let me (if tears and grief permit) relate
A nearer woe, a sister's stranger fate.
No nymph of all Œchalia could compare
For beauteous form with Dryope the fair,
Her tender mother's only hope and pride
(Myself the offspring of a second bride). 10
This nymph compress'd by him who rules
the day,
Whom Delphi and the Delian isle obey,
Andræmon lov'd ; and bless'd in all those
charms
That pleas'd a God, succeeded to her arms.
' A lake there was with shelving banks
around,
Whose verdant summit fragrant myrtles
crown'd.

These shades, unknowing of the fates, she
    sought,
And to the Naiads flowery garlands
    brought:
Her smiling babe (a pleasing charge) she
    prest
Within her arms, and nourish'd at her
    breast.   20
Not distant far a wat'ry lotos grows;
The spring was new, and all the verdant
    boughs
Adorn'd with blossoms, promis'd fruits that
    vie
In glowing colours with the Tyrian dye.
Of these she cropp'd, to please her infant
    son,
And I myself the same rash act had done:
But, lo! I saw (as near her side I stood)
The violated blossoms drop with blood;
Upon the tree I cast a frightful look;
The trembling tree with sudden horror
    shook.   30
Lotis the nymph (if rural tales be true)
As from Priapus' lawless lust she flew,
Forsook her form, and, fixing here, became
A flowery plant, which still preserves her
    name.
  'This change unknown, astonish'd at the
    sight,
My trembling sister strove to urge her
    flight;
And first the pardon of the Nymphs im-
    plor'd,
And those offended sylvan Powers ador'd:
But when she backward would have fled,
    she found
Her stiff'ning feet were rooted in the
    ground: 40
In vain to free her fasten'd feet she strove,
And as she struggles only moves above;
She feels th' encroaching bark around her
    grow
By quick degrees, and cover all below:
Surprised at this, her trembling hand she
    heaves
To rend her hair; her hand is fill'd with
    leaves:
Where late was hair the shooting leaves
    are seen
To rise, and shade her with a sudden green.
The child Amphissus, to her bosom prest,
Perceiv'd a colder and a harder breast, 50
And found the springs, that ne'er till then
    denied
Their milky moisture, on a sudden dried

I saw, unhappy! what I now relate,
And stood the helpless witness of thy fate;
Embraced thy boughs, thy rising bark de-
    lay'd,
There wish'd to grow, and mingle shade
    with shade.
  'Behold Andræmon and th' unhappy
    sire
Appear, and for their Dryope inquire:
A springing tree for Dryope they find,
And print warm kisses on the panting rind;
Prostrate, with tears, their kindred plant
    bedew,   61
And close embrace as to the roots they
    grew.
The face was all that now remain'd of
    thee,
No more a woman, nor yet quite a tree;
Thy branches hung with humid pearls ap-
    pear,
From ev'ry leaf distils a trickling tear;
And straight a voice, while yet a voice re-
    mains,
Thus thro' the trembling boughs in sighs
    complains.
  'If to the wretched any faith be giv'n,
I swear by all th' unpitying powers of
    Heav'n,   70
No wilful crime this heavy vengeance bred;
In mutual innocence our lives we led:
If this be false, let these new greens de-
    cay,
Let sounding axes lop my limbs away,
And crackling flames on all my honours
    prey.
But from my branching arms this infant
    bear;
Let some kind nurse supply a mother's
    care;
And to his mother let him oft be led,
Sport in her shades, and in her shades be
    fed.
Teach him, when first his infant voice shall
    frame   80
Imperfect words, and lisp his mother's
    name,
To hail this tree, and say with weeping
    eyes,
"Within this plant my hapless parent lies:"
And when in youth he seeks the shady
    woods,
Oh! let him fly the crystal lakes and floods,
Nor touch the fatal flowers; but, warn'd by
    me,
Believe a Goddess shrined in every tree.

My sire, my sister, and my spouse, farewell!
If in your breasts or love or pity dwell,
Protect your plant, nor let my branches
  feel 90
The browsing cattle or the piercing steel.
Farewell! and since I cannot bend to join
My lips to yours, advance at least to mine.
My son, thy mother's parting kiss receive,
While yet thy mother has a kiss to give.
I can no more; the creeping rind invades
My closing lips, and hides my head in
  shades:
Remove your hands; the bark shall soon
  suffice
Without their aid to seal these dying eyes.'
  'She ceas'd at once to speak and ceas'd
  to be, 100
And all the Nymph was lost within the
  tree;
Yet latent life thro' her new branches reign'd
And long the plant a human heat retain'd.'

VERTUMNUS AND POMONA

FROM THE FOURTEENTH BOOK OF OVID'S
METAMORPHOSES

THE fair Pomona flourish'd in his reign;
Of all the virgins of the sylvan train
None taught the trees a nobler race to
  bear,
Or more improv'd the vegetable care.
To her the shady grove, the flowery field,
The streams and fountains no delights
  could yield;
'T was all her joy the ripening fruits to
  tend,
And see the boughs with happy burdens
  bend.
The hook she bore instead of Cynthia's
  spear.
To lop the growth of the luxuriant year, 10
To decent form the lawless shoots to bring,
And teach th' obedient branches where to
  spring.
Now the cleft rind inserted grafts receives,
And yields an offspring more than Nature
  gives;
Now sliding streams the thirsty plants re-
  new,
And feed their fibres with reviving dew.
  These cares alone her virgin breast em-
  ploy,
Averse from Venus and the nuptial joy.

Her private orchards, wall'd on every side,
To lawless sylvans all access denied. 20
How oft the Satyrs and the wanton Fauns,
Who haunt the forests or frequent the
  lawns,
The God whose ensign scares the birds of
  prey,
And old Silenus, youthful in decay,
Employ'd their wiles and unavailing care
To pass the fences, and surprise the Fair?
Like these Vertumnus own'd his faithful
  flame,
Like these rejected by the scornful dame.
To gain her sight a thousand forms he
  wears;
And first a reaper from the field appears: 30
Sweating he walks, while loads of golden
  grain
O'ercharge the shoulders of the seeming
  swain:
Oft o'er his back a crooked scythe is laid,
And wreaths of hay his sunburnt temples
  shade:
Oft in his harden'd hand a goad he bears,
Like one who late unyoked the sweating
  steers:
Sometimes his pruning-hook corrects the
  vines,
And the loose stragglers to their ranks
  confines:
Now gath'ring what the bounteous year
  allows,
He pulls ripe apples from the bending
  boughs: 40
A soldier now, he with his sword appears;
A fisher next, his trembling angle bears:
Each shape he varies, and each art he
  tries,
On her bright charms to feast his longing
  eyes.
  A female form at last Vertumnus wears,
With all the marks of rev'rend age ap-
  pears,
His temples thinly spread with silver hairs:
Propp'd on his staff, and stooping as he
  goes,
A painted mitre shades his furrow'd brows.
The God in this decrepit form array'd, 50
The gardens enter'd, and the fruit sur-
  vey'd;
And, 'Happy you!' he thus address'd the
  maid,
'Whose charms as far all other nymphs
  outshine,
As other gardens are excell'd by thine!'

Then kiss'd the Fair; (his kisses warmer
grow
Than such as women on their sex bestow)
Then placed beside her on the flowery
ground,
Beheld the trees with autumn's bounty
crown'd.
An elm was near, to whose embraces led,
The curling vine her swelling clusters
spread: 60
He view'd her twining branches with de-
light,
And prais'd the beauty of the pleasing sight.
' Yet this tall elm, but for this vine,' he
said,
" Had stood neglected, and a barren shade;
And this fair vine, but that her arms sur-
round
Her married elm, had crept along the
ground.
Ah! beauteous maid! let this example move
Your mind, averse from all the joys of
love.
Deign to be lov'd, and every heart subdue!
What Nymph could e'er attract such crowds
as you ?   70
Not she whose beauty urged the Centaur's
arms,
Ulysses' queen, nor Helen's fatal charms.
Ev'n now, when silent scorn is all they
gain,
A thousand court you, tho' they court in
vain,
A thousand Sylvans, Demigods, and Gods,
That haunt our mountains and our Alban
woods.
But if you 'll prosper, mark what I advise,
Whom age and long experience render wise,
And one whose tender care is far above
All that these lovers ever felt of love   80
(Far more than e'er can by yourself be
guess'd);
Fix on Vertumnus, and reject the rest:
For his firm faith I dare engage my own;
Scarce to himself himself is better known.
To distant lands Vertumnus never roves;
Like you, contented with his native groves;
Nor at first sight, like most, admires the ⎤
Fair;   ⎬
For you he lives; and you alone shall share ⎮
His last affection as his early care.   ⎦

Besides, he 's lovely far above the rest,   90
With youth immortal, and with beauty
blest.
Add, that he varies every shape with ease,
And tries all forms that may Pomona
please.
But what should most excite a mutual flame,
Your rural cares and pleasures are the
same.
To him your orchard's early fruits are due
(A pleasing off'ring when 't is made by
you);
He values these; but yet, alas! complains
That still the best and dearest gift remains
Not the fair fruit that on yon branches
glows   100
With that ripe red th' autumnal sun be-
stows;
Nor tasteful herbs that in these gardens
rise,
Which the kind soil with milky sap sup-
plies;
You, only you, can move the God's desire.
O crown so constant and so pure a fire!
Let soft compassion touch your gentle
mind;
Think 't is Vertumnus begs you to be kind:
So may no frost, when early buds appear,
Destroy the promise of the youthful year;
Nor winds, when first your florid orchard
blows,   110
Shake the light blossoms from their blasted
boughs!'
This, when the various God had urged in
vain,
He straight assumed his native form again:
Such, and so bright an aspect now he
bears,
As when thro' clouds th' emerging sun ap-
pears,
And thence exerting his refulgent ray,
Dispels the darkness, and reveals the day.
Force he prepared, but check'd the rash
design;
For when, appearing in a form divine,
The Nymph surveys him, and beholds the
grace   120
Of charming features and a youthful face,
In her soft breast consenting passions move,
And the warm maid confess'd a mutual
love.

AN ESSAY ON CRITICISM

This, the first mature original work of the author, was written in 1709, when Pope was in his twentieth year. It was not published till 1711.

PART I

INTRODUCTION. That it is as great a fault to judge ill as to write ill, and a more dangerous one to the public. That a true Taste is as rare to be found as a true Genius. That most men are born with some Taste, but spoiled by false education. The multitude of Critics, and causes of them. That we are to study our own Taste, and know the limits of it. Nature the best guide of judgment. Improved by Art and rules, which are but methodized Nature. Rules derived from the practice of the ancient poets. That therefore the ancients are necessary to be studied by a Critic, particularly Homer and Virgil. Of licenses, and the use of them by the ancients. Reverence due to the ancients, and praise of them.

'T is hard to say if greater want of skill
Appear in writing or in judging ill;
But of the two less dangerous is th' of-
    fence
To tire our patience than mislead our sense :
Some few in that, but numbers err in this;
Ten censure wrong for one who writes
    amiss ;
A fool might once himself alone expose;
Now one in verse makes many more in
    prose.
'T is with our judgments as our watches,
    none
Go just alike, yet each believes his own. 10
In Poets as true Genius is but rare,
True Taste as seldom is the Critic's share;
Both must alike from Heav'n derive their
    light,
These born to judge, as well as those to
    write.
Let such teach others who themselves ex-
    cel,
And censure freely who have written well ;
Authors are partial to their wit, 't is true,
But are not Critics to their judgment
    too ?
Yet if we look more closely, we shall
    find
Most have the seeds of judgment in their
    mind: 20

Nature affords at least a glimm'ring light;
The lines, tho' touch'd but faintly, are drawn
    right:
But as the slightest sketch, if justly traced, ⎫
Is by ill col'ring but the more disgraced, ⎬
So by false learning is good sense defaced: ⎭
Some are bewilder'd in the maze of
    schools,
And some made coxcombs Nature meant
    but fools:
In search of wit these lose their common
    sense,
And then turn Critics in their own defence:
Each burns alike, who can or cannot write,
Or with a rival's or an eunuch's spite. 31
All fools have still an itching to deride,
And fain would be upon the laughing side.
If Mævius scribble in Apollo's spite,
There are who judge still worse than he
    can write.
Some have at first for Wits, then Poets
    pass'd;
Turn'd Critics next, and prov'd plain Fools
    at last.
Some neither can for Wits nor Critics pass,
As heavy mules are neither horse nor ass.
Those half-learn'd witlings, numerous in
    our isle, 40
As half-form'd insects on the banks of
    Nile ;
Unfinish'd things, one knows not what to
    call,
Their generation 's so equivocal;
To tell them would a hundred tongues re-
    quire,
Or one vain Wit's, that might a hundred
    tire.
But you who seek to give and merit
    fame,
And justly bear a Critic's noble name,
Be sure yourself and your own reach to
    know,
How far your Genius, Taste, and Learning
    go,
Launch not beyond your depth, but be dis-
    creet, 50
And mark that point where Sense and Dul-
    ness meet.

Nature to all things fix'd the limits fit,
And wisely curb'd proud man's pretending
    wit.
As on the land while here the ocean
    gains,
In other parts it leaves wide sandy plains;
Thus in the soul while Memory prevails,
The solid power of Understanding fails;
Where beams of warm Imagination play,
The Memory's soft figures melt away.
One Science only will one genius fit;   60
So vast is Art, so narrow human wit:
Not only bounded to peculiar arts,
But oft in those confin'd to single parts.
Like Kings we lose the conquests gain'd
    before,
By vain ambition still to make them more :
Each might his sev'ral province well com-
    mand,
Would all but stoop to what they under-
    stand.
  First follow Nature, and your judgment
    frame
By her just standard, which is still the
    same ;
Unerring Nature, still divinely bright,   70
One clear, unchanged, and universal light,
Life, force, and beauty must to all impart,
At once the source, and end, and test of
    Art.
Art from that fund each just supply pro-
    vides,
Works without show, and without pomp
    presides.
In some fair body thus th' informing soul
With spirits feeds, with vigour fills the
    whole;
Each motion guides, and every nerve sus-
    tains,
Itself unseen, but in th' effects remains.
Some, to whom Heav'n in wit has been pro-
    fuse,   80
Want as much more to turn it to its use ;
For Wit and Judgment often are at strife,
Tho' meant each other's aid, like man and
    wife.
'T is more to guide than spur the Muse's
    steed,
Restrain his fury than provoke his speed:
The winged courser, like a gen'rous horse,
Shows most true mettle when you check
    his course.
  Those rules of old, discover'd, not de-
    vised,
Are Nature still, but Nature methodized;

Nature, like Liberty, is but restrain'd   90
By the same laws which first herself or-
    dain'd.
  Hear how learn'd Greece her useful rules
    indites
When to repress and when indulge our
    flights:
High on Parnassus' top her sons she
    show'd,
And pointed out those arduous paths they
    trod;
Held from afar, aloft, th' immortal prize,
And urged the rest by equal steps to rise.
Just precepts thus from great examples
    giv'n,
She drew from them what they derived
    from Heav'n.
The gen'rous Critic fann'd the poet's fire,
And taught the world with reason to ad-
    mire.   101
Then Criticism the Muse's handmaid
    prov'd,
To dress her charms, and make her more
    belov'd:
But following Wits from that intention
    stray'd:
Who could not win the mistress woo'd the
    maid;
Against the Poets their own arms they
    turn'd,
Sure to hate most the men from whom
    they learn'd.
So modern 'pothecaries, taught the art
By doctors' bills to play the doctor's part,
Bold in the practice of mistaken rules,   110
Prescribe, apply, and call their masters
    fools.
Some on the leaves of ancient authors prey;
Nor time nor moths e'er spoil'd so much as
    they;
Some drily plain, without invention's aid,
Write dull receipts how poems may be
    made;
These leave the sense their learning to
    display,
And those explain the meaning quite away.
  You then whose judgment the right course
    would steer,
Know well each ancient's proper character;
His fable, subject, scope in every page;   120
Religion, country, genius of his age:
Without all these at once before your eyes,
Cavil you may, but never criticise.
Be Homer's works your study and delight,
Read them by day, and meditate by night;

Thence form your judgment, thence your
   maxims bring,
And trace the Muses upward to their spring.
Still with itself compared, his text peruse;
And let your comment be the Mantuan
   Muse.
When first young Maro in his boundless
   mind   130
A work t' outlast immortal Rome design'd,
Perhaps he seem'd above the critic's law,
And but from Nature's fountains scorn'd to
   draw;
But when t' examine ev'ry part he came,
Nature and Homer were, he found, the
   same.
Convinced, amazed, he checks the bold ⎫
   design,   ⎪
And rules as strict his labour'd work con- ⎬
   fine   ⎪
As if the Stagyrite o'erlook'd each line. ⎭
Learn hence for ancient rules a just es-
   teem;
To copy Nature is to copy them.   140
   Some beauties yet no precepts can de-
   clare,
For there 's a happiness as well as care.
Music resembles poetry; in each   ⎫
Are nameless graces which no methods ⎬
   teach,   ⎪
And which a master-hand alone can reach. ⎭
If, where the rules not far enough extend,
(Since rules were made but to promote their
   end)
Some lucky license answer to the full
Th' intent proposed, that license is a rule.
Thus Pegasus, a nearer way to take,   150
May boldly deviate from the common track.
Great Wits sometimes may gloriously of-
   fend,
And rise to faults true Critics dare not
   mend;
From vulgar bounds with brave disorder
   part,
And snatch a grace beyond the reach of Art,
Which, without passing thro' the judg-
   ment, gains
The heart, and all its end at once attains.
In prospects thus some objects please our ⎫
   eyes,   ⎬
Which out of Nature's common order rise, ⎪
The shapeless rock, or hanging precipice. ⎭
But tho' the ancients thus their rules in-
   vade,   161
(As Kings dispense with laws themselves
   have made)

Moderns, beware! or if you must offend
Against the precept, ne'er transgress its end;
Let it be seldom, and compell'd by need;
And have at least their precedent to plead;
The Critic else proceeds without remorse,
Seizes your fame, and puts his laws in
   force.
   I know there are to whose presumptu-
   ous thoughts
Those freer beauties, ev'n in them, seem
   faults.   170
Some figures monstrous and misshaped ap-
   pear,
Consider'd singly, or beheld too near,
Which, but proportion'd to their light or
   place,
Due distance reconciles to form and grace.
A prudent chief not always must display
His powers in equal ranks and fair array,
But with th' occasion and the place comply,
Conceal his force, nay, seem sometimes to
   fly.
Those oft are stratagems which errors
   seem,
Nor is it Homer nods, but we that dream.
   Still green with bays each ancient altar
   stands   181
Above the reach of sacrilegious hands,
Secure from flames, from Envy's fiercer
   rage,
Destructive war, and all-involving Age.
See from each clime the learn'd their incense
   bring!
Hear in all tongues consenting pæans ring!
In praise so just let ev'ry voice be join'd,
And fill the gen'ral chorus of mankind.
Hail, Bards triumphant! born in happier
   days,
Immortal heirs of universal praise!   190
Whose honours with increase of ages grow,
As streams roll down, enlarging as they
   flow;
Nations unborn your mighty names shall
   sound,
And worlds applaud that must not yet be
   found!
O may some spark of your celestial fire
The last, the meanest of your sons inspire,
(That on weak wings, from far, pursues
   your flights,
Glows while he reads, but trembles as he
   writes)
To teach vain Wits a science little known,
T' admire superior sense, and doubt their
   own.   200

PART II

Causes hindering a true judgment. Pride.
Imperfect learning. Judging by parts, and
not by the whole. Critics in wit, language,
versification only. Being too hard to please,
or too apt to admire. Partiality — too much
love to a sect — to the ancients or moderns. Prejudice or prevention. Singularity.
Inconstancy. Party spirit. Envy. Against
envy, and in praise of good-nature. When
severity is chiefly to be used by critics.

Of all the causes which conspire to blind
Man's erring judgment, and misguide the
  mind,
What the weak head with strongest bias
  rules,
Is Pride, the never failing vice of fools.
Whatever Nature has in worth denied
She gives in large recruits of needful Pride:
For as in bodies, thus in souls, we find
What wants in blood and spirits swell'd
  with wind:
Pride, where Wit fails, steps in to our de-
  fence,
And fills up all the mighty void of Sense: 10
If once right Reason drives that cloud away,
Truth breaks upon us with resistless day.
Trust not yourself; but your defects to
  know,
Make use of ev'ry friend — and ev'ry foe.
— A little learning is a dangerous thing;
Drink deep, or taste not the Pierian spring:
There shallow draughts intoxicate the brain,
And drinking largely sobers us again.
Fired at first sight with what the Muse
  imparts,
In fearless youth we tempt the heights of
  arts, 20
While from the bounded level of our mind
Short views we take, nor see the lengths
  behind:
But more advanc'd, behold with strange
  surprise
New distant scenes of endless science rise!
So pleas'd at first the tow'ring Alps we
  try,
Mount o'er the vales, and seem to tread the
  sky;
Th' eternal snows appear already past,
And the first clouds and mountains seem the
  last:
But those attain'd, we tremble to survey
The growing labours of the lengthen'd
  way; 30

Th' increasing prospect tires our wand'ring
  eyes,
Hills peep o'er hills, and Alps on Alps
  arise!
A perfect judge will read each work of
  wit
With the same spirit that its author writ;
Survey the whole, nor seek slight faults to
  find
Where Nature moves, and Rapture warms
  the mind:
Nor lose, for that malignant dull delight,
The gen'rous pleasure to be charm'd with
  wit.
But in such lays as neither ebb nor flow,
Correctly cold, and regularly low, 40
That shunning faults one quiet tenor keep,
We cannot blame indeed — but we may
  sleep.
In Wit, as Nature, what affects our hearts
Is not th' exactness of peculiar parts;
'T is not a lip or eye we beauty call,
But the joint force and full result of all.
Thus when we view some well proportion'd
  dome,
(The world's just wonder, and ev'n thine, O
  Rome!)
No single parts unequally surprise,
All comes united to th' admiring eyes; 50
No monstrous height, or breadth, or length,
  appear;
The whole at once is bold and regular.
  Whoever thinks a faultless piece to see,
Thinks what ne'er was, nor is, nor e'er shall
  be.
In every work regard the writer's end,
Since none can compass more than they in-
  tend;
And if the means be just, the conduct true,
Applause, in spite of trivial faults, is due.
As men of breeding, sometimes men of
  wit,
T' avoid great errors must the less commit;
Neglect the rules each verbal critic lays, 6.
For not to know some trifles is a praise.
Most critics, fond of some subservient art,
Still make the whole depend upon a part:
They talk of Principles, but Notions prize,
And all to one lov'd folly sacrifice.
  Once on a time La Mancha's Knight,
  they say,
A certain bard encount'ring on the way,
Discours'd in terms as just, with looks as
  sage,
As e'er could Dennis, of the Grecian Stage.

Concluding all were desperate sots and
    fools 71
Who durst depart from Aristotle's rules.
Our author, happy in a judge so nice,
Produced his play, and begg'd the knight's
    advice;
Made him observe the Subject and the Plot,
The Manners, Passions, Unities; what not?
All which exact to rule were brought about,
Were but a combat in the lists left out.
'What! leave the combat out?' exclaims
    the knight.
'Yes, or we must renounce the Stagyrite.'
'Not so, by Heaven! (he answers in a
    rage) 81
Knights, squires, and steeds must enter on
    the stage.'
'So vast a throng the stage can ne'er con-
    tain.'
'Then build a new, or act it in a plain.'
    Thus critics of less judgment than ca-
    price,
Curious, not knowing, not exact, but nice,
Form short ideas, and offend in Arts
(As most in Manners), by a love to parts.
    Some to Conceit alone their taste confine,
And glitt'ring thoughts struck out at every
    line; 90
Pleas'd with a work where nothing's just or
    fit,
One glaring chaos and wild heap of wit.
Poets, like painters, thus unskill'd to trace
The naked nature and the living grace,
With gold and jewels cover every part,
And hide with ornaments their want of Art.
True Wit is Nature to advantage dress'd,
What oft was thought, but ne'er so well ex-
    press'd;
Something whose truth convinced at sight
    we find,
That gives us back the image of our mind.
As shades more sweetly recommend the
    light, 101
So modest plainness sets off sprightly wit:
For works may have more wit than does
    them good,
As bodies perish thro' excess of blood.
    Others for language all their care express,
And value books, as women men, for dress:
Their praise is still — the Style is excel-
    lent;
The Sense they humbly take upon content.
Words are like leaves; and where they
    most abound,
Much fruit of sense beneath is rarely found.

False eloquence, like the prismatic glass, 111
Its gaudy colours spreads on every place;
The face of Nature we no more survey,
All glares alike, without distinction gay;
But true expression, like th' unchanging ⎤
    sun,   ⎟
Clears and improves whate'er it shines ⎬
    upon;   ⎟
It gilds all objects, but it alters none. ⎦
Expression is the dress of thought, and still
Appears more decent as more suitable.
A vile Conceit in pompous words express'd
Is like a clown in regal purple dress'd. 121
For diff'rent styles with diff'rent subjects
    sort,
As sev'ral garbs with country, town, and
    court.
Some by old words to fame have made
    pretence,
Ancients in phrase, mere moderns in their
    sense;
Such labour'd nothings, in so strange a
    style,
Amaze th' unlearn'd, and make the learned
    smile;
Unlucky as Fungoso in the play,
These sparks with awkward vanity display
What the fine gentleman wore yesterday;
And but so mimic ancient wits at best, 131
As apes our grandsires in their doublets
    drest.
In words as fashions the same rule will hold,
Alike fantastic if too new or old:
Be not the first by whom the new are tried,
Nor yet the last to lay the old aside.
    But most by Numbers judge a poet's
    song,
And smooth or rough with them is right or
    wrong.
In the bright Muse tho' thousand charms
    conspire, 139
Her voice is all these tuneful fools admire;
Who haunt Parnassus but to please their ⎤
    ear,   ⎟
Not mend their minds; as some to church ⎬
    repair,   ⎟
Not for the doctrine, but the music there. ⎦
These equal syllables alone require,
Tho' oft the ear the open vowels tire,
While expletives their feeble aid do join,
And ten low words oft creep in one dull
    line:
While they ring round the same unvaried
    chimes,
With sure returns of still expected rhymes,

Where'er you find 'the cooling western
   breeze,'   150
In the next line, it 'whispers thro' the
   trees;'
If crystal streams 'with pleasing murmurs
   creep,'
The reader's threaten'd (not in vain) with
   'sleep;'
Then, at the last and only couplet, fraught
With some unmeaning thing they call a
   thought,
A needless Alexandrine ends the song,
That, like a wounded snake, drags its slow
   length along.
Leave such to tune their own dull rhymes,
   and know
What's roundly smooth, or languishingly
   slow ;
And praise the easy vigour of a line   160
Where Denham's strength and Waller's
   sweetness join.
True ease in writing comes from Art, not
   Chance,
As those move easiest who have learn'd to
   dance.
'T is not enough no harshness gives offence;
The sound must seem an echo to the sense.
Soft is the strain when zephyr gently blows,
And the smooth stream in smoother num-
   bers flows ;
But when loud surges lash the sounding
   shore,
The hoarse rough verse should like the tor-
   rent roar.
When Ajax strives some rock's vast weight
   to throw,   170
The line, too, labours, and the words move
   slow:
Not so when swift Camilla scours the plain,
Flies o'er th' unbending corn, and skims
   along the main.
Hear how Timotheus' varied lays surprise,
And bid alternate passions fall and rise!
While at each change the son of Libyan
   Jove
Now burns with glory, and then melts with
   love;
Now his fierce eyes with sparkling fury
   glow,
Now sighs steal out, and tears begin to
   flow:
Persians and Greeks like turns of nature
   found,   180
And the world's Victor stood subdued by
   sound.

The power of music all our hearts allow,
And what Timotheus was is Dryden now.
  Avoid extremes, and shun the fault of
   such
Who still are pleas'd too little or too much.
At ev'ry trifle scorn to take offence;
That always shows great pride or little
   sense:
Those heads, as stomachs, are not sure the
   best
Which nauseate all, and nothing can digest.
Yet let not each gay turn thy rapture
   move;   190
For fools admire, but men of sense ap-
   prove:
As things seem large which we thro' mist
   descry,
Dulness is ever apt to magnify.
  Some foreign writers, some our own de-
   spise;
The ancients only, or the moderns prize.
Thus Wit, like Faith, by each man is ap-
   plied
To one small sect, and all are damn'd be-
   side.
Meanly they seek the blessing to confine,
And force that sun but on a part to shine,
Which not alone the southern wit sub-
   limes,   200
But ripens spirits in cold northern climes;
Which from the first has shone on ages
   past,
Enlights the present, and shall warm the
   last;
Tho' each may feel increases and decays,
And see now clearer and now darker days.
Regard not then if wit be old or new,
But blame the False and value still the
   True.
  Some ne'er advance a judgment of their
   own,
But catch the spreading notion of the town;
They reason and conclude by precedent, 210
And own stale nonsense which they ne'er
   invent.
Some judge of authors' names, not works,
   and then
Nor praise nor blame the writings, but the
   men.
Of all this servile herd, the worst is he
That in proud dulness joins with quality;
A constant critic at the great man's board,
To fetch and carry nonsense for my lord.
What woful stuff this madrigal would be
In some starv'd hackney sonneteer or me !

But let a lord once own the happy lines,
How the Wit brightens! how the Style re-
fines! 221
Before his sacred name flies every fault,
And each exalted stanza teems with
thought!
The vulgar thus thro' imitation err,
As oft the learn'd by being singular;
So much they scorn the crowd, that if the
throng
By chance go right, they purposely go
wrong.
So schismatics the plain believers quit,
And are but damn'd for having too much
wit.
Some praise at morning what they blame
at night, 230
But always think the last opinion right.
A Muse by these is like a mistress used,
This hour she 's idolized, the next abused;
While their weak heads, like towns unfor-
tified,
'Twixt sense and nonsense daily change
their side.
Ask them the cause; they 're wiser still
they say;
And still to-morrow 's wiser than to-day.
We think our fathers fools, so wise we
grow;
Our wiser sons no doubt will think us so.
Once school-divines this zealous isle o'er-
spread; 240
Who knew most sentences was deepest
read.
Faith, Gospel, all seem'd made to be dis-
puted,
And none had sense enough to be confuted.
Scotists and Thomists now in peace re-
main
Amidst their kindred cobwebs in Duck-
lane.
If Faith itself has diff'rent dresses worn,
What wonder modes in Wit should take
their turn ?
Oft, leaving what is natural and fit,
The current Folly proves the ready Wit;
And authors think their reputation safe, 250
Which lives as long as fools are pleas'd to
laugh.
Some, valuing those of their own side or
mind,
Still make themselves the measure of man-
kind:
Fondly we think we honour merit then,
When we but praise ourselves in other men.

Parties in wit attend on those of state,
And public faction doubles private hate.
Pride, Malice, Folly, against Dryden rose,
In various shapes of parsons, critics, beaux:
But sense survived when merry jests were
past; 260
For rising merit will buoy up at last.
Might he return and bless once more our
eyes,
New Blackmores and new Milbournes
must arise.
Nay, should great Homer lift his awful
head,
Zoilus again would start up from the dead.
Envy will Merit as its shade pursue,
But like a shadow proves the substance
true;
For envied Wit, like Sol eclips'd, makes
known
Th' opposing body's grossness, not its own.
When first that sun too powerful beams
displays, 270
It draws up vapours which obscure its
rays;
But ev'n those clouds at last adorn its way,
Reflect new glories, and augment the day.
Be thou the first true merit to befriend;
His praise is lost who stays till all com-
mend.
Short is the date, alas ! of modern rhymes,
And 't is but just to let them live betimes.
No longer now that Golden Age appears,
When patriarch wits survived a thousand
years:
Now length of fame (our second life) is
lost, 280
And bare threescore is all ev'n that can
boast:
Our sons their fathers' failing language see,
And such as Chaucer is shall Dryden be.
So when the faithful pencil has design'd
Some bright idea of the master's mind,
Where a new world leaps out at his com-
mand,
And ready Nature waits upon his hand;
When the ripe colours soften and unite,
And sweetly melt into just shade and
light;
When mellowing years their full perfection
give, 290
And each bold figure just begins to live,
The treach'rous colours the fair art be-
tray,
And all the bright creation fades away !
Unhappy Wit, like most mistaken things,

Atones not for that envy which it brings:
In youth alone its empty praise we boast,
But soon the short-lived vanity is lost;
Like some fair flower the early Spring sup-
plies,
That gaily blooms, but ev'n in blooming
dies.
What is this Wit, which must our cares em-
ploy?   300
The owner's wife that other men enjoy;
Then most our trouble still when most ad-
mired,
And still the more we give, the more re-
quired;
Whose fame with pains we guard, but lose
with ease,
Sure some to vex, but never all to please,
'T is what the vicious fear, the virtuous
shun;
By fools 't is hated, and by knaves un-
done!
  If Wit so much from Ignorance un-
dergo,
Ah, let not Learning too commence its
foe!
Of old those met rewards who could ex-
cel,   310
And such were prais'd who but endeavour'd
well;
Tho' triumphs were to gen'rals only due,
Crowns were reserv'd to grace the soldiers
too.
Now they who reach Parnassus' lofty
crown
Employ their pains to spurn some others
down;
And while self-love each jealous writer
rules,
Contending wits become the sport of fools;
But still the worst with most regret com-
mend,
For each ill author is as bad a friend.
To what base ends, and by what abject
ways,   320
Are mortals urged thro' sacred lust of
praise!
Ah, ne'er so dire a thirst of glory boast,
Nor in the critic let the man be lost!
Good nature and good sense must ever
join;
To err is human, to forgive divine.
  But if in noble minds some dregs re-
main,
Not yet purged off, of spleen and sour dis-
dain,

Discharge that rage on more provoking
crimes,
Nor fear a dearth in these flagitious times.
No pardon vile obscenity should find,   330
Tho' Wit and Art conspire to move your
mind;
But dulness with obscenity must prove
As shameful sure as impotence in love.
In the fat age of pleasure, wealth, and
ease
Sprung the rank weed, and thrived with
large increase:
When love was all an easy monarch's care,
Seldom at council, never in a war;
Jilts ruled the state, and statesmen farces
writ;
Nay wits had pensions, and young lords had
wit;   339
The Fair sat panting at a courtier's play,
And not a mask went unimprov'd away;
The modest fan was lifted up no more,
And virgins smil'd at what they blush'd
before.
The following license of a foreign reign
Did all the dregs of bold Socinus drain;
Then unbelieving priests reform'd the na-
tion,
And taught more pleasant methods of sal-
vation;
Where Heav'n's free subjects might their
rights dispute,
Lest God himself should seem too abso-
lute;   349
Pulpits their sacred satire learn'd to spare,
And vice admired to find a flatt'rer there!
Encouraged thus, Wit's Titans braved the
skies,
And the press groan'd with licens'd blas-
phemies.
These monsters, Critics! with your darts
engage,
Here point your thunder, and exhaust your
rage!
Yet shun their fault, who, scandalously
nice,
Will needs mistake an author into vice:
All seems infected that th' infected spy,
As all looks yellow to the jaundic'd eye.

PART III

Rules for the conduct and manners in a Critic.
Candour. Modesty. Good breeding. Sin-
cerity and freedom of advice. When one's
counsel is to be restrained. Character of an

incorrigible poet. And of an impertinent critic. Character of a good critic. The history of criticism, and characters of the best critics ; Aristotle. Horace. Dionysius. Petronius. Quintilian. Longinus. Of the decay of Criticism, and its revival. Erasmus. Vida. Boileau. Lord Roscommon, &c. Conclusion.

Learn then what morals Critics ought to show,
For 't is but half a judge's task to know.
'T is not enough Taste, Judgment, Learning join;
In all you speak let Truth and Candour shine;
That not alone what to your Sense is due
All may allow, but seek your friendship too.
Be silent always when you doubt your Sense,
And speak, tho' sure, with seeming diffidence.
Some positive persisting fops we know,
Who if once wrong will needs be always so;　10
But you with pleasure own your errors past,
And make each day a critique on the last.
'T is not enough your counsel still be true ;
Blunt truths more mischief than nice falsehoods do.
Men must be taught as if you taught them not,
And things unknown proposed as things forgot.
Without good breeding truth is disapprov'd ;
That only makes superior Sense belov'd.
Be niggards of advice on no pretence,
For the worst avarice is that of Sense.　20
With mean complacence ne'er betray your trust,
Nor be so civil as to prove unjust.
Fear not the anger of the wise to raise ;
Those best can bear reproof who merit praise.
'T were well might critics still this freedom take,
But Appius reddens at each word you speak,
And stares tremendous, with a threat'ning eye,
Like some fierce tyrant in old tapestry.
Fear most to tax an honourable fool,

Whose right it is, uncensured to be dull :　30
Such without Wit, are poets when they please,
As without Learning they can take degrees.
Leave dangerous truths to unsuccessful satires,
And flattery to fulsome dedicators ;
Whom, when they praise, the world believes no more
Than when they promise to give scribbling o'er.
'T is best sometimes your censure to restrain,
And charitably let the dull be vain ;
Your silence there is better than your spite,
For who can rail so long as they can write ?　40
Still humming on their drowsy course they keep,
And lash'd so long, like tops, are lash'd asleep.
False steps but help them to renew the race,
As, after stumbling, jades will mend their pace.
What crowds of these, impenitently bold,
In sounds and jingling syllables grown old,
Still run on poets, in a raging vein,
Ev'n to the dregs and squeezings of the brain,
Strain out the last dull droppings of their sense,
And rhyme with all the rage of impotence !　50
Such shameless bards we have ; and yet 't is true
There are as mad abandon'd critics too.
The bookful blockhead ignorantly read,
With loads of learned lumber in his head,
With his own tongue still edifies his ears,
And always list'ning to himself appears.
All books he reads, and all he reads assails,
From Dryden's Fables down to Durfey's Tales.
With him most authors steal their works, or buy ;
Garth did not write his own Dispensary.　60
Name a new play, and he 's the poet's friend;
Nay, show'd his faults — but when would poets mend ?
No place so sacred from such fops is barr'd,
Nor is Paul's church more safe than Paul's churchyard :

Nay, fly to altars ; there they 'll talk you
dead ;
For fools rush in where angels fear to tread.
Distrustful sense with modest caution ⎫
speaks, ⎪
It still looks home, and short excursions ⎬
makes; ⎪
But rattling nonsense in full volleys breaks ⎭
And never shock'd, and never turn'd
aside, 70
Bursts out, resistless, with a thund'ring
tide.
But where 's the man who counsel can
bestow,
Still pleas'd to teach, and yet not proud to
know ?
Unbiass'd or by favour or by spite;
Not dully prepossess'd nor blindly right;
Tho' learn'd, well bred, and tho' well bred
sincere;
Modestly bold, and humanly severe;
Who to a friend his faults can freely show,
And gladly praise the merit of a foe;
Bless'd with a taste exact, yet unconfin'd,
A knowledge both of books and human-
kind; 81
Gen'rous converse; a soul exempt from
pride;
And love to praise, with reason on his
side ?
Such once were critics; such the happy
few
Athens and Rome in better ages knew.
The mighty Stagyrite first left the shore,
Spread all his sails, and durst the deeps
explore;
He steer'd securely, and discover'd far,
Led by the light of the Mæonian star.
Poets, a race long unconfin'd and free, 90
Still fond and proud of savage liberty,
Receiv'd his laws, and stood convinc'd
't was fit
Who conquer'd Nature should preside o'er
Wit.
Horace still charms with graceful negli-
gence,
And without method talks us into sense;
Will, like a friend, familiarly convey
The truest notions in the easiest way.
He who, supreme in judgment as in wit,
Might boldly censure as he boldly writ,
Yet judg'd with coolness, though he sung
with fire; 100
His precepts teach but what his works in-
spire.

Our critics take a contrary extreme,
They judge with fury, but they write with
phlegm;
Nor suffers Horace more in wrong transla-
tions
By Wits, than Critics in as wrong quota-
tions.
See Dionysius Homer's thoughts refine,
And call new beauties forth from ev'ry
line !
Fancy and art in gay Petronius please,
The Scholar's learning with the courtier's
ease.
In grave Quintilian's copious work we
find 110
The justest rules and clearest method
join'd.
Thus useful arms in magazines we place,
All ranged in order, and disposed with
grace;
But less to please the eye than arm the
hand,
Still fit for use, and ready at command.
Thee, bold Longinus ! all the Nine in-
spire,
And bless their critic with a poet's fire:
An ardent judge, who, zealous in his trust,
With warmth gives sentence, yet is always
just;
Whose own example strengthens all his
laws, 120
And is himself that great sublime he draws.
Thus long succeeding critics justly
reign'd,
License repress'd, and useful laws ordain'd:
Learning and Rome alike in empire grew,
And arts still follow'd where her eagles
flew;
From the same foes at last both felt their
doom,
And the same age saw learning fall and
Rome.
With tyranny then superstition join'd,
As that the body, this enslaved the mind;
Much was believ'd, but little understood,
And to be dull was construed to be good;
A second deluge learning thus o'errun, 132
And the monks finish'd what the Goths
begun.
At length Erasmus, that great injur'd
name,
(The glory of the priesthood and the
shame !)
Stemm'd the wild torrent of a barb'rous
age,

And drove those holy Vandals off the
  stage.
But see! each Muse in Leo's golden
  days
Starts from her trance, and trims her with-
  er'd bays.
Rome's ancient genius, o'er its ruins
  spread, 140
Shakes off the dust, and rears his rev'rend
  head.
Then sculpture and her sister arts re-
  vive;
Stones leap'd to form, and rocks began to
  live;
With sweeter notes each rising temple
  rung;
A Raphael painted and a Vida sung:
Immortal Vida! on whose honour'd brow
The poet's bays and critic's ivy grow:
Cremona now shall ever boast thy name,
As next in place to Mantua, next in fame!
  But soon by impious arms from Latium
  chased, 150
Their ancient bounds the banish'd Muses
  pass'd;
Thence arts o'er all the northern world ad-
  vance,
But critic learning flourish'd most in France;
The rules a nation born to serve obeys,
And Boileau still in right of Horace sways.
But we, brave Britons, foreign laws de-
  spised,
And kept unconquer'd and uncivilized;
Fierce for the liberties of wit, and bold,
We still defied the Romans, as of old.
Yet some there were, among the sounder
  few 160
Of those who less presumed and better
  knew,

Who durst assert the juster ancient cause,
And here restor'd Wit's fundamental laws.
Such was the Muse whose rules and prac-
  tice tell
'Nature's chief masterpiece is writing
  well.'
Such was Roscommon, not more learn'd
  than good,
With manners gen'rous as his noble blood;
To him the wit of Greece and Rome was
  known,
And every author's merit but his own.
Such late was Walsh — the Muse's judge
  and friend, 170
Who justly knew to blame or to com-
  mend;
To failings mild but zealous for desert,
The clearest head, and the sincerest heart.
This humble praise, lamented Shade! re-
  ceive;
This praise at least a grateful Muse may
  give:
The Muse whose early voice you taught to
  sing,
Prescribed her heights, and pruned her
  tender wing,
(Her guide now lost), no more attempts to
  rise,
But in low numbers short excursions tries;
Content if hence th' unlearn'd their wants
  may view, 180
The learn'd reflect on what before they
  knew;
Careless of censure, nor too fond of fame;
Still pleas'd to praise, yet not afraid to
  blame;
Averse alike to flatter or offend;
Not free from faults, nor yet too vain to
  mend.

POEMS WRITTEN BETWEEN 1708 AND 1712

ODE FOR MUSIC ON ST. CECILIA'S DAY

This ode was written at the suggestion of Richard Steele, in 1708. It was recast in 1730 in briefer form so that it might be set to music; and the first four stanzas were considerably changed.

I

DESCEND, ye Nine, descend and sing:
The breathing instruments inspire,
Wake into voice each silent string,
And sweep the sounding lyre.
    In a sadly pleasing strain
    Let the warbling lute complain;
    Let the loud trumpet sound,
    Till the roofs all around
    The shrill echoes rebound;
While in more lengthen'd notes and slow
The deep, majestic, solemn organs blow.   11
    Hark! the numbers soft and clear
    Gently steal upon the ear;
    Now louder, and yet louder rise,
    And fill with spreading sounds the skies:
Exulting in triumph now swell the bold notes,
In broken air, trembling, the wild music floats:
    Till by degrees, remote and small,
    The strains decay,
    And melt away   20
    In a dying, dying fall.

II

By Music minds an equal temper know,
    Nor swell too high, nor sink too low.
If in the breast tumultuous joys arise,
Music her soft assuasive voice applies;
    Or when the soul is press'd with cares,
    Exalts her in enlivening airs.
Warriors she fires with animated sounds,
Pours balm into the bleeding lover's wounds;
    Melancholy lifts her head,   30
    Morpheus rouses from his bed,
    Sloth unfolds her arms and wakes,
    List'ning Envy drops her snakes;
Intestine war no more our passions wage,
And giddy Factions hear away their rage.

III

But when our country's cause provokes to arms,
How martial music ev'ry bosom warms!
So when the first bold vessel dared the seas,
High on the stern the Thracian rais'd his strain,
    While Argo saw her kindred trees   40
    Descend from Pelion to the main:
    Transported demigods stood round,
    And men grew heroes at the sound,
        Inflamed with Glory's charms:
    Each chief his sev'nfold shield display'd,
    And half unsheath'd the shining blade;
    And seas, and rocks, and skies rebound
        To arms, to arms, to arms!

IV

But when thro' all th' infernal bounds,
Which flaming Phlegethon surrounds,   50
Love, strong as Death, the Poet led
To the pale nations of the dead,
    What sounds were heard,
    What scenes appear'd,
    O'er all the dreary coasts!
        Dreadful gleams,
        Dismal screams,
        Fires that glow,
        Shrieks of woe,
        Sullen moans,   60
        Hollow groans,
    And cries of tortured ghosts!
But hark! he strikes the golden lyre,
And see! the tortured ghosts respire!
    See, shady forms advance!
Thy stone, O Sisyphus, stands still,
    Ixion rests upon his wheel,
        And the pale spectres dance;
The Furies sink upon their iron beds,
And snakes uncurl'd hang list'ning round their heads.   70

V

By the streams that ever flow,
By the fragrant winds that blow
O'er th' Elysian flowers;
By those happy souls who dwell
In yellow meads of Asphodel,
Or Amaranthine bowers·

By the heroes' armed shades,
Glitt'ring thro' the gloomy glades;
By the youths that died for love,
Wand'ring in the myrtle grove, 80
Restore, restore Eurydice to life !
Oh, take the husband, or return the wife !
He sung, and Hell consented
To hear the Poet's prayer :
Stern Proserpine relented,
And gave him back the Fair.
Thus song could prevail
O'er Death and o'er Hell,
A conquest how hard and how glorious !
Tho' fate had fast bound her, 90
With Styx nine times round her,
Yet music and love were victorious.

VI

But soon, too soon, the lover turns his eyes:
Again she falls, again she dies, she dies !
How wilt thou now the fatal sisters move ?
No crime was thine, if 't is no crime to love.
Now under hanging mountains,
Beside the falls of fountains,
Or where Hebrus wanders,
Rolling in meanders, 100
All alone,
Unheard, unknown,
He makes his moan;
And calls her ghost,
For ever, ever, ever lost !
Now with Furies surrounded,
Despairing, confounded,
He trembles, he glows,
Amidst Rhodope's snows.
See, wild as the winds, o'er the desert he
flies ! 110
Hark ! Hæmus resounds with the Baccha-
nals' cries —
Ah see, he dies !
Yet ev'n in death Eurydice he sung,
Eurydice still trembled on his tongue ;
Eurydice the woods,
Eurydice the floods,
Eurydice the rocks and hollow mountains
rung.

VII

Music the fiercest grief can charm,
And Fate's severest rage disarm:
Music can soften pain to ease, 120
And make despair and madness
please :
Our joys below it can improve,
And antedate the bliss above.

This the divine Cecilia found,
And to her Maker's praise confin'd the
sound.
When the full organ joins the tuneful quire,
Th' immortal Powers incline their ear ;
Borne on the swelling notes our souls aspire,
While solemn airs improve the sacred fire,
And Angels lean from Heav'n to hear. 130
Of Orpheus now no more let poets tell;
To bright Cecilia greater power is giv'n:
His numbers rais'd a shade from Hell,
Hers lift the soul to Heav'n.

ARGUS

Written in 1709 and sent in a letter to Henry
Cromwell in 1711.

WHEN wise Ulysses, from his native coast
Long kept by wars, and long by tempests
toss'd,
Arrived at last, poor, old, disguised, alone,
To all his friends, and ev'n his Queen un-
known,
Changed as he was, with age, and toils,
and cares,
Furrow'd his rev'rend face, and white his
hairs,
In his own palace forc'd to ask his bread,
Scorn'd by those slaves his former bounty
fed,
Forgot of all his own domestic crew,
The faithful Dog alone his rightful master
knew !
Unfed, unhous'd, neglected, on the clay,
Like an old servant now cashier'd, he lay ;
Touch'd with resentment of ungrateful
man,
And longing to behold his ancient lord
again.
Him when he saw he rose, and crawl'd to
meet,
('T was all he could) and fawn'd and kiss'd
his feet,
Seiz'd with dumb joy ; then falling by his
side,
Own'd his returning lord, look'd up, and
died !

THE BALANCE OF EUROPE

Now Europe balanc'd, neither side prevails :
For nothing 's left in either of the scales.

THE TRANSLATOR

'Egbert Sanger,' says Warton, 'served his apprenticeship with Jacob Tonson, and succeeded Bernard Lintot in his shop at Middle Temple Gate, Fleet Street. Lintot printed Ozell's translation of Perrault's *Characters*, and Sanger his translation of Boileau's *Lutrin*, recommended by Rowe, in 1709.'

OZELL, at Sanger's call, invoked his
    Muse —
For who to sing for Sanger could refuse?
His numbers such as Sanger's self might use.
Reviving Perrault, murd'ring Boileau, he
Slander'd the ancients first, then Wycher-
    ley ;
Which yet not much that old bard's anger
    rais'd,
Since those were slander'd most whom
    Ozell prais'd.
Nor had the gentle satire caused complain-
    ing,
Had not sage Rowe pronounc'd it enter-
    taining ;
How great must be the judgment of that
    writer,
Who The Plain Dealer damns, and prints
    The Biter !

ON MRS. TOFTS, A FAMOUS OPERA-SINGER

Katharine Tofts was an English opera singer popular in London between 1703 and 1709.

So bright is thy beauty, so charming thy
    song,
As had drawn both the beasts and their
    Orpheus along:
But such is thy av'rice, and such is thy
    pride,
That the beasts must have starv'd, and the
    poet have died.

EPISTLE TO MRS. BLOUNT, WITH THE WORKS OF VOI-TURE.

To Teresa Blount. First published in Lin-tot's *Miscellany*, in 1712. See note.

IN these gay thoughts the Loves and Graces
    shine,
And all the writer lives in ev'ry line;

His easy Art may happy Nature seem,
Trifles themselves are elegant in him.
Sure to charm all was his peculiar fate,
Who without flatt'ry pleas'd the Fair and
    Great ;
Still with esteem no less convers'd than
    read,
With wit well-natured, and with books well-
    bred:
His heart his mistress and his friend did
    share,   9
His time the Muse, the witty, and the fair.
Thus wisely careless, innocently gay,
Cheerful he play'd the trifle, Life, away;
Till Fate scarce felt his gentle breath sup-
    prest,
As smiling infants sport themselves to rest.
Ev'n rival Wits did Voiture's death deplore,
And the gay mourn'd who never mourn'd
    before;
The truest hearts for Voiture heav'd with
    sighs,
Voiture was wept by all the brightest
    eyes:
The Smiles and Loves had died in Voiture's
    death,   19
But that for ever in his lines they breathe.
Let the strict life of graver mortals be
A long, exact, and serious Comedy;
In ev'ry scene some Moral let it teach,
And, if it can, at once both please and
    preach.
Let mine an innocent gay farce appear,
And more diverting still than regular,
Have Humour, Wit, a native Ease and
    Grace,
Tho' not too strictly bound to Time and
    Place:
Critics in Wit, or Life, are hard to please,
Few write to those, and none can live to
    these.   30
Too much your Sex is by their forms
    confin'd,
Severe to all, but most to Womankind ;
Custom, grown blind with Age, must be
    your guide;
Your pleasure is a vice, but not your pride;
By Nature yielding, stubborn but for fame,
Made slaves by honour, and made fools by
    shame ;
Marriage may all those petty tyrants chase;
But sets up one, a greater, in their place;
Well might you wish for change by those
    accurst,   39
But the last tyrant ever proves the worst.

Still in constraint your suff'ring Sex re-
    mains,
Or bound in formal, or in real chains:
Whole years neglected, for some months
    ador'd,
The fawning Servant turns a haughty Lord.
Ah, quit not the free innocence of life,
For the dull glory of a virtuous Wife;
Nor let false shows, or empty titles please;
Aim not at Joy, but rest content with
    Ease.
    The Gods, to curse Pamela with her
        pray'rs,
Gave the gilt coach and dappled Flanders
    mares,   50
The shining robes, rich jewels, beds of state,
And, to complete her bliss, a fool for
    mate.
She glares in Balls, front Boxes, and the
    Ring,
A vain, unquiet, glitt'ring, wretched thing!
Pride, Pomp, and State but reach her out-
    ward part ;
She sighs, and is no Duchess at her heart.
    But, Madam, if the fates withstand, and
        you
Are destin'd Hymen's willing victim too;
Trust not too much your now resistless
    charms,
Those Age or Sickness soon or late dis-
    arms: 60
Good humour only teaches charms to last,
Still makes new conquests, and maintains
    the past;
Love, rais'd on Beauty, will like that decay,
Our hearts may bear its slender chain a
    day;
As flow'ry bands in wantonness are worn,
A morning's pleasure, and at evening torn;
This binds in ties more easy, yet more
    strong,
The willing heart, and only holds it long.
    Thus Voiture's early care still shone the
        same,   69
And Montausier was only changed in name;
By this, ev'n now they live, ev'n now they
    charm,
Their wit still sparkling, and their flames
    still warm.
    Now crown'd with myrtle, on th' Elysian
        coast,
Amid those lovers, joys his gentle Ghost:
Pleas'd, while with smiles his happy lines
    you view,
And finds a fairer Rambouillet in you.

The brightest eyes of France inspired his
    Muse;
The brightest eyes of Britain now peruse;
And dead, as living, 't is our Author's pride
Still to charm those who charm the world
    beside.   80

THE DYING CHRISTIAN TO HIS SOUL

This Ode was written, we find [in 1712], at
the desire of Steele ; and our Poet, in a letter
to him on that occasion, says, — ' You have it,
as Cowley calls it, just warm from the brain ;
it came to me the first moment I waked this
morning ; yet you 'll see, it was not so absolutely inspiration, but that I had in my head,
not only the verses of Hadrian, but the fine
fragment of Sappho.' It is possible, however,
that our Author might have had another composition in his head, besides those he here refers to: for there is a close and surprising
resemblance between this Ode of Pope, and
one of an obscure and forgotten rhymer of the
age of Charles the Second, Thomas Flatman.
(Warton). Pope's version of the *Adriani mo-
rientis ad Animam* was written at about this
date, and sent to Steele for publication in The
Spectator. It ran as follows : —

    ' Ah, fleeting Spirit ! wand'ring fire,
        That long hast warm'd my tender breast,
    Must thou no more this frame inspire,
        No more a pleasing cheerful guest ?
    Whither, ah whither, art thou flying,
        To what dark undiscover'd shore ?
    Thou seem'st all trembling, shiv'ring, dying,
        And Wit and Humour are no more ! '

I

VITAL spark of heav'nly flame,
Quit, oh quit, this mortal frame !
Trembling, hoping, ling'ring, flying,
Oh, the pain, the bliss of dying !
Cease, fond Nature, cease thy strife,
And let me languish into life !

II

Hark ! they whisper; Angels say,
Sister Spirit, come away.
What is this absorbs me quite,
Steals my senses, shuts my sight,
Drowns my spirits, draws my breath ?
Tell me, my Soul ! can this be Death ?

III

The world recedes; it disappears ;
Heav'n opens on my eyes; my ears

With sounds seraphic ring :
Lend, lend your wings ! I mount ! I fly !
O Grave ! where is thy Victory ?
O Death ! where is thy Sting ?

EPISTLE TO MR. JERVAS

WITH DRYDEN'S TRANSLATION OF FRES-
NOY'S ART OF PAINTING

Charles Jervas was an early and firm friend
of Pope's, and, himself an indifferent painter,
at one time gave Pope some instruction in
painting. Dryden's translation of Fresnoy appears to have been a hasty and perfunctory
piece of work. The poem was first published in
1712.

THIS verse be thine, my friend, nor thou
refuse
This from no venal or ungrateful Muse.
Whether thy hand strike out some free de-
sign,
Where life awakes, and dawns at ev'ry
line,
Or blend in beauteous tints the colour'd
mass,
And from the canvas call the mimic face:
Read these instructive leaves, in which con-
spire
Fresnoy's close Art and Dryden's native
Fire;
And reading wish like theirs our fate and
fame,
So mix'd our studies, and so join'd our
name;   10
Like them to shine thro' long succeeding
age,
So just thy skill, so regular my rage.
Smit with the love of Sister-Arts we came,
And met congenial, mingling flame with
flame;
Like friendly colours found them both
unite,
And each from each contract new strength
and light.
How oft in pleasing tasks we wear the
day,
While summer suns roll unperceiv'd away !
How oft our slowly growing works impart,
While images reflect from art to art !   20
How oft review; each finding, like a friend,
Something to blame, and something to
commend.

What flatt'ring scenes our wand'ring
fancy wrought,
Rome's pompous glories rising to our
thought!
Together o'er the Alps methinks we fly,
Fired with ideas of fair Italy.
With thee on Raphael's monument I mourn,
Or wait inspiring dreams at Maro's urn:
With thee repose where Tully once was laid,
Or seek some ruin's formidable shade: 30
While Fancy brings the vanish'd piles to
view,
And builds imaginary Rome anew.
Here thy well-studied marbles fix our eye;
A fading fresco here demands a sigh;
Each heav'nly piece unwearied we compare,
Match Raphael's grace with thy lov'd
Guido's air,
Carracci's strength, Correggio's softer line,
Paulo's free stroke, and Titian's warmth
divine.
How finish'd with illustrious toil appears
This small well-polish'd Gem, the work of
years,   40
Yet still how faint by precept is exprest
The living image in the painter's breast!
Thence endless streams of fair ideas flow,
Strike in the sketch, or in the picture glow;
Thence Beauty, waking all her forms, sup-
plies
An Angel's sweetness, or Bridgewater's
eyes.
Muse! at that name thy sacred sorrows
shed
Those tears eternal that embalm the dead;
Call round her tomb each object of desire,
Each purer frame inform'd with purer
fire ;   50
Bid her be all that cheers or softens life,
The tender sister, daughter, friend, and
wife;
Bid her be all that makes mankind adore,
Then view this marble, and be vain no
more !
Yet still her charms in breathing paint
engage,
Her modest cheek shall warm a future age.
Beauty, frail flower, that ev'ry season fears,
Blooms in thy colours for a thousand years.
Thus Churchill's race shall other hearts
surprise,
And other beauties envy Worsley's eyes; 60
Each pleasing Blount shall endless smiles
bestow,
And soft Belinda's blush for ever glow.

O, lasting as those colours may they
   shine,
Free as thy stroke, yet faultless as thy
   line;
New graces yearly like thy works display,
Soft without weakness, without glaring
   gay!
Led by some rule that guides, but not con-
   strains,
And finish'd more thro' happiness than
   pains.
The kindred arts shall in their praise con-
   spire,   69
One dip the pencil, and one string the lyre.
Yet should the Graces all thy figures place,
And breathe an air divine on ev'ry face;
Yet should the Muses bid my numbers roll
Strong as their charms, and gentle as their
   soul;
With Zeuxis' Helen thy Bridgewater vie,
And these be sung till Granville's Myra die;
Alas! how little from the grave we claim!
Thou but preserv'st a Face and I a Name!

IMPROMPTU TO LADY WIN-
CHILSEA

OCCASIONED BY FOUR SATIRICAL
VERSES ON WOMEN WITS, IN THE
RAPE OF THE LOCK

'The four verses,' says Ward, 'are apparently Canto IV. vv. 59–62. The Countess of
Winchilsea, a poetess whom Rowe hailed as inspired by 'more than Delphic ardour,' replied
by some pretty lines, where she declares that
"disarmed with so genteel an air," she gives
over the contest.'

IN vain you boast poetic names of yore,
And cite those Sapphos we admire no
   more:
Fate doom'd the fall of every female wit;
But doom'd it then, when first Ardelia
   writ.
Of all examples by the world confess'd,
I knew Ardelia could not quote the best;
Who, like her mistress on Britannia's
   throne,
Fights and subdues in quarrels not her
   own.
To write their praise you but in vain essay:
Ev'n while you write, you take that praise
   away.

Light to the stars the sun does thus restore,
But shines himself till they are seen no
   more.

ELEGY TO THE MEMORY OF
AN UNFORTUNATE LADY

It was long rumored that this poem was
literally founded on fact: that the unfortunate lady was a maiden with whom Pope was
in love, and from whom he was separated.
The fact seems to be that the poem's only
basis in truth lay in Pope's sympathy for an
unhappy married woman about whom he wrote
to Caryll in 1712. The verses were not published till 1717, but were probably written
several years earlier.

WHAT beck'ning ghost along the moon-
   light shade
Invites my steps, and points to yonder
   glade?
'T is she! — but why that bleeding bosom
   gor'd?
Why dimly gleams the visionary sword?
Oh ever beauteous, ever friendly! tell,
Is it, in Heav'n, a crime to love too well?
To bear too tender or too firm a heart,
To act a lover's or a Roman's part?
Is there no bright reversion in the sky
For those who greatly think, or bravely
   die?   10
   Why bade ye else, ye Powers! her soul
     aspire
Above the vulgar flight of low desire?
Ambition first sprung from your blest
   abodes,
The glorious fault of Angels and of Gods:
Thence to their images on earth it flows,
And in the breasts of Kings and Heroes
   glows.
Most souls, 't is true, but peep out once an
   age,
Dull sullen pris'ners in the body's cage;
Dim lights of life, that burn a length of
   years
Useless, unseen, as lamps in sepulchres; 20
Like eastern Kings a lazy state they keep,
And, close confin'd to their own palace,
   sleep.
   From these, perhaps (ere Nature bade
     her die),
Fate snatch'd her early to the pitying
   sky.

As into air the purer spirits flow,
And sep'rate from their kindred dregs be-
low;
So flew the soul to its congenial place,
Nor left one virtue to redeem her race.
But thou, false guardian of a charge too
good,
Thou, mean deserter of thy brother's
blood !   30
See on these ruby lips the trembling
breath,
These cheeks now fading at the blast of
death;
Cold is that breast which warm'd the world
before,
And those love-darting eyes must roll no
more.
Thus, if eternal justice rules the ball,
Thus shall your wives, and thus your chil-
dren fall;
On all the line a sudden vengeance waits,
And frequent hearses shall besiege your
gates;
There passengers shall stand, and pointing
say
(While the long funerals blacken all the
way),   40
Lo ! these were they whose souls the fu-
ries steel'd,
And cursed with hearts unknowing how to
yield.
Thus unlamented pass the proud away,
The gaze of fools, and pageant of a day !
So perish all, whose breast ne'er learn'd to
glow
For others' good, or melt at others' woe.
What can atone, O ever injured shade !
Thy fate unpitied, and thy rites unpaid ?
No friend's complaint, no kind domestic
tear
Pleas'd thy pale ghost, or graced thy
mournful bier;   50
By foreign hands thy dying eyes were
closed,
By foreign hands thy decent limbs com-
posed,
By foreign hands thy humble grave
adorn'd,
By strangers honour'd, and by strangers
mourn'd.
What tho' no friends in sable weeds appear,
Grieve for an hour, perhaps, then mourn a
year,
And bear about the mockery of woe
To midnight dances, and the public show ?

What tho' no weeping loves thy ashes
grace,
Nor polish'd marble emulate thy face ?   60
What tho' no sacred earth allow thee
room,
Nor hallow'd dirge be mutter'd o'er thy
tomb ?
Yet shall thy grave with rising flowers be
dress'd,
And the green turf lie lightly on thy
breast:
There shall the morn her earliest tears be-
stow,
There the first roses of the year shall
blow;
While angels with their silver wings o'er-
shade
The ground, now sacred by thy relics
made.
So peaceful rests, without a stone, a
name,
What once had Beauty, Titles, Wealth and
Fame.   70
How lov'd, how honour'd once, avails thee
not,
To whom related, or by whom begot;
A heap of dust alone remains of thee;
'Tis all thou art, and all the proud shall
be !
Poets themselves must fall like those
they sung,
Deaf the prais'd ear, and mute the tuneful
tongue.
Ev'n he whose soul now melts in mourn-
ful lays,
Shall shortly want the gen'rous tear he
pays;
Then from his closing eyes thy form shall
part,
And the last pang shall tear thee from his
heart;   80
Life's idle bus'ness at one gasp be o'er,
The Muse forgot, and thou belov'd no
more !

MESSIAH

Written, according to Courthope, in 1712.

ADVERTISEMENT

In reading several passages of the prophet
Isaiah, which foretell the coming of Christ, and
the felicities attending it, I could not but observe a remarkable parity between many of

the thoughts and those in the Pollio of Virgil. This will not seem surprising, when we reflect that the Eclogue was taken from a Sibylline prophecy on the same subject. One may judge that Virgil did not copy it line by line, but selected such ideas as best agreed with the nature of Pastoral Poetry, and disposed them in that manner which served most to beautify his piece. I have endeavoured the same in this imitation of him, though without admitting any thing of my own; since it was written with this particular view, that the reader, by comparing the several thoughts, might see how far the images and descriptions of the Prophet are superior to those of the Poet. But as I fear I have prejudiced them by my management, I shall subjoin the passages of Isaiah, and those of Virgil, under the same disadvantage of a literal translation.

YE Nymphs of Solyma! begin the song:
To heav'nly themes sublimer strains belong.
The mossy fountains, and the sylvan shades,
The dreams of Pindus, and th' Aonian maids,
Delight no more — O Thou my voice inspire
Who touch'd Isaiah's hallow'd lips with fire!
Rapt into future times, the bard begun:
A virgin shall conceive, a virgin bear a son![1]

IMITATIONS

[1] Virg. Ecl. iv. ver. 6.

'Jam redit et Virgo, redeunt Saturnia regna;
Jam nova progenies cœlo demittitur alto.
Te duce, si qua manent sceleris vestigia nostri,
Irrita perpetua solvent formidine terras. . . .
Pacatumque reget patriis virtutibus orbem.'

'Now the virgin returns, now the kingdom of Saturn returns, now a new progeny is sent down from high heaven. By means of thee, whatever relics of our crimes remain, shall be wiped away, and free the world from perpetual fears. He shall govern the earth in peace, with the virtues of his father.'
Isaiah, ch. vii. ver. 14. 'Behold, a virgin shall conceive and bear a son.' Chap. ix. ver. 6, 7. 'Unto us a child is born, unto us a son is given . . . the Prince of Peace: of the increase of his government, and of his peace, there shall be no end, upon the throne of David, and upon his kingdom, to order it, and to establish it, with judgment and with justice from henceforth even for ever.'

From Jesse's [2] root behold a branch arise,
Whose sacred flower with fragrance fills
the skies; 10
Th' ethereal spirit o'er its leaves shall move,
And on its top descends the mystic dove.
Ye Heav'ns! [3] from high the dewy nectar pour,
And in soft silence shed the kindly shower!
The sick [4] and weak the healing plant shall aid,
From storms a shelter, and from heat a shade.
All crimes shall cease, and ancient fraud shall fail,
Returning Justice [5] lift aloft her scale;
Peace o'er the world her olive wand extend,
And white-robed Innocence from Heav'n descend. 20
Swift fly the years, and rise th' expected morn!
O spring to light, auspicious babe! be born.
See Nature hastes her earliest wreaths to bring,[6]
With all the incense of the breathing spring:
See lofty Lebanon [7] his head advance,
See nodding forests on the mountains dance:

---

[2] Isaiah, ch. xi. ver. 1.
[3] Ch. xlv. ver. 8.
[4] Ch. xxv. ver. 4.
[5] Ch. ix. ver. 7.
[6] Virg. Ecl. iv. ver. 18.

'At tibi prima, puer, nullo munuscula cultu,
Errantes hederas passim cum baccare tellus,
Mixtaque ridenti colocasia fundet acantho —
Ipsa tibi blandos fundent cunabula flores.'

'For thee, O child, shall the earth, without being tilled, produce her early offerings; winding ivy, mixed with baccar, and colocasia with smiling acanthus. Thy cradle shall pour forth pleasing flowers about thee.'
Isaiah, ch. xxxv. ver. 1. 'The wilderness and the solitary place shall be glad . . . and the desert shall rejoice and blossom as the rose.' Ch. lx. ver. 13. 'The glory of Lebanon shall come unto thee, the fir-tree, the pine-tree, and the box together to beautify the place of my sanctuary.'
[7] Isaiah, ch. xxxv. ver. 2.

See spicy clouds from lowly Saron rise,
And Carmel's flow'ry top perfumes the
　skies!
Hark! a glad voice the lonely desert
　cheers; [1]
Prepare the way! [2] a God, a God appears!
A God, a God! the vocal hills reply;　31
The Rocks proclaim th' approaching Deity.
Lo, Earth receives him from the bending
　skies!
Sink down, ye Mountains, and, ye valleys,
　rise;
With heads declin'd, ye Cedars, homage
　pay;
Be smooth, ye Rocks; ye rapid floods, give
　way;
The Saviour comes, by ancient bards fore-
　told!
Hear him, [3] ye deaf, and all ye blind, be-
　hold!

He from thick films shall purge the visual
　ray,
And on the sightless eyeball pour the
　day:　40
'T is he th' obstructed paths of sound shall
　clear,
And bid new music charm th' unfolding
　ear:
The dumb shall sing, the lame his crutch
　forego,
And leap exulting like the bounding roe.
No sigh, no murmur, the wide world shall
　hear,
From every face he wipes off every tear.

IMITATIONS

[1] Virg. Ecl. iv. ver. 48, Ecl. v. ver. 62.

'Aggredere o magnos, aderit jam tempus, ho-
　nores,
Cara deum soboles, magnum Jovis incremen-
　tum!

Ipsi lætitia voces ad sidera jactant
Intonsi montes, ipsæ jam carmina rupes,
Ipsa sonant arbusta, Deus, deus ille, Menalca!'

'O come and receive the mighty honours:
the time draws nigh, O beloved offspring of the
Gods, O great increase of Jove! . . . The un-
cultivated mountains send shouts of joy to the
stars, the very rocks sing in verse, the very
shrubs cry out, A God, a God.'
　Isaiah, chap. xl. ver. 3, 4. 'The voice of
him that crieth in the wilderness, Prepare ye
the way of the Lord, make straight in the desert a high way for our God. Every valley

In [4] adamantine chains shall Death be
　bound,
And Hell's grim tyrant feel th' eternal
　wound.
As the good Shepherd [5] tends his fleecy care,
Seeks freshest pasture and the purest air,
Explores the lost, the wand'ring sheep
　directs,　51
By day o'ersees them, and by night pro-
　tects;
The tender lambs he raises in his arms,
Feeds from his hand, and in his bosom
　warms;
Thus shall mankind his guardian care en-
　gage,
The promis'd Father [6] of the future age.
No more shall [7] nation against nation rise,
Nor ardent warriors meet with hateful
　eyes,
Nor fields with gleaming steel be cover'd
　o'er,
The brazen trumpets kindle rage no more;
But useless lances into scythes shall bend, 61
And the broad falchion in a ploughshare
　end.
Then palaces shall rise; the joyful [8] son
Shall finish what his short-lived sire begun;
Their vines a shadow to their race shall
　yield,
And the same hand that sow'd shall reap
　the field:
The swain in barren [9] deserts with surprise
See lilies spring, and sudden verdure rise; [10]
And start, amidst the thirsty wilds, to hear
New falls of water murm'ring in his ear.　70

shall be exalted, and every mountain and hill
shall be made low, and the crooked shall be
made straight, and the rough places plain.'
Chap. xliv. ver. 23. 'Break forth into singing, ye mountains! O forest, and every tree
therein! for the Lord hath redeemed Jacob.'
　[2] Ch. xl. ver. 3, 4.
　[3] Isaiah, ch. xlii. ver. 18; ch. xxxv. ver. 5, 6.
　[4] Ch. xxv. ver. 8.
　[5] Ch. xl. ver. 11.
　[6] Ch. ix. ver. 6.
　[7] Isaiah, ch. ii. ver. 4.
　[8] Ch. lxv. ver. 21, 22.
　[9] Ch. xxxv. ver. 1, 7.
　[10] Virg. Ecl. iv. ver. 28.

'Molli paulatim flavescet campus arista,
Incultisque rubens pendebit sentibus uva,
Et duræ quercus sudabunt roscida mella.'

'The fields shall grow yellow with ripened
ears, and the red grape shall hang upon the

On rifted rocks, the dragon's late abodes,
The green reed trembles, and the bulrush
  nods;
Waste [1] sandy valleys, once perplex'd with
  thorn,
The spiry fir and shapely box adorn;
To leafless shrubs the flow'ring palms suc-
  ceed,
And od'rous myrtle to the noisome weed.
The lambs [2] with wolves shall graze the
  verdant mead,
And boys in flow'ry bands the tiger lead; [3]
The steer and lion at one crib shall meet,
And harmless serpents [4] lick the pilgrim's
  feet;   80
The smiling infant in his hand shall take
The crested basilisk and speckled snake,
Pleas'd, the green lustre of the scales
  survey,
And with their forky tongue shall inno-
  cently play.
Rise, crown'd with light, imperial Salem, [5]
  rise! [6]
Exalt thy tow'ry head, and lift thy eyes!
See a long race [7] thy spacious courts adorn;
See future sons and daughters, yet unborn,
In crowding ranks on every side arise,
Demanding life, impatient for the skies! 90

See barb'rous nations [8] at thy gates attend,
Walk in thy light, and in thy temple bend!
See thy bright altars throng'd with pros-
  trate kings,
And heap'd with products of Sabæan [9]
  springs;
For thee Idume's spicy forests blow,
And seeds of gold in Ophir's mountains
  glow;
See Heav'n its sparkling portals wide dis-
  play,
And break upon thee in a flood of day!
No more the rising sun [10] shall gild the
  morn,
Nor ev'ning Cynthia fill her silver horn;
But lost, dissolv'd in thy superior rays, 101
One tide of glory, one unclouded blaze
O'erflow thy courts: the light himself shall
  shine
Reveal'd, and God's eternal day be thine!
The seas [11] shall waste, the skies in smoke
  decay,
Rocks fall to dust, and mountains melt
  away;
But fix'd his word, his saving power re-
  mains; —
Thy realm for ever lasts, thy own Messiah
  reigns!

---

wild brambles, and the hard oaks shall distil
honey like dew.'
  Isaiah, chap. xxxv. ver. 7. ' The parched
ground shall become a pool, and the thirsty
land springs of water: in the habitation of
dragons, where each lay, shall be grass with
reeds and rushes.' — Chap. lv. ver. 13. ' Instead of the thorn shall come up the fir-tree,
and instead of the brier shall come up the myrtle tree.'
  [1] Isaiah, ch. xli. ver. 19, and ch. lv. ver. 13.
  [2] Ch. xi. ver. 6, 7, 8.
  [3] Virg. Ecl. iv. ver. 21.

' Ipsæ lacte domum referent distenta capellæ
Ubera, nec magnos metuent armenta leones. . . .
Occidet et serpens, et fallax herba veneni
Occidet.' —
  ' The goats shall bear to the fold their udders distended with milk: nor shall the herds be
afraid of the greatest lions. The serpent shall
die, and the herb that conceals poison shall
die.'
  Isaiah, chap. xi. ver. 6, &c. ' The wolf also
shall dwell with the lamb, and the leopard
shall lie down with the kid, and the calf, and

the young lion, and the fatling together; and a
little child shall lead them. — And the lion
shall eat straw like the ox. And the sucking
child shall play on the hole of the asp, and the
weaned child shall put his hand on the cocka-
trice' den.'
  [4] Ch. lxv. ver. 25.
  [5] Isaiah, ch. lx. ver. 1.
  [6] The thoughts of Isaiah, which compose the
latter part of the poem, are wonderfully elevated, and much above those general exclama-
tions of Virgil, which make the loftiest parts
of his Pollio.

' Magnus ab integro sæclorum nascitur ordo
— toto surget gens aurea mundo !
— incipient magni procedere menses !
Aspice, venturo lætantur ut omnia sæclo !' &c.

  The reader needs only to turn to the passages
of Isaiah here cited.
  [7] Ch. lx. ver. 4.
  [8] Ch. lx. ver. 3.
  [9] Ch. lx. ver. 6.
  [10] Isaiah ch. lx. ver. 19, 20.
  [11] Ch. li. ver. 6, and ch. liv. ver. 10.

THE RAPE OF THE LOCK

AN HEROI-COMICAL POEM

Nolueram, Belinda, tuos violare capillos;
Sed juvat, hoc precibus me tribuisse tuis.
Mart. Epig. xii. 84.

'It appears by this motto,' says Pope, in a footnote supplied for Warburton's edition, 'that the following poem was written or published at the lady's request. But there are some other circumstances not unworthy relating. Mr. Caryll (a gentleman who was secretary to Queen Mary, wife of James II., whose fortunes he followed into France, author of the comedy of *Sir Solomon Single*, and of several translations in Dryden's *Miscellanies*) originally proposed it to him in a view of putting an end, by this piece of ridicule, to a quarrel that was risen between two noble families, those of Lord Petre and Mrs. Fermor, on the trifling occasion of his having cut off a lock of her hair. The author sent it to the lady, with whom he was acquainted ; and she took it so well as to give about copies of it. That first sketch (we learn from one of his letters) was written in less than a fortnight, in 1711, in two cantos only, and it was so printed first, in a *Miscellany* of Bern. Lintot's, without the name of the author. But it was received so well that he made it more considerable the next year by the addition of the machinery of the Sylphs, and extended it to five cantos.'

TO MRS. ARABELLA FERMOR

MADAM, — It will be in vain to deny that I have some regard for this piece, since I dedicate it to you. Yet you may bear me witness it was intended only to divert a few young ladies, who have good sense and good humour enough to laugh not only at their sex's little unguarded follies, but at their own. But as it was communicated with the air of a secret, it soon found its way into the world. An imperfect copy having been offer'd to a bookseller, you had the good-nature for my sake, to consent to the publication of one more correct : this I was forced to, before I had executed half my design, for the Machinery was entirely wanting to complete it. The Machinery, Madam, is a term invented by the critics, to signify that part which the Deities, Angels, or Dæmons, are made to act in

a poem : for the ancient poets are in one respect like many modern ladies ; let an action be never so trivial in itself, they always make it appear of the utmost importance. These Machines I determined to raise on a very new and odd foundation, the Rosicrucian doctrine of Spirits.

I know how disagreeable it is to make use of hard words before a lady ; but it is so much the concern of a poet to have his works understood, and particularly by your sex, that you must give me leave to explain two or three difficult terms. The Rosicrucians are a people I must bring you acquainted with. The best account I know of them is in a French book called *La Comte de Gabalis*, which, both in its title and size, is so like a novel, that many of the fair sex have read it for one by mistake. According to these gentlemen, the four elements are inhabited by Spirits, which they call Sylphs, Gnomes, Nymphs, and Salamanders. The Gnomes, or Dæmons of earth, delight in mischief ; but the Sylphs, whose habitation is in the air, are the best-conditioned creatures imaginable ; for, they say, any mortal may enjoy the most intimate familiarities with these gentle spirits, upon a condition very easy to all true adepts, — an inviolate preservation of chastity.

As to the following cantos, all the passages of them are as fabulous as the Vision at the beginning, or the Transformation at the end (except the loss of your hair, which I always mention with reverence). The human persons are as fictitious as the airy ones ; and the character of Belinda, as it is now managed, resembles you in nothing but in beauty.

If this poem had as many graces as there are in your person or in your mind, yet I could never hope it should pass thro' the world half so uncensured as you have done. But let its fortune be what it will, mine is happy enough, to have given me this occasion of assuring you that I am, with the truest esteem, Madam,

Your most obedient, humble servant,
A. POPE.

CANTO I

WHAT dire offence from am'rous causes
    springs,
What mighty contests rise from trivial
    things,
I sing — This verse to *Caryll,* muse ! is
    due:
This, ev'n Belinda may vouchsafe to view :
Slight is the subject, but not so the praise,
If she inspire, and he approve my lays.
    Say what strange motive, Goddess ! could
    compel
A well-bred Lord t' assault a gentle Belle ?
O say what stranger cause, yet unex-
    plor'd,
Could make a gentle Belle reject a Lord ? 10
In tasks so bold can little men engage,
And in soft bosoms dwells such mighty
    rage ?
    Sol thro' white curtains shot a tim'rous
    ray,
And oped those eyes that must eclipse the
    day.
Now lapdogs give themselves the rousing
    shake,
And sleepless lovers just at twelve awake:
Thrice rung the bell, the slipper knock'd
    the ground,
And the press'd watch return'd a silver
    sound.
Belinda still her downy pillow prest,
Her guardian Sylph prolong'd the balmy
    rest. 20
'T was he had summon'd to her silent bed
The morning-dream that hover'd o'er her
    head;
A youth more glitt'ring than a Birthnight
    Beau
(That ev'n in slumber caus'd her cheek to
    glow)
Seem'd to her ear his winning lips to lay,
And thus in whispers said, or seem'd to
    say :
    ' Fairest of mortals, thou distinguish'd
    care
Of thousand bright Inhabitants of Air !
If e'er one vision touch'd thy infant thought,
Of all the nurse and all the priest have
    taught — 30
Of airy elves by moonlight shadows seen,
The silver token, and the circled green,
Or virgins visited by Angel-powers,
With golden crowns and wreaths of heav'nly
    flowers;

Hear and believe ! thy own importance
    know,
Nor bound thy narrow views to things be-
    low.
Some secret truths, from learned pride con-
    ceal'd,
To maids alone and children are reveal'd:
What tho' no credit doubting Wits may
    give ?
The fair and innocent shall still believe. 40
Know, then, unnumber'd Spirits round thee
    fly,
The light militia of the lower sky:
These, tho' unseen, are ever on the wing,
Hang o'er the Box, and hover round the
    Ring.
Think what an equipage thou hast in air,
And view with scorn two pages and a chair.
As now your own, our beings were of old,
And once inclosed in woman's beauteous
    mould;
Thence, by a soft transition, we repair
From earthly vehicles to these of air. 50
Think not, when woman's transient breath
    is fled,
That all her vanities at once are dead ;
Succeeding vanities she still regards,
And, tho' she plays no more, o'erlooks the
    cards.
Her joy in gilded chariots, when alive,
And love of Ombre, after death survive.
For when the Fair in all their pride expire,
To their first elements their souls retire.
The sprites of fiery termagants in flame 59
Mount up, and take a Salamander's name.
Soft yielding minds to water glide away,
And sip, with Nymphs, their elemental tea.
The graver prude sinks downward to a
    Gnome
In search of mischief still on earth to roam.
The light coquettes in Sylphs aloft repair,
And sport and flutter in the fields of air.
    ' Know further yet: whoever fair and
    chaste
Rejects mankind, is by some Sylph em-
    braced;
For spirits, freed from mortal laws, with
    ease
Assume what sexes and what shapes they
    please. 70
What guards the purity of melting maids,
In courtly balls, and midnight masquerades,
Safe from the treach'rous friend, the dar-
    ing spark,
The glance by day, the whisper in the dark:

When kind occasion prompts their warm
   desires,
When music softens, and when dancing
   fires ?
'Tis but their Sylph, the wise Celestials
   know,
Tho' Honour is the word with men below.
  'Some nymphs there are, too conscious
   of their face,
For life predestin'd to the Gnome's em-
   brace.   80
These swell their prospects and exalt their
   pride,
When offers are disdain'd, and love denied:
Then gay ideas crowd the vacant brain,
While peers, and dukes, and all their
   sweeping train,
And garters, stars, and coronets appear,
And in soft sounds, " Your Grace " salutes
   their ear.
'Tis these that early taint the female soul,
Instruct the eyes of young coquettes to roll,
Teach infant cheeks a bidden blush to know,
And little hearts to flutter at a Beau.   90
 "Oft, when the world imagine women
   stray,
The Sylphs thro' mystic mazes guide their
   way;
Thro' all the giddy circle they pursue,
And old impertinence expel by new.
What tender maid but must a victim fall
To one man's treat, but for another's ball ?
When Florio speaks, what virgin could
   withstand,
If gentle Damon did not squeeze her hand ?
With varying vanities, from every part,
They shift the moving toyshop of their
   heart;   100
Where wigs with wigs, with sword-knots
   sword-knots strive,
Beaux banish beaux, and coaches coaches
   drive.
This erring mortals levity may call;
Oh blind to truth! the Sylphs contrive it
   all.
  'Of these am I, who thy protection claim,
A watchful sprite, and Ariel is my name.
Late, as I ranged the crystal wilds of air,
In the clear mirror of thy ruling star
I saw, alas ! some dread event impend,
Ere to the main this morning sun descend,
But Heav'n reveals not what, or how or
   where.   111
Warn'd by the Sylph, O pious maid, be-
   ware!

This to disclose is all thy guardian can:
Beware of all, but most beware of Man!'
  He said; when Shock, who thought she
   slept too long,
Leap'd up, and waked his mistress with his
   tongue.
'T was then, Belinda, if report say true,
Thy eyes first open'd on a billet-doux;
Wounds, charms, and ardours were no
   sooner read,   119
But all the vision vanish'd from thy head.
  And now, unveil'd, the toilet stands dis-
   play'd,
Each silver vase in mystic order laid.
First, robed in white, the nymph intent
   adores,
With head uncover'd, the cosmetic powers.
A heav'nly image in the glass appears;
To that she bends, to that her eyes she
   rears.
Th' inferior priestess, at her altar's side,
Trembling begins the sacred rites of Pride.
Unnumber'd treasures ope at once, and here
The various off'rings of the world appear;
From each she nicely culls with curious
   toil,   131
And decks the Goddess with the glitt'ring
   spoil.
This casket India's glowing gems unlocks,
And all Arabia breathes from yonder box.
The tortoise here and elephant unite,
Transform'd to combs, the speckled, and
   the white.
Here files of pins extend their shining rows,
Puffs, powders, patches, bibles, billet-doux.
Now awful beauty puts on all its arms; 139
The Fair each moment rises in her charms,
Repairs her smiles, awakens every grace,
And calls forth all the wonders of her face;
Sees by degrees a purer blush arise,
And keener lightnings quicken in her eyes.
The busy Sylphs surround their darling
   care,
These set the head, and those divide the
   hair,
Some fold the sleeve, whilst others plait the
   gown;
And Betty's prais'd for labours not her
   own.

CANTO II

Not with more glories, in th' ethereal plain,
The sun first rises o'er the purpled main,
Than, issuing forth, the rival of his beams

Launch'd on the bosom of the silver Thames.
Fair nymphs, and well-dress'd youths
around her shone,
But every eye was fix'd on her alone.
On her white breast a sparkling cross she
wore,
Which Jews might kiss, and infidels adore.
Her lively looks a sprightly mind disclose,
Quick as her eyes, and as unfix'd as those:
Favours to none, to all she smiles extends; 11
Oft she rejects, but never once offends.
Bright as the sun, her eyes the gazers
strike,
And, like the sun, they shine on all alike.
Yet graceful ease, and sweetness void of
pride,
Might hide her faults, if belles had faults
to hide;
If to her share some female errors fall,
Look on her face, and you'll forget 'em
all.
This nymph, to the destruction of man-
kind,
Nourish'd two locks, which graceful hung
behind 20
In equal curls, and well conspired to deck
With shining ringlets the smooth iv'ry
neck.
Love in these labyrinths his slaves detains,
And mighty hearts are held in slender
chains.
With hairy springes we the birds betray,
Slight lines of hair surprise the finny prey,
Fair tresses man's imperial race ensnare,
And beauty draws us with a single hair.
Th' adventurous Baron the bright locks
admired;
He saw, he wish'd, and to the prize aspired.
Resolv'd to win, he meditates the way, 31
By force to ravish, or by fraud betray;
For when success a lover's toil attends,
Few ask if fraud or force attain'd his
ends.
For this, ere Phœbus rose, he had im-
plor'd
Propitious Heav'n, and every Power ador'd,
But chiefly Love — to Love an altar built
Of twelve vast French romances, neatly
gilt.
There lay three garters, half a pair of
gloves,
And all the trophies of his former loves; 40
With tender billet-doux he lights the pyre,
And breathes three am'rous sighs to raise
the fire.

Then prostrate falls, and begs with ardent
eyes
Soon to obtain, and long possess the prize:
The Powers gave ear, and granted half his
prayer,
The rest the winds dispers'd in empty air.
But now secure the painted vessel
glides,
The sunbeams trembling on the floating
tides;
While melting music steals upon the sky,
And soften'd sounds along the waters die:
Smooth flow the waves, the zephyrs gently
play, 51
Belinda smil'd, and all the world was
gay.
All but the Sylph — with careful thoughts
opprest
Th' impending woe sat heavy on his breast.
He summons straight his denizens of air;
The lucid squadrons round the sails re-
pair:
Soft o'er the shrouds aërial whispers
breathe
That seem'd but zephyrs to the train be-
neath.
Some to the sun their insect-wings unfold,
Waft on the breeze, or sink in clouds of
gold; 60
Transparent forms too fine for mortal
sight,
Their fluid bodies half dissolv'd in light,
Loose to the wind their airy garments
flew,
Thin glitt'ring textures of the filmy dew,
Dipt in the richest tincture of the skies,
Where light disports in ever-mingling
dyes,
While ev'ry beam new transient colours
flings,
Colours that change whene'er they wave
their wings.
Amid the circle, on the gilded mast,
Superior by the head was Ariel placed; 70
His purple pinions opening to the sun,
He raised his azure wand, and thus begun:
'Ye Sylphs and Sylphids, to your chief
give ear.
Fays, Fairies, Genii, Elves, and Dæmons,
hear!
Ye know the spheres and various tasks
assign'd
By laws eternal to th' aërial kind.
Some in the fields of purest ether play,
And bask and whiten in the blaze of day:

Some guide the course of wand'ring orbs
   on high,
Or roll the planets thro' the boundless
   sky: 80
Some, less refin'd, beneath the moon's pale
   light
Pursue the stars that shoot athwart the
   night,
Or suck the mists in grosser air below,
Or dip their pinions in the painted bow,
Or brew fierce tempests on the wintry
   main,
Or o'er the glebe distil the kindly rain.
Others, on earth, o'er human race preside,
Watch all their ways, and all their actions
   guide:
Of these the chief the care of nations own,
And guard with arms divine the British
   Throne.   90
  'Our humbler province is to tend the
   Fair,
Not a less pleasing, tho' less glorious care;
To save the Powder from too rude a gale;
Nor let th' imprison'd Essences exhale;
To draw fresh colours from the vernal
   flowers;
To steal from rainbows ere they drop in
   showers
A brighter Wash; to curl their waving
   hairs,
Assist their blushes and inspire their airs;
Nay oft, in dreams invention we bestow,
To change a Flounce, or add a Furbelow.
  'This day black omens threat the bright-
   est Fair,   101
That e'er deserv'd a watchful spirit's care;
Some dire disaster, or by force or slight;
But what, or where, the Fates have wrapt
   in night.
Whether the nymph shall break Diana's
   law,
Or some frail China jar receive a flaw;
Or stain her honour, or her new brocade,
Forget her prayers, or miss a masquerade,
Or lose her heart, or necklace, at a ball;
Or whether Heav'n has doom'd that Shock
   must fall.   110
Haste, then, ye Spirits! to your charge re-
   pair:
The flutt'ring fan be Zephyretta's care;
The drops to thee, Brillante, we consign;
And, Momentilla, let the watch be thine;
Do thou, Crispissa, tend her fav'rite
   Lock;
Ariel himself shall be the guard of Shock.

'To fifty chosen sylphs, of special note,
We trust th' important charge, the petti-
   coat;
Oft have we known that sev'n-fold fence to
   fail,
Tho' stiff with hoops, and arm'd with ribs
   of whale: 120
Form a strong line about the silver bound,
And guard the wide circumference around.
  'Whatever spirit, careless of his charge,
His post neglects, or leaves the Fair at
   large,
Shall feel sharp vengeance soon o'ertake
   his sins:
Be stopp'd in vials, or transfix'd with
   pins,
Or plunged in lakes of bitter washes lie,
Or wedg'd whole ages in a bodkin's eye;
Gums and pomatums shall his flight re-
   strain,
While clogg'd he beats his silken wings in
   vain,   130
Or alum styptics with contracting power
Shrink his thin essence like a rivell'd
   flower:
Or, as Ixion fix'd, the wretch shall feel
The giddy motion of the whirling mill,
In fumes of burning chocolate shall glow,
And tremble at the sea that froths be-
   low!'
  He spoke; the spirits from the sails de-
   scend;
Some, orb in orb, around the nymph ex-
   tend;
Some thread the mazy ringlets of her hair;
Some hang upon the pendants of her ear;
With beating hearts the dire event they
   wait,   141
Anxious, and trembling for the birth of
   Fate.

CANTO III

Close by those meads, for ever crown'd
   with flowers,
Where Thames with pride surveys his rising towers
There stands a structure of majestic frame,
Which from the neighb'ring Hampton
   takes its name.
Here Britain's statesmen oft the fall foredoom
Of foreign tyrants, and of nymphs at
   home;

Here, thou, great ANNA! whom three
realms obey,
Dost sometimes counsel take — and some-
times tea.
Hither the Heroes and the Nymphs re-
sort,
To taste awhile the pleasures of a court; 10
In various talk th' instructive hours they
past,
Who gave the ball, or paid the visit last;
One speaks the glory of the British Queen,
And one describes a charming Indian
screen;
A third interprets motions, looks, and eyes;
At every word a reputation dies.
Snuff, or the fan, supply each pause of
chat,
With singing, laughing, ogling, *and all that*.
Meanwhile, declining from the noon of
day,
The sun obliquely shoots his burning ray;
The hungry judges soon the sentence
sign, 21
And wretches hang that jurymen may dine;
The merchant from th' Exchange returns
in peace,
And the long labours of the toilet cease.
Belinda now, whom thirst of fame invites,
Burns to encounter two adventurous
knights,
At Ombre singly to decide their doom,
And swells her breast with conquests yet
to come.
Straight the three bands prepare in arms
to join,
Each band the number of the sacred Nine.
Soon as she spreads her hand, th' aërial
guard 31
Descend, and sit on each important card:
First Ariel perch'd upon a Matadore,
Then each according to the rank they bore;
For Sylphs, yet mindful of their ancient
race,
Are, as when women, wondrous fond of
place.
Behold four Kings in majesty revered,
With hoary whiskers and a forky beard;
And four fair Queens, whose hands sustain
a flower
Th' expressive emblem of their softer
power; 40
Four Knaves, in garbs succinct, a trusty
band,
Caps on their heads, and halberts in their
hand

And party-colour'd troops, a shining train,
Draw forth to combat on the velvet plain.
The skilful nymph reviews her force with
care;
'Let Spades be trumps!' she said, and
trumps they were.
Now move to war her sable Matadores,
In show like leaders of the swarthy Moors.
Spadillio first, unconquerable lord!
Led off two captive trumps, and swept the
board. 50
As many more Manillio forced to yield,
And march'd a victor from the verdant
field.
Him Basto follow'd, but his fate more hard
Gain'd but one trump and one plebeian card.
With his broad sabre next, a chief in years,
The hoary Majesty of Spades appears,
Puts forth his manly leg, to sight reveal'd;
The rest his many colour'd robe conceal'd.
The rebel Knave, who dares his prince en-
gage,
Proves the just victim of his royal rage. 60
Ev'n mighty Pam, that kings and queens
o'erthrew,
And mow'd down armies in the fights of
Loo,
Sad chance of war! now destitute of aid,
Falls undistinguish'd by the victor Spade.
Thus far both armies to Belinda yield;
Now to the Baron Fate inclines the field.
His warlike amazon her host invades,
Th' imperial consort of the crown of Spades.
The Club's black tyrant first her victim
died,
Spite of his haughty mien and barb'rous
pride: 70
What boots the regal circle on his head,
His giant limbs, in state unwieldy spread;
That long behind he trails his pompous
robe,
And of all monarchs only grasps the globe?
The Baron now his Diamonds pours
apace;
Th' embroider'd King who shows but half
his face,
And his refulgent Queen, with powers com-
bin'd,
Of broken troops an easy conquest find.
Clubs, Diamonds, Hearts, in wild disorder
seen,
With throngs promiscuous strew the level
green. 80
Thus when dispers'd a routed army runs,
Of Asia's troops, and Afric's sable sons,

With like confusion diff'rent nations fly,
Of various habit, and of various dye;
The pierced battalions disunited fall
In heaps on heaps ; one fate o'erwhelms
   them all.
  The Knave of Diamonds tries his wily
   arts,
And wins (oh shameful chance !) the Queen
   of Hearts.
At this, the blood the virgin's cheek for-
   sook,
A livid paleness spreads o'er all her look;
She sees, and trembles at th' approaching
   ill,   91
Just in the jaws of ruin, and Codille.
And now (as oft in some distemper'd state)
On one nice trick depends the gen'ral
   fate!
An Ace of Hearts steps forth: the King
   unseen
Lurk'd in her hand, and mourn'd his cap-
   tive Queen.
He springs to vengeance with an eager pace,
And falls like thunder on the prostrate
   Ace.
The nymph, exulting, fills with shouts the
   sky;
The walls, the woods, and long canals re-
   ply.   100
  Oh thoughtless mortals ! ever blind to
   fate,
Too soon dejected, and too soon elate:
Sudden these honours shall be snatch'd
   away,
And curs'd for ever this victorious day.
  For lo ! the board with cups and spoons
   is crown'd,
The berries crackle, and the mill turns
   round;
On shining altars of japan they raise
The silver lamp; the fiery spirits blaze:
From silver spouts the grateful liquors
   glide,
While China's earth receives the smoking
   tide.   110
At once they gratify their scent and taste,
And frequent cups prolong the rich repast.
Straight hover round the Fair her airy
   band;
Some, as she sipp'd, the fuming liquor
   fann'd,
Some o'er her lap their careful plumes dis-
   play'd,
Trembling, and conscious of the rich bro-
   cade.

Coffee (which makes the politician wise,
And see thro' all things with his half-shut
   eyes)
Sent up in vapors to the Baron's brain
New stratagems, the radiant Lock to gain.
Ah, cease, rash youth ! desist ere 't is too
   late,   121
Fear the just Gods, and think of Scylla's
   fate !
Changed to a bird, and sent to flit in air,
She dearly pays for Nisus' injured hair !
  But when to mischief mortals bend their
   will,
How soon they find fit instruments of ill!
Just then, Clarissa drew with tempting
   grace
A two-edg'd weapon from her shining case:
So ladies in romance assist their knight,
Present the spear, and arm him for the
   fight.   130
He takes the gift with rev'rence, and ex-
   tends
The little engine on his fingers' ends;
This just behind Belinda's neck he spread,
As o'er the fragrant steams she bends her
   head.
Swift to the Lock a thousand sprites re-
   pair;
A thousand wings, by turns, blow back the
   hair;
And thrice they twitch'd the diamond in her
   ear;
Thrice she look'd back, and thrice the foe
   drew near.   138
Just in that instant, anxious Ariel sought
The close recesses of the virgin's thought:
As on the nosegay in her breast reclin'd,
He watch'd th' ideas rising in her mind,
Sudden he view'd, in spite of all her art,
An earthly Lover lurking at her heart.
Amazed, confused, he found his power ex-
   pired,
Resign'd to fate, and with a sigh retired.
  The Peer now spreads the glitt'ring for-
   fex wide,
T' inclose the Lock; now joins it, to di-
   vide.
Ev'n then, before the fatal engine closed,
A wretched Sylph too fondly interposed;
Fate urged the shears, and cut the Sylph
   in twain   151
(But airy substance soon unites again).
The meeting points the sacred hair dissever
From the fair head, for ever, and for
   ever !

Then flash'd the living lightning from
 her eyes,
And screams of horror rend th' affrighted
 skies.
Not louder shrieks to pitying Heav'n are
 cast,
When husbands, or when lapdogs breathe
 their last;
Or when rich China vessels, fall'n from
 high,
In glitt'ring dust and painted fragments
 lie!   160
'Let wreaths of triumph now my temples
 twine,'
The Victor cried, 'the glorious prize is
 mine!
While fish in streams, or birds delight in
 air,
Or in a coach and six the British Fair,
As long as Atalantis shall be read,
Or the small pillow grace a lady's bed,
While visits shall be paid on solemn days,
When numerous wax-lights in bright order
 blaze:
While nymphs take treats, or assignations
 give,
So long my honour, name, and praise shall
 live!   170
What Time would spare, from Steel re-
 ceives its date,
And monuments, like men, submit to Fate!
Steel could the labour of the Gods destroy,
And strike to dust th' imperial towers of
 Troy;
Steel could the works of mortal pride con-
 found
And hew triumphal arches to the ground.
What wonder, then, fair Nymph! thy hairs
 should feel
The conquering force of unresisted steel?'

CANTO IV

But anxious cares the pensive nymph op-
 prest,
And secret passions labour'd in her breast.
Not youthful kings in battle seiz'd alive,
Not scornful virgins who their charms sur-
 vive,
Not ardent lovers robb'd of all their bliss,
Not ancient ladies when refused a kiss,
Not tyrants fierce that unrepenting die,
Not Cynthia when her mantua's pinn'd
 awry,

E'er felt such rage, resentment, and de-
 spair,
As thou, sad Virgin! for thy ravish'd hair.
For, that sad moment, when the Sylphs
 withdrew,   11
And Ariel weeping from Belinda flew,
Umbriel, a dusky, melancholy sprite
As ever sullied the fair face of light,
Down to the central earth, his proper scene,
Repair'd to search the gloomy cave of
 Spleen.
Swift on his sooty pinions flits the
 Gnome,
And in a vapour reach'd the dismal dome.
No cheerful breeze this sullen region knows,
The dreaded East is all the wind that
 blows.   20
Here in a grotto shelter'd close from air,
And screen'd in shades from day's de-
 tested glare,
She sighs for ever on her pensive bed,
Pain at her side, and Megrim at her head.
Two handmaids wait the throne; alike in
 place,
But diff'ring far in figure and in face.
Here stood Ill-nature, like an ancient
 maid,
Her wrinkled form in black and white ar-
 ray'd!
With store of prayers for mornings, nights,
 and noons,
Her hand is fill'd; her bosom with lam-
 poons.   30
There Affectation, with a sickly mien,
Shows in her cheek the roses of eighteen,
Practis'd to lisp, and hang the head aside,
Faints into airs, and languishes with pride;
On the rich quilt sinks with becoming woe,
Wrapt in a gown for sickness and for
 show.
The fair ones feel such maladies as these,
When each new night-dress gives a new
 disease.
A constant vapour o'er the palace flies
Strange phantoms rising as the mists arise;
Dreadful as hermits' dreams in haunted
 shades,   41
Or bright as visions of expiring maids:
Now glaring fiends, and snakes on rolling
 spires,
Pale spectres, gaping tombs, and purple
 fires;
Now lakes of liquid gold, Elysian scenes,
And crystal domes, and angels in ma-
 chines.

Unnumber'd throngs on ev'ry side are
  seen,
Of bodies changed to various forms by
  Spleen.
Here living Teapots stand, one arm held
  out,
One bent; the handle this, and that the
  spout: 50
A Pipkin there, like Homer's Tripod walks;
Here sighs a Jar, and there a Goose-pie
  talks;
Men prove with child, as powerful fancy
  works,
And maids turn'd bottles call aloud for
  corks.
  Safe pass'd the Gnome thro' this fantastic
  band,
A branch of healing spleenwort in his
  hand.
Then thus address'd the Power — 'Hail,
  wayward Queen!
Who rule the sex to fifty from fifteen:
Parent of Vapours and of female wit,
Who give th' hysteric or poetic fit,   60
On various tempers act by various ways,
Make some take physic, others scribble
  plays;
Who cause the proud their visits to delay,
And send the godly in a pet to pray.
A nymph there is that all your power dis-
  dains,
And thousands more in equal mirth main-
  tains.
But oh! if e'er thy Gnome could spoil a
  grace,
Or raise a pimple on a beauteous face,
Like citron-waters matrons' cheeks inflame,
Or change complexions at a losing game; 70
If e'er with airy horns I planted heads,
Or rumpled petticoats, or tumbled beds,
Or caused suspicion when no soul was rude,
Or discomposed the head-dress of a prude,
Or e'er to costive lapdog gave disease,
Which not the tears of brightest eyes could
  ease,
Hear me, and touch Belinda with chagrin;
That single act gives half the world the
  spleen.'
  The Goddess, with a discontented air,
Seems to reject him tho' she grants his
  prayer.   80
A wondrous Bag with both her hands she
  binds,
Like that where once Ulysses held the
  winds:

There she collects the force of female lungs,
Sighs, sobs, and passions, and the war of
  tongues.
A Vial next she fills with fainting fears,
Soft sorrows, melting griefs, and flowing
  tears.
The Gnome rejoicing bears her gifts away,
Spreads his black wings, and slowly mounts
  to day.
  Sunk in Thalestris' arms the nymph he
  found,
Her eyes dejected, and her hair unbound. 90
Full o'er their heads the swelling Bag he
  rent,
And all the Furies issued at the vent.
Belinda burns with more than mortal ire,
And fierce Thalestris fans the rising fire.
'O wretched maid!' she spread her hands,
  and cried
(While Hampton's echoes, 'Wretched
  maid!' replied),
Was it for this you took such constant care
The bodkin, comb, and essence to prepare?
For this your locks in paper durance
  bound?
For this with torturing irons wreathed
  around?   100
For this with fillets strain'd your tender
  head,
And bravely bore the double loads of lead?
Gods! shall the ravisher display your hair,
While the fops envy, and the ladies stare!
Honour forbid! at whose unrivall'd shrine
Ease, Pleasure, Virtue, all, our sex resign.
Methinks already I your tears survey,
Already hear the horrid things they say,
Already see you a degraded toast,
And all your honour in a whisper lost!   110
How shall I, then, your hapless fame de-
  fend?
'T will then be infamy to seem your friend!
And shall this prize, th' inestimable prize,
Exposed thro' crystal to the gazing eyes,
And heighten'd by the diamond's circling
  rays,
On that rapacious hand for ever blaze?
Sooner shall grass in Hyde Park Circus grow,
And Wits take lodgings in the sound of
  Bow;
Sooner let earth, air, sea, to chaos fall,
Men, monkeys, lapdogs, parrots, perish
  all!'   120
  She said; then raging to Sir Plume re-
  pairs,
And bids her beau demand the precious hairs

(Sir Plume, of amber snuff-box justly vain,
And the nice conduct of a clouded cane):
With earnest eyes, and round unthinking
  face,
He first the snuff-box open'd, then the case,
And thus broke out — 'My lord, why, what
  the devil!
Z—ds! damn the Lock! 'fore Gad, you
  must be civil!
Plague on 't! 't is past a jest — nay, prithee,
  pox!
Give her the hair.' — He spoke, and rapp'd
  his box.   130
'It grieves me much,' replied the Peer
  again,
'Who speaks so well should ever speak in
  vain:
But by this Lock, this sacred Lock, I swear
(Which never more shall join its parted
  hair;
Which never more its honours shall renew,
Clipp'd from the lovely head where late it
  grew),
That, while my nostrils draw the vital air,
This hand, which won it, shall for ever
  wear.'
He spoke, and speaking, in proud triumph
  spread
The long-contended honours of her head. 140
But Umbriel, hateful Gnome, forbears
  not so;
He breaks the Vial whence the sorrows
  flow.
Then see! the nymph in beauteous grief ap-
  pears,
Her eyes half-languishing, half drown'd in
  tears;
On her heav'd bosom hung her drooping
  head,
Which with a sigh she rais'd, and thus she
  said:
'For ever curs'd be this detested day,
Which snatch'd my best, my fav'rite curl
  away!
Happy! ah, ten times happy had I been,
If Hampton Court these eyes had never
  seen!   150
Yet am not I the first mistaken maid,
By love of courts to numerous ills betray'd.
O had I rather unadmired remain'd
In some lone isle, or distant northern land;
Where the gilt chariot never marks the
  way,
Where none learn Ombre, none e'er taste
  Bohea!

There kept my charms conceal'd from
  mortal eye,
Like roses, that in deserts bloom and die.
What mov'd my mind with youthful lords
  to roam?
O had I stay'd, and said my prayers at
  home;   160
'T was this the morning omens seem'd to
  tell,
Thrice from my trembling hand the patch-
  box fell;
The tott'ring china shook without a wind;
Nay, Poll sat mute, and Shock was most
  unkind!
A Sylph, too, warn'd me of the threats of
  fate,
In mystic visions, now believ'd too late!
See the poor remnants of these slighted
  hairs!
My hands shall rend what ev'n thy rapine
  spares.
These, in two sable ringlets taught to
  break,
Once gave new beauties to the snowy neck;
The sister-lock now sits uncouth alone, 171
And in its fellow's fate foresees its own;
Uncurl'd it hangs, the fatal shears de-
  mands,
And tempts once more thy sacrilegious
  hands.
O hadst thou, cruel! been content to seize
Hairs less in sight, or any hairs but these!'

CANTO V

She said: the pitying audience melt in
  tears;
But Fate and Jove had stopp'd the Baron's
  ears.
In vain Thalestris with reproach assails,
For who can move when fair Belinda fails?
Not half so fix'd the Trojan could remain,
While Anna begg'd and Dido raged in
  vain.
Then grave Clarissa graceful waved her
  fan;
Silence ensued, and thus the nymph began:
'Say, why are beauties prais'd and hon-
  our'd most,
The wise man's passion, and the vain
  man's toast?   10
Why deck'd with all that land and sea af-
  ford,
Why angels call'd, and angel-like ador'd?

Why round our coaches crowd the white-
glov'd beaux ?
Why bows the side-box from its inmost
rows ?
How vain are all these glories, all our
pains,
Unless Good Sense preserve what Beauty
gains;
That men may say when we the front-box
grace,
" Behold the first in virtue as in face ! "
Oh ! if to dance all night, and dress all
day,
Charm'd the smallpox, or chased old age
away; 20
Who would not scorn what housewife's
cares produce,
Or who would learn one earthly thing of
use ?
To patch, nay, ogle, might become a saint,
Nor could it sure be such a sin to paint.
But since, alas ! frail beauty must decay,
Curl'd or uncurl'd, since locks will turn to
gray;
Since painted, or not painted, all shall
fade,
And she who scorns a man must die a
maid;
What then remains, but well our power to
use,
And keep good humour still whate'er we
lose ? 30
And trust me, dear, good humour can pre-
vail,
When airs, and flights, and screams, and
scolding fail.
Beauties in vain their pretty eyes may roll;
Charms strike the sight, but merit wins
the soul.'
 So spoke the dame, but no applause en-
sued;
Belinda frown'd, Thalestris call'd her
prude.
'To arms, to arms ! ' the fierce virago cries,
And swift as lightning to the combat flies.
All side in parties, and begin th' attack;
Fans clap, silks rustle, and tough whale-
bones crack; 40
Heroes' and heroines' shouts confusedly
rise,
And bass and treble voices strike the skies.
No common weapons in their hands are
found,
Like Gods they fight nor dread a mortal
wound.

 So when bold Homer makes the Gods
engage,
And heav'nly breasts with human passions
rage;
'Gainst Pallas, Mars ; Latona, Hermes
arms;
And all Olympus rings with loud alarms;
Jove's thunder roars, Heav'n trembles all
around,
Blue Neptune storms, the bell'wing deeps
resound: 50
Earth shakes her nodding towers, the
ground gives way,
And the pale ghosts start at the flash of
day !
 Triumphant Umbriel, on a sconce's
height,
Clapp'd his glad wings, and sat to view the
fight:
Propp'd on their bodkin-spears, the sprites
survey
The growing combat, or assist the fray.
 While thro' the press enraged Thalestris
flies,
And scatters death around from both her
eyes,
A Beau and Witling perish'd in the throng,
One died in metaphor, and one in song: 60
'O cruel Nymph ! a living death I bear,'
Cried Dapperwit, and sunk beside his
chair.
A mournful glance Sir Fopling upwards
cast,
'Those eyes are made so killing ' — was his
last.
Thus on Mæander's flowery margin lies
Th' expiring swan, and as he sings he
dies.
 When bold Sir Plume had drawn Clar-
issa down,
Chloe stepp'd in, and kill'd him with a
frown;
She smiled to see the doughty hero slain,
But, at her smile, the beau revived again.
Now Jove suspends his golden scales in
air, 71
Weighs the men's wits against the lady's
hair;
The doubtful beam long nods from side to
side;
At length the wits mount up, the hairs sub-
side.
See fierce Belinda on the Baron flies,
With more than usual lightning in her
eyes;

Nor fear'd the chief th' unequal fight to try,
Who sought no more than on his foe to die.
But this bold lord, with manly strength en-
dued,
She with one finger and a thumb subdued:
Just where the breath of life his nostrils
drew, 81
A charge of snuff the wily virgin threw;
The Gnomes direct, to every atom just,
The pungent grains of titillating dust.
Sudden, with starting tears each eye o'er-
flows,
And the high dome reëchoes to his nose.
'Now meet thy fate,' incens'd Belinda
cried,
And drew a deadly bodkin from her side.
(The same, his ancient personage to deck,
Her great-great-grandsire wore about his
neck, 90
In three seal-rings; which after, melted
down,
Form'd a vast buckle for his widow's gown:
Her infant grandame's whistle next it grew,
The bells she jingled, and the whistle blew;
Then in a bodkin graced her mother's hairs,
Which long she wore and now Belinda
wears.)
'Boast not my fall,' he cried, 'insulting
foe!
Thou by some other shalt be laid as low;
Nor think to die dejects my lofty mind:
All that I dread is leaving you behind! 100
Rather than so, ah, let me still survive,
And burn in Cupid's flames — but burn
alive.'
'Restore the Lock!' she cries; and all
around
'Restore the Lock!' the vaulted roofs re-
bound.
Not fierce Othello in so loud a strain
Roar'd for the handkerchief that caus'd his
pain.
But see how oft ambitious aims are cross'd,
And chiefs contend till all the prize is lost!
The lock, obtain'd with guilt, and kept
with pain,
In ev'ry place is sought, but sought in
vain: 110
With such a prize no mortal must be blest.
So Heav'n decrees! with Heav'n who can
contest?
Some thought it mounted to the lunar
sphere,
Since all things lost on earth are treasured
there.

There heroes' wits are kept in pond'rous
vases,
And beaux' in snuffboxes and tweezer-
cases.
There broken vows, and deathbed alms are
found,
And lovers' hearts with ends of riband
bound,
The courtier's promises, and sick man's
prayers,
The smiles of harlots, and the tears o.
heirs, 120
Cages for gnats, and chains to yoke a flea,
Dried butterflies, and tomes of casuistry.
But trust the Muse — she saw it upward
rise,
Tho' mark'd by none but quick poetic eyes
(So Rome's great founder to the heav'ns
withdrew,
To Proculus alone confess'd in view):
A sudden star, it shot thro' liquid air,
And drew behind a radiant trail of hair.
Not Berenice's locks first rose so bright,
The heav'ns bespangling with dishevell'd
light. 130
The Sylphs behold it kindling as it flies,
And pleas'd pursue its progress thro' the
skies.
This the beau monde shall from the Mall
survey,
And hail with music its propitious ray;
This the blest lover shall for Venus take,
And send up vows from Rosamonda's lake;
This Partridge soon shall view in cloudless
skies,
When next he looks thro' Galileo's eyes;
And hence th' egregious wizard shall fore
doom
The fate of Louis, and the fall of Rome. 140
Then cease, bright Nymph! to mourn th
ravish'd hair,
Which adds new glory to the shinin
sphere!
Not all the tresses that fair head can boast
Shall draw such envy as the Lock you lost.
For after all the murders of your eye,
When, after millions slain, yourself shall
die;
When those fair suns shall set, as set they
must,
And all those tresses shall be laid in dust,
This Lock the Muse shall consecrate to
fame,
And 'midst the stars inscribe Belinda's
name. 150

POEMS WRITTEN BETWEEN 1713 AND 1717

PROLOGUE TO MR. ADDISON'S CATO

This prologue was written in 1713, after Addison had given Pope two of the main causes which led to their estrangement; and itself led the way for the third. Addison's faint praise of the *Pastorals*, and disagreement with Pope as to the advisability of revising *The Rape of the Lock*, had not as yet led to their estrangement. But when not long after the presentation of *Cato*, Pope ventured to become its champion against the attacks of John Dennis, Addison's quiet disclaimer of responsibility for his anonymous defender cut Pope to the quick.

To wake the soul by tender strokes of art,
To raise the genius, and to mend the heart;
To make mankind, in conscious virtue bold,
Live o'er each scene, and be what they behold:
For this the Tragic Muse first trod the stage,
Commanding tears to stream thro' ev'ry age:
Tyrants no more their savage nature kept,
And foes to virtue wonder'd how they wept.
Our author shuns by vulgar springs to move
The Hero's glory, or the Virgin's love; 10
In pitying Love, we but our weakness show,
And wild Ambition well deserves its woe.
Here tears shall flow from a more gen'rous cause,
Such tears as patriots shed for dying laws.
He bids your breasts with ancient ardour rise,
And calls forth Roman drops from British eyes:
Virtue confess'd in human shape he draws,
What Plato thought, and godlike Cato was:
No common object to your sight displays,
But what with pleasure Heav'n itself surveys, 20
A brave man struggling in the storms of fate,
And greatly falling with a falling state.
While Cato gives his little senate laws,
What bosom beats not in his country's cause?

Who sees him act, but envies ev'ry deed?
Who hears him groan, and does not wish to bleed?
Ev'n when proud Cæsar, midst triumphal cars,
The spoils of nations, and the pomp of wars,
Ignobly vain, and impotently great,
Show'd Rome her Cato's figure drawn in state; 30
As her dead father's rev'rend image past,
The pomp was darken'd, and the day o'ercast;
The triumph ceas'd, tears gush'd from ev'ry eye,
The world's great Victor pass'd unheeded by;
Her last good man dejected Rome ador'd,
And honour'd Cæsar's less than Cato's sword.
  Britons, attend: be worth like this approv'd,
And show you have the virtue to be mov'd.
With honest scorn the first famed Cato view'd
Rome learning arts from Greece, whom she subdued; 40
Your scene precariously subsists too long
On French translation and Italian song.
Dare to have sense yourselves; assert the stage;
Be justly warm'd with your own native rage:
Such plays alone should win a British ear
As Cato's self had not disdain'd to hear.

EPILOGUE TO MR. ROWE'S JANE SHORE

DESIGNED FOR MRS. OLDFIELD

Nicholas Rowe's play was acted at Drury Lane in February, 1714. Mrs. Oldfield played the leading part, but Pope's Epilogue was not used.

PRODIGIOUS this! the Frail-one of our play
From her own sex should mercy find to-day!

You might have held the pretty head aside,
Peep'd in your fans, been serious, thus, and
cried, —
'The play may pass — but that strange
creature, Shore,
I can't — indeed now — I so hate a whore!'
Just as a blockhead rubs his thoughtless
skull,
And thanks his stars he was not born a
fool;
So from a sister sinner you shall hear,
'How strangely you expose yourself, my
dear!   10
But let me die, all raillery apart,
Our sex are still forgiving at their heart;
And, did not wicked custom so contrive,
We'd be the best good-natured things
alive.'
  There are, 'tis true, who tell another
tale,
That virtuous ladies envy while they rail;
Such rage without betrays the fire within;
In some close corner of the soul they sin;
Still hoarding up, most scandalously nice,
Amidst their virtues a reserve of vice.   20
The godly dame, who fleshly failings
damns,
Scolds with her maid, or with her chaplain
crams.
Would you enjoy soft nights and solid
dinners?
Faith, gallants, board with saints, and bed
with sinners.
Well, if our author in the Wife offends,
He has a Husband that will make amends:
He draws him gentle, tender, and forgiv-
ing;
And sure such kind good creatures may be
living.
In days of old, they pardon'd breach of
vows;   29
Stern Cato's self was no relentless spouse.
Plu — Plutarch, what's his name that
writes his life,
Tells us, that Cato dearly lov'd his wife:
Yet if a friend, a night or so, should need
her,
He'd recommend her as a special breeder.
To lend a wife, few here would scruple
make;
But, pray, which of you all would take her
back?
Tho' with the Stoic Chief our stage may
ring,
The Stoic Husband was the glorious thing.

The man had courage, was a sage, 'tis
true,
And lov'd his country — but what's that
to you?   40
Those strange examples ne'er were made
to fit ye,
But the kind cuckold might instruct the
city:
There, many an honest man may copy Cato
Who ne'er saw naked sword, or look'd in
Plato.
  If, after all, you think it a disgrace,
That Edward's Miss thus perks it in your
face,
To see a piece of failing flesh and blood,
In all the rest so impudently good:
Faith, let the modest matrons of the town
Come here in crowds, and stare the strum-
pet down.   50

TO A LADY, WITH THE TEM-
PLE OF FAME

WHAT's Fame with men, by custom of the
nation,
Is call'd, in women, only Reputation:
About them both why keep we such a
pother?
Part you with one, and I'll renounce the
other.

UPON THE DUKE OF MARLBOR-
OUGH'S HOUSE AT WOOD-
STOCK

Atria longa patent; sed nec coenantibus usquam,
  Nec somno, locus est: quam bene non habitas.
                                        Martial.

These verses were first published in 1714.
There is no actual proof that they are Pope's,
but as his editors have always retained them,
they are here given.

SEE, Sir, here's the grand approach,
This way is for his Grace's coach;
There lies the bridge, and here's the clock;
Observe the lion and the cock,
The spacious court, the colonnade,
And mark how wide the hall is made!
The chimneys are so well design'd,
They never smoke in any wind.
This gallery's contrived for walking,
The windows to retire and talk in:

The council-chamber for debate,
And all the rest are rooms of state.
Thanks, Sir, cried I, 't is very fine,
But where d' ye sleep, or where d' ye
    dine ?
I find by all you have been telling
That 't is a house, but not a dwelling.

LINES TO LORD BATHURST

In illustration Mitford refers to Pope's letter
to Lord Bathurst of September 13, 1732, where
' Mr. L.' is spoken of as ' more inclined to admire God in his greater works, the tall timber.'
(Ward.) Proof is lacking that these lines belong to Pope. They were printed by E. Curll
in 1714.

' A Wood!' quoth Lewis, and with that
He laugh'd, and shook his sides of fat.
His tongue, with eye that mark'd his cun-
    ning,
Thus fell a-reas'ning, not a-running :
' Woods are — not to be too prolix —
Collective bodies of straight sticks.
It is, my lord, a mere conundrum
To call things woods for what grows under
    'em.
For shrubs, when nothing else at top is,
Can only constitute a coppice.
But if you will not take my word,
See anno quint. of Richard Third;
And that 's a coppice call'd, when dock'd,
Witness an. prim. of Harry Oct.
If this a wood you will maintain,
Merely because it is no plain,
Holland, for all that I can see,
May e'en as well be term'd the sea,
Or C[onings]by be fair harangued
An honest man, because not hang'd.'

MACER

A CHARACTER

This was first printed in 1727 in the *Miscellanies* of Pope and Swift, but was probably
written in 1715. *Macer* is supposed to be Ambrose Philips. The ' borrow'd Play ' of the
eighth line would then have been *The Distrest
Mother*, adapted by Philips from Racine.

WHEN simple *Macer*, now of high renown,
First sought a poet's fortune in the town,

'T was all th' ambition his high soul could
    feel
To wear red stockings, and to dine with
    Steele.
Some ends of verse his betters might af-
    ford,
And gave the harmless fellow a good word:
Set up with these he ventured on the town,
And with a borrow'd play outdid poor
    Crowne.
There he stopp'd short, nor since has writ
    a tittle,
But has the wit to make the most of little;
Like stunted hide-bound trees, that just
    have got   11
Sufficient sap at once to bear and rot.
Now he begs verse, and what he gets com-
    mends,
Not of the Wits his foes, but Fools his
    friends.
  So some coarse country wench, almost
    decay'd,
Trudges to town and first turns chamber-
    maid;
Awkward and supple each devoir to pay,
She flatters her good lady twice a day;
Thought wondrous honest, tho' of mean
    degree,
And strangely liked for her simplicity: 20
In a translated suit then tries the town,
With borrow'd pins and patches not her
    own:
But just endured the winter she began,
And in four months a batter'd harridan:
Now nothing left, but wither'd, pale, and
    shrunk,
To bawd for others, and go shares with
    punk.

EPISTLE TO MRS. TERESA
BLOUNT

ON HER LEAVING THE TOWN AFTER THE
CORONATION

This was written shortly after the coronation
of George I. ' Zephalinda' was a fanciful
name employed by Teresa Blount in correspondence.

As some fond virgin, whom her mother's
    care
Drags from the town to wholesome country
    air,

Just when she learns to roll a melting
eye,
And hear a spark, yet think no danger
nigh —
From the dear man unwilling she must
sever,
Yet takes one kiss before she parts for
ever —
Thus from the world fair Zephalinda flew,
Saw others happy, and with sighs with-
drew;
Not that their pleasures caus'd her dis-
content ;
She sigh'd not that they stay'd, but that
she went.   10
  She went to plain-work, and to purling
brooks,
Old-fashion'd halls, dull aunts, and croak-
ing rooks:
She went from Op'ra, Park, Assembly,
Play,
To morning walks, and prayers three hours
a day;
To part her time 'twixt reading and Bohea,
To muse, and spill her solitary tea;
Or o'er cold coffee trifle with the spoon,
Count the slow clock, and dine exact at
noon;
Divert her eyes with pictures in the fire,
Hum half a tune, tell stories to the squire;
Up to her godly garret after sev'n,   21
There starve and pray, for that 's the way
to Heav'n.
  Some Squire, perhaps, you take delight
to rack,
Whose game is Whist, whose treat a toast
in sack;
Who visits with a gun, presents you birds,
Then gives a smacking buss, and cries —
' No words! '
Or with his hounds comes hollowing from
the stable,
Makes love with nods, and knees beneath a
table;
Whose laughs are hearty, tho' his jests are
coarse,
And loves you best of all things — but his
horse.   30
  In some fair ev'ning, on your elbow laid,
You dream of triumphs in the rural shade;
In pensive thought recall the fancied scene,
See coronations rise on ev'ry green:
Before you pass th' imaginary sights
Of Lords and Earls and Dukes and garter'd
Knights,

While the spread fan o'ershades your clos-
ing eyes;
Then gives one flirt, and all the vision flies.
Thus vanish sceptres, coronets, and balls,
And leave you in lone woods, or empty
walls!   40
  So when your Slave, at some dear idle
time
(Not plagued with headaches or the want
of rhyme)
Stands in the streets, abstracted from the
crew,
And while he seems to study, thinks of
you;
Just when his fancy paints your sprightly
eyes,
Or sees the blush of soft Parthenia rise,
Gay pats my shoulder, and you vanish
quite,
Streets, Chairs, and Coxcombs rush upon
my sight;
Vext to be still in town, I knit my brow,
Look sour, and hum a tune, as you may
now.   50

LINES OCCASIONED BY SOME
VERSES OF HIS GRACE THE
DUKE OF BUCKINGHAM

MUSE, 't is enough, at length thy labour
ends,
And thou shalt live, for Buckingham commends.
Let crowds of critics now my verse assail,
Let Dennis write, and nameless numbers
rail:
This more than pays whole years of thankless pain;
Time, health, and fortune, are not lost in
vain.
Sheffield approves, consenting Phœbus
bends,
And I and malice from this hour are
friends.

A FAREWELL TO LONDON

IN THE YEAR 1715

DEAR, damn'd, distracting town, farewell!
  Thy fools no more I 'll tease:
This year in peace, ye Critics, dwell,
  Ye Harlots, sleep at ease!

Soft B——s and rough C[ragg]s, adieu!
　　Earl Warwick, make your moan;
The lively H[inchenbroo]k and you
　　May knock up whores alone.

To drink and droll be Rowe allow'd
　　Till the third watchman's toll;
Let Jervas gratis paint, and Froude
　　Save threepence and his soul.

Farewell Arbuthnot's raillery
　　On every learned sot;
And Garth, the best good Christian he,
　　Although he knows it not.

Lintot, farewell! thy bard must go;
　　Farewell, unhappy Tonson!
Heav'n gives thee for thy loss of Rowe,
　　Lean Philips and fat Johnson.

Why should I stay? Both parties rage;
　　My vixen mistress squalls;
The Wits in envious feuds engage;
　　And Homer (damn him!) calls.

The love of arts lies cold and dead
　　In Halifax's urn;
And not one Muse of all he fed
　　Has yet the grace to mourn.

My friends, by turns, my friends con-
　　found,
　　Betray, and are betray'd:
Poor Y[ounge]r 's sold for fifty pounds,
　　And B[ickne]ll is a jade.

Why make I friendships with the great,
　　When I no favour seek?
Or follow girls seven hours in eight? —
　　I need but once a week.

Still idle, with a busy air,
　　Deep whimseys to contrive;
The gayest valetudinaire,
　　Most thinking rake alive.

Solicitous for others' ends,
　　Tho' fond of dear repose;
Careless or drowsy with my friends,
　　And frolic with my foes.

Luxurious lobster-nights, farewell,
　　For sober, studious days!
And Burlington's delicious meal,
　　For salads, tarts, and pease!

Adieu to all but Gay alone,
　　Whose soul sincere and free,
Loves all mankind but flatters none,
　　And so may starve with me.

IMITATION OF MARTIAL

Referred to in a letter from Trumbull to Pope dated January, 1716. The epigram imitated is the twenty-third of the tenth book.

At length, my Friend (while Time, with
　　still career,
Wafts on his gentle wing his eightieth
　　year),
Sees his past days safe out of Fortune's
　　power,
Nor dreads approaching Fate's uncertain
　　hour;
Reviews his life, and in the strict survey, ⎫
Finds not one moment he could wish away, ⎬
Pleased with the series of each happy day. ⎭
Such, such a man extends his life's short
　　space,
And from the goal again renews the race ;
For he lives twice, who can at once employ
The present well, and ev'n the past enjoy.

IMITATION OF TIBULLUS

See the fourth elegy of Tibullus, lines 55, 56. In the course of his high-flown correspondence with Lady Mary Wortley Montagu, after her departure for the East, Pope often suggests the possibility of his travelling to meet her. ' But if my fate be such,' he says on the occasion which brought forth this couplet, 'that this body of mine (which is as ill matched to my mind as any wife to her husband) be left behind in the journey, let the epitaph of Tibullus be set over it!'

Here, stopt by hasty Death, Alexis lies,
Who cross'd half Europe, led by Wortley's
　　eyes.

THE BASSET-TABLE

AN ECLOGUE

This mock pastoral was one of three which made up the original volume of *Town Eclogues*, published anonymously in 1716. Three more appeared in a later edition. It is now known that only the *Basset-Table* is Pope's the rest being the work of Lady Mary Wortley Montagu.

CARDELIA, SMILINDA, LOVET

CARD. The Basset-Table spread, the
Tallier come,
Why stays *Smilinda* in the dressing-room ?
Rise, pensive nymph ! the Tallier waits ⎤
for you. |
SMIL. Ah, madam ! since my *Sharper* ⎬
is untrue, |
I joyless make my once adored Alpeu. ⎦
I saw him stand behind *Ombrelia's* chair, ⎤
And whisper with that soft deluding air, ⎰
And those feign'd sighs which cheat the ⎱
list'ning Fair.   ⎦
CARD. Is this the cause of your roman-
tic strains ?
A mightier grief my heavy heart sustains:
As you by love, so I by Fortune crost;   11
One, one bad Deal, three Septlevas have
lost.
SMIL. Is that the grief which you com-
pare with mine ?
With ease the smiles of fortune I resign :
Would all my gold in one bad Deal were
gone,
Were lovely *Sharper* mine, and mine alone.
CARD. A lover lost is but a common
care,
And prudent nymphs against that change
prepare:
The Knave of Clubs thrice lost: Oh ! who
could guess   19
This fatal stroke, this unforeseen distress ?
SMIL. See Betty Lovet ! very *àpropos;*
She all the cares of love and play does
know.
Dear Betty shall th' important point de-
cide;
Betty ! who oft the pain of each has tried;
Impartial she shall say who suffers most,
By cards' ill usage, or by lovers lost.
LOV. Tell, tell your griefs; attentive
will I stay,
Though time is precious, and I want some
tea.
CARD. Behold this equipage, by Mathers
wrought,
With fifty guineas (a great pen'worth)
bought.   30
See on the toothpick Mars and Cupid
strive,
And both the struggling figures seem alive.
Upon the bottom shines the Queen's bright
face;
A myrtle foliage round the thimble case.

Jove, Jove himself does on the scissors
shine:
The metal, and the workmanship, divine.
SMIL. This snuff-box — once the pledge
of *Sharper's* love,
When rival beauties for the present strove;
At Corticelli's he the raffle won;   39
Then first his passion was in public shown:
Hazardia blush'd, and turn'd her head aside,
A rival's envy (all in vain) to hide.
This snuffbox — on the hinge see brilliants
shine —
This snuffbox will I stake, the Prize is
mine.
CARD. Alas! far lesser losses than I
bear
Have made a soldier sigh, a lover swear.
And oh! what makes the disappointment
hard,
'T was my own Lord that drew the fatal
card.
In complaisance I took the Queen he gave,
Tho' my own secret wish was for the
Knave.   50
The Knave won Sonica, which I had chose,
And the next pull my Septleva I lose.
SMIL. But ah! what aggravates the kill-
ing smart,
The cruel thought that stabs me to the
heart,
This curs'd *Ombrelia*, this undoing Fair,
By whose vile arts this heavy grief I
bear,
She, at whose name I shed these spiteful
tears,
She owes to me the very charms she wears.
An awkward thing when first she came to
town,
Her shape unfashion'd, and her face un-
known: 60
She was my friend; I taught her first to
spread
Upon her sallow cheeks enlivening red;
I introduced her to the park and plays,
And by my int'rest Cozens made her Stays.
Ungrateful wretch! with mimic airs grown
pert,
She dares to steal my favourite lover's
heart.
CARD. Wretch that I was, how often
have I swore,
When Winnall tallied, I would punt no
more!
I know the bite, yet to my ruin run,
And see the folly which I cannot shun.   70

SMIL. How many maids have *Sharper's* vows deceiv'd ?
How many curs'd the moment they believ'd ?
Yet his known falsehoods could no warning prove:
Ah! what is warning to a maid in love ?
CARD. But of what marble must that breast be form'd,
To gaze on Basset, and remain unwarm'd ?
When Kings, Queens, Knaves, are set in decent rank,
Exposed in glorious heaps the tempting Bank,
Guineas, half-guineas, all the shining train,
The winner's pleasure, and the loser's pain.   80
In bright confusion open Rouleaux lie,
They strike the soul, and glitter in the eye:
Fired by the sight, all reason I disdain,
My passions rise, and will not bear the rein.
Look upon Basset, you who reason boast,
And see if reason must not there be lost.
SMIL. What more than marble must that heart compose
Can harken coldly to my *Sharper's* vows ?
Then when he trembles! when his blushes rise!
When awful love seems melting in his eyes!   90
With eager beats his Mechlin cravat moves:
'He loves'—I whisper to myself, 'He loves!'
Such unfeign'd passion in his looks appears,
I lose all mem'ry of my former fears;
My panting heart confesses all his charms,
I yield at once, and sink into his arms.
Think of that moment, you who Prudence boast;
For such a moment Prudence well were lost.
CARD. At the Groom-Porter's batter'd bullies play,   99
Some dukes at Mary-bone bowl time away;
But who the Bowl or rattling Dice compares
To Basset's heav'nly joys and pleasing cares ?
SMIL. Soft *Simplicetta* dotes upon a beau;
Prudina likes a man, and laughs at show:
Their several graces in my *Sharper* meet,
Strong as the footman, as the master sweet.

LOV. Cease your contention, which has been too long;
I grow impatient, and the tea 's too strong.
Attend, and yield to what I now decide;
The equipage shall grace *Smilinda's* side; 110
The snuffbox to *Cardelia* I decree;
Now leave complaining, and begin your tea.

EPIGRAM ON THE TOASTS OF THE KIT-CAT CLUB

ANNO 1716

WHENCE deathless 'Kit-cat' took its name,
  Few critics can unriddle:
Some say from 'Pastrycook' it came,
  And some, from 'cat' and 'fiddle.'

From no trim Beaux its name it boasts,
  Gray Statesmen, or green wits;
But from this pellmell pack of Toasts
  Of old 'cats' and young 'kits.'

THE CHALLENGE

A COURT BALLAD

TO THE TUNE OF 'TO ALL YOU LADIES NOW AT LAND,' ETC.

This lively ballad, written in 1717, belongs to the period of Pope's intimacy with court society. The three ladies here addressed were attached to the court of the Prince and Princess of Wales.

I

To one fair lady out of Court,
  And two fair ladies in,
Who think the Turk and Pope a sport,
  And wit and love no sin;
Come these soft lines, with nothing stiff in,
To Bellenden, Lepell, and Griffin.
  With a fa, la, la.

II

What passes in the dark third row,
  And what behind the scene,
Couches and crippled chairs I know,
  And garrets hung with green;
I know the swing of sinful hack,
Where many damsels cry alack.
  With a fa, la, la.

III

Then why to Courts should I repair,
  Where's such ado with Townshend?
To hear each mortal stamp and swear,
  And every speech with Zounds end;
To hear 'em rail at honest Sunderland,
  And rashly blame the realm of Blunder-
    land.
  With a fa, la, la.

IV

Alas! like Schutz, I cannot pun,
  Like Grafton court the Germans;
Tell Pickenbourg how slim she's grown,
  Like Meadows run to sermons;
To Court ambitious men may roam,
But I and Marlbro' stay at home.
  With a fa, la, la.

V

In truth, by what I can discern,
  Of courtiers 'twixt you three,
Some wit you have, and more may learn
  From Court, than Gay or me;
Perhaps, in time, you'll leave high diet,
To sup with us on milk and quiet.
  With a fa, la, la.

VI

At Leicester-Fields, a house full high,
  With door all painted green,
Where ribbons wave upon the tie
  (A milliner I mean),
There may you meet us three to three,
For Gay can well make two of me.
  With a fa, la, la.

VII

But should you catch the prudish itch
  And each become a coward,
Bring sometimes with you lady Rich,
  And sometimes mistress Howard;
For virgins to keep chaste must go
Abroad with such as are not so.
  With a fa, la, la.

VIII

And thus, fair maids, my ballad ends:
  God send the King safe landing;
And make all honest ladies friends
  To armies that are standing;
Preserve the limits of those nations,
And take off ladies' limitations.
  With a fa, la, la.

THE LOOKING-GLASS

ON MRS. PULTENEY

Mrs. Pulteney was a daughter of one John Gumley, who had made a fortune by a glass manufactory.

WITH scornful mien, and various toss of air,
Fantastic, vain, and insolently fair,
Grandeur intoxicates her giddy brain,
She looks ambition, and she moves disdain.
Far other carriage graced her virgin life,
But charming Gumley's lost in Pulteney's
    wife.
Not greater arrogance in him we find,
And this conjunction swells at least her
    mind.
O could the sire, renown'd in glass, pro-
    duce
One faithful mirror for his daughter's use!
Wherein she might her haughty errors
    trace,
And by reflection learn to mend her face:
The wonted sweetness to her form restore,
Be what she was, and charm mankind once
    more.

PROLOGUE, DESIGNED FOR MR. D'URFEY'S LAST PLAY

'Tom' D'Urfey was a writer of popular farces under the Restoration. Through Addison's influence his play *The Plotting Sisters* was revived for his benefit; and the present prologue was possibly written for that occasion. It was first published in 1727.

GROWN old in rhyme, 't were barb'rous to
    discard
Your persevering, unexhausted Bard:
Damnation follows death in other men,
But your damn'd poet lives and writes
    again.
The adventurous lover is successful still,
Who strives to please the Fair against her
    will.
Be kind, and make him in his wishes easy,
Who in your own despite has strove to
    please ye.
He scorn'd to borrow from the Wits of yore,
But ever writ, as none e'er writ before.   10
You modern Wits, should each man bring
    his claim,
Have desperate debentures on your fame;

And little would be left you, I'm afraid,
If all your debts to Greece and Rome were
  paid.
From this deep fund our author largely
  draws,
Nor sinks his credit lower than it was.
Tho' plays for honour in old time he made,
'T is now for better reasons — to be paid.
Believe him, he has known the world too
  long,
And seen the death of much immortal
  song.   20
He says, poor poets lost, while players won,
As pimps grow rich while gallants are un-
  done.
Though Tom the poet writ with ease and
  pleasure,
The comic Tom abounds in other treasure.
Fame is at best an unperforming cheat;
But 't is substantial happiness to eat.
Let ease, his last request, be of your giving,
Nor force him to be damn'd to get his liv-
  ing.

PROLOGUE TO THE 'THREE HOURS AFTER MARRIAGE'

Three Hours after Marriage was a dull and
unsuccessful farce produced in January, 1717,
at the Drury Lane Theatre. Though it was
attributed to the joint authorship of Pope, Gay,
and Arbuthnot, direct proof is lacking not
only of Pope's share in the play, but of his
authorship of the *Prologue.* Of the latter fact,
at least, we have, however, indirect evidence in
Pope's resentment of the ridicule cast by Cibber, in a topical impromptu, upon the play;
the incident which first roused Pope's enmity
for Cibber, which resulted in his eventually dis-
placing Theobald as the central figure in *The
Dunciad.*

AUTHORS are judged by strange capricious
  rules,
The great ones are thought mad, the small
  ones fools:
Yet sure the best are most severely fated;
For Fools are only laugh'd at, Wits are
  hated.
Blockheads with reason men of sense abhor;
But fool 'gainst fool, is barb'rous civil war.
Why on all Authors then should Critics
  fall?
Since some have writ, and shown no wit at
  all.

Condemn a play of theirs, and they evade
  it;
Cry, 'Damn not us, but damn the French,
  who made it.'   10
By running goods these graceless Owlers
  gain;
Theirs are the rules of France, the plots of
  Spain:
But wit, like wine, from happier climates
  brought,
Dash'd by these rogues, turns English com-
  mon draught.
They pall Molière's and Lopez' sprightly
  strain,
And teach dull Harlequins to grin in vain.
  How shall our Author hope a gentler
  fate,
Who dares most impudently not translate?
It had been civil, in these ticklish times,
To fetch his fools and knaves from foreign
  climes.   20
Spaniards and French abuse to the world's
  end,
But spare old England, lest you hurt a
  friend.
If any fool is by our satire bit,
Let him hiss loud, to show you all he's hit.
Poets make characters, as salesmen clothes;
We take no measure of your Fops and
  Beaux;
But here all sizes and all shapes you meet,
And fit yourselves like chaps in Monmouth
  Street.
  Gallants, look here! this Foolscap has
  an air   29
Goodly and smart, with ears of Issachar.
Let no one fool engross it, or confine
A common blessing! now 't is yours, now
  mine.
But poets in all ages had the care
To keep this cap for such as will, to wear.
Our Author has it now (for every Wit
Of course resign'd it to the next that writ)
And thus upon the stage 't is fairly thrown;
Let him that takes it wear it as his own.

PRAYER OF BRUTUS

FROM GEOFFREY OF MONMOUTH

  The Rev. Aaron Thompson, of Queen's College, Oxon., translated the Chronicle of Geoffrey
of Monmouth. He submitted the translation to Pope, 1717, who gave him the follow-

ing lines, being a translation of a Prayer of
Brutus. (Carruthers.)

GODDESS of woods, tremendous in the
    chase
To mountain wolves and all the savage
    race,
Wide o'er th' aerial vault extend thy
    sway,
And o'er th' infernal regions void of day.

On thy Third Reign look down; disclose
    our fate;
In what new station shall we fix our
    seat ?
When shall we next thy hallow'd altars
    raise,
And choirs of virgins celebrate thy praise ?

TO LADY MARY WORTLEY MONTAGU

While there is no absolute date to be given
for this or the following poem, both evidently
belong to the period of Pope's somewhat fanciful attachment for Lady Mary.

I

IN beauty, or wit,
  No mortal as yet
To question your empire has dar'd;
    But men of discerning
    Have thought that in learning,
To yield to a lady was hard.

II

Impertinent schools,
  With musty dull rules,
Have reading to females denied:
    So Papists refuse
    The Bible to use,
Lest flocks should be wise as their guide.

III

'T was a woman at first,
  (Indeed she was curst)
In Knowledge that tasted delight,
    And sages agree
    The laws should decree
To the first possessor the right.

IV

Then bravely, fair Dame,
  Resume the old claim,
Which to your whole sex does belong;
    And let men receive,
    From a second bright Eve,
The knowledge of right and of wrong.

V

But if the first Eve
  Hard doom did receive,
When only one apple had she,
    What a punishment new
    Shall be found out for you,
Who tasting have robb'd the whole tree ?

EXTEMPORANEOUS LINES

ON A PORTRAIT OF LADY MARY WORT-
LEY MONTAGU, PAINTED BY KNELLER

THE playful smiles around the dimpled
    mouth,
That happy air of majesty and truth,
So would I draw (but oh! 't is vain to try;
My narrow Genius does the power deny;)
The equal lustre of the heav'nly mind,
Where ev'ry grace with ev'ry virtue 's
    join'd;
Learning not vain, and Wisdom not severe,
With Greatness easy, and with Wit sincere;
With just description show the work divine,
And the whole Princess in my work
    should shine.

ELOISA TO ABELARD

The origin of this famous poem seems to have lain jointly in Pope's perception of the poetic availability of the Héloïse-Abelard legend, and in his somewhat factitious grief in his separation from Lady Mary Wortley Montagu. They met in 1715, became friends, and in 1716 Lady Mary left England. In a letter of June, 1717, Pope commends the poem to her consideration, with a suggestion of the personal applicability of the concluding lines to his own suffering under the existing circumstance of their separation.

ELOISA TO ABELARD

ARGUMENT

Abelard and Eloisa flourished in the twelfth century; they were two of the most distinguished persons of their age in Learning and Beauty, but for nothing more famous than for their unfortunate passion. After a long course of calamities, they retired each to a several convent, and consecrated the remainder of their days to Religion. It was many years after this separation that a letter of Abelard's to a friend, which contained the history of his misfortune, fell into the hands of Eloisa. This, awakening all her tenderness, occasioned those celebrated letters (out of which the following is partly extracted), which give so lively a picture of the struggles of Grace and Nature, Virtue and Passion.

In these deep solitudes and awful cells,
Where heav'nly-pensive Contemplation dwells,
And ever-musing Melancholy reigns,
What means this tumult in a vestal's veins?
Why rove my thoughts beyond this last retreat?
Why feels my heart its long-forgotten heat?
Yet, yet I love! — From Abelard it came,
And Eloisa yet must kiss the name.
Dear fatal name! rest ever unreveal'd,
Nor pass these lips, in holy silence seal'd: 10
Hide it, my heart, within that close disguise,
Where, mix'd with God's, his lov'd idea lies:
O write it not, my hand — the name appears
Already written — wash it out, my tears!
In vain lost Eloisa weeps and prays,
Her heart still dictates, and her hand obeys.
Relentless walls! whose darksome round contains
Repentant sighs, and voluntary pains:

Ye rugged rocks, which holy knees have worn;
Ye grots and caverns shagg'd with horrid thorn! 20
Shrines! where their vigils pale-eyed virgins keep,
And pitying saints, whose statues learn to weep!
Tho' cold like you, unmov'd and silent grown,
I have not yet forgot myself to stone.
All is not Heav'n's while Abelard has part,
Still rebel Nature holds out half my heart;
Nor prayers nor fasts its stubborn pulse restrain,
Nor tears, for ages taught to flow in vain.
Soon as thy letters trembling I unclose,
That well-known name awakens all my woes. 30
Oh name for ever sad! for ever dear!
Still breathed in sighs, still usher'd with a tear.
I tremble too, where'er my own I find,
Some dire misfortune follows close behind.
Line after line my gushing eyes o'erflow,
Led thro' a safe variety of woe:
Now warm in love, now with'ring in my bloom,
Lost in a convent's solitary gloom!
There stern religion quench'd th' unwilling flame,
There died the best of passions, Love and Fame. 40
Yet write, O write me all, that I may join
Griefs to thy griefs, and echo sighs to thine.
Nor foes nor fortune take this power away;
And is my Abelard less kind than they?
Tears still are mine, and those I need not spare;
Love but demands what else were shed in prayer.
No happier task these faded eyes pursue;
To read and weep is all they now can do.

Then share thy pain, allow that sad re-
lief;
Ah, more than share it, give me all thy
grief. 50
Heav'n first taught letters for some wretch's
aid,
Some banish'd lover, or some captive maid;
They live, they speak, they breathe what
love inspires,
Warm from the soul, and faithful to its
fires;
The virgin's wish without her fears impart,
Excuse the blush, and pour out all the
heart,
Speed the soft intercourse from soul to soul,
And waft a sigh from Indus to the Pole.
Thou know'st how guiltless first I met
thy flame,
When Love approach'd me under Friend-
ship's name; 60
My fancy form'd thee of angelic kind,
Some emanation of th' all-beauteous Mind.
Those smiling eyes, attemp'ring every ray,
Shone sweetly lambent with celestial day,
Guiltless I gazed; Heav'n listen'd while
you sung;
And truths divine came mended from that
tongue.
From lips like those what precept fail'd to
move?
Too soon they taught me 't was no sin to
love:
Back thro' the paths of pleasing sense I
ran, 69
Nor wish'd an angel whom I loved a man.
Dim and remote the joys of saints I see;
Nor envy them that Heav'n I lose for thee.
How oft, when press'd to marriage, have
I said,
Curse on all laws but those which Love has
made!
Love, free as air, at sight of human ties,
Spreads his light wings, and in a moment
flies.
Let Wealth, let Honour, wait the wedded
dame,
August her deed, and sacred be her fame;
Before true passion all those views remove;
Fame, Wealth, and Honour! what are you
to Love? 80
The jealous God, when we profane his fires,
Those restless passions in revenge inspires,
And bids them make mistaken mortals
groan,
Who seek in love for aught but love alone.

Should at my feet the world's great master
fall,
Himself, his throne, his world, I'd scorn
'em all:
Not Cæsar's empress would I deign to
prove;
No, make me mistress to the man I love;
If there be yet another name more free,
More fond than mistress, make me that to
thee! 90
O happy state! when souls each other draw,
When Love is liberty, and Nature law:
All then is full, possessing and possess'd,
No craving void left aching in the breast:
Ev'n thought meets thought, ere from the
lips it part,
And each warm wish springs mutual from
the heart.
This sure is bliss (if bliss on earth there
be),
And once the lot of Abelard and me.
Alas, how changed! what sudden horrors
rise!
A naked lover bound and bleeding lies! 100
Where, where was Eloise? her voice, her
hand,
Her poniard had opposed the dire com-
mand.
Barbarian, stay! that bloody stroke re-
strain;
The crime was common, common be the
pain.
I can no more; by shame, by rage sup-
press'd,
Let tears and burning blushes speak the
rest.
Canst thou forget that sad, that solemn
day,
When victims at yon altar's foot we lay?
Canst thou forget what tears that moment
fell,
When, warm in youth, I bade the world
farewell? 110
As with cold lips I kiss'd the sacred veil,
The shrines all trembled, and the lamps
grew pale:
Heav'n scarce believ'd the conquest it sur-
vey'd,
And saints with wonder heard the vows I
made.
Yet then, to those dread altars as I drew,
Not on the cross my eyes were fix'd, but
you:
Not grace, or zeal, love only was my call.
And if I lose thy love, I lose my all.

Come! with thy looks, thy words, relieve
     my woe;   119
Those still at least are left thee to bestow.
Still on that breast enamour'd let me lie,
Still drink delicious poison from thy eye,
Pant on thy lip, and to thy heart be press'd;
Give all thou canst — and let me dream the
     rest.
Ah, no! instruct me other joys to prize,
With other beauties charm my partial eyes!
Full in my view set all the bright abode,
And make my soul quit Abelard for God.
     Ah, think at least thy flock deserves thy
     care,
Plants of thy hand, and children of thy
     prayer.   130
From the false world in early youth they
     fled,
By thee to mountains, wilds, and deserts led.
You raised these hallow'd walls; the desert
     smil'd,
And Paradise was open'd in the wild.
No weeping orphan saw his father's stores
Our shrines irradiate or emblaze the floors;
No silver saints, by dying misers giv'n,
Here bribed the rage of ill-requited Heav'n;
But such plain roofs as piety could raise,
And only vocal with the Maker's praise. 140
In these lone walls (their day's eternal
     bound),
These moss-grown domes with spiry turrets
     crown'd,
Where awful arches make a noonday night,
And the dim windows shed a solemn light,
Thy eyes diffused a reconciling ray,
And gleams of glory brighten'd all the day.
But now no face divine contentment wears,
'T is all blank sadness, or continual tears.
See how the force of others' prayers I try,
(O pious fraud of am'rous charity!)   150
But why should I on others' prayers de-
     pend?
Come thou, my father, brother, husband,
     friend!
Ah, let thy handmaid, sister, daughter,
     move,
And all those tender names in one, thy
     love!
The darksome pines, that o'er yon rocks
     reclin'd,
Wave high, and murmur to the hollow
     wind,
The wand'ring streams that shine between
     the hills,
The grots that echo to the tinkling rills,

The dying gales that pant upon the trees,
The lakes that quiver to the curling
     breeze —   160
No more these scenes my meditation aid,
Or lull to rest the visionary maid:
But o'er the twilight groves and dusky
     caves,
Long-sounding aisles and intermingled
     graves,
Black Melancholy sits, and round her
     throws
A death-like silence, and a dread repose:
Her gloomy presence saddens all the scene,
Shades every flower, and darkens every
     green,
Deepens the murmur of the falling floods,
And breathes a browner horror on the
     woods.   170
     Yet here for ever, ever must I stay;
Sad proof how well a lover can obey!
Death, only Death can break the lasting
     chain;
And here, ev'n then shall my cold dust re-
     main;
Here all its frailties, all its flames resign,
And wait till 't is no sin to mix with thine.
     Ah, wretch! believ'd the spouse of God
     in vain,
Confess'd within the slave of Love and man.
Assist me, Heav'n! but whence arose that
     prayer?
Sprung it from piety or from despair?   180
Ev'n here, where frozen Chastity retires,
Love finds an altar for forbidden fires.
I ought to grieve, but cannot what I ought;
I mourn the lover, not lament the fault;
I view my crime, but kindle at the view,
Repent old pleasures, and solicit new;
Now turn'd to Heav'n, I weep my past
     offence,
Now think of thee, and curse my innocence.
Of all affliction taught a lover yet,
'T is sure the hardest science to forget! 190
How shall I lose the sin, yet keep the
     sense,
And love th' offender, yet detest th' of-
     fence?
How the dear object from the crime re-
     move,
Or how distinguish Penitence from Love?
Unequal task! a passion to resign,
For hearts so touch'd, so pierced, so lost
     as mine!
Ere such a soul regains its peaceful state,
How often must it love, how often hate!

How often hope, despair, resent, regret,
Conceal, disdain — do all things but for-
    get! 200
But let Heav'n seize it, all at once 't is fired;
Not touch'd, but rapt; not waken'd, but
    inspired!
O come! O teach me Nature to subdue,
Renounce my love, my life, myself — and
    You:
Fill my fond heart with God alone, for he
Alone can rival, can succeed to thee.
    How happy is the blameless vestal's lot!
The world forgetting, by the world forgot;
Eternal sunshine of the spotless mind,
Each prayer accepted, and each wish re-
    sign'd; 210
Labour and rest, that equal periods keep;
Obedient slumbers that can wake and weep;
Desires composed, affections ever ev'n;
Tears that delight, and sighs that waft to
    Heav'n.
Grace shines around her with serenest
    beams,
And whisp'ring angels prompt her golden
    dreams.
For her th' unfading rose of Eden blooms,
And wings of seraphs shed divine per-
    fumes;
For her the spouse prepares the bridal ring;
For her white virgins hymeneals sing; 220
To sounds of heav'nly harps she dies away,
And melts in visions of eternal day.
    Far other dreams my erring soul employ,
Far other raptures of unholy joy.
When at the close of each sad, sorrowing
    day,
Fancy restores what vengeance snatch'd
    away,
Then conscience sleeps, and leaving Nature
    free,
All my loose soul unbounded springs to
    thee!
Oh curst, dear horrors of all-conscious night!
How glowing guilt exalts the keen delight!
Provoking demons all restraint remove, 231
And stir within me every source of love.
I hear thee, view thee, gaze o'er all thy
    charms,
And round thy phantom glue my clasping
    arms.
I wake: — no more I hear, no more I
    view,
The phantom flies me, as unkind as you.
I call aloud; it hears not what I say:
I stretch my empty arms; it glides away.

To dream once more I close my willing
    eyes;
Ye soft illusions, dear deceits, arise! 240
Alas, no more! methinks we wand'ring go
Thro' dreary wastes, and weep each other's
    woe,
Where round some mould'ring tower pale
    ivy creeps,
And low-brow'd rocks hang nodding o'er
    the deeps.
Sudden you mount, you beckon from the
    skies;
Clouds interpose, waves roar, and winds
    arise.
I shriek, start up, the same sad prospect
    find,
And wake to all the griefs I left behind.
    For thee the Fates, severely kind, ordain
A cool suspense from pleasure and from
    pain; 250
Thy life a long dead calm of fix'd repose;
No pulse that riots, and no blood that
    glows.
Still as the sea, ere winds were taught to
    blow,
Or moving spirit bade the waters flow;
Soft as the slumbers of a saint forgiv'n,
And mild as opening gleams of promised
    Heav'n.
    Come, Abelard! for what hast thou to
    dread ?
The torch of Venus burns not for the dead.
Nature stands check'd; Religion disap-
    proves;
Ev'n thou art cold — yet Eloisa loves. 260
Ah, hopeless, lasting flames; like those that
    burn
To light the dead, and warm th' unfruitful
    urn!
    What scenes appear where'er I turn my
    view;
The dear ideas, where I fly, pursue;
Rise in the grove, before the altar rise,
Stain all my soul, and wanton in my eyes.
I waste the matin lamp in sighs for thee,
Thy image steals between my God and me:
Thy voice I seem in every hymn to hear,
With every bead I drop too soft a tear. 270
When from the censer clouds of fragrance
    roll,
And swelling organs lift the rising soul,
One thought of thee puts all the pomp to
    flight,
Priests, tapers, temples, swim before my
    sight:

In seas of flame my plunging soul is
    drown'd,
While altars blaze, and angels tremble
    round.
While prostrate here in humble grief I
    lie,
Kind virtuous drops just gath'ring in my
    eye,
While praying, trembling, in the dust I roll,
And dawning grace is opening on my soul:
Come, if thou dar'st, all charming as thou
    art!   281
Oppose thyself to Heav'n; dispute my
    heart;
Come, with one glance of those deluding
    eyes
Blot out each bright idea of the skies;
Take back that grace, those sorrows and
    those tears,
Take back my fruitless penitence and
    prayers;
Snatch me, just mounting, from the blest
    abode:
Assist the fiends, and tear me from my
    God!
No, fly me, fly me, far as pole from pole;
Rise Alps between us! and whole oceans
    roll!   290
Ah, come not, write not, think not once of
    me,
Nor share one pang of all I felt for thee.
Thy oaths I quit, thy memory resign;
Forget, renounce me, hate whate'er was
    mine.
Fair eyes, and tempting looks (which yet I
    view),
Long lov'd, ador'd ideas, all adieu!
O Grace serene! O Virtue heav'nly fair!
Divine Oblivion of low-thoughted care!
Fresh blooming Hope, gay daughter of the
    sky!
And Faith, our early immortality!   300
Enter each mild, each amicable guest;
Receive, and wrap me in eternal rest!
    See in her cell sad Eloisa spread,
Propt on some tomb, a neighbour of the
    dead.
In each low wind methinks a spirit calls,
And more than echoes talk along the walls.
Here, as I watch'd the dying lamps around,
From yonder shrine I heard a hollow
    sound:
'Come, sister, come! (it said, or seem'd to
    say)
Thy place is here, sad sister, come away;

Once, like thyself, I trembled, wept, and
    pray'd,   311
Love's victim then, tho' now a sainted
    maid:
But all is calm in this eternal sleep;
Here grief forgets to groan, and love to
    weep;
Ev'n superstition loses ev'ry fear:
For God, not man, absolves our frailties
    here.'
    I come, I come! prepare your roseate
    bowers,
Celestial palms, and ever-blooming flowers.
Thither, where sinners may have rest, I go,
Where flames refin'd in breasts seraphic
    glow;   320
Thou, Abelard! the last sad office pay,
And smooth my passage to the realms of
    day:
See my lips tremble, and my eyeballs roll,
Suck my last breath, and catch my flying
    soul!
Ah, no — in sacred vestments mayst thou
    stand,
The hallow'd taper trembling in thy hand,
Present the cross before my lifted eye,
Teach me at once, and learn of me, to die.
Ah then, thy once lov'd Eloisa see!
It will be then no crime to gaze on me. 330
See from my cheek the transient roses fly!
See the last sparkle languish in my eye!
Till ev'ry motion, pulse, and breath be o'er,
And ev'n my Abelard be lov'd no more.
O Death, all-eloquent! you only prove
What dust we doat on, when 't is man we
    love.
    Then too, when Fate shall thy fair frame
    destroy
(That cause of all my guilt, and all my
    joy),
In trance ecstatic may thy pangs be
    drown'd,
Bright clouds descend, and angels watch
    thee round;   340
From opening skies may streaming glories
    shine,
And saints embrace thee with a love like
    mine.
    May one kind grave unite each hapless
    name,
And graft my love immortal on thy fame!
Then, ages hence, when all my woes are
    o'er,
When this rebellious heart shall beat no
    more;

If ever chance two wand'ring lovers brings,
To Paraclete's white walls and silver
　　springs,
O'er the pale marble shall they join their
　　heads,
And drink the falling tears each other
　　sheds; 350
Then sadly say, with mutual pity mov'd,
' O may we never love as these have lov'd ! '
From the full choir, when loud hosannas
　　rise,
And swell the pomp of dreadful sacrifice,
Amid that scene if some relenting eye
Glance on the stone where our cold relics
　　lie,

Devotion's self shall steal a thought from
　　Heav'n,
One human tear shall drop, and be forgiv'n.
And sure if Fate some future bard shall join
In sad similitude of griefs to mine, 360
Condemn'd whole years in absence to de-
　　plore,
And image charms he must behold no
　　more, —
Such if there be, who loves so long, so well,
Let him our sad, our tender story tell;
The well-sung woes will soothe my pensive
　　ghost;
He best can paint them who shall feel them
　　most.

POEMS WRITTEN BETWEEN 1718 AND 1727

AN INSCRIPTION UPON A PUNCH-BOWL

IN THE SOUTH SEA YEAR, FOR A CLUB:
CHASED WITH JUPITER PLACING CAL-
LISTO IN THE SKIES, AND EUROPA
WITH THE BULL

Pope himself became seriously involved in
the South Sea speculations, and while he does
not appear to have been a heavy loser in the
end, his unwise action for friends, notably for
Lady Mary Wortley seems to have gotten him
into some difficulties. This was of course written before the bursting of the bubble; pre-
sumably in 1720.

COME, fill the South Sea goblet full;
　　The gods shall of our stock take care;
Europa pleased accepts the *Bull*,
　　And Jove with joy puts off the *Bear*.

EPISTLE TO JAMES CRAGGS, ESQ.

SECRETARY OF STATE

Craggs was made Secretary of War in 1717,
when Addison was Secretary of State. He
succeeded Addison in 1720, and died in the
following year. He was an intimate friend and
correspondent of Pope's after 1711.

A SOUL as full of Worth as void of Pride,
Which nothing seeks to show, or needs to
　　hide,

Which nor to guilt nor fear its Caution
　　owes,
And boasts a Warmth that from no passion
　　flows;
A face untaught to feign; a judging eye,
That darts severe upon a rising lie,
And strikes a blush thro' frontless Flat-
　　tery —
All this thou wert; and being this before,
Know, Kings and Fortune cannot make
　　thee more.
Then scorn to gain a friend by servile
　　ways,
Nor wish to lose a foe these virtues raise;
But candid, free, sincere, as you began,
Proceed, a Minister, but still a Man.
Be not (exalted to whate'er degree)
Ashamed of any friend, not ev'n of me:
The patriot's plain but untrod path pursue;
If not, 't is I must be ashamed of you.

A DIALOGUE

POPE

SINCE my old friend is grown so great,
As to be Minister of State,
I 'm told, but 't is not true, I hope,
That Craggs will be ashamed of Pope.

CRAGGS

Alas! if I am such a creature,
To grow the worse for growing greater,
Why, faith, in spite of all my brags,
'T is Pope must be ashamed of Craggs.

VERSES TO MR. C.

ST. JAMES'S PALACE, LONDON, OCT. 22

Probably Craggs, who was in office at the
time when Pope established himself at Twickenham. (Ward.)

FEW words are best; I wish you well;
  Bethel, I'm told, will soon be here;
Some morning walks along the Mall,
  And ev'ning friends, will end the year.

If, in this interval, between
  The falling leaf and coming frost,
You please to see, on Twit'nam green,
  Your friend, your poet, and your host:

For three whole days you here may rest
  From Office bus'ness, news, and strife;
And (what most folks would think a jest)
  Want nothing else, except your wife.

TO MR. GAY

WHO HAD CONGRATULATED POPE ON
FINISHING HIS HOUSE AND GARDENS

Written early in 1722.

AH, friend! 't is true — this truth you lov-
  ers know —
In vain my structures rise, my gardens
  grow,
In vain fair Thames reflects the double
  scenes
Of hanging mountains, and of sloping
  greens;
Joy lives not here, to happier seats it flies,
And only dwells where Wortley casts her
  eyes.
What are the gay Parterre, the chequer'd
  Shade,
The morning Bower, the ev'ning Colon-
  nade,
But soft recesses of uneasy minds,
To sigh unheard in to the passing winds?
So the struck deer in some sequester'd
  part
Lies down to die, the arrow at his heart;
He stretch'd unseen in coverts hid from
  day,
Bleeds drop by drop, and pants his life
  away.

ON DRAWINGS OF THE STAT-UES OF APOLLO, VENUS, AND HERCULES

MADE FOR POPE BY SIR GODFREY
KNELLER

These drawings were made for the adorn-
ment of Pope's house at Twickenham.

WHAT god, what genius did the pencil
  move,
  When Kneller painted these?
'T was friendship, warm as Phœbus, kind
  as Love,
  And strong as Hercules.

EPISTLE TO ROBERT EARL OF OXFORD AND MORTIMER

PREFIXED TO PARNELL'S POEMS

SUCH were the notes thy once-lov'd Poet
  sung,
Till Death untimely stopp'd his tuneful
  tongue.
Oh, just beheld and lost! admired and
  mourn'd!
With softest manners, gentlest arts,
  adorn'd!
Bless'd in each science! bless'd in ev'ry
  strain!
Dear to the Muse! to Harley dear — in
  vain!
  For him thou oft hast bid the world
  attend,
Fond to forget the statesman in the friend;
For Swift and him despised the farce of
  state,
The sober follies of the wise and great,   10
Dext'rous the craving, fawning crowd to
  quit,
And pleas'd to 'scape from Flattery to
  Wit.
  Absent or dead, still let a friend be dear
(A sigh the absent claims, the dead a tear);
Recall those nights that closed thy toilsome
  days,
Still hear thy Parnell in his living lays;
Who, careless now of Int'rest, Fame, or
  Fate,
Perhaps forgets that Oxford e'er was great;
Or deeming meanest what we greatest
  call,
Beholds thee glorious only in thy fall.   20

And sure if aught below the seats divine
Can touch immortals, 't is a soul like thine;
A soul supreme, in each hard instance tried,
Above all pain, all passion, and all pride,
The rage of power, the blast of public
    breath,
The lust of lucre, and the dread of death.
  In vain to deserts thy retreat is made;
The Muse attends thee to thy silent shade;
'T is hers the brave man's latest steps to
    trace,
Rejudge his acts, and dignify disgrace. 30
When Int'rest calls off all her sneaking
    train,
And all th' obliged desert, and all the
    vain,
She waits, or to the scaffold or the cell,
When the last ling'ring friend has bid
    farewell.
Ev'n now she shades thy evening walk
    with bays
(No hireling she, no prostitute to praise);
Ev'n now, observant of the parting ray,
Eyes the calm sunset of thy various day,
Thro' fortune's cloud one truly great can
    see,
Nor fears to tell that Mortimer is he. 40

TWO CHORUSES TO THE TRA-GEDY OF BRUTUS

Brutus, says Pope, was a play 'altered
from Shakespeare by the Duke of Buckingham,
at whose desire these choruses were composed
to supply as many wanting in his play.'
Marcus Brutus was one of two plays (the other
retaining Shakespeare's title) manufactured by
John Sheffield, Duke of Buckinghamshire, out
of *Julius Cæsar*. Both were published in
1722. Pope's choruses stand after the first and
second acts of *Brutus*. The plays have no
literary merit.

CHORUS OF ATHENIANS

STROPHE I

YE shades, where sacred truth is sought,
Groves, where immortal sages taught,
Where heav'nly visions Plato fired,
And Epicurus lay inspired!
In vain your guiltless laurels stood
Unspotted long with human blood.
War, horrid war, your thoughtful walks in-
    vades,
And steel now glitters in the Muses' shades.

ANTISTROPHE I

O Heav'n-born sisters! source of Art!
Who charm the sense, or mend the heart;
Who lead fair Virtue's train along,
Moral Truth and mystic Song!
To what new clime, what distant sky,
Forsaken, friendless, shall ye fly?
Say, will ye bless the bleak Atlantic shore?
Or bid the furious Gaul be rude no more?

STROPHE II

When Athens sinks by fates unjust,
When wild Barbarians spurn her dust;
Perhaps ev'n Britain's utmost shore
Shall cease to blush with strangers' gore,
See Arts her savage sons control,
And Athens rising near the pole!
Till some new tyrant lifts his purple hand,
And civil madness tears them from the land.

ANTISTROPHE II

Ye Gods! what justice rules the ball?
Freedom and Arts together fall;
Fools grant whate'er Ambition craves,
And men, once ignorant, are slaves.
O curs'd effects of civil hate,
In ev'ry age, in ev'ry state!
Still, when the lust of tyrant Power suc-
    ceeds,
Some Athens perishes, some Tully bleeds.

CHORUS OF YOUTHS AND VIRGINS

SEMICHORUS

O tyrant Love! hast thou possest
The prudent, learned, and virtuous
    breast?
Wisdom and wit in vain reclaim,
And arts but soften us to feel thy flame.
Love, soft intruder, enters here,
But ent'ring learns to be sincere.
Marcus with blushes owns he loves,
And Brutus tenderly reproves.
Why, Virtue, dost thou blame desire
    Which Nature hath imprest?
Why, Nature, dost thou soonest fire
    The mild and gen'rous breast?

CHORUS

Love's purer flames the Gods approve;
The Gods and Brutus bend to love:
Brutus for absent Portia sighs,
And sterner Cassius melts at Junia's eyes.
What is loose love? a transient gust,
Spent in a sudden storm of lust,

A vapour fed from wild desire,
A wand'ring, self-consuming fire.
But Hymen's kinder flames unite,
    And burn for ever one;
Chaste as cold Cynthia's virgin light,
    Productive as the sun.

SEMICHORUS

O source of ev'ry social tie,
United wish, and mutual joy!
What various joys on one attend,
As son, as father, brother, husband, friend?
Whether his hoary sire he spies,
While thousand grateful thoughts arise;
Or meets his spouse's fonder eye,
Or views his smiling progeny;
    What tender passions take their turns!
    What home-felt raptures move!
    His heart now melts, now leaps, now
        burns,
With Rev'rence, Hope, and Love.

CHORUS

Hence guilty joys, distastes, surmises,
Hence false tears, deceits, disguises,
Dangers, doubts, delays, surprises,
    Fires that scorch, yet dare not shine!
Purest Love's unwasting treasure,
Constant faith, fair hope, long leisure,
Days of ease, and nights of pleasure,
    Sacred Hymen! these are thine.

TO MRS. M. B. ON HER BIRTH-DAY

Written to Martha Blount in 1723. Lines
5-10 were elsewhere adapted for a versified
celebration of his own birthday, and for an
epitaph on a suicide!

OH, be thou blest with all that Heav'n can
        send,
Long Health, long Youth, long Pleasure,
    and a Friend:
Not with those Toys the female world ad-
        mire,
Riches that vex, and Vanities that tire.
With added years if Life bring nothing new,
But, like a sieve, let ev'ry blessing thro',
Some joy still lost, as each vain year runs
        o'er,
And all we gain, some sad Reflection more;
Is that a birthday? 't is alas! too clear,
'T is but the funeral of the former year.

Let Joy or Ease, let Affluence or Con-
    tent,
And the gay Conscience of a life well spent,
Calm ev'ry thought, inspirit ev'ry grace,
Glow in thy heart, and smile upon thy face.
Let day improve on day, and year on year,
Without a Pain, a Trouble, or a Fear;
Till Death unfelt that tender frame de-
    stroy,
In some soft dream, or extasy of joy,
Peaceful sleep out the Sabbath of the
    Tomb,
And wake to raptures in a life to come.

ANSWER TO THE FOLLOWING QUESTION OF MRS. HOWE

Mary Howe was appointed Maid of Honour
to Queen Caroline, in 1720. ' Lepell ' was another Maid of Honour, referred to in *The Challenge.*

WHAT is Prudery?
        'T is a beldam,
Seen with Wit and Beauty seldom.
'T is a fear that starts at shadows;
'T is (no, 't is n't) like Miss Meadows.
'T is a virgin hard of feature,
Old, and void of all good-nature;
Lean and fretful; would seem wise,
Yet plays the fool before she dies.
'T is an ugly envious shrew,
That rails at dear Lepell and you.

ON A CERTAIN LADY AT COURT

Catharine Howard, one of Queen Caroline's
waiting-women; afterward Countess of Suffolk and mistress to George II. Her identification as the Chloe of *Moral Essays*, II., makes
it easier to believe Walpole's statement that
this lady once reprieved a condemned criminal
that ' an experiment might be made on his
ears for her benefit.'

I KNOW the thing that 's most uncommon;
(Envy, be silent, and attend!)
I know a reasonable Woman,
Handsome and witty, yet a friend:

Not warp'd by Passion, awed by Rumour,
Not grave thro' Pride, nor gay thro' Folly,
An equal mixture of Good-humour,
And sensible soft Melancholy.

'Has she no faults then (Envy says), sir?'
Yes, she has one, I must aver:
When all the world conspires to praise her,
The woman's deaf and does not hear.

TO MR. JOHN MOORE

AUTHOR OF THE CELEBRATED WORM-
POWDER

How much, egregious *Moore!* are we
Deceiv'd by shows and forms!
Whate'er we think, whate'er we see,
All humankind are Worms.

Man is a very Worm by birth,
Vile reptile, weak, and vain!
A while he crawls upon the earth,
Then shrinks to earth again.

That woman is a Worm we find,
E'er since our Grandam's evil:
She first convers'd with her own kind,
That ancient Worm, the Devil.

The learn'd themselves we Bookworms
name,
The blockhead is a Slowworm;
The nymph whose tail is all on flame,
Is aptly term'd a Glowworm.

The fops are painted Butterflies,
That flutter for a day;
First from a Worm they take their rise,
And in a Worm decay.

The flatterer an Earwig grows;
Thus worms suit all conditions;
Misers are Muckworms; Silkworms, beaux;
And Deathwatches, physicians.

That statesmen have the worm, is seen
By all their winding play;
Their conscience is a Worm within,
That gnaws them night and day.

Ah, Moore, thy skill were well employ'd,
And greater gain would rise,
If thou couldst make the courtier void
The Worm that never dies!

O learned friend of Abchurch-Lane,
Who sett'st our entrails free,
Vain is thy Art, thy Powder vain,
Since Worms shall eat ev'n thee.

Our fate thou only canst adjourn
Some few short years, no more!
Ev'n Button's Wits to Worms shall turn,
Who Maggots were before.

THE CURLL MISCELLANIES

UMBRA

Though speculation has connected several
other persons with this poem, it is probably still another hit at the luckless Ambrose
Philips. It, with the three following poems,
was first published in the *Miscellanies*, 1727.

CLOSE to the best known author Umbra
sits,
The constant index to old Button's Wits.
'Who's here?' cries Umbra. 'Only
Johnson.'—'O!
Your slave,' and exit; but returns with
Rowe.
'Dear Rowe, let's sit and talk of trage-
dies:'
Ere long Pope enters, and to Pope he
flies.
Then up comes Steele: he turns upon his
heel,
And in a moment fastens upon Steele;
But cries as soon, 'Dear Dick, I must be
gone,
For, if I know his tread, here's Addison.'
Says Addison to Steele, ''T is time to go:'
Pope to the closet steps aside with Rowe.
Poor Umbra, left in this abandon'd pickle,
Ev'n sits him down, and writes to honest
Tickell.
Fool! 't is in vain from Wit to Wit to
roam;
Know, Sense, like Charity, ' begins at
home.'

BISHOP HOUGH

A BISHOP, by his neighbors hated,
Has cause to wish himself translated;
But why should Hough desire translation,
Loved and esteem'd by all the nation?
Yet if it be the old man's case,
I'll lay my life I know the place:
'T is where God sent some that adore
him,
And whither Enoch went before him.

SANDYS' GHOST

OR, A PROPER NEW BALLAD ON THE NEW
OVID'S METAMORPHOSES : AS IT WAS
INTENDED TO BE TRANSLATED BY
PERSONS OF QUALITY

This refers to the translation undertaken by
Sir Samuel Garth, which aimed to complete
Dryden's translation of Ovid, avoiding the
rigidness of Sandys' method. The enterprise
was begun in 1718, when these verses were
probably written.

YE Lords and Commons, men of wit
  And pleasure about town,
Read this, ere you translate one bit
  Of books of high renown.

Beware of Latin authors, all,
  Nor think your verses sterling,
Tho' with a golden pen you scrawl,
  And scribble in a Berlin.

For not the desk with silver nails,
  Nor bureau of expense,
Nor standish well japann'd, avails
  To writing of good sense.

Hear how a Ghost in dead of night,
  With saucer eyes of fire,
In woful wise did sore affright
  A Wit and courtly Squire:

Rare imp of Phœbus, hopeful youth!
  Like puppy tame, that uses
To fetch and carry in his mouth
  The works of all the Muses.

Ah! why did he write poetry,
  That hereto was so civil;
And sell his soul for vanity
  To Rhyming and the Devil ?

A desk he had of curious work,
  With glitt'ring studs about;
Within the same did Sandys lurk,
  Tho' Ovid lay without.

Now, as he scratch'd to fetch up thought,
  Forth popp'd the sprite so thin,
And from the keyhole bolted out,
  All upright as a pin.

With whiskers, band, and pantaloon,
  And ruff composed most duly,

This Squire he dropp'd his pen full soon,
  While as the light burnt bluely.

Ho! master Sam, quoth Sandys' sprite,
  Write on, nor let me scare ye!
Forsooth, if rhymes fall not in right,
  To Budgell seek or Carey.

I hear the beat of Jacob's drums,
  Poor Ovid finds no quarter!
See first the merry P[embroke] comes
  In haste without his garter.

Then Lords and Lordlings, Squires and
    Knights,
  Wits, Witlings, Prigs, and Peers:
Garth at St. James's, and at White's,
  Beats up for volunteers.

What Fenton will not do, nor Gay,
  Nor Congreve, Rowe, nor Stanyan,
Tom B[urne]t, or Tom D'Urfey may,
  John Dunton, Steele, or any one.

If Justice Philips' costive head
  Some frigid rhymes disburses,
They shall like Persian tales be read,
  And glad both babes and nurses.

Let W[a]rw[ic]k's Muse with Ash[urs]t
    join,
  And Ozell's with Lord Hervey's,
Tickell and Addison combine,
  And P[o]pe translate with Jervas.

L[ansdowne] himself, that lively lord,
  Who bows to every lady,
Shall join with F[rowde] in one accord,
  And be like Tate and Brady.

Ye ladies, too, draw forth your pen;
  I pray, where can the hurt lie ?
Since you have brains as well as men,
  As witness Lady Wortley.

Now, Tonson, list thy forces all,
  Review them and tell noses;
For to poor Ovid shall befall
  A strange metamorphosis;

A metamorphosis more strange
  Than all his books can vapour —
' To what (quoth 'Squire) shall **Ovid**
    change ? '
  Quoth Sandys, ' To waste paper.'

EPITAPH

Imitated from a Latin couplet on Joannes
Mirandula : —

*Joannes jacet hic Mirandula : cætera norunt
Et Tagus et Ganges —forsan et Antipodes.*

First applied by Pope to Francis Chartres,
but published in this form in 1727.

HERE lies *Lord Coningsby* — be civil!
The rest God knows — perhaps the Devil.

THE THREE GENTLE SHEP-
HERDS

OF gentle Philips will I ever sing,
With gentle Philips shall the valleys ring.
My numbers too for ever will I vary,
With gentle Budgell, and with gentle Carey.
Or if in ranging of the names I judge ill,
With gentle Carey and with gentle Budgell.
Oh! may all gentle bards together place ye,
Men of good hearts, and men of delicacy.
May Satire ne'er befool ye or beknave ye,
And from all Wits that have a knack, God
 save ye!

ON THE COUNTESS OF BUR-
LINGTON CUTTING PAPER

PALLAS grew vapourish once and odd;
 She would not do the least right thing,
Either for Goddess or for God,
 Nor work, nor play, nor paint, nor sing.

Jove frown'd, and 'Use (he cried) those
 eyes
 So skilful, and those hands so taper;
Do something exquisite and wise — '
 She bow'd, obey'd him, and cut paper.

This vexing him who gave her birth,
 Thought by all Heav'n a burning shame,
What does she next, but bids, on earth,
 Her *Burlington* do just the same.

Pallas, you give yourself strange airs;
 But sure you 'll find it hard to spoil
The Sense and Taste of one that bears
 The name of Saville and of Boyle.

Alas! one bad example shown,
 How quickly all the sex pursue!
See, madam, see the arts o'erthrown
 Between John Overton and you!

EPIGRAM

AN EMPTY HOUSE

YOU beat your Pate, and fancy Wit will
 come:
Knock as you please, there 's nobody at
 home.

POEMS SUGGESTED BY
GULLIVER

ODE TO QUINBUS FLESTRIN

THE MAN MOUNTAIN, BY TITTY TIT, POET
LAUREATE TO HIS MAJESTY OF LILLI-
PUT. TRANSLATED INTO ENGLISH

This 'Ode' and the three following poems,
were written by Pope after reading *Gulliver's
Travels*, and first published in the *Miscellanies*
of Pope and Swift, in 1727.

IN amaze
Lost I gaze!
Can our eyes
Reach thy size!
May my lays
Swell with praise,
Worthy thee!
Worthy me!
Muse, inspire
All thy fire!
Bards of old
Of him told,
When they said
Atlas' head
Propp'd the skies:
See! and believe your eyes!
See him stride
Valleys wide,
Over woods,
Over floods!
When he treads,
Mountains' heads
Groan and shake,
Armies quake;
Lest his spurn
Overturn
Man and steed:
Troops, take heed!
Left and right,
Speed your flight!
Lest an host

Beneath his foot be lost;
Turn'd aside
From his hide
Safe from wound,
Darts rebound.
From his nose
Clouds he blows!
When he speaks,
Thunder breaks!
When he eats,
Famine threats!
When he drinks,
Neptune shrinks!
Nigh thy ear
In mid air,
On thy hand
Let me stand;
So shall I,
Lofty poet! touch the sky.

THE LAMENTATION OF GLUM-DALCLITCH FOR THE LOSS OF GRILDRIG

A PASTORAL

Soon as Glumdalclitch miss'd her pleasing care,
She wept, she blubber'd, and she tore her hair;
No British miss sincerer grief has known,
Her squirrel missing, or her sparrow flown.
She furl'd her sampler, and haul'd in her thread,
And stuck her needle into Grildrig's bed;
Then spread her hands, and with a bounce let fall
Her baby, like the giant in Guildhall.
In peals of thunder now she roars, and now
She gently whimpers like a lowing cow: 10
Yet lovely in her sorrow still appears:
Her locks dishevell'd, and her flood of tears,
Seem like the lofty barn of some rich swain,
When from the thatch drips fast a shower of rain.
In vain she search'd each cranny of the house,
Each gaping chink, impervious to a mouse.
' Was it for this (she cried) with daily care
Within thy reach I set the vinegar,
And fill'd the cruet with the acid tide,
While pepper-water worms thy bait supplied ?   20

Where twined the silver eel around thy hook,
And all the little monsters of the brook!
Sure in that lake he dropt; my Grilly's drown'd! '
She dragg'd the cruet, but no Grildrig found.
' Vain is thy courage, Grilly, vain thy boast!
But little creatures enterprise the most.
Trembling I 've seen thee dare the kitten's paw,
Nay, mix with children, as they play'd at taw,
Nor fear the marbles as they bounding flew;
Marbles to them, but rolling rocks to you!   30
' Why did I trust thee with that giddy youth ?
Who from a page can ever learn the truth ?
Versed in court tricks, that money-loving boy
To some lord's daughter sold the living toy;
Or rent him limb from limb in cruel play,
As children tear the wings of flies away.
From place to place o'er Brobdingnag I 'll roam,
And never will return, or bring thee home.
But who hath eyes to trace the passing wind ?
How then thy fairy footsteps can I find ?   40
Dost thou bewilder'd wander all alone
In the green thicket of a mossy stone;
Or, tumbled from the toadstool's slipp'ry round,
Perhaps, all maim'd, lie grovelling on the ground
Dost thou, embosom'd in the lovely rose,
Or, sunk within the peach's down repose ?
Within the kingcup if thy limbs are spread,
Or in the golden cowslip's velvet head,
O show me, Flora, midst those sweets, the flower
Where sleeps my Grildrig in the fragrant bower.   50
' But ah! I fear thy little fancy roves
On little females, and on little loves;
Thy pigmy children, and thy tiny spouse,
The baby playthings that adorn thy house,
Doors, windows, chimneys, and the spacious rooms,
Equal in size to cells of honeycombs.
Hast thou for these now ventured from the shore,
Thy bark a bean shell, and a straw thy oar ?

Or in thy box now bounding on the main,
Shall I ne'er bear thyself and house again?
And shall I set thee on my hand no more, 61
To see thee leap the lines, and traverse o'er
My spacious palm; of stature scarce a span,
Mimic the actions of a real man?
No more behold thee turn my watch's key,
As seamen at a capstan anchors weigh?
How wert thou wont to walk with cautious
    tread,
A dish of tea, like milkpail, on thy head!
How chase the mite that bore thy cheese
    away,
And keep the rolling maggot at a bay!' 70
    She spoke; but broken accents stopp'd
        her voice,
Soft as the speaking-trumpet's mellow
    noise:
She sobb'd a storm, and wiped her flowing
    eyes,
Which seem'd like two broad suns in misty
    skies.
O squander not thy grief! those tears com-
    mand
To weep upon our cod in Newfoundland;
The plenteous pickle shall preserve the fish,
And Europe taste thy sorrows in a dish.

TO MR. LEMUEL GULLIVER

THE GRATEFUL ADDRESS OF THE UN-
HAPPY HOUYHNHNMS NOW IN SLAVERY
AND BONDAGE IN ENGLAND

To thee, we wretches of the Houyhnhnm
    band,
Condemn'd to labour in a barb'rous land,
Return our thanks. Accept our humble
    lays,
And let each grateful Houyhnhnm neigh
    thy praise.
    O happy Yahoo, purged from human
        crimes,
By thy sweet sojourn in those virtuous
    climes,
Where reign our sires; there, to thy coun-
    try's shame,
Reason, you found, and Virtue were the
    same.
Their precepts razed the prejudice of youth,
And ev'n a Yahoo learn'd the love of
    Truth.   10
    Art thou the first who did the coast ex-
        plore?

Did never Yahoo tread that ground before?
Yes, thousands! But in pity to their kind,
Or sway'd by envy, or thro' pride of mind,
They hid their knowledge of a nobler race,
Which own'd, would all their sires and sons
    disgrace.
    You, like the Samian, visit lands un-
        known,
And by their wiser morals mend your own.
Thus Orpheus travell'd to reform his kind,
Came back, and tamed the brutes he left
    behind.   20
    You went, you saw, you heard: with
        virtue fought,
Then spread those morals which the Houy-
    hnhnms taught.
Our labours here must touch thy gen'rous
    heart,
To see us strain before the coach and
    cart;
Compell'd to run each knavish jockey's
    heat!
Subservient to Newmarket's annual cheat!
With what reluctance do we lawyers bear,
To fleece their country clients twice a year!
Or managed in your schools, for fops to
    ride,
How foam, how fret beneath a load of
    pride!   30
Yes, we are slaves — but yet, by reason's
    force,
Have learn'd to bear misfortune like a
    horse.
O would the stars, to ease my bonds
    ordain
That gentle Gulliver might guide my rein!
Safe would I bear him to his journey's end,
For 't is a pleasure to support a friend.
But if my life be doom'd to serve the bad,
Oh! mayst thou never want an easy pad!
                                HOUYHNHNM

MARY GULLIVER TO CAPTAIN
LEMUEL GULLIVER

AN EPISTLE

ARGUMENT

The captain, some time after his return,
being retired to Mr. Sympson's in the country,
Mrs. Gulliver, apprehending from his late behaviour some estrangement of his affections,
writes him the following expostulatory, soothing, and tenderly complaining epistle.

WELCOME, thrice welcome to thy native
    place!
What, touch me not? what, shun a wife's
    embrace?
Have I for this thy tedious absence borne,
And waked, and wish'd whole nights for
    thy return?
In five long years I took no second spouse;
What Redriff wife so long hath kept her
    vows?
Your eyes, your nose, inconstancy betray;
Your nose you stop, your eyes you turn
    away.
'T is said, that thou shouldst 'cleave unto
    thy wife;'
Once thou didst cleave, and I could cleave
    for life.   10
Hear, and relent! hark how thy children
    moan!
Be kind at least to these; they are thy
    own:
Behold, and count them all; secure to find
The honest number that you left behind.
See how they bat thee with their pretty
    paws:
Why start you? are they snakes? or have
    they claws?
Thy Christian seed, our mutual flesh and
    bone:
Be kind at least to these; they are thy
    own.
Biddel, like thee, might farthest India
    rove;
He changed his country, but retain'd his
    love.   20
There's Captain Pannel, absent half his
    life,
Comes back, and is the kinder to his wife;
Yet Pannel's wife is brown compared to
    me,
And Mrs. Biddel sure is fifty-three.
Not touch me! never neighbour call'd
    me slut!
Was Flimnap's dame more sweet in Lilli-
    put?
I've no red hair to breathe an odious
    fume;
At least thy Consort's cleaner than thy
    Groom.
Why then that dirty stable-boy thy care?
What mean those visits to the Sorrel
    Mare?   30
Say, by what witchcraft, or what demon
    led,
Preferr'st thou litter to the marriage-bed?

Some say the Devil himself is in that
    mare:
If so, our Dean shall drive him forth by
    prayer.
Some think you mad, some think you are
    possess'd,
That Bedlam and clean straw will suit you
    best.
Vain means, alas, this frenzy to appease!
That straw, that straw would heighten the
    disease.
My bed (the scene of all our former joys,
Witness two lovely girls, two lovely boys)
Alone I press: in dreams I call my dear, 41
I stretch my hand; no Gulliver is there!
I wake, I rise, and shiv'ring with the frost
Search all the house; my Gulliver is lost!
Forth in the street I rush with frantic cries;
The windows open, all the neighbours rise:
'Where sleeps my Gulliver? O tell me
    where.'
The neighbours answer, 'With the Sorrel
    Mare.'
At early morn I to the market haste
(Studious in every thing to please thy
    taste);   50
A curious fowl and 'sparagus I chose
(For I remember'd you were fond of those);
Three shillings cost the first, the last seven
    groats;
Sullen you turn from both, and call for oats.
Others bring goods and treasure to their
    houses,
Something to deck their pretty babes and
    spouses:
My only token was a cup like horn,
That's made of nothing but a lady's corn.
'T is not for that I grieve; O, 't is to see
The Groom and Sorrel Mare preferr'd to
    me!   60
These, for some moments when you deign
    to quit,
And at due distance sweet discourse ad-
    mit,
'T is all my pleasure thy past toil to know;
For pleas'd remembrance builds delight on
    woe.
At ev'ry danger pants thy consort's breast,
And gaping infants squall to hear the rest.
How did I tremble, when by thousands
    bound,
I saw thee stretch'd on Lilliputian ground!
When scaling armies climb'd up every
    part,
Each step they trod I felt upon my heart.

But when thy torrent quench'd the dreadful
 blaze, 71
King, Queen, and Nation staring with
 amaze,
Full in my view how all my husband came;
And what extinguish'd theirs increas'd my
 flame.
Those spectacles, ordain'd thine eyes to
 save,
Were once my present; love that armour
 gave.
How did I mourn at Bolgolam's decree!
For when he sign'd thy death, he sentenc'd
 me.
 When folks might see thee all the coun-
 try round
For sixpence, I'd have giv'n a thousand
 pound. 80
Lord! when the giant babe that head of
 thine
Got in his mouth, my heart was up in mine!
When in the marrow bone I see thee
 ramm'd,
Or on the housetop by the monkey
 cramm'd,
The piteous images renew my pain,
And all thy dangers I weep o'er again.
But on the maiden's nipple when you rid,
Pray Heav'n, 't was all a wanton maiden
 did!
Glumdalclitch, too! with thee I mourn her
 case,
Heaven guard the gentle girl from all dis-
 grace! 90

O may the king that one neglect for-
 give,
And pardon her the fault by which I live!
Was there no other way to set him free ?
My life, alas! I fear prov'd death to
 thee.
 O teach me, dear, new words to speak
 my flame;
Teach me to woo thee by thy best lov'd
 name!
Whether the style of Grildrig please thee
 most,
So call'd on Brobdingnag's stupendous
 coast,
When on the monarch's ample hand you
 sate, 99
And halloo'd in his ear intrigues of state;
Or Quinbus Flestrin more endearment
 brings,
When like a mountain you look'd down on
 kings:
If ducal Nardac, Lilliputian peer,
Or Glumglum's humbler title soothe thy
 ear:
Nay, would kind Jove my organs so dis-
 pose,
To hymn harmonious Houyhnhnm thro'
 the nose,
I'd call thee Houyhnhnm, that high sound-
 ing name
Thy children's noses all should twang the
 same;
So might I find my loving spouse of course
Endued with all the virtues of a horse. 110

LATER POEMS

ON CERTAIN LADIES

WHEN other fair ones to the shades go
 down,
Still Chloë, Flavia, Delia, stay in town:
Those ghosts of beauty wand'ring here reside,
And haunt the places where their honour
 died.

CELIA

CELIA, we know, is sixty-five,
 Yet Celia's face is seventeen;
Thus winter in her breast must live,
 While summer in her face is seen.

How cruel Celia's fate, who hence
 Our heart's devotion cannot try;
Too pretty for our reverence,
 Too ancient for our gallantry!

PROLOGUE

TO A PLAY FOR MR. DENNIS'S BENEFIT,
IN 1733, WHEN HE WAS OLD, BLIND,
AND IN GREAT DISTRESS, A LITTLE
BEFORE HIS DEATH

As when that hero, who in each campaign
Had braved the Goth, and many a Vandal
 slain,

Lay fortune-struck, a spectacle of woe,
Wept by each friend, forgiv'n by ev'ry
   foe;
Was there a gen'rous, a reflecting mind,
But pitied Belisarius old and blind ?
Was there a chief but melted at the sight ?
A common soldier but who clubb'd his
   mite ?
Such, such emotions should in Britons rise,
When, press'd by want and weakness, Den-
   nis lies;
Dennis! who long had warr'd with modern
   Huns,
Their quibbles routed, and defied their
   puns;
A desp'rate bulwark, sturdy, firm, and
   fierce,
Against the Gothic sons of frozen verse.
How changed from him who made the
   boxes groan,
And shook the stage with thunders all his
   own!
Stood up to dash each vain pretender's
   hope,
Maul the French tyrant, or pull down the
   Pope!
If there's a Briton, then, true bred and
   born,
Who holds dragoons and wooden shoes in
   scorn;
If there's a critic of distinguish'd rage;
If there's a senior who contemns this age;
Let him to-night his just assistance lend,
And be the Critic's, Briton's, old man's
   friend.

SONG, BY A PERSON OF QUALITY

WRITTEN IN THE YEAR 1733

The public astonished Pope by taking this
burlesque seriously, and praising it as poetry.

I

FLUTT'RING spread thy purple Pinions,
   Gentle *Cupid*, o'er my Heart;
I a Slave in thy Dominions;
   Nature must give Way to Art.

II

Mild *Arcadians*, ever blooming,
   Nightly nodding o'er your Flocks,
See my weary Days consuming,
   All beneath yon flow'ry Rocks.

III

Thus the Cyprian Goddess weeping,
   Mourn'd *Adonis*, darling Youth:
Him the Boar in Silence creeping,
   Gored with unrelenting Tooth.

IV

Cynthia, tune harmonious Numbers;
   Fair *Discretion*, string the Lyre;
Soothe my ever-waking Slumbers:
   Bright *Apollo*, lend thy Choir.

V

Gloomy *Pluto*, King of Terrors,
   Arm'd in adamantine Chains,
Lead me to the Crystal Mirrors,
   Wat'ring soft Elysian Plains.

VI

Mournful Cypress, verdant Willow,
   Gilding my *Aurelia's* Brows,
Morpheus hov'ring o'er my Pillow,
   Hear me pay my dying Vows.

VII

Melancholy smooth *Mœander*,
   Swiftly purling in a Round,
On thy Margin Lovers wander,
   With thy flow'ry Chaplets crown'd.

VIII

Thus when *Philomela* drooping,
   Softly seeks her silent Mate,
See the Bird of *Juno* stooping;
   Melody resigns to Fate.

VERSES LEFT BY MR. POPE

ON HIS LYING IN THE SAME BED WHICH
WILMOT, THE CELEBRATED EARL OF
ROCHESTER, SLEPT IN AT ADDERBURY,
THEN BELONGING TO THE DUKE OF
ARGYLE, JULY 9TH, 1739

WITH no poetic ardour fired
   I press the bed where Wilmot lay;
That here he lov'd, or here expired,
   Begets no numbers grave or gay.

Beneath thy roof, Argyle, are bred
   Such thoughts as prompt the brave to
     lie
Stretch'd out in honour's nobler bed,
   Beneath a nobler roof — the sky.

Such flames as high in patriots burn,
  Yet stoop to bless a child or wife;
And such as wicked kings may mourn,
  When Freedom is more dear than Life.

ON HIS GROTTO AT TWICKEN-HAM

COMPOSED OF MARBLES, SPARS, GEMS, ORES, AND MINERALS

These lines were enclosed in a letter to Bolingbroke, dated September 3, 1740.

THOU who shalt stop where Thames'
    translucent wave
Shines a broad mirror thro' the shadowy
    cave;
Where ling'ring drops from min'ral roofs
    distil,
And pointed crystals break the sparkling
    rill;
Unpolish'd gems no ray on pride bestow,
And latent metals innocently glow;
Approach. Great Nature studiously behold!
And eye the mine without a wish for gold.
Approach; but awful! lo! the Ægerian grot,
Where, nobly pensive, St. John sate and
    thought;
Where British sighs from dying Wyndham
    stole,
And the bright flame was shot thro' Marchmont's soul.
Let such, such only, tread this sacred floor,
Who dare to love their country, and be
    poor.

ON RECEIVING FROM THE RIGHT HON. THE LADY FRANCES SHIRLEY A STANDISH AND TWO PENS

Lady Frances Shirley was daughter of Earl Ferrers, a neighbor of Pope's at Twickenham.

YES, I beheld th' Athenian Queen
  Descend in all her sober charms;
' And take ' (she said, and smiled serene),
  ' Take at this hand celestial arms:

' Secure the radiant weapons wield;
This golden lance shall guard Desert,

And if a Vice dares keep the field,
  This steel shall stab it to the heart.'

Awed, on my bended knees I fell,
  Received the weapons of the sky;   10
And dipt them in the sable well,
  The fount of Fame or Infamy.

' What *well?* what *weapons?* ' (Flavia
    cries,)
  ' A standish, steel and golden pen!
It came from Bertrand's, not the skies;
  I gave it you to write again.

' But, Friend, take heed whom you attack;
  You 'll bring a House (I mean of Peers)
Red, blue, and green, nay white and
    black,
  L[ambeth] and all about your ears.

' You 'd write as smooth again on glass,
  And run, on ivory, so glib,
As not to stick at Fool or Ass,
  Nor stop at Flattery or Fib.

' *Athenian Queen!* and *sober charms!*
  I tell ye, fool, there 's nothing in 't:
'T is Venus, Venus gives these arms;
  In Dryden's Virgil see the print.

' Come, if you 'll be a quiet soul,
  That dares tell neither Truth nor Lies,
I 'll lift you in the harmless roll
  Of those that sing of these poor eyes.'

ON BEAUFORT HOUSE GATE AT CHISWICK

The Lord Treasurer Middlesex's house at Chelsea, after passing to the Duke of Beaufort, was called Beaufort House. It was afterwards sold to Sir Hans Sloane. When the house was taken down in 1740, its gateway, built by Inigo Jones, was given by Sir Hans Sloane to the Earl of Burlington, who removed it with the greatest care to his garden at Chiswick, where it may be still seen. (Ward.)

I WAS brought from Chelsea last year,
  Batter'd with wind and weather;
Inigo Jones put me together;
Sir Hans Sloane let me alone;
  Burlington brought me hither.

TO MR. THOMAS SOUTHERN

ON HIS BIRTHDAY, 1742

Southern was invited to dine on his birthday with Lord Orrery, who had prepared the entertainment, of which the bill of fare is here set down.

RESIGN'D to live, prepared to die,
With not one sin but poetry,
This day Tom's fair account has run
(Without a blot) to eighty-one.
Kind Boyle before his poet lays
A table with a cloth of bays;
And Ireland, mother of sweet singers,
Presents her harp still to his fingers.
The feast, his tow'ring Genius marks
In yonder wildgoose and the larks!
The mushrooms show his Wit was sudden!
And for his Judgment, lo, a pudden!
Roast beef, tho' old, proclaims him stout,
And grace, although a bard, devout.
May Tom, whom Heav'n sent down to raise
The price of Prologues and of Plays,
Be ev'ry birthday more a winner,
Digest his thirty-thousandth dinner,
Walk to his grave without reproach,
And scorn a Rascal and a Coach.

EPIGRAM

MY Lord complains that Pope, stark mad with gardens,
Has cut three trees, the value of three farthings.
'But he's my neighbour,' cries the Peer polite:
'And if he visit me, I'll waive the right.'
What! on compulsion, and against my will,
A lord's acquaintance? Let him file his bill!

EPIGRAM

Explained by Carruthers to refer to the large sums of money given in charity on account of the severity of the weather about the year 1740.

YES! 't is the time (I cried), impose the chain,
Destin'd and due to wretches self-enslaved;

But when I saw such charity remain,
I half could wish this people should be saved.

Faith lost, and Hope, our Charity begins;
And 't is a wise design in pitying Heav'n,
If this can cover multitude of sins,
To take the *only* way to be forgiv'n.

1740 : A POEM

'I shall here,' says Dr. Warton, 'present the reader with a valuable literary curiosity, a Fragment of an unpublished Satire of Pope, entitled, *One Thousand Seven Hundred and Forty;* communicated to me by the kindness of the learned and worthy Dr. Wilson, formerly fellow and librarian of Trinity College, Dublin; who speaks of the Fragment in the following terms: —
'"This poem I transcribed from a rough draft in Pope's own hand. He left many blanks for fear of the Argus eye of those who, if they cannot find, can fabricate treason; yet, spite of his precaution, it fell into the hands of his enemies. To the hieroglyphics there are direct allusions, I think, in some of the notes on the *Dunciad.* It was lent me by a grandson of Lord Chetwynd, an intimate friend of the famous Lord Bolingbroke, who gratified his curiosity by a boxful of the rubbish and sweepings of Pope's study, whose executor he was, in conjunction with Lord Marchmont."'

O WRETCHED B[ritain], jealous now of all,
What God, what Mortal shall prevent thy fall?
Turn, turn thy eyes from wicked men in place,
And see what succour from the patriot race.
C[ampbell], his own proud dupe, thinks Monarchs things
Made just for him, as other fools for Kings;
Controls, decides, insults thee ev'ry hour,
And antedates the hatred due to power.
Thro' clouds of passion P[ulteney]'s views are clear;
He foams a Patriot to subside a Peer;   10
Impatient sees his country bought and sold,
And damns the market where he takes no gold.
Grave, righteous S[andys] jogs on till, past belief,
He finds himself companion with a thief.
To purge and let thee blood with fire and sword
Is all the help stern S[hippen] would afford.

That those who bind and rob thee would
  not kill,
Good C[ornbury] hopes, and candidly sits
  still.
Of Ch[arle]s W[illiams] who speaks at
  all ? 19
No more than of Sir Har[r]y or Sir P[aul]:
Whose names once up, they thought it was
  not wrong
To lie in bed, but sure they lay too long.
  G[owe]r, C[obha]m, B[athurs]t, pay thee
  due regards.
Unless the ladies bid them mind their
  cards.
            with wit that must
And C[hesterfiel]d who speaks so well and
  writes,
Whom (saving W.) every S[harper bites,]
            must needs
Whose wit and . . . equally provoke one,
Finds thee, at best, the butt to crack his
  joke on.
  As for the rest, each winter up they
  run,
And all are clear, that something must be
  done. 30
Then urged by C[artere]t, or by C[artere]t
  stopp'd,
Inflamed by P[ultene]y, and by P[ultene]y
  dropp'd;
They follow rev'rently each wondrous
  wight,
Amazed that one can read, that one can
  write
(So geese to gander prone obedience keep,
Hiss if he hiss, and if he slumber, sleep);
Till having done whate'er was fit or fine,
Utter'd a speech, and ask'd their friends
  to dine,
Each hurries back to his paternal ground,
Content but for five shillings in the pound, 40
Yearly defeated, yearly hopes they give,
And all agree Sir Robert cannot live.
  Rise, rise, great W[alpole], fated to ap-
  pear,
Spite of thyself a glorious minister !
Speak the loud language princes . . .
And treat with half the . . .
At length to B[ritain] kind, as to thy . . .
Espouse the nation, you . . .
  What can thy H[orace] . . .
Dress in Dutch . . . 50
  Though still he travels on no bad pre-
  tence,
To show . . .

Or those foul copies of thy face and
  tongue,
Veracious W[innington] and frontless
  Yonge;
Sagacious Bub, so late a friend, and there
So late a foe, yet more sagacious H[are] ?
Hervey and Hervey's school, F[ox], H[en-
  le]y, H[into]n,
Yea, moral Ebor, or religious Winton.
How ! what can O[nslo]w, what can D[ela-
  ware],
The wisdom of the one and other chair, 60
N[ewcastle] laugh, or D[orset]'s sager
  [sneer],
Or thy dread truncheon M[arlboro]'s
  mighty Peer ?
What help from J[ekyl]l's opiates canst
  thou draw
Or H[ardwic]k's quibbles voted into law ?
C[ummins], that Roman in his nose alone.
Who hears all causes, B[ritain], but thy
  own,
Or those proud fools whom nature, rank,
  and fate
Made fit companions for the sword of state.
  Can the light Packhorse, or the heavy
  Steer, 69
The sowzing Prelate, or the sweating Peer,
Drag out with all its dirt and all its
  weight,
The lumb'ring carriage of thy broken
  state ?
Alas! the people curse, the carman swears,
The drivers quarrel, and the master stares.
  The plague is on thee, Britain, and who
  tries
To save thee, in th' infectious office dies.
The first firm P[ultene]y soon resign'd his
  breath,
Brave S[carboro] loved thee, and was lied
  to death.
Good M[arch]m[on]t's fate tore P[olwar]th
  from thy side,
And thy last sigh was heard when W[ynd-
  ha]m died. 80
  Thy nobles sl[ave]s, thy se[nate]s bought
  with gold,
Thy clergy perjured, thy whole people
  sold,
An atheist �miniⁿ, a ⊕'''s ad. . . . .
Blotch thee all o'er, and sink. . . . . .
  Alas! on one alone our all relies,
Let him be honest, and he must be wise.
Let him no trifler from his   school,
Nor like his. . . . . still a. . . .

Be but a man! unminister'd, alone,
And free at once the Senate and the
    Throne;   90
Esteem the public love his best supply,
A ☉'s true glory his integrity;
Rich *with* his. . . . . . *in* his. . . . . strong,

Affect no conquest, but endure no wrong.
Whatever his religion or his blood,
His public Virtue makes his title good.
Europe's just balance and our own may
    stand,
And one man's honesty redeem the land.

POEMS OF UNCERTAIN DATE

TO ERINNA

THO' sprightly Sappho force our love and
    praise,
A softer wonder my pleas'd soul surveys,
The mild Erinna, blushing in her bays.
So, while the sun's broad beam yet strikes
    the sight,
All mild appears the moon's more sober
    light;
Serene, in virgin majesty she shines,
And, unobserv'd, the glaring sun declines.

LINES WRITTEN IN WINDSOR FOREST

Sent in an undated letter to Martha Blount.

ALL hail, once pleasing, once inspiring shade,
Scene of my youthful loves, and happier
    hours!
Where the kind Muses met me as I stray'd,
    And gently press'd my hand, and said,
    'Be ours.'
Take all thou e'er shalt have, a constant
    Muse:
    At Court thou mayst be liked, but nothing
    gain:
Stocks thou mayst buy and sell, but always
    lose;
    And love the brightest eyes, but love in
    vain.

VERBATIM FROM BOILEAU

FIRST PUBLISHED BY WARBURTON IN
1751

Un jour, dit un auteur, etc.

ONCE (says an author, where I need not say)
Two travellers found an Oyster in their way:

Both fierce, both hungry, the dispute grew
    strong,
While, scale in hand, dame Justice pass'd
    along.
Before her each with clamour pleads the
    laws,
Explain'd the matter, and would win the
    cause.
Dame Justice weighing long the doubtful
    right,
Takes, opens, swallows it before their
    sight.
The cause of strife remov'd so rarely well,
' There take (says Justice), take ye each a
    shell.
We thrive at Westminster on fools like
    you:
'T was a fat Oyster — Live in peace —
    Adieu.'

LINES ON SWIFT'S ANCESTORS

Swift set up a plain monument to his grandfather, and also presented a cup to the church
of Goodrich, or Gotheridge (in Herefordshire).
He sent a pencilled elevation of the monument
(a simple tablet) to Mrs. Howard, who returned
it with the following lines, inscribed on the
drawing by Pope. The paper is endorsed, in
Swift's hand: ' Model of a monument for my
grandfather. with Pope's roguery.' (Scott's
Life of Swift.)

JONATHAN SWIFT
Had the gift,
By fatherige, motherige,
And by brotherige
To come from Gotherige,
But now is spoil'd clean,
And an Irish dean;

In this church he has put
A stone of two foot,

With a cup and a can, sir,
In respect to his grandsire;
So, Ireland, change thy tone,
And cry, O hone! O hone!
For England hath its own.

ON SEEING THE LADIES AT CRUX EASTON WALK IN THE WOODS BY THE GROTTO

EXTEMPORE BY MR. POPE

AUTHORS the world and their dull brains
  have traced
To fix the ground where Paradise was
  placed;
Mind not their learned whims and idle
  talk;
Here, here 's the place where these bright
  angels walk.

INSCRIPTION ON A GROTTO, THE WORK OF NINE LADIES

HERE, shunning idleness at once and praise,
This radiant pile nine rural sisters raise;
The glitt'ring emblem of each spotless
  dame,
Clear as her soul and shining as her frame;

Beauty which Nature only can impart,
And such a polish as disgraces Art;
But Fate disposed them in this humble
  sort,
And hid in deserts what would charm a
  Court.

TO THE RIGHT HON. THE EARL OF OXFORD

UPON A PIECE OF NEWS IN MIST [MIST'S JOURNAL] THAT THE REV. MR. W. RE- FUSED TO WRITE AGAINST MR. POPE BECAUSE HIS BEST PATRON HAD A FRIENDSHIP FOR THE SAID POPE

WESLEY, if Wesley 't is they mean,
  They say on Pope would fall,
Would his best Patron let his Pen
  Discharge his inward gall.

What Patron this, a doubt must be,
  Which none but you can clear,
Or father Francis, 'cross the sea,
  Or else Earl Edward here.

That both were good must be confess'd,
  And much to both he owes;
But which to him will be the best
  The Lord of Oxford knows.

EPIGRAMS AND EPITAPHS

ON A PICTURE OF QUEEN CAROLINE

DRAWN BY LADY BURLINGTON

It is not known who the Bishop was. The 'lying Dean' refers to Dr. Alured Clarke, who preached a fulsome sermon upon the Queen's death.

PEACE, flatt'ring Bishop! lying Dean!
This portrait only paints the Queen!

EPIGRAM ENGRAVED ON THE COLLAR OF A DOG WHICH I GAVE TO HIS ROYAL HIGH- NESS

'His Highness' was Frederick, Prince of Wales.

I AM his Highness' dog at Kew;
Pray tell me, Sir, whose dog are you?

LINES WRITTEN IN EVELYN'S BOOK ON COINS

First printed in the *Gentleman's Magazine* in 1735.

TOM WOOD of Chiswick, deep divine,
To Painter Kent gave all this coin.
'T is the first coin, I 'm bold to say,
That ever churchman gave to lay.

FROM THE GRUB–STREET JOURNAL

This Journal was established in January 1730, and carried on for eight years by Pope

and his friends, in answer to the attacks provoked by the *Dunciad*. It corresponds in some
measure to the *Xenien* of Goethe and Schiller.
Only such pieces are here inserted as bear
Pope's distinguishing signature A.; several
others are probably his. (Ward.)

I

EPIGRAM

Occasioned by seeing some sheets of Dr.
Bentley's edition of Milton's *Paradise Lost*.

Did Milton's prose, O Charles, thy death
   defend ?
A furious Foe unconscious proves a Friend.
On Milton's verse does Bentley comment ?
   — Know
A weak officious Friend becomes a Foe.
While he but sought his Author's fame to
   further,
The murd'rous critic has avenged thy
   murder.

II

EPIGRAM

Should D[enni]s print, how once you
   robb'd your brother,
Traduced your monarch, and debauch'd
   your mother;
Say, what revenge on D[enni]s can be had;
Too dull for laughter, for reply too mad ?
Of one so poor you cannot take the law;
On one so old your sword you scorn to
   draw.
Uncaged then let the harmless monster
   rage,
Secure in dulness, madness, want, and age.

III

MR. J. M. S[MYTH]E

CATECHISED ON HIS ONE EPISTLE TO
MR. POPE

What makes you write at this odd rate ?
Why, Sir, it is to imitate.
What makes you steal and trifle so ?
Why, 't is to do as others do.
But there 's no meaning to be seen.
Why, that 's the very thing I mean.

IV

EPIGRAM

ON MR. M[OO]RE'S GOING TO LAW WITH
MR. GILIVER : INSCRIBED TO ATTORNEY
TIBBALD

Once in his life M[oo]re judges right:
   His sword and pen not worth a straw,
An author that could never write,
A gentleman that dares not fight,
   Has but one way to tease — by law.
This suit, dear Tibbald, kindly hatch;
   Thus thou may'st help the sneaking
   elf;
And sure a printer is his match,
   Who 's but a publisher himself.

V

EPIGRAM

A gold watch found on cinder whore,
Or a good verse on J[emm]y M[oor]e,
Proves but what either should conceal,
Not that they 're rich, but that they steal.

VI

EPITAPH

ON JAMES MOORE-SMYTHE

Here lies what had nor birth, nor shape,
   nor fame;
No gentleman! no man! no-thing! no name!
For Jamie ne'er grew James; and what
   they call
More, shrunk to Smith — and Smith 's no
   name at all.
Yet die thou can'st not, phantom, oddly
   fated:
For how can no-thing be annihilated ?

VII

A QUESTION BY ANONYMOUS

Tell, if you can, which did the worse,
   Caligula or Gr[afto]n's Gr[a]ce ?
That made a Consul of a horse,
   And *this* a Laureate of an ass.

VIII

EPIGRAM

The sting of this epigram was for Cibber, then Poet Laureate.

GREAT G[eorge] such servants since thou well canst lack,
Oh! save the salary, and drink the sack.

IX

EPIGRAM

BEHOLD! ambitious of the British bays,
Cibber and Duck contend in rival lays,
But, gentle Colley, should thy verse prevail,
Thou hast no fence, alas! against his flail:
Therefore thy claim resign, allow his right:
For Duck can thresh, you know, as well as write.

EPITAPHS

His saltem accumulem donis, et fungar inani Munere !
VIRG. [Æn. vii. 885.]

ON CHARLES EARL OF DORSET

IN THE CHURCH OF WITHYAM, SUSSEX

DORSET, the Grace of Courts, the Muses' Pride,
Patron of Arts, and Judge of Nature, died.
The scourge of Pride, tho' sanctified or great,
Of Fops in Learning, and of Knaves in State:
Yet soft his Nature, tho' severe his Lay,
His Anger moral, and his Wisdom gay.
Bless'd Satirist! who touch'd the mean so true,
As show'd, Vice had his hate and pity too.
Bless'd Courtier! who could King and Country please,
Yet sacred keep his Friendships and his Ease.
Bless'd Peer! his great Forefathers' ev'ry grace
Reflecting, and reflected in his race;

Where other Buckhursts, other Dorsets shine,
And Patriots still, or Poets, deck the line.

ON SIR WILLIAM TRUMBULL

ONE OF THE PRINCIPAL SECRETARIES OF STATE TO KING WILLIAM III

Who, having resigned his Place, died in his retirement at Easthamsted, in Berkshire, 1716.

A PLEASING Form, a firm, yet cautious Mind;
Sincere, tho' prudent; constant, yet resign'd:
Honour unchanged, a Principle profest,
Fix'd to one side, but mod'rate to the rest:
An honest Courtier, yet a Patriot too,
Just to his Prince, and to his Country true:
Fill'd with the Sense of age, the Fire of youth,
A scorn of Wrangling, yet a zeal for Truth;
A gen'rous Faith, from superstition free,
A love to Peace, and hate of Tyranny;
Such this Man was, who now, from earth remov'd,
At length enjoys that Liberty he lov'd.

ON THE HON. SIMON HARCOURT

ONLY SON OF THE LORD CHANCELLOR HARCOURT

At the Church of Stanton-Harcourt, Oxfordshire, 1720.

To this sad shrine, whoe'er thou art, draw near;
Here lies the Friend most lov'd, the Son most dear;
Who ne'er knew Joy but Friendship might divide,
Or gave his father grief but when he died.
How vain is Reason, Eloquence how weak!
If Pope must tell what Harcourt cannot speak.
Oh, let thy once-lov'd friend inscribe thy stone,
And with a father's sorrows mix his own!

ON JAMES CRAGGS, ESQ.

IN WESTMINSTER ABBEY

JACOBUS CRAGGS

REGI MAGNÆ BRITANNIÆ A SECRETIS, ET CONSILIIS SANCTIORIBUS: PRINCIPIS PARITER AC POPULI AMOR ET DELICIÆ: VIXIT TITULIS ET INVIDIA MAJOR ANNOS, HEU PAUCOS, XXXV. OB. FEB. XIV. MDCCXX.

STATESMAN, yet Friend to Truth! of Soul
  sincere,
In Action faithful, and in Honour clear!
Who broke no Promise, served no private
  end,
Who gain'd no Title, and who lost no
  Friend;
Ennobled by himself, by all approv'd,
Prais'd, wept, and honour'd, by the Muse
  he lov'd.

ON MR. ROWE

IN WESTMINSTER ABBEY

THY reliques, ROWE! to this sad shrine we
  trust,
And near thy Shakspeare place thy hon-
  our'd bust,
Oh, next him, skill'd to draw the tender
  tear —
For never heart felt passion more sincere —
To nobler sentiment to fire the brave —
For never Briton more disdain'd a slave!
Peace to thy gentle shade, and endless rest;
Blest in thy Genius, in thy Love too blest!
And blest, that timely from our scene re-
  mov'd,
Thy soul enjoys the Liberty it lov'd.
  To these, so mourn'd in death, so lov'd
  in life,
The childless parent and the widow'd wife
With tears inscribes this monumental
  stone,
That holds their ashes and expects her own.

ON MRS. CORBET

WHO DIED OF A CANCER IN HER BREAST

HERE rests a Woman, good without pre-
  tence,
Bless'd with plain Reason and with sober
  Sense:

No Conquests she but o'er herself desired,
No Arts essay'd but not to be admired.
Passion and Pride were to her soul un-
  known,
Convinc'd that Virtue only is our own.
So unaffected, so composed, a mind,
So firm, yet soft, so strong, yet so refin'd,
Heav'n, as its purest gold, by Tortures
  tried:
The Saint sustain'd it, but the Woman died.

ON THE MONUMENT OF THE HON. R. DIGBY AND OF HIS SISTER MARY

ERECTED BY THEIR FATHER, LORD DIGBY, IN THE CHURCH OF SHERBORNE, IN DORSETSHIRE, 1727.

Go! fair example of untainted youth,
Of modest Wisdom and pacific Truth:
Composed in Suff'rings, and in Joy sedate,
Good without noise, without pretension
  great:
Just of thy word, in ev'ry thought sincere,
Who knew no wish but what the world
  might hear:
Of softest Manners, unaffected Mind,
Lover of Peace, and Friend of humankind!
Go live! for Heav'n's eternal year is thine;
Go, and exalt thy Mortal to Divine.
  And thou, bless'd Maid! attendant on
  his doom,
Pensive hath follow'd to the silent Tomb,
Steer'd the same course to the same quiet
  shore,
Not parted long, and now to part no more!
Go then, where only bliss sincere is known!
Go where to love and to enjoy are one!
  Yet take these tears, mortality's relief,
And till we share your joys, forgive our
  grief:
These little rites, a Stone, a Verse, receive;
'T is all a Father, all a Friend can give!

ON SIR GODFREY KNELLER

IN WESTMINSTER ABBEY, 1723

KNELLER, by Heav'n, and not a master,
  taught,
Whose Art was Nature, and whose pictures thought:

Now for two ages having snatch'd from
    fate
Whate'er was beauteous, or whate'er was
    great,
Lies crown'd with Princes' honours, Poets'
    lays,
Due to his Merit and brave thirst of Praise.
    Living, great Nature fear'd he might
    outvie
Her works; and, dying, fears herself may
    die.

ON GENERAL HENRY WITHERS

IN WESTMINSTER ABBEY, 1729

HERE, WITHERS! rest; thou bravest, gen-
    tlest mind,
Thy Country's friend, but more of Human-
    kind.
O born to Arms! O Worth in youth ap-
    prov'd!
O soft Humanity, in age belov'd!
For thee the hardy Vet'ran drops a tear,
And the gay Courtier feels the sigh sincere.
    WITHERS, adieu! yet not with thee re-
    move
Thy martial spirit or thy social love!
Amidst Corruption, Luxury, and Rage,
Still leave some ancient Virtues to our
    age;
Nor let us say (those English glories gone)
The last true Briton lies beneath this stone.

ON MR. ELIJAH FENTON

AT EASTHAMSTEAD, BERKS, 1729

THIS modest stone, what few vain marbles
    can,
May truly say, Here lies an Honest Man;
A Poet bless'd beyond the Poet's fate,
Whom Heav'n kept sacred from the proud
    and great;
Foe to loud Praise, and friend to learned
    Ease,
Content with Science in the vale of peace.
Calmly he look'd on either life, and here
Saw nothing to regret, or there to fear;
From Nature's temp'rate feast rose satis-
    fied,
Thank'd Heav'n that he had lived, and that
    he died.

ON MR. GAY

IN WESTMINSTER ABBEY, 1730

OF Manners gentle, of Affections mild;
In Wit a man; Simplicity a child:
With native Humour temp'ring virtuous
    Rage,
Form'd to delight at once and lash the
    age:
Above temptation, in a low estate,
And uncorrupted ev'n among the Great:
A safe Companion, and an easy Friend,
Unblamed thro' life, lamented in thy
    End.
These are thy Honours ! not that here thy
    bust
Is mix'd with Heroes, or with Kings thy
    dust:
But that the Worthy and the Good shall
    say,
Striking their pensive bosoms — ' Here lies
    GAY ! '

INTENDED FOR SIR ISAAC
NEWTON

IN WESTMINSTER ABBEY

ISAACUS NEWTONUS

QUEM IMMORTALEM TESTANTUR TEMPUS,
    NATURA, CŒLUM : MORTALEM HOC MAR-
    MOR FATETUR

NATURE and Nature's laws lay hid in
    Night:
God said, *Let* NEWTON *be!* and all was
    Light.

ON DR. FRANCIS ATTERBURY

BISHOP OF ROCHESTER, WHO DIED IN
EXILE AT PARIS, 1732

His only daughter having expired in his
arms immediately after she arrived in France
to see him.

DIALOGUE

She. YES, we have liv'd — One pang,
    and then we part !
May Heav'n, dear Father ! now have all
    thy heart.

Yet ah ! how once we lov'd, remember
  still,
Till you are dust like me.
    He.   Dear Shade ! I will:
Then mix this dust with thine — O spotless
  Ghost !
O more than Fortune, Friends, or Country
  lost !
Is there on earth one care, one wish be-
  side ?
Yes — 'Save my country, Heav'n !' he said,
  and died.

ON EDMUND DUKE OF BUCK-INGHAM

WHO DIED IN THE NINETEENTH YEAR
OF HIS AGE, 1735

IF modest Youth, with cool Reflection
  crown'd,
And ev'ry opening Virtue blooming round,
Could save a Parent's justest Pride from
  fate,
Or add one Patriot to a sinking state,
This weeping marble had not ask'd thy
  tear,
Or sadly told, how many hopes lie here !
The living Virtue now had shone approv'd;
The Senate heard him, and his country
  lov'd.
Yet softer honours and less noisy fame
Attend the shade of gentle BUCKINGHAM:
In whom a race, for Courage famed and
  Art,
Ends in the milder merit of the Heart;
And, Chiefs or Sages long to Britain giv'n,
Pays the last tribute of a Saint to Heav'n.

FOR ONE WHO WOULD NOT BE BURIED IN WESTMIN-STER ABBEY

HEROES and KINGS ! your distance keep;
In peace let one poor Poet sleep,
Who never flatter'd folks like you:
Let Horace blush, and Virgil too.

ANOTHER ON THE SAME

UNDER this Marble, or under this Sill,
Or under this Turf, or ev'n what they will,

Whatever an Heir, or a Friend in his stead,
Or any good creature shall lay o'er my
  head,
Lies one who ne'er cared, and still cares
  not, a pin
What they said, or may say, of the mortal
  within;
But who, living and dying, serene, still and
  free,
Trusts in God that as well as he was he
  shall be.

ON TWO LOVERS STRUCK DEAD BY LIGHTNING

John Hughes and Sarah Drew. See Pope's
letter to Lady Mary written in September, 1718.

I

WHEN Eastern lovers feed the Funeral
  Fire,
On the same pile their faithful Fair ex-
  pire;
Here pitying Heav'n that Virtue mutual
  found,
And blasted both, that it might neither
  wound.
Hearts so sincere th' Almighty saw well
  pleas'd,
Sent his own lightning, and the victims
  seiz'd.

II

Think not by rig'rous judgment seiz'd,
  A pair so faithful could expire;
Victims so pure Heav'n saw well pleas'd,
  And snatch'd them in celestial fire

III

Live well, and fear no sudden fate:
  When God calls Virtue to the grave,
Alike 't is Justice, soon or late,
  Mercy alike to kill or save.
Virtue unmov'd can hear the call,
And face the flash that melts the ball.

EPITAPH

The subject is supposed to be John Gay.

WELL, then, poor G—— lies underground!
  So there's an end of honest Jack —
So little justice here be found,
  'T is ten to one he'll ne'er come back.

AN ESSAY ON MAN

IN FOUR EPISTLES TO LORD BOLINGBROKE

The first two epistles of the *Essay on Man* were written in 1732, the third in the year following, and the fourth in 1734, when the complete *Essay* was published as we have it.

THE DESIGN

Having proposed to write some pieces on Human Life and Manners, such as, to use my Lord Bacon's expression, ' come home to men's business and bosoms,' I thought it more satisfactory to begin with considering Man in the abstract, his nature and his state: since to prove any moral duty, to enforce any moral precept, or to examine the perfection or imperfection of any creature whatsoever, it is necessary first to know what condition and relation it is placed in, and what is the proper end and purpose of its being.

The science of Human Nature is, like all other sciences, reduced to a few clear points: there are not many certain truths in this world. It is therefore in the anatomy of the mind, as in that of the body; more good will accrue to mankind by attending to the large, open, and perceptible parts, than by studying too much such finer nerves and vessels, the conformations and uses of which will for ever escape our observation. The disputes are all upon these last; and, I will venture to say, they have less sharpened the wits than the hearts of men against each other, and have diminished the practice more than advanced the theory of morality. If I could flatter myself that this Essay has any merit, it is in steering betwixt the extremes of doctrines seemingly opposite, in passing over terms utterly unintelligible and in forming a temperate, yet not inconsistent, and a short, yet not imperfect, system of ethics.

This I might have done in prose; but I chose verse, and even rhyme, for two reasons. The one will appear obvious; that principles, maxims, or precepts, so written, both strike the reader more strongly at first, and are more easily retained by him afterwards: the other may seem odd, but it is true: I found I could express them more shortly this way than in prose itself; and nothing is more certain than that much of the force as well as grace of arguments or instructions depends on their conciseness. I was unable to treat this part of my subject more in detail without becoming dry and tedious; or more poetically without sacrificing perspicuity to ornament, without wandering from the precision, or breaking the chain of reasoning. If any man can unite all these without diminution of any of them, I freely confess he will compass a thing above my capacity.

What is now published is only to be considered as a general Map of Man, marking out no more than the greater parts, their extent, their limits, and their connexion, but leaving the particular to be more fully delineated in the charts which are to follow; consequently these epistles in their progress (if I have health and leisure to make any progress) will be less dry, and more susceptible of poetical ornament. I am here only opening the fountains, and clearing the passage: to deduce the rivers, to follow them in their course, and to observe their effects, may be a task more agreeable.

EPISTLE I

OF THE NATURE AND STATE OF MAN, WITH RESPECT TO THE UNIVERSE

ARGUMENT

Of Man in the abstract. I. That we can judge only with regard to our own system, being ignorant of the relations of systems and things, verse 17, etc. II. That Man is not to be deemed imperfect, but a being suited to his place and rank in the creation, agreeable to the general order of things, and conformable to ends and relations to him unknown, verse 35, etc. III. That it is partly upon his ignorance of future events, and partly upon the hope of a future state, that all his happiness in the present depends, verse 77, etc. IV. The pride of aiming at more knowledge, and pretending to more perfection, the cause of Man's error and misery. The impiety of putting himself in the place of God, and judging of the fitness or unfitness, perfection or imperfection, justice or injustice, of his dispensations, verse 113, etc. V. The absurdity of conceiting himself the final cause of the creation, or expecting that perfection in the moral world which is not in the natural, verse 131, etc. VI. The unreasonableness of his complaints against Providence, while, on the one hand, he demands the perfections of the angels, and, on the other, the bodily qualifications of the brutes; though to possess any of the sensitive faculties in a higher degree would render him miserable, verse 173, etc. VII. That throughout the whole visible world a universal order and gradation in the sensual and mental faculties is observed, which causes a subordination of creature to creature, and of all creatures to man. The gradations of Sense, Instinct, Thought, Reflection, Reason: that Reason alone countervails all the other faculties, verse 207, etc. VIII. How much further this order and subordination of living creatures may extend above and below us; were any part of which broken, not that part only, but the whole connected creation must be destroyed, verse 213, etc. IX. The extravagance, madness, and pride of such a desire, verse 209, etc. X. The consequence of all, the absolute submission due to Providence, both as to our present and future state, verse 281, etc., to the end.

AWAKE, my ST. JOHN! leave all meaner things
To low ambition and the pride of Kings.
Let us, since life can little more supply
Than just to look about us and to die,
Expatiate free o'er all this scene of man;
A mighty maze! but not without a plan;
A wild, where weeds and flowers promiscuous shoot,
Or garden, tempting with forbidden fruit.
Together let us beat this ample field,
Try what the open, what the covert yield; 10
The latent tracts, the giddy heights, explore
Of all who blindly creep or sightless soar;
Eye Nature's walks, shoot folly as it flies,
And catch the manners living as they rise;
Laugh where we must, be candid where we can,
But vindicate the ways of God to man.
  I. Say first, of God above or Man below
What can we reason but from what we know?
Of man what see we but his station here,
From which to reason, or to which refer? 20
Thro' worlds unnumber'd tho' the God be known,
'T is ours to trace him only in our own.
He who thro' vast immensity can pierce,
See worlds on worlds compose one universe,
Observe how system into system runs,
What other planets circle other suns,

What varied being peoples every star,
May tell why Heav'n has made us as we are:
But of this frame, the bearings and the ties,
The strong connexions, nice dependencies,
Gradations just, has thy pervading soul 31
Look'd thro'; or can a part contain the whole?
  Is the great chain that draws all to agree,
And drawn supports, upheld by God or thee?
  II. Presumptuous man! the reason wouldst thou find,
Why form'd so weak, so little, and so blind?
First, if thou canst, the harder reason guess
Why form'd no weaker, blinder, and no less!
Ask of thy mother earth why oaks are made
Taller or stronger than the weeds they shade! 40
Or ask of yonder argent fields above
Why Jove's satellites are less than Jove!
  Of systems possible, if 't is confest
That wisdom infinite must form the best,
Where all must fall or not coherent be,
And all that rises rise in due degree;
Then in the scale of reas'ning life 't is plain
There must be, somewhere, such a rank as Man:
And all the question (wrangle e'er so long)
Is only this, — if God has placed him wrong? 50
Respecting Man, whatever wrong we call,
May, must be right, as relative to all.
In human works, tho' labour'd on with pain,
A thousand movements scarce one purpose gain;
In God's, one single can its end produce,
Yet serve to second too some other use:
So man, who here seems principal alone,
Perhaps acts second to some sphere unknown,
Touches some wheel, or verges to some goal:
'T is but a part we see, and not a whole. 60
  When the proud steed shall know why man restrains
His fiery course, or drives him o'er the plains;
When the dull ox, why now he breaks the clod,
Is now a victim, and now Egypt's God;

Then shall man's pride and dulness com-
    prehend
His actions', passions', being's, use and end;
Why doing, suff'ring, check'd, impell'd;
    and why
This hour a Slave, the next a Deity.
    Then say not man's imperfect, Heav'n
    in fault;
Say rather man's as perfect as he ought; 70
His knowledge measured to his state and
    place,
His time a moment, and a point his space.
If to be perfect in a certain sphere,
What matter soon or late, or here or there ?
The blest to-day is as completely so
As who began a thousand years ago.
    III. Heav'n from all creatures hides the
    book of Fate,
All but the page prescribed, their present
    state;
From brutes what men, from men what
    spirits know;
Or who could suffer being here below ?   80
The lamb thy riot dooms to bleed to-day,
Had he thy reason would he skip and play ?
Pleas'd to the last he crops the flowery
    food,
And licks the hand just rais'd to shed his
    blood.
O blindness to the future ! kindly giv'n,
That each may fill the circle mark'd by
    Heav'n;
Who sees with equal eye, as God of all,
A hero perish or a sparrow fall,
Atoms or systems into ruin hurl'd,   89
And now a bubble burst, and now a world.
    Hope humbly then; with trembling pin-
    ions soar;
Wait the great teacher Death, and God
    adore.
What future bliss He gives not thee to
    know,
But gives that hope to be thy blessing
    now.
Hope springs eternal in the human breast:
Man never is, but always to be, blest.
The soul, uneasy and confin'd from home,
Rests and expatiates in a life to come.
    Lo, the poor Indian ! whose untutor'd
    mind
Sees God in clouds, or hears him in the
    wind;   100
His soul proud Science never taught to
    stray
Far as the solar walk or milky way;

Yet simple nature to his hope has giv'n,
Behind the cloud-topt hill, an humbler
    Heav'n,
Some safer world in depth of woods em-
    braced,
Some happier island in the wat'ry waste,
Where slaves once more their native land
    behold,
No fiends torment, no Christians thirst for
    gold.
To be, contents his natural desire;   109
He asks no Angel's wing, no Seraph's fire;
But thinks, admitted to that equal sky,
His faithful dog shall bear him company.
    IV. Go, wiser thou ! and in thy scale of
    sense
Weigh thy opinion against Providence;
Call imperfection what thou fanciest such;
Say, here he gives too little, there too
    much;
Destroy all creatures for thy sport or gust,
Yet cry, if man 's unhappy, God 's unjust;
If man alone engross not Heav'n's high
    care,   119
Alone made perfect here, immortal there:
Snatch from his hand the balance and the
    rod,
Rejudge his justice, be the god of God.
In pride, in reas'ning pride, our error lies;
All quit their sphere, and rush into the
    skies!
Pride still is aiming at the bless'd abodes,
Men would be Angels, Angels would be
    Gods.
Aspiring to be Gods if Angels fell,
Aspiring to be Angels men rebel:
And who but wishes to invert the laws
Of order, sins against th' Eternal Cause. 130
    V. Ask for what end the heav'nly bodies
    shine,
Earth for whose use, — Pride answers,
    ' 'T is for mine:
For me kind Nature wakes her genial
    power,
Suckles each herb, and spreads out ev'ry
    flower;
Annual for me the grape, the rose, renew
The juice nectareous and the balmy dew;
For me the mine a thousand treasures
    brings;
For me health gushes from a thousand
    springs;
Seas roll to waft me, suns to light me
    rise;
My footstool earth, my canopy the skies.'

But errs not Nature from this gracious end, 141
From burning suns when livid deaths descend,
When earthquakes swallow, or when tempests sweep
Towns to one grave, whole nations to the deep?
'No,' 't is replied, 'the first Almighty Cause
Acts not by partial but by gen'ral laws;
Th' exceptions few; some change since all began
And what created perfect?' — Why then man?
If the great end be human happiness,
Then Nature deviates; and can man do less? 150
As much that end a constant course requires
Of showers and sunshine, as of man's desires;
As much eternal springs and cloudless skies,
As men for ever temp'rate, calm, and wise.
If plagues or earthquakes break not Heav'n's design,
Why then a Borgia or a Catiline?
Who knows but He, whose hand the lightning forms,
Who heaves old ocean, and who wings the storms;
Pours fierce ambition in a Cæsar's mind,
Or turns young Ammon loose to scourge mankind? 160
From pride, from pride, our very reas'ning springs;
Account for moral as for natural things:
Why charge we Heav'n in those, in these acquit?
In both, to reason right is to submit.
Better for us, perhaps, it might appear,
Were there all harmony, all virtue here;
That never air or ocean felt the wind,
That never passion discomposed the mind:
But all subsists by elemental strife;
And passions are the elements of life. 170
The gen'ral order, since the whole began,
Is kept in Nature, and is kept in Man.
VI. What would this Man? Now upward will he soar,
And little less than Angel, would be more;
Now looking downwards, just as griev'd appears
To want the strength of bulls, the fur of bears.

Made for his use all creatures if he call,
Say what their use, had he the powers of all?
Nature to these without profusion kind, 179
The proper organs, proper powers assign'd;
Each seeming want compensated of course,
Here with degrees of swiftness, there of force;
All in exact proportion to the state;
Nothing to add, and nothing to abate;
Each beast, each insect, happy in its own:
Is Heav'n unkind to man, and man alone?
Shall he alone, whom rational we call,
Be pleas'd with nothing if not bless'd with all?
The bliss of man (could pride that blessing find)
Is not to act or think beyond mankind; 190
No powers of body or of soul to share,
But what his nature and his state can bear.
Why has not man a microscopic eye?
For this plain reason, man is not a fly.
Say, what the use, were finer optics giv'n,
T' inspect a mite, not comprehend the Heav'n?
Or touch, if tremblingly alive all o'er,
To smart and agonize at every pore?
Or quick effluvia darting thro' the brain,
Die of a rose in aromatic pain? 200
If Nature thunder'd in his opening ears,
And stunn'd him with the music of the spheres,
How would he wish that Heav'n had left him still
The whisp'ring zephyr and the purling rill?
Who finds not Providence all good and wise,
Alike in what it gives and what denies?
VII. Far as creation's ample range extends,
The scale of sensual, mental powers ascends.
Mark how it mounts to man's imperial race
From the green myriads in the peopled grass: 210
What modes of sight betwixt each wide extreme,
The mole's dim curtain and the lynx's beam:
Of smell, the headlong lioness between
And hound sagacious on the tainted green:
Of hearing, from the life that fills the flood
To that which warbles thro' the vernal wood.

The spider's touch, how exquisitely fine,
Feels at each thread, and lives along the line:
In the nice bee what sense so subtly true,
From pois'nous herbs extracts the healing
 dew!   220
How instinct varies in the grovelling swine,
Compared, half-reas'ning elephant, with
 thine!
'Twixt that and reason what a nice barrier!
For ever separate, yet for ever near!
Remembrance and reflection how allied!
What thin partitions Sense from Thought
 divide!
And middle natures how they long to join,
Yet never pass th' insuperable line!
Without this just gradation could they be
Subjected these to those, or all to thee! 230
The powers of all subdued by thee alone,
Is not thy Reason all these powers in one?
 VIII. See thro' this air, this ocean, and
 this earth
All matter quick, and bursting into birth:
Above, how high progressive life may go!
Around, how wide! how deep extend below!
Vast chain of being! which from God be-
 gan;
Natures ethereal, human, angel, man,
Beast, bird, fish, insect, who no eye can see,
No glass can reach; from infinite to thee;
From thee to nothing. — On superior
 powers   241
Were we to press, inferior might on ours;
Or in the full creation leave a void,
Where, one step broken, the great scale's
 destroy'd:
From Nature's chain whatever link you like,
Tenth, or ten thousandth, breaks the chain
 alike.
And if each system in gradation roll,
Alike essential to th' amazing Whole,
The least confusion but in one, not all
That system only, but the Whole must
 fall.   250
Let earth unbalanced from her orbit fly,
Planets and stars run lawless thro' the sky;
Let ruling angels from their spheres be
 hurl'd,
Being on being wreck'd, and world on
 world;
Heav'n's whole foundations to their centre
 nod,
And Nature tremble to the throne of God!
All this dread order break — for whom?
 for thee?
Vile worm! — O madness! pride! impiety!

 IX. What if the foot, ordain'd the dust
 to tread,
Or hand to toil, aspired to be the head? 260
What if the head, the eye, or ear repin'd
To serve mere engines to the ruling mind?
Just as absurd for any part to claim
To be another in this gen'ral frame;
Just as absurd to mourn the tasks or pains
The great directing Mind of All ordains.
All are but parts of one stupendous
 Whole,
Whose body Nature is, and God the soul;
That changed thro' all, and yet in all the
 same,   269
Great in the earth as in th' ethereal frame,
Warms in the sun, refreshes in the breeze,
Glows in the stars, and blossoms in the
 trees;
Lives thro' all life, extends thro' all extent,
Spreads undivided, operates unspent;
Breathes in our soul, informs our mortal
 part,
As full, as perfect, in a hair as heart;
As full, as perfect, in vile man that mourns,
As the rapt Seraph that adores and burns.
To him no high, no low, no great, no small;
He fills, he bounds, connects, and equals all!
 X. Cease, then, nor Order imperfection
 name;   281
Our proper bliss depends on what we blame.
Know thy own point: this kind, this due
 degree
Of blindness, weakness, Heav'n bestows on
 thee.
Submit: in this or any other sphere,
Secure to be as bless'd as thou canst bear;
Safe in the hand of one disposing Power,
Or in the natal or the mortal hour.
All Nature is but Art unknown to thee;
All chance direction, which thou canst not
 see;   290
All discord, harmony not understood;
All partial evil, universal good:
And spite of Pride, in erring Reason's spite,
One truth is clear, *Whatever is, is right.*

EPISTLE II

OF THE NATURE AND STATE OF MAN WITH
RESPECT TO HIMSELF AS AN INDIVIDUAL

ARGUMENT

I. The business of Man not to pry into God, but
to study himself. His middle nature; his
powers and frailties, verses 1 to 19. The

limits of his capacity, verse 19, etc. II. The two principles of Man, Self-love and Reason, both necessary. Self-love the stronger, and why. Their end the same, verse 81, etc. III. The Passions, and their use. The predominant passion, and its force. Its necessity, in directing men to different purposes. Its providential use, in fixing our principle, and ascertaining our virtue, verse 93, etc. IV. Virtue and Vice joined in our mixed nature; the limits near, yet the things separate and evident : what is the office of Reason, verse 203, etc. V. How odious Vice in itself, and how we deceive ourselves into it, verse 217, etc. VI. That, however, the ends of Providence, and general goods, are answered in our passions and imperfections. How usefully these are distributed to all orders of men : how useful they are to Society; and to individuals; in every state, and every age of life, verse 238, etc., to the end.

I. KNOW then thyself, presume not God to scan,
The proper study of mankind is Man.
Placed on this isthmus of a middle state,
A being darkly wise and rudely great:
With too much knowledge for the Sceptic side,
With too much weakness for the Stoic's pride,
He hangs between, in doubt to act or rest;
In doubt to deem himself a God or Beast;
In doubt his mind or body to prefer;
Born but to die, and reas'ning but to err; 10
Alike in ignorance, his reason such,
Whether he thinks too little or too much;
Chaos of thought and passion, all confused;
Still by himself abused or disabused;
Created half to rise, and half to fall;
Great lord of all things, yet a prey to all;
Sole judge of truth, in endless error hurl'd;
The glory, jest, and riddle of the world!
  Go, wondrous creature! mount where Science guides;
Go, measure earth, weigh air, and state the tides; 20
Instruct the planets in what orbs to run,
Correct old Time, and regulate the sun;
Go, soar with Plato to th' empyreal sphere,
To the first good, first perfect, and first fair;
Or tread the mazy round his followers trod,
And quitting sense call imitating God;
As eastern priests in giddy circles run,
And turn their heads to imitate the sun.

Go, teach Eternal Wisdom how to rule —
Then drop into thyself, and be a fool! 30
  Superior beings, when of late they saw
A mortal man unfold all Nature's law,
Admired such wisdom in an earthly shape,
And show'd a NEWTON as we show an ape.
Could he, whose rules the rapid comet bind,
Describe or fix one movement of his mind ?
Who saw its fires here rise, and there descend,
Explain his own beginning or his end ?
Alas ! what wonder ! Man's superior part
Uncheck'd may rise, and climb from art to art; 40
But when his own great work is but begun,
What Reason weaves, by Passion is undone.
  Trace Science then, with modesty thy guide;
First strip off all her equipage of pride;
Deduct what is but vanity or dress,
Or learning's luxury, or idleness,
Or tricks to show the stretch of human brain,
Mere curious pleasure, or ingenious pain;
Expunge the whole, or lop th' excrescent parts;
Of all our vices have created arts; 50
Then see how little the remaining sum,
Which serv'd the past, and must the times to come !
  II. Two principles in Human Nature reign,
Self-love to urge, and Reason to restrain;
Nor this a good, nor that a bad we call;
Each works its end, to move or govern all:
And to their proper operation still
Ascribe all good, to their improper, ill.
  Self-love, the spring of motion, acts the soul;
Reason's comparing balance rules the whole. 60
Man but for that no action could attend,
And but for this were active to no end:
Fix'd like a plant on his peculiar spot,
To draw nutrition, propagate, and rot;
Or meteor-like, flame lawless thro' the void,
Destroying others, by himself destroy'd.
  Most strength the moving principle requires;
Active its task, it prompts, impels, inspires:
Sedate and quiet the comparing lies,

Form'd but to check, delib'rate, and ad-
    vise.   70
Self-love still stronger, as its objects nigh;
Reason's at distance and in prospect lie:
That sees immediate good by present sense;
Reason, the future and the consequence.
Thicker than arguments, temptations
    throng;
At best more watchful this, but that more
    strong.
The action of the stronger to suspend,
Reason still use, to Reason still attend.
Attention habit and experience gains;
Each strengthens Reason, and Self-love re-
    strains.   80
Let subtle schoolmen teach these friends to
    fight,
More studious to divide than to unite;
And Grace and Virtue, Sense and Reason
    split,
With all the rash dexterity of Wit.
Wits, just like fools, at war about a name,
Have full as oft no meaning, or the same.
Self-love and Reason to one end aspire,
Pain their aversion, Pleasure their desire;
But greedy that, its object would devour;
This taste the honey, and not wound the
    flower: 90
Pleasure, or wrong or rightly understood,
Our greatest evil or our greatest good.
   III. Modes of Self-love the passions we
    may call;
'T is real good or seeming moves them
    all:
But since not every good we can divide,
And Reason bids us for our own provide,
Passions, tho' selfish, if their means be fair,
List under Reason, and deserve her care;
Those that imparted court a nobler aim,
Exalt their kind, and take some virtue's
    name.   100
   In lazy apathy let Stoics boast
Their virtue fix'd; 't is fix'd as in a frost;
Contracted all, retiring to the breast;
But strength of mind is Exercise, not Rest:
The rising tempest puts in act the soul,
Parts it may ravage, but preserves the
    whole.
On life's vast ocean diversely we sail,
Reason the card, but Passion is the gale;
Nor God alone in the still calm we find,
He mounts the storm, and walks upon the
    wind.   110
   Passions, like elements, tho' born to fight,
Yet, mix'd and soften'd, in his work unite:

These 't is enough to temper and employ;
But what composes man can man destroy?
Suffice that Reason keep to Nature's road;
Subject, compound them, follow her and
    God.
Love, Hope, and Joy, fair Pleasure's smil-
    ing train,
Hate, Fear, and Grief, the family of Pain,
These mix'd with art, and to due bounds
    confin'd,
Make and maintain the balance of the
    mind;   120
The lights and shades, whose well-accorded
    strife
Gives all the strength and colour of our life.
   Pleasures are ever in our hands or eyes,
And when in act they cease, in prospect
    rise:
Present to grasp, and future still to find,
The whole employ of body and of mind.
All spread their charms, but charm not all
    alike;
On diff'rent senses diff'rent objects strike;
Hence diff'rent passions more or less in-
    flame,   129
As strong or weak the organs of the frame;
And hence one Master-passion in the breast,
Like Aaron's serpent, swallows up the rest.
   As man, perhaps, the moment of his
    breath,
Receives the lurking principle of death,
The young disease, that must subdue at
    length,
Grows with his growth, and strengthens
    with his strength:
So, cast and mingled with his very frame,
The mind's disease, its Ruling Passion,
    came;
Each vital humour, which should feed the
    whole,
Soon flows to this in body and in soul;   140
Whatever warms the heart or fills the
    head,
As the mind opens and its functions spread,
Imagination plies her dangerous art,
And pours it all upon the peccant part.
Nature its mother, Habit is its nurse;
Wit, spirit, faculties, but make it worse;
Reason itself but gives it edge and power,
As Heav'n's bless'd beam turns vinegar
    more sour.
   We, wretched subjects, tho' to lawful
    sway,   149
In this weak queen some fav'rite still
    obey:

Ah ! if she lend not arms as well as rules,
What can she more than tell us we are
　fools ?
Teach us to mourn our nature, not to
　mend,
A sharp accuser, but a helpless friend!
Or from a judge turn pleader, to persuade
The choice we make, or justify it made;
Proud of an easy conquest all along,
She but removes weak passions for the
　strong:
So when small humours gather to a gout,
The doctor fancies he has driv'n them out.
　Yes, Nature's road must ever be pre-
　ferr'd;　161
Reason is here no guide, but still a guard;
'T is hers to rectify, not overthrow,
And treat this passion more as friend than
　foe:
A mightier Power the strong direction
　sends,
And sev'ral men impels to sev'ral ends:
Like varying winds, by other passions
　toss'd,
This drives them constant to a certain
　coast.
Let Power or Knowledge, Gold or Glory,
　please,
Or (oft more strong than all) the love of
　ease;　170
Thro' life 't is follow'd, ev'n at life's ex-
　pense;
The merchant's toil, the sage's indolence,
The monk's humility, the hero's pride,
All, all alike, find Reason on their side.
Th' Eternal Art educing good from ill,
Grafts on this passion our best principle:
'T is thus the mercury of man is fix'd,
Strong grows the virtue with his nature
　mix'd;
The dross cements what else were too re-
　fin'd,
And in one int'rest body acts with mind. 180
　As fruits ungrateful to the planter's care,
On savage stocks inserted, learn to bear,
The surest Virtues thus from Passions
　shoot,
Wild Nature's vigour working at the root.
What crops of wit and honesty appear
From spleen, from obstinacy, hate, or fear!
See anger, zeal, and fortitude supply;
Ev'n av'rice prudence, sloth philosophy;
Lust, thro' some certain strainers well re-
　fin'd,　189
Is gentle love, and charms all womankind;

Envy, to which th' ignoble mind 's a slave,
Is emulation in the learn'd or brave;
Nor virtue male or female can we name,
But what will grow on pride or grow on
　shame.
　Thus Nature gives us (let it check our
　pride)
The Virtue nearest to our Vice allied:
Reason the bias turns to good from ill,
And Nero reigns a Titus if he will.
The fiery soul abhorr'd in Catiline,
In Decius charms, in Curtius is divine: 200
The same ambition can destroy or save,
And makes a patriot as it makes a knave.
　IV. This light and darkness in our chaos
　join'd,
What shall divide ? — the God within the
　mind.
　Extremes in Nature equal ends produce;
In Man they join to some mysterious use;
Tho' each by turns the other's bounds in-
　vade,
As in some well-wrought picture light and
　shade;
And oft so mix, the diff'rence is too nice
Where ends the Virtue or begins the Vice.
　Fools! who from hence into the notion
　fall　211
That Vice or Virtue there is none at all.
If white and black blend, soften, and unite
A thousand ways, is there no black or white?
Ask your own heart, and nothing is so
　plain;
'T is to mistake them costs the time and
　pain.
　V. Vice is a monster of so frightful
　mien,
As to be hated needs but to be seen;
Yet seen too oft, familiar with her face,
We first endure, then pity, then embrace.
But where th' extreme of Vice was ne'er
　agreed:　221
Ask where 's the north ? — at York 't is on
　the Tweed;
In Scotland at the Orcades; and there
At Greenland, Zembla, or the Lord knows
　where.
No creature owns it in the first degree,
But thinks his neighbour farther gone than
　he;
Ev'n those who dwell beneath its very zone,
Or never feel the rage or never own;
What happier natures shrink at with af-
　fright,
The hard inhabitant contends is right. 230

Virtuous and vicious ev'ry man must be,
Few in th' extreme, but all in the degree:
The rogue and fool by fits is fair and wise,
And ev'n the best by fits what they despise.
'T is but by parts we follow good or ill;
For Vice or Virtue, Self directs it still;
Each individual seeks a sev'ral goal;
But Heav'n's great view is one, and that
   the Whole.
That counterworks each folly and caprice;
That disappoints th' effect of every vice; 240
That, happy frailties to all ranks applied,
Shame to the virgin, to the matron pride,
Fear to the statesman, rashness to the
   chief,
To kings presumption, and to crowds be-
   lief:
That, virtue's ends from vanity can raise,
Which seeks no int'rest, no reward but
   praise;
And build on wants, and on defects of mind,
The joy, the peace, the glory of mankind.
Heav'n forming each on other to depend,
A master, or a servant, or a friend,   250
Bids each on other for assistance call,
Till one man's weakness grows the strength
   of all.
Wants, frailties, passions, closer still ally
The common int'rest, or endear the tie.
To these we owe true friendship, love sin-
   cere,
Each home-felt joy that life inherits here;
Yet from the same we learn, in its decline,
Those joys, those loves, those int'rests to re-
   sign;
Taught, half by Reason, half by mere de-
   cay,
To welcome Death, and calmly pass away.
Whate'er the passion — knowledge, fame
   or pelf —   261
Not one will change his neighbour with
   himself.
The learn'd is happy Nature to explore,
The fool is happy that he knows no more;
The rich is happy in the plenty giv'n,
The poor contents him with the care of
   Heav'n.
See the blind beggar dance, the cripple sing,
The sot a hero, lunatic a king,
The starving chymist in his golden views
Supremely bless'd, the poet in his Muse. 270
See some strange comfort ev'ry state
   attend,
And Pride bestow'd on all, a common
   friend:

See some fit passion every age supply;
Hope travels thro', nor quits us when we
   die.
Behold the child, by Nature's kindly
   law,
Pleas'd with a rattle, tickled with a straw:
Some livelier plaything gives his youth
   delight,
A little louder, but as empty quite:
Scarfs, garters, gold, amuse his riper stage,
And beads and prayer-books are the toys
   of age: 280
Pleas'd with this bauble still, as that be-
   fore,
Till tired he sleeps, and life's poor play is
   o'er.
Meanwhile opinion gilds with varying
   rays
Those painted clouds that beautify our
   days;
Each want of happiness by Hope supplied,
And each vacuity of sense by Pride:
These build as fast as Knowledge can de-
   stroy;
In Folly's cup still laughs the bubble joy;
One prospect lost, another still we gain,
And not a vanity is giv'n in vain: 290
Ev'n mean Self-love becomes, by force
   divine,
The scale to measure others' wants by
   thine.
See! and confess one comfort still must
   rise;
'T is this, *Though Man's a fool, yet God is
wise.*

EPISTLE III

OF THE NATURE AND STATE OF MAN WITH
RESPECT TO SOCIETY

ARGUMENT

I. The whole Universe one system of Society.
Nothing made wholly for itself, nor yet
wholly for another. The happiness of animals mutual, verse 7, etc. II. Reason or Instinct operates alike to the good of each individual. Reason or Instinct operates also to
Society in all animals, verse 49, etc. III. How
far Society carried by Instinct; — how much
farther by reason, verse 109, etc. IV. Of that
which is called the state of nature. Reason
instructed by Instinct in the invention of
arts; — and in the forms of Society, verse
144, etc. V. Origin of political societies; —

origin of Monarchy; — patriarchal government, verse 199, etc. VI. Origin of true Religion and Government, from the same principle of Love ; — origin of Superstition and Tyranny, from the same principle of Fear. The influence of Self-love operating to the social and public good. Restoration of true Religion and Government on their first principle. Mixed government. Various forms of each, and the true end of all, verse 215, etc.

HERE then we rest: — 'The Universal Cause
Acts to one end, but acts by various laws.'
In all the madness of superfluous Health,
The trim of Pride, the impudence of Wealth,
Let this great truth be present night and day:
But most be present, if we preach or pray.
I. Look round our world; behold the chain of love
Combining all below and all above.
See plastic Nature working to this end,
The single atoms each to other tend,   10
Attract, attracted to, the next in place,
Form'd and impell'd its neighbour to embrace.
See matter next, with various life endued,
Press to one centre still, the gen'ral good:
See dying vegetables life sustain,
See life dissolving vegetate again.
All forms that perish other forms supply
(By turns we catch the vital breath, and die),
Like bubbles on the sea of Matter borne,
They rise, they break, and to that sea return.   20
Nothing is foreign; parts relate to whole;
One all-extending, all-preserving, soul
Connects each being, greatest with the least;
Made beast in aid of man, and man of beast;
All serv'd, all serving: nothing stands alone;
The chain holds on, and where it ends unknown.
Has God, thou fool! work'd solely for thy good,
Thy joy, thy pastime, thy attire, thy food ?
Who for thy table feeds the wanton fawn,
For him as kindly spreads the flowery lawn.   30
Is it for thee the lark ascends and sings ?
Joy tunes his voice, joy elevates his wings.

Is it for thee the linnet pours his throat ?
Loves of his own and raptures swell the note.
The bounding steed you pompously bestride
Shares with his lord the pleasure and the pride.
Is thine alone the seed that strews the plain ?
The birds of Heav'n shall vindicate their grain.
Thine the full harvest of the golden year ?
Part pays, and justly, the deserving steer.   40
The hog that ploughs not, nor obeys thy call,
Lives on the labours of this lord of all.
Know Nature's children all divide her care;
The fur that warms a monarch warm'd a bear.
While Man exclaims, 'See all things for my use!'
'See man for mine !' replies a pamper'd goose:
And just as short of Reason he must fall,
Who thinks all made for one, not one for all.
Grant that the pow'rful still the weak control;
Be Man the wit and tyrant of the whole: 50
Nature that tyrant checks; he only knows,
And helps, another creature's wants and woes.
Say will the falcon, stooping from above,
Smit with her varying plumage, spare the dove ?
Admires the jay the insect's gilded wings ?
Or hears the hawk when Philomela sings ? —
Man cares for all: to birds he gives his woods,
To beasts his pastures, and to fish his floods.
For some his Int'rest prompts him to provide,
For more his Pleasure, yet for more his Pride: 60
All feed on one vain patron, and enjoy
Th' extensive blessing of his luxury.
That very life his learned hunger craves,
He saves from famine, from the savage saves;
Nay, feasts the animal he dooms his feast,
And till he ends the being makes it blest;

Which sees no more the stroke, or feels the
   pain,
Than favour'd man by touch ethereal slain.
The creature had his feast of life before;
Thou too must perish when thy feast is
   o'er !   70
  To each unthinking being, Heav'n, a
   friend,
Gives not the useless knowledge of its end:
To man imparts it, but with such a view
As while he dreads it, makes him hope it
   too;
The hour conceal'd, and so remote the fear,
Death still draws nearer, never seeming
   near.
Great standing miracle ! that Heav'n as-
   sign'd
Its only thinking thing this turn of mind.
  II. Whether with Reason or with In-
   stinct blest,
Know all enjoy that power which suits them
   best;   80
To bliss alike by that direction tend,
And find the means proportion'd to their
   end.
Say, where full Instinct is th' unerring
   guide,
What Pope or Council can they need beside?
Reason, however able, cool at best,
Cares not for service, or but serves when
   prest,
Stays till we call, and then not often near;
But honest Instinct comes a volunteer,
Sure never to o'ershoot, but just to hit,   89
While still too wide or short is human wit;
Sure by quick Nature happiness to gain,
Which heavier Reason labours at in vain.
This, too, serves always; Reason, never
   long;
One must go right, the other may go
   wrong.
See then the acting and comparing powers
One in their nature, which are two in ours;
And Reason raise o'er Instinct as you can,
In this 't is God directs, in that 't is Man.
  Who taught the nations of the field and
   wood
To shun their poison and to choose their
   food ?   100
Prescient, the tides or tempests to with-
   stand,
Build on the wave, or arch beneath the
   sand ?
Who made the spider parallels design,
Sure as Demoivre, without rule or line ?

Who bade the stork, Columbus-like, ex-
   plore
Heav'ns not his own, and worlds unknown
   before ?
Who calls the council, states the certain
   day,
Who forms the phalanx, and who points
   the way ?
  III. God in the nature of each being
   founds   109
Its proper bliss, and sets its proper bounds;
But as he framed a whole the whole to
   bless,
On mutual wants built mutual happiness:
So from the first eternal order ran,
And creature link'd to creature, man to
   man.
Whate'er of life all-quick'ning ether keeps,
Or breathes thro' air, or shoots beneath the
   deeps,
Or pours profuse on earth, one Nature feeds
The vital flame, and swells the genial
   seeds.
Not man alone, but all that roam the wood,
Or wing the sky, or roll along the flood, 120
Each loves itself, but not itself alone,
Each sex desires alike, till two are one.
Nor ends the pleasure with the fierce em-
   brace:
They love themselves a third time in their
   race.
Thus beast and bird their common charge
   attend,
The mothers nurse it, and the sires defend;
The young dismiss'd to wander earth or air,
There stops the instinct, and there ends the
   care;
The link dissolves, each seeks a fresh em-
   brace,
Another love succeeds, another race.   130
A longer care man's helpless kind de-
   mands;
That longer care contracts more lasting
   bands:
Reflection, Reason, still the ties improve,
At once extend the int'rest and the love;
With choice we fix, with sympathy we
   burn;
Each virtue in each passion takes its turn;
And still new needs, new helps, new habits
   rise,
That graft benevolence on charities.
Still as one brood and as another rose.
These natural love maintain'd, habitual
   those: 140

The last, scarce ripen'd into perfect man,
Saw helpless him from whom their life be-
gan:
Mem'ry and forecast just returns engage,
That pointed back to youth, this on to age;
While pleasure, gratitude, and hope, com-
bin'd,
Still spread the int'rest, and preserv'd the
kind.
   IV. Nor think in Nature's state they
blindly trod;
The state of Nature was the reign of God:
Self-love and Social at her birth began,
Union the bond of all things, and of Man;
Pride then was not, nor arts, that pride to
aid;   151
Man walk'd with beast, joint tenant of the
shade;
The same his table, and the same his bed;
No murder clothed him, and no murder fed.
In the same temple, the resounding wood,
All vocal beings hymn'd their equal God:
The shrine with gore unstain'd, with gold
undrest,
Unbribed, unbloody, stood the blameless
priest:
Heav'n's attribute was universal care,
And man's prerogative to rule, but spare. 160
Ah! how unlike the man of times to come!
Of half that live the butcher and the tomb;
Who, foe to Nature, hears the gen'ral groan,
Murders their species, and betrays his own.
But just disease to luxury succeeds,
And ev'ry death its own avenger breeds;
The fury-passions from that blood began,
And turn'd on man a fiercer savage, man.
  See him from Nature rising slow to Art!
To copy Instinct then was Reason's part: 170
Thus then to man the voice of Nature
spake —
'Go, from the creatures thy instructions
take:
Learn from the birds what food the thick-
ets yield,
Learn from the beasts the physic of the
field;
Thy arts of building from the bee receive;
Learn of the mole to plough, the worm to
weave;
Learn of the little nautilus to sail,
Spread the thin oar, and catch the driving
gale.
Here too all forms of social union find,
And hence let Reason late instruct man-
kind.   180

Here subterranean works and cities see;
There towns aërial on the waving tree;
Learn each small people's genius, policies,
The ants' republic, and the realm of bees:
How those in common all their wealth be-
stow,
And anarchy without confusion know;
And these for ever, tho' a monarch reign,
Their sep'rate cells and properties maintain.
Mark what unvaried laws preserve each
state,   189
Laws wise as Nature, and as fix'd as Fate.
In vain thy Reason finer webs shall draw,
Entangle justice in her net of law,
And right, too rigid, harden into wrong,
Still for the strong too weak, the weak too
strong.
Yet go! and thus o'er all the creatures
sway,
Thus let the wiser make the rest obey;
And for those arts mere Instinct could af-
ford,
Be crown'd as Monarchs, or as Gods
ador'd.'
  V. Great Nature spoke; observant man
obey'd;
Cities were built, societies were made: 200
Here rose one little state; another near
Grew by like means, and join'd thro' love
or fear.
Did here the trees with ruddier burdens
bend,
And there the streams in purer rills de-
scend?
What war could ravish, commerce could
bestow,
And he return'd a friend who came a foe.
Converse and love mankind might strongly
draw,
When Love was liberty, and Nature law.
Thus states were form'd, the name of King
unknown,
Till common int'rest placed the sway in
one.   210
'T was Virtue only (or in arts or arms,
Diffusing blessings, or averting harms),
The same which in a sire the sons obey'd,
A prince the father of a people made.
  VI. Till then, by Nature crown'd, each
patriarch sate
King, priest, and parent of his growing
state;
On him, their second Providence, they
hung,
Their law his eye, their oracle his tongue.

He from the wond'ring furrow call'd the
food,
Taught to command the fire, control the
flood, 220
Draw forth the monsters of th' abyss pro-
found,
Or fetch th' aërial eagle to the ground;
Till drooping, sick'ning, dying, they began
Whom they revered as God to mourn as
Man:
Then, looking up from sire to sire, explor'd
One great first Father, and that first ador'd:
Or plain tradition that this all begun,
Convey'd unbroken faith from sire to son;
The worker from the work distinct was
known,
And simple Reason never sought but one.
Ere Wit oblique had broke that steady
light, 231
Man, like his Maker, saw that all was
right;
To virtue in the paths of pleasure trod,
And own'd a father when he own'd a God.
Love all the faith, and all th' allegiance
then,
For Nature knew no right divine in men;
No ill could fear in God, and understood
A sov'reign being but a sov'reign good;
True faith, true policy, united ran;
That was but love of God, and this of
Man. 240
  Who first taught souls enslaved, and
realms undone,
Th' enormous faith of many made for one;
That proud exception to all Nature's laws,
T' invert the world, and counterwork its
cause ?
Force first made conquest, and that con-
quest law;
Till Superstition taught the tyrant awe,
Then shared the tyranny, then lent it aid,
And Gods of conquerors, Slaves of subjects
made.
She, 'midst the lightning's blaze and thun-
der's sound,
When rock'd the mountains, and when
groan'd the ground, 250
She taught the weak to bend, the proud to
pray,
To Power unseen, and mightier far than
they:
She, from the rending earth and bursting
skies,
Saw Gods descend, and Fiends infernal
rise:

Here fix'd the dreadful, there the bless'd
abodes;
Fear made her Devils, and weak hope her
Gods;
Gods, partial, changeful, passionate, un-
just,
Whose attributes were rage, revenge, or
lust;
Such as the souls of cowards might con-
ceive,
And, form'd like tyrants, tyrants would be-
lieve. 260
Zeal then, not Charity, became the guide,
And Hell was built on spite, and Heav'n on
pride:
Then sacred seem'd th' ethereal vault no
more;
Altars grew marble then, and reek'd with
gore:
Then first the flamen tasted living food,
Next his grim idol smear'd with human
blood;
With Heav'n's own thunders shook the
world below,
And play'd the God an engine on his foe.
  So drives Self-love thro' just and thro'
unjust, 269
To one man's power, ambition, lucre, lust:
The same Self-love in all becomes the cause
Of what restrains him, government and
laws.
For, what one likes if others like as well,
What serves one will, when many wills re-
bel ?
How shall he keep what, sleeping or awake,
A weaker may surprise, a stronger take ?
His safety must his liberty restrain:
All join to guard what each desires to gain.
Forc'd into virtue thus by self-defence,
Ev'n kings learn'd justice and benevo-
lence: 280
Self-love forsook the path it first pursued,
And found the private in the public good.
'Twas then the studious head, or gen'-
rous mind
Follower of God, or friend of human kind,
Poet or patriot, rose but to restore
The faith and moral Nature gave before;
Relumed her ancient light, not kindled
new;
If not God's image, yet his shadow drew;
Taught power's due use to people and to
kings,
Taught nor to slack nor strain its tender
strings, 290

The less or greater set so justly true,
That touching one must strike the other too;
Till jarring int'rests of themselves create
Th' according music of a well-mix'd state.
Such is the world's great harmony, that springs
From order, union, full consent of things;
Where small and great, where weak and mighty made
To serve, not suffer, strengthen, not invade;
More powerful each as needful to the rest,
And, in proportion as it blesses, blest;   300
Draw to one point, and to one centre bring
Beast, man, or angel, servant, lord, or king.
For forms of government let fools contest;
Whate'er is best administer'd is best:
For modes of faith let graceless zealots fight;
His can't be wrong whose life is in the right.
In Faith and Hope the world will disagree,
But all mankind's concern is Charity:
All must be false that thwart this one great end,
And all of God that bless mankind or mend.   310
  Man, like the gen'rous vine, supported lives;
The strength he gains is from th' embrace he gives.
On their own axis as the planets run,
Yet make at once their circle round the sun;
So two consistent motions act the soul,
And one regards itself, and one the Whole.
  Thus God and Nature link'd the gen'ral frame,
And bade Self-love and Social be the same.

EPISTLE IV

OF THE NATURE AND STATE OF MAN, WITH
RESPECT TO HAPPINESS

ARGUMENT

I. False notions of Happiness, philosophical
and popular, answered, from verses 19 to 26.
II. It is the end of all men, and attainable
by all. God intends Happiness to be equal;
and, to be so, it must be social, since all particular Happiness depends on general, and
since he governs by general, not particular
laws. As it is necessary for order, and the
peace and welfare of Society, that external
goods should be unequal, Happiness is not
made to consist in these. But notwithstanding that inequality, the balance of Happiness
among mankind is kept even by Providence,
by the two passions of Hope and Fear, verse
29, etc. III. What the Happiness of individuals is, as far as is consistent with the
constitution of this world; and that the good
man has here the advantage. The error of
imputing to virtue what are only the calamities of Nature, or of Fortune, verse 77, etc.
IV. The folly of expecting that God should
alter his general laws in favour of particulars, verse 123, etc. V. That we are not
judges who are good; but that whoever
they are, they must be happiest, verse 131,
etc. VI. That external goods are not the
proper rewards, but often inconsistent with,
or destructive of Virtue. That even these
can make no man happy without Virtue:
— instanced in Riches; Honours; Nobility;
Greatness; Fame; Superior Talents, with
pictures of human infelicity in men possessed
of them all, verse 149, etc. VII. That Virtue only constitutes a Happiness, whose object is universal, and whose prospect eternal.
That the perfection of Virtue and Happiness
consists in a conformity to the Order of Providence here, and a resignation to it here
and hereafter, verse 327, etc.

O HAPPINESS! our being's end and aim!
Good, Pleasure, Ease, Content! whate'er thy name,
That something still which prompts th' eternal sigh,
For which we bear to live, or dare to die;
Which still so near us, yet beyond us lies,
O'erlook'd, seen double, by the fool and wise:
Plant of celestial seed! if dropt below,
Say in what mortal soil thou deign'st to grow?
Fair opening to some court's propitious shine,
Or deep with diamonds in the flaming mine?   10
Twin'd with the wreaths Parnassian laurels yield,
Or reap'd in iron harvests of the field?
Where grows? — where grows it not? If vain our toil,
We ought to blame the culture, not the soil:
Fix'd to no spot is Happiness sincere;
'T is nowhere to be found, or ev'rywhere:

'T is never to be bought, but always free,
And fled from monarchs, St. John!
　　　dwells with thee.
　I. Ask of the Learn'd the way? the
　　　Learn'd are blind,
This bids to serve, and that to shun man-
　　　kind:　　　　　　　　　　20
Some place the bliss in Action, some in
　　　Ease,
Those call it Pleasure, and Contentment
　　　these;
Some sunk to beasts, find pleasure end in
　　　Pain;
Some swell'd to Gods, confess ev'n Virtue
　　　vain;
Or indolent, to each extreme they fall,
To trust in everything, or doubt of all.
　Who thus define it, say they more or less
Than this, that happiness is happiness?
　II. Take Nature's path and mad Opin-
　　　ion's leave;
All states can reach it, and all heads con-
　　　ceive;　　　　　　　　　　30
Obvious her goods, in no extreme they
　　　dwell;
There needs but thinking right and mean-
　　　ing well:
And, mourn our various portions as we
　　　please,
Equal is common sense and common ease.
　Remember, Man, 'the Universal Cause
Acts not by partial but by gen'ral laws,'
And makes what Happiness we justly call
Subsist not in the good of one, but all.
There 's not a blessing individuals find,
But some way leans and hearkens to the
　　　kind;　　　　　　　　　　40
No bandit fierce, no tyrant mad with pride,
No cavern'd hermit, rests self-satisfied;
Who most to shun or hate mankind pretend,
Seek an admirer, or would fix a friend.
Abstract what others feel, what others think,
All pleasures sicken, and all glories sink:
Each has his share; and who would more
　　　obtain,
Shall find the pleasure pays not half the
　　　pain.
　Order is Heav'n's first law; and, this
　　　confest,
Some are and must be greater than the
　　　rest,　　　　　　　　　　50
More rich, more wise: but who infers from
　　　hence
That such are happier, shocks all common
　　　sense.

Heav'n to mankind impartial we confess,
If all are equal in their happiness:
But mutual wants this happiness increase;
All Nature's diff'rence keeps all Nature's
　　　peace.
Condition, circumstance, is not the thing;
Bliss is the same in subject or in king,
In who obtain defence, or who defend,　59
In him who is, or him who finds a friend:
Heav'n breathes thro' every member of the
　　　whole
One common blessing, as one common soul.
But Fortune's gifts, if each alike possest,
And each were equal, must not all contest?
If then to all men happiness was meant,
God in externals could not place content.
　Fortune her gifts may variously dispose,
And these be happy call'd, unhappy those;
But Heav'n's just balance equal will appear,
While those are placed in hope and these
　　　in fear:　　　　　　　　　70
Not present good or ill the joy or curse,
But future views of better or of worse.
　O sons of earth! attempt ye still to rise
By mountains piled on mountains to the
　　　skies?
Heav'n still with laughter the vain toil sur-
　　　veys,
And buries madmen in the heaps they raise.
　Know all the good that individuals find,
Or God and Nature meant to mere man-
　　　kind,
Reason's whole pleasure, all the joys of
　　　sense,
Lie in three words — Health, Peace, and
　　　Competence.　　　　　　80
But health consists with temperance alone,
And peace, O Virtue! peace is all thy own.
The good or bad the gifts of fortune gain;
But these less taste them as they worse ob-
　　　tain.
Say, in pursuit of profit or delight,
Who risk the most, that take wrong means
　　　or right?
Of vice or virtue, whether blest or curst,
Which meets contempt, or which compas-
　　　sion first?
Count all th' advantage prosp'rous vice at-
　　　tains,
'T is but what virtue flies from and dis-
　　　dains:　　　　　　　　　90
And grant the bad what happiness they
　　　would,
One they must want, which is, to pass for
　　　good.

O blind to truth and God's whole scheme
   below,
Who fancy bliss to vice, to virtue woe!
Who sees and follows that great scheme
   the best,
Best knows the blessing, and will most be
   blest.
But fools the good alone unhappy call,
For ills or accidents that chance to all.
See Falkland dies, the virtuous and the
   just!   99
See Godlike Turenne prostrate on the dust!
See Sidney bleeds amid the martial
   strife! —
Was this their virtue, or contempt of life?
Say, was it virtue, more tho' Heav'n ne'er
   gave,
Lamented Digby! sunk thee to the grave?
Tell me, if virtue made the son expire,
Why full of days and honour lives the sire?
Why drew Marseilles' good bishop purer
   breath
When Nature sicken'd, and each gale was
   death?
Or why so long (in life if long can be) 109
Lent Heav'n a parent to the poor and
   me?
   What makes all physical or moral ill?
There deviates Nature, and here wanders
   Will.
God sends not ill, if rightly understood,
Or partial ill is universal good,
Or change admits, or Nature lets it fall,
Short and but rare till man improv'd it all.
We just as wisely might of Heav'n com-
   plain
That Righteous Abel was destroy'd by
   Cain,
As that the virtuous son is ill at ease
When his lewd father gave the dire dis-
   ease.   120
Think we, like some weak prince, th' Eter-
   nal Cause
Prone for his fav'rites to reverse his laws?
   IV. Shall burning Ætna, if a sage re-
     quires,
Forget to thunder, and recall her fires?
On air or sea new motions be imprest,
O blameless Bethel! to relieve thy breast?
When the loose mountain trembles from on
   high,
Shall gravitation cease if you go by?
Or some old temple, nodding to its fall,
For Chartres' head reserve the hanging
   wall?   130

   V. But still this world, so fitted for the
     knave,
Contents us not. — A better shall we have?
A kingdom of the just then let it be;
But first consider how those just agree.
The good must merit God's peculiar care;
But who but God can tell us who they are?
One thinks on Calvin Heav'n's own spirit
   fell;
Another deems him instrument of Hell:
If Calvin feel Heav'n's blessing or its rod,
This cries there is, and that, there is no
   God.   140
What shocks one part will edify the rest;
Nor with one system can they all be blest.
The very best will variously incline,
And what rewards your virtue punish mine.
Whatever is, is right. — This world, 't is true,
Was made for Cæsar — but for Titus too:
And which more bless'd? who chain'd his
   country, say,
Or he whose virtue sigh'd to lose a day?
   VI. 'But sometimes Virtue starves while
     Vice is fed.'   149
What then? is the reward of virtue bread?
That vice may merit; 't is the price of toil;
The knave deserves it when he tills the soil,
The knave deserves it when he tempts the
   main,
Where Folly fights for kings or dives for
   gain.
The good man may be weak, be indolent;
Nor is his claim to plenty but content.
But grant him riches, your demand is o'er.
'No: shall the good want health, the good
   want power?'
Add health and power, and every earthly
   thing.
'Why bounded power? why private? why
   no king?   160
Nay, why external for internal giv'n?
Why is not man a God, and earth a
   Heav'n?'
Who ask and reason thus will scarce con-
   ceive
God gives enough while he has more to
   give:
Immense the power, immense were the
   demand;
Say at what part of Nature will they
   stand?
   What nothing earthly gives or can de-
   stroy,
The soul's calm sunshine and the heartfelt
   joy,

Is Virtue's prize. A better would you fix ?
Then give humility a coach and six,   170
Justice a conqueror's sword, or truth a
    gown,
Or public spirit its great cure, a crown.
Weak, foolish man! will Heav'n reward us
    there
With the same trash mad mortals wish for
    here ?
The boy and man an individual makes,
Yet sigh'st thou now for apples and for
    cakes ?
Go, like the Indian, in another life
Expect thy dog, thy bottle, and thy wife;
As well as dream such trifles are assign'd,
As toys and empires, for a godlike mind: 180
Rewards, that either would to Virtue bring
No joy, or be destructive of the thing:
How oft by these at sixty are undone
The virtues of a saint at twenty-one!
    To whom can Riches give repute or trust,
Content or pleasure, but the good and just ?
Judges and senates have been bought for
    gold,
Esteem and Love were never to be sold.
O fool! to think God hates the worthy
    mind,
The lover and the love of humankind,   190
Whose life is healthful, and whose con-
    science clear,
Because he wants a thousand pounds a
    year.
Honour and shame from no condition rise;
Act well your part: there all the honour lies.
Fortune in men has some small diff'rence
    made;
One flaunts in rags, one flutters in brocade,
The cobbler apron'd, and the parson gown'd;
The friar hooded, and the monarch crown'd.
' What differ more,' you cry, ' than crown
    and cowl ? '
I 'll tell you, friend! a wise man and a
    fool.   200
You 'll find, if once the monarch acts the
    monk,
Or, cobbler-like, the parson will be drunk,
Worth makes the man, and want of it the
    fellow,
The rest is all but leather or prunella.
    Stuck o'er with titles, and hung round
        with strings,
That thou mayst be by kings, or whores of
    kings,
Boast the pure blood of an illustrious race,
In quiet flow from Lucrece to Lucrece:

But by your fathers' worth if yours you
    rate,
Count me those only who were good and
    great.   210
Go! if your ancient but ignoble blood
Has crept thro' scoundrels ever since the
    flood,
Go! and pretend your family is young,
Nor own your fathers have been fools so
    long.
What can ennoble sots, or slaves, or cow-
    ards ?
Alas! not all the blood of all the *Howards*.
    Look next on Greatness: say where
        Greatness lies.
' Where but among the heroes and the
    wise ? '
Heroes are much the same, the point 's
    agreed,   219
From Macedonia's madman to the Swede;
The whole strange purpose of their lives to
    find,
Or make, an enemy of all mankind!
Not one looks backward, onward still he
    goes,
Yet ne'er looks forward further than his
    nose.
No less alike the politic and wise;
All sly slow things with circumspective
    eyes:
Men in their loose unguarded hours they
    take,
Not that themselves are wise, but others
    weak.
But grant that those can conquer, these can
    cheat: 229
'T is phrase absurd to call a villain great.
Who wickedly is wise, or madly brave,
Is but the more a fool, the more a knave.
Who noble ends by noble means obtains,
Or failing, smiles in exile or in chains,
Like good Aurelius let him reign, or bleed
Like Socrates: — that man is great in-
    deed!
    What 's fame ? a fancied life in others'
        breath;
A thing beyond us, ev'n before our death.
Just what you hear you have; and what 's
    unknown
The same, my lord, if Tully's or your
    own.   240
All that we feel of it begins and ends
In the small circle of our foes or friends;
To all beside as much an empty shade,
An Eugene living as a Cæsar dead;

Alike or when or where, they shone or
   shine,
Or on the Rubicon or on the Rhine.
A Wit's a feather, and a Chief a rod;
An Honest Man's the noblest work of God.
Fame but from death a villain's name can
   save,   249
As Justice tears his body from the grave;
When what t' oblivion better were resign'd
Is hung on high, to poison half mankind.
All fame is foreign but of true desert,
Plays round the head, but comes not to the
   heart:
One self-approving hour whole years out-
   weighs
Of stupid starers and of loud huzzas:
And more true joy Marcellus exiled feels
Than Cæsar with a senate at his heels.
  In Parts superior what advantage lies ?
Tell (for you can) what is it to be wise ? 260
'T is but to know how little can be known,
To see all others' faults, and feel our own:
Condemn'd in bus'ness or in arts to drudge,
Without a second, or without a judge.
Truths would you teach, or save a sinking
   land ?
All fear, none aid you, and few understand.
Painful preëminence! yourself to view
Above life's weakness, and its comforts too.
  Bring then these blessings to a strict
   account;
Make fair deductions; see to what they
   mount;   270
How much of other each is sure to cost;
How each for other oft is wholly lost;
How inconsistent greater goods with these;
How sometimes life is risk'd, and always
   ease.
Think, and if still the things thy envy call,
Say, wouldst thou be the man to whom
   they fall ?
To sigh for ribands if thou art so silly,
Mark how they grace Lord Umbra or Sir
   Billy.
Is yellow dirt the passion of thy life ?
Look but on Gripus or on Gripus' wife. 280
If parts allure thee, think how Bacon shined,
The wisest, brightest, meanest of mankind!
Or, ravish'd with the whistling of a name,
See Cromwell damn'd to everlasting fame!
If all united thy ambition call,
From ancient story learn to scorn them all:
There in the rich, the honour'd, famed, and
   great,
See the false scale of Happiness complete!

In hearts of Kings or arms of Queens who
   lay,
How happy those to ruin, these betray. 290
Mark by what wretched steps their glory
   grows,
From dirt and sea-weed, as proud Venice
   rose;
In each how guilt and greatness equal ran,
And all that rais'd the Hero sunk the Man:
Now Europe's laurels on their brows be-
   hold,
But stain'd with blood, or ill-exchanged
   for gold;
Then see them broke with toils, or sunk in
   ease,
Or infamous for plunder'd provinces.
O wealth ill-fated! which no act of fame
E'er taught to shine, or sanctified from
   shame!   300
What greater bliss attends their close of
   life ?
Some greedy minion, or imperious wife,
The trophied arches, storied halls invade,
And haunt their slumbers in the pompous
   shade.
Alas! not dazzled with their noontide ray,
Compute the morn and ev'ning to the
   day;
The whole amount of that enormous fame,
A tale that blends their glory with their
   shame!
  VII. Know then this truth (enough for
   man to know),
' Virtue alone is happiness below;'   310
The only point where human bliss stands
   still,
And tastes the good without the fall to ill;
Where only merit constant pay receives,
Is bless'd in what it takes and what it
   gives;
The joy unequall'd if its end it gain,
And, if it lose, attended with no pain;
Without satiety, tho' e'er so bless'd,
And but more relish'd as the more dis-
   tress'd:
The broadest mirth unfeeling Folly wears,
Less pleasing far than Virtue's very tears:
Good from each object, from each place
   acquired,   321
For ever exercised, yet never tired;
Never elated while one man 's oppress'd;
Never dejected while another 's bless'd:
And where no wants, no wishes can re-
   main,
Since but to wish more virtue is to gain.

See the sole bliss Heav'n could on all be-
stow!
Which who but feels can taste, but thinks
can know:
Yet poor with fortune, and with learning
blind,
The bad must miss, the good untaught will
find: 330
Slave to no sect, who takes no private
road,
But looks thro' Nature up to Nature's
God;
Pursues that chain which links th' immense
design,
Joins Heav'n and earth, and mortal and
divine;
Sees that no being any bliss can know,
But touches some above and some below;
Learns from this union of the rising whole
The first, last purpose of the human soul;
And knows where faith, law, morals, all
began,
All end, in love of God and love of Man.
For him alone Hope leads from goal to
goal, 341
And opens still and opens on his soul,
Till lengthen'd on to faith, and unconfin'd,
It pours the bliss that fills up all the mind.
He sees why Nature plants in man alone
Hope of known bliss, and faith in bliss un-
known
(Nature, whose dictates to no other kind
Are giv'n in vain, but what they seek they
find):
Wise is her present; she connects in this
His greatest virtue with his greatest bliss;
At once his own bright prospect to be
blest, 351
And strongest motive to assist the rest.
Self-love thus push'd to social, to Divine,
Gives thee to make thy neighbour's bless-
ing thine.
Is this too little for the boundless heart?
Extend it, let thy enemies have part:
Grasp the whole world of reason, life, and
sense,
In one close system of benevolence:
Happier as kinder, in whate'er degree,
And height of Bliss but height of Charity.
God loves from whole to parts: but hu-
man soul 361
Must rise from individual to the whole.

Self-love but serves the virtuous mind to
wake,
As the small pebble stirs the peaceful lake;
The centre mov'd, a circle straight suc-
ceeds,
Another still, and still another spreads;
Friends, parent, neighbour, first it will em-
brace;
His country next; and next all human race;
Wide and more wide, th' o'erflowings of the
mind
Take ev'ry creature in of ev'ry kind: 370
Earth smiles around, with boundless bounty
blest,
And Heav'n beholds its image in his breast,
Come then, my Friend! my Genius!
come along,
O master of the poet and the song!
And while the Muse now stoops, or now
ascends,
To man's low passions, or their glorious
ends,
Teach me, like thee, in various nature wise,
To fall with dignity, with temper rise:
Form'd by thy converse, happily to steer
From grave to gay, from lively to severe;
Correct with spirit, eloquent with ease, 381
Intent to reason, or polite to please.
O! while along the stream of time thy
name
Expanded flies, and gathers all its fame,
Say, shall my little bark attendant sail,
Pursue the triumph, and partake the gale?
When statesmen, heroes, kings, in dust re-
pose,
Whose sons shall blush their fathers were
thy foes,
Shall then this verse to future age pretend
Thou wert my guide, philosopher, and
friend? 390
That, urged by thee, I turn'd the tuneful
art
From sounds to things, from fancy to the
heart:
For Wit's false mirror held up Nature's
light,
Show'd erring pride, *Whatever is, is right;*
That Reason, Passion, answer one great aim;
That true Self-love and Social are the
same;
That Virtue only makes our bliss below,
And all our knowledge is, *ourselves to know.*

MORAL ESSAYS

Est brevitate opus, ut currat sententia, neu se
Impediat verbis lassas onerantibus aures:
Et sermone opus est modo tristi, sæpe jocoso,
Defendente vicem modo rhetoris atque poetæ,
Interdum urbani, parcentis viribus, atque
Extenuantis eas consulto.

HORACE.

The present order of the *Moral Essays* is very different from that of their original publication. The fifth epistle (to Addison) was written in 1715, and published five years later in Tickell's edition of Addison's works. The fourth epistle (to the Earl of Burlington) was published in 1731, under the title *Of Taste*. The third epistle (to Lord Bathurst) was published in 1732, and followed in 1733 by the first epistle (to Lord Cobham). The second epistle (to a Lady) was published in 1735. The whole series appeared in their present order, under the direction of Warburton, after Pope's death.

Though it is doubtful how far it suggests Pope's primary intention, Warburton's *Advertisement* is here printed because Pope undoubtedly wished it, with its flattering implication of his philosophical breadth, to be accepted as a true statement of a plan which was plainly broader than its execution.

ADVERTISEMENT

BY DR. WARBURTON

The Essay on Man was intended to be comprised in four books : —

The first of which the author has given us under that title in four epistles.

The second was to have consisted of the same number : 1. Of the extent and limits of human reason. 2. Of those arts and sciences, and of the parts of them, which are useful, and therefore attainable ; together with those which are unuseful, and therefore unattainable. 3. Of the nature, ends, use, and application of the different capacities of men. 4. Of the use of learning ; of the science of the world ; and of wit ; concluding with a satire against the misapplication of them, illustrated by pictures, characters, and examples.

The third book regarded civil regimen, or the science of politics ; in which the several forms of a republic were to be examined and explained ; together with the several modes of religious worship, as far forth as they affect society : between which the author always supposed there was the most interesting relation and closest connection. So that this part would have treated of civil and religious society in their full extent.

The fourth and last book concerned private ethics, or practical morality, considered in all the circumstances, orders, professions, and stations of human life.

The scheme of all this had been maturely digested, and communicated to Lord Bolingbroke, Dr. Swift, and one or two more ; and was intended for the only work of his riper years ; but was, partly through ill health, partly through discouragements from the depravity of the times ; and partly on prudential and other considerations, interrupted, postponed, and lastly, in a manner, laid aside.

But as this was the author's favourite work, which more exactly reflected the image of his strong capacious mind, and as we can have but a very imperfect idea of it from the *disjecta membra poetæ* that now remain, it may not be amiss to be a little more particular concerning each of these projected books.

The first, as it treats of man in the abstract, and considers him in general under every one of his relations, becomes the foundation, and furnishes out the subjects of the three following : so that —

The second book was to take up again the first and second epistles of the first book, and to treat of man in his intellectual capacity at large, as has been explained above. Of this only a small part of the conclusion (which, as we said, was to have contained a satire against the misapplication of wit and learning) may be found in the fourth book of the *Dunciad ;* and up and down, occasionally, in the other three.

The third book, in like manner, was to reassume the subject of the third epistle of the first, which treats of man in his social, political, and religious capacity. But this part the poet afterwards conceived might be best executed in an epic poem, as the action would make it more animated, and the fable less invidious ; in which all the great principles of true and false governments and religious should be chiefly delivered in feigned examples.

The fourth and last book was to pursue the

subject of the fourth epistle of the first, and to
treat of ethics, or practical morality; and would
have consisted of many members, of which the
four following epistles are detached portions;
the two first, on the characters of men and women, being the introductory part of this concluding book.

EPISTLE I

TO SIR RICHARD TEMPLE, LORD COBHAM

OF THE KNOWLEDGE AND CHARACTERS
OF MEN

ARGUMENT

I. That it is not sufficient for this knowledge to
consider Man in the abstract; Books will not
serve the purpose, nor yet our own Experience singly. General maxims, unless they
be formed upon both, will be but notional.
Some peculiarity in every man, characteristic
to himself, yet varying from himself. Difficulties arising from our own Passions, Fancies, Faculties, &c. The shortness of Life
to observe in, and the uncertainty of the
Principles of action in men to observe by.
Our own Principle of action often hid from
ourselves. Some few Characters plain, but
in general confounded, dissembled, or inconsistent. The same man utterly different in
different places and seasons. Unimaginable
weaknesses in the greatest. Nothing constant
and certain but God and Nature. No judging of the Motives from the actions; the
same actions proceeding from contrary Motives, and the same Motives influencing contrary actions. II. Yet to form Characters
we can only take the strongest actions of a
man's life, and try to make them agree: the
utter uncertainty of this, from Nature itself,
and from Policy. Characters given according to the rank of men of the world; and
some reason for it. Education alters the Nature, or at least the Character, of many. Actions, Passions, Opinions, Manners, Humours,
or Principles, all subject to change. No
judging by Nature. III. It only remains to
find (if we can) his *Ruling Passion:* that
will certainly influence all the rest, and can
reconcile the seeming or real inconsistency
of all his actions. Instanced in the extraordinary character of Clodio. A caution
against mistaking second qualities for first,
which will destroy all possibility of the knowledge of mankind. Examples of the strength
of the Ruling Passion, and its continuation
to the last breath.

YES, you despise the man to books con-
  fin'd,
Who from his study rails at humankind;
Tho' what he learns he speaks, and may
  advance
Some gen'ral maxims, or be right by
  chance.
The coxcomb bird, so talkative and grave,
That from his cage cries cuckold, whore,
  and knave,
Tho' many a passenger he rightly call,
You hold him no philosopher at all.
  And yet the fate of all extremes is such,
Men may be read, as well as books, too
  much.   10
To observations which ourselves we make,
We grow more partial for th' observer's
  sake;
To written wisdom, as another's, less:
Maxims are drawn from Notions, those
  from Guess.
There 's some peculiar in each leaf and
  grain,
Some unmark'd fibre, or some varying vein.
Shall only man be taken in the gross ?
Grant but as many sorts of mind as moss.
  That each from other differs, first confess;
Next, that he varies from himself no less:
And Nature's, Custom's, Reason's, Pas-
  sion's strife,   21
And all Opinion's colours cast on life.
  Our depths who fathoms, or our shallows
  finds,
Quick whirls and shifting eddies of our
  minds ?
On human actions reason tho' you can,
It may be Reason, but it is not Man:
His Principle of action once explore,
That instant 't is his Principle no more.
Like following life thro' creatures you dis-
  sect,
You lose it in the moment you detect.   30
  Yet more; the diff'rence is as great be-
  tween
The optics seeing as the objects seen.
All Manners take a tincture from our own,
Or come discolour'd thro' our Passions
  shown;
Or Fancy's beam enlarges, multiplies,
Contracts, inverts, and gives ten thousand
  dyes.
  Nor will life's stream for observation
  stay,
It hurries all too fast to mark their way:

In vain sedate reflections we would make,
When half our knowledge we must snatch,
    not take.   40
Oft in the Passions' wide rotation toss'd,
Our spring of action to ourselves is lost:
Tired, not determin'd, to the last we yield,
And what comes then is master of the field.
As the last image of that troubled heap,
When Sense subsides, and Fancy sports in
    sleep
(Tho' past the recollection of the thought),
Becomes the stuff of which our dream is
    wrought:
Something as dim to our internal view   49
Is thus, perhaps, the cause of most we do.
    True, some are open, and to all men
        known;
Others so very close they're hid from none
(So darkness strikes the sense no less than
    light):
Thus gracious Chandos is belov'd at sight;
And ev'ry child hates Shylock, tho' his
    soul
Still sits at squat, and peeps not from its
    hole.
At half mankind when gen'rous Manly
    raves,
All know 't is virtue, for he thinks them
    knaves:
When universal homage Umbra pays,
All see 't is vice, and itch of vulgar praise.
When Flatt'ry glares, all hate it in a
    Queen,   61
While one there is who charms us with his
    spleen.
    But these plain Characters we rarely
        find;
Tho' strong the bent, yet quick the turns
    of mind:
Or puzzling contraries confound the whole;
Or affectations quite reverse the soul.
The dull flat falsehood serves for policy;
And in the cunning truth itself 's a lie:
Unthought-of frailties cheat us in the wise:
The fool lies hid in inconsistencies.   70
    See the same man, in vigour, in the gout;
Alone, in company, in place, or out;
Early at bus'ness, and at hazard late,
Mad at a fox-chase, wise at a debate,
Drunk at a Borough, civil at a Ball,
Friendly at Hackney, faithless at White-
    hall!
    Catius is ever moral, ever grave,
Thinks who endures a knave is next a
    knave,

Save just at dinner — then prefers, no
    doubt,
A rogue with ven'son to a saint without. 80
    Who would not praise Patricio's high
        desert,
His hand unstain'd, his uncorrupted heart,
His comprehensive head? all int'rests
    weigh'd,
All Europe saved, yet Britain not betray'd!
He thanks you not, his pride is in Piquet,
Newmarket fame, and judgment at a bet.
    What made (say, Montaigne, or more
        sage Charron)
Otho a warrior, Cromwell a buffoon?
A perjured prince a leaden saint revere,
A godless regent tremble at a star?   9?
The throne a bigot keep, a genius quit,
Faithless thro' piety, and duped thro' wit?
Europe a woman, child, or dotard, rule;
And just her wisest monarch made a fool?
    Know, God and Nature only are the
        same:
In man the judgment shoots at flying game;
A bird of passage! gone as soon as found;
Now in the moon, perhaps now under
    ground.

In vain the sage, with retrospective eye,
Would from th' apparent What conclude
    the Why,   100
Infer the Motive from the Deed, and show
That what we chanced was what we meant
    to do.
Behold! if Fortune or a Mistress frowns,
Some plunge in bus'ness, others shave their
    crowns:
To ease the soul of one oppressive weight,
This quits an empire, that embroils a state.
The same adust complexion has impell'd
Charles to the convent, Philip to the field.
    Not always Actions show the man: we
        find   109
Who does a kindness is not therefore kind;
Perhaps Prosperity becalm'd his breast;
Perhaps the wind just shifted from the
    east:
Not therefore humble he who seeks retreat;
Pride guides his steps, and bids him shun
    the great:
Who combats bravely is not therefore
    brave;
He dreads a death-bed like the meanest
    slave:
Who reasons wisely is not therefore wise;
His pride in reas'ning, not in acting, lies.

But grant that Actions best discover
    man;
Take the most strong, and sort them as you
    can: 120
The few that glare each character must
    mark;
You balance not the many in the dark.
What will you do with such as disagree ?
Suppress them, or miscall them Policy ?
Must then at once (the character to save)
The plain rough hero turn a crafty knave ?
Alas! in truth the man but changed his
    mind;
Perhaps was sick, in love, or had not din'd.
Ask why from Britain Cæsar would re-
    treat ?   129
Cæsar himself might whisper he was beat.
Why risk the world's great empire for a
    punk ?
Cæsar perhaps might answer, he was
    drunk.
But, sage historians! 't is your task to prove
One action, Conduct, one, heroic Love.
'T is from high life high characters are
    drawn;
A saint in crape is twice a saint in lawn;
A judge is just, a chancellor juster still;
A gownman learn'd; a bishop what you
    will;
Wise if a minister; but if a king,
More wise, more learn'd, more just, more
    ev'rything.   140
Court-virtues bear, like gems, the highest
    rate,
Born where Heav'n's influence scarce can
    penetrate.
In life's low vale, the soil the virtues like,
They please as beauties, here as wonders
    strike.
Tho' the same sun, with all-diffusive
    rays,
Blush in the rose, and in the diamond
    blaze,
We prize the stronger effort of his power,
And justly set the gem above the flower.
'T is education forms the common mind;
Just as the twig is bent the tree's inclin'd.
Boastful and rough, your first son is a
    Squire;   151
The next a Tradesman, meek, and much a
    liar;
Tom struts a Soldier, open, bold, and
    brave;
Will sneaks a Scriv'ner, an exceeding
    knave.

Is he a Churchman ? then he 's fond of
    power:
A Quaker ? sly: a Presbyterian ? sour:
A smart Free-thinker ? all things in an
    hour.
    Ask men's opinions! Scoto now shall tell
How trade increases, and the world goes
    well:
Strike off his pension by the setting sun, 160
And Britain, if not Europe, is undone.
    That gay Free-thinker, a fine talker once,
What turns him now a stupid silent dunce ?
Some god or spirit he has lately found,
Or chanced to meet a Minister that
    frown'd.
    Judge we by Nature ? Habit can efface,
Int'rest o'ercome, or Policy take place:
By Actions ? those Uncertainty divides:
By Passions ? these Dissimulation hides:
Opinions ? they still take a wider range:
Find, if you can, in what you cannot
    change.   171
    Manners with Fortunes, Humours turn
    with Climes,
Tenets with Books, and Principles with
    Times.

Search then the RULING PASSION: there
    alone,
The wild are constant, and the cunning
    known;
The fool consistent, and the false sincere;
Priests, princes, women, no dissemblers
    here.
This clue once found unravels all the rest,
The prospect clears, and Wharton stands
    confest:
Wharton! the scorn and wonder of our
    days,   180
Whose Ruling Passion was the lust of
    praise:
Born with whate'er could win it from the
    wise,
Women and fools must like him, or he dies:
Tho' wond'ring Senates hung on all he
    spoke,
The Club must hail him master of the joke.
Shall parts so various aim at nothing new ?
He 'll shine a Tully and a Wilmot too:
Then turns repentant, and his God adores
With the same spirit that he drinks and
    whores;
Enough if all around him but admire,   190
And now the Punk applaud, and now the
    Friar.

Thus with each gift of Nature and of Art,
And wanting nothing but an honest heart;
Grown all to all, from no one vice exempt,
And most contemptible, to shun contempt;
His passion still to covet gen'ral praise,
His life, to forfeit it a thousand ways;
A constant bounty which no friend has
     made;
An angel tongue which no man can per-
     suade!
A fool with more of wit than half man-
     kind,   200
Too rash for thought, for action too refin'd;
A tyrant to the wife his heart approves;
A rebel to the very king he loves —
He dies, sad outcast of each church and
     state,
And, harder still! flagitious, yet not great!
Ask you why Wharton broke thro' ev'ry
     rule ?
'T was all for fear the Knaves should call
     him Fool.
     Nature well known, no prodigies remain;
Comets are regular, and Wharton plain.
     Yet in this search the wisest may mis-
     take,   210
If second qualities for first they take.
When Catiline by rapine swell'd his store,
When Cæsar made a noble dame a whore,
In this the Lust, in that the Avarice
Were means, not ends; Ambition was the
     vice.
That very Cæsar, born in Scipio's days,
Had aim'd, like him, by chastity at praise,
Lucullus, when Frugality could charm,
Had roasted turnips in the Sabine farm.
In vain th' observer eyes the builder's toil,
But quite mistakes the scaffold for the
     pile.   221
     In this one passion man can strength en-
     joy,
As fits give vigour just when they destroy.
Time, that on all things lays his lenient
     hand,
Yet tames not this; it sticks to our last
     sand.
Consistent in our follies and our sins,
Here honest Nature ends as she begins.
     Old politicians chew on wisdom past,
And totter on in bus'ness to the last;
As weak, as earnest, and as gravely out 230
As sober Lanesb'row dancing in the gout.
     Behold a rev'rend sire, whom want of
     grace
Has made the father of a nameless race,

Shov'd from the wall perhaps, or rudely
     press'd
By his own son, that passes by unbless'd;
Still to his wench he crawls on knocking
     knees,
And envies ev'ry sparrow that he sees.
     A salmon's belly, Helluo, was thy fate;
The doctor call'd, declares all help too
     late.
'Mercy!' cries Helluo, 'mercy on my soul!
Is there no hope ? — Alas! — then bring
     the jowl.'   241
     The frugal crone, whom praying priests
     attend,
Still strives to save the hallow'd taper's
     end,
Collects her breath, as ebbing life retires,
For one puff more, and in that puff ex-
     pires.
     'Odious! in woollen! 't would a saint
     provoke '
(Were the last words that poor Narcissa
     spoke);
'No, let a charming chintz and Brussels
     lace
Wrap my cold limbs, and shade my life-
     less face:
One would not, sure, be frightful when
     one 's dead —   250
And — Betty — give this cheek a little red.'
     The courtier smooth, who forty years
     had shined
An humble servant to all humankind,
Just brought out this, when scarce his
     tongue could stir: —
'If — where I 'm going — I could serve
     you, sir ?'
'I give and I devise (old Euclio said,
And sigh'd) my lands and tenements to
     Ned.'
'Your money, sir ?' — 'My money, sir!
     what, all ?
Why — if I must — (then wept) I give it
     Paul.'
'The manor, sir ?' — 'The manor! hold,'
     he cried,   260
'Not that — I cannot part with that !' —
     and died.
     And you, brave COBHAM! to the latest
     breath
Shall feel your Ruling Passion strong in
     death;
Such in those moments as in all the past,
'O save my country, Heav'n!' shall be
     your last.

EPISTLE II

TO A LADY

OF THE CHARACTERS OF WOMEN

ARGUMENT

That the particular Characters of women are not so strongly marked as those of men, seldom so fixed, and still more inconsistent with themselves. Instances of contrarieties given, even from such Characters as are more strongly marked, and seemingly, therefore, most consistent : as, 1. In the affected. 2. In the soft-natured. 3. In the cunning and artful. 4 In the whimsical. 5. In the lewd and vicious. 6. In the witty and refined. 7. In the stupid and simple. The former part having shown that the particular characters of women are more various than those of men, it is nevertheless observed that the general characteristic of the sex, as to the *Ruling Passion*, is more uniform. This is occasioned partly by their Nature, partly by their Education, and in some degree by Necessity. What are the aims and the fate of this sex : 1. As to Power. 2. As to Pleasure. Advice for their true interest. The picture of an estimable woman, with the best kind of contrarieties.

Nothing so true as what you once let fall,
' Most women have no Characters at all : '
Matter too soft a lasting mark to bear,
And best distinguish'd by black, brown, or fair.
 How many pictures of one nymph we view,
And how unlike each other, all how true!
Arcadia's countess here, in ermined pride,
Is there, Pastora by a fountain side:
Here Fannia, leering on her own good man,
And there a naked Leda with a swan. 10
Let then the fair one beautifully cry,
In Magdalen's loose hair and lifted eye;
Or drest in smiles of sweet Cecilia shine,
With simp'ring angels, palms, and harps divine;
Whether the charmer sinner it, or saint it,
If folly grow romantic, I must paint it.
 Come, then, the colours and the ground prepare;
Dip in the rainbow. trick her off in air;
Choose a firm cloud before it fall, and in it
Catch, ere she change, the Cynthia of this minute. 20

Rufa, whose eye quick glancing o'er the park,
Attracts each light gay meteor of a spark,
Agrees as ill with Rufa studying Locke,
As Sappho's diamonds with her dirty smock,
Or Sappho at her toilet's greasy task,
With Sappho fragrant at an ev'ning Masque:
So morning insects, that in muck begun,
Shine, buzz, and fly-blow in the setting sun.
 How soft is Silia! fearful to offend;
The frail one's advocate, the weak one's friend. 30
To her Calista proved her conduct nice,
And good Simplicius asks of her advice.
Sudden she storms! she raves! you tip the wink:
But spare your censure; Silia does not drink.
All eyes may see from what the change arose;
All eyes may see — a Pimple on her nose.
 Papillia, wedded to her am'rous spark,
Sighs for the shades — ' How charming is a park! '
A park is purchased; but the Fair he sees
All bathed in tears — ' Oh, odious, odious trees! ' 40
Ladies, like variegated tulips, show;
'T is to their changes half their charms we owe:
Fine by defect, and delicately weak,
Their happy spots the nice admirer take.
'T was thus Calypso once each heart alarm'd,
Awed without virtue, without beauty charm'd;
Her tongue bewitch'd as oddly as her eyes;
Less Wit than Mimic, more a Wit than wise.
Strange graces still, and stranger flights, she had,
Was just not ugly, and was just not mad; 50
Yet ne'er so sure our passion to create,
As when she touch'd the brink of all we hate.
 Narcissa's nature, tolerably mild,
To make a wash would hardly stew a child;
Has ev'n been prov'd to grant a lover's prayer,
And paid a tradesman once to make him stare;
Gave alms at Easter in a Christian trim,
And made a widow happy for a whim.

Why then declare Good-nature is her
    scorn,   59
When 't is by that alone she can be borne?
Why pique all mortals, yet affect a name?
A fool to Pleasure, yet a slave to Fame:
Now deep in Taylor and the Book of Mar-
    tyrs,
Now drinking citron with his Grace and
    Chartres:
Now conscience chills her, and now passion
    burns,
And atheism and religion take their turns:
A very heathen in the carnal part,
Yet still a sad good Christian at her heart.
  See Sin in state, majestically drunk,
Proud as a peeress, prouder as a punk;   70
Chaste to her husband, frank to all beside,
A teeming mistress, but a barren bride.
What then? let blood and body bear the
    fault;
Her head 's untouch'd, that noble seat of
    Thought:
Such this day's doctrine — in another fit
She sins with poets thro' pure love of Wit.
What has not fired her bosom or her brain?
Cæsar and Tall-boy, Charles and Charle-
    magne.
As Helluo, late dictator of the feast,
The nose of Hautgout, and the tip of Taste,
Critiqued your wine, and analyzed your
    meat,   81
Yet on plain pudding deign'd at home to
    eat:
So Philomede, lecturing all mankind
On the soft passion, and the taste refin'd,
The address, the delicacy — stoops at once,
And makes her hearty meal upon a dunce.
  Flavia 's a Wit, has too much sense to
    pray;
To toast our wants and wishes is her way;
Nor asks of God, but of her stars, to give
The mighty blessing 'while we live to
    live.'   90
Then all for death, that opiate of the
    soul!
Lucretia's dagger, Rosamonda's bowl.
Say, what can cause such impotence of
    mind?
A Spark too fickle, or a Spouse too kind.
Wise wretch! with pleasures too refin'd to
    please;
With too much spirit to be e'er at ease;
With too much quickness ever to be taught;
With too much thinking to have common
    thought:

You purchase Pain with all that Joy can
    give,
And die of nothing but a rage to live.   100
  Turn then from Wits, and look on Simo's
    mate,
No ass so meek, no ass so obstinate:
Or her that owns her faults but never
    mends,
Because she 's honest, and the best of
    friends:
Or her whose life the church and scandal
    share,
For ever in a Passion or a Prayer:
Or her who laughs at Hell, but (like her
    Grace)
Cries, 'Ah! how charming if there 's no
    such place!'
Or who in sweet vicissitude appears   109
Of Mirth and Opium, Ratifie and Tears;
The daily anodyne and nightly draught,
To kill those foes to fair ones, Time and
    Thought.
Woman and fool are two hard things to
    hit;
For true No-meaning puzzles more than
    Wit.
  But what are these to great Atossa's
    mind?
Scarce once herself, by turns all woman-
    kind!
Who with herself, or others, from her
    birth
Finds all her life one warfare upon earth;
Shines in exposing knaves and painting
    fools,
Yet is whate'er she hates and ridicules;   120
No thought advances, but her eddy brain
Whisks it about, and down it goes again.
Full sixty years the World has been her
    Trade,
The wisest fool much time has ever made:
From loveless youth to unrespected age,
No passion gratified except her rage:
So much the Fury still outran the Wit,
The pleasure miss'd her, and the scandal
    hit.
Who breaks with her provokes revenge
    from Hell,
But he 's a bolder man who dares be well.
Her ev'ry turn with violence pursued,   131
Nor more a storm her hate than gratitude:
To that each Passion turns or soon or
    late;
Love, if it makes her yield, must make her
    hate.

Superiors ? death! and equals ? what a
   curse!
But an inferior not dependent ? worse.
Offend her, and she knows not to forgive;
Oblige her, and she 'll hate you while you
   live:
But die, and she 'll adore you — then the
   bust
And temple rise — then fall again to dust.
Last night her lord was all that 's good and
   great;   141
A knave this morning, and his will a
   cheat.
Strange! by the means defeated of the
   ends,
By Spirit robb'd of power, by Warmth of
   friends,
By Wealth of foll'wers! without one dis-
   tress,
Sick of herself thro' very selfishness!
Atossa, curs'd with ev'ry granted prayer,
Childless with all her children, wants an
   heir:
To heirs unknown descends th' unguarded
   store,
Or wanders, Heav'n-directed, to the poor.
   Pictures like these, dear Madam! to de-
   sign,   151
Asks no firm hand and no unerring line;
Some wand'ring touches, some reflected
   light,
Some flying stroke, alone can hit 'em right:
For how should equal colours do the knack ?
Chameleons who can paint in white and
   black ?
' Yet Chloë sure was form'd without a
   spot.'
Nature in her then err'd not, but forgot.
' With ev'ry pleasing, ev'ry prudent part,
Say, what can Chloë want ? ' — She wants
   a Heart,   160
She speaks, behaves, and acts just as she
   ought,
But never, never reach'd one gen'rous
   thought.
Virtue she finds too painful an endeavour,
Content to dwell in decencies for ever.
So very reasonable, so unmov'd,
As never yet to love or to be lov'd.
She, while her lover pants upon her breast,
Can mark the figures on an Indian chest;
And when she sees her friend in deep de-
   spair,
Observes how much a chintz exceeds mo-
   hair.   170

Forbid it, Heav'n! a favour or a debt
She e'er should cancel! — but she may for-
   get.
Safe is your secret still in Chloë's ear;
But none of Chloë's shall you ever hear.
Of all her Dears she never slander'd one,
But cares not if a thousand are undone.
Would Chloë know if you 're alive or dead ?
She bids her footman put it in her head.
Chloë is prudent — Would you too be wise ?
Then never break your heart when Chloë
   dies.   180
   One certain portrait may (I grant) be
   seen,
Which Heav'n has varnish'd out and made
   a queen;
The same for ever! and described by all
With truth and goodness, as with crown
   and ball.
Poets heap virtues, painters gems, at will,
And show their zeal, and hide their want of
   skill.
'T is well — but, artists! who can paint or
   write,
To draw the naked is your true delight.
That robe of Quality so struts and swells,
None see what parts of Nature it conceals:
Th' exactest traits of body or of mind, 191
We owe to models of an humble kind.
If Queensbury to strip there 's no compel-
   ling,
'T is from a handmaid we must take a
   Helen.
From peer or bishop 't is no easy thing
To draw the man who loves his God or
   king.
Alas! I copy (or my draught would fail)
From honest Mah'met or plain parson Hale.
But grant, in public, men sometimes are
   shown;
A woman 's seen in private life alone: 200
Our bolder talents in full light display'd;
Your virtues open fairest in the shade.
Bred to disguise, in public 't is you hide;
There none distinguish 'twixt your shame
   or pride,
Weakness or delicacy; all so nice,
That each may seem a Virtue or a Vice.
   In men we various Ruling Passions find;
In women two almost divide the kind;
Those only fix'd, they first or last obey,
The love of Pleasure, and the love of Sway.
   That Nature gives; and where the lesson
   taught   211
Is but to please, can Pleasure seem a fault ?

Experience this: by man's oppression curst,
They seek the second not to lose the first.
  Men some to bus'ness, some to pleasure take;
But ev'ry woman is at heart a rake:
Men some to quiet, some to public strife;
But ev'ry lady would be queen for life.
  Yet mark the fate of a whole sex of queens!
Power all their end, but Beauty all the means.   220
In youth they conquer with so wild a rage,
As leaves them scarce a subject in their age:
For foreign glory, foreign joy they roam;
No thought of peace or happiness at home.
But wisdom's triumph is well-timed retreat,
As hard a science to the Fair as Great!
Beauties, like tyrants, old and friendless grown,
Yet hate repose, and dread to be alone;
Worn out in public, weary ev'ry eye,
Nor leave one sigh behind them when they die.   230
  Pleasures the sex, as children birds, pursue,
Still out of reach, yet never out of view;
Sure, if they catch, to spoil the toy at most,
To covet flying, and regret when lost:
At last to follies youth could scarce defend,
It grows their age's prudence to pretend;
Ashamed to own they gave delight before,
Reduced to feign it when they give no more.
As hags hold Sabbaths less for joy than spite,
So these their merry miserable night;   240
Still round and round the Ghosts of Beauty glide,
And haunt the places where their Honour died.
  See how the world its veterans rewards!
A youth of frolics, an old age of cards;
Fair to no purpose, artful to no end,
Young without lovers, old without a friend;
A Fop their passion, but their prize a Sot,
Alive ridiculous, and dead forgot!
  Ah! friend! to dazzle let the vain design;
To raise the thought and touch the heart be thine!   250
That charm shall grow, while what fatigues the Ring
Flaunts and goes down an unregarded thing.

So when the sun's broad beam has tired the sight,
All mild ascends the moon's more sober light,
Serene in virgin modesty she shines,
And unobserv'd the glaring orb declines.
  O! blest with temper, whose unclouded ray   257
Can make to-morrow cheerful as to-day;
She who can love a sister's charms, or hear
Sighs for a daughter with unwounded ear;
She who ne'er answers till a husband cools,
Or, if she rules him, never shows she rules;
Charms by accepting, by submitting sways,
Yet has her humour most when she obeys;
Let Fops or Fortune fly which way they will,
Disdains all loss of tickets or Codille;
Spleen, Vapours, or Smallpox, above them all,
And mistress of herself, tho' china fall.
  And yet believe me, good as well as ill,
Woman's at best a contradiction still.   270
Heav'n when it strives to polish all it can
Its last best work, but forms a softer Man;
Picks from each sex to make the fav'rite blest,
Your love of pleasure, our desire of rest;
Blends, in exception to all gen'ral rules,
Your taste of follies with our scorn of fools;
Reserve with Frankness, Art with Truth allied,
Courage with Softness, Modesty with Pride;
Fix'd principles, with fancy ever new: 279
Shakes all together, and produces — You.
  Be this a woman's fame; with this unblest,
Toasts live a scorn, and Queens may die a jest.
This Phœbus promis'd (I forget the year)
When those blue eyes first open'd on the sphere;
Ascendant Phœbus watch'd that hour with care,
Averted half your parents' simple prayer,
And gave you beauty, but denied the pelf
That buys your sex a tyrant o'er itself.
The gen'rous God, who wit and gold refines,
And ripens spirits as he ripens mines,   290
Kept dross for Duchesses, the world shall know it,
To you gave Sense, Good-humour, and a Poet.

EPISTLE III

TO ALLEN, LORD BATHURST

OF THE USE OF RICHES

ARGUMENT

That it is known to few, most falling into one of the extremes, Avarice or Profusion. The point discussed, whether the invention of money has been more commodious or pernicious to mankind. That Riches, either to the Avaricious or the Prodigal, cannot afford happiness, scarcely necessaries. That Avarice is an absolute frenzy, without an end or purpose. Conjectures about the motives of avaricious men. That the conduct of men, with respect to Riches, can only be accounted for by the Order of Providence, which works the general good out of extremes, and brings all to its great end by perpetual revolutions. How a Miser acts upon principles which appear to him reasonable. How a Prodigal does the same. The due medium and true use of riches. The Man of Ross. The fate of the Profuse and the Covetous, in two examples; both miserable in life and in death. The story of Sir Balaam.

P. Who shall decide when doctors disagree,
And soundest casuists doubt, like you and me ?
You hold the word from Jove to Momus giv'n,
That Man was made the standing jest of Heav'n,
And gold but sent to keep the fools in play,
For some to heap, and some to throw away.
　But I, who think more highly of our kind
(And surely Heav'n and I are of a mind),
Opine that Nature, as in duty bound,
Deep hid the shining mischief under ground:　　　　10
But when by man's audacious labour won,
Flamed forth this rival to its sire the sun,
Then careful Heav'n supplied two sorts of men,
To squander these, and those to hide again.
　Like doctors thus, when much dispute has past,
We find our tenets just the same at last:
Both fairly owning riches, in effect,
No grace of Heav'n, or token of th' elect;

Giv'n to the fool, the mad, the vain, the evil,
To Ward, to Waters, Chartres, and the Devil.　　　　20
　B. What Nature wants, commodious gold bestows;
'T is thus we eat the bread another sows.
　P. But how unequal it bestows, observe;
'T is thus we riot, while who sow it starve.
What Nature wants (a phrase I much distrust)
Extends to luxury, extends to lust.
Useful I grant, it serves what life requires,
But dreadful too, the dark assassin hires.
　B. Trade it may help, Society extend.
　P. But lures the pirate, and corrupts the friend.　　　　30
　B. It raises armies in a nation's aid.
　P. But bribes a senate, and the land 's betray'd.
In vain may heroes fight and patriots rave,
If secret gold sap on from knave to knave.
Once, we confess, beneath the patriot's cloak,
From the crack'd bag the dropping guinea spoke,
And jingling down the back-stairs, told the crew
' Old Cato is as great a rogue as you.'
Blest paper-credit ! last and best supply !
That lends Corruption lighter wings to fly !　　　　40
Gold imp'd by thee, can compass hardest things,
Can pocket states, can fetch or carry kings;
A single leaf shall waft an army o'er,
Or ship off senates to some distant shore;
A leaf, like Sibyl's, scatter to and fro
Our fates and fortunes as the winds shall blow;
Pregnant with thousands flits the scrap unseen,
And silent sells a King or buys a Queen.
　Oh, that such bulky bribes as all might see,
Still, as of old, incumber'd villany !　　　　50
Could France or Rome divert our brave designs
With all their brandies or with all their wines ?
What could they more than Knights and Squires confound,
Or water all the Quorum ten miles round ?
A statesman's slumbers how this speech would spoil,
' Sir, Spain has sent a thousand jars of oil,

Huge bales of British cloth blockade the
   door;
A hundred oxen at your levee roar.'
  Poor Avarice one torment more would
   find,   59
Nor could Profusion squander all in kind.
Astride his cheese Sir Morgan might we
   meet;
And Worldly crying coals from street to
   street,
Whom with a wig so wild and mien so
   'mazed,
Pity mistakes for some poor tradesman
   crazed.
Had Colepepper's whole wealth been hops
   and hogs,
Could he himself have sent it to the dogs ?
His Grace will game: to White's a bull be
   led,
With spurning heels and with a butting
   head.
To White's be carried, as to ancient games,
Fair coursers, vases, and alluring dames. 70
Shall then Uxorio, if the stakes he sweep,
Bear home six whores, and make his lady
   weep ?
Or soft Adonis, so perfumed and fine,
Drive to St. James's a whole herd of
   swine ?
Oh, filthy check on all industrious skill,
To spoil the nation's last great trade, —
   Quadrille!
Since then, my lord, on such a world we
   fall,
What say you ? B. Say ? Why, take it,
   gold and all.
  P. What Riches give us let us then in-
   quire:
Meat, Fire, and Clothes. B. What more ?
   P. Meat, Clothes, and Fire.   80
Is this too little ? would you more than
   live ?
Alas! 't is more than Turner finds, they
   give.
Alas! 't is more than (all his visions past)
Unhappy Wharton waking found at last!
What can they give ? To dying Hopkins,
   heirs ?
To Chartres, vigour ? Japhet, nose and
   ears ?
Can they in gems bid pallid Hippia glow ?
In Fulvia's buckle ease the throbs below ?
Or heal, old Narses, thy obscener ail,
With all th' embroidery plaster'd at thy
   tail ?   90

They might (were Harpax not too wise to
   spend)
Give Harpax' self the blessing of a friend;
Or find some doctor that would save the
   life
Of wretched Shylock, spite of Shylock's
   wife.
But thousands die without or this or that,
Die, and endow a College or a Cat.
To some indeed Heav'n grants the happier
   fate
T' enrich a bastard; or a son they hate.
Perhaps you think the poor might have
   their part ?
Bond damns the poor, and hates them from
   his heart: 100
The grave Sir Gilbert holds it for a rule
That ev'ry man in want is knave or fool.
'God cannot love (says Blunt, with tearless
   eyes)
The wretch he starves ' — and piously de-
   nies:
But the good bishop, with a meeker air,
Admits, and leaves them, Providence's
   care.
  Yet, to be just to these poor men of
   pelf,
Each does but hate his neighbour as him-
   self:
Damn'd to the mines, an equal fate betides
The slave that digs it and the slave that
   hides.   110
  B. Who suffer thus, mere charity should
   own,
Must act on motives powerful tho' un-
   known.
  P. Some war, some plague or famine,
   they foresee,
Some revelation hid from you and me.
Why Shylock wants a meal the cause is
   found;
He thinks a loaf will rise to fifty pound.
What made directors cheat in South-sea
   year ?
To live on ven'son, when it sold so dear.
Ask you why Phryne the whole auction
   buys ?
Phryne foresees a general excise.   120
Why she and Sappho raise that monstrous
   sum ?
Alas! they fear a man will cost a plum.
  Wise Peter sees the world's respect for
   gold,
And therefore hopes this nation may be
   sold.

Glorious ambition! Peter, swell thy store,
And be what Rome's great Didius was
   before.
The crown of Poland, venal twice an age,
To just three millions stinted modest Gage.
But nobler scenes Maria's dreams unfold,
Hereditary realms, and worlds of gold. 130
Congenial souls! whose life one av'rice
   joins,
And one fate buries in th' Asturian mines.
   Much-injured Blunt! why bears he Brit-
   ain's hate?
A wizard told him in these words our
   fate:
'At length Corruption, like a gen'ral flood
(So long by watchful ministers withstood),
Shall deluge all; and Av'rice, creeping on,
Spread like a low-born mist and blot the
   sun;
Statesman and Patriot ply alike the stocks,
Peeress and Butler share alike the Box, 140
And judges job, and bishops bite the town,
And mighty Dukes pack cards for half a
   crown:
See Britain sunk in lucre's sordid charms,
And France revenged of Anne's and Ed-
   ward's arms!'
'T was no court-badge, great Scriv'ner! fired
   thy brain,
Nor lordly luxury, nor city gain:
No, 't was thy righteous end, ashamed to
   see
Senates degen'rate, patriots disagree,
And nobly wishing party-rage to cease,
To buy both sides, and give thy country
   peace. 150
   'All this is madness,' cries a sober sage:
'But who, my friend, has Reason in his
   rage?
The Ruling Passion, be it what it will,
The Ruling Passion conquers Reason still.'
Less mad the wildest whimsy we can
   frame
Than ev'n that Passion, if it has no aim;
For tho' such motives folly you may call,
The folly 's greater to have none at all.
   Hear then the truth:— ''T is Heav'n
   each Passion sends, 159
And diff'rent men directs to diff'rent ends.
Extremes in Nature equal good produce;
Extremes in Man concur to gen'ral use.'
Ask me what makes one keep, and one be-
   stow?
That power who bids the ocean ebb and
   flow,

Bids seed-time, harvest, equal course main-
   tain,
Thro' reconciled extremes of drought and
   rain;
Builds life on death, on change duration
   founds,
And gives th' eternal wheels to know their
   rounds.
Riches, like insects, when conceal'd they
   lie, 169
Wait but for wings, and in their season fly.
Who sees pale Mammon pine amidst his
   store,
Sees but a backward steward for the poor;
This year a reservoir to keep and spare;
The next a fountain spouting thro' his heir
In lavish streams to quench a country's
   thirst,
And men and dogs shall drink him till they
   burst.
   Old Cotta shamed his fortune and his
   birth,
Yet was not Cotta void of wit or worth.
What tho' (the use of barb'rous spits for-
   got)
His kitchen vied in coolness with his grot?
His court with nettles, moats with cresses
   stor'd, 181
With soups unbought, and salads, bless'd
   his board;
If Cotta lived on pulse, it was no more
Than Bramins, Saints, and Sages did before;
To cram the rich was prodigal expense,
And who would take the poor from Provi-
   dence?
Like some lone Chartreux stands the good
   old hall,
Silence without, and fasts within the wall;
No rafter'd roofs with dance and tabor
   sound,
No noontide bell invites the country round;
Tenants with sighs the smokeless towers
   survey, 191
And turn th' unwilling steeds another way;
Benighted wanderers, the forest o'er,
Curse the saved candle and unopening door;
While the gaunt mastiff, growling at the
   gate,
Affrights the beggar whom he longs to eat.
   Not so his son; he mark'd this oversight,
And then mistook reverse of wrong for
   right:
(For what to shun will no great knowledge
   need
But what to follow is a task indeed!) 200

Yet sure, of qualities deserving praise,
More go to ruin fortunes than to raise.
What slaughter'd hecatombs, what floods
    of wine,
Fill the capacious Squire and deep Divine!
Yet no mean motive this profusion draws;
His oxen perish in his country's cause;
'Tis George and Liberty that crowns the
    cup,
And zeal for that great House which eats
    him up.
The woods recede around the naked seat,
The sylvans groan — no matter — for the
    fleet;   210
Next goes his wool — to clothe our valiant
    bands;
Last, for his country's love, he sells his
    lands.
To town he comes, completes the nation's
    hope,
And heads the bold train-bands, and burns
    a pope.
And shall not Britain now reward his toils,
Britain, that pays her patriots with her
    spoils ?
In vain at court the bankrupt pleads his
    cause;
His thankless country leaves him to her laws.
    The sense to value Riches, with the art
T' enjoy them, and the virtue to impart;
Not meanly nor ambitiously pursued,   221
Not sunk by sloth, nor raised by servitude;
To balance fortune by a just expense,
Join with economy magnificence;
With splendour charity, with plenty health;
O teach us, Bathurst! yet unspoil'd by
    wealth,
That secret rare, between th' extremes to
    move
Of mad Good-nature and of mean Self-love.
    B. To worth or want well weigh'd be
    bounty giv'n
And ease or emulate the care of Heav'n
(Whose measure full o'erflows on human
    race):   231
Mend Fortune's fault, and justify her grace.
Wealth in the gross is death, but life dif-
    fused,
As poison heals in just proportion used:
In heaps, like ambergris, a stink it lies,
But well dispers'd is incense to the skies.
    P. Who starves by nobles, or with nobles
    eats ?
The wretch that trusts them, and the rogue
    that cheats.

Is there a lord who knows a cheerful noon
Without a fiddler, flatt'rer, or buffoon ? 240
Whose table Wit or modest Merit share,
Unelbow'd by a gamester, pimp, or player ?
Who copies yours or Oxford's better part,
To ease th' oppress'd, and raise the sinking
    heart ?
Where'er he shines, O Fortune! gild the
    scene,
And angels guard him in the golden mean!
There English bounty yet a while may
    stand,
And honour linger ere it leaves the land.
    But all our praises why should Lords en-
    gross ?
Rise, honest Muse! and sing the Man of
    Ross: 250
Pleas'd Vaga echoes thro' her winding
    bounds,
And rapid Severn hoarse applause resounds.
Who hung with woods yon mountain's sul-
    try brow ?
From the dry rock who bade the waters
    flow ?
Not to the skies in useless columns tost,
Or in proud falls magnificently lost,
But clear and artless, pouring thro' the
    plain
Health to the sick, and solace to the swain.
Whose causeway parts the vale with shady
    rows ?
Whose seats the weary traveller repose ? 260
Who taught that Heav'n-directed spire to
    rise ?
The Man of Ross, each lisping babe replies.
Behold the market-place with poor o'er-
    spread!
The Man of Ross divides the weekly bread:
He feeds yon almshouse, neat, but void of
    state,
Where age and want sit smiling at the
    gate:
Him portion'd maids, apprenticed orphans
    blest,
The young who labour, and the old who
    rest.
Is any sick ? the Man of Ross relieves,
Prescribes, attends, the medicine makes
    and gives: 270
Is there a variance ? enter but his door,
Balk'd are the courts, and contest is no
    more:
Despairing quacks with curses fled the
    place,
And vile attorneys, now a useless race.

B. Thrice happy man! enabled to pursue
What all so wish, but want the power to
  do!
Oh say, what sums that gen'rous hand
  supply ?
What mines to swell that boundless
  charity ?
P. Of debts and taxes, wife and children
  clear,
This man possess'd — five hundred pounds
  a year.   280
Blush, Grandeur, blush! proud courts, with-
  draw your blaze!
Ye little stars, hide your diminish'd rays!
B. And what? no monument, inscrip-
  tion, stone,
His race, his form, his name almost un-
  known ?
P. Who builds a church to God, and not
  to Fame,
Will never mark the marble with his name:
Go, search it there, where to be born and
  die,
Of rich and poor makes all the history;
Enough that Virtue fill'd the space be-
  tween,
Prov'd by the ends of being to have been.
When Hopkins dies, a thousand lights at-
  tend   291
The wretch who living saved a candle's
  end:
Should'ring God's altar a vile image stands,
Belies his features, nay, extends his hands;
That livelong wig, which Gorgon's self
  might own,
Eternal buckle takes in Parian stone.
  Behold what blessings Wealth to life can
  lend!
And see what comfort it affords our end.
In the worst inn's worst room, with mat
  half-hung,
The floors of plaster, and the walls of dung,
On once a flock-bed, but repair'd with
  straw,   301
With tape-tied curtains, never meant to
  draw,
The George and Garter dangling from that
  bed
Where tawdry yellow strove with dirty red,
Great Villiers lies — alas! how changed
  from him,
That life of pleasure and that soul of
  whim!
Gallant and gay, in Cliveden's proud alcove,
The bower of wanton Shrewsbury and Love;

Or just as gay at council, in a ring
Of mimic statesmen and their merry King.
No Wit to flatter, left of all his store — 311
No Fool to laugh at, which he valued
  more —
There, victor of his health, of fortune,
  friends,
And fame, this lord of useless thousands
  ends!
  His Grace's fate sage Cutler could fore-
  see,
And well (he thought) advised him, 'Live
  like me.'
And well his Grace replied, 'Like you,
  Sir John ?
That I can do when all I have is gone ! '
Resolve me, Reason, which of these is worse,
Want with a full or with an empty purse ?
Thy life more wretched, Cutler! was con-
  fess'd;   321
Arise, and tell me, was thy death more
  bless'd ?
Cutler saw tenants break and houses fall,
For very want; he could not build a wall:
His only daughter in a stranger's power,
For very want; he could not pay a dower:
A few gray hairs his rev'rend temples
  crown'd;
'T was very want that sold them for two
  pound.
What ev'n denied a cordial at his end,
Banish'd the doctor, and expell'd the
  friend ?   330
What but a want, which you perhaps think
  mad,
Yet numbers feel, — the want of what he
  had!
Cutler and Brutus dying both exclaim,
' Virtue! and wealth! what are ye but a
  name! '
  Say, for such worth are other worlds
  prepared ?
Or are they both in this their own reward ?
A knotty point! to which we now proceed.
But you are tired — I 'll tell a tale — *B.*
  Agreed.
P. Where London's column, pointing at
  the skies,
Like a tall bully, lifts the head and lies, 340
There dwelt a citizen of sober fame,
A plain good man, and Balaam was his
  name.
Religious, punctual, frugal, and so forth,
His word would pass for more than he was
  worth;

One solid dish his week-day meal affords,
An added pudding solemnized the Lord's;
Constant at Church and 'Change; his gains
   were sure,
His givings rare, save farthings to the poor.
  The Devil was piqued such saintship to
   behold,
And long'd to tempt him like good Job of
   old;   350
But Satan now is wiser than of yore,
And tempts by making rich, not making
   poor.
Rous'd by the Prince of Air, the whirl-
   winds sweep
The surge, and plunge his father in the
   deep;
Then full against his Cornish lands they
   roar,
And two rich shipwrecks bless the lucky
   shore.
Sir Balaam now, he lives like other folks,
He takes his chirping pint, and cracks his
   jokes.
'Live like yourself,' was soon my lady's
   word;
And lo! two puddings smoked upon the
   board.   360
  Asleep and naked as an Indian lay,
An honest factor stole a gem away:
He pledg'd it to the knight; the knight had
   wit,
So kept the diamond, and the rogue was bit.
Some scruple rose, but thus he eas'd his
   thought:
'I'll now give sixpence where I gave a
   groat;
Where once I went to church I'll now go
   twice —
And am so clear too of all other vice.'
  The tempter saw his time; the work he
   plied;
Stocks and subscriptions pour on ev'ry
   side,   370
Till all the demon makes his full descent
In one abundant shower of cent per cent,
Sinks deep within him, and possesses whole,
Then dubs Director, and secures his soul.
  Behold Sir Balaam, now a man of Spirit,
Ascribes his gettings to his parts and merit;
What late he call'd a blessing now was wit,
And God's good providence a lucky hit.
Things change their titles as our manners
   turn,
His counting-house employ'd the Sunday
   morn: 380

Seldom at church ('t was such a busy
   life),
But duly sent his family and wife.
There (so the Devil ordain'd) one Christ-
   mas-tide
My good old lady catch'd a cold and died.
  A nymph of quality admires our knight;
He marries, bows at court, and grows po-
   lite;
Leaves the dull cits, and joins (to please
   the fair)
The well-bred cuckolds in St. James's air:
First for his son a gay commission buys,
Who drinks, whores, fights, and in a duel
   dies;   390
His daughter flaunts a viscount's tawdry
   wife;
She bears a coronet and p—x for life.
In Britain's senate he a seat obtains,
And one more pensioner St. Stephen
   gains.
My lady falls to play; so bad her chance,
He must repair it; takes a bribe from
   France:
The house impeach him; Coningsby ha-
   rangues;
The court forsake him, and Sir Balaam
   hangs.
Wife, son, and daughter, Satan! are thy
   own,
His wealth, yet dearer, forfeit to the
   crown: 400
The Devil and the King divide the prize,
And sad Sir Balaam curses God and dies.

EPISTLE IV

TO RICHARD BOYLE, EARL OF BURLINGTON

OF THE USE OF RICHES

ARGUMENT

The vanity of Expense in people of wealth and
quality. The abuse of the word Taste. That
the first principle and foundation in this, as
in every thing else, is Good Sense. The chief
proof of it is to follow Nature, even in works
of mere luxury and elegance. Instanced in
Architecture and Gardening, where all must
be adapted to the genius and use of the
place, and the beauties not forced into it,
but resulting from it. How men are disappointed in their most expensive undertak-
ings for want of this true foundation, without
which nothing can please long, if at all; and

the best examples and rules will but be perverted into something burdensome and ridicculous. A description of the false taste of Magnificence; the first grand error of which is to imagine that greatness consists in the size and dimension, instead of the proportion and harmony, of the whole; and the second, either in joining together parts incoherent, or too minutely resembling, or, in the repetition of the same too frequently. A word or two of false taste in books, in music, in painting, even in preaching and prayer, and lastly in entertainments. Yet Providence is justified in giving wealth to be squandered in this manner, since it is dispersed to the poor and laborious part of mankind. [Recurring to what is laid down in the first book, ep. ii. and in the epistle preceding this.] What are the proper objects of Magnificence, and a proper field for the expense of great men. And, finally, the great and public works which become a Prince.

'T is strange the Miser should his cares
employ
To gain those riches he can ne'er enjoy:
Is it less strange the Prodigal should waste
His wealth to purchase what he ne'er can
taste ?
Not for himself he sees, or hears, or eats;
Artists must choose his pictures, music,
meats:
He buys for Topham drawings and designs;
For Pembroke statues, dirty gods, and
coins;
Rare monkish manuscripts for Hearne
alone,
And books for Mead, and butterflies for
Sloane.   10
Think we all these are for himself ? no
more
Than his fine wife, alas ! or finer whore.
For what has Virro painted, built, and
planted ?
Only to show how many tastes he wanted.
What brought Sir Visto's ill-got wealth to
waste ?
Some demon whisper'd, ' Visto ! have a
Taste.'
Heav'n visits with a Taste the wealthy fool,
And needs no rod but Ripley with a rule.
See ! sportive Fate, to punish awkward
pride,
Bids Bubo build, and sends him such a
guide: 20
A standing sermon at each year's expense,
That never coxcomb reach'd Magnificence !

You show us Rome was glorious, not
profuse,
And pompous buildings once were things
of use;
Yet shall, my Lord, your just, your noble
rules
Fill half the land with imitating fools;
Who random drawings from your sheets
shall take,
And of one Beauty many Blunders make;
Load some vain church with old theatric
state,
Turn arcs of triumph to a garden gate; 30
Reverse your ornaments, and hang them all
On some patch'd dog-hole eked with ends
of wall,
Then clap four slices of pilaster on 't,
That laced with bits of rustic makes a front;
Shall call the winds thro' long arcades to
roar,
Proud to catch cold at a Venetian door:
Conscious they act a true Palladian part,
And if they starve, they starve by rules of
Art.
Oft have you hinted to your brother peer
A certain truth, which many buy too dear:
Something there is more needful than expense,   41
And something previous ev'n to Taste —
't is Sense;
Good Sense, which only is the gift of
Heav'n,
And tho' no science, fairly worth the sev'n;
A light which in yourself you must perceive;
Jones and Le Nôtre have it not to give.
To build, to plant, whatever you intend,
To rear the column, or the arch to bend,
To swell the terrace, or to sink the grot,
In all, let Nature never be forgot.   50
But treat the Goddess like a modest Fair,
Nor overdress, nor leave her wholly bare;
Let not each beauty everywhere be spied,
Where half the skill is decently to hide.
He gains all points who pleasingly confounds,
Surprises, varies, and conceals the bounds.
Consult the genius of the place in all;
That tells the waters or to rise or fall;
Or helps th' ambitious hill the heav'ns to
scale,
Or scoops in circling theatres the vale, 60
Calls in the country, catches opening glades,
Joins willing woods, and varies shades from
shades,

Now breaks, or now directs, th' intending
　　lines;
Paints as you plant, and as you work de-
　　signs.
Still follow Sense, of every art the soul;
Parts answering parts shall slide into a
　　whole,
Spontaneous beauties all around advance,
Start ev'n from difficulty, strike from
　　chance:
Nature shall join you; time shall make it
　　grow
A work to wonder at — perhaps a Stowe. 70
　　Without it, proud Versailles! thy glory
　　falls,
And Nero's terraces desert their walls:
The vast parterres a thousand hands shall
　　make,
Lo! Cobham comes, and floats them with
　　a lake;
Or cut wide views thro' mountains to the
　　plain,
You 'll wish your hill or shelter'd seat
　　again.
Ev'n in an ornament its place remark,
Nor in a hermitage set Dr. Clarke.
　　Behold Villario's ten years' toil com-
　　plete:
His quincunx darkens, his espaliers meet,
The wood supports the plain, the parts
　　unite, 81
And strength of shade contends with
　　strength of light;
A waving glow the bloomy beds display,
Blushing in bright diversities of day,
With silver quiv'ring rills meander'd o'er —
Enjoy them, you! Villario can no more:
Tired of the scene parterres and fountains
　　yield,
He finds at last he better likes a field.
　　Thro' his young woods how pleased
　　Sabinus stray'd,
Or sat delighted in the thick'ning shade, 90
With annual joy the redd'ning shoots to
　　greet,
Or see the stretching branches long to meet.
His son's fine Taste an opener vista loves,
Foe to the dryads of his father's groves;
One boundless green or flourish'd carpet
　　views,
With all the mournful family of yews;
The thriving plants, ignoble broomsticks
　　made,
Now sweep those alleys they were born to
　　shade.

At Timon's villa let us pass a day,
Where all cry out, ' What sums are thrown
　　away;' 100
So proud, so grand; of that stupendous
　　air,
Soft and agreeable come never there;
Greatness with Timon dwells in such a
　　draught
As brings all Brobdingnag before your
　　thought.
To compass this, his building is a town,
His pond an ocean, his parterre a down:
Who but must laugh, the master when he
　　sees,
A puny insect shiv'ring at a breeze! 108
Lo, what huge heaps of littleness around!
The whole a labour'd quarry above ground.
Two Cupids squirt before: a lake behind
Improves the keenness of the northern
　　wind.
His gardens next your admiration call;
On every side you look, behold the wall!
No pleasing intricacies intervene;
No artful wildness to perplex the scene;
Grove nods at grove, each alley has a
　　brother,
And half the platform just reflects the
　　other.
The suff'ring eye inverted Nature sees, 119
Trees cut to statues, statues thick as trees;
With here a fountain never to be play'd,
And there a summer-house that knows no
　　shade,
Here Amphitrite sails thro' myrtle bowers,
There gladiators fight or die in flowers;
Unwater'd, see the drooping seahorse
　　mourn,
And swallows roost in Nilus' dusty urn.
　　My Lord advances with majestic mien,
Smit with the mighty pleasure to be seen:
But soft! by regular approach — not yet —
First thro' the length of yon hot terrace
　　sweat; 130
And when up ten steep slopes you 've
　　dragg'd your thighs,
Just at his study door he 'll bless your eyes.
　　His study! with what authors is it stor'd ?
In books, not authors, curious is my lord.
To all their dated backs he turns you
　　round;
These Aldus printed, those Du Sueil has
　　bound;
Lo, some are vellum, and the rest as good,
For all his lordship knows, — but they are
　　wood.

For Locke or Milton 't is in vain to look;
These shelves admit not any modern book.
  And now the chapel's silver bell you
      hear,   141
That summons you to all the pride of
      prayer.
Light quirks of music, broken and unev'n,
Make the soul dance upon a jig to Heav'n:
On painted ceilings you devoutly stare,
Where sprawl the saints of Verrio or La-
      guerre,
On gilded clouds in fair expansion lie,
And bring all paradise before your eye:
To rest, the cushion and soft dean invite,
Who never mentions Hell to ears polite.   150
But hark! the chiming clocks to dinner
      call:
A hundred footsteps scrape the marble hall;
The rich buffet well-colour'd serpents
      grace,
And gaping Tritons spew to wash your
      face.
Is this a dinner? this a genial room?
No, 't is a temple and a hecatomb;
A solemn sacrifice perform'd in state;
You drink by measure, and to minutes eat.
So quick retires each flying course, you 'd
      swear
Sancho's dread doctor and his wand were
      there.   160
Between each act the trembling salvers
      ring,
From soup to sweet wine, and God bless
      the King.
In plenty starving, tantalized in state,
And complaisantly help'd to all I hate,
Treated, caress'd, and tired, I take my
      leave,
Sick of his civil pride from morn to eve;
I curse such lavish Cost and little Skill,
And swear no day was ever pass'd so ill.
  Yet hence the poor are clothed, the hun-
      gry fed;   169
Health to himself, and to his infants bread
The lab'rer bears; what his hard heart de-
      nies,
His charitable vanity supplies.
  Another age shall see the golden ear
Imbrown the slope, and nod on the parterre,
Deep harvests bury all his pride has plann'd,
And laughing Ceres reassume the land.
  Who then shall grace, or who improve
      the soil?
Who plants like Bathurst, or who builds
      like Boyle?

'T is use alone that sanctifies expense,
And splendour borrows all her rays from
      sense.   180
His father's acres who enjoys in peace,
Or makes his neighbours glad if he increase;
Whose cheerful tenants bless their yearly
      toil,
Yet to their Lord owe more than to the
      soil;
Whose ample lawns are not ashamed to
      feed
The milky heifer and deserving steed;
Whose rising forests, not for pride or show,
But future buildings, future navies, grow:
Let his plantations stretch from down to
      down,
First shade a country, and then raise a
      town.   190
  You, too, proceed! make falling arts
      your care;
Erect new wonders, and the old repair;
Jones and Palladio to themselves restore
And be whate'er Vitruvius was before,
Till kings call forth th' ideas of your mind
(Proud to accomplish what such hands
      design'd),
Bid harbours open, public ways extend,
Bid temples, worthier of the God, ascend,
Bid the broad arch the dangerous flood
      contain,
The mole projected break the roaring
      main,   200
Back to his bounds their subject sea com-
      mand,
And roll obedient rivers thro'the land.
These honours Peace to happy Britain
      brings;
These are imperial works, and worthy
      Kings.

EPISTLE V

TO MR. ADDISON

OCCASIONED BY HIS DIALOGUES ON MEDALS

'This was originally written,' says Pope, 'in
the year 1715, when Mr. Addison intended to
publish his book *Of Medals*; it was some time
before he was Secretary of State; but not published till Mr. Tickell's edition of his works;
at which time the verses on Mr. Craggs, which
conclude the poem, were added, viz., in 1720.'
  Warburton connects the epistle with the preceding Essays in this ingenious way: 'As the

third epistle treated the extremes of Avarice and Profusion, and the fourth took up one particular branch of the latter, namely the *vanity of expense* in people of wealth and quality, and was therefore corollary to the third; so this treats of one circumstance of that vanity, as it appears in the common collections of old coins; and is therefore a corollary to the fourth.'

See the wild waste of all-devouring years!
How Rome her own sad sepulchre appears!
With nodding arches, broken temples
    spread,
The very tombs now vanish'd like their
    dead!
Imperial wonders raised on nations spoil'd,
Where mix'd with slaves the groaning
    martyr toil'd;
Huge theatres, that now unpeopled woods,
Now drain'd a distant country of her floods;
Fanes, which admiring Gods with pride
    survey,   9
Statues of men, scarce less alive than they!
Some felt the silent stroke of mould'ring
    age,
Some hostile fury, some religious rage:
Barbarian blindness, Christian zeal con-
    spire,
And Papal piety, and Gothic fire.
Perhaps, by its own ruins saved from flame,
Some buried marble half preserves a name:
That name the learn'd with fierce disputes
    pursue
And give to Titus old Vespasian's due.
    Ambition sigh'd: she found it vain to
    trust
The faithless column and the crumbling
    bust;   20
Huge moles, whose shadow stretch'd from
    shore to shore,
Their ruins perish'd, and their place no
    more!
Convinced, she now contracts her vast de-
    sign,
And all her triumphs shrink into a coin.
A narrow orb each crowded conquest
    keeps,
Beneath her palm here sad Judea weeps:
Now scantier limits the proud arch con-
    fine,
And scarce are seen the prostrate Nile or
    Rhine:
A small Euphrates thro' the piece is
    roll'd,   29
And little eagles wave their wings in gold.

The Medal, faithful to its charge of
    fame,
Thro' climes and ages bears each form
    and name:
In one short view subjected to our eye,
Gods, Emp'rors, Heroes, Sages, Beauties,
    lie.
With sharpen'd sight pale antiquaries pore,
Th' inscription value, but the rust adore.
This the blue varnish, that the green en-
    dears,
The sacred rust of twice ten hundred
    years!
To gain Pescennius one employs his
    schemes,
One grasps a Cecrops in ecstatic dreams. 40
Poor Vadius, long with learned spleen de-
    vour'd,
Can taste no pleasure since his shield was
    scour'd;
And Curio, restless by the fair one's side,
Sighs for an Otho, and neglects his bride.
    Theirs is the vanity, the learning thine:
Touch'd by thy hand, again Rome's glories
    shine;
Her Gods and godlike Heroes rise to view,
And all her faded garlands bloom anew.
Nor blush these studies thy regard engage:
These pleas'd the fathers of poetic rage; 50
The verse and sculpture bore an equal part,
And art reflected images to art.
    Oh, when shall Britain, conscious of her
    claim,
Stand emulous of Greek and Roman fame?
In living medals see her wars enroll'd,
And vanquish'd realms supply recording
    gold?
Here, rising bold, the patriot's honest face,
There warriors frowning in historic brass.
Then future ages with delight shall see
How Plato's, Bacon's, Newton's looks
    agree;   60
Or in fair series laurell'd bards be shown,
A Virgil there, and here an Addison.
Then shall thy Craggs (and let me call him
    mine)
On the cast ore another Pollio shine;
With aspect open shall erect his head,
And round the orb in lasting notes be read,
'Statesman, yet friend to truth; of soul
    sincere,
In action faithful, and in honour clear;
Who broke no promise, serv'd no private
    end,   69
Who gain'd no title, and who lost no friend;

Ennobled by himself, by all approv'd
And prais'd, unenvied by the Muse he
    lov'd.'

UNIVERSAL PRAYER

DEO OPT. MAX.

This was written in 1738 to correct the impression of fatalism which Warburton's ingenious exposition had failed to remove. Pope
had really as little mind for dogma as most
poets; but these verses represent what, in view
of the instructions of Bolingbroke, corrected
by Warburton, he now believed himself to believe.

FATHER of all ! in ev'ry age,
    In ev'ry clime ador'd,
By saint, by savage, and by sage,
    Jehovah, Jove, or Lord !

Thou Great First Cause, least understood,
    Who all my sense confin'd
To know but this, that thou art good,
    And that myself am blind:

Yet gave me, in this dark estate,
    To see the good from ill;
And binding Nature fast in Fate,
    Left free the human Will.

What Conscience dictates to be done,
    Or warns me not to do;
This teach me more than Hell to shun,
    That more than Heav'n pursue.

What blessings thy free bounty gives
    Let me not cast away;
For God is paid when man receives;
    T' enjoy is to obey.

Yet not to earth's contracted span
    Thy goodness let me bound,
Or think thee Lord alone of man,
    When thousand worlds are round

Let not this weak unknowing hand
    Presume thy bolts to throw,
And deal damnation round the land
    On each I judge thy foe.

If I am right, thy grace impart,
    Still in the right to stay;
If I am wrong, O teach my heart
    To find that better way.

Save me alike from foolish Pride
    Or impious Discontent,
At aught thy wisdom has denied,
    Or aught thy goodness lent.

Teach me to feel another's woe
    To hide the fault I see:
That mercy I to others show,
    That mercy show to me.

Mean tho' I am, not wholly so,
    Since quicken'd by thy breath,
O lead me, whereso'er I go,
    Thro' this day's life or death!

This day be bread and peace my lot:
    All else beneath the sun
Thou know'st if best bestow'd or not
    And let thy will be done.

To Thee, whose temple is all Space,
    Whose altar earth, sea, skies,
One chorus let all Being raise,
    All Nature's incense rise !

SATIRES

The *Satires* retain nearly the order of their original publication. They appeared between 1733 and 1738. It is said that Bolingbroke suggested the translation of the First Satire of the Second Book of Horace, and that the translation of the others was done somewhat at random, as Pope saw his opportunity of adapting them to his own day.

EPISTLE TO DR. ARBUTHNOT

BEING THE PROLOGUE TO THE SATIRES

ADVERTISEMENT

This paper is a sort of bill of complaint, begun many years since, and drawn up by snatches, as the several occasions offered. I had no thoughts of publishing it, till it pleased some Persons of Rank and Fortune (the authors of 'Verses to the Imitator of Horace,' and of an 'Epistle to a Doctor of Divinity from a Nobleman at Hampton Court') to attack, in a very extraordinary manner, not only my Writings (of which, being public, the Public is judge), but my Person, Morals, and Family; whereof, to those who know me not, a truer information may be requisite. Being divided between the necessity to say something of myself, and my own laziness to undertake so awkward a task, I thought it the shortest way to put the last hand to this epistle. If it have any thing pleasing, it will be that by which I am most desirous to please, the Truth and the Sentiment; and if any thing offensive, it will be only to those I am least sorry to offend, the vicious or the ungenerous.

Many will know their own pictures in it, there being not a circumstance but what is true; but I have, for the most part, spared their names, and they may escape being laughed at if they please.

I would have some of them know it was owing to the request of the learned and candid Friend to whom it is inscribed, that I make not as free use of theirs as they have done of mine. However, I shall have this advantage and honour on my side, that whereas, by their proceeding, any abuse may be directed at any man, no injury can possibly be done by mine, since a nameless character can never be found out but by its truth and likeness.

P. 'SHUT, shut the door, good John!'
    fatigued, I said;
'Tie up the knocker, say I'm sick, I'm
    dead.'

The Dog-star rages! nay, 'tis past a doubt
All Bedlam or Parnassus is let out:
Fire in each eye, and papers in each hand,
They rave, recite, and madden round the
    land.
    What walls can guard me, or what
      shades can hide?
They pierce my thickets, thro' my grot they
    glide,
By land, by water, they renew the charge,
They stop the chariot, and they board the
    barge.   10
No place is sacred, not the church is free,
Ev'n Sunday shines no Sabbath-day to
    me:
Then from the Mint walks forth the man
    of rhyme,
Happy to catch me just at dinner time.
    Is there a Parson much bemused in beer,
A maudlin Poetess, a rhyming Peer,
A clerk foredoom'd his father's soul to cross,
Who pens a stanza when he should engross?
Is there who, lock'd from ink and paper,
    scrawls
With desp'rate charcoal round his darken'd
    walls?   20
All fly to TWIT'NAM, and in humble strain
Apply to me to keep them mad or vain,
Arthur, whose giddy son neglects the laws,
Imputes to me and my damn'd works the
    cause:
Poor Cornus sees his frantic wife elope,
And curses Wit and Poetry, and Pope.
    Friend to my life (which did not you
      prolong,
The world had wanted many an idle song)!
What Drop or Nostrum can this plague
    remove?
Or which must end me, a fool's wrath or
    love?   30
A dire dilemma! either way I'm sped;
If foes, they write, if friends, they read me
    dead.
Seiz'd and tied down to judge, how wretched
    I!
Who can't be silent, and who will not lie.

To laugh were want of goodness and of
grace,
And to be grave exceeds all power of face.
I sit with sad civility, I read
With honest anguish and an aching head,
And drop at last, but in unwilling ears,
This saving counsel, ' Keep your piece nine
years.'   40
  ' Nine years ! ' cries he, who, high in
Drury lane,
Lull'd by soft zephyrs thro' the broken
pane,
Rhymes ere he wakes, and prints before
Term ends,
Obliged by hunger and request of friends:
' The piece, you think, is incorrect ? why,
take it !
I 'm all submission: what you 'd have it —
make it.'
    Three things another's modest wishes
bound,
' My friendship, and a Prologue, and ten
pound.'
    Pitholeon sends to me: " You know his
Grace,
I want a patron ; ask him for a place.'   50
Pitholeon libell'd me — ' But here 's a
letter
Informs you, Sir, 'twas when he knew no
better.
Dare you refuse him ? Curll invites to dine,
He 'll write a *Journal*, or he 'll turn Divine.'
Bless me! a packet. — 'T is a stranger sues,
A Virgin Tragedy, an Orphan Muse.
If I dislike it, ' Furies, death, and rage ! '
If I approve, ' Commend it to the stage.'
There (thank my stars) my whole commis-
sion ends,   59
The players and I are, luckily, no friends.
Fired that the house rejects him, ' 'Sdeath,
I 'll print it,
And shame the fools — your int'rest, Sir,
with Lintot.'
Lintot, dull rogue, will think your price too
much:
' Not, Sir, if you revise it, and retouch.'
All my demurs but double his attacks;
At last he whispers, ' Do, and we go
snacks.'
Glad of a quarrel, straight I clap the door;
' Sir, let me see your works and you no
more.'
    'T is sung, when Midas' ears began to
spring
(Midas, a sacred person and a king),   70

His very Minister who spied them first
(Some say his Queen) was forc'd to speak
or burst.
And is not mine, my friend, a sorer case,
When ev'ry coxcomb perks them in my
face ?
  A. Good friend, forbear! you deal in
dangerous things;
I 'd never name Queens, Ministers, or
Kings;
Keep close to ears, and those let asses
prick,
'T is nothing —   *P*. Nothing! if they bite
and kick ?
Out with it, DUNCIAD! let the secret pass,
That secret to each fool, that he 's an ass:
The truth once told (and wherefore should
we lie ?)   81
The Queen of Midas slept, and so may I.
    You think this cruel ? take it for a
rule,
No creature smarts so little as a fool.
Let peals of laughter, Codrus! round thee
break,
Thou unconcern'd canst hear the mighty
crack:
Pit, Box, and Gall'ry in convulsions hurl'd,
Thou stand'st unshook amidst a bursting
world.
Who shames a Scribbler ? break one cob-
web thro',
He spins the slight self-pleasing thread
anew: 90
Destroy his fib, or sophistry — in vain!
The creature 's at his dirty work again,
Throned in the centre of his thin designs,
Proud of a vast extent of flimsy lines.
Whom have I hurt ? has Poet yet or Peer
Lost the arch'd eyebrow or Parnassian
sneer ?
And has not Colley still his lord and whore ?
His butchers Henley ? his freemasons
Moore ?
Does not one table Bavius still admit ?
Still to one Bishop Philips seem a wit ? 100
Still Sappho —   *A*. Hold! for God's sake
— you 'll offend.
No names — be calm — learn prudence of
a friend:
I too could write, and I am twice as tall;
But foes like these —   *P*. One flatt'rer 's
worse than all.
Of all mad creatures, if the learn'd are
right,
It is the slaver kills, and not the bite.

A fool quite angry is quite innocent:
Alas! 't is ten times worse when they re-
   pent.
  One dedicates in high heroic prose,
And ridicules beyond a hundred foes;   110
One from all Grub-street will my fame
   defend,
And, more abusive, calls himself my friend:
This prints my *Letters*, that expects a bribe,
And others roar aloud, 'Subscribe, sub-
   scribe!'
  There are who to my person pay their
   court:
I cough like Horace; and tho' lean, am
   short;
Ammon's great son one shoulder had too
   high,
Such Ovid's nose, and 'Sir! you have an
   eye —'
Go on, obliging creatures! make me see
All that disgraced my betters met in me.
Say, for my comfort, languishing in bed, 121
'Just so immortal Maro held his head:'
And when I die, be sure you let me know
Great Homer died three thousand years
   ago.
  Why did I write? what sin to me un-
   known
Dipp'd me in ink, my parents', or my own?
As yet a child, nor yet a fool to fame,
I lisp'd in numbers, for the numbers came:
I left no calling for this idle trade,
No duty broke, no father disobey'd: 130
The Muse but serv'd to ease some friend,
   not wife,
To help me thro' this long disease my life,
To second, ARBUTHNOT! thy art and care,
And teach the being you preserv'd, to bear.
  A. But why then publish? *P.* Granville
   the polite,
And knowing Walsh, would tell me I could
   write;
Well-natured Garth inflamed with early
   praise,
And Congreve lov'd, and Swift endured my
   lays;
The courtly Talbot, Somers, Sheffield, read;
Ev'n mitred Rochester would nod the
   head,   140
And St. John's self (great Dryden's friends
   before)
With open arms receiv'd one poet more.
Happy my studies, when by these approv'd!
Happier their author, when by these be-
   lov'd!

From these the world will judge of men
   and books,
Not from the Burnets, Oldmixons, and
   Cookes.
  Soft were my numbers; who could take
   offence
While pure description held the place of
   sense?
Like gentle Fanny's was my flowery theme,
'A painted mistress, or a purling stream.'
Yet then did Gildon draw his venal quill; 151
I wish'd the man a dinner, and sat still:
Yet then did Dennis rave in furious fret;
I never answer'd; I was not in debt.
If want provoked, or madness made them
   print,
I waged no war with Bedlam or the Mint.
  Did some more sober critic come abroad;
If wrong, I smiled, if right, I kiss'd the
   rod.
Pains, reading, study, are their just pre-
   tence,
And all they want is spirit, taste, and
   sense.   160
Commas and points they set exactly right,
And 't were a sin to rob them of their mite.
Yet ne'er one sprig of laurel graced these
   ribalds,
From slashing Bentleys down to piddling
   Tibbalds.
Each wight who reads not, and but scans
   and spells,
Each word-catcher that lives on syllables,
Ev'n such small critics some regard may
   claim,
Preserv'd in Milton's or in Shakspeare's
   name.
Pretty! in amber to observe the forms
Of hairs, or straws, or dirt, or grubs, or
   worms!   170
The things, we know, are neither rich nor
   rare,
But wonder how the devil they got there.
  Were others angry: I excused them too;
Well might they rage, I gave them but
   their due.
A man's true merit 't is not hard to find;
But each man's secret standard in his
   mind,
That casting-weight Pride adds to empti-
   ness,
This, who can gratify? for who can guess?
The bard whom pilfer'd pastorals renown,
Who turns a Persian tale for half-a-
   crown,   180

Just writes to make his barrenness appear,
And strains from hard-bound brains eight
  lines a year;
He who still wanting, tho' he lives on theft,
Steals much, spends little, yet has nothing
  left;
And he who now to sense, now nonsense,
  leaning,
Means not, but blunders round about a
  meaning:
And he whose fustian 's so sublimely bad,
It is not poetry, but prose run mad:
All these my modest satire bade translate,
And own'd that nine such poets made a
  Tate.   190
How did they fume, and stamp, and roar,
  and chafe!
And swear not ADDISON himself was safe.
    Peace to all such! but were there one
      whose fires
True Genius kindles, and fair Fame in-
  spires,
Bless'd with each talent and each art to
  please,
And born to write, converse, and live with
  ease;
Should such a man, too fond to rule alone,
Bear, like the Turk, no brother near the
  throne;
View him with scornful, yet with jealous
  eyes,
And hate for arts that caus'd himself to
  rise;   200
Damn with faint praise, assent with civil
  leer,
And without sneering teach the rest to
  sneer;
Willing to wound, and yet afraid to strike,
Just hint a fault, and hesitate dislike;
Alike reserv'd to blame or to commend,
A tim'rous foe, and a suspicious friend;
Dreading ev'n fools; by flatterers besieged,
And so obliging that he ne'er obliged;
Like Cato, give his little Senate laws,
And sit attentive to his own applause: 210
While Wits and Templars ev'ry sentence
  raise,
And wonder with a foolish face of praise —
Who but must laugh if such a man there be ?
Who would not weep, if Atticus were he ?
    What tho' my name stood rubric on the
      walls,
Or plaster'd posts, with claps, in capitals ?
Or smoking forth, a hundred hawkers load,
On wings of winds came flying all abroad ?

I sought no homage from the race that
  write;
I kept, like Asian Monarchs, from their
  sight: 220
Poems I heeded (now berhymed so long)
No more than thou, great George! a birth-
  day song.
I ne'er with Wits or Witlings pass'd my
  days
To spread about the itch of verse and
  praise;
Nor like a puppy daggled thro' the town
To fetch and carry sing-song up and down;
Nor at rehearsals sweat, and mouth'd, and
  cried,
With handkerchief and orange at my side;
But sick of fops, and poetry, and prate,
To Bufo left the whole Castalian state. 230
    Proud as Apollo on his forked hill
Sat full-blown Bufo, puff'd by ev'ry
  quill:
Fed with soft dedication all day long,
Horace and he went hand in hand in song.
His library (where busts of poets dead,
And a true Pindar stood without a head)
Receiv'd of Wits an undistinguish'd race,
Who first his judgment ask'd, and then a
  place:
Much they extoll'd his pictures, much his
  seat,
And flatter'd ev'ry day, and some days
  eat: 240
Till grown more frugal in his riper days,
He paid some bards with port, and some
  with praise;
To some a dry rehearsal was assign'd,
And others (harder still) he paid in kind.
Dryden alone (what wonder ?) came not
  nigh;
Dryden alone escaped this judging eye:
But still the great have kindness in re-
  serve;
He help'd to bury whom he help'd to
  starve.
May some choice patron bless each gray
  goose quill!
May every Bavius have his Bufo still!   250
So when a statesman wants a day's de-
  fence,
Or Envy holds a whole week's war with
  Sense,
Or simple Pride for flatt'ry makes de-
  mands,
May dunce by dunce be whistled off my
  hands!

Bless'd be the great! for those they take
    away,
And those they left me — for they left me
    Gay;
Left me to see neglected Genius bloom,
Neglected die, and tell it on his tomb:
Of all thy blameless life the sole return
My Verse, and Queensb'ry weeping o'er
    thy urn!   260
  Oh let me live my own, and die so too
(To live and die is all I have to do)!
Maintain a poet's dignity and ease,
And see what friends, and read what books
    I please;
Above a Patron, tho' I condescend
Sometimes to call a minister my Friend.
I was not born for courts or great affairs;
I pay my debts, believe, and say my
    prayers;
Can sleep without a poem in my head,
Nor know if Dennis be alive or dead.   270
  Why am I ask'd what next shall see the
    light ?
Heav'ns! was I born for nothing but to
    write ?
Has life no joys for me ? or (to be grave)
Have I no friend to serve, no soul to save ?
'I found him close with Swift' — 'Indeed ?
    no doubt
(Cries prating Balbus) something will come
    out.'
'T is all in vain, deny it as I will;
'No, such a genius never can lie still:'
And then for mine obligingly mistakes   279
The first lampoon Sir Will or Bubo makes.
Poor guiltless I! and can I choose but smile,
When ev'ry coxcomb knows me by my
    style ?
  Curst be the verse, how well soe'er it
    flow,
That tends to make one worthy man my foe,
Give Virtue scandal, Innocence a fear,
Or from the soft-eyed virgin steal a tear!
But he who hurts a harmless neighbour's
    peace,
Insults fall'n Worth, or Beauty in distress,
Who loves a lie, lame Slander helps about,
Who writes a libel, or who copies out;   290
That fop whose pride affects a patron's
    name,
Yet absent, wounds an author's honest
    fame;
Who can your merit selfishly approve,
And show the sense of it without the
    love:

Who has the vanity to call you friend,
Yet wants the honour, injured, to defend;
Who tells whate'er you think, whate'er you
    say,
And, if he lie not, must at least betray;
Who to the Dean and Silver Bell can
    swear,   299
And sees at Canons what was never there;
Who reads but with a lust to misapply,
Make satire a lampoon, and fiction lie:
A lash like mine no honest man shall dread,
But all such babbling blockheads in his
    stead.
  Let Sporus tremble — A. What ? that
    thing of silk,
Sporus, that mere white curd of Ass's
    milk ?
Satire or sense, alas ! can Sporus feel ?
Who breaks a butterfly upon a wheel ?
  P. Yet let me flap this bug with gilded
    wings,
This painted child of dirt, that stinks and
    stings;   310
Whose buzz the witty and the fair annoys,
Yet Wit ne'er tastes, and Beauty ne'er en-
    joys;
So well-bred spaniels civilly delight
In mumbling of the game they dare not bite.
Eternal smiles his emptiness betray,
As shallow streams run dimpling all the
    way,
Whether in florid impotence he speaks,
And, as the prompter breathes, the puppet
    squeaks,
Or at the ear of Eve, familiar toad,
Half froth, half venom, spits himself
    abroad,   320
In puns, or politics, or tales, or lies,
Or spite, or smut, or rhymes, or blasphem-
    ies;
His wit all see-saw between *that* and *this*,⎫
Now high, now low, now master up, now ⎬
    miss, ⎭
And he himself one vile Antithesis.
Amphibious thing ! that acting either part,
The trifling head, or the corrupted heart;
Fop at the toilet, flatt'rer at the board,
Now trips a lady, and now struts a lord.
Eve's tempter thus the Rabbins have ex-
    prest,   330
A cherub's face, a reptile all the rest;
Beauty that shocks you, Parts that none
    will trust,
Wit that can creep, and Pride that licks
    the dust.

Not Fortune's worshipper, nor Fashion's
    fool,
Not Lucre's madman, nor Ambition's tool,
Not proud nor servile; — be one poet's
    praise,
That if he pleas'd, he pleas'd by manly
    ways:
That flatt'ry ev'n to Kings, he held a
    shame,
And thought a lie in verse or prose the
    same;   339
That not in fancy's maze he wander'd long,
But stoop'd to truth, and moralized his
    song;
That not for Fame, but Virtue's better end,
He stood the furious foe, the timid friend,
The damning critic, half approving wit,
The coxcomb hit, or fearing to be hit;
Laugh'd at the loss of friends he never had,
The dull, the proud, the wicked, and the
    mad;
The distant threats of vengeance on his
    head,
The blow unfelt, the tear he never shed; 349
The tale revived, the lie so oft o'erthrown,
Th' imputed trash and dulness not his
    own;
The morals blacken'd when the writings
    'scape,
The libell'd person, and the pictured shape;
Abuse on all he lov'd, or lov'd him, spread,
A friend in exile, or a father dead;
The whisper, that, to greatness still too
    near,
Perhaps yet vibrates on his SOV'REIGN'S
    ear —
Welcome for thee, fair Virtue! all the
    past:
For thee, fair Virtue! welcome ev'n the
    last!
    A. But why insult the poor? affront the
    great?   360
    P. A knave 's a knave to me in ev'ry state;
Alike my scorn, if he succeed or fail,
Sporus at court, or Japhet in a jail;
A hireling scribbler, or a hireling peer,
Knight of the post corrupt, or of the shire;
If on a Pillory, or near a Throne,
He gain his prince's ear, or lose his own.
    Yet soft by nature, more a dupe than
    wit,
Sappho can tell you how this man was bit:
This dreaded Satirist Dennis will confess
Foe, to his pride, but friend to his dis-
    tress: 371

So humble, he has knock'd at Tibbald's
    door,
Has drunk with Cibber, nay, has rhymed for
    Moore.
Full ten years slander'd, did he once re-
    ply?
Three thousand suns went down on Wel-
    sted's lie.
To please a mistress one aspers'd his life;
He lash'd him not, but let her be his wife:
Let Budgell charge low Grub-street on his
    quill,
And write whate'er he pleased, except his
    will;   379
Let the two Curlls of town and court abuse
His father, mother, body, soul, and muse:
Yet why? that father held it for a rule,
It was a sin to call our neighbour fool;
That harmless mother thought no wife a
    whore:
Hear this, and spare his family, James
    Moore!
Unspotted names, and memorable long,
If there be force in Virtue, or in Song.
    Of gentle blood (part shed in honour's
    cause,
While yet in Britain honour had applause)
Each parent sprung — A. What fortune,
    pray? —
    P.   Their own;   390
And better got than Bestia's from the
    throne.
Born to no pride, inheriting no strife,
Nor marrying discord in a noble wife,
Stranger to civil and religious rage,
The good man walk'd innoxious thro' his
    age.
No courts he saw, no suits would ever try,
Nor dared an oath, nor hazarded a lie.
Unlearn'd, he knew no schoolman's subtle
    art,
No language but the language of the heart.
By Nature honest, by Experience wise, 400
Healthy by Temp'rance and by Exercise;
His life, tho' long, to sickness pass'd un-
    known,
His death was instant and without a groan.
O grant me thus to live, and thus to die!
Who sprung from kings shall know less joy
    than I.
    O friend! may each domestic bliss be
    thine!
Be no unpleasing melancholy mine:
Me, let the tender office long engage
To rock the cradle of reposing Age,   409

With lenient arts extend a Mother's breath,
Make Languor smile, and smooth the bed
of Death;
Explore the thought, explain the asking
eye,
And keep a while one parent from the sky !
On cares like these if length of days attend,
May Heav'n, to bless those days, preserve
my friend !
Preserve him social, cheerful, and serene,
And just as rich as when he serv'd a Queen.
A. Whether that blessing be denied or
giv'n,
Thus far was right; — the rest belongs to
Heav'n.

SATIRES, EPISTLES, AND ODES OF HORACE IMITATED

Ludentis speciem dabit, et torquebitur. — HOR.

ADVERTISEMENT

The occasion of publishing these Imitations
was the clamour raised on some of my Epistles. An answer from Horace was both more
full and of more dignity than any I could
have made in my own person ; and the example of much greater freedom in so eminent a divine as Dr. Donne, seemed a proof
with what indignation and contempt a Christian may treat Vice or Folly, in ever so low
or ever so high a station. Both these authors
were acceptable to the Princes and Ministers
under whom they lived. The satires of Dr.
Donne I versified at the desire of the Earl of
Oxford, while he was Lord Treasurer, and of
the Duke of Shrewsbury, who had been Secretary of State ; neither of whom looked
upon a satire on vicious courts as any reflection on those they served in. And indeed
there is not in the world a greater error than
that which fools are so apt to fall into, and
knaves with good reason to encourage, — the
mistaking a Satirist for a Libeller; whereas
to a true Satirist nothing is so odious as a
Libeller, for the same reason as to a man
truly virtuous nothing is so hateful as a
hypocrite.

Uni æquus virtuti atque ejus amicis.

THE FIRST SATIRE OF THE SECOND BOOK OF HORACE

This satire was first published in 1733, under
the title *A Dialogue between Alexander Pope of*

*Twickenham, on the one part, and the Learned
Counsel on the other.*

TO MR. FORTESCUE

P. THERE are (I scarce can think it, but
am told),
There are to whom my satire seems too
bold;
Scarce to wise Peter complaisant enough,
And something said of Chartres much too
rough.
The lines are weak, another 's pleas'd to
say;
Lord Fanny spins a thousand such a day.
Tim'rous by nature, of the rich in awe,
I come to counsel learned in the law:
You 'll give me, like a friend both sage and
free,
Advice; and (as you use) without a fee. 10
F. I'd write no more.
         P. Not write ? but then I think,
And for my soul I cannot sleep a wink.
I nod in company, I wake at night;
Fools rush into my head, and so I write.
    F. You could not do a worse thing for
your life.
Why, if the night seem tedious — take a
wife:
Or rather, truly, if your point be rest,
Lettuce and cowslip wine: *probatum est.*
But talk with Celsus, Celsus will advise
Hartshorn, or something that shall close
your eyes. 20
Or if you needs must write, write Cæsar's
praise;
You 'll gain at least a Knighthood or the
Bays.
    P. What ? like Sir Richard, rumbling,
rough, and fierce,
With Arms, and GEORGE, and Brunswick,
crowd the verse;
Rend with tremendous sound your ears
asunder,
With gun, drum, trumpet, blunderbuss, and
thunder ?
Or nobly wild, with Budgell's fire and
force,
Paint angels trembling round his falling
horse ?
    F. Then all your Muse's softer art dis-
play,
Let Carolina smooth the tuneful lay; 30
Lull with Amelia's liquid name the Nine,
And sweetly flow thro' all the royal line.

P. Alas! few verses touch their nicer ear;
They scarce can bear their Laureate twice a year;
And justly Cæsar scorns the poet's lays;
It is to history he trusts for praise.
F. Better be Cibber, I 'll maintain it still,
Than ridicule all Taste, blaspheme Quadrille,
Abuse the city's best good men in metre,
And laugh at peers that put their trust in Peter.   40
Ev'n those you touch not, hate you.
      P. What should ail 'em ?
F. A hundred smart in Timon and in Balaam.
The fewer still you name, you wound the more;
Bond is but one, but Harpax is a score.
P. Each mortal has his pleasure: none deny
Scarsdale his bottle, Darty his ham-pie:
Ridotta sips and dances till she see
The doubling lustres dance as fast as she:
F[ox] loves the Senate, Hockley-hole his brother,
Like in all else, as one egg to another.   50
I love to pour out all myself as plain
As downright Shippen, or as old Montaigne:
In them, as certain to be lov'd as seen,
The soul stood forth, nor kept a thought within;
In me what spots (for spots I have) appear,
Will prove at least the medium must be clear.
In this impartial glass my Muse intends
Fair to expose myself, my foes, my friends;
Publish the present age; but where my text
Is vice too high, reserve it for the next;   60
My foes shall wish my life a longer date,
And ev'ry friend the less lament my fate.
My head and heart thus flowing thro' my quill,
Verse-man or prose-man, term me which you will,
Papist or Protestant, or both between,
Like good Erasmus, in an honest mean,
In moderation placing all my glory,
While Tories call me Whig, and Whigs a Tory.
Satire 's my weapon, but I 'm too discreet
To run amuck, and tilt at all I meet;   70

I only wear it in a land of Hectors,
Thieves, supercargoes, sharpers, and directors.
Save but our Army! and let Jove incrust
Swords, pikes, and guns, with everlasting rust!
Peace is my dear delight — not Fleury's more:
But touch me, and no minister so sore.
Whoe'er offends, at some unlucky time
Slides into verse, and hitches in a rhyme,
Sacred to ridicule his whole life long,   79
And the sad burden of some merry song.
   Slander or poison dread from Delia's rage;
Hard words or hanging, if your judge be Page;
From furious Sappho scarce a milder fate,
Pox'd by her love, or libell'd by her hate.
Its proper power to hurt each creature feels;
Bulls aim their horns, and asses lift their heels;
'T is a bear's talent not to kick, but hug;
And no man wonders he 's not stung by Pug.
So drink with Walters, or with Chartres eat,
They 'll never poison you, they 'll only cheat.   90
   Then, learned Sir! (to cut the matter short)
Whate'er my fate, — or well or ill at court,
Whether old age, with faint but cheerful ray,
Attends to gild the ev'ning of my day,
Or death's black wing already be display'd,
To wrap me in the universal shade;
Whether the darken'd room to muse invite,
Or whiten'd wall provoke the skewer to write;
In durance, exile, Bedlam, or the Mint, —
Like Lee or Budgell I will rhyme and print.   100
   F. Alas, young man, your days can ne'er be long:
In flower of age you perish for a song!
Plums and directors, Shylock and his wife,
Will club their testers now to take your life.
   P. What ? arm'd for Virtue when I point the pen,
Brand the bold front of shameless guilty men.

Dash the proud Gamester in his gilded car,
Bare the mean heart that lurks beneath a
     Star;
Can there be wanting, to defend her cause,
Lights of the Church, or guardians of the
     Laws ?   110
Could pension'd Boileau lash in honest
     strain
Flatt'rers and bigots ev'n in Louis' reign ?
Could Laureate Dryden pimp and friar
     engage,
Yet neither Charles nor James be in a rage ?
And I not strip the gilding off a knave,
Unplaced, unpension'd, no man's heir or
     slave ?
I will, or perish in the gen'rous cause;
Hear this, and tremble! you who 'scape
     the laws.
Yes, while I live, no rich or noble knave
Shall walk the world in credit to his
     grave: 120
To VIRTUE only and her Friends a friend,
The world beside may murmur or com-
     mend.
Know, all the distant din that world can
     keep,
Rolls o'er my grotto and but soothes my
     sleep.
     There my retreat the best companions
     grace,
Chiefs out of war, and statesmen out of
     place:
There St. John mingles with my friendly
     bowl
The feast of reason and the flow of soul:
And he, whose lightning pierced th' Iberian
     lines,
Now forms my quincunx, and now ranks
     my vines;   130
Or tames the genius of the stubborn plain,
Almost as quickly as he conquer'd Spain.
     Envy must own I live among the great,
No pimp of Pleasure, and no spy of State,
With eyes that pry not, tongue that ne'er
     repeats,
Fond to spread friendships, but to cover
     heats;
To help who want, to forward who excel;
This all who know me, know; who love
     me, tell;
And who unknown defame me, let them be
Scribblers or peers, alike are Mob to me. 140
This is my plea, on this I rest my cause —
What saith my counsel, learned in the
     laws ?

F. Your plea is good; but still I say, be-
     ware!
Laws are explain'd by men — so have a
     care.
It stands on record, that in Richard's times
A man was hang'd for very honest rhymes.
Consult the statute; *quart.* I think it is,
Edwardi sext. or *prim. et quint. Eliz.*
See Libels, Satires — here you have it —
     read.
P. Libels and Satires! lawless things in-
     deed!   150
But grave epistles, bringing Vice to light,
Such as a King might read, a Bishop write,
Such as Sir Robert would approve — F.
     Indeed!
The case is alter'd — you may then pro-
     ceed:
In such a cause the Plaintiff will be hiss'd,
My Lords the Judges laugh, and you 're
     dismiss'd.

THE SECOND SATIRE OF THE
SECOND BOOK OF HORACE

TO MR. BETHEL

WHAT, and how great, the Virtue and the
     Art
To live on little with a cheerful heart!
(A doctrine sage, but truly none of mine)
Let 's talk, my friends, but talk before we
     dine;
Not when a gilt buffet's reflected pride
Turns you from sound Philosophy aside;
Not when from plate to plate your eyeballs
     roll,
And the brain dances to the mantling bowl.
     Hear Bethel's sermon, one not vers'd in
     schools
But strong in sense, and wise without the
     rules.   10
     'Go work, hunt, exercise! (he thus be-
     gan)
Then scorn a homely dinner if you can.
Your wine lock'd up, your butler stroll'd
     abroad,
Or fish denied (the river yet unthaw'd);
If then plain bread and milk will do the
     feat,
The pleasure lies in you, and not the meat.'
     Preach as I please, I doubt our curious
     men
Will choose a pheasant still before a hen;

Yet hens of Guinea full as good I hold,
Except you eat the feathers green and
    gold. 20
Of carps and mullets why prefer the great,
(Tho' cut in pieces ere my Lord can eat)
Yet for small turbots such esteem profess ?
Because God made these large, the other
    less.
Oldfield, with more than harpy throat
    endued,
Cries, 'Send me, Gods! a whole Hog bar-
    becued!'
O blast it, South-winds! till a stench ex-
    hale
Rank as the ripeness of a rabbit's tail.
By what criterion do you eat, d' ye think,
If this is prized for sweetness, that for
    stink ? 30
When the tired glutton labours thro' a
    treat,
He finds no relish in the sweetest meat;
He calls for something bitter, something
    sour,
And the rich feast concludes extremely
    poor:
Cheap eggs, and herbs, and olives, still we
    see;
Thus much is left of old Simplicity!
The robin-redbreast till of late had rest,
And children sacred held a martin's nest,
Till becaficos sold so devilish dear
To one that was, or would have been, a
    Peer. 40
Let me extol a cat on oysters fed;
I 'll have a party at the Bedford-head:
Or ev'n to crack live crawfish recommend;
I 'd never doubt at court to make a friend!
'T is yet in vain, I own, to keep a pother
About one vice, and fall into the other:
Between Excess and Famine lies a mean;
Plain, but not sordid; tho' not splendid,
    clean.
Avidien or his wife (no matter which, 49
For him you 'll call a dog, and her a bitch)
Sell their presented partridges and fruits,
And humbly live on rabbits and on roots:
One half-pint bottle serves them both to
    dine,
And is at once their vinegar and wine:
But on some lucky day (as when they
    found
A lost bank-bill, or heard their son was
    drown'd)
At such a feast, old vinegar to spare,
Is what two souls so gen'rous cannot bear:

Oil, tho' it stink, they drop by drop impart,
But souse the cabbage with a bounteous
    heart. 60
He knows to live who keeps the middle
    state,
And neither leans on this side nor on that;
Nor stops for one bad cork his butler's pay,
Swears, like Albutius, a good cook away;
Nor lets, like Nævius, ev'ry error pass,
The musty wine, foul cloth, or greasy glass.
    Now hear what blessings Temperance
    can bring
(Thus said our friend, and what he said I
    sing):
First Health: the stomach (cramm'd from
    ev'ry dish,
A tomb of boil'd and roast, and flesh and
    fish, 70
Where bile, and wind, and phlegm, and
    acid, jar,
And all the man is one intestine war)
Remembers oft the schoolboy's simple fare,
The temp'rate sleeps, and spirits light as
    air.
How pale each worshipful and rev'rend
    guest
Rise from a clergy or a city feast!
What life in all that ample body, say ?
What heav'nly particle inspires the clay ?
The Soul subsides, and wickedly inclines
To seem but mortal ev'n in sound Divines.
    On morning wings how active springs the
    mind 81
That leaves the load of yesterday behind!
How easy every labour it pursues!
How coming to the Poet ev'ry Muse!
Not but we may exceed, some holy-time,
Or tired in search of Truth or search of
    Rhyme:
Ill health some just indulgence may en-
    gage,
And more the sickness of long life, old age:
For fainting age what cordial drop remains,
If our intemp'rate youth the vessel drains ?
    Our fathers prais'd rank venison. You
    suppose, 91
Perhaps, young men! our fathers had no
    nose.
Not so: a buck was then a week's repast,
And 't was their point, I ween, to make it
    last;
More pleas'd to keep it till their friends
    could come,
Than eat the sweetest by themselves at
    home.

Why had not I in those good times my
    birth,
Ere coxcomb-pies or coxcombs were on
    earth ?
  Unworthy he the voice of Fame to hear,
That sweetest music to an honest ear   100
(For 'faith, Lord Fanny! you are in the
    wrong,
The world's good word is better than a
    song),
Who has not learn'd fresh sturgeon and
    ham-pie
Are no rewards for want and infamy!
When Luxury has lick'd up all thy pelf,
Curs'd by thy neighbours, thy trustees,
    thyself;
To friends, to fortune, to mankind a shame,
Think how posterity will treat thy name;
And buy a rope, that future times may tell
Thou hast at least bestow'd one penny well.
  ' Right,' cries his lordship, ' for a rogue
    in need   111
To have a taste is insolence indeed:
In me 't is noble, suits my birth and state,
My wealth unwieldy, and my heap too
    great.'
Then, like the sun, let Bounty spread her
    ray,
And shine that superfluity away.
Oh impudence of wealth! with all thy store
How darest thou let one worthy man be
    poor ?
Shall half the new-built churches round
    thee fall ?
Make quays, build bridges, or repair White-
    hall;   120
Or to thy country let that heap be lent,
As M[arlbor]o's was, but not at five per
    cent.
  ' Who thinks that Fortune cannot change
    her mind,
Prepares a dreadful jest for all mankind.
And who stands safest ? tell me, is it he
That spreads and swells in puff'd prosperity,
Or bless'd with little, whose preventing
    care
In peace provides fit arms against a war ? '
  Thus Bethel spoke, who always speaks
    his thought,
And always thinks the very thing he ought:
His equal mind I copy what I can,   131
And as I love, would imitate the man.
In South-Sea days, not happier, when sur-
    mised
The lord of thousands, than if now excised;

In forest planted by a father's hand,
Than in five acres now of rented land.
Content with little, I can piddle here
On brocoli and mutton round the year;
But ancient friends (tho' poor, or out of
    play)
That touch my bell, I cannot turn away.   140
'T is true, no turbots dignify my boards,
But gudgeons, flounders, what my Thames
    affords:
To Hounslow Heath I point, and Banstead
    Down,
Thence comes your mutton, and these
    chicks my own:
From yon old walnut tree a shower shall
    fall,
And grapes long ling'ring on my only wall;
And figs from standard and espalier join;
The devil is in you if you cannot dine:
Then cheerful healths (your Mistress shall
    have place),
And, what 's more rare, a Poet shall say
    grace.   150
  Fortune not much of humbling me can
    boast;
Tho' double tax'd, how little have I lost!
My life's amusements have been just the
    same,
Before and after standing armies came.
My lands are sold, my father's house is
    gone;
I 'll hire another's; is not that my own —
And yours, my friends — thro' whose free
    opening gate
None comes too early, none departs too
    late ?
(For I, who hold sage Homer's rule the
    best,
Welcome the coming, speed the going
    guest.)   160
  ' Pray Heav'n it last! (cries Swift) as
    you go on:
I wish to God this house had been your
    own!
Pity! to build without a son or wife:
Why, you 'll enjoy it only all your life.'
Well, if the use be mine, can it concern
    one
Whether the name belong to Pope or Ver-
    non ?
What 's property ? dear Swift! you see it
    alter
From you to me, from me to Peter Walter;
Or in a mortgage prove a lawyer's share,
Or in a jointure vanish from the heir;   170

Or in pure equity (the case not clear)
The Chancery takes your rents for twenty
    year:
At best it falls to some ungracious son,
Who cries, ' My father 's damn'd, and all 's
    my own.'
Shades, that to Bacon could retreat afford,
Become the portion of a booby lord;
And Hemsley, once proud Buckingham's
    delight,
Slides to a scriv'ner or a city knight.
Let lands and houses have what lords they
    will,   179
Let us be fix'd, and our own masters still.

THE FIRST EPISTLE OF THE FIRST BOOK OF HORACE

TO LORD BOLINGBROKE

St. John, whose love indulged my labours
    past,
Matures my present, and shall bound my
    last,
Why will you break the Sabbath of my
    days ?
Now sick alike of envy and of praise.
Public too long, ah ! let me hide my Age:
See modest Cibber now has left the Stage:
Our gen'rals now, retired to their estates,
Hang their old trophies o'er the garden
    gates;
In life's cool ev'ning satiate of applause,
Nor fond of bleeding ev'n in Brunswick's
    cause.   10
A voice there is, that whispers in my ear
('T is Reason's voice, which sometimes one
    can hear),
'Friend Pope! be prudent, let your Muse
    take breath,
And never gallop Pegasus to death;
Lest stiff and stately, void of fire or force,
You limp, like Blackmore, on a lord
    mayor's horse.'
Farewell then Verse, and Love, and ev'ry
    toy,
The rhymes and rattles of the Man or Boy;
What right, what true, what fit, we justly
    call,
Let this be all my care — for this is all; 20
To lay this harvest up, and hoard with
    haste
What ev'ry day will want, and most the
    last.

But ask not to what Doctors I apply;
Sworn to no master, of no sect am I:
As drives the storm, at any door I knock,
And house with Montaigne now, or now
    with Locke.
Sometimes a patriot, active in debate,
Mix with the world, and battle for the
    state;
Free as young Lyttleton, her cause pursue,
Still true to Virtue, and as warm as true: 30
Sometimes with Aristippus or St. Paul,
Indulge my candour, and grow all to all ;
Back to my native Moderation slide,
And win my way by yielding to the tide.
    Long as to him who works for debt the
    day,
Long as the night to her whose love 's away,
Long as the year's dull circle seems to run
When the brisk minor pants for twenty-
    one;
So slow th' unprofitable moments roll
That lock up all the functions of my soul, 40
That keep me from myself, and still delay
Life's instant business to a future day;
That task which as we follow or despise,
The eldest is a fool, the youngest wise;
Which done, the poorest can no wants en-
    dure;
And which not done, the richest must be
    poor.
    Late as it is, I put myself to school,
And feel some comfort not to be a fool.
Weak tho' I am of limb, and short of sight,
Far from a lynx, and not a giant quite, 50
I 'll do what Mead and Cheselden advise,
To keep these limbs, and to preserve these
    eyes.
Not to go back is somewhat to advance,
And men must walk, at least, before they
    dance.
    Say, does thy blood rebel, thy bosom
    move
With wretched Av'rice, or as wretched
    Love ?
Know there are words and spells which can
    control,
Between the fits, this fever of the soul;
Know there are rhymes which, fresh and
    fresh applied,   59
Will cure the arrant'st puppy of his pride.
Be furious, envious, slothful, mad, or drunk,
Slave to a wife, or vassal to a punk,
A Switz, a High-Dutch or a Low-Dutch
    bear;
All that we ask is but a patient ear.

'T is the first virtue vices to abhor,
And the first wisdom to be fool no more:
But to the world no bugbear is so great
As want of figure and a small Estate.
To either India see the merchant fly,
Scared at the spectre of pale Poverty! 70
See him with pains of body, pangs of
    soul,
Burn thro' the Tropics, freeze beneath the
    Pole!
Wilt thou do nothing for a nobler end,
Nothing to make Philosophy thy friend?
To stop thy foolish views, thy long desires,
And ease thy heart of all that it admires?
Here Wisdom calls, 'Seek Virtue first, be
    bold!
As gold to silver, Virtue is to gold.'
There London's voice, 'Get money, money
    still!
And then let Virtue follow if she will.' 80
This, this the saving doctrine preach'd to
    all,
From low St. James's up to high St. Paul;
From him whose quills stand quiver'd at
    his ear,
To him who notches sticks at Westmin-
    ster.
    Barnard in spirit, sense, and truth
        abounds;
'Pray then what wants he?' Fourscore
    thousand pounds;
A pension, or such harness for a slave
As Bug now has, and Dorimant would
    have.
Barnard, thou art a cit, with all thy worth;
But Bug and D*l their Honours! and so
    forth. 90
Yet ev'ry child another song will sing,
'Virtue, brave boys! 't is Virtue makes a
    King.'
True, conscious Honour is to feel no sin;
He's arm'd without that 's innocent within:
Be this thy screen, and this thy wall of
    brass;
Compared to this a Minister's an Ass.
    And say, to which shall our applause be-
        long,
This new Court jargon, or the good old
    song?
The modern language of corrupted peers,
Or what was spoke at Cressy and Poic-
    tiers? 100
Who counsels best? who whispers, 'Be
    but great,
With praise or infamy — leave that to Fate;

Get Place and Wealth, if possible with
    grace;
If not, by any means get Wealth and
    Place:'
(For what? to have a Box where eunuchs
    sing,
And foremost in the circle eye a King?)
Or he who bids thee face with steady view ⎫
Proud Fortune, and look shallow Great- ⎪
    ness thro',   ⎬
And, while he bids thee, sets th' example ⎪
    too?   ⎭
If such a doctrine, in St. James's air, 110
Should chance to make the well-drest
    rabble stare;
If honest S[chut]z take scandal at a spark
That less admires the Palace than the
    Park;
Faith, I shall give the answer Reynard
    gave:
'I cannot like, dread Sir! your royal cave;
Because I see, by all the tracks about,
Full many a beast goes in, but none come
    out.'
Adieu to Virtue, if you're once a slave:
Send her to Court, you send her to her
    grave.
    Well, if a King's a lion, at the least 120
The people are a many-headed beast;
Can they direct what measures to pursue,
Who know themselves so little what to
    do?
Alike in nothing but one lust of gold,
Just half the land would buy, and half be
    sold:
Their country's wealth our mightier misers
    drain,
Or cross, to plunder provinces, the main;
The rest, some farm the Poor-box, some
    the Pews;
Some keep Assemblies, and would keep the
    Stews;
Some with fat bucks on childless dotards
    fawn;   130
Some win rich widows by their chine and
    brawn;
While with the silent growth of ten per
    cent.,
In dirt and darkness, hundreds stink con-
    tent.
    Of all these ways, if each pursues his
        own,
Satire, be kind, and let the wretch alone;
But show me one who has it in his power
To act consistent with himself an hour.

Sir Job sail'd forth, the ev'ning bright and
still,
'No place on earth (he cried) like Green-
wich hill!'   139
Up starts a palace: lo, th' obedient base ⎤
Slopes at its foot, the woods its sides em- ⎥
brace,   ⎬
The silver Thames reflects its marble face. ⎦
Now let some whimsy, or that Devil ⎤
within   ⎥
Which guides all those who know not ⎥
what they mean,   ⎬
But give the Knight (or give his Lady) ⎥
spleen;   ⎦
'Away, away! take all your scaffolds down,
For snug's the word: My dear! we'll live
in town.'
    At am'rous Flavio is the stocking
thrown?
That very night he longs to lie alone.
The fool whose wife elopes some thrice a
quarter,   150
For matrimonial solace dies a martyr.
Did ever Proteus, Merlin, any witch, ⎤
Transform themselves so strangely as ⎥
the Rich?   ⎬
Well, but the Poor — the Poor have the ⎥
same itch;   ⎦
They change their weekly barber, weekly
news,
Prefer a new japanner to their shoes,
Discharge their garrets, move their beds,
and run
(They know not whither) in a chaise and
one;
They hire their sculler, and when once
aboard
Grow sick. and damn the climate — like a
Lord.   160
    You laugh, half Beau, half Sloven if I
stand,
My wig all powder, and all snuff my band;
You laugh if coat and breeches strangely
vary,
White gloves, and linen worthy Lady Mary!
But when no prelate's lawn, with hair-shirt
lin'd,
Is half so incoherent as my mind,
When (each opinion with the next at strife,
One ebb and flow of follies all my life)
I plant, root up, I build, and then confound;
Turn round to square, and square again to
round;   170
You never change one muscle of your face,
You think this madness but a common case;

Nor once to Chancery nor to Hale apply,
Yet hang your lip to see a seam awry!
Careless how ill I with myself agree,
Kind to my dress, my figure, — not to me.
Is this my Guide, Philosopher, and Friend?
This he who loves me, and who ought to
mend?
Who ought to make me (what he can, or
none)
That man divine whom Wisdom calls her
own;   180
Great without Title, without Fortune
bless'd;
Rich ev'n when plunder'd, honour'd while
oppress'd;
Lov'd without youth, and follow'd without
power;
At home tho' exiled, free tho' in the Tower;
In short, that reas'ning, high, immortal
thing,
Just less than Jove, and much above a
King;
Nay, half in Heav'n — except (what's
mighty odd)
A fit of Vapours clouds this Demigod.

THE SIXTH EPISTLE OF THE FIRST BOOK OF HORACE

TO MR. MURRAY

'Not to admire, is all the art I know,
To make men happy, and to keep them so.'
(Plain truth, dear Murray! needs no flow-
ers of speech,
So take it in the very words of Creech.)
    This vault of air, this congregated ball,
Self-centred sun, and stars that rise and
fall,
There are, my Friend! whose philosophic
eyes
Look thro', and trust the Ruler with his
skies;
To him commit the hour, the day, the
year,
And view this dreadful All — without a
fear.   10
    Admire we then what earth's low en- ⎤
trails hold,   ⎥
Arabian shores, or Indian seas infold; ⎬
All the mad trade of fools and slaves for ⎥
gold?   ⎦
Or Popularity? or Stars and Strings?
The Mob's applauses, or the gifts of Kings?

Say with what eyes we ought at courts to
  gaze,
And pay the great our homage of amaze ?
If weak the pleasure that from these
  can spring,
The fear to want them is as weak a thing:
Whether we dread, or whether we desire, 20
In either case, believe me, we admire:
Whether we joy or grieve, the same the
  curse,
Surprised at better, or surprised at worse.
Thus good or bad, to one extreme betray
Th' unbalanc'd mind, and snatch the man
  away;
For Virtue's self may too much zeal be had;
The worst of madmen is a saint run mad.
  Go then, and if you can, admire the state
Of beaming diamonds and reflected plate;
Procure a Taste to double the surprise, 30
And gaze on Parian charms with learned
  eyes;
Be struck with bright brocade or Tyrian dye,
Our birthday nobles' splendid livery.
If not so pleas'd, at council-board rejoice
To see their judgments hang upon thy
  voice;
From morn to night, at Senate, Rolls, and
  Hall,
Plead much, read more, dine late, or not at
  all.
But wherefore all this labour, all this strife ?
For Fame, for Riches, for a noble Wife ?
Shall one whom Nature, Learning, Birth,
  conspired   40
To form, not to admire, but be admired,
Sigh while his Chloë, blind to Wit and
  Worth,
Weds the rich dulness of some son of
  earth ?
Yet Time ennobles or degrades each line;
It brighten'd Craggs's, and may darken
  thine.
And what is Fame ? the meanest have their
  day;
The greatest can but blaze and pass away.
Graced as thou art with all the power of
  words,
So known, so honour'd, at the House of
  Lords:
Conspicuous scene! another yet is nigh 50
(More silent far), where Kings and Poets
  lie;
Where Murray (long enough his country's
  pride)
Shall be no more than Tully or than Hyde!

Rack'd with sciatics, martyr'd with the
  stone,
Will any mortal let himself alone ?
See Ward, by batter'd Beaux invited over,
And desp'rate misery lays hold on Dover.
The case is easier in the mind's disease;
There all men may be cured whene'er they
  please.
Would ye be bless'd ? despise low joys,⎫
  low gains;   60 ⎬
Disdain whatever Cornbury disdains;   ⎪
Be virtuous, and be happy for your pains. ⎭
  But art thou one whom new opinions
  sway,
One who believes as Tindal leads the way ?
Who Virtue and a Church alike disowns,
Thinks that but words, and this but brick
  and stones ?
Fly then on all the wings of wild desire,
Admire whate'er the maddest can admire.
Is Wealth thy passion ? hence ! from pole
  to pole,
Where winds can carry, or where waves
  can roll,   70
For Indian spices, for Peruvian gold,
Prevent the greedy, and outbid the bold:
Advance thy golden mountain to the skies;
On the broad base of fifty thousand rise;
Add one round hundred, and (if that's not
  fair)
Add fifty more, and bring it to a square:
For, mark th' advantage; just so many
  score
Will gain a wife with half as many more,
Procure her beauty, make that beauty
  chaste,
And then such friends — as cannot fail to
  last.   80
A man of Wealth is dubb'd a man of
  Worth;
Venus shall give him form, and Antis birth.
(Believe me, many a German Prince is
  worse,
Who proud of pedigree is poor of purse.)
His Wealth brave Timon gloriously con-
  founds;
Ask'd for a groat, he gives a hundred
  pounds;
Or if three ladies like a luckless play,
Takes the whole house upon the poet's day.
Now, in such exigencies not to need,
Upon my word you must be rich indeed: 90
A noble superfluity it craves,
Not for yourself, but for your fools and
  knaves:

Something which for your honour they may
cheat,
And which it much becomes you to forget.
If Wealth alone then make and keep us
blest,
Still, still be getting; never, never rest.
But if to Power and Place your passion
lie,
If in the pomp of life consist the joy;
Then hire a slave, or (if you will) a Lord,
To do the honours, and to give the word;
Tell at your Levee, as the crowds ap-
proach,   101
To whom to nod, whom take into your
coach,
Whom honour with your hand; to make
remarks,
Who rules in Cornwall, or who rules in
Berks:
'This may be troublesome, is near the
chair;
That makes three Members, this can choose
a Mayor.'
Instructed thus, you bow, embrace, pro-
test,
Adopt him son, or cousin at the least,
Then turn about, and laugh at your own
jest.
Or if your life be one continued treat, 110
If to live well means nothing but to eat;
Up, up! cries Gluttony, 't is break of day,
Go drive the deer, and drag the finny
prey:
With hounds and horns go hunt an appe-
tite —
So Russell did, but could not eat at night;
Call'd happy dog the beggar at his door,
And envied thirst and hunger to the poor.
Or shall we every decency confound,
Thro' Taverns, Stews, and Bagnios, take
our round?   119
Go dine with Chartres, in each vice outdo
K[innou]l's lewd cargo, or Ty[rawle]y's
crew,
From Latian Syrens, French Circean feasts,
Return well travell'd, and transform'd to
beasts;
Or for a titled punk, or foreign flame,
Renounce our country, and degrade our
name?
If, after all, we must with Wilmot own
The cordial drop of life is Love alone,
And Swift cry wisely, ' Vive la bagatelle!'
The man that loves and laughs must sure
do well.

Adieu — if this advice appear the worst, 130
Ev'n take the counsel which I gave you
first:
Or better precepts if you can impart,
Why do; I 'll follow them with all my
heart.

THE FIRST EPISTLE OF THE SECOND BOOK OF HORACE

The identification of Augustus with George
II. makes it necessary to take much of this poem
ironically. George II., since his accession ten
years before this was written (1737), had shown
absolute indifference to the literature of England. The critical portions of the satire undoubtedly present Pope's real judgment of contemporary literature.

ADVERTISEMENT

The reflections of Horace, and the judgments passed in his Epistle to Augustus,
seemed so seasonable to the present times, that
I could not help applying them to the use of
my own country. The author thought them
considerable enough to address them to his
prince, whom he paints with all the great and
good qualities of a monarch upon whom the
Romans depended for the increase of an absolute Empire; but to make the poem entirely
English, I was willing to add one or two of
those which contribute to the happiness of a
Free People, and are more consistent with the
welfare of our neighbours.

This epistle will show the learned world
to have fallen into two mistakes: one, that
Augustus was a Patron of poets in general;
whereas he not only prohibited all but the best
writers to name him, but recommended that
care even to the civil magistrate; Admonebat
prœtores. ne paterentur nomen suum obsolefieri,
&c.; the other, that this piece was only a
general Discourse of Poetry; whereas it was
an Apology for the Poets, in order to render
Augustus more their patron. Horace here
pleads the cause of his contemporaries; first,
against the Taste of the town, whose humour
it was to magnify the authors of the preceding
age; secondly, against the Court and Nobility,
who encouraged only the writers for the Theatre; and, lastly, against the Emperor himself,
who had conceived them of little use to the
Government. He shows (by a view of the
progress of Learning, and the change of Taste
among the Romans) that the introduction of
the Polite Arts of Greece had given the writers of his time great advantages over their pre-
decessors; that their Morals were much im-

proved, and the license of those ancient poets restrained; that Satire and Comedy were become more just and useful; that whatever extravagancies were left on the stage were owing to the ill taste of the nobility; that poets, under due regulations, were in many respects useful to the State; and concludes, that it was upon them the Emperor himself must depend for his Fame with posterity.

We may further learn from this Epistle, that Horace made his court to this great Prince, by writing with a decent freedom toward him, with a just contempt of his low flatterers, and with a manly regard to his own character.

TO AUGUSTUS

WHILE you, great Patron of Mankind! sustain
The balanced world, and open all the main;
Your country, chief, in Arms abroad defend,
At home with Morals, Arts, and Laws amend;
How shall the Muse, from such a monarch, steal
An hour, and not defraud the public weal?
  Edward and Henry, now the boast of Fame,
And virtuous Alfred, a more sacred name,
After a life of gen'rous toils endured, —
The Gaul subdued, or property secured, 10
Ambition humbled, mighty cities storm'd,
Or laws establish'd, and the world reform'd —
Closed their long glories with a sigh, to find
Th' unwilling gratitude of base Mankind!
All human Virtue, to its latest breath,
Finds Envy never conquer'd but by Death.
The great Alcides, ev'ry labour past,
Had still this monster to subdue at last:
Sure fate of all, beneath whose rising ray
Each star of meaner merit fades away! 20
Oppress'd we feel the beam directly beat;
Those suns of glory please not till they set.
  To thee the World its present homage pays,
The harvest early, but mature the praise:
Great friend of Liberty! in Kings a name
Above all Greek, above all Roman fame;
Whose word is truth, as sacred and revered
As Heav'n's own oracles from altars heard.
Wonder of Kings! like whom to mortal eyes
None e'er has risen, and none e'er shall rise. 30

Just in one instance, be it yet confest
Your people, sir, are partial in the rest;
Foes to all living worth except your own,
And advocates for folly dead and gone.
Authors, like coins, grow dear as they grow old;
It is the Rust we value, not the Gold.
Chaucer's worst ribaldry is learn'd by rote,
And beastly Skelton heads of houses quote;
One likes no language but the Faery Queen;
A Scot will fight for Christ's Kirk o' the Green; 40
And each true Briton is to Ben so civil,
He swears the Muses met him at the Devil.
Tho' justly Greece her eldest sons admires,
Why should not we be wiser than our sires?
In every public virtue we excel,
We build, we paint, we sing, we dance, as well;
And learned Athens to our art must stoop,
Could she behold us tumbling thro' a hoop.
  If time improve our Wit as well as Wine,
Say at what age a poet grows divine? 50
Shall we, or shall we not, account him so
Who died, perhaps, a hundred years ago?
End all dispute; and fix the year precise
When British bards begin t' immortalize?
' Who lasts a century can have no flaw;
I hold that Wit a classic, good in law.'
  Suppose he wants a year, will you compound?
And shall we deem him ancient, right, and sound,
Or damn to all eternity at once
At ninety-nine a modern and a dunce? 60
' We shall not quarrel for a year or two;
By courtesy of England he may do.'
  Then by the rule that made the horsetail bare,
I pluck out year by year, as hair by hair,
And melt down Ancients like a heap of snow,
While you, to measure merits, look in Stowe,
And estimating authors by the year,
Bestow a garland only on a bier.
  Shakespeare (whom you and every playhouse bill
Style the divine! the matchless! what you will) 70
For Gain, not Glory, wing'd his roving flight,
And grew immortal in his own despite.

Ben, old and poor, as little seem'd to heed
The life to come in every poet's creed.
Who now reads Cowley ? if he pleases yet,
His Moral pleases, not his pointed Wit:
Forgot his Epic, nay, Pindaric art,
But still I love the language of his heart.
'Yet surely, surely these were famous
  men!
What boy but hears the sayings of old Ben ?
In all debates where Critics bear a part, 81
Not one but nods, and talks of Jonson's
  Art,
Of Shakespeare's Nature, and of Cowley's
  Wit;
How Beaumont's judgment check'd what
  Fletcher writ;
How Shadwell hasty, Wycherley was slow;
But for the passions, Southern sure, and
  Rowe!
These, only these, support the crowded
  stage,
From eldest Heywood down to Cibber's
  age.'
All this may be; the People's voice is odd;
It is, and it is not, the voice of God.   90
To Gammer Gurton if it give the bays,
And yet deny the Careless Husband praise,
Or say our fathers never broke a rule;
Why then, I say, the Public is a fool.
But let them own that greater faults than
  we
They had, and greater virtues, I 'll agree.
Spenser himself affects the obsolete,
And Sidney's verse halts ill on Roman
  feet;
Milton's strong pinion now not Heav'n can
  bound,
Now, serpent-like, in prose he sweeps the
  ground.   100
In quibbles Angel and Archangel join,
And God the Father turns a School-divine.
Not that I 'd lop the beauties from his
  book,
Like slashing Bentley with his desp'rate
  hook;
Or damn all Shakespeare, like th' affected
  fool
At Court, who hates whate'er he read at
  School.
But for the Wits of either Charles's days,
The mob of gentlemen who wrote with
  ease;
Sprat, Carew, Sedley, and a hundred more
(Like twinkling stars the Miscellanies
  o'er),   110

One simile that solitary shines
In the dry Desert of a thousand lines,
Or lengthen'd thought, that gleams thro
  many a page,
Has sanctified whole poems for an age.
I lose my patience, and I own it too,
When works are censured not as bad, but
  new;
While, if our elders break all Reason's laws,
These fools demand not pardon, but ap-
  plause.
  On Avon's bank, where flowers eternal
    blow,
If I but ask if any weed can grow,   120
One tragic sentence if I dare deride,
Which Betterton's grave action dignified,
Or well - mouth'd Booth with emphasis
  proclaims,
(Tho' but perhaps a muster-roll of names),
How will our fathers rise up in a rage,
And swear all shame is lost in GEORGE'S
  age!
You 'd think no fools disgraced the former
  reign,
Did not some grave examples yet remain,
Who scorn a lad should teach his father
  skill,
And having once been wrong, will be so
  still.   130
He who, to seem more deep than you or I,
Extols old bards, or Merlin's prophecy,
Mistake him not; he envies, not admires,
And to debase the sons exalts the sires.
Had ancient times conspired to disallow
What then was new, what had been ancient
  now ?
Or what remain'd, so worthy to be read
By learned critics of the mighty dead ?
  In days of ease, when now the weary
    sword
Was sheath'd, and luxury with Charles re-
  stor'd,   140
In every taste of foreign courts improv'd,
'All by the King's example liv'd and lov'd,'
Then peers grew proud in horsemanship
  t' excel;
Newmarket's glory rose, as Britain's fell;
The soldier breathed the gallantries of
  France,
And ev'ry flowery Courtier writ Romance.
Then marble, soften'd into life, grew warm,
And yielding metal flow'd to human form;
Lely on animated canvas stole
The sleepy eye, that spoke the melting
  soul.   150

No wonder then, when all was love and
    sport,
The willing Muses were debauch'd at
    court;
On each enervate string they taught the
    note
To pant, or tremble thro' a Eunuch's throat.
    But Britain, changeful as a child at
    play,
Now calls in princes, and now turns away.
Now Whig, now Tory, what we loved we
    hate;
Now all for Pleasure, now for Church and
    State;
Now for Prerogatives, and now for laws;
Effects unhappy, from a noble cause.   160
    Time was, a sober Englishman would
    knock
His servants up, and rise by five o'clock;
Instruct his family in ev'ry rule,
And send his wife to church, his son to
    school.
To worship like his fathers was his care;
To teach their frugal virtues to his heir;
To prove that Luxury could never hold,
And place on good security his gold.
Now times are changed, and one poetic
    itch
Has seized the Court and City, Poor and
    Rich;   170
Sons, sires, and grandsires, all will wear
    the bays;
Our wives read Milton, and our daughters
    plays;
To theatres and to rehearsals throng,
And all our grace at table is a song.
I, who so oft renounce the Muses, lie:
Not ** 's self e'er tells more fibs than I.
When sick of Muse, our follies we deplore,
And promise our best friends to rhyme no
    more,
We wake next morning in a raging fit,
And call for pen and ink to show our wit.
    He served a 'prenticeship who sets up
    shop;   181
Ward tried on puppies and the poor his
    drop;
Ev'n Radcliff's doctors travel first to
    France,
Nor dare to practise till they 've learn'd to
    dance.
Who builds a bridge that never drove a
    pile ?
(Should Ripley venture, all the world would
    smile),

But those who cannot write, and those who
    can,
All rhyme, and scrawl, and scribble, to a
    man.
    Yet, Sir, reflect; the mischief is not
    great;
These madmen never hurt the Church or
    State: 190
Sometimes the folly benefits mankind,
And rarely av'rice taints the tuneful mind.
Allow him but his plaything of a Pen,
He ne'er rebels, or plots, like other men:
Flight of cashiers, or mobs, he 'll never
    mind,
And knows no losses while the Muse is
    kind.
To cheat a friend or ward, he leaves to
    Peter;
The good man heaps up nothing but mere
    metre,
Enjoys his Garden and his Book in quiet;
And then — a perfect hermit in his diet. 200
    Of little use the man you may suppose
Who says in verse what others say in
    prose;
Yet let me show a Poet 's of some weight,
And (tho' no soldier) useful to the State.
What will a child learn sooner than a song ?
What better teach a foreigner the tongue —
What 's long or short, each accent where
    to place,
And speak in public with some sort of
    grace ?
I scarce can think him such a worthless
    thing,   209
Unless he praise some monster of a King;
Or virtue or religion turn to sport,
To please a lewd or unbelieving Court.
Unhappy Dryden ! — In all Charles's days
Roscommon only boasts unspotted bays;
And in our own (excuse some courtly
    stains)
No whiter page than Addison remains.
He from the taste obscene reclaims our
    youth,
And sets the passions on the side of Truth,
Forms the soft bosom with the gentlest
    Art,
And pours each human virtue in the heart. 219
Let Ireland tell how wit upheld her cause,
Her trade supported, and supplied her
    laws;
And leave on Swift this grateful verse en-
    graved,
'The rights a Court attack'd, a Poet saved.'

Behold the hand that wrought a Nation's cure,
Stretch'd to relieve the idiot and the poor;
Proud vice to brand, or injured worth adorn,
And stretch the ray to ages yet unborn.
Not but there are, who merit other palms;
Hopkins and Sternhold glad the heart with psalms;   230
The boys and girls whom charity maintains
Implore your help in these pathetic strains:
How could Devotion touch the country pews
Unless the Gods bestow'd a proper Muse?
Verse cheers their leisure, verse assists their work,
Verse prays for peace, or sings down pope and Turk.
The silenced preacher yields to potent strain,
And feels that Grace his prayer besought in vain;
The blessing thrills thro' all the lab'ring throng,
And Heav'n is won by violence of song. 240
Our rural ancestors, with little blest,
Patient of labour when the end was rest,
Indulged the day that housed their annual grain
With feasts, and off'rings, and a thankful strain.
The joy their wives, their sons, and servants share,
Ease of their toil, and partners of their care:
The Laugh, the Jest, attendants on the bowl,
Smooth'd ev'ry brow, and open'd ev'ry soul:
With growing years the pleasing license grew,
And taunts alternate innocently flew.   250
But Times corrupt, and Nature, ill inclin'd,
Produced the point that left a sting behind;
Till friend with friend, and families at strife,
Triumphant malice raged thro' private life.
Who felt the wrong, or fear'd it, took th' alarm,
Appeal'd to law, and Justice lent her arm.
At length by wholesome dread of statutes bound,
The poets learn'd to please, and not to wound:

Most warp'd to Flatt'ry's side; but some, more nice,
Preserv'd the freedom, and forbore the vice.   260
Hence Satire rose, that just the medium hit,
And heals with morals what it hurts with wit.
We conquer'd France, but felt our captive's charms,
Her arts victorious triumph'd o'er our arms;
Britain to soft refinements less a foe,
Wit grew polite, and numbers learn'd to flow.
Waller was smooth; but Dryden taught to join
The varying verse, the full resounding line,
The long majestic march, and energy divine:
Tho' still some traces of our rustic vein
And splay-foot verse remain'd, and will remain.   271
Late, very late, correctness grew our care,
When the tired nation breathed from civil war
Exact Racine and Corneille's noble fire
Show'd us that France had something to admire.
Not but the tragic spirit was our own,
And full in Shakespeare, fair in Otway, shone;
But Otway fail'd to polish or refine,
And fluent Shakespeare scarce effaced a line.
Ev'n copious Dryden wanted, or forgot, 280
The last and greatest art — the art to blot.
Some doubt if equal pains or equal fire
The humbler Muse of Comedy require.
But in known images of life I guess
The labour greater, as th' indulgence less.
Observe how seldom ev'n the best succeed:
Tell me if Congreve's fools are fools indeed?
What pert low dialogue has Farquhar writ!
How Van wants grace, who never wanted wit:
The stage how loosely does Astrea tread,
Who fairly puts all characters to bed! 291
And idle Cibber, how he breaks the laws,
To make poor Pinkey eat with vast applause!
But fill their purse, our poet's work is done,
Alike to them by pathos or by pun.

O you! whom Vanity's light bark con-
veys
On Fame's mad voyage by the wind of
praise,
With what a shifting gale your course you
ply,
For ever sunk too low, or borne too high.
Who pants for glory finds but short repose;
A breath revives him, or a breath o'er-
throws. 301
Farewell the Stage! if just as thrives the
play
The silly bard grows fat or falls away.
There still remains, to mortify a Wit,
The many-headed monster of the pit;
A senseless, worthless, and unhonour'd
crowd,
Who, to disturb their betters, mighty
proud,
Clatt'ring their sticks before ten lines are
spoke,
Call for the Farce, the Bear, or the Black-
joke. 309
What dear delight to Britons farce affords!
Ever the taste of Mobs, but now of Lords:
(Taste! that eternal wanderer, which flies
From heads to ears, and now from ears to
eyes.)
The play stands still; damn action and dis-
course!
Back fly the scenes, and enter foot and
horse;
Pageants on pageants, in long order drawn,
Peers, heralds, bishops, ermine, gold, and
lawn;
The Champion too! and, to complete the
jest,
Old Edward's armour beams on Cibber's
breast. 319
With laughter sure Democritus had died,
Had he beheld an audience gape so wide.
Let bear or elephant be e'er so white,
The people sure, the people are the sight!
Ah, luckless Poet! stretch thy lungs and
roar,
That bear or elephant shall heed thee
more;
While all its throats the gallery extends,
And all the thunder of the pit ascends!
Loud as the wolves on Orcas' stormy steep
Howl to the roarings of the northern deep,
Such is the shout, the long applauding
note, 330
At Quin's high plume, or Oldfield's petti-
coat;

Or when from court a birthday suit be-
stow'd,
Sinks the lost actor in the tawdry load.
Booth enters — hark! the universal peal!
'But has he spoken?' — Not a syllable.
'What shook the stage, and made the peo-
ple stare?'
Cato's long wig, flower'd gown, and lack-
er'd chair.
Yes, lest you think I rally more than
teach,
Or praise malignly arts I cannot reach,
Let me for once presume t' instruct the
times, 340
To know the Poet from the man of rhymes:
'T is he who gives my breast a thousand
pains,
Can make me feel each passion that he
feigns,
Enrage, compose, with more than magic art,
With pity and with terror tear my heart,
And snatch me o'er the earth, or thro' the
air,
To Thebes, to Athens, when he will, and
where.
But not this part of the poetic state
Alone deserves the favour of the great.
Think of those authors, Sir, who would
rely 350
More on a reader's sense than gazer's eye.
Or who shall wander where the Muses
sing?
Who climb their mountain, or who taste
their spring?
How shall we fill a library with Wit,
When Merlin's Cave is half unfurnish'd
yet?
My liege! why writers little claim your
thought
I guess, and, with their leave, will tell the
fault.
We Poets are (upon a poet's word)
Of all mankind the creatures most absurd:
The season when to come, and when to go,
To sing, or cease to sing, we never know;
And if we will recite nine hours in ten, 362
You lose your patience just like other men.
Then, too, we hurt ourselves when, to de-
fend
A single verse, we quarrel with a friend;
Repeat, unask'd; lament, the wit 's too fine
For vulgar eyes, and point out every line;
But most when straining with too weak a
wing
We needs will write epistles to the King;

And from the moment we oblige the town,
Expect a Place or Pension from the Crown;
Or dubb'd historians by express command,
T' enrol your triumphs o'er the seas and
   land, 373
Be call'd to Court to plan some work di-
   vine,
As once for Louis, Boileau and Racine.
   Yet think, great Sir! (so many virtues
     shown)
Ah! think what poet best may make them
   known;
Or choose at least some minister of grace,
Fit to bestow the Laureate's weighty place.
   Charles, to late times to be transmitted
     fair, 380
Assign'd his figure to Bernini's care;
And great Nassau to Kneller's hand de-
   creed
To fix him graceful on the bounding steed:
So well in paint and stone they judg'd of
   merit;
But Kings in Wit may want discerning
   spirit.
The hero William, and the martyr Charles,
One knighted Blackmore, and one pension'd
   Quarles,
Which made old Ben and surly Dennis
   swear
· No Lord's anointed, but a Russian bear.'
   Not with such majesty, such bold relief,
The forms august of King, or conquering
   Chief, 391
E'er swell'd on marble, as in verse have
   shined
(In polish'd verse) the manners and the
   mind.
O! could I mount on the Mæonian wing,
Your arms, your actions, your repose, to
   sing!
What seas you travers'd, and what fields
   you fought!
Your country's peace how oft, how dearly
   bought!
How barb'rous rage subsided at your word,
And nations wonder'd while they dropp'd
   the sword!
How, when you nodded, o'er the land and
   deep, 400
Peace stole her wing, and wrapt the world
   in sleep,
Till earth's extremes your mediation own,
And Asia's tyrants tremble at your throne!
But verse, alas! your Majesty disdains;
And I'm not used to panegyric strains.

The zeal of fools offends at any time,
But most of all the zeal of fools in rhyme.
Besides, a Fate attends on all I write,
That when I aim at praise they say I bite.
A vile encomium doubly ridicules: 410
There's nothing blackens like the ink of
   fools.
If true, a woful likeness; and, if lies,
' Praise undeserv'd is scandal in disguise.'
Well may he blush who gives it, or re-
   ceives;
And when I flatter, let my dirty leaves
(Like Journals, Odes, and such forgotten
   things,
As Eusden, Philips, Settle, writ of Kings)
Clothe spice, line trunk, or, flutt'ring in a
   row,
Befringe the rails of Bedlam and Soho.

THE SECOND EPISTLE OF THE
SECOND BOOK OF HORACE

Ludentis speciem dabit, et torquebitur. — Hor.

DEAR COLONEL, Cobham's and your coun-
   try's friend,
You love a verse; take such as I can send.
   A Frenchman comes, presents you with
     his boy,
Bows and begins — 'This lad, sir, is of
   Blois:
Observe his shape how clean! his locks how
   curl'd.
My only son, I'd have him see the world:
His French is pure; his voice too — you
   shall hear —
Sir, he's your slave for twenty pound a
   year.
Mere wax as yet, you fashion him with
   ease,
Your barber, cook, upholst'rer; what you
   please: 10
A perfect genius at an opera song —
To say too much might do my honour
   wrong.
Take him with all his virtues on my word;
His whole ambition was to serve a Lord.
But, Sir, to you with what would I not
   part?
Tho', faith, I fear, 't will break his mother's
   heart.
Once (and but once) I caught him in a lie,
And then, unwhipp'd, he had the grace to
   cry:

The fault he has I fairly shall reveal
(Could you o'erlook but that), it is — to
  steal.'   20
  If, after this, you took the graceless lad,
Could you complain, my friend, he prov'd
  so bad ?
Faith, in such case, if you should prosecute,
I think Sir Godfrey should decide the suit;
Who sent the thief that stole the cash
  away,
And punish'd him that put it in his way.
  Consider then, and judge me in this
  light;
I told you when I went I could not write;
You said the same; and are you discontent
With laws to which you gave your own
  assent ?   30
Nay, worse, to ask for verse at such a
  time!
D'ye think me good for nothing but to
  rhyme ?
  In Anna's wars a Soldier, poor and old,
Had dearly earn'd a little purse of gold:
Tired in a tedious march, one luckless
  night
He slept, (poor dog!) and lost it to a doit.
This put the man in such a desp'rate mind, ⎫
Between revenge, and grief, and hunger ⎬
  join'd   ⎭
Against the foe, himself, and all mankind,
He leap'd the trenches, scaled a castle
  wall,   40
Tore down a standard, took the fort and
  all.
' Prodigious well!' his great commander
  cried,
Gave him much praise, and some reward
  beside.
Next pleas'd His Excellence a town to
  batter
(Its name I know not, and 'tis no great
  matter);
' Go on, my friend (he cried), see yonder
  walls!
Advance and conquer ! go where Glory
  calls!
More honours, more rewards, attend the
  brave.'
Don't you remember what reply he
  gave ? —
' D'ye think me, noble Gen'ral, such a
  sot ?   50
Let him take castles who has ne'er a groat.'
  Bred up at home, full early I begun
To read in Greek the wrath of Peleus' son:

Besides, my father taught me from a lad
The better art, to know the good from bad
(And little sure imported to remove,
To hunt for truth in Maudlin's learned
  grove).
But knottier points we knew not half so
  well,
Deprived us soon of our paternal cell;
And certain laws, by suff'rers thought
  unjust,   60
Denied all posts of profit or of trust.
Hopes after hopes of pious papists fail'd,
While mighty William's thund'ring arm
  prevail'd;
For right hereditary tax'd and fin'd
He stuck to poverty with peace of mind;
And me, the Muses help'd to undergo it;
Convict a Papist he, and I a Poet.
But (thanks to Homer) since I live and
  thrive,
Indebted to no prince or peer alive,
Sure I should want the care of ten Mon-
  roes,   70
If I would scribble rather than repose.
Years foll'wing years steal something ev'ry
  day,
At last they steal us from ourselves away;
In one our frolics, one amusements end,
In one a Mistress drops, in one a Friend.
This subtle thief of life, this paltry time,
What will it leave me if it snatch my
  rhyme ?
If ev'ry wheel of that unwearied mill
That turn'd ten thousand verses, now stands
  still ?
  But, after all, what would ye have me
  do,   80
When out of twenty I can please not two ?
When this Heroics only deigns to praise,
Sharp Satire that, and that Pindaric lays ?
One likes the pheasant's wing, and one the
  leg;
The vulgar boil, the learned roast an egg:
Hard task to hit the palate of such guests,
When Oldfield loves what Dartineuf de-
  tests !
But grant I may relapse, for want of
  grace,
Again to rhyme, can London be the place ?
Who there his muse, or self, or soul at-
  tends,   90
In Crowds, and Courts, Law, Bus'ness,
  Feasts, and Friends ?
My counsel sends to execute a deed:
A poet begs me I will hear him read.

In Palace yard at nine you'll find me
  there —
At ten, for certain, sir, in Bloomsbury-
  square —
Before the Lords at twelve my cause comes
  on —
There's a rehearsal, Sir, exact at one. —
'Oh ! but a Wit can study in the streets,
And raise his mind above the mob he
  meets.'
Not quite so well, however, as one ought: 100
A hackney-coach may chance to spoil a
  thought,
And then a nodding beam, or pig of lead,
God knows, may hurt the very ablest
  head.
Have you not seen, at Guildhall's narrow
  pass,
Two Aldermen dispute it with an Ass ?
And Peers give way, exalted as they are,
Ev'n to their own s-r-v — nce in a car ?
Go, lofty Poet, and in such a crowd
Sing thy sonorous verse — but not aloud.
Alas ! to grottos and to groves we run, 110
To ease and silence, ev'ry Muse's son :
Blackmore himself, for any grand effort
Would drink and doze at Tooting or Earl's-
  court.
How shall I rhyme in this eternal roar ?
How match the bards whom none e'er
  match'd before ?
  The man who, stretch'd in Isis' calm re-
  treat,
To books and study gives sev'n years com-
  plete,
See ! strew'd with learned dust, his night-
  cap on,
He walks an object new beneath the sun !
The boys flock round him, and the peo-
  ple stare: 120
So stiff, so mute ; some Statue you would
  swear
Stept from its pedestal to take the air !
And here, while town, and court, and city
  roars,
With Mobs, and Duns, and Soldiers, at
  their doors,
Shall I, in London, act this idle part,
Composing songs for fools to get by heart ?
  The Temple late two brother sergeants
  saw,
Who deem'd each other oracles of law ;
With equal talents these congenial souls,
One lull'd th' Exchequer, and one stunn'd
  the Rolls ; 130

Each had a gravity would make you split,
And shook his head at Murray as a wit;
'T was, ' Sir, your law ' — and ' Sir, your
  eloquence,'
' Yours, Cowper's manner ' — and ' Yours,
  Talbot's sense.'
  Thus we dispose of all poetic merit,
Yours Milton's genius, and mine Homer's
  spirit.
Call Tibbald Shakespeare, and he 'll swear
  the Nine,
Dear Cibber ! never match'd one ode of
  thine.
Lord ! how we strut thro' Merlin's Cave, to
  see 139
No poets there but Stephen, you, and me.
Walk with respect behind, while we at ease
Weave laurel crowns, and take what names
  we please.
' My dear Tibullus ! (if that will not do)
Let me be Horace, and be Ovid you:
Or, I 'm content, allow me Dryden's strains,
And you shall rise up Otway for your
  pains.'
Much do I suffer, much, to keep in peace
This jealous, waspish, wrongbead, rhyming
  race ;
And much must flatter, if the whim should
  bite 149
To court applause by printing what I write :
But let the fit pass o'er ; I 'm wise enough
To stop my ears to their confounded stuff.
  In vain bad rhymers all mankind reject,
They treat themselves with most profound
  respect ;
'T is to small purpose that you hold your
  tongue,
Each, prais'd within, is happy all day long :
But how severely with themselves proceed
The men who write such verse as we can
  read ?
Their own strict judges, not a word they
  spare
That wants or force, or light, or weight, or
  care ; 160
Howe'er unwillingly it quits its place,
Nay, tho' at Court (perhaps) it may find
  grace.
Such they 'll degrade; and, sometimes in
  its stead,
In downright charity revive the dead ;
Mark where a bold expressive phrase ap-
  pears,
Bright thro' the rubbish of some hundred
  years ;

Command old words, that long have slept,
to wake,
Words that wise Bacon or brave Raleigh
spake;
Or bid the new be English ages hence
(For Use will father what 's begot by
Sense); 170
Pour the full tide of eloquence along, ⎫
Serenely pure, and yet divinely strong, ⎬
Rich with the treasures of each foreign ⎭
tongue;
Prune the luxuriant, the uncouth refine,
But show no mercy to an empty line;
Then polish all with so much life and ease,
You think 't is Nature, and a knack to
please;
But ease in writing flows from Art, not
Chance,
As those move easiest who have learn'd to
dance.
If such the plague and pains to write by
rule, 180
Better (say I) be pleas'd, and play the
fool;
Call, if you will, bad rhyming a disease,
It gives men happiness, or leaves them
ease.
There lived *in primo Georgii* (they record)
A worthy member, no small fool, a Lord;
Who, tho' the House was up, delighted
sate,
Heard, noted, answer'd, as in full debate:
In all but this a man of sober life,
Fond of his friend, and civil to his wife;
Not quite a madman tho' a pasty fell, 190
And much too wise to walk into a well.
Him the damn'd doctors and his friends
immured,
They bled, they cupp'd, they purged; in
short they cured;
Whereat the gentleman began to stare —
'My friends! (he cried) pox take you for
your care!
That, from a patriot of distinguish'd note,
Have bled and purged me to a simple vote.'
Well, on the whole, plain prose must be
my fate:
Wisdom (curse on it!) will come soon or
late.
There is a time when poets will grow
dull: 200
I 'll ev'n leave verses to the boys at school.
To rules of poetry no more confin'd,
I 'll learn to smooth and harmonize my
mind,

Teach ev'ry thought within its bounds to
roll,
And keep the equal measure of the soul.
Soon as I enter at my country door,
My mind resumes the thread it dropt be-
fore;
Thoughts which at Hyde-park Corner I
forgot,
Meet and rejoin me in the pensive grot:
There all alone, and compliments apart, 210
I ask these sober questions of my heart :
If, when the more you drink the more
you crave,
You tell the doctor; when the more you
have
The more you want, why not, with equal
ease,
Confess as well your folly as disease ?
The heart resolves this matter in a trice,
' Men only feel the smart, but not the vice.'
When golden angels cease to cure the
evil,
You give all royal witchcraft to the devil:
When servile Chaplains cry, that birth and
place 220
Endue a Peer with Honour, Truth, and
Grace,
Look in that breast, most dirty D[uke]! be
fair,
Say, can you find out one such lodger
there ?
Yet still, not heeding what your heart can
teach,
You go to church to hear these flatt'rers
preach.
Indeed, could wealth bestow or Wit or
Merit,
A grain of Courage, or a spark of Spirit,
The wisest man might blush, I must agree,
If D[evonshire] lov'd sixpence more than
he.
If there be truth in law, and use can
give 230
A property, that 's yours on which you live.
Delightful Abs-court, if its fields afford
Their fruits to you, confesses you its lord:
All Worldly's hens, nay, partridge, sold to
town,
His venison too, a guinea makes your own:
He bought at thousands what with better
wit
You purchase as you want, and bit by bit:
Now, or long since, what diff'rence will be
found ?
You pay a penny, and he paid a pound.

Heathcote himself, and such large-acred
  men, 240
Lords of fat E'sham, or of Lincoln Fen,
Buy every stick of wood that lends them
  heat,
Buy every pullet they afford to eat;
Yet these are wights who fondly call their
  own
Half that the Devil o'erlooks from Lincoln
  town.
The laws of God, as well as of the land,
Abhor a perpetuity should stand:
Estates have wings, and hang in Fortune's
  power,
Loose on the point of ev'ry wav'ring hour,
Ready by force, or of your own accord, 250
By sale, at least by death, to change their
  lord.
Man? and for ever? Wretch! what
  wouldst thou have?
Heir urges heir, like wave impelling wave.
All vast possessions (just the same the
  case
Whether you call them Villa, Park, or
  Chase),
Alas, my BATHURST! what will they avail?
Join Cotswood hills to Saperton's fair dale;
Let rising granaries and temples here,
There mingled farms and pyramids, ap-
  pear;
Link towns to towns with avenues of
  oak, 260
Enclose whole towns in walls; 't is all a
  joke!
Inexorable death shall level all,
And trees, and stones, and farms, and
  farmer fall.
  Gold, silver, ivory, vases sculptured high,
Paint, marble, gems, and robes of Persian
  dye,
There are who have not — and, thank
  Heav'n, there are
Who, if they have not, think not worth
  their care.
  Talk what you will of Taste, my friend,
  you 'll find
Two of a face as soon as of a mind.
Why, of two brothers, rich and restless
  one 270
Ploughs, burns, manures, and toils from
  sun to sun,
The other slights, for women, sports, and
  wines,
All Townshend's turnips, and all Grosve-
  nor's mines:

Why one, like Bubb, with pay and scorn
  content,
Bows and votes on in Court and Parlia-
  ment;
One, driv'n by strong benevolence of soul,
Shall fly, like Oglethorpe, from pole to pole;
Is known alone to that directing Power 278
Who forms the genius in the natal hour;
That God of Nature, who, within us still,
Inclines our action, not constrains our will;
Various of temper, as of face or frame,
Each individual: His great end the same.
  Yes, Sir, how small soever be my heap,
A part I will enjoy as well as keep.
My heir may sigh, and think it want of
  grace
A man so poor would live without a place;
But sure no statute in his favour says,
How free or frugal I shall pass my days;
I who at some times spend, at others spare,
Divided between carelessness and care. 291
'T is one thing, madly to disperse my store;
Another, not to heed to treasure more;
Glad, like a boy, to snatch the first good
  day,
And pleas'd, if sordid want be far away.
  What is 't to me (a passenger, God wot)
Whether my vessel be first-rate or not?
The ship itself may make a better figure,
But I that sail, am neither less nor bigger.
I neither strut with ev'ry fav'ring breath, 300
Nor strive with all the tempest in my
  teeth;
In Power, Wit, Figure, Virtue, Fortune,
  placed
Behind the foremost, and before the last.
  ' But why all this of Av'rice? I have
  none.'
I wish you joy, sir, of a tyrant gone:
But does no other lord it at this hour,
As wild and mad? the avarice of Pow'r?
Does neither Rage inflame nor Fear ap-
  pall?
Not the black fear of Death, that saddens
  all?
With terrors round, can Reason hold her
  throne, 310
Despise the known, nor tremble at th' un-
  known?
Survey both worlds, intrepid and entire,
In spite of witches, devils, dreams, and fire?
Pleas'd to look forward, pleas'd to look be-
  hind,
And count each birthday with a grateful
  mind?

Has life no sourness, drawn so near its
    end ?
Canst thou endure a foe, forgive a friend ?
Has age but melted the rough parts away,
As winter fruits grow mild ere they decay ?
Or will you think, my friend! your bus'ness
    done, 320
When of a hundred thorns you pull out
    one ?
    Learn to live well, or fairly make your
        will;
You 've play'd and lov'd, and ate and
    drank, your fill.
Walk sober off, before a sprightlier age
Comes titt'ring on, and shoves you from the
    stage;
Leave such to trifle with more grace and
    ease,
Whom Folly pleases, and whose follies
    please.

SATIRES OF DR. JOHN DONNE,
DEAN OF ST. PAUL'S, VERSI-
FIED

Quid vetat et nosmet Lucili scripta legentes
Quærere, num illius, num rerum dura negarit
Versiculos natura magis factos, et euntes
Mollius ?   HORACE.

The paraphrases of Donne were, by Pope's
statement, done several years before their publication in 1735.

SATIRE II

YES, thank my stars! as early as I knew
This town, I had the sense to hate it too;
Yet here, as ev'n in Hell, there must be
    still
One giant vice, so excellently ill,
That all beside one pities, not abhors;
As who knows Sappho, smiles at other
    whores.
    I grant that Poetry 's a crying sin;
It brought (no doubt) th' excise and army
    in:
Catch'd like the plague, or love, the Lord
    knows how,
But that the cure is starving, all allow. 10
Yet like the Papist's is the Poet's state,
Poor and disarm'd, and hardly worth your
    hate!
    Here a lean bard, whose wit could never
        give

Himself a dinner, makes an actor live:
The thief condemn'd, in law already dead,
So prompts and saves a rogue who cannot
    read.
Thus as the pipes of some carv'd organ
    move,
The gilded puppets dance and mount above,
Heav'd by the breath th' inspiring bellows
    blow:
Th' inspiring bellows lie and pant below. 20
One sings the Fair; but songs no longer
    move;
No rat is rhymed to death, nor maid to
    love:
In Love's, in Nature's spite the siege they
    hold,
And scorn the flesh, the Devil, and all but
    gold.
    These write to Lords, some mean re-
        ward to get,
As needy beggars sing at doors for meat:
Those write because all write, and so have
    still
Excuse for writing, and for writing ill.
    Wretched, indeed! but far more wretched
        yet
Is he who makes his meal on others' wit: 30
'T is changed, no doubt, from what it was
    before;
His rank digestion makes it wit no more:
Sense pass'd thro' him no longer is the
    same;
For food digested takes another name.
    I pass o'er all those confessors and
        martyrs,
Who live like S[u]tt[o]n, or who die like
    Chartres,
Out-cant old Esdras, or out-drink his heir,
Out-usure Jews, or Irishmen out-swear;
Wicked as pages, who in early years
Act sins which Prisca's confessor scarce
    hears. 40
Ev'n those I pardon, for whose sinful sake
Schoolmen new tenements in hell must
    make;
Of whose strange crimes no canonist can
    tell
In what commandment's large contents
    they dwell.
    One, one man only breeds my just of-
        fence,
Whom crimes gave wealth, and wealth gave
    impudence:
Time, that at last matures a clap to pox,
Whose gentle progress makes a calf an ox,

And brings all natural events to pass,
Hath made him an attorney of an ass.   50
No young Divine, new beneficed, can be
More pert, more proud, more positive than
    he.
What further could I wish the fop to do,
But turn a Wit, and scribble verses too ?
Pierce the soft labyrinth of a lady's ear
With rhymes of this *per cent.* and that *per
    year ;*
Or court a wife, spread out his wily parts,
Like nets, or lime twigs, for rich widows'
    hearts;
Call himself barrister to ev'ry wench,
And woo in language of the Pleas and
    Bench;   60
Language which Boreas might to Auster
    hold,
More rough than forty Germans when they
    scold.
    Curs'd be the wretch, so venal and so vain,
Paltry and proud as drabs in Drury Lane.
'T is such a bounty as was never known,
If Peter deigns to help you to your own.
What thanks, what praise, if Peter but
    supplies !
And what a solemn face if he denies !
Grave, as when pris'ners shake the head,
    and swear
'T was only suretyship that brought them
    there.   70
His office keeps your parchment fates en-
    tire,
He starves with cold to save them from the
    fire;
For you he walks the streets thro' rain or
    dust,
For not in chariots Peter puts his trust;
For you he sweats and labours at the laws,
Takes God to witness he affects your cause,
And lies to ev'ry Lord in ev'rything,
Like a King's favourite — or like a King.
These are the talents that adorn them all,
From wicked Waters ev'n to godly [Paul].
Not more of simony beneath black gowns,
Nor more of bastardy in heirs to crowns. 82
In shillings and in pence at first they deal,
And steal so little, few perceive they steal;
Till like the sea, they compass all the land,
From Scots to Wight, from Mount to Dover
    strand;
And when rank widows purchase luscious
    nights,
Or when a Duke to Jansen punts at
    White's,

Or city heir in mortgage melts away,
Satan himself feels far less joy than they. 90
Piecemeal they win this acre first, then
    that,
Glean on, and gather up the whole estate;
Then strongly fencing ill-got wealth by law,
Indentures, cov'nants, articles, they draw,
Large as the fields themselves, and larger
    far
Than civil codes, with all their glosses,
    are;
So vast, our new divines, we must confess,
Are fathers of the church for writing less.
But let them write; for you each rogue im-
    pairs   99
The deeds, and dext'rously omits *ses heires :*
No commentator can more slily pass
O'er a learn'd unintelligible place;
Or in quotation shrewd divines leave out
Those words that would against them clear
    the doubt.
    So Luther thought the Paternoster long,
When doom'd to say his beads and even-
    song;
But having cast his cowl, and left those
    laws,
Adds to Christ's prayer, the Power and
    Glory clause.
    The lands are bought; but where are to
    be found
Those ancient woods that shaded all the
    ground ?   110
We see no new-built palaces aspire,
No kitchens emulate the vestal fire.
Where are those troops of Poor, that
    throng'd of yore
The good old Landlord's hospitable door ?
Well I could wish that still, in lordly
    domes,
Some beasts were kill'd, tho' not whole
    hecatombs;
That both extremes were banish'd from
    their walls,
Carthusian fasts and fulsome Bacchanals;
And all mankind might that just mean ob-
    serve,
In which none e'er could surfeit, none could
    starve.   120
These are good works, 't is true, we all
    allow,
But, oh ! these works are not in fashion
    now :
Like rich old wardrobes, things extremely
    rare,
Extremely fine, but what no man will wear.

Thus much I've said, I trust without
offence;
Let no Court Sycophant pervert my sense,
Nor sly informer watch, these words to draw
Within the reach of Treason or the Law.

SATIRE IV

WELL, if it be my time to quit the stage,
Adieu to all the follies of the age !
I die in charity with fool and knave,
Secure of peace at least beyond the grave.
I've had my Purgatory here betimes,
And paid for all my satires, all my rhymes.
The poet's Hell, its tortures, fiends, and
flames,
To this were trifles, toys, and empty
names.
With foolish pride my heart was never
fired,   9
Nor the vain itch t' admire or be admired:
I hoped for no commission from His Grace;
I bought no benefice, I begg'd no place;
Had no new verses nor new suit to show,
Yet went to Court ! — the Devil would
have it so.
But as the fool that in reforming days
Would go to mass in jest (as story says)
Could not but think to pay his fine was odd,
Since 't was no form'd design of serving
God;
So was I punish'd, as if full as proud
As prone to ill, as negligent of good,   20
As deep in debt, without a thought to ⎤
pay,   ⎥
As vain, as idle, and as false as they   ⎬
Who live at Court, for going once that   ⎥
way !   ⎦
Scarce was I enter'd, when, behold! there
came
A thing which Adam had been posed to
name;
Noah had refused it lodging in his ark,
Where all the race of reptiles might em-
bark;
A verier monster than on Afric's shore
The sun e'er got, or slimy Nilus bore,
Or Sloane or Woodward's wondrous shelves
contain,   30
Nay, all that lying travellers can feign.
The watch would hardly let him pass at
noon,
At night would swear him dropp'd out of
the moon:

One whom the Mob, when next we find or
make
A Popish plot, shall for a Jesuit take,
And the wise justice, starting from his
chair,
Cry, 'By your priesthood, tell me what
you are!'
Such was the wight: th' apparel on his
back,
Tho' coarse, was rev'rend, and tho' bare,
was black.
The suit, if by the fashion one might
guess,   40
Was velvet in the youth of good Queen
Bess,
But mere tuff-taffety what now remain'd:
So Time, that changes all things, had or-
dain'd!
Our sons shall see it leisurely decay,
First turn plain rash, then vanish quite
away.
This thing has travell'd, speaks each lan-
guage too,
And knows what's fit for ev'ry state to
do;
Of whose best phrase and courtly accent
join'd
He forms one tongue, exotic and refin'd.
Talkers I've learn'd to bear; Motteux I
knew,   50
Henley himself I've heard, and Budgell
too,
The Doctor's wormwood style, the hash of
tongues
A Pedant makes, the storm of Gonson's
lungs,
The whole artill'ry of the terms of War,
And (all those plagues in one) the bawling
Bar:
These I could bear; but not a rogue so
civil
Whose tongue will compliment you to the
Devil:
A tongue that can cheat widows, cancel
scores,
Make Scots speak treason, cozen subtlest
whores,
With royal favourites in flatt'ry vie,   60
And Oldmixon and Burnet both outlie.
He spies me out; I whisper, 'Gracious
God!
What sin of mine could merit such a rod,
That all the shot of dulness now must be
From this thy blunderbuss discharged on
me!'

'Permit,' he cries, 'no stranger to your
  fame,
To crave your sentiment, if * * * 's your
  name.
What speech esteem you most ? 'The
  King's,' said I.
But the best words ? — 'O, sir, the Dic-
  tion'ry.'   69
You miss my aim; I mean the most acute,
And perfect speaker ? — 'Onslow, past
  dispute.'
But, Sir, of writers ? — 'Swift, for closer
  style,
But Hoadley for a period of a mile.'
Why, yes, 't is granted, these indeed may
  pass;
Good common linguists, and so Panurge
  was;
Nay, troth, th' Apostles (tho' perhaps too
  rough)
Had once a pretty gift of tongues enough:
Yet these were all poor gentlemen! I dare
Affirm 't was Travel made them what they
  were.
Thus others' talents having nicely shown, 80
He came by sure transition to his own;
Till I cried out, ' You prove yourself so
  able,
Pity you was not druggerman at Babel;
For had they found a linguist half so good,
I make no question but the tower had
  stood.'
' Obliging Sir! for courts you sure were
  made,
Why then for ever buried in the shade ?
Spirits like you should see and should be
  seen;
The King would smile on you — at least
  the Queen.
Ah, gentle Sir! you courtiers so cajole
  us —   90
But Tully has it *Nunquam minus solus :*
And as for courts, forgive me if I say,
No lessons now are taught the Spartan
  way.
Tho' in his pictures lust be full display'd,
Few are the converts Aretine has made;
And tho' the court show Vice exceeding
  clear,
None should, by my advice, learn Virtue
  there.'
At this entranc'd, he lifts his hands and
  eyes,
Squeaks like a high-stretch'd lutestring,
  and replies,

' Oh! 't is the sweetest of all earthly
  things   100
To gaze on Princes, and to talk of Kings! '
' Then, happy man who shows the tombs!
  (said I)
He dwells amidst the royal family;
He ev'ry day from King to King can walk,
Of all our Harries, all our Edwards talk,
And get, by speaking truth of monarchs
  dead,
What few can of the living: Ease and
  Bread.'
' Lord, Sir, a mere mechanic! strangely low,
And coarse of phrase — your English all
  are so.
How elegant your Frenchmen! ' — 'Mine,
  d' ye mean ?   110
I have but one; I hope the fellow 's clean.'
' O Sir, politely so! nay, let me die,
Your only wearing is your paduasoy.'
' Not, Sir, my only; I have better still,
And this you see is but my dishabille.' —
Wild to get loose, his patience I provoke,
Mistake, confound, object at all he spoke:
But as coarse iron, sharpen'd, mangles
  more,
And itch most hurts when anger'd to a
  sore,
So when you plague a fool, 't is still the
  curse,   120
You only make the matter worse and
  worse.
He pass'd it o'er; affects an easy smile
At all my peevishness, and turns his style.
He asks, ' What news ? ' I tell him of new
  Plays,
New Eunuchs, Harlequins, and Operas.
He hears, and as a still, with simples in it,
Between each drop it gives stays half a
  minute,
Loath to enrich me with too quick replies,
By little and by little drops his lies.
Mere household trash! of birthnights, balls,
  and shows,   130
More than ten Holinsheds, or Halls, or
  Stowes.
When the Queen frown'd or smiled he
  knows, and what
A subtle minister may make of that:
Who sins, with whom: who got his pension
  rug,
Or quicken'd a reversion by a drug:
Whose place is quarter'd but three parts in
  four,
And whether to a Bishop or a Whore:

Who having lost his credit, pawn'd his
rent,
Is therefore fit to have a government:
Who, in the secret, deals in stocks secure,
And cheats th' unknowing widow and the
poor: 141
Who makes a trust or charity a job,
And gets an act of Parliament to rob:
Why turnpikes rise, and how no cit nor
clown
Can gratis see the country or the town:
Shortly no lad shall chuck, or lady vole,
But some excising courtier will have toll:
He tells what strumpet places sells for
life,
What 'squire his lands, what citizen his
wife:
And last (which proves him wiser still than
all) 150
What lady's face is not a whited wall.
As one of Woodward's patients, sick, and
sore,
I puke, I nauseate — yet he thrusts in
more;
Trims Europe's balance, tops the states-
man's part,
And talks Gazettes and Postboys o'er by
heart.
Like a big wife at sight of loathsome meat
Ready to cast, I yawn, I sigh, and sweat.
Then as a licens'd spy, whom nothing can
Silence or hurt, he libels the great man;
Swears ev'ry place entail'd for years to
come, 160
In sure succession to the day of doom.
He names the price for every office paid,
And says our wars thrive ill because de-
lay'd:
Nay, hints 't is by connivance of the Court
That Spain robs on, and Dunkirk 's still a
port.
Not more amazement seiz'd on Circe's
guests
To see themselves fall endlong into beasts,
Than mine, to find a subject staid and wise
Already half turn'd traitor by surprise.
I felt th' infection slide from him to me, 170
As in the pox some give it to get free;
And quick to swallow me, methought I
saw
One of our Giant Statues ope its jaw.
In that nice moment, as another lie
Stood just a-tilt, the Minister came by.
To him he flies, and bows and bows again,
Then, close as Umbra, joins the dirty train,

Not Fannius' self more impudently near,
When half his nose is in his prince's ear.
I quaked at heart; and, still afraid to see
All the court fill'd with stranger things
than he, 181
Ran out as fast as one that pays his bail
And dreads more actions, hurries from a
jail.
Bear me, some God! Oh, quickly bear
me hence
To wholesome Solitude, the nurse of sense,
Where contemplation prunes her ruffled
wings,
And the free soul looks down to pity
Kings!
There sober thought pursued th' amusing
theme,
Till Fancy colour'd it, and form'd a dream:
A vision hermits can to Hell transport, 190
And forced ev'n me to see the damn'd at
court.
Not Dante, dreaming all th' infernal state,
Beheld such scenes of envy, sin, and hate.
Base fear becomes the guilty, not the free,
Suits tyrants, plunderers, but suits not me:
Shall I, the terror of this sinful town,
Care if a liv'ried Lord or smile or frown?
Who cannot flatter, and detest who can,
Tremble before a noble serving man?
O my fair mistress, Truth! shall I quit
thee 200
For huffing, braggart, puff nobility?
Thou who, since yesterday, hast roll'd o'er
all
The busy idle blockheads of the ball,
Hast thou, O sun! beheld an emptier sort
Than such as swell this bladder of a court?
Now pox on those who show a Court in
Wax!
It ought to bring all courtiers on their
backs;
Such painted puppets! such a varnish'd
race
Of hollow gewgaws, only dress and face!
Such waxen noses, stately staring things 210
No wonder some folks bow, and think them
Kings.
See! where the British youth, engaged
no more
At Fig's, at White's, with felons, or a
whore,
Pay their last duty to the Court, and come
All fresh and fragrant to the drawing room;
In hues as gay, and odours as divine,
As the fair fields they sold to look so fine.

'That's velvet for a king!' the flatt'rer
    swears;
'T is true, for ten days hence 't will be
    King Lear's.
Our Court may justly to our Stage give
    rules,   220
That helps it both to fools' coats and to
    fools.
And why not players strut in courtiers'
    clothes?
For these are actors too as well as those:
Wants reach all states; they beg but better
    drest,
And all is splendid poverty at best.
    Painted for sight, and essenced for the
    smell,
Like frigates fraught with spice and cochi-
    neal,
Sail in the Ladies: how each pirate eyes
So weak a vessel and so rich a prize!
Top-gallant he, and she in all her trim: 230
He boarding her, she striking sail to him.
'Dear countess! you have charms all
    hearts to hit!'
And, 'Sweet Sir Fopling! you have so
    much wit!'
Such wits and beauties are not prais'd for
    nought,
For both the beauty and the wit are
    bought.
'T would burst ev'n Heraclitus with the
    spleen
To see those antics, Fopling and Cour-
    tin:
The Presence seems, with things so richly
    odd,
The mosque of Mahound, or some queer
    pagod.
See them survey their limbs by Durer's
    rules,   240
Of all beau-kind the best proportion'd
    fools!
Adjust their clothes, and to confession
    draw
Those venial sins, an atom, or a straw:
But oh! what terrors must distract the
    soul
Convicted of that mortal crime, a hole;
Or should one pound of powder less be-
    spread
Those monkey tails that wag behind their
    head!
Thus finish'd, and corrected to a hair,
They march, to prate their hour before the
    Fair.

So first to preach a white-glov'd Chaplain
    goes,   250
With band of lily, and with cheek of rose,
Sweeter than Sharon, in immaculate trim,
Neatness itself impertinent in him.
Let but the ladies smile, and they are blest:
Prodigious! how the things *protest*, pro-
    test.
Peace, fools! or Gonson will for papists
    seize you,
If once he catch you at your *Jesu! Jesu!*
    Nature made ev'ry Fop to plague his
    brother,
Just as one Beauty mortifies another.
But here's the captain that will plague
    them both;   260
Whose air cries, Arm! whose very look 's
    an oath.
The captain's honest, Sirs, and that 's
    enough,
Tho' his soul's bullet, and his body buff.
He spits foreright; his haughty chest be-
    fore,
Like batt'ring rams, beats open ev'ry door;
And with a face as red, and as awry,
As Herod's hang-dogs in old tapestry,
Scarecrow to boys, the breeding woman's
    curse,
Has yet a strange ambition to look worse;
Confounds the civil, keeps the rude in awe,
Jests like a licens'd Fool, commands like
    law.   271
    Frighted, I quit the room, but leave it so
As men from jails to execution go;
For hung with deadly sins I see the wall,
And lin'd with giants deadlier than them
    all.
Each man an Ask apart, of strength to
    toss,
For quoits, both Temple-bar and Charing-
    cross.
Scared at the grisly forms, I sweat, I fly,
And shake all o'er, like a discover'd spy.
    Courts are too much for wits so weak as
    mine;   280
Charge them with Heav'n's Artill'ry, bold
    Divine!
From such alone the Great rebukes endure,
Whose satire's sacred, and whose rage se-
    cure:
'T is mine to wash a few light stains, but
    theirs
To deluge sin, and drown a Court in tears.
Howe'er, what's now apocrypha, my wit,
In time to come, may pass for Holy Writ.

EPILOGUE TO THE SATIRES

IN TWO DIALOGUES. WRITTEN IN 1738

The first dialogue was originally entitled
*One Thousand Seven Hundred and thirty-eight,
a Dialogue something like Horace.* Johnson's
London is said by Boswell to have been published on the same morning of May, 1738, and
in spite of its anonymity to have made more
stir than Pope's satire.

DIALOGUE I

Fr. NOT twice a twelvemonth you appear
    in print,
And when it comes, the Court see nothing
    in 't:
You grow correct, that once with rapture
    writ,
And are, besides, too moral for a Wit.
Decay of parts, alas ! we all must feel —
Why now, this moment, don't I see you
    steal ?
'T is all from Horace; Horace long before
    ye
Said 'Tories call'd him whig, and whigs a
    tory;'
And taught his Romans, in much better
    metre,
'To laugh at fools who put their trust in
    Peter.'   10
But Horace, sir, was delicate, was nice;
Bubo observes, he lash'd no sort of vice:
Horace would say, Sir Billy served the
    crown,
Blunt could do business, Higgins knew the
    town;
In Sappho touch the failings of the sex,
In rev'rend bishops note some small neg-
    lects,
And own the Spaniards did a waggish
    thing,
Who cropt our ears, and sent them to the
    King.
His sly, polite, insinuating style
Could please at court, and make Augustus
    smile: 20
An artful manager, that crept between
His friend and shame, and was a kind of
    screen.
But, 'faith, your very Friends will soon be
    sore;
Patriots there are who wish you 'd jest no
    more.

And where 's the glory ? 't will be only
    thought
The great man never offer'd you a groat.
Go see Sir Robert —

P.   See Sir Robert! — hum —
And never laugh — for all my life to come;
Seen him I have; but in his happier hour
Of social Pleasure, ill exchanged for Power;
Seen him, uncumber'd with a venal tribe,
Smile without art, and win without a bribe.
Would he oblige me ? let me only find 33
He does not think me what he thinks man-
    kind.
Come, come, at all I laugh he laughs, no
    doubt;
The only diff'rence is — I dare laugh out.
    F. Why, yes: with Scripture still you
    may be free;
A horse-laugh, if you please, at Honesty;
A joke on Jekyl, or some odd Old Whig,
Who never changed his principle or wig. 40
A patriot is a fool in ev'ry age,
Whom all Lord Chamberlains allow the
    stage:
These nothing hurts; they keep their fash-
    ion still,
And wear their strange old virtue as they
    will.
If any ask you, 'Who 's the man so near
His Prince, that writes in verse, and has
    his ear ?'
Why, answer, Lyttelton! and I 'll engage
The worthy youth shall ne'er be in a
    rage;
But were his verses vile, his whisper base,
You 'd quickly find him in Lord Fanny's
    case.   50
Sejanus, Wolsey, hurt not honest Fleury,
But well may put some statesmen in a
    fury.
Laugh then at any but at Fools or Foes;
These you but anger, and you mend not
    those.
Laugh at your friends, and if your friends
    are sore,
So much the better, you may laugh the
    more.
To Vice and Folly to confine the jest
Sets half the world, God knows, against
    the rest,
Did not the sneer of more impartial men
At Sense and Virtue, balance all again. 60
Judicious Wits spread wide the ridicule,
And charitably comfort knave and fool.

P. Dear sir, forgive the prejudice of
 youth:
Adieu Distinction, Satire, Warmth, and
 Truth!
Come, harmless characters that no one hit;
Come, Henley's oratory, Osborne's wit!
The honey dropping from Favonio's tongue,
The flowers of Bubo, and the flow of Yonge!
The gracious dew of pulpit Eloquence,
And all the well-whipt cream of courtly
 Sense 70
That first was H[er]vey's, F[ox]'s next,
 and then
The S[ena]te's, and then H[er]vey's once
 again,
O come! that easy Ciceronian style,
So Latin, yet so English all the while,
As, tho' the pride of Middleton and Bland,
All boys may read, and girls may under-
 stand!
Then might I sing without the least offence,
And all I sung should be the 'Nation's
 Sense;'
Or teach the melancholy Muse to mourn,
Hang the sad verse on Carolina's urn, 80
And hail her passage to the realms of
 rest,
All parts perform'd, and all her children
 blest!
So — Satire is no more — I feel it die —
No Gazetteer more innocent than I —
And let, a' God's name! ev'ry Fool and
 Knave
Be graced thro' life, and flatter'd in his
 grave.
 F. Why so? if Satire knows its time
 and place,
You still may lash the greatest — in dis-
 grace;
For merit will by turns forsake them all;
Would you know when? exactly when they
 fall. 90
But let all Satire in all changes spare
Immortal S[elkir]k, and grave De[lawa]re.
Silent and soft, as saints remove to Heav'n,
All ties dissolv'd, and ev'ry sin forgiv'n,
These may some gentle ministerial wing
Receive, and place for ever near a King!
There where no Passion, Pride, or Shame
 transport,
Lull'd with the sweet Nepenthe of a Court:
There where no father's, brother's, friend's
 disgrace
Once break their rest, or stir them from
 their place; 100

But past the sense of human miseries,
All tears are wiped for ever from all eyes;
No cheek is known to blush, no heart to
 throb,
Save when they lose a Question or a Job.
 P. Good Heav'n forbid that I should
 blast their glory,
Who know how like Whig ministers to
 Tory,
And when three Sov'reigns died could
 scarce be vext,
Consid'ring what a gracious Prince was
 next.
Have I, in silent wonder, seen such things
As pride in slaves, and avarice in Kings?
And at a peer or peeress shall I fret, 111
Who starves a sister or forswears a debt?
Virtue, I grant you, is an empty boast;
But shall the dignity of Vice be lost?
Ye Gods! shall Cibber's son, without re-
 buke,
Swear like a Lord; or Rich outwhore a
 Duke?
A fav'rite's porter with his master vie,
Be bribed as often, and as often lie?
Shall Ward draw contracts with a states-
 man's skill? 119
Or Japhet pocket, like His Grace, a will?
Is it for Bond or Peter (paltry things)
To pay their debts, or keep their faith, like
 Kings?
If Blount dispatch'd himself, he play'd the
 man,
And so mayst thou, illustrious Passeran!
But shall a printer, weary of his life,
Learn from their books to hang himself
 and wife?
This, this, my friend, I cannot, must not
 bear;
Vice thus abused demands a nation's care;
This calls the Church to deprecate our sin,
And hurls the thunder of the Laws on
 Gin. 130
 Let modest Foster, if he will, excel
Ten Metropolitans in preaching well;
A simple quaker, or a quaker's wife,
Outdo Landaff in doctrine — yea, in life;
Let humble Allen, with an awkward shame,
Do good by stealth, and blush to find it
 fame.
Virtue may choose the high or low degree,
'T is just alike to Virtue and to me;
Dwell in a monk, or light upon a King,
She 's still the same belov'd, contented
 thing. 140

Vice is undone, if she forgets her birth,
And stoops from angels to the dregs of
earth;
But 't is the Fall degrades her to a whore;
Let Greatness own her, and she 's mean no
more:
Her birth, her beauty, crowds and courts
confess;
Chaste Matrons praise her, and grave
Bishops bless;
In golden chains the willing world she
draws,
And hers the Gospel is, and hers the Laws;
Mounts the tribunal, lifts her scarlet head,
And sees pale Virtue carted in her stead.
Lo! at the wheels of her triumphal car, 151
Old England's genius, rough with many a
scar,
Dragg'd in the dust! his arms hang idly
round,
His flag inverted trails along the ground!
Our youth, all liv'ried o'er with foreign
gold,
Before her dance! behind her crawl the
old!
See thronging millions to the pagod run,
And offer country, parent, wife, or son!
Hear her black trumpet thro' the land pro-
claim,
That not to be corrupted is the shame. 160
In Soldier, Churchman, Patriot, Man in
Power,
'T is Av'rice all, Ambition is no more!
See all our nobles begging to be slaves!
See all our fools aspiring to be knaves!
The wit of cheats, the courage of a whore,
Are what ten thousand envy and adore:
All, all look up with reverential awe,
At crimes that 'scape, or triumph o'er the
law:
While Truth, Worth, Wisdom, daily they
decry —
'Nothing is sacred now but Villany.' 170
Yet may this verse (if such a verse re-
main)
Show there was one who held it in disdain.

DIALOGUE II

Fr. 'T is all a libel — Paxton, Sir, will
say. ⎫
P. Not yet, my friend! to morrow ⎬
'faith it may;
And for that very cause I print to-day. ⎭

How should I fret to mangle ev'ry line
In rev'rence to the sins of Thirty-nine!
Vice with such giant strides comes on
amain,
Invention strives to be before in vain;
Feign what I will, and paint it e'er so
strong,
Some rising genius sins up to my song.
F. Yet none but you by name the guilty
lash; 10
Ev'n Guthry saves half Newgate by a dash.
Spare then the Person, and expose the
Vice.
P. How, Sir! not damn the Sharper, but
the Dice?
Come on then, Satire! gen'ral, unconfin'd,
Spread thy broad wing, and souse on all
the kind.
Ye statesmen, priests, of one religion all!
Ye tradesmen vile, in army, court, or hall!
Ye rev'rend atheists! *F.* Scandal! name
them, who?
P. Why that 's the thing you bid me not
to do.
Who starv'd a sister, who forswore a debt,
I never named; the town 's inquiring yet. 21
The pois'ning Dame — *F.* You mean —
P. I don't. *F.* You do.
P. See, now I keep the secret, and not
you!
The bribing Statesman — *F.* Hold, too
high you go.
P. The bribed Elector — *F.* There you
stoop too low.
P. I fain would please you, if I knew
with what.
Tell me, which knave is lawful game,
which not?
Must great offenders, once escaped the
crown,
Like royal harts, be never more run down?
Admit your law to spare the Knight re-
quires, 30
As beasts of Nature may we hunt the
Squires?
Suppose I censure — you know what I
mean —
To save a Bishop, may I name a Dean?
F. A Dean, sir? no: his fortune is not
made;
You hurt a man that 's rising in the trade.
P. If not the tradesman who set up to-
day,
Much less the 'prentice who to-morrow
may.

Down, down, proud Satire! tho' a realm
  be spoil'd,
Arraign no mightier thief than wretched
  Wild;
Or, if a court or country 's made a job,   40
Go drench a pickpocket, and join the Mob.
  But, Sir, I beg you — for the love of
    Vice —
The matter's weighty, pray consider
    twice —
Have you less pity for the needy cheat,
The poor and friendless villain, than the
    great ?
Alas ! the small discredit of a bribe
Scarce hurts the Lawyer, but undoes the
    Scribe.
Then better sure it charity becomes
To tax Directors, who (thank God !) have
    plums;
Still better Ministers, or if the thing   50
May pinch ev'n there — why, lay it on a
    King.
  F. Stop ! stop !
  P.   Must Satire then nor rise nor fall ?
Speak out, and bid me blame no rogues at
    all.
  F. Yes, strike that Wild, I 'll justify the
    blow.
  P. Strike ? why the man was hang'd
    ten years ago:
Who now that obsolete example fears ?
Ev'n Peter trembles only for his ears.
  F. What, always Peter ? Peter thinks
    you mad;
You make men desp'rate, if they once are
    bad;
Else might he take to Virtue some years
    hence —   60
  P. As S[elkir]k, if he lives, will love the
    Prince.
  F. Strange spleen to S[elkir]k !
  P.   Do I wrong the man ?
God knows I praise a Courtier where I
    can.
When I confess there is who feels for fame,
And melts to goodness, need I Scarb'row
    name ?
Pleased let me own, in Esher's peaceful
    grove
(Where Kent and Nature vie for Pelham's
    love),
The scene, the master, opening to my view,
I sit and dream I see my Craggs anew !
  Ev'n in a Bishop I can spy desert;   70
Secker is decent, Rundel has a heart;

Manners with candour are to Benson giv'n;
To Berkley ev'ry virtue under Heav'n.
  But does the Court a worthy man re-
    move ?
That instant, I declare, he has my love:
I shun his zenith, court his mild decline.
Thus Somers once and Halifax were mine:
Oft in the clear still mirror of retreat
I studied Shrewsbury, the wise and great:
Carleton's calm sense and Stanhope's noble
    flame   80
Compared, and knew their gen'rous end
    the same;
How pleasing Atterbury's softer hour !
How shined the soul, unconquer'd, in the
    Tower !
How can I Pulteney, Chesterfield, forget,
While Roman Spirit charms, and Attic
    Wit ?
Argyle, the state's whole thunder born to
    wield,
And shake alike the senate and the field ?
Or Wyndham, just to freedom and the
    throne,
The Master of our Passions and his own ?
Names which I long have lov'd, nor lov'd
    in vain,   90
Rank'd with their friends, not number'd
    with their train;
And if yet higher the proud list should end,
Still let me say, — no foll'wer, but a
    Friend.
  Yet think not friendship only prompts
    my lays;
I follow Virtue; where she shines I praise,
Point she to priest or elder, Whig, or Tory,
Or round a quaker's beaver cast a glory.
I never (to my sorrow I declare)
Dined with the Man of Ross or my Lord
    Mayor.
Some in their choice of friends (nay, look
    not grave)   100
Have still a secret bias to a knave:
To find an honest man I beat about,
And love him, court him, praise him, in or
    out.
  F. Then why so few commended ?
  P.   Not so fierce;
Find you the Virtue, and I 'll find the
    Verse.
But random praise — the task can ne'er be
    done;
Each mother asks it for her booby son;
Each widow asks it for the best of men,
For him she weeps, for him she weds again.

Praise cannot stoop, like Satire, to the
ground; 110
The number may be hang'd, but not be
crown'd.
Enough for half the greatest of these days
To 'scape my Censure, not expect my
Praise.
Are they not rich ? what more can they
pretend ?
Dare they to hope a poet for their
friend ? —
What Richelieu wanted, Louis scarce could
gain,
And what young Ammon wish'd, but
wish'd in vain.
No power the Muse's friendship can com-
mand;
No power, when Virtue claims it, can with-
stand.
To Cato, Virgil paid one honest line; 120
O let my country's friends illumine mine!
— What are you thinking ? F. Faith, the
thought 's no sin;
I think your friends are out, and would be
in.
P. If merely to come in, Sir, they go out,
The way they take is strangely round about.
F. They too may be corrupted, you 'll
allow ?
P. I only call those knaves who are so
now.
Is that too little ? come, then, I 'll comply —
Spirit of Arnall, aid me while I lie! 129
Cobham 's a coward! Polworth is a slave!
And Lyttelton a dark designing knave!
St. John has ever been a wealthy fool! —
But let me add, Sir Robert 's mighty dull,
Has never made a friend in private life,
And was, besides, a tyrant to his wife!
But pray, when others praise him, do I
blame ?
Call Verres, Wolsey, any odious name ?
Why rail they then if but a wreath of mine,
O all-accomplish'd St. John! deck thy
shrine ?
What! shall each spur-gall'd hackney of
the day, 140
When Paxton gives him double pots and
pay,
Or each new-pension'd Sycophant, pretend
To break my windows if I treat a friend;
Then, wisely plead, to me they meant no
hurt,
But 't was my guest at whom they threw
the dirt ?

Sure if I spare the Minister, no rules
Of honour bind me not to maul his Tools;
Sure if they cannot cut, it may be said
His saws are toothless, and his hatchet 's
lead.
It anger'd Turenne, once upon a day, 150
To see a footman kick'd that took his
pay;
But when he heard th' affront the fellow
gave,
Knew one a Man of Honour, one a Knave,
The prudent Gen'ral turn'd it to a jest,
And begg'd he 'd take the pains to kick the
rest;
Which not at present having time to do —
F. Hold, Sir! for God's sake, where 's
th' affront to you ?
Against your worship when had S[herloc]k
writ,
Or P[a]ge pour'd forth the torrent of his
wit ?
Or grant the bard whose distich all com-
mend 160
(' In power a servant, out of power a friend ')
To W[alpo]le guilty of some venial sin,
What 's that to you who ne'er was out nor
in ?
The Priest whose flattery bedropp'd the
crown,
How hurt he you ? he only stain'd the
gown.
And how did, pray, the florid youth offend,
Whose speech you took, and gave it to a
friend ?
P. Faith, it imports not much from⎫
whom it came; ⎪
Whoever borrow'd could not be to blame, ⎬
Since the whole House did afterwards ⎪
the same. 170 ⎭
Let courtly Wits to Wits afford supply,
As hog to hog in huts of Westphaly:
If one, thro' Nature's bounty or his Lord's
Has what the frugal dirty soil affords,
From him the next receives it, thick or
thin,
As pure a mess almost as it came in;
The blessed benefit, not there confin'd,
Drops to the third, who nuzzles close be-
hind;
From tail to mouth they feed and they
carouse;
The last full fairly gives it to the House. 180
F. This filthy simile, this beastly line,
Quite turns my stomach — P. So does
flatt'ry mine;

And all your courtly civet-cats can vent,
Perfume to you, to me is excrement.
But hear me further — Japhet, 't is agreed,
Writ not, and Chartres scarce could write
   or read
In all the courts of Pindus, guiltless quite;
But pens can forge, my friend, that cannot
   write,
And must no egg in Japhet's face be
   thrown,
Because the deed he forged was not my
   own ?   190
Must never Patriot then declaim at Gin
Unless, good man! he has been fairly in ?
No zealous Pastor blame a failing spouse
Without a staring reason on his brows ?
And each blasphemer quite escape the
   rod,
Because the insult 's not on man but God ?
   Ask you what provocation I have had ?
The strong antipathy of good to bad.
When Truth or Virtue an affront endures,
Th' affront is mine, my friend, and should
   be yours.   200
Mine, as a foe profess'd to false pretence,
Who think a coxcomb's honour like his
   sense;
Mine, as a friend to ev'ry worthy mind;
And mine as man, who feel for all man-
   kind.
   F. You 're strangely proud.
        P. So proud, I am no slave;
So impudent, I own myself no knave;
So odd, my country's ruin makes me grave.
Yes, I am proud; I must be proud to see
Men, not afraid of God, afraid of me;
Safe from the Bar, the Pulpit, and the
   Throne,   210
Yet touch'd and shamed by Ridicule alone.
   O sacred weapon! left for Truth's de-
   fence,
Sole dread of Folly, Vice, and Insolence,
To all but Heav'n-directed hands denied,
The Muse may give thee, but the Gods
   must guide!
Rev'rent I touch thee! but with honest
   zeal,
To rouse the watchmen of the public
   weal,
To Virtue's work provoke the tardy hall,
And goad the Prelate, slumb'ring in his
   stall.
Ye tinsel insects! whom a Court maintains,
That counts your beauties only by your
   stains,   221

Spin all your cobwebs o'er the eye of
   day!
The Muse's wing shall brush you all away.
All His Grace preaches, all His Lordship
   sings,
All that makes Saints of Queens, and Gods
   of Kings;
All, all but Truth, drops dead-born from
   the press,
Like the last Gazette, or the last Address.
   When black Ambition stains a public
   cause,
A Monarch's sword when mad Vainglory
   draws,
Not Waller's wreath can hide the nation's
   scar,   230
Nor Boileau turn the feather to a star.
   Not so when, diadem'd with rays divine,
Touch'd with the flame that breaks from
   Virtue's shrine,
Her priestess Muse forbids the good to
   die,
And opes the Temple of Eternity.
There other trophies deck the truly brave
Than such as Anstis casts into the grave;
Far other stars than [Kent] and [Grafton]
   wear,
And may descend to Mordington from
   Stair; —
Such as on Hough's unsullied mitre shine,
Or beam, good Digby! from a heart like
   thine.   241
Let envy howl, while heav'n's whole chorus
   sings,
And bark at honour not conferr'd by Kings;
Let Flatt'ry sick'ning see the incense rise,
Sweet to the world, and grateful to the
   skies:
Truth guards the Poet, sanctifies the line,
And makes immortal, verse as mean as
   mine.
   Yes, the last pen for Freedom let me
   draw,
When Truth stands trembling on the edge
   of law
Here, last of Britons! let your names be
   read;   250
Are none, none living ? let me praise the
   dead;
And for that cause which made your fathers
   shine
Fall by the votes of their degen'rate line.
   F. Alas! alas! pray end what you began,
And write next winter more Essays on
   Man.

THE SIXTH SATIRE OF THE SECOND BOOK OF HORACE

THE FIRST PART IMITATED IN THE YEAR 1714 BY DR. SWIFT; THE LATTER PART ADDED AFTERWARDS

Of the following *Imitations of Horace* the first two are rather imitations of Swift, Horace merely supplying the text for the travesty. For (as previous editors have not failed to point out) no styles could be found less like one another than the bland and polite style of Horace and the downright, and often cynically plain, manner of Swift. With Pope the attempt to write in Swift's style was a mere *tour de force*, which he could indeed carry out with success through a few lines, but not further, without relapsing into his own more elaborate manner. Swift's marvellous precision and *netteté* of expression are something very different from Pope's pointed and rhetorical elegance. The *Ode to Venus*, which was first published in 1737, more nearly approaches the character of a translation. (Ward.)

I 've often wish'd that I had clear
For life six hundred pounds a year,
A handsome house to lodge a friend,
A river at my garden's end,
A terrace walk, and half a rood
Of land set out to plant a wood.
  Well, now I have all this, and more,
I ask not to increase my store;
But here a grievance seems to lie,
All this is mine but till I die;　　　　10
I can't but think 't would sound more
    clever,
To me and to my heirs for ever.
  If I ne'er got or lost a groat
By any trick or any fault;
And if I pray by Reason's rules,
And not like forty other fools,
As thus: ' Vouchsafe, O gracious Maker!
To grant me this and t' other acre;
Or, if it be thy will and pleasure,
Direct my plough to find a treasure;　　20
But only what my station fits,
And to be kept in my right wits,
Preserve, almighty Providence!
Just what you gave me, Competence;
And let me in these shades compose
Something in verse as true as prose,
Remov'd from all th' ambitious scene,
Nor puff'd by Pride, nor sunk by Spleen.'
  In short, I 'm perfectly content,
Let me but live on this side Trent,　　30

Nor cross the channel twice a year,
To spend six months with statesmen
    here.
I must by all means come to town,
'T is for the service of the Crown;
' Lewis, the Dean will be of use;
Send for him up; take no excuse.'
  The toil, the danger of the seas,
Great ministers ne'er think of these;
Or, let it cost five hundred pound,
No matter where the money 's found;　　40
It is but so much more in debt,
And that they ne'er consider'd yet.
  ' Good Mr. Dean, go change your gown,
Let my Lord know you 're come to town.'
I hurry me in haste away,
Not thinking it is Levee day,
And find His Honour in a pound,
Hemm'd by a triple circle round,
Chequer'd with ribbons blue and green:
How should I thrust myself between?　　50
Some wag observes me thus perplex'd,
And smiling, whispers to the next,
' I thought the Dean had been too proud
To jostle here among a crowd.'
Another, in a surly fit,
Tells me I have more zeal than wit;
' So eager to express your love,
You ne'er consider whom you shove,
But rudely press before a Duke.'
I own I 'm pleas'd with this rebuke,　　60
And take it kindly meant, to show
What I desire the world should know.
  I get a whisper, and withdraw;
When twenty fools I never saw
Come with petitions fairly penn'd,
Desiring I would stand their friend.
This humbly offers me his Case —
That begs my int'rest for a Place —
A hundred other men's affairs,
Like bees, are humming in my ears;　　70
' To-morrow my appeal comes on,
Without your help the cause is gone.'
' The Duke expects my Lord and you
About some great affair at two.'
' Put my Lord Bolingbroke in mind
To get my warrant quickly sign'd:
Consider, 't is my first request.' —
' Be satisfied, I 'll do my best: ' —
Then presently he falls to tease,
' You may be certain, if you please;　　80
I doubt not, if his Lordship knew —
And, Mr. Dean, one word from you.' —
'T is (let me see) three years and more
(October next it will be four)

Since Harley bid me first attend,
And chose me for an humble friend:
Would take me in his coach to chat,
And question me of this and that;
As, 'What's o'clock?' and, 'How's the
    wind?'
'Whose chariot's that we left behind?' 90
Or gravely try to read the lines
Writ underneath the country signs;
Or, 'Have you nothing new to-day
From Pope, from Parnell, or from Gay?'
Such tattle often entertains
My Lord and me as far as Staines,
As once a week we travel down
To Windsor, and again to town,
Where all that passes *inter nos*
Might be proclaim'd at Charing-cross. 100
    Yet some I know with envy swell
Because they see me used so well.
'How think you of our friend the Dean?
I wonder what some people mean;
My lord and he are grown so great,
Always together *tête-à-tête*.
What! they admire him for his jokes —
See but the fortune of some folks!'
There flies about a strange report
Of some express arrived at Court; 110
I'm stopp'd by all the fools I meet,
And catechised in every street.
'You, Mr. Dean, frequent the Great:
Inform us, will the Emp'ror treat?
Or do the prints and papers lie?'
'Faith, Sir, you know as much as I.'
'Ah, Doctor, how you love to jest!
'T is now no secret.' — 'I protest
'T is one to me.' — 'Then tell us, pray,
When are the troops to have their pay?' 120
And tho' I solemnly declare
I know no more than my Lord Mayor,
They stand amazed, and think me grown
The closest mortal ever known.
    Thus in a sea of folly tost,
My choicest hours of life are lost;
Yet always wishing to retreat:
O, could I see my country-seat!
There leaning near a gentle brook,
Sleep, or peruse some ancient book, 130
And there, in sweet oblivion drown
Those cares that haunt the Court and town.
O charming Noons! and Nights divine!
Or when I sup, or when I dine,
My friends above, my folks below,
Chatting and laughing all-a-row,
The beans and bacon set before 'em,
The grace-cup served with all decorum;

Each willing to be pleas'd, and please,
And ev'n the very dogs at ease! 140
Here no man prates of idle things,
How this or that Italian sings,
A Neighbour's madness, or his Spouse's,
Or what's in either of the Houses;
But something much more our concern,
And quite a scandal not to learn;
Which is the happier or the wiser,
A man of merit, or a miser?
Whether we ought to choose our friends
For their own worth or our own ends? 150
What good, or better, we may call,
And what the very best of all?
    Our friend Dan Prior told (you know)
A tale extremely *à-propos:*
Name a town life, and in a trice
He had a story of two mice.
Once on a time (so runs the Fable)
A Country Mouse right hospitable,
Received a Town Mouse at his board,
Just as a farmer might a Lord. 160
A frugal mouse, upon the whole,
Yet lov'd his friend, and had a soul;
Knew what was handsome, and would do 't,
On just occasion, *coûte qui coûte.*
He brought him bacon (nothing lean),
Pudding that might have pleas'd a Dean;
Cheese, such as men in Suffolk make,
But wish'd it Stilton for his sake;
Yet, to his guest tho' no way sparing,
He ate himself the rind and paring. 170
Our Courtier scarce could touch a bit,
But show'd his breeding and his wit;
He did his best to seem to eat,
And cried, 'I vow you 're mighty neat:
But lord, my friend, this savage scene!
For God's sake come and live with men;
Consider, mice, like men, must die,
Both small and great, both you and I;
Then spend your life in joy and sport,
(This doctrine, friend, I learn'd at court).'
    The veriest hermit in the nation 181
May yield, God knows, to strong tempta-
    tion.
Away they came, thro' thick and thin,
To a tall house near Lincoln's-Inn
('T was on the night of a debate,
When all their Lordships had sat late).
    Behold the place where if a poet
Shined in description he might show it;
Tell how the moonbeam trembling falls,
And tips with silver all the walls; 190
Palladian walls, Venetian doors,
Grotesco roofs. and stucco floors:

But let it (in a word) be said, ⎫
The moon was up, and men a-bed, ⎬
The napkins white, the carpet red: ⎭
The guests withdrawn had left the treat,
And down the Mice sat *tête-à-tête*.
Our Courtier walks from dish to dish,
Tastes for his friend of fowl and fish;
Tells all their names, lays down the law, 200
' *Que ça est bon ! Ah, goutez ça !*
That Jelly 's rich, this Malmsey healing,
Pray, dip your whiskers and your tail in.'
Was ever such a happy swain!
He stuffs and swills, and stuffs again.
' I 'm quite ashamed — 't is mighty rude
To eat so much — but all 's so good —
I have a thousand thanks to give —
My Lord alone knows how to live.'
No sooner said, but from the hall 210
Rush chaplain, butler, dogs, and all:
' A rat, a rat! clap to the door ' —
The cat comes bouncing on the floor.
O for the art of Homer's mice,
Or gods to save them in a trice!
(It was by Providence, they think,
For your damn'd stucco has no chink!)
' An 't please Your Honour,' quoth the
    peasant,
' This same dessert is not so pleasant:
Give me again my hollow tree, 220
A crust of bread and Liberty! '

THE SEVENTH EPISTLE OF THE FIRST BOOK OF HORACE

IN THE MANNER OF DR. SWIFT

'T is true, my Lord, I gave my word
I would be with you June the third;
Changed it to August, and (in short)
Have kept it — as you do at Court.
You humour me when I am sick,
Why not when I am splenetic ?
In Town what objects could I meet ?
The shops shut up in every street,
And funerals black'ning all the doors,
And yet more melancholy whores: 10
And what a dust in every place!
And a thin Court that wants your face,
And fevers raging up and down,
And W[ard] and H[enley] both in town!
' The dogdays are no more the case.'
'T is true, but winter comes apace:
Then southward let your bard retire,
Hold out some months 'twixt sun and fire,

And you shall see the first warm weather
Me and the butterflies together. 20
My Lord, your favours well I know;
'T is with distinction you bestow,
And not to every one that comes,
Just as a Scotchman does his plums.
' Pray take them, Sir — enough 's a feast:
Eat some, and pocket up the rest: '
What, rob your boys ? those pretty rogues!
' No, Sir, you 'll leave them to the hogs.'
Thus fools with compliments besiege ye,
Contriving never to oblige ye. 30
Scatter your favours on a Fop,
Ingratitude 's the certain crop;
And 't is but just, I 'll tell ye wherefore,
You give the things you never care for.
A wise man always is, or should,
Be mighty ready to be good,
But makes a diff'rence in his thought
Betwixt a guinea and a groat.
Now this I 'll say, you 'll find in me
A safe companion, and a free; 40
But if you 'd have me always near,
A word, pray, in Your Honour's ear:
I hope it is your resolution
To give me back my constitution,
The sprightly wit, the lively eye,
Th' engaging smile, the gayety
That laugh'd down many a summer sun,
And kept you up so oft till one;
And all that voluntary vein,
As when Belinda rais'd my strain. 50
A Weasel once made shift to slink
In at a corn-loft thro' a chink,
But having amply stuff'd his skin,
Could not get out as he got in;
Which one belonging to the house
('T was not a man, it was a mouse)
Observing, cried, ' You 'scape not so;
Lean as you came, Sir, you must go.'
Sir, you may spare your application;
I 'm no such beast, nor his relation, 60
Nor one that Temperance advance,
Cramm'd to the throat with ortolans;
Extremely ready to resign
All that may make me none of mine.
South-Sea subscriptions take who please,
Leave me but liberty and ease:
'T was what I said to Craggs and Child,
Who praised my modesty, and smil'd.
' Give me,' I cried (enough for me)
' My bread and independency! ' 70
So bought an annual rent or two,
And lived — just as you see I do;

Near fifty, and without a wife,
I trust that sinking fund, my life.
Can I retrench ? Yes, mighty well,
Shrink back to my paternal cell,
A little house, with trees a row,
And, like its master, very low;
There died my father, no man's debtor,
And there I 'll die, nor worse nor better. 8o
  To set this matter full before ye,
Our old friend Swift will tell his story.
'Harley, the nation's great support' —
But you may read it, I stop short.

THE FIRST ODE OF THE FOURTH BOOK OF HORACE

TO VENUS

AGAIN ? new tumults in my breast ?
Ah, spare me, Venus ! let me, let me rest !
I am not now, alas ! the man
As in the gentle reign of my Queen Anne.
Ah ! sound no more thy soft alarms,
Nor circle sober fifty with thy charms.
Mother too fierce of dear desires !
Turn, turn to willing hearts your wanton
    fires:
To *number five* direct your doves,
There spread round Murray all your bloom-
    ing Loves;   10
Noble and young, who strikes the heart
With ev'ry sprightly, ev'ry decent part;
Equal the injured to defend,
To charm the Mistress, or to fix the Friend.
He, with a hundred arts refin'd,
Shall stretch thy conquests over half the
    kind:
To him each rival shall submit,
Make but his Riches equal to his Wit.
Then shall thy form the marble grace,
(Thy Grecian form) and Chloe lend the
    face: 20
His house, embosom'd in the grove,
Sacred to social life and social love,
Shall glitter o'er the pendant green,
Where Thames reflects the visionary scene:
Thither, the silver-sounding lyres
Shall call the smiling Loves, and young De-
    sires;
There, ev'ry Grace and Muse shall throng,

Exalt the dance, or animate the song;
There Youths and Nymphs, in concert gay,
Shall hail the rising, close the parting day.
With me, alas ! those joys are o'er;   31
For me, the vernal garlands bloom no more.
Adieu, fond hope of mutual fire,
The still-believing, still-renew'd desire;
Adieu, the heart-expanding bowl,
And all the kind deceivers of the soul !
But why ? ah tell me, ah too dear !
Steals down my cheek th' involuntary
    Tear ?
Why words so flowing, thoughts so free,
Stop, or turn nonsense, at one glance of
    thee ?   40
Thee, drest in Fancy's airy beam,
Absent I follow thro' th' extended Dream;
Now, now I seize, I clasp thy charms,
And now you burst (ah cruel !) from my
    arms;
And swiftly shoot along the Mall,
Or softly glide by the Canal,
Now, shown by Cynthia's silver ray,
And now, on rolling waters snatch'd away.

THE NINTH ODE OF THE FOURTH BOOK OF HORACE

A FRAGMENT

LEST you should think that verse shall die
  Which sounds the silver Thames along,
Taught on the wings of truth to fly
  Above the reach of vulgar song;

Tho' daring Milton sits sublime,
  In Spenser native muses play;
Nor yet shall Waller yield to time,
  Nor pensive Cowley's moral lay —

Sages and Chiefs long since had birth
  Ere Cæsar was or Newton named;
These rais'd new empires o'er the earth,
  And those new heav'ns and systems
    framed.

Vain was the Chief's, the Sage's Pride !
  They had no Poet, and they died.
In vain they schemed, in vain they bled !
  They had no Poet, and are dead.

THE DUNCIAD

IN FOUR BOOKS

THE first edition of *The Dunciad* was published in the spring of 1728, and included the first three books. In 1729 an edition with notes and other illustrative matter appeared, the original frontispiece of the owl being superseded by a vignette of a donkey bearing a pile of books upon which an owl perched. In this edition appeared the Dedication to Swift and the Letter to the Publisher. William Cleland, whose name is signed to this letter, was a real person and an acquaintance of Pope's, but it is generally conceded that the letter is directly or indirectly the work of Pope himself. The fourth book, then called *The New Dunciad*, was published separately in 1742. In the complete edition of 1743, Cibber takes the place of Theobald as hero of the poem. During these fifteen years, public interest in the satire, which was undoubtedly great, was artificially stimulated by Pope. So subtle were his mystifications that the confusion into which he threw his commentators has only recently been set straight.

MARTINUS SCRIBLERUS OF THE POEM

This poem, as it celebrateth the most grave and ancient of things, Chaos, Night, and Dulness, so is it of the most grave and ancient kind. Homer (saith Aristotle) was the first who gave the form, and (saith Horace) who adapted the measure, to heroic poesy. But even before this may be rationally presumed, from what the ancients have left written, was a piece by Homer, composed of like nature and matter with this of our poet; for of epic sort it appeareth to have been, yet of matter surely not unpleasant; witness what is reported of it by the learned Archbishop Eustathius, in Odyssey X. And accordingly Aristotle, in his Poetic, chap. iv., doth further set forth, that as the Iliad and Odyssey gave an example to Tragedy, so did this poem to Comedy its first idea.

From these authors also it should seem that the hero, or chief personage of it, was no less obscure, and his understanding and sentiments no less quaint and strange (if indeed not more so) than any of the actors of our poem. Margites was the name of this personage, whom antiquity recordeth to have been Dunce the First; and surely, from what we hear of him, not unworthy to be the root of so spreading a tree, and so numerous a posterity. The poem, therefore, celebrating him, was properly and absolutely a Dunciad; which though now unhappily lost, yet is its nature sufficiently known by the infallible tokens aforesaid. And thus it doth appear that the first Dunciad was the first epic poem, written by Homer himself, and anterior even to the Iliad or Odyssey.

Now, forasmuch as our poet hath translated those two famous works of Homer which are yet left, he did conceive it in some sort his duty to imitate that also which was lost; and was therefore induced to bestow on it the same form which Homer's is reported to have had, namely, that of epic poem; with a title also framed after the ancient Greek manner, to wit, that of Dunciad.

Wonderful it is that so few of the moderns have been stimulated to attempt some Dunciad; since, in the opinion of the multitude, it might cost less pain and toil than an imitation of the greater epic. But possible it is also that, on due reflection, the maker might find it easier to paint a Charlemagne, a Brute, or a Godfrey, with just pomp and dignity heroic, than a Margites, a Codrus, or a Fleckno.

We shall next declare the occasion and the cause which moved our poet to this particular work. He lived in those days when (after Providence had permitted the invention of printing as a scourge for the sins of the learned) paper also became so cheap, and printers so numerous, that a deluge of authors covered the land: whereby not only the peace of the honest unwriting subject was daily molested, but unmerciful demands were made of his applause, yea, of his money, by such as would neither earn the one nor deserve the other. At the same time the license of the press was such, that it grew dangerous to refuse them either; for they would forthwith publish slanders unpunished, the authors being anonymous, and skulking under the wings of publishers, a set of men who never scrupled to vend either calumny or blasphemy, as long as the town would call for it.

[1] Now our author, living in those times, did conceive it an endeavour well worthy an honest satirist, to dissuade the dull, and punish the wicked, the only way that was left. In that public-spirited view he laid the Plan of this poem, as the greatest service he was

[1] Vide Bossu, du Poeme Epique, chap. viii.

capable (without much hurt, or being slain) to render his dear country. First, taking things from their original, he considereth the causes creative of such authors, namely, dulness and poverty; the one born with them, the other contracted by neglect of their proper talents, through self-conceit of greater abilities. This truth he wrappeth in an allegory [1] (as the construction of epic poesy requireth), and feigns that one of these goddesses had taken up her abode with the other, and that they jointly inspired all such writers and such works.[2] He proceedeth to show the qualities they bestow on these authors, and the effects they produce; [3] then the materials, or stock, with which they furnish them; [4] and (above all) that self-opinion [5] which causeth it to seem to themselves vastly greater than it is, and is the prime motive of their setting up in this sad and sorry merchandise. The great power of these goddesses acting in alliance (whereof as the one is the mother of industry, so is the other of plodding) was to be exemplified in some one great and remarkable action; [6] and none could be more so than that which our poet hath chosen, viz. the restoration of the reign of Chaos and Night, by the ministry of Dulness their daughter, in the removal of her imperial seat from the city to the polite world; as the action of the Æneid is the restoration of the empire of Troy, by the removal of the race from thence to Latium. But as Homer, singing only the wrath of Achilles, yet includes in his poem the whole history of the Trojan war; in like manner, our author has drawn into this single action the whole history of Dulness and her children.

A Person must next be fixed upon to support this action. This phantom, in the poet's mind, must have a name.[7] He finds it to be ———; and he becomes of course the hero of the poem.

The Fable being thus, according to the best example, one and entire, as contained in the proposition; the machinery is a continued chain of allegories, setting forth the whole power, ministry, and empire of Dulness, extended through her subordinate instruments, in all her various operations.

This is branched into Episodes, each of which hath its moral apart, though all conducive to the main end. The crowd assembled in the second Book demonstrates the design to be more extensive than to bad poets only, and that we may expect other episodes of the patrons, encouragers, or paymasters of such authors, as occasion shall bring them forth.

And the third Book, if well considered, seemeth to embrace the whole world. Each of the games relateth to some or other vile class of writers. The first concerneth the plagiary, to whom he giveth the name of Moore; the second the libellous novelist, whom he styleth Eliza; the third, the flattering dedicator; the fourth, the bawling critic, or noisy poet; the fifth the dark and dirty party-writer; and so of the rest; assigning to each some proper name or other, such as he could find.

As for the Characters, the public hath already acknowledged how justly they are drawn. The manners are so depicted, and the sentiments so peculiar to those to whom applied, that surely to transfer them to any other or wiser personages would be exceeding difficult; and certain it is that every person concerned, being consulted apart, hath readily owned the resemblance of every portrait, his own excepted. So Mr. Cibber calls them 'a parcel of poor wretches, so many silly flies;' but adds, 'our author's wit is remarkably more bare and barren whenever it would fall foul on Cibber than upon any other person whatever.'

The Descriptions are singular, the comparisons very quaint, the narrations various, yet of one colour, the purity and chastity of diction is so preserved, that in the places most suspicious, not the words, but only the images, have been censured; and yet are those images no other than have been sanctified by ancient and classical authority (though, as was the manner of those good times, not so curiously wrapped up), yea, and commented upon by the most grave doctors and approved critics.

As it beareth the name of Epic, it is thereby subjected to such severe indispensable rules as are laid on all neoterics, a strict imitation of the ancients; insomuch that any deviation, accompanied with whatever poetic beauties, hath always been censured by the sound critic. How exact that imitation hath been in this piece, appeareth not only by its general structure, but by particular allusions infinite, many whereof have escaped both the commentator and poet himself; yea divers, by his exceeding diligence, are so altered and interwoven with the rest, that several have already been, and more will be, by the ignorant abused, as altogether and originally his own.

In a word, the whole Poem proveth itself to be the work of our author, when his faculties were in full vigour and perfection; at that exact time when years have ripened the judgment without diminishing the imagination;

---

[1] Bossu, chap. vii.
[2] Book i. ver. 32, &c.
[3] Book i. ver. 45 to 54.
[4] Ver. 57 to 77.

[5] Ver. 80.
[6] Bossu, chap. vii., viii.
[7] Bossu, chap. viii. Vide Aristot. Poetic, cap. ix.

which, by good critics, is held to be punctually at forty : for at that season it was that Virgil finished his *Georgics;* and Sir Richard Blackmore, at the like age composing his *Arthurs,* declared the same to be the very acme and pitch of life for epic poesy; though, since, he hath altered it to sixty, the year in which he published his *Alfred.* True it is that the talents for criticism, namely, smartness, quick censure, vivacity of remark, certainty of asseveration, indeed all but acerbity, seem rather the gifts of youth than of riper age : but it is far otherwise in poetry; witness the works of Mr. Rymer and Mr. Dennis, who, beginning with criticism, became afterwards such poets as no age hath paralleled. With good reason, therefore, did our author choose to write his Essay on that subject at twenty, and reserve for his maturer years this great and wonderful work of THE DUNCIAD.

PREFACE

PREFIXED TO THE FIVE FIRST IMPERFECT EDITIONS OF THE DUNCIAD, IN THREE BOOKS, PRINTED AT DUBLIN AND LONDON, IN OCTAVO AND DUODECIMO, 1727.

THE PUBLISHER TO THE READER

It will be found a true observation, though somewhat surprising, that when any scandal is vented against a man of the highest distinction and character, either in the state or literature, the public in general afford it a most quiet reception, and the larger part accept it as favourably as if it were some kindness done to themselves : whereas, if a known scoundrel or blockhead but chance to be touched upon, a whole legion is up in arms, and it becomes the common cause of all scribblers, booksellers, and printers whatsoever.

Not to search too deeply into the reason hereof, I will only observe as a fact, that every week, for these two months past, the town has been persecuted with pamphlets, advertisements, letters, and weekly essays, not only against the wit and writings, but against the character and person of Mr. Pope; and that of all those men who have received pleasure from his works (which by modest computation may be about a hundred thousand in these kingdoms of England and Ireland, not to mention Jersey, Guernsey, the Orcades, those in the New World, and foreigners who have translated him into their languages), of all this number not a man hath stood up to say one word in his defence.

The only exception is the author of the following poem, who doubtless had either a better insight into the grounds of this clamour, or a better opinion of Mr. Pope's integrity, joined with a greater personal love for him than any other of his numerous friends and admirers.

Farther, that he was in his peculiar intimacy, appears from the knowledge he manifests of the most private authors of all the anonymous pieces against him, and from his having in this poem attacked no man living who had not before printed or published some scandal against this gentleman.

How I came possessed of it, is no concern to the reader; but it would have been a wrong to him had I detained the publication; since those names which are its chief ornaments die off daily so fast, as must render it too soon unintelligible. If it provoke the author to give us a more perfect edition, I have my end.

Who he is I cannot say, and (which is a great pity) there is certainly nothing in his style and manner of writing which can distinguish or discover him; for if it bears any resemblance to that of Mr. Pope, it is not improbable but it might be done on purpose, with a view to have it pass for his. But by the frequency of his allusions to Virgil, and a laboured (not to say affected) shortness in imitation of him, I should think him more an admirer of the Roman poet than of the Grecian, and in that not of the same taste with his friend.

I have been well informed that this work was the labour of full six years of his life, and that he wholly retired himself from all the avocations and pleasures of the world to attend diligently to its correction and perfection; and six years more he intended to bestow upon it, as it should seem by this verse of Statius, which was cited at the head of his manuscript : —

'Oh mihi bissenos multum vigilata per annos, Duncia ! '

Hence also we learn the true title of the poem; which, with the same certainty as we call that of Homer the Iliad, of Virgil the Æneid, of Camöens the Lusiad, we may pronounce could have been, and can be, no other than

THE DUNCIAD

It is styled heroic, as being doubly so; not only with respect to its nature, which, according to the best rules of the ancients, and strictest ideas of the moderns, is critically such ; but also with regard to the heroical disposition and high courage of the writer, who dared to stir up such a formidable, irritable, and implacable race of mortals.

There may arise some obscurity in chronology from the names in the poem, by the inevitable removal of some authors, and insertion of others in their niches: for, whoever will consider the unity of the whole design, will be sensible that the poem was not made for these authors, but these authors for the poem. I should judge that they were clapped in as they rose, fresh and fresh, and changed from day to day; in like manner as when the old boughs wither we thrust new ones into a chimney.

I would not have the reader too much troubled or anxious, if he cannot decipher them; since, when he shall have found them out, he will probably know no more of the persons than before.

Yet we judged it better to preserve them as they are, than to change them for fictitious names; by which the satire would only be multiplied, and applied to many instead of one. Had the hero, for instance, been called Codrus, how many would have affirmed him to have been Mr. T., Mr. E., Sir R. B.? &c., but now all that unjust scandal is saved, by calling him by a name which, by good luck, happens to be that of a real person.

A LETTER TO THE PUBLISHER

OCCASIONED BY THE FIRST CORRECT EDITION OF THE DUNCIAD

It is with pleasure I hear that you have procured a correct copy of the Dunciad, which the many surreptitious ones have rendered so necessary; and it is yet with more, that I am informed it will be attended with a Commentary; a work so requisite, that I cannot think the author himself would have omitted it, had he approved of the first appearance of this poem.

Such Notes as have occurred to me I herewith send you: you will oblige me by inserting them amongst those which are, or will be, transmitted to you by others; since not only the author's friends, but even strangers, appear engaged by humanity, to take some care of an orphan of so much genius and spirit, which its parent seems to have abandoned from the very beginning, and suffered to step into the world naked, unguarded, and unattended.

It was upon reading some of the abusive papers lately published, that my great regard to a person whose friendship I esteem as one of the chief honours of my life, and a much greater respect to truth than to him or any man living, engaged me in inquiries of which the enclosed Notes are the fruit.

I perceived that most of these authors had been (doubtless very wisely) the first aggressors. They had tried, till they were weary, what was to be got by railing at each other: nobody was either concerned or surprised if this or that scribbler was proved a dunce, but every one was curious to read what could be said to prove Mr. Pope one, and was ready to pay something for such a discovery; a stratagem which, would they fairly own it, might not only reconcile them to me, but screen them from the resentment of their lawful superiors, whom they daily abuse, only (as I charitably hope) to get that by them, which they cannot get from them.

I found this was not all: ill success in that had transported them to personal abuse, either of himself, or (what I think he could less forgive) of his friends. They had called men of virtue and honour bad men, long before he had either leisure or inclination to call them bad writers; and some of them had been such old offenders, that he had quite forgotten their persons, as well as their slanders, till they were pleased to revive them.

Now what had Mr. Pope done before to incense them? He had published those works which are in the hands of every body, in which not the least mention is made of any of them. And what has he done since? He has laughed, and written the Dunciad. What has that said of them? A very serious truth, which the public had said before, that they were dull; and what it had no sooner said, but they themselves were at great pains to procure, or even purchase, room in the prints to testify under their hands to the truth of it.

I should still have been silent, if either I had seen any inclination in my friend to be serious with such accusers, or if they had only meddled with his writings; since whoever publishes, puts himself on his trial by his country: but when his moral character was attacked, and in a manner from which neither truth nor virtue can secure the most innocent; in a manner which, though it annihilates the credit of the accusation with the just and impartial, yet aggravates very much the guilt of the accusers — I mean by authors without names — then I thought, since the danger was common to all, the concern ought to be so; and that it was an act of justice to detect the authors, not only on this account, but as many of them are the same who, for several years past, have made free with the greatest names in church and state, exposed to the world the private misfortunes of families, abused all, even to women; and whose prostituted papers (for one or other party in the unhappy divisions of their country) have insulted the fallen, the friendless, the exiled, and the dead.

Besides this, which I take to be public concern, I have already confessed I had a private one. I am one of that number who have long loved and esteemed Mr. Pope; and had often declared it was not his capacity or writings (which we ever thought the least valuable part of his character), but the honest, open, and beneficent man, that we most esteemed and loved in him. Now, if what these people say were believed, I must appear to all my friends either a fool or a knave; either imposed on myself, or imposing on them; so that I am as much interested in the confutation of these calumnies as he is himself.

I am no author, and consequently not to be suspected either of jealousy or resentment against any of the men, of whom scarce one is known to me by sight; and as for their writings, I have sought them (on this one occasion) in vain, in the closets and libraries of all my acquaintance. I had still been in the dark, if a gentleman had not procured me (I suppose from some of themselves, for they are generally much more dangerous friends than enemies) the passages I send you. I solemnly protest I have added nothing to the malice or absurdity of them; which it behoves me to declare, since the vouchers themselves will be so soon and so irrecoverably lost. You may, in some measure, prevent it, by preserving at least their titles, and discovering (as far as you can depend on the truth of your information) the names of the concealed authors.

The first objection I have heard made to the poem is, that the persons are too obscure for satire. The persons themselves, rather than allow the objection, would forgive the satire; and if one could be tempted to afford it a serious answer, were not all assassinates, popular insurrections, the insolence of the rabble without doors, and of domestics within, most wrongfully chastised, if the meanness of offenders indemnified them from punishment? On the contrary, obscurity renders them more dangerous, as less thought of: law can pronounce judgment only or open facts; morality alone can pass censure on intentions of mischief; so that for secret calumny, or the arrow flying in the dark, there is no public punishment left but what a good writer inflicts.

The next objection is, that these sort of authors are poor. That might be pleaded as an excuse at the Old Bailey for lesser crimes than defamation (for it is the case of almost all who are tried there), but sure it can be none here: for who will pretend that the robbing another of his reputation supplies the want of it in himself? I question not but such authors are poor, and heartily wish the objection were removed by any honest livelihood; but poverty is here the accident, not the subject. He who describes malice and villany to be pale and meagre, expresses not the least anger against paleness or leanness, but against malice and villany. The apothecary in Romeo and Juliet is poor; but is he therefore justified in vending poison? Not but poverty itself becomes a just subject of satire, when it is the consequence of vice, prodigality, or neglect of one's lawful calling; for then it increases the public burden, fills the streets and highways with robbers, and the garrets with clippers, coiners, and weekly journalists.

But admitting that two or three of these offend less in their morals than in their writings; must poverty make nonsense sacred? If so, the fame of bad authors would be much better consulted than that of all the good ones in the world; and not one of a hundred had ever been called by his right name.

They mistake the whole matter: it is not charity to encourage them in the way they follow, but to get them out of it; for men are not bunglers because they are poor, but they are poor because they are bunglers.

Is it not pleasant enough to hear our authors crying out on the one hand, as if their persons and characters were too sacred for satire; and the public objecting, on the other, that they are too mean even for ridicule? But whether bread or fame be their end, it must be allowed, our author, by and in this poem, has mercifully given them a little of both.

There are two or three who, by their rank and fortune, have no benefit from the former objections, supposing them good, and these I was sorry to see in such company: but if, without any provocation, two or three gentlemen will fall upon one, in an affair wherein his interest and reputation are equally embarked, they cannot, certainly, after they have been content to print themselves his enemies, complain of being put into the number of them.

Others, I am told, pretend to have been once his friends. Surely they are their enemies who say so, since nothing can be more odious than to treat a friend as they have done. But of this I cannot persuade myself, when I consider the constant and eternal aversion of all bad writers to a good one.

Such as claim a merit from being his admirers, I would gladly ask, if it lays him under a personal obligation. At that rate, he would be the most obliged humble servant in the world. I dare swear for these in particular, he never desired them to be his admirers, nor promised in return to be theirs: that had truly been a sign he was of their acquaintance; but would not the malicious world have suspected such an approbation of some motive worse than ignorance, in the author of the Essay on Criticism? Be it as it will, the reasons of their admiration and of his contempt are equally subsisting, for his works and theirs are the very same that they were.

One, therefore, of their assertions I believe may be true, 'that he has a contempt for their writings :' and there is another which would probably be sooner allowed by himself than by any good judge beside, 'that his own have found too much success with the public.' But as it cannot consist with his modesty to claim this as a justice, it lies not on him, but entirely on the public, to defend its own judgment.

There remains, what, in my opinion, might seem a better plea for these people than any they have made use of : — If obscurity or poverty were to exempt a man from satire, much more should folly or dulness, which are still more involuntary; nay, as much so as personal deformity. But even this will not help them : deformity becomes an object of ridicule when a man sets up for being handsome; and so must dulness, when he sets up for a wit. They are not ridiculed because ridicule in itself is, or ought to be, a pleasure; but because it is just to undeceive and vindicate the honest and unpretending part of mankind from imposition; because particular interest ought to yield to general, and a great number, who are not naturally fools, ought never to be made so, in complaisance to those who are. Accordingly we find that in all ages all vain pretenders, were they ever so poor, or ever so dull, have been constantly the topics of the most candid satirists, from the Codrus of Juvenal to the Damon of Boileau.

Having mentioned Boileau, the greatest poet and most judicious critic of his age and country, admirable for his talents, and yet perhaps more admirable for his judgment in the proper application of them, I cannot help remarking the resemblance betwixt him and our author, in qualities, fame, and fortune ; in the distinctions shown them by their superiors, in the general esteem of their equals, and in their extended reputation amongst foreigners ; in the latter of which ours has met with the better fate, as he has had for his translators persons of the most eminent rank and abilities in their respective nations.[1] But the resemblance holds in nothing more than in their being equally abused

by the ignorant pretenders to poetry of their times ; of which not the least memory will remain but in their own writings, and in the notes made upon them. What Boileau has done in almost all his poems, our author has only in this. I dare answer for him he will do it in no more ; and on this principle, of attacking few but who had slandered him, he could not have done it at all, had he been confined from censuring obscure and worthless persons : for scarce any other were his enemies. However, as the parity is so remarkable, I hope it will continue to the last ; and if ever he should give us an edition of this poem himself, I may see some of them treated as gently, on their repentance or better merit, as Perrault and Quinault were at last by Boileau.

In one point I must be allowed to think the character of our English poet the more amiable ; he has not been a follower of fortune or success ; he has lived with the great without flattery ; been a friend to men in power without pensions, from whom, as he asked, so he received, no favour, but what was done him in his friends. As his satires were the more just for being delayed, so were his panegyrics ; bestowed only on such persons as he had familiarly known, only for such virtues as he had long observed in them, and only at such times as others cease to praise, if not begin to calumniate them — I mean when out of power, or out of fashion.[2] A satire, therefore, on writers so notorious for the contrary practice, became no man so well as himself ; as none, it is plain, was so little in their friendships, or so much in that of those whom they had most abused ; namely, the greatest and best of all parties. Let me add a further reason, that though engaged in their friendships, he never espoused their animosities ; and can almost singly challenge this honour, not to have written a line of any man which, through guilt, through shame, or through fear, through variety of fortune, or change of interests, he was ever unwilling to own.

I shall conclude with remarking, what a pleasure it must be to every reader of humanity to see all along that our author, in his very laughter, is not indulging his own ill nature, but only punishing that of others. As to his poem, those alone are capable of doing it jus-

[1] *Essay on Criticism*, in French verse, by General Hamilton ; the same, in verse also, by Monsieur Roboton, counsellor and privy secretary to King George I., after by the Abbé Resnel, in verse, with notes. *Rape of the Lock*, in French, by the Princess of Conti, Paris, 1728 ; and in Italian verse by the Abbé Conti, a noble Venetian ; and by the Marquis Rangoni, envoy extraordinary from Modena to King George II. Others of his works by Salvini of Florence, &c. His *Essays and Dissertations on Homer*, several times translated into French. *Essay on Man*, by the Abbé Resnel, in verse, by Monsieur Silhouette, in prose, 1737 ; and since by others in French, Italian, and Latin.

[2] As Mr. Wycherley, at the time the town declaimed against his book of poems ; Mr. Walsh, after his death ; Sir William Trumbull, when he had resigned the office of Secretary of State ; Lord Bolingbroke, at his leaving England, after the Queen's death ; Lord Oxford, in his last decline of life ; Mr. Secretary Craggs, at the end of the South-Sea year, and after his death ; others only in Epitaphs.

tice who, to use the words of a great writer, know how hard it is (with regard both to his subject and his manner) *vetustis dare novitatem, obsoletis nitorem, obscuris lucem, fastiditis gratiam.* I am

Your most humble Servant,
WILLIAM CLELAND.[1]
St. James's, Dec. 22, 1728.

ADVERTISEMENT TO THE FIRST EDITION
WITH NOTES, QUARTO, 1729

It will be sufficient to say of this edition, that the reader has here a much more correct and complete copy of the Dunciad than has hitherto appeared. I cannot answer but some mistakes may have slipt into it, but a vast number of others will be prevented by the names being now not only set at length, but justified by the authorities and reasons given. I make no doubt the author's own motive to use real rather than feigned names, was his care to preserve the innocent from any false application; whereas, in the former editions, which had no more than the initial letters, he was made, by keys printed here, to hurt the inoffensive; and (what was worse) to abuse his friends, by an impression at Dublin.

The commentary which attends this poem was sent me from several hands, and consequently must be unequally written; yet will have one advantage over most commentaries, that it is not made upon conjectures, or at a remote distance of time: and the reader cannot but derive one pleasure from the very obscurity of the persons it treats of, that it partakes of the nature of a secret, which most people love to be let into, though the men or the things be ever so inconsiderable or trivial.

Of the persons, it was judged proper to give some account: for, since it is only in this monument that they must expect to survive (and here survive they will, as long as the English tongue shall remain such as it was in the reigns of Queen Anne and King George), it seemed but humanity to bestow a word or two upon each, just to tell what he was, what he writ, when he lived, and when he died.

If a word or two more are added upon the chief offenders, it is only as a paper pinned upon the breast to mark the enormities for which they suffered; lest the correction only

should be remembered, and the crime forgotten.

In some articles it was thought sufficient barely to transcribe from Jacob, Curll, and other writers of their own rank, who were much better acquainted with them than any of the authors of this comment can pretend to be. Most of them had drawn each other's characters on certain occasions; but the few here inserted are all that could be saved from the general destruction of such works.

Of the part of Scriblerus I need say nothing: his manner is well enough known, and approved by all but those who are too much concerned to be judges.

The imitations of the ancients are added, to gratify those who either never read, or may have forgotten them; together with some of the parodies and allusions to the most excellent of the moderns. If, from the frequency of the former, any man think the poem too much a cento, our poet will but appear to have done the same thing in jest which Boileau did in earnest, and upon which Vida, Fracastorius, and many of the most eminent Latin poets, professedly valued themselves.

ADVERTISEMENT TO THE FIRST EDITION OF
THE FOURTH BOOK OF THE DUNCIAD, WHEN
PRINTED SEPARATELY IN THE YEAR 1742

We apprehend it can be deemed no injury to the author of the three first books of the Dunciad that we publish this fourth. It was found merely by accident, in taking a survey of the library of a late eminent nobleman; but in so blotted a condition, and in so many detached pieces, as plainly showed it to be not only incorrect, but unfinished. That the author of the three first books had a design to extend and complete his poem in this manner, appears from the dissertation prefixed to it, where it is said, that 'The design is more extensive, and that we may expect other episodes to complete it;' and, from the declaration in the argument to the third book, that 'The accomplishment of the prophecies therein would be the theme hereafter of a greater Dunciad.' But whether or no he be the author of this, we declare ourselves ignorant. If he be, we are no more to be blamed for the publication of it, than Tucca and Varius for that of the last six books of

---

[1] This gentleman was of Scotland, and bred at the University of Utrecht with the Earl of Mar. He served in Spain under Earl Rivers. After the peace, he was made one of the commissioners of the customs in Scotland, and then of taxes in England; in which having shown himself for twenty years diligent, punctual, and incorruptible (though without any other assistance of fortune), he was suddenly displaced by the minister, in the sixty-eighth year of his age, and died two months after, in 1741. He was a person of universal learning, and an enlarged conversation; no man had a warmer heart for his friend, or a sincerer attachment to the constitution of his country; and yet, for all this, the public would never believe him to be the author of this *Letter*

the Æneid, though, perhaps, inferior to the former.

If any person be possessed of a more perfect copy of this work, or of any other fragments of it, and will communicate them to the publisher, we shall make the next edition more complete: in which we also promise to insert any criticisms that shall be published (if at all to the purpose), with the names of the authors; or any letters sent us (though not to the purpose) shall yet be printed, under the title of *Epistolæ obscurorum virorum;* which, together with some others of the same kind, formerly laid by for that end, may make no unpleasant addition to the future impressions of this poem.

ADVERTISEMENT TO THE COMPLETE EDITION OF 1743

I have long had a design of giving some sort of notes on the works of this poet. Before I had the happiness of his acquaintance, I had written a commentary on his Essay on Man, and have since finished another on the Essay on Criticism. There was one already on the Dunciad, which had met with general approbation; but I still thought some additions were wanting (of a more serious kind) to the humorous notes of Scriblerus, and even to those written by Mr. Cleland, Dr. Arbuthnot, and others. I had lately the pleasure to pass some months with the author in the country, where I prevailed upon him to do what I had long desired, and favour me with his explanation of several passages in his works. It happened, that just at that juncture was published a ridiculous book against him, full of personal reflections, which furnished him with a lucky opportunity of improving this poem, by giving it the only thing it wanted, a more considerable hero. He was always sensible of its defect in that particular, and owned he had let it pass with the hero it had, purely for want of a better, not entertaining the least expectation that such a one was reserved for this post as has since obtained the laurel: but since that had happened, he could no longer deny this justice either to him or the Dunciad.

And yet I will venture to say, there was another motive which had still more weight with our author: this person was one who, from every folly (not to say vice) of which another would be ashamed, has constantly derived a vanity; and therefore was the man in the world who would least be hurt by it.

W. W.

By virtue of the Authority in us vested by the Act for subjecting Poets to the power of a Licenser, we have revised this Piece; where finding the style and appellation of KING to have been given to a certain *Pretender, Pseudo-poet,* or *Phantom,* of the name of TIBBALD; and apprehending the same may be deemed in some sort a reflection on *Majesty,* or at least an insult on that Legal Authority which has bestowed on another person the Crown of Poesy: we have ordered the said *Pretender, Pseudo-poet,* or *Phantom,* utterly to vanish and evaporate out of this work; and do declare the said Throne of Poesy from henceforth to be abdicated and vacant, unless duly and lawfully supplied by the LAUREATE himself. And it is hereby enacted that no other person do presume to fill the same.

X. CH.

THE DUNCIAD

TO DR. JONATHAN SWIFT

BOOK I

ARGUMENT

The Proposition, the Invocation, and the Inscription. Then the original of the great Empire of Dulness, and cause of the continuance thereof. The College of the Goddess in the city, with her private academy for Poets in particular; the Governors of it, and the four Cardinal Virtues. Then the poem hastes into the midst of things, presenting her, on the evening of a Lord Mayor's day, revolving the long succession of her sons, and the glories past and to come. She fixes her eye on Bayes, to be the Instrument of that great event which is the Subject of the poem. He is described pensive among his books, giving up the Cause, and apprehending the Period of her Empire. After debating whether to betake himself to the Church, or to Gaming, or to Party-writing, he raises an altar of proper books, and (making first his solemn prayer and declaration) purposes thereon to sacrifice all his unsuccessful writings. As the pile is kindled, the Goddess, beholding the flame from her seat, flies and puts it out, by casting upon it the poem of Thulé. She forthwith reveals herself to him, transports him to her Temple, unfolds her Arts, and initiates him into her Mysteries; then announcing the death of Eusden, the Poet Laureate, anoints him, carries him to Court, and proclaims him Successor.

THE Mighty Mother, and her son who brings
The Smithfield Muses to the ear of Kings,
I sing. Say you, her instruments the great!
Call'd to this work by Dulness, Jove, and Fate;
You by whose care, in vain decried and curst,
Still Dunce the second reigns like Dunce the first;
Say how the Goddess bade Britannia sleep,
And pour'd her Spirit, o'er the land and deep.
In eldest time, ere mortals writ or read,
Ere Pallas issued from the Thund'rer's head,   10
Dulness o'er all possess'd her ancient right,
Daughter of Chaos and eternal Night:
Fate in their dotage this fair idiot gave,
Gross as her sire, and as her mother grave;
Laborious, heavy, busy, bold, and blind,
She ruled, in native anarchy, the mind.
Still her old empire to restore she tries,
For, born a Goddess, Dulness never dies.
O thou! whatever title please thine ear,
Dean, Drapier, Bickerstaff, or Gulliver!   20
Whether thou choose Cervantes' serious air,
Or laugh and shake in Rabelais' easy chair,
Or praise the Court, or magnify Mankind,
Or thy griev'd country's copper chains unbind;
From thy Bœotia tho' her power retires,
Mourn not, my Swift! at aught our realm requires.
Here pleas'd behold her mighty wings outspread
To hatch a new Saturnian age of Lead.
Close to those walls where Folly holds her throne,
And laughs to think Monroe would take her down,   30
Where o'er the gates, by his famed father's hand,
Great Cibber's brazen, brainless brothers stand;
One cell there is, conceal'd from vulgar eye,
The cave of Poverty and Poetry:
Keen hollow winds howl thro' the bleak recess,
Emblem of Music caus'd by Emptiness:
Hence bards, like Proteus long in vain tied down,
Escape in monsters, and amaze the town;

Hence Miscellanies spring, the weekly boast
Of Curll's chaste press, and Lintot's rubric post;   40
Hence hymning Tyburn's elegiac lines;
Hence Journals, Medleys, Merceries, Magazines;
Sepulchral Lies, our holy walls to grace,
And new-year Odes, and all the Grubstreet race.
In clouded majesty here Dulness shone,
Four guardian Virtues, round, support her throne:
Fierce champion Fortitude, that knows no fears
Of hisses, blows, or want, or loss of ears:
Calm Temperance, whose blessings those partake,
Who hunger and who thirst for scribbling sake: 50
Prudence, whose glass presents th' approaching jail:
Poetic Justice, with her lifted scale,
Where, in nice balance, truth with gold she weighs,
And solid pudding against empty praise.
Here she beholds the Chaos dark and deep,
Where nameless somethings in their causes sleep,
Till genial Jacob, or a warm third day,
Call forth each mass, a Poem or a Play :
How hints, like spawn, scarce quick in embryo lie,
How new-born nonsense first is taught to cry,   60
Maggots, half-form'd, in rhyme exactly meet,
And learn to crawl upon poetic feet.
Here one poor word a hundred clenches makes,
And ductile Dulness new meanders takes;
There motley images her fancy strike,
Figures ill pair'd, and Similes unlike.
She sees a Mob of Metaphors advance,
Pleas'd with the madness of the mazy dance;
How Tragedy and Comedy embrace;
How Farce and Epic get a jumbled race;   70
How Time himself stands still at her command,
Realms shift their place, and Ocean turns to land.
Here gay description Egypt glads with showers,
Or gives to Zembla fruits, to Barca flowers;

Glitt'ring with ice here hoary hills are seen,
There painted valleys of eternal green;
In cold December fragrant chaplets blow,
And heavy harvests nod beneath the snow.
    All these, and more, the cloud-compell-
      ing Queen   79
Beholds thro' fogs that magnify the scene.
She, tinsel'd o'er in robes of varying hues,
With self-applause her wild creation views;
Sees momentary monsters rise and fall,
And with her own fools-colours gilds them
    all.
    'T was on the day when Thorold, rich
      and grave,
Like Cimon, triumph'd both on land and
    wave
(Pomps without guilt, of bloodless swords
    and maces,
Glad chains, warm furs, broad banners, and
    broad faces):
Now Night descending, the proud scene
    was o'er,
But lived in Settle's numbers one day more.
Now Mayors and Shrieves all hush'd and
    satiate lay,   91
Yet eat, in dreams, the custard of the day;
While pensive Poets painful vigils keep,
Sleepless themselves to give their readers
    sleep.
Much to the mindful Queen the feast re-
    calls
What city swans once sung within the
    walls;
Much she revolves their arts, their ancient
    praise,
And sure succession down from Heywood's
    days.
She saw with joy the line immortal run,
Each sire imprest and glaring in his son. 100
So watchful Bruin forms, with plastic care,
Each growing lump, and brings it to a
    bear.
She saw old Prynne in restless Daniel
    shine,
And Eusden eke out Blackmore's endless
    line;
She saw slow Philips creep like Tate's poor
    page,
And all the mighty mad in Dennis rage.
In each she marks her image full exprest,
But chief in Bayes's monster-breeding
    breast;
Bayes, form'd by nature stage and town to
    bless,   109
And act, and be, a coxcomb with success;

Dulness with transport eyes the lively
    dunce,
Rememb'ring she herself was Pertness
    once.
Now (shame to Fortune !) an ill run at play
Blank'd his bold visage, and a thin third
    day :
Swearing and supperless the hero sate,
Blasphemed his gods the dice, and damn'd
    his fate;
Then gnaw'd his pen, then dash'd it on the
    ground,
Sinking from thought to thought, a vast
    profound !
Plunged for his sense, but found no bottom
    there,
Yet wrote and flounder'd on in mere de-
    spair.   120
Round him much Embryo, much Abortion
    lay,
Much future Ode, and abdicated Play;
Nonsense precipitate, like running lead,
That slipp'd thro' cracks and zigzags of
    the head;
All that on folly frenzy could beget,
Fruits of dull heat, and Sooterkins of wit.
Next o'er his books his eyes began to roll,
In pleasing memory of all he stole;
How here he sipp'd, how there he plunder'd
    snug,   129
And suck'd all o'er like an industrious bug.
Here lay poor Fletcher's half-eat scenes,
    and here
The frippery of crucified Molière;
There hapless Shakspeare, yet of Tibbald
    sore,
Wish'd he had blotted for himself before.
The rest on outside merit but presume,
Or serve (like other fools) to fill a room;
Such with their shelves as due proportion
    hold,
Or their fond parents dress'd in red and
    gold;
Or where the pictures for the page atone,
And Quarles is saved by beauties not his
    own.   140
Here swells the shelf with Ogilby the great;
There, stamp'd with arms, Newcastle shines
    complete:
Here all his suff'ring brotherhood retire,
And 'scape the martyrdom of jakes and
    fire:
A Gothic library! of Greece and Rome
Well purged, and worthy Settle, Banks,
    and Broome.

But, high above, more solid Learning
    shone,
The classics of an age that heard of none;
There Caxton slept, with Wynkyn at his
    side,
One clasp'd in wood, and one in strong
    cow-hide;   150
There, saved by spice, like mummies, many
    a year,
Dry bodies of Divinity appear:
De Lyra there a dreadful front extends,
And here the groaning shelves Philemon
    bends.
    Of these, twelve volumes, twelve of am-
      plest size,
Redeem'd from tapers and defrauded pies,
Inspired he seizes: these an altar raise;
A hecatomb of pure unsullied lays
That altar crowns; a folio Commonplace
Founds the whole pile, of all his works the
    base: 160
Quartos, octavos, shape the less'ning pyre,
A twisted Birth-day Ode completes the
    spire.
    Then he: 'Great tamer of all human art!
First in my care, and ever at my heart;
Dulness! whose good old cause I yet defend,
With whom my Muse began, with whom
    shall end,
E'er since Sir Fopling's periwig was praise,
To the last honours of the Butt and Bays:
O thou! of bus'ness the directing soul
To this our head, like bias to the bowl, 170
Which, as more pond'rous, made its aim
    more true,
Obliquely waddling to the mark in view:
Oh! ever gracious to perplex'd mankind,
Still spread a healing mist before the mind;
And, lest we err by Wit's wild dancing
    light,
Secure us kindly in our native night.
Or, if to Wit a coxcomb make pretence,
Guard the sure barrier between that and
    Sense!
Or quite unravel all the reas'ning thread,
And hang some curious cobweb in its stead!
As, forced from wind-guns, lead itself can
    fly,   181
And pond'rous slugs cut swiftly thro' the
    sky;
As clocks to weight their nimble motion
    owe,
The wheels above urged by the load below;
Me Emptiness and Dulness could inspire,
And were my elasticity and fire.

Some Daemon stole my pen (forgive th'
    offence),
And once betray'd me into common sense:
Else all my prose and verse were much the
    same;   189
This prose on stilts, that poetry fall'n lame.
Did on the stage my fops appear confin'd?
My life gave ampler lessons to mankind.
Did the dead letter unsuccessful prove?
The brisk example never fail'd to move.
Yet sure, had Heav'n decreed to save the
    state,
Heav'n had decreed these works a longer
    date.
Could Troy be saved by any single hand,
This gray-goose weapon must have made
    her stand.
What can I now? my Fletcher cast aside,
Take up the Bible, once my better guide?
Or tread the path by venturous heroes
    trod,   201
This box my Thunder, this right hand my
    God?
Or chair'd at White's, amidst the doctors
    sit,
Teach oaths to Gamesters, and to Nobles
    Wit?
O bidd'st thou rather Party to embrace?
(A friend to party thou, and all her race;
'T is the same rope at diff'rent ends they
    twist;
To Dulness Ridpath is as dear as Mist;)
Shall I, like Curtius, desp'rate in my zeal,
O'er head and ears plunge for the Com-
    monweal?   210
Or rob Rome's ancient geese of all their
    glories,
And cackling save the monarchy of Tories?
Hold — to the Minister I more incline;
To serve his cause, O Queen! is serving
    thine.
And see! thy very Gazetteers give o'er,
Ev'n Ralph repents, and Henley writes no
    more.
What then remains? Ourself. Still, still
    remain
Cibberian forehead, and Cibberian brain;
This brazen brightness to the 'Squire so
    dear;
This polish'd hardness that reflects the
    Peer;   220
This arch absurd, that wit and fool de-
    lights;
This mess, toss'd up of Hockley-hole and
    White's;

Where dukes and butchers join to wreathe
my crown,
At once the Bear and fiddle of the town.
' O born in sin, and forth in folly brought!
Works damn'd or to be damn'd (your fa-
ther's fault)!
Go, purified by flames, ascend the sky,
My better and more Christian progeny!
Unstain'd, untouch'd, and yet in maiden
sheets,
While all your smutty sisters walk the
streets. 230
Ye shall not beg, like gratis-given Bland,
Sent with a pass and vagrant thro' the
land;
Not sail with Ward to ape-and-monkey
climes,
Where vile Mundungus trucks for viler
rhymes;
Not sulphur-tipt, emblaze an alehouse fire!
Not wrap up oranges to pelt your sire!
O! pass more innocent, in infant state,
To the mild limbo of our Father Tate:
Or peaceably forgot, at once be blest
In Shadwell's bosom with eternal rest! 240
Soon to that mass of nonsense to return,
Where things destroy'd are swept to things
unborn.'
With that, a tear (portentous sign of
grace!)
Stole from the master of the sev'nfold
face;
And thrice he lifted high the Birthday
brand,
And thrice he dropt it from his quiv'ring
hand;
Then lights the structure with averted
eyes:
The rolling smoke involves the sacrifice.
The opening clouds disclose each work by
turns,
Now flames the Cid, and now Perolla
burns; 250
Great Cæsar roars and hisses in the fires;
King John in silence modestly expires:
No merit now the dear Nonjuror claims,
Molière's old stubble in a moment flames.
Tears gush'd again, as from pale Priam's
eyes,
When the last blaze sent Ilion to the
skies.
Rous'd by the light, old Dulness heav'd
the head,
Then snatch'd a sheet of Thulé from her
bed:

Sudden she flies, and whelms it o'er the
pyre:
Down sink the flames, and with a hiss
expire. 260
Her ample presence fills up all the
place;
A veil of fogs dilates her awful face:
Great in her charms! as when on Shrieves
and Mayors
She looks, and breathes herself into their
airs.
She bids him wait her to her sacred dome:
Well pleas'd he enter'd, and confess'd his
home.
So spirits ending their terrestrial race
Ascend, and recognize their Native Place.
This the Great Mother dearer held than
all
The clubs of Quidnuncs, or her own Guild-
hall: 270
Here stood her opium, here she nursed her
owls,
And here she plann'd th' imperial seat of
Fools.
Here to her chosen all her works she
shows,
Prose swell'd to verse, verse loit'ring into
prose:
How random thoughts now meaning chance
to find,
Now leave all memory of sense behind:
How Prologues into Prefaces decay,
And these to Notes are fritter'd quite
away:
How index-learning turns no student pale,
Yet holds the eel of science by the tail:
How, with less reading than makes felons
scape, 281
Less human genius than God gives an ape,
Small thanks to France, and none to Rome
or Greece,
A past, vamp'd future, old revived, new
piece,
'Twixt Plautus, Fletcher, Shakspeare, and
Corneille,
Can make a Cibber, Tibbald, or Ozell.
The Goddess then o'er his anointed head,
With mystic words, the sacred opium shed.
And lo! her bird (a monster of a fowl,
Something betwixt a heideggre and an
owl) 290
Perch'd on his crown: — ' All hail! and
hail again,
My son! the promised land expects thy
reign.

Know Eusden thirsts no more for sack or
  praise;
He sleeps among the dull of ancient days;
Safe where no critics damn, no duns
  molest,
Where wretched Withers, Ward, and Gil-
  don rest,
And high-born Howard, more majestic
  sire,
With fool of quality completes the quire.
Thou, Cibber! thou his laurel shalt sup-
  port;   299
Folly, my son, has still a Friend at Court.
Lift up your gates, ye princes, see him
  come!
Sound, sound ye viols, be the cat-call
  dumb!
Bring, bring the madding Bay, the drunken
  Vine,
The creeping, dirty, courtly Ivy join.
And thou! his Aid-de-camp, lead on my
  sons,
Light-arm'd with Points, Antitheses, and
  Puns.
Let Bawdry, Billingsgate, my daughters
  dear,
Support his front, and Oaths bring up the
  rear:
And under his, and under Archer's wing,
Gaming and Grub-street skulk behind the
  King.   310
  'Oh! when shall rise a monarch all our
  own,
And I, a nursing mother, rock the throne;
'Twixt Prince and People close the curtain
  draw,
Shade him from light, and cover him from
  law;
Fatten the Courtier, starve the learned
  band,
And suckle Armies, and dry-nurse the
  land;
Till Senates nod to lullabies divine,
And all be sleep, as at an Ode of thine?'
  She ceas'd. Then swells the Chapel-
  royal throat;
'God save King Cibber!' mounts in every
  note.   320
Familiar White's, 'God save King Colley!'
  cries,
'God save King Colley!' Drury-lane re-
  plies.
To Needham's quick the voice triumphant
  rode,
But pious Needham dropt the name of God;

Back to the Devil the last echoes roll,
And 'Coll!' each butcher roars at Hock-
  ley-hole.
So when Jove's block descended from on
  high
(As sings thy great forefather Ogilby),
Loud thunder to its bottom shook the
  bog,
And the hoarse nation croak'd, 'God save
  King Log!'   330

BOOK II

ARGUMENT

The King being proclaimed, the solemnity is
graced with public games and sports of various kinds; not instituted by the Hero, as by
Æneas in Virgil, but for greater honour by
the Goddess in person (in like manner as the
games Pythia, Isthmia, &c. were anciently
said to be ordained by the Gods, and as Thetis herself appearing, according to Homer,
Odyssey xxiv. proposed the prizes in honour
of her son Achilles). Hither flock the Poets
and Critics, attended, as is but just, with
their Patrons and Booksellers. The Goddess
is first pleased, for her disport, to propose
games to the Booksellers, and setteth up the
phantom of a Poet, which they contend to
overtake. The Races described, with their
divers accidents. Next, the game for a
Poetess. Then follow the exercises for the
Poets, of tickling, vociferating, diving; the
first holds forth the arts and practices of
Dedicators, the second of Disputants and
fustian Poets, the third of profound, dark,
and dirty Party-writers. Lastly, for the
Critics the Goddess proposes (with great propriety) an exercise, not of their parts, but
their patience, in hearing the works of two
voluminous authors, the one in verse and the
other in prose, deliberately read, without
sleeping; the various effects of which, with
the several degrees and manners of their operation, are here set forth, till the whole
number, not of Critics only, but of spectators, actors, and all present, fall fast asleep:
which naturally and necessarily ends the
games.

HIGH on a gorgeous seat, that far out-
  shone
Henley's gilt tub or Fleckno's Irish throne,
Or that whereon her Curlls the public
  pours,
All bounteous, fragrant grains and golden
  showers,

Great Cibber sate; the proud Parnassian
   sneer,
The conscious simper, and the jealous leer,
Mix on his look: all eyes direct their
   rays
On him, and crowds turn coxcombs as they
   gaze.
His peers shine round him with reflected
   grace,
New-edge their dulness, and new-bronze
   their face.   10
So from the sun's broad beam, in shallow
   urns,
Heav'n's twinkling sparks draw light, and
   point their horns.
  Not with more glee, by hands pontific
   crown'd,
With scarlet hats wide-waving circled
   round,
Rome, in her capitol saw Querno sit,
Throned on sev'n hills, the Antichrist of
   wit.
  And now the Queen, to glad her sons,
   proclaims
By herald hawkers, high heroic games.
They summon all her race: an endless
   band
Pours forth, and leaves unpeopled half the
   land;   20
A motley mixture! in long wigs, in bags,
In silks, in crapes, in Garters, and in Rags,
From drawing rooms, from colleges, from
   garrets,
On horse, on foot, in hacks, and gilded
   chariots;
All who true Dunces in her cause appear'd,
And all who knew those Dunces to reward.
  Amid that area wide they took their
   stand,
Where the tall Maypole once o'erlook'd the
   Strand,
But now (so ANNE and Piety ordain)
A Church collects the saints of Drury-lane.
  With Authors, Stationers obey'd the
   call   31
(The field of glory is a field for all);
Glory and gain th' industrious tribe pro-
   voke,
And gentle Dulness ever loves a joke.
A poet's form she placed before their eyes,
And bade the nimblest racer seize the
   prize;
No meagre, Muse-rid Mope, adust and
   thin,
In a dun nightgown of his own loose skin,

But such a bulk as no twelve bards could
   raise,
Twelve starveling bards of these degen'rate
   days.   40
All as a partridge plump, full fed and fair,
She form'd this image of well-bodied air;
With pert flat eyes she window'd well its
   head,
A brain of Feathers, and a heart of Lead;
And empty words she gave, and sounding
   strain,
But senseless, lifeless! idol void and vain!
Never was dash'd out, at one lucky hit,
A Fool so just a copy of a Wit;
So like, that Critics said, and Courtiers
   swore,
A Wit it was, and call'd the phantom
   Moore.   50
  All gaze with ardour: some a poet's
   name,
Others a swordknot and laced suit inflame.
But lofty Lintot in the circle rose:
' This prize is mine, who tempt it are my
   foes;
With me began this genius, and shall end.'
He spoke; and who with Lintot shall con-
   tend ?
  Fear held them mute. Alone untaught
   to fear,
Stood dauntless Curll: ' Behold that rival
   here!
The race by vigour, not by vaunts, is won;
So take the hindmost, Hell,' he said, and
   run.   60
Swift as a bard the bailiff leaves behind,
He left huge Lintot, and outstript the wind.
As when a dabchick waddles thro' the
   copse
On feet and wings, and flies, and wades,
   and hops;
So lab'ring on, with shoulders, hands, and
   head,
Wide as a windmill all his figure spread,
With arms expanded Bernard rows his state,
And left-legg'd Jacob seems to emulate.
Full in the middle way there stood a lake,
Which Curll's Corinna chanced that morn
   to make   70
(Such was her wont, at early dawn to drop
Her ev'ning cates before his neighbour's
   shop):
Here fortuned Curll to slide; loud shout
   the band,
And ' Bernard! Bernard! ' rings thro' all
   the Strand.

Obscene with filth the miscreant lies be-
  wray'd,
Fall'n in the plash his wickedness had laid:
Then first (if Poets aught of truth declare)
The caitiff Vaticide conceiv'd a prayer.
  'Hear, Jove! whose name my bards and
    I adore,
As much at least as any God's, or more; 80
And him and his, if more devotion warms,
Down with the Bible, up with the Pope's
    Arms.'
  A place there is betwixt earth, air, and
    seas,
Where, from ambrosia, Jove retires for
    ease.
There in his seat two spacious vents ap-
    pear,
On this he sits, to that he leans his ear,
And hears the various vows of fond Man-
    kind;
Some beg an eastern, some a western wind:
All vain petitions, mounting to the sky,
With reams abundant this abode supply: 90
Amused he reads, and then returns the bills,
Sign'd with that ichor which from Gods
    distils.
In office here fair Cloacina stands,
And ministers to Jove with purest hands.
Forth from the heap she pick'd her vot'ry's
    prayer,
And placed it next him, a distinction rare!
Oft had the Goddess heard her servant's
    call,
From her black grottos near the temple
    wall,
List'ning delighted to the jest unclean
Of linkboys vile, and watermen obscene; 100
Where as he fish'd her nether realms for
    wit,
She oft had favour'd him, and favours yet.
Renew'd by ordure's sympathetic force,
As oil'd with magic juices for the course,
Vig'rous he rises; from th' effluvia strong;
Imbibes new life, and scours and stinks
    along;
Repasses Lintot, vindicates the race,
Nor heeds the brown dishonours of his face.
  And now the victor stretch'd his eager
    hand
Where the tall Nothing stood, or seem'd to
    stand; 110
A shapeless shade, it melted from his
    sight,
Like forms in clouds, or visions of the
    night.

To seize his papers, Curll, was next thy care;
His papers light, fly diverse, toss'd in air;
Songs, Sonnets, Epigrams, the winds uplift,
And whisk 'em back to Evans, Young, and
    Swift.
Th' embroider'd suit at least he deem'd his
    prey;
That suit an unpaid tailor snatch'd away.
No rag, no scrap, of all the Beau or Wit,
That once so flutter'd and that once so
    writ. 120
  Heav'n rings with laughter: of the
    laughter vain,
Dulness, good Queen, repeats the jest
    again.
Three wicked imps of her own Grub-street
    choir,
She deck'd like Congreve, Addison, and
    Prior;
Mears, Warner, Wilkins, run; delusive
    thought!
Breval, Bond, Bezaleel, the varlets caught.
Curll stretches after Gay, but Gay is gone,
He grasps an empty Joseph for a John:
So Proteus, hunted in a nobler shape,
Became, when seized, a puppy or an ape.
  To him the Goddess: 'Son! thy grief lay
    down, 131
And turn this whole illusion on the town.
As the sage dame, experienced in her trade,
By names of toasts retails each batter'd
    jade
(Whence hapless Monsieur much complains
    at Paris
Of wrongs from Duchesses and Lady Ma-
    ries);
Be thine, my stationer! this magic gift;
Cook shall be Prior; and Concanen Swift;
So shall each hostile name become our own,
And we, too, boast our Garth and Addison.'
  With that she gave him (piteous of his
    case, 141
Yet smiling at his rueful length of face)
A shaggy tap'stry, worthy to be spread
On Codrus' old, or Dunton's modern bed;
Instructive work! whose wry-mouth'd por-
    traiture
Display'd the fates her confessors endure.
Earless on high stood unabash'd De Foe,
And Tutchin flagrant from the scourge be-
    low:
There Ridpath, Roper, cudgell'd might ye
    view,
The very worsted still look'd black and
    blue: 150

Himself among the storied chiefs he spies,
As, from the blanket, high in air he flies,
And, 'Oh! (he cried) what street, what
    lane but knows
Our purgings, pumpings, blanketings and
    blows ?
In every loom our labours shall be seen,
And the fresh vomit run for ever green!'
    See in the circle next Eliza placed,
Two babes of love close clinging to her
    waist;
Fair as before her works she stands con-
    fess'd,
In flowers and pearls by bounteous Kirkall
    dress'd.   160
    The Goddess then: ' Who best can send
    on high
The salient spout, far-streaming to the
    sky,
His be yon Juno of majestic size,
With cow-like udders, and with ox-like
    eyes.
This China Jordan let the chief o'er-
    come
Replenish, not ingloriously, at home.'
    Osborne and Curll accept the glorious
    strife
(Tho' this his son dissuades, and that his
    wife);
One on his manly confidence relies,
One on his vigour and superior size.   170
First Osborne lean'd against his letter'd
    post;
It rose, and labour'd to a curve at most:
So Jove's bright bow displays its wat'ry
    round
(Sure sign that no spectator shall be
    drown'd).
A second effort brought but new disgrace,
The wild mæander wash'd the Artist's
    face:
Thus the small jet, which hasty hands un-
    lock,
Spirts in the gard'ner's eyes who turns the
    cock.
Not so from shameless Curll; impetuous
    spread
The stream, and smoking flourish'd o'er his
    head: 180
So (famed like thee for turbulence and
    horns)
Eridanus his humble fountain scorns;
Thro' half the heav'ns he pours th' exalted
    urn;
His rapid waters in their passage burn.

Swift as it mounts, all follow with their
    eyes;
Still happy Impudence obtains the prize.
Thou triumph'st, victor of the high-wrought
    day,
And the pleas'd dame, soft smiling, lead'st
    away.
Osborne, thro' perfect modesty o'ercome,
Crown'd with the Jordan, walks contented
    home.   190
    But now for Authors nobler palms re-
    main;
Room for my Lord! three jockeys in his
    train;
Six huntsmen with a shout precede his
    chair:
He grins, and looks broad nonsense with a
    stare.
His honour's meaning Dulness thus exprest,
' He wins this patron who can tickle best.'
    He chinks his purse, and takes his seat
    of state;
With ready quills the dedicators wait;
Now at his head the dext'rous task com-
    mence,   199
And, instant, fancy feels th' imputed sense;
Now gentle touches wanton o'er his face,
He struts Adonis, and affects grimace;
Rolli the feather to his ear conveys,
Then his nice taste directs our operas;
Bentley his mouth with classic flatt'ry opes,
And the puff'd orator bursts out in tropes.
But Welsted most the poet's healing balm
Strives to extract from his soft, giving
    palm.
Unlucky Welsted! thy unfeeling master,
The more thou ticklest, gripes his fist the
    faster.   210
    While thus each hand promotes the pleas-
    ing pain,
And quick sensations skip from vein to vein,
A youth unknown to Phœbus, in despair,
Puts his last refuge all in Heav'n and
    prayer.
What force have pious vows! The Queen
    of Love
Her sister sends, her vot'ress from above.
As taught by Venus, Paris learn'd the art
To touch Achilles' only tender part;
Secure, thro' her, the noble prize to carry,
He marches off, his Grace's Secretary.   220
    ' Now turn to diff'rent sports (the God-
    dess cries),
And learn, my sons, the wondrous power
    of Noise.

To move, to raise, to ravish ev'ry heart,
With Shakespeare's nature, or with Jonson's
    art,
Let others aim; 't is yours to shake the soul
With thunder rumbling from the mustard
    bowl;
With horns and trumpets now to madness
    swell,
Now sink in sorrow with a tolling bell!
Such happy arts attention can command
When Fancy flags, and Sense is at a stand.
Improve we these.   Three Cat-calls be the
    bribe   231
Of him whose chatt'ring shames the mon-
    key tribe;
And his this drum, whose hoarse heroic bass
Drowns the loud clarion of the braying ass.'
  Now thousand tongues are heard in one
    loud din:
The monkey mimics rush discordant in;
'T was chatt'ring, grinning, mouthing, jab-
    b'ring all,
And noise and Norton, brangling and
    Breval,
Dennis and dissonance, and captious art,
And snipsnap short, and interruption
    smart,   240
And demonstration thin, and theses thick,
And Major, Minor, and Conclusion quick.
' Hold (cried the Queen), a Cat-call each
    shall win;
Equal your merits! equal is your din!
But that this well-disputed game may end,
Sound forth, my Brayers, and the welkin
    rend.'
  As when the long-ear'd milky mothers
    wait
At some sick miser's triple-bolted gate,
For their defrauded absent foals they make
A moan so loud, that all the guild awake;
Sore sighs Sir Gilbert, starting at the bray,
From dreams of millions, and three groats
    to pay,   252
So swells each windpipe; ass intones to ass,
Harmonic twang! of leather, horn, and
    brass;
Such as from lab'ring lungs th' Enthusi-
    ast blows,
High sound, attemper'd to the vocal nose;
Or such as bellow from the deep divine;
There Webster! peal'd thy voice, and,
    Whitefield! thine.
But far o'er all, sonorous Blackmore's strain;
Walls, steeples, skies, bray back to him
    again;   260

In Tot'nam Fields the brethren, with amaze,
Prick all their ears up, and forget to graze!
Long Chancery Lane retentive rolls the
    sound,
And courts to courts return it round and
    round;
Thames wafts it thence to Rufus' roaring
    hall,
And Hungerford reëchoes bawl for bawl.
All hail him victor in both gifts of song,
Who sings so loudly, and who sings so long.
  This labour past, by Bridewell all de-
    scend
(As morning prayer and flagellation end) 270
To where Fleet Ditch, with disemboguing
    streams,
Rolls the large tribute of dead dogs to
    Thames;
The king of dykes! than whom no sluice of
    mud
With deeper sable blots the silver flood.
' Here strip, my children! here at once
    leap in;
Here prove who best can dash thro' thick
    and thin,
And who the most in love of dirt excel,
Or dark dexterity of groping well:
Who flings most filth, and wide pollutes
    around
The stream, be his the Weekly Journals
    bound;   280
A Pig of Lead to him who dives the best;
A Peck of Coals apiece shall glad the rest.'
  In naked majesty Oldmixon stands,
And, Milo-like, surveys his arms and
    hands;
Then sighing, thus, ' And am I now three-
    score ?
Ah, why, ye Gods! should two and two
    make four ? '
He said, and climb'd a stranded lighter's
    height,
Shot to the black abyss, and plunged down-
    right.
The senior's judgment all the crowd ad-
    mire,   289
Who but to sink the deeper rose the higher.
  Next Smedley dived; slow circles dim-
    pled o'er
The quaking mud, that closed and oped no
    more.
All look, all sigh, and call on Smedley
    lost;
' Smedley! ' in vain resounds thro' all the
    coast.

Then [Hill] essay'd; scarce vanish'd out
  of sight,
He buoys up instant, and returns to light;
He bears no tokens of the sabler streams,
And mounts far off among the swans of
  Thames.
  True to the bottom, see Concanen creep,
A cold, long-winded native of the deep; 300
If perseverance gain the diver's prize,
Not everlasting Blackmore this denies:
No noise, no stir, no motion canst thou
  make;
Th' unconscious stream sleeps o'er thee
  like a lake.
  Next plunged a feeble, but a desp'rate
  pack,
With each a sickly brother at his back:
Sons of a Day! just buoyant on the flood,
Then number'd with the puppies in the
  mud.
Ask ye their names ? I could as soon dis-
  close
The names of these blind puppies as of
  those.   310
Fast by, like Niobe (her children gone),
Sits mother Osborne, stupefied to stone!
And monumental brass this record bears,
' These are, ah no! these were the Gazet-
  teers!'
  Not so bold Arnall; with a weight of skull
Furious he dives, precipitately dull.
Whirlpools and storms his circling arms
  invest,
With all the might of gravitation blest.
No crab more active in the dirty dance,
Downward to climb, and backward to ad-
  vance,   320
He brings up half the bottom on his head,
And loudly claims the Journals and the
  Lead.
  The plunging Prelate, and his pond'rous
  Grace,
With holy envy gave one layman place.
When lo! a burst of thunder shook the
  flood,
Slow rose a form in majesty of mud;
Shaking the horrors of his sable brows,
And each ferocious feature grim with ooze.
Greater he looks, and more than mortal
  stares;
Then thus the wonders of the deep de-
  clares.   330
  First he relates how, sinking to the chin,
Smit with his mien, the mud-nymphs suck'd
  him in;

How young Lutetia, softer than the down,
Nigrina black, and Merdamante brown,
Vied for his love in jetty bowers below,
As Hylas fair was ravish'd long ago.
Then sung, how shown him by the nut-
  brown maids
A branch of Styx here rises from the
  shades,
That tinctured as it runs with Lethe's
  streams,
And wafting vapours from the land of
  dreams   340
(As under seas Alpheus' secret sluice
Bears Pisa's offering to his Arethuse),
Pours into Thames; and hence the mingled
  wave
Intoxicates the pert, and lulls the grave:
Here, brisker vapours o'er the Temple
  creep;
There, all from Paul's to Algate drink and
  sleep.
  Thence to the banks where rev'rend
  bards repose
They led him soft; each rev'rend bard
  arose;
And Milbourn chief, deputed by the rest,
Gave him the cassock, surcingle, and vest.
' Receive (he said) these robes which once
  were mine;   351
Dulness is sacred in a sound divine.'
He ceas'd, and spread the robe; the crowd
  confess
The rev'rend flamen in his lengthen'd dress.
Around him wide a sable army stand,
A low-born, cell-bred, selfish, servile band,
Prompt or to guard or stab, or saint or
  damn,
Heav'n's Swiss, who fight for any God or
  Man.
  Thro' Lud's famed gates, along the well-
  known Fleet,
Rolls the black troop, and overshades the
  street,   360
Till showers of Sermons, Characters, Es-
  says,
In circling fleeces whiten all the ways.
So clouds replenish'd from some bog below,
Mount in dark volumes, and descend in
  snow.
Here stopt the Goddess; and in pomp pro-
  claims
A gentler exercise to close the games.
  ' Ye Critics! in whose heads, as equal
  scales,
I weigh what author's heaviness prevails;

Which most conduce to soothe the soul in
　　slumbers,
My Henley's periods, or my Blackmore's
　　numbers; 370
Attend the trial we propose to make:
If there be man who o'er such works can
　　wake,
Sleep's all subduing charms who dares defy,
And boasts Ulysses' ear with Argus' eye;
To him we grant our amplest powers to sit
Judge of all present, past, and future wit;
To cavil, censure, dictate, right or wrong,
Full and eternal privilege of tongue.'
　　Three college Sophs, and three pert
　　　　Templars came,
The same their talents, and their tastes the
　　same! 380
Each prompt to query, answer, and debate,
And smit with love of Poesy and Prate.
The pond'rous books two gentle readers
　　bring;
The heroes sit, the vulgar form a ring;
The clam'rous crowd is hush'd with mugs
　　of mum,
Till all tuned equal send a gen'ral hum.
Then mount the clerks, and in one lazy tone
Thro' the long, heavy, painful page drawl
　　on;
Soft creeping words on words the sense
　　compose,
At ev'ry line they stretch, they yawn, they
　　doze. 390
As to soft gales top-heavy pines bow low
Their heads, and lift them as they cease to
　　blow,
Thus oft they rear, and oft the head de-
　　cline,
As breathe, or pause, by fits, the airs
　　divine;
And now to this side, now to that they nod,
As verse, or prose, infuse the drowsy God.
Thrice Budgell aim'd to speak, but thrice
　　supprest
By potent Arthur, knock'd his chin and
　　breast.
Toland and Tindal, prompt at priests to
　　jeer,
Yet silent bow'd to 'Christ's no kingdom
　　here.' 400
Who sat the nearest, by the words o'ercome,
Slept first; the distant nodded to the hum,
Then down are roll'd the books; stretch'd
　　o'er 'em lies
Each gentle clerk, and mutt'ring seals his
　　eyes.

As what a Dutchman plumps into the lakes,
One circle first and then a second makes,
What Dulness dropt among her sons im-
　　prest
Like motion from one circle to the rest:
So from the midmost the nutation spreads,
Round and more round, o'er all the sea of
　　heads. 410
　　At last Centlivre felt her voice to fail;
Motteux himself unfinish'd left his tale;
Boyer the state, and Law the stage gave
　　o'er;
Morgan and Mandeville could prate no
　　more;
Norton, from Daniel and Ostrœa sprung,
Bless'd with his father's front and mother's
　　tongue,
Hung silent down his never-blushing head,
And all was hush'd, as Folly's self lay
　　dead.
　　Thus the soft gifts of sleep conclude the
　　　　day,
And stretch'd on bulks, as usual Poets lay.
Why should I sing what bards the nightly
　　Muse 421
Did slumb'ring visit, and convey to stews?
Who prouder march'd, with magistrates in
　　state,
To some famed roundhouse, ever-open
　　gate?
How Henley lay inspired beside a sink,
And to mere mortals seem'd a priest in
　　drink,
While others, timely, to the neighb'ring
　　Fleet
(Haunt of the Muses) made their safe re-
　　treat?

BOOK III

ARGUMENT

After the other persons are disposed in their
proper places of rest, the Goddess transports
the King to her Temple, and there lays him
to slumber with his head on her lap; a position of marvellous virtue, which causes all
the visions of wild enthusiasts, projectors,
politicians, inamoratos, castle-builders, chy-
mists, and poets. He is immediately carried on the wings of Fancy, and led by a
mad poetical Sibyl, to the Elysian shade;
where, on the banks of Lethe, the souls of
the dull are dipped by Bavius, before
their entrance into this world. There he
is met by the ghost of Settle, and by him

made acquainted with the wonders of the place, and with those which he himself is destined to perform. He takes him to a Mount of Vision, from whence he shows him the past triumphs of the Empire of Dulness; then, the present; and, lastly, the future: how small a part of the world was ever conquered by Science, how soon those conquests were stopped, and these very nations again reduced to her dominion. Then distinguishing the island of Great Britain, shows by what aids, by what persons, and by what degrees, it shall be brought to her empire. Some of the persons he causes to pass in review before his eyes, describing each by his proper figure, character, and qualifications. On a sudden the scene shifts, and a vast number of miracles and prodigies appear, utterly surprising and unknown to the King himself, till they are explained to be the wonders of his own reign now commencing. On this subject Settle breaks into a congratulation, yet not unmixed with concern, that his own times were but the types of these. He prophesies how first the nation shall be overrun with Farces, Operas, and Shows; how the throne of Dulness shall be advanced over the Theatres, and set up even at Court; then how her sons shall preside in the seats of Arts and Sciences; giving a glimpse, or Pisgah-sight, of the future fulness of her glory, the accomplishment whereof is the subject of the fourth and last book.

But in her temple's last recess inclosed,
On Dulness' lap th' anointed head reposed.
Him close she curtains round with vapours blue,
And soft besprinkles with Cimmerian dew:
Then raptures high the seat of Sense o'er-flow,
Which only heads refin'd from Reason know.
Hence from the straw where Bedlam's prophet nods,
He hears loud oracles, and talks with Gods;
Hence the fool's paradise, the statesman's scheme,
The air-built castle, and the golden dream,
The maid's romantic wish, the chymist's flame,   11
And poet's vision of eternal Fame.
    And now, on Fancy's easy wing convey'd,
The king descending views th' Elysian shade.
A slipshod Sibyl led his steps along,
In lofty madness meditating song;

Her tresses staring from poetic dreams,
And never wash'd but in Castalia's streams.
Taylor, their better Charon, lends an oar
(Once swan of Thames, tho' now he sings no more);   20
Benlowes, propitious still to blockheads, bows;
And Shadwell nods, the poppy on his brows.
Here in a dusky vale, where Lethe rolls,
Old Bavius sits to dip poetic souls,
And blunt the sense, and fit it for a skull
Of solid proof, impenetrably dull.
Instant, when dipt, away they wing their flight,
Where Browne and Mears unbar the gates of light,
Demand new bodies, and in calf's array
Rush to the world, impatient for the day.
Millions and millions on these banks he views,   31
Thick as the stars of night or morning dews,
As thick as bees o'er vernal blossoms fly,
As thick as eggs at Ward in pillory.
    Wond'ring he gazed: when, lo! a Sage appears,
By his broad shoulders known, and length of ears,
Known by the band and suit which Settle wore
(His only suit) for twice three years before:
All as the vest, appear'd the wearer's frame,
Old in new state — another, yet the same.
Bland and familiar, as in life, begun   41
Thus the great father to the greater son:
    'Oh! born to see what none can see awake,
Behold the wonders of th' oblivious lake!
Thou, yet unborn, hast touch'd this sacred shore;
The hand of Bavius drench'd thee o'er and o'er.
But blind to former as to future fate,
What mortal knows his preëxistent state?
Who knows how long thy transmigrating soul
Might from Bœotian to Bœotian roll?   50
How many Dutchmen she vouchsafed to thrid?
How many stages thro' old monks she rid?
And all who since, in mild benighted days,
Mix'd the Owl's ivy with the Poet's bays?

As man's mæanders to the vital spring
Roll all their tides, then back their circles
  bring;
Or whirligigs, twirl'd round by skilful
  swain,
Suck the thread in, then yield it out
  again;
All nonsense thus, of old or modern date,
Shall in thee centre, from thee circulate. 60
For this our Queen unfolds to vision true
Thy mental eye, for thou hast much to
  view:
Old scenes of glory, times long cast behind,
Shall, first recall'd, rush forward to thy
  mind:
Then stretch thy sight o'er all her rising
  reign,
And let the past and future fire thy brain.
  'Ascend this hill, whose cloudy point
    commands
Her boundless empire over seas and lands.
See, round the poles where keener spangles
  shine,
Where spices smoke beneath the burning
  Line   70
(Earth's wide extremes), her sable flag dis-
  play'd,
And all the nations cover'd in her shade!
  'Far eastward cast thine eye, from
    whence the sun
And orient Science their bright course be-
  gun:
One godlike monarch all that pride con-
  founds,
He whose long wall the wand'ring Tartar
  bounds:
Heav'ns! what a pile! whole ages perish
  there,
And one bright blaze turns learning into
  air.
  'Thence to the south extend thy glad-
    den'd eyes;
There rival flames with equal glory rise; 80
From shelves to shelves see greedy Vulcan
  roll,
And lick up all their physic of the soul.
  'How little, mark! that portion of the
    ball,
Where, faint at best, the beams of Science
  fall:
Soon as they dawn, from hyperborean skies
Embodied dark, what clouds of Vandals
  rise!
Lo! where Mæotis sleeps, and hardly flows
The freezing Tanais thro' a waste of snows,

The North by myriads pours her mighty
  sons,
Great nurse of Goths, of Alans, and of
  Huns!   90
See Alaric's stern port! the martial frame
Of Genseric! and Attila's dread name!
See the bold Ostrogoths on Latium fall!
See the fierce Visigoths on Spain and
  Gaul!
See where the morning gilds the palmy
  shore
(The soil that arts and infant letters bore),
His conqu'ring tribes th' Arabian prophet
  draws,
And saving Ignorance enthrones by laws!
See Christians, Jews, one heavy sabbath
  keep,
And all the western world believe and
  sleep!   100
  'Lo! Rome herself, proud mistress now
    no more
Of arts, but thund'ring against heathen
  lore;
Her gray-hair'd synods damning books un-
  read,
And Bacon trembling for his brazen head.
Padua, with sighs, beholds her Livy burn,
And ev'n th' Antipodes Virgilius mourn.
See the Cirque falls, th' unpillar'd Temple
  nods,
Streets paved with Heroes, Tiber choked
  with Gods;
Till Peter's keys some christen'd Jove
  adorn,
And Pan to Moses lends his Pagan horn. 110
See graceless Venus to a virgin turn'd,
Or Phidias broken, and Apelles burn'd!
  'Behold yon isle, by Palmers, Pilgrims
    trod,
Men bearded, bald, cowl'd, uncowl'd, shod,
  unshod,
Peel'd, patch'd, and piebald, linsey-woolsey
  brothers,
Grave Mummers! sleeveless some and
  shirtless others.
That once was Britain — Happy! had she
  seen
No fiercer sons, had Easter never been.
In peace, great Goddess, ever be ador'd;
How keen the war, if Dulness draw the
  sword!   120
Thus visit not thy own! on this bless'd
  age
O spread thy influence, but restrain thy
  rage.

'And see, my son! the hour is on its
    way
That lifts our Goddess to imperial sway;
This fav'rite isle, long sever'd from her
    reign,
Dove-like, she gathers to her wings again.
Now look thro' Fate! behold the scene she
    draws!
What aids, what armies, to assert her
    cause!
See all her progeny, illustrious sight!
Behold, and count them, as they rise to
    light.   130
As Berecynthia, while her offspring vie
In homage to the mother of the sky,
Surveys around her, in the bless'd abode,
A hundred sons, and every son a God,
Not with less glory mighty Dulness
    crown'd,
Shall take thro' Grub-street her triumphant
    round,
And her Parnassus glancing o'er at once,
Behold a hundred sons, and each a Dunce.
  'Mark first that youth who takes the
    foremost place,   139
And thrusts his person full into your face.
With all thy father's virtues bless'd, be
    born!
And a new Cibber shall the stage adorn.
  'A second see, by meeker manners
    known,
And modest as the maid that sips alone;
From the strong fate of drams if thou get
    free,
Another Durfey, Ward! shall sing in thee.
Thee shall each alehouse, thee each gill-
    house mourn,
And answering ginshops sourer sighs return.
  'Jacob, the scourge of grammar, mark
    with awe;   149
Nor less revere him, blunderbuss of law.
Lo Popple's brow, tremendous to the town,
Horneck's fierce eye, and Roome's funereal
    frown.
Lo sneering Goode, half malice and half
    whim,
A fiend in glee, ridiculously grim.
Each cygnet sweet, of Bath and Tunbridge
    race,
Whose tuneful whistling makes the waters
    pass:
Each songster, riddler, ev'ry nameless
    name,
All crowd, who foremost shall be damn'd
    to Fame.

Some strain in rhyme: the Muses, on their
    racks,
Scream like the winding of ten thousand
    jacks: 160
Some free from rhyme or reason, rule or
    check,
Break Priscian's head, and Pegasus's neck;
Down, down they larum, with impetuous
    whirl,
The Pindars and the Miltons of a Curll.
  'Silence, ye wolves! while Ralph to
    Cynthia howls,
And makes night hideous — Answer him,
    ye owls!
  'Sense, speech, and measure, living
    tongues and dead,
Let all give way — and Morris may be
    read.
Flow, Welsted, flow! like thine inspirer,
    beer,
Tho' stale, not ripe, tho' thin, yet never
    clear;   170
So sweetly mawkish, and so smoothly dull;
Heady, not strong; o'erflowing, tho' not
    full.
Ah, Dennis! Gildon, ah! what ill-starr'd
    rage
Divides a friendship long confirm'd by
    age ?
Blockheads with reason wicked wits abhor,
But fool with fool is barb'rous civil war.
Embrace, embrace, my sons! be foes no
    more!
Nor glad vile poets with true critics' gore.
  'Behold yon pair, in strict embraces
    join'd;
How like in manners, and how like in
    mind!   180
Equal in wit, and equally polite
Shall this a Pasquin, that a Grumbler
    write;
Like are their merits, like rewards they
    share,
That shines a Consul, this Commissioner.'
  'But who is he, in closet close y-pent,
Of sober face, with learned dust besprent ?
Right well mine eyes arede the myster
    wight,
On parchment scraps y-fed and Wormius
    hight.
To future ages may thy dulness last,
As thou preserv'st the dulness of the past!
  'There, dim in clouds, the poring scho-
    liasts mark,   191
Wits, who, like owls, see only in the dark,

A lumberhouse of books in ev'ry head,
For ever reading, never to be read!
  'But, where each science lifts its modern type,
Hist'ry her pot, Divinity her pipe,
While proud Philosophy repines to show,
Dishonest sight! his breeches rent below,
Imbrown'd with native bronze, lo! Henley stands,
Tuning his voice, and balancing his hands.
How fluent nonsense trickles from his tongue!   201
How sweet the periods, neither said nor sung!
Still break the benches, Henley! with thy strain,
While Sherlock, Hare, and Gibson preach in vain.
O great restorer of the good old stage,
Preacher at once, and Zany of thy age!
O worthy thou of Egypt's wise abodes,
A decent priest where monkeys were the gods!
But fate with butchers placed thy priestly stall,
Meek modern faith to murder, hack, and maul;   210
And bade thee live, to crown Britannia's praise,
In Toland's, Tindal's, and in Woolston's days.
  'Yet, oh, my sons! a father's words attend
(So may the Fates preserve the ears you lend):
'T is yours a Bacon or a Locke to blame,
A Newton's genius, or a Milton's flame:
But, oh! with One, immortal One, dispense,
The source of Newton's light, of Bacon's sense.
Content, each emanation of his fires
That beams on earth, each virtue he inspires,   220
Each art he prompts, each charm he can create,
Whate'er he gives, are giv'n for you to hate.
Persist, by all divine in man unawed,
But learn, ye Dunces! not to scorn your God.'
Thus he, for then a ray of Reason stole
Half thro' the solid darkness of his soul;
But soon the cloud return'd — and thus the sire:
'See now what Dulness and her sons admire!

See what the charms that smite the simple heart,
Not touch'd by Nature, and not reach'd by art.'   230
His never-blushing head he turn'd aside
(Not half so pleas'd when Goodman prophesied),
And look'd, and saw a sable sorcerer rise,
Swift to whose hand a winged volume flies:
All sudden, Gorgons hiss, and Dragons glare,
And ten-horn'd Fiends and Giants rush to war;
Hell rises, Heav'n descends, and dance on earth;
Gods, imps, and monsters, music, rage, and mirth,
A fire, a jig, a battle, and a ball,
Till one wide conflagration swallows all.   240
  Thence a new world, to Nature's laws unknown,
Breaks out refulgent, with a Heav'n its own:
Another Cynthia her new journey runs,
And other planets circle other suns.
The forests dance, the rivers upward rise,
Whales sport in woods, and dolphins in the skies:
And last, to give the whole creation grace,
Lo! one vast egg produces human race.
  Joy fills his soul, joy innocent of thought:
'What Power (he cries), what Power these wonders wrought?'   250
'Son, what thou seek'st is in thee! look and find
Each monster meets his likeness in thy mind.
Yet would'st thou more? in yonder cloud behold,
Whose sarsenet skirts are edged with flamy gold,
A matchless youth! his nod these worlds controls,
Wings the red lightning, and the thunder rolls.
Angel of Dulness, sent to scatter round
Her magic charms o'er all unclassic ground,
Yon stars, yon suns, he rears at pleasure higher,
Illumes their light, and sets their flames on fire.   260
Immortal Rich! how calm he sits at ease,
Midst snows of paper, and fierce hail of pease!

And proud his mistress' orders to perform,
Rides in the whirlwind, and directs the
  storm.
 'But lo! to dark encounter in mid air
New wizards rise; I see my Cibber there!
Booth in his cloudy tabernacle shrined;
On grinning dragons thou shalt mount the
  wind.
Dire is the conflict, dismal is the din,
Here shouts all Drury, there all Lincoln's-
  inn;   270
Contending theatres our empire raise,
Alike their labours, and alike their praise.
 'And are these wonders, Son, to thee
  unknown?
Unknown to thee! these wonders are thy
  own.
These Fate reserv'd to grace thy reign
  divine,
Foreseen by me, but ah! withheld from
  mine.
In Lud's old walls tho' long I ruled re-
  nown'd,
Far as loud Bow's stupendous bells resound;
Tho' my own aldermen confer'd the bays,
To me committing their eternal praise, 280
Their full-fed heroes, their pacific mayors,
Their annual trophies, and their monthly
  wars;
Tho' long my party built on me their
  hopes,
For writing pamphlets, and for roasting
  Popes;
Yet lo! in me what authors have to brag
  on!
Reduced at last to hiss in my own dragon.
Avert it, Heav'n! that thou, my Cibber,
  e'er
Shouldst wag a serpent-tail in Smithfield
  fair!
Like the vile straw that 's blown about the
  streets,
The needy poet sticks to all he meets, 290
Coach'd, carted, trod upon, now loose, now
  fast,
And carried off in some dog's tail at last.
Happier thy fortunes! like a rolling stone,
Thy giddy dulness still shall lumber on;
Safe in its heaviness, shall never stray,
But lick up every blockhead in the way.
Thee shall the patriot, thee the courtier
  taste,
And ev'ry year be duller than the last;
Till raised from booths, to theatre, to Court,
Her seat imperial Dulness shall transport.

Already Opera prepares the way,   301
The sure forerunner of her gentle sway:
Let her thy heart (next Drabs and Dice)
  engage,
The third mad passion of thy doting age.
Teach thou the warbling Polypheme to roar,
And scream thyself as none e'er scream'd
  before!
To aid our cause, if Heav'n thou canst not
  bend,
Hell thou shalt move; for Faustus is our
  friend:
Pluto with Cato thou for this shalt join,
And link the Mourning Bride to Proser-
  pine,   310
Grub-street! thy fall should men and Gods
  conspire,
Thy stage shall stand, insure it but from
  fire.
Another Æschylus appears! prepare
For new abortions, all ye pregnant fair!
In flames like Semele's, be brought to bed,
While opening Hell spouts wildfire at your
  head.
 'Now, Bavius, take the poppy from thy
  brow,
And place it here! here, all ye heroes,
  bow!
This, this is he foretold by ancient rhymes,
Th' Augustus born to bring Saturnian
  times.   320
Signs foll'wing signs lead on the mighty
  year!
See the dull stars roll round and reap-
  pear!
See, see, our own true Phœbus wears the
  bays!
Our Midas sits Lord Chancellor of plays!
On poets' tombs see Benson's titles writ!
Lo! Ambrose Philips is preferr'd for wit!
See under Ripley rise a new Whitehall,
While Jones' and Boyle's united labours
  fall;
While Wren with sorrow to the grave de-
  scends,
Gay dies unpension'd with a hundred
  friends,   330
Hibernian politics, O Swift! thy fate,
And Pope's, ten years to comment and
  translate!
 'Proceed, great days! till learning fly
  the shore,
Till birch shall blush with noble blood no
  more;
Till Thames see Eton's sons for ever play,

Till Westminster's whole year be holiday;
Till Isis' elders reel, their pupils' sport,
And Alma Mater lie dissolv'd in port!'
  'Enough! enough!' the raptured mon-
    arch cries,   339
And thro' the iv'ry gate the vision flies.

BOOK IV

ARGUMENT

The poet being, in this book, to declare the
Completion of the Prophecies mentioned at
the end of the former, makes a new Invocation; as the greater poets are wont, when
some high and worthy matter is to be sung.
He shows the Goddess coming in her majesty
to destroy Order and Science, and to substi-
tute the Kingdom of the Dull upon earth:
how she leads captive the Sciences, and si-
lences the Muses; and what they be who
succeed in their stead. All her children, by
a wonderful attraction, are drawn about her;
and bear along with them divers others, who
promote her empire by connivance, weak resistance, or discouragement of Arts; such as
Half-wits, tasteless Admirers, vain Pretenders, the Flatterers of Dunces, or the Patrons
of them. All these crowd round her; one of
them offering to approach her, is driven back
by a rival, but she commends and encourages
both. The first who speak in form are the
Geniuses of the Schools, who assure her of
their care to advance her cause by confin-
ing youth to words, and keeping them out of
the way of real knowledge. Their address,
and her gracious answer; with her charge
to them and the Universities. The Universities appear by their proper deputies, and assure her that the same method is observed in
the progress of Education. The speech of
Aristarchus on this subject. They are driven
off by a band of young Gentlemen returned
from travel with their tutors; one of whom
delivers to the Goddess, in a polite oration,
an account of the whole conduct and fruits
of their travels; presenting to her at the
same time a young Nobleman perfectly accomplished. She receives him graciously,
and endues him with the happy quality of
Want of Shame. She sees loitering about
her a number of indolent persons abandoning
all business and duty, and dying with laziness: to these approaches the antiquary
Annius, entreating her to make them Vir-
tuosos, and assign them over to him; but
Mummius, another antiquary, complaining
of his fraudulent proceeding, she finds a
method to reconcile their difference. Then
enter a troop of people fantastically adorned,

offering her strange and exotic Presents:
among them, one stands forth, and demands
justice on another who had deprived him of
one of the greatest curiosities in Nature; but
he justifies himself so well, that the Goddess
gives them both her approbation. She recommends to them to find proper employment for the Indolents before mentioned, in
the study of Butterflies, Shells, Birds-nests,
Moss, &c., but with particular caution not to
proceed beyond trifles, to any useful or extensive views of Nature, or of the Author of
Nature. Against the last of these apprehen-
sions, she is secured by a hearty address from
the Minute Philosophers and Freethinkers,
one of whom speaks in the name of the rest.
The Youth thus instructed and principled,
are delivered to her in a body, by the hands
of Silenus; and then admitted to taste the
cup of the Magus, her high priest, which
causes a total oblivion of all Obligations, divine, civil, moral, or rational. To these her
adepts she sends Priests, Attendants, and
Comforters, of various kinds; confers on
them Orders and Degrees; and then dismiss-
ing them with a speech, confirming to each
his privileges, and telling what she expects
from each, concludes with a Yawn of extraordinary virtue: the Progress and Effects
whereof on all orders of men, and the Con-
summation of all, in the restoration of Night
and Chaos, conclude the Poem.

Yet, yet a moment, one dim ray of light
Indulge, dread Chaos, and eternal Night!
Of darkness visible so much be lent,
As half to show, half veil the deep intent.
Ye Powers! Whose mysteries restor'd I
    sing,
To whom Time bears me on his rapid
    wing,
Suspend a while your force inertly strong,
Then take at once the Poet and the Song.
Now flamed the Dogstar's unpropitious
    ray,   9
Smote ev'ry brain, and wither'd ev'ry bay;
Sick was the sun, the owl forsook his
    bower,
The moon-struck prophet felt the madding
    hour:
Then rose the seed of Chaos, and of Night,
To blot out Order, and extinguish Light,
Of dull and venal a new world to mould,
And bring Saturnian days of Lead and
    Gold.
She mounts the Throne: her head a cloud
    conceal'd,
In broad effulgence all below reveal'd

('T is thus aspiring Dulness ever shines); 19
Soft on her lap her Laureate Son reclines:
Beneath her footstool Science groans in
  chains,
And Wit dreads exile, penalties, and pains.
There foam'd rebellious Logic, gagg'd and
  bound;
There, stript, fair Rhetoric languish'd on
  the ground;
His blunted arms by Sophistry are borne,
And shameless Billingsgate her robes adorn,
Morality, by her false guardians drawn,
Chicane in furs, and Casuistry in lawn,
Gasps, as they straiten at each end the
  cord,
And dies when Dulness gives her Page the
  word.   30
Mad Mathesis alone was unconfin'd,
Too mad for mere material chains to bind,
Now to pure Space lifts her ecstatic stare,
Now running round the Circle, finds it
  square.
But held in tenfold bonds the Muses lie,
Watch'd both by envy's and by flatt'ry's
  eye.
There to her heart sad Tragedy addrest
The dagger, wont to pierce the Tyrant's
  breast;
But sober History restrain'd her rage,
And promis'd vengeance on a barb'rous
  age.   40
There sunk Thalia, nerveless, cold, and
  dead,
Had not her sister Satire held her head:
Nor couldst thou, Chesterfield! a tear re-
  fuse,
Thou wept'st, and with thee wept each gen-
  tle Muse.
  When lo! a harlot form soft sliding by,
With mincing step, small voice, and lan-
  guid eye:
Foreign her air, her robe's discordant pride
In patchwork flutt'ring, and her head
  aside;
By singing peers upheld on either hand,
She tripp'd and laugh'd, too pretty much to
  stand;   50
Cast on the prostrate Nine a scornful look,
Then thus in quaint recitativo spoke:
  ' O cara! cara! silence all that train!
Joy to great Chaos! let Division reign!
Chromatic tortures soon shall drive them
  hence,
Break all their nerves, and fritter all their
  sense:

One Trill shall harmonize joy, grief, and
  rage,
Wake the dull Church, and lull the ranting
  Stage;
To the same notes thy sons shall hum, or
  snore,   59
And all thy yawning daughters cry encore.
Another Phœbus, thy own Phœbus, reigns,
Joys in my jigs, and dances in my chains.
But soon, ah, soon, rebellion will com-
  mence,
If Music meanly borrows aid from Sense:
Strong in new arms, lo! giant Handel
  stands,
Like bold Briareus, with a hundred hands;
To stir, to rouse, to shake the soul he
  comes,
And Jove's own thunders follow Mars's
  drums.
Arrest him, Empress, or you sleep no
  more ' ——
She heard, and drove him to th' Hibernian
  shore.   70
  And now had Fame's posterior trumpet
  blown,
And all the nations summon'd to the
  Throne:
The young, the old, who feel her inward
  sway,
One instinct seizes, and transports away.
None need a guide, by sure attraction led,
And strong impulsive gravity of head:
None want a place, for all their centre
  found,
Hung to the Goddess, and cohered around.
Not closer, orb in orb, conglobed are seen
The buzzing bees about their dusky
  queen.   80
  The gath'ring number, as it moves
  along,
Involves a vast involuntary throng,
Who gently drawn, and struggling less and
  less,
Roll in her vortex, and her power confess.
Not those alone who passive own her laws,
But who, weak rebels, more advance her
  cause:
Whate'er of Dunce in College or in Town
Sneers at another, in toupee or gown;
Whate'er of mongrel no one class admits,
A Wit with Dunces, and a Dunce with
  Wits.   90
Nor absent they, no members of her state,
Who pay her homage in her sons, the
  Great;

Who, false to Phœbus, bow the knee to
    Baal,
Or impious, preach his word without a call:
Patrons, who sneak from living worth to
    dead,
Withhold the pension, and set up the head;
Or vast dull Flatt'ry in the sacred gown,
Or give from fool to fool the laurel crown;
And (last and worst) with all the cant of
    wit,   99
Without the soul, the Muse's hypocrite.
    There march'd the Bard and Blockhead
    side by side,
Who rhymed for hire, and patronized for
    pride.
Narcissus, prais'd with all a parson's power,
Look'd a white lily sunk beneath a shower.
There moved Montalto with superior air;
His stretch'd-out arm display'd a volume
    fair;
Courtiers and Patriots in two ranks divide,
Thro' both he pass'd, and bow'd from
    side to side;
But as in graceful act, with awful eye,
Composed he stood, bold Benson thrust
    him by: 110
On two unequal crutches propt he came,
Milton's on this, on that one Johnston's
    name.
The decent knight retired with sober rage,
Withdrew his hand, and closed the pom-
    pous page:
But (happy for him as the times went
    then)
Appear'd Apollo's mayor and aldermen,
On whom three hundred gold-capp'd youths
    await,
To lug the pond'rous volume off in state.
    When Dulness, smiling — 'Thus revive
    the Wits!
But murder first, and mince them all to
    bits;   120
As erst Medea (cruel, so to save!)
A new edition of old Æson gave;
Let standard authors thus, like trophies
    borne,
Appear more glorious as more hack'd and
    torn.
And you, my Critics! in the chequer'd
    shade,
Admire new light thro' holes yourselves
    have made.
Leave not a foot of verse, a foot of stone,
A page, a grave, that they can call their
    own:

But spread, my sons, your glory thin or
    thick,
On passive paper, or on solid brick.   130
So by each Bard an Alderman shall sit,
A heavy Lord shall hang at every Wit,
And while on Fame's triumphal car they
    ride,
Some slave of mine be pinion'd to their
    side.'
    Now crowds on crowds around the God-
    dess press,
Each eager to present the first address.
Dunce scorning Dunce beholds the next
    advance,
But Fop shows Fop superior complaisance.
When lo! a spectre rose, whose index hand
Held forth the virtue of the dreadful wand;
His beaver'd brow a birchen garland
    wears,   141
Dropping with infants' blood and mothers'
    tears.
O'er ev'ry vein a shudd'ring horror runs,
Eton and Winton shake thro' all their
    sons.
All flesh is humbled, Westminster's bold
    race
Shrink, and confess the Genius of the
    place:
The pale boy-senator yet tingling stands,
And holds his breeches close with both his
    hands.
    Then thus: 'Since man from beast by
    words is known,
Words are man's province, words we teach
    alone.   150
When reason doubtful, like the Samian
    letter,
Points him two ways, the narrower is the
    better.
Placed at the door of learning, youth to
    guide,
We never suffer it to stand too wide.
To ask, to guess, to know, as they com-
    mence,
As Fancy opens the quick springs of Sense,
We ply the Memory, we load the Brain,
Bind rebel wit, and double chain on chain,
Confine the thought, to exercise the breath,
And keep them in the pale of words till
    death.   160
Whate'er the talents, or howe'er design'd,
We hang one jingling padlock on the
    mind:
A poet the first day he dips his quill;
And what the last ? a very poet still.

Pity! the charm works only in our wall,
Lost, lost too soon in yonder house or hall.
There truant Wyndham ev'ry Muse gave
o'er,
There Talbot sunk, and was a Wit no more!
How sweet an Ovid, Murray was our
boast!
How many Martials were in Pulteney lost!
Else sure some bard, to our eternal praise,
In twice ten thousand rhyming nights and
days,   172
Had reach'd the work, the all that mortal
can,
And South beheld that masterpiece of man.
  'O (cried the Goddess) for some pedant
reign!
Some gentle James, to bless the land again:
To stick the doctor's chair into the throne,
Give law to words, or war with words
alone,
Senates and Courts with Greek and Latin
rule,
And turn the Council to a grammar school!
For sure if Dulness sees a grateful day, 181
'T is in the shade of arbitrary sway.
O! if my sons may learn one earthly thing,
Teach but that one, sufficient for a King;
That which my priests, and mine alone,
maintain,
Which, as it dies, or lives, we fall, or reign:
May you, may Cam, and Isis, preach it
long!
  '"The right divine of Kings to govern
wrong."'
    Prompt at the call, around the Goddess
roll
Broad hats, and hoods, and caps, a sable
shoal: 190
Thick and more thick the black blockade
extends,
A hundred head of Aristotle's friends.
Nor wert thou, Isis! wanting to the day
(Tho' Christ Church long kept prudishly
away):
Each stanch polemic, stubborn as a rock,
Each fierce logician, still expelling Locke,
Came whip and spur, and dash'd thro' thin
and thick,
On German Crousaz, and Dutch Burgers-
dyck.
As many quit the streams that murm'ring
fall
To lull the sons of Marg'ret and Clare Hall,
Where Bentley late tempestuous wont to
sport   201

In troubled waters, but now sleeps in port.
Before them march'd that awful Aristarch;
Plough'd was his front with many a deep
remark;
His hat, which never veil'd to human pride,
Walker with rev'rence took, and laid aside.
Low bow'd the rest; he, kingly, did but nod;
So upright Quakers please both man and
God.
  'Mistress! dismiss that rabble from your
throne;
Avaunt — is Aristarchus yet unknown? 210
Thy mighty scholiast, whose unwearied
pains
Made Horace dull, and humbled Milton's
strains.
Turn what they will to verse, their toil is
vain,
Critics like me shall make it prose again.
Roman and Greek grammarians! know your
better;
Author of something yet more great than
letter;
While tow'ring o'er your alphabet, like
Saul,
Stands our Digamma, and o'ertops them
all.
'T is true, on words is still our whole debate,
Disputes of me or te, of aut or at,   220
To sound or sink in cano, O or A,
Or give up Cicero to C or K.
Let Friend affect to speak as Terence
spoke,
And Alsop never but like Horace joke:
For me what Virgil, Pliny, may deny,
Manilius or Solinus shall supply:
For Attic phrase in Plato let them seek,
I poach in Suidas for unlicens'd Greek.
In ancient sense if any needs will deal,
Be sure I give them fragments, not a meal;
What Gellius or Stobæus hash'd before, 231
Or chew'd by blind old scholiasts o'er and
o'er.
The critic eye, that microscope of wit,
Sees hairs and pores, examines bit by bit.
How parts relate to parts, or they to whole,
The Body's harmony, the beaming Soul,
Are things which Kuster, Burman, Wasse
shall see;
When man's whole frame is obvious to a
flea.
  'Ah, think not, Mistress! more true dul-
ness lies
In Folly's cap, than Wisdom's grave dis-
guise.   240

Like buoys, that never sink into the flood,
On learning's surface we but lie and nod.
Thine is the genuine head of many a house,
And much divinity without a νοῦς.
Nor could a Barrow work on ev'ry block,
Nor has one Atterbury spoil'd the flock !
See ! still thy own, the heavy Canon roll,
And metaphysic smokes involve the pole.
For thee we dim the eyes, and stuff the head
With all such reading as was never read:
For thee explain a thing till all men doubt
    it,   251
And write about it, Goddess, and about it:
So spins the silkworm small its slender store,
And labours till it clouds itself all o'er.
' What tho' we let some better sort of fool
Thrid ev'ry science, run thro' ev'ry school ?
Never by tumbler thro' the hoops was
    shown
Such skill in passing all, and touching none.
He may indeed (if sober all this time)
Plague with Dispute, or persecute with
    Rhyme.   260
We only furnish what he cannot use,
Or, wed to what he must divorce, a Muse:
Full in the midst of Euclid dip at once,
And petrify a Genius to a Dunce:
Or, set on metaphysic ground to prance,
Show all his paces, not a step advance.
With the same cement, ever sure to bind,
We bring to one dead level ev'ry mind:
Then take him to develop, if you can,
And hew the Block off, and get out the
    Man.   270
But wherefore waste I words ? I see ad-
    vance
Whore, pupil, and laced governor from
    France.
Walker ! our hat ! ' —— nor more he
    deign'd to say,
But stern as Ajax' spectre strode away.
In flow'd at once a gay embroider'd race,
And titt'ring push'd the pedants off the
    place:
Some would have spoken, but the voice was
    drown'd
By the French horn or by the opening
    hound.
The first came forwards with as easy mien,
As if he saw St. James's and the Queen.
When thus th' attendant orator begun: 281
' Receive, great Empress ! thy accomplish'd
    son;
Thine from the birth, and sacred from the
    rod,

A dauntless infant ! never scared with God.
The sire saw, one by one, his Virtues wake;
The mother begg'd the blessing of a Rake.
Thou gavest that ripeness, which so soon
    began,
And ceas'd so soon, he ne'er was boy nor
    man.
Thro' school and college, thy kind cloud
    o'ercast,
Safe and unseen the young Æneas past: 290
Thence bursting glorious, all at once let
    down,
Stunn'd with his giddy larum half the town.
Intrepid then, o'er seas and lands he flew;
Europe he saw, and Europe saw him too.
There all thy gifts and graces we display,
Thou, only thou, directing all our way !
To where the Seine, obsequious as she runs,
Pours at great Bourbon's feet her silken
    sons;
Or Tyber, now no longer Roman, rolls,
Vain of Italian arts, Italian souls: 300
To happy convents, bosom'd deep in vines,
Where slumber abbots, purple as their
    wines:
To isles of fragrance, lily-silver'd vales,
Diffusing languor in the panting gales:
To lands of singing, or of dancing, slaves,
Love-whisp'ring woods, and lute-resound-
    ing waves.
But chief her shrine where naked Venus
    keeps,
And Cupids ride the lion of the deeps;
Where, eas'd of fleets, the Adriatic main
Wafts the smooth eunuch and enamour'd
    swain.   310
Led by my hand, he saunter'd Europe round,
And gather'd ev'ry vice on Christian ground;
Saw every Court, heard every King declare
His royal sense of Op'ras or the Fair;
The Stews and Palace equally explored,
Intrigued with glory, and with spirit
    whored;
Tried all hors-d'œuvres, all liqueurs defined,
Judicious drank, and greatly daring dined;
Dropp'd the dull lumber of the Latin store,
Spoil'd his own language, and acquired no
    more;   320
All classic learning lost on classic ground;
And last — turn'd Air, the Echo of a
    Sound !
See now, half-cured, and perfectly well-
    bred,
With nothing but a solo in his head;
As much estate, and principle, and wit,

As Jansen, Fleetwood, Cibber shall think fit;
Stol'n from a Duel, follow'd by a Nun,
And, if a borough choose him not, undone;
See, to my country happy I restore
This glorious youth, and add one Venus
  more. 330
Her too receive (for her my soul adores);
So may the sons of sons of sons of whores
Prop thine, O Empress! like each neigh-
  bour Throne,
And make a long posterity thy own.'
  Pleas'd, she accepts the Hero and the
  Dame,
Wraps in her veil, and frees from sense of
  shame:
Then look'd, and saw a lazy lolling sort,
Unseen at Church, at Senate, or at Court,
Of ever listless loit'rers, that attend 339
No cause, no trust, no duty, and no friend.
Thee, too, my Paridell! she mark'd thee
  there,
Stretch'd on the rack of a too easy chair,
And heard thy everlasting yawn confess
The pains and penalties of Idleness.
She pitied! but her pity only shed
Benigner influence on thy nodding head.
  But Annius, crafty seer, with ebon wand,
And well-dissembled em'rald on his hand,
False as his gems, and canker'd as his coins,
Came, cramm'd with capon, from where
  Pollio dines. 350
Soft, as the wily fox is seen to creep,
Where bask on sunny banks the simple
  sheep,
Walk round and round, now prying here,
  now there,
So he, but pious, whisper'd first his prayer:
  'Grant, gracious Goddess! grant me still
  to cheat!
O may thy cloud still cover the deceit!
Thy choicer mists on this assembly shed,
But pour them thickest on the noble head.
So shall each youth, assisted by our eyes,
See other Cæsars, other Homers rise; 360
Thro' twilight ages hunt th' Athenian fowl,
Which Chalcis, Gods, and Mortals call an
  owl;
Now see an Attys, now a Cecrops clear,
Nay, Mahomet! the pigeon at thine ear;
Be rich in ancient brass, tho' not in gold,
And keep his Lares, tho' his House be sold;
To heedless Phœbe his fair bride postpone,
Honour a Syrian prince above his own;
Lord of an Otho, if I vouch it true;
Bless'd in one Niger, till he knows of two.'

Mummius o'erheard him; Mummius,
  fool renown'd, 371
Who, like his Cheops, stinks above the
  ground,
Fierce as a startled adder, swell'd and
  said,
Rattling an ancient Sistrum at his head:
  'Speak'st thou of Syrian Princes? trai-
  tor base!
Mine, Goddess! mine is all the horned race.
True, he had wit to make their value rise;
From foolish Greeks to steal them was as
  wise;
More glorious yet, from barb'rous hands to
  keep, 379
When Sallee rovers chased him on the deep.
Then taught by Hermes, and divinely bold,
Down his own throat he risk'd the Grecian
  gold,
Receiv'd each demigod, with pious care,
Deep in his entrails — I revered them there,
I bought them, shrouded in that living
  shrine,
And, at their second birth, they issue mine.'
'Witness, great Ammon! by whose horns
  I swore
(Replied soft Annius), this our paunch be-
  fore
Still bears them, faithful; and that thus I
  eat,
Is to refund the Medals with the Meat. 390
To prove me, Goddess! clear of all design,
Bid me with Pollio sup as well as dine:
There all the learn'd shall at the labour
  stand,
And Douglas lend his soft obstetric hand.'
  The Goddess, smiling, seem'd to give
  consent;
So back to Pollio hand in hand they went.
  Then thick as locusts black'ning all the
  ground,
A tribe with weeds and shells fantastic
  crown'd,
Each with some wondrous gift approach'd
  the Power,
A nest, a toad, a fungus, or a flower. 400
By far the foremost two, with earnest zeal
And aspect ardent, to the throne appeal.
The first thus open'd: 'Hear thy suppliant's
  call,
Great Queen, and common Mother of us all!
Fair from its humble bed I rear'd this
  flower,
Suckled, and cheer'd, with air, and sun,
  and shower.

Soft on the paper ruff its leaves I spread,
Bright with the gilded button tipp'd its head,
Then throned in glass, and named it CARO-
    LINE.
Each maid cried, " Charming! " and each
    youth, " Divine! "   410
Did Nature's pencil ever blend such rays,
Such varied light in one promiscuous blaze ?
Now prostrate! dead! behold that Caroline:
No maid cries, " Charming! " and no youth,
    " Divine! "
And lo, the wretch! whose vile, whose in-
    sect lust
Laid this gay daughter of the spring in dust.
O punish him, or to th' Elysian shades
Dismiss my soul, where no Carnation fades.'
He ceas'd, and wept. With innocence of
    mien
Th' accused stood forth, and thus address'd
    the Queen: 420
'Of all th' enamell'd race, whose silv'ry
    wing
Waves to the tepid zephyrs of the spring,
Or swims along the fluid atmosphere,
Once brightest shined this child of Heat
    and Air.
I saw, and started from its vernal bower
The rising game, and chased from flower
    to flower.
It fled, I follow'd; now in hope, now pain;
It stopt, I stopt; it mov'd, I mov'd again.
At last it fix'd, 't was on what plant it pleas'd.
And where it fix'd the beauteous bird I
    seiz'd: 430
Rose or Carnation was below my care;
I meddle, Goddess! only in my sphere.
I tell the naked fact without disguise,
And, to excuse it, need but show the prize;
Whose spoils this paper offers to your eye,
Fair ev'n in death, this peerless butterfly!'
' My sons! (she answer'd) both have
    done your parts:
Live happy both, and long promote our Arts.
But hear a mother when she recommends
To your fraternal care our sleeping friends.
The common soul, of Heav'n's more frugal
    make,   441
Serves but to keep Fools pert, and Knaves
    awake;
A drowsy watchman, that just gives a knock,
And breaks our rest, to tell us what 's o'clock.
Yet by some object ev'ry brain is stirr'd;
The dull may waken to a Humming-bird;
The most recluse, discreetly open'd, find
Congenial matter in the Cockle kind;

The mind, in metaphysics at a loss,
May wander in a wilderness of Moss;   450
The head that turns at superlunar things
Pois'd with a tail, may steer on Wilkins'
    wings.
' O! would the sons of men once think
    their eyes
And Reason giv'n them but to study flies!
See Nature in some partial narrow shape,
And let the Author of the whole escape:
Learn but to trifle; or, who most observe,
To wonder at their Maker, not to serve!'
  ' Be that my task (replies a gloomy Clerk,
Sworn foe to myst'ry, yet divinely dark; 460
Whose pious hope aspires to see the day
When moral evidence shall quite decay,
And damns implicit faith, and holy lies;
Prompt to impose, and fond to dogmatize):
Let others creep by timid steps, and slow,
On plain Experience lay foundations low,
By common sense to common knowledge
    bred,
And last, to Nature's Cause thro' Nature
    led.
All-seeing in thy mists, we want no guide,
Mother of Arrogance, and source of pride!
We nobly take the high *priori* road,   471
And reason downward, till we doubt of God:
Make Nature still encroach upon his plan,
And shove him off as far as e'er we can:
Thrust some Mechanic Cause into his place,
Or bind in Matter, or diffuse in Space:
Or, at one bound o'erleaping all his laws,
Make God man's image; man, the final
    Cause;
Find Virtue local, all Relation scorn,
See all in self, and but for self be born: 480
Of nought so certain as our Reason still,
Of nought so doubtful as of Soul and Will.
O hide the God still more ! and make us see
Such as Lucretius drew, a God like thee:
Wrapt up in self, a God without a thought,
Regardless of our merit or default.
Or that bright image to our fancy draw,
Which Theocles in raptured vision saw,
While thro' poetic scenes the Genius roves,
Or wanders wild in academic groves;   490
That Nature our society adores,
Where Tindal dictates, and Silenus snores!'
  Rous'd at his name, up rose the bousy
    Sire,
And shook from out his pipe the seeds of
    fire;
Then snapt his box, and stroked his belly
    down;

Rosy and rev'rend, tho' without a gown.
Bland and familiar to the Throne he came,
Led up the youth, and call'd the Goddess
   Dame;
Then thus: 'From priestcraft happily set
   free,
Lo ! every finish'd son returns to thee: 500
First slave to Words, then vassal to a
   Name,
Then dupe to Party; child and man the
   same;
Bounded by Nature, narrow'd still by Art,
A trifling head, and a contracted heart.
Thus bred, thus taught, how many have I
   seen,
Smiling on all, and smil'd on by a Queen !
Mark'd out for honours, honour'd for their
   birth,
To thee the most rebellious things on
   earth: 508
Now to thy gentle shadow all are shrunk,
All melted down in Pension or in Punk !
So K[ent] so B ** sneak'd into the grave,
A monarch's half, and half a harlot's slave.
Poor W[harton] nipt in Folly's broadest
   bloom,
Who praises now ? his chaplain on his tomb.
Then take them all, O take them to thy
   breast !
Thy Magus, Goddess ! shall perform the
   rest.'
With that a wizard old his Cup extends,
Which whoso tastes, forgets his former
   Friends,
Sire, Ancestors, Himself. One casts his eyes
Up to a star, and like Endymion dies: 520
A feather, shooting from another's head,
Extracts his brain, and Principle is fled;
Lost is his God, his Country, everything,
And nothing left but homage to a King !
The vulgar herd turn off to roll with hogs,
To run with horses, or to hunt with dogs;
But, sad example ! never to escape
Their infamy, still keep the human shape.
   But she, good Goddess, sent to every
   child
Firm Impudence, or Stupefaction mild; 530
And straight succeeded, leaving shame no
   room,
Cibberian forehead, or Cimmerian gloom.
   Kind Self-conceit to some her glass ap-
   plies,
Which no one looks in with another's eyes:
But as the Flatt'rer or Dependant paint,
Beholds himself a Patriot, Chief, or Saint.

On others Int'rest her gay liv'ry flings,
Int'rest, that waves on party-colour'd
   wings:
Turn'd to the sun, she casts a thousand
   dyes, 539
And, as she turns, the colours fall or rise.
   Others the Syren Sisters warble round,
And empty heads console with empty
   sound.
No more, alas ! the voice of Fame they
   hear,
The balm of Dulness trickling in their ear.
Great C **, H **, P **, R **, K *,
Why all your toils ? your sons have learn'd
   to sing.
How quick Ambition hastes to Ridicule:
The sire is made a Peer, the son a Fool.
   On some, a priest succinct in amice
   white 549
Attends; all flesh is nothing in his sight !
Beeves, at his touch, at once to jelly turn,
And the huge boar is shrunk into an urn:
The board with specious Miracles he loads,
Turns hares to larks, and pigeons into
   toads.
Another (for in all what one can shine ?)
Explains the *sève* and *verdeur* of the Vine.
What cannot copious sacrifice atone ?
Thy truffles, Périgord, thy hams, Bayonne,
With French libation, and Italian strain,
Wash Bladen white, and expiate Hays's
   stain, 560
Knight lifts the head; for, what are crowds
   undone,
To three essential partridges in one ?
Gone ev'ry blush, and silent all reproach,
Contending Princes mount them in their
   coach.
   Next bidding all draw near on bended
   knees,
The Queen confers her Titles and Degrees.
Her children first of more distinguish'd
   sort,
Who study Shakespeare at the Inns of
   Court,
Impale a glow-worm, or Vertù profess,
Shine in the dignity of F. R. S. 570
Some, deep Freemasons, join the silent race,
Worthy to fill Pythagoras's place:
Some Botanists, or florists at the least,
Or issue members of an annual feast.
Nor past the meanest unregarded; one
Rose a Gregorian, one a Gormogon.
The last, not least in honour or applause,
Isis and Cam made Doctors of her Laws.

Then, blessing all, 'Go children of my
  care !
To practice now from theory repair.   580
All my commands are easy, short and full:
My sons ! be proud, be selfish, and be dull.
Guard my Prerogative, assert my Throne:
This nod confirms each privilege your own.
The cap and switch be sacred to His Grace;
With staff and pumps the Marquis leads
  the race;
From stage to stage the licens'd Earl may
  run,
Pair'd with his fellow charioteer, the sun;
The learned Baron butterflies design,
Or draw to silk Arachne's subtle line;   590
The Judge to dance his brother sergeant
  call;
The Senator at cricket urge the ball:
The Bishop stow (pontific luxury !)
A hundred souls of turkeys in a pie;
The sturdy Squire to Gallic masters stoop,
And drown his lands and manors in a soup.
Others import yet nobler arts from France,
Teach Kings to fiddle, and make Senates
  dance.
Perhaps more high some daring son may
  soar,   599
Proud to my list to add one monarch more;
And nobly-conscious, Princes are but things
Born for first Ministers, as slaves for Kings,
Tyrant supreme ! shall three estates com-
  mand,
And make one mighty Dunciad of the land !'
  More she had spoke, but yawn'd — All
  nature nods:
What mortal can resist the yawn of Gods ?
Churches and chapels instantly it reach'd
(St. James's first, for leaden Gilbert
  preach'd);
Then catch'd the Schools; the Hall scarce
  kept awake;
The Convocation gaped, but could not
  speak.   610
Lost was the Nation's sense, nor could be
  found,
While the long solemn unison went round:
Wide, and more wide, it spread o'er all the
  realm;
Ev'n Palinurus nodded at the helm:
The vapour mild o'er each committee crept;

Unfinish'd treaties in each office slept;
And chiefless armies dozed out the cam-
  paign;
And navies yawn'd for orders on the main.
  O Muse! relate (for you can tell alone,
Wits have short memories, and Dunces
  none),   620
Relate who first, who last, resign'd to rest;
Whose heads she partly, whose completely
  blest;
What charms could Faction, what Ambition
  lull,
The venal quiet, and entrance the dull,
Till drown'd was Sense, and Shame, and
  Right, and Wrong;
O sing, and hush the nations with thy song!

. . . .
  In vain, in vain — the all-composing hour
Resistless falls; the Muse obeys the power.
She comes! she comes! the sable throne
  behold
Of Night primeval, and of Chaos old!   630
Before her Fancy's gilded clouds decay,
And all its varying rainbows die away.
Wit shoots in vain its momentary fires,
The meteor drops, and in a flash expires.
As one by one, at dread Medea's strain,
The sick'ning stars fade off th' ethereal
  plain;
As Argus' eyes, by Hermes' wand opprest,
Closed one by one to everlasting rest;
Thus at her felt approach, and secret might,
Art after Art goes out, and all is night.   640
See skulking Truth to her old cavern fled,
Mountains of casuistry heap'd o'er her head!
Philosophy, that lean'd on Heaven before,
Shrinks to her second cause, and is no more.
Physic of Metaphysic begs defence,
And Metaphysic calls for aid on Sense!
See Mystery to Mathematics fly!
In vain! they gaze, turn giddy, rave, and die.
Religion, blushing, veils her sacred fires,
And unawares Morality expires.   650
Nor public flame, nor private, dares to shine;
Nor human spark is left, nor glimpse divine!
Lo! thy dread empire, Chaos! is restor'd;
Light dies before thy uncreating word:
Thy hand, great Anarch! lets the **curtain**
  fall;
And universal Darkness buries all.

TRANSLATIONS FROM HOMER

THE ILIAD

POPE began the actual work of translating *The Iliad* in 1714. Swift not only strongly urged him to undertake the task, but by personal exertions secured for him a very large and distinguished list of subscribers. The first four books were published in 1715, and the succeeding books in 1717, 1718 and 1720.

POPE'S PREFACE

Homer is universally allowed to have had the greatest *Invention* of any writer whatever. The praise of judgment Virgil has justly contested with him, and others may have their pretensions as to particular excellencies; but his invention remains yet unrivalled. Nor is it a wonder if he has ever been acknowledged the greatest of poets, who most excelled in that which is the very foundation of poetry. It is the invention that in different degrees distinguishes all great geniuses : the utmost stretch of human study, learning, and industry, which masters everything besides, can never attain to this. It furnishes Art with all her materials, and without it, judgment itself can at best but *steal wisely :* for Art is only like a prudent steward, that lives on managing the riches of Nature. Whatever praises may be given to works of judgment, there is not even a single beauty in them but is owing to the invention : as in the most regular gardens, however Art may carry the greatest appearance, there is not a plant or flower but is the gift of Nature. The first can only reduce the beauties of the latter into a more obvious figure, which the common eye may better take in, and is therefore more entertained with them. And perhaps the reason why most critics are inclined to prefer a judicious and methodical genius to a great and fruitful one, is, because they find it easier for themselves to pursue their observations through an uniform and bounded walk of Art, than to comprehend the vast and various extent of Nature.

Our author's work is a wild paradise, where if we cannot see all the beauties so distinctly as in an ordered garden, it is only because the number of them is infinitely greater. It is like a copious nursery, which contains the seeds and first productions of every kind, out of which those who followed him have but selected some particular plants, each according to his fancy, to cultivate and beautify. If some things are too luxuriant, it is owing to the richness of the soil ; and if others are not arrived to perfection or maturity, it is only because they are over-run and oppressed by those of a stronger nature.

It is to the strength of this amazing invention we are to attribute that unequalled fire and rapture, which is so forcible in Homer, that no man of a true poetical spirit is master of himself while he reads him. What he writes is of the most animated nature imaginable ; everything moves, everything lives, and is put in action. If a council be called, or a battle fought, you are not coldly informed of what was said or done as from a third person ; the reader is hurried out of himself by the force of the poet's imagination, and turns in one place to a hearer, in another to a spectator. The course of his verses resembles that of the army he describes,

Οἱ δ' ἄρ' ἴσαν, ὡσεί τε πυρὶ χθὼν πᾶσα νέμοιτο.

They pour along like a fire that sweeps the whole earth before it. It is, however, remarkable that his fancy, which is everywhere vigorous, is not discovered immediately at the beginning of his poem in its fullest splendour ; it grows in the progress both upon himself and others, and becomes on fire, like a chariot-wheel, by its own rapidity. Exact disposition, just thought, correct elocution, polished numbers, may have been found in a thousand ; but this poetical fire, this *vivida vis animi,* in a very few. Even in works where all those are imperfect or neglected, this can overpower criticism, and make us admire even while we disapprove. Nay, where this appears, though attended with absurdities, it brightens all the rubbish about it, till we see nothing but its own splendour. This *fire* is discerned in Virgil, but discerned as through a glass, reflected from Homer, more shining than fierce, but everywhere equal and constant : in Lucan and Statius. it bursts out in sudden, short, and interrupted flashes : in Milton, it glows like a furnace kept up to an uncommon ardour by the force of art : in Shakespeare, it strikes before we are aware, like an accidental fire from heaven : but in Homer, and in him only, it burns everywhere clearly, and everywhere irresistibly.

I shall here endeavour to show how this vast

invention exerts itself in a manner superior to that of any poet, through all the main constituent parts of his work, as it is the great and peculiar characteristic which distinguishes him from all other authors.

This strong and ruling faculty was like a powerful star, which, in the violence of its course, drew all things within its vortex. It seemed not enough to have taken in the whole circle of arts, and the whole compass of Nature, to supply his maxims and reflections; all the inward passions and affections of mankind, to furnish his characters; and all the outward forms and images of things for his descriptions; but wanting yet an ampler sphere to expatiate in, he opened a new and boundless walk for his imagination, and created a world for himself in the invention of *Fable*. That which Aristotle calls the *soul of poetry*, was first breathed into it by Homer. I shall begin with considering him in this part, as it is naturally the first; and I speak of it both as it means the design of a poem, and as it is taken for fiction.

Fable may be divided into the probable, the allegorical, and the marvellous. The *probable Fable* is the recital of such actions as, though they did not happen, yet might, in the common course of Nature; or of such as, though they did, become fables by the additional episodes and manner of telling them. Of this sort is the main story of an Epic poem, the return of Ulysses, the settlement of the Trojans in Italy, or the like. That of the *Iliad*, is the anger of Achilles, the most short and single subject that ever was chosen by any poet. Yet this he has supplied with a vaster variety of incidents and events, and crowded with a greater number of councils, speeches, battles, and episodes of all kinds, than are to be found even in those poems whose schemes are of the utmost latitude and irregularity. The action is hurried on with the most vehement spirit, and its whole duration employs not so much as fifty days. Virgil, for want of so warm a genius, aided himself by taking in a more extensive subject, as well as a greater length of time, and contracting the design of both Homer's poems into one, which is yet but a fourth part as large as his. The other Epic poets have used the same practice, but generally carried it so far as to superinduce a multiplicity of fables, destroy the unity of action, and lose their readers in an unreasonable length of time. Nor is it only in the main design that they have been unable to add to his invention, but they have followed him in every episode and part of story. If he has given a regular catalogue of an army, they all draw up their forces in the same order. If he has funeral games for Patroclus, Virgil has

the same for Anchises, and Statius (rather than omit them) destroys the unity of his action for those of Archemorus. If Ulysses visit the shades, the Æneas of Virgil, and Scipio of Silius, are sent after him. If he be detained from his return by the allurements of Calypso, so is Æneas by Dido, and Rinaldo by Armida. If Achilles be absent from the army on the score of a quarrel through half the poem, Rinaldo must absent himself just as long, on the like account. If he gives his hero a suit of celestial armour, Virgil and Tasso make the same present to theirs. Virgil has not only observed this close imitation of Homer, but, where he had not led the way, supplied the want from other Greek authors. Thus the story of Sinon and the taking of Troy was copied (says Macrobius) almost word for word from Pisander, as the loves of Dido and Æneas are taken from those of Medea and Jason in Apollonius, and several others in the same manner.

To proceed to the *allegorical Fable*. If we reflect upon those innumerable knowledges, those secrets of Nature and Physical Philosophy, which Homer is generally supposed to have wrapped up in his *Allegories*, what a new and ample scene of wonder may this consideration afford us? How fertile will that imagination appear, which was able to clothe all the properties of elements, the qualifications of the mind, the virtues and vices, in forms and persons; and to introduce them into actions agreeable to the nature of the things they shadowed! This is a field in which no succeeding poets could dispute with Homer; and whatever commendations have been allowed them on this head, are by no means for their invention in having enlarged the circle, but for their judgment in having contracted it. For when the mode of learning changed in following ages, and Science was delivered in a plainer manner, it then became as reasonable in the more modern poets to lay it aside, as it was in Homer to make use of it. And perhaps it was no unhappy circumstance for Virgil, that there was not in his time that demand upon him of so great an invention, as might be capable of furnishing all those allegorical parts of a poem.

The *marvellous Fable* includes whatever is supernatural, and especially the machines of the Gods. If Homer was not the first who introduced the Deities (as Herodotus imagines) into the religion of Greece, he seems the first who brought them into a system of machinery for poetry, and such a one as makes its greatest importance and dignity. For we find those authors who have been offended at the literal notion of the Gods, constantly laying their accusation against Homer as the undoubted inventor of it. But whatever cause there might be to blame his *Machines* in a philosophical or religious view, they are so perfect in the poetic, that mankind have been ever since contented to follow them: none have been able to enlarge the sphere of poetry beyond the limits he has set: every attempt of this nature has proved unsuccessful; and after all the various changes of times and religions, his Gods continue to this day the Gods of poetry.

We come now to the *Characters* of his persons; and here we shall find no author has ever drawn so many, with so visible and surprising a variety, or given us such lively and affecting impressions of them. Every one has something so singularly his own, that no painter could have distinguished them more by their features, than the poet has by their manners. Nothing can be more exact than the distinctions he has observed in the different degrees of virtues and vices. The single quality of *Courage* is wonderfully diversified in the several characters of *The Iliad*. That of Achilles is furious and untractable; that of Diomed forward, yet listening to advice, and subject to command; that of Ajax is heavy, and self-confiding; of Hector, active and vigilant: the courage of Agamemnon is inspirited by love of empire and ambition; that of Menelaus mixed with softness and tenderness for his people: we find in Idomeneus a plain direct soldier, in Sarpedon a gallant and generous one. Nor is this judicious and astonishing diversity to be found only in the principal quality which constitutes the main of each character, but even in the under-parts of it, to which he takes care to give a tincture of that principal one. For example, the main characters of Ulysses and Nestor consist in *Wisdom*; and they are distinct in this, that the wisdom of one is artificial and various, of the other natural, open, and regular. But they have, besides, characters of *Courage*; and this quality also takes a different turn in each from the difference of his prudence; for one in the war depends still upon *Caution*, the other upon *Experience*. It would be endless to produce instances of these kinds. The characters of Virgil are far from striking us in this open manner; they lie in a great degree hidden and undistinguished, and where they are marked most evidently, affect us not in proportion to those of Homer. His characters of valour are much alike; even that of Turnus seems no way peculiar, but as it is in a superior degree; and we see nothing that differences the courage of Mnestheus from that of Sergestus, Cloanthus, or the rest. In like manner it may be remarked of Statius's heroes, that an air of impetuosity runs through them all; the same horrid and savage courage appears in his Capaneus, Tydeus, Hippomedon, &c. They have a parity of character, which makes them seem brothers of one family. I believe when the reader is led into this track of reflection, if he will pursue it through the Epic and Tragic writers, he will be convinced how infinitely superior in this point the invention of Homer was to that of all others.

The *Speeches* are to be considered as they flow from the characters, being perfect or defective as they agree or disagree with the manners of those who utter them. As there is more variety of characters in *The Iliad*, so there is of speeches, than in any other poem. *Every thing in it has manners* (as Aristotle expresses it); that is, everything is acted or spoken. It is hardly credible in a work of such length, how small a number of lines are employed in narration. In Virgil, the dramatic part is less in proportion to the narrative; and the speeches often consist of general reflections or thoughts, which might be equally just in any person's mouth upon the same occasion. As many of his persons have no apparent characters, so many of his speeches escape being applied and judged by the rule of propriety. We oftener think of the author himself when we read Virgil than when we are engaged in Homer: all which are the effects of a colder invention, that interests us less in the action described: Homer makes us hearers, and Virgil leaves us readers.

If in the next place we take a view of the *Sentiments*, the same presiding faculty is eminent in the sublimity and spirit of his thoughts. Longinus has given his opinion, that it was in this part Homer principally excelled. What were alone sufficient to prove the grandeur and excellence of his sentiments in general, is, that they have so remarkable a parity with those of the Scripture: Duport, in his Gnomologia Homerica, has collected innumerable instances of this sort. And it is with justice an excellent modern writer allows, that if Virgil has not so many thoughts that are low and vulgar, he has not so many that are sublime and noble; and that the Roman author seldom rises into very astonishing sentiments where he is not fired by *The Iliad*.

If we observe his *Descriptions, Images,* and *Similes,* we shall find the invention still predominant. To what else can we ascribe that vast comprehension of images of every sort, where we see each circumstance of art and individual of nature summoned together, by the extent and fecundity of his imagination; to which all things, in their various views, presented themselves in an instant, and had their impressions taken off to perfection, at a heat? Nay, he not only gives us the full prospects of things, but several unexpected peculiarities and side-views, unobserved by any painter but Homer. Nothing is so surprising as the description of his battles, which take up no less than half *The Iliad*, and are supplied with so vast a variety of incidents, that no one bears a likeness to another; such different kinds of deaths, that no two heroes are wounded in the same manner; and such a profusion of noble ideas, that every battle rises above the last in greatness, horror, and confusion. It is certain there is not near the number of images and descriptions in any Epic poet; though every one has assisted himself with a great quantity out of him: and it is evident of Virgil especially, that he has scarce any comparisons which are not drawn from his master.

If we descend from hence to the *Expression*, we see the bright imagination of Homer shining out in the most enlivened forms of it. We acknowledge him the father of poetical diction, the first who taught that language of the Gods to men. His expression is like the colouring of some great masters, which discovers itself to be laid on boldly, and executed with rapidity. It is indeed the strongest and most glowing imaginable, and touched with the greatest spirit. Aristotle had reason to say, he was the only poet who had found out living words; there are in him more daring figures and metaphors than in any good author whatever. An arrow is *impatient* to be on the wing, a weapon *thirsts* to drink the blood of an enemy, and the like. Yet his expression is never too big for the sense, but justly great in proportion to it. It is the sentiment that swells and fills out the diction, which rises with it, and forms itself about it; and in the same degree that a thought is warmer, an expression will be brighter; as that is more strong, this will become more perspicuous: like glass in the furnace, which grows to a greater magnitude, and refines to a greater clearness, only as the breath within is more powerful, and the heat more intense.

To throw his language more out of prose, Homer seems to have affected the *compound epithets*. This was a sort of composition peculiarly proper to poetry, not only as it heightened the diction, but as it assisted and filled the numbers with greater sound and pomp, and likewise conduced in some measure to thicken the images. On this last consideration I cannot but attribute these also to the fruitfulness of his invention; since (as he has managed them) they are a sort of supernumerary pictures of the persons or things to which they are joined. We see the motion of Hector's plumes in the epithet Κορυθαίολος, the landscape of Mount Neritus in that of Εἰνοσίφυλλος, and so of others; which particular images could

not have been insisted upon so long as to express them in a description (though but of a single line), without diverting the reader too much from the principal action or figure. As a metaphor is a short simile, one of these epithets is a short description.

Lastly, if we consider his *Versification*, we shall be sensible what a share of praise is due to his invention in that. He was not satisfied with his language as he found it settled in any one part of Greece, but searched through its differing dialects with this particular view, to beautify and perfect his numbers: he considered these as they had a greater mixture of vowels or consonants, and accordingly employed them as the verse required either a greater smoothness or strength. What he most affected was the Ionic, which has a peculiar sweetness from its never using contractions, and from its custom of resolving the diphthongs into two syllables; so as to make the words open themselves with a more spreading and sonorous fluency. With this he mingled the Attic contractions, the broader Doric, and the feebler Æolic, which often rejects its aspirate, or takes off its accent; and completed this variety by altering some letters with the license of poetry. Thus his measures, instead of being fetters to his sense, were always in readiness to run along with the warmth of his rapture, and even to give a farther representation of his notions, in the correspondence of their sounds to what they signified. Out of all these he has derived that harmony, which makes us confess he had not only the richest head, but the finest ear, in the world. This is so great a truth, that whoever will but consult the tune of his verses, even without understanding them (with the same sort of diligence as we daily see practised in the case of Italian operas), will find more sweetness, variety, and majesty of sound than in any other language or poetry. The beauty of his numbers is allowed by the critics to be copied but faintly by Virgil himself, though they are so just to ascribe it to the nature of the Latin tongue: indeed, the Greek has some advantages both from the natural sound of its words, and the turn and cadence of its verse, which agree with the genius of no other language. Virgil was very sensible of this, and used the utmost diligence in working up a more intractable language to whatsoever graces it was capable of; and in particular never failed to bring the sound of his line to a beautiful agreement with its sense. If the Grecian poet has not been so frequently celebrated on this account as the Roman, the only reason is, that fewer critics have understood one language than the other. Dionysius of Halicarnassus has pointed out many of our author's beauties in this kind, in his treatise of the *Composition of Words*, and others will be taken notice of in the course of my notes. It suffices at present to observe of his numbers, that they flow with so much ease, as to make one imagine Homer had no other care than to transcribe as fast as the Muses dictated; and at the same time with so much force and inspiriting vigour, that they awaken and raise us like the sound of a trumpet. They roll along as a plentiful river, always in motion, and always full; while we are borne away by a tide of verse, the most rapid, and yet the most smooth imaginable.

Thus, on whatever side we contemplate Homer, what principally strikes us is his *Invention*. It is that which forms the character of each part of his work; and accordingly we find it to have made his fable more extensive and copious than any other; his manners more lively and strongly marked, his speeches more affecting and transported, his sentiments more warm and sublime, his images and descriptions more full and animated, his expression more raised and daring, and his numbers more rapid and various. I hope, in what has been said of Virgil with regard to any of these heads, I have no way derogated from his character. Nothing is more absurd or endless, than the common method of comparing eminent writers by an opposition of particular passages in them, and forming a judgment from thence of their merit upon the whole. We ought to have a certain knowledge of the principal character and distinguishing excellence of each: it is in that we are to consider him, and in proportion to his degree in that we are to admire him. No author or man ever excelled all the world in more than one faculty, and as Homer has done this in *Invention*, Virgil has in *Judgment*. Not that we are to think Homer wanted Judgment, because Virgil had it in a more eminent degree; or that Virgil wanted Invention, because Homer possessed a larger share of it; each of these great authors had more of both than perhaps any man besides, and are only said to have less in comparison with one another. Homer was the greater genius, Virgil the better artist. In one we most admire the man, in the other the work. Homer hurries and transports us with a commanding impetuosity. Virgil leads us with an attractive majesty: Homer scatters with a generous profusion, Virgil bestows with a careful magnificence: Homer, like the Nile, pours out his riches with a boundless overflow; Virgil, like a river in its banks, with a gentle and constant stream. When we behold their battles, methinks the two poets resemble the heroes they celebrate: Homer, boundless and irresistible

as Achilles, bears all before him, and shines more and more as the tumult increases; Virgil, calmly daring like Æneas, appears undisturbed in the midst of the action, disposes all about him, and conquers with tranquillity. And when we look upon their machines, Homer seems like his own Jupiter in his terrors, shaking Olympus, scattering the lightnings, and firing the heavens; Virgil, like the same power in his benevolence, counselling with the Gods, laying plans for empires, and regularly ordering his whole creation.

But, after all, it is with great parts, as with great virtues; they naturally border on some imperfection; and it is often hard to distinguish exactly where the virtue ends, or the fault begins. As prudence may sometimes sink to suspicion, so may a great judgment decline to coldness; and as magnanimity may run up to profusion or extravagance, so may a great invention to redundancy or wildness. If we look upon Homer in this view, we shall perceive the chief objections against him to proceed from so noble a cause as the excess of this faculty.

Among these we may reckon some of his marvellous fictions, upon which so much criticism has been spent, as surpassing all the bounds of probability. Perhaps it may be with great and superior souls as with gigantic bodies, which, exerting themselves with unusual strength, exceed what is commonly thought the due proportion of parts, to become miracles in the whole; and, like the old heroes of that make, commit something near extravagance, amidst a series of glorious and inimitable performances. Thus Homer has his speaking horses, and Virgil his myrtles distilling blood; where the latter has not so much as contrived the easy intervention of a deity to save the probability.

It is owing to the same vast invention, that his *Similes* have been thought too exuberant and full of circumstances. The force of this faculty is seen in nothing more, than in its inability to confine itself to that single circumstance upon which the comparison is grounded: it runs out into embellishments of additional images, which, however, are so managed as not to overpower the main one. His similes are like pictures, where the principal figure has not only its proportion given agreeable to the original, but is also set off with occasional ornaments and prospects. The same will account for his manner of heaping a number of comparisons together in one breath, when his fancy suggested to him at once so many various and corresponding images. The reader will easily extend this observation to more objections of the same kind.

If there are others which seem rather to charge him with a defect or narrowness of genius, than an excess of it, those seeming defects will be found upon examination to proceed wholly from the nature of the times he lived in. Such are his grosser representations of the Gods, and the vicious and imperfect manners of his heroes; but I must here speak a word of the latter, as it is a point generally carried into extremes, both by the censurers and defenders of Homer. It must be a strange partiality to antiquity, to think with Madame Dacier, ' that those times and manners are so much the more excellent, as they are more contrary to ours.' Who can be so prejudiced in their favour as to magnify the felicity of those ages, when a spirit of revenge and cruelty, joined with the practice of rapine and robbery, reigned through the world; when no mercy was shewn for the sake of lucre; when the greatest princes were put to the sword, and their wives and daughters made slaves and concubines? On the other side, I would not be so delicate as those modern critics, who are shocked at the servile offices and mean employments in which we sometimes see the heroes of Homer engaged. There is a pleasure in taking a view of that simplicity, in opposition to the luxury of succeeding ages; in beholding monarchs without their guards, princes tending their flocks, and princesses drawing water from the springs. When we read Homer, we ought to reflect that we are reading the most ancient author in the heathen world; and those who consider him in this light, will double their pleasure in the perusal of him. Let them think they are growing acquainted with nations and people that are now no more; that they are stepping almost three thousand years back into the remotest antiquity, and entertaining themselves with a clear and surprising vision of things nowhere else to be found, the only true mirror of that ancient world. By this means alone their greatest obstacles will vanish; and what usually creates their dislike will become a satisfaction.

This consideration may farther serve to answer for the constant use of the same Epithets to his Gods and Heroes. such as the far-darting Phœbus, the blue-eyed Pallas, the swift-footed Achilles, &c., which some have censured as impertinent and tediously repeated. Those of the Gods depended upon the powers and offices then believed to belong to them, and had contracted a weight and veneration from the rites and solemn devotions in which they were used: they were a sort of attributes with which it was a matter of religion to salute them on all occasions, and which it was an irreverence to omit. As for the epithets of great men, Mons.

Boileau is of opinion, that they were in the nature of *surnames*, and repeated as such; for the Greeks, having no names derived from their fathers, were obliged to add some other distinction of each person; either naming his parents expressly, or his place of birth, profession, or the like: as Alexander, the son of Philip, Herodotus of Halicarnassus, Diogenes the Cynic, &c. Homer, therefore, complying with the custom of his country, used such distinctive additions as better agreed with poetry. And indeed we have something parallel to these in modern times, such as the names of Harold Harefoot, Edmund Ironside, Edward Longshanks. Edward the Black Prince, &c. If yet this be thought to account better for the propriety than for the repetition, I shall add a farther conjecture. Hesiod, dividing the world into its different ages, has placed a fourth age between the brazen and the iron one, of ' heroes distinct from other men, a divine race, who fought at Thebes and Troy, are called demi-gods, and live by the care of Jupiter in the islands of the blessed.' [1] Now among the divine honours which were paid them, they might have this also in common with the Gods, not to be mentioned without the solemnity of an epithet, and such as might be acceptable to them by its celebrating their families, actions, or qualities.

What other cavils have been raised against Homer, are such as hardly deserve a reply, but will yet be taken notice of as they occur in the course of the work. Many have been occasioned by an injudicious endeavour to exalt Virgil; which is much the same, as if one should think to raise the superstructure by undermining the foundation: one would imagine by the whole course of their parallels, that these critics never so much as heard of Homer's having written first; a consideration which whoever compares these two poets ought to have always in his eye. Some accuse him for the same things which they overlook or praise him in the other; as when they prefer the fable and moral of the *Æneis* to those of the *Iliad*, for the same reasons which might set the *Odyssey* above the *Æneis*; as that the hero is a wiser man and the action of the one more beneficial to his country than that of the other: or else they blame him for not doing what he never designed; as because Achilles is not as good and perfect a prince as Æneas, when the very moral of his poem required a contrary character; it is thus that Rapin judges in his comparison of Homer and Virgil. Others select those particular passages of Homer, which are not so laboured as some that Virgil drew out of them: this is the whole management of

[1] Hesiod, lib. i. ver. 155, &c.

Scaliger in his *Poetics*. Others quarrel with what they take for low and mean expressions, sometimes through a false delicacy and refinement, oftener from an ignorance of the graces of the original ; and then triumph in the awkwardness of their own translations : this is the conduct of Perrault in his *Parallels*. Lastly, there are others, who, pretending to a fairer proceeding, distinguish between the personal merit of Homer, and that of his work; but when they come to assign the causes of the great reputation of the *Iliad*, they found it upon the ignorance of his times, and the prejudice of those that followed ; and in pursuance of this principle, they make those accidents (such as the contention of the cities, &c.) to be the causes of his fame, which were in reality the consequences of his merit. The same might as well be said of Virgil, or any great author, whose general character will infallibly raise many casual additions to their reputation. This is the method of Mons. de la Motte ; who yet confesses upon the whole, that in whatever age Homer had lived, he must have been the greatest poet of his nation, and that he may be said in this sense to be the master even of those who surpassed him.

In all these objections we see nothing that contradicts his title to the honour of the chief *Invention ;* and as long as this (which is indeed the characteristic of poetry itself) remains unequalled by his followers, he still continues superior to them. A cooler judgment may commit fewer faults, and be more approved in the eyes of one sort of critics : but that warmth of fancy will carry the loudest and most universal applauses, which holds the heart of a reader under the strongest enchantment. Homer not only appears the inventor of poetry, but excels all the inventors of other arts in this, that he has swallowed up the honour of those who succeeded him. What he has done admitted no increase, it only left room for contraction or regulation. He showed all the stretch of fancy at once ; and if he has failed in some of his flights, it was but because he attempted every thing. A work of this kind seems like a mighty tree which rises from the most vigorous seed, is improved with industry, flourishes, and produces the finest fruit ; nature and art conspire to raise it ; pleasure and profit join to make it valuable ; and they who find the justest faults, have only said, that a few branches (which run luxuriant through a richness of Nature) might be lopped into form to give it a more regular appearance.

Having now spoken of the beauties and defects of the Original, it remains to treat of the Translation, with the same view to the chief characteristic. As far as that is seen in the main parts of the poem, such as the Fable, Manners, and Sentiments, no translator can prejudice it but by wilful omissions or contractions. As it also breaks out in every particular image, description, and simile ; whoever lessens or too much softens those, takes off from this chief character. It is the first grand duty of an interpreter to give his author entire and unmaimed : and for the rest, the diction and versification only are his proper province ; since these must be his own, but the others he is to take as he finds them.

It should then be considered what methods may afford some equivalent in our language for the graces of these in the Greek. It is certain no literal translation can be just to an excellent original in a superior language : but it is a great mistake to imagine (as many have done) that a rash paraphrase can make amends for this general defect : which is no less in danger to lose the spirit of an ancient, by deviating into the modern manners of expression. If there be sometimes a darkness, there is often a light in antiquity, which nothing better preserves than a version almost literal. I know no liberties one ought to take, but those which are necessary for transfusing the spirit of the original, and supporting the poetical style of the translation : and I will venture to say there have not been more men misled in former times by a servile dull adherence to the letter, than have been deluded in ours by a chimerical insolent hope of raising and improving their author. It is not to be doubted that the *fire* of the poem is what a translator should principally regard, as it is most likely to expire in his managing : however, it is his safest way to be content with preserving this to his utmost in the whole, without endeavouring to be more than he finds his author is, in any particular place. It is a great secret in writing to know when to be plain, and when poetical and figurative ; and it is what Homer will teach us, if we will but follow modestly in his footsteps. Where his diction is bold and lofty, let us raise ours as high as we can ; but where his is plain and humble, we ought not to be deterred from imitating him by the fear of incurring the censure of a mere English critic. Nothing that belongs to Homer seems to have been more commonly mistaken than the just pitch of his style: some of his translators having swelled into fustian in a proud confidence of the *Sublime ;* others sunk into flatness in a cold and timorous notion of *Simplicity*. Methinks I see these different followers of Homer, some sweating and straining after him by violent leaps and bounds (the certain signs of false mettle) ; others slowly and servilely creeping in his train, while the poet himself is all the time proceeding with an unaffected and equal majesty before them. However, of the two extremes one could sooner pardon frenzy than frigidity : no author is to be envied for such commendations as he may gain by that character of style, which his friends must agree together to call Simplicity, and the rest of the world will call Dulness. There is a graceful and dignified simplicity, as well as a bald and sordid one, which differ as much from each other as the air of a plain man from that of a sloven : it is one thing to be tricked up, and another not to be dressed at all. Simplicity is the mean between ostentation and rusticity.

This pure and noble simplicity is nowhere in such perfection as in the *Scripture* and our Author. One may affirm, with all respect to the inspired writings, that the divine Spirit made use of no other words but what were intelligible and common to men at that time, and in that part of the world; and as Homer is the author nearest to those, his style must of course bear a greater resemblance to the sacred books than that of any other writer. This consideration (together with what has been observed of the parity of some of his thoughts) may, methinks, induce a translator on the one hand to give into several of those general phrases and manners of expression, which have attained a veneration even in our language from being used in the Old Testament; as, on the other, to avoid those which have been appropriated to the Divinity, and in a manner consigned to mystery and religion.

For a farther preservation of this air of simplicity, a particular care should be taken to express with all plainness those moral sentences and proverbial speeches which are so numerous in this poet. They have something venerable, and, as I may say, oracular. in that unadorned gravity and shortness with which they are delivered : a grace which would be utterly lost by endeavouring to give them what we call a more ingenious (that is, a more modern) turn in the paraphrase.

Perhaps the mixture of some Græcisms and old words after the manner of Milton, if done without too much affectation, might not have an ill effect in a version of this particular work, which most of any other seems to require a venerable antique cast. But certainly the use of modern terms of war and government, such as *platoon, campaign, junto*, or the like (into which some of his translators have fallen), cannot be allowable ; those only excepted, without which it is impossible to treat the subjects in any living language.

There are two peculiarities in Homer's diction which are a sort of marks, or moles, by which every common eye distinguishes him at first sight: those who are not his greatest admirers look upon them as defects, and those who are, seem pleased with them as beauties. I speak of his Compound Epithets, and of his Repetitions. Many of the former cannot be done literally into English without destroying the purity of our language. I believe such should be retained as slide easily of themselves into an English compound, without violence to the ear or to the received rules of composition : as well as those which have received a sanction from the authority of our best poet, and are become familiar through their use of them ; such as 'the cloud-compelling Jove,' &c. As for the rest, whenever they can be as fully and significantly expressed in a single word as in a compound one, the course to be taken is obvious.

Some that cannot be so turned as to preserve their full image by one or two words, may have justice done them by circumlocution; as the epithet εἰνοσίφυλλος to a mountain, would appear little or ridiculous translated literally ' leaf-shaking,' but affords a majestic idea in the periphrasis : ' The lofty mountain shakes his waving woods.' Others that admit of differing significations, may receive an advantage by a judicious variation according to the occasions on which they are introduced. For example, the epithet of Apollo, ἑκηβόλος, or ' far-shooting.' is capable of two explications; one literal in respect of the darts and bow, the ensigns of that God ; the other allegorical, with regard to the rays of the sun : therefore in such places where Apollo is represented as a God in person, I would use the former interpretation, and where the effects of the sun are described, I would make choice of the latter. Upon the whole. it will be necessary to avoid that perpetual repetition of the same epithets which we find in Homer, and which, though it might be accommodated (as has been already shewn) to the ear of those times, is by no means so to ours : but one may wait for opportunities of placing them where they derive an additional beauty from the occasions on which they are employed ; and in doing this properly, a translator may at once shew his fancy and his judgment.

As for Homer's Repetitions, we may divide them into three sorts; of whole narrations and speeches, of single sentences, and of one verse or hemistich. I hope it is not impossible to have such a regard to these, as neither to lose so known a mark of the author on the one hand, nor to offend the reader too much on the other. The repetition is not ungraceful in those speeches where the dignity of the speaker renders it a sort of insolence to alter his words;

as in the messages from Gods to men, or from higher powers to inferiors in concerns of state, or where the ceremonial of religion seems to require it, in the solemn forms of prayers, oaths, or the like. In other cases, I believe the best rule is to be guided by the nearness or distance at which the repetitions are placed in the original: when they follow too close, one may vary the expression, but it is a question whether a professed translator be authorized to omit any; if they be tedious, the author is to answer for it.

It only remains to speak of the *Versification.* Homer (as has been said) is perpetually applying the sound to the sense, and varying it on every new subject. This is indeed one of the most exquisite beauties of poetry, and attainable by very few: I know only of Homer eminent for it in the Greek, and Virgil in Latin. I am sensible it is what may sometimes happen by chance, when a writer is warm, and fully possessed of his image: however, it may reasonably be believed they designed this, in whose verse it so manifestly appears in a superior degree to all others. Few readers have the ear to be judges of it, but those who have, will see I have endeavoured at this beauty.

Upon the whole, I must confess myself utterly incapable of doing justice to Homer. I attempt him in no other hope but that which one may entertain without much vanity, of giving a more tolerable copy of him than any entire translation in verse has yet done. We have only those of Chapman, Hobbes, and Ogilby. Chapman has taken the advantage of an immeasurable length of verse, notwithstanding which, there is scarce any paraphrase more loose and rambling than his. He has frequent interpolations of four or six lines, and I remember one in the thirteenth book of the *Odyssey,* ver. 312, where he has spun twenty verses out of two. He is often mistaken in so bold a manner, that one might think he deviated on purpose, if he did not in other places of his notes insist so much upon verbal trifles. He appears to have had a strong affectation of extracting new meanings out of his author, insomuch as to promise, in his rhyming preface, a poem of the mysteries he had revealed in Homer; and perhaps he endeavoured to strain the obvious sense to this end. His expression is involved in fustian; a fault for which he was remarkable in his original writings, as in the tragedy of Bussy d'Amboise, &c. In a word, the nature of the man may account for his whole performance; for he appears from his preface and remarks to have been of an arrogant turn, and an enthusiast in poetry. His own boast of having finished half the *Iliad* in less than fifteen weeks, shews with what negli-

gence his version was performed. But that which is to be allowed him, and which very much contributed to cover his defects, is a daring fiery spirit that animates his translation, which is something like what one might imagine Homer himself would have writ before he arrived to years of discretion.

Hobbes has given us a correct explanation of the sense in general; but for particulars and circumstances, he continually lops them, and often omits the most beautiful. As for its being esteemed a close translation, I doubt not many have been led into that error by the shortness of it, which proceeds not from his following the original line by line, but from the contractions above mentioned. He sometimes omits whole similes and sentences, and is now and then guilty of mistakes, into which no writer of his learning could have fallen, but through carelessness. His poetry, as well as Ogilby's, is too mean for criticism.

It is a great loss to the poetical world that Mr. Dryden did not live to translate the *Iliad.* He has left us only the first book, and a small part of the sixth; in which if he has in some places not truly interpreted the sense, or preserved the antiquities, it ought to be excused on account of the haste he was obliged to write in. He seems to have had too much regard to Chapman, whose words he sometimes copies, and has unhappily followed him in passages where he wanders from the original. However, had he translated the whole work, I would no more have attempted Homer after him than Virgil, his version of whom (notwithstanding some human errors) is the most noble and spirited translation I know in any language. But the fate of great geniuses is like that of great ministers: though they are confessedly the first in the commonwealth of letters, they must be envied and calumniated only for being at the head of it.

That which in my opinion ought to be the endeavour of any one who translates Homer, is above all things to keep alive that spirit and fire which makes his chief character: in particular places, where the sense can bear any doubt, to follow the strongest and most poetical, as most agreeing with that character; to copy him in all the variations of his style, and the different modulations of his numbers; to preserve, in the more active or descriptive parts, a warmth and elevation; in the more sedate or narrative, a plainness and solemnity; in the speeches, a fulness and perspicuity; in the sentences, a shortness and gravity: not to neglect even the little figures and turns on the words, nor sometimes the very cast of the periods; neither to omit nor confound any rites or customs of antiquity: perhaps, too, he ought to conclude the whole in a shorter compass than has hitherto been done by any translator who has tolerably preserved either the sense or poetry. What I would farther recommend to him, is to study his author rather from his own text, than from any commentaries, how learned soever, or whatever figure they may make in the estimation of the world; to consider him attentively in comparison with Virgil above all the ancients, and with Milton above all the moderns. Next these, the Archbishop of Cambray's Telemachus may give him the truest idea of the spirit and turn of our author, and Bossu's admirable treatise of the Epic Poem the justest notion of his design and conduct. But, after all, with whatever judgment and study a man may proceed, or with whatever happiness he may perform such a work, he must hope to please but a few; those only who have at once a taste of poetry, and competent learning. For to satisfy such as want either, is not in the nature of this undertaking; since a mere modern Wit can like nothing that is not *modern*, and a Pedant nothing that is not *Greek*.

What I have done is submitted to the public, from whose opinions I am prepared to learn; though I fear no judges so little as our best poets, who are most sensible of the weight of this task. As for the worst, whatever they shall please to say, they may give me some concern as they are unhappy men, but none as they are malignant writers. I was guided in this translation by judgments very different from theirs, and by persons for whom they can have no kindness, if an old observation be true, that the strongest antipathy in the world is that of fools to men of wit. Mr. Addison was the first whose advice determined me to undertake this task; who was pleased to write to me upon that occasion in such terms as I cannot repeat without vanity. I was obliged to Sir Richard Steele for a very early recommendation of my undertaking to the public. Dr. Swift promoted my interest with that warmth with which he always serves his friend. The humanity and frankness of Sir Samuel Garth are what I never knew wanting on any occasion. I must also acknowledge, with infinite pleasure, the many friendly offices, as well as sincere criticisms, of Mr. Congreve, who had led me the way in translating some parts of Homer. I must add the names of Mr. Rowe and Dr. Parnell, though I shall take a farther opportunity of doing justice to the last, whose good-nature (to give it a great panegyric) is no less extensive than his learning. The favour of these gentlemen is not entirely undeserved by one who bears them so true an affection. But what can I say of the honour so many of the

great have done me, while the *first names* of the age appear as my subscribers, and the most distinguished patrons and ornaments of learning, as my chief encouragers? Among these it is a particular pleasure to me to find, that my highest obligations are to such who have done most honour to the name of poet: That his grace the Duke of Buckingham was not displeased I should undertake the author to whom he has given (in his excellent *Essay*) so complete a praise:

Read Homer once, and you can read no more;
For all books else appear so mean, so poor,
Verse will seem prose; but still persist to read
And Homer will be all the books you need:

That the Earl of Halifax was one of the first to favour me, of whom it is hard to say whether the advancement of the Polite Arts is more owing to his generosity or his example: That such a genius as my Lord Bolingbroke, not more distinguished in the great scenes of business, than in all the useful and entertaining parts of learning, has not refused to be the critic of these sheets, and the patron of their writer: and that the noble author [1] of the tragedy of *Heroic Love* has continued his partiality to me, from my writing Pastorals, to my attempting the *Iliad*. I cannot deny myself the pride of confessing, that I have had the advantage not only of their advice for the conduct in general, but their correction of several particulars of this translation.

I could say a great deal of the pleasure of being distinguished by the Earl of Carnarvon, but it is almost absurd to particularize any one generous action in a person whose whole life is a continued series of them. Mr. Stanhope, the present secretary of state, will pardon my desire of having it known that he was pleased to promote this affair. The particular zeal of Mr. Harcourt (the son of the late Lord Chancellor) gave me a proof how much I am honoured in a share of his friendship. I must attribute to the same motive that of several others of my friends, to whom all acknowledgments are rendered unnecesary by the privileges of a familiar correspondence; and I am satisfied I can no way better oblige men of their turn than by my silence.

In short, I have found more patrons than ever Homer wanted. He would have thought himself happy to have met the same favour at Athens, that has been shown me by its learned rival, the university of Oxford. And I can hardly envy him those pompous honours he received after death, when I reflect on the enjoyment of so many agreeable obligations, and easy friendships, which make the satisfaction of life. This distinction is the more to be ac-

[1] George Granville, Lord Lansdowne.

knowledged, as it is shewn to one whose pen has never gratified the prejudices of particular *parties*, or the vanities of particular *men*. Whatever the success may prove, I shall never repent of an undertaking in which I have experienced the candour and friendship of so many persons of merit; and in which I hope to pass some of those years of youth that are generally lost in a circle of follies, after a manner neither wholly unuseful to others, nor disagreeable to myself.

BOOK I

THE CONTENTION OF ACHILLES AND AGAMEMNON

THE ARGUMENT

In the war of Troy, the Greeks having sacked some of the neighbouring towns, and taking from thence two beautiful captives, Chryseïs and Briseïs, allotted the first to Agamemnon, and the last to Achilles. Chryses, the father of Chryseïs, and priest of Apollo, comes to the Grecian camp to ransom her; with which the action of the poem opens, in the tenth year of the siege. The priest being refused and insolently dismissed by Agamemnon, entreats for vengeance from his god, who inflicts a pestilence on the Greeks. Achilles calls a council, and encourages Chalcas to declare the cause of it, who attributes it to the refusal of Chryseïs. The king being obliged to send back his captive, enters into a furious contest with Achilles, which Nestor pacifies; however, as he had the absolute command of the army, he seizes on Briseïs in revenge. Achilles in discontent withdraws himself and his forces from the rest of the Greeks; and complaining to Thetis, she supplicates Jupiter to render them sensible of the wrong done to her son, by giving victory to the Trojans. Jupiter granting her suit, incenses Juno, between whom the debate runs high, till they are reconciled by the address of Vulcan.

The time of two-and-twenty days is taken up in this book; nine during the plague, one in the council and quarrel of the Princes, and twelve for Jupiter's stay with the Ethiopians, at whose return Thetis prefers her petition. The scene lies in the Grecian camp, then changes to Chrysa, and lastly to Olympus.

ACHILLES' wrath, to Greece the direful spring
Of woes unnumber'd, heav'nly Goddess, sing!

That wrath which hurl'd to Pluto's gloomy reign
The souls of mighty chiefs untimely slain:
Whose limbs, unburied on the naked shore,
Devouring dogs and hungry vultures tore:
Since great Achilles and Atrides strove,
Such was the Sov'reign doom, and such the will of Jove!
  Declare, O Muse! in what ill-fated hour
Sprung the fierce strife, from what offended power ?   10
Latona's son a dire contagion spread,
And heap'd the camp with mountains of the dead;
The King of Men his rev'rend priest defied,
And for the King's offence, the people died.
  For Chryses sought with costly gifts to gain
His captive daughter from the victor's chain.
Suppliant the venerable father stands;
Apollo's awful ensigns grace his hands:
By these he begs: and, lowly bending down,   19
Extends the sceptre and the laurel crown.
He sued to all, but chief implored for grace
The brother-kings of Atreus' royal race:
  ' Ye Kings and Warriors! may your vows be crown'd,
And Troy's proud walls lie level with the ground;
May Jove restore you, when your toils are o'er,
Safe to the pleasures of your native shore.
But oh ! relieve a wretched parent's pain,
And give Chryseïs to these arms again;
If mercy fail, yet let my presents move,
And dread avenging Phœbus, son of Jove.'
  The Greeks in shouts their joint assent declare,   31
The Priest to rev'rence and release the Fair.
Not so Atrides: he, with kingly pride,
Repuls'd the sacred sire, and thus replied:
  ' Hence on thy life, and fly these hostile plains,
Nor ask, presumptuous, what the King detains:
Hence, with thy laurel crown, and golden rod,
Nor trust too far those ensigns of thy God.
Mine is thy daughter, Priest, and shall remain;
And prayers, and tears, and bribes, shall plead in vain;   40

Till time shall rifle ev'ry youthful grace,
And age dismiss her from my cold em-
brace,
In daily labours of the loom employ'd,
Or doom'd to deck the bed she once en-
joy'd.
Hence then! to Argos shall the maid re-
tire,
Far from her native soil, and weeping sire.'
The trembling priest along the shore
return'd,
And in the anguish of a father mourn'd.
Disconsolate, not daring to complain,
Silent he wander'd by the sounding main: 50
Till, safe at distance, to his God he prays,
The God who darts around the world his
rays.
'O Smintheus! sprung from fair Latona's
line,
Thou guardian power of Cilla the divine,
Thou source of light! whom Tenedos
adores,
And whose bright presence gilds thy
Chrysa's shores;
If e'er with wreaths I hung thy sacred
fane,
Or fed the flames with fat of oxen slain,
God of the silver bow! thy shafts employ,
Avenge thy servant, and the Greeks de-
stroy.' 60
Thus Chryses pray'd: the fav'ring power
attends,
And from Olympus' lofty tops descends.
Bent was his bow, the Grecian hearts to
wound;
Fierce, as he mov'd, his silver shafts re-
sound.
Breathing revenge, a sudden night he
spread,
And gloomy darkness roll'd around his
head.
The fleet in view, he twang'd his deadly
bow,
And hissing fly the feather'd fates below.
On mules and dogs th' infection first began;
And last, the vengeful arrows fix'd in
man. 70
For nine long nights, thro' all the dusky air
The pyres thick-flaming shot a dismal
glare.
But ere the tenth revolving day was run,
Inspired by Juno, Thetis' god-like son
Convened to council all the Grecian train;
For much the Goddess mourn'd her heroes
slain.

Th' assembly seated, rising o'er the rest,
Achilles thus the King of Men address'd:
'Why leave we not the fatal Trojan
shore,
And measure back the seas we cross'd
before ? 80
The Plague destroying whom the Sword
would spare,
'T is time to save the few remains of war.
But let some prophet or some sacred sage
Explore the cause of great Apollo's rage;
Or learn the wasteful vengeance to remove
By mystic dreams, for dreams descend
from Jove.
If broken vows this heavy curse have laid,
Let altars smoke, and hecatombs be paid.
So Heav'n atoned shall dying Greece re-
store,
And Phœbus dart his burning shafts no
more.' 90
He said, and sat: when Chalcas thus
replied:
Chalcas the wise, the Grecian priest and
guide,
That sacred seer, whose comprehensive
view
The past, the present, and the future
knew;
Uprising slow, the venerable sage
Thus spoke the prudence and the fears of
age:
'Belov'd of Jove, Achilles! would'st
thou know
Why angry Phœbus bends his fatal bow ?
First give thy faith, and plight a Prince's
word
Of sure protection, by thy power and
sword, 100
For I must speak what wisdom would con-
ceal,
And truths invidious to the great reveal.
Bold is the task, when subjects, grown too
wise,
Instruct a monarch where his error lies;
For tho' we deem the short-lived fury past,
'T is sure, the mighty will revenge at last.'
To whom Pelides: 'From thy inmost soul
Speak what thou know'st, and speak with-
out control.
Ev'n by that God I swear, who rules the
day,
To whom thy hands the vows of Greece
convey, 110
And whose blest oracles thy lips declare;
Long as Achilles breathes this vital air,

No daring Greek, of all the numerous band,
Against his priest shall lift an impious
  hand:
Not ev'n the Chief by whom our hosts are
  led,
The King of Kings, shall touch that sacred
  head.'
  Encouraged thus, the blameless man re-
  plies:
' Nor vows unpaid, nor slighted sacrifice,
But he, our Chief, provoked the raging
  pest,   119
Apollo's vengeance for his injured priest.
Nor will the God's awaken'd fury cease,
But plagues shall spread, and funeral fires
  increase,
Till the great King, without a ransom paid,
To her own Chrysa send the black-eyed
  maid.
Perhaps, with added sacrifice and prayer,
The Priest may pardon, and the God may
  spare.'
  The prophet spoke; when, with a gloomy
  frown,
The Monarch started from his shining
  throne;
Black choler fill'd his breast that boil'd
  with ire,
And from his eyeballs flash'd the living
  fire.   130
' Augur accurs'd! denouncing mischief still,
Prophet of plagues, for ever boding ill!
Still must that tongue some wounding mes-
  sage bring,
And still thy priestly pride provoke thy
  King ?
For this are Phœbus' oracles explor'd,
To teach the Greeks to murmur at their
  lord ?
For this with falsehoods is my honour
  stain'd;
Is Heav'n offended, and a priest profaned,
Because my prize, my beauteous maid, I
  hold,
And heav'nly charms prefer to proffer'd
  gold ?   140
A maid, unmatch'd in manners as in face,
Skill'd in each art, and crown'd with ev'ry
  grace:
Not half so dear were Clytæmnestra's
  charms,
When first her blooming beauties bless'd
  my arms.
Yet, if the Gods demand her, let her sail;
Our cares are only for the public weal:

Let me be deem'd the hateful cause of all,
And suffer, rather than my people fall.
The prize, the beauteous prize, I will re-
  sign,
So dearly valued, and so justly mine.   150
But since for common good I yield the Fair,
My private loss let grateful Greece repair;
Nor unrewarded let your Prince complain,
That he alone has fought and bled in vain.'
  ' Insatiate King!' (Achilles thus re-
  plies)
'Fond of the Power, but fonder of the
  Prize!
Wouldst thou the Greeks their lawful prey
  should yield,
The due reward of many a well-fought
  field ?
The spoils of cities razed, and warriors
  slain,
We share with justice, as with toil we
  gain: 160
But to resume whate'er thy av'rice craves
(That trick of tyrants) may be borne by
  slaves.
Yet if our Chief for plunder only fight,
The spoils of Ilion shall thy loss requite,
Whene'er, by Jove's decree, our conquer-
  ing powers
Shall humble to the dust her lofty towers.'
  Then thus the King: 'Shall I my prize
  resign
With tame content, and thou possess'd of
  thine ?
Great as thou art, and like a God in fight,
Think not to rob me of a soldier's right. 170
At thy demand shall I restore the maid ?
First let the just equivalent be paid;
Such as a King might ask; and let it be
A treasure worthy her, and worthy me.
Or grant me this, or with a monarch's
  claim
This hand shall seize some other captive
  dame.
The mighty Ajax shall his prize resign,
Ulysses' spoils, or ev'n thy own be mine.
The man who suffers, loudly may com-
  plain;
And rage he may, but he shall rage in
  vain.   180
But this when time requires: It now re-
  mains
We launch a bark to plough the wat'ry
  plains,
And waft the sacrifice to Chrysa's shores,
With chosen pilots, and with lab'ring oars.

Soon shall the Fair the sable ship ascend,
And some deputed prince the charge attend.
This Creta's king, or Ajax shall fulfil,
Or wise Ulysses see perform'd our will;
Or, if our royal pleasure shall ordain,   189
Achilles' self conduct her o'er the main;
Let fierce Achilles, dreadful in his rage,
The God propitiate, and the pest assuage.'
    At this, Pelides, frowning stern, replied:
' O tyrant, arm'd with insolence and pride!
Inglorious slave to int'rest, ever join'd
With fraud unworthy of a royal mind!
What gen'rous Greek, obedient to thy
        word,
Shall form an ambush, or shall lift the
        sword ?
What cause have I to war at thy decree ?
The distant Trojans never injured me;   200
To Phthia's realms no hostile troops they
        led :
Safe in her vales my warlike coursers fed;
Far hence remov'd, the hoarse-resounding
        main,
And walls of rocks, secure my native reign,
Whose fruitful soil luxuriant harvests
        grace,
Rich in her fruits, and in her martial race.
Hither we sail'd, a voluntary throng,
T' avenge a private, not a public wrong:
What else to Troy th' assembled nations
        draws,
But thine, ungrateful, and thy brother's
        cause ?   210
Is this the pay our blood and toils deserve,
Disgraced and injured by the man we
        serve ?
And darest thou threat to snatch my prize
        away,
Due to the deeds of many a dreadful day ?
A prize as small, O tyrant! match'd with
        thine,
As thy own actions if compared to mine.
Thine in each conquest is the wealthy prey,
Tho' mine the sweat and danger of the day.
Some trivial present to my ships I bear,
Or barren praises pay the wounds of war.
But know, proud Monarch, I 'm thy slave
        no more: 221
My fleet shall waft me to Thessalia's shore.
Left by Achilles on the Trojan plain,
What spoils, what conquests, shall Atrides
        gain ? '
    To this the King: ' Fly, mighty warrior!
        fly,
Thy aid we need not, and thy threats defy:

There want not chiefs in such a cause to
        fight,
And Jove himself shall guard a Monarch's
        right.
Of all the Kings (the Gods' distinguish'd
        care)   229
To pow'r superior none such hatred bear;
Strife and debate thy restless soul employ,
And wars and horrors are thy savage joy.
If thou hast strength, 't was Heav'n that
        strength bestow'd,
For know, vain man! thy valour is from
        God.
Haste, launch thy vessels, fly with speed
        away,
Rule thy own realms with arbitrary sway:
I heed thee not, but prize at equal rate
Thy short-lived friendship, and thy ground-
        less hate.
Go, threat thy earth-born Myrmidons; but
        here
'T is mine to threaten, Prince, and thine to
        fear.   240
Know, if the God the beauteous dame de-
        mand,
My bark shall waft her to her native land;
But then prepare, imperious Prince! pre-
        pare,
Fierce as thou art, to yield thy captive
        fair:
Ev'n in thy tent I 'll seize the blooming
        prize,
Thy loved Briseïs, with the radiant eyes.
Hence shalt thou prove my might, and
        curse the hour,
Thou stood'st a rival of imperial power;
And hence to all our host it shall be known
That Kings are subject to the Gods alone.'
    Achilles heard, with grief and rage op-
        press'd;   251
His heart swell'd high, and labour'd in his
        breast.
Distracting thoughts by turns his bosom
        ruled,
Now fired by wrath, and now by reason
        cool'd:
That prompts his hand to draw the deadly
        sword,
Force thro' the Greeks, and pierce their
        haughty lord;
This whispers soft, his vengeance to control,
And calm the rising tempest of his soul.
Just as in anguish of suspense he stay'd,
While half unsheathed appear'd the glitt'r-
        ing blade,   260

Minerva swift descended from above,
Sent by the sister and the wife of Jove
(For both the princes claim'd her equal
    care);
Behind she stood, and by the golden hair
Achilles seized; to him alone confess'd,
A sable cloud conceal'd her from the rest.
He sees, and sudden to the Goddess cries
(Known by the flames that sparkle from
    her eyes):
'Descends Minerva, in her guardian care,
A heav'nly witness of the wrongs I bear 270
From Atreus' son? Then let those eyes
    that view
The daring crime, behold the vengeance
    too.'
'Forbear!' (the progeny of Jove replies)
'To calm thy fury I forsake the skies:
Let great Achilles, to the Gods resign'd,
To reason yield the empire o'er his mind.
By awful Juno this command is giv'n;
The King and you are both the care of
    Heav'n.
The force of keen reproaches let him feel,
But sheathe, obedient, thy revenging steel.
For I pronounce (and trust a heav'nly
    Power)   281
Thy injured honour has its fated hour,
When the proud monarch shall thy arms
    implore,
And bribe thy friendship with a boundless
    store.
Then let revenge no longer bear the sway,
Command thy passions, and the Gods obey.'
    To her Pelides: 'With regardful ear,
'T is just, O Goddess! I thy dictates hear.
Hard as it is, my vengeance I suppress:
Those who revere the Gods, the Gods will
    bless.'   290
He said, observant of the blue-eyed maid;
Then in the sheath return'd the shining
    blade.
The Goddess swift to high Olympus flies,
And joins the sacred senate of the skies.
    Nor yet the rage his boiling breast for-
    sook;
Which thus redoubling on Atrides broke:
'O monster! mix'd of insolence and fear,
Thou dog in forehead, but in heart a deer!
When wert thou known in ambush'd fights
    to dare,
Or nobly face the horrid front of war? 300
'T is ours, the chance of fighting fields to
    try,
Thine to look on, and bid the valiant die.

So much 't is safer thro' the camp to go,
And rob a subject, than despoil a foe.
Scourge of thy people, violent and base!
Sent in Jove's anger on a slavish race,
Who, lost to sense of gen'rous freedom
    past,
Are tamed to wrongs, or this had been thy
    last.
Now by this sacred sceptre hear me swear,
Which never more shall leaves or blossoms
    bear,   310
Which, sever'd from the trunk (as I from
    thee)
On the bare mountains left its parent tree;
This sceptre, form'd by temper'd steel to
    prove
An ensign of the delegates of Jove,
From whom the power of laws and justice
    springs
(Tremendous oath! inviolate to Kings):
By this I swear, when bleeding Greece
    again
Shall call Achilles, she shall call in vain.
When, flush'd with slaughter, Hector comes
    to spread
The purpled shore with mountains of the
    dead,   320
Then shalt thou mourn th' affront thy mad-
    ness gave,
Forced to deplore, when impotent to save:
Then rage in bitterness of soul, to know
This act has made the bravest Greek thy
    foe.'
    He spoke; and furious hurl'd against
    the ground
His sceptre starr'd with golden studs
    around;
Then sternly silent sat. With like disdain,
The raging King return'd his frowns again.
    To calm their passion with the words
    of age,   329
Slow from his seat arose the Pylian sage.
Experienced Nestor, in persuasion skill'd;
Words sweet as honey from his lips dis-
    till'd:
Two generations now had pass'd away,
Wise by his rules, and happy by his sway;
Two ages o'er his native realm he reign'd,
And now th' example of the third remain'd.
All view'd with awe the venerable man;
Who thus, with mild benevolence, began:
    'What shame, what woe is this to Greece!
    what joy
To Troy's proud monarch, and the friends
    of Troy!   340

That adverse Gods commit to stern debate
The best, the bravest of the Grecian state.
Young as you are, this youthful heat re-
 strain,
Nor think your Nestor's years and wisdom
 vain.
A godlike race of heroes once I knew,
Such as no more these aged eyes shall view!
Lives there a chief to match Pirithous'
 fame,
Dryas the bold, or Ceneus' deathless name;
Theseus, endued with more than mortal
 might,   349
Or Polyphemus, like the Gods in fight?
With these of old to toils of battle bred,
In early youth my hardy days I led;
Fired with the thirst which virtuous envy
 breeds,
And smit with love of honourable deeds.
Strongest of men, they pierc'd the moun-
 tain boar,
Ranged the wild deserts red with mon-
 sters' gore,
And from their hills the shaggy Centaurs
 tore.
Yet these with soft persuasive arts I sway'd;
When Nestor spoke, they listen'd and
 obey'd.
If in my youth, ev'n these esteem'd me
 wise,   360
Do you, young warriors, hear my age advise.
Atrides, seize not on the beauteous slave;
That prize the Greeks by common suffrage
 gave:
Nor thou, Achilles, treat our Prince with
 pride;
Let Kings be just; and sov'reign power
 preside.
Thee, the first honours of the war adorn,
Like Gods in strength, and of a Goddess
 born;
Him, awful majesty exalts above
The powers of earth, and sceptred sons of
 Jove.   369
Let both unite with well-consenting mind,
So shall authority with strength be join'd.
Leave me, O King! to calm Achilles' rage;
Rule thou thyself, as more advanced in age.
Forbid it, Gods! Achilles should be lost,
The pride of Greece, and bulwark of our
 host.'
  This said, he ceas'd: the King of Men
 replies:
'Thy years are awful, and thy words are
 wise.

But that imperious, that unconquer'd soul,
No laws can limit, no respect control:
Before his pride must his superiors fall, 380
His word the law, and he the lord of all?
Him must our hosts, our chiefs, ourself,
 obey?
What King can bear a rival in his sway?
Grant that the Gods his matchless force
 have giv'n;
Has foul reproach a privilege from
 Heav'n?'
  Here on the Monarch's speech Achilles
 broke,
And furious, thus, and interrupting, spoke:
'Tyrant, I well deserv'd thy galling chain,
To live thy slave, and still to serve in vain,
Should I submit to each unjust decree: 390
Command thy vassals, but command not
 me.
Seize on Briseïs, whom the Grecians doom'd
My prize of war, yet tamely see resumed;
And seize secure; no more Achilles draws
His conquering sword in any woman's
 cause.
The Gods command me to forgive the past;
But let this first invasion be the last:
For know, thy blood, when next thou darest
 invade,
Shall stream in vengeance on my reeking
 blade.'
  At this they ceas'd; the stern debate ex-
 pired: 400
The Chiefs in sullen majesty retired.
  Achilles with Patroclus took his way,
Where near his tents his hollow vessels lay.
Meantime Atrides launch'd with numerous
 oars
A well-rigg'd ship for Chrysa's sacred
 shores:
High on the deck was fair Chryseïs placed,
And sage Ulysses with the conduct graced:
Safe in her sides the hecatomb they stow'd,
Then, swiftly sailing, cut the liquid road.
  The host to expiate, next the King pre-
 pares,   410
With pure lustrations and with solemn
 prayers.
Wash'd by the briny wave, the pious train
Are cleans'd; and cast th' ablutions in the
 main.
Along the shores whole hecatombs were
 laid,
And bulls and goats to Phœbus' altars paid.
The sable fumes in curling spires arise,
And waft their grateful odours to the skies.

The army thus in sacred rites engaged,
Atrides still with deep resentment raged.
To wait his will two sacred heralds stood,
Talthybius and Eurybates the good. 421
Haste to the fierce Achilles' tent' (he cries),
'Thence bear Briseïs as our royal prize:
Submit he must; or, if they will not part,
Ourself in arms shall tear her from his
    heart.'
Th' unwilling heralds act their lord's
    commands;
Pensive they walk along the barren sands:
Arrived, the hero in his tent they find,
With gloomy aspect, on his arm reclin'd.
At awful distance long they silent stand, 430
Loth to advance, or speak their hard com-
    mand;
Decent confusion! This the godlike man
Perceiv'd, and thus with accent mild be-
    gan:
'With leave and honour enter our
    abodes,
Ye sacred ministers of men and Gods!
I know your message; by constraint you
    came;
Not you, but your imperious lord, I blame.
Patroclus, haste, the fair Briseïs bring;
Conduct my captive to the haughty King.
But witness, Heralds, and proclaim my
    vow, 440
Witness to Gods above, and men below!
But first, and loudest, to your Prince de-
    clare,
That lawless tyrant whose commands you
    bear;
Unmov'd as death Achilles shall remain,
Tho' prostrate Greece should bleed at
    ev'ry vein:
The raging Chief in frantic passion lost,
Blind to himself, and useless to his host,
Unskill'd to judge the future by the past,
In blood and slaughter shall repent at last.'
Patroclus now th' unwilling beauty
    brought; 450
She, in soft sorrows, and in pensive thought,
Pass'd silent, as the heralds held her hand,
And oft look'd back, slow-moving o'er the
    strand.
Not so his loss the fierce Achilles bore;
But sad retiring to the sounding shore,
O'er the wild margin of the deep he hung,
That kindred deep from whence his mother
    sprung;
There, bathed in tears of anger and disdain,
Thus loud lamented to the stormy main:

'O parent Goddess! since in early bloom
Thy son must fall, by too severe a doom;
Sure, to so short a race of glory born, 462
Great Jove in justice should this span
    adorn.
Honour and Fame at least the Thund'rer
    owed;
And ill he pays the promise of a God,
If yon proud monarch thus thy son defies,
Obscures my glories, and resumes my
    prize.'
Far in the deep recesses of the main,
Where aged Ocean holds his wat'ry reign,
The Goddess-mother heard. The waves
    divide; 470
And like a mist she rose above the tide;
Beheld him mourning on the naked shores,
And thus the sorrows of his soul explores:
'Why grieves my son? thy anguish let me
    share,
Reveal the cause, and trust a parent's care.'
He deeply sighing said: 'To tell my woe,
Is but to mention what too well you know.
From Thebe, sacred to Apollo's name
(Eëtion's realm), our conquering army
    came,
With treasure loaded and triumphant
    spoils, 480
Whose just division crown'd the soldier's
    toils;
But bright Chryseïs, heav'nly prize! was
    led
By vote selected to the gen'ral's bed.
The priest of Phœbus sought by gifts to
    gain
His beauteous daughter from the victor's
    chain;
The fleet he reach'd, and, lowly bending
    down,
Held forth the sceptre and the laurel crown,
Entreating all; but chief implor'd for
    grace
The brother-kings of Atreus' royal race:
The gen'rous Greeks their joint consent
    declare, 490
The Priest to rev'rence, and release the
    Fair.
Not so Atrides: he, with wonted pride,
The sire insulted, and his gifts denied:
Th' insulted sire (his God's peculiar care)
To Phœbus pray'd, and Phœbus heard the
    prayer:
A dreadful plague ensues; th' avenging
    darts
Incessant fly, and pierce the Grecian hearts,

A prophet then, inspired by Heav'n, arose,
And points the crime, and thence derives
   the woes:
Myself the first th' assembled chiefs in-
   cline   500
T' avert the vengeance of the Power di-
   vine;
Then, rising in his wrath, the Monarch
   storm'd;
Incens'd he threaten'd, and his threats per-
   form'd:
The fair Chryseïs to her sire was sent,
With offer'd gifts to make the God relent;
But now he seized Briseïs' heav'nly charms,
And of my valour's prize defrauds my
   arms,
Defrauds the votes of all the Grecian train;
And Service, Faith, and Justice, plead in
   vain.
But, Goddess! thou thy suppliant son at-
   tend,   510
To high Olympus' shining court ascend,
Urge all the ties to former service owed,
And sue for vengeance to the thund'ring
   God.
Oft hast thou triumph'd in the glorious
   boast
That thou stood'st forth, of all th' ethereal
   host,
When bold rebellion shook the realms
   above,
Th' undaunted guard of cloud-compelling
   Jove.
When the bright partner of his awful
   reign,
The warlike maid, and Monarch of the
   Main,
The Traitor-gods, by mad ambition driv'n,
Durst threat with chains th' omnipotence
   of Heav'n,   521
Then call'd by thee, the monster Titan
   came
(Whom Gods Briareus, men Ægeon name);
Thro' wond'ring skies enormous stalk'd
   along;
Not he that shakes the solid earth so
   strong:
With giant pride at Jove's high throne he
   stands,
And brandish'd round him all his hundred
   hands.
Th' affrighted Gods confess'd their awful
   lord,
They dropp'd the fetters, trembled and
   adored.

This, Goddess, this to his rememb'rance
   call,   530
Embrace his knees, at his tribunal fall;
Conjure him far to drive the Grecian train,
To hurl them headlong to their fleet and
   main,
To heap the shores with copious death, and
   bring
The Greeks to know the curse of such a
   King:
Let Agamemnon lift his haughty head
O'er all his wide dominion of the dead,
And mourn in blood, that e'er he durst dis-
   grace
The boldest warrior of the Grecian race.'
' Unhappy son!' (fair Thetis thus re-
   plies,   540
While tears celestial trickle from her
   eyes)
' Why have I borne thee with a mother's
   throes,
To fates averse, and nurs'd for future
   woes ?
So short a space the light of Heav'n to
   view!
So short a space! and fill'd with sorrow
   too!
O might a parent's careful wish prevail,
Far, far from Ilion should thy vessels sail,
And thou, from camps remote, the danger
   shun,
Which now, alas! too nearly threats my
   son.
Yet (what I can) to move thy suit I 'll
   go   550
To great Olympus crown'd with fleecy
   snow.
Meantime, secure within thy ships from
   far
Behold the field, nor mingle in the war.
The Sire of Gods, and all th' ethereal train,
On the warm limits of the farthest main,
Now mix with mortals, nor disdain to
   grace
The feasts of Æthiopia's blameless race:
Twelve days the Powers indulge the genial
   rite,
Returning with the twelfth revolving light.
Then will I mount the brazen dome, and
   move   560
The high tribunal of immortal Jove.'
   The Goddess spoke: the rolling waves
   unclose;
Then down the deep she plunged, from
   whence she rose,

And left him sorrowing on the lonely coast
In wild resentment for the Fair he lost.
 In Chrysa's port now sage Ulysses rode;
Beneath the deck the destin'd victims
 stow'd:
The sails they furl'd, they lash'd the mast
 aside,
And dropp'd their anchors, and the pinnace
 tied.
Next on the shore their hecatomb they
 land, 570
Chryseïs last descending on the strand.
Her, thus returning from the furrow'd
 main,
Ulysses led to Phœbus' sacred fane;
Where at his solemn altar, as the maid
He gave to Chryses, thus the hero said:
 'Hail, rev'rend Priest! to Phœbus' awful
 dome
A suppliant I from great Atrides come:
Unransom'd here receive the spotless Fair;
Accept the hecatomb the Greeks prepare;
And may thy God who scatters darts
 around, 580
Atoned by sacrifice, desist to wound.'
 At this the sire embraced the maid again,
So sadly lost, so lately sought in vain.
Then near the altar of the darting King
Disposed in rank their hecatomb they
 bring:
With water purify their hands, and take
The sacred off'ring of the salted cake;
While thus with arms devoutly raised in
 air,
And solemn voice, the priest directs his
 prayer:
 'God of the Silver Bow, thy ear in-
 cline, 590
Whose power encircles Cilla the divine;
Whose sacred eye thy Tenedos surveys,
And gilds fair Chrysa with distinguish'd
 rays!
If, fired to vengeance at thy priest's re-
 quest,
Thy direful darts inflict the raging pest;
Once more attend! avert the wasteful woe,
And smile propitious, and unbend thy bow.'
 So Chryses pray'd, Apollo heard his
 prayer:
And now the Greeks their hecatomb pre-
 pare;
Between their horns the salted barley
 threw, 600
And with their heads to Heav'n the victims
 slew:

The limbs they sever from th' inclosing
 hide;
The thighs, selected to the Gods, divide:
On these, in double cauls involv'd with
 art,
The choicest morsels lay from every part.
The priest himself before his altar stands,
And burns the off'ring with his holy hands,
Pours the black wine, and sees the flames
 aspire;
The youths with instruments surround the
 fire:
The thighs thus sacrificed, and entrails
 drest, 610
Th' assistants part, transfix, and roast the
 rest:
Then spread the tables, the repast prepare,
Each takes his seat, and each receives his
 share.
When now the rage of hunger was re-
 press'd,
With pure libations they conclude the
 feast:
The youths with wine the copious goblets
 crown'd,
And, pleas'd, dispense the flowing bowls
 around.
With hymns divine the joyous banquet
 ends,
The Pæans lengthen'd till the sun de-
 scends:
The Greeks, restor'd, the grateful notes
 prolong: 620
Apollo listens, and approves the song.
 'T was night; the chiefs beside their
 vessel lie,
Till rosy morn had purpled o'er the sky:
Then launch, and hoist the mast; indulgent
 gales,
Supplied by Phœbus, fill the swelling sails;
The milk-white canvas bellying as they
 blow,
The parted ocean foams and roars below:
Above the bounding billows swift they
 flew,
Till now the Grecian camp appear'd in
 view.
Far on the beach they haul their barks to
 land, 630
(The crooked keel divides the yellow
 sand),
Then part, where stretch'd along the wind-
 ing bay
The ships and tents in mingled prospect
 lay.

But, raging still, amidst his navy sate
The stern Achilles, steadfast in his hate;
Nor mix'd in combat, nor in council join'd;
But wasting cares lay heavy on his mind:
In his black thoughts revenge and slaugh-
ter roll,
And scenes of blood rise dreadful in his
soul.
Twelve days were past, and now the
dawning light 640
The Gods had summon'd to th' Olympian
height:
Jove, first ascending from the wat'ry
bowers,
Leads the long order of ethereal Powers.
When like the morning mist, in early day,
Rose from the flood the Daughter of the
Sea;
And to the seats divine her flight ad-
dress'd.
There, far apart, and high above the rest,
The Thund'rer sat; where old Olympus
shrouds
His hundred heads in Heav'n, and props
the clouds.
Suppliant the Goddess stood: one hand she
placed 650
Beneath his beard, and one his knees em-
braced.
'If e'er, O father of the Gods!' she said,
'My words could please thee, or my actions
aid;
Some marks of honour on thy son bestow,
And pay in glory what in life you owe.
Fame is at least by heav'nly promise due
To life so short, and now dishonour'd too.
Avenge this wrong, oh ever just and wise!
Let Greece be humbled, and the Trojans
rise;
Till the proud King, and all th' Achaian
race 660
Shall heap with honours him they now dis-
grace.'
Thus Thetis spoke, but Jove in silence
held
The sacred councils of his breast conceal'd.
Not so repuls'd, the Goddess closer press'd,
Still grasp'd his knees, and urged the dear
request.
'O Sire of Gods and men! thy suppliant
hear,
Refuse, or grant; for what has Jove to
fear?
Or, oh! declare, of all the Powers above,
Is wretched Thetis least the care of Jove?'

She said, and sighing thus the God re-
plies, 670
Who rolls the thunder o'er the vaulted
skies:
'What hast thou ask'd? Ah, why should
Jove engage
In foreign contests, and domestic rage,
The Gods' complaints, and Juno's fierce
alarms,
While I, too partial, aid the Trojan arms?
Go, lest the haughty partner of my sway
With jealous eyes thy close access survey;
But part in peace, secure thy prayer is sped:
Witness the sacred honours of our head,
The nod that ratifies the will divine, 680
The faithful, fix'd, irrevocable sign;
This seals thy suit, and this fulfils thy
vows — '
He spoke, and awful bends his sable brows,
Shakes his ambrosial curls, and gives the
nod;
The stamp of Fate, and sanction of the
God:
High Heav'n with trembling the dread sig-
nal took,
And all Olympus to the centre shook.
Swift to the seas profound the Goddess
flies,
Jove to his starry mansion in the skies. 689
The shining Synod of th' Immortals wait
The coming God, and from their thrones
of state
Arising silent, rapt in holy fear,
Before the Majesty of Heav'n appear.
Trembling they stand, while Jove assumes
the throne,
All, but the God's imperious Queen alone:
Late had she view'd the silver-footed
dame,
And all her passions kindled into flame.
'Say, artful manager of Heav'n' (she cries),
'Who now partakes the secrets of the
skies?
Thy Juno knows not the decrees of Fate, 700
In vain the partner of imperial state.
What fav'rite Goddess then those cares
divides,
Which Jove in prudence from his consort
hides?'
To this the Thund'rer: 'Seek not thou
to find
The sacred counsels of almighty mind:
Involved in darkness lies the great decree,
Nor can the depths of Fate be pierc'd by
thee.

What fits thy knowledge, thou the first
   shalt know:
The first of Gods above and men below:
But thou, nor they, shall search the
   thoughts that roll   710
Deep in the close recesses of my soul.'
   Full on the Sire, the Goddess of the skies
Roll'd the large orbs of her majestic eyes,
And thus return'd: 'Austere Saturnius,
   say,
From whence this wrath, or who controls
   thy sway ?
Thy boundless will, for me, remains in
   force,
And all thy counsels take the destin'd
   course.
But 't is for Greece I fear: for late was
   seen
In close consult the Silver-footed Queen.
Jove to his Thetis nothing could deny,   720
Nor was the signal vain that shook the sky.
What fatal favour has the Goddess won,
To grace her fierce inexorable son ?
Perhaps in Grecian blood to drench the
   plain,
And glut his vengeance with my people
   slain.'
   Then thus the God: 'Oh restless fate of
   pride,
That strives to learn what Heav'n resolves
   to hide;
Vain is the search, presumptuous and
   abhorr'd,
Anxious to thee, and odious to thy Lord.
Let this suffice: th' immutable decree   730
No force can shake: what *is*, that *ought* to
   be.
Goddess, submit, nor dare our will with-
   stand,
But dread the power of this avenging hand;
Th' united strength of all the Gods above
In vain resist th' omnipotence of Jove.'
   The Thund'rer spoke, nor durst the
   Queen reply;
A rev'rend horror silenced all the sky.
The feast disturb'd, with sorrow Vulcan
   saw
His mother menaced, and the Gods in awe;
Peace at his heart, and pleasure his design,
Thus interposed the architect divine: 741
'The wretched quarrels of the mortal state
Are far unworthy, Gods! of your debate:
Let men their days in senseless strife em-
   ploy,
We, in eternal peace, and constant joy.

Thou, Goddess-mother, with our sire com-
   ply,
Nor break the sacred union of the sky:
Lest, rous'd to rage, he shake the blest
   abodes,
Launch the red lightning, and dethrone the
   Gods.
If you submit, the Thund'rer stands ap-
   peas'd;   750
The gracious Power is willing to be
   pleas'd.'
   Thus Vulcan spoke; and, rising with a
   bound,
The double bowl with sparkling nectar
   crown'd,
Which held to Juno in a cheerful way,
'Goddess' (he cried), 'be patient and obey.
Dear as you are, if Jove his arm extend,
I can but grieve, unable to defend.
What God so daring in your aid to move,
Or lift his hand against the force of Jove ?
Once in your cause I felt his matchless
   might,   760
Hurl'd headlong downward from th' ethe-
   real height;
Toss'd all the day in rapid circles round;
Nor, till the sun descended, touch'd the
   ground:
Breathless I fell, in giddy motion lost;
The Sinthians rais'd me on the Lemnian
   coast.'
   He said, and to her hands the goblet
   heav'd,
Which, with a smile, the white-arm'd Queen
   receiv'd.
Then to the rest he fill'd; and, in his
   turn,
Each to his lips applied the nectar'd urn.
Vulcan with awkward grace his office
   plies,   770
And unextinguish'd laughter shakes the
   skies.
   Thus the blest Gods the genial day pro-
   long,
In feasts ambrosial, and celestial song.
Apollo tuned the lyre; the Muses round
With voice alternate aid the silver sound.
Meantime the radiant sun, to mortal sight
Descending swift, roll'd down the rapid
   light.
Then to their starry domes the Gods de-
   part,
The shining monuments of Vulcan's art:
Jove on his couch reclin'd his awful head,
And Juno slumber'd on the golden bed.   781

BOOK II

THE TRIAL OF THE ARMY AND CATALOGUE
OF THE FORCES

THE ARGUMENT

Jupiter, in pursuance of the request of Thetis,
sends a deceitful vision to Agamemnon, persuading him to lead the army to battle; in
order to make the Greeks sensible of their
want of Achilles. The general, who is deluded with the hopes of taking Troy without
his assistance, but fears the army was discouraged by his absence and the late plague,
as well as by length of time, contrives to
make trial of their disposition by a stratagem. He first communicates his design to
the Princes in council, that he would propose
a return to the soldiers, and that they should
put a stop to them if the proposal was embraced. Then he assembles the whole host,
and upon moving for a return to Greece, they
unanimously agree to it, and run to prepare
the ships. They are detained by the management of Ulysses, who chastises the insolence
of Thersites. The assembly is recalled, several speeches made on the occasion, and
at length the advice of Nestor followed,
which was to make a general muster of the
troops, and to divide them into their several nations, before they proceeded to battle.
This gives occasion to the poet to enumerate
all the forces of the Greeks and Trojans, in a
large catalogue.
The time employed in this book consists not
entirely of one day. The scene lies in the
Grecian camp and upon the seashore; toward the end it removes to Troy.

Now pleasing sleep had seal'd each mortal
    eye,
Stretch'd in the tents the Grecian leaders
    lie,
Th' immortal slumber'd on their thrones
    above;
All but the ever-wakeful eyes of Jove.
To honour Thetis' son he bends his care,
And plunge the Greeks in all the woes of
    war:
Then bids an empty Phantom rise to sight,
And thus commands the Vision of the
    night:
  ' Fly hence, deluding Dream! and, light
    as air,
To Agamemnon's ample tent repair.   10
Bid him in arms draw forth th' embattled
    train,
Lead all his Grecians to the dusty plain.

Declare, ev'n now 't is given him to destroy
The lofty towers of wide-extended Troy.
For now no more the Gods with Fate con-
    tend,
At Juno's suit the heav'nly factions end.
Destruction hangs o'er yon devoted wall,
And nodding Ilion waits th' impending
    fall.'
  Swift as the word the vain Illusion fled,
Descends, and hovers o'er Atrides' head; 20
Clothed in the figure of the Pylian sage,
Renown'd for wisdom, and revered for
    age;
Around his temples spreads his golden
    wing,
And thus the flatt'ring Dream deceives the
    King:
  ' Canst thou, with all a Monarch's cares
    oppress'd,
O Atreus' son! canst thou indulge thy
    rest ?
Ill fits a chief who mighty nations guides,
Directs in council, and in war presides,
To whom its safety a whole people owes,
To waste long nights in indolent repose. 30
Monarch, awake! 't is Jove's command I
    bear,
Thou and thy glory claim his heav'nly
    care.
In just array draw forth th' embattled train,
Lead all thy Grecians to the dusty plain;
Ev'n now, O King! 't is given thee to de-
    stroy
The lofty towers of wide-extended Troy.
For now no more the Gods with Fate con-
    tend,
At Juno's suit the heav'nly factions end.
Destruction hangs o'er yon devoted wall,
And nodding Ilion waits th' impending
    fall,   40
Awake, but, waking, this advice approve,
And trust the vision that descends from
    Jove.'
  The Phantom said; then vanish'd from
    his sight,
Resolves to air, and mixes with the night.
A thousand schemes the Monarch's mind
    employ;
Elate in thought, he sacks untaken Troy;
Vain as he was, and to the future blind;
Nor saw what Jove and secret Fate de-
    sign'd;
What mighty toils to either host remain,
What scenes of grief, and numbers of the
    slain!   50

Eager he rises, and in fancy hears
The voice celestial murm'ring in his ears.
First on his limbs a slender vest he drew,
Around him next the regal mantle threw,
Th' embroider'd sandals on his feet were
　tied;
The starry falchion glitter'd at his side:
And last his arm the massy sceptre loads,
Unstain'd, immortal, and the gift of Gods.
　Now rosy Morn ascends the court of
　Jove,
Lifts up her light, and opens day above. 60
The King dispatch'd his heralds with com-
　mands
To range the camp and summon all the
　bands:
The gath'ring hosts the Monarch's word
　obey;
While to the fleet Atrides bends his way.
In his black ship the Pylian Prince he
　found;
There calls a senate of the peers around:
Th' assembly placed, the King of Men ex-
　press'd
The counsels lab'ring in his artful breast:
　'Friends and confed'rates! with atten-
　tive ear
Receive my words, and credit what you
　hear. 70
Late as I slumber'd in the shades of night,
A Dream divine appear'd before my sight;
Whose visionary form like Nestor came,
The same in habit, and in mien the same.
The heav'nly Phantom hover'd o'er my
　head,
And, "Dost thou sleep, O Atreus' son?"
　(he said)
"Ill fits a chief who mighty nations guides,
Directs in council, and in war presides,
To whom its safety a whole people owes,
To waste long nights in indolent repose. 80
Monarch, awake! 't is Jove's command I
　bear,
Thou and thy glory claim his heav'nly care;
In just array draw forth th' embattled train,
And lead the Grecians to the dusty plain.
Ev'n now, O King! 't is giv'n thee to de-
　stroy
The lofty towers of wide-extended Troy.
For now no more the Gods with Fate con-
　tend,
At Juno's suit the heav'nly factions end.
Destruction hangs o'er yon devoted wall,
And nodding Ilion waits th' impending
　fall. 90

This hear observant, and the Gods obey!"
The Vision spoke, and pass'd in air away.
Now, valiant chiefs! since Heav'n itself
　alarms,
Unite, and rouse the sons of Greece to
　arms.
But first, with caution, try what yet they
　dare,
Worn with nine years of unsuccessful war.
To move the troops to measure back the
　main,
Be mine; and yours the province to detain.'
　He spoke, and sat; when Nestor rising
　said
(Nestor, whom Pylos' sandy realms
　obey'd): 100
'Princes of Greece, your faithful ears in-
　cline,
Nor doubt the Vision of the Powers divine;
Sent by great Jove to him who rules the
　host,
Forbid it, Heav'n! this warning should be
　lost!
Then let us haste, obey the God's alarms,
And join to rouse the sons of Greece to
　arms.'
　Thus spoke the sage: the Kings without
　delay
Dissolve the council, and their Chief obey:
The sceptred rulers lead; the foll'wing
　host,
Pour'd forth by thousands, darkens all the
　coast. 110
As from some rocky cleft the shepherd
　sees
Clust'ring in heaps on heaps the driving
　bees,
Rolling and black'ning, swarms succeeding
　swarms
With deeper murmurs and more hoarse
　alarms;
Dusky they spread, a close - embodied
　crowd,
And o'er the vale descends the living
　cloud.
So, from the tents and ships, a length'ning
　train
Spreads all the beach, and wide o'ershades
　the plain;
Along the region runs a deaf'ning sound;
Beneath their footsteps groans the trem-
　bling ground. 120
Fame flies before, the messenger of Jove,
And shining soars, and claps her wings
　above.

Nine sacred heralds now proclaiming loud
The Monarch's will, suspend the list'ning
  crowd.
Soon as the throngs in order ranged ap-
  pear,
And fainter murmurs died upon the ear,
The King of Kings his awful figure raised;
High in his hand the golden sceptre blazed:
The golden sceptre, of celestial frame,
By Vulcan form'd, from Jove to Hermes
  came: 130
To Pelops he th' immortal gift resign'd;
Th' immortal gift great Pelops left behind,
In Atreus' hand, which not with Atreus
  ends,
To rich Thyestes next the prize descends;
And now, the mark of Agamemnon's reign,
Subjects all Argos, and controls the main.
  On this bright sceptre now the King re-
  clin'd,
And artful thus pronounced the speech de-
  sign'd;
'Ye sons of Mars! partake your leader's
  care,
Heroes of Greece, and brothers of the war!
Of partial Jove with justice I complain, 141
And heav'nly oracles believ'd in vain.
A safe return was promis'd to our toils,
Renown'd, triumphant, and enrich'd with
  spoils.
Now shameful flight alone can save the
  host,
Our blood, our treasure, and our glory lost.
So Jove decrees, resistless Lord of all!
At whose command whole empires rise or
  fall:
He shakes the feeble props of human trust,
And towns and armies humbles to the dust.
What shame to Greece a fruitless war to
  wage,   151
Oh lasting shame in ev'ry future age!
Once great in arms, the common scorn we
  grow,
Repuls'd and baffled by a feeble foe.
So small their number, that, if wars were
  ceas'd,
And Greece triumphant held a gen'ral
  feast,
All rank'd by tens; whole decades, when
  they dine,
Must want a Trojan slave to pour the wine.
But other forces have our hopes o'er-
  thrown,
And Troy prevails by armies not her
  own.   160

Now nine long years of mighty Jove are
  run,
Since first the labours of this war begun;
Our cordage torn, decay'd our vessels lie,
And scarce ensure the wretched power to
  fly.
Haste then, for ever leave the Trojan wall!
Our weeping wives, our tender children
  call;
Love, Duty, Safety, summon us away,
'T is Nature's voice, and Nature we obey.
Our shatter'd barks may yet transport us
  o'er,
Safe and inglorious, to our native shore. 170
Fly, Grecians, fly! your sails and oars em-
  ploy,
And dream no more of Heav'n-defended
  Troy.'
  His deep design unknown, the hosts ap-
  prove
Atrides' speech. The mighty numbers
  move.
So roll the billows to th' Icarian shore,
From east and south when winds begin to
  roar,
Burst their dark mansions in the clouds,
  and sweep
The whitening surface of the ruffled deep:
And as on corn when western gusts de-
  scend,
Before the blast the lofty harvests bend; 180
Thus o'er the field the moving host appears,
With nodding plumes and groves of wav-
  ing spears,
The gath'ring murmur spreads, their tram-
  pling feet
Beat the loose sands, and thicken to the
  fleet.
With long-resounding cries they urge the
  train
To fit the ships, and launch into the main.
They toil, they sweat, thick clouds of dust
  arise,
The doubling clamours echo thro' the
  skies.
Ev'n then the Greeks had left the hostile
  plain,
And Fate decreed the fall of Troy in vain;
But Jove's imperial Queen their flight sur-
  vey'd,   191
And sighing thus bespoke the blue-eyed
  maid:
  'Shall then the Grecians fly ? O dire dis-
  grace!
And leave unpunish'd this perfidious race ?

Shall Troy, shall Priam, and the adult'rous
  spouse,
In peace enjoy the fruits of broken vows?
And bravest chiefs, in Helen's quarrel slain,
Lie unavenged on yon detested plain?
No: let my Greeks, unmov'd by vain
  alarms,
Once more refulgent shine in brazen arms.
Haste, Goddess, haste! the flying host de-
  tain,   201
Nor let one sail be hoisted on the main.'
  Pallas obeys, and from Olympus' height
Swift to the ships precipitates her flight;
Ulysses, first in public cares, she found,
For prudent counsel like the Gods renown'd;
Oppress'd with gen'rous grief the hero
  stood;
Nor drew his sable vessels to the flood.
' And is it thus, divine Laertes' son!
Thus fly the Greeks?' (the Martial Maid
  begun)   210
' Thus to their country bear their own dis-
  grace,
And Fame eternal leave to Priam's race?
Shall beauteous Helen still remain unfreed,
Still unrevenged a thousand heroes bleed?
Haste, gen'rous Ithacus! prevent the
  shame,
Recall your armies, and your chiefs re-
  claim.
Your own resistless eloquence employ,
And to th' immortals trust the fall of
  Troy.'
  The voice divine confess'd the Warlike
  Maid,
Ulysses heard, nor uninspired obey'd: 220
Then, meeting first Atrides, from his hand
Receiv'd th' imperial sceptre of command.
Thus graced, attention and respect to gain,
He runs, he flies thro' all the Grecian
  train,
Each Prince of name, or Chief in arms
  approv'd,
He fired with praise, or with persuasion
  mov'd:
' Warriors like you, with strength and
  wisdom blest,
By brave examples should confirm the
  rest.
The Monarch's will not yet reveal'd ap-
  pears;
He tries our courage, but resents our
  fears.   230
Th' unwary Greeks his fury may provoke;
Not thus the King in secret council spoke.

Jove loves our Chief, from Jove his honour
  springs,
Beware! for dreadful is the wrath of
  Kings.'
  But if a clam'rous vile plebeian rose,
Him with reproof he check'd or tamed
  with blows.
' Be still, thou slave, and to thy betters
  yield;
Unknown alike in council and in field:
Ye Gods, what dastards would our host
  command?   239
Swept to the war, the number of a land.
Be silent, wretch, and think not here
  allow'd
That worst of tyrants, an usurping crowd.
To one sole monarch Jove commits the
  sway;
His are the laws, and him let all obey.'
  With words like these the troops Ulysses
  ruled,
The loudest silenc'd, and the fiercest cool'd.
Back to th' assembly roll the thronging
  train,
Desert the ships, and pour upon the plain.
Murm'ring they move, as when old Ocean
  roars,
And heaves huge surges to the trembling
  shores: 250
The groaning banks are burst with bellow-
  ing sound,
The rocks remurmur, and the deeps re-
  bound.
At length the tumult sinks, the noises cease,
And a still silence lulls the camp to peace.
  Thersites only clamour'd in the throng,
Loquacious, loud, and turbulent of tongue:
Awed by no shame, by no respect con-
  troll'd,
In scandal busy, in reproaches bold;
With witty malice studious to defame; 259
Scorn all his joy, and laughter all his aim.
But chief he gloried with licentious style
To lash the great, and monarchs to revile.
His figure such as might his soul pro-
  claim:
One eye was blinking, and one leg was
  lame:
His mountain-shoulders half his breast
  o'erspread;
Thin hairs bestrew'd his long misshapen
  head.
Spleen to mankind his envious heart
  possess'd,
And much he hated all, but most the best.

Ulysses or Achilles still his theme;
But royal scandal his delight supreme. 270
Long had he lived the scorn of ev'ry
    Greek;
Vex'd when he spoke, yet still they heard
    him speak.
Sharp was his voice; which, in the shrillest
    tone,
Thus with injurious taunts attack'd the
    throne:
'Amidst the glories of so bright a reign,
What moves the great Atrides to com-
    plain?
'T is thine whate'er the warrior's breast
    inflames,
The golden spoil, and thine the lovely
    dames.
With all the wealth our wars and blood
    bestow,
Thy tents are crowded, and thy chests
    o'erflow. 280
Thus at full ease, in heaps of riches roll'd,
What grieves the Monarch? Is it thirst of
    gold?
Say, shall we march with our unconquer'd
    powers
(The Greeks and I), to Ilion's hostile
    towers,
And bring the race of royal bastards here,
For Troy to ransom at a price too dear?
But safer plunder thy own host supplies;
Say, wouldst thou seize some valiant lead-
    er's prize?
Or, if thy heart to gen'rous love be led,
Some captive fair, to bless thy kingly
    bed? 290
Whate'er our master craves, submit we
    must,
Plagued with his pride, or punish'd for his
    lust.
Oh, women of Achaia! men no more!
Hence let us fly, and let him waste his
    store
In loves and pleasures on the Phrygian
    shore.
We may be wanted on some busy day,
When Hector comes: so great Achilles
    may:
From him be forced the prize we jointly
    gave,
From him, the fierce, the fearless, and the
    brave:
And durst he, as he ought, resent that
    wrong, 300
This mighty tyrant were no tyrant long.'

Fierce from his seat, at this, Ulysses
    springs
In gen'rous vengeance of the King of Kings.
With indignation sparkling in his eyes,
He views the wretch, and sternly thus re-
    plies:
'Peace, factious monster! born to vex
    the state,
With wrangling talents form'd for foul de-
    bate:
Curb that impetuous tongue, nor, rashly
    vain
And singly mad, asperse the sov'reign reign.
Have we not known thee, Slave! of all our
    host, 310
The man who acts the least, upbraids the
    most?
Think not the Greeks to shameful flight to
    bring,
Nor let those lips profane the name of
    King.
For our return we trust the heav'nly
    powers;
Be that their care; to fight like men be
    ours.
But grant the host with wealth the gen'ral
    load,
Except detraction, what hast thou be-
    stow'd?
Suppose some hero should his spoils resign,
Art thou that hero, could those spoils be
    thine? 319
Gods! let me perish on this hateful shore,
And let these eyes behold my son no more;
If, on thy next offence, this hand forbear
To strip those arms thou ill deserv'st to
    wear,
Expel the council where our Princes meet,
And send thee scourged, and howling
    thro' the fleet.'
He said, and cow'ring as the dastard
    bends,
The weighty sceptre on his back descends,
On the round bunch the bloody tumours
    rise;
The tears spring starting from his haggard
    eyes:
Trembling he sat, and, shrunk in abject
    fears, 330
From his vile visage wiped the scalding
    tears.
While to his neighbour each express'd his
    thought:
'Ye Gods! what wonders has Ulysses
    wrought!

What fruits his conduct and his courage
    yield,
Great in the council, glorious in the field!
Gen'rous he rises in the Crown's defence,
To curb the factious tongue of insolence.
Such just examples on offenders shewn
Sedition silence, and assert the throne.'
  'T was thus the gen'ral voice the hero
    praised   340
Who, rising high, th' imperial sceptre
    rais'd:
The blue-eyed Pallas, his celestial friend
(In form a herald), bade the crowds at-
    tend;
Th' expecting crowds in still attention
    hung,
To hear the wisdom of his heav'nly tongue.
Then, deeply thoughtful, pausing ere he
    spoke,
His silence thus the prudent hero broke:
' Unhappy Monarch! whom the Grecian
    race,
With shame deserting, heap with vile dis-
    grace,
Not such at Argos was their gen'rous
    vow,   350
Once all their voice, but ah! forgotten now:
Ne'er to return, was then the common cry,
Till Troy's proud structures should in ashes
    lie.
Behold them weeping for their native
    shore!
What could their wives or helpless children
    more ?
What heart but melts to leave the tender
    train,
And, one short month, endure the wintry
    main ?
Few leagues remov'd, we wish our peace-
    ful seat,
When the ship tosses and the tempests
    beat:
Then well may this long stay provoke their
    tears,   360
The tedious length of nine revolving years.
Not for their grief the Grecian host I
    blame;
But vanquish'd! baffled! oh eternal shame!
Expect the time to Troy's destruction giv'n,
And try the faith of Calchas and of
    Heav'n.
What pass'd at Aulis, Greece can witness
    bear,
And all who live to breathe this Phrygian
    air.

Beside a fountain's sacred brink we rais'd
Our verdant altars, and the victims blazed
('T was where the plane-tree spread its
    shades around);   370
The altars heav'd; and from the crumbling
    ground
A mighty dragon shot, of dire portent;
From Jove himself the dreadful sign was
    sent.
Straight to the tree his sanguine spires he
    roll'd,
And curl'd around in many a winding fold.
The topmost branch a mother-bird possess'd;
Eight callow infants fill'd the mossy nest;
Herself the ninth: the serpent, as he hung,
Stretch'd his black jaws, and crash'd the
    crying young;
While hov'ring near, with miserable moan,
The drooping mother wail'd her children
    gone.   381
The mother last, as round the nest she flew,
Seiz'd by the beating wing, the monster
    slew:
Nor long survived; to marble turn'd he
    stands
A lasting prodigy on Aulis' sands,
Such was the will of Jove; and hence we
    dare
Trust in his omen, and support the war.
For while around we gazed with wond'ring
    eyes,
And trembling sought the Powers with
    sacrifice,   389
Full of his God, the rev'rend Calchas cried;
" Ye Grecian warriors! lay your fears aside:
This wondrous signal Jove himself displays,
Of long, long labours, but eternal praise,
As many birds as by the snake were slain,
So many years the toils of Greece remain;
But wait the tenth, for Ilion's fall decreed: "
Thus spoke the prophet, thus the Fates
    succeed.
Obey, ye Grecians, with submission wait,
Nor let your flight avert the Trojan fate.'
  He said: the shores with loud applauses
    sound,   400
The hollow ships each deaf'ning shout re-
    bound.
Then Nestor thus: ' These vain debates
    forbear:
Ye talk like children, not like heroes dare.
Where now are all your high resolves at
    last ?
Your leagues concluded, your engagements
    past ?

Vow'd with libations and with victims
then,
Now vanish'd like their smoke: the faith
of men!
While useless words consume th' unactive
hours,
No wonder Troy so long resists our powers.
Rise, great Atrides! and with courage
sway;   410
We march to war, if thou direct the way.
But leave the few that dare resist thy laws,
The mean deserters of the Grecian cause,
To grudge the conquests mighty Jove pre-
pares,
And view, with envy, our successful wars.
On that great day when first the martial
train,
Big with the fate of Ilion, plough'd the
main;
Jove on the right a prosp'rous signal sent,
And thunder rolling shook the firmament.
Encouraged hence, maintain the glorious
strife,   420
Till ev'ry soldier grasp a Phrygian wife,
Till Helen's woes at full revenged appear,
And Troy's proud matrons render tear for
tear.
Before that day, if any Greek invite
His country's troops to base, inglorious
flight,
Stand forth that Greek! and hoist his sail
to fly;
And die the dastard first, who dreads to die.
But now, O monarch! all thy Chiefs advise:
Nor what they offer, thou thyself despise.
Among those counsels, let not mine be
vain;   430
In tribes and nations to divide thy train:
His sep'rate troops let ev'ry leader call,
Each strengthen each, and all encourage
all.
What Chief, or soldier, of the numerous
band,
Or bravely fights, or ill obeys command,
When thus distinct they war, shall soon be
known,
And what the cause of Ilion not o'erthrown;
If Fate resists, or if our arms are slow,
If Gods above prevent, or men below.'
  To him the King: 'How much thy years
excel   440
In arts of council, and in speaking well!
Oh would the Gods, in love to Greece, de-
cree
But ten such sages as they grant in thee;

Such wisdom soon should Priam's force
destroy,
And soon should fall the haughty towers of
Troy!
But Jove forbids, who plunges those he
hates
In fierce contention and in vain debates.
Now great Achilles from our aid withdraws,
By me provoked; a captive maid the cause:
If e'er as friends we join, the Trojan wall
Must shake, and heavy will the vengeance
fall!   451
But now, ye warriors, take a short repast;
And, well-refresh'd, to bloody conflict
haste.
His sharpen'd spear let every Grecian wield
And every Grecian fix his brazen shield;
Let all excite the fiery steeds of war,
And all for combat fit the rattling car.
This day, this dreadful day, let each con-
tend;
No rest, no respite, till the shades descend;
Till darkness, or till death shall cover all, 460
Let the war bleed, and let the mighty fall;
Till bathed in sweat be ev'ry manly breast,
With the huge shield each brawny arm de-
press'd,
Each aching nerve refuse the lance to
throw,
And each spent courser at the chariot blow.
Who dares, inglorious, in his ships to stay,
Who dares to tremble on this signal day,
That wretch, too mean to fall by martial
power,
The birds shall mangle and the dogs de-
vour.'
  The Monarch spoke: and straight a mur·
mur rose,   470
Loud as the surges when the tempest
blows,
That dash'd on broken rocks tumultuous
roar,
And foam and thunder on the stony shore.
Straight to the tents the troops dispersing
bend,
The fires are kindled, and the smokes
ascend;
With hasty feasts they sacrifice, and pray
T' avert the dangers of the doubtful day.
A steer of five years' age, large limb'd, and
fed,
To Jove's high altars Agamemnon led:
There bade the noblest of the Grecian
peers,   480
And Nestor first, as most advanc'd in years.

Next came Idomeneus and Tydeus' son,
Ajax the less, and Ajax Telamon;
Then wise Ulysses in his rank was placed;
And Menelaus came unbid, the last.
The Chiefs surround the destin'd beast, and
take
The sacred off'ring of the salted cake:
When thus the King prefers his solemn
prayer:
'Oh thou! whose thunder rends the clouded
air,
Who in the Heav'n of Heav'ns hast fix'd
thy throne,   490
Supreme of Gods! unbounded and alone!
Hear, and before the burning sun descends,
Before the night her gloomy veil extends,
Low in the dust be laid yon hostile spires,
Be Priam's palace sunk in Grecian fires,
In Hector's breast be plunged this shining
sword,
And slaughter'd heroes groan around their
lord!'
    Thus pray'd the Chief: his unavailing
prayer
Great Jove refused, and toss'd in empty
air:
The God, averse, while yet the fumes arose,
Prepar'd new toils, and doubled woes on
woes.   501
Their prayers perform'd, the Chiefs the
rites pursue,
The barley sprinkled, and the victim slew.
The limbs they sever from th' enclosing
hide,
The thighs, selected to the Gods, divide.
On these, in double cauls involv'd with
art,
The choicest morsels lie from every part.
From the cleft wood the crackling flames
aspire,
While the fat victim feeds the sacred fire.
The thighs thus sacrificed and entrails
dress'd,   510
Th' assistants part, transfix, and roast the
rest;
Then spread the tables, the repast prepare,
Each takes his seat, and each receives his
share.
Soon as the rage of hunger was suppress'd,
The gen'rous Nestor thus the Prince ad-
dress'd:
    'Now bid thy heralds sound the loud
alarms,
And call the squadrons sheathed in brazen
arms:

Now seize th' occasion, now the troops sur-
vey,
And lead to war when Heav'n directs the
way.'
He said; the Monarch issued his com-
mands;   520
Straight the loud heralds call the gath'ring
bands.
The Chiefs enclose their King: the hosts
divide,
In tribes and nations rank'd on either side.
High in the midst the blue-eyed Virgin flies;
From rank to rank she darts her ardent
eyes:
The dreadful ægis, Jove's immortal shield,
Blazed on her arm, and lighten'd all the
field:
Round the vast orb a hundred serpents
roll'd,
Form'd the bright fringe, and seem'd to
burn in gold.
With this each Grecian's manly breast she
warms,   530
Swells their bold hearts, and strings their
nervous arms;
No more they sigh inglorious to return,
But breathe revenge, and for the combat
burn.
    As on some mountain, thro' the lofty
grove,
The crackling flames ascend and blaze
above,
The fires, expanding as the winds arise,
Shoot their long beams, and kindle half the
skies,
So from the polish'd arms, and brazen
shields,
A gleamy splendour flash'd along the fields.
Not less their number than th' embodied
cranes,   540
Or milk-white swans in Asius' wat'ry
plains,
That o'er the windings of Caÿster's springs
Stretch their long necks, and clap their
rustling wings,
Now tower aloft, and course in airy rounds;
Now light with noise; with noise the field
resounds.
Thus numerous and confused, extending
wide,
The legions crowd Scamander's flow'ry side;
With rushing troops the plains are cover'd
o'er,
And thund'ring footsteps shake the sound-
ing shore;

Along the river's level meads they stand, 550
Thick as in spring the flowers adorn the
　　land,
Or leaves the trees; or thick as insects play,
The wand'ring nation of a summer's day,
That, drawn by milky steams, at ev'ning
　　hours,
In gather'd swarms surround the rural
　　bowers;
From pail to pail with busy murmur run
The gilded legions, glitt'ring in the sun.
So throng'd, so close, the Grecian squadrons
　　stood
In radiant arms, and thirst for Trojan
　　blood.
Each leader now his scatter'd force con-
　　joins　　　　　　　　　　　　　　560
In close array, and forms the deep'ning
　　lines.
Not with more ease the skilful shepherd
　　swain
Collects his flock from thousands on the
　　plain.
The King of Kings, majestically tall,
Towers o'er his armies, and outshines them
　　all:
Like some proud bull that round the pas-
　　tures leads
His subject - herds, the monarch of the
　　meads.
Great as the Gods th' exalted Chief was
　　seen,
His strength like Neptune, and like Mars
　　his mien;
Jove o'er his eyes celestial glories spread,
And dawning conquest play'd around his
　　head.　　　　　　　　　　　　　571
　　Say, Virgins, seated round the throne
　　divine,
All-knowing Goddesses! immortal Nine!
Since earth's wide regions, Heav'n's un-
　　measured height,
And Hell's abyss, hide nothing from your
　　sight
(We, wretched mortals! lost in doubts be-
　　low,
But guess by rumour, and but boast we
　　know),
Oh say what heroes, fired by thirst of
　　fame,
Or urged by wrongs, to Troy's destruction
　　came ?
To count them all, demands a thousand
　　tongues,　　　　　　　　　　　　580
A throat of brass, and adamantine lungs;

Daughters of Jove, assist! inspired by you,
The mighty labour dauntless I pursue:
What crowded armies, from what climes,
　　they bring,
Their names, their numbers, and their
　　Chiefs, I sing.
　　The hardy warriors whom Bœotia bred,
Peneleus, Leitus, Prothoënor led:
With these Arcesilaus and Clonius stand,
Equal in arms, and equal in command.
These head the troops that rocky Aulis
　　yields,　　　　　　　　　　　　590
And Eteon's hills, and Hyrie's wat'ry
　　fields,
And Schœnos, Scolos, Græa near the main,
And Mycalessia's ample piny plain.
Those who in Peteon or Ilesion dwell,
Or Harma, where Apollo's prophet fell;
Heleon and Hyle, which the springs o'er-
　　flow;
And Medeon lofty, and Ocalea low;
Or in the meads of Haliartus stray,
Or Thespia, sacred to the God of Day.
Onchestus, Neptune's celebrated groves; 600
Copæ, and Thisbè, famed for silver doves,
For flocks Erythræ, Glissa for the vine;
Platæa green, and Nisa the divine.
And they whom Thebes' well-built walls en-
　　close,
Where Myde, Eutresis, Coronè rose;
And Arne rich, with purple harvests
　　crown'd;
And Anthedon, Bœotia's utmost bound.
Full fifty ships they send, and each con-
　　veys
Twice sixty warriors thro' the foaming
　　seas.
　　To these succeed Asplendon's martial
　　train,　　　　　　　　　　　　610
Who plough the spacious Orchomenian
　　plain.
Two valiant brothers rule th' undaunted
　　throng,
Iälmen and Ascalaphus the strong,
Sons of Astyoche, the heav'nly Fair,
Whose virgin charms subdued the God of
　　War
(In Actor's court as she retired to rest,
The strength of Mars the blushing maid
　　compress'd):
Their troops in thirty sable vessels sweep,
With equal oars, the hoarse - resounding
　　deep.　　　　　　　　　　　　619
　　The Phocians next in forty barks repair,
Epistrophus and Schedius head the war;

From those rich regions where Cephissus
leads
His silver current thro' the flowery meads;
From Panopea, Chrysa the divine,
Where Anemoria's stately turrets shine,
Where Pytho, Daulis, Cyparissus stood,
And fair Lilæa views the rising flood.
These, ranged in order on the floating tide,
Close, on the left, the bold Bœotians' side.
  Fierce Ajax led the Locrian squadrons
on,   630
Ajax the less, Oïleus' valiant son;
Skill'd to direct the flying dart aright;
Swift in pursuit, and active in the fight.
Him, as their chief, the chosen troops at-
tend,
Which Bessa, Thronus, and rich Cynos
send;
Opus, Calliarus, and Scarphe's bands;
And those who dwell where pleasing
Augia stands,
And where Boägrius floats the lowly lands,
Or in fair Tarphe's sylvan seats reside;
In forty vessels cut the yielding tide.   640
  Eubœa next her martial sons prepares,
And sends the brave Abantes to the wars;
Breathing revenge, in arms they take their
way
From Chalcis' walls, and strong Eretria;
Th' Isteian fields for gen'rous vines re-
nown'd,
The fair Carystos, and the Styrian ground;
Where Dios from her towers o'erlooks the
plain,
And high Cerinthus views the neighb'ring
main,
Down their broad shoulders falls a length
of hair;
Their hands dismiss not the long lance in
air: 650
But with portended spears, in fighting
fields,
Pierce the tough corselets and the brazen
shields.
Twice twenty ships transport the warlike
bands,
Which bold Elphenor, fierce in arms, com-
mands.
  Full fifty more from Athens stem the
main,
Led by Menestheus thro' the liquid plain
(Athens the fair, where great Erectheus
sway'd,
That owed his nurture to the blue-eyed
maid,

But from the teeming furrow took his
birth,
The mighty offspring of the foodfull
earth.   660
Him Pallas placed amidst her wealthy
fane,
Ador'd with sacrifice and oxen slain;
Where as the years revolve her altars
blaze,
And all the tribes resound the Goddess'
praise).
No Chief like thee, Menestheus! Greece
could yield,
To marshal armies in the dusty field,
Th' extended wings of battle to display,
Or close th' embodied host in firm array.
Nestor alone, improv'd by length of days,
For martial conduct bore an equal
praise.   670
With these appear the Salaminian bands,
Whom the gigantic Telamon commands;
In twelve black ships to Troy they steer
their course,
And with the great Athenians join their
force.
  Next move to war the gen'rous Argive
train
From high Trœzene, and Maseta's plain,
And fair Ægina circled by the main:
Whom strong Tirynthe's lofty walls sur-
round,
And Epidaure with viny harvests crown'd:
And where fair Asinen and Hermion
shew   680
Their cliffs above, and ample bay below.
These by the brave Euryalus were led,
Great Sthenelus, and greater Diomed,
But Chief Tydides bore the sov'reign sway;
In fourscore barks they plough the wat'ry
way.
  The proud Mycene arms her martial
powers,
Cleone, Corinth, with imperial towers,
Fair Aræthyrea, Ornia's fruitful plain,
And Ægion, and Adrastus' ancient reign;
And those who dwell along the sandy
shore,   690
And where Pellene yields her fleecy store,
Where Helice and Hyperesia lie,
And Gonoëssa's spires salute the sky.
Great Agamemnon rules the numerous
band,
A hundred vessels in long order stand,
And crowded nations wait his dread com-
mand.

High on the deck the King of men appears,
And his refulgent arms in triumph wears;
Proud of his host, unrivall'd in his reign,
In silent pomp he moves along the
main.　　　700
　His brother follows, and to vengeance
warms
The hardy Spartans, exercised in arms:
Phares and Brysia's valiant troops, and
those
Whom Lacedæmon's lofty hills enclose:
Or Messe's towers for silver doves re-
nown'd,
Amyclæ, Laäs, Augia's happy ground,
And those whom Œtylos' low walls con-
tain,
And Helos on the margin of the main:
These o'er the bending ocean, Helen's
cause
In sixty ships with Menelaus draws:　710
Eager and loud, from man to man he flies,
Revenge and fury flaming in his eyes;
While, vainly fond, in fancy oft he hears
The fair one's grief, and sees her falling
tears.
　In ninety sail, from Pylos' sandy coast,
Nestor the sage conducts his chosen host:
From Amphigenia's ever-fruitful land;
Where Æpy high, and little Pteleon stand:
Where beauteous Arene her structures
shows,
And Thryon's walls Alpheüs' streams en-
close:　　　720
And Dorion, famed for Thamyris' disgrace,
Superior once of all the tuneful race,
Till, vain of mortal's empty praise, he
strove
To match the seed of cloud-compelling
Jove!
Too daring bard! whose unsuccessful pride
Th' immortal Muses in their art defied.
Th' avenging Muses of the light of day
Deprived his eyes, and snatch'd his voice
away;
No more his heav'nly voice was heard to
sing;
His hand no more awaked the silver
string.　　　730
Where under high Cyllenè, crown'd with
wood,
The shaded tomb of old Æpytus stood;
From Ripè, Stratie, Tegea's bord'ring
towns,
The Phenean fields, and Orchomenian
downs,

Where the fat herds in plenteous pasture
rove;
And Stymphelus with her surrounding
grove,
Parrhasia, on her snowy cliffs reclin'd,
And high Enispè shook by wintry wind,
And fair Mantinea's ever-pleasing site;
In sixty sail th' Arcadian bands unite.　740
Bold Agapenor, glorious at their head
(Ancæus' son), the mighty squadron led.
Their ships, supplied by Agamemnon's
care,
Thro' roaring seas the wond'ring warriors
bear;
The first to battle on th' appointed plain,
But new to all the dangers of the main.
　Those, where fair Elis and Buprasium
join;
Whom Hyrmin, here, and Myrsinus con-
fine,
And bounded there, where o'er the valleys
rose
Th' Olenian rock; and where Alisium
flows;　　　750
Beneath four Chiefs (a numerous army)
came:
The strength and glory of th' Epean name.
In sep'rate squadrons these their train
divide,
Each leads ten vessels thro' the yielding
tide.
One was Amphimachus, and Thalpius one;
(Eurytus' this, and that Teätus' son):
Diores sprung from Amarynceus' line;
And great Polyxenus, of force divine.
　But those who view fair Elis o'er the seas
From the blest islands of th' Echinades, 760
In forty vessels under Meges move,
Begot by Phyleus, the belov'd of Jove.
To strong Dulichium from his sire he fled,
And thence to Troy his hardy warriors led.
　Ulysses follow'd thro' the wat'ry road,
A Chief, in wisdom equal to a God.
With those whom Cephallenia's isle en-
closed,
Or till their fields along the coast opposed;
Or where fair Ithaca o'erlooks the floods,
Where high Neritos shakes his waving
woods,　　　770
Where Ægilipa's rugged sides are seen,
Crocylia rocky, and Zacynthus green.
These, in twelve galleys with vermillion
prores,
Beneath his conduct sought the Phrygian
shores.

Thoas came next, Andræmon's valiant
son,
From Pleuron's walls and chalky Calydon,
And rough Pylenè, and th' Olenian steep,
And Chalcis, beaten by the rolling deep.
He led the warriors from th' Ætolian
shore,
For now the sons of Œneus were no
more! 780
The glories of the mighty race were fled!
Œneus himself, and Meleager dead!
To Thoas' care now trust the martial train:
His forty vessels follow thro' the main.
Next eighty barks the Cretan King com-
mands,
Of Gnossus, Lyctus, and Gortyna's bands,
And those who dwell where Rhytion's
domes arise,
Or white Lycastus glitters to the skies,
Or where by Phæstus silver Jardan runs;
Crete's hundred cities pour forth all her
sons. 790
These march'd, Idomeneus, beneath thy
care,
And Merion, dreadful as the God of War.
Tlepolemus, the son of Hercules,
Led nine swift vessels thro' the foamy seas;
From Rhodes, with everlasting sunshine
bright,
Jalyssus, Lindus and Camirus white.
His captive mother fierce Alcides bore
From Ephyr's walls, and Sellè's winding
shore,
Where mighty towns in ruins spread the
plain,
And saw their blooming warriors early
slain. 800
The hero, when to manly years he grew,
Alcides' uncle, old Licymnius, slew;
For this constrain'd to quit his native
place,
And shun the vengeance of th' Herculean
race,
A fleet he built, and with a numerous
train
Of willing exiles, wander'd o'er the main;
Where, many seas and many suff'rings past,
On happy Rhodes the Chief arrived at last:
There in three tribes divides his native
band,
And rules them peaceful in a foreign
land; 810
Increas'd and prosper'd in their new
abodes
By mighty Jove, the sire of men and Gods:

With joy they saw the growing empire
rise,
And showers of wealth descending from
the skies.
Three ships with Nireus sought the Tro-
jan shore,
Nireus, whom Aglaë to Charopus bore,
Nireus, in faultless shape, and blooming
grace,
The loveliest youth of all the Grecian race;
Pelides only match'd his early charms;
But few his troops, and small his strength
in arms. 820
Next thirty galleys cleave the liquid
plain,
Of those Calydnæ's sea-girt isles contain;
With them the youth of Nisyrus repair,
Casus the strong, and Crapathus the fair;
Cos, where Eurypylus possess'd the sway,
Till great Alcides made the realms obey:
These Antiphus and bold Phidippus bring,
Sprung from the God by Thessalus the
King.
Now, Muse, recount Pelasgic Argos'
powers, 829
From Alos, Alopè, and Trechin's towers;
From Phthia's spacious vales; and Hella,
bless'd
With female beauty far beyond the rest.
Full fifty ships beneath Achilles' care
Th' Achaians, Myrmidons, Hellenians bear;
Thessalians all, tho' various in their name,
The same their nation, and their Chief the
same.
But now inglorious, stretch'd along the
shore,
They hear the brazen voice of war no more;
No more the foe they face in dire array:
Close in his fleet their angry leader lay; 840
Since fair Briseïs from his arms was torn,
The noblest spoil from sack'd Lyrnessus
borne,
Then, when the Chief the Theban walls o'er-
threw,
And the bold sons of great Evenus slew.
There mourn'd Achilles, plunged in depth
of care,
But soon to rise in slaughter, blood, and
war.
To these the youth of Phylacè succeed,
Itona, famous for her fleecy breed,
And grassy Pteleon deck'd with cheerful
greens,
The bowers of Ceres, and the sylvan
scenes, 850

Sweet Pyrrhasus, with blooming flowerets
    crown'd,
And Antron's wat'ry dens, and cavern'd
    ground.
These own'd as Chief Protesilas the brave,
Who now lay silent in the gloomy grave:
The first who boldly touch'd the Trojan
    shore,
And dyed a Phrygian lance with Grecian
    gore;
There lies, far distant from his native plain; ⎫
Unfinish'd his proud palaces remain,   ⎬
And his sad consort beats her breast in vain. ⎭
His troops in forty ships Podarces led, 860
Iphiclus' son, and brother to the dead;
Nor he unworthy to command the host;
Yet still they mourn'd their ancient leader
    lost.
    The men who Glaphyra's fair soil par-
    take,
Where hills encircle Bœbe's lowly lake,
Where Pheræ hears the neighb'ring waters
    fall,
Or proud Iolcus lifts her airy wall,
In ten black ships embark'd for Ilion's
    shore,
With bold Eumelus, whom Alcestè bore:
All Pelias' race Alcestè far outshined, 870
The grace and glory of the beauteous kind.
    The troops Methonè, or Thaumacia
    yields,
Olizon's rocks, or Melibœa's fields,
With Philoctetes sail'd, whose matchless
    art
From the tough bow directs the feather'd
    dart.
Seven were his ships: each vessel fifty row,
Skill'd in his science of the dart and bow.
But he lay raging on the Lemnian ground;
A pois'nous Hydra gave the burning
    wound;
There groan'd the Chief in agonizing pain,
Whom Greece at length shall wish, nor
    wish in vain. 881
His forces Medon led from Lemnos' shore,
Oïleus' son, whom beauteous Rhena bore.
    Th' Œchalian race, in those high towers
    contain'd,
Where once Eurytus in proud triumph
    reign'd,
Or where her humbler turrets Tricca rears,
Or where Ithomè, rough with rocks, ap-
    pears;
In thirty sail the sparkling waves divide,
Which Podalirius and Machaon guide.

To these his skill their Parent-god imparts,
Divine professors of the healing arts. 891
    The bold Ormenian and Asterian bands
In forty barks Eurypylus commands,
Where Titan hides his hoary head in snow,
And where Hyperia's silver fountains flow.
    Thy troops, Argissa, Polypœtes leads,
And Eleon, shelter'd by Olympus' shades,
Grytonè's warriors; and where Orthè lies,
And Oloösson's chalky cliffs arise.
Sprung from Pirithoüs of immortal race, 900
The fruit of fair Hippodame's embrace
(That day, when, hurl'd from Pelion's
    cloudy head,
To distant dens the shaggy Centaurs fled),
With Polypœtes join'd in equal sway,
Leonteus leads, and forty ships obey.
    In twenty sail the bold Perrhæbians came
From Cyphus, Guneus was their leader's
    name.
With these the Enians join'd, and those
    who freeze
Where cold Dodona lifts her holy trees;
Or where the pleasing Titaresius glides, 910
And into Peneus rolls his easy tides;
Yet o'er the silver surface pure they flow,
The sacred stream unmix'd with streams
    below,
Sacred and awful!   From the dark abodes
Styx pours them forth, the dreadful oath of
    Gods!
    Last under Prothous the Magnesians
    stood,
Prothous the swift, of old Tenthredon's
    blood;
Who dwell where Pelion, crown'd with piny
    boughs,
Obscures the glade, and nods his shaggy
    brows:
Or where thro' flowery Tempè Peneus
    stray'd 920
(The region stretch'd beneath his mighty
    shade):
In forty sable barks they stemm'd the
    main;
Such were the Chiefs, and such the Grecian
    train.
    Say next, O Muse! of all Achaia breeds,
Who bravest fought, or rein'd the noblest
    steeds?
Eumelus' mares were foremost in the chase,
As eagles fleet, and of Pheretian race;
Bred where Pieria's fruitful fountains flow,
And train'd by him who bears the silver
    bow.

Fierce in the fight, their nostrils breathed a
flame, 930
Their height, their colour, and their age,
the same;
O'er fields of death they whirl the rapid
car,
And break the ranks, and thunder thro' the
war.
Ajax in arms the first renown acquired,
While stern Achilles in his wrath retired
(His was the strength that mortal might
exceeds,
And his th' unrivall'd race of heav'nly
steeds):
But Thetis' son now shines in arms no
more;
His troops, neglected on the sandy shore,
In empty air their sportive jav'lins throw,
Or whirl the disk, or bend an idle bow: 941
Unstain'd with blood his cover'd chariots
stand;
Th' immortal coursers graze along the
strand;
But the brave Chiefs th' inglorious life de-
plor'd,
And, wand'ring o'er the camp, required
their lord.
Now, like a deluge, cov'ring all around,
The shining armies swept along the ground;
Swift as a flood of fire, when storms arise,
Floats the wide field, and blazes to the
skies.
Earth groan'd beneath them; as when an-
gry Jove 950
Hurls down the forky lightning from
above,
On Arimè when he the thunder throws,
And fires Typhœus with redoubled blows,
Where Typhon, press'd beneath the burn-
ing load,
Still feels the fury of th' avenging God.
But various Iris, Jove's commands to
bear,
Speeds on the wings of winds thro' liquid air;
In Priam's porch the Trojan Chiefs she
found,
The old consulting, and the youths around.
Polites' shape, the monarch's son, she chose,
Who from Æsetes' tomb observ'd the foes,
High on the mound; from whence in pro-
spect lay 962
The fields, the tents, the navy, and the bay.
In this dissembled form she hastes to bring
Th' unwelcome message to the Phrygian
King:

'Cease to consult, the time for action
calls,
War, horrid war, approaches to your walls!
Assembled armies oft have I beheld,
But ne'er till now such numbers charged a
field.
Thick as autumnal leaves, or driving sand,
The moving squadrons blacken all the
strand. 971
Thou, godlike Hector! all thy force em-
ploy,
Assemble all th' united bands of Troy;
In just array let every leader call
The foreign troops: this day demands them
all.'
The voice divine the mighty Chief alarms;
The council breaks, the warriors rush to
arms.
The gates unfolding pour forth all their
train,
Nations on nations fill the dusky plain,
Men, steeds, and chariots, shake the trem-
bling ground; 980
The tumult thickens, and the skies resound.
Amidst the plain in sight of Ilion stands
A rising mount, the work of human hands
(This for Myrinne's tomb th' immortals
know,
Tho' call'd Bateia in the world below);
Beneath their Chiefs in martial order here
Th' auxiliar troops and Trojan hosts ap-
pear.
The godlike Hector, high above the rest,
Shakes his huge spear, and nods his plumy
crest:
In throngs around his native bands appear,
And groves of lances glitter in the air. 991
Divine Æneas brings the Dardan race,
Anchises' son, by Venus' stol'n embrace,
Born in the shades of Ida's secret grove
(A mortal mixing with the Queen of Love);
Archilochus and Acamas divide
The warrior's toils, and combat by his side.
Who fair Zeleia's wealthy valleys till,
Fast by the foot of Ida's sacred hill;
Or drink, Æsepus, of thy sable flood; 1000
Were led by Pandarus, of royal blood.
To whom his art Apollo deign'd to shew,
Graced with the present of his shafts and
bow.
From rich Apæsus and Adrestia's towers,
High Teree's summits, and Pityea's bowers;
From these the congregated troops obey
Young Amphius and Adrastus' equal
sway;

Old Merops' sons; whom, skill'd in fates to
  come,
The sire forewarn'd, and prophesied their
  doom:
Fate urged them on! the sire forewarn'd in
  vain,   1010
They rush'd to war, and perish'd on the
  plain.
From Practius' stream, Percotè's pasture
  lands,
And Sestos and Abydos' neighb'ring strands,
From great Arisba's walls and Sellè's coast,
Asius Hyrtacides conducts his host:
High on his car he shakes the flowing reins,
His fiery coursers thunder o'er the plains.
  The fierce Pelasgi next, in war renown'd,
March from Larissa's ever-fertile ground:
In equal arms their brother leaders shine,
Hippothous bold, and Pyleus the divine. 1021
  Next Acamas and Pyroüs lead their
  hosts
In dread array, from Thracia's wintry
  coasts;
Round the black realms where Hellespon-
  tus roars,
And Boreas beats the hoarse-resounding
  shores.
  With great Euphemus the Ciconians
  move,
Sprung from Trœzenian Ceüs, lov'd by
  Jove.
Pyræchmes the Pæonian troops attend,
Skill'd in the fight their crooked bows to
  bend;
From Axius' ample bed he leads them on,
Axius, that laves the distant Amydon, 1031
Axius, that swells with all his neighb'ring
  rills,
And wide around the floating region fills.
The Paphlagonians Pylæmenes rules,
Where rich Henetia breeds her savage
  mules,
Where Erythinus' rising cliffs are seen,
Thy groves of box, Cytorus! ever green;
And where Ægialus and Cromna lie,
And lofty Sesamus invades the sky;
And where Parthenius roll'd thro' banks of
  flowers,   1040
Reflects her bord'ring palaces and bowers.
  Here march'd in arms the Halizonian
  band,
Whom Odius and Epistrophus command,
From those far regions where the sun re-
  fines
The ripening silver in Alybean mines.

There, mighty Chromis led the Mysian
  train,
And augur Ennomus, inspired in vain,
For stern Achilles lopp'd his sacred head,
Roll'd down Scamander with the vulgar
  dead.
Phorcys and brave Ascanius here unite
Th' Ascanian Phrygians, eager for the
  fight.   1051
  Of those who round Mæonia's realms
  reside,
Or whom the vales in shade of Tmolus
  hide,
Mestles and Antiphus the charge partake;
Born on the banks of Gyges' silent lake.
There, from the fields where wild Mæander
  flows,
High Mycalè, and Latmos' shady brows,
And proud Miletus, came the Carian
  throngs,
With mingled clamours, and with barb'rous
  tongues: 1059
Amphimachus and Naustes guide the train,
Naustes the bold, Amphimachus the vain,
Who, trick'd with gold, and glitt'ring on
  his car,
Rode like a woman to the field of war.
Fool that he was! by fierce Achilles slain,
The river swept him to the briny main:
There whelm'd with waves the gaudy war-
  rior lies;
The valiant victor seiz'd the golden prize.
  The forces last in fair array succeed,
Which blameless Glaucus and Sarpedon
  lead;
The warlike bands that distant Lycia
  yields   1070
Where gulfy Xanthus foams along the
  fields.

BOOK III

THE DUEL OF MENELAUS AND PARIS

THE ARGUMENT

The armies being ready to engage, a single
combat is agreed upon between Menelaus
and Paris (by the intervention of Hector) for
the determination of the war. Iris is sent to
call Helena to behold the fight. She leads
her to the walls of Troy, where Priam sat
with his counsellors, observing the Grecian
leaders on the plain below, to whom Helen
gives an account of the chief of them. The
Kings on either part take the solemn oath

for the conditions of the combat. The duel ensues, wherein Paris, being overcome, is snatched away in a cloud by Venus, and transported to his apartment. She then calls Helen from the walls, and brings the lovers together. Agamemnon, on the part of the Grecians, demands the restoration of Helen, and the performance of the articles.
The three-and-twentieth day still continues throughout this book. The scene is sometimes in the field before Troy, and sometimes in Troy itself.

Thus by their leader's care each martial band
Moves into ranks, and stretches o'er the land.
With shouts the Trojans, rushing from afar,
Proclaim their motions, and provoke the war:
So when inclement winters vex the plain
With piercing frosts, or thick-descending rain,
To warmer seas the cranes embodied fly,
With noise, and order, thro' the midway sky;
To pigmy nations wounds and death they bring,
And all the war descends upon the wing. 10
But silent, breathing rage, resolv'd, and skill'd
By mutual aids to fix a doubtful field,
Swift march the Greeks: the rapid dust around
Dark'ning arises from the labour'd ground.
Thus from his flaggy wings when Notus sheds
A night of vapours round the mountain-heads,
Swift-gliding mists the dusky fields invade,
To thieves more grateful than the midnight shade;
While scarce the swains their feeding flocks survey,
Lost and confused amidst the thicken'd day: 20
So, wrapt in gath'ring dust, the Grecian train,
A moving cloud, swept on, and hid the plain.
  Now front to front the hostile armies stand,
Eager of fight, and only wait command:
When, to the van, before the sons of fame
Whom Troy sent forth, the beauteous Paris came:

In form a God! the panther's speckled hide
Flow'd o'er his armour with an easy pride;
His bended bow across his shoulders flung,
His sword beside him negligently hung; 30
Two pointed spears he shook with gallant grace,
And dared the bravest of the Grecian race.
  As thus, with glorious air and proud disdain,
He boldly stalk'd, the foremost on the plain,
Him Menelaus, loved of Mars, espies,
With heart elated, and with joyful eyes:
So joys a lion, if the branching deer
Or mountain goat, his bulky prize, appear;
In vain the youths oppose, the mastiffs bay,
The lordly savage rends the panting prey.
Thus, fond of vengeance, with a furious bound, 41
In clanging arms he leaps upon the ground
From his high chariot: him, approaching near,
The beauteous champion views with marks of fear,
Smit with a conscious sense, retires behind,
And shuns the fate he well deserv'd to find.
As when some shepherd, from the rustling trees
Shot forth to view, a scaly serpent sees:
Trembling and pale, he starts with wild affright,
And, all confused, precipitates his flight: 50
So from the King the shining warrior flies,
And plunged amid the thickest Trojans lies.
  As godlike Hector sees the Prince retreat,
He thus upbraids him with a gen'rous heat:
' Unhappy Paris! but to women brave!
So fairly form'd, and only to deceive!
Oh, hadst thou died when first thou saw'st the light,
Or died at least before thy nuptial rite!
A better fate, than vainly thus to boast,
And fly, the scandal of thy Trojan host. 60
Gods! how the scornful Greeks exult to see
Their fears of danger undeceiv'd in thee!
Thy figure promis'd with a martial air,
But ill thy soul supplies a form so fair.
In former days, in all thy gallant pride,
When thy tall ships triumphant stemm'd the tide,

When Greece beheld thy painted canvas
  flow,
And crowds stood wond'ring at the passing
  show;
Say, was it thus, with such a baffled mien,
You met th' approaches of the Spartan
  Queen,   70
Thus from her realm convey'd the beaute-
  ous prize,
And both her warlike lords outshined in
  Helen's eyes?
This deed, thy foes' delight, thy own dis-
  grace,
Thy father's grief, and ruin of thy race;
This deed recalls thee to the proffer'd
  flight;
Or hast thou injured whom thou dar'st not
  right?
Soon to thy cost the field would make thee
  know
Thou keep'st the consort of a braver foe.
Thy graceful form instilling soft desire,
Thy curling tresses, and thy silver lyre, 80
Beauty and youth, in vain to these you
  trust,
When youth and beauty shall be laid in
  dust:
Troy yet may wake, and one avenging blow
Crush the dire author of his country's
  woe.'
  His silence here, with blushes, Paris
  breaks:
''T is just, my brother, what your anger
  speaks:
But who like thee can boast a soul sedate,
So firmly proof to all the shocks of Fate?
Thy force, like steel, a temper'd hardness
  shews,
Still edged to wound, and still untired with
  blows,   90
Like steel, uplifted by some strenuous
  swain,
With falling woods to strow the wasted
  plain.
Thy gifts I praise; nor thou despise the
  charms
With which a lover golden Venus arms;
Soft moving speech, and pleasing outward
  show,
No wish can gain them, but the Gods be-
  stow.
Yet wouldst thou have the proffer'd combat
  stand,
The Greeks and Trojans seat on either
  hand;

Then let a mid-way space our hosts divide,
And on that stage of war the cause be
  tried: 100
By Paris there the Spartan King be fought,
For beauteous Helen and the wealth she
  brought;
And who his rival can in arms subdue,
His be the fair, and his the treasure too.
Thus with a lasting league your toils may
  cease,
And Troy possess her fertile fields in peace;
Thus may the Greeks review their native
  shore,
Much famed for gen'rous steeds, for beauty
  more.'
  He said. The challenge Hector heard
  with joy,
Then with his spear restrain'd the youth of
  Troy,   110
Held by the midst, athwart; and near the
  foe
Advanced with steps majestically slow;
While round his dauntless head the Gre-
  cians pour
Their stones and arrows in a mingled
  shower.
  Then thus the Monarch, great Atrides,
  cried:
'Forbear, ye warriors! lay the darts aside:
A parley Hector asks, a message bears;
We know him by the various plume he
  wears.'
Awed by his high command the Greeks at-
  tend,   119
The tumult silence, and the fight suspend.
  While from the centre Hector rolls his
  eyes
On either host, and thus to both applies:
'Hear, all ye Trojan, all ye Grecian bands!
What Paris, author of the war, demands.
Your shining swords within the sheath re-
  strain,
And pitch your lances in the yielding plain.
Here, in the midst, in either army's sight,
He dares the Spartan King to single fight;
And wills, that Helen and the ravish'd spoil,
That caus'd the contest, shall reward the
  toil.   130
Let these the brave triumphant victor grace,
And diff'ring nations part in leagues of
  peace.'
  He spoke: in still suspense on either
  side
Each army stood. The Spartan Chief re-
  plied:

'Me too, ye warriors, hear, whose fatal
    right
A world engages in the toils of fight —
To me the labour of the field resign;
Me Paris injured; all the war be mine.
Fall he that must, beneath his rival's arms,
And live the rest secure of future harms.
Two lambs, devoted by your country's
    rite,   141
To Earth a sable, to the Sun a white,
Prepare, ye Trojans! while a third we
    bring
Select to Jove, th' inviolable King.
Let rev'rend Priam in the truce engage,
And add the sanction of consid'rate age;
His sons are faithless, headlong in debate,
And youth itself an empty wav'ring state:
Cool age advances venerably wise,
Turns on all hands its deep-discerning
    eyes;   150
Sees what befell, and what may yet befall,
Concludes from both, and best provides for
    all.'
    The nations hear, with rising hopes pos-
    sess'd,
And peaceful prospects dawn in every
    breast.
Within the lines they drew their steeds
    around,
And from their chariots issued on the
    ground:
Next all, unbuckling the rich mail they
    wore,
Laid their bright arms along the sable shore.
On either side the meeting hosts are seen
With lances fix'd, and close the space be-
    tween.   160
Two heralds now, despatch'd to Troy, in-
    vite
The Phrygian monarch to the peaceful rite;
Talthybius hastens to the fleet, to bring
The lamb for Jove, th' inviolable King.
    Meantime, to beauteous Helen, from the
    skies
The various Goddess of the Rainbow flies
(Like fair Laödicè in form and face,
The loveliest nymph of Priam's royal race);
Her in the palace, at her loom she found;
The golden web her own sad story crown'd.
The Trojan wars she weav'd (herself the
    prize),   171
And the dire triumphs of her fatal eyes.
To whom the Goddess of the Painted Bow:
'Approach, and view the wondrous scene
    below!

Each hardy Greek, and valiant Trojan
    knight,
So dreadful late, and furious for the fight,
Now rest their spears, or lean upon their
    shields;
Ceas'd is the war, and silent all the fields.
Paris alone and Sparta's King advance,
In single fight to toss the beamy lance; 180
Each met in arms, the fate of combat tries,
Thy love the motive, and thy charms the
    prize.'
    This said, the many-colour'd maid in-
    spires
Her husband's love, and wakes her former
    fires;
Her country, parents, all that once were
    dear,
Rush to her thought, and force a tender
    tear.
O'er her fair face a snowy veil she threw
And, softly sighing, from the loom with-
    drew.
Her handmaids Clymenè and Æthra wait
Her silent footsteps to the Scæan gate. 190
    There sat the seniors of the Trojan race
(Old Priam's Chiefs, and most in Priam's
    grace);
The King the first; Thymœtes at his side;
Lampus and Clytius, long in council tried;
Panthus, and Hicetaön, once the strong;
And next the wisest of the rev'rend throng,
Antenor grave, and sage Ucalegon,
Lean'd on the walls, and bask'd before the
    sun.
Chiefs, who no more in bloody fights en-
    gage,
But, wise thro' time, and narrative with
    age,   200
In summer-days like grasshoppers rejoice,
A bloodless race, that send a feeble voice.
These, when the Spartan Queen approach'd
    the tower,
In secret own'd resistless Beauty's power:
They cried, 'No wonder, such celestial
    charms
For nine long years have set the world in
    arms!
What winning graces! what majestic
    mien!
She moves a Goddess, and she looks a
    Queen.
Yet hence, oh Heav'n! convey that fatal
    face,
And from destruction save the Trojan
    race.'   210

The good old Priam welcom'd her, and
    cried,
'Approach, my child, and grace thy father's
    side.
See on the plain thy Grecian spouse ap-
    pears,
The friends and kindred of thy former
    years.
No crime of thine our present suff'rings
    draws,
Not thou, but Heav'n's disposing will, the
    cause;
The Gods these armies and this force em-
    ploy,
The hostile Gods conspire the fate of Troy.
But lift thine eyes, and say, what Greek is
    he
(Far as from hence these aged orbs can
    see),   220
Around whose brow such martial graces
    shine,
So tall, so awful, and almost divine?
Tho' some of larger stature tread the green,
None match his grandeur and exalted mien:
He seems a monarch and his country's
    pride.'
Thus ceas'd the King, and thus the Fair
    replied:
'Before thy presence, father, I appear
With conscious shame and reverential fear,
Ah! had I died, ere to these walls I fled,
False to my country, and my nuptial bed,
My brothers, friends, and daughter left be-
    hind,   231
False to them all, to Paris only kind!
For this I mourn, till grief or dire disease
Shall waste the form whose crime it was to
    please!
The King of Kings, Atrides, you survey,
Great in the war, and great in arts of sway:
My brother once, before my days of shame:
And oh! that still he bore a brother's
    name!'
  With wonder Priam view'd the godlike
    man,
Extoll'd the happy Prince, and thus began:
'O blest Atrides! born to prosp'rous fate, 241
Successful monarch of a mighty state!
How vast thy empire! Of yon matchless
    train
What numbers lost, what numbers yet re-
    main!
In Phrygia once were gallant armies known,
In ancient time, when Otreus fill'd the
    throne;

When godlike Mygdon led their troops of
    horse,
And I, to join them, rais'd the Trojan force;
Against the manlike Amazons we stood,
And Sangar's stream ran purple with their
    blood.   250
But far inferior those, in martial grace
And strength of numbers, to this Grecian
    race.'
  This said, once more he view'd the war-
    rior train:
'What's he, whose arms lie scatter'd on the
    plain?
Broad is his breast, his shoulders larger
    spread,
Tho' great Atrides overtops his head.
Nor yet appear his care and conduct small;
From rank to rank he moves, and orders
    all.
The stately ram thus measures o'er the
    ground,
And, master of the flocks, surveys them
    round.'   260
  Then Helen thus: 'Whom your discern-
    ing eyes
Have singled out, is Ithacus the wise:
A barren island boasts his glorious birth;
His fame for wisdom fills the spacious
    earth.'
  Antenor took the word, and thus began:
'Myself, O King! have seen that wondrous
    man;
When, trusting Jove and hospitable laws,
To Troy he came, to plead the Grecian
    cause
(Great Menelaus urged the same request);
My house was honour'd with each royal
    guest: 270
I knew their persons, and admired their
    parts,
Both brave in arms, and both approv'd in
    arts.
Erect, the Spartan most engaged our view,
Ulysses seated greater rev'rence drew.
When Atreus' son harangued the list'ning
    train,
Just was his sense, and his expression
    plain,
His words succinct, yet full, without a
    fault;
He spoke no more than just the thing he
    ought.
But when Ulysses rose, in thought pro-
    found,
His modest eyes he fix'd upon the ground;

As one unskill'd or dumb, he seem'd to
    stand,   281
Nor rais'd his head, nor stretch'd his scep-
    tred hand;
But when he speaks, what elocution flows!
Soft as the fleeces of descending snows,
The copious accents fall, with easy art;
Melting they fall, and sink into the heart!
Wond'ring we hear, and, fix'd in deep sur-
    prise,
Our ears refute the censure of our eyes.'
    The King then ask'd (as yet the camp
    he view'd),
'What Chief is that, with giant strength
    endued,   290
Whose brawny shoulders, and whose swell-
    ing chest,
And lofty stature, far exceed the rest ? '
'Ajax the great ' (the beauteous Queen re-
    plied),
'Himself a host: the Grecian strength and
    pride.
See! bold Idomeneus superior towers
Amidst yon circle of his Cretan powers,
Great as a God! I saw him once before,
With Menelaus on the Spartan shore.
The rest I know, and could in order name;
All valiant Chiefs, and men of mighty
    fame.   300
Yet two are wanting of the numerous train,
Whom long my eyes have sought, but
    sought in vain;
Castor and Pollux, first in martial force,
One bold on foot, and one renown'd for
    horse.
My brothers these; the same our native
    shore,
One house contain'd us, as one mother
    bore.
Perhaps the Chiefs, from warlike toils at
    ease,
For distant Troy refused to sail the seas :
Perhaps their sword some nobler quarrel
    draws,
Ashamed to combat in their sister's cause.'
    So spoke the Fair, nor knew her brothers'
    doom,   311
Wrapt in the cold embraces of the tomb;
Adorn'd with honours in their native shore,
Silent they slept, and heard of wars no
    more.
    Meantime, the heralds thro' the crowded
    town
Bring the rich wine and destin'd victims
    down.

Idæus' arms the golden goblets press'd,
Who thus the venerable King address'd:
'Arise, O father of the Trojan state!
The nations call, thy joyful people wait, 320
To seal the truce, and end the dire debate.
Paris, thy son, and Sparta's King advance,
In measured lists to toss the weighty lance;
And who his rival shall in arms subdue,
His be the dame, and his the treasure too.
Thus with a lasting league our toils may
    cease,
And Troy possess her fertile fields in
    peace:
So shall the Greeks review their native
    shore,
Much famed for gen'rous steeds, for beauty
    more.'
    With grief he heard, and bade the Chiefs
    prepare   330
To join his milk-white coursers to the car:
He mounts the seat, Antenor at his side;
The gentle steeds thro' Scæa's gates they
    guide:
Next from the car, descending on the plain,
Amid the Grecian host and Trojan train
Slow they proceed: the sage Ulysses then
Arose, and with him rose the King of men.
On either side a sacred herald stands;
The wine they mix, and on each monarch's
    hands
Pour the full urn; then draws the Grecian
    lord   340
His cutlass, sheathed beside his pond'rous
    sword;
From the sign'd victims crops the curling
    hair,
The heralds part it, and the Princes share;
Then loudly thus before th' attentive bands
He calls the Gods, and spreads his lifted
    hands:
    'O first and greatest Power! whom all
    obey,
Who high on Ida's holy mountain sway,
Eternal Jove! and you bright Orb that roll
From east to west, and view from pole to
    pole!
Thou mother Earth! and all ye living
    Floods!   350
Infernal Furies, and Tartarean Gods,
Who rule the dead, and horrid woes pre-
    pare
For perjured Kings, and all who falsely
    swear!
Hear, and be witness. If, by Paris slain,
Great Menelaus press the fatal plain;

The dame and treasures let the Trojan
keep;
And Greece returning plough the wat'ry
deep.
If by my brother's lance the Trojan bleed,
Be his the wealth and beauteous dame de-
creed:
Th' appointed fine let Ilion justly pay, 360
And age to age record the signal day.
This if the Phrygians shall refuse to yield,
Arms must revenge, and Mars decide the
field.'
 With that the Chief the tender victims
slew,
And in the dust their bleeding bodies
threw:
The vital spirit issued at the wound,
And left the members quiv'ring on the
ground.
From the same urn they drink the mingled
wine,
And add libations to the Powers divine.
While thus their prayers united mount the
sky: 370
'Hear, mighty Jove! and hear, ye Gods on
high!
And may their blood, who first the league
confound,
Shed like this wine, disdain the thirsty
ground;
May all their consorts serve promiscuous
lust,
And all their race be scatter'd as the dust!'
Thus either host their imprecations join'd,
Which Jove refused, and mingled with the
wind.
 The rites now finish'd, rev'rend Priam
rose,
And thus express'd a heart o'ercharged with
woes:
'Ye Greeks and Trojans, let the Chiefs en-
gage, 380
But spare the weakness of my feeble age:
In yonder walls that object let me shun,
Nor view the danger of so dear a son.
Whose arms shall conquer, and what Prince
shall fall,
Heav'n only knows, for Heav'n disposes
all.'
 This said, the hoary King no longer
stay'd,
But on his car the slaughter'd victims laid;
Then seiz'd the reins his gentle steeds to
guide,
And drove to Troy, Antenor at his side.

Bold Hector and Ulysses now dispose 390
The lists of combat, and the ground en-
close;
Next to decide by sacred lots prepare,
Who first shall lance his pointed spear in
air.
The people pray with elevated hands,
And words like these are heard thro' all
the bands:
'Immortal Jove! high Heav'n's superior
lord,
On lofty Ida's holy mount ador'd!
Whoe'er involv'd us in this dire debate,
Oh give that author of the war to Fate
And shades eternal! let division cease, 400
And joyful nations join in leagues of peace.'
 With eyes averted Hector hastes to turn
The lots of fight, and shakes the brazen
urn.
Then, Paris, thine leap'd forth; by fatal
chance
Ordain'd the first to whirl the mighty
lance.
Both armies sat, the combat to survey,
Beside each Chief his azure armour lay,
And round the lists the gen'rous coursers
neigh.
The beauteous warrior now arrays for fight,
In gilded arms magnificently bright: 410
The purple cuishes clasp his thighs around,
With flowers adorn'd, with silver buckles
bound:
Lycaön's corslet his fair body dress'd,
Braced in, and fitted to his softer breast;
A radiant baldric, o'er his shoulder tied,
Sustain'd the sword that glitter'd at his
side:
His youthful face a polish'd helm o'er-
spread;
The waving horse-hair nodded on his head:
His figured shield, a shining orb, he takes,
And in his hand a pointed jav'lin shakes. 420
With equal speed, and fired by equal
charms,
The Spartan hero sheathes his limbs in arms.
 Now round the lists th' admiring armies
stand,
With jav'lins fix'd, the Greek and Trojan
band.
Amidst the dreadful vale the Chiefs ad-
vance,
All pale with rage, and shake the threat'-
ning lance.
The Trojan first his shining jav'lin threw:
Full on Atrides' ringing shield it flew,

Nor pierc'd the brazen orb, but with a
   bound
Leap'd from the buckler blunted on the
   ground. 430
Atrides then his massy lance prepares,
In act to throw, but first prefers his
   prayers:
'Give me, great Jove! to punish lawless
   lust,
And lay the Trojan gasping in the dust;
Destroy th' aggressor, aid my righteous
   cause,
Avenge the breach of hospitable laws!
Let this example future times reclaim,
And guard from wrong fair friendship's
   holy name.'
He said, and, pois'd in air, the jav'lin sent;
Thro' Paris' shield the forceful weapon
   went, 440
His corslet pierces, and his garment rends,
And, glancing downward, near his flank
   descends.
The wary Trojan, bending from the blow,
Eludes the death, and disappoints his
   foe:
But fierce Atrides waved his sword, and
   struck
Full on his casque; the crested helmet
   shook;
The brittle steel, unfaithful to his hand,
Broke short: the fragments glitter'd on the
   sand;
The raging warrior to the spacious skies
Rais'd his upbraiding voice, and angry
   eyes: 450
'Then is it vain in Jove himself to trust?
And is it thus the Gods assist the just?
When crimes provoke us, Heav'n success
   denies:
The dart falls harmless, and the falchion
   flies.'
Furious he said, and toward the Grecian
   crew
(Seiz'd by the crest) th' unhappy warrior
   drew;
Struggling he follow'd, while th' em-
   broider'd thong,
That tied his helmet. dragg'd the Chief
   along.
Then had his ruin crown'd Atrides' joy,
But Venus trembled for the Prince of
   Troy: 460
Unseen she came, and burst the golden
   band;
And left an empty helmet in his hand.

The casque, enraged, amidst the Greeks he
   threw;
The Greeks with smiles the polish'd trophy
   view.
Then, as once more he lifts the deadly
   dart,
In thirst of vengeance, at his rival's heart,
The Queen of Love her favour'd champion
   shrouds
(For Gods can all things) in a veil of
   clouds.
Rais'd from the field the panting youth she
   led,
And gently laid him on the bridal bed, 470
With pleasing sweets his fainting sense re-
   news,
And all the dome perfumes with heav'nly
   dews.
   Meantime the brightest of the female
   kind,
The matchless Helen, o'er the walls re-
   clin'd:
To her, beset with Trojan beauties, came,
In borrow'd form, the laughter-loving
   dame
(She seem'd an ancient maid, well skill'd
   to cull
The snowy fleece, and wind the twisted
   wool).
The Goddess softly shook her silken vest
That shed perfumes, and whisp'ring thus
   address'd: 480
'Haste, happy nymph! for thee thy Paris
   calls
Safe from the fight, in yonder lofty walls,
Fair as a God! with odours round him
   spread
He lies, and waits thee on the well-known
   bed,
Not like a warrior parted from the foe,
But some gay dancer in the public show.'
   She spoke, and Helen's secret soul was
   mov'd;
She scorn'd the champion, but the man she
   lov'd.
Fair Venus' neck, her eyes that sparkled
   fire,
And breast, reveal'd the Queen of soft de-
   sire. 490
Struck with her presence, straight the
   lively red
Forsook her cheek; and trembling thus she
   said:
'Then is it still thy pleasure to deceive?
And woman's frailty always to believe?

Say, to new nations must I cross the main,
Or carry wars to some soft Asian plain ?
For whom must Helen break her second
vow ?
What other Paris is thy darling now ?
Left to Atrides (victor in the strife)
An odious conquest and a captive wife, 500
Hence let me sail: and, if thy Paris bear
My absence ill, let Venus ease his care.
A handmaid Goddess at his side to wait,
Renounce the glories of thy heav'nly state,
Be fix'd for ever to the Trojan shore,
His spouse, or slave; and mount the skies
no more.
For me, to lawless love no longer led,
I scorn the coward, and detest his bed;
Else should I merit everlasting shame,
And keen reproach from every Phrygian
dame: 510
Ill suits it now the joys of love to know,
Too deep my anguish, and too wild my woe.'
Then thus, incens'd, the Paphian Queen
replies:
'Obey the power from whom thy glories
rise:
Should Venus leave thee, ev'ry charm must
fly,
Fade from thy cheek, and languish in thy
eye.
Cease to provoke me, lest I make thee
more
The world's aversion, than their love before;
Now the bright prize for which mankind
engage,
Then, the sad victim of the public rage.' 520
At this, the fairest of her sex obey'd,
And veil'd her blushes in a silken shade;
Unseen, and silent, from the train she
moves,
Led by the Goddess of the smiles and loves.
Arrived, and enter'd at the palace gate,
The maids officious round their mistress
wait:
Then all, dispersing, various tasks attend;
The Queen and Goddess to the Prince as-
cend.
Full in her Paris' sight the Queen of Love
Had placed the beauteous progeny of Jove;
Where, as he view'd her charms, she turn'd
away 531
Her glowing eyes, and thus began to say:
'Is this the Chief, who, lost to sense of
shame,
Late fled the field, and yet survives his
fame ?

Oh hadst thou died beneath the righteous
sword
Of that brave man whom once I call'd my
lord!
The boaster Paris oft desired the day
With Sparta's King to meet in single fray:
Go now, once more thy rival's rage excite,
Provoke Atrides, and renew the fight: 540
Yet Helen bids thee stay, lest thou un-
skill'd
Shouldst fall an easy conquest on the field.'
The Prince replies: 'Ah cease, divinely
fair,
Nor add reproaches to the wounds I bear;
This day the foe prevail'd by Pallas' power;
We yet may vanquish in a happier hour:
There want not Gods to favour us above;
But let the bus'ness of our life be love:
These softer moments let delights employ,
And kind embraces snatch the hasty joy. 550
Not thus I lov'd thee, when from Sparta's
shore
My forced, my willing, heav'nly prize I
bore,
When first entranc'd in Cranae's isle I lay,
Mix'd with thy soul, and all dissolv'd
away!'
Thus having spoke, th' enamour'd Phrygian
boy
Rush'd to the bed, impatient for the joy.
Him Helen follow'd slow with bashful
charms,
And clasp'd the blooming hero in her arms.
While these to love's delicious rapture
yield,
The stern Atrides rages round the field: 560
So some fell lion whom the woods obey,
Roars thro' the desert, and demands his
prey.
Paris he seeks, impatient to destroy,
But seeks in vain along the troops of Troy;
Ev'n those had yielded to a foe so brave
The recreant warrior, hateful as the grave.
Then speaking thus, the King of Kings
arose:
'Ye Trojans, Dardans, all our gen'rous foes!
Hear and attest! from Heav'n with conquest
crown'd,
Our brother's arms the just success have
found. 570
Be therefore now the Spartan wealth re-
stor'd,
Let Argive Helen own her lawful lord;
Th' appointed fine let Ilion justly pay,
And age to age record this signal day.'

He ceas'd; his army's loud applauses
rise,
And the long shout runs echoing thro' the
skies.

BOOK IV

THE BREACH OF THE TRUCE, AND THE FIRST BATTLE

THE ARGUMENT

The Gods deliberate in council concerning the
Trojan war: they agree upon the continuation of it, and Jupiter sends down Minerva
to break the truce. She persuades Pandarus
to aim an arrow at Menelaus, who is wounded,
but cured by Machaon. In the mean time
some of the Trojan troops attack the Greeks.
Agamemnon is distinguished in all the parts
of a good general; he reviews the troops, and
exhorts the leaders, some by praises, and
others by reproofs. Nestor is particularly celebrated for his military discipline. The battle joins, and great numbers are slain on
both sides.
The same day continues through this, as
through the last book; as it does also through
the two following, and almost to the end of
the seventh book. The scene is wholly in the
field before Troy.

AND now Olympus' shining gates unfold;
The Gods, with Jove, assume their thrones
of gold:
Immortal Hebè, fresh with bloom divine,
The golden goblet crowns with purple wine:
While the full bowls flow round, the
Powers employ
Their careful eyes on long-contended Troy.
When Jove, disposed to tempt Saturnia's
spleen,
Thus waked the fury of his partial Queen:
'Two Powers divine the son of Atreus aid,
Imperial Juno, and the Martial Maid: 10
But high in Heav'n they sit, and gaze from
far,
The tame spectators of his deeds of war.
Not thus fair Venus helps her favour'd
knight,
The Queen of Pleasures shares the toils of
fight,
Each danger wards, and, constant in her
care,
Saves in the moment of the last despair.
Her act has rescued Paris' forfeit life,
Tho' great Atrides gain'd the glorious
strife.

Then say, ye Powers! what signal issue
waits
To crown this deed, and finish all the
Fates?   20
Shall Heav'n by peace the bleeding king-
doms spare,
Or rouse the Furies, and awake the war?
Yet, would the Gods for human good pro-
vide,
Atrides soon might gain his beauteous
bride,
Still Priam's walls in peaceful honours grow,
And thro' his gates the crowding nations
flow.'
    Thus while he spoke, the Queen of
Heav'n, enraged,
And Queen of War, in close consult en-
gaged:
Apart they sit, their deep designs employ,
And meditate the future woes of Troy.   30
Tho' secret anger swell'd Minerva's breast,
The prudent Goddess yet her wrath sup-
press'd;
But Juno, impotent of passion, broke
Her sullen silence, and with fury spoke:
    'Shall then, O Tyrant of th' ethereal
reign!
My schemes, my labours, and my hopes, be
vain?
Have I, for this, shook Ilion with alarms,
Assembled nations, set two worlds in arms?
To spread the war, I flew from shore to
shore;
Th' immortal coursers scarce the labour
bore.   40
At length ripe vengeance o'er their heads
impends,
But Jove himself the faithless race de-
fends;
Loth as thou art to punish lawless lust,
Not all the Gods are partial and unjust.'
    The Sire whose thunder shakes the
cloudy skies,
Sighs from his inmost soul, and thus replies:
'Oh lasting rancour! oh insatiate hate
To Phrygia's monarch and the Phrygian
state!
What high offence has fired the wife of
Jove?
Can wretched mortals harm the Powers
above?   50
That Troy and Troy's whole race thou
wouldst confound,
And yon fair structures level with the
ground?

Haste, leave the skies, fulfil thy stern desire,
Burst all her gates, and wrap her walls in
  fire!
Let Priam bleed! if yet thou thirst for
  more,
Bleed all his sons, and Ilion float with gore,
To boundless vengeance the wide realm be
  giv'n
Till vast destruction glut the Queen of
  Heav'n!
So let it be, and Jove his peace enjoy,
When Heav'n no longer hears the name of
  Troy.   60
But should this arm prepare to wreak our
  hate
On thy lov'd realms, whose guilt demands
  their fate,
Presume not thou the lifted bolt to stay,
Remember Troy, and give the vengeance
  way,
For know, of all the numerous towns that
  rise
Beneath the rolling sun, and starry skies,
Which Gods have rais'd, or earth-born
  men enjoy;
None stands so dear to Jove as sacred
  Troy.
No mortals merit more distinguish'd grace
Than godlike Priam, or than Priam's
  race: 70
Still to our name their hecatombs expire,
And altars blaze with unextinguish'd fire.'
  At this the Goddess roll'd her radiant
    eyes,
Then on the Thund'rer fix'd them, and re-
  plies:
'Three towns are Juno's on the Grecian
  plains,
More dear than all th' extended earth con-
  tains,
Mycenæ, Argos, and the Spartan wall;
These thou may'st raze, nor I forbid their
  fall:
'T is not in me the vengeance to remove;
The crime 's sufficient that they share my
  love.   80
Of power superior, why should I com-
  plain ?
Resent I may, but must resent in vain.
Yet some distinction Juno might require,
Sprung with thyself from one celestial
  sire,
A Goddess born to share the realms above,
And styled the consort of the thund'ring
  Jove:

Nor thou a wife and sister's right deny;
Let both consent, and both by turns
  comply;
So shall the Gods our joint decrees obey,
And Heav'n shall act as we direct the
  way.   90
See ready Pallas waits thy high commands,
To raise in arms the Greek and Phrygian
  bands;
Their sudden friendship by her arts may
  cease,
And the proud Trojans first infringe the
  peace.'
  The Sire of men, and Monarch of the
    sky,
Th' advice approv'd, and bade Minerva fly,
Dissolve the league, and all her arts em-
  ploy
To make the breach the faithless act of
  Troy.
  Fired with the charge, she headlong
    urged her flight
And shot like lightning from Olympus'
  height.   100
As the red comet, from Saturnius sent
To fright the nations with a dire portent
(A fatal sign to armies on the plain,
Or trembling sailors on the wintry main),
With sweeping glories glides along in air,
And shakes the sparkles from its blazing
  hair;
Between both armies thus, in open sight,
Shot the bright Goddess in a trail of light.
With eyes erect, the gazing hosts admire
The Power descending, and the Heav'ns on
  fire!   110
'The Gods' (they cried), 'the Gods this
  signal sent,
And Fate now labours with some vast
  event:
Jove seals the league, or bloodier scenes
  prepares;
Jove, the great arbiter of peace and wars!'
  They said, while Pallas thro' the Trojan
    throng
(In shape a mortal) pass'd disguised along.
Like bold Laödocus, her course she bent,
Who from Antenor traced his high descent.
Amidst the ranks Lycaön's son she found,
The warlike Pandarus, for strength re-
  nown'd;   120
Whose squadrons, led from black Æsepus'
  flood,
With flaming shields in martial circle
  stood.

To him the Goddess: 'Phrygian! canst thou hear
A well-timed counsel with a willing ear ?
What praise were thine, could'st thou direct thy dart,
Amidst his triumph, to the Spartan's heart ?
What gifts from Troy, from Paris, wouldst thou gain,
Thy country's foe, the Grecian glory, slain ?
Then seize th' occasion, dare the mighty deed,
Aim at his breast, and may that aim succeed!   130
But first, to speed the shaft, address thy vow
To Lycian Phœbus with the silver bow,
And swear the firstlings of thy flock to pay
On Zelia's altars, to the God of Day.'
  He heard, and madly at the motion pleas'd,
His polish'd bow with hasty rashness seiz'd.
'T was form'd of horn, and smooth'd with artful toil;
A mountain goat resign'd the shining spoil,
Who pierc'd long since beneath his arrows bled;
The stately quarry on the cliffs lay dead,   140
And sixteen palms his brow's large honours spread:
The workman join'd, and shaped the bended horns,
And beaten gold each taper point adorns.
This, by the Greeks unseen, the warrior bends,
Screen'd by the shields of his surrounding friends.
There meditates the mark, and, crouching low,
Fits the sharp arrow to the well-strung bow.
One, from a hundred feather'd deaths he chose,
Fated to wound, and cause of future woes.
Then offers vows with hecatombs to crown   150
Apollo's altars in his native town.
  Now with full force the yielding horn he bends,
Drawn to an arch, and joins the doubling ends;

Close to his breast he strains the nerve below,
Till the barb'd point approach the circling bow;
Th' impatient weapon whizzes on the wing;
Sounds the tough horn, and twangs the quiv'ring string.
  But thee, Atrides! in that dangerous hour
The Gods forget not, nor thy guardian Power.   159
Pallas assists, and (weaken'd in its force)
Diverts the weapon from its destin'd course:
So from her babe, when slumber seals his eye,
The watchful mother wafts th' envenom'd fly.
Just where his belt with golden buckles join'd,
Where linen folds the double corslet lin'd,
She turn'd the shaft, which, hissing from above,
Pass'd the broad belt, and thro' the corslet drove;
The folds it pierc'd, the plaited linen tore,
And razed the skin, and drew the purple gore.
As when some stately trappings are decreed   170
To grace a monarch on his bounding steed,
A nymph, in Caria or Mæönia bred,
Stains the pure iv'ry with a lively red;
With equal lustre various colours vie,
The shining whiteness, and the Tyrian dye:
So, great Atrides! shew'd thy sacred blood,
As down thy snowy thigh distill'd the streaming flood.
With horror seiz'd, the King of men descried
The shaft infix'd, and saw the gushing tide:
Nor less the Spartan fear'd, before he found   180
The shining barb appear above the wound.
Then, with a sigh that heav'd his manly breast,
The royal brother thus his grief express'd,
And grasp'd his hand; while all the Greeks around
With answering sighs return'd the plaintive sound:
  'Oh dear as life! did I for this agree
The solemn truce, a fatal truce to thee!

Wert thou exposed to all the hostile train,
To fight for Greece, and conquer to be
    slain ?
The race of Trojans in thy ruin join,   190
And faith is scorn'd by all the perjured line.
Not thus our vows, confirm'd with wine
    and gore,
Those hands we plighted, and those oaths
    we swore,
Shall all be vain: when Heav'n's revenge
    is slow,
Jove but prepares to strike the fiercer
    blow.
The day shall come, the great avenging day,
Which Troy's proud glories in the dust
    shall lay,
When Priam's powers and Priam's self
    shall fall,
And one prodigious ruin swallow all.
I see the God, already, from the pole,   200
Bare his red arm, and bid the thunder roll;
I see th' Eternal all his fury shed,
And shake his ægis o'er their guilty head.
Such mighty woes on perjured Princes
    wait;
But thou, alas! deserv'st a happier fate.
Still must I mourn the period of thy days,
And only mourn, without my share of
    praise ?
Deprived of thee, the heartless Greeks no
    more
Shall dream of conquests on the hostile
    shore;
Troy seized of Helen, and our glory
    lost,   210
Thy bones shall moulder on a foreign
    coast:
While some proud Trojan thus insulting
    cries
(And spurns the dust where Menelaus lies):
" Such are the trophies Greece from Ilion
    brings,
And such the conquest of her King of
    Kings!
Lo his proud vessels scatter'd o'er the
    main,
And unrevenged his mighty brother slain."
Oh, ere that dire disgrace shall blast my
    fame,
O'erwhelm me, earth! and hide a mon-
    arch's shame.'
  He said: a leader's and a brother's
    fears   220
Possess his soul, which thus the Spartan
    cheers:

' Let not thy words the warmth of Greece
    abate;
The feeble dart is guiltless of my fate:
Stiff with the rich embroider'd work around,
My varied belt repell'd the flying wound.'
  To whom the King: ' My brother and
    my friend,
Thus, always thus, may Heav'n thy life de-
    fend!
Now seek some skilful hand, whose power-
    ful art
May stanch th' effusion, and extract the
    dart.
Herald, be swift, and bid Machaon bring   230
His speedy succour to the Spartan King;
Pierced with a winged shaft (the deed of
    Troy),
The Grecian's sorrow and the Dardan's joy.'
  With hasty zeal the swift Talthybius
    flies;
Thro' the thick files he darts his searching
    eyes,
And finds Machaon, where sublime he
    stands
In arms encircled with his native bands.
Then thus: ' Machaon, to the King repair,
His wounded brother claims thy timely
    care;
Pierced by some Lycian or Dardanian
    bow,   240
A grief to us, a triumph to the foe.'
  The heavy tidings grieved the godlike
    man;
Swift to his succour through the ranks he
    ran:
The dauntless King yet standing firm he
    found,
And all the Chiefs in deep concern around.
Where to the steely point the reed was
    join'd,
The shaft he drew, but left the head be-
    hind.
Straight the broad belt, with gay em-
    broid'ry graced,
He loosed: the corslet from his breast un-
    braced;
Then suck'd the blood, and sov'reign balm
    infused,   250
Which Chiron gave, and Æsculapius used.
  While round the Prince the Greeks em-
    ploy their care,
The Trojans rush tumultuous to the war;
Once more they glitter in refulgent arms,
Once more the fields are fill'd with dire
    alarms.

Nor had you seen the King of Men appear
Confused, inactive, or surprised with fear;
But fond of glory, with severe delight,
His beating bosom claim'd the rising fight.
No longer with his warlike steeds he stay'd,
Or press'd the car with polish'd brass in-
    laid, 261
But left Eurymedon the reins to guide;
The fiery coursers snorted at his side.
On foot thro' all the martial ranks he
    moves,
And these encourages, and those reproves.
'Brave men!' he cries (to such who boldly
    dare
Urge their swift steeds to face the coming
    war),
'Your ancient valour on the foes approve;
Jove is with Greece, and let us trust in
    Jove.
'T is not for us, but guilty Troy, to
    dread, 270
Whose crimes sit heavy on her perjured
    head:
Her sons and matrons Greece shall lead in
    chains,
And her dread warriors strew the mourn-
    ful plains.'
    Thus with new ardour he the brave in-
    spires;
Or thus the fearful with reproaches fires:
'Shame to your country, scandal of your
    kind!
Born to the fate ye well deserve to find;
Why stand ye gazing round the dreadful
    plain,
Prepared for flight, but doom'd to fly in
    vain?
Confused and panting, thus the hunted
    deer 280
Falls as he flies, a victim to his fear.
Still must ye wait the foes, and still retire,
Till yon tall vessels blaze with Trojan fire?
Or trust ye, Jove a valiant foe shall chase,
To save a trembling, heartless, dastard
    race?'
    This said, he stalk'd with ample strides
    along,
To Crete's brave monarch and his martial
    throng;
High at their head he saw the Chief ap-
    pear,
And bold Meriones excite the rear.
At this the King his gen'rous joy express'd,
And clasp'd the warrior to his armèd
    breast: 291

'Divine Idomeneus! what thanks we owe
To worth like thine? what praise shall we
    bestow?
To thee the foremost honours are decreed,
First in the fight, and ev'ry graceful deed.
For this, in banquets, when the gen'rous
    bowls
Restore our blood, and raise the warriors'
    souls,
Tho' all the rest with stated rules we
    bound,
Unmix'd, unmeasured are thy goblets
    crown'd.
Be still thyself; in arms a mighty name; 300
Maintain thy honours, and enlarge thy
    fame.'
    To whom the Cretan thus his speech ad-
    dress'd:
'Secure of me, O King! exhort the rest:
Fix'd to thy side, in ev'ry toil I share,
Thy firm associate in the day of war.
But let the signal be this moment giv'n;
To mix in fight is all I ask of Heav'n.
The field shall prove how perjuries suc-
    ceed,
And chains or death avenge their impious
    deed.'
    Charm'd with this heat, the King his
    course pursues, 310
And next the troops of either Ajax views:
In one firm orb the bands were ranged
    around,
A cloud of heroes blacken'd all the ground.
Thus from the lofty promontory's brow
A swain surveys the gath'ring storm below;
Slow from the main the heavy vapours rise,
Spread in dim streams, and sail along the
    skies,
Till black as night the swelling tempest
    shews,
The cloud condensing as the west-wind
    blows:
He dreads th' impending storm, and drives
    his flock 320
To the close covert of an arching rock.
    Such, and so thick, th' embattled squad-
    rons stood,
With spears erect, a moving iron wood;
A shady light was shot from glimm'ring
    shields,
And their brown arms obscured the dusky
    fields.
    'O Heroes! worthy such a dauntless
    train,
Whose godlike virtue we but urge in vain'

(Exclaim'd the King), 'who raise your
eager bands
With great examples, more than loud
commands.
Ah would the Gods but breathe in all the
rest   330
Such souls as burn in your exalted breast!
Soon should our arms with just success be
crown'd,
And Troy's proud walls lie smoking on the
ground.'
    Then to the next the gen'ral bends his
course
(His heart exults, and glories in his force);
There rev'rend Nestor ranks his Pylian
bands,
And with inspiring eloquence commands;
With strictest order sets his train in arms,
The Chiefs advises, and the soldiers warms.
Alastor, Chromius, Hæmon, round him
wait,   340
Bias the good, and Pelagon the great.
The horse and chariots to the front as-
sign'd,
The foot (the strength of war) he ranged
behind:
The middle space suspected troops supply,
Enclosed by both, nor left the power to fly:
He gives command to curb the fiery steed,
Nor cause confusion, nor the ranks exceed:
'Before the rest let none too rashly ride;
No strength nor skill, but just in time, be
tried:
The charge once made, no warrior turn the
rein,   350
But fight, or fall; a firm, embodied train.
He whom the fortune of the field shall cast
From forth his chariot, mount the next in
haste;
Nor seek unpractis'd to direct the car,
Content with jav'lins to provoke the war.
Our great forefathers held this prudent
course,
Thus ruled their ardour, thus preserv'd
their force,
By laws like these immortal conquests
made,
And earth's proud tyrants low in ashes laid.'
    So spoke the master of the martial art,
And touch'd with transport great Atrides'
heart.   361
'Oh! hadst thou strength to match thy
brave desires,
And nerves to second what thy soul in-
spires!

But wasting years that wither human race,
Exhaust thy spirits, and thy arms un-
brace.
What once thou wert, oh ever might'st
thou be!
And age the lot of any Chief but thee.'
    Thus to th' experienc'd Prince Atrides
cried;
He shook his hoary locks, and thus replied:
'Well might I wish, could mortal wish re-
new   370
That strength which once in boiling youth
I knew;
Such as I was, when Ereuthalion slain
Beneath this arm fell prostrate on the
plain.
But Heav'n its gifts not all at once bestows,
These years with wisdom crowns, with ac-
tion those:
The field of combat fits the young and
bold,
The solemn council best becomes the old:
To you the glorious conflict I resign,
Let sage advice, the palm of age, be mine.'
    He said. With joy the Monarch march'd
before   380
And found Menestheus on the dusty shore,
With whom the firm Athenian phalanx
stands;
And next Ulysses, with his subject bands.
Remote their forces lay, nor knew so far
The peace infringed, nor heard the sounds
of war;
The tumult late begun, they stood intent
To watch the motion, dubious of th' event.
The King, who saw their squadrons yet un-
mov'd,
With hasty ardour thus the Chiefs re-
prov'd:
    'Can Peteus' son forget a warrior's part,
And fears Ulysses, skill'd in every art ? 391
Why stand you distant, and the rest expect
To mix in combat which yourselves neg-
lect ?
From you 't was hoped among the first to
dare
The shock of armies, and commence the
war.
For this your names are call'd before the
rest,
To share the pleasures of the genial feast:
And can you, Chiefs! without a blush sur-
vey
Whole troops before you lab'ring in the
fray ?   399

Say, is it thus those honours you requite?
The first in banquets, but the last in fight.'
  Ulysses heard: the hero's warmth o'er-
    spread
His cheek with blushes; and, severe, he
  said:
'Take back th' unjust reproach! Behold
  we stand
Sheathed in bright arms, and but expect
  command.
If glorious deeds afford thy soul delight,
Behold me plunging in the thickest fight.
Then give thy warrior-chief a warrior's
  due,
Who dares to act whate'er thou darest to
  view.'
  Struck with his gen'rous wrath, the King
    replies: 410
'Oh great in action, and in council wise!
With ours, thy care and ardour are the
  same,
Nor need I to command, nor ought to
  blame.
Sage as thou art, and learn'd in human
  kind,
Forgive the transport of a martial mind.
Haste to the fight, secure of just amends;
The Gods that make shall keep the wor-
  thy friends.'
  He said, and pass'd where great Tydides
    lay,
His steeds and chariots wedg'd in firm
  array 419
(The warlike Sthenelus attends his side);
To whom with stern reproach the Monarch
  cried:
'Oh son of Tydeus' (he whose strength
  could tame
The bounding steed, in arms a mighty
  name),
'Canst thou, remote, the mingling hosts
  decry,
With hands inactive, and a careless eye?
Not thus thy sire the fierce encounter
  fear'd;
Still first in front the matchless Prince ap-
  pear'd:
What glorious toils, what wonders they re-
  cite,
Who view'd him lab'ring thro' the ranks of
  fight!
I saw him once, when, gath'ring martial
  powers, 430
A peaceful guest he sought Mycenæ's towers;

Armies he ask'd, and armies had been
  giv'n,
Not we denied, but Jove forbade from
  Heav'n;
While dreadful comets glaring from afar
Forewarn'd the horrors of the Theban war.
Next, sent by Greece from where Asopus
  flows,
A fearless envoy, he approach'd the foes;
Thebes' hostile walls, unguarded and alone,
Dauntless he enters and demands the
  throne.
The tyrant, feasting with his Chiefs he
  found, 440
And dared to combat all those Chiefs
  around;
Dared and subdued, before their haughty
  lord;
For Pallas strung his arm, and edg'd his
  sword.
Stung with the shame, within the winding
  way,
To bar his passage fifty warriors lay;
Two heroes led the secret squadron on,
Mæon the fierce, and hardy Lycophon;
Those fifty slaughter'd in the gloomy vale,
He spared but one to bear the dreadful
  tale.
Such Tydeus was, and such his martial
  fire; 450
Gods! how the son degen'rates from the
  sire!'
  No words the godlike Diomed return'd,
But heard respectful, and in secret burn'd:
Not so fierce Capaneus' undaunted son;
Stern as his sire, the boaster thus begun:
'What needs, O Monarch, this invidious
  praise,
Ourselves to lessen, while our sires you
  raise?
Dare to be just, Atrides! and confess
Our valour equal, tho' our fury less.
With fewer troops we storm'd the Theban
  wall, 460
And, happier, saw the sev'nfold city fall.
In impious acts the guilty fathers died;
The sons subdued, for Heav'n was on their
  side.
Far more than heirs of all our parents'
  fame,
Our glories darken their diminish'd name.'
  To him Tydides thus: 'My friend, for-
    bear,
Suppress thy passion, and the King re-
  vere:

His high concern may well excuse this rage,
Whose cause we follow, and whose war we wage;
His the first praise, were Ilion's towers o'erthrown, 470
And, if we fail, the chief disgrace his own.
Let him the Greeks to hardy toils excite,
'T is ours to labour in the glorious fight.'
He spoke, and ardent on the trembling ground
Sprung from his car; his ringing arms resound.
Dire was the clang, and dreadful from afar,
Of arm'd Tydides rushing to the war.
As when the winds, ascending by degrees,
First move the whitening surface of the seas,
The billows float in order to the shore, 480
The wave behind rolls on the wave before;
Till, with the growing storm, the deeps arise,
Foam o'er the rocks, and thunder to the skies:
So to the fight the thick battalions throng,
Shields urged on shields, and men drove men along.
Sedate and silent move the numerous bands;
No sound, no whisper, but their Chief's commands.
Those only heard; with awe the rest obey,
As if some God had snatch'd their voice away.
Not so the Trojans; from their host ascends 490
A gen'ral shout that all the region rends.
As when the fleecy flocks unnumber'd stand
In wealthy folds, and wait the milker's hand,
The hollow vales incessant bleating fills,
The lambs reply from all the neighb'ring hills:
Such clamours rose from various nations round,
Mix'd was the murmur, and confused the sound.
Each host now joins, and each a God inspires,
These Mars incites, and those Minerva fires.
Pale Flight around, and dreadful Terror reign; 500
And Discord raging bathes the purple plain:

Discord! dire sister of the slaught'ring Power,
Small at her birth, but rising ev'ry hour;
While scarce the skies her horrid head can bound,
She stalks on earth, and shakes the world around;
The nations bleed, where'er her steps she turns;
The groan still deepens, and the combat burns.
Now shield with shield, with helmet helmet closed,
To armour armour, lance to lance opposed,
Host against host with shadowy squadrons drew, 510
The sounding darts in iron tempests flew.
Victors and vanquish'd join promiscuous cries,
And shrilling shouts and dying groans arise;
With streaming blood the slipp'ry fields are dyed,
And slaughter'd heroes swell the dreadful tide.
As torrents roll, increas'd by numerous rills,
With rage impetuous down their echoing hills;
Rush to the vales, and, pour'd along the plain,
Roar thro' a thousand channels to the main;
The distant shepherd trembling hears the sound: 520
So mix both hosts, and so their cries rebound.
The bold Antilochus the slaughter led,
The first who struck a valiant Trojan dead:
At great Echepolus the lance arrives,
Razed his high crest and thro' his helmet drives;
Warm'd in the brain the brazen weapon lies,
And shades eternal settle o'er his eyes.
So sinks a tower that long assaults had stood
Of force and fire, its walls besmear'd with blood.
Him, the bold leader of th' Abantian throng
Seized to despoil, and dragg'd the corpse along: 531
But, while he strove to tug th' inserted dart,
Agenor's jav'lin reach'd the hero's heart.

His flank, unguarded by his ample shield,
Admits the lance: he falls, and spurns the
    field;
The nerves unbraced support his limbs no
    more:
The soul comes floating in a tide of gore.
Trojans and Greeks now gather round the
    slain;   538
The war renews, the warriors bleed again;
As o'er their prey rapacious wolves engage,
Man dies on man, and all is blood and rage.
    In blooming youth fair Simoïsius fell,
Sent by great Ajax to the shades of Hell:
Fair Simoïsius, whom his mother bore
Amid the flocks, on silver Simoïs' shore:
The nymph, descending from the hills of
    Ide,
To seek her parents on his flowery side,
Brought forth the babe, their common care
    and joy,
And thence from Simoïs named the lovely
    boy.
Short was his date! by dreadful Ajax slain
He falls, and renders all their cares in
    vain!   551
So falls a poplar, that in wat'ry ground
Rais'd high the head, with stately branches
    crown'd
(Fell'd by some artist with his shining steel,
To shape the circle of the bending wheel);
Cut down it lies, tall, smooth, and largely
    spread,
With all its beauteous honours on its head;
There, left a subject to the wind and rain,
And scorch'd by suns, it withers on the
    plain.
Thus, pierc'd by Ajax, Simoïsius lies   560
Stretch'd on the shore, and thus neglected
    dies.
    At Ajax, Antiphus his jav'lin threw: ⎫
The pointed lance with erring fury flew, ⎬
And Leucus, loved by wise Ulysses, slew. ⎭
He drops the corpse of Simoïsius slain,
And sinks a breathless carcass on the plain.
This saw Ulysses, and, with grief enraged,
Strode where the foremost of the foes en-
    gaged;
Arm'd with his spear, he meditates the
    wound,
In act to throw; but, cautious, look'd
    around.   570
Struck at his sight the Trojans backward
    drew,
And trembling heard the jav'lin as it
    flew.

A Chief stood nigh, who from Abydos
    came,
Old Priam's son, Democoön was his name;
The weapon enter'd close above his ear,
Cold thro' his temples glides the whizzing
    spear;
With piercing shrieks the youth resigns his
    breath,
His eye-balls darken with the shades of
    death;
Pond'rous he falls; his clanging arms re-
    sound;
And his broad buckler rings against the
    ground.   580
    Seiz'd with affright the boldest foes ap-
    pear;
Ev'n godlike Hector seems himself to fear;
Slow he gave way, the rest tumultuous fled;
The Greeks with shouts press on, and spoil
    the dead.
But Phœbus now from Ilion's tow'ring
    height
Shines forth reveal'd, and animates the
    fight.
' Trojans, be bold, and force with force
    oppose;
Your foaming steeds urge headlong on the
    foes!
Nor are their bodies rocks, nor ribb'd with
    steel;
Your weapons enter, and your strokes they
    feel.   590
Have you forgot what seem'd your dread
    before ?
The great, the fierce Achilles fights no
    more.'
    Apollo thus from Ilion's lofty towers,
Array'd in terrors, rous'd the Trojan pow-
    ers:
While war's fierce Goddess fires the Grecian
    foe,
And shouts and thunders in the fields below.
    Then great Diores fell, by doom divine;
In vain his valour and illustrious line.
A broken rock the force of Pirus threw
(Who from cold Ænus led the Thracian
    crew);   600
Full on his ankle dropp'd the pond'rous
    stone,
Burst the strong nerves, and crash'd the
    solid bone:
Supine he tumbles on the crimson sands, ⎫
Before his helpless friends, and native ⎬
    bands,   ⎭
And spreads for aid his unavailing hands.

The foe rush'd furious as he pants for
   breath,
And thro' his navel drove the pointed
   death:
His gushing entrails smoked upon the
   ground,
And the warm life came issuing from the
   wound.
His lance bold Thoas at the conqu'ror
   sent, 610
Deep in his breast above the pap it went,
Amid the lungs was fix'd the winged
   wood,
And quiv'ring in his heaving bosom stood:
Till from the dying Chief, approaching
   near,
Th' Ætolian warrior tugg'd his weighty
   spear:
Then sudden waved his flaming falchion
   round,
And gash'd his belly with a ghastly wound.
The corpse now breathless on the bloody
   plain,
To spoil his arms the victor strove in
   vain;
The Thracian bands against the victor
   press'd; 620
A grove of lances glitter'd at his breast.
Stern Thoas, glaring with revengeful eyes,
In sullen fury slowly quits the prize.
   Thus fell two heroes, one the pride of
   Thrace,
And one the leader of th' Epeian race;
Death's sable shade at once o'ercast their
   eyes,
In dust the vanquish'd and the victor
   lies.
With copious slaughter all the fields are
   red,
And heap'd with growing mountains of the
   dead.
   Had some brave Chief this martial scene
   beheld, 630
By Pallas guarded thro' the dreadful field,
Might darts be bid to turn their points
   away,
And swords around him innocently play,
The war's whole art with wonder had he
   seen,
And counted heroes where he counted
   men.
   So fought each host, with thirst of glory
   fired,
And crowds on crowds triumphantly ex-
   pired.

OBSERVATIONS ON HOMER'S BATTLES

It may be necessary, at the opening of Homer's battles, to give some explanatory observations upon them. When we reflect that no less than the compass of twelve books is taken up in these, we shall have reason to wonder by what method the author could prevent descriptions of such a length from being tedious. It is not enough to say, that though the subject itself be the same, the actions are always different; that we have now distinct combats, now promiscuous fights, now single duels, now general engagements; or that the scenes are perpetually varied; we are now in the fields, now at the fortification of the Greeks, now at the ships, now at the gates of Troy, now at the river Scamander: but we must look farther into the art of the poet to find the reasons of this astonishing variety.

We first observe that diversity in the deaths of his warriors, which he has supplied by the vastest fertility of invention. These he distinguishes several ways: sometimes by the *Characters* of the men, their *age, office, profession, nation, family,* etc. One is a blooming Youth, whose father dissuaded him from the war; one is a Priest, whose piety could not save him: one is a Sportsman, whom Diana taught in vain; one is the native of a far distant country, who is never to return; one is descended from a Noble Line, which ends in his death; one is made remarkable by his Boasting; another by his Beseeching; and another, who is distinguished no way else, is marked by his Habit, and the singularity of his armour.

Sometimes he varies these by the several *Postures* in which his heroes are represented either fighting or falling. Some of these are so exceedingly exact, that one may guess, from the very position of the combatant, whereabouts the wound will light: others so very peculiar and uncommon, that they could only be the effect of an imagination which had searched through all the ideas of nature. Such is that picture of Mydon in the fifth book, whose arm being numbed by a blow on the elbow, drops the reins, that trail on the ground; and then being suddenly struck on the temples, falls headlong from the chariot, in a soft and deep place, where he sinks up to the shoulders in the sands, and continues a while fixed by the weight of his armour, with his legs quivering in the air, till he is trampled down by his horses.

Another cause of this variety is the difference of the *Wounds* that are given in the *Iliad:* they are by no means like the wounds described by most other poets, which are commonly made in the self-same obvious places: the heart and head serve for all those in general who understand no anatomy, and sometimes, for variety, they kill men by wounds that are nowhere mortal but in their poems. As the whole human body is the subject of these, so nothing is more necessary to him who would describe them well, than a thorough knowledge of its structure, even though the poet is not professedly to write of them as an anatomist; in the same manner as an exact skill in anatomy is necessary to those painters that would excel in drawing the naked body, though they are not to make every muscle as visible as in a book of chirurgery. It appears from so many passages in Homer, that he was perfectly master of this science, that it would be needless to cite any in particular.

It may be necessary to take notice of some customs of antiquity relating to the Arms and Art Military of those times, which are proper to be known, in order to form a right notion of our author's descriptions of war.

That Homer copied the manners and customs of the age he wrote of, rather than of that he lived in, has been observed in some instances. As that he nowhere represents Cavalry or Trumpets to have been used in the Trojan wars, though they apparently were in his own time. It is not therefore impossible but there may be found in his works some deficiencies in the art of war, which are not to be imputed to his ignorance, but to his judgment.

Horses had not been brought into Greece long before the siege of Troy. They were originally eastern animals, and if we find at that very period so great a number of them reckoned up in the wars of the Israelites, it is the less a wonder, considering they came from Asia. The practice of riding them was so little known in Greece a few years before, that they looked upon the Centaurs who first used it, as monsters compounded of men and horses. Nestor, in the first *Iliad*, says he had seen these Centaurs in his youth, and Polypœtes in the second is said to have been born on the day that his father expelled them from Pelion to the deserts of Æthica. They had no other use of horses than to draw their chariots in battle, so that whenever Homer speaks of *fighting from a horse, taming a horse*, or the like, it is constantly to be understood of fighting from a chariot, or taming horses to that service. This was a piece of decorum in the poet; for in his own time they were arrived to such a perfection in horsemanship, that in the fifteenth *Iliad*, ver. 822, we have a simile taken from an extraordinary feat of activity, where one man manages four horses at once, and leaps from the back of one to another at full speed.

If we consider in what high esteem among warriors these noble animals must have been at their first coming into Greece, we shall the less wonder at the frequent occasions Homer has taken to describe and celebrate them. It is not so strange to find them set almost upon a level with men, at the time when a horse in the prizes was of equal value with a captive.

The Chariots were in all probability very low. For we frequently find in the *Iliad*, that a person who stands erect on a chariot is killed (and sometimes by a stroke on the head), by a foot soldier with a sword. This may farther appear from the ease and readiness with which they alight or mount on every occasion, to facilitate which, the chariots were made open behind. That the wheels were but small, may be guessed from a custom they had of taking them off and setting them on as they were laid by, or made use of. Hebe in the fifth book puts on the wheels of Juno's chariot when she calls for it in haste: and it seems to be with allusion to the same practice that it is said in *Exodus*, ch. xiv., *The Lord took off their chariot-wheels, so that they drove them heavily*. The sides were also low; for whoever is killed in his chariot throughout the poem, constantly falls to the ground, as having nothing to support him. That the whole machine was very small and light, is evident from a passage in the tenth *Iliad*, where Diomed debates whether he shall draw the chariot of Rhesus out of the way, or carry it on his shoulders to a place of safety. All the particulars agree with the representations of the chariots on the most ancient Greek coins; where the tops of them reached not so high as the backs of the horses; the wheels are yet lower, and the heroes who stand in them are seen from the knee upwards.

There were generally two persons in each chariot, one of whom was wholly employed in guiding the horses. They used, indifferently, two, three, or four horses: from whence it happens, that sometimes when a horse is killed, the hero continues the fight with the two or more that remain; and at other times a warrior retreats upon the loss of one; not that he had less courage than the other, but that he has fewer horses.

Their Swords were all broad cutting swords, for we find they never stab but with their spears. The Spears were used two ways, either to push with, or to cast from them, like the missive javelins. It seems surprising, that a man should throw a dart or spear with such force, as to pierce through both sides of the armour and the body (as is often described in Homer): for if the strength of the men was gigantic, the armour must have been strong in proportion. Some solution might be given for

this, if we imagined the armour was generally
brass, and the weapons pointed with iron; and
if we could fancy that Homer called the spears
and swords *brazen*, in the same manner that he
calls the reins of a bridle *ivory*, only from the
ornaments about them. But there are passages where the point of the spear is expressly
said to be of brass, as in the description of that
of Hector in *Iliad* vi. Pausanias (Laconicis)
takes it for granted, that the arms, as well
offensive as defensive, were brass. He says
the spear of Achilles was kept in his time in
the temple of Minerva, the top and point of
which were of brass; and the sword of Meriones, in that of Æsculapius among the Nico-
medians, was entirely of the same metal. But
be it as it will, there are examples even at this
day of such a prodigious force in casting darts,
as almost exceeds credibility. The Turks and
Arabs will pierce through thick planks with
darts of hardened wood; which can only be
attributed to their being bred (as the ancients
were) to that exercise, and to the strength and
agility acquired by a constant practice of it.

We may ascribe to the same cause their
power of casting stones of a vast weight, which
appears a common practice in these battles.
It is an error to imagine this to be only a fictitious embellishment of the poet, which was one
of the exercises of war among the ancient
Greeks and Orientals. St. Jerome tells us, it
was an old custom in Palestine, and in use in
his own time, to have round stones of a great
weight kept in the castles and villages, for the
youth to try their strength with.

BOOK V

THE ACTS OF DIOMED

THE ARGUMENT

Diomed, assisted by Pallas, performs wonders
in this day's battle. Pandarus wounds him
with an arrow, but the Goddess cures him,
enables him to discern Gods from mortals,
and prohibits him from contending with any
of the former, excepting Venus. Æneas joins
Pandarus to oppose him. Pandarus is killed,
and Æneas in great danger but for the assistance of Venus; who, as she is removing
her son from the fight, is wounded on the
hand by Diomed. Apollo seconds her in his
rescue, and, at length, carries off Æneas to
Troy, where he is healed in the temple of
Pergamus. Mars rallies the Trojans, and
assists Hector to make a stand. In the mean
time Æneas is restored to the field, and they
overthrow several of the Greeks; among the

rest Tlepolemus is slain by Sarpedon. Juno
and Minerva descend to resist Mars; the
latter incites Diomed to go against that God;
he wounds him, and sends him groaning to
Heaven.

The first battle continues through this book.
The scene is the same as in the former.

But Pallas now Tydides' soul inspires,
Fills with her force, and warms with all
     her fires,
Above the Greeks his deathless fame to
     raise,
And crown her hero with distinguish'd
     praise.
High on his helm celestial lightnings play,
His beamy shield emits a living ray;
Th' unwearied blaze incessant streams sup-
     plies,
Like the red star that fires th' autumnal
     skies,
When fresh he rears his radiant orb to
     sight,
And bathed in Ocean shoots a keener light.
Such glories Pallas on the Chief bestow'd,   11
Such, from his arms, the fierce effulgence
     flow'd:
Onward she drives him, furious to engage,
Where the fight burns, and where the
     thickest rage.
     The sons of Dares first the combat
        sought,
A wealthy priest, but rich without a fault;
In Vulcan's fane the father's days were
     led;
The sons to toils of glorious battle bred;
These, singled from their troops, the fight
     maintain;
These from their steeds, Tydides on the
     plain.   20
Fierce for renown the brother Chiefs draw
     near,
And first bold Phegeus casts his sounding
     spear,
Which o'er the warrior's shoulder took its
     course,
And spent in empty air its erring force.
Not so, Tydides, flew thy lance in vain,
But pierced his breast, and stretch'd him
     on the plain.
Seiz'd with unusual fear, Idæus fled,
Left the rich chariot, and his brother dead;
And had not Vulcan lent celestial aid,
He too had sunk to death's eternal shade; 30
But in a smoky cloud the God of Fire
Preserv'd the son, in pity to the sire.

The steeds and chariot, to the navy led,
Increas'd the spoils of gallant Diomed.
  Struck with amaze and shame, the Trojan
    crew
Or slain, or fled, the sons of Dares view;
When by the blood-stain'd hand Minerva
    press'd
The God of Battles, and this speech ad-
    dress'd:
  'Stern Power of War! by whom the
    mighty fall,
Who bathe in blood, and shake the lofty
    wall!   40
Let the brave Chiefs their glorious toils
    divide;
And whose the conquest mighty Jove de-
    cide:
While we from interdicted fields retire,
Nor tempt the wrath of Heav'n's avenging
    Sire.'
  Her words allay th' impetuous warrior's
    heat,
The God of Arms and Martial Maid re-
    treat;
Remov'd from fight, on Xanthus' flowery
    bounds
They sat, and listen'd to the dying sounds.
  Meantime, the Greeks the Trojan race
    pursue,
And some bold chieftain every leader slew:
First Odius falls and bites the bloody
    sand,   51
His death ennobled by Atrides' hand;
As he to flight his wheeling car address'd,
The speedy jav'lin drove from back to
    breast.
In dust the mighty Halizonian lay,
His arms resound, the spirit wings its way.
  Thy fate was next, O Phæstus! doom'd
    to feel
The great Idomeneus' protended steel;
Whom Borus sent (his son and only joy)
From fruitful Tarne to the fields of Troy. 60
The Cretan jav'lin reach'd him from afar,
And pierc'd his shoulder as he mounts his
    car;
Back from the car he tumbles to the
    ground,
And everlasting shades his eyes surround.
  Then died Scamandrius, expert in the
    chase,
In woods and wilds to wound the savage
    race;
Diana taught him all her sylvan arts,
To bend the bow, and aim unerring darts;

But vainly here Diana's arts he tries,
The fatal lance arrests him as he flies;   70
From Menelaus' arm the weapon sent,
Thro' his broad back and heaving bosom
    went:
Down sinks the warrior with a thund'ring
    sound,
His brazen armour rings against the
    ground.
  Next artful Phereclus untimely fell;
Bold Merion sent him to the realms of
    Hell.
Thy father's skill, O Phereclus, was thine,
The graceful fabric and the fair design;
For, lov'd by Pallas, Pallas did impart
To him the shipwright's and the builder's
    art.   80
Beneath his hand the fleet of Paris rose,
The fatal cause of all his country's woes;
But he, the mystic will of Heav'n un-
    known,
Nor saw his country's peril, nor his own.
The hapless artist, while confused he fled,
The spear of Merion mingled with the
    dead.
Thro' his right hip, with forceful fury cast,
Between the bladder and the bone it pass'd;
Prone on his knees he falls with fruitless
    cries,
And death in lasting slumber seals his
    eyes.   90
  From Meges' force the swift Pedæus fled,
Antenor's offspring from a foreign bed;
Whose gen'rous spouse, Theano, heav'nly
    fair,
Nurs'd the young stranger with a mother's
    care.
How vain those cares! when Meges in the
    rear
Full in his nape infix'd the fatal spear;
Swift thro' his crackling jaws the
    weapon glides,
And the cold tongue and grinning teeth
    divides.
  Then died Hypsenor, gen'rous and divine,
Sprung from the brave Dolopion's mighty
    line,   100
Who near ador'd Scamander made abode,
Priest of the stream, and honour'd as a God.
On him, amidst the flying numbers found,
Eurypylus inflicts a deadly wound;
On his broad shoulder fell the forceful
    brand,
Thence glancing downward lopp'd his holy
    hand,

Which stain'd with sacred blood the blush-
ing sand.
Down sunk the priest: the purple hand of
death
Closed his dim eye, and Fate suppress'd his
breath.
  Thus toil'd the Chiefs, in diff'rent parts
engaged, 110
In ev'ry quarter fierce Tydides raged,
Amid the Greek, amid the Trojan train,
Rapt thro' the ranks he thunders o'er the
plain;
Now here, now there, he darts from place
to place,
Pours on the rear, or lightens in their face.
Thus from high hills the torrents swift and
strong
Deluge whole fields, and sweep the trees
along;
Thro' ruin'd moles the rushing wave re-
sounds,
O'erwhelms the bridge, and bursts the
lofty bounds;
The yellow harvests of the ripen'd year, 120
And flatted vineyards, one sad waste ap-
pear!
While Jove descends in sluicy sheets of
rain,
And all the labours of mankind are vain.
  So raged Tydides, boundless in his ire,
Drove armies back, and made all Troy re-
tire.
With grief the leader of the Lycian band
Saw the wide waste of his destructive
hand:
His bended bow against the Chief he drew;
Swift to the mark the thirsty arrow flew,
Whose forky point the hollow breastplate
tore, 130
Deep in his shoulder pierc'd, and drank the
gore;
The rushing stream his brazen armour dyed,
While the proud archer thus exulting cried:
'Hither, ye Trojans, hither drive your
steeds!
Lo! by our hand the bravest Grecian bleeds.
Not long the deathful dart he can sustain;
Or Phœbus urged me to these fields in
vain.'
  So spoke he, boastful; but the winged
dart
Stopp'd short of life, and mock'd the shoot-
er's art. 139
The wounded Chief, behind his car retired,
The helping hand of Sthenelus required;

Swift from his seat he leap'd upon the
ground,
And tugg'd the weapon from the gushing
wound;
When thus the King his guardian Power
address'd,
The purple current wand'ring o'er his
vest:
'O progeny of Jove! unconquer'd maid!
If e'er my godlike sire deserv'd thy aid,
If e'er I felt thee in the fighting field;
Now, Goddess, now, thy sacred succour
yield.
Oh give my lance to reach the Trojan
knight, 150
Whose arrow wounds the Chief thou
guard'st in fight;
And lay the boaster grov'ling on the shore,
That vaunts these eyes shall view the light
no more.'
  Thus pray'd Tydides, and Minerva
heard,
His nerves confirm'd, his languid spirits
cheer'd;
He feels each limb with wonted vigour
light;
His beating bosom claims the promis'd
fight.
'Be bold' (she cried), 'in every combat
shine,
War be thy province, thy protection mine;
Rush to the fight, and every foe control; 160
Wake each paternal virtue in thy soul:
Strength swells thy boiling breast infused
by me,
And all thy godlike father breathes in
thee!
Yet more, from mortal mists I purge thy
eyes,
And set to view the warring deities.
These see thou shun, thro' all th' em-
battled plain,
Nor rashly strive where human force is
vain.
If Venus mingle in the martial band,
Her shalt thou wound: so Pallas gives
command.'
  With that, the Blue-eyed Virgin wing'd
her flight; 170
The hero rush'd impetuous to the fight;
With tenfold ardour now invades the plain,
Wild with delay, and more enraged by
pain.
As on the fleecy flocks, when hunger calls,
Amidst the field a brindled lion falls;

If chance some shepherd with a distant
    dart
The savage wound, he rouses at the smart,
He foams, he roars; the shepherd dares not
    stay,
But trembling leaves the scatt'ring flocks a
    prey.
Heaps fall on heaps; he bathes with blood
    the ground,   180
Then leaps victorious o'er the lofty mound.
Not with less fury stern Tydides flew,
And two brave leaders at an instant slew;
Astynous breathless fell, and by his side
His people's pastor, good Hypenor, died;
Astynous' breast the deadly lance receives,
Hypenor's shoulder his broad falchion
    cleaves.
Those slain he left; and sprung with noble
    rage
Abas and Polyïdus to engage;
Sons of Eurydamas, who, wise and old,   190
Could fates foresee, and mystic dreams un-
    fold;
The youths return'd not from the doubtful
    plain,
And the sad father tried his arts in vain;
No mystic dream could make their fates
    appear,
Tho' now determin'd by Tydides' spear.
    Young Xanthus next, and Thoön felt his
    rage,
The joy and hope of Phænops' feeble age;
Vast was his wealth, and these the only
    heirs
Of all his labours, and a life of cares.
Cold death o'ertakes them in their bloom-
    ing years,   200
And leaves the father unavailing tears:
To strangers now descends his heapy store,
The race forgotten, and the name no more.
    Two sons of Priam in one chariot ride,
Glitt'ring in arms, and combat side by
    side.
As when the lordly lion seeks his food
Where grazing heifers range the lonely
    wood,
He leaps amidst them with a furious bound,
Bends their strong necks, and tears them
    to the ground:
So from their seats the brother Chiefs are
    torn,   210
Their steeds and chariots to the navy
    borne.
    With deep concern divine Æneas view'd
The foe prevailing and his friends pursued;

Thro' the thick storm of singing spears he
    flies,
Exploring Pandarus with careful eyes.
At length he found Lycaön's mighty son;
To whom the Chief of Venus' race begun:
    ' Where, Pandarus, are all thy honours
    now,
Thy winged arrows and unerring bow,
Thy matchless skill, thy yet unrivall'd
    fame,   220
And boasted glory of the Lycian name ?
Oh pierce that mortal! if we mortal call
That wondrous force by which whole armies
    fall;
Or God incens'd, who quits the distant
    skies
To punish Troy for slighted sacrifice;
(Which oh avert from our unhappy state!
For what so dreadful as celestial hate) ?
Whoe'er he be, propitiate Jove with prayer;
If man, destroy; if God, entreat to spare.'
    To him the Lycian: ' Whom your eyes
    behold,   230
If right I judge, is Diomed the bold.
Such coursers whirl him o'er the dusty
    field,
So towers his helmet, and so flames his
    shield.
If 't is a God, he wears that Chief's dis-
    guise;
Or if that Chief, some guardian of the
    skies,
Involv'd in clouds, protects him in the
    fray,
And turns unseen the frustrate dart away.
I wing'd an arrow, which not idly fell;
The stroke had fix'd him to the gates of
    Hell;
And, but some God, some angry God with-
    stands,   240
His fate was due to these unerring hands.
Skill'd in the bow, on foot I sought the
    war,
Nor join'd swift horses to the rapid car.
Ten polish'd chariots I possess'd at home,
And still they grace Lycaön's princely
    dome:
There veil'd in spacious coverlets they
    stand;
And twice ten coursers wait their lord's
    command.
The good old warrior bade me trust to
    these,
When first for Troy I sail'd the sacred
    seas;

In fields, aloft, the whirling car to guide, 250
And thro' the ranks of death triumphant
    ride.
But vain with youth, and yet to thrift in-
    clin'd,
I heard his counsels with unheedful mind,
And thought the steeds (your large sup-
    plies unknown)
Might fail of forage in the straiten'd town;
So took my bow and pointed darts in hand,
And left the chariots in my native land.
    'Too late, O friend! my rashness I de-
    plore;
These shafts, once fatal, carry death no
    more.
Tydeus' and Atreus' sons their points have
    found, 260
And undissembled gore pursued the wound.
In vain they bled: this unavailing bow
Serves not to slaughter, but provoke the
    foe.
In evil hour these bended horns I strung,
And seiz'd the quiver where it idly hung.
Curs'd be the fate that sent me to the field,
Without a warrior's arms, the spear and
    shield!
If e'er with life I quit the Trojan plain,
If e'er I see my spouse and sire again,
This bow, unfaithful to my glorious aims,
Broke by my hand, shall feed the blazing
    flames.' 271
    To whom the leader of the Dardan race:
'Be calm, nor Phœbus' honour'd gift dis-
    grace.
The distant dart be prais'd, tho' here we
    need
The rushing chariot, and the bounding
    steed.
Against yon hero let us bend our course,
And, hand to hand, encounter force with
    force.
Now mount my seat, and from the chariot's
    height
Observe my father's steeds, renown'd in
    fight; 279
Practis'd alike to turn, to stop, to chase,
To dare the shock, or urge the rapid race:
Secure with these, thro' fighting fields we go,
Or safe to Troy, if Jove assist the foe.
Haste, seize the whip, and snatch the guid-
    ing rein;
The warrior's fury let this arm sustain:
Or if to combat thy bold heart incline,
Take thou the spear the chariot's care be
    mine.'

'O Prince' (Lycaön's valiant son re-
    plied),
'As thine the steeds, be thine the task to
    guide.
The horses, practis'd to their lord's com-
    mand, 290
Shall hear the rein and answer to thy hand.
But if, unhappy, we desert the fight,
Thy voice alone can animate their flight:
Else shall our fates be number'd with the
    dead,
And these, the victor's prize, in triumph
    led.
Thine be the guidance then: with spear and
    shield
Myself will charge this terror of the field.'
    And now both heroes mount the glitt-
    t'ring car;
The bounding coursers rush amidst the war.
Their fierce approach bold Sthenelus es-
    pied, 300
Who thus, alarm'd, to great Tydides cried:
'O friend! two Chiefs of force immense
    I see,
Dreadful they come, and bend their rage
    on thee:
Lo the brave heir of old Lycaön's line,
And great Æneas, sprung from race di-
    vine!
Enough is giv'n to Fame. Ascend thy car;
And save a life, the bulwark of our war.'
    At this the hero cast a gloomy look,
Fix'd on the Chief with scorn, and thus he
    spoke:
'Me dost thou bid to shun the coming
    fight? 310
Me wouldst thou move to base, inglorious
    flight?
Know, 't is not honest in my soul to fear,
Nor was Tydides born to tremble here
I hate the cumbrous chariot's slow ad-
    vance,
And the long distance of the flying lance:
But while my nerves are strong, my force
    entire,
Thus front the foe, and emulate my sire.
Nor shall yon steeds, that fierce to fight
    convey
Those threat'ning heroes, bear them both
    away;
One Chief at least beneath this arm shall
    die: 320
So Pallas tells me, and forbids to fly.
But if she dooms, and if no God withstand,
That both shall fall by one victorious hand;

Then heed my words: my horses here de-
tain,
Fix'd to the chariot by the straiten'd rein;
Swift to Æneas' empty seat proceed,
And seize the coursers of ethereal breed,
The race of those, which once the Thun-
d'ring God
For ravish'd Ganymede on Tros bestow'd,
The best that e'er on earth's broad surface
run 330
Beneath the rising or the setting sun.
Hence great Anchises stole a breed, un-
known
By mortal mares, from fierce Laömedon:
Four of this race his ample stalls contain,
And two transport Æneas o'er the plain.
These, were the rich immortal prize our
own,
Thro' the wide world should make our glory
known.'
Thus while they spoke, the foe came
furious on,
And stern Lycaön's warlike race begun:
'Prince, thou art met. Tho' late in vain
assail'd, 340
The spear may enter where the arrow
fail'd.'
He said, then shook the pond'rous ⎫
lance, and flung; ⎪
On his broad shield the sounding weapon ⎬
rung, ⎪
Pierc'd the tough orb, and in his cuirass ⎪
hung. ⎭
'He bleeds! the pride of Greece' (the
boaster cries),
'Our triumph now the mighty warrior
lies!'
'Mistaken vaunter!' Diomed replied;
'Thy dart has err'd, and now my spear be
tried:
Ye 'scape not both; one headlong from his
car,
With hostile blood shall glut the God of
War.' 350
He spoke, and, rising, hurl'd his forceful
dart,
Which, driv'n by Pallas, pierc'd a vital
part;
Full in his face it enter'd, and betwixt
The nose and eyeball the proud Lycian
fix'd:
Crash'd all his jaws, and cleft the tongue
within,
Till the bright point look'd out beneath the
chin.

Headlong he falls, his helmet knocks the
ground;
Earth groans beneath him, and his arms
resound;
The starting coursers tremble with af-
fright;
The soul indignant seeks the realms of
night. 360
To guard his slaughter'd friend, Æneas
flies,
His spear extending where the carcass lies,
Watchful he wheels, protects it every way,
As the grim lion stalks around his prey.
O'er the fall'n trunk his ample shield dis-
play'd,
He hides the hero with his mighty shade,
And threats aloud: the Greeks with long-
ing eyes
Behold at distance, but forbear the prize.
Then fierce Tydides stoops; and, from the
fields
Heav'd with vast force, a rocky fragment
wields. 370
Not two strong men th' enormous weight
could raise,
Such men as live in these degen'rate days.
He swung it round; and, gath'ring strength
to throw,
Discharged the pond'rous ruin at the foe.
Where to the hip th' inserted thigh unites,
Full on the bone the pointed marble lights;
Thro' both the tendons broke the rugged
stone.
And stripp'd the skin, and crack'd the solid
bone.
Sunk on his knees, and stagg'ring with his
pains,
His falling bulk his bended arms sustains;
Lost in a dizzy mist the warrior lies; 381
A sudden cloud comes swimming o'er his
eyes.
There the brave Chief, who mighty numbers
sway'd,
Oppress'd had sunk to death's eternal
shade:
But heav'nly Venus, mindful of the love
She bore Anchises in th' Idæan grove,
His danger views with anguish and de-
spair,
And guards her offspring with a mother's
care.
About her much-lov'd son her arms she
throws,
Her arms whose whiteness match the fall-
ing snows. 390

Screen'd from the foe behind her shining
    veil,
The swords wave harmless, and the jav'lins
    fail:
Safe thro' the rushing horse, and feather'd
    flight
Of sounding shafts, she bears him from the
    fight.
    Nor Sthenelus, with unassisting hands,
Remain'd unheedful of his lord's com-
    mands:
His panting steeds, remov'd from out the
    war,
He fix'd with straiten'd traces to the car.
Next, rushing to the Dardan spoil, detains
The heav'nly coursers with the flowing
    manes: 400
These, in proud triumph to the fleet con-
    vey'd,
No longer now a Trojan lord obey'd.
That charge to bold Deïpylus he gave
(Whom most he lov'd, as brave men love
    the brave),
Then, mounting on his car, resumed the
    rein,
And follow'd where Tydides swept the
    plain.
    Meanwhile (his conquest ravish'd from
    his eyes)
The raging Chief in chase of Venus flies:
No Goddess she commission'd to the field,
Like Pallas dreadful with her sable shield,
Or fierce Bellona thund'ring at the wall, 411
While flames ascend, and mighty ruins fall;
He knew soft combats suit the tender
    dame,
New to the field, and still a foe to fame.
Thro' breaking ranks his furious course he
    bends,
And at the Goddess his broad lance ex-
    tends;
Thro' her bright veil the daring weapon
    drove,
Th' ambrosial veil, which all the Graces
    wove:
Her snowy hand the razing steel profaned,
And the transparent skin with crimson
    stain'd.   420
From the clear vein a stream immortal
    flow'd,
Such stream as issues from a wounded
    God;
Pure emanation! uncorrupted flood;
Unlike our gross, diseas'd, terrestrial
    blood;

(For not the bread of man their life sus-
    tains,
Nor wine's inflaming juice supplies their
    veins).
With tender shrieks the Goddess fill'd the
    place;
And dropp'd her offspring from her weak
    embrace.
Him Phœbus took: he casts a cloud around
The fainting Chief, and wards the mortal
    wound.   430
    Then with a voice that shook the vaulted
    skies,
The King insults the Goddess as she flies:
' Ill with Jove's daughter bloody fights
    agree,
The field of combat is no scene for thee:
Go, let thy own soft sex employ thy care,
Go, lull the coward, or delude the fair.
Taught by this stroke, renounce the war's
    alarms,
And learn to tremble at the name of arms.'
    Tydides thus. The Goddess, seiz'd with
    dread,
Confused, distracted, from the conflict fled.
To aid her, swift the winged Iris flew, 441
Wrapt in a mist above the warring crew.
The Queen of Love with faded charms she
    found,
Pale was her cheek, and livid look'd the
    wound.
To Mars, who sat remote, they bent their
    way;
Far on the left, with clouds involv'd he
    lay;
Beside him stood his lance, distain'd with
    gore,
And, rein'd with gold, his foaming steeds
    before:
Low at his knee, she begg'd, with stream-
    ing eyes,
Her brother's car, to mount the distant
    skies,   450
And shew'd the wound by fierce Tydides
    giv'n,
A mortal man, who dares encounter Heav'n.
Stern Mars attentive hears the Queen com-
    plain,
And to her hand commits the golden
    rein:
She mounts the seat, oppress'd with silent
    woe,
Driv'n by the Goddess of the Painted Bow.
The lash resounds, the rapid chariot flies,
And in a moment scales the lofty skies.

There stopp'd the car, and there the
  coursers stood,
Fed by fair Iris with ambrosial food.   460
Before her mother, Love's bright Queen
  appears,
O'erwhelm'd with anguish and dissolv'd in
  tears;
She rais'd her in her arms, beheld her
  bleed,
And ask'd what God had wrought this
  guilty deed ?
  Then she: ' This insult from no God I
  found,
An impious mortal gave the daring wound!
Behold the deed of haughty Diomed!
'T was in the son's defence the mother
  bled.
The war with Troy no more the Grecians
  wage;
But with the Gods (th' immortal Gods) en-
  gage.'   470
  Dione then: ' Thy wrongs with patience
  bear,
And share those griefs inferior Powers must
  share;
Unnumber'd woes mankind from us sustain,
And men with woes afflict the Gods again.
The mighty Mars, in mortal fetters bound,
And lodg'd in brazen dungeons under
  ground,
Full thirteen moons imprison'd roar'd in
  vain;
Otus and Ephialtes held the chain;
Perhaps had perish'd, had not Hermes'
  care
Restored the groaning God to upper air. 480
Great Juno's self has borne her weight of
  pain,
Th' imperial partner of the heav'nly reign;
Amphitryon's son infix'd the deadly dart,
And fill'd with anguish her immortal heart.
Ev'n Hell's grim King Alcides' power con-
  fess'd,
The shaft found entrance in his iron breast;
To Jove's high palace for a cure he
  fled,
Pierc'd in his own dominions of the dead;
Where Pæon, sprinkling heav'nly balm
  around,
Assuaged the glowing pangs and closed the
  wound.   490
Rash, impious man! to stain the bless'd
  abodes,
And drench his arrows in the blood of
  Gods!

But thou (tho' Pallas urged thy frantic
  deed),
Whose spear ill-fated makes a Goddess
  bleed,
Know thou, whoe'er with heav'nly power
  contends,
Short is his date, and soon his glory
  ends;
From fields of death when late he shall re-
  tire,
No infant on his knees shall call him sire.
Strong as thou art, some God may yet be
  found,
To stretch thee pale and gasping on the
  ground;   500
Thy distant wife, Ægiale the fair,
Starting from sleep with a distracted air,
Shall rouse thy slaves, and her lost lord de-
  plore,
The brave, the great, the glorious, now no
  more!'
  This said, she wiped from Venus'
  wounded palm
The sacred ichor, and infused the balm.
Juno and Pallas with a smile survey'd,
And thus to Jove began the Blue-eyed
  Maid:
' Permit thy daughter, gracious Jove! to
  tell
How this mischance the Cyprian Queen
  befel.   510
As late she tried with passion to inflame
The tender bosom of a Grecian dame,
Allured the Fair with moving thoughts of
  joy,
To quit her country for some youth of
  Troy;
The clasping zone, with golden buckles
  bound,
Razed her soft hand with this lamented
  wound.'
  The Sire of Gods and men superior
  smiled,
And, calling Venus, thus address'd his
  child:
' Not these, O daughter, are thy proper
  cares,
Thee milder arts befit, and softer wars; 520
Sweet smiles are thine, and kind endearing
  charms;
To Mars and Pallas leave the deeds of
  arms.'
  Thus they in Heav'n. While on the
  plain below
The fierce Tydides charged his Dardan foe,

Flush'd with celestial blood pursued his way,
And fearless dared the threat'ning God of Day;
Already in his hopes he saw him kill'd,
Tho' screen'd behind Apollo's mighty shield.
Thrice, rushing furious, at the Chief he struck;
His blazing buckler thrice Apollo shook: 530
He tried the fourth: when, breaking from the cloud,
A more than mortal voice was heard aloud:
'O son of Tydeus, cease! be wise, and see
How vast the diff'rence of the Gods and thee;
Distance immense! between the Powers that shine
Above, eternal, deathless, and divine,
And mortal man! a wretch of humble birth,
A short-lived reptile in the dust of earth.'
So spoke the God who darts celestial fires;
He dreads his fury, and some steps retires.
Then Phœbus bore the chief of Venus' race 541
To Troy's high fane, and to his holy place;
Latona there and Phœbe heal'd the wound;
With vigour arm'd him, and with glory crown'd.
This done, the patron of the silver bow
A phantom rais'd, the same in shape and show
With great Æneas; such the form he bore,
And such in fight the radiant arms he wore.
Around the spectre bloody wars are waged,
And Greece and Troy with clashing shields engaged. 550
Meantime on Ilion's tower Apollo stood,
And, calling Mars, thus urged the raging God:
'Stern Power of Arms, by whom the mighty fall,
Who bathe in blood, and shake th' embattled wall!
Rise in thy wrath! to Hell's abhorr'd abodes
Despatch yon Greek, and vindicate the Gods.
First rosy Venus felt his brutal rage;
Me next he charged, and dares all Heav'n engage:
The wretch would brave high Heav'n's immortal Sire,
His triple thunder, and his bolts of fire.' 560

The God of Battles issues on the plain,
Stirs all the ranks, and fires the Trojan train:
In form like Acamas, the Thracian guide,
Enraged, to Troy's retiring Chiefs he cried:
'How long, ye sons of Priam! will ye fly,
And unrevenged see Priam's people die?
Still unresisted shall the foe destroy,
And stretch the slaughter to the gates of Troy?
Lo, brave Æneas sinks beneath his wound,
Not godlike Hector more in arms renown'd: 570
Haste all, and take the gen'rous warrior's part.'
He said; new courage swell'd each hero's heart.
Sarpedon first his ardent soul express'd,
And, turn'd to Hector, these bold words address'd:
'Say, Chief, is all thy ancient valour lost?
Where are thy threats, and where thy glorious boast,
That, propp'd alone by Priam's race should stand
Troy's sacred walls, nor need a foreign hand?
Now, now thy country calls her wanted friends,
And the proud vaunt in just derision ends.
Remote they stand, while alien troops engage, 581
Like trembling hounds before the lion's rage.
Far distant hence I held my wide command,
Where foaming Xanthus laves the Lycian land,
With ample wealth (the wish of mortals) bless'd,
A beauteous wife, and infant at her breast;
With those I left whatever dear could be;
Greece, if she conquers, nothing wins from me.
Yet first in fight my Lycian bands I cheer,
And long to meet this mighty man ye fear;
While Hector idle stands, nor bids the brave 591
Their wives, their infants, and their altars, save.
Haste, Warrior, haste! preserve thy threaten'd state;
Or one vast burst of all-involving Fate

Full o'er your towers shall fall, and sweep
    away
Sons, sires, and wives, an undistinguish'd
    prey.
Rouse all thy Trojans, urge thy aids to
    fight;
These claim thy thoughts by day, thy watch
    by night:
With force incessant the brave Greece op-
    pose;
Such care thy friends deserve, and such
    thy foes.' 600
    Stung to the heart the gen'rous Hector
    hears,
But just reproof with decent silence bears.
From his proud car the Prince impetuous
    springs;
On earth he leaps; his brazen armour rings.
Two shining spears are brandish'd in his
    hands;
Thus arm'd, he animates his drooping
    bands,
Revives their ardour, turns their steps
    from flight,
And wakes anew the dying flames of fight.
They turn, they stand: the Greeks their
    fury dare,
Condense their powers, and wait the grow-
    ing war. 610
    As when, on Ceres' sacred floor, the
    swain
Spreads the wide fan to clear the golden
    grain,
And the light chaff, before the breezes
    borne,
Ascends in clouds from off the heapy corn;
The grey dust, rising with collected winds,
Drives o'er the barn, and whitens all the
    hinds:
So, white with dust, the Grecian host ap-
    pears,
From trampling steeds, and thund'ring
    charioteers
The dusky clouds from labour'd earth arise,
And roll in smoking volumes to the skies.
Mars hovers o'er them with his sable
    shield, 621
And adds new horrors to the darken'd field;
Pleas'd with this charge, and ardent to ful-
    fil,
In Troy's defence, Apollo's heav'nly will:
Soon as from fight the Blue-eyed Maid re-
    tires,
Each Trojan bosom with new warmth he
    fires.

And now the God, from forth his sacred
    fane,
Produced Æneas to the shouting train;
Alive, unharm'd, with all his peers around,
Erect he stood, and vig'rous from his
    wound: 630
Inquiries none they made; the dreadful
    day
No pause of words admits, no dull delay;
Fierce Discord storms, Apollo loud ex-
    claims,
Fame calls, Mars thunders, and the field's
    in flames.
Stern Diomed with either Ajax stood,
And great Ulysses, bathed in hostile blood.
Embodied close, the lab'ring Grecian train
The fiercest shock of charging hosts sus-
    tain;
Unmov'd and silent, the whole war they
    wait,
Serenely dreadful, and as fix'd as Fate. 640
So, when th' embattled clouds in dark
    array
Along the skies their gloomy lines display,
When now the North his boist'rous rage
    has spent,
And peaceful sleeps the liquid element,
The low-hung vapours, motionless and still,
Rest on the summits of the shaded hill;
Till the mass scatters as the winds arise,
Dispers'd and broken thro' the ruffled
    skies.
    Nor was the Gen'ral wanting to his train;
From troop to troop he toils thro' all the
    plain: 650
'Ye Greeks, be men! the charge of battle
    bear;
Your brave associates and yourselves re-
    vere!
Let glorious acts more glorious acts in-
    spire,
And catch from breast to breast the noble
    fire!
On valour's side the odds of combat lie,
The brave live glorious, or lamented die:
The wretch who trembles in the field of
    fame,
Meets death, and worse than death, eternal
    shame.'
    These words he seconds with his flying
    lance,
To meet whose point was strong Deicoön's
    chance: 660
Æneas' friend, and in his native place
Honour'd and lov'd like Priam's royal race:

Long had he fought, the foremost in the
   field;
But now the monarch's lance transpierc'd
   his shield:
His shield too weak the furious dart to stay,
Thro' his broad belt the weapon forced its
   way;
The grisly wound dismiss'd his soul to Hell,
His arms around him rattled as he fell.
   Then fierce Æneas, brandishing his blade,
In dust Orsilochus and Crethon laid,   670
Whose sire Diocleus, wealthy, brave, and
   great,
In well-built Pheræ held his lofty seat:
Sprung from Alpheus, plenteous stream!
   that yields
Increase of harvests to the Pylian fields:
He got Orsilochus, Diocleus he,
And these descended in the third degree.
Too early expert in the martial toil,
In sable ships they left their native soil,
T' avenge Atrides; now, untimely slain,
They fell with glory on the Phrygian plain.
So two young mountain lions, nurs'd with
   blood   681
In deep recesses of the gloomy wood,
Rush fearless to the plains, and uncontroll'd
Depopulate the stalls and waste the fold;
Till, pierc'd at distance from their native
   den,
O'erpower'd they fall beneath the force of
   men.
Prostrate on earth their beauteous bodies
   lay,
Like mountain firs, as tall and straight as
   they.
Great Menelaus views with pitying eyes,
Lifts his bright lance, and at the victor
   flies;   690
Mars urged him on; yet, ruthless in his
   hate,
The God but urged him to provoke his fate.
He thus advancing, Nestor's valiant son
Shakes for his danger, and neglects his own;
Struck with the thought, should Helen's
   lord be slain,
And all his country's glorious labours vain.
Already met, the threat'ning heroes stand;
The spears already tremble in their hand;
In rush'd Antilochus, his aid to bring,
And fall or conquer by the Spartan King. 700
These seen, the Dardan backward turn'd
   his course,
Brave as he was, and shunn'd unequal
   force.

The breathless bodies to the Greeks they
   drew;
Then mix in combat, and their toils renew.
   First Pylæmenes, great in battle, bled,
Who, sheathed in brass, the Paphlagonians
   led.
Atrides mark'd him where sublime he stood;
Fix'd in his throat, the jav'lin drank his
   blood.
The faithful Mydon, as he turn'd from
   fight   709
His flying coursers, sunk to endless night:
A broken rock by Nestor's son was thrown;
His bended arm receiv'd the falling stone;
From his numb'd hand the ivory-studded
   reins,
Dropp'd in the dust, are trail'd along the
   plains:
Meanwhile his temples feel a deadly
   wound;
He groans in death, and pond'rous sinks to
   ground:
Deep drove his helmet in the sands, and
   there
The head stood fix'd, the quiv'ring legs in
   air,
Till trampled flat beneath the coursers'
   feet:
The youthful victor mounts his empty seat,
And bears the prize in triumph to the
   fleet.   721
   Great Hector saw, and, raging at the
   view,
Pours on the Greeks; the Trojan troops
   pursue
He fires his host with animating cries,
And brings along the furies of the skies.
Mars, stern destroyer! and Bellona dread,
Flame in the front, and thunder at their
   head:
This swells the tumult and the rage of
   fight;
That shakes a spear that casts a dreadful
   light;
Where Hector march'd, the God of Battles
   shined,   730
Now storm'd before him, and now raged
   behind.
   Tydides paus'd amidst his full career;
Then first the hero's manly breast knew
   fear.
As when some simple swain his cot for-
   sakes,
And wide thro' fens an unknown journey
   takes;

If chance a swelling brook his passage stay,
And foam impervious cross the wand'rer's
  way,
Confused he stops, a length of country past,
Eyes the rough waves, and, tired, returns
  at last:
Amazed no less the great Tydides stands;
He stay'd, and, turning, thus address'd his
  bands: 741
  'No wonder, Greeks, that all to Hector
  yield:
Secure of fav'ring Gods, he takes the field;
His strokes they second, and avert our
  spears:
Behold where Mars in mortal arms ap-
  pears!
Retire then, warriors, but sedate and slow;
Retire, but with your faces to the foe.
Trust not too much your unavailing might;
'T is not with Troy, but with the Gods, ye
  fight.'
  Now near the Greeks the black battalions
  drew; 750
And first, two leaders valiant Hector slew:
His force Anchialus and Mnesthes found,
In ev'ry art of glorious war renown'd:
In the same car the Chiefs to combat
  ride,
And fought united, and united died.
Struck at the sight, the mighty Ajax glows
With thirst of vengeance, and assaults the
  foes.
His massy spear, with matchless fury sent,
Thro' Amphius' belt and heaving belly
  went:
Amphius Apæsus' happy soil possess'd, 760
With herds abounding, and with treasure
  bless'd;
But fate resistless from his country led
The Chief, to perish at his people's head.
Shook with his fall, his brazen armour
  rung,
And fierce, to seize it, conqu'ring Ajax
  sprung;
Around his head an iron tempest rain'd;
A wood of spears his ample shield sus-
  tain'd;
Beneath one foot the yet warm corpse he
  press'd,
And drew his jav'lin from the bleeding
  breast:
He could no more; the show'ring darts de-
  nied 770
To spoil his glitt'ring arms, and plumy
  pride.

Now foes on foes came pouring on the
  fields,
With bristling lances, and compacted
  shields;
Till, in the steely circle straiten'd round,
Forc'd he gives way, and sternly quits the
  ground.
  While thus they strive, Tlepolemus the
  great,
Urged by the force of unresisted Fate,
Burns with desire Sarpedon's strength to
  prove;
Alcides' offspring meets the son of Jove.
Sheathed in bright arms each adverse Chief
  came on, 780
Jove's great descendant, and his greater
  son.
Prepared for combat, ere the lance he
  toss'd,
The daring Rhodian vents his haughty
  boast:
  'What brings this Lycian counsellor so
  far,
To tremble at our arms, not mix in war?
Know thy vain self; nor let their flatt'ry
  move,
Who style thee son of cloud-compelling
  Jove.
How far unlike those Chiefs of race divine!
How vast the diff'rence of their deeds and
  thine!
Jove got such heroes as my sire, whose
  soul 790
No fear could daunt, nor Earth nor Hell
  control.
Troy felt his arm, and yon proud ramparts
  stand,
Rais'd on the ruins of his vengeful hand:
With six small ships, and but a slender
  train,
He left the town a wide deserted plain.
But what art thou, who deedless look'st
  around,
While unrevenged thy Lycians bite the
  ground?
Small aid to Troy thy feeble force can
  be;
But wert thou greater, thou must yield to
  me,
Pierc'd by my spear, to endless darkness
  go! 800
I make this present to the shades below.'
  The son of Hercules, the Rhodian guide,
Thus haughty spoke. The Lycian King
  replied:

' Thy sire, O Prince! o'erturn'd the
    Trojan state,
Whose perjured monarch well deserv'd his
    fate;
Those heav'nly steeds the hero sought so
    far,
False he detain'd, the just reward of war:
Nor so content, the gen'rous Chief defied,
With base reproaches and unmanly pride.
But you, unworthy the high race you boast,
Shall raise my glory when thy own is lost:
Now meet thy fate, and, by Sarpedon slain,
Add one more ghost to Pluto's gloomy
    reign.'   813
He said: both jav'lins at an instant
    flew:
Both struck, both wounded, but Sarpedon's
    slew:
Full in the boaster's neck the weapon
    stood,
Transfix'd his throat, and drank the vital
    blood;
The soul disdainful seeks the caves of
    night,
And his seal'd eyes for ever lose the light.
Yet not in vain, Tlepolemus, was thrown
Thy angry lance; which, piercing to the
    bone   821
Sarpedon's thigh, had robb'd the Chief of
    breath,
But Jove was present, and forbade the
    death.
Borne from the conflict by his Lycian
    throng,
The wounded hero dragg'd the lance along
(His friends, each busied in his sev'ral
    part,
Thro' haste, or danger, had not drawn the
    dart).
The Greeks with slain Tlepolemus retired;
Whose fall Ulysses view'd, with fury fired;
Doubtful if Jove's great son he should pur-
    sue,   830
Or pour his vengeance on the Lycian
    crew.
But Heav'n and Fate the first design with-
    stand,
Nor this great death must grace Ulysses'
    hand.
Minerva drives him on the Lycian train;
Alastor, Cromius, Halius, strew'd the
    plain,
Albander, Prytanis, Noëmon fell;
And numbers more his sword had sent to
    Hell,

But Hector saw; and, furious at the sight,
Rush'd terrible amidst the ranks of fight.
With joy Sarpedon view'd the wish'd re-
    lief,   840
And faint, lamenting, thus implored the
    Chief:
' Oh, suffer not the foe to bear away
My helpless corpse, an unassisted prey!
If I, unbless'd, must see my son no more,
My much-lov'd consort, and my native
    shore,
Yet let me die in Ilion's sacred wall;
Troy, in whose cause I fell, shall mourn
    my fall.'
He said, nor Hector to the Chief replies,
But shakes his plume, and fierce to combat
    flies,
Swift as a whirlwind drives the scatt'ring
    foes,   850
And dyes the ground with purple as he
    goes.
Beneath a beech, Jove's consecrated
    shade,
His mournful friends divine Sarpedon
    laid:
Brave Pelagon, his fav'rite Chief, was
    nigh,
Who wrench'd the jav'lin from his sinewy
    thigh.
The fainting soul stood ready wing'd for
    flight,
And o'er his eyeballs swam the shades of
    night;
But Boreas rising fresh, with gentle breath,
Recall'd his spirit from the gates of death.
The gen'rous Greeks recede with tardy
    pace,   860
Tho' Mars and Hector thunder in their
    face;
None turn their backs to mean ignoble
    flight,
Slow they retreat, and, ev'n retreating,
    fight.
Who first, who last, by Mars' and Hector's
    hand,
Stretch'd in their blood, lay gasping on the
    sand ?
Teuthras the great, Orestes the renown'd
For managed steeds, and Trechus, press'd
    the ground;
Next Œnomaus, and Œnops' offspring
    died;
Oresbius last fell groaning at their side:
Oresbius, in his painted mitre gay,   870
In fat Bœotia held his wealthy sway;

Where lakes surround low Hyle's wat'ry
plain;
A Prince and people studious of their gain.
The carnage Juno from the skies sur-
vey'd,
And touch'd with grief, bespoke the Blue-
eyed Maid:
'Oh sight accurs'd! shall faithless Troy
prevail,
And shall our promise to our people fail?
How vain the word to Menelaus giv'n
By Jove's great daughter and the Queen
of Heav'n,
Beneath his arms that Priam's towers
should fall, 880
If warring Gods for ever guard the wall!
Mars, red with slaughter, aids our hated
foes:
Haste, let us arm, and force with force op-
pose!'
She spoke; Minerva burns to meet the
war:
And now Heav'n's Empress calls her blaz-
ing car.
At her command rush forth the steeds
divine;
Rich with immortal gold their trappings
shine.
Bright Hebe waits; by Hebe, ever young,
The whirling wheels are to the chariot
hung. 889
On the bright axle turns the bidden wheel
Of sounding brass; the polish'd axle steel.
Eight brazen spokes in radiant order flame;
The circles gold, of uncorrupted frame,
Such as the Heav'ns produce: and round
the gold
Two brazen rings of work divine were
roll'd.
The bossy naves of solid silver shone;
Braces of gold suspend the moving throne:
The car behind an arching figure bore;
The bending concave form'd an arch before.
Silver the beam, th' extended yoke was
gold, 900
And golden reins th' immortal coursers
hold.
Herself, impatient, to the ready car
The coursers joins, and breathes revenge
and war.
Pallas disrobes; her radiant veil untied,
With flowers adorn'd, with art diversified
(The labour'd veil her heav'nly fingers
wove),
Flows on the pavement of the court of Jove.

Now Heav'n's dread arms her mighty limbs
invest,
Jove's cuirass blazes on her ample breast;
Deck'd in sad triumph for the mournful
field, 910
O'er her broad shoulders hangs his horrid
shield,
Dire, black, tremendous! round the margin
roll'd,
A fringe of serpents hissing guards the
gold:
Here all the terrors of grim war appear,
Here rages Force, here tremble Flight and
Fear,
Here storm'd Contention, and here Fury
frown'd,
And the dire orb portentous Gorgon
crown'd.
The massy golden helm she next assumes,
That dreadful nods with four o'ershading
plumes:
So vast, the broad circumference contains
A hundred armies on a hundred plains. 921
The Goddess thus th' imperial car ascends;
Shook by her arm the mighty jav'lin bends,
Pond'rous and huge; that, when her fury
burns,
Proud tyrants humbles, and whole hosts
o'erturns.
Swift at the scourge th' ethereal coursers
fly,
While the smooth chariot cuts the liquid sky:
Heav'n's gates spontaneous open to the
Powers,
Heav'n's golden gates, kept by the winged
Hours;
Commission'd in alternate watch they
stand, 930
The sun's bright portals and the skies com-
mand,
Involve in clouds th' eternal gates of day,
Or the dark barrier roll with ease away.
The sounding hinges ring: on either side
The gloomy volumes, pierc'd with light,
divide.
The chariot mounts, where deep in ambient
skies
Confused, Olympus' hundred heads arise;
Where far apart the Thund'rer fills his
throne,
O'er all the Gods, superior and alone.
There with her snowy hand the Queen re-
strains 940
The fiery steeds, and thus to Jove com-
plains:

'O Sire! can no resentment touch thy
    soul?
Can Mars rebel, and does no thunder roll?
What lawless rage on yon forbidden plain!
What rash destruction! and what heroes
    slain!
Venus, and Phœbus with the dreadful bow,
Smile on the slaughter, and enjoy my woe.
Mad, furious Power! whose unrelenting
    mind
No God can govern, and no justice bind.
Say, mighty Father! shall we scourge his
    pride,   950
And drive from fight th' impetuous homi-
    cide?'
    To whom assenting, thus the Thund'rer
    said:
'Go! and the great Minerva be thy aid.
To tame the monster-God Minerva knows,
And oft afflicts his brutal breast with
    woes.'
He said: Saturnia, ardent to obey,
Lash'd her white steeds along th' aërial
    way.
Swift down the steep of Heav'n the chariot
    rolls,
Between th' expanded earth and starry
    poles.
Far as a shepherd from some point on high,
O'er the wide main extends his boundless
    eye;   961
Thro' such a space of air, with thund'ring
    sound,
At ev'ry leap th' immortal coursers bound.
Troy now they reach'd, and touch'd those
    banks divine
Where silver Simoïs and Scamander join.
There Juno stopp'd, and (her fair steeds
    unloos'd)
Of air condensed a vapour circumfused:
For these, impregnate with celestial dew,
On Simoïs' brink ambrosial herbage grew.
Thence to relieve the fainting Argive
    throng,   970
Smooth as the sailing doves, they glide along.
    The best and bravest of the Grecian
    band
(A warlike circle) round Tydides stand:
Such was their look as lions bathed in
    blood,
Or foaming boars, the terror of the wood.
Heav'n's Empress mingles with the mortal
    crowd,
And shouts, in Stentor's sounding voice,
    aloud:

Stentor the strong, endued with brazen
    lungs,
Whose throat surpass'd the force of fifty
    tongues:
    'Inglorious Argives! to your race a
    shame,   980
And only men in figure and in name!
Once from the walls your tim'rous foes en-
    gaged,
While fierce in war divine Achilles raged;
Now, issuing fearless, they possess the
    plain,
Now win the shores, and scarce the seas
    remain.'
    Her speech new fury to their hearts con-
    vey'd;
While near Tydides stood th' Athenian
    Maid:
The King beside his panting steeds she
    found,
O'erspent with toil, reposing on the ground:
To cool his glowing wound he sat apart   990
(The wound inflicted by the Lycian dart);
Large drops of sweat from all his limbs
    descend,
Beneath his pond'rous shield his sinews
    bend,
Whose ample belt, that o'er his shoulder
    lay,
He eased; and wash'd the clotted gore
    away.
The Goddess, leaning o'er the bending yoke
Beside his coursers, thus her silence broke:
    'Degen'rate Prince! and not of Tydeus'
    kind:
Whose little body lodg'd a mighty mind;
Foremost he press'd in glorious toils to
    share,   1000
And scarce refrain'd when I forbade the
    war.
Alone, unguarded, once he dared to go,
And feast encircled by the Theban foe;
There braved and vanquish'd many a
    hardy knight;
Such nerves I gave him, and such force in
    fight.
Thou too no less hast been my constant
    care;
Thy hands I arm'd, and sent thee forth to
    war:
But thee or fear deters or sloth detains;
No drop of all thy father warms thy veins.'
    The Chief thus answer'd mild: 'Im-
    mortal Maid!   1010
I own thy presence, and confess thy aid.

Not fear, thou know'st, withholds me from
    the plains,
Nor sloth hath seiz'd me, but thy word re-
    strains:
From warring Gods thou bad'st me turn
    my spear,
And Venus only found resistance here.
Hence, Goddess ! heedful of thy high com-
    mands,
Loth I gave way, and warn'd our Argive
    bands:
For Mars, the homicide, these eyes beheld,
With slaughter red, and raging round the
    field.'
    Then thus Minerva: 'Brave Tydides,
    hear!   1020
Not Mars himself, nor aught immortal,
    fear.
Full on the God impel thy foaming horse:
Pallas commands, and Pallas lends thee
    force.
Rash, furious, blind, from these to those he
    flies,
And ev'ry side of wavering combat tries:
Large promise makes, and breaks the
    promise made;
Now gives the Grecians, now the Trojans
    aid.'
    She said, and to the steeds approaching
    near,
Drew from his seat the martial charioteer.
The vig'rous Power the trembling car
    ascends,   1030
Fierce for revenge; and Diomed attends.
The groaning axle bent beneath the load;
So great a Hero, and so great a God.
She snatch'd the reins, she lash'd with all
    her force,
And full on Mars impell'd the foaming
    horse:
But first to hide her heav'nly visage spread
Black Orcus' helmet o'er her radiant head.
    Just then gigantic Periphas lay slain,
The strongest warrior of th' Ætolian train;
The God who slew him leaves his prostrate
    prize   1040
Stretch'd where he fell, and at Tydides flies.
Now rushing fierce, in equal arms, appear
The daring Greek, the dreadful God of
    War !
Full at the Chief, above his courser's head,
From Mars's arm th' enormous weapon fled:
Pallas opposed her hand, and caus'd to
    glance
Far from the car the strong immortal lance.

Then threw the force of Tydeus' warlike
    son;
The jav'lin hiss'd; the Goddess urged it on:
Where the broad cincture girt his armour
    round,   1050
It pierc'd the God: his groin receiv'd the
    wound.
From the rent skin the warrior tugs again
The smoking steel. Mars bellows with the
    pain:
Loud, as the roar encount'ring armies
    yield,
When shouting millions shake the thun-
    d'ring field.
Both armies start, and trembling gaze
    around;
And Earth and Heaven rebellow to the
    sound.
As vapours blown by Auster's sultry
    breath,
Pregnant with plagues and shedding seeds
    of death,
Beneath the rage of burning Sirius rise,
Choke the parch'd earth, and blacken all
    the skies;   1061
In such a cloud the God, from combat
    driv'n,
High o'er the dusty whirlwind scales the
    Heav'n.
Wild with his pain, he sought the bright
    abodes,
There sullen sat beneath the Sire of Gods,
Shew'd the celestial blood, and with a
    groan
Thus pour'd his plaints before th' immortal
    throne:
    'Can Jove, supine, flagitious facts sur-
    vey,
And brook the furies of this daring day ?
For mortal men celestial Powers engage,
And Gods on Gods exert eternal rage. 1071
From thee, O Father! all these ills we
    bear,
And thy fell daughter with the shield and
    spear:
Thou gavest that fury to the realms of
    light,
Pernicious, wild, regardless of the right.
All Heav'n beside reveres thy sov'reign
    sway,
Thy voice we hear, and thy behests obey:
'T is hers t' offend, and ev'n offending,
    share
Thy breast, thy counsels, thy distinguish'd
    care·

So boundless she, and thou so partial grown,
Well may we deem the wondrous birth thy
   own.   1081
Now frantic Diomed, at her command,
Against th' immortals lifts his raging hand:
The heav'nly Venus first his fury found,
Me next encount'ring, me he dared to
   wound;
Vanquish'd I fled: ev'n I, the God of Fight,
From mortal madness scarce was saved by
   flight.
Else hadst thou seen me sink on yonder
   plain,
Heap'd round, and heaving under loads of
   slain;   1089
Or, pierc'd with Grecian darts, for ages lie,
Condemn'd to pain, tho' fated not to die.'
   Him thus upbraiding, with a wrathful
   look
The Lord of Thunders view'd, and stern
   bespoke:
'To me, perfidious! this lamenting strain?
Of lawless force shall lawless Mars com-
   plain?
Of all the Gods who tread the spangled
   skies,
Thou most unjust, most odious in our eyes!
Inhuman discord is thy dire delight,
The waste of slaughter, and the rage of
   fight:
No bound, no law, thy fiery temper quells,
And all thy mother in thy soul rebels. 1101
In vain our threats, in vain our power, we
   use:
She gives th' example, and her son pur-
   sues.
Yet long th' inflicted pangs thou shalt not
   mourn,
Sprung since thou art from Jove, and
   heav'nly born.
Else, singed with lightning, hadst thou
   hence been thrown,
Where chain'd on burning rocks the Titans
   groan.'
   Thus he who shakes Olympus with his
   nod;
Then gave to Pæon's care the bleeding
   God.
With gentle hand the balm he pour'd
   around,   1110
And heal'd th' immortal flesh, and closed
   the wound.
As when the fig's press'd juice, infused in
   cream,
To curds coagulates the liquid stream,

Sudden the fluids fix, the parts combin'd;
Such and so soon th' ethereal texture join'd.
Cleans'd from the dust and gore, fair Hebe
   dress'd
His mighty limbs in an immortal vest.
Glorious he sat, in majesty restor'd,
Fast by the throne of Heav'n's superior
   Lord.
Juno and Pallas mount the blest abodes,
Their task perform'd, and mix among the
   Gods.   1121

BOOK VI

THE EPISODES OF GLAUCUS AND DIOMED,
AND OF HECTOR AND ANDROMACHE

THE ARGUMENT

The Gods having left the field, the Grecians
prevail. Helenus, the chief augur of Troy,
commands Hector to return to the city, in
order to appoint a solemn procession of the
Queen and the Trojan matrons to the temple
of Minerva, to entreat her to remove Diomed
from the fight. The battle relaxing during
the absence of Hector, Glaucus and Diomed
have an interview between the two armies;
where, coming to the knowledge of the
friendship and hospitality past between their
ancestors, they make exchange of their arms.
Hector, having performed the orders of
Helenus, prevailed upon Paris to return to
the battle, and taken a tender leave of his
wife Andromache, hastens again to the
field.
The scene is first in the field of battle, between
the river Simoïs and Scamander, and then
changes to Troy.

Now Heav'n forsakes the fight; th' im-
   mortals yield
To human force and human skill the field:
Dark showers of jav'lins fly from foes to
   foes;
Now here, now there, the tide of combat
   flows;
While Troy's famed streams, that bound
   the deathful plain,
On either side run purple to the main.
   Great Ajax first to conquest led the way,
Broke the thick ranks, and turn'd the
   doubtful day.
The Thracian Acamas his falchion found,
And hew'd th' enormous giant to the
   ground;   10

His thund'ring arm a deadly stroke im-
    press'd
Where the black horse-hair nodded o'er his
    crest:
Fix'd in his front the brazen weapon lies,
And seals in endless shades his swimming
    eyes.
Next Teuthras' son distain'd the sands
    with blood,
Axylus, hospitable, rich, and good:
In fair Arisba's walls (his native place)
He held his seat; a friend to human race.
Fast by the road, his ever-open door
Obliged the wealthy, and reliev'd the
    poor.   20
To stern Tydides now he falls a prey,
No friend to guard him in the dreadful
    day!
Breathless the good man fell, and by his
    side
His faithful servant, Old Calesius, died.
By great Euryalus was Dresus slain,
And next he laid Opheltius on the plain.
Two twins were near, bold, beautiful, and
    young,
From a fair Naiad and Bucolion sprung
(Laömedon's white flocks Bucolion fed,
That monarch's first-born by a foreign
    bed;   30
In secret woods he won the Naiad's grace,
And two fair infants crown'd his strong
    embrace):
Here dead they lay in all their youthful
    charms;
The ruthless victor stripp'd their shining
    arms.
Astyalus by Polypœtes fell;
Ulysses' spear Pidytes sent to Hell;
By Teucer's shaft brave Aretaön bled,
And Nestor's son laid stern Ablerus dead;
Great Agamemnon, leader of the brave,
The mortal wound of rich Elatus gave,   40
Who held in Pedasus his proud abode,
And till'd the banks where silver Satnio
    flow'd.
Melanthius by Eurypylus was slain;
And Phylacus from Leitus flies in vain.
Unbless'd Adrastus next at mercy lies
Beneath the Spartan spear, a living prize.
Scared with the din and tumult of the fight,
His headlong steeds, precipitate in flight,
Rush'd on a tamarisk's strong trunk, and
    broke
The shatter'd chariot from the crooked
    yoke: 50

Wide o'er the field, resistless as the wind,
For Troy they fly, and leave their lord be-
    hind.
Prone on his face he sinks beside the wheel:
Atrides o'er him shakes his vengeful steel;
The fallen Chief in suppliant posture press'd
The victor's knees, and thus his prayer
    address'd:
    'Oh spare my youth, and for the life I
        owe
Large gifts of price my father shall be-
    stow:
When Fame shall tell, that not in battle
    slain
Thy hollow ships his captive son detain, 60
Rich heaps of brass shall in thy tent be
    told,
And steel well-temper'd, and persuasive
    gold.'
    He said: compassion touch'd the hero's
        heart;
He stood suspended with the lifted dart:
As pity pleaded for his vanquish'd prize,
Stern Agamemnon swift to vengeance flies,
And furious thus: 'Oh impotent of mind!
Shall these, shall these, Atrides' mercy
    find ?
Well hast thou known proud Troy's per-
    fidious land,
And well her natives merit at thy hand! 70
Not one of all the race, nor sex, nor age,
Shall save a Trojan from our boundless
    rage:
Ilion shall perish whole, and bury all;
Her babes, her infants at the breast, shall
    fall.
A dreadful lesson of exampled fate,
To warn the nations, and to curb the great.'
    The Monarch spoke; the words, with
        warmth address'd,
To rigid justice steel'd his brother's breast.
Fierce from his knees the hapless Chief he
    thrust;
The Monarch's jav'lin stretch'd him in the
    dust.   80
Then, pressing with his foot his panting
    heart,
Forth from the slain he tugg'd the reeking
    dart.
Old Nestor saw, and rous'd the warriors'
    rage;
'Thus, heroes! thus the vig'rous combat
    wage !
No son of Mars descend, for servile gains,
To touch the booty, while a foe remains.

Behold yon glitt'ring host, your future
    spoil!
First gain the conquest, then reward the
    toil.'
    And now had Greece eternal Fame
        acquired,
And frighted Troy within her walls re-
    tired;   90
Had not sage Helenus her state redress'd,
Taught by the Gods that mov'd his sacred
    breast:
Where Hector stood, with great Æneas
    join'd,
The seer reveal'd the counsels of his mind:
    'Ye gen'rous Chief! on whom th' im-
        mortals lay
The cares and glories of this doubtful day,
On whom your aids, your country's hopes
    depend,
Wise to consult, and active to defend!
Here, at our gates, your brave efforts
    unite,
Turn back the routed, and forbid the
    flight;   100
Ere yet their wives' soft arms the cowards
    gain,
The sport and insult of the hostile train.
When your commands have hearten'd
    ev'ry band,
Ourselves, here fix'd, will make the dan-
    gerous stand;
Press'd as we are, and sore of former
    fight,
These straits demand our last remains of
    might.
Meanwhile, thou, Hector, to the town
    retire
And teach our mother what the Gods re-
    quire:
Direct the Queen to lead th' assembled
    train
Of Troy's chief matrons to Minerva's
    fane;   110
Unbar the sacred gates, and seek the
    Power
With offer'd vows, in Ilion's topmost
    tower.
The largest mantle her rich wardrobes
    hold,
Most prized for art, and labour'd o'er with
    gold,
Before the Goddess' honour'd knees be
    spread;
And twelve young heifers to her altars
    led.

If so the Power atoned by fervent prayer,
Our wives, our infants, and our city spare,
And far avert Tydides' wasteful ire,
That mows whole troops, and makes all
    Troy retire.   120
Not thus Achilles taught our hosts to
    dread,
Sprung tho' he was from more than mortal
    bed;
Not thus resistless ruled the stream of
    fight,
In rage unbounded, and unmatch'd in
    might.'
    Hector obedient heard; and, with a
        bound,
Leap'd from his trembling chariot to the
    ground;
Thro' all his host, inspiring force, he flies,
And bids the thunder of the battle rise.
With rage recruited the bold Trojans glow,
And turn the tide of conflict on the foe: 130
Fierce in the front he shakes two dazzling
    spears;
All Greece recedes, and 'midst her triumph
    fears:
Some God, they thought, who ruled the
    fate of wars,
Shot down avenging from the vault of
    stars.
    Then thus, aloud: 'Ye dauntless Dar-
        dans, hear!
And you whom distant nations send to war;
Be mindful of the strength your fathers
    bore;
Be still yourselves, and Hector asks no
    more.
One hour demands me in the Trojan wall,
To bid our altars flame, and victims
    fall: 140
Nor shall, I trust, the matrons' holy train,
And rev'rend elders, seek the Gods in vain.'
    This said, with ample strides the hero
        pass'd;
The shield's large orb behind his shoulder
    cast,
His neck o'ershading, to his ankle hung;
And as he march'd the brazen buckler
    rung.
    Now paus'd the battle (godlike Hector
        gone),
When daring Glaucus and great Tydeus' son
Between both armies met; the Chiefs from
    far
Observ'd each other, and had mark'd for
    war.   150

Near as they drew, Tydides thus began:
'What art thou, boldest of the race of
man ?
Our eyes, till now, that aspect ne'er beheld,
Where fame is reap'd amid th' embattled
field;
Yet far before the troops thou darest ap-
pear,
And meet a lance the fiercest heroes fear.
Unhappy they, and born of luckless sires,
Who tempt our fury when Minerva fires!
But if from Heav'n, celestial, thou de-
scend,
Know, with immortals we no more con-
tend.   160
Not long Lycurgus view'd the golden
light,
That daring man who mix'd with Gods in
fight;
Bacchus, and Bacchus' votaries, he drove
With brandish'd steel from Nyssa's sacred
grove;
Their consecrated spears lay scatter'd
round,
With curling vines and twisted ivy bound;
While Bacchus headlong sought the briny
flood,
And Thetis' arms received the trembling
God.
Nor fail'd the crime th' immortals' wrath
to move
(Th' immortals bless'd with endless ease
above);   170
Deprived of sight, by their avenging doom,
Cheerless he breathed, and wander'd in the
gloom:
Then sunk unpitied to the dire abodes,
A wretch accurs'd, and hated by the
Gods!
I brave not Heav'n; but if the fruits of
earth
Sustain thy life, and human be thy birth,
Bold as thou art, too prodigal of breath,
Approach, and enter the dark gates of
death.'
'What, or from whence I am, or who my
sire '
(Replied the Chief), 'can Tydeus' son in-
quire ?   180
Like leaves on trees the race of man is
found,
Now green in youth, now with'ring on the
ground:
Another race the foll'wing spring supplies,
They fall successive, and successive rise;

So generations in their course decay,
So flourish these, when those are past
away.
But if thou still persist to search my birth,
Then hear a tale that fills the spacious
earth:
'A city stands on Argos' utmost bound
(Argos the fair, for warlike steeds re-
nown'd);   190
Æolian Sisyphus, with wisdom bless'd,
In ancient time the happy walls possess'd,
Then call'd Ephyre: Glaucus was his
son;
Great Glaucus, father of Bellerophon,
Who o'er the sons of men in beauty shined,
Loved for that valour which preserves
mankind.
Then mighty Prœtus Argos' sceptre
sway'd,
Whose hard commands Bellerophon obey'd.
With direful jealousy the monarch raged,
And the brave Prince in numerous toils en-
gaged,   200
For him, Antea burn'd with lawless flame,
And strove to tempt him from the paths of
fame:
In vain she tempted the relentless youth,
Endued with wisdom, sacred fear, and
truth.
Fired at his scorn, the Queen to Prœtus
fled,
And begg'd revenge for her insulted bed:
Incens'd he heard, resolving on his fate;
But hospitable laws restrain'd his hate:
To Lycia the devoted youth he sent,
With tablets seal'd, that told his dire in-
tent.   210
Now, bless'd by ev'ry Power who guards
the good,
The Chief arrived at Xanthus' silver flood:
There Lycia's Monarch paid him honours
due;
Nine days he feasted, and nine bulls he
slew.
But when the tenth bright morning orient
glow'd
The faithful youth his Monarch's mandate
shew'd:
The fatal tablets, till that instant seal'd,
The deathful secret to the King reveal'd.
First, dire Chimæra's conquest was en-
join'd;
A mingled monster, of no mortal kind;   220
Behind, a dragon's fiery tail was spread;
A goat's rough body bore a lion's head;

Her pitchy nostrils flaky flames expire;
Her gaping throat emits infernal fire.
  'This pest he slaughter'd (for he read
      the skies,
And trusted Heav'n's informing pro-
      digies);
Then met in arms the Solymæan crew
(Fiercest of men), and those the warrior
      slew.
Next the bold Amazons' whole force de-
      fied;
And conquer'd still, for Heav'n was on his
      side.   230
  'Nor ended here his toils: his Lycian
      foes,
At his return, a treach'rous ambush rose,
With levell'd spears along the winding
      shore:
There fell they breathless, and return'd no
      more.
  'At length the Monarch with repentant
      grief
Confess'd the Gods, and god-descended
      Chief;
His daughter gave, the stranger to detain,
With half the honours of his ample reign.
The Lycians grant a chosen space of
      ground,
With woods, with vineyards, and with har-
      vests crown'd.   240
There long the Chief his happy lot possess'd,
With two brave sons and one fair daughter
      bless'd:
(Fair ev'n in heav'nly eyes; her fruitful
      love
Crown'd with Sarpedon's birth th' embrace
      of Jove).
But when at last, distracted in his mind,
Forsook by Heav'n, forsaking human kind,
Wide o'er th' Aleian field he chose to
      stray,
A long, forlorn, uncomfortable way !
Woes heap'd on woes consumed his wasted
      heart;
His beauteous daughter fell by Phœbe's
      dart;   250
His eldest-born by raging Mars was slain,
In combat on the Solymæan plain.
Hippolochus survived; from him I came,
The honour'd author of my birth and
      name;
By his decree I sought the Trojan town,
By his instructions learn to win renown;
To stand the first in worth as in command,
To add new honours to my native land;

Before my eyes my mighty sires to place,
And emulate the glories of our race.'   260
  He spoke, and transport fill'd Tydides'
      heart;
In earth the gen'rous warrior fix'd his
      dart,
Then friendly, thus, the Lycian prince ad-
      dress'd:
'Welcome, my brave hereditary guest!
Thus ever let us meet with kind embrace,
Nor stain the sacred friendship of our
      race.
Know, Chief, our grandsires have been
      guests of old,
Œneus the strong, Bellerophon the bold;
Our ancient seat his honour'd presence
      graced,
Where twenty days in genial rites he
      pass'd.   270
The parting heroes mutual presents left;
A golden goblet was thy grandsire's gift;
Œneus a belt of matchless work bestow'd,
That rich with Tyrian dye refulgent
      glow'd
(This from his pledge I learn'd, which,
      safely stored
Among my treasures, still adorns my
      board:
For Tydeus left me young, when Thebes'
      wall
Beheld the sons of Greece untimely fall).
Mindful of this, in friendship let us
      join;
If Heav'n our steps to foreign lands in-
      cline,   280
My guest in Argos thou, and I in Lycia
      thine.
Enough of Trojans to this lance shall
      yield,
In the full harvest of yon ample field;
Enough of Greeks shall dye thy spear with
      gore;
But thou and Diomed be foes no more.
Now change we arms, and prove to either
      host
We guard the friendship of the line we
      boast.'
  Thus having said, the gallant Chiefs
      alight,
Their hands they join, their mutual faith
      they plight;
Brave Glaucus then each narrow thought
      resign'd   290
(Jove warm'd his bosom and enlarged his
      mind);

For Diomed's brass arms, of mean device,
For which nine oxen paid (a vulgar
 price),
He gave his own, of gold divinely wrought;
A hundred beeves the shining purchase
 bought.
Meantime the guardian of the Trojan
 state,
Great Hector, enter'd at the Scæan gate.
Beneath the beech-trees' consecrated
 shades,
The Trojan matrons and the Trojan maids
Around him flock'd, all press'd with pious
 care   300
For husbands, brothers, sons, engaged in
 war.
He bids the train in long procession go,
And seek the Gods, t' avert th' impending
 woe.
And now to Priam's stately courts he
 came,
Rais'd on arch'd columns of stupendous
 frame;
O'er these a range of marble structure
 runs;
The rich pavilions of his fifty sons,
In fifty chambers lodg'd: and rooms of
 state
Opposed to those, where Priam's daughters
 sate:
Twelve domes for them and their lov'd
 spouses shone,   310
Of equal beauty, and of polish'd stone.
Hither great Hector pass'd, nor pass'd
 unseen
Of royal Hecuba, his mother Queen
(With her Laödicè, whose beauteous face
Surpass'd the nymphs of Troy's illustrious
 race).
Long in a strict embrace she held her
 son,
And press'd his hand, and tender thus
 begun:
'O Hector! say, what great occasion
 calls
My son from fight, when Greece surrounds
 our walls ?
Com'st thou to supplicate th' almighty
 Power,   320
With lifted hands from Ilion's lofty tower ?
Stay, till I bring the cup with Bacchus
 crown'd,
In Jove's high name, to sprinkle on the
 ground,
And pay due vows to all the Gods around.

Then with a plenteous draught refresh thy
 soul,
And draw new spirits from the gen'rous
 bowl;
Spent as thou art with long laborious fight,
The brave defender of thy country's right.'
'Far hence be Bacchus' gifts' (the
 Chief rejoin'd);
'Inflaming wine, pernicious to mankind, 330
Unnerves the limbs, and dulls the noble
 mind.
Let Chiefs abstain, and spare the sacred
 juice,
To sprinkle to the Gods, its better use.
By me that holy office were profaned;
Ill fits it me, with human gore distain'd,
To the pure skies these horrid hands to
 raise,
Or offer Heav'n's great Sire polluted
 praise.
You with your matrons, go, a spotless
 train !
And burn rich odours in Minerva's fane.
The largest mantle your full wardrobes
 hold,   340
Most prized for art, and labour'd o'er with
 gold,
Before the Goddess' honour'd knees be
 spread,
And twelve young heifers to her altar
 led.
So may the Power, atoned by fervent
 prayer,
Our wives, our infants, and our city spare,
And far avert Tydides' wasteful ire,
Who mows whole troops, and makes all
 Troy retire.
Be this, O mother, your religious care;
I go to rouse soft Paris to the war;
If yet, not lost to all the sense of shame, 350
The recreant warrior hear the voice of
 Fame.
Oh would kind earth the hateful wretch
 embrace,
That pest of Troy, that ruin of our race !
Deep to the dark abyss might he descend,
Troy yet should flourish, and my sorrows
 end.'
 This heard, she gave command; and
 summon'd came
Each noble matron, and illustrious dame.
The Phrygian Queen to her rich wardrobe
 went,
Where treasured odours breathed a costly
 scent.

There lay the vestures of no vulgar art, 360
Sidonian maids embroider'd ev'ry part,
Whom from soft Sidon youthful Paris bore,
With Helen touching on the Tyrian shore.
Here as the Queen revolv'd with careful
    eyes
The various textures and the various dyes.
She chose a veil that shone superior far,
And glowed refulgent as the morning star,
Herself with this the long procession
    leads;
The train majestically slow proceeds.
Soon as to Ilion's topmost tower they
    come,   370
And awful reach the high Palladian dome,
Antenor's consort, fair Theano, waits
As Pallas' priestess, and unbars the gates.
With hands uplifted, and imploring eyes,
They fill the dome with supplicating cries.
The priestess then the shining veil dis-
    plays,
Placed on Minerva's knees, and thus she
    prays:
  'Oh awful Goddess! ever-dreadful Maid,
Troy's strong defence, unconquer'd Pallas,
    aid!
Break thou Tydides' spear, and let him
    fall   380
Prone on the dust before the Trojan wall.
So twelve young heifers, guiltless of the
    yoke,
Shall fill thy temple with a grateful
    smoke.
But thou, atoned by penitence and prayer,
Ourselves, our infants, and our city spare!'
So pray'd the priestess in her holy fane;
So vow'd the matrons, but they vow'd in
    vain.
  While these appear before the Power
    with prayers,
Hector to Paris' lofty dome repairs.
Himself the mansion rais'd, from every
    part   390
Assembling architects of matchless art.
Near Priam's court and Hector's palace
    stands
The pompous structure, and the town com-
    mands.
A spear the hero bore of wondrous
    strength,
Of full ten cubits was the lance's length;
The steely point with golden ringlets
    join'd,
Before him brandish'd, at each motion
    shined.

Thus ent'ring, in the glitt'ring rooms he
    found
His brother-Chief, whose useless arms lay
    round.
His eyes delighting with their splendid
    show,   400
Bright'ning the shield, and polishing the
    bow.
Beside him Helen with her virgins stands,
Guides their rich labours, and instructs
    their hands.
  Him thus inactive, with an ardent look
The Prince beheld, and high resenting
    spoke:
' Thy hate to Troy is this the time to
    shew ?
(Oh wretch ill-fated, and thy country's
    foe!)
Paris and Greece against us both conspire,
Thy close resentment, and their vengeful
    ire.
For thee great Ilion's guardian heroes
    fall,   410
Till heaps of dead alone defend her wall;
For thee the soldier bleeds, the matron
    mourns,
And wasteful war in all its fury burns.
Ungrateful man! deserves not this thy
    care,
Our troops to hearten, and our toils to
    share ?
Rise, or behold the conqu'ring flames as-
    cend,
And all the Phrygian glories at an end.'
  ' Brother, 't is just ' (replied the beauteous
    youth),
' Thy free remonstrance proves thy worth
    and truth:
Yet charge my absence less, oh gen'rous
    Chief !   420
On hate to Troy, than conscious shame
    and grief.
Here, hid from human eyes, thy brother
    sate,
And mourn'd in secret his and Ilion's fate.
'T is now enough: now glory spreads her
    charms,
And beauteous Helen calls her Chief to
    arms.
Conquest to-day my happier sword may
    bless,
'T is man's to fight, but Heav'n's to give
    success.
But while I arm, contain thy ardent mind;
Or go, and Paris shall not lag behind.'

He said, nor answer'd Priam's warlike
son; 430
When Helen thus with lowly grace begun:
'Oh gen'rous brother! if the guilty
dame
That caus'd these woes deserves a sister's
name !
Would Heav'n, ere all these dreadful deeds
were done,
The day that shew'd me to the golden sun
Had seen my death! Why did not whirl-
winds bear
The fatal infant to the fowls of air ?
Why sunk I not beneath the whelming
tide,
And midst the roarings of the waters
died ?
Heav'n fill'd up all my ills, and I ac-
curst 440
Bore all, and Paris of those ills the
worst.
Helen at least a braver spouse might claim,
Warm'd with some Virtue, some regard of
Fame !
Now, tired with toils, thy fainting limbs
recline,
With toils sustain'd for Paris' sake and
mine:
The Gods have link'd our miserable doom,
Our present woe and infamy to come:
Wide shall it spread, and last thro' ages
long,
Example sad! and theme of future song.'
The Chief replied: 'This Time forbids
to rest: 450
The Trojan bands, by hostile fury press'd,
Demand their Hector, and his arm re-
quire;
The combat urges, and my soul 's on fire.
Urge thou thy knight to march where
glory calls,
And timely join me, ere I leave the walls.
Ere yet I mingle in the direful fray,
My wife, my infant, claim a moment's
stay:
This day (perhaps the last that sees me
here)
Demands a parting word, a tender tear:
This day some God, who hates our Trojan
land, 460
May vanquish Hector by a Grecian hand.'
He said, and pass'd with sad presaging
heart
To seek his spouse, his soul's far dearer
part;

At home he sought her, but he sought in
vain:
She, with one maid of all her menial train,
Had thence retired; and, with her second
joy,
The young Astyanax, the hope of Troy,
Pensive she stood on Ilion's tow'ry height,
Beheld the war, and sicken'd at the sight;
There her sad eyes in vain her lord ex-
plore, 470
Or weep the wounds her bleeding country
bore.
But he who found not whom his soul
desired,
Whose virtue charm'd him as her beauty
fired,
Stood in the gates, and asked what way she
bent
Her parting steps ? If to the fane she
went,
Where late the mourning matrons made
resort;
Or sought her sisters in the Trojan court ?
'Not to the court' (replied th' attendant
train),
'Nor, mixed with matrons, to Minerva's
fane:
To Ilion's steepy tower she bent her
way, 480
To mark the fortunes of the doubtful
day.
Troy fled, she heard, before the Grecian
sword:
She heard, and trembled for her distant
lord;
Distracted with surprise, she seemed to
fly,
Fear on her cheek, and sorrow in her eye.
The nurse attended with her infant boy,
The young Astyanax, the hope of Troy.'
Hector, this heard, return'd without
delay;
Swift thro' the town he trod his former
way,
Thro' streets of palaces and walks of
state; 490
And met the mourner at the Scæan gate.
With haste to meet him sprung the joyful
fair,
His blameless wife, Eëtion's wealthy heir
(Cicilian Thebé great Eëtion sway'd,
And Hippoplacus' wide-extended shade):
The nurse stood near, in whose embraces
press'd,
His only hope hung smiling at her breast,

Whom each soft charm and early grace
　　adorn,
Fair as the new-born star that gilds the
　　morn.
To this lov'd infant Hector gave the
　　name　　　　　　　　　　　　　　500
Scamandrius, from Scamander's honour'd
　　stream:
Astyanax the Trojans call'd the boy,
From his great father, the defence of
　　Troy.
Silent the warrior smil'd, and, pleas'd, re-
　　sign'd
To tender passions all his mighty mind:
His beauteous Princess cast a mournful
　　look,
Hung on his hand, and then dejected
　　spoke;
Her bosom labour'd with a boding sigh,
And the big tear stood trembling in her eye.
　'Too daring Prince! ah, whither dost
　　thou run?　　　　　　　　　　　510
Ah too forgetful of thy wife and son!
And think'st thou not how wretched we
　　shall be,
A widow I, a helpless orphan he!
For sure such courage length of life de-
　　nies,
And thou must fall, thy virtue's sacrifice.
Greece in her single heroes strove in vain;
Now hosts oppose thee, and thou must be
　　slain!
Oh grant me, Gods! ere Hector meets his
　　doom,
All I can ask of Heav'n, an early tomb!
So shall my days in one sad tenor run,　520
And end with sorrows as they first begun.
No parent now remains, my griefs to
　　share,
No father's aid, no mother's tender care.
The fierce Achilles wrapt our walls in fire,
Laid Thebé waste, and slew my warlike
　　sire!
His fate compassion in the victor bred;
Stern as he was, he yet revered the dead,
His radiant arms preserv'd from hostile
　　spoil,
And laid him decent on the funeral pile;
Then raised a mountain where his bones
　　were burn'd;　　　　　　　　530
The mountain nymphs the rural tomb
　　adorn'd;
Jove's sylvan daughters bade their elms
　　bestow
A barren shade, and in his honour grow.

'By the same arm my sev'n brave bro-
　　thers fell;
In one sad day beheld the gates of Hell;
While the fat herds and snowy flocks they
　　fed,
Amid their fields the hapless heroes bled!
My mother lived to bear the victor's bands,
The Queen of Hippoplacia's sylvan lands:
Redeem'd too late, she scarce beheld
　　again　　　　　　　　　　　　　540
Her pleasing empire and her native plain,
When, ah! oppress'd by life-consuming
　　woe,
She fell a victim to Diana's bow.
　'Yet while my Hector still survives, I see
My father, mother, brethren, all, in thee.
Alas! my parents, brothers, kindred, all,
Once more will perish if my Hector fall.
Thy wife, thy infant, in thy danger share;
Oh prove a husband's and a father's care!
That quarter most the skilful Greeks
　　annoy,　　　　　　　　　　　550
Where yon wild fig-trees join the wall of
　　Troy:
Thou, from this tower defend th' important
　　post;
There Agamemnon points his dreadful
　　host,
That pass Tydides, Ajax, strive to gain,
And there the vengeful Spartan fires his
　　train.
Thrice our bold foes the fierce attack have
　　giv'n,
Or led by hopes, or dictated from Heav'n.
Let others in the field their arms employ,
But stay my Hector here, and guard his
　　Troy.'
　　The Chief replied: 'That post shall be
　　my care,　　　　　　　　　　560
Nor that alone, but all the works of war.
How would the sons of Troy, in arms re-
　　nown'd,
And Troy's proud dames, whose garments
　　sweep the ground,
Attaint the lustre of my former name,
Should Hector basely quit the field of
　　fame?
My early youth was bred to martial pains,
My soul impels me to th' embattled plains:
Let me be foremost to defend the throne,
And guard my father's glories, and my own.
Yet come it will, the day decreed by
　　Fates　　　　　　　　　　　570
(How my heart trembles while my tongue
　　relates)!

The day when thou, imperial Troy! must
    bend,
And see thy warriors fall, thy glories end.
And yet no dire presage so wounds my
    mind,
My mother's death, the ruin of my kind,
Not Priam's hoary hairs defiled with gore,
Not all my brothers gasping on the shore;
As thine, Andromache! thy griefs I dread;
I see thee trembling, weeping, captive led!
In Argive looms our battles to design,   580
And woes of which so large a part was
    thine!
To bear the victor's hard commands, or
    bring
The weight of waters from Hyperia's
    spring.
There, while you groan beneath the load of
    life,
They cry, Behold the mighty Hector's
    wife!
Some haughty Greek, who lives thy tears
    to see,
Embitters all thy woes by naming me.
The thoughts of glory past, and present
    shame,
A thousand griefs, shall waken at the
    name!
May I lie cold before that dreadful day, 590
Press'd with a load of monumental clay!
Thy Hector, wrapp'd in everlasting sleep,
Shall neither hear thee sigh, nor see thee
    weep.'
    Thus having spoke, th' illustrious Chief
    of Troy
Stretch'd his fond arms to clasp the lovely
    boy.
The babe clung crying to his nurse's breast,
Scared at the dazzling helm, and nodding
    crest.
With secret pleasure each fond parent
    smil'd,
And Hector hasted to relieve his child;
The glitt'ring terrors from his brows un-
    bound,   600
And placed the beaming helmet on the
    ground.
Then kiss'd the child, and, lifting high in
    air,
Thus to the Gods preferr'd a father's
    prayer:
  'O thou! whose glory fills th' ethereal
    throne,
And all ye deathless Powers! protect my
    son!

Grant him, like me, to purchase just re-
    nown,
To guard the Trojans, to defend the crown,
Against his country's foes the war to
    wage,
And rise the Hector of the future age ! 609
So when, triumphant from successful toils
Of heroes slain he bears the reeking spoils,
Whole hosts may hail him with deserv'd
    acclaim,
And say, This Chief transcends his father's
    fame:
While pleas'd, amidst the gen'ral shouts of
    Troy,
His mother's conscious heart o'erflows with
    joy.'
  He spoke, and fondly gazing on her
    charms,
Restor'd the pleasing burden to her arms;
Soft on her fragrant breast the babe she
    laid,
Hush'd to repose, and with a smile sur-
    vey'd.
The troubled pleasure soon chastised by
    fear,   620
She mingled with the smile a tender tear.
The soften'd Chief with kind compassion
    view'd,
And dried the falling drops, and thus pur-
    sued:
  'Andromache! my soul's far better part,
Why with untimely sorrows heaves thy
    heart ?
No hostile hand can antedate my doom,
Till Fate condemns me to the silent tomb.
Fix'd is the term to all the race of earth,
And such the hard condition of our birth.
No force can then resist, no flight can save;
All sink alike, the fearful and the brave.
No more — but hasten to thy tasks at
    home,   632
There guide the spindle, and direct the
    loom:
Me glory summons to the martial scene,
The field of combat is the sphere for
    men.
Where heroes war, the foremost place I
    claim,
The first in danger as the first in fame.'
  Thus having said, the glorious Chief re-
    sumes
His tow'ry helmet, black with shading
    plumes.
His Princess parts with a prophetic sigh, 640
Unwilling parts, and oft reverts her eye,

That stream'd at ev'ry look: then, moving
   slow,
Sought her own palace, and indulged her
   woe.
There, while her tears deplor'd the god-
   like man,
Thro' all her train the soft infection ran;
The pious maids their mingled sorrows
   shed,
And mourn the living Hector as the dead.
   But now, no longer deaf to honour's call,
Forth issues Paris from the palace wall.
In brazen arms that cast a gleamy ray, 650
Swift thro' the town the warrior bends his
   way.
The wanton courser thus, with reins un-
   bound,
Breaks from his stall, and beats the trem-
   bling ground;
Pamper'd and proud he seeks the wonted
   tides,
And laves, in height of blood, his shining
   sides:
His head now freed he tosses to the skies;
His mane dishevell'd o'er his shoulders
   flies;
He snuffs the females in the distant plain,
And springs, exulting, to his fields again.
With equal triumph, sprightly, bold, and
   gay,   660
In arms refulgent as the God of Day,
The son of Priam, glorying in his might,
Rush'd forth with Hector to the fields of
   fight.
   And now the warriors passing on the
   way,
The graceful Paris first excused his stay.
To whom the noble Hector thus replied:
'O Chief! in blood, and now in arms, al-
   lied!
Thy power in war with justice none con-
   test;
Known is thy courage, and thy strength
   confess'd.
What pity, sloth should seize a soul so
   brave,   670
Or godlike Paris live a woman's slave!
My heart weeps blood at what the Trojans
   say,
And hopes thy deeds shall wipe the stain
   away.
Haste then, in all their glorious labours
   share;
For much they suffer, for thy sake, in
   war.

These ills shall cease, whene'er by Jove's
   decree
We crown the bowl to Heav'n and Liberty:
While the proud foe his frustrate triumphs
   mourns,
And Greece indignant thro' her seas returns.'

BOOK VII

THE SINGLE COMBAT OF HECTOR AND AJAX

THE ARGUMENT

The battle renewing with double ardour upon
   the return of Hector, Minerva is under ap-
   prehensions for the Greeks. Apollo, seeing
   her descend from Olympus, joins her near
   the Scæan gate. They agree to put off the
   general engagement for that day, and incite
   Hector to challenge the Greeks to a single
   combat. Nine of the Princes accepting the
   challenge, the lot is cast, and falls upon
   Ajax. These heroes, after several attacks,
   are parted by the night. The Trojans calling a council, Antenor proposes the delivery
   of Helen to the Greeks, to which Paris will
   not consent, but offers to restore them her
   riches. Priam sends a herald to make this
   offer, and to demand a truce for burning the
   dead, the last of which only is agreed to by
   Agamemnon. When the funerals are performed, the Greeks, pursuant to the advice
   of Nestor, erect a fortification to protect their
   fleet and camp, flanked with towers, and defended by a ditch and palisades. Neptune
   testifies his jealousy at this work, but is
   pacified by a promise from Jupiter. Both
   armies pass the night in feasting, but Jupiter disheartens the Trojans with thunder and
   other signs of his wrath.
The three-and-twentieth day ends with the
   duel of Hector and Ajax; the next day the
   truce is agreed: another is taken up in the
   funeral rites of the slain; and one more in
   building the fortification before the ships;
   so that somewhat above three days is employed in this book. The scene lies wholly
   in the field.

So spoke the guardian of the Trojan state,
Then rush'd impetuous thro' the Scæan
   gate.
Him Paris follow'd to the dire alarms;
Both breathing slaughter, both resolv'd in
   arms.
As when to sailors lab'ring thro' the main,
That long had heav'd the weary oar in vain,

Jove bids at length th' expected gales arise;
The gales blow grateful, and the vessel flies:
So welcome these to Troy's desiring train:
The bands are cheer'd, the war awakes
  again. 10
Bold Paris first the work of death begun
On great Menestheus, Areïthous' son;
Sprung from the fair Philomeda's embrace,
The pleasing Arne was his native place.
Then sunk Eioneus to the shades below;
Beneath his steely casque he felt the blow
Full on his neck, from Hector's weighty
  hand;
And roll'd, with limbs relax'd, along the
  land.
By Glaucus' spear the bold Iphinous bleeds,
Fix'd in the shoulder as he mounts his
  steeds; 20
Headlong he tumbles: his slack nerves un-
  bound
Drop the cold useless members on the
  ground.
When now Minerva saw her Argives
  slain,
From vast Olympus to the gleaming plain
Fierce she descends: Apollo mark'd her
  flight,
Nor shot less swift from Ilion's tow'ry
  height:
Radiant they met, beneath the beechen
  shade;
When thus Apollo to the Blue-eyed Maid:
  'What cause, O daughter of almighty
    Jove!
Thus wings thy progress from the realms
  above? 30
Once more impetuous dost thou bend thy
  way,
To give to Greece the long-divided day?
Too much has Troy already felt thy hate,
Now breathe thy rage, and hush the stern
  debate:
This day the bus'ness of the field suspend;
War soon shall kindle, and great Ilion bend;
Since vengeful Goddesses confed'rate join
To raze her walls, tho' built by hands di-
  vine.'
To whom the progeny of Jove replies:
'I left for this the council of the skies: 40
But who shall bid conflicting hosts forbear,
What art shall calm the furious sons of
  war?'
  To her the God: 'Great Hector's soul
    incite
To dare the boldest Greek to single fight,

Till Greece, provoked, from all her num-
  bers shew
A warrior worthy to be Hector's foe.'
  At this agreed, the heav'nly Powers
    withdrew;
Sage Helenus their secret counsels knew:
Hector inspired he sought: to him ad-
  dress'd,
Thus told the dictates of his sacred breast:
'O son of Priam! let thy faithful ear 51
Receive my words; thy friend and brother
  hear!
Go forth persuasive, and awhile engage
The warring nations to suspend their rage;
Then dare the boldest of the hostile train
To mortal combat on the listed plain,
For not this day shall end thy glorious
  date;
The Gods have spoke it, and their voice is
  Fate.'
  He said: the warrior heard the word
    with joy;
Then with his spear restrain'd the youth of
  Troy, 60
Held by the midst athwart. On either
  hand
The squadrons part; th' expecting Trojans
  stand.
Great Agamemnon bids the Greeks for-
  bear;
They breathe, and hush the tumult of the
  war.
Th' Athenian Maid, and glorious God of
  Day,
With silent joy the settling hosts survey:
In form of vultures, on the beech's height
They sit conceal'd, and wait the future
  fight.
  The thronging troops obscure the dusky
    fields,
Horrid with bristling spears, and gleaming
  shields. 70
As when a gen'ral darkness veils the main
(Soft Zephyr curling the wide wat'ry
  plain),
The waves scarce heave, the face of ocean
  sleeps,
And a still horror saddens all the deeps:
Thus in thick orders settling wide around,
At length composed they sit, and shade the
  ground.
Great Hector first amidst both armies
  broke
The solemn silence, and their powers be-
  spoke:

'Hear all ye Trojan, all ye Grecian
   bands,
What my soul prompts, and what some
   God commands.   80
Great Jove, averse our warfare to compose,
O'erwhelms the nations with new toils and
   woes;
War with a fiercer tide once more returns,
Till Ilion falls, or till yon navy burns.
You then, O Princes of the Greeks! ap-
   pear;
'T is Hector speaks, and calls the Gods to
   hear:
From all your troops select the boldest
   knight,
And him, the boldest, Hector dares to
   fight.
Here if I fall, by chance of battle slain,
Be his my spoil, and his these arms re-
   main;   90
But let my body, to my friends return'd,
By Trojan hands, and Trojan flames be
   burn'd.
And if Apollo, in whose aid I trust,
Shall stretch your daring champion in the
   dust;
If mine the glory to despoil the foe,
On Phœbus' temple I 'll his arms bestow;
The breathless carcass to your navy sent,
Greece on the shore shall raise a monu-
   ment;
Which when some future mariner surveys,
Wash'd by broad Hellespont's resounding
   seas,   100
Thus shall he say, A valiant Greek lies
   there,
By Hector slain, the mighty man of war.
The stone shall tell your vanquish'd hero's
   name,
And distant ages learn the victor's fame.'
   This fierce defiance Greece astonish'd
      heard,
Blush'd to refuse, and to accept it fear'd.
Stern Menelaus first the silence broke,
And, inly groaning, thus opprobrious spoke:
   'Women of Greece! Oh scandal of your
      race,
Whose coward souls your manly forms dis-
   grace,   110
How great the shame, when ev'ry age shall
   know
That not a Grecian met this noble foe !
Go then, resolve to earth from whence ye
   grew,
A heartless, spiritless, inglorious crew !

Be what ye seem, unanimated clay!
Myself will dare the danger of the day.
'T is man's bold task the gen'rous strife to
   try,
But in the hands of God is victory.'
   These words scarce spoke, with gen'rous
      ardour press'd,
His manly limbs in azure arms he dress'd:
That day, Atrides! a superior hand   121
Had stretch'd thee breathless on the hostile
   strand;
But all at once, thy fury to compose,
The Kings of Greece, an awful band, arose:
Ev'n he their Chief, great Agamemnon,
   press'd
Thy daring hand, and this advice ad-
   dress'd:
' Whither, O Menelaus! wouldst thou run,
And tempt a fate which prudence bids thee
   shun ?
Griev'd tho' thou art, forbear the rash de-
   sign;
Great Hector's arm is mightier far than
   thine.   130
Ev'n fierce Achilles learn'd its force to
   fear,
And trembling met this dreadful son of
   war.
Sit thou secure amidst thy social band;
Greece in our cause shall arm some power-
   ful hand.
The mightiest warrior of th' Achaian name,
Tho' bold, and burning with desire of
   Fame,
Content, the doubtful honour might forego,
So great the danger, and so brave the
   foe.'
   He said, and turn'd his brother's venge-
      ful mind;
He stoop'd to reason, and his rage resign'd,
No longer bent to rush on certain harms: 141
His joyful friends unbrace his azure arms.
   He, from whose lips divine persuasion
      flows,
Grave Nestor then, in graceful act arose.
Thus to the Kings he spoke: 'What grief,
   what shame,
Attend on Greece, and all the Grecian
   name!
How shall, alas! her hoary heroes mourn
Their sons degen'rate, and their race a
   scorn;
What tears shall down thy silver beard be
   roll'd,
Oh Peleus, old in arms, in wisdom old!   150

Once with what joy the gen'rous Prince
would hear
Of ev'ry Chief, who fought this glorious
war,
Participate their fame, and pleas'd inquire
Each name, each action, and each hero's
sire !
Gods! should he see our warriors trembling
stand,
And trembling all before one hostile hand;
How would he lift his aged arms on high,
Lament inglorious Greece, and beg to die!
Oh! would to all th' immortal Powers
above,
Minerva, Phœbus, and almighty Jove! 160
Years might again roll back, my youth re-
new,
And give this arm the spring which once it
knew:
When, fierce in war, where Jardan's waters
fall
I led my troops to Phea's trembling wall,
And with th' Arcadian spears my prowess
tried,
Where Celadon rolls down his rapid tide.
There Ereuthalion braved us in the field,
Proud Areïthous' dreadful arms to wield;
Great Areïthous, known from shore to shore
By the huge, knotted, iron mace he bore; 170
No lance he shook, nor bent the twanging
bow,
But broke, with this, the battle of the foe.
Him not by manly force Lycurgus slew,
Whose guileful jav'lin from the thicket
flew,
Deep in a winding way his breast assail'd,
Nor aught the warrior's thund'ring mace
avail'd:
Supine he fell: those arms which Mars be-
fore
Had giv'n the vanquish'd, now the victor
bore:
But when old age had dimm'd Lycurgus'
eyes,
To Ereuthalion he consign'd the prize. 180
Furious with this, he crush'd our levell'd
bands,
And dared the trial of the strongest hands;
Nor could the strongest hands his fury
stay;
All saw, and fear'd, his huge tempestuous
sway;
Till I, the youngest of the host, appear'd,
And, youngest, met whom all our army
fear'd.

I fought the Chief; my arms Minerva
crown'd:
Prone fell the giant o'er a length of
ground.
What then he was, oh were your Nestor
now !
Not Hector's self should want an equal foe.
But, warriors, you that youthful vigour
boast,   191
The flower of Greece, th' examples of our
host,
Sprung from such fathers, who such
numbers sway,
Can you stand trembling, and desert the
day ? '
    His warm reproofs the list'ning Kings
inflame;
And nine, the noblest of the Grecian name,
Upstarted fierce: but far before the rest
The King of men advanc'd his dauntless
breast;
Then bold Tydides, great in arms, appear'd;
And next his bulk gigantic Ajax rear'd. 200
Oïleus follow'd: Idomen was there,
And Merion, dreadful as the God of War:
With these Eurypylus and Thoas stand,
And wise Ulysses closed the daring band.
All these, alike inspired with noble rage,
Demand the fight. To whom the Pylian
sage:
    ' Lest thirst of glory your brave souls
divide,
What Chief shall combat, let the lots de-
cide.
Whom Heav'n shall choose, be his the
chance to raise
His country's fame, his own immortal
praise.'   210
    The lots produced, each hero signs his
own;
Then in the Gen'ral's helm the fates are
thrown.
The people pray with lifted eyes and hands,
And vows like these ascend from all the
bands:
' Grant thou, Almighty! in whose hand is
fate,
A worthy champion for the Grecian state.
This task let Ajax or Tydides prove,
Or he, the King of Kings, belov'd by
Jove.'
    Old Nestor shook the casque. By
Heav'n inspired,
Leap'd forth the lot, of ev'ry Greek de-
sired.   220

This from the right to left the herald
    bears,
Held out in order to the Grecian peers;
Each to his rival yields the mark unknown,
Till godlike Ajax finds the lot his own;
Surveys th' inscription with rejoicing eyes,
Then casts before him, and with transport
    cries:
'Warriors! I claim the lot, and arm with
    joy;
Be mine the conquest of this Chief of Troy.
Now, while my brightest arms my limbs
    invest,
To Saturn's son be all your vows ad-
    dress'd: 230
But pray in secret, lest the foes should
    hear,
And deem your prayers the mean effect of
    fear.
Said I in secret ? No, your vows declare,
In such a voice as fills the earth and air.
Lives there a Chief, whom Ajax ought to
    dread,
Ajax, in all the toils of battle bred ?
From warlike Salamis I drew my birth,
And, born to combats, fear no force of
    earth.'
He said. The troops with elevated eyes,
Implore the God whose thunder rends the
    skies: 240
'O Father of Mankind, superior Lord!
On lofty Ida's holy hill ador'd;
Who in the highest Heav'n hast fix'd thy
    throne,
Supreme of Gods! unbounded, and alone:
Grant thou, that Telamon may bear away
The praise and conquest of this doubtful
    day;
Or if illustrious Hector be thy care,
That both may claim it, and that both may
    share.'
Now Ajax braced his dazzling armour
    on;
Sheathed in bright steel the giant warrior
    shone: 250
He moves to combat with majestic pace;
So stalks in arms the grisly God of Thrace,
When Jove to punish faithless men pre-
    pares,
And gives whole nations to the waste of
    wars.
Thus march'd the Chief, tremendous as a
    God;
Grimly he smil'd: earth trembled as he
    strode:

His massy jav'lin quiv'ring in his hand,
He stood, the bulwark of the Grecian band.
Thro' every Argive heart new transport
    ran;
All Troy stood trembling at the mighty
    man.   260
Ev'n Hector paus'd; and, with new doubt
    oppress'd,
Felt his great heart suspended in his breast:
'T was vain to seek retreat, and vain to
    fear;
Himself had challenged, and the foe drew
    near.
Stern Telamon behind his ample shield,
As from a brazen tower, o'erlook'd the
    field.
Huge was its orb, with seven thick folds
    o'ercast
Of tough bull-hides; of solid brass the last
(The work of Tychius, who in Hyle dwell'd,
And all in arts of armoury excell'd).   270
This Ajax bore before his manly breast,
And, threat'ning, thus his adverse Chief
    address'd:
'Hector! approach my arm, and singly
    know
What strength thou hast, and what the
    Grecian foe.
Achilles shuns the fight; yet some there
    are
Not void of soul, and not unskill'd in war:
Let him, inactive on the sea-beat shore,
Indulge his wrath, and aid our arms no
    more;
Whole troops of heroes Greece has yet to
    boast,   279
And sends thee one, a sample of her host.
Such as I am, I come to prove thy might;
No more — be sudden, and begin the fight.'
'O son of Telamon, thy country's pride'
(To Ajax thus the Trojan Prince replied),
'Me, as a boy or woman, would'st thou
    fright,
New to the field, and trembling at the
    fight ?
Thou meet'st a Chief deserving of thy
    arms,
To combat born, and bred amidst alarms:
I know to shift my ground, remount the car,
Turn, charge, and answer every call of
    war: 290
To right, to left, the dext'rous lance I
    wield,
And bear thick battle on my sounding
    shield.

But open be our fight, and bold each blow;
I steal no conquest from a noble foe.'
　He said, and, rising high above the field,
Whirl'd the long lance against the sev'n-
　　fold shield.
Full on the brass descending from above
Thro' six bull-hides the furious weapon
　　drove,
Till in the sev'nth it fix'd.　Then Ajax
　　threw;
Thro' Hector's shield the forceful jav'lin
　　flew;　　　　　　　　　　　　　　300
His corslet enters, and his garment rends,
And glancing downwards, near his flank
　　descends.
The wary Trojan shrinks, and, bending
　　low
Beneath his buckler, disappoints the blow.
From their bored shields the Chiefs their
　　jav'lins drew,
Then close impetuous, and the charge re-
　　new:
Fierce as the mountain lions bathed in
　　blood,
Or foaming boars, the terror of the wood.
At Ajax, Hector his long lance extends;
The blunted point against the buckler
　　bends.　　　　　　　　　　　　　310
But Ajax, watchful as his foe drew near,
Drove thro' the Trojan targe the knotty
　　spear;
It reach'd his neck, with matchless strength
　　impell'd;
Spouts the black gore, and dims the shining
　　shield.
Yet ceas'd not Hector thus; but, stooping
　　down,
In his strong hand upheav'd a flinty stone,
Black, craggy, vast: to this his force he
　　bends;
Full on the brazen boss the stone descends;
The hollow brass resounded with the
　　shock.
Then Ajax seiz'd the fragment of a rock,
Applied each nerve, and, swinging round
　　on high,　　　　　　　　　　　321
With force tempestuous let the ruin fly:
The huge stone thund'ring thro' his buckler
　　broke;
His slacken'd knees receiv'd the numbing
　　stroke;
Great Hector falls extended on the field,
His bulk supporting on the shatter'd shield:
Nor wanted heav'nly aid: Apollo's might
Confirm'd his sinews, and restored to fight.

And now both heroes their broad falchions
　　drew;
In flaming circles round their heads they
　　flew;　　　　　　　　　　　　　330
But then by heralds' voice the word was
　　giv'n,
The sacred Ministers of earth and Heav'n:
Divine Talthybius whom the Greeks em‧
　　ploy,
And sage Idæus on the part of Troy,
Between the swords their peaceful sceptres
　　rear'd;
And first Idæus' awful voice was heard:
　'Forbear, my sons! your farther force
　　to prove,
Both dear to men, and both belov'd of
　　Jove.
To either host your matchless worth is
　　known,
Each sounds your praise, and war is all
　　your own.　　　　　　　　　　340
But now the Night extends her awful shade:
The Goddess parts you: be the night
　　obey'd.'
　To whom great Ajax his high soul ex-
　　press'd:
'O sage! to Hector be these words ad-
　　dress'd.
Let him, who first provoked our Chiefs to
　　fight,
Let him demand the sanction of the night;
If first he ask it, I content obey,
And cease the strife when Hector shews
　　the way.'
　'O first of Greeks' (his noble foe re-
　　join'd),
'Whom Heav'n adorns, superior to thy
　　kind,　　　　　　　　　　　　350
With strength of body, and with worth
　　of mind !
Now martial law commands us to forbear;
Hereafter we shall meet in glorious war;
Some future day shall lengthen out the
　　strife,
And let the Gods decide of death or life!
Since then the Night extends her gloomy
　　shade,
And Heav'n enjoins it, be the night obey'd.
Return, brave Ajax, to thy Grecian friends,
And joy the nations whom thy arm de-
　　fends;
As I shall glad each Chief, and Trojan
　　wife,　　　　　　　　　　　　360
Who wearies Heav'n with vows for Hec‧
　　tor's life.

But let us, on this memorable day,
Exchange some gift; that Greece and
　　Troy may say,
"Not hate, but glory, made these Chiefs
　　contend;
And each brave foe was in his soul a
　　friend." '
　　With that, a sword with stars of silver
　　　graced,
The baldrick studded, and the sheath en-
　　chased,
He gave the Greek. The gen'rous Greek
　　bestow'd
A radiant belt that rich with purple glow'd.
Then with majestic grace they quit the
　　plain;　　　　　　　　　　　　　370
This seeks the Grecian, that the Phrygian
　　train.
The Trojan bands returning Hector wait,
And hail with joy the champion of their
　　state:
Escaped great Ajax, they survey'd him
　　round,
Alive, unharm'd, and vig'rous from his
　　wound.
To Troy's high gates the godlike man they
　　bear,
Their present triumph, as their late de-
　　spair.
But Ajax, glorying in his hardy deed,
The well-arm'd Greeks to Agamemnon
　　lead.
A steer for sacrifice the King design'd,　380
Of full five years, and of the nobler kind.
The victim falls; they strip the smoking
　　hide,
The beast they quarter, and the joints di-
　　vide;
Then spread the tables, the repast pre-
　　pare,
Each takes his seat, and each receives his
　　share.
The King himself (an honorary sign)
Before great Ajax placed the mighty chine.
When now the rage of hunger was re-
　　mov'd,
Nestor, in each persuasive art approv'd,
The sage whose counsels long had sway'd
　　the rest,　　　　　　　　　　　　390
In words like these his prudent thought ex-
　　press'd:
　　'How dear, O King! this fatal day has
　　　cost !
What Greeks are perish'd ! what a people
　　lost !

What tides of blood have drench'd Sca-
　　mander's shore!
What crowds of heroes sunk, to rise no
　　more!
Then hear me, Chief! nor let the morrow's
　　light
Awake thy squadrons to new toils of fight:
Some space at least permit the war to
　　breathe,
While we to flames our slaughter'd friends
　　bequeath,
From the red field their scatter'd bodies
　　bear,　　　　　　　　　　　　　400
And nigh the fleet a funeral structure
　　rear:
So decent urns their snowy bones may
　　keep,
And pious children o'er their ashes weep.
Here, where on one promiscuous pile they
　　blaz'd,
High o'er them all a gen'ral tomb be
　　rais'd;
Next, to secure our camp, and naval
　　powers,
Raise an embattled wall, with lofty towers;
From space to space be ample gates
　　around,
For passing chariots, and a trench pro-
　　found.
So Greece to combat shall in safety go,　410
Nor fear the fierce incursions of the foe.'
'T was thus the sage his wholesome coun-
　　sel mov'd;
The sceptred Kings of Greece his words
　　approv'd.
　　Meanwhile, convened at Priam's palace
　　　gate,
The Trojan peers in nightly council sate:
A senate void of order, as of choice,
Their hearts were fearful, and confused
　　their voice.
Antenor rising, thus demands their ear:
'Ye Trojans, Dardans, and auxiliars, hear!
'T is Heav'n the counsel of my breast in-
　　spires,　　　　　　　　　　　　420
And I but move what ev'ry God requires:
Let Sparta's treasures be this hour re-
　　stor'd,
And Argive Helen own her ancient lord.
The ties of faith, the sworn alliance
　　broke
Our impious battles the just Gods pro-
　　voke.
As this advice ye practise, or reject,
So hope success, or dread the dire effect.'

The senior spoke, and sat. To whom replied
The graceful husband of the Spartan bride:
'Cold counsels, Trojan, may become thy
    years,   430
But sound ungrateful in a warrior's ears:
Old man, if void of fallacy or art,
Thy words express the purpose of thy
    heart,
Thou, in thy time, more sound advice hast
    giv'n;
But wisdom has its date, assign'd by
    Heav'n.
Then hear me, Princes of the Trojan
    name!
Their treasures I 'll restore, but not the
    dame;
My treasures, too, for peace I will resign;
But be this bright possession ever mine.'
'T was then, the growing discord to com-
    pose,   440
Slow from his seat the rev'rend Priam
    rose:
His godlike aspect deep attention drew:
He paus'd, and these pacific words ensue:
'Ye Trojans, Dardans, and auxiliar
    bands!
Now take refreshment as the hour de-
    mands;
Guard well the walls, relieve the watch of
    night,
Till the new sun restores the cheerful
    light:
Then shall our herald, to th' Atrides sent,
Before their ships proclaim my son's intent.
Next let a truce be ask'd, that Troy may
    burn   450
Her slaughter'd heroes, and their bones
    inurn;
That done, once more the fate of war be tried,
And whose the conquest, mighty Jove de-
    cide!'
The Monarch spoke: the warriors snatch'd
    with haste
(Each at his post in arms) a short repast.
Soon as the rosy morn had waked the day,
To the black ships Idæus bent his way;
There, to the sons of Mars, in council
    found,
He rais'd his voice: the hosts stood lis-
    t'ning round:
'Ye sons of Atreus, and ye Greeks, give
    ear!   460
The words of Troy, and Troy's great mon-
    arch, hear.

Pleas'd may ye hear (so Heav'n succeed
    my prayers)
What Paris, author of the war, declares.
The spoils and treasures he to Ilion bore
(O had he perish'd ere they touch'd our
    shore)
He proffers injured Greece; with large in-
    crease
Of added Trojan wealth, to buy the peace.
But, to restore the beauteous bride again,
This Greece demands, and Troy requests
    in vain.
Next, O ye Chiefs! we ask a truce to
    burn   470
Our slaughter'd heroes, and their bones
    inurn.
That done, once more the fate of war be
    tried,
And whose the conquest, mighty Jove de-
    cide!'
The Greeks give ear, but none the silence
    broke;
At length Tydides rose, and rising spoke:
'O take not, friends! defrauded of your
    fame,
Their proffer'd wealth, nor ev'n the Spar-
    tan dame.
Let conquest make them ours: Fate shakes
    their wall,
And Troy already totters to her fall.'
Th' admiring Chiefs, and all the Grecian
    name,   480
With gen'ral shouts return'd him loud ac-
    claim.
Then thus the King of Kings rejects the
    peace:
'Herald! in him thou hear'st the voice of
    Greece.
For what remains, let funeral flames be
    fed
With hero's corpse: I war not with the
    dead:
Go, search your slaughter'd Chiefs on yon-
    der plain,
And gratify the Manes of the slain.
Be witness, Jove, whose thunder rolls on
    high!'
He said, and rear'd his sceptre to the sky.
To sacred Troy, where all her Princes
    lay   490
To wait th' event, the herald bent his
    way.
He came, and, standing in the midst, ex-
    plain'd;
The peace rejected, but the truce obtain'd,

Straight to their sev'ral cares the Trojans
   move;
Some search the plain, some fell the sound-
   ing grove:
Nor less the Greeks, descending on the
   shore,
Hew'd the green forests, and the bodies
   bore.
And now from forth the chambers of the
   main,
To shed his sacred light on earth again,
Arose the golden chariot of the day,   500
And tipp'd the mountains with a purple
   ray.
In mingled throngs the Greek and Trojan
   train
Thro' heaps of carnage search'd the mourn-
   ful plain.
Scarce could the friend his slaughter'd
   friend explore,
With dust dishonour'd, and deform'd with
   gore.
The wounds they wash'd, their pious tears
   they shed,
And, laid along their cars, deplored the
   dead.
Sage Priam check'd their grief: with silent
   haste
The bodies decent on the piles were placed:
With melting hearts the cold remains they
   burn'd;   510
And sadly slow to sacred Troy return'd.
Nor less the Greeks their pious sorrows
   shed,
And decent on the pile dispose the dead;
The cold remains consume with equal care;
And slowly, sadly, to their fleet repair.
Now, ere the morn had streak'd with red-
   d'ning light
The doubtful confines of the day and night;
About the dying flames the Greeks ap-
   pear'd,
And round the pile a gen'ral tomb they
   rear'd.
Then, to secure the camp and naval
   powers,   520
They rais'd embattled walls with lofty
   towers:
From space to space were ample gates
   around,
For passing chariots; and a trench pro-
   found,
Of large extent: and deep in earth below
Strong piles infix'd stood adverse to the
   foe.

So toil'd the Greeks: meanwhile the
   Gods above,
In shining circle round their father Jove,
Amazed beheld the wondrous works of man:
Then he whose trident shakes the earth
   began:
  'What mortals henceforth shall our
   power adore,   530
Our fanes frequent, our oracles implore,
If the proud Grecians thus successful
   boast
Their rising bulwarks on the sea-beat
   coast ?
See the long walls extending to the main,
No God consulted, and no victim slain!
Their fame shall fill the world's remotest
   ends;
Wide as the morn her golden beam ex-
   tends:
While old Laömedon's divine abodes,
Those radiant structures rais'd by lab'ring
   Gods,
Shall, razed and lost, in long oblivion
   sleep.'   540
Thus spoke the hoary monarch of the deep.
  Th' almighty Thund'rer with a frown
   replies,
That clouds the world, and blackens half
   the skies:
'Strong God of Ocean! thou, whose rage
   can make
The solid earth's eternal basis shake!
What cause of fear from mortal works
   could move
The meanest subject of our realms above ?
Where'er the sun's refulgent rays are cast,
Thy power is honour'd and thy fame shall
   last.
But yon proud work no future age shall
   view,   550
No trace remain where once the glory grew.
The sapp'd foundations by thy force shall
   fall,
And, whelm'd beneath thy waves, drop
   the huge wall;
Vast drifts of sand shall change the former
   shore;
The ruin vanish'd, and the name no more.'
  Thus they in Heav'n: while o'er the
   Grecian train
The rolling sun descending to the main
Beheld the finish'd work. Their bulls they
   slew;
Black from the tents the sav'ry vapours
   flew.

And now the fleet, arrived from Lemnos'
   strands, 560
With Bacchus' blessings cheer'd the gen'-
   rous bands.
Of fragrant wines the rich Eunæus sent
A thousand measures to the royal tent
(Eunæus, whom Hypsipyle of yore
To Jason, shepherd of his people, bore).
The rest they purchas'd at their proper
   cost,
And well the plenteous freight supplied
   the host:
Each, in exchange, proportion'd treasures
   gave,
Some brass, or iron, some an ox or slave.
All night they feast, the Greek and Trojan
   powers; 570
Those on the fields, and these within their
   towers.
But Jove averse the signs of wrath dis-
   play'd,
And shot red lightnings thro' the gloomy
   shade:
Humbled they stood; pale horror seized
   on all,
While the deep thunder shook th' aërial
   hall.
Each pour'd to Jove, before the bowl was
   crown'd,
And large libations drench'd the thirsty
   ground;
Then late, refresh'd with sleep from toils
   of fight,
Enjoy'd the balmy blessings of the night.

BOOK VIII

THE SECOND BATTLE, AND THE DISTRESS
OF THE GREEKS

THE ARGUMENT

Jupiter assembles a council of the deities, and
threatens them with the pains of Tartarus,
if they assist either side: Minerva only obtains of him that she may direct the Greeks
by her counsels. The armies join battle;
Jupiter on Mount Ida weighs in his balances
the fates of both, and affrights the Greeks
with his thunders and lightnings. Nestor
alone continues in the field in great danger;
Diomed relieves him; whose exploits, and
those of Hector, are excellently described.
Juno endeavours to animate Neptune to the
assistance of the Greeks, but in vain. The

acts of Teucer, who is at length wounded by
Hector, and carried off. Juno and Minerva
prepare to aid the Grecians, but are restrained by Iris, sent from Jupiter. The
night puts an end to the battle. Hector
continues in the field (the Greeks being
driven to their fortifications before the
ships), and gives orders to keep the watch
all night in the camp, to prevent the enemy
from reëmbarking and escaping by flight.
They kindle fires through all the field, and
pass the night under arms.
The time of seven-and-twenty days is employed
from the opening of the poem to the end of
this book. The scene here (except of the
celestial machines) lies in the field toward
the sea-shore.

AURORA now, fair Daughter of the
   Dawn,
Sprinkled with rosy light the dewy lawn:
When Jove convened the senate of the
   skies
Where high Olympus' cloudy tops arise.
The Sire of Gods his awful silence broke;
The Heav'ns attentive trembled as he
   spoke:
'Celestial states, immortal Gods! give
   ear,
Hear our decree, and rev'rence what ye
   hear;
The fix'd decree which not all Heav'n can
   move!
Thou, Fate! fulfil it! and ye, Powers! ap-
   prove! 10
What God but enters yon forbidden field,
Who yields assistance, or but wills to
   yield;
Back to the skies with shame he shall be
   driv'n,
Gash'd with dishonest wounds, the scorn of
   Heav'n:
Or far, oh far from steep Olympus thrown,
Low in the dark Tartarean gulf shall
   groan,
With burning chains fix'd to the brazen
   floors,
And lock'd by Hell's inexorable doors;
As deep beneath th' infernal centre hurl'd,
As from that centre to th' ethereal world. 20
Let him who tempts me, dread those dire
   abodes;
And know, th' Almighty is the God of
   Gods.
League all your forces then, ye Powers
   above,
Join all, and try th' omnipotence of Jove:

Let down our golden everlasting chain,
Whose strong embrace holds Heav'n and
　Earth and Main:
Strive all, of mortal and immortal birth,
To drag, by this, the Thund'rer down to
　earth,
Ye strive in vain! if I but stretch this
　hand,
I heave the Gods, the Ocean, and the Land;
I fix the chain to great Olympus' height, 31
And the vast world hangs trembling in my
　sight!
For such I reign, unbounded and above;
And such are men and Gods, compared to
　Jove.'
　Th' Almighty spoke, nor durst the
　Powers reply;
A rev'rent horror silenc'd all the sky;
Trembling they stood before their sov'-
　reign's look;
At length his best belov'd, the Power of
　Wisdom, spoke:
　'Oh first and greatest! God, by Gods
　ador'd!
We own thy might, our father and our
　Lord!　　　　　　　　　　　40
But ah! permit to pity human state:
If not to help, at least lament their fate.
From fields forbidden we submiss refrain,
With arms unaiding mourn our Argives slain;
Yet grant my counsels still their breasts
　may move,
Or all must perish in the wrath of Jove.'
　The cloud-compelling God her suit ap-
　prov'd,
And smil'd superior on his best-belov'd.
Then call'd his coursers, and his chariot
　took;
The steadfast firmament beneath them
　shook:　　　　　　　　　　　50
Rapt by th' ethereal steeds the chariot
　roll'd;
Brass were their hoofs, their curling manes
　of gold.
Of Heav'n's undrossy gold the God's array,
Refulgent, flash'd intolerable day.
High on the throne he shines: his coursers fly
Between th' extended earth and starry sky.
But when to Ida's topmost height he came
(Fair nurse of fountains, and of savage
　game),
Where, o'er her pointed summits proudly
　rais'd,
His fane breathed odours, and his altar
　blazed:　　　　　　　　　　　60

There, from his radiant car, the sacred Sire
Of Gods and men released the steeds of
　fire:
Blue ambient mists th' immortal steeds
　embraced;
High on the cloudy point his seat he
　placed;
Thence his broad eye the subject world
　surveys,
The town, and tents, and navigable seas.
　Now had the Grecians snatch'd a short
　repast,
And buckled on their shining arms with
　haste.
Troy rous'd as soon; for on this dreadful
　day
The fate of fathers, wives, and infants lay.
The gates unfolding pour forth all their
　train;　　　　　　　　　　　71
Squadrons on squadrons cloud the dusky
　plain:
Men, steeds, and chariots, shake the trem-
　bling ground,
The tumult thickens, and the skies re-
　sound.
And now with shouts the shocking armies
　closed,
To lances lances, shields to shields op-
　posed;
Host against host with shadowy legions
　drew,
The sounding darts in iron tempests flew;
Victors and vanquish'd join promiscuous
　cries,
Triumphant shouts and dying groans arise;
With streaming blood the slipp'ry fields are
　dyed,　　　　　　　　　　　81
And slaughter'd heroes swell the dreadful
　tide.
Long as the morning beams, increasing
　bright,
O'er Heav'n's clear azure spread the sacred
　light,
Commutual death the fate of war con-
　founds,
Each adverse battle gored with equal
　wounds.
But when the sun the height of Heav'n
　ascends,
The Sire of Gods his golden scales sus-
　pends,
With equal hand; in these explored the
　fate
Of Greece and Troy, and pois'd the mighty
　weight.　　　　　　　　　　　90

Press'd with its load, the Grecian balance lies
Low sunk on earth, the Trojan strikes the skies.
Then Jove from Ida's top his horrors spreads;
The clouds burst dreadful o'er the Grecian heads;
Thick lightnings flash; the mutt'ring thunder rolls;
Their strength he withers, and unmans their souls.
Before his wrath the trembling hosts retire,
The Gods in terrors, and the skies on fire.
Nor great Idomeneus that sight could bear.
Nor each stern Ajax, thunderbolts of war;
Nor he, the King of Men, th' alarm sustain'd; 101
Nestor alone amidst the storm remain'd.
Unwilling he remain'd, for Paris' dart
Had pierc'd his courser in a mortal part;
Fix'd in the forehead where the springing mane
Curl'd o'er the brow, it stung him to the brain;
Mad with his anguish, he begins to rear,
Paw with his hoofs aloft, and lash the air.
Scarce had his falchion cut the reins, and freed
Th' incumbent chariot from the dying steed, 110
When dreadful Hector, thund'ring thro' the war,
Pour'd to the tumult on his whirling car.
That day had stretch'd beneath his matchless hand
The hoary Monarch of the Pylian band,
But Diomed beheld; from forth the crowd
He rush'd, and on Ulysses call'd aloud:
'Whither, oh whither does Ulysses run?
O flight unworthy great Laertes' son!
Mix'd with the vulgar shall thy fate be found,
Pierc'd in the back, a vile, dishonest wound? 120
Oh turn and save from Hector's direful rage
The glory of the Greeks, the Pylian sage.'
His fruitless words are lost unheard in air;
Ulysses seeks the ships, and shelters there.
But bold Tydides to the rescue goes,
A single warrior 'midst a host of foes;

Before the coursers with a sudden spring
He leap'd, and anxious thus bespoke the King:
'Great perils, Father! wait th' unequal fight;
These younger champions will oppress thy might. 130
Thy veins no more with ancient vigour glow,
Weak is thy servant, and thy coursers slow.
Then haste, ascend my seat, and from the car
Observe the steeds of Tros, renown'd in war,
Practis'd alike to turn, to stop, to chase,
To dare the fight, or urge the rapid race:
These late obey'd Æneas' guiding rein;
Leave thou thy chariot to our faithful train:
With these against yon Trojans will we go,
Nor shall great Hector want an equal foe;
Fierce as he is, ev'n he may learn to fear
The thirsty fury of my flying spear.' 142
Thus said the Chief; and Nestor, skill'd in war,
Approves his counsel, and ascends the car:
The steeds he left, their trusty servants hold;
Eurymedon, and Sthenelus the bold.
The rev'rend charioteer directs the course,
And strains his aged arm to lash the horse.
Hector they face; unknowing how to fear,
Fierce he drove on: Tydides whirl'd his spear. 150
The spear with erring haste mistook its way,
But plunged in Eniopeus' bosom lay.
His opening hand in death forsakes the rein;
The steeds fly back: he falls, and spurns the plain.
Great Hector sorrows for his servant kill'd,
Yet unrevenged permits to press the field;
Till to supply his place and rule the car,
Rose Archeptolemus, the fierce in war.
And now had death and horror cover'd all;
Like tim'rous flocks the Trojans in their wall 160
Enclosed had bled: but Jove with awful sound
Roll'd the big thunder o'er the vast profound:
Full in Tydides' face the lightning flew;
The ground before him flamed with sulphur blue:

The quiv'ring steeds fell prostrate at the
   sight;
And Nestor's trembling hand confess'd his
   fright:
He dropp'd the reins; and, shook with
   sacred dread,
Thus, turning, warn'd th' intrepid Diomed:
   ' O Chief ! too daring in thy friend's de-
     fence,   169
Retire advised, and urge the chariot hence.
This day, averse, the Sov'reign of the Skies
Assists great Hector, and our palm denies.
Some other sun may see the happier hour,
When Greece shall conquer by his heav'nly
   power.
'T is not in man his fix'd decree to move:
The great will glory to submit to Jove.'
   ' O rev'rend Prince! ' (Tydides thus re-
     plies)
' Thy years are awful, and thy words are
   wise.
But ah, what grief! should haughty Hector
   boast,
I fled inglorious to the guarded coast.   180
Before that dire disgrace shall blast my
   fame,
O'erwhelm me, earth! and hide a warrior's
   shame.'
   To whom Gerenian Nestor thus replied:
' Gods! can thy courage fear the Phrygian's
   pride ?
Hector may vaunt, but who shall heed ⎤
   the boast ?   ⎟
Not those who felt thy arm, the Dardan ⎬
   host,   ⎟
Nor Troy, yet bleeding in her heroes lost; ⎦
Not ev'n a Phrygian dame, who dreads the
   sword
That laid in dust her lov'd, lamented lord.'
   He said: and hasty o'er the gasping
     throng   190
Drives the swift steeds; the chariot smokes
   along.
The shouts of Trojans thicken in the wind;
The storm of hissing jav'lins pours behind.
Then with a voice that shakes the solid
   skies,
Pleas'd Hector braves the warrior as he
   flies:
' Go, mighty Hero! graced above the rest
In seats of council and the sumptuous
   feast:
Now hope no more those honours from thy
   train;
Go, less than woman, in the form of man !

To scale our walls, to wrap our towers in
   flames,   200
To lead in exile the fair Phrygian dames,
Thy once proud hopes, presumptuous
   Prince! are fled;
This arm shall reach thy heart, and stretch
   thee dead.'
   Now fears dissuade him, and now hopes
   invite,
To stop his coursers, and to stand the
   fight;
Thrice turn'd the Chief, and thrice imperial
   Jove
On Ida's summit thunder'd from above.
Great Hector heard; he saw the flashing
   light
(The sign of conquest), and thus urged the
   fight:
   ' Hear, ev'ry Trojan, Lycian, Dardan
   band,   210
All famed in war, and dreadful hand to
   hand,
Be mindful of the wreaths your arms have
   won,
Your great forefathers' glories, and your
   own.
Heard ye the voice of Jove ?   Success and
   fame
Await on Troy, on Greece eternal shame.
In vain they skulk behind their boasted
   wall,
Weak bulwarks! destin'd by this arm to
   fall.
High o'er their slighted trench our steeds
   shall bound,
And pass victorious o'er the levell'd
   mound.
Soon as before yon hollow ships we stand,
Fight each with flames, and toss the blazing
   brand;   221
Till, their proud navy wrapt in smoke and
   fires,
All Greece, encompass'd, in one blaze ex-
   pires.'
   Furious he said: then, bending o'er the
   yoke,
Encouraged his proud steeds, while thus he
   spoke.
' Now Xanthus, Æthon, Lampus! urge the
   chase,
And thou, Podargus! prove thy gen'rous
   race.
Be fleet, be fearless, this important day,
And all your master's well-spent care re-
   pay.

For this, high fed in plenteous stalls ye
   stand,   230
Serv'd with pure wheat, and by a Princess'
   hand;
For this, my spouse, of great Eëtion's
   line,
So oft has steep'd the strength'ning grain
   in wine.
Now swift pursue, now thunder uncon-
   troll'd;
Give me to seize rich Nestor's shield of
   gold;
From Tydeus' shoulders strip the costly
   load,
Vulcanian arms, the labour of a God:
These if we gain, then victory, ye Powers!
This night, this glorious night, the fleet is
   ours.'
   That heard, deep anguish stung Satur-
   nia's soul;   240
She shook her throne that shook the starry
   pole:
And thus to Neptune: ' Thou whose force
   can make
The steadfast earth from her foundations
   shake,
Seest thou the Greeks by Fates unjust op-
   press'd,
Nor swells thy heart in that immortal
   breast ?
Yet Ægæ, Helice, thy power obey,
And gifts unceasing on thine altars lay.
Would all the deities of Greece com-
   bine,
In vain the gloomy Thund'rer might re-
   pine:
Sole should he sit, with scarce a God to
   friend,   250
And see his Trojans to the shades descend:
Such be the scene from his Idæan bower:
Ungrateful prospect to the sullen Power ! '
   Neptune with wrath rejects the rash de-
   sign:
' What rage, what madness, furious Queen !
   is thine ?
I war not with the highest. All above
Submit and tremble at the hand of Jove.'
   Now godlike Hector, to whose matchless
   might
Jove gave the glory of the destin'd
   fight,
Squadrons on squadrons drives, and fills
   the fields   260
With close-ranged chariots, and with thick-
   en'd shields.

Where the deep trench in length extended
   lay,
Compacted troops stand wedg'd in firm
   array,
A dreadful front! they shake the bands,
   and threat
With long-destroying flames the hostile fleet.
The King of men, by Juno's self inspired,
Toil'd thro' the tents, and all his army
   fired.
Swift as he mov'd, he lifted in his hand
His purple robe, bright ensign of com-
   mand.
High on the midmost bark the King ap-
   pear'd;   270
There, from Ulysses' deck, his voice was
   heard:
To Ajax and Achilles reach'd the sound,
Whose distant ships the guarded navy
   bound.
' Oh Argives! shame of human race! ' he
   cried
(The hollow vessels to his voice replied),
' Where now are all your glorious boasts of
   yore,
Your hasty triumphs on the Lemnian shore ?
Each fearless hero dares a hundred foes,
While the feast lasts, and while the goblet
   flows;
But who to meet one martial man is found,
When the fight rages, and the flames sur-
   round ?   281
O mighty Jove! oh Sire of the distress'd!
Was ever King like me, like me oppress'd ?
With power immense, with justice arm'd
   in vain;
My glory ravish'd, and my people slain!
To thee my vows were breathed from ev'ry
   shore;
What altar smoked not with our victims'
   gore ?
With fat of bulls I fed the constant flame,
And ask'd destruction to the Trojan name.
Now, gracious God! far humbler our de-⎫
   mand;   290 ⎪
Give these at least to 'scape from Hec- ⎬
   tor's hand, ⎪
And save the relics of the Grecian land!'⎭
   Thus pray'd the King, and Heav'n's
   great Father heard
His vows, in bitterness of soul preferr'd;
The wrath appeas'd by happy signs de-
   clares,
And gives the people to their Monarch's
   prayers.

His eagle, sacred bird of Heav'n! he sent,
A fawn his talons truss'd (divine portent),
High o'er the wond'ring hosts he soar'd
  above,
Who paid their vows to Panomphæan Jove;
Then let the prey before his altar fall: 301
The Greeks beheld, and transport seiz'd on
  all:
Encouraged by the sign, the troops revive,
And fierce on Troy with double fury drive.
Tydides first, of all the Grecian force,
O'er the broad ditch impell'd his foaming
  horse,
Pierc'd the deep ranks, their strongest bat-
  tle tore,
And dyed his jav'lin red with Trojan gore.
Young Agelaüs (Phradmon was his sire)
With flying coursers shunn'd his dreadful
  ire: 310
Struck thro' the back the Phrygian fell op-
  press'd;
The dart drove on, and issued at his breast:
Headlong he quits the car; his arms re-
  sound;
His pond'rous buckler thunders on the
  ground.
Forth rush a tide of Greeks, the passage
  freed;
Th' Atridæ first, th' Ajaces next succeed:
Meriones, like Mars in arms renown'd,
And godlike Idomen, now pass'd the
  mound;
Evæmon's son next issues to the foe,
And last, young Teucer with his bended
  bow. 320
Secure behind the Telamonian shield
The skilful archer wide survey'd the field,
With ev'ry shaft some hostile victim slew,
Then close beneath the sev'n-fold orb with-
  drew:
The conscious infant so, when fear alarms,
Retires for safety to the mother's arms.
Thus Ajax guards his brother in the field,
Moves as he moves, and turns the shining
  shield.
Who first by Teucer's mortal arrows bled?
Orsilochus; then fell Ormenus dead: 330
The godlike Lycophon next press'd the
  plain,
With Chromius, Dætor, Ophelestes slain:
Bold Hamopaon breathless sunk to ground:
The bloody pile great Melanippus crown'd.
Heaps fell on heaps, sad trophies of his
  art,
A Trojan ghost attending every dart.

Great Agamemnon views with joyful eye
The ranks grow thinner as his arrows
  fly:
'Oh youth, for ever dear' (the Monarch
  cried),
'Thus, always thus, thy early worth be
  tried; 340
Thy brave example shall retrieve our host,
Thy country's saviour, and thy father's
  boast!
Sprung from an alien's bed thy sire to
  grace,
The vig'rous offspring of a stol'n embrace.
Proud of his boy, he own'd the gen'rous
  flame,
And the brave son repays his cares with
  fame.
Now hear a Monarch's vow: If Heav'n's
  high Powers
Give me to raze Troy's long-defended
  towers;
Whatever treasures Greece for me design,
The next rich honorary gift be thine: 350
Some golden tripod, or distinguish'd car,
With coursers dreadful in the ranks of
  war;
Or some fair captive whom thy eyes ap-
  prove,
Shall recompense the warrior's toils with
  love.'
  To this the Chief: 'With praise the rest
  inspire,
Nor urge a soul already fill'd with fire.
What strength I have, be now in battle
  tried,
Till ev'ry shaft in Phrygian blood be
  dyed.
Since, rallying, from our wall we forced
  the foe,
Still aim'd at Hector have I bent my
  bow; 360
Eight forky arrows from this hand have
  fled,
And eight bold heroes by their points lie
  dead:
But sure some God denies me to destroy
This fury of the field, this dog of Troy.'
  He said, and twang'd the string. The
  weapon flies
At Hector's breast, and sings along the
  skies:
He miss'd the mark; but pierc'd Gor-
  gythio's heart
And drench'd in royal blood the thirsty
  dart

(Fair Castianira, nymph of form divine,
This offspring added to King Priam's
	line).							370
As full-blown poppies overcharged with
	rain
Decline the head, and drooping kiss the
	plain;
So sinks the youth: his beauteous head,
	depress'd
Beneath his helmet, drops upon his breast.
Another shaft the raging archer drew:
That other shaft with erring fury flew
(From Hector Phœbus turn'd the flying
	wound),
Yet fell not dry or guiltless to the ground:
Thy breast, brave Archeptolemus! it tore,
And dipp'd its feathers in no vulgar
	gore.							380
Headlong he falls: his sudden fall alarms
The steeds, that startle at his sounding
	arms.
Hector with grief his charioteer beheld
All pale and breathless on the sanguine
	field.
Then bids Cebriones direct the rein,
Quits his bright car, and issues on the
	plain.
Dreadful he shouts: from earth a stone he
	took,
And rush'd on Teucer with a lifted rock.
The youth already strain'd the forceful yew;
The shaft already to his shoulder drew;		390
The feather in his hand, just wing'd for
	flight,
Touch'd where the neck and hollow chest
	unite;
There, where the juncture knits the chan-
	nel bone,
The furious Chief discharged the craggy
	stone;
The bow-string burst beneath the pon-
	d'rous blow,
And his numb'd hand dismiss'd his useless
	bow.
He fell; but Ajax his broad shield dis-
	play'd,
And screen'd his brother with a mighty
	shade;
Till great Alastor and Mecistheus bore
The batter'd archer groaning to the
	shore.							400
	Troy yet found grace before th' Olym-
		pian sire;
He arm'd their hands, and fill'd their
	breasts with fire.

The Greeks, repuls'd, retreat behind their
	wall,
Or in the trench on heaps confusedly fall.
First of the foe, great Hector march'd
	along,
With terror clothed, and more than mortal
	strong.
As the bold hound that gives the lion
	chase,
With beating bosom, and with eager pace,
Hangs on his haunch, or fastens on his
	heels,
Guards as he turns, and circles as he
	wheels;						410
Thus oft the Grecians turn'd, but still they
	flew;
Thus following, Hector still the hindmost
	slew.
When, flying, they had pass'd the trench
	profound,
And many a Chief lay gasping on the
	ground;
Before the ships a desp'rate stand they
	made;
And fired the troops, and call'd the Gods
	to aid.
Fierce on his rattling chariot Hector came;
His eyes like Gorgon shot a sanguine
	flame
That wither'd all their host: like Mars he
	stood,
Dire as the monster, dreadful as the
	God!							420
Their strong distress the wife of Jove sur-
	vey'd;
Then pensive thus to War's triumphant
	Maid:
	'Oh, Daughter of that God, whose arm
		can wield
Th' avenging bolt, and shake the sable
	shield!
Now, in this moment of her last despair,
Shall wretched Greece no more confess
	our care,
Condemn'd to suffer the full force of Fate,
And drain the dregs of Heav'n's relentless
	hate ?
Gods! shall one raging hand thus level
	all ?
What numbers fell! what numbers yet
	shall fall!						430
What Power divine shall Hector's wrath
	assuage ?
Still swells the slaughter, and still grows
	the rage!'

So spoke th' imperial Regent of the
    Skies;
To whom the Goddess with the azure eyes:
'Long since had Hector stain'd these fields
    with gore,
Stretch'd by some Argive on his native
    shore:
But he above, the Sire of Heav'n, with-
    stands,
Mocks our attempts, and slights our just
    demands.
The stubborn God, inflexible and hard,
Forgets my service and deserv'd re-
    ward;   440
Saved I, for this, his fav'rite son distress'd,
By stern Eurystheus with long labours
    press'd?
He begg'd, with tears he begg'd, in deep
    dismay;
I shot from Heav'n, and gave his arm the
    day.
Oh had my wisdom known this dire event,
When to grim Pluto's gloomy gates he
    went;
The triple dog had never felt his chain,
Nor Styx been cross'd, nor Hell explor'd
    in vain.
Averse to me of all his Heav'n of Gods,
At Thetis' suit the partial Thund'rer
    nods.   450
To grace her gloomy, fierce, resenting son,
My hopes are frustrate, and my Greeks
    undone.
Some future day, perhaps, he may be
    mov'd
To call his Blue-eyed Maid his best-be-
    lov'd.
Haste, launch thy chariot, thro' yon ranks
    to ride;
Myself will arm, and thunder at thy side.
Then, Goddess! say, shall Hector glory
    then
(That terror of the Greeks, that Man of
    men),
When Juno's self, and Pallas shall appear,
All dreadful in the crimson walks of
    war?   460
What mighty Trojan then, on yonder shore,⎫
Expiring, pale, and terrible no more,   ⎬
Shall feast the fowls, and glut the dogs   ⎪
    with gore?'   ⎭
    She ceas'd, and Juno rein'd the steeds
        with care
(Heav'n's awful Empress, Saturn's other
    heir):

Pallas, meanwhile, her various veil un-
    bound,
With flowers adorn'd, with art immortal
    crown'd;
The radiant robe her sacred fingers wove
Floats in rich waves, and spreads the court
    of Jove.
Her father's arms her mighty limbs in-
    vest,   470
His cuirass blazes on her ample breast.
The vig'rous Power the trembling car
    ascends;
Shook by her arm, the massy jav'lin bends;
Huge, pond'rous, strong! that, when her
    fury burns,
Proud tyrants humbles, and whole hosts
    o'erturns.
    Saturnia lends the lash; the coursers fly;
Smooth glides the chariot thro' the liquid
    sky.
Heav'n's gates spontaneous open to the
    Powers,
Heav'n's golden gates, kept by the winged
    Hours:
Commission'd in alternate watch they
    stand,   480
The sun's bright portals and the skies com-
    mand;
Close or unfold th' eternal gates of day,
Bar Heav'n with clouds, or roll those clouds
    away:
The sounding hinges ring, the clouds
    divide;
Prone down the steep of Heav'n their
    course they guide.
But Jove, incens'd, from Ida's top survey'd,
And thus enjoin'd the many-colour'd Maid:
'Thaumantia! mount the winds, and
    stop their car;
Against the highest who shall wage the
    war?
If furious yet they dare the vain debate, 490
Thus have I spoke, and what I speak is
    Fate.
Their coursers crush'd beneath the wheels
    shall lie,
Their car in fragments scatter'd o'er the
    sky;
My lightning these rebellious shall con-
    found,
And hurl them flaming, headlong to the
    ground,
Condemn'd for ten revolving years to weep
The wounds impress'd by burning Thunder
    deep.

So shall Minerva learn to fear our ire,
Nor dare to combat hers and Nature's
    Sire.
For Juno, headstrong and imperious still, 500
She claims some title to transgress our
    will.'
  Swift as the wind, the various-colour'd
    Maid
From Ida's top her golden wings display'd;
To great Olympus' shining gates she flies,
There meets the chariot rushing down the
    skies,
Restrains their progress from the bright
    abodes,
And speaks the mandate of the Sire of
    Gods:
  ' What frenzy, Goddesses ! what rage
    can move
Celestial minds to tempt the wrath of
    Jove ?
Desist, obedient to his high command; 510
This is his word: and know his word shall
    stand.
His lightning your rebellion shall confound,
And hurl ye headlong, flaming to the
    ground:
Your horses crush'd beneath the wheels
    shall lie,
Your car in fragments scatter'd o'er the
    sky;
Yourselves condemn'd ten rolling years to
    weep
The wounds impress'd by burning Thunder
    deep.
So shall Minerva learn to fear his ire,
Nor dare to combat hers and Nature's
    Sire.
For Juno, headstrong and imperious
    still,   520
She claims some title to transgress his
    will:
But thee what desp'rate insolence has
    driv'n,
To lift thy lance against the King of
    Heav'n ? '
  Then, mounting on the pinions of the
    wind,
She flew; and Juno thus her rage resign'd:
  ' O Daughter of that God, whose arm
    can wield
Th' avenging bolt, and shake the dreadful
    shield!
No more let beings of superior birth
Contend with Jove for this low race of
    earth:

Triumphant now, now miserably slain, 530
They breathe or perish as the Fates ordain.
But Jove's high counsels full effect shall
    find,
And, ever constant, ever rule mankind.'
  She spoke, and backward turn'd her
    steeds of light,
Adorn'd with manes of gold, and heav'nly
    bright.
The Hours unloos'd them, panting as they
    stood,
And heap'd their mangers with ambrosial
    food.
There tied, they rest in high celestial stalls;
The chariot propp'd against the crystal
    walls.
The pensive Goddesses, abash'd, controll'd,
Mix with the Gods, and fill their seats of
    gold.   541
  And now the Thund'rer meditates his
    flight
From Ida's summits to th' Olympian
    height.
Swifter than thought the wheels instinctive
    fly,
Flame thro' the vast of air, and reach the sky.
'T was Neptune's charge his coursers to
    unbrace,
And fix the car on its immortal base;
There stood the chariot, beaming forth its
    rays,
Till with a snowy veil he screen'd the
    blaze.
He, whose all-conscious eyes the world be-
    hold,   550
Th' eternal Thunderer, sat throned in gold.
High Heav'n the footstool of his feet he
    makes,
And wide beneath him all Olympus shakes.
Trembling afar th' offending Powers ap-
    pear'd,
Confused and silent, for his frown they
    fear'd.
He saw their soul, and thus his word im-
    parts:
  ' Pallas and Juno! say, why heave your
    hearts ?
Soon was your battle o'er: proud Troy re-
    tired
Before your face, and in your wrath ex-
    pired.
But know, whoe'er almighty Power with-
    stand!   560
Unmatch'd our force, unconquer'd is our
    hand:

Who shall the Sov'reign of the Skies con-
  trol ?
Not all the Gods that crown the starry pole.
Your hearts shall tremble, if our arms we
  take,
And each immortal nerve with horror
  shake.
For thus I speak, and what I speak shall
  stand,
What Power soe'er provokes our lifted
  hand,
On this our hill no more shall hold his
  place,
Cut off, and exil'd from th' ethereal race.'
  Juno and Pallas grieving hear the doom,
But feast their souls on Ilion's woes to
  come.   571
Tho' secret anger swell'd Minerva's breast,
The prudent Goddess yet her wrath re-
  press'd:
But Juno, impotent of rage, replies:
' What hast thou said, oh Tyrant of the
  Skies!
Strength and omnipotence invest thy
  throne;
'T is thine to punish; ours to grieve alone.
For Greece we grieve, abandon'd by her
  Fate
To drink the dregs of thy unmeasured
  hate: 579
From fields forbidden we submiss refrain,
With arms unaiding see our Argives slain;
Yet grant our counsels still their breasts
  may move,
Lest all should perish in the rage of Jove.'
  The Goddess thus: and thus the God re-
  plies;
Who swells the clouds, and blackens all the
  skies:
' The morning sun, awaked by loud alarms,
Shall see th' almighty Thunderer in arms.
What heaps of Argives then shall load the
  plain,
Those radiant eyes shall view, and view in
  vain.
Nor shall great Hector cease the rage of
  fight,   590
The navy flaming, and thy Greeks in flight,
Ev'n till the day, when certain Fates ordain ⎫
That stern Achilles (his Patroclus slain) ⎬
Shall rise in vengeance, and lay waste the ⎭
  plain.
For such is Fate, nor canst thou turn its
  course
With all thy rage, with all thy rebel force.

Fly, if thou wilt, to earth's remotest bound,
Where on her utmost verge the seas re-
  sound;
Where curs'd Iäpetus and Saturn dwell,
Fast by the brink, within the steams of
  Hell;   600
No sun e'er gilds the gloomy horrors there,
No cheerful gales refresh the lazy air:
There arm once more the bold Titanian
  band,
And arm in vain: for what I will shall
  stand.'
  Now deep in ocean sunk the lamp of
  light,
And drew behind the cloudy veil of night:
The conquering Trojans mourn his beams
  decay'd;
The Greeks rejoicing bless the friendly
  shade.
  The victors keep the field; and Hector
  calls
A martial council near the navy walls: 610
These to Scamander's bank apart he led,
Where thinly scatter'd lay the heaps of
  dead.
Th' assembled Chiefs, descending on the
  ground,
Attend his order, and their Prince sur-
  round.
A massy spear he bore of mighty strength,
Of full ten cubits was the lance's length;
The point was brass, refulgent to behold,
Fix'd to the wood with circling rings of
  gold:
The noble Hector on this lance reclin'd,
And, bending forward, thus reveal'd his
  mind: 620
  ' Ye valiant Trojans, with attention hear!
Ye Dardan bands, and gen'rous aids, give
  ear!
This day, we hoped, would wrap in con-
  quering flame
Greece with her ships, and crown our toils
  with fame:
But darkness now, to save the cowards,
  falls,
And guards them trembling in their wooden
  walls.
Obey the night, and use her peaceful hours
Our steeds to forage, and refresh our
  powers.
Straight from the town be sheep and oxen
  sought,
And strength'ning bread and gen'rous wine
  be brought.   630

Wide o'er the field, high blazing to the sky,
Let numerous fires the absent sun supply,
The flaming piles with plenteous fuel raise,
Till the bright morn her purple beam displays:
Lest in the silence and the shades of night,
Greece on her sable ships attempt her flight.
Not unmolested let the wretches gain
Their lofty decks, or safely cleave the main:
Some hostile wound let ev'ry dart bestow,
Some lasting token of the Phrygian foe, 640
Wounds, that long hence may ask their spouses' care,
And warn their children from a Trojan war.
Now thro' the circuit of our Ilion wall,
Let sacred heralds sound the solemn call;
To bid the sires with hoary honours crown'd,
And beardless youths, our battlements surround.
Firm be the guard, while distant lie our powers,
And let the matrons hang with lights the towers:
Lest, under covert of the midnight shade,
Th' insidious foe the naked town invade. 650
Suffice, to-night, these orders to obey;
A nobler charge shall rouse the dawning day.
The Gods, I trust, shall give to Hector's hand,
From these detested foes to free the land,
Who plough'd, with Fates averse, the wat'ry way;
For Trojan vultures a predestin'd prey.
Our common safety must be now the care;
But, soon as morning paints the fields of air,
Sheathed in bright arms let every troop engage,
And the fired fleet behold the battle rage.
Then, then shall Hector and Tydides prove, 661
Whose Fates are heaviest in the scale of Jove.
To-morrow's light (oh haste the glorious morn!)
Shall see his bloody spoils in triumph borne;
With this keen jav'lin shall his breast be gored,
And prostrate heroes bleed around their lord.

Certain as this, oh! might my days endure,
From age inglorious, and black death, secure;
So might my life and glory know no bound,
Like Pallas worshipp'd, like the sun renown'd, 670
As the next dawn, the last they shall enjoy,
Shall crush the Greeks, and end the woes of Troy.'
    The leader spoke. From all his hosts around
Shouts of applause along the shores resound.
Each from the yoke the smoking steeds untied,
And fix'd their headstalls to his chariot-side.
Fat sheep and oxen from the town are led,
With gen'rous wine, and all-sustaining bread.
Full hecatombs lay burning on the shore;
The winds to Heav'n the curling vapours bore. 680
Ungrateful off'ring to th' immortal Powers!
Whose wrath hung heavy o'er the Trojan towers;
Nor Priam nor his sons obtain'd their grace;
Proud Troy they hated, and her guilty race.
    The troops exulting sat in order round,
And beaming fires illumin'd all the ground.
As when the moon, refulgent lamp of night,
O'er Heav'n's clear azure spreads her sacred light,
When not a breath disturbs the deep serene,
And not a cloud o'ercasts the solemn scene; 690
Around her throne the vivid planets roll,
And stars unnumber'd gild the glowing pole,
O'er the dark trees a yellower verdure shed,
And tip with silver ev'ry mountain's head;
Then shine the vales, the rocks in prospect rise,
A flood of glory bursts from all the skies:
The conscious swains, rejoicing in the sight,
Eye the blue vault and bless the useful light.

So many flames before proud Ilion blaze,
And lighten glimm'ring Xanthus with
   their rays: 700
The long reflections of the distant fires
Gleam on the walls, and tremble on the
   spires.
A thousand piles the dusky horrors gild,
And shoot a shady lustre o'er the field.
Full fifty guards each flaming pile attend,
Whose umber'd arms, by fits, thick flashes
   send.
Loud neigh the coursers o'er their heaps
   of corn,
And ardent warriors wait the rising morn.

BOOK IX

THE EMBASSY TO ACHILLES

THE ARGUMENT

Agamemnon, after the last day's defeat, proposes to the Greeks to quit the siege, and return to their country. Diomed opposes this,
and Nestor seconds him, praising his wisdom
and resolution. He orders the guard to be
strengthened, and a council summoned to deliberate what measures were to be followed in
this emergency. Agamemnon pursues this
advice, and Nestor farther prevails upon him
to send ambassadors to Achilles, in order to
move him to a reconciliation. Ulysses and
Ajax are made choice of, who are accompanied by old Phœnix. They make, each
of them, very moving and pressing speeches,
but are rejected with roughness by Achilles,
who notwithstanding retains Phœnix in his
tent. The ambassadors return unsuccess-
fully to the camp, and the troops betake
themselves to sleep.
This book, and the next following, take up the
space of one night, which is the twenty-
seventh from the beginning of the poem.
The scene lies on the sea-shore, the station of
the Grecian ships.

THUS joyful Troy maintain'd the watch
   of night:
While Fear, pale comrade of inglorious
   Flight,
And heav'n-bred Horror, on the Grecian
   part,
Sat on each face, and sadden'd ev'ry
   heart.
As from its cloudy dungeon issuing forth,
A double tempest of the west and north

Swells o'er the sea, from Thracia's frozen
   shore,
Heaps waves on waves, and bids th' Ægean
   roar;
This way and that the boiling deeps are
   toss'd;
Such various passions urged the troubled
   host.   10
Great Agamemnon griev'd above the rest;
Superior sorrows swell'd his royal breast;
Himself his orders to the heralds bears,
To bid to council all the Grecian peers,
But bid in whispers: these surround their
   Chief,
In solemn sadness and majestic grief.
The King amidst the mournful circle rose;
Down his wan cheek a briny torrent flows:
So silent fountains, from a rock's tall head,
In sable streams soft-trickling waters
   shed.   20
With more than vulgar grief he stood op-
   press'd;
Words, mix'd with sighs, thus bursting
   from his breast:
   'Ye sons of Greece! partake your leader's
   care,
Fellows in arms, and Princes of the war!
Of partial Jove too justly we complain,
And heav'nly oracles believ'd in vain.
A safe return was promis'd to our toils
With conquest honour'd, and enrich'd with
   spoils:
Now shameful flight alone can save the
   host,
Our wealth, our people, and our glory,
   lost.   30
So Jove decrees, almighty Lord of all!
Jove, at whose nod whole empires rise or
   fall,
Who shakes the feeble props of human
   trust,
And towers and armies humbles to the
   dust.
Haste then, for ever quit these fatal fields,
Haste to the joys our native country yields;
Spread all your canvas, all your oars
   employ,
Nor hope the fall of Heav'n-defended
   Troy.'
   He said; deep silence held the Grecian
   band;
Silent, unmov'd, in dire dismay they
   stand,   40
A pensive scene! till Tydeus' warlike son
Roll'd on the King his eyes, and thus begun:

'When Kings advise us to renounce our
  fame,
First let him speak, who first has suffer'd
  shame.
If I oppose thee, Prince! thy wrath with-
  hold;
The laws of council bid my tongue be
  bold.
Thou first, and thou alone, in fields of
  fight,
Durst brand my courage, and defame my
  might;
Nor from a friend th' unkind reproach ap-
  pear'd,
The Greeks stood witness, all our army
  heard.   50
The Gods, O Chief! from whom our
  honours spring,
The Gods have made thee but by halves a
  King:
They gave thee sceptres and a wide com-
  mand,
They gave dominion o'er the seas and
  land;
The noblest power that might the world
  control
They gave thee not — a brave and virtuous
  soul.
Is this a gen'ral's voice, that would sug-
  gest
Fears like his own in ev'ry Grecian breast?
Confiding in our want of worth he stands,
And if we fly, 't is what our King com-
  mands.   60
Go thou, inglorious! from th' embattled
  plain,
Ships thou hast, store, and nearest to the
  main;
A nobler care the Grecians shall employ,
To combat, conquer, and extirpate Troy.
Here Greece shall stay; or, if all Greece
  retire,
Myself will stay, till Troy or I expire;
Myself, and Sthenelus, will fight for
  fame;
God bade us fight, and 't was with God we
  came.'
  He ceas'd; the Greeks loud acclamations
  raise,
And voice to voice resounds Tydides'
  praise.   70
Wise Nestor then his rev'rend figure
  rear'd;
He spoke: the host in still attention
  heard:

'O truly great! in whom the Gods have
  join'd
Such strength of body with such force of
  mind;
In conduct, as in courage, you excel,
Still first to act what you advise so well.
Those wholesome counsels which thy wis-
  dom moves,
Applauding Greece, with common voice,
  approves.
Kings thou canst blame; a bold, but prudent
  youth;
And blame ev'n Kings with praise, because
  with truth.   80
And yet those fears that since thy birth
  have run,
Would hardly style thee Nestor's youngest
  son.
Then let me add what yet remains behind,
A thought unfinish'd in that gen'rous mind;
Age bids me speak; nor shall th' advice I
  bring
Distaste the people, or offend the King:
  'Curs'd is the man, and void of law and
  right,
Unworthy property, unworthy light,
Unfit for public rule, or private care,
That wretch, that monster, that delights in
  war: 90
Whose lust is murder, and whose horrid
  joy
To tear his country, and his kind destroy!
This night refresh and fortify thy train;
Between the trench and wall let guards
  remain:
Be that the duty of the young and bold;
But thou, O King, to council call the old:
Great is thy sway, and weighty are thy
  cares;
Thy high commands must spirit all our
  wars:
With Thracian wines recruit thy honour'd
  guests,
For happy counsels flow from sober feasts.
Wise, weighty counsels aid a state dis-
  tress'd   101
And such a monarch as can choose the
  best.
See! what a blaze from hostile tents aspires,
How near our fleet approach the Trojan
  fires!
Who can, unmov'd, behold the dreadful
  light?
What eye beholds them, and can close to-
  night?

This dreadful interval determines all;
To-morrow, Troy must flame, or Greece
   must fall.'
    Thus spoke the hoary Sage: the rest
     obey;
Swift thro' the gates the guards direct
   their way.   110
His son was first to pass the lofty mound,
The gen'rous Thrasymed, in arms re-
   nown'd:
Next him Ascalaphus, Ialmen, stood,
The double offspring of the Warrior-God.
Deïpyrus, Aphareus, Merion join,
And Lycomed, of Creon's noble line.
Sev'n were the leaders of the nightly
   bands,
And each bold Chief a hundred spears
   commands.
The fires they light, to short repasts they
   fall,
Some line the trench, and others man the
   wall.   120
    The King of Men, on public counsels
    bent,
Convened the Princes in his ample tent;
Each seiz'd a portion of the kingly feast,
But stay'd his hand when thirst and hunger
   ceas'd.
Then Nestor spoke, for wisdom long ap-
   prov'd,
And, slowly rising, thus the council mov'd:
   'Monarch of nations! whose superior sway
Assembled states and lords of earth obey,
The laws and sceptres to thy hand are giv'n,
And millions own the care of thee and
   Heav'n.   130
O King! the counsels of my age attend;
With thee my cares begin, with thee must
   end;
Thee, Prince! it fits alike to speak and
   hear,
Pronounce with judgment, with regard
   give ear,
To see no wholesome motion be withstood,
And ratify the best for public good.
Nor, tho' a meaner give advice, repine,
But follow it, and make the wisdom thine.
Hear then a thought, not now conceiv'd in
   haste,
At once my present judgment, and my
   past: 140
When from Pelides' tent you forced the
   Maid,
I first opposed, and, faithful, durst dis-
   suade;

But, bold of soul, when headlong fury fired,
You wrong'd the man, by men and Gods
   admired:
Now seek some means his fatal wrath to
   end,
With prayers to move him, or with gifts to
   bend.'
    To whom the King: 'With justice hast
    thou shewn
A Prince's faults, and I with reason own.
That happy man whom Jove still honours
   most,
Is more than armies, and himself a host. 150
Bless'd in his love, this wondrous Hero
   stands;
Heav'n fights his war, and humbles all our
   bands.
Fain would my heart, which err'd thro'
   frantic rage,
The wrathful Chief and angry Gods as-
   suage.
If gifts immense his mighty soul can bow,
Hear, all ye Greeks, and witness what I
   vow:
Ten weighty talents of the purest gold,
And twice ten vases of refulgent mould;
Sev'n sacred tripods, whose unsullied
   frame
Yet knows no office, nor has felt the
   flame: 160
Twelve steeds unmatch'd in fleetness and
   in force,
And still victorious in the dusty course
(Rich were the man whose ample stores
   exceed
The prizes purchas'd by their winged
   speed):
Sev'n lovely captives of the Lesbian line,
Skill'd in each art, unmatch'd in form
   divine,
The same I chose for more than vulgar
   charms,
When Lesbos sunk beneath the hero's
   arms:
All these, to buy his friendship, shall be
   paid,
And join'd with these the long-contested
   maid;   170
With all her charms, Briseïs I resign,
And solemn swear those charms were never
   mine;
Untouch'd she staid, uninjured she re-
   moves,
Pure from my arms, and guiltless of my
   loves.

These instant shall be his; and if the Powers
Give to our arms proud Ilion's hostile towers,
Then shall he store (when Greece the spoil divides)
With gold and brass his loaded navy's sides.
Besides, full twenty nymphs of Trojan race
With copious love shall crown his warm embrace; 180
Such as himself will choose; who yield to none,
Or yield to Helen's heav'nly charms alone.
Yet hear me farther: when our wars are o'er,
If safe we land on Argos' fruitful shore,
There shall he live my son, our honours share,
And with Orestes' self divide my care.
Yet more — three daughters in my court are bred,
And each well worthy of a royal bed,
Laodice and Iphigenia fair,
And bright Chrysothemis with golden hair: 190
Her let him choose whom most his eyes approve,
I ask no presents, no reward for love;
Myself will give the dower; so vast a store,
As never father gave a child before.
Sev'n ample cities shall confess his sway,
Him Enopé, and Pheræ him obey,
Cardamylé with ample turrets crown'd,
And sacred Pedasus for vines renown'd;
Æpea fair, the pastures Hira yields,
And rich Antheia with her flowery fields:
The whole extent to Pylos' sandy plain, 201
Along the verdant margin of the main.
There heifers graze, and lab'ring oxen toil;
Bold are the men, and gen'rous is the soil;
There shall he reign with power and justice crown'd,
And rule the tributary realms around.
All this I give, his vengeance to control,
And sure all this may move his mighty soul.
Pluto, the grisly God, who never spares,
Who feels no mercy, and who hears no prayers, 210
Lives dark and dreadful in deep Hell's abodes,

And mortals hate him as the worst of Gods.
Great tho' he be, it fits him to obey:
Since more than his my years, and more my sway.'
The Monarch thus: the rev'rend Nestor then:
'Great Agamemnon! glorious King of Men!
Such are thy offers as a Prince may take,
And such as fits a gen'rous King to make.
Let chosen delegates this hour be sent
(Myself will name them) to Pelides' tent: 220
Let Phœnix lead, revered for hoary age,
Great Ajax next, and Ithacus the sage.
Yet more to sanctify the word you send,
Let Hodius and Eurybates attend.
Now pray to Jove to grant what Greece demands;
Pray, in deep silence, and with purest hands.'
He said, and all approv'd. The heralds bring
The cleansing water from the living spring,
The youth with wine the sacred goblets crown'd,
And large libations drench'd the sands around. 230
The rite perform'd, the Chiefs their thirst allay,
Then from the royal tent they take their way;
Wise Nestor turns on each his careful eye,
Forbids t' offend, instructs them to apply:
Much he advised them all, Ulysses most,
To deprecate the Chief, and save the host.
Thro' the still night they march, and hear the roar
Of murm'ring billows on the sounding shore.
To Neptune, ruler of the seas profound,
Whose liquid arms the mighty globe surround, 240
They pour forth vows, their embassy to bless,
And calm the rage of stern Æacides.
And now arrived, where, on the sandy bay
The Myrmidonian tents and vessels lay,
Amused at ease, the godlike man they found,
Pleas'd with the solemn harp's harmonious sound
(The well-wrought harp from conquer'd Thebæ came,
Of polish'd silver was its costly frame):

With this he soothes his angry soul, and
   sings
Th' immortal deeds of heroes and of
   Kings.   250
Patroclus only of the royal train,
Placed in his tent, attends the lofty strain:
Full opposite he sat, and listen'd long
In silence waiting till he ceas'd the song.
Unseen the Grecian embassy proceeds
To his high tent; the great Ulysses leads.
Achilles starting, as the Chiefs he spied,
Leap'd from his seat, and laid the harp
   aside.
With like surprise arose Menœtius' son:
Pelides grasp'd their hands, and thus
   begun: 260
' Princes, all hail! whatever brought you
   here,
Or strong necessity, or urgent fear;
Welcome, tho' Greeks! for not as foes ye
   came;
To me more dear than all that bear the
   name.'
   With that, the Chiefs beneath his roof he
   led,
And placed in seats with purple carpets
   spread.
Then thus: ' Patroclus, crown a larger bowl,
Mix purer wine, and open every soul.
Of all the warriors yonder host can send,
Thy friend most honours these, and these
   thy friend.'   270
   He said: Patroclus, o'er the blazing fire
Heaps in a brazen vase three chines entire:
The brazen vase Automedon sustains,
Which flesh of porket, sheep, and goat
   contains:
Achilles at the genial feast presides,
The parts transfixes, and with skill divides.
Meanwhile Patroclus sweats the fire to
   raise;
The tent is brighten'd with the rising
   blaze:
Then, when the languid flames at length
   subside,   279
He strews a bed of glowing embers wide,
Above the coals the smoking fragments
   turns,
And sprinkles sacred salt from lifted urns;
With bread the glitt'ring canisters they
   load,
Which round the board Menœtius' son be-
   stow'd:
Himself, opposed t' Ulysses full in sight,
Each portion parts, and orders every rite.

The first fat off'rings, to th' immortals due,
Amidst the greedy flames Patroclus threw;
Then each indulging in the social feast,   289
His thirst and hunger soberly repress'd.
That done, to Phœnix Ajax gave the sign;
Not unperceiv'd; Ulysses crown'd with
   wine
The foaming bowl, and instant thus began,
His speech addressing to the godlike man:
  ' Health to Achilles! happy are thy
   guests!
Not those more honour'd whom Atrides
   feasts:
Tho' gen'rous plenty crown thy loaded
   boards,
That, Agamemnon's regal tent affords;
But greater cares sit heavy on our souls,
Not eased by banquets or by flowing
   bowls.   300
What scenes of slaughter in yon fields ap-
   pear!
The dead we mourn, and for the living
   fear;
Greece on the brink of fate all doubtful
   stands,
And owns no help but from thy saving
   hands:
Troy and her aids for ready vengeance
   call;
Their threat'ning tents already shade our
   wall:
Hear how with shouts their conquest they
   proclaim,
And point at ev'ry ship their vengeful
   flame!
For them the Father of the Gods declares,
Theirs are his omens, and his Thunder
   theirs.   310
See, full of Jove, avenging Hector rise! ⎤
See! Heav'n and Earth the raging Chief ⎟
   defies;   ⎬
What fury in his breast, what lightning ⎟
   in his eyes!   ⎦
He waits but for the morn, to sink in flame
The ships, the Greeks, and all the Grecian
   name.
Heav'ns! how my country's woes distract
   my mind,
Lest Fate accomplish all his rage design'd.
And must we, Gods! our heads inglorious
   lay
In Trojan dust, and this the fatal day ?
Return, Achilles! oh return, tho' late,   320
To save thy Greeks, and stop the course of
   Fate:

If in that heart or grief or courage lies,
Rise to redeem; ah yet, to conquer, rise!
The day may come, when, all our warriors
　　slain,
That heart shall melt, that courage rise in
　　vain.
Regard in time, O Prince divinely brave!
Those wholesome counsels which thy father
　　gave.
When Peleus in his aged arms embraced
His parting son, these accents were his
　　last:
" My child! with strength, with glory and
　　success,　　　　　　　　　　　　330
Thy arms may Juno and Minerva bless!
Trust that to Heav'n: but thou thy cares
　　engage
To calm thy passions, and subdue thy rage:
From gentler manners let thy glory grow,
And shun contention, the sure source of
　　woe;
That young and old may in thy praise com-
　　bine,
The virtues of humanity be thine."
This now despised advice thy father gave;
Ah! check thy anger, and be truly brave.
If thou wilt yield to great Atrides' prayers,
Gifts worthy thee his royal hand prepares;
If not —— but hear me, while I number
　　o'er,　　　　　　　　　　　　　342
The proffer'd presents, an exhaustless
　　store.
Ten weighty talents of the purest gold,
And twice ten vases of refulgent mould;
Sev'n sacred tripods, whose unsullied
　　frame
Yet knows no office, nor has felt the flame:
Twelve steeds unmatch'd in fleetness and
　　in force,
And still victorious in the dusty course
(Rich were the man whose ample stores
　　exceed　　　　　　　　　　　　350
The prizes purchas'd by their winged
　　speed):
Sev'n lovely captives of the Lesbian line,
Skill'd in each art, unmatch'd in form
　　divine,
The same he chose for more than vulgar
　　charms,
When Lesbos sunk beneath thy conquering
　　arms;
All these, to buy thy friendship, shall be
　　paid,
And join'd with these the long-contested
　　maid;

With all her charms, Briseïs he 'll resign,
And solemn swear those charms were only
　　thine;
Untouch'd she stay'd, uninjured she re-
　　moves,　　　　　　　　　　　　360
Pure from his arms, and guiltless of his
　　loves.
These instant shall be thine: and if the
　　Powers
Give to our arms proud Ilion's hostile
　　towers,
Then shalt thou store (when Greece the
　　spoil divides)
With gold and brass thy loaded navy's
　　sides.
Besides, full twenty nymphs of Trojan race
With copious love shall crown thy warm
　　embrace;
Such as thyself shalt choose; who yield to
　　none,
Or yield to Helen's heav'nly charms alone.
Yet hear me farther: when our wars are
　　o'er,　　　　　　　　　　　　　370
If safe we land on Argos' fruitful shore,
There shalt thou live his son, his honours
　　share,
And with Orestes' self divide his care.
Yet more — three daughters in his court
　　are bred,
And each well worthy of a royal bed;
Laodice and Iphigenia fair,
And bright Chrysothemis with golden hair;
Her shalt thou wed whom most thy eyes
　　approve;
He asks no presents, no reward for love:
Himself will give the dower: so vast a
　　store,　　　　　　　　　　　　380
As never father gave a child before.
Sev'n ample cities shall confess thy sway,
Thee Enope, and Pheræ thee obey,
Cardamyle with ample turrets crown'd,
And sacred Pedasus, for vines renown'd:
Æpea fair, the pastures Hira yields,
And rich Antheia with her flowery fields:
The whole extent to Pylos' sandy plain
Along the verdant margin of the main.
There heifers graze, and lab'ring oxen
　　toil;　　　　　　　　　　　　　390
Bold are the men, and gen'rous is the soil.
There shalt thou reign with power and
　　justice crown'd,
And rule the tributary realms around.
Such are the proffers which this day we
　　bring,
Such the repentance of a suppliant King.

But if all this, relentless, thou disdain,
If honour and if int'rest plead in vain;
Yet some redress to suppliant Greece af-
ford,
And be, amongst her guardian Gods, ador'd.
If no regard thy suff'ring country claim, 400
Hear thy own glory, and the voice of
Fame:
For now that Chief, whose unresisted ire
Made nations tremble, and whole hosts re-
tire,
Proud Hector, now, th' unequal fight de-
mands,
And only triumphs to deserve thy hands.'
Then thus the Goddess-born: 'Ulysses,
hear
A faithful speech, that knows nor art nor
fear;
What in my secret soul is understood,
My tongue shall utter, and my deeds make
good.
Let Greece then know, my purpose I re-
tain, 410
Nor with new treaties vex my peace in
vain.
Who dares think one thing, and another
tell,
My heart detests him as the gates of Hell.
' Then thus in short my fix'd resolves at-
tend,
Which nor Atrides, nor his Greeks, can
bend:
Long toils, long perils, in their cause I
bore;
But now th' unfruitful glories charm no
more.
Fight or not fight, a like reward we claim,
The wretch and hero find their prize the
same,
Alike regretted in the dust he lies, 420
Who yields ignobly, or who bravely dies.
Of all my dangers, all my glorious pains,
A life of labours, lo! what fruit remains?
As the bold bird her helpless young at-
tends,
From danger guards them, and from want
defends;
In search of prey she wings the spacious
air,
And with th' untasted food supplies her
care:
For thankless Greece such hardships have
I braved,
Her wives, her infants, by my labours
saved;

Long sleepless nights in heavy arms I
stood, 430
And sweat laborious days in dust and
blood.
I sack'd twelve ample cities on the main,
And twelve lay smoking on the Trojan
plain:
Then at Atrides' haughty feet were laid
The wealth I gather'd, and the spoils I
made.
Your mighty monarch these in peace pos-
sess'd;
Some few my soldiers had, himself the
rest.
Some present too to ev'ry Prince was paid;
And ev'ry Prince enjoys the gift he made;
I only must refund of all his train; 440
See what preëminence our merits gain!
My spoil alone his greedy soul delights;
My spouse alone must bless his lustful
nights:
The woman, let him (as he may) enjoy;
But what's the quarrel then of Greece to
Troy?
What to these shores th' assembled nations
draws,
What calls for vengeance but a woman's
cause?
Are fair endowments and a beauteous face
Belov'd by none but those of Atreus' race?
The wife whom choice and passion both ap-
prove, 450
Sure ev'ry wise and worthy man will love.
Nor did my fair one less distinction claim;
Slave as she was, my soul ador'd the
dame.
Wrong'd in my love, all proffers I disdain;
Deceiv'd for once, I trust not Kings again.
Ye have my answer. What remains to
do,
Your King, Ulysses, may consult with you.
What needs he the defence this arm can
make?
Has he not walls no human force can
shake?
Has he not fenc'd his guarded navy round
With piles, with ramparts, and a trench
profound? 461
And will not these (the wonders he has
done)
Repel the rage of Priam's single son?
There was a time ('t was when for Greece
I fought)
When Hector's prowess no such wonders
wrought;

He kept the verge of Troy, nor dared to
    wait
Achilles' fury at the Scæan gate;
He tried it once, and scarce was saved by
    Fate.
But now those ancient enmities are o'er;
To-morrow we the fav'ring Gods implore;
Then shall you see our parting vessels
    crown'd,   471
And hear with oars the Hellespont resound.
The third day hence, shall Phthia greet our
    sails,
If mighty Neptune send propitious gales;
Phthia to her Achilles shall restore
The wealth he left for this detested shore:
Thither the spoils of this long war shall pass,
The ruddy gold, the steel, and shining
    brass;
My beauteous captives thither I'll convey,
And all that rests of my unravish'd prey, 480
One only valued gift your tyrant gave,
And that resumed; the fair Lyrnessian
    slave.
Then tell him, loud, that all the Greeks
    may hear,
And learn to scorn the wretch they basely
    fear
(For, arm'd in impudence, mankind he
    braves,
And meditates new cheats on all his slaves;
Tho', shameless as he is, to face these eyes
Is what he dares not; if he dares, he dies);
Tell him, all terms, all commerce I decline,
Nor share his council, nor his battle join;
For once deceiv'd, was his; but twice,
    were mine.   491
No — let the stupid Prince, whom Jove de-
    prives
Of sense and justice, run where frenzy
    drives;
His gifts are hateful: Kings of such a kind
Stand but as slaves before a noble mind.
Not tho' he proffer'd all himself possess'd,
And all his rapine could from others wrest:
Not all the golden tides of wealth that
    crown
The many-peopled Orchomenian town;
Not all proud Thebes' unrivall'd walls con-
    tain,   500
The world's great Empress on th' Egyptian
    plain
(That spreads her conquests o'er a thou-
    sand states,
And pours her Heroes thro' a hundred
    gates,

Two hundred horsemen and two hundred
    cars
From each wide portal issuing to the wars);
Tho' bribes were heap'd on bribes, in num-
    ber more
Than dust in fields, or sands along the
    shore;
Should all these offers for my friendship call;
'T is he that offers, and I scorn them all.
Atrides' daughter never shall be led   510
(An ill-match'd consort) to Achilles' bed;
Like golden Venus tho' she charm'd the
    heart,
And vied with Pallas in the works of art.
Some greater Greek let those high nuptials
    grace,
I hate alliance with a tyrant's race.
If Heav'n restore me to my realms with
    life,
The rev'rend Peleus shall elect my wife;
Thessalian nymphs there are, of form di-
    vine,
And Kings that sue to mix their blood with
    mine.
Bless'd in kind love, my years shall glide
    away,   520
Content with just hereditary sway;
There, deaf forever to the martial strife,
Enjoy the dear prerogative of life.
Life is not to be bought with heaps of gold;
Not all Apollo's Pythian treasures hold,
Or Troy once held, in peace and pride of
    sway,
Can bribe the poor possession of a day!
Lost herds and treasures we by arms re-
    gain,
And steeds unrivall'd on the dusty plain:
But from our lips the vital spirit fled,   530
Returns no more to wake the silent dead.
My Fates long since by Thetis were dis-
    closed,
And each alternate, Life or Fame, pro-
    posed:
Here if I stay, before the Trojan town,
Short is my date, but deathless my renown;
If I return, I quit immortal praise
For years on years, and long-extended
    days.
Convinc'd, tho' late, I find my fond mis-
    take,
And warn the Greeks the wiser choice to
    make;
To quit these shores, their native seats en-
    joy,   540
Nor hope the fall of Heav'n-defended Troy.

Jove's arm display'd asserts her from the
skies;
Her hearts are strengthen'd, and her glo-
ries rise.
Go then, to Greece report our fix'd design:
Bid all your councils, all your armies join,
Let all your forces, all your arts conspire,
To save the ships, the troops, the Chiefs,
from fire.
One stratagem has fail'd, and others will:
Ye find Achilles is unconquer'd still.
Go then: digest my message as ye may:
But here this night let rev'rend Phœnix
stay: 551
His tedious toils and hoary hairs demand
A peaceful death in Phthia's friendly land.
But whether he remain, or sail with me,
His age be sacred, and his will be free.'
  The son of Peleus ceas'd: the Chiefs
around
In silence wrapp'd, in consternation
drown'd,
Attend the stern reply. Then Phœnix
rose
(Down his white beard a stream of sorrow
flows),
And while the fate of suff'ring Greece he
mourn'd, 560
With accent weak these tender words re-
turn'd:
  ' Divine Achilles! wilt thou then retire,
And leave our hosts in blood, our fleets on
fire ?
If wrath so dreadful fill thy ruthless mind,
How shall thy friend, thy Phœnix, stay be-
hind ?
The royal Peleus, when from Phthia's coast
He sent thee early to th' Achaian host;
Thy youth as then in sage debates un-
skill'd,
And new to perils of the direful field;
He bade me teach thee all the ways of
war; 570
To shine in councils, and in camps to dare.
Never, ah never, let me leave thy side!
No time shall part us, and no Fate divide.
Not tho' the God, that breathed my life,
restore
The bloom I boasted, and the port I bore,
When Greece of old beheld my youthful
flames
(Delightful Greece, the land of lovely
dames).
My father, faithless to my mother's arms,
Old as he was, ador'd a stranger's charms.

I tried what youth could do (at her desire)
To win the damsel, and prevent my sire. 581
My sire with curses loads my hated head,
And cries, " Ye Furies! barren be his bed."
Infernal Jove, the vengeful fiends below,
And ruthless Proserpine, confirm'd his
vow.
Despair and grief attract my lab'ring
mind;
Gods! what a crime my impious heart de-
sign'd!
I thought (but some kind God that thought
suppress'd)
To plunge the poniard in my father's breast:
Then meditate my flight; my friends in
vain 590
With prayers entreat me, and with force
detain.
On fat of rams, black bulls, and brawny
swine,
They daily feast, with draughts of fragrant
wine:
Strong guards they placed, and watch'd
nine nights entire:
The roofs and porches flamed with constant
fire.
The tenth, I forc'd the gates, unseen of
all:
And, favour'd by the night, o'erleap'd the
wall.
My travels thence thro' spacious Greece
extend:
In Phthia's court at last my labours end.
Your sire receiv'd me, as his son caress'd,
With gifts enrich'd, and with possessions
bless'd. 601
The strong Dolopians thenceforth own'd
my reign,
And all the coast that runs along the main.
By love to thee his bounties I repaid,
And early wisdom to thy soul convey'd:
Great as thou art, my lessons made thee
brave,
A child I took thee, but a hero gave.
Thy infant breast a like affection shew'd:
Still in my arms (an ever-pleasing load),
Or at my knee, by Phœnix wouldst thou
stand; 610
No food was grateful but from Phœnix'
hand.
I pass my watchings o'er thy helpless years,
The tender labours, the compliant cares;
The Gods (I thought) revers'd their hard
decree,
And Phœnix felt a father's joys in thee:

Thy growing virtues justified my cares,
And promis'd comfort to my silver hairs.
Now be thy rage, thy fatal rage, resign'd;
A cruel heart ill suits a manly mind: 619
The Gods (the only great, and only wise)
Are mov'd by off'rings, vows, and sacrifice;
Offending man their high compassion wins,
And daily prayers atone for daily sins.
Prayers are Jove's daughters, of celestial
 race,
Lame are their feet, and wrinkled is their
 face;
With humble mien, and with dejected eyes,
Constant they follow where Injustice flies:
Injustice, swift, erect, and unconfin'd,
Sweeps the wide earth, and tramples o'er
 mankind,
While Prayers, to heal her wrongs, move
 slow behind. 630
Who hears these daughters of almighty
 Jove,
For him they mediate to the throne above:
When man rejects the humble suit they
 make,
The sire revenges for the daughters' sake;
From Jove commission'd, fierce Injustice
 then
Descends, to punish unrelenting men.
Oh let not headlong passion bear the sway;
These reconciling Goddesses obey:
Due honours to the seed of Jove belong;
Due honours calm the fierce and bend the
 strong. 640
Were these not paid thee by the terms we
 bring,
Were rage still harbour'd in the haughty
 King,
Nor Greece, nor all her fortunes, should
 engage
Thy friend to plead against so just a rage.
But since what honour asks, the Gen'ral
 sends,
And sends by those whom most thy heart
 commends,
The best and noblest of the Grecian train;
Permit not these to sue, and sue in vain!
Let me (my son) an ancient fact unfold,
A great example drawn from times of old;
Hear what our fathers were, and what
 their praise, 651
Who conquer'd their revenge in former days.
 'Where Calydon on rocky mountains
 stands,
Once fought th' Ætolian and Curetian
 bands;

To guard it those, to conquer these, ad-
 vance;
And mutual deaths were dealt with mutual
 chance.
The silver Cynthia bade Contention rise,
In vengeance of neglected sacrifice;
On Œneus' fields she sent a monstrous
 boar,
That levell'd harvests and whole forests
 tore: 660
This beast (when many a Chief his tusks
 had slain)
Great Meleager stretch'd along the plain.
Then, for his spoils, a new debate arose,
The neighbour nations thence commencing
 foes.
Strong as they were, the bold Curetes
 fail'd,
While Meleager's thund'ring arm pre-
 vail'd:
Till rage at length inflamed his lofty breast
(For rage invades the wisest and the best).
Curs'd by Althæa, to his wrath he yields,
And, in his wife's embrace, forgets the
 fields. 670
 '(She from Marpessa sprung, divinely
 fair,
And matchless Idas, more than man in
 war;
The God of Day adored the mother's
 charms;
Against the God the father bent his arms:
Th' afflicted pair, their sorrows to pro-
 claim,
From Cleopatra changed this daughter's
 name,
And call'd Alcyone; a name to shew
The father's grief, the mourning mother's
 woe.)
To her the Chief retired from stern debate,
But found no peace from fierce Althæa's
 hate: 680
Althæa's hate th' unhappy warrior drew,
Whose luckless hand his royal uncle slew;
She beat the ground, and call'd the Powers
 beneath
On her own son to wreak her brother's
 death:
Hell heard her curses from the realms pro-
 found,
And the red fiends that walk'd the nightly
 round.
In vain Ætolia her deliv'rer waits,
War shakes her walls, and thunders at her
 gates.

She sent ambassadors, a chosen band,
Priests of the Gods, and elders of the
   land,   690
Besought the Chief to save the sinking
   state:
Their prayers were urgent, and their
   proffers great;
(Full fifty acres of the richest ground,
Half pasture green, and half with vineyards
   crown'd).
His suppliant father, aged Œneus, came;
His sisters follow'd: ev'n the vengeful
   dame
Althæa sues; his friends before him fall:
He stands relentless, and rejects them all.
Meanwhile the victors' shouts ascend the
   skies;
The walls are scaled; the rolling flames
   arise;   700
At length his wife (a form divine) appears,
With piercing cries, and supplicating tears;
She paints the horrors of a conquer'd
   town,
The heroes slain, the palaces o'erthrown,
The matrons ravish'd, the whole race en-
   slaved:
The warrior heard, he vanquish'd, and he
   saved.
Th' Ætolians, long disdain'd, now took
   their turn,
And left the Chief their broken faith to
   mourn.
Learn hence, betimes to curb pernicious
   ire,
Nor stay, till yonder fleets ascend in fire:
Accept the presents; draw thy conquering
   sword;   711
And be amongst our guardian Gods
   ador'd.'
   Thus he: the stern Achilles thus re-
   plied:
'My second father, and my rev'rend guide!
Thy friend, believe me, no such gifts de-
   mands,
And asks no honours from a mortal's
   hands:
Jove honours me, and favours my designs:
His pleasure guides me, and his will con-
   fines:
And here I stay (if such his high behest)
While life's warm spirit beats within my
   breast.   720
Yet hear one word, and lodge it in thy
   heart;
No more molest me on Atrides' part:

Is it for him these tears are taught to
   flow,
For him these sorrows? for my mortal
   foe?
A gen'rous friendship no cold medium
   knows,
Burns with one love, with one resentment
   glows;
One should our int'rests, and our passions,
   be;
My friend must hate the man that injures
   me.
Do this, my Phœnix, 't is a gen'rous part,
And share my realms, my honours, and my
   heart.   730
Let these return: our voyage, or our stay,
Rest undetermin'd till the dawning day.'
   He ceas'd: then order'd for the sage's
   bed
A warmer couch with numerous carpets
   spread.
With that, stern Ajax his long silence
   broke,
And thus, impatient, to Ulysses spoke:
   ' Hence let us go — why waste we time in
   vain?
See what effect our low submissions gain!
Liked or not liked, his words we must re-
   late,
The Greeks expect them, and our heroes
   wait.   740
Proud as he is, that iron heart retains
Its stubborn purpose, and his friends dis-
   dains.
Stern, and unpitying! if a brother bleed,
On just atonement, we remit the deed;
A sire the slaughter of his son forgives;
The price of blood discharged, the mur-
   d'rer lives:
The haughtiest hearts at length their rage
   resign,
And gifts can conquer ev'ry soul but thine:
The Gods that unrelenting breast have
   steel'd,
And curs'd thee with a mind that cannot
   yield.   750
One woman-slave was ravish'd from thy
   arms:
Lo, sev'n are offer'd, and of equal charms.
Then hear, Achilles! be of better mind;
Revere thy roof, and to thy guests be kind;
And know the men, of all the Grecian
   host
Who honour worth, and prize thy valour
   most.'

'Oh Soul of Battles, and thy people's
　　guide!'
(To Ajax thus the first of Greeks replied)
'Well hast thou spoke; but at the tyrant's
　　name　　　　　　　　　　　759
My rage rekindles and my soul's on flame;
'T is just resentment, and becomes the
　　brave;
Disgraced, dishonour'd, like the vilest
　　slave!
Return then, Heroes! and our answer bear,
The glorious combat is no more my care;
Not till amidst yon sinking navy slain,
The blood of Greeks shall dye the sable
　　main;
Not till the flames, by Hector's fury
　　thrown,
Consume your vessels, and approach my
　　own;
Just there, th' impetuous homicide shall
　　stand,
There cease his battle, and there feel our
　　hand.'　　　　　　　　　　770
　　This said, each Prince a double goblet
　　crown'd,
And cast a large libation on the ground:
Then to their vessels, thro' the gloomy
　　shades,
The Chiefs return; divine Ulysses leads.
Meantime Achilles' slaves prepared a bed,
With fleeces, carpets, and soft linen spread:
There, till the sacred morn restor'd the
　　day,
In slumbers sweet the rev'rend Phœnix lay,
But in his inner tent, an ampler space, ⎫
Achilles slept: and in his warm embrace ⎬
Fair Diomede of the Lesbian race.　781 ⎭
Last, for Patroclus was the couch prepared,
Whose nightly joys the beauteous Iphis
　　shared:
Achilles to his friend consign'd her charms,
When Scyros fell before his conquering
　　arms.
　　And now th' elected Chiefs, whom
　　Greece had sent,
Pass'd thro' the hosts, and reach'd the
　　royal tent.
Then rising all, with goblets in their hands,
The peers, and leaders of th' Achaian
　　bands,
Hail'd their return: Atrides first begun: 790
'Say, what success? divine Laertes'
　　son!
Achilles' high resolves declare to all:
Returns the Chief, or must our navy fall?'

'Great King of Nations!' (Ithacus re-
　　plied)
'Fix'd is his wrath, unconquer'd is his
　　pride;
He slights thy friendship, thy proposals
　　scorns,
And, thus implor'd, with fiercer fury
　　burns.
To save our army, and our fleets to free,
Is not his care; but left to Greece and
　　thee.
Your eyes shall view, when morning paints
　　the sky,　　　　　　　　　　800
Beneath his oars the whitening billows
　　fly.
Us too he bids our oars and sails employ,
Nor hope the fall of Heav'n-protected
　　Troy;
For Jove o'ershades her with his arm
　　divine,
Inspires her war, and bids her glory shine.
Such was his word: what farther he de-
　　clared,
These sacred heralds and great Ajax heard.
But Phœnix in his tent the Chief retains,
Safe to transport him to his native plains,
When morning dawns; if other he decree,
His age is sacred, and his choice is free.' 811
　　Ulysses ceas'd: the great Achaian host,
With sorrow seiz'd, in consternation lost,
Attend the stern reply.　Tydides broke
The gen'ral silence, and undaunted spoke:
'Why should we gifts to proud Achilles
　　send?
Or strive with prayers his haughty soul to
　　bend?
His country's woes he glories to deride,
And prayers will burst that swelling heart
　　with pride.
Be the fierce impulse of his rage obey'd; 820
Our battles let him or desert or aid;
Then let him arm when Jove or he think
　　fit;
That, to his madness, or to Heav'n, com-
　　mit:
What for ourselves we can, is always ours:
This night, let due repast refresh our
　　powers;
(For strength consists in spirits and in
　　blood,
And those are owed to gen'rous wine and
　　food);
But when the rosy Messenger of Day
Strikes the blue mountains with her golden
　　ray,

Ranged at the ships let all our squadrons
    shine,   830
In flaming arms, a long extended line:
In the dread front let great Atrides stand,
The first in danger, as in high command.'
  Shouts of acclaim the list'ning heroes
    raise,
Then each to Heav'n the due libations
    pays;
Till sleep, descending o'er the tents, be-
    stows
The grateful blessings of desired repose.

BOOK X

THE NIGHT ADVENTURE OF DIOMEDE AND
ULYSSES

THE ARGUMENT

Upon the refusal of Achilles to return to the
army, the distress of Agamemnon is described
in the most lively manner. He takes no rest
that night, but passes through the camp,
awaking the leaders, and contriving all possible methods for the public safety. Menelaus,
Nestor, Ulysses, and Diomede, are employed
in raising the rest of the captains. They call
a council of war, and determine to send
scouts into the enemy's camp, to learn their
posture, and discover their intentions. Diomede undertakes this hazardous enterprise,
and makes choice of Ulysses for his companion. In their passage they surprise Dolon,
whom Hector had sent on a like design to the
camp of the Grecians. From him they are
informed of the situation of the Trojan and
auxiliary forces, and particularly of Rhesus,
and the Thracians, who were lately arrived.
They pass on with success; kill Rhesus with
several of his officers, and seize the famous
horses of that Prince, with which they return
in triumph to the camp.
The same night continues; the scene lies in
the two camps.

ALL night the Chiefs before their vessels
    lay,
And lost in sleep the labours of the day:
All but the King; with various thoughts
    oppress'd,
His country's cares lay rolling in his
    breast.
As when by lightnings Jove's ethereal
    Power
Foretells the rattling hail, or weighty
    shower,

Or sends soft snows to whiten all the shore,
Or bids the brazen throat of war to roar;
By fits one flash succeeds as one expires,
And Heav'n flames thick with momentary
    fires: 10
So bursting frequent from Atrides' breast,
Sighs foll'wing sighs his inward fears con-
    fess'd.
  Now, o'er the fields, dejected, he surveys
From thousand Trojan fires the mounting
    blaze;
Hears in the passing wind their music blow,
And marks distinct the voices of the foe.
  Now, looking backwards to the fleet and
    coast,
Anxious he sorrows for th' endanger'd host.
He rends his hairs, in sacrifice to Jove,
And sues to him that ever lives above: 20
Inly he groans; while glory and despair
Divide his heart, and wage a doubtful war.
  A thousand cares his lab'ring breast re-
    volves;
To seek sage Nestor now the Chief re-
    solves,
With him, in wholesome counsels, to debate
What yet remains to save th' afflicted state.
He rose, and first he cast his mantle round,
Next on his feet the shining sandals bound;
A lion's yellow spoils his back conceal'd;
His warlike hand a pointed jav'lin held.   30
  Meanwhile his brother, press'd with equal
    woes,
Alike denied the gift of soft repose,
Laments for Greece; that in his cause be-
    fore
So much had suffer'd, and must suffer more.
A leopard's spotted hide his shoulders
    spread;
A brazen helmet glitter'd on his head:
Thus (with a jav'lin in his hand) he went
To wake Atrides in the royal tent.
  Already waked, Atrides he descried
His armour buckling at his vessel's side.   40
Joyful they met; the Spartan thus begun:
'Why puts my brother this bright armour
    on?
Sends he some spy, amidst these silent
    hours,
To try yon camp, and watch the Trojan
    powers?
But say, what hero shall sustain the task?
Such bold exploits uncommon courage ask,
Guideless, alone, thro' night's dark shade to
    go,
And 'midst a hostile camp explore the foe.'

To whom the King: 'In such distress we
stand,
No vulgar counsels our affairs demand; 50
Greece to preserve is now no easy part,
But asks high wisdom, deep design, and art.
For Jove averse our humble prayer denies,
And bows his head to Hector's sacrifice.
What eye has witness'd, or what ear be-
liev'd,
In one great day, by one great arm
achiev'd,
Such wondrous deeds as Hector's hand has
done,
And we beheld, the last revolving sun?
What honours the belov'd of Jove adorn!
Sprung from no God, and of no Goddess
born, 60
Yet such his acts, as Greeks unborn shall
tell,
And curse the battle where their fathers
fell.
Now speed thy hasty course along the
fleet,
There call great Ajax, and the Prince of
Crete;
Ourself to hoary Nestor will repair;
To keep the guards on duty, be his care:
(For Nestor's influence best that quarter
guides,
Whose son, with Merion, o'er the watch
presides.')
To whom the Spartan: 'These thy orders
borne,
Say, shall I stay, or with despatch re-
turn?' 70
'There shalt thou stay (the King of
Men replied),
Else may we miss to meet without a guide,
The paths so many, and the camp so wide.
Still, with your voice, the slothful soldiers
raise,
Urge by their fathers' fame, their future
praise.
Forget we now our state and lofty birth;
Not titles here, but works, must prove our
worth.
To labour is the lot of man below;
And when Jove gave us life, he gave us
woe.'
This said, each parted to his sev'ral
cares; 80
The King to Nestor's sable ship repairs;
The sage protector of the Greeks he found
Stretch'd in his bed, with all his arms
around;

The various-colour'd scarf, the shield he
rears,
The shining helmet, and the pointed spears;
The dreadful weapons of the warrior's
rage,
That, old in arms, disdain'd the peace of
age.
Then, leaning on his hand his watchful
head,
The hoary Monarch rais'd his eyes, and
said:
'What art thou, speak, that on designs
unknown, 90
While others sleep, thus range the camp
alone?
Seek'st thou some friend, or nightly sen-
tinel?
Stand off, approach not, but thy purpose
tell.'
'O son of Neleus! (thus the King re-
join'd)
Pride of the Greeks, and glory of thy kind!
Lo here the wretched Agamemnon stands,
Th' unhappy Gen'ral of the Grecian bands;
Whom Jove decrees with daily cares to
bend,
And woes, that only with his life shall end!
Scarce can my knees these trembling limbs
sustain, 100
And scarce my heart support its load of
pain.
No taste of sleep these heavy eyes have
known;
Confused, and sad, I wander thus alone,
With fears distracted, with no fix'd design;
And all my people's miseries are mine.
If aught of use thy waking thought sug-
gest,
(Since cares, like mine, deprive thy soul of
rest,
Impart thy counsel, and assist thy friend:
Now let us jointly to the trench descend,
At every gate the fainting guard excite, 110
Tired with the toils of day, and watch of
night:
Else may the sudden foe our works invade,
So near, and favour'd by the gloomy shade.'
To him thus Nestor: 'Trust the Powers
above,
Nor think proud Hector's hopes confirm'd
by Jove:
How ill agree the views of vain mankind,
And the wise counsels of th' eternal mind!
Audacious Hector, if the Gods ordain
That great Achilles rise and rage again,

What toils attend thee, and what woes
　　remain!　　　　　　　　　　　120
Lo ! faithful Nestor thy command obeys;
The care is next our other Chiefs to raise:
Ulysses, Diomed, we chiefly need;
Meges for strength, Oïleus famed for
　　speed,
Some other be despatch'd of nimbler feet, ⎫
To those tall ships, remotest of the fleet, ⎬
Where lie great Ajax, and the King of ⎭
　　Crete.
To rouse the Spartan I myself decree;
Dear as he is to us, and dear to thee,
Yet must I tax his sloth, that claims no
　　share,　　　　　　　　　　　130
With his great brother, in this martial
　　care:
Him it behoved to ev'ry Chief to sue,
Preventing ev'ry part perform'd by you;
For strong necessity our toils demands,
Claims all our hearts, and urges all our
　　hands.'
　　To whom the King: ' With rev'rence we
　　allow
Thy just rebukes, yet learn to spare them
　　now.
My gen'rous brother is of gentle kind,
He seems remiss, but bears a valiant mind;
Thro' too much def'rence to our sov'reign
　　sway,　　　　　　　　　　　140
Content to follow when we lead the way.
But now, our ills industrious to prevent,
Long ere the rest he rose, and sought my
　　tent.
The Chiefs you named, already, at his call,
Prepare to meet us at the navy-wall;
Assembling there, between the trench and
　　gates,
Near the night-guards our chosen council
　　waits.'
　　'Then none (said Nestor) shall his rule
　　withstand,
For great examples justify command.'　149
　　With that, the venerable warrior rose;
The shining greaves his manly legs enclose;
His purple mantle golden buckles join'd,
Warm with the softest wool, and doubly
　　lin'd.
Then, rushing from his tent, he snatch'd in
　　haste
His steely lance, that lighten'd as he
　　pass'd.
The camp he travers'd thro' the sleeping
　　crowd,
Stopp'd at Ulysses' tent, and call'd aloud.

Ulysses, sudden as the voice was sent,
Awakes, starts up, and issues from his
　　tent:
　　' What new distress, what sudden cause
　　of fright,　　　　　　　　　　160
Thus leads you wand'ring in the silent
　　night ? '
　　' O prudent Chief! (the Pylian Chief re-
　　plied)
Wise as thou art, be now thy wisdom tried:
Whatever means of safety can be sought,
Whatever counsels can inspire our thought,
Whatever methods, or to fly or fight;
All, all depend on this important night! '
　　He heard, return'd, and took his painted
　　shield:
Then join'd the Chiefs, and follow'd thro'
　　the field.　　　　　　　　　　169
Without his tent, bold Diomed they found,
All sheath'd in arms, his brave companions
　　round:
Each sunk in sleep, extended on the field,
His head reclining on his bossy shield:
A wood of spears stood by, that, fix'd up-
　　right,
Shot from their flashing points a quiv'ring
　　light.
A bull's black hide composed the hero's
　　bed;
A splendid carpet roll'd beneath his head.
Then, with his foot, old Nestor gently
　　shakes
The slumb'ring Chief, and in these words
　　awakes:
　　' Rise, son of Tydeus! to the brave and
　　strong　　　　　　　　　　180
Rest seems inglorious, and the night too
　　long.
But sleep'st thou now ? when from yon hill
　　the foe
Hangs o'er the fleet, and shades our walls
　　below ? '
　　At this, soft slumber from his eyelids fled;
The warrior saw the hoary Chief, and said:
' Wondrous old man! whose soul no respite
　　knows,
Tho' years and honours bid thee seek re-
　　pose.
Let younger Greeks our sleeping warriors
　　wake;
Ill fits thy age these toils to undertake.'
　　' My friend ' (he answer'd), ' gen'rous is
　　thy care,　　　　　　　　　　190
These toils, my subjects and my sons might
　　bear,

Their loyal thoughts and pious loves con-
spire
To ease a Sov'reign, and relieve a Sire.
But now the last despair surrounds our
host;
No hour must pass, no moment must be
lost;
Each single Greek, in this conclusive strife,
Stands on the sharpest edge of death or
life:
Yet if my years thy kind regard engage,
Employ thy youth as I employ my age;
Succeed to these my cares, and rouse the
rest; 200
He serves me most, who serves his country
best.'
This said, the Hero o'er his shoulder ⎫
flung ⎪
A lion's spoils, that to his ankles hung; ⎬
Then seiz'd his pond'rous lance, and strode ⎪
along. ⎭
Meges the bold, with Ajax famed for
speed,
The warrior rous'd, and to th' entrench-
ments led.
And now the Chiefs approach the nightly
guard;
A wakeful squadron, each in arms pre-
pared:
Th' unwearied watch their list'ning leaders
keep, 209
And, couching close, repel invading sleep.
So faithful dogs their fleecy charge main-
tain,
With toil protected from the prowling
train;
When the gaunt lioness, with hunger bold,
Springs from the mountains tow'rd the
guarded fold:
Thro' breaking woods her rustling course
they hear;
Loud, and more loud, the clamours strike
their ear
Of hounds, and men; they start, they gaze
around;
Watch ev'ry side, and turn to ev'ry sound.
Thus watch'd the Grecians, cautious of
surprise,
Each voice, each motion, drew their ears
and eyes; 220
Each step of passing feet increas'd th'
affright;
And hostile Troy was ever full in sight.
Nestor with joy the wakeful band sur-
vey'd,

And thus accosted thro' the gloomy shade:
' 'T is well, my sons! your nightly cares
employ,
Else must our host become the scorn of
Troy.
' Watch thus, and Greece shall live.' The
hero said;
Then o'er the trench the foll'wing Chief-
tains led.
His son, and godlike Merion, march'd be-
hind;
(For these the Princes to their council
join'd); 230
The trenches pass'd, th' assembled Kings
around
In silent state the consistory crown'd.
A place there was yet undefil'd with gore,
The spot where Hector stopp'd his rage
before,
When night, descending, from his vengeful
hand
Repriev'd the relics of the Grecian band.
(The plain beside with mangled corps was
spread,
And all his progress mark'd by heaps of
dead.)
There sat the mournful kings: when Ne-
leus' son,
The Council opening, in these words be-
gun: 240
' Is there ' (said he) ' a Chief so greatly
brave,
His life to hazard, and his country save?
Lives there a man, who singly dares to go
To yonder camp, or seize some straggling
foe?
Or, favour'd by the night, approach so
near,
Their speech, their counsels, and designs
to hear?
If to besiege our navies they prepare,
Or Troy once more must be the seat of
war?
This could he learn and to our peers recite,
And pass unharm'd the dangers of the
night: 250
What fame were his thro' all succeeding
days,
While Phœbus shines, or men have tongues
to praise!
What gifts his grateful country would be-
stow!
What must not Greece to her deliv'rer owe!
A sable ewe each leader should provide,
With each a sable lambkin by her side;

At ev'ry rite his share should be increas'd,
And his the foremost honours of the feast.'
　Fear held them mute: alone, untaught
　　to fear,
Tydides spoke: 'The man you seek is
　here.　　　　　　　　　　　　　　　260
Thro' yon black camps to bend my danger-
　ous way,
Some God within commands, and I obey.
But let some other chosen warrior join,
To raise my hopes and second my design.
By mutual confidence and mutual aid,
Great deeds are done, and great discov'ries
　made;
The wise new prudence from the wise
　acquire,
And one brave hero fans another's fire.'
　Contending leaders at the word arose;
Each gen'rous breast with emulation
　glows:　　　　　　　　　　　　　　270
So brave a task each Ajax strove to share,
Bold Merion strove, and Nestor's valiant
　heir;
The Spartan wish'd the second place to
　gain,
And great Ulysses wish'd, nor wish'd in
　vain.
Then thus the King of Men the contest
　ends:
'Thou first of warriors, and thou best of
　friends,
Undaunted Diomed! what Chief to join
In this great enterprise, is only thine.
Just be thy choice, without affection made,
To birth or office no respect be paid;　280
Let worth determine here.'　The Monarch
　spake,
And inly trembled for his brother's sake.
　Then thus (the godlike Diomed re-
　join'd):
'My choice declares the impulse of my
　mind.
How can I doubt, while great Ulysses
　stands
To lend his counsels, and assist our hands?
A Chief, whose safety is Minerva's care:
So famed, so dreadful in the works of
　war:
Bless'd in his conduct, I no aid require,
Wisdom like his might pass thro' flames of
　fire.'　　　　　　　　　　　　　　290
　'It fits thee not, before these Chiefs of
　fame '
(Replied the Sage), 'to praise me, or to
　blame:

Praise from a friend, or censure from a
　foe,
Are lost on hearers that our merits know.
But let us haste.　Night rolls the hours
　away,
The redd'ning Orient shows the coming
　day,
The stars shine fainter on th' ethereal
　plains,
And of Night's empire but a third re-
　mains.'
　Thus having spoke, with gen'rous ardour
　press'd,
In arms terrific their huge limbs they
　dress'd.　　　　　　　　　　　　　300
A two-edged falchion Thrasymed the brave,
And ample buckler, to Tydides gave:
Then. in a leathern helm he cased his
　head,
Short of its crest, and with no plume o'er-
　spread:
(Such as by youths, unused to arms, are
　worn;
No spoils enrich it, and no studs adorn.)
Next him Ulysses took a shining sword,
A bow and quiver, with bright arrows
　stor'd:
A well-prov'd casque, with leather braces
　bound　　　　　　　　　　　　　309
(Thy gift, Meriones), his temple crown'd:
Soft wool within; without, in order spread,
A boar's white teeth grinn'd horrid o'er his
　head.
This from Amyntor, rich Ormenus' son,
Autolycus by fraudful rapine won,
And gave Amphidamas; from him the
　prize
Molus receiv'd, the pledge of social ties;
The helmet next by Merion was possess'd,
And now Ulysses' thoughtful temples
　press'd.
Thus sheath'd in arms, the council they
　forsake,
And dark thro' paths oblique their progress
　take.　　　　　　　　　　　　　320
Just then, in sign she favour'd their intent,
A long-wing'd heron great Minerva sent:
This, tho' surrounding shades obscured
　their view,
By the shrill clang and whistling wings
　they knew.
As from the right she soar'd, Ulysses
　pray'd,
Hail'd the glad omen, and address'd the
　Maid:

'O Daughter of that God, whose arm
  can wield
Th' avenging bolt, and shake the dreadful
  shield!
O thou! for ever present in my way,   329
Who all my motions, all my toils, survey!
Safe may we pass beneath the gloomy
  shade,
Safe by thy succour to our ships convey'd;
And let some deed this signal night adorn,
To claim the tears of Trojans yet unborn.'
  Then godlike Diomed preferr'd his
    prayer:
'Daughter of Jove, unconquer'd Pallas!
  hear,
Great Queen of Arms, whose favour Ty-
  deus won,
As thou defend'st the sire, defend the son.
When on Æsopus' banks the banded powers
Of Greece he left, and sought the Theban
  towers,   340
Peace was his charge; receiv'd with peace-
  ful show,
He went a legate, but return'd a foe:
Then help'd by thee, and cover'd by thy
  shield,
He fought with numbers, and made num-
  bers yield.
So now be present, O celestial Maid!
So still continue to the race thine aid!
A youthful steer shall fall beneath the
  stroke,
Untamed, unconscious of the galling yoke,
With ample forehead, and with spreading
  horns,   349
Whose taper tops refulgent gold adorns.'
  The heroes pray'd, and Pallas, from the
    skies,
Accords their vow, succeeds their enter-
  prise.
Now like two lions panting for the prey,
With deathful thoughts they trace the
  dreary way,
Thro' the black horrors of th' ensanguin'd
  plain,
Thro' dust, thro' blood, o'er arms, and hills
  of slain.
  Nor less bold Hector, and the sons of
    Troy,
On high designs the wakeful hours em-
  ploy;
Th' assembled peers their lofty Chief en-
  closed;
Who thus the counsels of his breast pro-
  posed: 360

'What glorious man, for high attempts
  prepared,
Dares greatly venture for a rich reward?
Of yonder fleet a bold discov'ry make,
What watch they keep, and what resolves
  they take?
If now, subdued, they meditate their flight,
And, spent with toil, neglect the watch of
  night?
His be the chariot that shall please him
  most,
Of all the plunder of the vanquish'd host;
His the fair steeds that all the rest excel,
And his the glory to have serv'd so well.'
  A youth there was among the tribes of
    Troy,   371
Dolon his name, Eumedes' only boy,
(Five girls beside the rev'rend Herald told):
Rich was the son in brass, and rich in gold:
Not bless'd by Nature with the charms of
  face,
But swift of foot, and matchless in the race.
'Hector!' (he said) 'my courage bids me
  meet
This high achievement, and explore the fleet:
But first exalt thy sceptre to the skies,
And swear to grant me the demanded prize;
Th' immortal coursers, and the glitt'ring
  car   381
That bear Pelides thro' the ranks of war.
Encouraged thus, no idle scout I go,
Fulfil thy wish, their whole intention know,
Ev'n to the royal tent pursue my way,
And all their councils, all their aims, be-
  tray.'
  The Chief then heav'd the golden scep-
    tre high,
Attesting thus the Monarch of the Sky:
'Be witness, thou!' immortal Lord of All!
Whose thunder shakes the dark aërial hall:
By none but Dolon shall this prize be
  borne,   391
And him alone th' immortal steeds adorn.'
  Thus Hector swore: the Gods were call'd
    in vain;
But the rash youth prepares to scour the
  plain:
Across his back the bended bow he flung,
A wolf's grey hide around his shoulders
  hung,
A ferret's downy fur his helmet lined,
And in his hand a pointed jav'lin shined.
Then (never to return) he sought the shore,
And trod the path his feet must tread no
  more.   400

Scarce had he pass'd the steeds and Trojan
   throng,
(Still bending forward as he cours'd along),
When, on the hollow way, th' approaching
   tread
Ulysses mark'd, and thus to Diomed:
  'O friend! I hear some step of hostile
   feet,
Moving this way, or hast'ning to the fleet;
Some spy, perhaps, to lurk beside the main;
Or nightly pillager that strips the slain.
Yet let him pass, and win a little space;
Then rush behind him, and prevent his
   pace.   410
But if, too swift of foot, he flies before,
Confine his course along the fleet and shore,
Betwixt the camp and him our spears em-
   ploy,
And intercept his hoped return to Troy.'
   With that they stepp'd aside, and stoop'd
   their head
(As Dolon pass'd), behind a heap of dead:
Along the path the spy unwary flew:
Soft, at just distance, both the Chiefs pur-
   sue.
So distant they, and such the space between,
As when two teams of mules divide the
   green   420
(To whom the hind like shares of land al-
   lows),
When now new furrows part th' approach-
   ing ploughs.
Now Dolon list'ning heard them as they
   pass'd;
Hector (he thought) had sent, and check'd
   his haste:
Till scarce at distance of a jav'lin's throw,
No voice succeeding, he perceiv'd the foe.
As when two skilful hounds the lev'ret
   wind,
Or chase thro' woods obscure the trembling
   hind,
Now lost, now seen, they intercept his way,
And from the herd still turn the flying
   prey: 430
So fast, and with such fears, the Trojan
   flew;
So close, so constant, the bold Greeks pur-
   sue.
Now almost on the fleet the dastard falls,
And mingles with the guards that watch
   the walls:
When brave Tydides stopp'd: a gen'rous
   thought
(Inspired by Pallas) in his bosom wrought,

Lest on the foe some forward Greek ad-
   vance,
And snatch the glory from his lifted lance.
Then thus aloud: 'Whoe'er thou art, re-
   main;
This jav'lin else shall fix thee to the
   plain.'   440
He said, and high in air the weapon cast,
Which wilful err'd, and o'er his shoulder
   pass'd:
Then fix'd in earth. Against the trembling
   wood
The wretch stood propp'd, and quiver'd as
   he stood;
A sudden palsy seiz'd his turning head;
His loose teeth chatter'd, and his colour
   fled:
The panting warriors seize him, as he
   stands,
And, with unmanly tears, his life demands:
  'O spare my youth, and, for the breath
   I owe,
Large gifts of price my father shall be-
   stow: 450
Vast heaps of brass shall in your ships be
   told,
And steel well-temper'd, and refulgent
   gold.'
   To whom Ulysses made this wise reply:
'Whoe'er thou art, be bold, nor fear to die.
What moves thee, say, when sleep has closed
   the sight,
To roam the silent fields in dead of night?
Camest thou the secrets of our camp to
   find,
By Hector prompted, or thy daring mind?
Or art some wretch by hopes of plunder
   led
Thro' heaps of carnage to despoil the
   dead?'   460
   Then thus pale Dolon with a fearful look
(Still as he spoke his limbs with horror
   shook):
'Hither I came, by Hector's words deceiv'd:
Much did he promise, rashly I believ'd:
No less a bribe than great Achilles' car,
And those swift steeds that sweep the ranks
   of war,
Urged me, unwilling, this attempt to make;
To learn what counsels, what resolves, you
   take:
If now, subdued, you fix your hopes on
   flight,
And, tired with toils, neglect the watch of
   night?'   470

'Bold was thy aim, and glorious was the
    prize'
(Ulysses, with a scornful smile, replies):
'Far other rulers those proud steeds de-
    mand,
And scorn the guidance of a vulgar hand;
Ev'n great Achilles scarce their rage can
    tame,
Achilles sprung from an immortal dame.
But say, be faithful, and the truth recite:
Where lies encamp'd the Trojan Chief to-
    night ?
Where stand his coursers ? in what quarter
    sleep
Their other princes ? tell what watch they
    keep.   480
Say, since this conquest, what their coun-
    sels are;
Or here to combat, from their city far,
Or back to Ilion's walls transfer the war ?'
    Ulysses thus, and thus Eumedes' son:
'What Dolon knows, his faithful tongue
    shall own.
Hector, the peers assembling in his tent,
A council holds at Ilus' monument.
No certain guards the nightly watch par-
    take:
Where'er yon fires ascend, the Trojans
    wake:
Anxious for Troy, the guard the natives
    keep: 490
Safe in their cares, th' auxiliar forces sleep,
Whose wives and infants, from the danger
    far,
Discharge their souls of half the fears of
    war.'
  'Then sleep these aids among the Trojan
    train,'
(Inquired the Chief), 'or scatter'd o'er the
    plain ? '
  To whom the spy: 'Their powers they
    thus dispose;
The Pæons, dreadful with their bended
    bows,
The Carians, Caucons, the Pelasgian host,
And Leleges, encamp along the coast.
Not distant far, lie higher on the land   500
The Lycian, Mysian, and Mæonian band,
And Phrygia's horse, by Thymbra's ancient
    wall;
The Thracians utmost, and apart from all.
These Troy but lately to her succour won,
Led on by Rhesus, great Eioneus' son:
I saw his coursers in proud triumph go,
Swift as the wind, and white as winter snow:

Rich silver plates his shining car infold;
His solid arms, refulgent, flame with gold;
No mortal shoulders suit the glorious load,
Celestial panoply, to grace a God!   511
Let me, unhappy, to your fleet be borne,
Or leave me here, a captive's fate to mourn,
In cruel chains; till your return reveal
The truth or falsehood of the news I tell.'
  To this Tydides, with a gloomy frown:
'Think not to live, tho' all the truth be
    shewn;
Shall we dismiss thee, in some future strife
To risk more bravely thy now forfeit life ?
Or that again our camps thou may'st ex-
    plore ?   520
No — once a traitor, thou betray'st no
    more.'
  Sternly he spoke, and, as the wretch pre-
    pared
With humble blandishment to stroke his
    beard,
Like lightning swift the wrathful falchion
    flew,
Divides the neck, and cuts the nerves in
    two;
One instant snatch'd his trembling soul to
    Hell,
The head, yet speaking, mutter'd as it fell.
The furry helmet from his brow they tear,
The wolf's grey hide, th' unbended bow and
    spear;
These great Ulysses lifting to the skies, 530
To fav'ring Pallas dedicates the prize:
  'Great Queen of Arms! receive this hos-
    tile spoil,
And let the Thracian steeds reward our
    toil;
Thee first of all the heav'nly host we
    praise;
O speed our labours, and direct our ways! '
This said, the spoils, with dropping gore
    defaced,
High on a spreading tamarisk he placed;
Then heap'd with reeds and gather'd boughs
    the plain,
To guide their footsteps to the place again.
  Thro' the still night they cross the devi-
    ous fields,   540
Slipp'ry with blood, o'er arms and heaps of
    shields.
Arriving where the Thracian squadrons lay,
And eased in sleep the labours of the day.
Ranged in three lines they view the pros-
    trate band:
The horses yoked beside each warrior stand;

Their arms in order on the ground reclined,
Thro' the brown shade the fulgid weapons
　　shined;
Amidst, lay Rhesus, stretch'd in sleep pro-
　　found,
And the white steeds behind his chariot
　　bound.
The welcome sight Ulysses first descries, 550
And points to Diomed the tempting prize:
' The man, the coursers, and the car be-
　　hold!
Described by Dolon, with the arms of gold.
Now, brave Tydides! now thy courage try,
Approach the chariot, and the steeds untie;
Or if thy soul aspire to fiercer deeds,
Urge thou the slaughter, while I seize the
　　steeds.'
　　Pallas (this said) her hero's bosom
　　warms,
Breathed in his heart, and strung his ner-
　　vous arms;
Where'er he pass'd, a purple stream pur-
　　sued;　　　　　　　　　　　　　560
His thirsty falchion, fat with hostile blood,
Bathed all his footsteps, dyed the fields
　　with gore,
And a low groan remurmur'd thro' the
　　shore.
So the grim lion, from his nightly den,
O'erleaps the fences, and invades the pen;
On sheep or goats, resistless in his way,
He falls, and foaming rends the guardless
　　prey.
Nor stopp'd the fury of his vengeful hand,
Till twelve lay breathless of the Thracian
　　band.
Ulysses foll'wing as his partner slew,　570
Back by the foot each slaughter'd warrior
　　drew;
The milk-white coursers studious to convey
Safe to the ships, he wisely clear'd the way;
Lest the fierce steeds, not yet to battles
　　bred,
Should start and tremble at the heaps of
　　dead.
Now twelve despatch'd, the Monarch last
　　they found;
Tydides' falchion fix'd him to the ground.
Just then a dreadful dream Minerva sent;
A warlike form appear'd before his tent,
Whose visionary steel his bosom tore:　580
So dream'd the Monarch, and awaked no
　　more.
　　Ulysses now the snowy steeds detains,
And leads them fasten'd by the silver reins;

These, with his bow unbent, he lash'd along
(The scourge, forgot, on Rhesus' chariot
　　hung).
Then gave his friend the signal to retire;
But him new dangers, new achievements,
　　fire:
Doubtful he stood, or with his reeking blade
To send more heroes to th' infernal shade,
Drag off the car where Rhesus' armour
　　lay,　　　　　　　　　　　　　590
Or heave with manly force, and lift away.
While unresolv'd the son of Tydeus stands,
Pallas appears, and thus her Chief com-
　　mands:
' Enough, my son; from farther slaugh-
　　ter cease,
Regard thy safety, and depart in peace;
Haste to the ships, the gotten spoils enjoy,
Nor tempt too far the hostile Gods of Troy.'
　　The voice divine confess'd the Martial
　　Maid;
In haste he mounted, and her word obey'd;
The coursers fly before Ulysses' bow,　600
Swift as the wind, and white as winter
　　snow.
　　Not unobserv'd they pass'd: the God of
　　Light
Had watch'd his Troy, and mark'd Miner-
　　va's flight,
Saw Tydeus' son with heav'nly succour
　　bless'd,
And vengeful anger fill'd his sacred breast.
Swift to the Trojan camp descends the
　　power,
And wakes Hippocoön in the morning hour
(On Rhesus' side accustom'd to attend,
A faithful kinsman and instructive friend).
He rose, and saw the field deform'd with
　　blood,　　　　　　　　　　　　610
An empty space where late the coursers
　　stood,
The yet warm Thracians panting on the
　　coast;
For each he wept, but for his Rhesus most.
Now, while on Rhesus' name he calls in vain,
The gath'ring tumult spreads o'er all the
　　plain;
On heaps the Trojans rush, with wild af-
　　fright,
And wond'ring view the slaughter of the
　　night.
　　Meanwhile the Chiefs arriving at the
　　shade
Where late the spoils of Hector's spy were
　　laid,

Ulysses stopp'd; to him Tydides bore   620
The trophy, dropping yet with Dolon's
  gore:
Then mounts again; again their nimble
  feet
The coursers ply, and thunder towards the
  fleet.
Old Nestor first perceiv'd th' approach-
  ing sound,
Bespeaking thus the Grecian peers around:
'Methinks the noise of trampling steeds I
  hear,
Thick'ning this way, and gath'ring on my
  ear;
Perhaps some horses of the Trojan breed
(So may, ye Gods! my pious hopes succeed)
The great Tydides and Ulysses bear,   630
Return'd triumphant with this prize of war.
Yet much I fear (ah may that fear be
  vain)!
The Chiefs outnumber'd by the Trojan
  train;
Perhaps, ev'n now pursued, they seek the
  shore;
Or, oh! perhaps those heroes are no more.'
  Scarce had he spoke, when lo! the Chiefs
  appear,
And spring to earth; the Greeks dismiss
  their fear:
With words of friendship and extended
  hands
They greet the Kings; and Nestor first de-
  mands:
'Say thou, whose praises all our host
  proclaim,   640
Thou living glory of the Grecian name!
Say, whence these coursers? by what
  chance bestow'd,
The spoil of foes, or present of a God?
Not those fair steeds so radiant and so gay,
That draw the burning chariot of the day.
Old as I am, to age I scorn to yield,
And daily mingle in the martial field;
But sure till now no coursers struck my
  sight
Like these, conspicuous thro' the ranks of
  fight.
Some God, I deem, conferr'd the glorious
  prize,   650
Bless'd as ye are, and fav'rites of the skies:
The care of him who bids the thunder roar,
And her, whose fury bathes the world with
  gore!'
  'Father! not so (sage Ithacus rejoin'd),
The gifts of Heav'n are of a nobler kind.

Of Thracian lineage are the steeds ye view,
Whose hostile King the brave Tydides
  slew;
Sleeping he died, with all his guards around,
And twelve beside lay gasping on the
  ground.
These other spoils from conquer'd Dolon
  came,   660
A wretch, whose swiftness was his only
  fame;
By Hector sent our forces to explore,
He now lies headless on the sandy shore.'
  Then o'er the trench the bounding cours-
  ers flew;
The joyful Greeks with loud acclaim pur-
  sue.
Straight to Tydides' high pavilion borne,
The matchless steeds his ample stalls adorn:
The neighing coursers their new fellows
  greet,
And the full racks are heap'd with gen'-
  rous wheat.   669
But Dolon's armour to his ships convey'd, ⎫
High on the painted stern Ulysses laid,   ⎬
A trophy destin'd to the blue-eyed maid. ⎭
  Now from nocturnal sweat, and sanguine
  stain,
They cleanse their bodies in the neighb'ring
  main:
Then in the polish'd bath, refresh'd from
  toil,
Their joints they supple with dissolving oil,
In due repast indulge the genial hour,
And first to Pallas the libations pour:
They sit rejoicing in her aid divine,
And the crown'd goblet foams with floods
  of wine.   680

BOOK XI

THE THIRD BATTLE, AND THE ACTS OF
AGAMEMNON

THE ARGUMENT

Agamemnon, having armed himself, leads the
  Grecians to battle; Hector prepares the Trojans to receive them: while Jupiter, Juno,
  and Minerva give the signals of war. Agamemnon bears all before him; and Hector is
  commanded by Jupiter (who sends Iris for
  that purpose) to decline the engagement, till
  the king should be wounded and retire from
  the field. He then makes a great slaughter
  of the enemy; Ulysses and Diomede put a
  stop to him for a time; but the latter, being

wounded by Paris, is obliged to desert his companion, who is encompassed by the Trojans, wounded, and in the utmost danger, till Menelaus and Ajax rescue him. Hector comes against Ajax, but that hero alone opposes multitudes and rallies the Greeks. In the meantime Machaon, in the other wing of the army, is pierced with an arrow by Paris, and carried from the fight in Nestor's chariot. Achilles (who overlooked the action from his ship) sends Patroclus to inquire which of the Greeks was wounded in that manner. Nestor entertains him in his tent with an account of the accidents of the day, and a long recital of some former wars which he had remembered, tending to put Patroclus upon persuading Achilles to fight for his countrymen, or at least to permit him to do it clad in Achilles' armour. Patroclus in his return meets Eurypylus also wounded, and assists in that distress.

This book opens with the eight-and-twentieth day of the poem; and the same day, with its various actions and adventures, is extended through the twelfth, thirteenth, fourteenth, fifteenth, sixteenth, seventeenth, and part of the eighteenth books. The scene lies in the field near the monument of Ilus.

THE saffron Morn, with early blushes spread,
Now rose refulgent from Tithonus' bed;
With new-born day to gladden mortal sight,
And gild the courts of Heav'n with sacred light:
When baleful Eris, sent by Jove's command,
The torch of discord blazing in her hand,
Thro' the red skies her bloody sign extends,
And, wrapp'd in tempests, o'er the fleet descends.
High on Ulysses' bark her horrid stand
She took, and thunder'd thro' the seas and land.　10
Ev'n Ajax and Achilles heard the sound,
Whose ships, remote, the guarded navy bound.
Thence the black fury thro' the Grecian throng
With horror sounds the loud Orthian song:
The navy shakes, and at the dire alarms
Each bosom boils, each warrior starts to arms:
No more they sigh inglorious to return,
But breathe revenge, and for the combat burn.

The King of Men his hardy host inspires
With loud command, with great example fires:　20
Himself first rose, himself before the rest
His mighty limbs in radiant armour dress'd.
And first he cased his manly legs around
In shining greaves, with silver buckles bound:
The beaming cuirass next adorn'd his breast,
The same which once King Cinyras possess'd:
(The fame of Greece and her assembled host
Had reach'd that Monarch on the Cyprian coast;
'T was then, the friendship of the Chief to gain,
This glorious gift he sent, nor sent in vain.)　30
Ten rows of azure steel the work infold,
Twice ten of tin, and twelve of ductile gold;
Three glitt'ring dragons to the gorget rise,
Whose imitated scales against the skies
Reflected various light, and arching bow'd,
Like colour'd rainbows o'er a showery cloud
(Jove's wondrous bow, of three celestial dyes,
Placed as a sign to man amid the skies).
A radiant baldrick, o'er his shoulder tied,
Sustain'd the sword that glitter'd at his side;　40
Gold was the hilt, a silver sheath encased
The shining blade, and golden hangers graced.
His buckler's mighty orb was next display'd,
That round the warrior cast a dreadful shade;
Ten zones of brass its ample brim surround,
And twice ten bosses the bright convex crown'd;
Tremendous Gorgon frown'd upon its field,
And circling terrors fill th' expressive shield:
Within its concave hung a silver thong,
On which a mimic serpent creeps along,　50
His azure length in easy waves extends,
Till in three heads th' embroider'd monster ends.
Last o'er his brows his fourfold helm he placed,

With nodding horse-hair formidably graced;
And in his hands two steely jav'lins wields,
That blaze to Heav'n, and lighten all the
    fields.
That instant Juno and the Martial Maid
In happy thunders promis'd Greece their
    aid;
High o'er the Chief they clash'd their arms
    in air,
And, leaning from the clouds, expect the
    war.   60
    Close to the limits of the trench and
    mound,
The fiery coursers, to their chariots bound,
The squires restrain'd; the foot, with those
    who wield
The lighter arms, rush forward to the
    field.
To second these, in close array combin'd,
The squadrons spread their sable wings
    behind.
Now shouts and tumults wake the tardy
    sun,
As with the light the warriors' toils begun;
Ev'n Jove, whose thunder spoke his wrath,
    distill'd
Red drops of blood o'er all the fatal
    field;   70
The woes of men unwilling to survey,
And all the slaughters that must stain the
    day.
    Near Ilus' tomb in order ranged around,
The Trojan lines possess'd the rising
    ground.
There wise Polydamas and Hector stood;
Æneas, honour'd as a guardian God;
Bold Polybus, Agenor the divine;
The brother-warriors of Antenor's line;
With youthful Acamas, whose beauteous
    face,
And fair proportions, match'd th' ethereal
    race.   80
Great Hector, cover'd with his spacious
    shield,
Plies all the troops, and orders all the field.
As the red star now shews his sanguine
    fires,
Thro' the dark clouds, and now in night
    retires;
Thus thro' the ranks appear'd the godlike
    man,
Plunged in the rear, or blazing in the van;
While streamy sparkles, restless as he flies,
Flash from his arms, as lightning from the
    skies.

As sweating reapers in some wealthy field,
Ranged in two bands, their crooked wea-
    pons wield,   90
Bear down the furrows till their labours
    meet;
Thick fall the heapy harvests at their
    feet:
So Greece and Troy the field of war divide,
And falling ranks are strew'd on ev'ry
    side.
None stoop'd a thought to base inglorious
    flight;
But horse to horse and man to man they
    fight.
Not rabid wolves more fierce contest their
    prey;
Each wounds, each bleeds, but none resign
    the day.
Discord with joy the scene of death de-
    scries,
And drinks large slaughter at her sanguine
    eyes: 100
Discord alone, of all th' immortal train,
Swells the red horrors of this direful plain:
The Gods in peace their golden mansions
    fill,
Ranged in bright order on th' Olympian
    hill;
But gen'ral murmurs told their griefs
    above,
And each accused the partial will of Jove.
Meanwhile apart, superior, and alone,
Th' Eternal Monarch, on his awful throne,
Wrapp'd in the blaze of boundless glory
    sat:
And, fix'd, fulfill'd the just decrees of
    fate.   110
On earth he turn'd his all-consid'ring eyes,
And mark'd the spot where Ilion's towers
    arise;
The sea with ships, the field with armies
    spread,
The victor's rage, the dying, and the dead.
    Thus while the morning beams increas-
    ing bright
O'er Heav'n's pure azure spread the glow-
    ing light,
Commutual Death the fate of War con-
    founds,
Each adverse battle gored with equal
    wounds.
But now (what time in some sequester'd
    vale
The weary woodman spreads his sparing
    meal,   120

When his tired arms refuse the axe to
    rear,
And claim a respite from the sylvan war;
But not till half the prostrate forests lay
Stretch'd in long ruin, and exposed to
    day;)
Then, nor till then, the Greeks' impulsive
    might
Pierc'd the black phalanx, and let in the
    light.
Great Agamemnon then the slaughter led,
And slew Bienor at his people's head;
Whose squire Oïleus, with a sudden spring,
Leap'd from the chariot to revenge his
    King, 130
But in his front he felt the fatal wound,
Which pierc'd his brain, and stretch'd him
    on the ground:
Atrides spoil'd, and left them on the plain:
Vain was their youth, their glitt'ring ar-
    mour vain:
Now soil'd with dust, and naked to the sky,
Their snowy limbs and beauteous bodies
    lie.
Two sons of Priam next to battle move,
The product one of marriage, one of love;
In the same car the brother warriors
    ride,
This took the charge to combat, that to
    guide: 140
Far other task, than when they went to
    keep,
On Ida's tops, their father's fleecy sheep!
These on the mountains once Achilles
    found,
And captive led, with pliant osiers bound;
Then to their sire for ample sums restor'd;
But now to perish by Atrides' sword:
Pierc'd in the breast the base-born Isus
    bleeds:
Cleft thro' the head, his brother's fate suc-
    ceeds.
Swift to the spoil the hasty victor falls,
And, stripp'd, their features to his mind
    recalls. 150
The Trojans see the youths untimely die,
But helpless tremble for themselves, and
    fly.
So when a lion, ranging o'er the lawns,
Finds, on some grassy lair, the couching
    fawns,
Their bones he cracks, their reeking vitals
    draws,
And grinds the quiv'ring flesh with bloody
    jaws;

The frighted hind beholds, and dares not
    stay,
But swift thro' rustling thickets bursts her
    way;
All drown'd in sweat the panting mother
    flies,
And the big tears roll trickling from her
    eyes. 160
Amidst the tumult of the routed train,
The sons of false Antimachus were slain,
He, who for bribes his faithless counsels
    sold,
And voted Helen's stay for Paris' gold.
Atrides mark'd, as these their safety
    sought,
And slew the children for the father's
    fault;
Their headstrong horse unable to restrain,
They shook with fear, and dropp'd the
    silken rein;
Then in their chariot on their knees they
    fall,
And thus with lifted hands for mercy
    call: 170
' O spare our youth, and, for the life we
    owe,
Antimachus shall copious gifts bestow;
Soon as he hears, that, not in battle slain,
The Grecian ships his captive sons detain,
Large heaps of brass in ransom shall be
    told,
And steel well-temper'd, and persuasive
    gold.'
These words, attended with a flood of
    tears,
The youths address'd to unrelenting ears:
The vengeful Monarch gave this stern
    reply:
' If from Antimachus ye spring, ye die: 180
The daring wretch who once in council
    stood
To shed Ulysses' and my brother's blood,
For proffer'd peace! and sues his seed for
    grace ?
No, die, and pay the forfeit of your race.'
This said, Pisander from the car he
    cast,
And pierc'd his breast: supine he breathed
    his last.
His brother leap'd to earth; but, as he lay,
The trenchant falchion lopp'd his hands
    away:
His sever'd head was toss'd among the
    throng,
And rolling drew a bloody trail along. 190

Then, where the thickest fought, the victor
   flew;
The King's example all his Greeks pursue.
Now by the foot the flying foot were slain,
Horse trod by horse lay foaming on the
   plain.
From the dry fields thick clouds of dust
   arise,
Shade the black host, and intercept the
   skies.
The brass-hoof'd steeds tumultuous plunge
   and bound,
And the thick thunder beats the lab'ring
   ground.
Still, slaught'ring on, the King of Men pro-
   ceeds;
The distanced army wonders at his deeds.
As when the winds with raging flames con-
   spire,   201
And o'er the forests roll the flood of fire,
In blazing heaps the grove's old honours
   fall,
And one refulgent ruin levels all:
Before Atrides' rage so sinks the foe,
Whole squadrons vanish, and proud heads
   lie low.
The steeds fly trembling from his waving
   sword;
And many a car, now lighten'd of its lord,
Wide o'er the fields with guideless fury
   rolls,
Breaking their ranks, and crushing out
   their souls: 210
While his keen falchion drinks the war-
   riors' lives;
More grateful now to vultures than their
   wives!
   Perhaps great Hector then had found his
   fate,
But Jove and Destiny prolong'd his date.
Safe from the darts, the care of Heav'n, he
   stood,
Amidst alarms, and death, and dust, and
   blood.
   Now past the tomb where ancient Ilus
   lay,
Thro' the mid field the routed urge their
   way
Where the wild figs th' adjoining summit
   crown,
That path they take, and speed to reach
   the town.   220
As swift Atrides with loud shouts pursued,
Hot with his toil, and bathed in hostile
   blood.

Now near the beech-tree, and the Scæan
   gates,
The hero halts, and his associates waits.
Meanwhile, on ev'ry side, around the plain,
Dispers'd, disorder'd, fly the Trojan train.
So flies a herd of beeves, that hear dis-
   may'd
The lion's roaring thro' the midnight shade:
On heaps they tumble with successless
   haste:
The savage seizes, draws, and rends the
   last: 230
Not with less fury stern Atrides flew,
Still press'd the rout, and still the hind-
   most slew;
Hurl'd from their cars the bravest Chiefs
   are kill'd,
And rage, and death, and carnage, load the
   field.
   Now storms the victor at the Trojan
   wall;
Surveys the towers, and meditates their
   fall.
But Jove, descending, shook th' Idæan hills,
And down their summits pour'd a hundred
   rills:
Th' unkindled lightning in his hand he
   took,
And thus the many-colour'd maid bespoke:
'Iris, with haste thy golden wings dis-
   play,   241
To godlike Hector this our word convey.
While Agamemnon wastes the ranks
   around,
Fights in the front, and bathes with blood
   the ground,
Bid him give way; but issue forth com-
   mands,
And trust the war to less important hands:
But when, or wounded by the spear or
   dart,
That Chief shall mount his chariot and de-
   part:
Then Jove shall string his arm, and fire his
   breast,
Then to her ships shall flying Greece be
   press'd,   250
Till to the main the burning sun descend,
And sacred night her awful shade extend.'
   He spoke, and Iris at his word obey'd;
On wings of winds descends the various
   Maid.
The Chief she found amidst the ranks of
   war,
Close to the bulwarks, on his glitt'ring car.

The Goddess then: ' O son of Priam, hear!
From Jove I come, and his high mandate
  bear.
While Agamemnon wastes the ranks
  around,
Fights in the front, and bathes with blood
  the ground, 260
Abstain from fight, yet issue forth com-
  mands,
And trust the war to less important hands:
But when, or wounded by the spear or dart,
The Chief shall mount his chariot, and de-
  part;
Then Jove shall string thy arm, and fire
  thy breast,
Then to her ships shall flying Greece be
  press'd,
Till to the main the burning sun descend,
And sacred night her awful shade extend.'
  She said, and vanish'd: Hector with a
  bound,
Springs from his chariot on the trembling
  ground, 270
In clanging arms: he grasps in either hand
A pointed lance, and speeds from band to
  band;
Revives their ardour, turns their steps from
  flight,
And wakes anew the dying flames of fight.
They stand to arms; the Greeks their onset
  dare,
Condense their powers, and wait the com-
  ing war.
New force, new spirit, to each breast re-
  turns;
The fight renew'd, with fiercer fury burns:
The King leads on; all fix on him their
  eye,
And learn, from him, to conquer, or to die.
  Ye sacred Nine, celestial Muses! tell, 281
Who faced him first, and by his prowess
  fell ?
The great Iphidamas, the bold and young:
From sage Antenor and Theano sprung;
Whom from his youth his grandsire Cisseus
  bred,
And nurs'd in Thrace, where snowy flocks
  are fed.
Scarce did the down his rosy cheeks invest,
And early honour warm his gen'rous breast,
When the kind sire consign'd his daughter's
  charms
(Theano's sister) to his youthful arms: 290
But, call'd by glory to the wars of Troy,
He leaves untasted the first fruits of joy;

From his lov'd bride departs with melting
  eyes,
And swift to aid his dearer country flies.
With twelve black ships he reach'd Per-
  cope's strand,
Thence took the long laborious march by
  land.
Now fierce for Fame, before the ranks he
  springs,
Tow'ring in arms, and braves the King of
  Kings.
Atrides first discharged the missive spear;
The Trojan stoop'd, the jav'lin pass'd in
  air. 300
Then near the corslet, at the Monarch's
  heart,
With all his strength the youth directs his
  dart:
But the broad belt, with plates of silver
  bound,
The point rebated, and repell'd the wound.
Encumber'd with the dart, Atrides stands,
Till, grasp'd with force, he wrench'd it from
  his hands.
At once his weighty sword discharged a
  wound
Full on his neck, that fell'd him to the
  ground.
Stretch'd in the dust th' unhappy warrior
  lies,
And sleep eternal seals his swimming eyes.
Oh worthy better fate! oh early slain! 311
Thy country's friend; and virtuous, tho' in
  vain!
No more the youth shall join his consort's
  side,
At once a virgin, and at once a bride!
No more with presents her embraces meet,
Or lay the spoils of conquest at her feet,
On whom his passion, lavish of his store,
Bestow'd so much, and vainly promis'd
  more!
Unwept, uncover'd, on the plain he lay, 319
While the proud victor bore his arms away.
  Coön, Antenor's eldest hope, was nigh:
Tears at the sight came starting from his
  eye,
While pierc'd with grief the much-lov'd
  youth he view'd,
And the pale features now deform'd with
  blood.
Then with his spear, unseen, his time he
  took,
Aim'd at the King, and near his elbow
  struck.

The thrilling steel transpierc'd the brawny part,
And thro' his arm stood forth the barbed dart.
Surprised the Monarch feels, yet void of fear
On Coön rushes with his lifted spear: 330
His brother's corpse the pious Trojan draws,
And calls his country to assert his cause,
Defends him breathless on the sanguine field,
And o'er the body spreads his ample shield.
Atrides, marking an unguarded part,
Transfix'd the warrior with his brazen dart;
Prone on his brother's bleeding breast he lay
The Monarch's falchion lopp'd his head away:
The social shades the same dark journey go,
And join each other in the realms below.
  The vengeful victor rages round the fields, 341
With ev'ry weapon art or fury yields:
By the long lance, the sword, or pond'rous stone,
Whole ranks are broken, and whole troops o'erthrown.
This, while yet warm, distill'd the purple flood;
But when the wound grew stiff with clotted blood,
Then grinding tortures his strong bosom rend;
Less keen those darts the fierce Ilythiæ send
(The Powers that cause the teeming matron's throes,
Sad mothers of unutterable woes!), 350
Stung with the smart, all panting with the pain,
He mounts the car, and gives his squire the rein:
Then with a voice which fury made more strong,
And pain augmented, thus exhorts the throng:
  'O friends! O Greeks! assert your honours won;
Proceed, and finish what this arm begun:
Lo! angry Jove forbids your Chief to stay,
And envies half the glories of the day.'
  He said, the driver whirls his lengthful thong:
The horses fly, the chariot smokes along 360

Clouds from their nostrils the fierce coursers blow,
And from their sides the foam descends in snow;
Shot thro' the battle in a moment's space,
The wounded Monarch at his tent they place.
No sooner Hector saw the King retired,
But thus his Trojans and his aids he fired:
' Hear, all ye Dardan, all ye Lycian race!
Famed in close fight, and dreadful face to face;
Now call to mind your ancient trophies won,
Your great forefathers' virtues, and your own. 370
Behold, the gen'ral flies, deserts his powers!
Lo, Jove himself declares the conquest ours!
Now on yon ranks impel your foaming steeds;
And, sure of glory, dare immortal deeds.'
  With words like these the fiery Chief alarms
His fainting host, and ev'ry bosom warms.
As the bold hunter cheers his hounds to tear
The brindled lion, or the tusky bear,
With voice and hand provokes their doubting heart.
And springs the foremost with his lifted dart: 380
So godlike Hector prompts his troops to dare:
Nor prompts alone, but leads himself the war.
On the black body of the foes he pours;
As from the cloud's deep bosom, swell'd with showers,
A sudden storm the purple ocean sweeps,
Drives the wild waves, and tosses all the deeps.
Say, Muse! when Jove the Trojan's glory crown'd,
Beneath his arm what heroes bit the ground ?
Assæus, Dolops, and Autonous died,
Opites next was added to their side, 390
Then brave Hipponous, famed in many a fight,
Opheltius, Orus, sunk to endless night,
Æsymnus, Agelaus; all Chiefs of name·
The rest were vulgar deaths, unknown to fame.
As when a western whirlwind, charged with storms.

Dispels the gather'd clouds that Notus
   forms;
The gust continued, violent, and strong,
Rolls sable clouds in heaps on heaps along;
Now to the skies the foaming billows rears,
Now breaks the surge, and wide the bot-
   tom bares: 400
Thus raging Hector, with resistless hands,
O'erturns, confounds, and scatters all their
   bands.
Now the last ruin the whole host appalls;
Now Greece had trembled in her wooden
   walls;
But wise Ulysses call'd Tydides forth,
His soul rekindled, and awaked his worth:
' And stand we deedless, O eternal shame!
Till Hector's arm involve the ships in
   flame ?
Haste, let us join, and combat side by side.'
The warrior thus, and thus the friend re-
   plied: 410
' No martial toil I shun, no danger fear;
Let Hector come; I wait his fury here.
But Jove with conquest crowns the Trojan
   train;
And, Jove our foe, all human force is vain.'
He sigh'd; but, sighing, rais'd his venge-
   ful steel,
And from his car the proud Thymbræus
   fell:
Molion, the charioteer, pursued his lord,
His death ennobled by Ulysses' sword.
There slain, they left them in eternal night;
Then plunged amidst the thickest ranks of
   fight.   420
So two wild boars outstrip the foll'wing
   hounds,
Then swift revert, and wounds return for
   wounds.
Stern Hector's conquests in the middle
   plain
Stood check'd awhile, and Greece respired
   again.
   The sons of Merops shone amidst the war;
Tow'ring they rode in one refulgent car;
In deep prophetic arts their father skill'd,
Had warn'd his children from the Trojan
   field;
Fate urged them on; the father warn'd in
   vain,
They rush'd to fight, and perish'd on the
   plain!   430
Their breasts no more the vital spirit
   warms;
The stern Tydides strips their shining arms.

Hypirochus by great Ulysses dies,
And rich Hippodamus becomes his prize.
Great Jove from Ide with slaughter fills
   his sight,
And level hangs the doubtful scale of fight.
By Tydeus' lance Agastrophus was slain,
The far-famed hero of Pæonian strain;
Wing'd with his fears, on foot he strove to
   fly,   439
His steeds too distant, and the foe too nigh;
Thro' broken orders, swifter than the wind,
He fled, but, flying, left his life behind.
This Hector sees, as his experienced eyes
Traverse the files, and to the rescue flies;
Shouts, as he pass'd, the crystal regions
   rend,
And moving armies on his march attend.
Great Diomed himself was seiz'd with fear,
And thus bespoke his brother of the war:
' Mark how this way yon bending squad-
   rons yield!
The storm rolls on, and Hector rules the
   field: 450
Here stand his utmost force ' — The war-
   rior said:
Swift at the word his pond'rous jav'lin fled;
Nor miss'd its aim, but, where the plumage
   danced,
Razed the smooth cone, and thence obliquely
   glanced.
Safe in his helm (the gift of Phœbus'
   hands)
Without a wound the Trojan hero stands;
But yet so stunn'd, that, stagg'ring on the
   plain,
His arm and knee his sinking bulk sustain;
O'er his dim sight the misty vapours rise,
And a short darkness shades his swimming
   eyes.   460
Tydides follow'd to regain his lance;
While Hector rose, recover'd from the
   trance,
Remounts his car, and herds amidst the
   crowd;
The Greek pursues him, and exults aloud:
' Once more thank Phœbus for thy forfeit
   breath,
Or thank that swiftness which outstrips the
   death.
Well by Apollo are thy prayers repaid,
And oft that partial power has lent his
   aid.
Thou shalt not long the death deserv'd
   withstand,
If any God assist Tydides' hand.   47c

Fly then, inglorious! but thy flight, this day,
Whole hecatombs of Trojan ghosts shall
    pay.'
Him, while he triumph'd, Paris eyed from
    far,
(The spouse of Helen, the fair cause of
    war):
Around the fields his feather'd shafts he
    sent,
From ancient Ilus' ruin'd monument;
Behind the column placed, he bent his bow,
And wing'd an arrow at th' unwary foe:
Just as he stoop'd, Agastrophus's crest
To seize, and draw the corslet from his
    breast,   480
The bow-string twang'd; nor flew the shaft
    in vain,
But pierc'd his foot, and nail'd it to the
    plain.
The laughing Trojan, with a joyful spring,
Leaps from his ambush, and insults the
    King:
  'He bleeds!' (he cries) 'some God has
    sped my dart;
Would the same God had fix'd it in his
    heart!
So Troy, reliev'd from that wide-wasting
    hand,
Should breathe from slaughter, and in com-
    bat stand,
Whose sons now tremble at his darted spear,
As scatter'd lambs the rushing lion fear.'
  He dauntless thus: 'Thou conqueror of
    the Fair,   491
Thou woman-warrior with the curling hair;
Vain archer! trusting to the distant dart,
Unskill'd in arms to act a manly part!
Thou hast but done what boys or women
    can;
Such hands may wound, but not incense a
    man.
Nor boast the scratch thy feeble arrow
    gave,
A coward's weapon never hurts the brave.
Not so this dart, which thou may'st one day
    feel:
Fate wings its flight, and death is on the
    steel.   500
Where this but lights, some noble life ex-
    pires,
Its touch makes orphans, bathes the cheeks
    of sires,
Steeps earth in purple, gluts the birds of
    air,
And leaves such objects as distract the fair.'

Ulysses hastens with a trembling heart,
Before him steps, and bending draws the
    dart:
Forth flows the blood; an eager pang suc-
    ceeds:
Tydides mounts, and to the navy speeds.
  Now on the field Ulysses stands alone,
The Greeks all fled, the Trojans pouring
    on: 510
But stands collected in himself and whole,
And questions thus his own unconquer'd
    soul:
  'What farther subterfuge, what hopes
    remain?
What shame, inglorious if I quit the plain?
What danger, singly if I stand the ground,
My friends all scatter'd, all the foes
    around?
Yet wherefore doubtful? let this truth suf-
    fice:
The brave meets danger, and the coward
    flies;
To die, or conquer, proves a hero's heart;
And, knowing this, I know a soldier's part.'
  Such thoughts revolving in his careful
    breast,   521
Near, and more near, the shady cohorts
    press'd;
These, in the warrior, their own fate en-
    close:
And round him deep the steely circle grows.
So fares a boar, whom all the troop sur-
    rounds
Of shouting huntsmen, and of clam'rous
    hounds;
He grinds his iv'ry tusks; he foams with
    ire;
His sanguine eyeballs glare with living fire;
By these, by those, on every part is plied;
And the red slaughter spreads on every
    side.   530
Pierc'd thro' the shoulder, first Deiopis
    fell;
Next Ennomus and Thoön sunk to hell;
Chersidamas, beneath the navel thrust,
Falls prone to earth, and grasps the bloody
    dust.
Charops, the son of Hippasus, was near;
Ulysses reach'd him with the fatal spear;
But to his aid his brother Socus flies,
Socus, the brave, the gen'rous, and the
    wise:
Near as he drew, the warrior thus began:
  'O great Ulysses, much-enduring man!
Not deeper skill'd in every martial sleight,

Than worn to toils, and active in the
   fight!   542
This day two brothers shall thy conquest
   grace,
And end at once the great Hippasian race,
Or thou beneath this lance must press the
   field.'
He said, and forceful pierc'd his spacious
   shield;
Thro' the strong brass the ringing jav'lin
   thrown,
Plough'd half his side, and bared it to the
   bone.
By Pallas' care, the spear, tho' deep infix'd,
Stopp'd short of life, nor with his entrails
   mix'd,   550
The wound not mortal wise Ulysses knew,
Then furious thus (but first some steps
   withdrew):
  'Unhappy man! whose death our hands
     shall grace!
Fate calls thee hence, and finish'd is thy
   race.
No longer check my conquests on the foe:
But, pierc'd by this, to endless darkness
   go,
And add one spectre to the realms below !'
  He spoke, while Socus, seiz'd with sud-
   den fright,
Trembling gave way, and turn'd his back
   to flight,
Between his shoulders pierc'd the foll'wing
   dart,   560
And held its passage thro' the panting
   heart.
Wide in his breast appear'd the grizzly
   wound;
He falls: his armour rings against the
   ground.
Then thus Ulysses, gazing on the slain:
'Famed son of Hippasus! there press the
   plain;
There ends thy narrow span assign'd by
   fate:
Heav'n owes Ulysses yet a longer date.
Ah wretch! no father shall thy corpse com-
   pose,
Thy dying eyes no tender mother close,
But hungry birds shall tear those balls
   away,   570
And hov'ring vultures scream around their
   prey.
Me Greece shall honour, when I meet my
   doom,
With solemn funerals, and a lasting tomb.'

Then, raging with intolerable smart,
He writhes his body, and extracts the dart.
The dart a tide of spouting gore pursued,
And gladden'd Troy with sight of hostile
   blood.
Now troops on troops the fainting Chief
   invade;
Forced he recedes, and loudly calls for
   aid.
Thrice to its pitch his lofty voice he
   rears;   580
The well-known voice thrice Menelaus
   hears;
Alarm'd, to Ajax Telamon he cried,
Who shares his labours, and defends his
   side:
'O friend! Ulysses' shouts invade my ear;
Distress'd he seems, and no assistance
   near:
Strong as he is, yet, one opposed to all,
Oppress'd by multitudes, the best may fall.
Greece, robb'd of him, must bid her host
   despair,
And feel a loss not ages can repair.'
Then, where the cry directs, his course he
   bends,   590
Great Ajax, like the God of War, attends.
The prudent Chief in sore distress they
   found,
With bands of furious Trojans compass'd
   round,
As when some huntsman, with a flying
   spear,
From the blind thicket wounds a stately
   deer;
Down his cleft side while fresh the blood
   distils,
He bounds aloft, and scuds from hills to
   hills:
Till, life's warm vapour issuing thro' the
   wound,
Wild mountain-wolves the fainting beast
   surround;
Just as their jaws his prostrate limbs in-
   vade,   600
The lion rushes thro' the woodland shade;
The wolves, tho' hungry, scour dispers'd
   away;
The lordly savage vindicates his prey.
Ulysses thus, unconquer'd by his pains,
A single warrior, half a host sustains:
But soon as Ajax heaves his tower-like
   shield,
The scatter'd crowds fly frighted o'er the
   field:

Atrides' arm the sinking hero stays,
And, saved from numbers, to his car con-
    veys. 609
Victorious Ajax plies the routed crew;
And first Doryclus, Priam's son, he slew:
On strong Pandocus next inflicts a wound,
And lays Lysander bleeding on the ground.
As when a torrent, swell'd with wintry rains,
Pours from the mountains o'er the deluged
    plains,
And pines and oaks, from their foundation
    torn,
A country's ruins! to the seas are borne:
Fierce Ajax thus o'erwhelms the yielding
    throng;
Men, steeds, and chariots, roll in heaps
    along.
    But Hector, from this scene of slaughter
    far, 620
Raged on the left, and ruled the tide of
    war:
Loud groans proclaim his progress thro'
    the plain,
And deep Scamander swells with heaps of
    slain.
There Nestor and Idomeneus oppose
The warrior's fury; there the battle glows;
There fierce on foot, or from the chariot's
    height,
His sword deforms the beauteous ranks of
    fight.
The spouse of Helen, dealing darts around,
Had pierc'd Machaon with a distant wound:
In his right shoulder the broad shaft ap-
    pear'd, 630
And trembling Greece for her physician
    fear'd.
To Nestor then Idomeneus begun:
'Glory of Greece, old Neleus' valiant son!
Ascend thy chariot, haste with speed away,
And great Machaon to the ships convey.
A wise physician, skill'd our wounds to heal,
Is more than armies to the public weal.'
    Old Nestor mounts the seat. Beside
    him rode
The wounded offspring of the healing God.
He lends the lash; the steeds with sound-
    ing feet 640
Shake the dry field, and thunder toward
    the fleet.
    But now Cebriones, from Hector's car,
Survey'd the various fortune of the war.
' While here' (he cried) ' the flying Greeks
    are slain,
Trojans on Trojans yonder load the plain.

Before great Ajax, see the mingled throng
Of men and chariots driv'n in heaps along!
I know him well, distinguish'd o'er the
    field
By the broad glitt'ring of the sev'nfold
    shield.
Thither, O Hector, thither urge thy
    steeds, 650
There danger calls, and there the combat
    bleeds;
There horse and foot in mingled deaths
    unite,
And groans of slaughter mix with shouts of
    fight.'
    Thus having spoke, the driver's lash re-
    sounds;
Swift thro' the ranks the rapid chariot
    bounds;
Stung by the stroke, the coursers scour the
    fields,
O'er heaps of carcases, and hills of shields.
The horses' hoofs are bathed in heroes'
    gore,
And, dashing, purple all the car before:
The groaning axle sable drops distils, 660
And mangled carnage clogs the rapid
    wheels.
Here Hector, plunging thro' the thickest
    fight,
Broke the dark phalanx, and let in the
    light:
(By the long lance, the sword, or pond'rous
    stone,
The ranks lie scatter'd, and the troops o'er-
    thrown.)
Ajax he shuns, thro' all the dire debate,
And fears that arm whose force he felt so
    late.
But partial Jove, espousing Hector's part,
Shot Heav'n-bred horror thro' the Grecian's
    heart;
Confused, unnerv'd in Hector's presence
    grown, 670
Amazed he stood, with terrors not his own.
O'er his broad back his moony shield he
    threw,
And, glaring round, by tardy steps with-
    drew.
Thus the grim lion his retreat maintains,
Beset with watchful dogs and shouting
    swains,
Repuls'd by numbers from the nightly
    stalls,
Tho' rage impels him, and tho' hunger
    calls,

Long stands the show'ring darts, and mis-
  sile fires;
Then sourly slow th' indignant beast re-
  tires.
So turn'd stern Ajax, by whole hosts re-
  pell'd,   680
While his swoln heart at every step re-
  bell'd.
  As the slow beast, with heavy strength
    endued,
In some wide field by troops of boys pur-
  sued,
Tho' round his sides a wooden tempest
  rain,
Crops the tall harvest, and lays waste the
  plain;
Thick on his hide the hollow blows re-
  sound;
The patient animal maintains his ground;
Scarce from the field with all their efforts
  chased,
And stirs but slowly when he stirs at last.
On Ajax thus a weight of Trojans hung, 690
The strokes redoubled on his buckler rung;
Confiding now in bulky strength he stands,
Now turns, and backward bears the yield-
  ing bands;
Now stiff recedes, yet hardly seems to fly,
And threats his foll'wers with retorted
  eye.
Fix'd as the bar between two warring
  powers,
While hissing darts descend in iron
  showers:
In his broad buckler many a weapon stood,
Its surface bristled with a quiv'ring wood;
And many a jav'lin, guiltless on the
  plain,   700
Marks the dry dust, and thirsts for blood
  in vain.
But bold Eurypylus his aid imparts,
And dauntless springs beneath a cloud of
  darts;
Whose eager jav'lin launch'd against the
  foe,
Great Apisaon felt the fatal blow;
From his torn liver the red current flow'd,
And his slack knees desert their dying
  load.
The victor rushing to despoil the dead,
From Paris' bow a vengeful arrow fled:
Fix'd in his nervous thigh the weapon
  stood,   710
Fix'd was the point, but broken was the
  wood.

Back to the lines the wounded Greek re-
  tired,
Yet thus, retreating, his associates fired :
' What God, O Grecians! has your hearts
  dismay'd ?
Oh, turn to arms; 't is Ajax claims your
  aid.
This hour he stands the mark of hostile
  rage,
And this the last brave battle he shall
  wage:
Haste, join your forces; from the gloomy
  grave
The warrior rescue, and your country
  save.'
  Thus urged the Chief; a gen'rous troop
    appears,   720
Who spread their bucklers, and advance
  their spears,
To guard their wounded friend: while thus
  they stand
With pious care, great Ajax joins the band:
Each takes new courage at the hero's sight;
The hero rallies and renews the fight.
  Thus raged both armies like conflicting
    fires,
While Nestor's chariot far from fight re-
  tires:
His coursers steep'd in sweat, and stain'd
  with gore,
The Greeks' preserver, great Machaon,
  bore.
That hour, Achilles, from the topmost
  height   730
Of his proud fleet, o'erlook'd the fields of
  fight;
His feasted eyes beheld around the plain
The Grecian rout, the slaying, and the
  slain.
His friend Machaon singled from the rest,
A transient pity touch'd his vengeful breast.
Straight to Menœtius' much-lov'd son he
  sent;
Graceful as Mars, Patroclus quits his tent:
In evil hour! then Fate decreed his doom;
And fix'd the date of all his woes to come!
  ' Why calls my friend ? thy lov'd injunc-
    tions lay;   740
Whate'er thy will, Patroclus shall obey.'
  ' O first of friends ! ' (Pelides thus re-
    plied)
' Still at my heart, and ever at my side!
The time is come, when yon despairing
  host
Shall learn the value of the man they lost:

Now at my knees the Greeks shall pour
    their moan,
And proud Atrides tremble on his throne.
Go now to Nestor, and from him be taught
What wounded warrior late his chariot
    brought?   749
For, seen at distance, and but seen behind,
His form recall'd Machaon to my mind;
Nor could I, thro' yon cloud, discern his
    face,
The coursers pass'd me with so swift a
    pace.'
    The hero said. His friend obey'd with
    haste;
Thro' intermingled ships and tents he
    pass'd;
The Chiefs descending from their car he
    found;
The panting steeds Eurymedon unbound.
The warriors, standing on the breezy shore,
To dry their sweat, and wash away the
    gore,
Here paus'd a moment, while the gentle
    gale   760
Convey'd that freshness the cool seas ex-
    hale;
Then to consult on farther methods went,
And took their seats beneath the shady
    tent.
The draught prescribed fair Hecamede
    prepares,
Arsinous' daughter, graced with golden
    hairs;
(Whom to his aged arms, a royal slave,
Greece, as the prize of Nestor's wisdom,
    gave;)
A table first with azure feet she placed;
Whose ample orb a brazen charger graced:
Honey new press'd, the sacred flower of
    wheat,   770
And wholesome garlicks crown'd the sav'ry
    treat.
Next her white hand an antique goblet
    brings,
A goblet sacred to the Pylian Kings,
From eldest times: emboss'd with studs of
    gold,
Two feet support it, and four handles hold;
On each bright handle, bending o'er the
    brink,
In sculptured gold, two turtles seem to
    drink:
A massy weight, yet heav'd with ease by
    him,
When the brisk nectar overlook'd the brim.

Temper'd in this, the nymph of form
    divine   780
Pours a large portion of the Pramnian
    wine;
With goat's-milk cheese a flav'rous taste
    bestows,
And last with flour the smiling surface
    strews.
This for the wounded Prince the dame pre-
    pares;
The cordial bev'rage rev'rend Nestor shares:
Salubrious draughts the warrior's thirst
    allay,
And pleasing conference beguiles the day.
    Meantime Patroclus, by Achilles sent,
Unheard approach'd, and stood before the
    tent.
Old Nestor, rising then, the hero led   790
To his high seat; the Chief refused, and said:
    ' 'Tis now no season for these kind de-
    lays;
The great Achilles with impatience stays.
To great Achilles this respect I owe;
Who asks what hero, wounded by the foe,
Was borne from combat by thy foaming
    steeds?
With grief I see the great Machaon bleeds.
This to report, my hasty course I bend;
Thou know'st the fiery temper of my
    friend.'
    'Can then the sons of Greece' (the sage
    rejoin'd)   800
' Excite compassion in Achilles' mind?
Seeks he the sorrows of our host to know?
This is not half the story of our woe.
Tell him, not great Machaon bleeds alone,
Our bravest heroes in the navy groan;
Ulysses, Agamemnon, Diomed,
And stern Eurypylus, already bleed.
But ah! what flatt'ring hopes I entertain!
Achilles heeds not, but derides our pain;
Ev'n till the flames consume our fleet he
    stays,   810
And waits the rising of the fatal blaze.
Chief after Chief the raging foe destroys;
Calm he looks on, and ev'ry death enjoys.
Now the slow course of all-impairing time
Unstrings my nerves, and ends my manly
    prime;
Oh! had I still that strength my youth
    possess'd,
When this bold arm th' Epeian powers op-
    press'd,
The bulls of Elis in glad triumph led,
And stretch'd the great Itymonæus dead!

'Then, from my fury fled the trembling
swains,   820
And ours was all the plunder of the plains:
Fifty white flocks, full fifty herds of swine,
As many goats, as many lowing kine:
And thrice the number of unrivall'd steeds,
All teeming females, and of gen'rous
breeds.
These, as my first essay of arms, I won;
Old Neleus gloried in his conquering son.
Thus Elis forc'd, her long arrears restor'd,
And shares were parted to each Pylian
lord.
The state of Pyle was sunk to last despair,
When the proud Elians first commenced
the war.   831
For Neleus' sons Alcides' rage had slain;
Of twelve bold brothers, I alone remain !
Oppress'd, we arm'd; and now, this con-
quest gain'd,
My sire three hundred chosen sheep ob-
tain'd.
(That large reprisal he might justly claim,
For prize defrauded, and insulted fame;
When Elis' monarch at the public course
Detain'd his chariot, and victorious horse.)
The rest the people shared; myself sur-
vey'd   840
The just partition, and due victims paid.
Three days were past, when Elis rose to
war,
With many a courser, and with many a car;
The sons of Actor at their army's head
(Young as they were) the vengeful squad-
rons led.
High on a rock fair Thryoëssa stands,
Our utmost frontier on the Pylian lands;
Not far the streams of famed Alphæus
flow;
The stream they pass'd, and pitch'd their
tents below;
Pallas, descending in the shades of night,
Alarms the Pylians, and commands the
fight.   851
Each burns for Fame, and swells with
martial pride;
Myself the foremost; but my sire denied;
Fear'd for my youth, exposed to stern
alarms,
And stopp'd my chariot, and detain'd my
arms.
My sire denied in vain: on foot I fled
Amidst our chariots: for the Goddess led.
   ' Along fair Arene's delightful plain,
Soft Minyas rolls his waters to the main.

There, horse and foot, the Pylian troops
unite,   860
And, sheathed in arms, expect the dawning
light.
Thence, ere the sun advanc'd his noon-day
flame,
To great Alphæus' sacred source we came.
There first to Jove our solemn rites were
paid;
An untamed heifer pleas'd the Blue-eyed
Maid,
A bull Alphæus; and a bull was slain
To the blue Monarch of the wat'ry Main.
In arms we slept, beside the winding flood,
While round the town the fierce Epeians
stood.
Soon as the sun, with all-revealing ray,   870
Flamed in the front of Heav'n, and gave
the day,
Bright scenes of arms, and works of war
appear;
The nations meet; there Pylos, Elis here.
The first who fell, beneath my jav'lin bled;
King Augias' son, and spouse of Agamede:
(She that all simples' healing virtues knew,
And every herb that drinks the morning
dew.)
I seiz'd his car, the van of battle led;
Th' Epeians saw, they trembled, and they
fled.
The foe dispers'd, their bravest warrior
kill'd,   880
Fierce as a whirlwind now I swept the
field:
Full fifty captive chariots graced my train;
Two Chiefs from each fell breathless to the
plain.
Then Actor's sons had died, but Neptune
shrouds
The youthful heroes in a veil of clouds.
O'er heapy shields, and o'er the prostrate
throng,
Collecting spoils, and slaught'ring all
along,
Thro' wide Buprasian fields we forc'd the ⎫
foes,   ⎪
Where o'er the vales th' Olenian rocks   ⎬
arose;   ⎪
Till Pallas stopp'd us where Alisium flows. ⎭
Ev'n there, the hindmost of their rear I ⎫
slay,   891   ⎪
And the same arm that led, concludes the ⎬
day;   ⎪
Then back to Pyle triumphant take my ⎭
way.

There to high Jove were public thanks as-
sign'd
As first of Gods; to Nestor, of mankind.
Such then I was, impell'd by youthful
blood:
So prov'd my valour for my country's good.
Achilles with inactive fury glows,
And gives to passion what to Greece he
owes.
How shall he grieve, when to th' eternal
shade 900
Her hosts shall sink, nor his the power to
aid ?
O friend! my memory recalls the day,
When, gath'ring aids along the Grecian sea,
I, and Ulysses, touch'd at Phthia's port,
And enter'd Peleus' hospitable court.
A bull to Jove he slew in sacrifice,
And pour'd libations on the flaming thighs.
Thyself, Achilles, and thy rev'rend sire
Menœtius, turn'd the fragments on the fire.
Achilles sees us, to the feast invites; 910
Social we sit, and share the genial rites.
We then explain'd the cause on which we
came,
Urged you to arms, and found you fierce
for fame.
Your ancient fathers gen'rous precepts gave:
Peleus said only this: " My son! be brave,"
Menœtius thus: " Tho' great Achilles shine
In strength superior, and of race divine,
Yet cooler thoughts thy elder years attend;
Let thy just counsels aid, and rule thy
friend."
Thus spoke your father at Thessalia's
court; 920
Words now forgot, tho' now of vast import.
Ah! try the utmost that a friend can say,
Such gentle force the fiercest minds obey;
Some fav'ring God Achilles' heart may
move;
Tho' deaf to glory, he may yield to love.
If some dire oracle his breast alarm,
If aught from Heav'n withhold his saving
arm;
Some beam of comfort yet on Greece may
shine,
If thou but lead the Myrmidonian line;
Clad in Achilles' arms, if thou appear, 930
Proud Troy may tremble, and desist from
war!
Press'd by fresh forces, her o'erlabour'd
train
Shall seek their walls, and Greece respire
again.'

This touch'd his gen'rous heart, and from
the tent
Along the shore with hasty strides he went,
Soon as he came, where, on the crowded
strand,
The public mart and courts of justice stand,
Where the tall fleet of great Ulysses lies,
And altars to the guardian Gods arise;
There sad he met the brave Evæmon's son;
Large painful drops from all his members
run; 941
An arrow's head yet rooted in his wound,
The sable blood in circles mark'd the
ground,
As, faintly reeling, he confess'd the smart:
Weak was his pace, but dauntless was his
heart.
Divine compassion touch'd Patroclus'
breast,
Who, sighing, thus his bleeding friend ad-
dress'd:
' Ah, hapless leaders of the Grecian host!
Thus must ye perish on a barb'rous coast ?
Is this your fate, to glut the dogs with
gore, 950
Far from your friends, and from your na-
tive shore ?
Say, great Eurypylus! shall Greece yet
stand ?
Resists she yet the raging Hector's hand ?
Or are her heroes doom'd to die with
shame,
And this the period of our wars and fame ? '
Eurypylus replies: ' No more, my friend,
Greece is no more! this day her glories end.
Ev'n to the ships victorious Troy pursues,
Her force increasing as her toil renews.
Those Chiefs, that used her utmost rage to
meet, 960
Lie pierc'd with wounds, and bleeding in
the fleet.
But thou, Patroclus! act a friendly part,
Lead to my ships, and draw this deadly
dart;
With lukewarm water wash the gore away,
With healing balms the raging smart allay,
Such as sage Chiron, sire of pharmacy,
Once taught Achilles, and Achilles thee.
Of two famed surgeons, Podalirius stands
This hour surrounded by the Trojan bands;
And great Machaon, wounded in his tent,
Now wants that succour which so oft he
lent.' 97-
To whom the Chief: ' What then remains
to do ?

Th' event of things the Gods alone can
　　view.
Charged by Achilles' great command I
　　fly,
And bear with haste the Pylian King's re-
　　ply:
But thy distress this instant claims relief.'
He said, and in his arms upheld the Chief.
The slaves their master's slow approach
　　survey'd,
And hides of oxen on the floor displayed:
There stretch'd at length the wounded hero
　　lay;　　　　　　　　　　　　　　　　980
Patroclus cut the forky steel away.
Then in his hands a bitter root he bruis'd;
The wound he wash'd, the styptic juice in-
　　fused.
The closing flesh that instant ceas'd to
　　glow,
The wound to torture, and the blood to
　　flow.

BOOK XII

THE BATTLE AT THE GRECIAN WALL

THE ARGUMENT

The Greeks being retired into their entrench-
ments, Hector attempts to force them; but
it proving impossible to pass the ditch, Polydamas advises to quit their chariots, and
manage the attack on foot. The Trojans
follow his counsel, and having divided their
army into five bodies of foot, begin the assault. But upon the signal of an eagle with
a serpent in his talons, which appeared on
the left hand of the Trojans, Polydamas endeavours to withdraw them again. This Hector opposes, and continues the attack; in
which, after many actions, Sarpedon makes
the first breach in the wall: Hector also,
casting a stone of a vast size, forces open one
of the gates, and enters at the head of his
troops, who victoriously pursue the Grecians
even to their ships.

WHILE thus the hero's pious cares at-
　　tend
The cure and safety of his wounded friend,
Trojans and Greeks with clashing shields
　　engage,
And mutual deaths are dealt with mutual
　　rage.
Nor long the trench or lofty walls oppose;
With Gods averse th' ill-fated works arose;

Their powers neglected, and no victim slain,
The walls are rais'd, the trenches sunk, in
　　vain.
　Without the Gods, how short a period
　　stands
The proudest monument of mortal hands!
This stood, while Hector and Achilles
　　raged,　　　　　　　　　　　　　　　　11
While sacred Troy the warring hosts en-
　　gaged;
But when her sons were slain, her city
　　burn'd,
And what survived of Greece to Greece re-
　　turn'd;
Then Neptune and Apollo shook the shore,
Then Ida's summits pour'd their wat'ry
　　store;
Rhesus and Rhodius then unite their rills,
Caresus roaring down the stony hills,
Æsepus, Granicus, with mingled force,
And Xanthus foaming from his fruitful
　　source;　　　　　　　　　　　　　　　20
And gulfy Simois, rolling to the main
Helmets, and shields, and godlike heroes
　　slain:
These, turn'd by Phœbus from their wonted
　　ways,
Deluged the rampire nine continual days;
The weight of waters saps the yielding
　　wall,
And to the sea the floating bulwarks fall.
Incessant cataracts the Thund'rer pours,
And half the skies descend in sluicy show-
　　ers.
　The God of Ocean, marching stern be-
　　fore,
With his huge trident wounds the trembling
　　shore,　　　　　　　　　　　　　　　　30
Vast stones and piles from their foundation
　　heaves,
And whelms the smoky ruin in the waves.
Now, smooth'd with sand, and levell'd by
　　the flood,
No fragment tells where once the wonder
　　stood;
In their old bounds the rivers roll again,
Shine 'twixt the hills, or wander o'er the
　　plain.
　But this the Gods in later times perform;
As yet the bulwark stood, and braved the
　　storm!
The strokes yet echoed of contending
　　powers;
War thunder'd at the gates, and blood dis-
　　tain'd the towers.　　　　　　　　　　40

Smote by the arm of Jove, and dire dis-
　may,
Close by their hollow ships the Grecians lay;
Hector's approach in every wind they hear,
And Hector's fury every moment fear.
He, like a whirlwind, toss'd the scatt'ring
　throng,
Mingled the troops, and drove the field
　along,
So, 'midst the dogs and hunters' daring
　bands,
Fierce of his might, a boar or lion stands;
Arm'd foes around a dreadful circle form,
And hissing jav'lins rain an iron storm;　50
His powers untamed their bold assault defy,
And, where he turns, the rout disperse, or
　die:
He foams, he glares, he bounds against
　them all,
And, if he falls, his courage makes him fall.
With equal rage encompass'd Hector glows;
Exhorts his armies, and the trenches shows.
The panting steeds impatient fury breathe,
But snort and tremble at the gulf beneath;
Just on the brink, they neigh, and paw the
　ground,
And the turf trembles, and the skies re-
　sound.　60
Eager they view'd the prospect dark and
　deep,
Vast was the leap, and headlong hung the
　steep;
The bottom bare (a formidable show)!
And bristled thick with sharpen'd stakes
　below.
The foot alone this strong defence could
　force,
And try the pass impervious to the horse.
This saw Polydamas; who, wisely brave,
Restrain'd great Hector, and this counsel
　gave:
'O thou! bold leader of our Trojan
　bands,
And you, confed'rate Chiefs from foreign
　lands!　70
What entrance here can cumbrous chariots
　find,
The stakes beneath, the Grecian walls be-
　hind ?
No pass thro' those without a thousand
　wounds;
No space for combat in yon narrow bounds.
Proud of the favours mighty Jove has
　shown,
On certain dangers we too rashly run:

If 't is his will our haughty foes to tame,
O may this instant end the Grecian name!
Here, far from Argos, let their heroes
　fall,　79
And one great day destroy, and bury all!
But should they turn, and here oppress our
　train,
What hopes, what methods of retreat re-
　main ?
Wedg'd in the trench, by our own troops
　confused,
In one promiscuous carnage crush'd and
　bruis'd,
All Troy must perish, if their arms pre-
　vail,
Nor shall a Trojan live to tell the tale.
Hear then, ye warriors! and obey with
　speed;
Back from the trenches let your steeds be
　led;
Then all alighting, wedg'd in firm array,
Proceed on foot, and Hector lead the
　way.　90
So Greece shall stoop before our conquer-
　ing power,
And this (if Jove consent) her fatal hour.'
　This counsel pleas'd: the godlike Hector
　sprung
Swift from his seat; his clanging armour
　rung.
The Chief's example follow'd by his train,
Each quits his car, and issues on the plain.
By orders strict the charioteers enjoin'd,
Compel the coursers to their ranks behind.
The forces part in five distinguish'd bands,
And all obey their sev'ral Chiefs' com-
　mands,　100
The best and bravest in the first conspire,
Pant for the fight, and threat the fleet with
　fire:
Great Hector glorious in the van of these,
Polydamas, and brave Cebriones.
Before the next the graceful Paris shines,
And bold Alcathoüs, and Agenor joins.
The sons of Priam with the third appear,
Deïphobus, and Helenus the seer;
In arms with these the mighty Asius stood,
Who drew from Hyrtacus his noble
　blood,　110
And whom Arisba's yellow coursers bore,
The coursers fed on Selle's winding shore.
Antenor's sons the fourth battalion guide,
And great Æneas, born on fountful Ide.
Divine Sarpedon the last band obey'd,
Whom Glaucus and Asteropæus aid;

Next him, the bravest at their army's
   head,
But he more brave than all the hosts he
   led.
Now, with compacted shields, in close
   array,
The moving legions speed their headlong
   way: 120
Already in their hopes they fire the fleet,
And see the Grecians gasping at their feet.
While every Trojan thus, and every aid,
Th' advice of wise Polydamas obey'd;
Asius alone, confiding in his car,
His vaunted coursers urged to meet the
   war.
Unhappy hero! and advised in vain!
Those wheels returning ne'er shall mark
   the plain;
No more those coursers with triumphant
   joy
Restore their master to the gates of
   Troy!   130
Black death attends behind the Grecian
   wall,
And great Idomeneus shall boast thy fall!
Fierce to the left he drives, where from the
   plain
The flying Grecians strove their ships to
   gain;
Swift thro' the wall their horse and chari-
   ots past,
The gates half-open'd to receive the last.
Thither, exulting in his force, he flies;
His foll'wing host with clamours rend the
   skies:
To plunge the Grecians headlong in the
   main,
Such their proud hopes, but all their hopes
   were vain!   140
   To guard the gates, two mighty Chiefs
   attend,
Who from the Lapiths' warlike race de-
   scend;
This Polypœtes, great Perithous' heir,
And that Leonteus, like the God of War.
As two tall oaks, before the wall they rise;
Their roots in earth, their heads amidst
   the skies:
Whose spreading arms, with leafy honours
   crown'd,
Forbid the tempest, and protect the
   ground;
High on the hills appears their stately form,
And their deep roots for ever brave the
   storm.   150

So graceful these, and so the shock they
   stand
Of raging Asius, and his furious band.
Orestes, Acamas, in front appear,
And Œnomaus and Thoön close the rear.
In vain their clamours shake the ambient
   fields,
In vain around them beat their hollow
   shields;
The fearless brothers on the Grecians call,
To guard their navies, and defend their
   wall.
Ev'n when they saw Troy's sable troops
   impend,
And Greece tumultuous from her towers
   descend,   160
Forth from the portals rush'd th' intrepid
   pair.
Opposed their breasts, and stood them-
   selves the war.
So two wild boars spring furious from their
   den,
Rous'd with the cries of dogs, and voice of
   men;
On every side the crackling trees they tear,
And root the shrubs, and lay the forest
   bare;
They gnash their tusks, with fire their eye-
   balls roll,
Till some wide wound lets out their mighty
   soul.
Around their heads the whistling jav'lins
   sung;
With sounding strokes their brazen targets
   rung: 170
Fierce was the fight, while yet the Grecian
   powers
Maintain'd the walls, and mann'd the lofty
   towers:
To save their fleet, the last efforts they
   try,
And stones and darts in mingled tempests
   fly.
   As when sharp Boreas blows abroad, and
   brings
The dreary winter on his frozen wings;
Beneath the low-hung clouds the sheets of
   snow
Descend, and whiten all the fields below:
So fast the darts on either army pour,
So down the rampires rolls the rocky
   shower;   180
Heavy, and thick, resound the batter'd
   shields,
And the deaf echo rattles round the fields.

With shame repuls'd, with grief and fury
  driv'n,
The frantic Asius thus accuses Heav'n:
' In powers immortal who shall now be-
  lieve ?
Can those too flatter, and can Jove de-
  ceive ?
What man can doubt but Troy's victorious
  power
Should humble Greece, and this her fatal
  hour ?
But like when wasps from hollow crannies
  drive,
To guard the entrance of their common
  hive, 190
Dark'ning the rock, while, with unwearied
  wings,
They strike th' assailants, and infix their
  stings;
A race determin'd, that to death contend:
So fierce, these Greeks their last retreat
  defend.
Gods! shall two warriors only guard their
  gates,
Repel an army, and defraud the fates ? '
  These empty accents mingled with the
  wind,
Nor mov'd great Jove's unalterable mind;
To godlike Hector and his matchless
  might 199
Was owed the glory of the destin'd fight.
Like deeds of arms thro' all the forts were
  tried,
And all the gates sustain'd an equal tide;
Thro' the long walls the stony showers
  were heard,
The blaze of flames, the flash of arms, ap-
  pear'd.
The spirit of a God my breast inspire,
To raise each act to life, and sing with fire!
While Greece unconquer'd kept alive the
  war,
Secure of death, confiding in despair;
And all her guardian Gods, in deep dis-
  may, 209
With unassisting arms deplor'd the day.
  Ev'n yet the dauntless Lapithæ maintain
The dreadful pass, and round them heap
  the slain.
First Damasus, by Polypœtes' steel
Pierc'd thro' his helmet's brazen vizor, fell;
The weapon drank the mingled brains and
  gore;
The warrior sinks, tremendous now no
  more!

Next Ormenus and Pylon yield their
  breath:
Nor less Leonteus strews the field with
  death;
First thro' the belt Hippomachus he
  gor'd, 219
Then sudden waved his unresisted sword;
Antiphates, as thro' the ranks he broke,
The falchion struck, and Fate pursued the
  stroke;
Iämenus, Orestes, Menon, bled;
And round him rose a monument of dead.
  Meantime, the bravest of the Trojan
  crew
Bold Hector and Polydamas pursue;
Fierce with impatience on the works to
  fall,
And wrap in rolling flames the fleet and
  wall.
These on the farther bank now stood and
  gazed, 229
By Heav'n alarm'd, by prodigies amazed:
A signal omen stopp'd the passing host,
Their martial fury in their wonder lost.
Jove's bird on sounding pinions beat the
  skies,
A bleeding serpent of enormous size
His talons truss'd; alive, and curling
  round,
He stung the bird, whose throat receiv'd
  the wound:
Mad with the smart, he drops the fatal prey,
In airy circles wings his painful way,
Floats on the winds, and rends the Heav'ns
  with cries;
Amidst the host the fallen serpent lies: 240
They, pale with terror, mark its spires un-
  roll'd
And Jove's portent with beating hearts
  behold.
Then first Polydamas the silence broke,
Long weigh'd the signal, and to Hector
  spoke:
  ' How oft, my brother, thy reproach I
  bear,
For words well meant, and sentiments sin-
  cere ?
True to those counsels which I judge the
  best,
I tell the faithful dictates of my breast.
To speak his thoughts, is every freeman's
  right, 249
In peace and war, in council and in fight;
And all I move, deferring to thy sway,
But tends to raise that power which I obey.

Then hear my words, nor may my words
    be vain;
Seek not, this day, the Grecian ships to
    gain;
For sure to warn us Jove his omen sent,
And thus my mind explains its clear event.
The victor eagle, whose sinister flight
Retards our host, and fills our hearts with
    fright,
Dismiss'd his conquest in the middle skies,
Allow'd to seize, but not possess, the prize;
Thus, tho' we gird with fires the Grecian
    fleet,   261
Tho' these proud bulwarks tumble at our
    feet,
Toils unforeseen, and fiercer, are decreed;
More woes shall follow, and more heroes
    bleed.
So bodes my soul, and bids me thus advise;
For thus a skilful seer would read the
    skies.'
    To him then Hector with disdain re-
    turn'd:
(Fierce as he spoke, his eyes with fury
    burn'd):
'Are these the faithful counsels of thy
    tongue?   269
Thy will is partial, not thy reason wrong:
Or if the purpose of thy heart thou vent,
Sure Heav'n resumes the little sense it
    lent.
What coward counsels would thy madness
    move,
Against the word, the will reveal'd of
    Jove?
The leading sign, th' irrevocable nod,
And happy thunders of the fav'ring God,
These shall I slight? and guide my wav'r-
    ing mind
By wand'ring birds, that flit with ev'ry
    wind?
Ye vagrants of the sky! your wings ex-
    tend,   279
Or where the suns arise, or where descend;
To right, to left, unheeded take your way,
While I the dictates of high Heav'n obey.
Without a sign, his sword the brave man
    draws,
And asks no omen but his country's cause.
But why shouldst thou suspect the war's
    success?
None fears it more, as none promotes it
    less:
Tho' all our Chiefs amid yon ships expire,
Trust thy own cowardice t' escape their fire.

Troy and her sons may find a gen'ral
    grave,
But thou canst live, for thou canst be a
    slave.   290
Yet should the fears that wary mind sug-
    gests
Spread their cold poison thro' our soldiers'
    breasts,
My jav'lin can revenge so base a part,
And free the soul that quivers in thy heart.'
    Furious he spoke, and, rushing to the
    wall,
Calls on his host; his host obey the call;
With ardour follow where their leader
    flies:
Redoubling clamours thunder in the skies.
Jove breathes a whirlwind from the hills of
    Ide,   299
And drifts of dust the clouded navy hide:
He fills the Greeks with terror and dismay,
And gives great Hector the predestin'd
    day.
Strong in themselves, but stronger in his
    aid,
Close to the works their rigid siege they
    laid.
In vain the mounds and massy beams de-
    fend,
While these they undermine, and those they
    rend;
Upheave the piles that prop the solid wall;
And heaps on heaps the smoky ruins fall.
Greece on her ramparts stands the fierce
    alarms;
The crowded bulwarks blaze with waving
    arms,   310
Shield touching shield, a long refulgent
    row;
Whence hissing darts, incessant, rain be-
    low.
The bold Ajaces fly from tower to tower,
And rouse, with flame divine, the Grecian
    power.
The gen'rous impulse every Greek obeys;
Threats urge the fearful; and the valiant,
    praise.
    'Fellows in arms! whose deeds are known
    to Fame,
And you whose ardour hopes an equal
    name!   318
Since not alike endued with force or art,
Behold a day when each may act his part!
A day to fire the brave, and warm the
    cold,
To gain new glories, or augment the old.

Urge those who stand, and those who faint,
excite,
Drown Hector's vaunts in loud exhorts of
fight;
Conquest, not safety, fill the thoughts of
all;
Seek not your fleet, but sally from the
wall;
So Jove once more may drive their routed
train,
And Troy lie trembling in her walls again.'
Their ardour kindles all the Grecian
powers;
And now the stones descend in heavier
showers.   330
As when high Jove his sharp artillery
forms,
And opes his cloudy magazine of storms;
In winter's bleak uncomfortable reign,
A snowy inundation hides the plain;
He stills the winds, and bids the skies to
sleep;
Then pours the silent tempest, thick and
deep:
And first the mountain tops are cover'd o'er,
Then the green fields, and then the sandy
shore;
Bent with the weight the nodding woods
are seen,
And one bright waste hides all the works of
men: 340
The circling seas alone absorbing all,
Drink the dissolving fleeces as they fall.
So from each side increas'd the stony rain,
And the white ruin rises o'er the plain.
    Thus godlike Hector and his troops con-
tend
To force the ramparts, and the gates to
rend;
Nor Troy could conquer, nor the Greeks
would yield,
Till great Sarpedon tower'd amid the field;
For mighty Jove inspired with martial flame
His matchless son, and urged him on to
fame.   350
In arms he shines, conspicuous from afar,
And bears aloft his ample shield in air;
Within whose orb the thick bull-hides were
roll'd,
Pond'rous with brass, and bound with duc-
tile gold:
And while two pointed jav'lins arm his
hands,
Majestic moves along, and leads his Lycian
bands.

So press'd with hunger, from the moun-
tain's brow,
Descends a lion on the flocks below:
So stalks the lordly savage o'er the plain,
In sullen majesty, and stern disdain: 360
In vain loud mastiffs bay him from afar,
And shepherds gall him with an iron war;
Regardless, furious, he pursues his way;
He foams, he roars, he rends the panting
prey.
Resolv'd alike, divine Sarpedon glows
With gen'rous rage that drives him on the
foes.
He views the towers, and meditates their
fall;
To sure destruction dooms th' aspiring wall:
Then, casting on his friend an ardent look,
Fired with the thirst of glory, thus he
spoke: 370
    'Why boast we, Glaucus! our extended
reign,
Where Xanthus' streams enrich the Lycian
plain,
Our numerous herds that range the fruitful
field,
And hills where vines their purple harvest
yield,
Our foaming bowls with purer nectar
crown'd,
Our feasts enhanc'd with music's sprightly
sound ?
Why on those shores are we with joy sur-
vey'd,
Admired as heroes, and as Gods obey'd
Unless great acts superior merit prove,
And vindicate the bounteous Powers
above ?   380
'T is ours, the dignity they give to grace;
The first in valour, as the first in place:
That when, with wond'ring eyes, our mar-
tial bands
Behold our deeds transcending our com-
mands,
Such, they may cry, deserve the sov'reign
state,
Whom those that envy dare not imitate!
Could all our care elude the gloomy grave,
Which claims no less the fearful than the
brave,
For lust of fame I should not vainly dare
In fighting fields, nor urge thy soul to war
But since, alas! ignoble age must come, 391
Disease, and death's inexorable doom;
The life which others pay, let us bestow,
And give to Fame what we to Nature owe;

Brave tho' we fall, and honour'd if we live,
Or let us glory gain, or glory give!'
  He said: his words the list'ning Chief
    inspire
With equal warmth, and rouse the war-
    rior's fire;
The troops pursue their leaders with de-
    light,
Rush to the foe, and claim the promis'd
    fight.   400
Menestheus from on high the storm beheld,
Threat'ning the fort, and black'ning in the
    field;
Around the walls he gazed, to view from
    far
What aid appear'd t' avert th' approaching
    war,
And saw where Teucer with th' Ajaces
    stood,
Of fight insatiate, prodigal of blood.
In vain he calls; the din of helms and
    shields
Rings to the skies, and echoes thro' the
    fields;
The brazen hinges fly, the walls resound,
Heav'n trembles, roar the mountains, thun-
    ders all the ground.   410
  Then thus to Thoös: — 'Hence with
    speed' (he said),
' And urge the bold Ajaces to our aid;
Their strength united best may help to bear
The bloody labours of the doubtful war:
Hither the Lycian princes bend their
    course,
The best and bravest of the hostile force.
But if too fiercely there the foes contend,
Let Telamon, at least, our towers defend,
And Teucer haste with his unerring bow,
To share the danger, and repel the foe.' 420
  Swift as the word, the herald speeds
    along
The lofty ramparts, thro' the martial
    throng;
And finds the heroes, bathed in sweat and
    gore,
Opposed in combat on the dusty shore.
' Ye valiant leaders of our warlike bands!
Your aid,' (said Thoös), 'Peleus' son de-
    mands.
Your strength, united, best may help to
    bear
The bloody labours of the doubtful war:
Thither the Lycian princes bend their
    course,   429
The best and bravest of the hostile force.

But if too fiercely here the foes contend,
At least let Telamon these towers defend,
And Teucer haste with his unerring bow,
To share the danger, and repel the foe.'
  Straight to the fort great Ajax turn'd his
    care,
And thus bespoke his brothers of the war:
'Now, valiant Lycomede! exert your might,
And, brave Oïleus, prove your force in
    fight:
To you I trust the fortune of the field,
Till by this arm the foe shall be repell'd: 440
That done, expect me to complete the
    day — '
Then, with his sev'n-fold shield, he strode
    away.
With equal steps bold Teucer press'd the
    shore,
Whose fatal bow the strong Pandion bore.
  High on the walls appear'd the Lycian
    powers,
Like some black tempest gath'ring round
    the towers;
The Greeks, oppress'd, their utmost force
    unite,
Prepared to labour in th' unequal fight;
The war renews, mix'd shouts and groans
    arise;
Tumultuous clamour mounts, and thickens
    in the skies.   450
Fierce Ajax first th' advancing host in-
    vades,
And sends the brave Epicles to the shades,
Sarpedon's friend; across the warrior's
    way,
Rent from the walls a rocky fragment
    lay;
In modern ages not the strongest swain
Could heave th' unwieldy burthen from the
    plain.
He pois'd, and swung it round; then toss'd
    on high;
It flew with force, and labour'd up the sky:
Full on the Lycian's helmet thund'ring
    down,
The pond'rous ruin crush'd his batter'd
    crown.   460
As skilful divers from some airy steep
Headlong descend, and shoot into the deep,
So falls Epicles; then in groans expires,
And murm'ring to the shades the soul
    retires.
  While to the ramparts daring Glaucus
    drew,
From Teucer's hand a winged arrow flew;

The bearded shaft the destin'd passage
 found;
And on his naked arm inflicts a wound.
The Chief, who fear'd some foe's insulting
 boast
Might stop the progress of his warlike
 host,   470
Conceal'd the wound, and, leaping from his
 height,
Retired reluctant from th' unfinish'd fight.
Divine Sarpedon with regret beheld
Disabled Glaucus slowly quit the field:
His beating breast with gen'rous ardour
 glows,
He springs to fight, and flies upon the foes.
Alcmaön first was doom'd his force to feel:
Deep in his breast he plunged the pointed
 steel;
Then, from the yawning wound with fury
 tore
The spear, pursued by gushing streams of
 gore: 480
Down sinks the warrior with a thund'ring
 sound,
His brazen armour rings against the
 ground.
 Swift to the battlement the victor flies,
Tugs with full force, and ev'ry nerve ap-
 plies;
It shakes; the pond'rous stones disjointed
 yield:
The rolling ruins smoke along the field.
A mighty breach appears: the walls lie
 bare,
And, like a deluge, rushes in the war.
At once bold Teucer draws the twanging
 bow,
And Ajax sends his jav'lin at the foe: 490
Fix'd in his belt the feather'd weapon
 stood,
And thro' his buckler drove the trembling
 wood;
But Jove was present in the dire debate,
To shield his offspring, and avert his fate.
The Prince gave back, not meditating flight,
But urging vengeance and severer fight;
Then, rais'd with hope, and fired with
 glory's charms,
His fainting squadrons to new fury warms:
'O where, ye Lycians! is the strength you
 boast ?
Your former fame, and ancient virtue lost!
The breach lies open, but your Chief in
 vain   501
Attempts alone the guarded pass to gain:

Unite, and soon that hostile fleet shall
 fall;
The force of powerful union conquers all.'
 This just rebuke inflamed the Lycian
 crew,
They join, they thicken, and th' assault re-
 new:
Unmov'd th' embodied Greeks their fury
 dare,
And fix'd support the weight of all the war!
Nor could the Greeks repel the Lycian
 powers,
Nor the bold Lycians force the Grecian
 towers.   510
As on the confines of adjoining grounds,
Two stubborn swains with blows dispute
 their bounds;
They tug, they sweat: but neither gain, nor
 yield,
One foot, one inch, of the contended field:
Thus obstinate to death, they fight, they
 fall:
Nor these can keep, nor those can win, the
 wall.
Their manly breasts are pierc'd with many
 a wound,
Loud strokes are heard, and rattling arms
 resound;
The copious slaughter covers all the shore,
And the high ramparts drop with human
 gore.   520
 As when two scales are charged with
 doubtful loads,
From side to side the trembling balance
 nods
(While some laborious matron, just and
 poor,
With nice exactness weighs her woolly
 store,)
Till, pois'd aloft, the resting beam suspends
Each equal weight; nor this nor that de-
 scends:
So stood the war, till Hector's matchless
 might,
With fates prevailing, turn'd the scale of
 fight.
Fierce as a whirlwind up the walls he flies,
And fires his host with loud repeated cries:
'Advance, ye Trojans! lend your valiant
 hands,   531
Haste to the fleet, and toss the blazing
 brands!'
They hear, they run, and, gath'ring at his
 call,
Raise scaling engines, and ascend the wall:

Around the works a wood of glitt'ring
  spears
Shoots up, and all the rising host appears.
A pond'rous stone bold Hector heav'd to
  throw,
Pointed above, and rough and gross below:
Not two strong men th' enormous weight
  could raise,
Such men as live in these degen'rate days.
Yet this, as easy as a swain could bear   541
The snowy fleece, he toss'd and shook in
  air:
For Jove upheld, and lighten'd of its load
Th' unwieldy rock, the labour of a God.
Thus arm'd, before the folded gates he
  came,
Of massy substance, and stupendous frame;
With iron bars and brazen hinges strong,
On lofty beams of solid timber hung:
Then thund'ring thro' the planks, with
  forceful sway,
Drives the sharp rock: the solid beams
  give way;   550
The folds are shatter'd; from the crackling
  door
Lead the resounding bars, the flying hinges
  roar.
Now, rushing in, the furious Chief appears,
Gloomy as night! and shakes two shining
  spears:
A dreadful gleam from his bright armour
  came,
And from his eye-balls flash'd the living
  flame.
He moves a God, resistless in his course,
And seems a match for more than mortal
  force.
Then, pouring after, thro' the gaping space,
A tide of Trojans flows, and fills the place;
The Greeks behold, they tremble, and they
  fly: 561
The shore is heap'd with death, and tumult
  rends the sky.

BOOK XIII

THE FOURTH BATTLE CONTINUED, IN WHICH
  NEPTUNE ASSISTS THE GREEKS.   THE ACTS
  OF IDOMENEUS

THE ARGUMENT

Neptune, concerned for the loss of the Grecians,
upon seeing the fortification forced by Hector
(who had entered the gate near the station

of the Ajaces), assumes the shape of Calchas,
and inspires those heroes to oppose him;
then, in the form of one of the generals, encourages the other Greeks who had retired
to their vessels.   The Ajaces form their
troops into a close phalanx, and put a stop
to Hector and the Trojans.   Several deeds
of valour are performed; Meriones, losing
his spear in the encounter, repairs to seek
another at the tent of Idomeneus: this occasions a conversation between these two
warriors, who return together to the battle.
Idomeneus signalizes his courage above the
rest; he kills Othryoneus, Asius, and Alca-
thous: Deiphobus and Æneas march against
him, and at length Idomeneus retires.
Menelaus wounds Helenus, and kills Pisander.   The Trojans are repulsed in the
left wing.   Hector still keeps his ground
against the Ajaces, till, being galled by the
Locrian slingers and archers, Polydamas
advises to call a council of war: Hector approves his advice, but goes first to rally the
Trojans; upbraids Paris, rejoins Polydamas,
meets Ajax again, and renews the attack.
The eight-and-twentieth day still continues.
The scene is between the Grecian wall and
the sea-shore.

WHEN now the Thund'rer on the sea-
    beat coast
Had fix'd great Hector and his conquering
    host,
He left them to the fates, in bloody fray
To toil and struggle thro' the well-fought
    day.
Then turned to Thracia from the field of
    fight
Those eyes that shed insufferable light,
To where the Mysians prove their martial
    force,
And hardy Thracians tame the savage
    horse;
And where the far-famed Hippemolgian
    strays,
Renown'd for justice and for length of
    days.   10
Thrice happy race! that, innocent of blood,
From milk innoxious seek their simple food:
Jove sees delighted; and avoids the scene
Of guilty Troy, of arms, and dying men:
No aid, he deems, to either host is giv'n,
While his high law suspends the Powers
    of Heav'n.
Meantime the Monarch of the wat'ry
    main
Observ'd the Thund'rer, nor observ'd in vain.
In Samothracia, on a mountain's brow,

Whose waving woods o'erhung the deeps
    below,   20
He sat; and round him cast his azure
    eyes,
Where Ida's misty tops confusedly rise;
Below, fair Ilion's glitt'ring spires were
    seen;
The crowded ships, and sable seas between.
There, from the crystal chambers of the
    main
Emerged, he sat; and mourn'd his Argives
    slain.
At Jove incens'd, with grief and fury
    stung,
Prone down the rocky steep he rush'd
    along;
Fierce as he pass'd, the lofty mountains
    nod,
The forests shake; earth trembled as he
    trod,   30
And felt th' footsteps of the immortal
    God.
From realm to realm three ample strides
    he took,
And, at the fourth, the distant Ægæ
    shook.
    Far in the bay his shining palace stands,
Eternal frame! not rais'd by mortal hands:
This having reach'd, his brass-hoof'd steeds
    he reins,
Fleet as the winds, and deck'd with golden
    manes.
Refulgent arms his mighty limbs infold,
Immortal arms of adamant and gold.
He mounts the car, the golden scourge
    applies,   40
He sits superior, and the chariot flies;
His whirling wheels the glassy surface
    sweep;
Th' enormous monsters, rolling o'er the
    deep,
Gambol around him on the wat'ry way;
And heavy whales in awkward measures
    play:
The sea subsiding spreads a level plain,
Exults, and owns the monarch of the main;
The parting waves before his coursers fly;
The wond'ring waters leave his axle dry.
    Deep in the liquid regions lies a cave, 50
Between where Tenedos the surges lave,
And rocky Imbrus breaks the rolling
    wave:
There the great ruler of the azure round
Stopp'd his swift chariot, and his steeds
    unbound,

Fed with ambrosial herbage from his hand,
And link'd their fetlocks with a golden
    band,
Infrangible, immortal: there they stay;
The Father of the Floods pursues his way,
Where, like a tempest dark'ning Heav'n
    around,
Or fiery deluge that devours the ground, 60
Th' impatient Trojans, in a gloomy throng,
Embattled roll'd, as Hector rush'd along:
To the loud tumult and the barb'rous cry,
The Heav'ns re-echo, and the shores reply;
They vow destruction to the Grecian name,
And in their hopes the fleets already flame.
    But Neptune, rising from the seas pro-
    found,
The God whose earthquakes rock the solid
    ground,
Now wears a mortal form; like Calchas seen,
Such his loud voice, and such his manly
    mien;   70
His shouts incessant every Greek inspire,
But most th' Ajaces, adding fire to fire:
    ' 'T is yours, O warriors, all our hopes to
    raise;
Oh recollect your ancient worth and praise!
'T is yours to save us if you cease to fear;
Flight, more than shameful, is destructive
    here.
On other works tho' Troy with fury fall,
And pour her armies o'er our batter'd
    wall;
There, Greece has strength: but this, this
    part o'erthrown,
Her strength were vain; I dread for you
    alone.   80
Here Hector rages like the force of fire,
Vaunts of his Gods, and calls high Jove his
    sire.
If yet some heav'nly power your breast
    excite,
Breathe in your hearts and string your
    arms to fight,
Greece yet may live, her threaten'd fleet
    maintain,
And Hector's force, and Jove's own aid, be
    vain.'
    Then with his sceptre that the deep con-
    trols,
He touch'd the Chiefs, and steel'd their
    manly souls:
Strength, not their own, the touch divine
    imparts,
Prompts their light limbs, and swells their
    daring hearts.   90

Then, as a falcon from the rocky height,
Her quarry seen, impetuous at the sight,
Forth-springing instant, darts herself from
high,
Shoots on the wing, and skims along the
sky:
Such, and so swift, the power of ocean
flew;
The wide horizon shut him from their
view.
Th' inspiring God Oïleus' active son
Perceiv'd the first, and thus to Telamon:
'Some God, my friend, some God in
human form,
Fav'ring descends, and wills to stand the
storm;   100
Not Calchas this, the venerable seer;
Short as he turn'd, I saw the Power ap-
pear:
I mark'd his parting, and the steps he
trod,
His own bright evidence reveals a God.
Ev'n now some energy divine I share,
And seem to walk on wings, and tread in
air!'
'With equal ardour' (Telamon returns),
'My soul is kindled, and my bosom
burns;
New rising spirits all my force alarm,
Lift each impatient limb, and brace my
arm.   110
This ready arm, unthinking, shakes the
dart;
The blood pours back, and fortifies my
heart;
Singly, methinks, yon tow'ring Chief I
meet,
And stretch the dreadful Hector at my
feet.'
Full of the God that urged their burning
breast,
The heroes thus their mutual warmth ex-
press'd.
Neptune meanwhile the routed Greeks in-
spired;
Who, breathless, pale, with length of labours tired,
Pant in the ships; while Troy to conquest
calls,
And swarms victorious o'er their yielding
walls: 120
Trembling before th' impending storm
they lie,
While tears of rage stand burning in their
eye.

Greece sunk they thought, and this their
fatal hour;
But breathe new courage as they feel the
power.
Teucer and Leitus first his words excite;
Then stern Peneleus rises to the fight;
Thoas, Deipyrus, in arms renown'd,
And Merion next, th' impulsive fury found;
Last Nestor's son the same bold ardour
takes,
While thus the God the martial fire
awakes: 130
'Oh lasting infamy, oh dire disgrace
To Chiefs of vig'rous youth, and manly
race!
I trusted in the Gods, and you, to see
Brave Greece victorious, and her navy
free:
Ah no — the glorious combat you disclaim,
And one black day clouds all her former
fame.
Heav'ns! what a prodigy these eyes sur-
vey,
Unseen, unthought, till this amazing day!
Fly we at length from Troy's oft-con-
quer'd bands?
And falls our fleet by such inglorious
hands?   140
A rout undisciplin'd, a straggling train,
Not born to glories of the dusty plain;
Like frighted fawns from hill to hill pur-
sued,
A prey to every savage of the wood;
Shall these, so late who trembled at your
name,
Invade your camps, involve your ships in
flame?
A change so shameful, say, what cause has
wrought?
The soldier's baseness, or the gen'ral's
fault?
Fools! will ye perish for your leader's
vice?   149
The purchase infamy, and life the price!
'T is not your cause, Achilles' injur'd
fame:
Another's is the crime, but yours the
shame.
Grant that our Chief offend thro' rage or
lust,
Must you be cowards if your king's un-
just?
Prevent this evil, and your country save:
Small thought retrieves the spirits of the
brave.

Think, and subdue! on dastards dead to
fame
I waste no anger, for they feel no shame:
But you, the pride, the flower of all our
host,
My heart weeps blood to see your glory
lost! 160
Nor deem this day, this battle, all you lose:
A day more black, a fate more vile, en-
sues.
Let each reflect, who prizes fame or
breath,
On endless infamy, on instant death.
For lo! the fated time, th' appointed shore;
Hark! the gates burst, the brazen barriers
roar!
Impetuous Hector thunders at the wall;
The hour, the spot, to conquer or to fall.'
These words the Grecians' fainting hearts
inspire,
And list'ning armies catch the godlike
fire. 170
Fix'd at his post was each bold Ajax found,
With well-ranged squadrons strongly cir-
cled round:
So close their order, so disposed their fight,
As Pallas' self might view with fix'd de-
light;
Or had the God of War inclin'd his eyes,
The God of War had own'd a just sur-
prise.
A chosen phalanx, firm, resolv'd as Fate,
Descending Hector and his battle wait.
An iron scene gleams dreadful o'er the
fields,
Armour in armour lock'd, and shields in
shields, 180
Spears lean on spears, on targets targets
throng,
Helms stuck to helms, and man drove man
along.
The floating plumes unnumber'd wave
above,
As when an earthquake stirs the nodding
grove;
And, levell'd at the skies with pointing
rays,
Their brandish'd lances at each motion
blaze.
Thus breathing death, in terrible array,
The close-compacted legions urged their
way:
Fierce they drove on, impatient to destroy;
Troy charged the first, and Hector first of
Troy. 190

As from some mountain's craggy forehead
torn,
A rock's round fragment flies with fury
borne,
(Which from the stubborn stone a torrent
rends,)
Precipitate the pond'rous mass descends:
From steep to steep the rolling ruin
bounds;
At every shock the crackling wood re-
sounds;
Still gath'ring force, it smokes; and, urged
amain,
Whirls, leaps, and thunders down, impetu-
ous to the plain:
There stops — So Hector. Their whole
force he prov'd,
Resistless when he raged, and, when he
stopp'd, unmov'd. 200
On him the war is bent, the darts are
shed,
And all their faulchions wave around his
head:
Repuls'd he stands, nor from his stand re-
tires;
But with repeated shouts his army fires.
'Trojans! be firm; this arm shall make
your way
Thro' yon square body, and that black
array;
Stand, and my spear shall rout their scat-
t'ring power,
Strong as they seem, embattled like a
tower.
For he that Juno's heav'nly bosom warms,
The first of Gods, this day inspires our
arms.' 210
He said, and rous'd the soul in ev'ry
breast;
Urged with desire of fame, beyond the rest,
Forth march'd Deïphobus ; but marching
held
Before his wary steps his ample shield.
Bold Merion aim'd a stroke, nor aim'd it
wide;
The glitt'ring jav'lin pierc'd the tough
bull-hide;
But pierc'd not thro' : unfaithful to his
hand,
The point broke short, and sparkled in the
sand.
The Trojan warrior, touch'd with timely
fear,
On the rais'd orb to distance bore the
spear: 220

The Greek retreating mourn'd his frustrate
blow,
And curs'd the treach'rous lance that spared
a foe;
Then to the ships with surly speed he went,
To seek a surer jav'lin in his tent.
  Meanwhile with rising rage the battle
glows,
The tumult thickens, and the clamour
grows.
By Teucer's arm the warlike Imbrius
bleeds,
The son of Mentor, rich in gen'rous steeds.
Ere yet to Troy the sons of Greece were
led,
In fair Pedæus' verdant pastures bred,   230
The youth had dwelt; remote from war's
alarms,
And bless'd in bright Medesicaste's arms:
(This nymph, the fruit of Priam's ravish'd
joy,
Allied the warrior to the house of Troy.)
To Troy, when glory call'd his arms, he
came:
And match'd the bravest of her Chiefs in
fame:
With Priam's sons, a guardian of the
throne,
He liv'd, belov'd and honour'd as his own.
Him Teucer pierc'd between the throat and
ear:
He groans beneath the Telamonian spear.
As from some far-seen mountain's airy
crown,   241
Subdued by steel, a tall ash tumbles
down,
And soils its verdant tresses on the ground:
So falls the youth; his arms the fall re-
sound.
Then, Teucer rushing to despoil the dead,
From Hector's hand a shining jav'lin fled:
He saw, and shunn'd the death; the force-
ful dart
Sung on, and pierc'd Amphimachus's heart,
Cteatus' son, of Neptune's forceful line;
Vain was his courage, and his race divine!
Prostrate he falls; his clanging arms re-
sound,   251
And his broad buckler thunders on the
ground.
To seize his beamy helm the victor flies,
And just had fasten'd on the dazzling prize,
When Ajax' manly arm a jav'lin flung;
Full on the shield's round boss the weapon
rung;

He felt the shock, nor more was doom'd
to feel,
Secure in mail, and sheathed in shining
steel.
Repuls'd he yields; the victor Greeks ob-
tain   259
The spoils contested, and bear off the slain.
Between the leaders of th' Athenian line,
(Stichius the brave, Menestheus the di-
vine,)
Deplor'd Amphimachus, sad object! lies;
Imbrius remains the fierce Ajaces' prize.
As two grim lions bear across the lawn,
Snatch'd from devouring hounds, a slaugh-
ter'd fawn
In their fell jaws high lifting thro' the
wood,
And sprinkling all the shrubs with drops of
blood;
So these the Chief: great Ajax from the
dead
Strips his bright arms, Oïleus lops his
head: 270
Toss'd like a ball, and whirl'd in air away,
At Hector's feet the gory visage lay.
  The God of Ocean, fired with stern dis-
dain,
And pierc'd with sorrow for his grandson
slain,
Inspires the Grecian hearts, confirms their
hands,
And breathes destruction to the Trojan
bands.
Swift as a whirlwind rushing to the fleet,
He finds the lance-famed Idomen of Crete;
His pensive brow the gen'rous care ex-
press'd
With which a wounded soldier touch'd his
breast,   280
Whom in the chance of war a jav'lin tore,
And his sad comrades from the battle bore;
Him to the surgeons of the camp he sent;
That office paid, he issued from his tent,
Fierce for the fight: to him the God begun,
In Thoas' voice, Andræmon's valiant son,
Who ruled where Calydon's white rocks
arise,
And Pleuron's chalky cliffs emblaze the
skies:
' Where 's now th' impetuous vaunt, the
daring boast,
Of Greece victorious, and proud Ilion
lost ? '   290
  To whom the King: ' On Greece no blame
be thrown,

Arms are her trade, and war is all her
 own.
Her hardy heroes from the well-fought
 plains
Nor Fear withholds, nor shameful Sloth
 detains.
'T is Heav'n, alas! and Jove's all-powerful
 doom,
That far, far distant from our native home
Wills us to fall, inglorious! Oh, my
 friend!
Once foremost in the fight, still prone to
 lend
Or arms, or counsels; now perform thy
 best,
And what thou canst not singly, urge the
 rest.' 300
 Thus he; and thus the God whose force
 can make
The solid globe's eternal basis shake:
' Ah! never may he see his native land,
But feed the vultures on this hateful
 strand,
Who seeks ignobly in his ships to stay,
Nor dares to combat on this signal day!
For this, behold! in horrid arms I shine,
And urge thy soul to rival acts with mine;
Together let us battle on the plain;
Two, not the worst; nor ev'n this succour
 vain: 310
Not vain the weakest, if their force unite;
But ours, the bravest have confess'd in
 fight.'
 This said, he rushes where the combat
 burns;
Swift to his tent the Cretan King returns.
From thence, two jav'lins glitt'ring in his
 hand,
And clad in arms that lighten'd all the
 strand,
Fierce on the foe th' impetuous hero drove;
Like lightning bursting from the arm of
 Jove,
Which to pale man the wrath of Heav'n
 declares, 319
Or terrifies th' offending world with wars;
In streamy sparkles, kindling all the skies,
From pole to pole the trail of glory flies.
Thus his bright armour o'er the dazzled
 throng
Gleam'd dreadful as the Monarch flash'd
 along.
 Him, near his tent, Meriones attends;
Whom thus he questions: ' Ever best of
 friends!

O say, in every art of battle skill'd,
What holds thy courage from so brave a
 field ?
On some important message art thou
 bound,
Or bleeds my friend by some unhappy
 wound ? 330
Inglorious here, my soul abhors to stay,
And glows with prospects of th' approach-
 ing day.'
 ' O Prince!' (Meriones replies), ' whose
 care
Leads forth th' embattled sons of Crete to
 war;
This speaks my grief: this headless lance I
 wield;
The rest lies rooted in a Trojan shield.'
 To whom the Cretan: ' Enter, and re-
 ceive
The wanted weapons; those my tent can
 give;
Spears I have store (and Trojan lances
 all),
That shed a lustre round th' illumin'd wall.
Tho' I, disdainful of the distant war, 341
Nor trust the dart, nor aim th' uncertain
 spear,
Yet hand to hand I fight, and spoil the
 slain;
And thence these trophies, and these arms
 I gain.
Enter, and see on heaps the helmets roll'd,
And high-hung spears, and shields that
 flame with gold.'
 ' Nor vain ' (said Merion) ' are our mar-
 tial toils;
We too can boast of no ignoble spoils.
But those my ship contains, whence dis-
 tant far,
I fight conspicuous in the van of war. 350
What need I more ? If any Greek there
 be
Who knows not Merion, I appeal to thee.'
 To this Idomeneus : ' The fields of fight
Have prov'd thy valour, and unconquer'd
 might:
And were some ambush for the foes de-
 sign'd,
Ev'n there thy courage would not lag be-
 hind.
In that sharp service, singled from the rest,
The fear of each, or valour, stands con-
 fess'd.
No force, no firmness, the pale coward
 shews;

He shifts his place; his colour comes and
   goes;   360
A dropping sweat creeps cold on ev'ry
   part;
Against his bosom beats his quiv'ring
   heart;
Terror and death in his wild eye-balls ⎫
   stare;   ⎪
With chatt'ring teeth he stands, and ⎬
   stiff'ning hair,   ⎪
And looks a bloodless image of despair! ⎭
Not so the brave; still dauntless, still the
   same,
Unchanged his colour, and unmov'd his
   frame;
Composed his thought, determin'd is his
   eye,
And fix'd his soul, to conquer or to die:
If aught disturb the tenor of his breast, 370
'Tis but the wish to strike before the rest.
   'In such assays thy blameless worth is
   known,
And ev'ry art of dangerous war thy own.
By chance of fight whatever wounds you
   bore,
Those wounds were glorious all, and all
   before:
Such as may teach, 't was still thy brave
   delight
T' oppose thy bosom where the foremost
   fight.
But why, like infants, cold to honour's
   charms,
Stand we to talk, when glory calls to arms?
Go — from my conquer'd spears the choi-
   cest take,   380
And to their owners send them nobly
   back.'
   Swift as the word bold Merion snatch'd
   a spear,
And, breathing slaughter, follow'd to the
   war.
So Mars armipotent invades the plain,
(The wide destroyer of the race of man;)
Terror, his best-lov'd son, attends his
   course,
Arm'd with stern boldness, and enormous
   force;
The pride of haughty warriors to confound,
And lay the strength of tyrants on the
   ground.
From Thrace they fly, call'd to the dire
   alarms   390
Of warring Phlegians, and Ephyrian
   arms:

Invoked by both, relentless they dispose
To these glad conquest, murd'rous rout to
   those.
So march'd the leaders of the Cretan train,
And their bright arms shot horror o'er the
   plain.
   Then first spake Merion: 'Shall we join
   the right,
Or combat in the centre of the fight?
Or to the left our wanted succour lend?
Hazard and Fame all parts alike attend.'
   'Not in the centre' (Idomen replied),
'Our ablest Chieftains the main battle
   guide;   401
Each godlike Ajax makes that post his
   care,
And gallant Teucer deals destruction there:
Skill'd, or with shafts to gall the distant
   field
Or bear close battle on the sounding shield.
These can the rage of haughty Hector
   tame;
Safe in their arms, the navy fears no flame;
Till Jove himself descends, his bolts to
   shed,
And hurl the blazing ruin at our head.
Great must he be, of more than human
   birth,   410
Nor feed like mortals on the fruits of
   earth,
Him neither rocks can crush, nor steel can
   wound,
Whom Ajax fells not on th' ensanguin'd
   ground.
In standing fight he mates Achilles' force,
Excell'd alone in swiftness in the course.
Then to the left our ready arms apply,
And live with glory, or with glory die.'
   He said: and Merion to th' appointed
   place,
Fierce as the God of Battles, urged his
   pace.   419
Soon as the foe the shining chiefs beheld
Rush like a fiery torrent round the field,
Their force embodied in a tide they pour;
The rising combat sounds along the shore:
As warring winds, in Sirius' sultry reign,
From diff'rent quarters sweep the sandy
   plain;
On every side the dusty whirlwinds rise,
And the dry fields are lifted to the skies:
Thus, by despair, hope, rage, together
   driv'n,
Met the black hosts, and, meeting, darken'd
   Heav'n.

All dreadful glared the iron face of war, 430
Bristled with upright spears, that flash'd
  afar;
Dire was the gleam of breast-plates, helms,
  and shields,
And polish'd arms emblazed the flaming
  fields:
Tremendous scene! that gen'ral horror
  gave,
But touch'd with joy the bosoms of the
  brave.
  Saturn's great sons in fierce contention
  vied,
And crowds of heroes in their anger died.
The Sire of Earth and Heav'n, by Thetis
  won
To crown with glory Peleus' godlike son,
Will'd not destruction to the Grecian
  powers, 440
But spared awhile the destin'd Trojan
  towers:
While Neptune, rising from his azure ⎫
  main, ⎪
Warr'd on the King of Heav'n with stern ⎬
  disdain, ⎪
And breathed revenge, and fired the Gre- ⎭
  cian train.
Gods of one source, of one ethereal race,
Alike divine, and Heav'n their native place;
But Jove the greater; first-born of the
  skies,
And more than men, or Gods, supremely
  wise.
For this, of Jove's superior might afraid,
Neptune in human form conceal'd his aid.
These Powers infold the Greek and Trojan
  train 451
In War and Discord's adamantine chain;
Indissolubly strong, the fatal tie
Is stretch'd on both, and close-compell'd
  they die.
  Dreadful in arms, and grown in combat
  grey,
The bold Idomeneus controls the day.
First by his hand Othryoneus was slain,
Swell'd with false hopes, with mad ambi-
  tion vain;
Call'd by the voice of war to martial fame,
From high Cabesus' distant walls he came;
Cassandra's love he sought, with boasts of
  power, 461
And promis'd conquest was the proffer'd
  dower.
The King consented, by his vaunts abused;
The King consented, but the Fates refused.

Proud of himself, and of th' imagin'd
  bride,
The field he measured with a larger stride.
Him, as he stalk'd, the Cretan jav'lin found;
Vain was his breast-plate to repel the
  wound:
His dream of glory lost, he plunged to
  Hell;
The plains resounded as the boaster fell. 470
  The great Idomeneus bestrides the dead:
' And thus ' (he cries) ' behold thy promise
  sped ! '
' Such is the help thy arms to Ilion bring,
And such the contract of the Phrygian
  King!
Our offers now, illustrious Prince! receive;
For such an aid what will not Argos give ?
To conquer Troy, with ours thy forces join,
And count Atrides' fairest daughter thine.
Meantime, on farther methods to advise,
Come, follow to the fleet thy new allies; 480
There hear what Greece has on her part to
  say.'
He spoke, and dragg'd the gory corse away.
  This Asius view'd, unable to contain,
Before his chariot warring on the plain;
(His valued coursers, to his squire con-
  sign'd,
Impatient panted on his neck behind):
To vengeance rising with a sudden spring,
He hoped the conquest of the Cretan King.
The wary Cretan, as his foe drew near,
Full on his throat discharged the forceful
  spear: 490
Beneath the chin the point was seen to
  glide,
And, glitter'd, extant, at the farther side
As when the mountain oak, or poplar tall,
Or pine, fit mast for some great admiral,
Groans to the oft-heav'd axe, with many
  a wound,
Then spreads a length of ruin o'er the
  ground:
So sunk proud Asius in that dreadful day,
And stretch'd before his much-lov'd
  coursers lay.
He grinds the dust distain'd with stream-
  ing gore,
And, fierce in death, lies foaming on the
  shore. 500
Deprived of motion, stiff with stupid fear,
Stands all aghast his trembling charioteer,
Nor shuns the foe, nor turns the steeds
  away,
But falls transfix'd, an unresisting prey:

Pierc'd by Antilochus, he pants beneath
The stately car, and labours out his breath.
Thus Asius' steeds (their mighty master
  gone)
Remain the prize of Nestor's youthful son.
  Stabb'd at the sight, Deïphobus drew
  nigh,
And made, with force, the vengeful weapon
  fly: 510
The Cretan saw; and, stooping, caus'd to
  glance,
From his slope shield, the disappointed
  lance.
Beneath the spacious targe (a blazing
  round,
Thick with bull-hides, and brazen orbits
  bound,
On his rais'd arm by two strong braces
  stay'd),
He lay collected in defensive shade;
O'er his safe head the jav'lin idly sung,
And on the tinkling verge more faintly
  rung.
Ev'n then, the spear the vig'rous arm con-
  fess'd,
And pierc'd, obliquely, King Hypsenor's
  breast;   520
Warm'd in his liver, to the ground it bore
The Chief, his people's guardian now no
  more!
  'Not unattended' (the proud Trojan
  cries)
'Nor unrevenged, lamented Asius lies:
For thee, tho' Hell's black portals stand
  display'd,
This mate shall joy thy melancholy shade.'
  Heart-piercing anguish, at the haughty
  boast,
Touch'd every Greek, but Nestor's son the
  most:
Griev'd as he was, his pious arms attend,
And his broad buckler shields his slaugh-
  ter'd friend: 530
Till sad Mecistheus and Alastor bore
His honour'd body to the tented shore.
  Nor yet from fight Idomeneus with-
  draws;
Resolv'd to perish in his country's cause,
Or find some foe, whom Heav'n and he
  shall doom
To wail his fate in death's eternal gloom.
He sees Alcathoüs in the front aspire:
Great Æsyetes was the hero's sire:
His spouse Hippodame, divinely fair,
Anchises' eldest hope, and darling care: 540

Who charm'd her parent's and her hus-
  band's heart,
With beauty, sense, and every work of art:
He, once, of Ilion's youth the loveliest boy,
The fairest she, of all the fair of Troy.
By Neptune now the hapless hero dies,
Who covers with a cloud those beauteous
  eyes,
And fetters every limb: yet bent to meet
His fate, he stands; nor shuns the lance of
  Crete.
Fix'd as some column, or deep-rooted oak,
(While the winds sleep,) his breast receiv'd
  the stroke.   550
Before the pond'rous stroke his corslet
  yields,
Long used to ward the death in fighting
  fields.
The riven armour sends a jarring sound: ⎫
His lab'ring heart heaves with so strong ⎪
  a bound,   ⎬
The long lance shakes, and vibrates in   ⎪
  the wound: ⎭
Fast flowing from its source, as prone he
  lay,
Life's purple tide impetuous gush'd away.
  Then Idomen, insulting o'er the slain:
'Behold, Deïphobus! nor vaunt in vain:
See! on one Greek three Trojan ghosts at-
  tend,   560
This, my third victim, to the shades I send.
Approaching now, thy boasted might ap-
  prove,
And try the prowess of the seed of Jove.
From Jove, enamour'd on a mortal dame,
Great Minos, guardian of his country,
  came;
Deucalion, blameless Prince! was Minos'
  heir;
His first-born I, the third from Jupiter:
O'er spacious Crete and her bold sons I
  reign,
And thence my ships transport me thro'
  the main:
Lord of a host, o'er all my host I shine, 570
A scourge to thee, thy father, and thy line.'
  The Trojan heard; uncertain, or to meet
Alone, with venturous arms, the King of
  Crete;
Or seek auxiliar force; at length decreed
To call some hero to partake the deed.
Forthwith Æneas rises to his thought;
For him, in Troy's remotest lines he sought,
Where he, incens'd at partial Priam, stands,
And sees superior posts in meaner hands.

To him, ambitious of so great an aid, 580
The bold Deïphobus approach'd, and said:
'Now, Trojan Prince, employ thy pious
arms,
If e'er thy bosom felt fair honour's charms.
Alcathoüs dies, thy brother and thy friend.
Come, and the warrior's lov'd remains de-
fend.
Beneath his cares thy early youth was
train'd,
One table fed you, and one roof contain'd.
This deed to fierce Idomeneus we owe;
Haste, and revenge it on th' insulting foe.'
Æneas heard, and for a space resign'd 590
To tender pity all his manly mind;
Then, rising in his rage, he burns to fight:
The Greek awaits him, with collected
might.
As the fell boar on some rough mountain's
head,
Arm'd with wild terrors, and to slaughter
bred,
When the loud rustics rise, and shout from
far,
Attends the tumult, and expects the war;
O'er his bent back the bristly horrors rise,
Fires stream in lightning from his sanguine
eyes;
His foaming tusks both dogs and men en-
gage, 600
But most his hunters rouse his mighty rage:
So stood Idomeneus, his jav'lin shook,
And met the Trojan with a low'ring look.
Antilochus, Deïpyrus, were near,
The youthful offspring of the God of War;
Merion, and Aphareus, in field renown'd:
To these the warrior sent his voice around:
'Fellows in arms! your timely aid unite:
Lo, great Æneas rushes to the fight:
Sprung from a God, and more than mortal
bold: 610
He fresh in youth, and I in arms grown
old.
Else should this hand, this hour, decide the
strife,
The great dispute, of glory, or of life.'
He spoke, and all as with one soul
obey'd;
Their lifted bucklers cast a dreadful shade
Around the Chief. Æneas too demands
Th' assisting forces of his native bands:
Paris, Deïphobus, Agenor join;
(Co-aids and captains of the Trojan line;)
In order follow all th' embodied train; 620
Like Ida's flocks proceeding o'er the plain:

Before his fleecy care, erect and bold,
Stalks the proud ram, the father of the
fold:
With joy the swain surveys them, as he
leads
To the cool fountains thro' the well-known
meads:
So joys Æneas, as his native band
Moves on in rank, and stretches o'er the
land.
Round dead Alcathoüs now the battle
rose;
On ev'ry side the steely circle grows ;
Now batter'd breast-plates and hack'd hel-
mets ring, 630
And o'er their heads unheeded jav'lins
sing.
Above the rest, two tow'ring Chiefs ap-
pear,
There great Idomeneus, Æneas here.
Like Gods of War, dispensing fate, they
stood,
And burn'd to drench the ground with
mutual blood.
The Trojan weapon whizz'd along in air:
The Cretan saw, and shunn'd the brazen
spear,
Sent from an arm so strong, the missive
wood
Stuck deep in earth, and quiver'd where it
stood. 639
But Œnomas receiv'd the Cretan's stroke;
The forceful spear his hollow corslet broke;
It ripp'd his belly with a ghastly wound,
And roll'd the smoking entrails to the
ground.
Stretch'd on the plain, he sobs away his
breath,
And furious grasps the bloody dust in
death.
The victor from his breast the weapon
tears
(His spoils he could not, for the shower of
spears);
Tho' now unfit an active war to wage,
Heavy with cumbrous arms, stiff with cold
age,
His listless limbs unable for the course; 650
In standing fight he yet maintains his
force:
Till, faint with labour, and by foes repell'd,
His tired slow steps he drags along the
field.
Deïphobus beheld him as he pass'd,
And, fired with hate, a parting jav'lin cast:

The jav'lin err'd, but held its course along,
And pierc'd Ascalaphus, the brave and
   young:
The son of Mars fell gasping on the
   ground,
And gnash'd the dust all bloody with his
   wound.
Nor knew the furious father of his fall;
High-throned amidst the great Olympian
   hall, 661
On golden clouds th' immortal synod sat;
Detain'd from bloody war by Jove and
   Fate.
Now, where in dust the breathless hero
   lay,
For slain Ascalaphus commenc'd the fray.
Deïphobus to seize his helmet flies,
And from his temples rends the glitt'ring
   prize:
Valiant as Mars, Meriones drew near,
And on his loaded arm discharged his spear.
He drops the weight, disabled with the
   pain; 670
The hollow helmet rings against the plain.
Swift as a vulture leaping on his prey,
From his torn arm the Grecian rent away
The reeking jav'lin, and rejoin'd his friends.
His wounded brother good Polites tends;
Around his waist his pious arms he threw,
And from the rage of combat gently drew:
Him his swift coursers, on his splendid car,
Rapt from the less'ning thunder of the
   war;
To Troy they drove him, groaning, from
   the shore, 680
And sprinkling, as he pass'd, the sands with
   gore.
Meanwhile fresh slaughter bathes the
   sanguine ground,
Heaps fall on heaps, and Heav'n and Earth
   resound.
Bold Aphareus by great Æneas bled;
As toward the Chief he turn'd his daring
   head,
He pierc'd his throat; the bending head,
   depress'd
Beneath his helmet, nods upon his breast;
His shield revers'd o'er the fall'n warrior
   lies;
And everlasting slumber seals his eyes.
Antilochus, as Thoön turn'd him round, 690
Transpierc'd his back with a dishonest
   wound:
The hollow vein that to the neck extends
Along the chine, his eager jav'lin rends:

Supine he falls, and to his social train
Spreads his imploring arms, but spreads in
   vain.
Th' exulting victor, leaping where he lay,
From his broad shoulders tore the spoils
   away;
His time observ'd; for, closed by foes
   around,
On all sides thick, the peals of arms re-
   sound.
His shield, emboss'd, the ringing storm sus-
   tains, 700
But he impervious and untouch'd remains.
(Great Neptune's care preserv'd from hos-
   tile rage
This youth, the joy of Nestor's glorious
   age.)
In arms intrepid with the first he fought,
Faced ev'ry foe, and ev'ry danger sought;
His winged lance, resistless as the wind,
Obeys each motion of the master's mind:
Restless it flies, impatient to be free,
And meditates the distant enemy.
The son of Asius, Adamas, drew near, 710
And struck his target with the brazen
   spear,
Fierce in his front; but Neptune wards the
   blow,
And blunts the jav'lin of th' eluded foe.
In the broad buckler half the weapon stood;
Splinter'd on earth flew half the broken
   wood.
Disarm'd, he mingled in the Trojan crew;
But Merion's spear o'ertook him as he flew,
Deep in the belly's rim an entrance found,
Where sharp the pang, and mortal is the
   wound.
Bending he fell, and, doubled to the
   ground, 720
Lay panting. Thus an ox, in fetters tied,
While death's strong pangs distend his la-
   b'ring side,
His bulk enormous on the field displays;
His heaving heart beats thick, as ebbing
   life decays.
The spear the conqueror from his body
   drew,
And death's dim shadows swam before his
   view.
Next brave Deïpyrus in dust was laid:
King Helenus waved high the Thracian
   blade,
And smote his temples with an arm so strong,
The helm fell off, and roll'd amid the
   throng; 730

There, for some luckier Greek it rests a
    prize,
For dark in death the godlike owner lies!
With raging grief great Menelaus burns,
And, fraught with vengeance, to the victor
    turns;
That shook the pond'rous lance, in act to
    throw,
And this stood adverse with the bended
    bow:
Full on his breast the Trojan arrow fell,
But harmless bounded from the plated
    steel.
As on some ample barn's well-harden'd
    floor,   739
(The winds collected at each open door,)
While the broad fan with force is whirl'd
    around,
Light leaps the golden grain, resulting from
    the ground:
So from the steel that guards Atrides'
    heart,
Repell'd to distance flies the bounding dart.
Atrides, watchful of th' unwary foe,
Pierc'd with his lance the hand that grasp'd
    the bow,
And nail'd it to the yew: the wounded
    hand
Trail'd the long lance that mark'd with
    blood the sand;
But good Agenor gently from the wound
The spear solicits, and the bandage bound;
A sling's soft wool, snatch'd from a sol-
    dier's side,   751
At once the tent and ligature supplied.
    Behold! Pisander, urged by Fate's de-
    cree,
Springs thro' the ranks to fall, and fall by
    thee,
Great Menelaus! to enhance thy fame;
High tow'ring in the front, the warrior
    came.
First the sharp lance was by Atrides
    thrown;
The lance far distant by the winds was
    blown.
Nor pierc'd Pisander thro' Atrides' shield;
Pisander's spear fell shiver'd on the
    field.   760
Not so discouraged, to the future blind,
Vain dreams of conquest swell his haughty
    mind;
Dauntless he rushes where the Spartan lord
Like lightning brandish'd his far-beaming
    sword.

His left arm high opposed the shining
    shield;
His right, beneath, the cover'd pole-axe
    held;
(An olive's cloudy grain the handle made,
Distinct with studs; and brazen was the
    blade);
This on the helm discharged a noble blow;
The plume dropp'd nodding to the plain
    below,   770
Shorn from the crest. Atrides waved his
    steel;
Deep thro' his front the weighty falchion
    fell;
The crashing bones before its force gave
    way;
In dust and blood the groaning hero lay;
Forc'd from their ghastly orbs, and spout-
    ing gore,
The clotted eye-balls tumble on the shore.
The fierce Atrides spurn'd him as he bled,
Tore off his arms, and loud exulting said:
    ' Thus, Trojans, thus, at length be taught
    to fear;
O race perfidious, who delight in war! 780
Already noble deeds ye have perform'd,
A Princess raped transcends a navy
    storm'd:
In such bold feats your impious might ap-
    prove,
Without th' assistance or the fear of Jove.
The violated rites, the ravish'd dame,
Our heroes slaughter'd, and our ships on
    flame,
Crimes heap'd on crimes, shall bend your
    glory down,
And whelm in ruins yon flagitious town.
O thou, great Father, lord of earth and
    skies,
Above the thought of man, supremely
    wise!   790
If from thy hand the fates of mortals
    flow,
From whence this favour to an impious
    foe,
A godless crew, abandon'd and unjust,
Still breathing rapine, violence, and lust ?
The best of things, beyond their measure,
    cloy;
Sleep's balmy blessing, love's endearing
    joy;
The feast, the dance; whate'er mankind
    desire,
Ev'n the sweet charms of sacred numbers
    tire.

But Troy for ever reaps a dire delight
In thirst of slaughter, and in lust of
fight.'   800
This said, he seiz'd (while yet the car-
cass heav'd)
The bloody armour, which his train re-
ceiv'd:
Then sudden mix'd among the warring crew,
And the bold son of Pylæmenes slew.
Harpalion had thro' Asia travell'd far,
Following his martial father to the war;
Thro' filial love he left his native shore,
Never, ah never, to behold it more!
His unsuccessful spear he chanc'd to fling
Against the target of the Spartan king; 810
Thus of his lance disarm'd, from death he
flies,
And turns around his apprehensive eyes.
Him, thro' the hip transpiercing as he fled,
The shaft of Merion mingled with the
dead.
Beneath the bone the glancing point de-
scends,
And, driving down, the swelling bladder
rends:
Sunk in his sad companions' arms he lay,
And in short pantings sobb'd his soul away
(Like some vile worm extended on the
ground),
While life's red torrent gush'd from out
the wound.   820
Him on his car the Paphlagonian train
In slow procession bore from off the plain.
The pensive father, father now no more!
Attends the mournful pomp along the
shore;
And unavailing tears profusely shed,
And unrevenged deplor'd his offspring
dead.
Paris from far the moving sight beheld,
With pity soften'd, and with fury swell'd:
His honour'd host, a youth of matchless
grace,
And lov'd of all the Paphlagonian race! 830
With his full strength he bent his angry
bow,
And wing'd the feather'd vengeance at the
foe.
A Chief there was, the brave Euchenor
named,
For riches much, and more for virtue,
famed,
Who held his seat in Corinth's stately
town;
Polydus' son, a seer of old renown.

Oft had the father told his early doom,
By arms abroad, or slow disease at home:
He climb'd his vessel, prodigal of breath,
And chose the certain glorious path to
death.   840
Beneath his ear the pointed arrow went;
The soul came issuing at the narrow vent;
His limbs, unnerv'd, drop useless on the
ground,
And everlasting darkness shades him
round.
Nor knew great Hector how his legions
yield
(Wrapp'd in the cloud and tumult of the
field);
Wide on the left the force of Greece com-
mands,
And conquest hovers o'er th' Achaian
bands:
With such a tide superior virtue sway'd,
And he that shakes the solid earth, gave
aid.   850
But in the centre Hector fix'd remain'd,
Where first the gates were forc'd, and bul-
warks gain'd;
There, on the margin of the hoary deep
(Their naval station where th' Ajaces
keep,
And where low walls confine the beating
tides,
Whose humble barrier scarce the foe di-
vides;
Where late in fight both foot and horse
engaged,
And all the thunder of the battle raged),
There join'd, the whole Bœotian strength
remains,
The proud Ionians with their sweeping
trains,   860
Locrians and Phthians, and th' Epeian
force;
But, join'd, repel not Hector's fiery course.
The flower of Athens, Stichius, Phidas led,
Bias and great Menestheus at their head.
Meges the strong th' Epeian bands con-
troll'd,
And Dracius prudent, and Amphion bold;
The Phthians Medon, famed for martial
might,
And brave Podarces, active in the fight.
This drew from Phylacus his noble line,
Iphiclus' son; and that, Oïleus, thine 870
(Young Ajax' brother, by a stol'n em-
brace;
He dwelt far distant from his native place;

By his fierce stepdame from his father's
reign
Expell'd and exiled for her brother slain):
These rule the Phthians, and their arms
employ,
Mix'd with Bœotians, on the shores of
Troy.
Now side by side, with like unwearied
care,
Each Ajax labour'd thro' the field of
war.
So when two lordly bulls, with equal toil,
Force the bright ploughshare thro' the fal-
low soil, 880
Join'd to one yoke, the stubborn earth they
tear,
And trace large furrows with the shining
share:
O'er their huge limbs the foam descends in
snow,
And streams of sweat down their sour fore-
heads flow.
A train of heroes follow'd thro' the field,
Who bore by turns great Ajax' seven-fold
shield;
Whene'er he breathed, remissive of his
might,
Tired with th' incessant slaughters of the
fight.
No foll'wing troops his brave associate
grace ; 889
In close engagement an unpractis'd race,
The Locrian squadrons nor the jav'lin
wield,
Nor bear the helm, nor lift the moony
shield;
But skill'd from far the flying shaft to
wing,
Or whirl the sounding pebble from the
sling;
Dext'rous with these they aim a certain
wound,
Or fell the distant warrior to the ground.
Thus in the van, the Telamonian train,
Throng'd in bright arms, a pressing fight
maintain;
Far in the rear the Locrian archers lie,
Whose stones and arrows intercept the
sky: 900
The mingled tempest on the foes they
pour;
Troy's scatt'ring orders open to the shower.
Now had the Greeks eternal fame
acquired,
And the gall'd Ilians to their walls retired;

But sage Polydamas, discreetly brave,
Address'd great Hector, and this counsel
gave:
'Tho' great in all, thou seem'st averse to
lend
Impartial audience to a faithful friend:
To Gods and men thy matchless worth is
known,
And ev'ry art of glorious war thy own; 910
But in cool thought and counsel to excel,
How widely differs this from warring well!
Content with what the bounteous Gods have
giv'n,
Seek not alone t' engross the gifts of
Heav'n.
To some the powers of bloody war belong,
To some, sweet music, and the charm of
song;
To few, and wondrous few, has Jove as-
sign'd
A wise, extensive, all-consid'ring mind;
Their guardians these the nations round
confess,
And towns and empires for their safety
bless. 920
If Heav'n have lodg'd this virtue in my
breast,
Attend, O Hector, what I judge the best.
See, as thou mov'st, on dangers dangers
spread,
And war's whole fury burns around thy head:
Behold! distress'd within yon hostile wall,
How many Trojans yield, disperse, or fall!
What troops, out-number'd, scarce the war
maintain!
And what brave heroes at the ships lie slain!
Here cease thy fury; and, the Chiefs and
Kings
Convoked to council, weigh the sum of
things. 930
Whether (the Gods succeeding our desires)
To yon tall ships to bear the Trojan fires;
Or quit the fleet, and pass unhurt away,
Contented with the conquest of the day.
I fear, I fear, lest Greece (not yet undone)
Pay the large debt of last revolving sun.
Achilles, great Achilles, yet remains
On yonder decks, and yet o'erlooks the
plains!'
The counsel pleas'd; and Hector, with
a bound,
Leap'd from his chariot on the trembling
ground; 940
Swift as he leap'd, his clanging arms re-
sound.

'To guard this post' (he cried) 'thy art
     employ,
And here detain the scatter'd youth of
     Troy;
Where yonder heroes faint, I bend my way,
And hasten back to end the doubtful day.'
This said, the tow'ring Chief prepares ⎤
     to go,   ⎟
Shakes his white plumes that to the   ⎟
     breezes flow,   ⎬
And seems a moving mountain topp'd   ⎟
     with snow.   ⎦
Thro' all his host inspiring force, he flies,
And bids anew the martial thunder
     rise.   950
To Panthus' son, at Hector's high com-
     mand,
Haste the bold leaders of the Trojan band:
But round the battlements, and round the
     plain,
For many a Chief he look'd, but look'd in
     vain;
Deïphobus, nor Helenus the seer,
Nor Asius' son, nor Asius' self appear.
For these were pierc'd with many a ghastly
     wound,
Some cold in death, some groaning on the
     ground;
Some low in dust (a mournful object) lay,
High on the wall some breathed their souls
     away.   960
    Far on the left, amidst the throng he
     found
(Cheering the troops, and dealing deaths
     around),
The graceful Paris: whom, with fury
     mov'd,
Opprobrious, thus th' impatient Chief re-
     prov'd:
'Ill-fated Paris! slave to womankind,
As smooth of face as fraudulent of mind!
Where is Deïphobus, where Asius gone?
The godlike father, and th' intrepid son?
The force of Helenus, dispensing fate,   969
And great Othryoneus, so fear'd of late?
Black fate hangs o'er thee from th' aveng-
     ing Gods,
Imperial Troy from her foundation nods;
Whelm'd in thy country's ruins shalt thou
     fall,
And one devouring vengeance swallow all.'
    When Paris thus: 'My brother and my
     friend,
Thy warm impatience makes thy tongue
     offend.

In other battles I deserv'd thy blame,
Tho' then not deedless, nor unknown to
     Fame:
But since yon rampart by thy arms lay
     low,   979
I scatter'd slaughter from my fatal bow.
The Chiefs you seek on yonder shore lie
     slain;
Of all those heroes, two alone remain;
Deïphobus, and Helenus the seer:
Each now disabled by a hostile spear.
Go then, successful, where thy soul inspires;
This heart and hand shall second all thy
     fires:
What with this arm I can, prepare to
     know,
Till death for death be paid, and blow for
     blow.
But 't is not ours, with forces not our own
To combat; strength is of the Gods
     alone.'   990
    These words the hero's angry mind as-
     suage:
Then fierce they mingle where the thickest
     rage.
Around Polydamas, distain'd with blood,
Cebrion, Phalces, stern Orthæus, stood;
Palmus, with Polypœtes the divine,
And two bold brothers of Hippotion's line:
(Who reach'd fair Ilion, from Ascania far,
The former day; the next, engaged in
     war).
As when from gloomy clouds a whirlwind
     springs,
That bears Jove's thunder on its dreadful
     wings,   1000
Wide o'er the blasted fields the tempest
     sweeps,
Then, gather'd, settles on the hoary deeps;
Th' afflicted deeps tumultuous mix and ⎤
     roar;   ⎟
The waves behind impel the waves before, ⎬
Wide-rolling, foaming high, and tum-   ⎟
     bling to the shore: ⎦
Thus rank on rank the chief battalions
     throng,
Chief urged on Chief, and man drove man
     along:
Far o'er the plains in dreadful order
     bright,
The brazen arms reflect a beamy light.
Full in the blazing van great Hector
     shined,   1010
Like Mars commission'd to confound man-
     kind.

Before him flaming, his enormous shield,
Like the broad sun, illumin'd all the field;
His nodding helm emits a streamy ray;
His piercing eyes thro' all the battle stray,
And, while beneath his targe he flash'd
along,
Shot terrors round, that wither'd ev'n the
strong.
Thus stalk'd he dreadful; death was in
his look;
Whole nations fear'd; but not an Argive
shook. 1019
The tow'ring Ajax, with an ample stride,
Advanc'd the first, and thus the Chief de-
fied:
'Hector! come on, thy empty threats
forbear:
'T is not thy arm, 't is thund'ring Jove, we
fear:
The skill of war to us not idly giv'n,
Lo! Greece is humbled, not by Troy, but
Heav'n.
Vain are the hopes that haughty mind im-
parts
To force our fleet: the Greeks have hands
and hearts.
Long ere in flames our lofty navy fall,
Your boasted city, and your god-built wall,
Shall sink beneath us, smoking on the
ground; 1030
And spread a long unmeasured ruin round.
The time shall come, when, chased along
the plain,
Ev'n thou shalt call on Jove, and call in
vain;
Ev'n thou shalt wish, to aid thy desp'rate
course,
The wings of falcons for thy flying horse;
Shalt run, forgetful of a warrior's fame,
While clouds of friendly dust conceal thy
shame.'
As thus he spoke, behold, in open view,
On sounding wings a dexter eagle flew.
To Jove's glad omen all the Grecians
rise, 1040
And hail, with shouts, his progress thro'
the skies.
Far-echoing clamours bound from side to
side;
They ceas'd; and thus the Chief of Troy
replied:
'From whence this menace, this insult-
ing strain?
Enormous boaster! doom'd to vaunt in
vain.

So may the Gods on Hector life bestow
(Not that short life which mortals lead
below,
But such as those of Jove's high lineage
born,
The Blue-eyed Maid, or He that gilds the
morn),
As this decisive day shall end the fame 1050
Of Greece, and Argos be no more a name.
And thou, imperious! if thy madness wait
The lance of Hector, thou shalt meet thy
fate:
That giant-corpse, extended on the shore,
Shall largely feast the fowls with fat and
gore.'
He said, and like a lion stalk'd along:
With shouts incessant earth and ocean
rung,
Sent from his foll'wing host. The Grecian
train
With answering thunders fill'd the echoing
plain;
A shout that tore Heav'n's concave, and
above 1060
Shook the fix'd splendours of the throne of
Jove.

BOOK XIV

JUNO DECEIVES JUPITER BY THE GIRDLE OF
VENUS

THE ARGUMENT

Nestor, sitting at the table with Machaon, is
alarmed with the increasing clamour of the
war, and hastens to Agamemnon: on his
way he meets that Prince with Diomed and
Ulysses, whom he informs of the extremity
of the danger. Agamemnon proposes to
make their escape by night, which Ulysses
withstands; to which Diomed adds his advice, that, wounded as they were, they
should go forth and encourage the army
with their presence; which advice is pursued. Juno seeing the partiality of Jupiter
to the Trojans, forms a design to overreach
him; she sets off her charms with the utmost care, and (the more surely to enchant
him) obtains the magic girdle of Venus. She
then applies herself to the God of Sleep, and
with some difficulty persuades him to seal
the eyes of Jupiter; this done, she goes to
Mount Ida, where the God, at first sight, is
ravished with her beauty, sinks in her embraces, and is laid asleep. Neptune takes
advantage of his slumber, and succours the

Greeks; Hector is struck to the ground with a prodigious stone by Ajax, and carried off from the battle: several actions succeed; till the Trojans, much distressed, are obliged to give way; the lesser Ajax signalizes himself in a particular manner.

But nor the genial feast, nor flowing bowl,
Could charm the cares of Nestor's watchful soul;
His startled ears th' increasing cries attend;
Then thus, impatient, to his wounded friend:
'What new alarms, divine Machaon, say,
What mix'd events attend this mighty day?
Hark! how the shouts divide, and how they meet,
And now come full, and thicken to the fleet!
Here, with the cordial draught dispel thy care,
Let Hecamede the strength'ning bath prepare, 10
Refresh thy wound, and cleanse the clotted gore,
While I th' adventures of the day explore.'
He said: and, seizing Thrasymedes' shield
(His valiant offspring), hasten'd to the field
(That day, the son his father's buckler bore);
Then snatch'd a lance, and issued from the door.
Soon as the prospect open'd to his view,
His wounded eyes the scene of sorrow knew;
Dire disarray! the tumult of the fight,
The wall in ruins, and the Greeks in flight. 20
As when old Ocean's silent surface sleeps,
The waves just heaving on the purple deeps;
While yet th' expected tempest hangs on high,
Weighs down the cloud, and blackens in the sky,
The mass of waters will no wind obey;
Jove sends one gust, and bids them roll away.
While wav'ring counsels thus his mind engage,
Fluctuates in doubtful thought the Pylian sage;

To join the host, or to the Gen'ral haste;
Debating long, he fixes on the last: 30
Yet, as he moves, the fight his bosom warms;
The field rings dreadful with the clang of arms;
The gleaming falchions flash, the jav'lins fly;
Blows echo blows, and all or kill or die.
 Him, in his march, the wounded Princes meet,
By tardy steps ascending from the fleet;
The King of Men, Ulysses the divine,
And who to Tydeus owes his noble line.
(Their ships at distance from the battle stand,
In lines advanc'd along the shelving strand;
Whose bay the fleet unable to contain 41
At length, beside the margin of the main,
Rank above rank, the crowded ships they moor:
Who landed first, lay highest on the shore.)
Supported on their spears they took their way,
Unfit to fight, but anxious for the day.
Nestor's approach alarm'd each Grecian breast,
Whom thus the Gen'ral of the host address'd:
 'O grace and glory of th' Achaian name!
What drives thee, Nestor, from the Field of Fame? 50
Shall then proud Hector see his boast fulfill'd,
Our fleets in ashes, and our heroes kill'd?
Such was his threat, ah! now too soon made good,
On many a Grecian bosom writ in blood.
Is every heart inflamed with equal rage
Against your King, nor will one Chief engage?
And have I liv'd to see with mournful eyes
In ev'ry Greek a new Achilles rise?'
 Gerenian Nestor then: 'So Fate has will'd; 59
And all confirming time has Fate fulfill'd,
Not he that thunders from th' aërial bower,
Not Jove himself, upon the past has power.
The wall, our late inviolable bound,
And best defence, lies smoking on the ground:
Ev'n to the ships their conquering arms extend,
And groans of slaughter'd Greeks to Heav'n ascend.

On speedy measures then employ your
    thought;
In such distress if counsel profit aught;
Arms cannot much: tho' Mars our souls
    incite,
These gaping wounds withhold us from the
    fight.'   70
    To him the Monarch: 'That our army
    bends,
That Troy triumphant our high fleet as-
    cends,
And that the rampart, late our surest trust,
And best defence, lies smoking in the dust:
All this, from Jove's afflictive hand we bear,
Who, far from Argos, wills our ruin here,
Past are the days when happier Greece was
    bless'd,
And all his favour, all his aid, confess'd;
Now Heav'n, averse, our hands from bat-
    tle ties,
And lifts the Trojan glory to the skies. 80
Cease we at length to waste our blood in
    vain,
And launch what ships lie nearest to the
    main;
Leave these at anchor till the coming ⎤
    night; |
Then, if impetuous Troy forbear the fight, ⎬
Bring all to sea, and hoist each sail for |
    flight.   ⎦
Better from evils, well foreseen, to run,
Than perish in the danger we may shun.'
    Thus he. The sage Ulysses thus replies,
While anger flash'd from his disdainful
    eyes:
'What shameful words (unkingly as thou
    art)   90
Fall from that trembling tongue and tim'-
    rous heart!
Oh were thy sway the curse of meaner
    powers,
And thou the shame of any host but ours!
A host, by Jove endued with martial might,
And taught to conquer, or to fall in fight:
Adventurous combats and bold wars to
    wage,
Employ'd our youth, and yet employs our
    age.
And wilt thou thus desert the Trojan plain?
And have whole streams of blood been
    spilt in vain?
In such base sentence if thou couch thy
    fear,   100
Speak it in whispers, lest a Greek should
    hear.

Lives there a man so dead to fame, who
    dares
To think such meanness, or the thought de-
    clares?
And comes it ev'n from him whose sov'-
    reign sway
The banded legions of all Greece obey?
Is this a Gen'ral's voice, that calls to flight?
While war hangs doubtful, while his sol-
    diers fight?
What more could Troy? What yet their
    fate denies
Thou giv'st the foe: all Greece becomes
    their prize.
No more the troops (our hoisted sails in
    view,   110
Themselves abandon'd) shall the fight pur-
    sue;
But thy ships flying with despair shall see,
And owe destruction to a Prince like thee.'
    'Thy just reproofs' (Atrides calm re-
    plies)
'Like arrows pierce me, for thy words are
    wise.
Unwilling as I am to lose the host,
I force not Greece to quit this hateful
    coast.
Glad I submit, whoe'er, or young or old,
Aught, more conducive to our weal, un-
    fold.'   119
    Tydides cut him short, and thus began:
'Such counsel if ye seek, behold the man
Who boldly gives it, and what he shall say,
Young tho' he be, disdain not to obey:
A youth, who from the mighty Tydeus
    springs,
May speak to councils and assembled
    Kings.
Hear then in me the great Œnides' son,
Whose honour'd dust (his race of glory
    run)
Lies whelm'd in ruins of the Theban wall;
Brave in his life, and glorious in his fall.
With three bold sons was gen'rous Pro-
    thous bless'd,   130
Who Pleuron's walls and Calydon possess'd:
Melas and Agrius, but (who far surpass'd
The rest in courage) Œneus was the last:
From him, my sire. From Calydon ex-
    pell'd,
He pass'd to Argos, and in exile dwell'd;
The Monarch's daughter there (so Jove
    ordain'd)
He won, and flourish'd where Adrastus
    reign'd:

There, rich in fortune's gifts, his acres
 till'd,
Beheld his vines their liquid harvest yield,
And numerous flocks that whiten'd all
 the field.   140
Such Tydeus was, the foremost once in
 fame !
Nor lives in Greece a stranger to his name.
Then, what for common good my thoughts
 inspire,
Attend, and in the son respect the sire.
Tho' sore of battle, tho' with wounds op-
 prest,
Let each go forth, and animate the rest,
Advance the glory which he cannot share,
Tho' not partaker, witness of the war.
But lest new wounds on wounds o'erpower
 us quite,   149
Beyond the missile jav'lin's sounding flight,
Safe let us stand; and, from the tumult
 far,
Inspire the ranks, and rule the distant war.'
 He added not: the list'ning Kings obey,
Slow moving on; Atrides leads the way.
The God of Ocean (to inflame their rage)
Appears a warrior furrow'd o'er with age;
Press'd in his own, the Gen'ral's hand he
 took,
And thus the venerable hero spoke:
 ' Atrides, lo ! with what disdainful eye
Achilles sees his country's forces fly: 160
Blind impious man ! whose anger is his
 guide,
Who glories in unutterable pride.
So may he perish, so may Jove disclaim
The wretch relentless, and o'erwhelm with
 shame !
But Heav'n forsakes not thee: o'er yonder
 sands
Soon shalt thou view the scatter'd Trojan
 bands
Fly diverse; while proud Kings, and Chiefs
 renown'd,
Driv'n heaps on heaps, with clouds involv'd
 around
Of rolling dust, their winged wheels em-
 ploy
To hide their ignominious heads in Troy.'
 He spoke, then rush'd among the war-
 rior crew: 171
And sent his voice before him as he flew,
Loud, as the shout encount'ring armies
 yield,
When twice ten thousand shake the la-
 b'ring field;

Such was the voice, and such the thun-
 d'ring sound
Of him whose trident rends the solid
 ground.
Each Argive bosom beats to meet the fight,
And grisly war appears a pleasing sight.
 Meantime Saturnia from Olympus' brow,
High-throned in gold, beheld the fields be-
 low;   180
With joy the glorious conflict she survey'd,
Where her great brother gave the Grecians
 aid.
But placed aloft, on Ida's shady height
She sees her Jove, and trembles at the
 sight.
Jove to deceive, what methods shall she
 try,
What arts, to blind his all-beholding eye ?
At length she trusts her power; resolv'd
 to prove
The old, yet still successful, cheat of love;
Against his wisdom to oppose her charms,
And lull the Lord of Thunders in her
 arms.   190
 Swift to her bright apartment she re-
 pairs,
Sacred to dress, and beauty's pleasing
 cares:
With skill divine had Vulcan form'd the
 bower,
Safe from access of each intruding power.
Touch'd with her secret key, the doors un-
 fold
Self-closed, behind her shut the valves of
 gold.
Here first she bathes; and round her body
 pours
Soft oils of fragrance, and ambrosial
 showers:
The winds, perfumed, the balmy gale con-
 vey
Thro' Heav'n, thro' earth, and all th' aërial
 way;   200
Spirit divine ! whose exhalation greets
The sense of Gods with more than mortal
 sweets.
Thus while she breathed of Heav'n, with
 decent pride
Her artful hands the radiant tresses tied;
Part on her head in shining ringlets roll'd,
Part o'er her shoulders waved like melted
 gold.
Around her next a heav'nly mantle flow'd,
That rich with Pallas' labour'd colours
 glow'd;

Large clasps of gold the foldings gather'd
   round, 209
A golden zone her swelling bosom bound.
Far-beaming pendants tremble in her ear,
Each gem illumin'd with a triple star.
Then o'er her head she cast a veil more
   white
Than new-fall'n snow, and dazzling as the
   light.
Last her fair feet celestial sandals grace.
Thus issuing radiant, with majestic pace,
Forth from the dome th' imperial Goddess
   moves,
And calls the mother of the smiles and loves.
  'How long' (to Venus thus apart she
   cried)
'Shall human strife celestial minds divide?
Ah yet, will Venus aid Saturnia's joy, 221
And set aside the cause of Greece and
   Troy?'
'Let Heav'n's dread Empress' (Cytherea
   said)
'Speak her request, and deem her will
   obey'd.'
  'Then grant me' (said the Queen) 'those
   conquering charms,
That Power, which mortals and immortals
   warms,
That love, which melts mankind in fierce
   desires,
And burns the sons of Heav'n with sacred
   fires!
For lo! I haste to those remote abodes,
Where the great parents (sacred source of
   Gods!) 230
Ocean and Tethys their old empire keep,
On the last limits of the land and deep.
In their kind arms my tender years were
   pass'd;
What time old Saturn, from Olympus cast,
Of upper Heav'n to Jove resign'd the
   reign,
Whelm'd under the huge mass of earth and
   main.
For strife, I hear, has made the union
   cease,
Which held so long that ancient pair in
   peace.
What honour, and what love, shall I ob-
   tain,
If I compose those fatal feuds again? 240
Once more their minds in mutual ties en-
   gage,
And what my youth has owed, repay their
   age.'

She said. With awe divine the Queen
   of Love
Obey'd the sister and the wife of Jove;
And from her fragrant breast the zone un-
   braced,
With various skill and high embroid'ry
   graced.
In this was ev'ry art, and ev'ry charm,
To win the wisest, and the coldest warm:
Fond love, the gentle vow, the gay desire,
The kind deceit, the still reviving fire; 250
Persuasive speech, and more persuasive
   sighs,
Silence that spoke, and eloquence of eyes.
This on her hand the Cyprian Goddess laid;
'Take this, and with it all thy wish,' she
   said:
With smiles she took the charm; and smil-
   ing press'd
The powerful cestus to her snowy breast.
  Then Venus to the courts of Jove with-
   drew;
Whilst from Olympus pleas'd Saturnia
   flew.
O'er high Pieria thence her course she bore,
O'er fair Emathia's ever-pleasing shore, 260
O'er Hæmus' hills with snows eternal
   crown'd:
Nor once her flying foot approach'd the
   ground.
Then taking wing from Athos' lofty steep,
She speeds to Lemnos o'er the rolling
   deep,
And seeks the cave of Death's half-
   brother, Sleep.
  'Sweet pleasing Sleep!' (Saturnia thus
   began)
'Who spread'st thy empire o'er each God
   and man;
If e'er obsequious to thy Juno's will,
O Power of Slumbers! hear, and favour still.
Shed thy soft dews on Jove's immortal
   eyes, 270
While sunk in love's entrancing joys he
   lies.
A splendid footstool, and a throne, that
   shine
With gold unfading, Somnus, shall be thine;
The work of Vulcan, to indulge thy ease,
When wine and feasts thy golden humours
   please.'
  'Imperial Dame' (the balmy Power re-
   plies),
'Great Saturn's heir, and Empress of the
   Skies!

O'er other Gods I spread my easy chain;⎫
The sire of all, old Ocean, owns my reign, ⎬
And his hush'd waves lie silent on the ⎪
   main.   280⎭
But how, unbidden, shall I dare to steep
Jove's awful temples in the dew of sleep?
Long since, too venturous, at thy bold com-
   mand,
On those eternal lids I laid my hand;
What time, deserting Ilion's wasted plain,
His conquering son, Alcides, plough'd the
   main:
When lo! the deeps arise, the tempests
   roar,
And drive the hero to the Coan shore;
Great Jove, awaking, shook the bless'd
   abodes
With rising wrath, and tumbled Gods on
   Gods;   290
Me chief he sought, and from the realms
   on high
Had hurl'd indignant to the nether sky,
But gentle Night, to whom I fled for aid
(The friend of Earth and Heav'n), her
   wings display'd;
Empower'd the wrath of Gods and men to
   tame,
Ev'n Jove revered the venerable dame.'
  'Vain are thy fears' (the Queen of
   Heav'n replies,
And, speaking, rolls her large majestic
   eyes);
'Think'st thou that Troy has Jove's high
   favour won,   299
Like great Alcides, his all-conquering son?
Hear, and obey the Mistress of the Skies,
Nor for the deed expect a vulgar prize:
For know, thy lov'd-one shall be ever
   thine,
The youngest Grace, Pasithaë the divine.'
  'Swear then' (he said) 'by those tre-
   mendous floods,
That roar thro' Hell, and bind th' invoking
   Gods:
Let the great parent earth one hand sustain,
And stretch the other o'er the sacred main:
Call the black Titans that with Cronos
   dwell,
To hear and witness from the depths of
   Hell;   310
That she, my lov'd-one, shall be ever mine,
The youngest Grace, Pasithaë the divine.'
  The Queen assents, and from th' infernal
   bowers
Invokes the sable subtartarean powers,

And those who rule th' inviolable floods,
Whom mortals name the dread Titanian
   Gods.
  Then, swift as wind, o'er Lemnos' smoky
   isle,
They wing their way, and Imbrus' sea-
   beat soil,
Thro' air, unseen, involv'd in darkness
   glide,   319
And light on Lectos, on the point of Ide
(Mother of savages, whose echoing hills
Are heard resounding with a hundred rills);
Fair Ida trembles underneath the God;
Hush'd are her mountains, and her forests
   nod.
There, on a fir, whose spiry branches rise
To join its summit to the neighb'ring skies,
Dark in embow'ring shade, conceal'd from
   sight,
Sat Sleep, in likeness of the bird of night
(Chalcis his name with those of heav'nly
   birth,
But called Cymindis by the race of earth).
  To Ida's top successful Juno flies;   331
Great Jove surveys her with desiring eyes:
The God, whose lightning sets the Heav'ns
   on fire,
Thro' all his bosom feels the fierce desire;
Fierce as when first by stealth he seiz'd her
   charms,
Mix'd with her soul, and melted in her
   arms.
Fix'd on her eyes he fed his eager look,
Then press'd her hand, and then with trans-
   port spoke:
'Why comes my Goddess from th' ethereal
   sky,
And not her steeds and flaming chariot
   nigh!'   340
  Then she—'I haste to those remote
   abodes,
Where the great parents of the deathless
   Gods,
The rev'rend Ocean and great Tethys,
   reign,
On the last limits of the land and main.
I visit these, to whose indulgent cares
I owe the nursing of my tender years.
For strife, I hear, has made that union
   cease,
Which held so long this ancient pair in
   peace.
The steeds, prepared my chariot to convey
O'er earth and seas, and thro' th' aërial
   way,   350

Wait under Ide: of thy superior power
To ask consent, I leave th' Olympian
  bower;
Nor seek, unknown to thee, the sacred cells
Deep under seas, where hoary Ocean
  dwells.'
'For that' (said Jove) 'suffice another
  day;
But eager love denies the least delay.
Let softer cares the present hour employ,
And be these moments sacred all to joy.
Ne'er did my soul so strong a passion
  prove,
Or for an earthly, or a heav'nly love;   360
Not when I press'd Ixion's matchless dame,
Whence rose Pirithous, like the Gods in
  fame.
Not when fair Danaë felt the shower of
  gold
Stream into life, whence Perseus brave and
  bold.
Not thus I burn'd for either Theban dame
(Bacchus from this, from that Alcides
  came),
Not Phœnix' daughter, beautiful and
  young,
Whence Godlike Rhadamanth and Minos
  sprung;
Not thus I burn'd for fair Latona's face,
Nor comelier Ceres' more majestic grace.
Not thus ev'n for thyself I felt desire,   371
As now my veins receive the pleasing
  fire.'
  He spoke; the Goddess with the charm-
    ing eyes
Glows with celestial red, and thus replies:
'Is this a scene for love? On Ida's height,
Exposed to mortal and immortal sight;
Our joys profaned by each familiar eye;
The sport of Heav'n, and fable of the sky!
How shall I e'er review the bless'd abodes,
Or mix among the Senate of the Gods?   380
Shall I not think, that, with disorder'd
  charms,
All Heav'n beholds me recent from thy
  arms?
With skill divine has Vulcan form'd thy
  bower,
Sacred to love and to the genial hour;
If such thy will, to that recess retire,
And secret there indulge thy soft desire.'
  She ceas'd: and smiling with superior
    love,
Thus answer'd mild the cloud-compelling
  Jove:

'Not God nor mortal shall our joys be-
  hold,
Shaded with clouds, and circumfused in
  gold;   390
Not ev'n the sun, who darts thro' Heav'n
  his rays,
And whose broad eye th' extended earth
  surveys.'
  Gazing he spoke, and, kindling at the
    view,
His eager arms around the Goddess threw.
Glad Earth perceives, and from her bosom
  pours
Unbidden herbs, and voluntary flowers;
Thick new-born violets a soft carpet
  spread,
And clust'ring lotos swell'd the rising bed,
And sudden hyacinths the turf bestrow,
And flamy crocus made the mountain
  glow.   400
There golden clouds conceal the heav'nly
  pair,
Steep'd in soft joys, and circumfused with
  air;
Celestial dews, descending o'er the ground,
Perfume the mount, and breathe ambrosia
  round.
At length with Love and Sleep's soft power
  oppress'd,
The panting Thund'rer nods, and sinks to
  rest.
  Now to the navy borne on silent wings,
To Neptune's ear soft Sleep his message
  brings;
Beside him sudden, unperceiv'd he stood,
And thus with gentle words address'd the
  God: 410
'Now, Neptune! now, th' important hour
  employ,
To check awhile the haughty hopes of
  Troy:
While Jove yet rests, while yet my va-
  pours shed
The golden vision round his sacred head;
For Juno's love, and Somnus' pleasing ties,
Have closed those awful and eternal eyes.'
  Thus having said, the Power of Slumber
    flew,
On human lids to drop the balmy dew.
Neptune, with zeal increas'd, renews his
  care,
And tow'ring in the foremost ranks of
  war,   420
Indignant thus: 'Oh once of martial fame!
O Greeks! if yet ye can deserve the name!

This half-recover'd day shall Troy obtain?
Shall Hector thunder at your ships again?
Lo, still he vaunts, and threats the fleet
  with fires,
While stern Achilles in his wrath retires.
One hero's loss too tamely you deplore,
Be still yourselves, and we shall need no
  more.
Oh yet, if glory any bosom warms,
Brace on your firmest helms, and stand to
  arms: 430
His strongest spear each valiant Grecian
  wield,
Each valiant Grecian seize his broadest
  shield;
Let to the weak the lighter arms belong,
The pond'rous targe be wielded by the
  strong.
Thus arm'd, not Hector shall our presence
  stay;
Myself, ye Greeks! myself will lead the
  way.'
  The troops assent; their martial arms
  they change,
The busy chiefs their banded legions range.
The Kings, tho' wounded, and oppress'd
  with pain,
With helpful hands themselves assist the
  train.   440
The strong and cumbrous arms the valiant
  wield,
The weaker warrior takes a lighter shield.
Thus sheathed in shining brass, in bright
  array
The legions march, and Neptune leads the
  way:
His brandish'd falchion flames before their
  eyes,
Like lightning flashing thro' the frighted
  skies.
Clad in his might th' earth-shaking Power
  appears;
Pale mortals tremble, and confess their
  fears.
  Troy's great defender stands alone un-
  aw'd,
Arms his proud host, and dares oppose a
  God: 450
And lo! the God and wondrous man ap-
  pear;
The sea's stern ruler there, and Hector here.
The roaring main, at her great master's
  call,
Rose in huge ranks, and form'd a wat'ry
  wall

Around the ships, seas hanging o'er the
  shores;
Both armies join; earth thunders, ocean
  roars.
Not half so loud the bell'wing deeps re-
  sound,
When stormy winds disclose the dark pro-
  found;
Less loud the winds that from th' Æolian
  hall
Roar thro' the woods, and make whole
  forests fall;   460
Less loud the woods, when flames in tor-
  rents pour,
Catch the dry mountain and its shades de-
  vour.
With such a rage the meeting hosts are
  driv'n,
And such a clamour shakes the sounding
  Heav'n.
  The first bold jav'lin, urged by Hector's
  force,
Direct at Ajax' bosom wing'd its course;
But there no pass the crossing belts afford
(One braced his shield, and one sustain'd
  his sword).
Then back the disappointed Trojan drew,
And curs'd the lance that unavailing flew: 470
But 'scaped not Ajax; his tempestuous
  hand
A pond'rous stone up-heaving from the
  sand
(Where heaps, laid loose beneath the war-
  rior's feet,
Or serv'd to ballast, or to prop the fleet),
Toss'd round and round, the missive mar-
  ble flings;
On the rais'd shield the falling ruin rings,
Full on his breast and throat with force de-
  scends;
Nor deaden'd there its giddy fury spends,
But, whirling on, with many a fiery round,
Smokes in the dust, and ploughs into the
  ground.   480
As when the bolt, red-hissing from above,
Darts on the consecrated plant of Jove,
The mountain-oak in flaming ruin lies,
Black from the blow, and smokes of sulphur
  rise:
Stiff with amaze the pale beholders stand,
And own the terrors of th' almighty hand!
So lies great Hector prostrate on the
  shore;
His slacken'd hand deserts the lance it
  bore:

His foll'wing shield the fallen chief o'er-
  spread;
Beneath his helmet dropp'd his fainting
  head;   490
His load of armour, sinking to the ground,
Clanks on the field: a dead and hollow
  sound.
Loud shouts of triumph fill the crowded
  plain;
Greece sees, in hope, Troy's great defender
  slain:
All spring to seize him: storms of arrows
  fly;
And thicker jav'lins intercept the sky.
In vain an iron tempest hisses round:
He lies protected and without a wound.
Polydamas, Agenor the divine,
The pious warrior of Anchises' line,   500
And each bold leader of the Lysian band,
With cov'ring shields (a friendly circle)
  stand.
His mournful foll'wers, with assistant care,
The groaning hero to his chariot bear;
His foaming coursers, swifter than the
  wind
Speed to the town, and leave the war be-
  hind.
  When now they touch'd the mead's
    enamell'd side,
Where gentle Xanthus rolls his easy tide,
With wat'ry drops the chief they sprinkle
  round,
Placed on the margin of the flowery
  ground.   510
Rais'd on his knees, he now ejects the gore;
Now faints anew, low sinking on the shore:
By fits he breathes, half views the fleeting
  skies,
And seals again, by fits, his swimming
  eyes.
  Soon as the Greeks the chief's retreat
    beheld,
With double fury each invades the field.
Oïlean Ajax first his jav'lin sped,
Pierc'd by whose point the son of Enops
  bled
(Satnius the brave, whom beauteous Neïs
  bore
Amidst her flocks, on Satnio's silver
  shore).   520
Struck thro' the belly's rim, the warrior lies
Supine, and shades eternal veil his eyes.
An arduous battle rose around the dead;
By turns the Greeks, by turns the Trojans,
  bled.

Fired with revenge, Polydamas drew
  near,
And at Prothœnor shook the trembling
  spear:
The driving jav'lin thro' his shoulder thrust,
He sinks to earth, and grasps the bloody
  dust.
'Lo! thus' (the Victor cries) 'we rule
  the field,
And thus their arms the race of Panthus
  wield: 530
From this unerring hand there flies no
  dart,
But bathes its point within a Grecian heart.
Propp'd on that spear to which thou ow'st
  thy fall,
Go, guide thy darksome steps to Pluto's
  dreary hall.'
  He said, and sorrow touch'd each Argive
    breast;
The soul of Ajax burn'd above the rest.
As by his side the groaning warrior fell,
At the fierce foe he lanc'd his piercing
  steel;
The foe, reclining, shunn'd the flying death;
But Fate, Archilochus, demands thy
  breath;   540
Thy lofty birth no succour could impart,
The wings of death o'ertook thee on the
  dart:
Swift to perform Heav'n's fatal will it fled,
Full on the juncture of the neck and head,
And took the joint, and cut the nerves in
  twain;
The drooping head first tumbled to the
  plain:
So just the stroke, that yet the body stood
Erect, then roll'd along the sands in blood.
  'Here, proud Polydamas, here turn thy
    eyes!'
The tow'ring Ajax loud-insulting cries: 550
'Say, is this chief, extended on the plain,
A worthy vengeance for Prothœnor slain?
Mark well his port! his figure and his face
Nor speak him vulgar, nor of vulgar race;
Some lines, methinks, may make his lineage
  known,
Antenor's brother, or perhaps his son.'
  He spake, and smil'd severe, for well he
    knew
The bleeding youth: Troy sadden'd at the
  view.
But furious Acamas avenged his cause;
As Promachus his slaughter'd brother
  draws,   560

He pierc'd his heart — 'Such fate attends
you all,
Proud Argives! destin'd by our arms to
fall.
Not Troy alone, but haughty Greece, shall
share
The toils, the sorrows, and the wounds of
war.
Behold your Promachus deprived of breath,
A victim owed to my brave brother's death.
Not unappeas'd he enters Pluto's gate,
Who leaves a brother to revenge his fate.'
   Heart-piercing anguish struck the Gre-
cian host,
But touch'd the breast of bold Peneleus
most: 570
At the proud boaster he directs his course;
The boaster flies, and shuns superior force.
But young Ilioneus receiv'd the spear;
Ilioneus, his father's only care
(Phorbas the rich, of all the Trojan train
Whom Hermes lov'd, and taught the arts
of gain):
Full in his eye the weapon chanc'd to fall,
And from the fibres scoop'd the rooted ball,
Drove thro' the neck, and hurl'd him to
the plain:
He lifts his miserable arms in vain! 580
Swift his broad falchion fierce Peneleus
spread,
And from the spouting shoulders struck his
head;
To earth at once the head and helmet fly:
The lance, yet sticking thro' the bleeding
eye,
The victor seiz'd; and as aloft he shook
The gory visage, thus insulting spoke:
'Trojans! your great Ilioneus beheld!
Haste, to his father let the tale be told.
Let his high roofs resound with frantic woe,
Such as the house of Promachus must
know; 590
Let doleful tidings greet his mother's ear,
Such as to Promachus' sad spouse we bear;
When we victorious shall to Greece return,
And the pale matron in our triumphs
mourn.'
   Dreadful he spoke, then toss'd the head
on high;
The Trojans hear, they tremble, and they fly:
Aghast they gaze around the fleet and wall,
And dread the ruin that impends on all.
   Daughters of Jove! that on Olympus
shine,
Ye all beholding, all-recording Nine! 600

O say, when Neptune made proud Ilion
yield,
What Chief, what hero, first imbrued the
field?
Of all the Grecians, what immortal name,
And whose bless'd trophies, will ye raise to
Fame?
   Thou first, great Ajax! on th' ensan-
guin'd plain
Laid Hyrtius, leader of the Mysian train.
Phalces and Mermer, Nestor's son o'er-
threw,
Bold Merion, Morys and Hippotion slew.
Strong Periphætes and Prothoön bled,
By Teucer's arrows mingled with the
dead. 610
Pierc'd in the flank by Menelaus' steel,
His people's pastor, Hyperenor fell;
Eternal darkness wrapp'd the warrior
round,
And the fierce soul came rushing thro' the
wound.
But stretch'd in heaps before Oïleus' son,
Fall mighty numbers, mighty numbers
run,
Ajax the less, of all the Grecian race
Skill'd in pursuit, and swiftest in the chase.

BOOK XV

THE FIFTH BATTLE, AT THE SHIPS; AND
THE ACTS OF AJAX

THE ARGUMENT

Jupiter, awaking, sees the Trojans repulsed
from the trenches, Hector in a swoon, and
Neptune at the head of the Greeks; he is
highly incensed at the artifice of Juno, who
appeases him by her submissions; she is
then sent to Iris and Apollo. Juno, repair-
ing to the assembly of the Gods, attempts
with extraordinary address to incense them
against Jupiter; in particular she touches
Mars with a violent resentment; he is ready
to take arms, but is prevented by Minerva.
Iris and Apollo obey the orders of Jupiter;
Iris commands Neptune to leave the battle,
to which, after much reluctance and passion,
he consents. Apollo reinspires Hector with
vigour, brings him back to the battle,
marches before him with his ægis, and turns
the fortune of the fight. He breaks down a
great part of the Grecian wall; the Trojans
rush in, and attempt to fire the first line of
the fleet, but are yet repelled by the greater
Ajax with a prodigious slaughter.

Now in swift flight they pass the trench
  profound,
And many a Chief lay gasping on the ground;
Then stopp'd and panted, where the chariots
  lie;
Fear on their cheek, and horror in their eye.
Meanwhile, awaken'd from his dream of
  love,
On Ida's summit sat imperial Jove;
Round the wide fields he cast a careful
  view,
There saw the Trojans fly, the Greeks pur-
  sue;
These proud in arms, those scatter'd o'er
  the plain;
And, midst the war, the Monarch of the
  Main.   10
Not far, great Hector on the dust he spies
(His sad associates round with weeping
  eyes),
Ejecting blood, and panting yet for breath,
His senses wand'ring to the verge of death.
The God beheld him with a pitying look,
And thus, incens'd, to fraudful Juno spoke:
  'O thou, still adverse to th' eternal will,
For ever studious in promoting ill!
Thy arts have made the godlike Hector
  yield,
And driv'n his conquering squadrons from
  the field.   20
Canst thou, unhappy in thy wiles! with-
  stand
Our power immense, and brave th' almighty
  hand?
Hast thou forgot, when, bound and fix'd on
  high,
From the vast concave of the spangled sky,
I hung thee trembling in a golden chain;
And all the raging Gods opposed in vain?
Headlong I hurl'd them from th' Olympian
  hall,
Stunn'd in the whirl, and breathless with
  the fall.
For godlike Hercules these deeds were
  done,
Nor seem'd the vengeance worthy such a
  son;   30
When, by thy wiles induced, fierce Boreas
  toss'd
The shipwreck'd hero on the Coan coast:
Him thro' a thousand forms of death I bore,
And sent to Argos, and his native shore.
Hear this, remember, and our fury dread,
Nor pull th' unwilling vengeance on thy
  head;

Lest arts and blandishments successless
  prove,
Thy soft deceits, and well-dissembled love.'
The Thund'rer spoke: imperial Juno
  mourn'd,
And, trembling, these submissive words re-
  turn'd: 40
  'By ev'ry oath that powers immortal ties,
The foodful earth, and all infolding skies,
By thy black waves, tremendous Styx! that
  flow
Thro' the drear realms of gliding ghosts
  below:
By the dread honours of thy sacred head,
And that unbroken vow, our virgin bed!
Not by my arts the ruler of the main
Steeps Troy in blood, and ranges round the
  plain:
By his own ardour, his own pity, sway'd
To help his Greeks; he fought, and dis-
  obey'd: 50
Else had thy Juno better counsels giv'n,
And taught submission to the Sire of
  Heav'n.'
  'Thinkst thou with me? fair Empress of
  the Skies!'
Th' immortal Father with a smile replies:
'Then soon the haughty Sea-God shall obey,
Nor dare to act, but when we point the way.
If truth inspires thy tongue, proclaim our
  will
To yon bright Synod on th' Olympian Hill,
Our high decree let various Iris know,
And call the God that bears the silver bow.
Let her descend, and from th' embattled
  plain   61
Command the Sea-God to his wat'ry reign:
While Phœbus hastes great Hector to pre-
  pare
To rise afresh, and once more wake the war;
His lab'ring bosom re-inspires with breath,
And calls his senses from the verge of
  death.
Greece, chased by Troy ev'n to Achilles'
  fleet,
Shall fall by thousands at the hero's feet.
He, not untouch'd with pity, to the plain
Shall send Patroclus, but shall send in vain.
What youths he slaughters under Ilion's
  walls!   71
Ev'n my lov'd son, divine Sarpedon, falls!
Vanquish'd at last by Hector's lance he
  lies,
Then, not till then, shall great Achilles
  rise:

And lo ! that instant, godlike Hector dies.
From that great hour the war's whole for-
    tune turns,
Pallas assists, and lofty Ilion burns.
Not till that day shall Jove relax his rage,
Nor one of all the heav'nly host engage
In aid of Greece.   The promise of a God 80
I gave, and seal'd it with th' almighty nod,
Achilles' glory to the stars to raise;
Such was our word, and Fate the word
    obeys.'
    The trembling Queen (th' almighty
    order given)
Swift from th' Idæan summit shot to
    Heav'n.
As some wayfaring man, who wanders
    o'er,
In thought, a length of lands he trod be-
    fore,
Sends forth his active mind from place to
    place,
Joins hill to dale, and measures space with
    space:
So swift flew Juno to the blest abodes, 90
If thought of man can match the speed of
    Gods.
There sat the Powers in awful Synod
    placed:
They bow'd, and made obeisance as she
    pass'd,
Thro' all the brazen dome: with goblets
    crown'd
They hail her queen; the nectar streams
    around.
Fair Themis first presents the golden bowl,
And anxious asks what cares disturb her
    soul ?
    To whom the white-arm'd Goddess thus
    replies:
'Enough thou know'st the Tyrant of the
    Skies;
Severely bent his purpose to fulfil,   100
Unmov'd his mind, and unrestrain'd his
    will.
Go thou, the feasts of Heav'n attend thy
    call;
Bid the crown'd nectar circle round the
    hall;
But Jove shall thunder thro' th' ethereal
    dome
Such stern decrees, such threaten'd woes to
    come,
As soon shall freeze mankind with dire sur-
    prise,
And damp th' eternal banquets of the skies.'

    The Goddess said, and sullen took her
    place:
Blank horror sadden'd each celestial face.
To see the gath'ring grudge in every
    breast,   110
Smiles on her lips a spleenful joy express'd.
While on her wrinkled front, and eyebrow
    bent,
Sat steadfast care, and low'ring discon-
    tent.
Thus she proceeds: ' Attend, ye Powers
    above!
But know, 't is madness to contest with
    Jove:
Supreme he sits; and sees, in pride of
    sway,
Your vassal Godheads grudgingly obey;
Fierce in the majesty of power controls,
Shakes all the thrones of Heav'n, and bends
    the poles.
Submiss, immortals! all he wills, obey; 120
And thou, great Mars, begin and show the
    way.
Behold Ascalaphus! behold him die,
But dare not murmur, dare not vent a sigh;
Thy own lov'd boasted offspring lies o'er-
    thrown,
If that lov'd boasted offspring be thy own.'
    Stern Mars, with anguish for his slaugh-
    ter'd son,
Smote his rebelling breast, and fierce be-
    gun:
'Thus then, Immortals! thus shall Mars
    obey ?
Forgive me, Gods, and yield my vengeance
    way:
Descending first to yon forbidden plain, 130
The God of Battles dares avenge the slain;
Dares, tho' the thunder bursting o'er my
    head
Should hurl me blazing on those heaps of
    dead.'
    With that, he gives command to Fear
    and Flight
To join his rapid coursers for the fight:
Then grim in arms, with hasty vengeance
    flies;
Arms, that reflect a radiance thro' the
    skies.
And now had Jove, by bold rebellion driv'n,
Discharged his wrath on half the host of
    Heav'n;   139
But Pallas springing thro' the bright abode,
Starts from her azure throne to calm the
    God.

Struck for th' immortal race with timely
fear,
From frantic Mars she snatch'd the shield
and spear;
Then the huge helmet lifting from his
head,
Thus to th' impetuous homicide she said:
'By what wild passion, furious! art thou
toss'd ?
Strivest thou with Jove ? thou art already
lost.
Shall not the Thund'rer's dread command
restrain,
And was imperial Juno heard in vain ?
Back to the skies would'st thou with shame
be driv'n, 150
And in thy guilt involve the host of Heav'n?
Ilion and Greece no more shall Jove en-
gage;
The skies would yield an ampler scene of
rage,
Guilty and guiltless find an equal fate,
And one vast ruin whelm th' Olympian
state.
Cease then thy offspring's death unjust to
call;
Heroes as great have died, and yet shall
fall.
Why should Heav'n's law with foolish man
comply,
Exempted from the race ordain'd to die ?'
This menace fix'd the warrior to his
throne; 160
Sullen he sat, and curb'd the rising groan.
Then Juno call'd (Jove's orders to obey)
The winged Iris, and the God of Day.
'Go wait the Thund'rer's will' (Saturnia
cried),
'On yon tall summit of the fountful Ide:
There in the Father's awful presence stand,
Receive and execute his dread command.'
She said, and sat. The God that gilds
the day,
And various Iris, wing their airy way.
Swift as the wind, to Ida's hills they came
(Fair nurse of fountains, and of savage
game); 171
There sat th' Eternal; he whose nod con-
trols
The trembling world, and shakes the steady
poles.
Veil'd in a mist of fragrance him they
found,
With clouds of gold and purple circled
round.

Well-pleas'd the Thund'rer saw their ear-
nest care,
And prompt obedience to the Queen of
Air;
Then (while a smile serenes his awful brow)
Commands the Goddess of the Showery
Bow:
'Iris! descend, and what we here ordain
Report to yon mad tyrant of the main, 181
Bid him from fight to his own deeps repair,
Or breathe from slaughter in the fields of
air.
If he refuse, then let him timely weigh
Our elder birthright, and superior sway.
How shall his rashness stand the dire
alarms,
If Heav'n's omnipotence descend in arms ?
Strives he with me, by whom his power
was giv'n,
And is there equal to the Lord of Heav'n ?'
Th' Almighty spoke; the Goddess wing'd
her flight 190
To sacred Ilion from th' Idæan height.
Swift as the rattling hail or fleecy snows
Drive thro' the skies, when Boreas fiercely
blows;
So from the clouds descending Iris falls;
And to blue Neptune thus the Goddess
calls:
'Attend the mandate of the Sire above,
In me behold the Messenger of Jove:
He bids thee from forbidden wars repair
To thy own deeps, or to the fields of air.
This if refused, he bids thee timely weigh
His elder birthright, and superior sway. 201
How shall thy rashness stand the dire
alarms,
If Heav'n's omnipotence descend in arms ?
Strivest thou with him, by whom all power
is giv'n ?
And art thou equal to the lord of Heav'n ?'
'What means the haughty Sov'reign of
the Skies ? '
(The King of Ocean thus, incens'd, replies):
'Rule as he will his portion'd realms on
high,
No vassal God, nor of his train, am I. 209
Three brother deities from Saturn came,
And ancient Rhea, earth's immortal dame:
Assign'd by lot, our triple rule we know:
Infernal Pluto sways the shades below;
O'er the wide clouds, and o'er the starry
plain,
Ethereal Jove extends his high domain;
My court beneath the hoary waves I keep,

And hush the roarings of the sacred deep:
Olympus, and this earth, in common lie;
What claim has here the Tyrant of the
Sky ?
Far in the distant clouds let him control,
And awe the younger brothers of the pole;
There to his children his commands be
giv'n, 222
The trembling, servile, second race of
Heav'n.'
' And must I then ' (said she), ' O Sire of
floods!
Bear this fierce answer to the King of
Gods ?
Correct it yet, and change thy rash intent;
A noble mind disdains not to repent.
To elder brothers guardian fiends are giv'n,
To scourge the wretch insulting them and
Heav'n.'
' Great is the profit ' (thus the God re-
join'd), 230
' When ministers are bless'd with prudent
mind:
Warn'd by thy words, to powerful Jove I
yield,
And quit, tho' angry, the contended field.
Not but his threats with justice I disclaim,
The same our honours, and our birth the
same.
If yet, forgetful of his promise giv'n
To Hermes, Pallas, and the queen of
Heav'n,
To favour Ilion, that perfidious place,
He breaks his faith with half th' ethereal
race; 239
Give him to know, unless the Grecian train
Lay yon proud structures level with the
plain,
Howe'er th' offence by other Gods be
pass'd,
The wrath of Neptune shall for ever last.'
Thus speaking, furious from the field he
strode,
And plunged into the bosom of the flood.
The Lord of Thunders from his lofty
height
Beheld, and thus bespoke the source of
light:
' Behold! the God whose liquid arms are
hurl'd
Around the globe, whose earthquakes rock
the world,
Desists at length his rebel-war to wage, 250
Seeks his own seas, and trembles at our
rage:

Else had my wrath, Heav'n's thrones all
shaking round,
Burn'd to the bottom of his seas profound;
And all the Gods that round old Saturn
dwell,
Had heard the thunders to the deeps of
Hell.
Well was the crime, and well the ven-
geance spared,
Ev'n power immense had found such battle
hard.
Go thou, my son! the trembling Greeks
alarm,
Shake my broad ægis on thy active arm:
Be godlike Hector thy peculiar care, 260
Swell his bold heart, and urge his strength
to war:
Let Ilion conquer, till the Achaian train
Fly to their ships and Hellespont again:
Then Greece shall breathe from toils.' The
Godhead said;
His will divine the Son of Jove obey'd.
Not half so swift the sailing falcon flies,
That drives a turtle thro' the liquid skies;
As Phœbus, shooting from th' Idæan brow,
Glides down the mountain to the plain
below.
There Hector seated by the stream he
sees, 270
His sense returning with the coming breeze;
Again his pulses beat, his spirits rise;
Again his lov'd companions meet his eyes;
Jove thinking of his pains, they pass'd
away.
To whom the God who gives the golden day:
' Why sits great Hector from the field
so far,
What grief, what wound, withholds him
from the war ? '
The fainting hero, as the vision bright
Stood shining o'er him, half unseal'd his
sight:
' What bless'd immortal, with commanding
breath, 280
Thus wakens Hector from the sleep of
death ?
Has fame not told, how, while my trusty
sword
Bathed Greece in slaughter, and her battle
gored,
The mighty Ajax with a deadly blow
Had almost sunk me to the shades below ?
Ev'n yet, methinks, the gliding ghosts I spy,
And Hell's black horrors swim before my
eye.'

To him Apollo: 'Be no more dismay'd;
See, and be strong ! the Thund'rer sends
    thee aid:
Behold ! thy Phœbus shall his arms em-
    ploy, 290
Phœbus, propitious still to thee and Troy.
Inspire thy warriors then with manly
    force,
And to the ships impel thy rapid horse:
Ev'n I will make thy fiery coursers' way,
And drive the Grecians headlong to the
    sea.'
    Thus to bold Hector spoke the Son of
    Jove,
And breathed immortal ardour from above.
As when the pamper'd steed, with reins
    unbound,
Breaks from his stall, and pours along the
    ground;
With ample strokes he rushes to the
    flood, 300
To bathe his sides and cool his fiery blood:
His head, now freed, he tosses to the skies:
His mane dishevell'd o'er his shoulders
    flies:
He snuffs the females in the well-known
    plain,
And springs, exulting, to his fields again:
Urged by the voice divine, thus Hector
    flew,
Full of the God; and all his hosts pursue.
As when the force of men and dogs com-
    bin'd
Invade the mountain - goat or branching
    hind;
Far from the hunter's rage secure they
    lie 310
Close in the rock (not fated yet to die);
When lo ! a lion shoots across the way !
They fly: at once the chasers and the prey:
So Greece, that late in conquering troops
    pursued,
And mark'd their progress thro' the ranks
    in blood,
Soon as they see the furious Chief appear,
Forget to vanquish, and consent to fear.
    Thoas with grief observ'd his dreadful
    course,
Thoas, the bravest of th' Ætolian force; 319
Skill'd to direct the jav'lin's distant flight,
And bold to combat in the standing fight;
Nor more in counsels famed for solid
    sense,
Than winning words and heav'nly elo-
    quence.

'Gods ! what portent' (he cried) 'these
    eyes invades ?
Lo, Hector rises from the Stygian shades !
We saw him, late, by Thund'ring Ajax
    kill'd;
What God restores him to the frighted
    field;
And not content that half of Greece lie
    slain,
Pours new destruction on her sons again ?
He comes not, Jove ! without thy powerful
    will; 330
Lo ! still he lives, pursues, and conquers
    still !
Yet hear my counsel, and his worst with-
    stand;
The Greek's main body to the fleet com-
    mand:
But let the few whom brisker spirits warm,
Stand the first onset, and provoke the
    storm:
Thus point your arms; and when such foes
    appear,
Fierce as he is, let Hector learn to fear.'
    The warrior spoke, the list'ning Greeks
    obey,
Thick'ning their ranks, and form a deep
    array.
Each Ajax, Teucer, Merion gave com-
    mand, 340
The valiant leader of the Cretan band,
And Mars-like Meges: these the Chiefs
    excite,
Approach the foe, and meet the coming
    fight.
Behind, unnumber'd multitudes attend
To flank the navy, and the shores defend.
Full on the front the pressing Trojans
    bear,
And Hector first came tow'ring to the war.
Phœbus himself the rushing battle led;
A veil of clouds involv'd his radiant head:
High-held before him, Jove's enormous
    shield 350
Portentous shone, and shaded all the field:
Vulcan to Jove th' immortal gift con-
    sign'd,
To scatter hosts, and terrify mankind.
The Greeks expect the shock; the clam-
    ours rise
From diff'rent parts, and mingle in the
    skies.
Dire was the hiss of darts, by heroes flung,
And arrows leaping from the bow-string
    sung;

These drink the life of gen'rous warriors
   slain;
Those guiltless fall, and thirst for blood in
   vain.
As long as Phœbus bore unmov'd the
   shield,   360
Sat doubtful Conquest hov'ring on the field;
But when aloft he shakes it in the skies,
Shouts in their ears, and lightens in their
   eyes,
Deep horror seizes ev'ry Grecian breast,
Their force is humbled, and their fear con-
   fess'd.
So flies a herd of oxen, scatter'd wide,
No swain to guard them, and no day to
   guide,
When two fell lions from the mountain
   come,
And spread the carnage thro' the shady
   gloom.
Impending Phœbus pours around them
   fear,   370
And Troy and Hector thunder in the rear.
Heaps fall on heaps: the slaughter Hector
   leads;
First, great Arcesilas, then Stichius bleeds;
One to the bold Bœotians ever dear,
And one Menestheus' friend, and famed
   compeer.
Medon and Iäsus, Æneas sped;
This sprung from Phelus, and th' Athe-
   nians led;
But hapless Medon from Oïleus came;
Him Ajax honour'd with a brother's name,
Tho' born of lawless love: from home ex-
   pell'd,   380
A banish'd man, in Phylace he dwell'd,
Press'd by the vengeance of an angry wife;
Troy ends, at last, his labours and his life.
Mecystes next, Polydamas o'erthrew;
And thee, brave Clonius ! great Agenor
   slew.
By Paris, Deiochus inglorious dies,
Pierc'd thro' the shoulder as he basely
   flies.
Polites' arm laid Echius on the plain;
Stretch'd on one heap, the victors spoil the
   slain.
The Greeks dismay'd, confused, disperse
   or fall,   390
Some seek the trench, some skulk behind
   the wall;
While these fly trembling, others pant for
   breath,
And o'er the slaughter stalks gigantic death.

On rush'd bold Hector, gloomy as the
   night,
Forbids to plunder, animates the fight.
Points to the fleet: 'For, by the Gods, who
   flies,
Who dares but linger, by this hand he
   dies;
No weeping sister his cold eye shall close,
No friendly hand his funeral pyre compose.
Who stops to plunder at this signal
   hour,   400
The birds shall tear him, and the dogs de-
   vour.'
   Furious he said; the smarting scourge
   resounds;
The coursers fly; the smoking chariot
   bounds;
The hosts rush on; loud clamours shake
   the shore;
The horses thunder, earth and ocean roar !
Apollo, planted at the trench's bound,
Push'd at the bank; down sunk th' enor-
   mous mound:
Roll'd in the ditch the heapy ruin lay;
A sudden road ! a long and ample way.
O'er the dread fosse (a late impervious
   space)   410
Now steeds, and men, and cars tumultuous
   pass.
The wond'ring crowds the downward level
   trod;
Before them flamed the shield, and march'd
   the God.
Then with his hand he shook the mighty
   wall;
And lo ! the turrets nod, the bulwarks fall.
Easy, as when ashore an infant stands,
And draws imagin'd houses in the sands;
The sportive wanton, pleas'd with some
   new play,
Sweeps the slight works and fashion'd
   domes away.
Thus vanish'd, at thy touch, the towers
   and walls;   420
The toil of thousands in a moment falls.
   The Grecians gaze around with wild de-
   spair,
Confused, and weary all the powers with
   prayer;
Exhort their men, with praises, threats,
   commands;
And urge the Gods, with voices, eyes, and
   hands.
Experienc'd Nestor chief obtests the skies,
And weeps his country with a father's eyes:

'O Jove ! if ever, on his native shore,
One Greek enrich'd thy shrine with offer'd
gore;
If e'er in hope our country to behold,   430
We paid the fatted firstlings of the fold;
If e'er thou sign'st our wishes with thy
nod;
Perform the promise of a gracious God !
This day preserve our navies from the
flame,
And save the reliques of the Grecian name.'
   Thus pray'd the sage: th' Eternal gave
consent,
And peals of Thunder shook the firmament.
Presumptuous Troy mistook th' accepting
sign,
And catch'd new fury at the voice divine.
As, when black tempests mix the seas and
skies,   440
The roaring deeps in wat'ry mountains
rise,
Above the sides of some tall ship ascend,
Its womb they deluge, and its ribs they
rend:
Thus loudly roaring, and o'erpowering all,
Mount the thick Trojans up the Grecian
wall;
Legions on legions from each side arise:
Thick sound the keels; the storm of arrows
flies:
Fierce on the ships above, the cars below,
These wield the mace, and those the jav'lin
throw.
   While thus the thunder of the battle
raged,   450
And lab'ring armies round the works en-
gaged;
Still in the tent Patroclus sat, to tend
The good Eurypylus, his wounded friend.
He sprinkles healing balms, to anguish
kind,
And adds discourse, the med'cine of the
mind.
But when he saw, ascending up the fleet,
Victorious Troy; then, starting from his
seat,
With bitter groans his sorrows he express'd;
He wrings his hands, he beats his manly
breast.
'Tho' yet thy state require redress' (he
cries),   460
'Depart I must: what horrors strike my
eyes !
Charged with Achilles' high commands I go,
A mournful witness of this scene of woe:

I haste to urge him, by his country's care,
To rise in arms, and shine again in war.
Perhaps some fav'ring God his soul may
bend:
The voice is powerful of a faithful friend.'
   He spoke; and, speaking, swifter than
the wind
Sprung from the tent, and left the war be-
hind.
Th' embodied Greeks the fierce attack sus-
tain,   470
But strive, tho' numerous, to repulse in
vain:
Nor could the Trojans, thro' that firm ar-
ray,
Force, to the fleet and tents, th' impervious
way.
As when a shipwright, with Palladian art,
Smooths the rough wood, and levels ev'ry
part:
With equal hand he guides his whole de-
sign,
By the just rule, and the directing line:
The martial leaders, with like skill and
care,
Preserv'd their line, and equal kept the
war.
Brave deeds of arms thro' all the ranks
were tried,   480
And ev'ry ship sustain'd an equal tide.
At one proud bark, high-tow'ring o'er the
fleet,
Ajax the great and Godlike Hector meet:
For one bright prize the matchless Chiefs
contend,
Nor this the ships can fire, nor that defend;
One kept the shore, and one the vessel
trod;
That fix'd as fate, this acted by a God.
The son of Clytius in his daring hand,
The deck approaching, shakes a flaming
brand;
But pierc'd by Telamon's huge lance ex-
pires;   490
Thund'ring he falls, and drops th' extin-
guish'd fires.
Great Hector view'd him with a sad sur-
vey,
As stretch'd in dust before the stern he
lay.
'Oh ! all of Trojan, all of Lycian race !
Stand to your arms, maintain this arduous
space.
Lo ! where the son of royal Clytius lies,
Ah, save his arms, secure his obsequies !'

This said, his eager jav'lin sought the foe:
But Ajax shunn'd the meditated blow.
Not vainly yet the forceful lance was thrown; 500
It stretch'd in dust unhappy Lycophron:
An exile long, sustain'd at Ajax' board,
A faithful servant to a foreign lord;
In peace, in war, for ever at his side,
Near his lov'd master, as he liv'd, he died.
From the high poop he tumbles on the sand,
And lies, a lifeless load, along the land.
With anguish Ajax views the piercing sight,
And thus inflames his brother to the fight:
' Teucer, behold ! extended on the shore, 510
Our friend, our lov'd companion ! now no more!
Dear as a parent, with a parent's care
To fight our wars, he left his native air.
This death deplor'd to Hector's rage we owe;
Revenge, revenge it on the cruel foe !
Where are those darts on which the fates attend ?
And where the bow which Phœbus taught to bend ? '
Impatient Teucer, hast'ning to his aid,
Before the Chief his ample bow display'd;
The well-stored quiver on his shoulders hung: 520
Then hiss'd his arrow, and the bow-string sung.
Clytus, Pisenor's son, renown'd in fame
(To thee, Polydamas ! an honour'd name),
Drove thro' the thickest of th' embattled plains
The startling steeds, and shook his eager reins.
As all on glory ran his ardent mind,
The pointed death arrests him from behind:
Thro' his fair neck the thrilling arrow flies;
In youth's first bloom reluctantly he dies.
Hurl'd from the lofty seat, at distance far, 530
The headlong coursers spurn his empty car;
Till sad Polydamas the steeds restrain'd,
And gave, Astynous, to thy careful hand;
Then, fired to vengeance, rush'd amidst the foe;
Rage edg'd his sword, and strengthen'd ev'ry blow.

Once more bold Teucer, in his country's cause,
At Hector's breast a chosen arrow draws:
And had the weapon found the destin'd way,
Thy fall, great Trojan ! had renown'd that day.
But Hector was not doom'd to perish then: 540
Th' all-wise disposer of the fates of men
(Imperial Jove) his present death withstands;
Nor was such glory due to Teucer's hands.
At his full stretch as the tough string he drew,
Struck by an arm unseen, it burst in two:
Down dropp'd the bow: the shaft with brazen head
Fell innocent, and on the dust lay dead.
Th' astonish'd archer to great Ajax cries:
' Some God prevents our destin'd enterprise:
Some God propitious to the Trojan foe, 550
Has, from my arm unfailing, struck the bow,
And broke the nerve my hands had twined with art,
Strong to impel the flight of many a dart.'
' Since Heav'n commands it ' (Ajax made reply),
' Dismiss the bow, and lay thy arrows by:
Thy arms no less suffice the lance to wield,
And quit the quiver for the pond'rous shield.
In the first ranks indulge thy thirst of fame,
Thy brave example shall the rest inflame.
Fierce as they are, by long successes vain, 560
To force our fleet, or ev'n a ship to gain,
Asks toil, and sweat, and blood: their utmost might
Shall find its match — No more; 't is ours to fight.'
Then Teucer laid his faithless bow aside:
The fourfold buckler o'er his shoulder tied;
On his brave head a crested helm he placed,
With nodding horsehair formidably graced;
A dart, whose point with brass refulgent shines,
The warrior wields; and his great brother joins.
This Hector saw, and thus express'd his joy; 570
' Ye troops of Lycia, Dardanus, and Troy !

Be mindful of yourselves, your ancient
   fame,
And spread your glory with the navy's
   flame.
Jove is with us; I saw his hand, but now,
From the proud archer strike his vaunted
   bow.
Indulgent Jove ! how plain thy favours
   shine,
When happy nations bear the marks di-
   vine !
How easy then to see the sinking state
Of realms accurs'd, deserted, reprobate !
Such is the fate of Greece, and such is
   ours: 580
Behold, ye warriors, and exert your powers.
Death is the worst; a fate which all must
   try;
And for our country 't is a bliss to die.
The gallant man, tho' slain in fight he be,
Yet leaves his nation safe, his children free;
Entails a debt on all the grateful state;
His own brave friends shall glory in his fate;
His wife live honour'd, all his race succeed,
And late posterity enjoy the deed ! '
   This rous'd the soul in ev'ry Trojan
   breast.   590
The godlike Ajax next his Greeks ad-
   dress'd:
' How long, ye warriors of the Argive race,
(To gen'rous Argos what a dire disgrace !)
How long on these curs'd confines will ye
   lie,
Yet undetermin'd, or to live, or die ?
What hopes remain, what methods to re-
   tire,
If once your vessels catch the Trojan fire ?
Mark how the flames approach, how near
   they fall,
How Hector calls, and Troy obeys his
   call !
Not to the dance that dreadful voice in-
   vites;   600
It calls to death, and all the rage of
   fights.
'T is now no time for wisdom or debates;
To your own hands are trusted all your
   fates:
And better far, in one decisive strife,
One day should end our labour, or our
   life,
Than keep this hard-got inch of barren
   sands,
Still press'd, and press'd by such inglori-
   ous hands.'

The list'ning Grecians feel their leader's
   flame,
And ev'ry kindling bosom pants for fame.
Then mutual slaughters spread on either
   side;   610
By Hector here the Phocian Schedius
   died;
There, pierc'd by Ajax, sank Laodamas,
Chief of the foot, of old Antenor's race.
Polydamas laid Otus on the sand,
The fierce commander of th' Epeian band.
His lance bold Meges at the victor threw;
The victor stooping, from the death with-
   drew
(That valued life, O Phœbus ! was thy
   care),
But Crœsmus' bosom took the flying spear:
His corpse fell bleeding on the slipp'ry
   shore: 620
His radiant arms triumphant Meges bore.
Dolops, the son of Lampus, rushes on,
Sprung from the race of old Laomedon,
And famed for prowess in a well-fought
   field;
He pierc'd the centre of his sounding
   shield:
But Meges Phyleus' ample breast-plate
   wore
(Well known in fight on Selles' winding
   shore:
For King Euphetes gave the golden mail,
Compact, and firm with many a jointed
   scale),
Which oft, in cities storm'd, and battles
   won,   630
Had saved the father, and now saves the
   son.
Full at the Trojan's head he urged his
   lance,
Where the high plumes above the helmet
   dance,
New-tinged with Tyrian dye: in dust be-
   low,
Shorn from the crest, the purple honours
   glow;
Meantime their fight the Spartan King
   survey'd,
And stood by Meges' side, a sudden aid,
Thro' Dolops' shoulder urged his forceful
   dart,
Which held its passage thro' the panting
   heart,
And issued at his breast. With thund'ring
   sound   640
The warrior falls extended on the ground.

In rush the conquering Greeks to spoil the
slain;
But Hector's voice excites his kindred
train;
The hero most from Hicetaon sprung,
Fierce Melanippus, gallant, brave, and
young.
He (e'er to Troy the Grecians cross'd the
main)
Fed his large oxen on Percote's plain;
But when oppress'd, his country claim'd
his care,
Return'd to Ilion, and excell'd in war: 649
For this in Priam's court he held his place,
Belov'd no less than Priam's royal race.
Him Hector singled, as his troops he led,
And thus inflamed him, pointing to the dead:
'Lo, Melanippus! lo where Dolops lies;
And is it thus our royal kinsman dies?
O'ermatch'd he falls; to two at once a prey,
And lo, they bear the bloody arms away!
Come on — a distant war no longer wage,
But hand to hand thy country's foes en-
gage: 659
Till Greece at once, and all her glory, end;
Or Ilion from her tow'ry height descend,
Heav'd from the lowest stone; and bury all
In one sad sepulchre, one common fall.'
Hector (this said) rush'd forward on the
foes:
With equal ardour Melanippus glows:
Then Ajax thus: 'O Greeks! respect your
fame,
Respect yourselves, and learn an honest
shame:
Let mutual rev'rence mutual warmth in-
spire,
And catch from breast to breast the noble
fire.
On valour's side the odds of combat lie, 670
The brave live glorious, or lamented die;
The wretch that trembles in the Field of
Fame,
Meets death, and worse than death, eternal
shame.'
His gen'rous sense he not in vain im-
parts;
It sunk, and rooted in the Grecian hearts.
They join, they throng, they thicken at his
call,
And flank the navy with a brazen wall;
Shields touching shields, in order blaze
above,
And stop the Trojans, tho' impell'd by
Jove. 679

The fiery Spartan first, with loud applause,
Warms the bold son of Nestor in his cause.
'Is there' (he said) 'in arms a youth like
you,
So strong to fight, so active to pursue?
Why stand you distant, nor attempt a
deed?
Lift the bold lance, and make some Trojan
bleed.'
He said, and backwards to the lines re-
tired;
Forth rush'd the youth, with martial fury
fired,
Beyond the foremost ranks; his lance he
threw
And round the black battalions cast his
view.
The troops of Troy recede with sudden
fear, 690
While the swift jav'lin hiss'd along in air.
Advancing Melanippus met the dart
With his bold breast, and felt it in his
heart:
Thund'ring he falls; his falling arms re-
sound,
And his broad buckler rings against the
ground.
The victor leaps upon his prostrate prize;
Thus on a roe the well-breathed beagle flies,
And rends his side, fresh-bleeding with the
dart
The distant hunter sent into his heart.
Observing Hector to the rescue flew; 700
Bold as he was, Antilochus withdrew:
So when a savage, ranging o'er the plain,
Has torn the shepherd's dog, or shepherd
swain;
While, conscious of the deed, he glares
around,
And hears the gath'ring multitude resound,
Timely he flies the yet untasted food,
And gains the friendly shelter of the wood.
So fears the youth; all Troy with shouts
pursue,
While stones and darts in mingled tem-
pests flew;
But, enter'd in the Grecian ranks, he
turns 710
His manly breast, and with new fury burns.
Now on the fleet the tides of Trojans
drove,
Fierce to fulfil the stern decrees of Jove:
The Sire of Gods, confirming Thetis' prayer,
The Grecian ardour quench'd in deep de-
spair;

But lifts to glory Troy's prevailing bands,
Swells all their hearts, and strengthens all
  their hands.
On Ida's top he waits with longing eyes,
To view the navy blazing to the skies;
Then, nor till then, the scale of war shall
  turn, 720
The Trojans fly, and conquer'd Ilion burn.
These fates revolv'd in his almighty mind,
He raises Hector to the work design'd,
Bids him with more than mortal fury glow,
And drives him, like a lightning, on the foe.
So Mars, when human crimes for vengeance
  call,
Shakes his huge jav'lin, and whole armies
  fall.
Not with more rage a conflagration rolls,
Wraps the vast mountains, and involves the
  poles.
He foams with wrath; beneath his gloomy
  brow 730
Like fiery meteors his red eye-balls glow:
The radiant helmet on his temple burns,
Waves when he nods, and lightens as he
  turns:
For Jove his splendour round the Chief
  had thrown,
And cast the blaze of both the hosts on one.
Unhappy glories! for his fate was near,
Due to stern Pallas, and Pelides' spear:
Yet Jove deferr'd the death he was to
  pay,
And gave what Fate allow'd, the honours
  of a day!
  Now all on fire for fame, his breast, his
  eyes 740
Burn at each foe, and single ev'ry prize;
Still at the closest ranks, the thickest fight,
He points his ardour, and exerts his might.
The Grecian phalanx, moveless as a tower,
On all sides batter'd, yet resists his power:
So some tall rock o'erhangs the hoary
  main,
By winds assail'd, by billows beat in vain;
Unmov'd it hears, above, the tempest blow,
And sees the wat'ry mountains break be-
  low.
Girt in surrounding flames, he seems to
  fall 750
Like fire from Jove, and bursts upon them
  all;
Bursts as a wave that from the clouds im-
  pends,
And swell'd with tempests on the ship de-
  scends;

White are the decks with foam; the winds
  aloud
Howl o'er the masts, and sing thro' ev'ry
  shroud:
Pale, trembling, tired, the sailors freeze
  with fears;
And instant death on ev'ry wave appears.
So pale the Greeks the eyes of Hector
  meet,
The Chief so thunders, and so shakes the
  fleet.
  As when a lion rushing from his den, 760
Amidst the plain of some wide-water'd fen
(Where numerous oxen, as at ease they
  feed,
At large expatiate o'er the ranker mead),
Leaps on the herds before the herdsman's
  eyes:
The trembling herdsman far to distance
  flies:
Some lordly bull (the rest dispers'd and fled)
He singles out; arrests, and lays him dead.
Thus from the rage of Jove-like Hector
  flew
All Greece in heaps; but one he seiz'd, and
  slew.
Mycenean Periphes, a mighty name, 770
In wisdom great, in arms well-known to
  fame:
The minister of stern Eurystheus' ire,
Against Alcides; Copreus was his sire:
The son redeem'd the honours of the race,
A son as gen'rous as the sire was base;
O'er all his country's youth conspicuous far
In ev'ry virtue, or of peace or war:
But doom'd to Hector's stronger force to
  yield!
Against the margin of his ample shield
He struck his hasty foot: his heels up-
  sprung; 780
Supine he fell, his brazen helmet rung.
On the fall'n Chief th' invading Trojan
  press'd,
And plunged the pointed jav'lin in his
  breast.
His circling friends, who strove to guard
  too late
Th' unhappy hero, fled, or shared his fate.
  Chased from the foremost line, the Gre-
  cian train
Now man the next, receding toward the
  main:
Wedg'd in one body at the tents they stand,
Wall'd round with sterns, a gloomy, des-
  p'rate band.

Now manly shame forbids th' inglorious
   flight;   790
Now fear itself confines them to the fight:
Man courage breathes in man; but Nestor
   most
(The sage preserver of the Grecian host)
Exhorts, adjures, to guard these utmost
   shores;
And by their parents, by themselves, im-
   plores:
'O friends! be men: your gen'rous
   breasts inflame
With mutual honour, and with mutual
   shame!
Think of your hopes, your fortunes; all the
   care
Your wives, your infants, and your parents,
   share: 799
Think of each living father's rev'rend head;
Think of each ancestor with glory dead;
Absent, by me they speak, by me they sue;
They ask their safety and their fame from
   you:
The Gods their fates on this one action lay,
And all are lost if you desert the day.'
   He spoke, and round him breathed heroic
   fires;
Minerva seconds what the sage inspires.
The mist of darkness Jove around them
   threw,
She clear'd, restoring all the war to view:
A sudden ray shot beaming o'er the plain,
And shew'd the shores, the navy, and the
   main.   811
Hector they saw, and all who fly or fight,
The scene wide opening to the blaze of light.
First of the field, great Ajax strikes their
   eyes,
His port majestic, and his ample size:
A pond'rous mace, with studs of iron
   crown'd,
Full twenty cubits long, he swings around.
Nor fights like others fix'd to certain stands,
But looks a moving tower above the bands;
High on the decks, with vast gigantic
   stride,   820
The godlike hero stalks from side to side.
So when a horseman from the wat'ry mead
(Skill'd in the manage of the bounding
   steed)
Drives four fair coursers, practis'd to obey,
To some great city thro' the public way;
Safe in his art, as side by side they run,
He shifts his seat, and vaults from one to
   one;

And now to this, and now to that he
   flies;
Admiring numbers follow with their eyes.
From ship to ship thus Ajax swiftly flew,
No less the wonder of the warring crew.
As furious, Hector thunder'd threats
   aloud,   832
And rush'd enraged before the Trojan
   crowd;
Then swift invades the ships, whose beaky
   prores
Lay rank'd contiguous on the bending
   shores.
So the strong eagle from his airy height,
Who marks the swans' or cranes' embodied
   flight,
Stoops down impetuous, while they light
   for food,
And stooping darkens with his wings the
   flood.   839
Jove leads him on with his almighty hand,
And breathes fierce spirits in his foll'wing
   band.
The warring nations meet, the battle roars,
Thick beats the combat on the sounding
   prores.
Thou would'st have thought, so furious was
   their fire,
No force could tame them, and no toil
   could tire;
As if new vigour from new fights they won,
And the long battle was but then begun.
Greece, yet unconquer'd, kept alive the
   war,
Secure of death, confiding in despair;
Troy in proud hopes already view'd the
   main   850
Bright with the blaze, and red with heroes
   slain:
Like strength is felt from hope, and from
   despair,
And each contends, as his were all the war.
'T was thou, bold Hector! whose resist-
   less hand
First seiz'd a ship on that contested strand;
The same which dead Protesilaüs bore,
The first that touch'd th' unhappy Trojan
   shore.
For this in arms the warring nations stood,
And bathed their gen'rous breasts with
   mutual blood.
No room to poise the lance, or bend the
   bow;   860
But hand to hand, and man to man they
   grow:

Wounded, they wound; and seek each
    other's hearts
With falchions, axes, swords, and short-
    en'd darts.
The falchions ring, shields rattle, axes
    sound,
Swords flash in air, or glitter on the ground:
With streaming blood the slipp'ry shores
    are dyed,
And slaughter'd heroes swell the dreadful
    tide.
  Still raging Hector with his ample hand
Grasps the high stern, and gives his loud
    command:
  ' Haste, bring the flames! the toil of ten
    long years   870
Is finish'd; and the day desired appears!
This happy day with acclamations greet,
Bright with destruction of yon hostile fleet.
The coward counsels of a tim'rous throng
Of rev'rend dotards, check'd our glory
    long:
Too long Jove lull'd us with lethargic
    charms,
But now in peals of thunder calls to arms;
In this great day he crowns our full de-
    sires,
Wakes all our force, and seconds all our
    fires.'
  He spoke. The warriors, at his fierce
    command,   880
Pour a new deluge on the Grecian band.
Ev'n Ajax paus'd (so thick the jav'lins fly),
Stepp'd back, and doubted or to live, or
    die.
Yet where the oars are placed, he stands to
    wait
What Chief approaching dares attempt his
    fate:
Ev'n to the last his naval charge defends,
Now shakes his spear, now lifts, and now
    protends;
Ev'n yet, the Greeks with piercing shouts
    inspires,
Amidst attacks, and deaths, and darts, and
    fires:
  ' O friends! O heroes! names for ever
    dear,   890
Once sons of Mars, and thunderbolts of war!
Ah! yet be mindful of your old renown,
Your great forefathers' virtues and your
    own.
What aids expect you in this utmost strait ?
What bulwarks rising between you and
    fate ?

No aids, no bulwarks, your retreat attend,
No friends to help, no city to defend.
This spot is all you have, to lose or keep;
There stand the Trojans, and here rolls
    the deep.
'T is hostile ground you tread; your native
    lands   900
Far, far from hence: your fates are in your
    hands.'
  Raging he spoke; nor farther wastes his
    breath,
But turns his jav'lin to the work of death.
Whate'er bold Trojan arm'd his daring
    bands
Against the sable ships with flaming
    brands,
So well the Chief his naval weapon sped,
The luckless warrior at his stern lay dead:
Full twelve, the boldest, in a moment fell,
Sent by great Ajax to the shades of hell.

BOOK XVI

THE SIXTH BATTLE : THE ACTS AND DEATH
OF PATROCLUS

THE ARGUMENT

Patroclus (in pursuance of the request of Nestor in the eleventh book) entreats Achilles
to suffer him to go to the assistance of the
Greeks with Achilles' troops and armour.
He agrees to it, but at the same time charges
him to content himself with rescuing the
fleet, without farther pursuit of the enemy.
The armour, horses, soldiers, and officers of
Achilles are described. Achilles offers a
libation for the success of his friend, after
which Patroclus leads the Myrmidons to battle. The Trojans, at the sight of Patroclus
in Achilles' armour, taking him for that
hero, are cast into the utmost consternation :
he beats them off from the vessels, Hector
himself flies, Sarpedon is killed, though Jupiter was averse to his fate. Several other
particulars of the battle are described ; in
the heat of which, Patroclus, neglecting the
orders of Achilles, pursues the foe to the
walls of Troy; where Apollo repulses and
disarms him. Euphorbus wounds him, and
Hector kills him : which concludes the book.

So warr'd both armies on th' ensanguin'd
    shore,
While the black vessels smoked with hu-
    man gore.
Meantime Patroclus to Achilles flies;

The streaming tears fall copious from his
　　eyes;
Not faster, trickling to the plains below,
From the tall rock the sable waters flow.
Divine Pelides, with compassion mov'd,
Thus spoke, indulgent to his best belov'd:
　'Patroclus, say, what grief thy bosom
　　bears,　　　　　　　　　　　　　9
That flows so fast in these unmanly tears?
No girl, no infant whom the mother keeps
From her lov'd breast, with fonder passion
　　weeps;
Not more the mother's soul that infant
　　warms,
Clung to her knees, and reaching at her
　　arms,
Than thou hast mine! Oh tell me to what
　　end
Thy melting sorrows thus pursue thy
　　friend?
　'Griev'st thou for me, or for my martial
　　band?
Or come sad tidings from our native land?
Our fathers live (our first, most tender
　　care,)　　　　　　　　　　　　　19
Thy good Menœtius breathes the vital
　　air,
And hoary Peleus yet extends his days;
Pleas'd in their age to hear their children's
　　praise.
　'Or may some meaner cause thy pity
　　claim?
Perhaps yon relics of the Grecian name,
Doom'd in their ships to sink by fire and
　　sword,
And pay the forfeit of their haughty lord?
Whate'er the cause, reveal thy secret
　　care,
And speak those sorrows which a friend
　　would share.'
　A sigh, that instant, from his bosom
　　broke,
Another follow'd, and Patroclus spoke: 30
　'Let Greece at length with pity touch
　　thy breast,
Thyself a Greek; and, once, of Greeks the
　　best!
Lo! ev'ry Chief that might her fate pre-
　　vent,
Lies pierc'd with wounds, and bleeding in
　　his tent:
Eurypylus, Tydides, Atreus' son,
And wise Ulysses, at the navy groan,
More for their country's wounds, than for
　　their own.

Their pain soft arts of pharmacy can ease;
Thy breast alone no lenitives appease.
　'May never rage like thine my soul en-
　　slave,　　　　　　　　　　　　　40
O great in vain! unprofitably brave!
Thy country slighted in her last distress,
What friend, what man, from thee shall
　　hope redress?
No: men unborn, and ages yet behind,
Shall curse that fierce, that unforgiving
　　mind.
　'O man unpitying! if of man thy race;
But sure thou spring'st not from a soft
　　embrace,
Nor ever am'rous hero caus'd thy birth,
Nor ever tender Goddess brought thee
　　forth.
Some rugged rock's hard entrails gave thee
　　form,　　　　　　　　　　　　　50
And raging seas produced thee in a storm;
A soul well suiting that tempestuous kind,
So rough thy manners, so untamed thy
　　mind.
　'If some dire oracle thy breast alarm,
If aught from Jove, or Thetis, stop thy
　　arm,
Some beam of comfort yet on Greece may
　　shine,
If I but lead the Myrmidonian line:
Clad in thy dreadful arms if I appear,
Proud Troy shall tremble and desert the
　　war:
Without thy person Greece shall win the
　　day,　　　　　　　　　　　　　60
And thy mere image chase her foes away.
Press'd by fresh forces, her o'erlabour'd
　　train
Shall quit the ships, and Greece respire
　　again.'
　Thus, blind to fate! with supplicating
　　breath,
Thou begg'st his arms, and in his arms thy
　　death.
Unfortunately good! a boding sigh
Thy friend return'd; and with it, this re-
　　ply:
　'Patroclus! thy Achilles knows no fears;
Nor words from Jove, nor oracles, he
　　hears;
Nor aught a mother's caution can sug-
　　gest;　　　　　　　　　　　　　70
The tyrant's pride lies rooted in my breast.
My wrongs, my wrongs, my constant
　　thought engage,
Those, my sole oracles, inspire my rage:

I made him tyrant; gave him power to
    wrong
Ev'n me: I felt it; and shall feel it long.
The maid, my black-eyed maid, he forc'd
    away.
Due to the toils of many a well-fought day;
Due to my conquest of her father's reign;
Due to the votes of all the Grecian train.
From me he forc'd her, me the bold and
    brave; 80
Disgraced, dishonour'd, like the meanest
    slave.
But bear we this —— The wrongs I grieve
    are past;
'T is time our fury should relent at last:
I fix'd its date; the day I wish'd appears;⎫
Now Hector to my ships his battle bears, ⎪
The flames my eyes, the shouts invade ⎬
    my ears. ⎭
Go, then, Patroclus! court fair honour's
    charms
In Troy's famed fields, and in Achilles'
    arms:
Lead forth my martial Myrmidons to
    fight,
Go, save the fleets, and conquer in my
    right. 90
See the thin relics of their baffled band,
At the last edge of yon deserted land!
Behold all Ilion on their ships descends;
How the cloud blackens, how the storm
    impends!
It was not thus, when, at my sight amazed,
Troy saw and trembled as this helmet
    blazed:
Had not th' injurious king our friendship
    lost,
You ample trench had buried half her
    host.
No camps, no bulwarks, now the Trojans
    fear,
Those are not dreadful, no Achilles
    there: 100
No longer flames the lance of Tydeus' son;
No more your Gen'ral calls his heroes on:
Hector alone I hear; his dreadful breath
Commands your slaughter, or proclaims
    your death.
Yet now, Patroclus, issue to the plain; ⎫
Now save the ships, the rising fires re- ⎬
    strain, ⎪
And give the Greeks to visit Greece again. ⎭
But heed my words, and mark a friend's
    command,
Who trusts his fame and honours in thy hand,

And from thy deeds expects th' Achaian
    host 110
Shall render back the beauteous maid he
    lost:
Rage uncontroll'd thro' all the hostile crew,
But touch not Hector, Hector is my due.
Tho' Jove in thunder should command the
    war,
Be just, consult my glory, and forbear.
The fleet once saved, desist from farther
    chase,
Nor lead to Ilion's walls the Grecian race;
Some adverse God thy rashness may de-
    stroy;
Some God, like Phœbus, ever kind to
    Troy.
Let Greece, redeem'd from this destructive
    strait, 120
Do her own work, and leave the rest to
    fate.
Oh! would to all th' immortal powers above,
Apollo, Pallas, and almighty Jove!
That not one Trojan might be left alive,
And not a Greek of all the race survive;
Might only we the vast destruction shun,
And only we destroy th' accursed town!'
    Such conf'rence held the Chiefs: while,
    on the strand,
Great Jove with conquest crown'd the Tro-
    jan band.
Ajax no more the sounding storm sus-
    tain'd, 130
So thick the darts an iron tempest rain'd:
On his tired arm the weighty buckler hung;
His hollow helm with falling jav'lins rung:
His breath, in quick short pantings, comes
    and goes;
And painful sweat from all his members
    flows.
Spent and o'erpower'd, he barely breathes
    at most;
Yet scarce an army stirs him from his
    post:
Dangers on dangers all around him grow,
And toil to toil, and woe succeeds to woe.
    Say, Muses, throned above the starry
    frame, 140
How first the navy blazed with Trojan
    flame?
    Stern Hector waved his sword, and,
    standing near
Where furious Ajax plied his ashen spear,
Full on the lance a stroke so justly sped,
That the broad falchion lopp'd its brazen
    head:

His pointless spear the warrior shakes in
     vain;
The brazen head falls sounding on the plain.
Great Ajax saw, and own'd the hand divine,
Confessing Jove, and trembling at the sign;
Warn'd he retreats. Then swift from all
     sides pour   150
The hissing brands; thick streams the fiery
     shower;
O'er the high stern the curling volumes
     rise,
And sheets of rolling smoke involve the
     skies.
Divine Achilles view'd the rising flames,
And smote his thigh, and thus aloud ex-
     claims:
'Arm, arm, Patroclus! lo, the blaze aspires!
The glowing ocean reddens with the fires.
Arm, ere our vessels catch the spreading
     flame;
Arm, ere the Grecians be no more a name;
I haste to bring the troops.' The Hero
     said;   160
The friend with ardour and with joy
     obey'd.
He cased his limbs in brass; and first
     around
His manly legs with silver buckles bound
The clasping greaves: then to his breast
     applies
The flamy cuirass, of a thousand dyes;
Emblazed with studs of gold, his falchion
     shone
In the rich belt, as in a starry zone.
Achilles' shield his ample shoulders spread,
Achilles' helmet nodded o'er his head.
Adorn'd in all his terrible array,   170
He flash'd around intolerable day.
Alone, untouch'd, Pelides' jav'lin stands,
Not to be pois'd but by Pelides' hands:
From Pelion's shady brow the plant entire
Old Chiron rent, and shaped it for his sire;
Whose son's great arm alone the weapon
     wields,
The death of heroes, and the dread of
     fields.
Then brave Automedon (an honour'd
     name,
The second to his lord in love and fame,
In peace his friend, and partner of the
     war)   180
The winged coursers harness'd to the car.
Xanthus and Balius, of immortal breed,
Sprung from the wind, and like the wind
     in speed;

Whom the wing'd harpy, swift Podarge,
     bore,
By Zephyr pregnant on the breezy shore.
Swift Pedasus was added to their side
(Once great Eëtion's, now Achilles' pride),
Who, like in strength, in swiftness, and in
     grace,
A mortal courser, match'd th' immortal
     race.
Achilles speeds from tent to tent, and
     warms   190
His hardy Myrmidons to blood and arms.
All breathing death, around their Chief
     they stand,
A grim, terrific, formidable band;
Grim as voracious wolves that seek the
     springs,
When scalding thirst their burning bowels
     wrings
(When some tall stag, fresh slaughter'd in
     the wood,
Has drench'd their wide insatiate throats
     with blood);
To the black fount they rush, a hideous
     throng,
With paunch distended and with lolling
     tongue;
Fire fills their eyes, their black jaws belch
     the gore,   200
And, gorged with slaughter, still they thirst
     for more.
Like furious rush'd the Myrmidonian crew,
Such their dread strength, and such their
     dreadful view.
     High in the midst the great Achilles
     stands,
Directs their order, and the war com-
     mands.
He, lov'd of Jove, had launch'd for Ilion's
     shores
Full fifty vessels, mann'd with fifty oars:
Five chosen leaders the fierce bands obey,
Himself supreme in valour, as in sway.
     First march'd Menestheus, of celestial
     birth,   210
Derived from thee, whose waters wash the
     earth,
Divine Sperchius! Jove-descended flood!
A mortal mother mixing with a God.
Such was Menestheus, but miscall'd by
     Fame
The son of Borus, that espous'd the dame.
     Eudorus next; whom Polymele the gay,
Famed in the graceful dance, produced to
     day.

Her, sly Cyllenius lov'd; on her would
    gaze,
As with swift step she form'd the running
    maze:
To her high chamber, from Diana's quire, 220
The God pursued her, urged, and crown'd
    his fire.
The son confess'd his father's heav'nly
    race,
And heir'd his mother's swiftness in the
    chase.
Strong Echecleüs, bless'd in all those
    charms
That pleas'd a God, succeeded to her arms;
Not conscious of those loves, long hid from
    fame,
With gifts of price he sought and won the
    dame;
Her secret offspring to her sire she bare;
Her sire caress'd him with a parent's
    care. 229
    Pisander follow'd; matchless in his art
To wing the spear, or aim the distant
    dart;
No hand so sure of all th' Emathian line,
Or if a surer, great Patroclus ! thine.
    The fourth by Phœnix' grave command
    was graced:
Laërces' valiant offspring led the last.
    Soon as Achilles with superior care
Had call'd the Chiefs, and order'd all the
    war,
This stern remembrance to his troops he
    gave:
'Ye far-famed Myrmidons, ye fierce and
    brave !
Think with what threats you dared the
    Trojan throng, 240
Think what reproach these ears endured so
    long:
" Stern son of Peleus " (thus ye used to
    say,
While restless, raging, in your ships you
    lay),
" Oh nurs'd with gall, unknowing how to
    yield !
Whose rage defrauds us of so famed a
    field,
If that dire fury must for ever burn,
What make we here ? Return, ye Chiefs,
    return ! "
Such were your words. Now, warriors,
    grieve no more,
Lo there the Trojans ! bathe your swords in
    gore !

This day shall give you all your soul de-
    mands; 250
Glut all your hearts ! and weary all your
    hands ! '
    Thus while he rous'd the fire in ev'ry
    breast,
Close, and more close, the list'ning cohorts
    press'd;
Ranks wedg'd in ranks, of arms a steely
    ring
Still grows and spreads and thickens round
    the King.
As when a circling wall the builder forms,
Of strength defensive against winds and
    storms,
Compacted stones the thick'ning work com-
    pose,
And round him wide the rising structure
    grows:
So helm to helm, and crest to crest they
    throng, 260
Shield urged on shield, and man drove man
    along:
Thick undistinguish'd plumes, together
    join'd,
Float in one sea, and wave before the
    wind.
    Far o'er the rest, in glitt'ring pomp ap-
    pear,
There bold Automedon, Patroclus here;
Brothers in arms, with equal fury fired;
Two friends, two bodies with one soul in-
    spired.
    But, mindful of the Gods, Achilles went
To the rich coffer in his shady tent:
There lay on heaps his various garments
    roll'd, 270
And costly furs, and carpets stiff with
    gold
(The presents of the silver-footed dame);
From thence he took a bowl of antique
    frame,
Which never man had stain'd with ruddy
    wine,
Nor rais'd in offerings to the Powers di-
    vine,
But Peleus' son; and Peleus' son to none
Had rais'd in offerings, but to Jove alone.
This, tinged with sulphur, sacred first to
    flame,
He purged; and wash'd it in the running
    stream.
Then cleans'd his hands; and, fixing for a
    space 280
His eyes on Heav'n, his feet upon the place

Of sacrifice, the purple draught he pour'd
Forth in the midst; and thus the God
   implor'd:
  'Oh thou Supreme ! high - throned all
   height above !
Oh great Pelasgic, Dodonean Jove !
Who, 'midst surrounding frosts, and va-
   pours chill,
Presid'st on bleak Dodona's vocal hill
(Whose groves the Selli, race austere !
   surround,
Their feet unwash'd, their slumbers on the
   ground;
Who hear from rustling oaks thy dark de-
   crees;   290
And catch the fates low-whisper'd in the
   breeze):
Hear, as of old: Thou gavest at Thetis'
   prayer,
Glory to me, and to the Greeks despair:
Lo, to the dangers of the fighting field
The best, the dearest of my friends, I
   yield:
Tho' still determin'd, to my ships confin'd,
Patroclus gone, I stay but half behind.
Oh be his guard thy providential care,
Confirm his heart, and string his arm to war;
Press'd by his single force, let Hector
   see   300
His fame in arms not owing all to me.
But when the fleets are saved from foes
   and fire,
Let him with conquest and renown retire;
Preserve his arms, preserve his social train,
And safe return him to these eyes again !'
  Great Jove consents to half the Chief's
   request,
But Heav'n's eternal doom denies the rest:
To free the fleet was granted to his prayer;
His safe return the winds dispers'd in air.
Back to his tent the stern Achilles flies, 310
And waits the combat with impatient eyes.
  Meanwhile the troops, beneath Patroclus'
   care,
Invade the Trojans, and commence the war.
As wasps, provoked by children in their
   play,
Pour from their mansions by the broad
   highway,
In swarms the guiltless traveller engage,
Whet all their stings, and call forth all
   their rage:
All rise in arms, and with a gen'ral cry
Assert their waxen domes, and buzzing
   progeny.

Thus from the tents the fervent legion
   swarms,   320
So loud their clamours, and so keen their
   arms;
Their rising rage Patroclus' breath inspires,
Who thus inflames them with heroic fires:
  'Oh warriors, partners of Achilles' praise !
Be mindful of your deeds in ancient days:
Your Godlike master let your acts pro-
   claim,
And add new glories to his mighty name.
Think your Achilles sees you fight: be
   brave,
And humble the proud Monarch whom you
   save.'
  Joyful they heard, and, kindling as he
   spoke,   330
Flew to the fleet, involv'd in fire and
   smoke.
From shore to shore the doubling shouts
   resound,
The hollow ships return a deeper sound.
The war stood still, and all around them
   gazed,
When great Achilles' shining armour
   blazed :
Troy saw, and thought the dread Achilles
   nigh;
At once they see, they tremble, and they fly.
  Then first thy spear, divine Patroclus !
   flew,
Where the war raged, and where the tu-
   mult grew.
Close to the stern of that famed ship,
   which bore   340
Unbless'd Protesilaus to Ilion's shore,
The great Pæonian, bold Pyræchmes, stood,
Who led his bands from Axius' winding
   flood:
His shoulder - blade receives the fatal
   wound;
The groaning warrior pants upon the
   ground.
His troops, that see their country's glory
   slain,
Fly diverse, scatter'd o'er the distant plain.
Patroclus' arm forbids the spreading fires,
And from the half-burn'd ship proud Troy
   retires,
Clear'd from the smoke the joyful navy
   lies,   350
In heaps on heaps the foe tumultuous flies;
Triumphant Greece her rescued decks as-
   cends,
And loud acclaim the starry region rends

So when thick clouds enwrap the moun-
tain's head,
O'er Heav'n's expanse like one black ceil-
ing spread:
Sudden the Thund'rer, with a flashing ray,
Bursts thro' the darkness, and lets down
the day:
The hills shine out, the rocks in prospect
rise,
And streams, and vales, and forests strike
the eyes;
The smiling scene wide opens to the
sight, 360
And all th' unmeasur'd ether flames with
light.
But Troy repuls'd, and scatter'd o'er the
plains,
Forc'd from the navy, yet the fight main-
tains.
Now ev'ry Greek some hostile hero slew,
But still the foremost bold Patroclus flew:
As Areïlycus had turn'd him round,
Sharp in his thigh he felt the piercing
wound;
The brazen-pointed spear, with vigour
thrown,
The thigh transfix'd, and broke the brittle
bone:
Headlong he fell. Next, Thoas, was thy
chance, 370
Thy breast, unarm'd, receiv'd the Spartan
lance.
Phylides' dart, as Amphiclus drew nigh,
His blow prevented, and transpierc'd his
thigh,
Tore all the brawn, and rent the nerves
away;
In darkness and in death the warrior lay.
In equal arms two sons of Nestor stand,
And two bold brothers of the Lycian band:
By great Antilochus, Antymnius dies,
Pierc'd in the flank, lamented youth! he
lies.
Kind Maris, bleeding in his brother's
wound, 380
Defends the breathless carcass on the
ground.
Furious he flies, his murd'rer to engage,
But godlike Thrasymed prevents his rage:
Between his arm and shoulder aims a blow;
His arm falls spouting on the dust below:
He sinks, with endless darkness cover'd
o'er,
And vents his soul, effused with gushing
gore.

Slain by two brothers, thus two brothers
bleed,
Sarpedon's friends, Amisodarus' seed;
Amisodarus, who, by Furies led, 390
The bane of man, abhorr'd Chimæra bred:
Skill'd in the dart in vain, his sons expire,
And pay the forfeit of their guilty sire.
Stopp'd in the tumult Cleobulus lies,
Beneath Oïleus' arm, a living prize;
A living prize not long the Trojan stood:
The thirsty falchion drank his reeking
blood;
Plunged in his throat the smoking weapon
lies:
Black Death, and Fate unpitying, seal his
eyes.
Amid the ranks, with mutual thirst of
fame, 400
Lycon the brave, and fierce Peneleus came;
In vain their jav'lins at each other flew;
Now, met in arms, their eager swords they
drew:
On the plumed crest of his Bœotian foe
The daring Lycon aim'd a noble blow;
The sword broke short; but his, Peneleus
sped
Full on the juncture of the neck and head:
The head, divided by a stroke so just,
Hung by the skin; the body sunk to dust.
O'ertaken Acamas by Merion bleeds, 410
Pierc'd thro' the shoulders as he mounts his
steeds:
Back from the car he tumbles to the
ground;
His swimming eyes eternal shades sur-
round.
Next Erymas was doom'd his fate to feel:
His open'd mouth receiv'd the Cretan steel;
Beneath the brain the point a passage
tore,
Crash'd the thin bones, and ground the
teeth in gore.
His mouth, his eyes, his nostrils, pour a
flood;
He sobs his soul out in the gush of blood.
As when the flocks neglected by the
swain 420
(Or kids, or lambs) lie scatter'd o'er the
plain,
A troop of wolves th' unguarded charge
survey,
And rend the trembling, unresisting prey.
Thus on the foe the Greeks impetuous
came :
Troy fled, unmindful of her former fame.

But still at Hector godlike Ajax aim'd,
Still, pointed at his breast, his jav'lin
 flamed:
The Trojan Chief, experienc'd in the field,
O'er his broad shoulders spread the massy
 shield,
Observ'd the storm of darts the Grecians
 pour,   430
And on his buckler caught the ringing
 shower.
He sees for Greece the scale of conquest
 rise,
Yet stops, and turns, and saves his lov'd
 allies.
 As when the hand of Jove a tempest
 forms,
And rolls the clouds to blacken Heav'n
 with storms,
Dark o'er the fields th' ascending vapour
 flies,
And shades the sun, and blots the golden
 skies:
So from the ships, along the dusky plain,
Dire Fright and Terror drove the Trojan
 train.
Ev'n Hector fled; thro' heaps of disarray 440
The fiery coursers forc'd their lord away:
While far behind his Trojans fall confused,
Wedg'd in the trench, in one vast carnage
 bruis'd.
Chariots on chariots roll; the clashing
 spokes
Shock; while the madd'ning steeds break
 short their yokes.
In vain they labour up the steepy mound;
Their charioteers lie foaming on the ground.
Fierce on the rear, with shouts, Patroclus
 flies;
Tumultuous clamour fills the fields and
 skies;
Thick drifts of dust involve their rapid
 flight;   450
Clouds rise on clouds, and Heav'n is
 snatch'd from sight.
Th' affrighted steeds, their dying lords
 cast down,
Scour o'er the fields, and stretch to reach
 the town.
Loud o'er the rout was heard the victor's
 cry,
Where the war bleeds, and where the
 thickest die;
Where horse, and arms, and chariots, lie
 o'erthrown,
And bleeding heroes under axles groan.

No stop, no check, the steeds of Peleus
 knew;
From bank to bank th' immortal coursers
 flew,
High-bounding o'er the fosse: the whirling
 car   460
Smokes thro' the ranks, o'ertakes the flying
 war,
And thunders after Hector; Hector flies,
Patroclus shakes his lance; but Fate denies.
Not with less noise, with less impetuous
 force,
The tide of Trojans urge their desperate
 course,
Than when in autumn Jove his fury pours,
And earth is laden with incessant showers
(When guilty mortals break th' eternal
 laws,
Or judges, bribed, betray the righteous
 cause);
From their deep beds he bids the rivers
 rise,   470
And opens all the floodgates of the skies:
Th' impetuous torrents from their hills obey,
Whole fields are drown'd, and mountains
 swept away;
Loud roars the deluge till it meets the main;
And trembling man sees all his labours
 vain.
 And now the Chief (the foremost troops
 repell'd)
Back to the ships his destin'd progress held,
Bore down half Troy in his resistless way,
And forc'd the routed ranks to stand the
 day.
Between the space where silver Simois
 flows,   480
Where lay the fleets, and where the ram-
 pires rose,
All grim with dust and blood, Patroclus
 stands,
And turns the slaughter on the conquering
 bands.
First Pronoüs died beneath his fiery dart,
Which pierc'd below the shield his valiant
 heart.
Thestor was next; who saw the Chief ap-
 pear,
And fell the victim of his coward fear:
Shrunk up he sat, with wild and haggard
 eye,
Nor stood to combat, nor had force to fly:
Patroclus mark'd him as he shunn'd the
 war,   490
And with unmanly trembling shook the car,

And dropp'd the flowing reins. Him 'twixt
    the jaws
The jav'lin sticks, and from the chariot
    draws.
As on a rock that overhangs the main,
An angler, studious of the line and cane,
Some mighty fish draws panting on the
    shore;
Not with less ease the barbed jav'lin bore
The gaping dastard; as the spear was
    shook,
He fell, and life his heartless breast for-
    sook.
    Next on Eryalus he flies; a stone,   500
Large as a rock, was by his fury thrown:
Full on his crown the pond'rous fragment
    flew,
And burst the helm, and cleft the head in
    two:
Prone to the ground the breathless warrior
    fell,
And death involv'd him with the shades of
    hell.
Then low in dust Epaltes, Echius, lie;
Ipheas, Evippus, Polymelus, die;
Amphoterus and Erymas succeed;
And last Tlepolemus and Pyres bleed.
Where'er he moves, the growing slaughters
    spread   510
In heaps on heaps; a monument of dead.
    When now Sarpedon his brave friends
    beheld
Grovelling in dust, and gasping on the field,
With this reproach his flying host he warms;
' Oh stain to honour! oh disgrace to arms!
Forsake, inglorious, the contended plain;
This hand, unaided, shall the war sustain;
The task be mine, this hero's strength to
    try,
Who mows whole troops, and makes an
    army fly.'
    He spake; and, speaking, leaps from off
    the car;   520
Patroclus lights, and sternly waits the war.
As when two vultures on the mountain's
    height
Stoop with resounding pinions to the fight;
They cuff, they tear, they raise a screaming
    cry;
The desert echoes, and the rocks reply:
The warriors thus, opposed in arms, engage
With equal clamours, and with equal rage.
    Jove view'd the combat, whose event
    foreseen,
He thus bespoke his Sister and his Queen:

' The hour draws on; the destinies ordain
My godlike son shall press the Phrygian
    plain: 531
Already on the verge of death he stands,
His life is ow'd to fierce Patroclus' hands.
What passions in a parent's breast debate!
Say, shall I snatch him from impending
    fate,
And send him safe to Lycia, distant far
From all the dangers and the toils of war ?
Or to his doom my bravest offspring yield,
And fatten with celestial blood the field ? '
    Then thus the Goddess with the radiant
    eyes: 540
' What words are these ? O Sov'reign of
    the Skies!
Short is the date prescribed to mortal
    man;
Shall Jove, for one, extend the narrow
    span,
Whose bounds were fix'd before his race
    began ?
How many sons of Gods, foredoom'd to
    death,
Before proud Ilion must resign their
    breath!
Were thine exempt, debate would rise
    above,
And murm'ring Powers condemn their
    partial Jove.
Give the bold Chief a glorious fate in fight;
And when th' ascending soul has wing'd
    her flight,   550
Let Sleep and Death convey, by thy com-
    mand,
The breathless body to his native land.
His friends and people, to his future praise,
A marble tomb and pyramid shall raise,
And lasting honours to his ashes give;
His fame ('t is all the dead can have) shall
    live.'
    She said; the Cloud-compeller, over-
    come,
Assents to Fate, and ratifies the doom.
Then, touch'd with grief, the weeping Hea-
    v'ns distill'd   559
A shower of blood o'er all the fatal field;
The God, his eyes averting from the plain,
Laments his son, predestin'd to be slain,
Far from the Lycian shores, his happy
    native reign.
    Now met in arms, the combatants ap-
    pear,
Each heav'd the shield, and pois'd the
    lifted spear;

From strong Patroclus' hand the jav'lin fled,
And pass'd the groin of valiant Thrasy-
    med;
The nerves unbraced no more his bulk sus-
    tain;
He falls, and falling bites the bloody plain.
Two sounding darts the Lycian leader
    threw;   570
The first aloof with erring fury flew,
The next transpierc'd Achilles' mortal
    steed,
The gen'rous Pedasus, of Theban breed,
Fix'd in the shoulder-joint; he reel'd
    around,
Roll'd in the bloody dust, and paw'd the
    slipp'ry ground.
His sudden fall th' entangled harness
    broke;
Each axle crackled, and the chariot shook:
When bold Automedon, to disengage
The starting coursers, and restrain their
    rage,
Divides the traces with his sword, and
    freed   580
Th' encumber'd chariot from the dying
    steed:
The rest move on, obedient to the rein;
The car rolls slowly o'er the dusty plain.
    The tow'ring Chiefs to fiercer fight ad-
    vance,
And first Sarpedon whirl'd his mighty
    lance,
Which o'er the warrior's shoulder took its
    course,
And spent in empty air its dying force.
Not so Patroclus' never-erring dart;
Aim'd at his breast, it pierc'd the mortal
    part,
Where the strong fibres bind the solid
    heart.   590
Then, as the mountain oak, or poplar tall,
Or pine (fit mast for some great admiral),
Nods to the axe, till with a groaning sound
It sinks, and spreads its honours on the
    ground;
Thus fell the King; and, laid on earth
    supine,
Before his chariot stretch'd his form divine:
He grasp'd the dust distain'd with stream-
    ing gore,
And, pale in death, lay groaning on the
    shore.
So lies a bull beneath the lion's paws,
While the grim savage grinds with foam-
    ing jaws   600

The trembling limbs, and sucks the smok-
    ing blood;
Deep groans, and hollow roars, rebellow
    thro' the wood.
    Then to the leader of the Lycian band
The dying Chief address'd his last com-
    mand:
' Glaucus, be bold; thy task be first to dare
The glorious dangers of destructive war,
To lead my troops, to combat at their head,
Incite the living, and supply the dead.
Tell them, I charged them with my latest
    breath   609
Not unrevenged to bear Sarpedon's death.
What grief, what shame, must Glaucus
    undergo,
If these spoil'd arms adorn a Grecian foe !
Then as a friend, and as a warrior, fight;
Defend my body, conquer in my right;
That, taught by great examples, all may try
Like thee to vanquish, or like me to die.'
    He ceas'd; the Fates suppress'd his la-
    b'ring breath,
And his eyes darken'd with the shades of
    death.
Th' insulting victor with disdain bestrode
The prostrate Prince, and on his bosom
    trod;   620
Then drew the weapon from his panting
    /heart,
The reeking fibres clinging to the dart;
From the wide wound gush'd out a stream
    of blood,
And the soul issued in the purple flood.
His flying steeds the Myrmidons detain,
Unguided now, their mighty master slain.
All-impotent of aid, transfix'd with grief,
Unhappy Glaucus heard the dying Chief.
His painful arm, yet useless with the smart
Inflicted late by Teucer's deadly dart,   630
Supported on his better hand he stay'd;
To Phœbus then ('t was all he could) he
    pray'd:
    ' All-seeing Monarch ! whether Lycia's
    coast,
Or sacred Ilion, thy bright presence boast,
Powerful alike to ease the wretch's smart;
O hear me ! God of ev'ry healing art !
Lo ! stiff with clotted blood, and pierc'd
    with pain,
That thrills my arm, and shoots thro' ev'ry
    vein:
I stand unable to sustain the spear,
And sigh, at distance from the glorious
    war.   640

Low in the dust is great Sarpedon laid,
Nor Jove vouchsafed his hapless offspring
aid.
But thou, O God of health! thy succour
lend,
To guard the reliques of my slaughter'd
friend.
For thou, tho' distant, canst restore my
might,
To head my Lycians, and support the fight.'
Apollo heard; and, suppliant as he stood,
His heav'nly hand restrain'd the flux of
blood;
He drew the dolours from the wounded
part,
And breathed a spirit in his rising heart. 650
Renew'd by art divine, the hero stands,
And owns th' assistance of immortal hands.
First to the fight his native troops he
warms,
Then loudly calls on Troy's vindictive
arms;
With ample strides he stalks from place to
place,
Now fires Agenor, now Polydamas;
Æneas next, and Hector he accosts;
Inflaming thus the rage of all their hosts:
'What thoughts, regardless Chief! thy
breast employ,
Oh too forgetful of the friends of Troy! 660
Those gen'rous friends, who, from their
country far,
Breathe their brave souls out in another's
war.
See! where in dust the great Sarpedon lies,
In action valiant, and in council wise,
Who guarded right, and kept his people
free;
To all his Lycians lost, and lost to thee!
Stretch'd by Patroclus' arm on yonder
plains;
Oh save from hostile rage his lov'd re-
mains!
Ah! let not Greece his conquer'd trophies
boast, 669
Nor on his corse revenge her heroes lost.'
He spoke: each leader in his grief par-
took;
Troy, at the loss, thro' all her legions
shook;
Transfix'd with deep regret, they view o'er-
thrown
At once his country's pillar, and their own;
A Chief, who led to Troy's beleaguered wall
A host of heroes, and outshined them all.

Fired, they rush on; first Hector seeks the
foes,
And with superior vengeance greatly glows.
But o'er the head the fierce Patroclus
stands,
And, rousing Ajax, rous'd the list'ning
bands: 680
'Heroes, be men! be what you were be-
fore;
Or weigh the great occasion, and be more.
The Chief who taught our lofty walls to
yield,
Lies pale in death, extended on the field:
To guard his body, Troy in numbers flies;
'T is half the glory to maintain our prize.
Haste, strip his arms, the slaughter round
him spread,
And send the living Lycians to the dead.'
The heroes kindle at his fierce command;
The martial squadrons close on either
hand: 690
Here Troy and Lycia charge with loud
alarms,
Thessalia there and Greece oppose their
arms.
With horrid shouts they circle round the
slain;
The clash of armour rings o'er all the plain.
Great Jove, to swell the horrors of the
fight,
O'er the fierce armies pours pernicious
night,
And round his son confounds the warring
hosts,
His fate ennobling with a crowd of ghosts.
Now Greece gives way, and great Epi-
geus falls; 699
Agacleus' son, from Budium's lofty walls:
Who, chased for murder thence, a sup-
pliant came
To Peleus and the silver-footed dame;
Now sent to Troy, Achilles' arms to aid,
He pays the vengeance to his kinsman's
shade.
Soon as his luckless hand had touch'd the
dead,
A rock's large fragment thunder'd on his
head;
Hurl'd by Hectorean force, it cleft in
twain
His shatter'd helm, and stretch'd him o'er
the slain.
Fierce to the van of fight Patroclus
came;
And, like an eagle darting at his game, 710

Sprung on the Trojan and the Lycian band:
What grief thy heart, what fury urged thy
   hand,
Oh gen'rous Greek! when with full vigour
   thrown
At Sthenelaüs flew the weighty stone,
Which sunk him to the dead: when Troy,
   too near
That arm, drew back; and Hector learn'd
   to fear.
Far as an able hand a lance can throw,
Or at the lists, or at the fighting foe,   718
So far the Trojans from their lines retired;
Till Glaucus, turning, all the rest inspired.
Then Bathycleüs fell beneath his rage,
The only hope of Chalcon's trembling age:
Wide o'er the land was stretch'd his large
   domain,
With stately seats and riches bless'd in
   vain.
Him, bold with youth, and eager to pursue
The flying Lycians, Glaucus met, and slew;
Pierc'd thro' the bosom with a sudden
   wound,
He fell, and, falling, made the fields re-
   sound.
Th' Achaians sorrow for their hero slain;
With conquering shouts the Trojans shake
   the plain,   730
And crowd to spoil the dead: the Greeks
   oppose:
An iron circle round the carcass grows.
   Then brave Laogonus resign'd his breath,
Despatch'd by Merion to the shades of
   death:
On Ida's holy hill he made abode,
The priest of Jove, and honour'd like his
   God.
Between the jaw and ear the jav'lin went:
The soul, exhaling, issued at the vent.
   His spear Æneas at the victor threw,
Who, stooping forward, from the death
   withdrew;   740
The lance hiss'd harmless o'er his cov'ring
   shield,
And trembling struck, and rooted in the
   field;
There yet scarce spent, it quivers on the
   plain,
Sent by the great Æneas' arm in vain.
'Swift as thou art' (the raging hero cries),
'And skill'd in dancing to dispute the prize,
My spear, the destin'd passage had it
   found,
Had fix'd thy active vigour to the ground.'

'Oh valiant leader of the Dardan host!'
(Insulted Merion thus retorts the boast);
'Strong as you are, 't is mortal force you
   trust,   751
An arm as strong may stretch thee in the
   dust.
And if to this my lance thy fate be giv'n,
Vain are thy vaunts; success is still from
   Heav'n:
This, instant, sends thee down to Pluto's
   coast:
Mine is the glory, his thy parting ghost.'
   'O friend!' (Menœtius' son this answer
   gave)
'With words to combat ill befits the brave:
Not empty boasts the sons of Troy repel,
Your swords must plunge them to the
   shades of Hell.   760
To speak, beseems the council: but to dare
In glorious action, is the task of war.'
This said, Patroclus to the battle flies;
Great Merion follows, and new shouts
   arise:
Shields, helmets rattle, as the warriors
   close;
And thick and heavy sounds the storm of
   blows.
As thro' the shrilling vale, or mountain
   ground,
The labours of the woodman's axe re-
   sound;
Blows following blows are heard re-echo-
   ing wide,
While crackling forests fall on ev'ry
   side: 770
Thus echoed all the fields with loud alarms,
So fell the warriors, and so rung their
   arms.
   Now great Sarpedon on the sandy shore,
His heav'nly form defaced with dust and
   gore,
And stuck with darts by warring heroes
   shed,
Lies undistinguish'd from the vulgar dead.
His long-disputed corse the chiefs enclose,
On ev'ry side the busy combat grows;
Thick as beneath some shepherd's thatch'd
   abode,
(The pails high foaming with a milky
   flood),   780
The buzzing flies, a persevering train,
Incessant swarm, and chased return again.
   Jove view'd the combat with a stern sur-
   vey,
And eyes that flash'd intolerable day;

Fix'd on the field his sight, his breast debates
The vengeance due, and meditates the fates:
Whether to urge their prompt effect, and call
The force of Hector to Patroclus' fall,
This instant see his short-lived trophies won,
And stretch him breathless on his slaughter'd son; 790
Or yet, with many a soul's untimely flight,
Augment the fame and horror of the fight.
To crown Achilles' valiant friend with praise
At length he dooms: and that his last of days
Shall set in glory; bids him drive the foe;
Nor unattended see the shades below.
Then Hector's mind he fills with dire dismay:
He mounts his car, and calls his hosts away;
Sunk with Troy's heavy fates, he sees decline
The scales of Jove, and pants with awe divine. 800
Then, nor before, the hardy Lycians fled,
And left their Monarch with the common dead:
Around, in heaps on heaps, a dreadful wall
Of carnage rises, as the heroes fall.
(So Jove decreed!) At length the Greeks obtain
The prize contested, and despoil the slain.
The radiant arms are by Patroclus borne,
Patroclus' ships the glorious spoils adorn.
Then thus to Phœbus in the realms above,
Spoke from his throne the cloud-compelling Jove: 810
'Descend, my Phœbus! on the Phrygian plain,
And from the fight convey Sarpedon slain:
Then bathe his body in the crystal flood,
With dust dishonour'd, and deform'd with blood:
O'er all his limbs ambrosial odours shed,
And with celestial robes adorn the dead.
Those rites discharged, his sacred corse bequeath
To the soft arms of silent Sleep and Death:
They to his friends the mournful charge shall bear
His friends a tomb and pyramid shall rear; 820

What honours mortals after death receive,
Those unavailing honours we may give.'
Apollo bows, and from Mount Ida's height,
Swift to the field precipitates his flight;
Thence from the war the breathless hero bore,
Veil'd in a cloud to silver Simois' shore;
There bathed his honourable wounds, and dress'd
His manly members in th' immortal vest
And with perfumes of sweet ambrosial dews,
Restores his freshness, and his form renews. 830
Then Sleep and Death, two twins of winged race,
Of matchless swiftness, but of silent pace,
Receiv'd Sarpedon at the God's command,
And in a moment reach'd the Lycian land;
The corse amidst his weeping friends they laid,
Where endless honours wait the sacred shade.
Meanwhile Patroclus pours along the plains,
With foaming coursers, and with loosen'd reins:
Fierce on the Trojan and the Lycian crew,
Ah blind to Fate! thy headlong fury flew: 840
Against what Fate and powerful Jove ordain,
Vain was thy friend's command, thy courage vain.
For he, the God, whose counsels uncontroll'd
Dismay the mighty, and confound the bold;
The God, who gives, resumes, and orders all,
He urged thee on, and urged thee on to fall.
Who first, brave hero! by that arm was slain,
Who last beneath thy vengeance press'd the plain,
When Heav'n itself thy fatal fury led,
And call'd to fill the number of the dead? 850
Adrestus first; Autonoüs then succeeds;
Echeclus follows; next young Megas bleeds;
Epistor, Menalippus, bite the ground:
The slaughter Elasus and Mulius crown'd:
Then sunk Pylartes to eternal night;
The rest, dispersing, trust their fates to flight.

Now Troy had stoop'd beneath his
   matchless power
But flaming Phœbus kept the sacred tower.
Thrice at the battlements Patroclus struck,
His blazing ægis thrice Apollo shook: 860
He tried the fourth; when, bursting from
   the cloud,
A more than mortal voice was heard aloud:
'Patroclus! cease; this Heav'n-defended
   wall
Defies thy lance, not fated yet to fall;
Thy friend, thy greater far, it shall with-
   stand,
Troy shall not stoop, ev'n to Achilles' hand.'
   So spoke the God who darts celestial
   fires:
The Greek obeys him, and with awe re-
   tires:
While Hector, checking at the Scæan gates
His panting coursers, in his breast de-
   bates,   870
Or in the field his forces to employ,
Or draw the troops within the walls of
   Troy.
   Thus while he thought, beside him
   Phœbus stood,
In Asius' shape, who reign'd by Sangar's
   flood
(Thy brother, Hecuba! from Dymas
   sprung,
A valiant warrior, haughty, bold and
   young):
Thus he accosts him: 'What a shameful
   sight!
Gods! is it Hector that forbears the fight?
Were thine my vigour, this successful spear
Should soon convince thee of so false a
   fear.   880
Turn thee, ah turn thee to the Field of
   Fame,
And in Patroclus' blood efface thy shame.
Perhaps Apollo shall thy arms succeed,
And Heav'n ordains him by thy lance to
   bleed.'
   So spoke th' inspiring God: then took
   his flight,
And plunged amidst the tumult of the
   fight.
He bids Cebrion drive the rapid car;
The lash resounds, the coursers rush to
   war:
The God the Grecians' sinking souls de-
   press'd,
And pour'd swift spirits thro' each Trojan
   breast.   890

Patroclus lights, impatient for the fight;
A spear his left, a stone employs his right:
With all his nerves he drives it at the foe;
Pointed above, and rough and gross below:
The falling ruin crush'd Cebrion's head,
The lawless offspring of King Priam's bed;
His front, brows, eyes, one undistinguish'd
   wound;
The bursting balls drop sightless to the
   ground.
The charioteer, while yet he held the rein,
Struck from the car, falls headlong on the
   plain.   900
To the dark shades the soul unwilling
   glides,
While the proud victor thus his fall de-
   rides:
'Good Heav'ns! what active feats yon
   artist shews!
What skilful divers are our Phrygian foes!
Mark with what ease they sink into the
   sand!
Pity, that all their practice is by land!'
   Then rushing sudden on his prostrate
   prize,
To spoil the carcass fierce Patroclus flies:
Swift as a lion, terrible and bold,
That sweeps the fields, depopulates the
   fold;   910
Pierc'd thro' the dauntless heart, then
   tumbles slain;
And from his fatal courage finds his bane.
At once bold Hector, leaping from his car,
Defends the body, and provokes the war.
Thus for some slaughter'd hind, with equal
   rage,
Two lordly rulers of the wood engage;
Stung with fierce hunger each the prey in-
   vades,
And echoing roars rebellow thro' the
   shades.
Stern Hector fastens on the warrior's head,
And by the foot Patroclus drags the
   dead;   920
While all around, confusion, rage, and fright
Mix the contending hosts in mortal fight.
So, pent by hills, the wild winds roar aloud
In the deep bosom of some gloomy wood;
Leaves, arms, and trees, aloft in air are
   blown,
The broad oaks crackle, and the Sylvans
   groan;
This way and that the rattling thicket
   bends,
And the whole forest in one crash descends.

Not with less noise, with less tumultuous
rage,
In dreadful shock the mingled hosts en-
gage. 930
Darts shower'd on darts now round the car-
cass ring;
Now flights of arrows bounding from the
string:
Stones follow stones; some clatter on the
fields,
Some, hard and heavy, shake the sounding
shields.
But where the rising whirlwind clouds
the plains,
Sunk in soft dust the mighty Chief re-
mains,
And, stretch'd in death, forgets the guid-
ing reins!
Now, flaming from the zenith, Sol had
driv'n
His fervid orb thro' half the vault of
Heav'n; 939
While on each host with equal tempest fell
The show'ring darts, and numbers sunk to
hell.
But when his evening wheels o'erhung the
main,
Glad conquest rested on the Grecian train,
Then, from amidst the tumult and alarms,
They draw the conquer'd corse and radiant
arms.
Then rash Patroclus with new fury glows,
And, breathing slaughter, pours amid the
foes.
Thrice on the press like Mars himself he
flew,
And thrice three heroes at each onset
slew.
There ends thy glory! there the Fates un-
twine 950
The last black remnant of so bright a line;
Apollo dreadful stops thy middle way;
Death calls, and Heav'n allows no longer
day!
For lo! the God in dusky clouds en-
shrin'd,
Approaching, dealt a stagg'ring blow be-
hind.
The weighty shock his neck and shoulders
feel;
His eyes flash sparkles, his stunn'd senses
reel
In giddy darkness; far to distance flung,
His bounding helmet on the champaign
rung.

Achilles' plume is stain'd with dust and
gore, 960
That plume which never stoop'd to earth
before;
Long used, untouch'd, in fighting fields to
shine,
And shade the temples of the man divine.
Jove dooms it now on Hector's helm to nod;
Not long — for Fate pursues him, and the
God.
His spear in shivers falls: his ample
shield
Drops from his arm: his baldric strews the
field:
The corslet his astonish'd breast forsakes;
Loose is each joint; each nerve with horror
shakes, 969
Stupid he stares, and all assistless stands:
Such is the force of more than mortal
hands!
A Dardan youth there was, well known
to fame,
From Panthus sprung, Euphorbus was his
name;
Famed for the manage of the foaming
horse,
Skill'd in the dart, and matchless in the
course:
Full twenty knights he tumbled from the
car,
While yet he learn'd his rudiments of war.
His venturous spear first drew the hero's
gore;
He struck, he wounded, but he durst no
more; 979
Nor, tho' disarm'd, Patroclus' fury stood,
But swift withdrew the long-protended
wood,
And turn'd him short, and herded in the
crowd.
Thus by an arm divine, and mortal spear,
Wounded at once, Patroclus yields to fear,
Retires for succour to his social train,
And flies the fate which Heav'n decreed, in
vain.
Stern Hector, as the bleeding Chief he
views,
Breaks thro' the ranks, and his retreat pur-
sues:
The lance arrests him with a mortal wound;
He falls, earth thunders, and his arms re-
sound. 990
With him all Greece was sunk; that mo-
ment all
Her yet surviving heroes seem'd to fall.

So, scorch'd with heat, along the desert
  shore,
The roaming lion meets a bristly boar,
Fast by the spring; they both dispute the
  flood.
With flaming eyes and jaws besmear'd with
  blood;
At length the sov'reign savage wins the
  strife,
And the torn boar resigns his thirst and
  life.
Patroclus thus, so many Chiefs o'erthrown,
So many lives effused, expires his own. 1000
As dying now at Hector's feet he lies,
He sternly views him, and triumphing cries:
  'Lie there, Patroclus! and with thee the
    joy,
Thy pride once promis'd, of subverting
    Troy;
The fancied scenes of Ilion wrapp'd in
    flames,
And thy soft pleasures serv'd with captive
    dames!
Unthinking man! I fought those towers to
    free,
And guard that beauteous race from lords
    like thee:
But thou a prey to vultures shalt be made;
Thy own Achilles cannot lend thee aid; 1010
Tho' much at parting that great Chief
    might say,
And much enjoin thee, this important day:
"Return not, my brave friend" (perhaps
    he said),
"Without the bloody arms of Hector
    dead."
He spoke, Patroclus march'd, and thus
    he sped.'
  Supine, and wildly gazing on the skies,
With faint expiring breath, the Chief replies:
  'Vain Boaster! cease, and know the
    Powers divine:
Jove's and Apollo's is this deed, not thine;
To Heav'n is owed whate'er your own you
    call, 1020
And Heav'n itself disarm'd me ere my fall.
Had twenty mortals, each thy match in
    might,
Opposed me fairly, they had sunk in fight:
By Fate and Phœbus was I first o'erthrown,
Euphorbus next; the third mean part thy
    own.
But thou, Imperious! hear my latest breath;
The Gods inspire it, and it sounds thy
    death.

Insulting man, thou shalt be soon as I;
Black Fate hangs o'er thee, and thy hour
    draws nigh;
Ev'n now on life's last verge I see thee
    stand. 1030
I see thee fall, and by Achilles' hand.'
  He faints; the soul unwilling wings her
    way
(The beauteous body left a load of clay),
Flits to the lone, uncomfortable coast;
A naked, wand'ring, melancholy ghost!
  Then Hector pausing, as his eyes he fed
On the pale carcass, thus address'd the
    dead:
  'From whence this boding speech, the
    stern decree
Of death denounc'd, or why denounc'd to
    me?
Why not as well Achilles' fate be giv'n 1040
To Hector's lance? who knows the will of
    Heav'n?'
  Pensive he said: then, pressing as he lay
His breathless bosom, tore the lance away,
And upwards cast the corse: the reeking
    spear
He shakes, and charges the bold charioteer.
But swift Automedon with loosen'd reins,
Rapt in the chariot o'er the distant plains,
Far from his rage th' immortal coursers
    drove;
Th' immortal coursers were the gift of
    Jove.

BOOK XVII

THE SEVENTH BATTLE, FOR THE BODY OF
PATROCLUS. — THE ACTS OF MENELAUS

THE ARGUMENT

Menelaus, upon the death of Patroclus, defends his body from the enemy: Euphorbus,
who attempts it, is slain. Hector advancing,
Menelaus retires; but soon returns with
Ajax, and drives him off. This Glaucus
objects to Hector as a flight, who thereupon
puts on the armour he had won from Patroclus, and renews the battle. The Greeks
give way, till Ajax rallies them: Æneas sustains the Trojans. Æneas and Hector attempt the chariot of Achilles, which is borne
off by Automedon. The horses of Achilles
deplore the loss of Patroclus; Jupiter covers
his body with a thick darkness: the noble
prayer of Ajax on that occasion. Menelaus
sends Antilochus to Achilles, with the news

of Patroclus's death: then returns to the fight, where, though attacked with the utmost fury, he and Meriones, assisted by the Ajaces, bear off the body to the ships. The time is the evening of the eight-and-twentieth day. The scene lies in the fields before Troy.

On the cold earth divine Patroclus spread,
Lies pierc'd with wounds among the vulgar dead.
Great Menelaus, touch'd with gen'rous woe,
Springs to the front, and guards him from the foe:
Thus, round her new-fall'n young the heifer moves,
Fruit of her throes, and first-born of her loves;
And anxious (helpless as he lies, and bare)
Turns and re-turns her, with a mother's care.
Opposed to each that near the carcass came,
His broad shield glimmers, and his lances flame.   10
The son of Panthus, skill'd the dart to send,
Eyes the dead hero, and insults the friend:
'This hand, Atrides, laid Patroclus low;
Warrior! desist, nor tempt an equal blow.
To me the spoils my prowess won, resign;
Depart with life, and leave the glory mine.'
The Trojan thus: the Spartan Monarch burn'd
With gen'rous anguish, and in scorn return'd:
'Laugh'st thou not, Jove! from thy superior throne,
When mortals boast of prowess not their own ?   20
Not thus the lion glories in his might,
Nor panther braves his spotted foe in fight;
Nor thus the boar (those terrors of the plain);
Man only vaunts his force, and vaunts in vain.
But far the vainest of the boastful kind
These sons of Panthus vent their haughty mind.
Yet 't was but late, beneath my conquering steel
This boaster's brother, Hyperenor, fell: 28
Against our arm, which rashly he defied,
Vain was his vigour, and as vain his pride.

These eyes beheld him on the dust expire,
No more to cheer his spouse, or glad his sire.
Presumptuous youth! like his shall be thy doom,
Go, wait thy brother to the Stygian gloom;
Or, while thou may'st, avoid the threaten'd fate;
Fools stay to feel it, and are wise too late.'
Unmov'd, Euphorbus thus: 'That action known,
Come, for my brother's blood repay thy own.
His weeping father claims thy destin'd head,
And spouse, a widow in her bridal bed. 40
On these thy conquer'd spoils I shall bestow,
To soothe a consort's and a parent's woe.
No longer then defer the glorious strife,
Let Heav'n decide our Fortune, Fame, and Life.'
Swift as the word the missile lance he flings,
The well-aim'd weapon on the buckler rings,
But, blunted by the brass, innoxious falls:
On Jove, the father, great Atrides calls;
Nor flies the jav'lin from his arm in vain;
It pierc'd his throat, and bent him to the plain;   50
Wide thro' the neck appears the grisly wound,
Prone sinks the warrior, and his arms resound.
The shining circlets of his golden hair,
Which ev'n the Graces might be proud to wear,
Instarr'd with gems and gold, bestrew the shore,
With dust dishonour'd, and deform'd with gore.
As the young olive, in some sylvan scene,
Crown'd by fresh fountains with eternal green,
Lifts the gay head, in snowy flow'rets fair,
And plays and dances to the gentle air; 60
When lo ! a whirlwind from high Heav'n invades
The tender plant, and withers all its shades;
It lies uprooted from its genial bed,
A lovely ruin now defaced and dead :

Thus young, thus beautiful, Euphorbus lay,
While the fierce Spartan tore his arms
    away.
Proud of his deed, and glorious in the
    prize,
Affrighted Troy the tow'ring victor flies;
Flies, as before some mountain lion's ire
The village curs and trembling swains re-
    tire;   70
When o'er the slaughter'd bull they hear
    him roar,
And see his jaws distil with smoking gore;
All pale with fear, at distance scatter'd
    round,
They shout incessant, and the vales re-
    sound.
    Meanwhile Apollo view'd with envious
    eyes,
And urged great Hector to dispute the
    prize
(In Mentes' shape, beneath whose martial
    care
The rough Ciconians learn'd the trade of
    war):
'Forbear,' he cried, 'with fruitless speed
    to chase
Achilles' coursers, of ethereal race;   80
They stoop not, these, to mortal man's
    command,
Or stoop to none but great Achilles' hand.
Too long amused with a pursuit so vain,
Turn, and behold the brave Euphorbus
    slain!
By Sparta slain; for ever now suppress'd
The fire which burn'd in that undaunted
    breast!'
    Thus having spoke, Apollo wing'd his
    flight,
And mix'd with mortals in the toils of
    fight:
His words infix'd unutterable care
Deep in great Hector's soul: thro' all the
    war   90
He darts his anxious eye: and instant
    view'd
The breathless hero in his blood imbrued
(Forth welling from the wound, as prone
    he lay),
And in the victor's hand the shining prey.
Sheathed in bright arms, thro' cleaving
    ranks he flies,
And sends his voice in thunder to the
    skies:
Fierce as a flood of flame by Vulcan sent,
It flew, and fired the nations as it went.

Atrides from the voice the storm divin'd,
And thus explor'd his own unconquer'd
    mind: 100
'Then shall I quit Patroclus on the
    plain,
Slain in my cause, and for my honour
    slain;
Desert the arms, the relics of my friend?
Or singly Hector and his troops attend?
Sure, where such partial favour Heav'n
    bestow'd,
To brave the Hero were to brave the God:
Forgive me, Greece, if once I quit the
    field;
'T is not to Hector, but to Heav'n, I yield.
Yet, nor the God nor Heav'n should give
    me fear,
Did but the voice of Ajax reach my ear: 110
Still would we turn, still battle on the
    plains,
And give Achilles all that yet remains
Of his and our Patroclus.' This, no more,
The time allow'd: Troy thicken'd on the
    shore;
A sable scene! The terrors Hector led;
Slow he recedes, and sighing quits the dead.
    So from the fold th' unwilling lion parts,
Forc'd by loud clamours, and a storm of
    darts;
He flies indeed, but threatens as he
    flies,   119
With heart indignant and retorted eyes.
Now, enter'd in the Spartan ranks, he
    turn'd
His manly breast, and with new fury
    burn'd:
O'er all the black battalions sent his view,
And thro' the cloud the godlike Ajax
    knew;
Where lab'ring on the left the warrior
    stood,
All grim in arms, and cover'd o'er with
    blood;
There breathing courage, where the God
    of Day
Had sunk each heart with terror and
    dismay.
    To him the King: 'Oh! Ajax, oh my
    friend!
Haste, and Patroclus' lov'd remains de-
    fend: 130
The body to Achilles to restore,
Demands our care; alas! we can no more!
For naked now, despoil'd of arms, he lies;
And Hector glories in the dazzling prize.'

He said, and touch'd his heart. The raging pair
Pierce the thick battle, and provoke the war.
Already had stern Hector seiz'd his head,
And doom'd to Trojan dogs th' unhappy dead;
But soon as Ajax rear'd his tower-like shield,
Sprung to his car, and measured back the field. 140
His train to Troy the radiant armour bear,
To stand a trophy of his fame in war.
Meanwhile great Ajax (his broad shield display'd)
Guards the dead hero with the dreadful shade;
And now before, and now behind he stood:
Thus, in the centre of some gloomy wood,
With many a step the lioness surrounds
Her tawny young, beset by men and hounds;
Elate her heart, and rousing all her powers,
Dark o'er the fiery balls each hanging eye-brow lowers. 150
Fast by his side the gen'rous Spartan glows
With great revenge, and feeds his inward woes.
But Glaucus, leader of the Lycian aids,
On Hector frowning, thus his flight up-braids:
'Where now in Hector shall we Hector find?
A manly form, without a manly mind!
Is this, O Chief! a hero's boasted fame?
How vain, without the merit, is the name!
Since battle is renounc'd, thy thoughts employ
What other methods may preserve thy Troy: 160
'T is time to try if Ilion's state can stand
By thee alone, nor ask a foreign hand;
Mean, empty boast! but shall the Lycians stake
Their lives for you? those Lycians you forsake?
What from thy thankless arms can we expect?
Thy friend Sarpedon proves thy base neglect:
Say, shall our slaughter'd bodies guard your walls,
While unrevenged the great Sarpedon falls?

Ev'n where he died for Troy, you left him there,
A feast for dogs, and all the fowls of air. 170
On my command if any Lycian wait,
Hence let him march, and give up Troy to fate.
Did such a spirit as the Gods impart
Impel one Trojan hand, or Trojan heart
(Such as should burn in every soul that draws
The sword for glory, and his country's cause),
Ev'n yet our mutual arms we might employ,
And drag yon carcass to the walls of Troy.
Oh! were Patroclus ours, we might obtain
Sarpedon's arms, and honour'd corse, again! 180
Greece with Achilles' friend should be repaid,
And thus due honours purchas'd to his shade.
But words are vain. Let Ajax once appear,
And Hector trembles and recedes with fear;
Thou darest not meet the terrors of his eye;
And lo, already thou preparest to fly.'
The Trojan Chief with fix'd resentment eyed
The Lycian leader, and sedate replied:
'Say, is it just (my friend) that Hector's ear
From such a warrior such a speech should hear? 190
I deem'd thee once the wisest of thy kind,
But ill this insult suits a prudent mind.
I shun great Ajax? I desert my train?
'T is mine to prove the rash assertion vain;
I joy to mingle where the battle bleeds,
And hear the thunder of the sounding steeds.
But Jove's high will is ever uncontroll'd,
The strong he withers, and confounds the bold:
Now crowns with fame the mighty man, and now
Strikes the fresh garland from the victor's brow! 200
Come, thro' yon squadrons let us hew the way,
And thou be witness if I fear to-day:

If yet a Greek the sight of Hector dread,
Or yet their hero dare defend the dead.'
Then, turning to the martial hosts, he
cries,
' Ye Trojans, Dardans, Lycians, and allies !
Be men (my friends) in action as in name,
And yet be mindful of your ancient fame.
Hector in proud Achilles' arms shall shine,
Torn from his friend, by right of conquest
mine.'   210
He strode along the field as thus he
said
(The sable plumage nodded o'er his head):
Swift thro' the spacious plain he sent a look;
One instant saw, one instant overtook
The distant band, that on the sandy shore
The radiant spoils to sacred Ilion bore.
There his own mail unbraced the field be-
strew'd;
His train to Troy convey'd the massy load.
Now blazing in th' immortal arms he
stands,   219
The work and present of celestial hands;
By aged Peleus to Achilles giv'n,
As first to Peleus by the court of Heav'n:
His father's arms not long Achilles wears,
Forbid by Fate to reach his father's years.
Him, proud in triumph, glitt'ring from
afar,
The God whose thunder rends the troubled
air
Beheld with pity ! as apart he sat,
And, conscious, look'd thro' all the scene of
fate,
He shook the sacred honours of his head;
Olympus trembled, and the Godhead said:
' Ah, wretched man ! unmindful of thy
end !   231
A moment's glory, and what fates attend !
In heav'nly panoply, divinely bright
Thou stand'st, and armies tremble at thy
sight,
As at Achilles' self ! beneath thy dart
Lies slain the great Achilles' dearer part:
Thou from the mighty dead those arms
hast torn,
Which once the greatest of mankind had
worn.
Yet live ! I give thee one illustrious day,
A blaze of glory ere thou fadest away.   240
For ah ! no more Andromache shall come,
With joyful tears to welcome Hector home;
No more officious, with endearing charms,
From thy tired limbs unbrace Pelides'
arms ! '

Then with his sable brow he gave the
nod,
That seals his word; the sanction of the
God.
The stubborn arms (by Jove's command
disposed)
Conform'd spontaneous, and around him
closed:
Fill'd with the God, enlarged his members
grew,
Thro' all his veins a sudden vigour flew: 250
The blood in brisker tides began to roll,
And Mars himself came rushing on his
soul.
Exhorting loud thro' all the field he strode,
And look'd, and mov'd, Achilles, or a God.
Now Mesthles, Glaucus, Medon he in-
spires,
Now Phorcys, Chromius, and Hippothoüs
fires;
The great Thersilochus like fury found, ⎫
Asteropæus kindled at the sound,   ⎬
And Ennomus, in augury renown'd.   ⎭
' Hear, all ye hosts, and hear, unnumber'd
bands   260
Of neighb'ring nations, or of distant lands !
'T was not for state we summon'd you so
far,
To boast our numbers, and the pomp of
war;
Ye came to fight; a valiant foe to chase,
To save our present and our future race.
For this, our wealth, our products, you en-
joy,
And glean the relics of exhausted Troy.
Now, then, to conquer or to die prepare,
To die or conquer are the terms of war.
Whatever hand shall win Patroclus slain,
Whoe'er shall drag him to the Trojan
train,   271
With Hector's self shall equal honours
claim;
With Hector part the spoil, and share the
fame.'
Fired by his words, the troops dismiss
their fears,
They join, they thicken, they protend thei
spears;
Full on the Greeks they drive in firm array,
And each from Ajax hopes the glorious
prey;
Vain hope ! what numbers shall the field
o'erspread,
What victims perish round the mighty
dead !

Great Ajax mark'd the growing storm
   from far,   280
And thus bespoke his brother of the war:
'Our fatal day, alas! is come, my friend,
And all our wars and glories at an end!
'Tis not this corse alone we guard in vain,
Condemn'd to vultures on the Trojan
   plain;
We too must yield; the same sad fate must
   fall
On thee, on me, perhaps (my friend) on all.
See what a tempest direful Hector spreads,
And lo! it bursts, it thunders on our
   heads!
Call on our Greeks, if any hear the call, 290
The bravest Greeks: this hour demands
   them all.'
   The warrior rais'd his voice, and wide
   around
The field re-echoed the distressful sound:
'Oh Chiefs! oh Princes! to whose hand is
   giv'n
The rule of men; whose glory is from
   Heav'n!
Whom with due honours both Atrides
   grace:
Ye guides and guardians of our Argive
   race!
All, whom this well-known voice shall
   reach from far,
All, whom I see not thro' this cloud of war,
Come all! let gen'rous rage your arms
   employ,   300
And save Patroclus from the dogs of Troy.'
   Oïlean Ajax first the voice obey'd,
Swift was his pace and ready was his aid;
Next him Idomeneus, more slow with age,
And Merion, burning with a hero's rage.
The long-succeeding numbers who can
   name?
But all were Greeks, and eager all for
   fame.
Fierce to the charge great Hector led the
   throng;
Whole Troy, embodied, rush'd with shouts
   along.
Thus, when a mountain billow foams and
   raves,   310
Where some swoln river disembogues his
   waves,
Full in the mouth is stopp'd the rushing
   tide,
The boiling ocean works from side to side,
The river trembles to his utmost shore,
And distant rocks rebellow to the roar.

Nor less resolv'd, the firm Achaian band
With brazen shields in horrid circle stand:
Jove, pouring darkness o'er the mingled
   fight,
Conceals the warriors' shining helms in
   night:
To him the Chief, for whom the hosts con-
   tend,   320
Had liv'd not hateful, for he liv'd a friend:
Dead he protects him with superior care,
Nor dooms his carcass to the birds of air.
   The first attack the Grecians scarce sus-
   tain,
Repuls'd, they yield; the Trojans seize the
   slain:
Then fierce they rally, to revenge led on
By the swift rage of Ajax Telamon
(Ajax, to Peleus' son the second name,
In graceful stature next, and next in fame).
With headlong force the foremost ranks he
   tore: 330
So thro' the thicket bursts the mountain
   boar,
And rudely scatters, far to distance round,
The frighted hunter and the baying hound.
The son of Lethus, brave Pelasgus' heir,
Hippothoüs, dragg'd the carcass thro' the
   war;
The sinewy ancles bored, the feet he bound
With thongs, inserted thro' the double
   wound;
Inevitable Fate o'ertakes the deed;
Doom'd by great Ajax' vengeful lance to
   bleed;
It cleft the helmet's brazen cheeks in
   twain;   340
The shatter'd crest and horsehair strew the
   plain:
With nerves relax'd he tumbles to the
   ground,
The brain comes gushing thro' the ghastly
   wound:
He drops Patroclus' foot, and, o'er him
   spread,
Now lies a sad companion of the dead:
Far from Larissa lies, his native air,
And ill requites his parent's tender care.
Lamented youth! in life's first bloom he
   fell,
Sent by great Ajax to the shades of Hell.
   Once more at Ajax Hector's jav'lin flies;
The Grecian marking as it cut the skies, 351
Shunn'd the descending death, which, hiss-
   ing on,
Stretch'd in the dust the great Iphitus' son,

Schedius the brave, of all the Phocian
  kind
The boldest warrior, and the noblest mind:
In little Panope, for strength renown'd,
He held his seat, and ruled the realms
  around.
Plunged in his throat, the weapon drank
  his blood,
And, deep transpiercing, thro' the shoulder
  stood;
In clanging arms the hero fell, and all 360
The fields resounded with his weighty fall.
  Phorcys, as slain Hippothous he defends,
The Telamonian lance his belly rends;
The hollow armour burst before the stroke,
And thro' the wound the rushing entrails
  broke.
In strong convulsions panting on the sands
He lies, and grasps the dust with dying
  hands.
  Struck at the sight, recede the Trojan
  train:
The shouting Argives strip the heroes
  slain.
And now had Troy, by Greece compell'd
  to yield, 370
Fled to her ramparts, and resign'd the field;
Greece, in her native fortitude elate,
With Jove averse, had turn'd the scale of
  Fate;
But Phœbus urged Æneas to the fight;
He seem'd like aged Periphas to sight
(A herald in Anchises' love grown old,
Revered for prudence, and, with prudence,
  bold).
  Thus he: 'What methods yet, oh Chief!
  remain,
To save your Troy, tho' Heav'n its fall
  ordain?
There have been heroes, who, by virtuous
  care, 380
By valour, numbers, and by arts of war,
Have forc'd the Powers to spare a sinking
  state,
And gain'd at length the glorious odds of
  Fate.
But you, when Fortune smiles, when Jove
  declares
His partial favour, and assists your wars,
Your shameful efforts 'gainst yourselves
  employ,
And force th' unwilling God to ruin Troy.'
  Æneas, thro' the form assumed, descries
The power conceal'd, and thus to Hector
  cries:

'Oh lasting shame! to our own fears a
  prey, 390
We seek our ramparts, and desert the day.
A God (nor is he less) my bosom warms,
And tells me Jove asserts the Trojan
  arms.'
  He spoke, and foremost to the combat
  flew;
The bold example all his hosts pursue.
Then first Leocritus beneath him bled,
In vain beloved by valiant Lycomede;
Who view'd his fall, and, grieving at the
  chance,
Swift to revenge it, sent his angry lance:
The whirling lance, with vig'rous force ad-
  dress'd, 400
Descends, and pants in Apisaon's breast:
From rich Pæonia's vales the warrior came;
Next thee, Asteropeus! in place and fame,
Asteropeus with grief beheld the slain,
And rush'd to combat, but he rush'd in vain:
Indissolubly firm, around the dead,
Rank within rank, on buckler buckler
  spread,
And hemm'd with bristled spears, the Gre-
  cians stood;
A brazen bulwark, and an iron wood. 409
Great Ajax eyes them with incessant care,
And in an orb contracts the crowded war,
Close in their ranks commands to fight or
  fall,
And stands the centre and the soul of all:
Fix'd on the spot they war, and wounded,
  wound;
A sanguine torrent steeps the reeking
  ground;
On heaps the Greeks, on heaps the Trojans
  bled,
And, thick'ning round them, rise the hills
  of dead.
  Greece, in close order and collected
  might,
Yet suffers least, and sways the wav'ring
  fight;
Fierce as conflicting fires, the combat burns,
And now it rises, now it sinks, by turns. 421
In one thick darkness all the fight was lost:
The sun, the moon, and all th' ethereal
  host,
Seem'd as extinct; day ravish'd from their
  eyes,
And all Heav'n's splendours blotted from
  the skies.
Such o'er Patroclus' body hung the night,
The rest in sunshine fought, and open light:

Unclouded there, th' aërial azure spread,
No vapour rested on the mountain's head,
The golden sun pour'd forth a stronger
ray, 430
And all the broad expansion flamed with
day.
Dispers'd around the plain, by fits they
fight,
And here, and there, their scatter'd arrows
light:
But death and darkness o'er the carcass
spread,
There burn'd the war, and there the mighty
bled.
Meanwhile the sons of Nestor, in the rear
(Their fellows routed), toss the distant
spear,
And skirmish wide: so Nestor gave com-
mand,
When from the ships he sent the Pylian
band.
The youthful brothers thus for fame con-
tend, 440
Nor knew the fortune of Achilles' friend;
In thought they view'd him still, with mar-
tial joy,
Glorious in arms, and dealing deaths to
Troy.
But round the corse the heroes pant for
breath,
And thick and heavy grows the work of
death:
O'erlabour'd now, with dust, and sweat,
and gore,
Their knees, their legs, their feet, are cov-
er'd o'er;
Drops follow drops, the clouds on clouds
arise,
And carnage clogs their hands, and dark-
ness fills their eyes.
As when a slaughter'd bull's yet reeking
hide, 450
Strain'd with full force, and tugg'd from
side to side,
The brawny curriers stretch; and labour
o'er
Th' extended surface, drunk with fat and
gore;
So tugging round the corse both armies
stood;
The mangled body bathed in sweat and
blood:
While Greeks and Ilians equal strength
employ,
Now to the ships to force it, now to Troy.

Not Pallas' self, her breast when fury
warms,
Nor he whose anger sets the world in arms,
Could blame this scene; such rage, such
horror, reign'd; 460
Such Jove to honour the great dead or-
dain'd.
Achilles in his ships at distance lay,
Nor knew the fatal fortune of the day;
He, yet unconscious of Patroclus' fall,
In dust extended under Ilion's wall,
Expects him glorious from the conquer'd
plain,
And for his wish'd return prepares in vain;
Tho' well he knew, to make proud Ilion
bend,
Was more than Heav'n had destin'd to his
friend, 469
Perhaps to him: this Thetis had reveal'd;
The rest, in pity to her son, conceal'd.
Still raged the conflict round the hero
dead,
And heaps on heaps by mutual wounds
they bled.
'Curs'd be the man' (ev'n private Greeks
would say)
'Who dares desert this well-disputed day!
First may the cleaving earth before our
eyes
Gape wide, and drink our blood for sacri-
fice!
First perish all, ere haughty Troy shall
boast
We lost Patroclus, and our glory lost.'
Thus they. While with one voice the
Trojans said, 480
'Grant this day, Jove! or heap us on the
dead!'
Then clash their sounding arms; the
clangors rise,
And shake the brazen concave of the skies.
Meantime, at distance from the scene of
blood,
The pensive steeds of great Achilles stood;
Their godlike master slain before their eyes,
They wept, and shared in human miseries.
In vain Automedon now shakes the rein,
Now plies the lash, and soothes and threats
in vain; 489
Nor to the fight, nor Hellespont they go;
Restive they stood, and obstinate in woe:
Still as a tombstone, never to be mov'd,
On some good man, or woman unreprov'd,
Lays its eternal weight; or fix'd as stands
A marble courser by the sculptor's hands

Placed on the hero's grave. Along their face
The big round drops cours'd down with silent pace,
Conglobing on the dust. Their manes, that late
Circled their arched necks, and waved in state,
Trail'd on the dust beneath the yoke were spread, 500
And prone to earth was hung their languid head:
Nor Jove disdain'd to cast a pitying look,
While thus relenting to the steeds he spoke:
'Unhappy coursers of immortal strain!
Exempt from age, and deathless now in vain;
Did we your race on mortal man bestow,
Only, alas! to share in mortal woe?
For ah! what is there, of inferior birth,
That breathes or creeps upon the dust of earth;
What wretched creature of what wretched kind, 510
Than man more weak, calamitous, and blind?
A miserable race! but cease to mourn:
For not by you shall Priam's son be borne
High on the splendid car: one glorious prize
He rashly boasts; the rest our will denies.
Ourself will swiftness to your nerves impart,
Ourself with rising spirits swell your heart.
Automedon your rapid flight shall bear
Safe to the navy thro' the storm of war.
For yet 't is given to Troy, to ravage o'er
The field, and spread her slaughters to the shore; 521
The sun shall see her conquer, till his fall
With sacred darkness shades the face of all.'
He said; and breathing in th' immortal horse
Excessive spirit, urged them to the course;
From their high manes they shake the dust, and bear
The kindling chariot thro' the parted war.
So flies a vulture thro' the clam'rous train
Of geese, that scream, and scatter round the plain.
From danger now with swiftest speed they flew, 530
And now to conquest with like speed pursue;

Sole in the seat the charioteer remains,
Now plies the jav'lin, now directs the reins:
Him brave Alcimedon beheld distress'd,
Approach'd the chariot, and the Chief address'd:
'What God provokes thee, rashly thus to dare,
Alone, unaided, in the thickest war?
Alas! thy friend is slain, and Hector wields
Achilles' arms triumphant in the fields.'
'In happy time (the charioteer replies),
The bold Alcimedon now greets my eyes;
No Greek like him the heav'nly steeds restrains, 542
Or holds their fury in suspended reins:
Patroclus, while he liv'd, their rage could tame,
But now Patroclus is an empty name!
To thee I yield the seat, to thee resign
The ruling charge: the task of fight be mine.'
He said. Alcimedon, with active heat,
Snatches the reins, and vaults into the seat.
His friend descends. The Chief of Troy descried, 550
And call'd Æneas fighting near his side:
'Lo, to my sight beyond our hope restor'd,
Achilles' car, deserted of its lord!
The glorious steeds our ready arms invite,
Scarce their weak drivers guide them thro' the fight:
Can such opponents stand, when we assail?
Unite thy force, my friend, and we prevail.'
The son of Venus to the counsel yields:
Then o'er their backs they spread their solid shields;
With brass refulgent the broad surface shin'd, 560
And thick bull-hides the spacious concave lin'd.
Them Chromius follows, Aretus succeeds,
Each hopes the conquest of the lofty steeds;
In vain, brave youths, with glorious hopes ye burn,
In vain advance! not fated to return.
Unmov'd, Automedon attends the fight,
Implores th' Eternal, and collects his might.
Then, turning to his friend, with dauntless mind:
'Oh keep the foaming coursers close behind!
Full on my shoulders let their nostrils blow, 570
For hard the fight, determin'd is the foe;

'T is Hector comes; and when he seeks the
prize,
War knows no mean: he wins it, or he dies.'
  Then thro' the field he sends his voice
    aloud,
And calls th' Ajaces from the warring
    crowd,
With great Atrides. 'Hither turn' (he
    said),
'Turn where distress demands immediate
    aid;
The dead, encircled by his friends, forego,
And save the living from a fiercer foe.
Unhelp'd we stand, unequal to engage 580
The force of Hector and Æneas' rage:
Yet mighty as they are, my force to prove
Is only mine; th' event belongs to Jove.'
  He spoke, and high the sounding jav'lin
    flung,
Which pass'd the shield of Aretus the
    young;
It pierc'd his belt, emboss'd with curious
    art;
Then in the lower belly stuck the dart.
As when a pond'rous axe, descending full,
Cleaves the broad forehead of some brawny
    bull;
Struck 'twixt the horns, he springs with
    many a bound, 590
Then tumbling rolls enormous on the
    ground:
Thus fell the youth; the air his soul re-
    ceiv'd,
And the spear trembled as his entrails
    heav'd.
  Now at Automedon the Trojan foe
Discharged his lance; the meditated blow,
Stooping, he shunn'd; the jav'lin idly fled,
And hiss'd innoxious o'er the hero's head:
Deep rooted in the ground, the forceful
    spear
In long vibrations spent its fury there.
With clashing falchions now the Chiefs had
    closed, 600
But each brave Ajax heard, and inter-
    posed;
Nor longer Hector with his Trojans stood,
But left their slain companion in his blood:
His arms Automedon divests, and cries,
'Accept, Patroclus, this mean sacrifice.
Thus have I soothed my griefs, and thus
    have paid,
Poor as it is, some off'ring to thy shade.'
  So looks the lion o'er a mangled boar,
All grim with rage, and horrible with gore:

High on the chariot at one bound he
    sprung, 610
And o'er his seat the bloody trophies hung.
  And now Minerva, from the realms of
    air,
Descends impetuous, and renews the war;
For, pleas'd at length the Grecian arms to
    aid,
The Lord of Thunders sent the Blue-eyed
    Maid.
As when high Jove, denouncing future
    woe,
O'er the dark clouds extends his purple
    bow
(In sign of tempests from the troubled air,
Or, from the rage of man, destructive
    war);
The drooping cattle dread th' impending
    skies, 620
And from his half-till'd field the lab'rer
    flies:
In such a form the Goddess round her
    drew
A livid cloud, and to the battle flew.
Assuming Phœnix' shape, on earth she
    falls,
And in his well-known voice to Sparta
    calls:
'And lies Achilles' friend, belov'd by all,
A prey to dogs beneath the Trojan wall ?
What shame to Greece for future times to
    tell,
To thee the greatest, in whose cause he
    fell ! '
  'O Chief, oh Father ! ' (Atreus' son re-
    plies) 630
'O full of days ! by long experience wise !
What more desires my soul, than here,
    unmov'd,
To guard the body of the man I lov'd ?
Ah would Minerva send me strength to
    rear
This wearied arm, and ward the storm of
    war !
But Hector, like the rage of fire, we dread,
And Jove's own glories blaze around his
    head.'
  Pleas'd to be first of all the Powers ad-
    dress'd,
She breathes new vigour in her hero's
    breast,
And fills with keen revenge, with fell de-
    spite, 640
Desire of blood, and rage, and lust of
    fight.

So burns the vengeful hornet (soul all
  o'er),
Repuls'd in vain, and thirsty still of gore
(Bold son of air and heat), on angry wings
Untamed, untired, he turns, attacks, and
  stings:
Fired with like ardour fierce Atrides flew,
And sent his soul with every lance he
  threw.
There stood a Trojan, not unknown to
  Fame,
Eëtion's son, and Podes was his name;
With riches honour'd, and with courage
  bless'd, 650
By Hector lov'd, his comrade, and his
  guest;
Thro' his broad belt the spear a passage
  found,
And, pond'rous as he falls, his arms re-
  sound.
Sudden at Hector's side Apollo stood,
Like Phænops, Asius' son, appear'd the
  God
(Asius the great, who held his wealthy
  reign
In fair Abydos, by the rolling main).
'Oh Prince' (he cried), 'oh foremost
  once in Fame!
What Grecian now shall tremble at thy
  name?
Dost thou at length to Menelaüs yield? 660
A Chief, once thought no terror of the
  field!
Yet singly, now, the long-disputed prize
He bears victorious, while our army flies.
By the same arm illustrious Podes bled,
The friend of Hector, unrevenged, is
  dead!'
This heard, o'er Hector spreads a cloud of
  woe,
Rage lifts his lance, and drives him on the
  foe.
But now th' Eternal shook his sable
  shield,
That shaded Ide, and all the subject field,
Beneath its ample verge.   A rolling
  cloud 670
Involv'd the mount, the thunder roar'd
  aloud:
Th' affrighted hills from their foundations
  nod,
And blaze beneath the lightnings of the
  God:
At one regard of his all-seeing eye,
The vanquish'd triumph, and the victors fly.

Then trembled Greece: the flight Pene-
  leus led;
For, as the brave Bœotian turn'd his head
To face the foe, Polydamas drew near,
And razed his shoulder with a shorten'd
  spear: 679
By Hector wounded, Leitus quits the plain,⎫
Pierc'd thro' the wrist; and, raging with ⎬
  the pain, ⎪
Grasps his once formidable lance in vain. ⎭
  As Hector follow'd, Idomen address'd
The flaming jav'lin to his manly breast;
The brittle point before his corslet yields;
Exulting Troy with clamour fills the fields:
High on his chariot as the Cretan stood,
The son of Priam whirl'd the missive
  wood:
But, erring from its aim, th' impetuous
  spear
Struck to the dust the squire and chari-
  oteer 690
Of martial Merion: Cœranus his name,
Who left fair Lyctus for the fields of fame.
On foot bold Merion fought; and now, laid
  low,
Had graced the triumphs of his Trojan
  foe;
But the brave squire the ready coursers
  brought,
And with his life his master's safety bought.
Between his cheek and ear the weapon
  went,
The teeth it shatter'd, and the tongue it
  rent.
Prone from the seat he tumbles to the
  plain;
His dying hand forgets the falling rein: 700
This Merion reaches, bending from the car,
And urges to desert the hopeless war;
Idomeneus consents; the lash applies;
And the swift chariot to the navy flies.
  Nor Ajax less the will of Heav'n de-
  scried,
And conquest shifting to the Trojan side,
Turn'd by the hand of Jove.   Then thus
  begun,
To Atreus' seed, the godlike Telamon:
'Alas! who sees not Jove's almighty
  hand 709
Transfers the glory to the Trojan band!
Whether the weak or strong discharge the
  dart,
He guides each arrow to a Grecian heart:
Not so our spears: incessant tho' they rain,
He suffers ev'ry lance to fall in vain.

Deserted of the God, yet let us try
What human strength and prudence can
  supply;
If yet this honour'd corse, in triumph
  borne,
May glad the fleets that hope not our re-
  turn,
Who tremble yet, scarce rescued from their
  fates,
And still hear Hector thund'ring at their
  gates.   720
Some hero too must be despatch'd to bear
The mournful message to Pelides' ear;
For sure he knows not, distant on the
  shore,
His friend, his lov'd Patroclus, is no more.
But such a Chief I spy not thro' the host:
The men, the steeds, the armies, all are
  lost
In gen'ral darkness: Lord of earth and
  air !
Oh King ! oh Father ! hear my humble
  prayer :
Dispel this cloud, the light of Heav'n re-
  store ;
Give me to see, and Ajax asks no more: 730
If Greece must perish, we thy will obey,
But let us perish in the face of day ! '
  With tears the Hero spoke, and at his
  prayer
The God relenting, clear'd the clouded air;
Forth burst the sun with all-enlight'ning
  ray;
The blaze of armour flash'd against the day.
' Now, now, Atrides ! cast around thy
  sight,
If yet Antilochus survives the fight,
Let him to great Achilles' ear convey   739
The fatal news.' Atrides hastes away.
  So turns the lion from the nightly fold,
Tho' high in courage, and with hunger
  bold,
Long gall'd by herdsmen, and long vex'd
  by hounds,
Stiff with fatigue, and fretted sore with
  wounds;
The darts fly round him from a hundred
  hands,
And the red terrors of the blazing brands:
Till late, reluctant, at the dawn of day
Sour he departs, and quits th' untasted
  prey.
So mov'd Atrides from his dangerous place,
With weary limbs, but with unwilling
  pace;   750

The foe, he fear'd, might yet Patroclus
  gain,
And much admonish'd, much adjur'd his
  train:
' Oh, guard these relics to your charge
  consign'd,
And bear the merits of the dead in mind;
How skill'd he was in each obliging art;
The mildest manners, and the gentlest
  heart:
He was, alas ! but Fate decreed his end,
In death a hero, as in life a friend ! '
  So parts the Chief, from rank to rank he
  flew,
And round on all sides sent his piercing
  view.   760
As the bold bird, endued with sharpest
  eye
Of all that wing the mid aërial sky,
The sacred eagle, from his walks above
Looks down, and sees the distant thicket
  move;
Then stoops, and sousing on the quiv'ring
  hare,
Snatches his life amid the clouds of air:
Not with less quickness his exerted sight
Pass'd this and that way, thro' the ranks of
  fight;
Till on the left the Chief he sought, he
  found,
Cheering his men, and spreading deaths
  around.   770
  To him the King: ' Belov'd of Jove !
  draw near,
For sadder tidings never touch'd thy ear.
Thy eyes have witness'd what a fatal turn !
How Ilion triumphs, and th' Achaians
  mourn.
This is not all: Patroclus, on the shore
Now pale and dead, shall succour Greece
  no more.
Fly to the fleet, this instant fly, and tell
The sad Achilles how his lov'd one fell:
He too may haste the naked corse to gain;
The arms are Hector's, who despoil'd the
  slain.'   780
  The youthful warrior heard with silent
  woe,
From his fair eyes the tears began to flow;
Big with the mighty grief, he strove to say
What sorrow dictates, but no word found
  way.
To brave Laodocus his arms he flung,
Who, near him wheeling, drove his steeds
  along;

Then ran, the mournful message to impart,
With tearful eyes, and with dejected heart.
Swift fled the youth: nor Menelaüs
 stands
(Tho' sore distress'd) to aid the Pylian
 bands; 790
But bids bold Thrasymede those troops
 sustain;
Himself returns to his Patroclus slain.
'Gone is Antilochus' (the hero said),
'But hope not, warriors, for Achilles' aid:
Tho' fierce his rage, unbounded be his
 woe,
Unarm'd he fights not with the Trojan
 foe.
'T is in our hands alone our hopes remain,
'T is our own vigour must the dead regain;
And save ourselves, while with impetuous
 hate
Troy pours along, and this way rolls our
 fate.' 800
''T is well' (said Ajax); 'be it then thy
 care,
With Merion's aid, the weighty corse to
 rear;
Myself and my bold brother will sustain
The shock of Hector and his charging
 train:
Nor fear we armies, fighting side by side;
What Troy can dare, we have already
 tried,
Have tried it, and have stood.' The hero
 said:
High from the ground the warriors heave
 the dead.
A gen'ral clamour rises at the sight:
Loud shout the Trojans, and renew the
 fight; 810
Not fiercer rush along the gloomy wood,
With rage insatiate, and with thirst of
 blood,
Voracious hounds, that many a length be-
 fore
Their furious hunters, drive the wounded
 boar;
But if the savage turns his glaring eye,
They howl aloof, and round the forest fly.
Thus on retreating Greece the Trojans
 pour,
Wave their thick falchions, and their jav'-
 lins shower:
But, Ajax turning, to their fears they
 yield,
All pale they tremble, and forsake the
 field. 820

While thus aloft the hero's corse they
 bear,
Behind them rages all the storm of war;
Confusion, tumult, horror, o'er the throng
Of men, steeds, chariots, urged the rout
 along:
Less fierce the winds with rising flames
 conspire,
To whelm some city under waves of fire;
Now sink in gloomy clouds the proud
 abodes;
Now crack the blazing temples of the Gods;
The rumbling torrent thro' the ruin rolls,
And sheets of smoke mount heavy to the
 poles. 830
The heroes sweat beneath their honour'd
 load:
As when two mules, along the rugged road,
From the steep mountain with exerted
 strength
Drag some vast beam, or mast's unwieldly
 length;
Inly they groan, big drops of sweat distil,
Th' enormous timber lumb'ring down the
 hill;
So these: Behind, the bulk of Ajax stands,
And breaks the torrent of the rushing
 bands.
Thus when a river, swell'd with sudden
 rains,
Spreads his broad waters o'er the level
 plains, 840
Some interposing hill the stream divides,
And breaks its force, and turns the wind-
 ing tides.
Still close they follow, close the rear en-
 gage;
Æneas storms, and Hector foams with rage:
While Greece a heavy thick retreat main-
 tains,
Wedg'd in one body, like a flight of cranes,
That shriek incessant while the falcon, hung
High on pois'd pinions, threats their callow
 young.
So from the Trojan Chiefs the Grecians
 fly, 849
Such the wild terror, and the mingled cry;
Within, without the trench, and all the
 way,
Strew'd in bright heaps, their arms and
 armour lay;
Such horror Jove impress'd ! yet still pro-
 ceeds
The work of death, and still the battle
 bleeds.

BOOK XVIII

THE GRIEF OF ACHILLES, AND NEW AR-
MOUR MADE HIM BY VULCAN

THE ARGUMENT

The news of the death of Patroclus is brought
to Achilles by Antilochus. Thetis, hearing
his lamentations, comes with all her sea-
nymphs to comfort him. The speeches of
the mother and son on this occasion. Iris
appears to Achilles by the command of Juno,
and orders him to show himself at the head
of the intrenchments. The sight of him
turns the fortune of the day, and the body
of Patroclus is carried off by the Greeks.
The Trojans call a council, where Hector
and Polydamas disagree in their opinions;
but the advice of the former prevails, to remain encamped in the field. The grief of
Achilles over the body of Patroclus.
Thetis goes to the palace of Vulcan, to obtain
new arms for her son. The description of
the wonderful works of Vulcan ; and, lastly,
that noble one of the shield of Achilles.
The latter part of the nine-and-twentieth day,
and the night ensuing, take up this book.
The scene is at Achilles' tent on the sea-
shore, from whence it changes to the palace
of Vulcan.

THUS like the rage of fire the combat
        burns,
And now it rises, now it sinks, by turns.
Meanwhile, where Hellespont's broad
        waters flow,
Stood Nestor's son, the messenger of woe.
There sat Achilles, shaded by his sails,
On hoisted yards extended to the gales;
Pensive he sat; for all that Fate design'd
Rose in sad prospect to his boding mind.
Thus to his soul he said: ' Ah what con-
        strains
The Greeks, late victors, now to quit the
        plains ?   10
Is this the day, which Heav'n so long ago
Ordain'd, to sink me with the weight of woe
(So Thetis warn'd), when, by a Trojan
        hand,
The bravest of the Myrmidonian band
Should lose the light ? Fulfill'd is that de-
        cree ?
Fall'n is the warrior, and Patroclus he ?
In vain I charged him soon to quit the
        plain,
And warn'd to shun Hectorean force in
        vain ! '

Thus while he thinks, Antilochus ap-
        pears,
And tells the melancholy tale with tears: 20
' Sad tidings, son of Peleus ! thou must
        hear;
And wretched I, th' unwilling messenger !
Dead is Patroclus ! for his corse they
        fight;
His naked corse: his arms are Hector's
        right.'
A sudden horror shot thro' all the Chief,
And wrapt his senses in the cloud of grief;
Cast on the ground, with furious hand he
        spread
The scorching ashes o'er his graceful head;
His purple garments, and his golden hairs,
Those he deforms with dust, and these he
        tears: 30
On the hard soil his groaning breast he
        threw,
And roll'd and grovell'd, as to earth he
        grew.
The virgin captives, with disorder'd charms
(Won by his own, or by Patroclus' arms),
Rush'd from the tents with cries; and,
        gath'ring round,
Beat their white breasts, and fainted on the
        ground :
While Nestor's son sustains a manlier part,
And mourns the warrior with a warrior's
        heart;
Hangs on his arms, amidst his frantic woe,
And oft prevents the meditated blow.   40
    Far in the deep abysses of the main,
With hoary Nereus, and the wat'ry train,
The Mother-Goddess from her crystal
        throne
Heard his loud cries, and answered groan
        for groan.
The circling Nereids with their mistress
        weep,
And all the sea-green Sisters of the Deep.
Thalia, Glauce (every wat'ry name),
Nesæa mild, and silver Spio came:
Cymothoë and Cymodoce were nigh,
And the blue languish of soft Alia's eye: 50
Their locks Actæa and Limnoria rear,
Then Proto, Doris, Panope appear,
Thoa, Pherusa, Doto, Melita;
Agave gentle, and Amphithoë gay;
Next Callianira, Callianassa shew
Their sister looks; Dexamene the slow,
And swift Dynamene, now cut the tides:
Iæra now the verdant wave divides:
Nemertes with Apseudes lifts the head,

Bright Galatea quits her pearly bed;   60
These Orythia, Clymene, attend,
Mæra, Amphinome, the train extend,
And black Janira, and Janassa fair,
And Amatheia with her amber hair.
All these, and all that deep in ocean held
Their sacred seats, the glimm'ring grotto
   fill'd;
Each beat her iv'ry breast with silent woe,
Till Thetis' sorrows thus began to flow:
   'Hear me, and judge, ye Sisters of the
     Main !
How just a cause has Thetis to com-
   plain !   70
How wretched, were I mortal, were my
   fate !
How more than wretched in th' immortal
   state !
Sprung from my bed a godlike Hero came,
The bravest far that ever bore the name;
Like some fair olive, by my careful hand
He grew, he flourish'd, and adorn'd the
   land.
To Troy I sent him; but the Fates ordain
He never, never must return again.
So short a space the light of Heav'n to
   view,
So short, alas ! and fill'd with anguish
   too.   80
Hear how his sorrows echo thro' the shore!
I cannot ease them, but I must deplore ;
I go at least to bear a tender part,
And mourn my lov'd one with a mother's
   heart.'
   She said, and left the caverns of the
   main.
All bathed in tears, the melancholy train
Attend her way. Wide-opening part the
   tides,
While the long pomp the silver wave
   divides,
Approaching now, they touch'd the Trojan
   land;
Then, two by two, ascended up the strand.
Th' immortal mother, standing close be-
   side   91
Her mournful offspring, to his sighs re-
   plied;
Along the coast their mingled clamours
   ran,
And thus the Silver-footed Dame began:
   'Why mourns my son ? thy late-pre-
     ferr'd request
The God has granted, and the Greeks dis-
   tress'd:

Why mourns my son ? thy anguish let me
   share,
Reveal the cause, and trust a parent's
   care.'
He, deeply groaning, 'To this cureless
   grief
Not ev'n the Thund'rer's favour brings re-
   lief.   100
Patroclus — Ah ! say, Goddess, can I
   boast
A pleasure now ? Revenge itself is lost;
Patroclus, lov'd of all my martial train,
Beyond mankind, beyond myself, is slain !
Lost are those arms the Gods themselves
   bestow'd
On Peleus; Hector bears the glorious load.
Curs'd be that day, when all the powers
   above
Thy charms submitted to a mortal love:
Oh hadst thou still, a sister of the main,
Pursued the pleasures of the wat'ry reign;
And happier Peleus, less ambitious, led   111
A mortal beauty to his equal bed !
Ere the sad fruit of thy unhappy womb
Had caus'd such sorrows past, and woes to
   come.
For soon, alas ! that wretched offspring
   slain,
New woes, new sorrows, shall create again.
'T is not in Fate th' alternate now to give;
Patroclus dead, Achilles hates to live.
Let me revenge it on proud Hector's heart,
Let his last spirit smoke upon my dart; 120
On these conditions will I breathe: till
   then,
I blush to walk among the race of men.'
   A flood of tears, at this, the Goddess
   shed:
'Ah then, I see thee dying, see thee dead !
When Hector falls, thou diest.' — 'Let
   Hector die,
And let me fall !' (Achilles made reply.)
'Far lies Patroclus from his native plain;
He fell, and, falling, wish'd my aid in
   vain.
Ah then, since from this miserable day
I cast all hope of my return away;   130
Since, unrevenged, a hundred ghosts de-
   mand
The fate of Hector from Achilles' hand;
Since here, for brutal courage far re-
   nown'd,
I live an idle burden to the ground
(Others in council famed for nobler skill,
More useful to preserve than I to kill);

Let me — But oh ! ye gracious Powers
above !
Wrath and revenge from men and Gods
remove:
Far, far too dear to ev'ry mortal breast,
Sweet to the soul, as honey to the taste; 140
Gath'ring like vapours of a noxious kind
From fiery blood, and dark'ning all the
mind.
Me Agamemnon urged to deadly hate;
'T is past — I quell it; I resign to Fate.
Yes — I will meet the murd'rer of my
friend,
Or (if the Gods ordain it) meet my end.
The stroke of Fate the bravest cannot shun:
The great Alcides, Jove's unequall'd son,
To Juno's hate at length resign'd his
breath,
And sunk the victim of all-conquering
death. 150
So shall Achilles fall ! stretch'd pale and
dead,
No more the Grecian hope, or Trojan
dread !
Let me, this instant, rush into the fields,
And reap what glory life's short harvest
yields.
Shall I not force some widow'd dame to
tear,
With frantic hands, her long dishevell'd
hair ?
Shall I not force her breast to heave with
sighs,
And the soft tears to trickle from her
eyes ?
Yes, I shall give the fair those mournful
charms —
In vain you hold me — Hence ! my arms,
my arms ! 160
Soon shall the sanguine torrent spread so
wide,
That all shall know Achilles swells the tide.'
' My son ' (cœrulean Thetis made reply,
To Fate submitting with a secret sigh),
' The host to succour and thy friends to save,
Is worthy thee; the duty of the brave.
But canst thou, naked, issue to the plains ?
Thy radiant arms the Trojan foe detains.
Insulting Hector bears the spoils on high,
But vainly glories, for his fate is nigh. 170
Yet, yet, awhile, thy gen'rous ardour stay,
Assured I meet thee at the dawn of day,
Charged with refulgent arms (a glorious
load),
Vulcanian arms, the labour of a God.'

Then turning to the Daughters of the
Main,
The Goddess thus dismiss'd her azure train:
' Ye sister Nereids ! to your deeps de-
scend;
Haste, and our father's sacred seat attend;
I go to find the architect divine,
Where vast Olympus' starry summits
shine: 180
So tell our hoary Sire.' This charge she
gave:
The sea-green Sisters plunge beneath the
wave:
Thetis once more ascends the blest abodes,
And treads the brazen threshold of the
Gods.
And now the Greeks, from furious Hec-
tor's force,
Urge to broad Hellespont their headlong
course:
Nor yet their Chiefs Patroclus' body bore
Safe thro' the tempest, to the tented shore.
The horse, the foot, with equal fury join'd,
Pour'd on the rear, and thunder'd close be-
hind; 190
And like a flame thro' fields of ripen'd corn,
The rage of Hector o'er the ranks was
borne.
Thrice the slain hero by the foot he drew:
Thrice to the skies the Trojan clamours
flew
As oft th' Ajaces his assault sustain;
But check'd, he turns; repuls'd, attacks
again.
With fiercer shouts his ling'ring troops he
fires,
Nor yields a step, nor from his post re-
tires:
So watchful shepherds strive to force, in
vain,
The hungry lion from a carcass slain. 200
Ev'n yet, Patroclus had he borne away,
And all the glories of th' extended day;
Had not high Juno, from the realms of air,
Secret despatch'd her trusty messenger,
The various Goddess of the Showery Bow,
Shot in a whirlwind to the shore below;
To great Achilles at his ships she came,
And thus began the Many-coloured Dame:
' Rise, son of Peleus ! rise, divinely brave!
Assist the combat, and Patroclus save: 210
For him the slaughter to the fleet they
spread,
And fall with mutual wounds around the
dead.

To drag him back to Troy the foe con-
tends;
Nor with his death the rage of Hector
ends;
A prey to dogs he dooms the corse to lie,
And marks the place to fix his head on
high.
Rise, and prevent (if yet you think of fame)
Thy friend's disgrace; thy own eternal
shame !'
'Who sends thee, Goddess ! from th'
ethereal skies ? '
Achilles thus: and Iris thus replies: 220
'I come, Pelides, from the Queen of Jove,
Th' immortal Empress of the realms above:
Unknown to him who sits remote on high,
Unknown to all the Synod of the Sky.'
'Thou com'st in vain,' he cries (with fury
warm'd),
'Arms I have none, and can I fight un-
arm'd ?
Unwilling as I am, of force I stay,
Till Thetis bring me at the dawn of day
Vulcanian arms: what other can I wield,
Except the mighty Telamonian shield ?   230
That, in my friend's defence, has Ajax
spread,
While his strong lance around him heaps
the dead:
The gallant Chief defends Menœtius' son,
And does what his Achilles should have
done.'
'Thy want of arms' (said Iris) 'well we
know;
But, tho' unarm'd, yet, clad in terrors, go !
Let but Achilles o'er yon trench appear,
Proud Troy shall tremble, and consent to
fear;
Greece from one glance of that tremendous
eye   239
Shall take new courage, and disdain to fly.'
  She spoke, and pass'd in air. The hero
rose:
Her ægis Pallas o'er his shoulder throws:
Around his brows a golden cloud she spread;
A stream of glory flamed above his head.
As when from some beleaguer'd town arise
The smokes, high curling to the shaded
skies
(Seen from some island, o'er the main afar,
When men distress'd hang out the sign of
war):
Soon as the sun in ocean hides his rays,
Thick on the hills the flaming beacons
blaze;   250

With long-projected beams the seas are
bright,
And Heav'n's high arch reflects the ruddy
light:
So from Achilles' head the splendours rise,
Reflecting blaze on blaze, against the skies.
Forth march'd the Chief, and, distant from
the crowd,
High on the rampart rais'd his voice aloud;
With her own shout Minerva swells the
sound;
Troy starts astonish'd, and the shores re-
bound.
As the loud trumpet's brazen mouth from far
With shrilling clangour sounds th' alarm
of war,   260
Struck from the walls, the echoes float on
high,
And the round bulwarks and thick towers
reply;
So high his brazen voice the hero rear'd:
Hosts dropt their arms, and trembled as
they heard;
And back the chariots roll, and coursers
bound,
And steeds and men lie mingled on the
ground.
Aghast they see the living lightnings play,
And turn their eye-balls from the flashing
ray.
Thrice from the trench his dreadful voice
he raised:
And thrice they fled, confounded and
amazed.   270
Twelve in the tumult wedg'd, untimely
rush'd
On their own spears, by their own chariots
crush'd;
While, shielded from the darts, the Greeks
obtain
The long-contended carcass of the slain.
A lofty bier the breathless warrior bears:
Around, his sad companions melt in tears.
But chief Achilles, bending down his head,
Pours unavailing sorrows o'er the dead,
Whom late, triumphant with his steeds and
car,
He sent refulgent to the Field of War   280
(Unhappy change !): now senseless, pale,
he found,
Stretch'd forth. and gash'd with many a
gaping wound.
  Meantime, unwearied with his heav'nly
way,
In ocean's waves th' unwilling light of day

Quench'd his red orb, at Juno's high command,
And from their labours eas'd th' Achaian band.
The frighted Trojans (panting from the war,
Their steeds unharness'd from the weary car)
A sudden council call'd : each Chief appear'd
In haste, and standing ; for to sit they fear'd. 290
'T was now no season for prolong'd debate;
They saw Achilles, and in him their fate.
Silent they stood: Polydamas at last,
Skill'd to discern the future by the past,
The son of Panthus, thus express'd his fears
(The friend of Hector, and of equal years:
The self-same night to both a being gave,
One wise in council, one in action brave):
  ' In free debate, my friends, your sentence speak:
For me, I move, before the morning break, 300
To raise our camp: too dangerous here our post,
Far from Troy walls, and on a naked coast.
I deem'd not Greece so dreadful, while engaged
In mutual feuds her King and Hero raged;
Then, while we hoped our armies might prevail,
We boldly camp'd beside a thousand sail.
I dread Pelides now: his rage of mind
Not long continues to the shores confin'd,
Nor to the fields, where long in equal fray
Contending nations won and lost the day; 310
For Troy, for Troy, shall henceforth be the strife,
And the hard contest, not for Fame, but Life.
Haste then to Ilion, while the fav'ring night
Detains those terrors, keeps that arm from fight;
If but the morrow's sun behold us here,
That arm, those terrors, we shall feel, not fear;
And hearts that now disdain, shall leap with joy,
If Heav'n permits them then to enter Troy.
Let not my fatal prophecy be true,
Nor what I tremble but to think, ensue. 320

Whatever be our fate, yet let us try
What force of thought and reason can supply;
Let us on council for our guard depend;
The town, her gates and bulwarks shall defend.
When morning dawns, our well-appointed powers,
Array'd in arms, shall line the lofty towers.
Let the fierce hero then, when fury calls,
Vent his mad vengeance on our rocky walls,
Or fetch a thousand circles round the plain,
Till his spent coursers seek the fleet again: 330
So may his rage be tired, and labour'd down;
And dogs shall tear him ere he sack the town.'
  ' Return ? ' (said Hector, fired with stern disdain),
' What ! coop whole armies in our walls again ?
Was 't not enough, ye valiant warriors say,
Nine years imprison'd in those towers ye lay ?
Wide o'er the world was Ilion famed of old
For brass exhaustless, and for mines of gold;
But while inglorious in her walls we stay'd,
Sunk were her treasures, and her stores decay'd; 340
The Phrygians now her scatter'd spoils enjoy,
And proud Mæonia wastes the fruits of Troy.
Great Jove at length my arms to conquest calls,
And shuts the Grecians in their wooden walls:
Darest thou dispirit whom the Gods incite ?
Flies any Trojan ? I shall stop his flight.
To better counsel then attention lend;
Take due refreshment, and the watch attend.
If there be one whose riches cost him care,
Forth let him bring them for the troops to share; 350
'T is better gen'rously bestow'd on those,
Than left the plunder of our country's foes.
Soon as the morn the purple orient warms,
Fierce on yon navy will we pour our arms.
If great Achilles rise in all his might,
His be the danger: I shall stand the fight.

Honour, ye Gods ? or let me gain, or give;
And live he glorious, whosoe'er shall live !
Mars is our common Lord, alike to all:
And oft the victor triumphs, but to fall.' 360
   The shouting host in loud applauses join'd:
So Pallas robb'd the many of their mind;
To their own sense condemn'd, and left to choose
The worst advice, the better to refuse.
   While the long night extends her sable reign,
Around Patroclus mourn'd the Grecian train.
Stern in superior grief Pelides stood;
Those slaught'ring arms, so used to bathe in blood,
Now clasp his clay-cold limbs: then, gushing, start
The tears, and sighs burst from his swelling heart. 370
The lion thus, with dreadful anguish stung,
Roars thro' the desert, and demands his young;
When the grim savage, to his rifled den
Too late returning, snuffs the track of men,
And o'er the vales and o'er the forest bounds;
His clam'rous grief the bell'wing wood resounds.
So grieves Achilles; and impetuous vents
To all his Myrmidons, his loud laments:
   ' In what vain promise, Gods ! did I engage,
When, to console Menœtius' feeble age, 380
I vow'd his much-lov'd offspring to restore,
Charged with rich spoils, to fair Opuntia's shore ?
But mighty Jove cuts short, with just disdain,
The long, long views of poor designing man !
One fate the warrior and the friend shall strike,
And Troy's black sands must drink our blood alike:
Me, too, a wretched mother shall deplore,
An aged father never see me more !
Yet, my Patroclus ! yet a space I stay,
Then swift pursue thee on the darksome way. 390
Ere thy dear relics in the grave are laid,
Shall Hector's head be offer'd to thy shade:
That, with his arms, shall hang before thy shrine;
And twelve, the noblest of the Trojan line,

Sacred to vengeance, by this hand expire,
Their lives effused around thy flaming pyre.
Thus let me lie till then ! thus, closely press'd,
Bathe thy cold face, and sob upon thy breast !
While Trojan captives here thy mourners stay,
Weep all the night, and murmur all the day, 400
Spoils of my arms, and thine ; when, wasting wide,
Our swords kept time, and conquer'd side by side.'
   He spoke, and bid the sad attendants round
Cleanse the pale corse, and wash each honour'd wound.
A massy cauldron of stupendous frame
They brought, and placed it o'er the rising flame;
Then heap the lighted wood; the flame divides
Beneath the vase, and climbs around the sides.
In its wide womb they pour the rushing stream;
The boiling water bubbles to the brim. 410
The body then they bathe with pious toil,
Embalm the wounds, anoint the limbs with oil;
High on a bed of state extended laid,
And decent cover'd with a linen shade;
Last o'er the dead the milk-white veil they threw;
That done, their sorrows and their sighs renew.
   Meanwhile to Juno, in the realms above
(His wife and sister) spoke almighty Jove:
' At last thy will prevails: great Peleus' son
Rises in arms: such grace thy Greeks have won. 420
Say (for I know not), is their race divine,
And thou the mother of that martial line ?'
   ' What words are these ? ' (th' Imperial Dame replies,
While anger flash'd from her majestic eyes);
' Succour like this a mortal arm might lend,
And such success mere human wit attend:
And shall not I, the second Power above,
Heav'n's Queen, and Consort of the thund'ring Jove,

Say, shall not I one nation's fate command,
Not wreak my vengeance on one guilty
   land ? '   430
So they. Meanwhile the Silver-footed
   Dame
Reach'd the Vulcanian dome, eternal frame !
High-eminent amid the works divine,
Where Heav'n's far-beaming brazen man-
   sions shine.
There the lame architect the Goddess
   found,
Obscure in smoke, his forges flaming round,
While bathed in sweat from fire to fire he
   flew,
And, puffing loud, the roaring bellows
   blew.
That day no common task his labour
   claim'd:
Full twenty tripods for his hall he
   framed,   440
That, placed on living wheels of massy
   gold
(Wondrous to tell) ! instinct with spirit
   roll'd
From place to place, around the blest
   abodes,
Self-mov'd, obedient to the beck of Gods:
For their fair handles now, o'erwrought
   with flowers,
In moulds prepared, the glowing ore he
   pours.
Just as, responsive to his thought, the
   frame
Stood prompt to move, the azure Goddess
   came:
Charis, his spouse, a Grace divinely fair
(With purple fillets round her braided
   hair),   450
Observ'd her ent'ring; her soft hand she
   press'd,
And, smiling, thus the wat'ry Queen ad-
   dress'd:
' What, Goddess! this unusual favour
   draws ?
All hail, and welcome! whatsoe'er the
   cause:
Till now a stranger, in a happy hour
Approach, and taste the dainties of the
   bower.'
   High on a throne, with stars of silver
   graced,
And various artifice, the Queen she placed;
A footstool at her feet: then, calling, said,
' Vulcan, draw near, 't is Thetis asks your
   aid.'   460

' Thetis ' (replied the God) ' our powers
   may claim,
An ever-dear, an ever-honour'd name!
When my proud mother hurl'd me from
   the sky
(My awkward form, it seems, displeas'd
   her eye),
She, and Eurynome, my griefs redress'd,
And soft receiv'd me on their silver breast.
Ev'n then, these arts employ'd my infant
   thought;
Chains, bracelets, pendants, all their toys
   I wrought.   468
Nine years kept secret in the dark abode,
Secure I lay, conceal'd from man and God:
Deep in a cavern'd rock my days were led;
The rushing ocean murmur'd o'er my head.
Now since her presence glads our mansion,
   say,
For such desert what service can I pay ?
Vouchsafe, O Thetis! at our board to share
The genial rites, and hospitable fare;
While I the labours of the forge forego,
And bid the roaring bellows cease to blow.'
   Then from his anvil the lame artist rose;
Wide with distorted legs oblique he goes,
And stills the bellows, and (in order laid)
Locks in their chests his instruments of
   trade: 482
Then with a sponge the sooty workman
   dress'd
His brawny arms imbrown'd, and hairy
   breast.
With his huge sceptre graced, and red at-
   tire,
Came halting forth the Sov'reign of the
   Fire:
The Monarch's steps two female forms
   uphold,
That mov'd, and breathed, in animated
   gold;
To whom was voice, and sense, and science
   giv'n
Of works divine (such wonders are in
   Heav'n!):   490
On these supported, with unequal gait,
He reach'd the throne where pensive The-
   tis sat;
There placed beside her on the shining
   frame,
He thus address'd the Silver-footed Dame:
' Thee, welcome Goddess! what occasion
   calls
(So long a stranger) to these honour'd
   walls ?

'T is thine, fair Thetis, the command to lay,
And Vulcan's joy and duty to obey.'
　To whom the mournful mother thus re-
　　plies
　(The crystal drops stood trembling in her
　　eyes): 500
·Oh Vulcan! say, was ever breast divine
So pierc'd with sorrows, so o'erwhelm'd as
　　mine ?
Of all the Goddesses, did Jove prepare
For Thetis only such a weight of care ?
I, only I, of all the wat'ry race,
By force subjected to a man's embrace,
Who, sinking now with age and sorrow,
　　pays
The mighty fine imposed on length of days.
Sprung from my bed, a godlike Hero came,
The bravest sure that ever bore the name;
Like some fair plant, beneath my careful
　　hand, 511
He grew, he flourish'd, and he graced the
　　land:
To Troy I sent him; but his native shore
Never, ah never, shall receive him more !
Ev'n while he lives, he wastes with secret
　　woe,
Nor I, a Goddess, can retard the blow!
Robb'd of the prize the Grecian suffrage
　　gave,
The King of Nations forc'd his royal slave:
For this he griev'd; and, till the Greeks
　　oppress'd 519
Required his arm, he sorrow'd unredress'd.
Large gifts they promise, and their elders
　　send;
In vain — he arms not, but permits his
　　friend
His arms, his steeds, his forces, to employ;
He marches, combats, almost conquers
　　Troy:
Then slain by Phœbus (Hector had the
　　name),
At once resigns his armour, life, and fame.
But thou, in pity, by my prayer be won;
Grace with immortal arms this short-lived
　　son,
And to the field in martial pomp restore,
To shine with glory, till he shines no
　　more! ' 530
　To her the Artist-God: 'Thy griefs re-
　　sign,
Secure, what Vulcan can, is ever thine.
O could I hide him from the Fates as well,
Or with these hands the cruel stroke
　　repel,

As I shall forge most envied arms, the
　　gaze
Of wond'ring ages, and the world's amaze!'
　Thus having said, the Father of the Fires
To the black labours of his forge retires.
Soon as he bade them blow, the bellows
　　turn'd
Their iron mouths, and, where the furnace
　　burn'd, 540
Resounding breathed: at once the blast
　　expires,
And twenty forges catch at once the fires;
Just as the God directs, now loud, now
　　low,
They raise a tempest, or they gently blow.
In hissing flames huge silver bars are roll'd,
And stubborn brass, and tin, and solid
　　gold:
Before, deep fix'd, th' eternal anvils stand;
The pond'rous hammer loads his better
　　hand,
His left with tongs turns the vex'd metal
　　round;
And thick strong strokes the doubling
　　vaults rebound. 550
　Then first he form'd th' immense and
　　solid shield;
Rich various artifice emblazed the field;
Its utmost verge a threefold circle bound;
A silver chain suspends the massy round:
Five ample plates the broad expanse com-
　　pose,
And godlike labours on the surface rose.
There shone the image of the master-mind:
There Earth, there Heav'n, there Ocean,
　　he design'd;
Th' unwearied sun, the moon completely
　　round;
The starry lights that Heav'n's high convex
　　crown'd; 560
The Pleiads, Hyads, with the Northern
　　Team);
And great Orion's more refulgent beam;
To which, around the axle of the sky,
The Bear revolving points his golden eye;
Still shines exalted on th' ethereal plain,
Nor bathes his blazing forehead in the
　　main.
　Two cities radiant on the shield appear,
The image one of peace, and one of war.
Here sacred pomp and genial feast delight,
And solemn dance, and Hymeneal rite; 570
Along the street the new-made brides are
　　led,
With torches flaming, to the nuptial bed:

The youthful dancers in a circle bound
To the soft flute, and cittern's silver sound:
Thro' the fair streets, the matrons in a row
Stand in their porches, and enjoy the show.
    There, in the Forum swarm a numerous
      train;
The subject of debate, a townsman slain:
One pleads the fine discharged, which one
    denied,   579
And bade the public and the laws decide:
The witness is produced on either hand:
For this, or that, the partial people stand:
Th' appointed heralds still the noisy bands,
And form a ring, with sceptres in their
    hands;
On seats of stone, within the sacred place,
The rev'rend elders nodded o'er the case;
Alternate, each th' attending sceptre took,
And, rising solemn, each his sentence spoke.
Two golden talents lay amidst, in sight,
The prize of him who best adjudg'd the
    right.   590
    Another part (a prospect diff'ring far)
Glow'd with refulgent arms, and horrid
    war.
Two mighty hosts a leaguer'd town em-
    brace,
And one would pillage, one would burn,
    the place.
Meantime the townsmen, arm'd with silent
    care,
A secret ambush on the foe prepare:
Their wives, their children, and the watch-
    ful band
Of trembling parents, on the turrets stand.
They march, by Pallas and by Mars made
    bold;
Gold were the Gods, their radiant garments
    gold,   600
And gold their armour; these the squadron
    led,
August, divine, superior by the head!
A place for ambush fit they found, and
    stood
Cover'd with shields, beside a silver flood.
Two spies at distance lurk, and watchful
    seem
If sheep or oxen seek the winding stream.
Soon the white flocks proceeded o'er the
    plains,
And steers slow-moving, and two shepherd
    swains;
Behind them, piping on their reeds, they
    go,
Nor fear an ambush, nor suspect a foe.   610

In arms the glitt'ring squadron rising
    round,
Rush sudden; hills of slaughter heap the
    ground:
Whole flocks and herds lie bleeding on the
    plains,
And, all amidst them, dead, the shepherd
    swains!
The bell'wing oxen the besiegers hear;
They rise, take horse, approach, and meet
    the war;
They fight, they fall, beside the silver flood;
The waving silver seem'd to blush with
    blood.
There tumult, there contention, stood con-
    fess'd;   619
One rear'd a dagger at a captive's breast,
One held a living foe, that freshly bled
With new-made wounds; another dragg'd
    a dead;
Now here, now there, the carcasses they
    tore:
Fate stalk'd amidst them, grim with hu-
    man gore.
And the whole war came out, and met the
    eye:
And each bold figure seem'd to live, or die.
    A field deep furrow'd next the God de-
    sign'd,
The third time labour'd by the sweating
    hind;
The shining shares full many ploughmen
    guide,
And turn their crooked yokes on ev'ry
    side.   630
Still as at either end they wheel around,
The master meets them with his goblet
    crown'd;
The hearty draught rewards, renews their
    toil;
Then back the turning ploughshares cleave
    the soil:
Behind, the rising earth in ridges roll'd,
And sable look'd, tho' form'd of molten
    gold.
    Another field rose high with waving
    grain;
With bended sickles stand the reaper-train.
Here stretch'd in ranks the levell'd swaths
    are found,
Sheaves, heap'd on sheaves, here thicken
    up the ground.   640
With sweeping stroke the mowers strew the
    lands;
The gath'rers follow, and collect in bands;

And last the children, in whose arms are
borne
(Too short to gripe them) the brown
sheaves of corn.
The rustic Monarch of the Field descries,
With silent glee, the heaps around him
rise.
A ready banquet on the turf is laid,
Beneath an ample oak's expanded shade.
The victim ox the sturdy youth prepare; 649
The reaper's due repast, the women's care.
  Next ripe, in yellow gold, a vineyard
shines,
Bent with the pond'rous harvest of its
vines;
A deeper dye the dangling clusters shew,
And, curl'd on silver props, in order glow:
A darker metal mix'd, intrench'd the
place;
And pales of glitt'ring tin th' enclosure
grace.
To this, one pathway gently winding leads,
Where march a train with baskets on their
heads
(Fair maids and blooming youths), that
smiling bear   659
The purple product of th' autumnal year.
To these a youth awakes the warbling
strings,
Whose tender lay the fate of Linus sings;
In measured dance behind him move the
train,
Tune soft the voice, and answer to the
strain.
  Here, herds of oxen march, erect and
bold,
Rear high their horns, and seem to low in
gold,
And speed to meadows, on whose sounding
shores
A rapid torrent thro' the rushes roars:
Four golden herdsmen as their guardians
stand,
And nine sour dogs complete the rustic
band.   670
Two lions rushing from the wood appear'd;
And seized a bull, the master of the herd;
He roar'd: in vain the dogs, the men, with-
stood;
They tore his flesh, and drank the sable
blood.
The dogs (oft cheer'd in vain) desert the
prey,
Dread the grim terrors, and at distance
bay.

  Next this, the eye the art of Vulcan
leads
Deep thro' fair forests, and a length of
meads;
And stalls, and folds, and scatter'd cots
between;
And fleecy flocks, that whiten all the
scene.   680
  A figured dance succeeds: such once was
seen
In lofty Gnossus, for the Cretan Queen,
Form'd by Dædalean art: A comely band
Of youths and maidens, bounding hand in
hand;
The maids in soft cymars of linen dress'd;
The youths all graceful in the glossy
vest;
Of those the locks with flowery wreaths
inroll'd,
Of these the sides adorn'd with swords of
gold,
That, glitt'ring gay, from silver belts de-
pend.
Now all at once they rise, at once de-
scend,   690
With well-taught feet: now shape, in
oblique ways,
Confusedly regular, the moving maze:
Now forth at once, too swift for sight, they
spring,
And undistinguish'd blend the flying ring:
So whirls a wheel, in giddy circle toss'd,
And, rapid as it runs, the single spokes are
lost.
The gazing multitudes admire around;
Two active tumblers in the centre bound;
Now high, now low, their pliant limbs they
bend,   699
And gen'ral songs the sprightly revel
end.
  Thus the broad shield complete the artist
crown'd
With his last hand, and pour'd the ocean
round:
In living silver seem'd the waves to roll,
And beat the buckler's verge, and bound
the whole.
  This done, whate'er a warrior's use re-
quires
He forged; the cuirass that outshines the
fires,
The greaves of ductile tin, the helm im-
press'd
With various sculpture, and the golden
crest.

At Thetis' feet the finish'd labour lay;
She, as a falcon, cuts th' aërial way, 710
Swift from Olympus' snowy summit flies,
And bears the blazing present thro' the
skies.

BOOK XIX

THE RECONCILIATION OF ACHILLES AND
AGAMEMNON

THE ARGUMENT

Thetis brings to her son the armour made by
Vulcan. She preserves the body of his friend
from corruption, and commands him to assemble the army, to declare his resentment
at an end. Agamemnon and Achilles are
solemnly reconciled: the speeches, presents,
and ceremonies on that occasion. Achilles
is with great difficulty persuaded to refrain
from the battle till the troops have refreshed
themselves, by the advice of Ulysses. The
presents are conveyed to the tent of Achilles:
where Briseis laments over the body of Patroclus. The hero obstinately refuses all
repast, and gives himself up to lamentations for his friend. Minerva descends to
strengthen him, by the order of Jupiter. He
arms for the fight; his appearance described.
He addresses himself to his horses, and reproaches them with the death of Patroclus.
One of them is miraculously endued with
voice, and inspired to prophesy his fate; but
the hero, not astonished by that prodigy,
rushes with fury to the combat.
The thirtieth day. The scene is on the sea-
shore.

SOON as Aurora heav'd her orient head
Above the waves that blush'd with early
red
(With new-born day to gladden mortal
sight,
And gild the courts of Heav'n with sacred
light),
Th' immortal arms the Goddess-mother
bears
Swift to her son: her son she finds in
tears,
Stretch'd o'er Patroclus' corse, while all the
rest
Their Sov'reign's sorrows in their own ex-
press'd.
A ray divine her heav'nly presence shed,
And thus, his hand soft touching, Thetis
said: 10

'Suppress, my son, this rage of grief, and
know
It was not man, but Heav'n, that gave the
blow:
Behold what arms by Vulcan are bestow'd,
Arms worthy thee, or fit to grace a God.'
Then drops the radiant burden on the
ground;
Clang the strong arms, and ring the shores
around;
Back shrink the Myrmidons with dread
surprise,
And from the broad effulgence turn their
eyes.
Unmov'd, the hero kindles at the show,
And feels with rage divine his bosom
glow; 20
From his fierce eye-balls living flames ex-
pire,
And flash incessant like a stream of fire:
He turns the radiant gift, and feeds his
mind
On all th' immortal artist had design'd.
'Goddess' (he cried), 'these glorious
arms that shine
With matchless art, confess the hand di-
vine.
Now to the bloody battle let me bend:
But ah! the relics of my slaughter'd
friend!
In those wide wounds thro' which his
spirit fled,
Shall flies, and worms obscene, pollute the
dead?' 30
'That unavailing care be laid aside'
(The azure Goddess to her son replied);
'Whole years untouch'd, uninjured shall
remain,
Fresh as in life, the carcass of the slain.
But go, Achilles (as affairs require),
Before the Grecian peers renounce thine
ire:
Then uncontroll'd in boundless war engage,
And Heav'n with strength supply the
mighty rage!'
Then in the nostrils of the slain she
pour'd
Nectareous drops, and rich ambrosia show-
er'd 40
O'er all the corse: the flies forbid their
prey,
Untouch'd it rests, and sacred from decay.
Achilles to the strand obedient went;
The shores resounded with the voice he
sent.

The heroes heard, and all the naval train
That tend the ships, or guide them o'er the main,
Alarm'd, transported, at the well-known sound,
Frequent and full, the great assembly crown'd;
Studious to see that terror of the plain,
Long lost to battle, shine in arms again. 50
Tydides and Ulysses first appear,
Lame with their wounds, and leaning on the spear:
These on the sacred seats of council placed,
The King of Men, Atrides, came the last:
He too sore wounded by Agenor's son.
Achilles (rising in the midst) begun:
'Oh Monarch! better far had been the fate
Of thee, of me, of all the Grecian state,
If (ere the day when by mad passion sway'd,
Rash we contended for the black-eyed maid) 60
Preventing Dian had despatch'd her dart,
And shot the shining mischief to the heart!
Then many a hero had not press'd the shore,
Nor Troy's glad fields been fatten'd with our gore:
Long, long shall Greece the woes we caus'd bewail,
And sad posterity repeat the tale.
But this, no more the subject of debate,
Is past, forgotten, and resign'd to Fate:
Why should, alas! a mortal man, as I,
Burn with a fury that can never die? 70
Here then my anger ends: let war succeed,
And ev'n as Greece hath bled, let Ilion bleed.
Now call the hosts, and try, if in our sight,
Troy yet shall dare to camp a second night?
I deem their mightiest, when this arm he knows,
Shall 'scape with transport, and with joy repose.'
He said; his finish'd wrath with loud acclaim
The Greeks accept, and shout Pelides' name.
When thus, not rising from his lofty throne,
In state unmov'd, the King of Men begun:
'Hear me, ye sons of Greece! with silence hear! 81
And grant your Monarch an impartial ear:

Awhile your loud untimely joy suspend,
And let your rash injurious clamours end:
Unruly murmurs, or ill-timed applause,
Wrong the best speaker, and the justest cause.
Nor charge on me, ye Greeks, the dire debate;
Know, angry Jove, and all-compelling Fate,
With fell Erinnys, urged my wrath that day
When from Achilles' arms I forc'd the prey.
What then could I, against the will of 90
Heav'n?
Not by myself, but vengeful Até driv'n;
She, Jove's dread daughter, fated to infest
The race of mortals, enter'd in my breast.
Not on the ground that haughty Fury treads,
But prints her lofty footsteps on the heads
Of mighty men; inflicting as she goes
Long-fest'ring wounds, inextricable woes!
Of old, she stalk'd amidst the bright abodes;
And Jove himself, the sire of men and Gods, 100
The world's great ruler, felt her venom'd dart;
Deceiv'd by Juno's wiles and female art.
For when Alcmena's nine long months were run,
And Jove expected his immortal son,
To Gods and Goddesses th' unruly joy
He shew'd, and vaunted of his matchless boy:
"From us" (he said) "this day an infant springs,
Fated to rule, and born a King of Kings."
Saturnia ask'd an oath, to vouch the truth,
And fix dominion on the favour'd youth. 110
The Thund'rer, unsuspicious of the fraud,
Pronounc'd those solemn words that bind a God.
The joyful Goddess, from Olympus' height,
Swift to Achaian Argos bent her flight.
Scarce seven moons gone, lay Sthenelus's wife;
She push'd her ling'ring infant into life:
Her charms Alcmena's coming labours stay,
And stop the babe just issuing to the day.
Then bids Saturnius bear his oath in mind;
"A youth" (said she) "of Jove's immortal kind
20

Is this day born: from Sthenelus he
    springs,
And claims thy promise to be King of
    Kings."
Grief seiz'd the Thund'rer, by his oath en-
    gaged;
Stung to the soul, he sorrow'd and he raged.
From his ambrosial head, where perch'd she
    sat,
He snatch'd the Fury-Goddess of Debate,
The dread, th' irrevocable oath he swore,
Th' immortal seats should ne'er behold her
    more;
And whirl'd her headlong down, for ever
    driv'n
From bright Olympus and the starry
    Heav'n; 130
Thence on the nether world the Fury
    fell;
Ordain'd with man's contentious race to
    dwell.
Full oft the God his son's hard toils be-
    moan'd,
Curs'd the dire Fury, and in secret groan'd.
Ev'n thus, like Jove himself, was I misled,
While raging Hector heap'd our camps
    with dead.
What can the errors of my rage atone ?
My martial troops, my treasures, are thy
    own:
This instant from the navy shall be sent
Whate'er Ulysses promis'd at thy tent; 140
But thou ! appeas'd, propitious to our
    prayer,
Resume thy arms, and shine again in war.'
   ' O King of Nations ! whose superior
    sway '
(Returns Achilles) ' all our hosts obey !
To keep or send the presents be thy care;
To us, 't is equal: all we ask is war.
While yet we talk, or but an instant shun
The fight, our glorious work remains un-
    done.
Let ev'ry Greek who sees my spear con-
    found
The Trojan ranks, and deal destruction
    round, 150
With emulation, what I act, survey,
And learn from thence the business of the
    day.'
   The son of Peleus thus: and thus replies
The great in councils, Ithacus the wise:
' Tho', godlike, thou art by no toils op-
    press'd,
At least our armies claim repast and rest :

Long and laborious must the combat be,
When by the Gods inspired, and led by
    thee.
Strength is derived from spirits and from
    blood,
And those augment by gen'rous wine and
    food; 160
What boastful son of war, without that
    stay,
Can last a hero thro' a single day ?
Courage may prompt; but, ebbing out his
    strength
Mere unsupported man must yield at
    length;
Shrunk with dry famine, and with toils de-
    clin'd,
The drooping body will desert the mind:
But built anew, with strength-conferring
    fare,
With limbs and soul untamed, he tires a
    war.
Dismiss the people then, and give com-
    mand, 169
With strong repast to hearten ev'ry band;
But let the presents to Achilles made,
In full assembly of all Greece be laid.
The King of Men shall rise in public
    sight,
And solemn swear (observant of the rite),
That, spotless as she came, the maid re-
    moves,
Pure from his arms, and guiltless of his
    loves.
That done, a sumptuous banquet shall be
    made,
And the full price of injured honour paid.
Stretch not henceforth, O Prince ! thy
    sov'reign might, 179
Beyond the bounds of reason and of right;
'T is the chief praise that e'er to Kings
    belong'd,
To right with justice whom with power
    they wrong'd.'
   To him the Monarch: ' Just is thy de-
    cree,
Thy words give joy, and wisdom breathes
    in thee.
Each due atonement gladly I prepare;
And Heav'n regard me as I justly swear !
Here then awhile let Greece assembled
    stay,
Nor great Achilles grudge this short delay;
Till from the fleet our presents be convey'd,
And, Jove attesting, the firm compact
    made. 190

A train of noble youth the charge shall
    bear;
These to select, Ulysses, be thy care;
In order rank'd let all our gifts appear,
And the fair train of captives close the
    rear:
Talthybius shall the victim boar convey,
Sacred to Jove, and yon bright orb of
    day.'
    'For this' (the stern Æacides replies)
'Some less important season may suffice,
When the stern fury of the war is o'er,
And wrath extinguish'd burns my breast
    no more.   200
By Hector slain, their faces to the sky,
All grim with gaping wounds our heroes
    lie:
Those call to war! and, might my voice
    incite,
Now, now this instant should commence
    the fight.
Then, when the day's complete, let gen'-
    rous bowls,
And copious banquets, glad your weary
    souls.
Let not my palate know the taste of food,
Till my insatiate rage be cloy'd with blood:
Pale lies my friend, with wounds disfigured
    o'er,   209
And his cold feet are pointed to the door.
Revenge is all my soul! no meaner care,
Int'rest, or thought, has room to harbour
    there;
Destruction be my feast, and mortal
    wounds,
And scenes of blood, and agonizing sounds.'
    'O first of Greeks!' (Ulysses thus re-
    join'd)
'The best and bravest of the warrior-kind!
Thy praise it is in dreadful camps to shine,
But old experience and calm wisdom, mine.
Then hear my counsel, and to reason yield;
The bravest soon are satiate of the field;
Tho' vast the heaps that strew the crimson
    plain,   221
The bloody harvest brings but little gain:
The scale of conquest ever wav'ring lies,
Great Jove but turns it, and the victor dies!
The great, the bold, by thousands daily fall,
And endless were the grief to weep for all.
Eternal sorrows what avails to shed?
Greece honours not with solemn fasts the
    dead:
Enough, when death demands the brave, to
    pay

The tribute of a melancholy day.   230
One Chief with patience to the grave re-
    sign'd,
Our care devolves on others left behind.
Let gen'rous food supplies of strength pro-
    duce,
Let rising spirits flow from sprightly juice,
Let their warm heads with scenes of bat-
    tle glow,
And pour new furies on the feebler foe.
Yet a short interval, and none shall dare
Expect a second summons to the war;
Who waits for that, the dire effect shall
    find,
If trembling in the ships he lags behind. 240
Embodied, to the battle let us bend,
And all at once on haughty Troy descend.'
    And now the delegates Ulysses sent,
To bear the presents from the royal tent.
The sons of Nestor, Phyleus' valiant heir,
Thoas and Merion, thunderbolts of war,
With Lycomedes of Creiontian strain,
And Melanippus, form'd the chosen train.
Swift as the word was giv'n, the youths
    obey'd;
Twice ten bright vases in the midst they
    laid;   250
A row of six fair tripods then succeeds;
And twice the number of high-bounding
    steeds;
Sev'n captives next a lovely line compose;
The eighth Briseïs, like the blooming rose,
Closed the bright band: great Ithacus be-
    fore,
First of the train, the golden talents bore:
The rest in public view the Chiefs dispose,
A splendid scene! Then Agamemnon rose:
The boar Talthybius held: the Grecian lord
Drew the broad cutlass sheathed beside his
    sword;   260
The stubborn bristles from the victim's
    brow
He crops, and, off'ring, meditates his vow.
His hands uplifted to th' attesting skies,
On Heav'n's broad marble roof were fix'd
    his eyes;
The solemn words a deep attention draw,
And Greece around sat thrill'd with sacred
    awe.
    'Witness, thou first! thou greatest Power
    above;
All-good, all-wise, and all-surveying Jove!
And mother Earth, and Heav'n's revolving
    light,
And ye fell Furies of the realms of night, 270

Who rule the dead, and horrid woes pre-
pare
For perjured kings, and all who falsely
swear !
The black-eyed maid inviolate removes,
Pure and unconscious of my manly loves.
If this be false, Heav'n all its vengeance
shed,
And levell'd thunder strike my guilty
head !'
  With that, his weapon deep inflicts the
wound:
The bleeding savage tumbles to the ground:
The sacred Herald rolls the victim slain
(A feast for fish) into the foaming main. 280
  Then thus Achilles: 'Hear, ye Greeks !
and know
Whate'er we feel, 't is Jove inflicts the woe:
Not else Atrides could our rage inflame,
Nor from my arms, unwilling, force the
dame.
'T was Jove's high will alone, o'er-ruling all,
That doom'd our strife, and doom'd the
Greeks to fall.
Go then, ye Chiefs ! indulge the genial rite:
Achilles waits ye, and expects the fight.'
  The speedy council at his word ad-
journ'd;
To their black vessels all the Greeks re-
turn'd: 290
Achilles sought his tent. His train before
March'd onward, bending with the gifts
they bore.
Those in the tents the squires industrious
spread;
The foaming coursers to the stalls they led.
To their new seats the female captives
move:
Briseïs, radiant as the Queen of Love,
Slow as she pass'd, beheld with sad survey
Where, gash'd with cruel wounds, Patroclus
lay.
Prone on the body fell the heav'nly Fair,
Beat her sad breast, and tore her golden
hair;   300
All-beautiful in grief, her humid eyes,
Shining with tears, she lifts, and thus she
cries:
  'Ah youth ! for ever dear, for ever kind,
Once tender friend of my distracted mind !
I left thee fresh in life, in beauty gay;
Now find thee cold, inanimated clay !
What woes my wretched race of life at-
tend !
Sorrows on sorrows, never doom'd to end !

The first lov'd consort of my virgin bed
Before these eyes in fatal battle bled: 310
My three brave brothers in one mournful
day
All trod the dark irremeable way:
Thy friendly arm uprear'd me from the
plain,
And dried my sorrows for a husband slain;
Achilles' care you promis'd I should prove,
The first, the dearest partner of his love;
That rites divine should ratify the band,
And make me Empress in his native land.
Accept these grateful tears ! for thee they
flow,
For thee, that ever felt another's woe !' 320
  Her sister captives echoed groan for
groan,
Nor mourn'd Patroclus' fortunes, but their
own.
The leaders press'd the Chief on ev'ry side;
Unmov'd he heard them, and with sighs
denied:
  'If yet Achilles have a friend, whose care
Is bent to please him, this request forbear:
Till yonder sun descend, ah, let me pay
To grief and anguish one abstemious day.'
  He spoke, and from the warriors turn'd
his face:
Yet still the Brother-Kings of Atreus'
race,   330
Nestor, Idomeneus, Ulysses sage,
And Phœnix, strive to calm his grief and
rage:
His rage they calm not, nor his grief con-
trol:
He groans, he raves, he sorrows from his
soul.
  'Thou too, Patroclus' (thus his heart
he vents) !
'Hast spread th' inviting banquet in our
tents;
Thy sweet society, thy winning care,
Oft stay'd Achilles, rushing to the war.
But now, alas ! to death's cold arms re-
sign'd,
What banquet but revenge can glad my
mind ?   340
What greater sorrow could afflict my
breast,
What more, if hoary Peleus were deceas'd ?
Who now, perhaps, in Phthia dreads to
hear
His son's sad fate, and drops a tender tear.
What more, should Neoptolemus the brave
(My only offspring) sink into the grave ?

If yet that offspring lives (I distant far,
Of all neglectful, wage a hateful war).
I could not this, this cruel stroke attend;
Fate claim'd Achilles, but might spare his
   friend. 350
I hoped Patroclus might survive to rear
My tender orphan with a parent's care,
From Scyros' isle conduct him o'er the ⎫
   main,   ⎬
And glad his eyes with his paternal reign, ⎪
The lofty palace, and the large domain. ⎭
For Peleus breathes no more the vital air;
Or drags a wretched life of age and care,
But till the news of my sad fate invades
His hast'ning soul, and sinks him to the
   shades.'
   Sighing he said: his grief the heroes
   join'd, 360
Each stole a tear, for what he left behind.
Their mingled grief the Sire of Heav'n
   survey'd,
And thus, with pity, to his Blue-eyed Maid:
' Is then Achilles now no more thy care,
And dost thou thus desert the great in war?
Lo, where yon sails their canvas wings ex-
   tend,
All comfortless he sits, and wails his friend:
Ere thirst and want his forces have op-
   press'd,
Haste and infuse ambrosia in his breast.'
   He spoke, and sudden at the word of
   Jove 370
Shot the descending Goddess from above.
So swift thro' ether the shrill Harpy
   springs,
The wide air floating to her ample wings.
To great Achilles she her flight address'd,
And pour'd divine ambrosia in his breast,
With nectar sweet (refection of the Gods)!
Then, swift ascending, sought the bright
   abodes.
   Now issued from the ships the warrior
   train,
And like a deluge pour'd upon the plain.
As when the piercing blasts of Boreas
   blow, 380
And scatter o'er the fields the driving
   snow;
From dusky clouds the fleecy winter flies,
Whose dazzling lustre whitens all the
   skies:
So helms succeeding helms, so shields from
   shields
Catch the quick beams, and brighten all the
   fields;

Broad glitt'ring breast-plates, spears with
   pointed rays,
Mix in one stream, reflecting blaze on
   blaze:
Thick beats the centre as the coursers
   bound,
With splendour flame the skies, and laugh
   the fields around.
   Full in the midst, high-tow'ring o'er the
   rest, 390
His limbs in arms divine Achilles dress'd;
Arms which the Father of the Fire be-
   stow'd,
Forged on th' eternal anvils of the God.
Grief and revenge his furious heart inspire,
His glowing eye-balls roll with living
   fire;
He grinds his teeth, and furious with delay
O'erlooks th' embattled host, and hopes
   the bloody day.
The silver cuishes first his thighs infold;
Then o'er his breast was braced the hollow
   gold:
The brazen sword a various baldric tied, 400
That, starr'd with gems, hung glitt'ring
   at his side;
And, like the moon, the broad refulgent
   shield
Blazed with long rays, and gleam'd athwart
   the field.
   So to night-wand'ring sailors, pale with
   fears,
Wide o'er the wat'ry waste a light appears,
Which on the far-seen mountain blazing
   high,
Streams from some lonely watch-tower to
   the sky:
With mournful eyes they gaze and gaze
   again;
Loud howls the storm, and drives them
   o'er the main.
   Next, his high head the helmet graced;
   behind 410
The sweepy crest hung floating in the
   wind:
Like the red star, that from his flaming
   hair
Shakes down diseases, pestilence, and war;
So stream'd the golden honours from his
   head,
Trembled the sparkling plumes, and the
   loose glories shed.
   The Chief beholds himself with wond'ring
   eyes;
His arms he poises, and his motions tries;

Buoy'd by some inward force, he seems to
swim,
And feels a pinion lifting ev'ry limb.
And now he shakes his great paternal
spear,   420
Pond'rous and huge ! which not a Greek
could rear:
From Pelion's cloudy top an ash entire
Old Chiron fell'd, and shaped it for his
sire;
A spear which stern Achilles only wields,
The death of heroes, and the dread of
fields.
Automedon and Alcimus prepare
Th' immortal coursers and the radiant car
(The silver traces sweeping at their side);
Their fiery mouths resplendent bridles
tied;   429
The iv'ry-studded reins, return'd behind,
Waved o'er their backs, and to the chariot
join'd.
The charioteer then whirl'd the lash
around,
And swift ascended at one active bound.
All bright in heav'nly arms, above his
squire
Achilles mounts, and sets the field on fire;
Not brighter Phœbus in th' ethereal way
Flames from his chariot, and restores the
day.
High o'er the host, all terrible he stands,
And thunders to his steeds these dread
commands:
' Xanthus and Balius ! of Podarges'
strain   440
(Unless ye boast that heav'nly race in
vain),
Be swift, be mindful of the load ye bear,
And learn to make your master more your
care:
Thro' falling squadrons bear my slaught'-
ring sword,
Nor, as ye left Patroclus, leave your lord.'
The gen'rous Xanthus, as the words he
said,
Seem'd sensible of woe, and droop'd his
head:
Trembling he stood before the golden wain,
And bow'd to dust the honours of his
mane;
When, strange to tell (so Juno will'd !), he
broke   450
Eternal silence, and portentous spoke:
' Achilles ! yes ! this day at least we bear
Thy rage in safety thro' the files of war:

But come it will, the fatal time must come,
Not ours the fault, but God decrees thy
doom.
Not thro' our crime, or slowness in the
course,
Fell thy Patroclus, but by heav'nly force:
The bright far-shooting God who gilds the
day
(Confess'd we saw him) tore his arms
away.
No: could our swiftness o'er the winds pre-
vail,   460
Or beat the pinions of the western gale,
All were in vain: the Fates thy death de-
mand,
Due to a mortal and immortal hand.'
Then ceas'd for ever, by the Furies
tied,
His fateful voice. Th' intrepid Chief re-
plied
With unabated rage: ' So let it be !
Portents and prodigies are lost on me.
I know my fates: to die, to see no more
My much-lov'd parents, and my native
shore —
Enough: when Heav'n ordains, I sink in
night;   470
Now perish Troy !' He said, and rush'd
to fight.

BOOK XX

THE BATTLE OF THE GODS, AND THE ACTS
OF ACHILLES

THE ARGUMENT

Jupiter, upon Achilles' return to the battle,
calls a council of the gods, and permits them
to assist either party. The terrors of the
combat described when the deities are engaged. Apollo encourages Æneas to meet
Achilles. After a long conversation, these
two heroes encounter ; but Æneas is preserved by the assistance of Neptune. Achilles falls upon the rest of the Trojans, and is
upon the point of killing Hector, but Apollo
conveys him away in a cloud. Achilles pursues the Trojans with a great slaughter.
The same day continues. The scene is in the
field before Troy.

THUS round Pelides breathing war and
blood,
Greece, sheathed in arms, beside her vessels stood;

While, near impending from a neighb'ring
    height,
Troy's black battalions wait the shock of
    fight.
Then Jove to Themis gives command, to
    call
The Gods to council in tho starry hall:
Swift o'er Olympus' hundred hills she
    flies,
And summons all the Senate of the Skies.
These, shining on, in long procession come
To Jove's eternal adamantine dome.   10
Not one was absent, not a rural Power
That haunts the verdant gloom, or rosy
    bower;
Each fair-hair'd Dryad of the shady wood,
Each azure sister of the silver flood;
All but old Ocean, hoary Sire! who keeps
His ancient seat beneath the sacred deeps.
On marble thrones with lucid columns
    crown'd
(The work of Vulcan) sat the Powers
    around.
Ev'n he, whose trident sways the wat'ry
    reign,
Heard the loud summons, and forsook the
    main,   20
Assumed his throne amid the bright abodes,
And question'd thus the Sire of men and
    Gods:
   'What moves the God who Heav'n and
    earth commands,
And grasps the thunder in his awful
    hands,
Thus to convene the whole ethereal state?
Is Greece and Troy the subject in debate?
Already met, the low'ring hosts appear,
And death stands ardent on the edge of
    war.'
   ''T is true' (the Cloud-compelling Power
    replies),
'This day we call the Council of the
    Skies   30
In care of human race; ev'n Jove's own
    eye
Sees with regret unhappy mortals die.
Far on Olympus' top in secret state
Ourself will sit, and see the hand of Fate
Work out our will. Celestial Powers! de-
    scend,
And, as your minds direct, your succour
    lend
To either host. Troy soon must lie o'er-
    thrown,
If uncontroll'd Achilles fights alone:

Their troops but lately durst not meet his
    eyes;
What can they now, if in his rage he
    rise?   40
Assist them, Gods! or Ilion's sacred wall
May fall this day, tho' Fate forbids the
    fall.'
   He said, and fired their Heav'nly breasts
    with rage;
On adverse parts the warring Gods en-
    gage.
Heav'n's awful Queen; and he whose azure
    round
Girds the vast globe; the Maid in arms
    renown'd;
Hermes, of profitable arts the sire,
And Vulcan, the black Sov'reign of the
    Fire:
These to the fleet repair with instant flight;
The vessels tremble as the Gods alight.   50
In aid of Troy, Latona, Phœbus came,
Mars fiery - helm'd, the Laughter-loving
    Dame,
Xanthus, whose streams in golden currents
    flow,
And the chaste Huntress of the Silver
    Bow.
Ere yet the Gods their various aid employ,
Each Argive bosom swell'd with manly
    joy,
While great Achilles (terror of the plain)
Long lost to battle, shone in arms again.
Dreadful he stood in front of all his host;
Pale Troy beheld, and seem'd already
    lost;   60
Her bravest heroes pant with inward fear,
And trembling see another God of War.
   But when the Powers descending swell'd
    the fight,
Then tumult rose; fierce rage and pale
    affright
Varied each face; then discord sounds
    alarms,
Earth echoes, and the nations rush to
    arms.
Now thro' the trembling shores Minerva
    calls,
And now she thunders from the Grecian
    walls.
Mars, hov'ring o'er his Troy, his terror
    shrouds   69
In gloomy tempests, and a night of clouds:
Now thro' each Trojan heart he fury pours
With voice divine from Ilion's topmost
    towers;

Now shouts to Simois, from her beauteous
  hill;
The mountain shook, the rapid stream stood
  still.
Above, the Sire of Gods his thunder rolls,
And peals on peals redoubled rend the
  poles.
Beneath, stern Neptune shakes the solid
  ground;
The forests wave, the mountains nod
  around;
Thro' all their summits tremble Ida's
  woods,
And from their sources boil her hundred
  floods.   80
Troy's turrets totter on the rocking plain;
And the toss'd navies beat the heaving
  main.
Deep in the dismal regions of the dead,
Th' Infernal Monarch rear'd his horrid
  head,
Leap'd from his throne, lest Neptune's
  arm should lay
His dark dominions open to the day,
And pour in light on Pluto's drear abodes,
Abhorr'd by men, and dreadful ev'n to
  Gods.
  Such war th' Immortals wage: such hor-
    rors rend
The world's vast concave, when the Gods
  contend.   90
First silver-shafted Phœbus took the plain
Against blue Neptune, Monarch of the
  Main:
The God of Arms his giant bulk display'd,
Opposed to Pallas, War's triumphant Maid.
Against Latona march'd the son of May;
The quiver'd Dian, sister of the Day
(Her golden arrows sounding at her side),
Saturnia, Majesty of Heav'n, defied.
With fiery Vulcan last in battle stands
The sacred flood that rolls on golden
  sands;   100
Xanthus his name with those of heav'nly
  birth,
But call'd Scamander by the sons of earth.
  While thus the Gods in various league
    engage,
Achilles glow'd with more than mortal rage:
Hector he sought; in search of Hector
  turn'd
His eyes around, for Hector only burn'd;
And burst like lightning thro' the ranks,
  and vow'd
To glut the God of Battles with his blood.

Æneas was the first who dared to stay;
Apollo wedg'd him in the warrior's
  way,   110
But swell'd his bosom with undaunted
  might,
Half-forc'd and half-persuaded to the
  fight.
Like young Lycaon, of the royal line,
In voice and aspect, seem'd the Power
  divine;
And bade the Chief reflect, how late with
  scorn
In distant threats he braved the Goddess-
  born.
  Then thus the hero of Anchises' strain:
' To meet Pelides you persuade in vain;
Already have I met, nor void of fear
Observ'd the fury of his flying spear;   120
From Ida's woods he chased us to the field,
Our force he scatter'd, and our herds he
  kill'd.
Lyrnessus, Pedasus in ashes lay;
But (Jove assisting) I survived the day.
Else had I sunk oppress'd in fatal fight,
By fierce Achilles and Minerva's might.
Where'er he mov'd, the Goddess shone be-
  fore,
And bathed his brazen lance in hostile
  gore.
What mortal man Achilles can sustain ?
Th' Immortals guard him thro' the dread-
  ful plain,   130
And suffer not his dart to fall in vain.
Were God my aid, this arm should check
  his power,
Tho' strong in battle as a brazen tower.'
  To whom the Son of Jove: ' That God
    implore,
And be what great Achilles was before.
From heav'nly Venus thou derivest thy
  strain,
And he but from a Sister of the Main;
An aged Sea-God father of his line,
But Jove himself the sacred source of
  thine.
Then lift thy weapon for a noble blow,   140
Nor fear the vaunting of a mortal foe.'
  This said, and spirit breathed into his
    breast,
Thro' the thick troops th' embolden'd hero
  press'd:
His venturous act the White-arm'd Queen
  survey'd,
And thus, assembling all the Powers, she
  said:

'Behold an action, Gods! that claims
    your care,
Lo, great Æneas rushing to the war;
Against Pelides he directs his course;
Phœbus impels, and Phœbus gives him
    force.
Restrain his bold career; at least, t' at-
    tend   150
Our favour'd Hero, let some Power de-
    scend.
To guard his life, and add to his renown,
We, the great Armament of Heav'n, came
    down.
Hereafter let him fall, as Fates design,
That spun so short his life's illustrious line;
But lest some adverse God now cross his
    way,
Give him to know what Powers assist this
    day:
For how shall mortal stand the dire alarms,
When Heav'n's refulgent host appear in
    arms?'
    Thus she, and thus the God whose force
    can make   160
The solid globe's eternal basis shake:
'Against the might of man, so feeble
    known,
Why should celestial Powers exert their
    own?
Suffice, from yonder mount to view the
    scene;
And leave to war the fates of mortal men.
But if th' Armipotent, or God of Light,
Obstruct Achilles, or commence the fight,
Thence on the Gods of Troy we swift de-
    scend:
Full soon, I doubt not, shall the conflict
    end;
And these, in ruin and confusion hurl'd, 170
Yield to our conquering arms the lower
    world.'
    Thus having said, the Tyrant of the Sea,
Cœrulean Neptune, rose, and led the way.
Advanc'd upon the field there stood a
    mound
Of earth congested, wall'd, and trench'd
    around;
In elder times to guard Alcides made
(The work of Trojans with Minerva's aid),
What time a vengeful monster of the main
Swept the wide shore, and drove him to the
    plain.
    Here Neptune and the Gods of Greece
    repair,   180
With clouds encompass'd, and a veil of air:

The adverse Powers, around Apollo laid,
Crown the fair hills that silver Simois
    shade.
In circle close each heav'nly party sat,
Intent to form the future scheme of Fate;
But mix not yet in fight, tho' Jove on high
Gives the loud signal, and the Heav'ns
    reply.
    Meanwhile the rushing armies hide the
    ground;
The trampled centre yields a hollow sound:
Steeds cased in mail, and Chiefs in armour
    bright,   190
The gleamy champaign glows with brazen
    light.
Amidst both hosts (a dreadful space!) ap-
    pear
There, great Achilles; bold Æneas here.
With tow'ring strides Æneas first ad-
    vanc'd;
The nodding plumage on his helmet
    danc'd;
Spread o'er his breast the fencing shield he
    bore,
And, as he mov'd, his jav'lin flamed before.
Not so Pelides: furious to engage,
He rush'd impetuous. Such the lion's rage,
Who, viewing first his foes with scornful
    eyes,   200
Tho' all in arms the peopled city rise,
Stalks careless on, with unregarding pride;
Till at the length, by some brave youth de-
    fied,
To his bold spear the savage turns alone;
He murmurs fury with a hollow groan:
He grins, he foams, he rolls his eyes
    around;
Lash'd by his tail, his heaving sides re-
    sound;
He calls up all his rage, he grinds his teeth,
Resolv'd on vengeance, or resolv'd on
    death.
So fierce Achilles on Æneas flies;   210
So stands Æneas, and his force defies.
Ere yet the stern encounter join'd, begun
The seed of Thetis thus to Venus' son:
    'Why comes Æneas thro' the ranks so
    far?
Seeks he to meet Achilles' arm in war,
In hope the realms of Priam to enjoy,
And prove his merits to the throne of
    Troy?
Grant that beneath thy lance Achilles dies,
The partial Monarch may refuse the
    prize;

Sons he has many: those thy pride may
   quell; 220
And 't is his fault to love those sons too
   well.
Or, in reward of thy victorious hand,
Has Troy proposed some spacious tract of
   land ?
An ample forest, or a fair domain,
Of hills for vines, and arable for grain ?
Ev'n this, perhaps, will hardly prove thy
   lot.
But can Achilles be so soon forgot ?
Once (as I think) you saw this brandish'd
   spear,
And then the great Æneas seem'd to fear.
With hearty haste from Ida's mount he
   fled, 230
Nor, till he reach'd Lyrnessus, turn'd his
   head.
Her lofty walls not long our progress
   stay'd;
Those, Pallas, Jove, and we, in ruins laid:
In Grecian chains her captive race were
   cast;
'T is true, the great Æneas fled too fast.
Defrauded of my conquest once before,
What then I lost, the Gods this day re-
   store.
Go; while thou may'st, avoid the threaten'd
   fate;
Fools stay to feel it, and are wise too late.'
   To this Anchises' son: ' Such words em-
   ploy 240
To one that fears thee, some unwarlike
   boy;
Such we disdain; the best may be defied
With mean reproaches, and unmanly pride:
Unworthy the high race from which we
   came,
Proclaim'd so loudly by the voice of Fame;
Each from illustrious fathers draws his
   line;
Each Goddess-born; half human, half
   divine.
Thetis' this day, or Venus' offspring dies,
And tears shall trickle from celestial eyes:
For when two heroes, thus derived, con-
   tend, 250
'T is not in words the glorious strife can
   end.
If yet thou farther seek to learn my birth
(A tale resounded thro' the spacious earth),
Hear how the glorious orgin we prove
From ancient Dardanus. the first from
   Jove:

Dardania's walls he rais'd; for Ilion then
(The city since of many-languaged men)
Was not. The natives were content to till
The shady foot of Ida's fountful hill.
From   Dardanus,   great   Erichthonius
   springs, 260
The richest once of Asia's wealthy Kings;
Three thousand mares his spacious pastures
   bred,
Three thousand foals beside their mothers
   fed.
Boreas, enamour'd of the sprightly train,
Conceal'd his Godhead in a flowing mane,
With voice dissembled to his loves he
   neigh'd,
And cours'd the dappled beauties o'er the
   mead:
Hence sprung twelve others of unrivall'd
   kind,
Swift as their mother mares and father
   wind.
These lightly skimming, when they swept
   the plain, 270
Nor plied the grass, nor bent the tender
   grain;
And when along the level seas they flew,
Scarce on the surface curl'd the briny dew.
Such Erichthonius was: From him there
   came
The sacred Tros, of whom the Trojan name.
Three sons renown'd adorn'd his nuptial bed,
Ilus, Assaracus, and Ganymed:
The matchless Ganymed, divinely fair,
Whom Heav'n, enamour'd, snatch'd to up-
   per air,
To bear the cup of Jove (ethereal guest, 280
The grace and glory of th' ambrosial feast).
The two remaining sons the line divide:
First rose Laomedon from Ilus' side:
From him Tithonus, now in cares grown
   old,
And Priam (blest with Hector, brave and
   bold);
Clytius and Lampus, ever-honour'd pair;
And Hicetaon, thunderbolt of war.
From great Assaracus sprung Capys, he
Begat Anchises, and Anchises me,
Such is our race: 't is Fortune gives us
   birth, 290
But Jove alone endues the soul with worth:
He, source of power and might! with bound-
   less sway
All human courage gives or takes away.
Long in the field of words we may contend,
Reproach is infinite, and knows no end,

Arm'd or with truth or falsehood, right or
    wrong,
So voluble a weapon is the tongue;
Wounded, we wound; and neither side can
    fail,
For ev'ry man has equal strength to rail:
Women alone, when in the streets they
    jar,   300
Perhaps excel us in this wordy war;
Like us they stand, encompass'd with the
    crowd,
And vent their anger, impotent and loud.
Cease then: our bus'ness in the Field of
    Fight
Is not to question, but to prove our might.
To all those insults thou hast offer'd here
Receive this answer: 't is my flying spear.'
    He spoke. With all his force the jav'lin
    flung,
Fix'd deep, and loudly in the buckler rung.
Far on his outstretch'd arm Pelides held 310
(To meet the thund'ring lance) his dread-
    ful shield,
That trembled as it struck ; nor void of fear
Saw, ere it fell, th' immeasurable spear.
His fears were vain; impenetrable charms
Secured the temper of th' ethereal arms.
Thro' two strong plates the point its pas-
    sage held,
But stopp'd and rested, by the third re-
    pell'd;
Five plates of various metal, various ⎫
    mould,   ⎬
Composed the shield; of brass each out- ⎪
    ward fold,   319 ⎪
Of tin each inward, and the middle gold: ⎭
There stuck the lance. Then, rising ere he
    threw,
The forceful spear of great Achilles flew,
And pierc'd the Dardan shield's extremest
    bound,
Where the shrill brass return'd a sharper
    sound:
Thro' the thin verge the Pelian weapon
    glides,
And the slight cov'ring of expanded hides.
Æneas his contracted body bends,
And o'er him high the riven targe extends,
Sees, thro' its parting plates, the upper air,
And at his back perceives the quiv'ring
    spear: 330
A fate so near him chills his soul with
    fright,
And swims before his eyes the many-col-
    our'd light.

Achilles, rushing in with dreadful cries,
Draws his broad blade, and at Æneas flies:
Æneas, rousing as the foe came on
(With force collected), heaves a mighty
    stone;
A mass enormous! which, in modern days
No two of earth's degen'rate sons could
    raise.
But ocean's God, whose earthquakes rock
    the ground,
Saw the distress, and mov'd the Powers
    around: 340
' Lo! on the brink of fate Æneas stands,
An instant victim to Achilles' hands;
By Phœbus urged; but Phœbus has bestow'd
His aid in vain: the man o'erpowers the
    God.
And can ye see this righteous Chief atone,
With guiltless blood, for vices not his own ?
To all the Gods his constant vows were
    paid;
Sure, tho' he wars for Troy, he claims our
    aid.
Fate wills not this; nor thus can Jove re-
    sign
The future father of the Dardan line: 350
The first great ancestor obtain'd his grace,
And still his love descends on all the race.
For Priam now, and Priam's faithless kind,
At length are odious to th' all-seeing mind;
On great Æneas shall devolve the reign,
And sons succeeding sons the lasting line
    sustain.'
    The great earth-shaker thus: to whom
    replies
Th' imperial Goddess with the radiant eyes:
' Good as he is, to immolate or spare
The Dardan Prince, O Neptune, be thy
    care;   360
Pallas and I, by all that Gods can bind,
Have sworn destruction to the Trojan kind;
Not ev'n an instant to protract their fate,
Or save one member of the sinking state;
Till her last flame be quench'd with her
    last gore,
And ev'n her crumbling ruins are no more.'
    The King of Ocean to the fight descends;
Thro' all the whistling darts his course he
    bends,
Swift interposed between the warriors flies,
And casts thick darkness o'er Achilles'
    eyes.   370
From great Æneas' shield the spear he
    drew,
And at its master's feet the weapon threw.

That done, with force divine he snatch'd
    on high
The Dardan Prince, and bore him thro' the
    sky,
Smooth-gliding without step, above the
    heads
Of warring heroes and of bounding steeds.
Till at the battle's utmost verge they light,
Where the slow Caucons close the rear of
    fight:
The Godhead there (his heav'nly form con-
    fess'd)
With words like these the panting Chief
    address'd: 380
   'What Power, O Prince, with force in-
    ferior far
Urged thee to meet Achilles' arm in war ?
Henceforth beware, nor antedate thy doom,
Defrauding Fate of all thy fame to come.
But when the day decreed (for come it
    must),
Shall lay this dreadful hero in the dust,
Let then the furies of that arm be known,
Secure no Grecian force transcends thy
    own.'
   With that, he left him wond'ring as he
    lay,   389
Then from Achilles chased the mist away:
Sudden, returning with the stream of light,
The scene of war came rushing on his sight.
Then thus amazed: 'What wonders strike
    my mind!
My spear, that parted on the wings of
    wind,
Laid here before me! and the Dardan lord,
That fell this instant, vanish'd from my
    sword!
I thought alone with mortals to contend,
But Powers celestial sure this foe defend.
Great as he is, our arm he scarce will try,
Content for once, with all his Gods, to fly.
Now then let others bleed.' This said,
    aloud   401
He vents his fury, and inflames the crowd:
'O Greeks' (he cries, and every rank
    alarms),
'Join battle, man to man, and arms to arms!
'T is not in me, tho' favour'd by the sky,
To mow whole troops, and make whole
    armies fly:
No God can singly such a host engage,
Not Mars himself, nor great Minerva's
    rage.
But whatsoe'er Achilles can inspire,
Whate'er of active force, or acting fire, 410

Whate'er this heart can prompt, or hand
    obey;
All, all Achilles, Greeks, is yours to-day.
Thro' yon wide host this arm shall scatter
    fear,
And thin the squadrons with my single
    spear.'
   He said: nor less elate with martial joy,
The godlike Hector warm'd the troops of
    Troy:
'Trojans, to war! think Hector leads you on;
Nor dread the vaunts of Peleus' haughty
    son.
Deeds must decide our fate. Ev'n those
    with words
Insult the brave, who tremble at their
    swords;   420
The weakest atheist-wretch all Heav'n de-
    fies,
But shrinks and shudders, when the thun-
    der flies.
Nor from yon boaster shall your Chief
    retire,
Not tho' his heart were steel, his hands
    were fire;
That fire, that steel, your Hector should
    withstand,
And brave that vengeful heart, that dread-
    ful hand.'
   Thus (breathing rage thro' all) the hero
    said;
A wood of lances rises round his head,
Clamours on clamours tempest all the air;
They join, they throng, they thicken to the
    war.   430
But Phœbus warns him from high Heav'n
    to shun
The single fight with Thetis' godlike son:
More safe to combat in the mingled band,
Nor tempt too near the terrors of his hand.
He hears, obedient to the God of Light,
And, plunged within the ranks, awaits the
    fight.
   Then fierce Achilles, shouting to the
    skies,
On Troy's whole force with boundless fury
    flies.
First falls Iphytion, at his army's head;
Brave was the Chief, and brave the host he
    led;   440
From great Otrynteus he derived his blood,
His mother was a Naïs of the flood;
Beneath the shades of Tmolus, crown'd
    with snow,
From Hyde's walls he ruled the lands below.

Fierce as he springs, the sword his head
  divides;
The parted visage falls on equal sides:
With loud resounding arms he strikes the
  plain;
While thus Achilles glories o'er the slain:
 ' Lie there, Otryntides ! the Trojan earth
Receives thee dead, tho' Gygæ boast thy
  birth;   450
Those beauteous fields where Hyllus' waves
  are roll'd,
And plenteous Hermus swells with tides of
  gold,
Are thine no more.' Th' insulting hero said,
And left him sleeping in eternal shade.
The rolling wheels of Greece the body tore,
And dash'd their axles with no vulgar gore.
  Demoleon next, Antenor's offspring, laid
Breathless in dust, the price of rashness
  paid.
Th' impatient steel with full descending
  sway
Forc'd thro' his brazen helm its furious
  way,   460
Resistless drove the batter'd skull before,
And dash'd and mingled all the brains with
  gore.
This sees Hippodamas, and, seiz'd with
  fright,
Deserts his chariot for a swifter flight:
The lance arrests him; an ignoble wound
The panting Trojan rivets to the ground.
He groans away his soul: not louder roars
At Neptune's shrine on Helicé's high shores
The victim bull; the rocks rebellow round,
And ocean listens to the grateful sound. 470
  Then fell on Polydore his vengeful rage,
The youngest hope of Priam's stooping age
(Whose feet for swiftness in the race sur-
  pass'd) ;
Of all his sons, the dearest and the last.
To the forbidden field he takes his flight
In the first folly of a youthful knight;
To vaunt his swiftness wheels around the
  plain,
But vaunts not long, with all his swiftness
  slain;
Struck where the crossing belts unite be-
  hind,
And golden rings the double back-plate
  join'd.   480
Forth thro' the navel burst the thrilling
  steel;
And on his knees with piercing shrieks he
  fell;

The rushing entrails pour'd upon the
  ground
His hands collect: and darkness wraps him
  round.
When Hector view'd, all ghastly in his gore,
Thus sadly slain, th' unhappy Polydore;
A cloud of sorrow overcast his sight,
His soul no longer brook'd the distant fight;
Full in Achilles' dreadful front he came,
And shook his jav'lin like a waving
  flame.   490
The son of Peleus sees, with joy possess'd,
His heart high-bounding in his rising
  breast:
And, ' Lo ! the man, on whom black fates
  attend ;
The man that slew Achilles in his friend !
No more shall Hector's and Pelides' spear
Turn from each other in the walks of war.'
Then with revengeful eyes he scann'd him
  o'er —
' Come, and receive thy Fate !' He spake
  no more.
  Hector, undaunted, thus: ' Such words
  employ
To one that dreads thee, some unwarlike
  boy: 500
Such we could give, defying and defied,
Mean intercourse of obloquy and pride !
I know thy force to mine superior far;
But Heav'n alone confers success in war;
Mean as I am, the Gods may guide my
  dart,
And give it entrance in a braver heart.'
  Then parts the lance: but Pallas' heav'nly
  breath
Far from Achilles wafts the winged death:
The bidden dart again to Hector flies,
And at the feet of its great master lies. 510
Achilles closes with his hated foe,
His heart and eyes with flaming fury glow:
But, present to his aid, Apollo shrouds
The favour'd hero in a veil of clouds.
Thrice struck Pelides with indignant heart,
Thrice in impassive air he plunged the
  dart:
The spear a fourth time buried in the cloud,
He foams with fury, and exclaims aloud:
 ' Wretch ! thou hast 'scaped again, once
  more thy flight
Has saved thee, and the partial God of
  Light;   520
But long thou shalt not thy just Fate with-
  stand,
If any Power assist Achilles' hand.

Fly then inglorious; but thy flight this day
Whole hecatombs of Trojan ghosts shall
    pay.'
With that he gluts his rage on numbers
    slain:
Then Dryops tumbled to th' ensanguin'd
    plain
Pierc'd thro' the neck: he left him panting
    there,
And stopp'd Demuchus, great Philetor's
    heir,
Gigantic Chief! deep gash'd th' enormous
    blade,
And for the soul an ample passage made. 530
Laogonus and Dardanus expire,
The valiant sons of an unhappy sire;
Both in one instant from the chariot hurl'd,
Sunk in one instant to the nether world;
This diff'rence only their sad fates afford,
That one the spear destroy'd, and one the
    sword.
    Nor less unpitied, young Alastor bleeds;
In vain his youth, in vain his beauty pleads:
In vain he begs thee, with a suppliant's
    moan
To spare a form and age so like thy
    own! 540
Unhappy boy! no prayer, no moving art
E'er bent that fierce inexorable heart!
While yet he trembled at his knees, and
    cried,
The ruthless faichion oped his tender side;
The panting liver pours a flood of gore,
That drowns his bosom till he pants no
    more.
    Thro' Mulius' head then drove th' impet-
    uous spear;
The warrior falls transfix'd from ear to ear.
Thy life, Echeclus! next the sword be-
    reaves;
Deep thro' the front the pond'rous falchion
    cleaves; 550
Warm'd in the brain the smoking weapon
    lies,
The purple death comes floating o'er his
    eyes.
Then brave Deucalion died: the dart was
    flung
Where the knit nerves the pliant elbow
    strung:
He dropp'd his arm, an unassisting weight,
And stood all impotent expecting Fate:
Full on his neck the falling falchion sped,
From his broad shoulders hew'd his crested
    head:

Forth from the bone the spinal marrow
    flies,
And sunk in dust the corpse extended
    lies. 560
Rhigmus, whose race from fruitful Thracia
    came
(The son of Pireus, an illustrious name),
Succeeds to Fate: the spear his belly rends;
Prone from his car the thund'ring Chief de-
    scends;
The squire who saw expiring on the ground
His prostrate master, rein'd the steeds
    around.
His back scarce turn'd, the Pelian jav'lin
    gored,
And stretch'd the servant o'er his dying
    lord.
As when a flame the winding valley fills,
And runs on crackling shrubs between the
    hills; 570
Then o'er the stubble up the mountain
    flies,
Fires the high woods, and blazes to the
    skies,
This way and that the spreading torrent
    roars;
So sweeps the hero thro' the wasted shores:
Around him wide immense destruction
    pours,
And earth is deluged with the sanguine
    showers.
As with autumnal harvests cover'd o'er,
And thick bestrown, lies Ceres' sacred
    floor,
When round and round, with never-wearied
    pain,
The trampling steers beat out th' unnum-
    ber'd grain: 580
So the fierce coursers, as the chariot
    rolls,
Tread down whole ranks, and crush out
    heroes' souls.
Dash'd from their hoofs, while o'er the
    dead they fly,
Black, bloody drops the smoking chariot
    dye:
The spiky wheels thro' heaps of carnage
    tore;
And thick the groaning axles dropp'd with
    gore.
High o'er the scene of death Achilles
    stood,
All grim with dust, all horrible in blood:
Yet still insatiate, still with rage on flame;
Such is the lust of never-dying Fame! 590

BOOK XXI

THE BATTLE IN THE RIVER SCAMANDER

THE ARGUMENT.

The Trojans fly before Achilles, some towards the town, others to the river Scamander; he falls upon the latter with great slaughter, takes twelve captives alive, to sacrifice to the shade of Patroclus; and kills Lycaon and Asteropæus. Scamander attacks him with all his waves; Neptune and Pallas assist the hero; Simois joins Scamander; at length Vulcan, by the instigation of Juno, almost dries up the river. This combat ended, the other gods engage each other. Meanwhile Achilles continues the slaughter, and drives the rest into Troy: Agenor only makes a stand, and is conveyed away in a cloud by Apollo: who (to delude Achilles) takes upon him Agenor's shape, and while he pursues him in that disguise, gives the Trojans an opportunity of retiring into their city. The same day continues. The scene is on the banks and in the stream of Scamander.

AND now to Xanthus' gliding stream they drove,
Xanthus, immortal progeny of Jove.
The river here divides the flying train:
Part to the town fly diverse o'er the plain,
Where late their troops triumphant bore the fight,
Now chased and trembling in ignoble flight
(These with a gather'd mist Saturnia shrouds,
And rolls behind the rout a heap of clouds);
Part plunge into the stream: old Xanthus roars;
The flashing billows beat the whiten'd shores: 10
With cries promiscuous all the banks resound,
And here and there, in eddies whirling round,
The flouncing steeds and shrieking warriors drown'd,
As the scorch'd locusts from their fields retire,
While fast behind them runs the blaze of fire;
Driv'n from the land before the smoky cloud,
The clust'ring legions rush into the flood:
So plunged in Xanthus by Achilles' force,
Roars the resounding surge with men and horse.

His bloody lance the hero casts aside 20
(Which spreading tam'risks on the margin hide),
Then, like a God, the rapid billows braves,
Arm'd with his sword, high brandish'd o'er the waves;
Now down he plunges, now he whirls it round,
Deep groan the waters with the dying sound;
Repeated wounds the redd'ning river dyed,
And the warm purple circled on the tide.
Swift thro' the foamy flood the Trojans fly,
And close in rocks or winding caverns lie:
So the huge dolphin tempesting the main, 30
In shoals before him fly the scaly train;
Confusedly heap'd, they seek their inmost caves,
Or pant and heave beneath the floating waves.
Now, tired with slaughter, from the Trojan band
Twelve chosen youths he drags alive to land;
With their rich belts their captive arms constrains
(Late their proud ornaments, but now their chains);
These his attendants to the ships convey'd,
Sad victims! destin'd to Patroclus' shade.
Then, as once more he plunged amid the flood, 40
The young Lycaon in his passage stood;
The son of Priam, whom the hero's hand
But late made captive in his father's land
(As from a sycamore his sounding steel
Lopp'd the green arms to spoke a chariot wheel),
To Lemnos' isle he sold the royal slave,
Where Jason's son the price demanded gave:
But kind Eëtion, touching on the shore,
The ransom'd Prince to fair Arisbe bore.
Ten days were past, since in his father's reign 50
He felt the sweets of liberty again:
The next, that God whom men in vain withstand,
Gives the same youth to the same conquering hand:
Now never to return! and doom'd to go
A sadder journey to the shades below.
His well-known face when great Achilles eyed
(The helm and vizor he had cast aside

With wild affright, and dropp'd upon the
   field
His useless lance and unavailing shield),
As trembling, panting, from the stream he
   fled,   60
And knock'd his falt'ring knees, the hero
   said:
   'Ye mighty Gods! what wonders strike
   my view!
Is it in vain our conquering arms subdue?
Sure I shall see yon heaps of Trojans kill'd,
Rise from the shade, and brave me on the
   field:
As now the captive, whom so late I bound
And sold to Lemnos, stalks on Trojan
   ground!
Not him the sea's unmeasur'd deeps de-
   tain,
That bar such numbers from their native
   plain:
Lo! he returns. Try then my flying
   spear!   70
Try, if the grave can hold the wanderer:
If earth at length this active Prince can
   seize,
Earth, whose strong grasp has held down
   Hercules.'
   Thus while he spake, the Trojan, pale
   with fears,
Approach'd, and sought his knees with sup-
   pliant tears;
Loath as he was to yield his youthful
   breath,
And his soul shiv'ring at th' approach of
   death.
Achilles rais'd the spear, prepared to
   wound;
He kiss'd his feet, extended on the ground:
And while above the spear suspended
   stood,   80
Longing to dip its thirsty point in blood,
One hand embraced them close, one stopp'd
   the dart;
While thus these melting words attempt
   his heart:
   'Thy well-known captive, great Achilles!
   see;
Once more Lycaon trembles at thy knee;
Some pity to a suppliant's name afford,
Who shared the gifts of Ceres at thy
   board;
Whom late thy conquering arm to Lemnos
   bore,
Far from his father, friends, and native
   shore;

A hundred oxen were his price that day, 90
Now sums immense thy mercy shall repay.
Scarce respited from woes I yet appear,
And scarce twelve morning suns have seen
   me here:
Lo! Jove again submits me to thy hands,
Again, her victim cruel Fate demands!
I sprung from Priam, and Laothoë fair
(Old Altes' daughter, and Lelegia's heir;
Who held in Pedasus his famed abode,
And ruled the fields where silver Satnio
   flow'd);   99
Two sons (alas! unhappy sons) she bore;⎫
For ah! one spear shall drink each bro- ⎬
   ther's gore,   ⎭
And I succeed to slaughter'd Polydore.
How from that arm of terror shall I fly?
Some demon urges, 't is my doom to die!
If ever yet soft pity touch'd thy mind,
Ah! think not me too much of Hector's
   kind!
Not the same mother gave thy suppliant
   breath,
With his, who wrought thy lov'd Patroclus'
   death.'
   These words, attended with a shower of
   tears,
The youth address'd to unrelenting ears: 110
'Talk not of life, or ransom' (he replies),
'Patroclus dead, whoever meets me, dies:
In vain a single Trojan sues for grace;
But least, the sons of Priam's hateful race.
Die then, my friend! what boots it to de-
   plore?
The great, the good Patroclus is no more!
He, far thy better, was foredoom'd to die,
And thou, dost thou bewail mortality?
Seest thou not me, whom Nature's gifts
   adorn,   119
Sprung from a Hero, from a Goddess born?
The day shall come (which nothing can
   avert)
When by the spear, the arrow, or the dart,
By night, or day, by force or by design,
Impending death and certain fate are mine.
Die then:' he said, and as the word he
   spoke,
The fainting stripling sunk before the
   stroke;
His hand forgot its grasp, and left the
   spear;
While all his trembling frame confess'd
   his fear.
Sudden Achilles his broad sword display'd,
And buried in his neck the reeking blade.

Prone fell the youth; and, panting on the
   land, 131
The gushing purple dyed the thirsty sand:
The victor to the stream the carcass gave,
And thus insults him, floating on the wave:
'Lie there, Lycaon! let the fish surround
Thy bloated corse, and suck thy gory
   wound:
There no sad mother shall thy funerals
   weep,
But swift Scamander roll thee to the deep,
Whose ev'ry wave some wat'ry monster
   brings,
To feast unpunish'd on the fat of Kings. 140
So perish Troy, and all the Trojan line!
Such ruin theirs, and such compassion
   mine.
What boots ye now Scamander's worshipp'd
   stream,
His earthly honours, and immortal name?
In vain your immolated bulls are slain,
Your living coursers glut his gulfs in vain:
Thus he rewards you with this bitter fate;
Thus, till the Grecian vengeance is com-
   plete;
Thus is atoned Patroclus' honour'd shade,
And the short absence of Achilles paid.' 150
   These boastful words provoke the raging
   God;
With fury swells the violated flood.
What means divine may yet the Power
   employ,
To check Achilles, and to rescue Troy?
Meanwhile the hero springs in arms, to
   dare
The great Asteropæus to mortal war;
The son of Pelagon, whose lofty line
Flows from the source of Axius, stream
   divine! 158
(Fair Peribœa's love the God had crown'd,
With all his refluent waters circled round.)
On him Achilles rush'd: he fearless stood,
And shook two spears, advancing from the
   flood:
The flood impell'd him, on Pelides' head
T' avenge his waters choked with heaps of
   dead.
Near as they drew, Achilles thus began:
'What art thou, boldest of the race of man?
Who, or from whence? Unhappy is the
   sire,
Whose son encounters our resistless ire.'
   'O son of Peleus! what avails to trace'
(Replied the warrior) 'our illustrious
   race? 170

From rich Pæonia's valleys I command,
Arm'd with protended spears, my native
   band;
Now shines the tenth bright morning since
   I came
In aid of Ilion to the Fields of Fame:
Axius, who swells with all the neighb'ring
   rills,
And wide around the floated region fills,
Begot my sire, whose spear such glory won:
Now lift thy arm, and try that hero's son!'
   Threat'ning he said: the hostile Chiefs
   advance; 179
At once Asteropæus discharged each lance;
(For both his dext'rous hands the lance
   could wield);
One struck, but pierc'd not the Vulcanian
   shield;
One razed Achilles' hand; the spouting
   blood
Spun forth, in earth the fasten'd weapon
   stood.
Like lightning next the Pelian jav'lin flies;
Its erring fury hiss'd along the skies;
Deep in the swelling bank was driv'n the
   spear,
Ev'n to the middle earth; and quiver'd
   there.
Then from his side the sword Pelides drew,
And on his foe with double fury flew; 190
The foe thrice tugg'd, and shook the rooted
   wood,
Repulsive of his might the weapon stood:
The fourth, he tries to break the spear, in
   vain;
Bent as he stands he tumbles to the plain;
His belly open'd with a ghastly wound,
The reeking entrails pour upon the ground.
Beneath the hero's feet he panting lies,
And his eye darkens, and his spirit flies:
While the proud victor thus triumphing
   said, 199
His radiant armour tearing from the dead:
   'So ends thy glory! such the fate they
   prove
Who strive presumptuous with the sons of
   Jove.
Sprung from a river didst thou boast thy
   line?
But great Saturnius is the source of mine.
How durst thou vaunt thy wat'ry progeny?
Of Peleus, Æacus, and Jove, am I;
The race of these superior far to those,
As he that thunders to the stream that
   flows.

What rivers can, Scamander might have
  shewn:
But Jove he dreads, nor wars against his
  son. 210
Ev'n Acheloüs might contend in vain,
And all the roaring billows of the main.
Th' eternal ocean, from whose fountains
  flow
The seas, the rivers, and the springs below,
The thund'ring voice of Jove abhors to
  hear,
And in his deep abysses shakes with fear.'
  He said: then from the bank his jav'lin
  tore,
And left the breathless warrior in his gore.
The floating tides the bloody carcass lave,
And beat against it, wave succeeding wave:
Till, roll'd between the banks, it lies the
  food 221
Of curling eels, and fishes of the flood.
All scatter'd round the stream (their might-
  iest slain)
Th' amazed Pæonians scour along the plain:
He vents his fury on the flying crew,
Thrasius, Astypylus, and Mnesus, slew;
Mydon, Thersilochus, with Ænius fell;
And numbers more his lance had plunged
  to Hell,
But from the bottom of his gulfs profound,
Scamander spoke; the shores return'd the
  sound: 230
  'O first of mortals (for the Gods are
  thine) !
In valour matchless, and in force divine!
If Jove have giv'n thee ev'ry Trojan head,
'T is not on me thy rage should heap the
  dead.
See! my choked streams no more their
  course can keep,
Nor roll their wonted tribute to the deep.
Turn then, impetuous! from our injured
  flood;
Content, thy slaughters could amaze a God.'
  In human form confess'd, before his
  eyes 239
The River thus; and thus the Chief replies:
'O sacred stream! thy word we shall obey;
But not till Troy the destin'd vengeance
  pay;
Nor till within her towers the perjur'd train
Shall pant, and tremble at our arms again;
Not till proud Hector, guardian of her wall,
Or stain this lance, or see Achilles fall.'
  He said: and drove with fury on the foe.
Then to the Godhead of the Silver Bow

The yellow Flood began: 'O Son of Jove!
Was not the mandate of the Sire above
Full and express ? that Phœbus should em-
  ploy 251
His sacred arrows in defence of Troy,
And make her conquer, till Hyperion's fall
In awful darkness hide the face of all ? '
  He spoke in vain: the Chief without dis-
  may
Ploughs thro' the boiling surge his des-
  p'rate way.
Then, rising in his rage above the shores,
From all his deep the bell'wing river roars;
Huge heaps of slain disgorges on the coast,
And round the banks the ghastly dead are
  toss'd; 260
While all before, the billows ranged on
  high
(A wat'ry bulwark) screen the bands who
  fly.
Now bursting on his head with thund'ring
  sound,
The falling deluge whelms the hero round:
His loaded shield bends to the rushing tide;
His feet, upborne, scarce the strong flood
  divide,
Slidd'ring, and stagg'ring. On the border
  stood
A spreading elm, that overhung the flood;
He seiz'd a bending bough, his steps to
  stay; 269
The plant uprooted to his weight gave way,
Heaving the bank, and undermining all;
Loud flash the waters to the rushing fall
Of the thick foliage. The large trunk dis-
  play'd
Bridg'd the rough flood across: the hero
  stayed
On this his weight, and, rais'd upon his
  hand,
Leap'd from the channel, and regain'd the
  land.
Then blacken'd the wild waves; the mur-
  mur rose;
The God pursues, a huger billow throws,
And burst the bank, ambitious to destroy
The man whose fury is the Fate of Troy. 280
He, like the warlike eagle, speeds his pace
(Swiftest and strongest of the aërial race).
Far as a spear can fly, Achilles springs
At every bound; his clanging armour rings·
Now here, now there, he turns on ev'ry
  side,
And winds his course before the foll'wing
  tide;

The waves flow after, wheresoe'er he
    wheels,
And gather fast, and murmur at his heels.
So when a peasant to his garden brings
Soft rills of water from the bubbling
    springs,   290
And calls the floods from high to bless his
    bowers,
And feed with pregnant streams the plants
    and flowers;
Soon as he clears whate'er their passage
    stay'd,
And marks the future current with his
    spade,
Swift o'er the rolling pebbles, down the
    hills
Louder and louder purl the falling rills;
Before him scatt'ring, they prevent his
    pains,
And shine in mazy wand'rings o'er the
    plains.   298
    Still flies Achilles, but before his eyes
Still swift Scamander rolls where'er he flies:
Not all his speed escapes the rapid floods;
The first of men, but not a match for Gods:
Oft as he turn'd the torrent to oppose,
And bravely try if all the Powers were
    foes;
So oft the surge, in wat'ry mountains
    spread,
Beats on his back, or bursts upon his head.
Yet dauntless still the adverse flood he
    braves,
And still indignant bounds above the waves.
Tired by the tides, his knees relax with
    toil;
Wash'd from beneath him slides the slimy
    soil;   310
When thus (his eyes on Heav'n's expansion
    thrown)
Forth bursts the hero with an angry groan:
    ' Is there no God Achilles to befriend,
No power t' avert his miserable end ?
Prevent, oh Jove! this ignominious date,
And make my future life the sport of Fate:
Of all Heav'n's oracles believ'd in vain,
But most of Thetis, must her son complain:
By Phœbus' darts she prophesied my fall,
In glorious arms before the Trojan wall. 320
Oh ! had I died in fields of battle warm,
Stretch'd like a Hero, by a Hero's arm;
Might Hector's spear this dauntless bosom
    rend,
And my swift soul o'ertake my slaughter'd
    friend !

Ah no ! Achilles meets a shameful fate,
Oh how unworthy of the brave and great !
Like some vile swain, whom, on a rainy ⎤
    day,   ⎟
Crossing a ford, the torrent sweeps away, ⎬
An unregarded carcass to the sea.'   ⎦
    Neptune and Pallas haste to his relief, 330
And thus in human form address the Chief:
The Power of Ocean first: ' Forbear thy
    fear,
O son of Peleus ! lo, thy Gods appear !
Behold ! from Jove descending to thy aid,
Propitious Neptune, and the Blue-eyed
    Maid.
Stay, and the furious flood shall cease to
    rave:
'T is not thy fate to glut his angry wave.
But thou the counsel Heav'n suggests at-
    tend;
Nor breathe from combat, nor thy sword
    suspend,
Till Troy receive her flying sons, till all 340
Her routed squadrons pant behind their
    wall:
Hector alone shall stand his fatal chance,
And Hector's blood shall smoke upon thy
    lance;
Thine is the glory doom'd.' Thus spake
    the Gods:
Then swift ascended to the bright abodes.
    Stung with new ardour, thus by Heav'n
    impell'd,
He springs impetuous, and invades the
    field:
O'er all th' expanded plain the waters
    spread;
Heav'd on the bounding billows danc'd the
    dead,
Floating 'midst scatter'd arms: while
    casques of gold,   350
And turn'd-up bucklers, glitter'd as they
    roll'd.
High o'er the surging tide, by leaps and
    bounds,
He wades, and mounts; the parted wave
    resounds.
Not a whole river stops the hero' course,
While Pallas fills him with immortal force.
With equal rage indignant Xanthus roars,
And lifts his billows, and o'erwhelms his
    shores.
    Then thus to Sïmois: ' Haste, my bro-
    ther flood !
And check this mortal that controls a God:
Our bravest heroes else shall quit the fight,

And Ilion tumble from her tow'ry height. 361
Call then thy subject streams, and bid
  them roar;
From all thy fountains swell thy wat'ry
  store ;
With broken rocks, and with a load of
  dead
Charge the black surge, and pour it on his
  head.
Mark how resistless thro' the floods he
  goes,
And boldly bids the warring Gods be foes !
But nor that force, nor form divine to
  sight,
Shall aught avail him, if our rage unite:
Whelm'd under our dark gulfs those harms
  shall lie, 370
That blaze so dreadful in each Trojan eye;
And deep beneath a sandy mountain hurl'd,
Immers'd remain this terror of the world.
Such pond'rous ruin shall confound the
  place,
No Greeks shall e'er his perish'd relics
  grace,
No hand his bones shall gather or inhume;
These his cold rites, and this his wat'ry
  tomb.'
He said; and on the Chief descends amain,
Increas'd with gore, and swelling with the
  slain.
Then, murm'ring from his beds, he boils,
  he raves, 380
And a foam whitens on the purple waves:
At ev'ry step, before Achilles stood
The crimson surge, and deluged him with
  blood.
Fear touch'd the Queen of Heav'n: she
  saw dismay'd,
She call'd aloud, and summon'd Vulcan's
  aid.
  ' Rise to the war ! th' insulting Flood re-
  quires
Thy wasteful arm: assemble all thy fires !
While to their aid, by our command en-
  join'd,
Rush the swift eastern and the western
  wind:
These from old ocean at my word shall
  blow, 390
Pour the red torrent on the wat'ry foe,
Corses and arms to one bright ruin turn,
And hissing rivers to their bottoms burn.
Go, mighty in thy rage ! display thy power;
Drink the whole flood, the crackling trees
  devour;

Scorch all the banks ! and (till our voice
  reclaim)
Exert th' unwearied furies of the flame ! '
  The Power Ignipotent her word obeys:
Wide o'er the plain he pours the boundless
  blaze;
At once consumes the dead, and dries the
  soil; 400
And the shrunk waters in their channel boil.
As when autumnal Boreas sweeps the sky,
And instant blows the water'd gardens dry:
So look'd the field, so whiten'd was the
  ground,
While Vulcan breathed the fiery blast
  around.
Swift on the sedgy reeds the ruin preys;
Along the margin winds the running blaze:
The trees in flaming rows to ashes turn,
The flow'ry lotos and the tam'risk burn,
Broad elm, and cypress rising in a spire;
The wat'ry willows hiss before the fire. 411
Now glow the waves, the fishes pant for
  breath:
The eels lie twisting in the pangs of death:
Now flounce aloft, now dive the scaly fry,
Or gasping, turn their bellies to the sky.
At length the River rear'd his languid head,
And thus, short panting, to the God he
  said:
  ' Oh Vulcan ! oh ! what Power resists
  thy might ?
I faint, I sink, unequal to the fight ——
I yield — let Ilion fall; if Fate de-
  cree —— 420
Ah bend no more thy fiery arms on me ! '
  He ceas'd; while, conflagration blazing
  round,
The bubbling waters yield a hissing sound.
As when the flames beneath a caldron rise,
To melt the fat of some rich sacrifice,
Amid the fierce embrace of circling fires
The waters foam, the heavy smoke aspires:
So boils th' imprison'd flood, forbid to flow,
And, choked with vapours, feels his bottom
  glow.
To Juno then, imperial Queen of Air, 430
The burning River sends his earnest prayer:
  ' Ah why, Saturnia ! must thy son engage
Me, only me, with all his wasteful rage ?
On other Gods his dreadful arm employ,
For mightier Gods assert the cause of Troy.
Submissive I desist, if thou command,
But ah ! withdraw this all-destroying hand.
Hear then my solemn oath, to yield to Fate
Unaided Ilion, and her destin'd state,

Till Greece shall gird her with destructive
    flame,   440
And in one ruin sink the Trojan name.'
  His warm entreaty touch'd Saturnia's
    ear:
She bade th' Ignipotent his rage forbear,
Recall the flame, nor in a mortal cause
Infest a God: th' obedient flame withdraws:
Again, the branching streams begin to
    spread,
And soft re-murmur in their wonted bed.
  While these by Juno's will the strife
    resign,
The warring Gods in fierce contention join:
Rekindling rage each heav'nly breast
    alarms;   450
With horrid clangour shock th' ethereal
    arms:
Heav'n in loud thunder bids the trumpet
    sound;
And wide beneath them groans the rending
    ground.
Jove, as his sport, the dreadful scene de-
    scries,
And views contending Gods with careless
    eyes.
The Power of Battles lifts his brazen
    spear,
And first assaults the radiant Queen of
    War.
  'What mov'd thy madness, thus to dis-
    unite
Ethereal minds, and mix all Heav'n in
    fight?
What wonder this, when in thy frantic
    mood   460
Thou drovest a mortal to insult a God?
Thy impious hand Tydides' jav'lin bore,
And madly bathed it in celestial gore.'
  He spoke, and smote the loud-resound-
    ing shield,
Which bears Jove's thunder on its dread-
    ful field;
The adamantine ægis of her sire,
That turns the glancing bolt, and forked
    fire.
Then heav'd the Goddess in her mighty
    hand
A stone, the limit of the neighb'ring land,
There fix'd from eldest times; black,
    craggy, vast.   470
This at the heav'nly homicide she cast.
Thund'ring he falls; a mass of monstrous
    size,
And sev'n broad acres covers as he lies.

The stunning stroke his stubborn nerves
    unbound;
Loud o'er the fields his ringing arms re-
    sound:
The scornful Dame her conquest views
    with smiles,
And, glorying, thus the prostrate God re-
    viles:
  'Hast thou not yet, insatiate fury!
    known
How far Minerva's force transcends thy
    own?
Juno, whom thou rebellious dar'st with-
    stand,   480
Corrects thy folly thus by Pallas' hand;
Thus meets thy broken faith with just dis-
    grace,
And partial aid to Troy's perfidious race.'
  The Goddess spoke, and turn'd her eyes
    away,
That, beaming round, diffused celestial
    day.
Jove's Cyprian daughter, stooping on the
    land,
Lent to the wounded God her tender hand:
Slowly he rises, scarcely breathes with
    pain,
And propt on her fair arm forsakes the
    plain:
This the bright Empress of the Heav'ns
    survey'd,   490
And scoffing thus to War's victorious
    Maid:
  'Lo, what an aid on Mars's side is seen!
The smiles' and loves' unconquerable
    Queen!
Mark with what insolence, in open view,
She moves: let Pallas, if she dares, pursve.'
  Minerva smiling heard, the pair o'ertook,
And slightly on her breast the wanton
    struck:
She, unresisting, fell (her spirits fled);
On earth together lay the lovers spread.
  'And like these heroes, be the fate of
    all'   500
(Minerva cries) 'who guard the Trojan
    wall!
To Grecian Gods such let the Phrygian be,
So dread, so fierce, as Venus is to me;
Then from the lowest stone shall Troy be
    mov'd:'
  Thus she, and Juno with a smile approv'd.
  Meantime, to mix in more than mortal
    fight,
The God of Ocean dares the God of Light.

'What sloth has seiz'd us, when the fields
around
Ring with conflicting Powers, and Heav'n
returns the sound ?   509
Shall, ignominious, we with shame retire,
No deed perform'd, to our Olympian sire ?
Come, prove thy arm ! for first the war to
wage,
Suits not my greatness, or superior age;
Rash as thou art, to prop the Trojan ⎤
throne   ⎥
(Forgetful of my wrongs, and of thy own), ⎬
And guard the race of proud Laomedon! ⎦
Hast thou forgot, how, at the Monarch's
prayer,
We shared the lengthen'd labours of a
year ?
Troy's walls I rais'd (for such were Jove's
commands),
And yon proud bulwarks grew beneath my
hands;   520
Thy task it was to feed the bell'wing
droves
Along fair Ida's vales, and pendent groves.
But when the circling seasons in their train
Brought back the grateful day that crown'd
our pain;
With menace stern the fraudful King de-
fied
Our latent Godhead, and the prize denied:
Mad as he was, he threaten'd servile bands,
And doom'd us exiles far in barb'rous
lands.
Incens'd, we heavenward fled with swiftest
wing,
And destin'd vengeance on the perjur'd
King.   530
Dost thou, for this, afford proud Ilion
grace,
And not, like us, infest the faithless race ?
Like us, their present, future sons destroy,
And from its deep foundations heave their
Troy ? '
Apollo thus: ' To combat for mankind
Ill suits the wisdom of celestial mind:
For what is man ? Calamitous by birth,
They owe their life and nourishment to
earth:
Like yearly leaves, that now, with beauty
crown'd,
Smile on the sun; now, wither on the
ground;   540
To their own hands commit the frantic
scene,
Nor mix Immortals in a cause so mean.'

Then turns his face, far beaming heav'nly
fires,
And from the senior Power submiss re-
tires;
Him, thus retreating, Artemis upbraids,
The quiver'd Huntress of the sylvan
Shades:
' And is it thus the youthful Phœbus
flies,
And yields to Ocean's hoary Sire the
prize ?
How vain that martial pomp, and dreadful
show
Of pointed arrows, and the silver bow ! 550
Now boast no more in yon celestial bower,
Thy force can match the great earth-shak-
ing Power.'
Silent he heard the Queen of Woods
upbraid:
Not so Saturnia bore the vaunting maid;
But furious thus: ' What insolence has
driv'n
Thy pride to face the Majesty of Heav'n ?
What tho' by Jove the female plague de-
sign'd,
Fierce to the feeble race of womankind,
The wretched matron feels thy piercing
dart;
Thy sex's tyrant, with a tiger's heart ? 560
What tho', tremendous in the woodland
chase,
Thy certain arrows pierce the savage race ?
How dares thy rashness on the Powers
divine
Employ those arms, or match thy force
with mine ?
Learn hence, no more unequal war to
wage ' —
She said, and seiz'd her wrists with eager
rage;
These in her left hand lock'd, her right
untied
The bow, the quiver, and its plumy pride.
About her temples flies the busy bow;
Now here, now there, she winds her from
the blow;   570
The scatt'ring arrows, rattling from the
case,
Drop round, and idly mark the dusty place.
Swift from the field the baffled huntress
flies,
And scarce restrains the torrent in her
eyes:
So when the falcon wings her way above
To the cleft cavern speeds the gentle dove

(Not fated yet to die), there safe retreats,
Yet still her heart against the marble
beats.
To her Latona hastes with tender care;
Whom Hermes viewing thus declines the
war: 580
'How shall I face the Dame who gives
delight
To him whose thunders blacken Heav'n
with night?
Go, matchless Goddess! triumph in the
skies,
And boast my conquest, while I yield the
prize.'
He spoke, and pass'd: Latona, stooping
low,
Collects the scatter'd shafts, and fallen
bow,
That, glitt'ring on the dust, lay here and
there;
Dishonour'd relics of Diana's war.
Then swift pursued her to her blest abode,
Where, all confused, she sought the sov'-
reign God; 590
Weeping she grasp'd his knees: th' ambro-
sial vest
Shook with her sighs, and panted on her
breast.
The Sire superior smiled; and bade her
shew
What heav'nly hand had caus'd his daugh-
ter's woe?
Abash'd she names his own imperial spouse;
And the pale cresent fades upon her brows.
Thus they above; while, swiftly gliding
down,
Apollo enters Ilion's sacred town:
The guardian God now trembled for her
wall,
And fear'd the Greeks, tho' Fate forbade
her fall. 600
Back to Olympus, from the war's alarms,
Return the shining bands of Gods in arms;
Some proud in triumph, some with rage on
fire;
And take their thrones around th' ethereal
Sire.
Thro' blood, thro' death, Achilles still
proceeds,
O'er slaughter'd heroes, and o'er rolling
steeds.
As when avenging flames, with fury driv'n,
On guilty towns exert the wrath of Heav'n;
The pale inhabitants, some fall, some fly;
And the red vapours purple all the sky: 610

So raged Achilles: death, and dire dismay,
And toils, and terror, fill'd the dreadful
day.
High on a turret hoary Priam stands,
And marks the waste of his destructive
hands;
Views, from his arm, the Trojans' scatter'd
flight,
And the near hero rising on his sight.
No stop, no check, no aid! With feeble
pace,
And settled sorrow on his aged face,
Fast as he could, he sighing quits the
walls!
And thus, descending, on the guards he
calls: 620
'You, to whose care our city gates be-
long,
Set wide your portals to the flying throng.
For lo! he comes, with unresisted sway;
He comes, and desolation marks his way!
But when within the walls our troops take
breath,
Lock fast the brazen bars, and shut out
death.'
Thus charged the rev'rend Monarch: wide
were flung
The opening folds! the sounding hinges
rung.
Phœbus rush'd forth, the flying bands to
meet,
Struck slaughter back, and cover'd the re-
treat. 630
On heaps the Trojans crowd to gain the
gate,
And gladsome see their last escape from
Fate:
Thither, all parch'd with thirst, a heart-
less train,
Hoary with dust, they beat the hollow
plain;
And gasping, panting, fainting, labour on
With heavier strides, that lengthen tow'rd
the town.
Enraged Achilles follows with his spear;
Wild with revenge, insatiable of war.
Then had the Greeks eternal praise
acquired,
And Troy inglorious to her walls retired; 640
But he, the God who darts ethereal flame,
Shot down to save her, and redeem her
fame.
To young Agenor force divine he gave
(Antenor's offspring, haughty, bold, and
brave):

In aid of him, beside the beech he sat,
And, wrapt in clouds, restrain'd the hand
  of Fate.
When now the gen'rous youth Achilles
  spies,
Thick beats his heart, the troubled motions
  rise
(So, ere a storm, the waters heave and
  roll):
He stops, and questions thus his mighty
  soul: 650
  'What! shall I fly this terror of the
  plain?
Like others fly, and be like others slain?
Vain hope! to shun him by the self-same
  road
Yon line of slaughter'd Trojans lately trod.
No: with the common heap I scorn to
  fall —
What if they pass'd me to the Trojan wall,
While I decline to yonder path that leads
To Ida's forests and surrounding shades?
So may I reach, conceal'd, the cooling
  flood,
From my tired body wash the dirt and
  blood,   660
And, soon as Night her dusky veil extends,
Return in safety to my Trojan friends.
What if — ? But wherefore all this vain
  debate?
Stand I to doubt within the reach of Fate?
Ev'n now perhaps, ere yet I turn the wall,
The fierce Achilles sees me, and I fall:
Such is his swiftness, 't is in vain to fly,
And such his valour, that who stands must
  die.
Howe'er 't is better, fighting for the state,
Here, and in public view, to meet my
  fate.   670
Yet sure he too is mortal; he may feel
(Like all the sons of earth) the force of
  steel:
One only soul informs that dreadful frame;
And Jove's sole favour gives him all his
  fame.'
  He said, and stood, collected in his
  might;
And all his beating bosom claim'd the fight.
So from some deep-grown wood a panther
  starts,
Rous'd from his thicket by a storm of
  darts:
Untaught to fear or fly, he hears the sounds
Of shouting hunters, and of clam'rous
  hounds;   680

Tho' struck, tho' wounded, scarce perceives
  the pain,
And the barb'd jav'lin stings his breast in
  vain;
On their whole war, untamed the savage
  flies;
And tears his hunter, or beneath him dies.
Not less resolv'd Antenor's valiant heir
Confronts Achilles, and awaits the war,
Disdainful of retreat: high-held before,
His shield (a broad circumference) he
  bore;
Then, graceful as he stood, in act to throw
The lifted jav'lin, thus bespoke the foe: 690
  'How proud Achilles glories in his fame!
And hopes this day to sink the Trojan
  name
Beneath her ruins! Know, that hope is
  vain;
A thousand woes, a thousand toils, remain.
Parents and children our just arms employ,
And strong, and many, are the sons of
  Troy:
Great as thou art, ev'n thou may'st stain
  with gore
These Phrygian fields, and press a foreign
  shore.'
  He said; with matchless force the jav'lin
  flung
Smote on his knee, the hollow cuishes
  rung   700
Beneath the pointed steel; but safe from
  harms
He stands impassive in th' ethereal arms.
Then, fiercely rushing on the daring foe,
His lifted arm prepares the fatal blow;
But, jealous of his fame, Apollo shrouds
The godlike Trojan in a veil of clouds:
Safe from pursuit, and shut from mortal
  view,
Dismiss'd with fame, the favour'd youth
  withdrew.
Meanwhile the God, to cover their escape,
Assumes Agenor's habit, voice, and shape,
Flies from the furious Chief in this dis-
  guise;   711
The furious Chief still follows where he
  flies.
Now o'er the fields they stretch with
  lengthen'd strides,
Now urge the course where swift Sca-
  mander glides:
The God, now distant scarce a stride before,
Tempts his pursuit, and wheels about the
  shore,

While all the flying troops their speed em-
ploy,
And pour on heaps into the walls of Troy:
No stop, no stay: no thought to ask or tell,
Who 'scaped by flight, or who by battle
fell. 720
'T was tumult all, and violence of flight;
And sudden joy confused, and mix'd af-
fright:
Pale Troy against Achilles shuts her gate;
And nations breathe, deliver'd from their
Fate.

BOOK XXII

THE DEATH OF HECTOR

THE ARGUMENT

The Trojans being safe within the walls, Hector only stays to oppose Achilles. Priam is
struck at his approach, and tries to persuade
his son to re-enter the town. Hecuba joins
her entreaties, but in vain. Hector consults
within himself what measures to take; but,
at the advance of Achilles, his resolution
fails him, and he flies: Achilles pursues
him thrice round the walls of Troy. The
Gods debate concerning the fate of Hector;
at length Minerva descends to the aid of
Achilles. She deludes Hector in the shape
of Deïphobus; he stands the combat, and is
slain. Achilles drags the dead body at his
chariot, in the sight of Priam and Hecuba.
Their lamentations, tears, and despair. Their
cries reach the ears of Andromache, who,
ignorant of this, was retired into the inner
part of the palace; she mounts up to the
walls, and beholds her dead husband. She
swoons at the spectacle. Her excess of grief
and lamentation.
The thirtieth day still continues. The scene
lies under the walls, and on the battlements
of Troy.

THUS to their bulwarks, smit with panic
fear,
The herded Ilians rush like driven deer;
There safe, they wipe the briny drops
away,
And drown in bowls the labours of the day.
Close to the walls, advancing o'er the fields,
Beneath one roof of well-compacted shields,
March, bending on, the Greeks' embodied
powers,
Far-stretching in the shade of Trojan
towers.

Great Hector singly stay'd; chain'd down
by Fate,
There fix'd he stood before the Scæan
gate; 10
Still his bold arms determin'd to employ,
The guardian still of long-defended Troy.
　Apollo now to tired Achilles turns
(The Power confess'd in all his glory
burns),
'And what' (he cries) 'has Peleus' son in
view,
With mortal speed a Godhead to pursue?
For not to thee to know the Gods is giv'n,
Unskill'd to trace the latent marks of
Heav'n.
What boots thee now, that Troy forsook
the plain? 19
Vain thy past labour, and thy present
vain:
Safe in their walls are now her troops
bestow'd,
While here thy frantic rage attacks a
God.'
　The Chief incens'd: 'Too partial God of
Day!
To check my conquest in the middle
way:
How few in Ilion else had refuge found!
What gasping numbers now had bit the
ground!
Thou robb'st me of a glory justly mine,
Powerful of Godhead, and of fraud divine:
Mean fame, alas! for one of heav'nly
strain,
To cheat a mortal who repines in vain.' 30
　Then to the city, terrible and strong,
With high and haughty steps he tower'd
along:
So the proud courser, victor of the prize,
To the near goal with double ardour flies.
Him, as he blazing shot across the field,
The careful eyes of Priam first beheld.
Not half so dreadful rises to the sight,
Thro' the thick gloom of some tempestuous
night,
Orion's dog (the year when autumn
weighs),
And o'er the feebler stars exerts his rays; 40
Terrific glory! for his burning breath
Taints the red air with fevers, plagues, and
death.
So flamed his fiery mail. Then wept the
sage:
He strikes his rev'rend head, now white
with age;

He lifts his wither'd arms; obtests the
    skies;
He calls his much-lov'd son with feeble
    cries:
The son, resolv'd Achilles' force to dare,
Full at the Scæan gate expects the war:
While the sad father on the rampart
    stands,   49
And thus adjures him with extended hands:
' Ah stay not, stay not ! guardless and
    alone;
Hector, my lov'd, my dearest, bravest son !
Methinks already I behold thee slain,
And stretch'd beneath that fury of the
    plain.
Implacable Achilles ! might'st thou be
To all the Gods no dearer than to me !
Thee, vultures wild should scatter round
    the shore,
And bloody dogs grow fiercer from thy gore !
How many valiant sons I late enjoy'd,
Valiant in vain ! by thy curs'd arm de-
    stroy'd: 60
Or, worse than slaughter'd, sold in distant
    isles
To shameful bondage and unworthy toils.
Two, while I speak, my eyes in vain ex-⎫
    plore,   ⎬
Two from one mother sprung, my Poly-
    dore   ⎭
And loved Lycaon; now perhaps no more !
Oh ! if in yonder hostile camp they live,
What heaps of gold, what treasures would
    I give !
(Their grandsire's wealth, by right of birth
    their own,
Consign'd his daughter with Lelegia's
    throne):   69
But if (which Heav'n forbid) already lost,
All pale they wander on the Stygian coast,
What sorrows then must their sad mother
    know,
What anguish I ! unutterable woe !
Yet less that anguish, less to her, to me,
Less to all Troy, if not deprived of thee.
Yet shun Achilles ! enter yet the wall;
And spare thyself, thy father, spare us all !
Save thy dear life: or if a soul so brave
Neglect that thought, thy dearer glory save.
Pity, while yet I live, these silver hairs; 80
While yet thy father feels the woes he
    bears,
Yet curs'd with sense ! a wretch, whom in
    his rage
(All trembling on the verge of helpless age)

Great Jove has placed, sad spectacle of
    pain !
The bitter dregs of fortune's cup to drain:
To fill with scenes of death his closing
    eyes,
And number all his days by miseries !
My heroes slain, my bridal bed o'erturn'd,
My daughters ravish'd, and my city burn'd,
My bleeding infants dash'd against the
    floor;   90
These I have yet to see, perhaps yet more !
Perhaps ev'n I, reserv'd by angry Fate
The last sad relic of my ruin'd state
(Dire pomp of sovereign wretchedness !),
    must fall
And stain the pavement of my regal hall;
Where famish'd dogs, late guardians of my
    door,
Shall lick their mangled master's spatter'd
    gore.
Yet for my sons I thank ye, Gods ! 't was
    well:
Well have they perish'd, for in fight they
    fell.
Who dies in youth and vigour, dies the
    best,   100
Struck thro' with wounds, all honest on
    the breast.
But when the Fates, in fulness of their
    rage,
Spurn the hoar head of unresisting age,
In dust the rev'rend lineaments deform,
And pour to dogs the life-blood scarcely
    warm;
This, this is misery ! the last, the worst,
That man can feel: man, fated to be
    curs'd ! '
    He said, and acting what no words could
    say,
Rent from his head the silver locks away.
With him the mournful mother bears a
    part: 110
Yet all their sorrows turn not Hector's
    heart:
The zone unbraced, her bosom she dis-
    play'd;
And thus, fast-falling the salt tears, she
    said:
    ' Have mercy on me, O my son ! revere
The words of age; attend a parent's prayer !
If ever thee in these fond arms I press'd,
Or still'd thy infant clamours at this
    breast;
Ah ! do not thus our helpless years forego,
But, by our walls secured, repel the foe.

Against his rage if singly thou proceed, 120
Should'st thou (but Heav'n avert it !)
    should'st thou bleed,
Nor must thy corse lie honour'd on the
    bier,
Nor spouse, nor mother, grace thee with a
    tear;
Far from our pious rites, those dear re-
    mains
Must feast the vultures on the naked
    plains.'
    So they, while down their cheeks the
    torrents roll:
But fix'd remains the purpose of his soul;
Resolv'd he stands, and with a fiery glance
Expects the hero's terrible advance.   129
So, roll'd up in his den, the swelling snake
Beholds the traveller approach the brake;
When, fed with noxious herbs, his turgid
    veins
Have gather'd half the poisons of the
    plains;
He burns, he stiffens with collected ire,
And his red eyeballs glare with living
    fire.
Beneath a turret, on his shield reclin'd,
He stood, and question'd thus his mighty
    mind:
    ' Where lies my way ?   To enter in the
    wall ?
Honour and shame th' ungen'rous thought
    recall:
Shall proud Polydamas before the gate 140
Proclaim, his counsels are obey'd too late,
Which timely follow'd but the former
    night,
What numbers had been saved by Hector's
    flight ?
That wise advice rejected with disdain,
I feel my folly in my people slain.
Methinks my suff'ring country's voice I
    hear,
But most, her worthless sons insult my
    ear,
On my rash courage charge the chance of
    war,
And blame those virtues which they can-
    not share.
No — If I e'er return, return I must   150
Glorious, my country's terror laid in dust:
Or if I perish, let her see my fall
In field at least, and fighting for her wall.
And yet suppose these measures I forego,
Approach unarm'd, and parley with the
    foe,

The warrior-shield, the helm, and lance lay
    down,
And treat on terms of peace to save the
    town :
The wife withheld, the treasure ill-de-
    tain'd
(Cause of the war, and grievance of the
    land),
With honourable justice to restore;   160
And add half Ilion's yet remaining store,
Which Troy shall, sworn, produce; that
    injur'd Greece
May share our wealth, and leave our walls
    in peace.
But why this thought ?   unarm'd if I ⎫
    should go, ⎪
What hope of mercy from this vengeful ⎬
    foe, ⎪
But woman-like to fall, and fall without ⎪
    a blow ? ⎭
We greet not here, as man conversing
    man,
Met at an oak, or journeying o'er a plain;
No season now for calm, familiar talk,
Like youths and maidens in an ev'ning
    walk: 170
War is our business, but to whom is
    giv'n
To die or triumph, that determine Heav'n!'
    Thus pond'ring, like a God the Greek
    drew nigh:
His dreadful plumage nodded from on
    high;
The Pelian jav'lin, in his better hand,
Shot trembling rays that glitter'd o'er the
    land;
And on his breast the beamy splendours
    shone
Like Jove's own lightning, or the rising
    sun.
As Hector sees, unusual terrors rise,
Struck by some God, he fears, recedes, and
    flies: 180
He leaves the gates, he leaves the walls
    behind;
Achilles follows like the winged wind.
Thus at the panting dove the falcon flies
(The swiftest racer of the liquid skies);
Just when he holds, or thinks he holds, his
    prey,
Obliquely wheeling thro' th' aërial way,
With open beak and shrilling cries he
    springs,
And aims his claws, and shoots upon his
    wings:

No less fore-right the rapid chase they
   held, 189
One urged by fury, one by fear impell'd;
Now circling round the walls their course
   maintain,
Where the high watch-tower overlooks the
   plain;
Now where the fig-trees spread their um-
   brage broad
(A wider compass), smoke along the road.
Next by Scamander's double source they
   bound,
Where two famed fountains burst the
   parted ground:
This hot thro' scorching clefts is seen to
   rise,
With exhalations steaming to the skies;
That the green banks in summer's heat
   o'erflows,
Like crystal clear, and cold as winter
   snows. 200
Each gushing fount a marble cistern fills,
Whose polish'd bed receives the falling
   rills;
Where Trojan dames (ere yet alarm'd by
   Greece)
Wash'd their fair garments in the days of
   peace.
By these they pass'd, one chasing, one in
   flight
(The mighty fled, pursued by stronger
   might);
Swift was the course; no vulgar prize they
   play,
No vulgar victim must reward the day
(Such as in races crown the speedy strife);
The prize contended was great Hector's
   life. 210
  As when some hero's funerals are de-
   creed,
In grateful honour of the mighty dead;
Where high rewards the vig'rous youth
   inflame
(Some golden tripod, or some lovely dame),
The panting coursers swiftly turn the
   goal,
And with them turns the rais'd spectator's
   soul:
Thus three times round the Trojan wall
   they fly;
The gazing Gods lean forward from the
   sky:
To whom, while eager on the chase they
   look, 219
The Sire of mortals and immortals spoke:

'Unworthy sight ! the man, belov'd of
   Heav'n,
Behold, inglorious round yon city driv'n !
My heart partakes the gen'rous Hector's
   pain;
Hector, whose zeal whole hecatombs has
   slain,
Whose grateful fumes the Gods receiv'd
   with joy,
From Ida's summits, and the towers of
   Troy:
Now see him flying ! to his fears resign'd,
And Fate, and fierce Achilles, close be-
   hind.
Consult, ye Powers ('t is worthy your de-
   bate)
Whether to snatch him from impending
   Fate, 230
Or let him bear, by stern Pelides slain
(Good as he is), the lot imposed on man ? '
  Then Pallas thus: 'Shall he whose ven-
   geance forms
The forky bolt, and blackens Heav'n with
   storms,
Shall he prolong one Trojan's forfeit
   breath,
A man a mortal, pre-ordain'd to death ?
And will no murmurs fill the courts above ?
No Gods indignant blame their partial
   Jove ? '
  'Go then' (return'd the Sire), 'without
   delay;
Exert thy will: I give the Fates their
   way.' 240
Swift at the mandate pleas'd Tritonia flies,
And stoops impetuous from the cleaving
   skies.
  As thro' the forest, o'er the vale and
   lawn,
The well-breathed beagle drives the flying
   fawn;
In vain he tries the covert of the brakes,
Or deep beneath the trembling thicket
   shakes:
Sure of the vapour in the tainted dews,
The certain hound his various maze pur-
   sues:
Thus step by step, where'er the Trojan
   wheel'd,
There swift Achilles compass'd round the
   field. 250
Oft as to reach the Dardan gates he
   bends,
And hopes th' assistance of his pitying
   friends

(Whose show'ring arrows, as he cours'd
  below,
From the high turrets might oppress the
  foe),
So oft Achilles turns him to the plain:
He eyes the city, but he eyes in vain.
As men in slumbers seem with speedy
  pace
One to pursue, and one to lead the chase,
Their sinking limbs the fancied course for-
  sake,
Nor this can fly, nor that can overtake: 260
No less the lab'ring heroes pant and strain;
While that but flies, and this pursues, in
  vain.
  What God, O Muse! assisted Hector's
    force,
With Fate itself so long to hold the course?
Phœbus it was: who, in his latest hour,
Endued his knees with strength, his nerves
  with power;
And great Achilles, lest some Greek's
  advance
Should snatch the glory from his lifted
  lance,
Sign'd to the troops, to yield his foe the
  way,
And leave untouch'd the honours of the
  day. 270
  Jove lifts the golden balances, that show
The fates of mortal men, and things below:
Here each contending hero's lot he tries,
And weighs, with equal hand, their des-
  tinies.
Low sinks the scale surcharg'd with Hec-
  tor's fate;
Heavy with death it sinks, and Hell re-
  ceives the weight.
  Then Phœbus left him. Fierce Minerva
    flies
To stern Pelides, and, triumphing, cries:
'Oh lov'd of Jove! this day our labours
  cease,
And conquest blazes with full beams on
  Greece. 280
Great Hector falls; that Hector famed so
  far,
Drunk with renown, insatiable of war,
Falls by thy hand, and mine! nor force nor
  flight
Shall more avail him, nor his God of Light.
See, where in vain he supplicates above,
Roll'd at the feet of unrelenting Jove!
Rest here: myself will lead the Trojan on,
And urge to meet the fate he cannot shun.'

Her voice divine the Chief with joyful
  mind
Obey'd, and rested, on his lance reclin'd. 290
While like Deïphobus the Martial Dame
(Her face, her gesture, and her arms, the
  same),
In show an aid, by hapless Hector's side
Approach'd, and greets him thus with voice
  belied:
'Too long, O Hector! have I borne the
  sight
Of this distress, and sorrow'd in thy flight:
It fits us now a noble stand to make,
And here, as brothers, equal fates par-
  take.'
  Then he: 'O Prince! allied in blood and
    fame, 299
Dearer than all that own a brother's name;
Of all that Hecuba to Priam bore,
Long tried, long lov'd; much lov'd, but
  honour'd more!
Since you of all our numerous race alone
Defend my life, regardless of your own.'
  Again the Goddess: 'Much my father's
    prayer,
And much my mother's, press'd me to for-
  bear:
My friends embraced my knees, adjured
  my stay,
But stronger love impell'd, and I obey.
Come then, the glorious conflict let us try,
Let the steel sparkle and the jav'lin fly; 310
Or let us stretch Achilles on the field,
Or to his arm our bloody trophies yield.'
  Fraudful she said; then swiftly march'd
    before;
The Dardan hero shuns his foe no more.
Sternly they met. The silence Hector
  broke;
His dreadful plumage nodded as he spoke:
'Enough, O son of Peleus! Troy has
  view'd
Her walls thrice circled, and her Chief
  pursued.
But now some God within me bids me try
Thine, or my fate: I kill thee, or I die. 320
Yet on the verge of battle let us stay,
And for a moment's space suspend the
  day:
Let Heav'n's high Powers be call'd to arbi-
  trate
The just conditions of this stern debate
(Eternal witnesses of all below,
And faithful guardians of the treasured
  vow)!

To them I swear : if, victor in the strife,
Jove by these hands shall shed thy noble
life,
No vile dishonour shall thy corse pursue;
Stripp'd of its arms alone (the conqueror's
due), 330
The rest to Greece uninjur'd I 'll restore:
Now plight thy mutual oath, I ask no
more.'
  'Talk not of oaths' (the dreadful Chief
replies,
While anger flash'd from his disdainful
eyes),
'Detested as thou art, and ought to be,
Nor oath nor pact Achilles plights with
thee;
Such pacts, as lambs and rabid wolves
combine,
Such leagues, as men and furious lions
join,
To such I call the Gods! one constant
state
Of lasting rancour and eternal hate: 340
No thought but rage, and never-ceasing
strife,
Till death extinguish rage, and thought,
and life.
Rouse then thy forces this important hour,
Collect thy soul, and call forth all thy
power.
No farther subterfuge, no farther chance;
'T is Pallas, Pallas gives thee to my lance.
Each Grecian ghost by thee deprived of
breath,
Now hovers round, and calls thee to thy
death.'
  He spoke, and launch'd his jav'lin at the
foe;
But Hector shunn'd the meditated blow: 350
He stoop'd, while o'er his head the flying
spear
Sung innocent, and spent its force in air.
Minerva watch'd it falling on the land,
Then drew, and gave to great Achilles'
hand,
Unseen of Hector, who, elate with joy,
Now shakes his lance, and braves the dread
of Troy:
'The life you boasted to that jav'lin giv'n,
Prince! you have miss'd. My fate de-
pends on Heav'n.
To thee (presumptuous as thou art) un-
known
Or what must prove my fortune, or thy
own. 360

Boasting is but an art, our fears to blind,
And with false terrors sink another's mind.
But know, whatever fate I am to try,
By no dishonest wound shall Hector die;
I shall not fall a fugitive at least,
My soul shall bravely issue from my breast.
But first, try thou my arm; and may this
dart
End all my country's woes, deep buried in
thy heart !'
  The weapon flew, its course unerring
held; 369
Unerring, but the heav'nly shield repell'd
The mortal dart; resulting with a bound
From off the ringing orb, it struck the
ground.
Hector beheld his jav'lin fall in vain,
Nor other lance nor other hope remain;
He calls Deïphobus, demands a spear,
In vain, for no Deïphobus was there.
All comfortless he stands: then, with a
sigh,
' 'T is so — Heav'n wills it, and my hour is
nigh !
I deem'd Deïphobus had heard my call,
But he secure lies guarded in the wall. 380
A God deceiv'd me; Pallas, 't was thy
deed:
Death and black Fate approach! 't is I
must bleed:
No refuge now, no succour from above,
Great Jove deserts me, and the son of
Jove,
Propitious once, and kind ! Then welcome
Fate!
'T is true I perish, yet I perish great:
Yet in a mighty deed I shall expire,
Let future ages hear it, and admire !'
  Fierce, at the word, his weighty sword
he drew,
And, all collected, on Achilles flew. 390
So Jove's bold bird, high balanc'd in the
air,
Stoops from the clouds to truss the quiv'ring
hare.
Nor less Achilles his fierce soul prepares;
Before his breast the flaming shield he
bears,
Refulgent orb ! above his fourfold cone
The gilded horse-hair sparkled in the sun,
Nodding at ev'ry step (Vulcanian frame)!
And as he mov'd, his figure seem'd on
flame.
As radiant Hesper shines with keener light,
Far-beaming o'er the silver host of night,

When all the starry train emblaze the
   sphere: 401
So shone the point of great Achilles' spear.
In his right hand he waves the weapon
   round,
Eyes the whole man, and meditates the
   wound:
But the rich mail Patroclus lately wore,
Securely cased the warrior's body o'er.
One place at length he spies, to let in Fate,
Where 'twixt the neck and throat the
   jointed plate
Gave entrance: thro' that penetrable part
Furious he drove the well-directed dart: 410
Nor pierc'd the windpipe yet, nor took the
   power
Of speech, unhappy! from thy dying hour.
Prone on the field the bleeding warrior lies,
While thus, triumphing, stern Achilles
   cries:
'At last is Hector stretch'd upon the
   plain,
Who fear'd no vengeance for Patroclus
   slain:
Then, Prince! you should have fear'd,
   what now you feel;
Achilles absent was Achilles still.
Yet a short space the great avenger stay'd,
Then low in dust thy strength and glory
   laid.   420
Peaceful he sleeps, with all our rites adorn'd,
For ever honour'd, and for ever mourn'd:
While, cast to all the rage of hostile power,
Thee birds shall mangle, and thee dogs
   devour.'
   Then Hector, fainting at th' approach of
   death:
'By thy own soul! by those who gave thee
   breath!
By all the sacred prevalence of prayer;
Ah, leave me not for Grecian dogs to tear!
The common rites of sepulture bestow, 429
To soothe a father's and a mother's woe;
Let their large gifts procure an urn at
   least,
And Hector's ashes in his country rest.'
   'No, wretch accurs'd!' relentless he re-
   plies
(Flames, as he spoke, shot flashing from
   his eyes),
'Not those who gave me breath should bid
   me spare,
Nor all the sacred prevalence of prayer.
Could I myself the bloody banquet join!
No — to the dogs that carcass I resign.

Should Troy to bribe me bring forth all
   her store,
And, giving thousands, offer thousands
   more;   440
Should Dardan Priam, and his weeping
   dame,
Drain their whole realm to buy one funeral
   flame;
Their Hector on the pile they should not
   see,
Nor rob the vultures of one limb of thee.'
   Then thus the Chief his dying accents
   drew:
'Thy rage, implacable! too well I knew:
The Furies that relentless breast have
   steel'd,
And curs'd thee with a heart that cannot
   yield.
Yet think, a day will come, when Fate's
   decree
And angry Gods shall wreak this wrong on
   thee;   450
Phœbus and Paris shall avenge my fate,
And stretch thee here, before this Scæan
   gate.'
   He ceas'd: the Fates suppress'd his la-
   b'ring breath,
And his eyes stiffen'd at the hand of
   death;
To the dark realm the spirit wings its way
(The manly body left a load of clay),
And plaintive glides along the dreary
   coast,
A naked, wand'ring, melancholy ghost!
   Achilles, musing as he roll'd his eyes
O'er the dead hero, thus (unheard) re-
   plies: 460
'Die thou the first! when Jove and Heav'n
   ordain,
I follow thee.' He said, and stripp'd the
   slain.
Then, forcing backward from the gaping
   wound
The reeking jav'lin, cast it on the ground.
The thronging Greeks behold with won-
   d'ring eyes
His manly beauty and superior size:
While some, ignobler, the great dead de-
   face
With wounds ungen'rous, or with taunts
   disgrace.
'How changed that Hector! who, like
   Jove, of late
Sent lightning on our fleets and scatter'd
   Fate!'   470

High o'er the slain the great Achilles
  stands,
Begirt with heroes and surrounding bands;
And thus aloud, while all the host attends:
'Princes and leaders! countrymen and
  friends!
Since now at length the powerful will of
  Heav'n
The dire destroyer to our arm has giv'n,
Is not Troy fall'n already? Haste, ye
  Powers!
See if already their deserted towers
Are left unmann'd; or if they yet retain
The souls of heroes, their great Hector
  slain?   480
But what is Troy, or glory what to me?
Or why reflects my mind on aught but
  thee,
Divine Patroclus! Death has seal'd his
  eyes;
Unwept, unhonour'd, uninterr'd he lies!
Can his dear image from my soul depart,
Long as the vital spirit moves my heart?
If, in the melancholy shades below,
The flames of friends and lovers cease to
  glow,
Yet mine shall sacred last; mine, unde-
  cay'd,
Burn on thro' death, and animate my
  shade.   490
Meanwhile, ye sons of Greece, in triumph
  bring
The corse of Hector, and your Pæans
  sing.
Be this the song, slow moving tow'rd the
  shore,
" Hector is dead, and Ilion is no more." '
  Then his fell soul a thought of vengeance
  bred
(Unworthy of himself, and of the dead);
The nervous ancles bored, his feet he
  bound
With thongs inserted thro' the double
  wound;
These fix'd up high behind the rolling
  wain,
His graceful head was trail'd along the
  plain.   500
Proud on his car th' insulting victor stood,
And bore aloft his arms, distilling blood.
He smites the steeds; the rapid chariot
  flies;
The sudden clouds of circling dust arise.
Now lost is all that formidable air;
The face divine, and long-descending hair,

Purple the ground, and streak the sable
  sand;
Deform'd, dishonour'd, in his native land i
Giv'n to the rage of an insulting throng!
And, in his parents' sight, now dragg'd
  along.   510
  The mother first beheld with sad sur-
  vey;
She rent her tresses, venerably grey,
And cast far off the regal veils away.
With piercing shrieks his bitter fate she
  moans,
While the sad father answers groans with
  groans;
Tears after tears his mournful cheeks o'er-
  flow,
And the whole city wears one face of woe:
No less than if the rage of hostile fires,
From her foundations curling to her spires,
O'er the proud citadel at length should
  rise,   520
And the last blaze send Ilion to the skies.
The wretched Monarch of the falling state,
Distracted, presses to the Dardan gate:
Scarce the whole people stop his desp'rate
  course,
While strong affliction gives the feeble
  force:
Grief tears his heart, and drives him to
  and fro,
In all the raging impotence of woe.
At length he roll'd in dust, and thus
  begun,
Imploring all, and naming one by one:
' Ah! let me, let me go where sorrow
  calls;   530
I, only I, will issue from your walls
(Guide or companion, friends! I ask ye
  none),
And bow before the murd'rer of my son:
My grief perhaps his pity may engage;
Perhaps at least he may respect my age.
He has a father too; a man like me;
One not exempt from age and misery
(Vig'rous no more, as when his young em-
  brace
Begot this pest of me, and all my race).
How many valiant sons, in early bloom, 540
Has that curs'd hand sent headlong to the
  tomb!
Thee, Hector! last; thy loss (divinely
  brave)!
Sinks my sad soul with sorrow to the grave
Oh had thy gentle spirit pass'd in peace,
The son expiring in the sire's embrace,

While both thy parents wept thy fatal
    hour,
And, bending o'er thee, mix'd the tender
    shower!
Some comfort that had been, some sad
    relief,
To melt in full satiety of grief!'
    Thus wail'd the father, grov'ling on the
      ground,   550
And all the eyes of Ilion stream'd around.
    Amidst her matrons Hecuba appears
(A mourning Princess, and a train in
    tears):
'Ah! why has Heav'n prolong'd this hated
    breath,
Patient of horrors, to behold thy death?
O Hector! late thy parents' pride and joy,
The boast of nations! the defence of Troy!
To whom her safety and her fame she
    owed,
Her Chief, her hero, and almost her God!
O fatal change! become in one sad day 560
A senseless corse! inanimated clay!'
    But not as yet the fatal news had spread
To fair Andromache, of Hector dead;
As yet no messenger had told his Fate,
Nor ev'n his stay without the Scæan gate.
Far in the close recesses of the dome
Pensive she plied the melancholy loom;
A growing work employ'd her secret hours,
Confusedly gay with intermingled flowers.
Her fair-hair'd handmaids heat the brazen
    urn,   570
The bath preparing for her lord's return:
In vain: alas! her lord returns no more!
Unbathed he lies, and bleeds along the
    shore!
Now from the walls the clamours reach
    her ear
And all her members shake with sudden
    fear;
Forth from her iv'ry hand the shuttle
    falls,
As thus, astonish'd, to her maids she calls:
'Ah, follow me' (she cried)! 'what
    plaintive noise
Invades my ear? 'T is sure my mother's
    voice.
My falt'ring knees their trembling frame
    desert,   580
A pulse unusual flutters at my heart.
Some strange disaster, some reverse of
    fate
(Ye Gods avert it!) threats the Trojan
    state.

Far be the omen which my thoughts sug-
    gest!
But much I fear my Hector's dauntless
    breast
Confronts Achilles; chased along the plain,
Shut from our walls! I fear, I fear him
    slain!
Safe in the crowd he ever scorn'd to wait,
And sought for glory in the jaws of Fate:
Perhaps that noble heat has cost his
    breath,   590
Now quench'd for ever in the arms of
    death.'
    She spoke; and, furious, with distracted
    pace,
Fears in her heart, and anguish in her face,
Flies thro' the dome (the maids her step
    pursue),
And mounts the walls, and sends around
    her view.
Too soon her eyes the killing object found,
The godlike Hector dragg'd along the
    ground.
A sudden darkness shades her swimming
    eyes:
She faints, she falls; her breath, her colour,
    flies.
Her hair's fair ornaments, the braids that
    bound,   600
The net that held them, and the wreath
    that crown'd,
The veil and diadem, flew far away
(The gift of Venus on her bridal day).
Around, a train of weeping sisters stands,
To raise her sinking with assistant hands.
Scarce from the verge of death recall'd,
    again
She faints, or but recovers to complain:
    'O wretched husband of a wretched
    wife!
Born with one fate, to one unhappy life!
For sure one star its baneful beam dis-
    play'd   610
On Priam's roof, and Hippoplacia's shade.
From diff'rent parents, diff'rent climes, we
    came,
At diff'rent periods, yet our fate the same!
Why was my birth to great Eëtion owed,
And why was all that tender care be-
    stow'd?
Would I had never been!—Oh thou, the
    ghost
Of my dead husband! miserably lost!
Thou to the dismal realms for ever gone!
And I abandon'd, desolate, alone!

An only child, once comfort of my pains, 620
Sad product now of hapless love, remains !
No more to smile upon his sire ! no friend
To help him now ! no father to defend !
For should he 'scape the sword, the common
    doom,
What wrongs attend him, and what griefs
    to come !
Ev'n from his own paternal roof expell'd,
Some stranger ploughs his patrimonial
    field.
The day that to the shades the father
    sends,
Robs the sad orphan of his father's friends:
He, wretched outcast of mankind ! ap-
    pears   630
For ever sad, for ever bathed in tears;
Amongst the happy, unregarded he
Hangs on the robe or trembles at the knee;
While those his father's former bounty fed,
Nor reach the goblet, nor divide the bread:
The kindest but his present wants allay,
To leave him wretched the succeeding day.
Frugal compassion ! Heedless, they who
    boast
Both parents still, nor feel what he has
    lost,
Shall cry, Begone ! thy father feasts not
    here: 640
The wretch obeys, retiring with a tear.
Thus wretched, thus retiring all in tears,
To my sad soul Astyanax appears !
Forc'd by repeated insults to return,
And to his widow'd mother vainly mourn.
He who, with tender delicacy bred,
With Princes sported, and on dainties fed,
And, when still ev'ning gave him up to
    rest,
Sunk soft in down upon the nurse's breast,
Must — ah what must he not ? Whom
    Ilion calls   650
Astyanax, from her well-guarded walls,
Is now that name no more, unhappy boy !
Since now no more thy father guards his
    Troy.
But thou, my Hector ! liest exposed in air,
Far from thy parents' and thy consort's
    care,
Whose hand in vain, directed by her love,
The martial scarf and robe of triumph
    wove.
Now to devouring flames be these a prey,
Useless to thee, from this accursed day !
Yet let the sacrifice at least be paid,   660
An honour to the living, not the dead ! '

So spake the mournful dame: her ma-
    trons hear,
Sigh back her sighs, and answer tear with
    tear.

BOOK XXIII

FUNERAL GAMES IN HONOUR OF PATROCLUS

THE ARGUMENT

Achilles and the Myrmidons do honours to the
    body of Patroclus. After the funeral feast
    he retires to the sea-shore, where, falling
    asleep, the ghost of his friend appears to
    him, and demands the rites of burial : the
    next morning the soldiers are sent with
    mules and wagons to fetch wood for the
    pyre. The funeral procession, and the of-
    fering their hair to the dead. Achilles
    sacrifices several animals, and lastly, twelve
    Trojan captives, at the pile ; then sets fire to
    it. He pays libations to the winds, which
    (at the instance of Iris) rise, and raise the
    flame. When the pile has burned all night,
    they gather the bones, place them in an urn
    of gold, and raise the tomb. Achilles in-
    stitutes the funeral games : the chariot-race,
    the fight of the cæstus, the wrestling, the
    foot-race, the single combat, the discus, the
    shooting with arrows, the darting the javelin :
    the various descriptions of which, and the
    various success of the several antagonists,
    make the greatest part of the book.
In this book ends the thirtieth day : the night
    following, the ghost of Patroclus appears to
    Achilles : the one-and-thirtieth day is em-
    ployed in felling the timber for the pile ; the
    two-and-thirtieth in burning it ; and the
    three-and-thirtieth in the games. The
    scene is generally on the sea-shore.

THUS humbled in the dust, the pensive
    train
Thro' the sad city mourn'd her hero slain.
The body soil'd with dust, and black with
    gore,
Lies on broad Hellespont's resounding
    shore:
The Grecians seek their ships, and clear
    the strand,
All but the martial Myrmidonian band:
These yet assembled great Achilles holds,
And the stern purpose of his mind unfolds:
' Not yet (my brave companions of the
    war)
Release your smoking coursers from the
    car;   10

But with his chariot each in order led,
Perform due honours to Patroclus dead;
Ere yet from rest or food we seek relief,
Some rites remain, to glut our rage of
grief.'
The troops obey'd; and thrice in order
led
(Achilles first) their coursers round the
dead
And thrice their sorrows and laments re-
new;
Tears bathe their arms, and tears the sands
bedew.
For such a warrior Thetis aids their woe,
Melts their strong hearts, and bids their
eyes to flow.   20
But chief, Pelides; thick-succeeding sighs
Burst from his heart, and torrents from his
eyes:
His slaught'ring hands, yet red with blood,
he laid
On his dead friend's cold breast, and thus
he said:
'All hail, Patroclus! let thy honour'd
ghost
Hear and rejoice on Pluto's dreary coast;
Behold! Achilles' promise is complete;
The bloody Hector stretch'd before thy
feet.
Lo! to the dogs his carcass I resign;   29
And twelve sad victims of the Trojan line,
Sacred to vengeance, instant shall expire,
Their lives effused around thy funeral
pyre.'
Gloomy he said, and (horrible to view)
Before the bier the bleeding Hector threw,
Prone on the dust. The Myrmidons
around
Unbraced their armour, and the steeds un-
bound.
All to Achilles' sable ship repair,
Frequent and full, the genial feast to
share.
Now from the well-fed swine black smokes
aspire,
The bristly victims hissing o'er the fire; 40
The huge ox bell'wing falls; with feebler
cries
Expires the goat; the sheep in silence dies.
Around the hero's prostrate body flow'd,
In one promiscuous stream, the reeking
blood.
And now a band of Argive Monarchs
brings
The glorious victor to the King of Kings.

From his dead friend the pensive warrior
went,
With steps unwilling, to the regal tent.
Th' attending heralds, as by office bound,
With kindled flames the tripod-vase sur-
round;   50
To cleanse his conquering hands from hos-
tile gore,
They urged in vain; the Chief refused, and
swore,
'No drop shall touch me, by Almighty
Jove!
The first and greatest of the Gods above!
Till on the pyre I place thee; till I rear
The grassy mound, and clip thy sacred
hair.
Some ease at least those pious rites may
give,
And soothe my sorrows, while I bear to
live.
Howe'er, reluctant as I am, I stay,
And share your feast; but, with the dawn
of day   60
(O King of Men!) it claims thy royal care,
That Greece the warrior's funeral pile pre-
pare,
And bid the forests fall (such rites are
paid
To heroes slumb'ring in eternal shade).
Then, when his earthly part shall mount in
fire,
Let the leagued squadrons to their posts
retire.'
He spoke: they hear him, and the word⎫
obey;   ⎪
The rage of hunger and of thirst allay, ⎬
Then ease in sleep the labours of the day.⎭
But great Pelides, stretch'd along the
shore,   70
Where dash'd on rocks the broken billows
roar,
Lies inly groaning; while on either hand
The martial Myrmidons confusedly stand:
Along the grass his languid members fall,
Tired with his chase around the Trojan
wall;
Hush'd by the murmurs of the rolling
deep,
At length he sinks in the soft arms of
sleep.
When lo! the shade before his closing eyes
Of sad Patroclus rose, or seem'd to rise:
In the same robe he living wore, he came, 80
In stature, voice, and pleasing look, the
same.

The form familiar hover'd o'er his head,
And, 'Sleeps Achilles' (thus the phan-
tom said),
'Sleeps my Achilles, his Patroclus dead ?
Living, I seem'd his dearest, tenderest
care,
But now forgot, I wander in the air:
Let my pale corse the rites of burial know,
And give me entrance in the realms below;
Till then, the spirit finds no resting-place,
But here and there th' unbodied spectres
chase   90
The vagrant dead around the dark abode,
Forbid to cross th' irremeable flood.
Now give thy hand; for to the farther
shore
When once we pass, the soul returns no
more.
When once the last funereal flames ascend,
No more shall meet Achilles and his friend;
No more our thoughts to those we love
make known,
Or quit the dearest to converse alone.
Me Fate has sever'd from the sons of earth,
The Fate foredoom'd that waited from my
birth: 100
Thee too it waits; before the Trojan wall
Ev'n great and godlike thou art doom'd to
fall.
Hear then; and as in Fate and love we join,
Ah, suffer that my bones may rest with
thine !
Together have we liv'd, together bred,
One house receiv'd us, and one table fed !
That golden urn thy goddess-mother gave,
May mix our ashes in one common grave.'
'And is it thou ? ' (he answers) 'To my
sight
Once more return'st thou from the realms
of night ?   110
Oh more than brother ! think each office
paid
Whate'er can rest a discontented shade;
But grant one last embrace, unhappy boy !
Afford at least that melancholy joy.'
He said, and with his longing arms es-
say'd
In vain to grasp the visionary shade;
Like a thin smoke he sees the spirit fly,
And hears a feeble, lamentable cry.
Confused he wakes; amazement breaks
the bands
Of golden sleep, and, starting from the
sands,   120
Pensive he muses with uplifted hands:

' 'T is true, 't is certain; man, tho' dead,
retains
Part of himself; th' immortal mind re-
mains:
The form subsists, without the body's aid,
Aërial semblance, and an empty shade !
This night, my friend, so late in battle
lost,
Stood at my side a pensive, plaintive ghost;
Ev'n now familiar, as in life, he came,
Alas, how different ! yet how like the
same ! '
Thus while he spoke, each eye grew big
with tears;   130
And now the rosy-finger'd morn appears,
Shows every mournful face with tears o'er-
spread,
And glares on the pale visage of the dead.
But Agamemnon, as the rites demand,
With mules and wagons sends a chosen
band
To load the timber, and the pile to rear;
A charge consign'd to Merion's faithful
care.
With proper instruments they take the
road,
Axes to cut, and ropes to sling the load. 139
First march the heavy mules, securely slow,
O'er hills, o'er dales, o'er crags, o'er rocks
they go:
Jumping, high o'er the shrubs of the rough
ground,
Rattle the clatt'ring cars, and the shock'd
axles bound,
But when arrived at Ida's spreading woods
(Fair Ida, water'd with descending floods),
Loud sounds the axe, redoubling strokes on
strokes;
On all sides round the forest hurls her
oaks
Headlong. Deep-echoing groan the thick-
ets brown;
Then rustling, crackling, crashing, thunder
down:
The wood the Grecians cleave, prepared to
burn;   150
And the slow mules the same rough road
return.
The sturdy woodmen equal burthens bore
(Such charge was giv'n them) to the sandy
shore;
There on the spot which great Achilles
show'd,
They eas'd their shoulders and disposed
the load;

Circling around the place, where times to
    come
Shall view Patroclus' and Achilles' tomb.
The hero bids his martial troops appear
High on their cars, in all the pomp of war:
Each in refulgent arms his limbs attires, 160
All mount their chariots, combatants and
    squires.
The chariots first proceed, a shining train;
Then clouds of foot that smoke along the
    plain;
Next these a melancholy band appear;
Amidst, lay dead Patroclus on the bier:
O'er all the corse their scatter'd locks they
    throw:
Achilles next, oppress'd with mighty woe,
Supporting with his hands the hero's head,
Bends o'er th' extended body of the dead. 169
Patroclus decent on th' appointed ground
They place, and heap the sylvan pile
    around.
But great Achilles stands apart in prayer,
And from his head divides the yellow hair;
Those curling locks which from his youth
    he vow'd,
And sacred grew to Sperchius' honour'd
    flood:
Then, sighing, to the deep his looks he
    cast,
And roll'd his eyes around the wat'ry
    waste:
   ' Sperchius ! whose waves, in mazy
    errors lost,
Delightful roll along my native coast ! 179
To whom we vainly vow'd, at our return,
These locks to fall, and hecatombs to burn;
Full fifty rams to bleed in sacrifice,
Where to the day thy silver fountains rise,
And where in shade of consecrated bowers
Thy altars stand, perfumed with native
    flowers !
So vow'd my father, but he vow'd in vain;
No more Achilles sees his native plain;
In that vain hope these hairs no longer
    grow, 188
Patroclus bears them to the shades below.'
   Thus o'er Patroclus while the hero pray'd,
On his cold hand the sacred lock he laid.
Once more afresh the Grecian sorrows flow:
And now the sun had set upon their woe;
But to the King of Men thus spoke the
    Chief:
' Enough, Atrides ! give the troops relief:
Permit the mourning legions to retire,
And let the Chiefs alone attend the pyre;

The pious care be ours, the dead to burn.'
He said: the people to their ships re-
    turn: 199
While those deputed to inter the slain,
Heap with a rising pyramid the plain;
A hundred foot in length, a hundred wide,
The growing structure spreads on ev'ry
    side;
High on the top the manly corse they lay,
And well-fed sheep and sable oxen slay:
Achilles cover'd with their fat the dead,
And the piled victims round the body
    spread;
Then jars of honey and of fragrant oil
Suspends around, low-bending o'er the pile.
Four sprightly coursers, with a deadly
    groan, 210
Pour forth their lives, and on the pyre are
    thrown.
Of nine large dogs, domestic at his board,
Fall two, selected to attend their lord.
Then last of all, and horrible to tell,
Sad sacrifice ! twelve Trojan captives fell:
On these the rage of fire victorious preys,
Involves, and joins them in one common
    blaze.
Smear'd with the bloody rites he stands on
    high,
And calls the spirit with a dreadful cry:
   ' All hail, Patroclus ! let thy vengeful
    ghost 220
Hear and exult on Pluto's dreary coast.
Behold Achilles' promise fully paid,
Twelve Trojan heroes offer'd to thy shade;
But heavier fates on Hector's corse attend,
Saved from the flames, for hungry dogs to
    rend.'
   So spake he, threat'ning: but the Gods
    made vain
His threat, and guard inviolate the slain:
Celestial Venus hover'd o'er his head,
And roseate unguents, heav'nly fragrance !
    shed:
She watch'd him all the night, and all the
    day, 230
And drove the bloodhounds from their des-
    tin'd prey.
Nor sacred Phœbus less employ'd his care:
He pour'd around a veil of gather'd air,
And kept the nerves undried, the flesh
    entire,
Against the solar beam and Sirian fire.
Nor yet the pile, where dead Patroclus
    lies,
Smokes, nor as yet the sullen flames arise;

But, fast beside, Achilles stood in prayer,
Invoked the Gods whose spirit moves the
    air,
And victims promis'd, and libations cast, 240
To gentle Zephyr and the Boreal blast:
He call'd th' aërial Powers, along the skies
To breathe, and whisper to the fires to rise.
The winged Iris heard the hero's call,
And instant hasten'd to their airy hall,
Where, in old Zephyr's open courts on high,
Sat all the blust'ring brethren of the sky.
She shone amidst them, on her painted
    bow;
The rocky pavement glitter'd with the
    show. 249
All from the banquet rise, and each invites
The various Goddess to partake the rites.
'Not so' (the Dame replied), 'I haste to
    go
To sacred Ocean, and the floods below;
Ev'n now our solemn hecatombs attend,
And Heav'n is feasting on the world's
    green end,
With righteous Æthiops (uncorrupted
    train)!
Far on th' extremest limits of the main.
But Peleus' son entreats, with sacrifice,
The Western spirit, and the North to rise;
Let on Patroclus' pile your blast be
    driv'n, 260
And bear the blazing honours high to
    Heav'n.'
    Swift as the word, she vanish'd from
    their view:
Swift as the word, the winds tumultuous
    flew;
Forth burst the stormy band with thun-
    d'ring roar,
And heaps on heaps the clouds are toss'd
    before.
To the wide main then stooping from the
    skies,
The heaving deeps in wat'ry mountains
    rise:
Troy feels the blast along her shaking
    walls,
Till on the pile the gather'd tempest falls.
The structure crackles in the roaring
    fires, 270
And all the night the plenteous flame as-
    pires:
All night Achilles hails Patroclus' soul,
With large libation from the golden bowl,
As a poor father, helpless and undone,
Mourns o'er the ashes of an only son,

Takes a sad pleasure the last bones to
    burn,
And pour in tears, ere yet they close the
    urn:
So stay'd Achilles, circling round the shore,
So watch'd the flames, till now they flame
    no more.
'T was when, emerging thro' the shades of
    night, 280
The morning planet told th' approach of
    light;
And, fast behind, Aurora's warmer ray
O'er the broad ocean pour'd the golden
    day:
Then sunk the blaze, the pile no longer
    burn'd,
And to their caves the whistling winds
    return'd:
Across the Thracian seas their course they
    bore;
The ruffled seas beneath their passage roar.
    Then, parting from the pile, he ceas'd to
    weep,
And sunk to quiet in th' embrace of sleep,
Exhausted with his grief: meanwhile the
    crowd 290
Of thronging Grecians round Achilles
    stood:
The tumult waked him: from his eyes he
    shook
Unwilling slumber, and the Chief bespoke:
    'Ye Kings and Princes of th' Achaian
    name!
First let us quench the yet remaining flame
With sable wine; then (as the rites direct)
The hero's bones with careful view select
(Apart, and easy to be known they lie,
Amidst the heap, and obvious to the eye:
The rest around the margins will be seen,
Promiscuous, steeds and immolated men).
These, wrapp'd in double cauls of fat, pre-
    pare; 302
And in the golden vase dispose with care;
There let them rest, with decent honour
    laid,
Till I shall follow to th' infernal shade.
Meantime erect the tomb with pious hands,
A common structure on the humble sands;
Hereafter Greece some nobler work may
    raise,
And late posterity record our praise.'
    The Greeks obey; where yet the embers
    glow, 310
Wide o'er the pile the sable wine they
    throw,

And deep subsides the ashy heap below.
Next the white bones his sad companions
   place,
With tears collected, in the golden vase.
The sacred relics to the tent they bore;
The urn a veil of linen cover'd o'er.
That done, they bid the sepulchre aspire,
And cast the deep foundations round the
   pyre;
High in the midst they heap the swelling
   bed
Of rising earth, memorial of the dead.   320
  The swarming populace the Chief de-
   tains,
And leads amidst a wide extent of plains;
There placed them round; then from the
   ships proceeds
A train of oxen, mules, and stately steeds,
Vases and tripods, for the funeral games,
Resplendent brass, and more resplendent
   dames.
First stood the prizes to reward the force
Of rapid racers in the dusty course:
A woman for the first, in beauty's bloom,
Skill'd in the needle, and the lab'ring
   loom;   330
And a large vase, where two bright handles
   rise,
Of twenty measures its capacious size.
The second victor claims a mare unbroke,
Big with a mule, unknowing of the yoke;
The third, a charger yet untouch'd by
   flame;
Four ample measures held the shining
   frame:
Two golden talents for the fourth were
   placed;
An ample double bowl contents the last.
These in fair order ranged upon the plain,
The hero, rising, thus address'd the train:
  'Behold the prizes, valiant Greeks! de-
   creed   341
To the brave rulers of the racing steed;
Prizes which none beside ourself could
   gain,
Should our immortal coursers take the
   plain
(A race unrivall'd, which from Ocean's God
Peleus receiv'd, and on his son bestow'd).
But 't is no time our vigour to display,
Nor suit with them the games of this sad
   day:
Lost is Patroclus now, that wont to deck
Their flowing manes, and sleek their glossy
   neck.   350

Sad, as they shared in human grief, they
   stand,
And trail those graceful honours on the
   sand!
Let others for the noble task prepare,
Who trust the courser, and the flying car.'
  Fired at his word, the rival racers rise;
But, far the first, Eumelus hopes the prize;
Famed thro' Pieria for the fleetest breed,
And skill'd to manage the high-bounding
   steed.
With equal ardour bold Tydides swell'd,
The steeds of Tros beneath his yoke com-
   pell'd   360
(Which late obey'd the Dardan Chief's
   command,
When scarce a God redeem'd him from his
   hand).
Then Menelaüs his Podargus brings,
And the famed courser of the King of
   Kings:
Whom rich Echepolus (more rich than
   brave),
To 'scape the wars, to Agamemnon gave
(Æthe her name), at home to end his days,
Base wealth preferring to eternal praise.
Next him Antilochus demands the course,
With beating heart, and cheers his Pylian
   horse.   370
Experienc'd Nestor gives his son the reins,
Directs his judgment, and his heat re-
   strains;
Nor idly warns the hoary sire, nor hears
The prudent son with unattending ears:
  'My son! tho' youthful ardour fire thy
   breast,
The Gods have lov'd thee, and with arts
   have bless'd.
Neptune and Jove on thee conferr'd the
   skill
Swift round the goal to turn the flying
   wheel.
To guide thy conduct, little precept needs;
But slow, and past their vigour, are my
   steeds.   380
Fear not thy rivals, tho' for swiftness known,
Compare those rivals' judgment, and thy
   own:
It is not strength, but art, obtains the
   prize,
And to be swift is less than to be wise:
'T is more by art, than force of numerous
   strokes,
The dext'rous woodman shapes the stub-
   born oaks;

By art the pilot, thro' the boiling deep
And howling tempests, steers the fearless
　ship;
And 't is the artist wins the glorious course,
Not those who trust in chariots and in
　horse. 390
In vain, unskilful, to the goal they strive,
And short, or wide, th' ungovern'd courser
　drive:
While with sure skill, tho' with inferior
　steeds,
The knowing racer to his end proceeds;
Fix'd on the goal his eye fore-runs the
　course,
His hand unerring steers the steady horse,
And now contracts, or now extends, the
　rein,
Observing still the foremost on the plain.
Mark then the goal, 't is easy to be found;
You aged trunk, a cubit from the ground,
Of some once-stately oak the last remains,
Or hardy fir, unperish'd with the rains: 402
Enclosed with stones, conspicuous from
　afar,
And round, a circle for the wheeling car
(Some tomb perhaps of old, the dead to
　grace;
Or then, as now, the limit of a race).
Bear close to this, and warily proceed,
A little bending to the left-hand steed;
But urge the right, and give him all the
　reins;
While thy strict hand his fellow's head
　restrains, 410
And turns him short; till, doubling as they
　roll,
The wheel's round naves appear to brush
　the goal;
Yet (not to break the car, or lame the
　horse),
Clear of the stony heap direct the course;
Lest, thro' incaution failing, thou may'st be
A joy to others, a reproach to me.
So shalt thou pass the goal, secure of mind,
And leave unskilful swiftness far behind,
Tho' thy fierce rival drove the matchless
　steed 419
Which bore Adrastus, of celestial breed;
Or the famed race thro' all the regions
　known,
That whirl'd the car of proud Laomedon.'
　Thus (nought unsaid) the much-advising
　　sage
Concludes; then sat, stiff with unwieldy
　age.

Next bold Meriones was seen to rise,
The last, but not least ardent for the prize.
They mount their seats; the lots their place
　dispose
(Roll'd in his helmet, these Achilles
　throws);
Young Nestor leads the race; Eumelus
　then;
And next, the brother of the King of
　Men: 430
Thy lot, Meriones, the fourth was cast;
And, far the bravest, Diomed, was last.
They stand in order, an impatient train;
Pelides points the barrier on the plain,
And sends before old Phœnix to the place,
To mark the racers, and to judge the race.
At once the coursers from the barrier
　bound;
The lifted scourges all at once resound;
Their heart, their eyes, their voice, they
　send before;
And up the champaign thunder from the
　shore: 440
Thick, where they drive, the dusty clouds
　arise,
And the lost courser in the whirlwind flies;
Loose on their shoulders the long manes
　reclin'd,
Float in their speed, and dance upon the
　wind:
The smoking chariots, rapid as they bound,
Now seem to touch the sky, and now the
　ground;
While hot for Fame, and conquest all their
　care
(Each o'er his flying courser hung in air),
Erect with ardour, pois'd upon the rein,
They pant, they stretch, they shout along
　the plain: 450
Now (the last compass fetch'd around the
　goal)
At the near prize each gathers all his soul,
Each burns with double hope, with double
　pain
Tears up the shore, and thunders tow'rd
　the main.
First flew Eumelus on Pheretian steeds;
With those of Tros, bold Diomed succeeds:
Close on Eumelus' back they puff the wind,
And seem just mounting on his car behind;
Full on his neck he feels the sultry breeze,
And, hov'ring o'er, their stretching shadows
　sees. 460
Then had he lost, or left a doubtful prize;
But angry Phœbus to Tydides flies,

Strikes from his hand the scourge, and ren-
　　ders vain
His matchless horses' labour on the plain.
Rage fills his eye with anguish, to survey,
Snatch'd from his hope, the glories of the
　　day.
The fraud celestial Pallas sees with pain,
Springs to her knight, and gives the scourge
　　again,
And fills his steeds with vigour.   At a
　　stroke,
She breaks his rival's chariot from the
　　yoke: 470
No more their way the startled horses
　　held;
The car revers'd came rattling on the
　　field;
Shot headlong from his seat, beside the
　　wheel,
Prone on the dust th' unhappy master
　　fell;
His batter'd face and elbows strike the
　　ground:
Nose, mouth, and front one undistinguish'd
　　wound:
Grief stops his voice, a torrent drowns his
　　eyes;
Before him far the glad Tydides flies;
Minerva's spirit drives his matchless pace,
And crowns him victor of the labour'd
　　race.   480
　　The next, tho' distant, Menelaus suc-
　　ceeds;
While thus young Nestor animates his
　　steeds:
'Now, now, my gen'rous pair, exert your
　　force;
Not that we hope to match Tydides' horse;
Since great Minerva wings their rapid
　　way,
And gives their lord the honours of the
　　day.
But reach Atrides ! shall his mare out-go
Your swiftness ? vanquish'd by a female
　　foe ?
Thro' your neglect, if, lagging on the
　　plain,
The last ignoble gift be all we gain,   490
No more shall Nestor's hand your food
　　supply;
The old man's fury rises, and ye die.
Haste then ! yon narrow road before our
　　sight
Presents th' occasion, could we use it
　　right.'

Thus he.   The coursers at their master's
　　threat
With quicker steps the sounding cham-
　　paign beat.
And now Antilochus, with nice survey,
Observes the compass of the hollow way.
'T was where by force of wintry torrents
　　torn,
Fast by the road a precipice was worn: 500
Here, where but one could pass, to shun
　　the throng,
The Spartan hero's chariot smoked along.
Close up the venturous youth resolves to
　　keep,
Still edging near, and bears him tow'rd
　　the steep.
Atrides, trembling, casts his eye below,
And wonders at the rashness of his foe:
' Hold, stay your steeds — what madness
　　thus to ride
This narrow way !   Take larger field ' (he
　　cried),
' Or both must fall.'   Atrides cried in vain;
He flies more fast, and throws up all the
　　rein.   510
Far as an able arm the disc can send,
When youthful rivals their full force ex-
　　tend,
So far, Antilochus ! thy chariot flew
Before the King :   he, cautious, backward
　　drew
His horse compell'd; foreboding in his
　　fears
The rattling ruin of the clashing cars,
The flound'ring coursers rolling on the
　　plain,
And conquest lost thro' frantic haste to
　　gain.
But thus upbraids his rival as he flies:
' Go, furious youth ! ungen'rous and un-
　　wise !   520
Go, but expect not I 'll the prize resign;
Add perjury to fraud, and make it thine.'
Then to his steeds with all his force he
　　cries:
' Be swift, be vig'rous, and regain the
　　prize !
Your rivals, destitute of youthful force,
With fainting knees shall labour in the
　　course,
And yield the glory yours.'   The steeds ⎫
　　obey;   ⎪
Already at their heels they wing their ⎬
　　way,   ⎪
And seem already to retrieve the day.   ⎭

Meantime the Grecians in a ring be-
held   530
The coursers bounding o'er the dusty field.
The first who mark'd them was the Cretan
King;
High on a rising ground, above the ring,
The Monarch sat; from whence with sure
survey
He well observ'd the Chief who led the
way,
And heard from far his animating cries,
And saw the foremost steed with sharpen'd
eyes;
On whose broad front a blaze of shining
white,
Like the full moon, stood obvious to the
sight.   539
He saw; and, rising, to the Greeks begun:
'Are yonder horse discern'd by me alone?
Or can ye, all, another Chief survey,
And other steeds, than lately led the way?
Those, tho' the swiftest, by some God with-
held,
Lie sure disabled in the middle field:
For since the goal they doubled, round the
plain
I search to find them, but I search in vain.
Perchance the reins forsook the driver's
hand,
And, turn'd too short, he tumbled on the
strand,
Shot from the chariot; while his coursers
stray   550
With frantic fury from the destin'd way.
Rise then some other, and inform my
sight
(For these dim eyes, perhaps, discern not
right);
Yet sure he seems (to judge by shape and
air)
The great Ætolian Chief, renown'd in war.'
'Old man!' (Oïleus rashly thus replies),
'Thy tongue too hastily confers the prize.
Of those who view the course, not sharpest
eyed,
Nor youngest, yet the readiest to decide.
Eumelus' steeds high-bounding in the
chase,   560
Still, as at first, unrivall'd lead the race;
I well discern him, as he shakes the rein,
And hear his shouts victorious o'er the
plain.'
Thus he. Idomeneus incens'd rejoin'd:
'Barb'rous of words! and arrogant of
mind!

Contentious Prince! of all the Greeks be-
side
The last in merit, as the first in pride!
To vile reproach what answer can we
make?
A goblet or a tripod let us stake,
And be the King the judge. The most
unwise   570
Will learn their rashness, when they pay
the price.'
He said: and Ajax, by mad passion
borne,
Stern had replied; fierce scorn enhancing
scorn
To fell extremes. But Thetis' godlike son,
Awful, amidst them rose; and thus begun:
'Forbear, ye Chiefs! reproachful to
contend:
Much would ye blame, should others thus
offend:
And lo! th' approaching steeds your con-
test end.'
No sooner had he spoke, but, thund'ring
near,
Drives, thro' a stream of dust, the chario-
teer;   580
High o'er his head the circling lash he
wields;
His bounding horses scarcely touch the
fields:
His car amidst the dusty whirlwind roll'd,
Bright with the mingled blaze of tin and
gold,
Refulgent thro' the cloud: no eye could
find
The track his flying wheels had left be-
hind:
And the fierce coursers urged their rapid
pace
So swift, it seem'd a flight, and not a race.
Now victor at the goal Tydides stands,
Quits his bright car, and springs upon the
sands;   590
From the hot steeds the sweaty torrents
stream;
The well-plied whip is hung athwart the
beam:
With joy brave Sthenelus receives the
prize,
The tripod-vase, and dame with radiant
eyes:
These to the ships his train triumphant
leads,
The Chief himself unyokes the panting
steeds.

Young Nestor follows (who by art, not
   force,
O'erpass'd Atrides), second in the course.
Behind, Atrides urged the race, more near
Than to the courser in his swift career 600
The foll'wing car, just touching with his
   heel
And brushing with his tail the whirling
   wheel:
Such, and so narrow, now the space be-
   tween
The rivals, late so distant on the green;
So soon swift Æthe her lost ground re-
   gain'd,
One length, one moment, had the race ob-
   tain'd.
   Merion pursued, at greater distance
   still,
With tardier coursers, and inferior skill.
Last came, Admetus ! thy unhappy son;
Slow dragg'd the steeds his batter'd
   chariot on; 610
Achilles saw, and pitying thus begun:
   'Behold ! the man whose matchless art
   surpass'd
The sons of Greece ! the ablest, yet the
   last !
Fortune denies, but justice bids us pay
(Since great Tydides bears the first away)
To him the second honours of the day.'
   The Greeks consent with loud applaud-
   ing cries,
And then Eumelus had receiv'd the prize,
But youthful Nestor, jealous of his fame,
Th' award opposes, and asserts his claim: 620
'Think not ' (he cries), ' I tamely will re-
   sign,
O Peleus' son ! the mare so justly mine.
What if the Gods, the skilful to confound,
Have thrown the horse and horseman to
   the ground ?
Perhaps he sought not Heav'n by sacrifice,
And vows omitted forfeited the prize.
If yet (distinction to thy friend to show,
And please a soul desirous to bestow)
Some gift must grace Eumelus, view thy
   store
Of beauteous handmaids, steeds, and shin-
   ing ore; 630
An ample present let him thence receive,
And Greece shall praise thy gen'rous thirst
   to give.
But this, my prize, I never shall forego;
This, who but touches, Warriors ! is my
   foe.'

Thus spake the youth, nor did his words
   offend;
Pleas'd with the well-turn'd flattery of a
   friend,
Achilles smiled: ' The gift proposed ' (he
   cried),
' Antilochus ! we shall ourselves provide.
With plates of brass the corslet cover'd
   o'er
(The same renown'd Asteropæus wore), 640
Whose glitt'ring margins rais'd with silver
   shine
(No vulgar gift), Eumelus, shall be thine.'
He said : Automedon at his command
The corslet brought, and gave it to his
   hand.
Distinguish'd by his friend, his bosom glows
With gen'rous joy; then Menelaus rose;
The herald placed the sceptre in his hands,
And still'd the clamour of the shouting
   bands.
Not without cause incens'd at Nestor's son,
And inly grieving, thus the King begun:
   'The praise of wisdom, in thy youth ob-
   tain'd, 651
An act so rash, Antilochus, has stain'd.
Robb'd of my glory and my just reward,
To you, O Grecians! be my wrong de-
   clared:
So not a leader shall our conduct blame,
Or judge me envious of a rival's fame.
But shall not we, ourselves, the truth
   maintain ?
What needs appealing in a fact so plain ?
What Greek shall blame me, if I bid thee
   rise
And vindicate by oath th' ill-gotten prize?
Rise, if thou darest, before thy chariot
   stand, 661
The driving scourge high lifted in thy hand,
And touch thy steeds, and swear thy whole
   intent
Was but to conquer, not to circumvent.
Swear by that God whose liquid arms sur-
   round
The globe, and whose dread earthquakes
   heave the ground.'
   The prudent Chief with calm attention
   heard;
Then mildly thus: 'Excuse, if youth have
   err'd;
Superior as thou art, forgive th' offence,
Nor I thy equal, or in years, or sense. 670
Thou know'st the errors of unripen'd age,
Weak are its counsels, headlong is its rage.

The prize I quit, if thou thy wrath resign;
The mare, or aught thou ask'st, be freely
thine,
Ere I become (from thy dear friendship
torn)
Hateful to thee, and to the Gods forsworn.'
So spoke Antilochus; and at the word
The mare contested to the King restor'd.
Joy swells his soul, as when the vernal grain
Lifts the green ear above the springing
plain, 680
The fields their vegetable life renew,
And laugh and glitter with the morning
dew:
Such joy the Spartan's shining face o'er-
spread,
And lifted his gay heart, while thus he said:
' Still may our souls, O gen'rous youth !
agree;
'T is now Atrides' turn to yield to thee.
Rash heat perhaps a moment might con-
trol,
Not break, the settled temper of thy soul.
Not but (my friend) t' is still the wiser way
To waive contention with superior sway:
For ah ! how few, who should like thee
offend, 691
Like thee, have talents to regain the friend?
To plead indulgence, and thy fault atone,
Suffice thy father's merits, and thy own:
Gen'rous alike, for me the sire and son
Have greatly suffer'd, and have greatly
done.
I yield that all may know my soul can
bend,
Nor is my pride preferr'd before my
friend.'
He said: and pleas'd his passion to com-
mand,
Resign'd the courser to Noëmon's hand, 700
Friend of the youthful Chief: himself con-
tent,
The shining charger to his vessel sent.
The golden talents Merion next obtain'd;
The fifth reward, the double bowl, re-
main'd.
Achilles this to rev'rend Nestor bears,
And thus the purpose of his gift declares:
' Accept thou this, O sacred Sire ' (he
said),
' In dear memorial of Patroclus dead;
Dead, and for ever lost, Patroclus lies, 709
For ever snatch'd from our desiring eyes!
Take thou this token of a grateful heart:
Tho' 't is not thine to hurl the distant dart,

The quoit to toss, the pond'rous mace to
wield,
Or urge the race, or wrestle on the field:
Thy pristine vigour age has overthrown,
But left the glory of the past thy own.'
He said, and placed the goblet at his
side:
With joy the venerable King replied:
' Wisely and well, my son, thy words have
prov'd
A senior honour'd and a friend belov'd! 720
Too true it is, deserted of my strength,
These wither'd arms and limbs have fail'd
at length.
Oh ! had I now that force I felt of yore,
Known thro' Buprasium and the Pylian
shore !
Victorious then in ev'ry solemn game,
Ordain'd to Amarynces' mighty name;
The brave Epeians gave my glory way,
Ætolians, Pylians, all resign'd the day.
I quell'd Clytomedes in fights of hand,
And backward hurled Ancæus on the
sand, 730
Surpassed Iphiclus in the swift career,
Phyleus and Polydorus, with the spear:
The sons of Actor won the prize of horse,
But won by numbers, not by art or force:
For the famed twins, impatient to survey
Prize after prize by Nestor borne away,
Sprung to their car; and with united pains
One lash'd the coursers, while one ruled
the reins.
Such once I was ! Now to these tasks suc-
ceeds 739
A younger race, that emulate our deeds:
I yield, alas ! (to age who must not yield?)
Tho' once the foremost hero of the field.
Go thou, my son ! by gen'rous friendship
led,
With martial honours decorate the dead;
While pleas'd I take the gift thy hands
present
(Pledge of benevolence, and kind intent);
Rejoic'd, of all the numerous Greeks, to see
Not one but honours sacred age and me:
Those due distinctions thou so well canst
pay, 749
May the just Gods return another day.'
Proud of the gift, thus spake the Full of
Days:
Achilles heard him, prouder of the praise.
The prizes next are order'd to the field,
For the bold champions who the cæstus
wield.

A stately mule, as yet by toils unbroke,
Of six years' age, unconscious of the yoke,
Is to the circus led, and firmly bound;
Next stands a goblet, massy, large, and
    round.
Achilles rising thus: ' Let Greece excite
Two heroes equal to this hardy fight;   760
Who dares his foe with lifted arms pro-
    voke,
And rush beneath the long - descending
    stroke.
On whom Apollo shall the palm bestow,
And whom the Greeks supreme by con-
    quest know,
This mule his dauntless labour shall re-
    pay;
The vanquish'd bear the massy bowl away.'
  The dreadful combat great Epeüs chose:
High o'er the crowd, enormous bulk ! he
    rose,
And seiz'd the beast, and thus began to say:
' Stand forth some man, to bear the bowl
    away !   770
(Price of his ruin) for who dares deny
This mule my right ? th' undoubted vic-
    tor I.
Others, 't is own'd, in fields of battle shine,
But the first honours of this fight are mine;
For who excels in all?   Then let my foe
Draw near, but first his certain fortune
    know,
Secure, this hand shall his whole frame
    confound,
Mash all his bones, and all his body
    pound:
So let his friends be nigh, a needful train,
To heave the batter'd carcass off the
    plain.'   780
  The Giant spoke; and in a stupid gaze
The host beheld him, silent with amaze !
'T was thou, Euryalus ! who durst aspire
To meet his might, and emulate thy sire,
The great Mecistheus; who in days of yore
In Theban games the noblest trophy bore
(The games ordain'd dead Œdipus to
    grace),
And singly vanquish'd the Cadmean race.
Him great Tydides urges to contend,
Warm with the hopes of conquest for his
    friend;   790
Officious with the cincture girds him round;
And to his wrist the gloves of death are
    bound.
Amid the circle now each champion stands,
And poises high in air his iron hands:

With clashing gauntlets now they fiercely ⎤
    close,   ⎟
Their crackling jaws re-echo to the blows, ⎬
And painful sweat from all their mem- ⎟
    bers flows. ⎦
At length Epeüs dealt a weighty blow
Full on the cheek of his unwary foe;   799
Beneath that pond'rous arm's resistless sway
Down dropp'd he, nerveless, and extended
    lay.
As a large fish, when winds and waters
    roar,
By some huge billow dash'd against the
    shore,
Lies panting : not less batter'd with his
    wound,
The bleeding hero pants upon the ground.
To rear his fallen foe the victor lends,
Scornful, his hand; and gives him to his
    friends;
Whose arms support him, reeling thro' the
    throng.
And dragging his disabled legs along;
Nodding, his head hangs down, his shoulder
    o'er;   810
His mouth and nostrils pour the clotted
    gore;
Wrapp'd round in mists he lies, and lost to
    thought;
His friends receive the bowl, too dearly
    bought.
  The third bold game Achilles next de-
    mands,
And calls the wrestlers to the level sands :
A massy tripod for the victor lies,
Of twice six oxen its reputed price:
And next, the loser's spirits to restore,
A female captive, valued but at four;
Scarce did the Chief the vig'rous strife pro-
    pose,   820
When tower-like Ajax and Ulysses rose.
Amid the ring each nervous rival stands,
Embracing rigid with implicit hands:
Close lock'd above, their heads and arms
    are mix'd;
Below, their planted feet at distance fix'd:
Like two strong rafters, which the builder
    forms
Proof to the wintry winds and howling
    storms,
Their tops connected, but at wider space
Fix'd on the centre stands their solid base.
Now to the grasp each manly body
    bends;   830
The humid sweat from every pore descends;

Their bones resound with blows : sides,
  shoulders, thighs,
Swell to each gripe, and bloody tumours
  rise.
Nor could Ulysses, for his art renown'd,
O'erturn the strength of Ajax on the
  ground;
Nor could the strength of Ajax overthrow
The watchful caution of his artful foe.
While the long strife ev'n tired the lookers-
  on,
Thus to Ulysses spoke great Telamon:
  'Or let me lift thee, Chief, or lift thou
    me: 840
Prove we our force, and Jove the rest de-
  cree.'
  He said: and, straining, heav'd him off
  the ground
With matchless strength: that time Ulysses
  found
The strength t' evade, and where the nerves
  combine
His ankle struck: the giant fell supine;
Ulysses foll'wing, on his bosom lies;
Shouts of applause run rattling thro' the
  skies.
Ajax to lift, Ulysses next essays,
He barely stirr'd him, but he could not
  raise;
His knee lock'd fast, the foe's attempt de-
  nied;   850
And, grappling close, they tumble side by
  side.
Defiled with honourable dust, they roll,
Still breathing strife, and unsubdued of
  soul:
Again they rage, again to combat rise;
When great Achilles thus divides the prize:
  'Your noble vigour, oh my friends, re-
    strain;
Nor weary out your gen'rous strength in
  vain.
Ye both have won: let others who excel,
Now prove that prowess you have prov'd
  so well.'   859
  The hero's words the willing Chiefs
    obey,
From their tired bodies wipe the dust
    away,
And, clothed anew, the foll'wing games
    survey.
  And now succeed the gifts ordain'd to grace
The youths contending in the rapid race:
A silver urn that full six measures held,
By none in weight or workmanship excell'd:

Sidonian artists taught the frame to shine,
Elaborate, with artifice divine;
Whence Tyrian sailors did the prize trans-
  port,   869
And gave to Thoas at the Lemnian port:
From him descended, good Eunæus heir'd
The glorious gift; and, for Lycaon spared,
To brave Patroclus gave the rich reward.
Now, the same hero's funeral rites to grace,
It stands the prize of swiftness in the race.
A well-fed ox was for the second placed;
And half a talent must content the last.
Achilles rising then bespoke the train:
  'Who hope the palm of swiftness to ob-
    tain,
Stand forth, and bear these prizes from the
  plain.'   880
  The hero said, and, starting from his
  place,
Oïlean Ajax rises to the race;
Ulysses next; and he whose speed sur-
  pass'd
His youthful equals, Nestor's son the last.
Ranged in a line the ready racers stand;
Pelides points the barrier with his hand:
All start at once; Oïleus led the race;
The next Ulysses, measuring pace with pace:
Behind him, diligently close, he sped,   889
As closely foll'wing as the running thread
The spindle follows, and displays the
  charms
Of the fair spinster's breast, and moving
  arms:
Graceful in motion thus, his foe he plies,
And treads each footstep ere the dust can
  rise:
His glowing breath upon his shoulders
  plays;
Th' admiring Greeks loud acclamations
  raise:
To him they give their wishes, hearts, and
  eyes,
And send their souls before him as he flies.
Now three times turn'd in prospect of the
  goal,
The panting chief to Pallas lifts his soul: 900
  'Assist, O Goddess!' (thus in thought he
    pray'd)
And, present at his thought, descends the
  maid.
Buoy'd by her heav'nly force, he seems to
  swim,
And feels a pinion lifting ev'ry limb.
All fierce, and ready now the prize to gain,
Unhappy Ajax stumbles on the plain

(O'erturn'd by Pallas) where the slipp'ry
   shore
Was clogg'd with slimy dung, and mingled
   gore
(The self-same place beside Patroclus' pyre,
Where late the slaughter'd victims fed the
   fire):   910
Besmear'd with filth, and blotted o'er with
   clay,
Obscene to sight, the rueful racer lay:
The well-fed bull (the second prize) he
   shared,
And left the urn Ulysses' rich reward.
Then, grasping by the horn the mighty
   beast,
The baffled hero thus the Greeks address'd:
  'Accursed Fate! the conquest I forego;
A mortal I, a Goddess was my foe:
She urged her fav'rite on the rapid way,
And Pallas, not Ulysses, won the day.' 920
  Thus sourly wail'd he, sputt'ring dirt and
   gore;
A burst of laughter echoed thro' the shore.
Antilochus, more humorous than the rest,
Takes the last prize and takes it with a
   jest:
  'Why with our wiser elders should we
   strive?
The Gods still love them, and they always
   thrive.
Ye see, to Ajax I must yield the prize;
He to Ulysses, still more aged and wise
(A green old age unconscious of decays,
That proves the hero born in better
   days);   930
Behold his vigour in this active race!
Achilles only boasts a swifter pace:
For who can match Achilles? He who
   can,
Must yet be more than hero, more than
   man.'
  Th' effect succeeds the speech. Pelides
   cries,
'Thy artful praise deserves a better prize.
Nor Greece in vain shall hear thy friend
   extoll'd;
Receive a talent of the purest gold.'
The youth departs content. The host ad-
   mire
The son of Nestor, worthy of his sire. 940
  Next these a buckler, spear, and helm he
   brings;
Cast on the plain the brazen burthen rings:
Arms, which of late divine Sarpedon wore,
And great Patroclus in short triumph bore.

'Stand forth, the bravest of our host' (he
   cries),
'Whoever dares deserve so rich a prize!
Now grace the lists before our army's
   sight,
And, sheathed in steel, provoke his foe to
   fight.
Who first the jointed armour shall ex-
   plore,
And stain his rival's mail with issuing
   gore;   950
The sword Asteropæus possess'd of old
(A Thracian blade, distinct with studs of
   gold),
Shall pay the stroke, and grace the strik-
   er's side;
These arms in common let the chiefs
   divide:
For each brave champion, when the com-
   bat ends,
A sumptuous banquet at our tent attends.'
  Fierce at the word, up rose great Tydeus'
   son,
And the huge bulk of Ajax Telamon:
Clad in refulgent steel, on either hand, 959
The dreadful chiefs amid the circle stand:
Low'ring they meet, tremendous to the
   sight;
Each Argive bosom beats with fierce de-
   light.
Opposed in arms not long they idly stood,
But thrice they closed, and thrice the charge
   renew'd.
A furious pass the spear of Ajax made
Thro' the broad shield, but at the corslet
   stay'd:
Not thus the foe; his jav'lin aim'd above
The buckler's margin, at the neck he drove.
But Greece, now trembling for her hero's
   life,
Bade share the honours, and surcease the
   strife.   970
Yet still the victor's due Tydides gains,
With him the sword and studded belt re-
   mains.
  Then hurl'd the hero, thund'ring on the
   ground,
A mass of iron (an enormous round),
Whose weight and size the circling Greeks
   admire,
Rude from the furnace, and but shaped by
   fire.
This mighty quoit Eëtion wont to rear,
And from his whirling arm dismiss in
   air:

The giant by Achilles slain, he stow'd
Among his spoils this memorable load. 980
For this he bids those nervous artists vie,
That teach the disc to sound along the sky:
'Let him whose might can hurl this bowl,
   arise;
Who farthest hurls it, takes it as his
   prize:
If he be one enrich'd with large domain
Of downs for flocks, and arable for grain,
Small stock of iron needs that man pro-
   vide;
His hinds and swains whole years shall be
   supplied
From hence ; nor ask the neighb'ring city's
   aid
For ploughshares, wheels, and all the ru-
   ral trade.'   990
   Stern Polypœtes stepp'd before the
      throng,
And great Leonteus, more than mortal
   strong:
Whose force with rival forces to oppose,
Up rose great Ajax; up Epeüs rose.
Each stood in order: first Epeüs threw;
High o'er the wond'ring crowds the whirl-
   ing circle flew.
Leonteus next a little space surpass'd,
And third, the strength of godlike Ajax
   cast:
O'er both their marks it flew; till, fiercely
   flung
From Polypœtes' arm, the discus sung: 1000
Far as a swain his whirling sheephook
   throws,
That distant falls among the grazing cows,
So past them all the rapid circle flies:
His friends (while loud applauses shake
   the skies)
With force conjoin'd heave off the
   weighty prize.
   Those who in skilful archery contend
He next invites, the twanging bow to bend:
And twice ten axes casts amidst the round
(Ten double-edg'd, and ten that singly
   wound).
The mast, which late a first-rate galley
   bore,   1010
The hero fixes in the sandy shore:
To the tall top a milk-white dove they tie,
The trembling mark at which their arrows
   fly.
'Whose weapon strikes yon flutt'ring bird
   shall bear
These two-edg'd axes, terrible in war:

The single, he whose shaft divides the
   cord.'
He said: experienc'd Merion took the word;
And skilful Teucer: in the helm they threw
Their lots inscribed, and forth the latter
   flew.
Swift from the string the sounding arrow
   flies;   1020
But flies unblest ! No grateful sacrifice,
No firstling lambs, unheedful ! didst thou
   vow
To Phœbus, patron of the shaft and bow.
For this, thy well-aim'd arrow, turn'd
   aside,
Err'd from the dove, yet cut the cord that
   tied:
Adown the main-mast fell the parted
   string,
And the free bird to Heav'n displays her
   wing:
Seas, shores, and skies with loud applause
   resound,
And Merion eager meditates the wound:
He takes the bow, directs the shaft above,
And, foll'wing with his eye the soaring
   dove,   1031
Implores the God to speed it thro' the
   skies,
With vows of firstling lambs, and grateful
   sacrifice.
The dove, in airy circles as she wheels,
Amid the clouds the piercing arrow feels;
Quite thro' and thro' the point its passage
   found,
And at his feet fell bloody to the ground.
The wounded bird, ere yet she breathed
   her last
With flagging wings alighted on the mast,
A moment hung, and spread her pinions
   there,   1040
Then sudden dropp'd, and left her life in
   air.
From the pleas'd crowd new peals of thun-
   der rise,
And to the ships brave Merion bears the
   prize.
   To close the funeral games, Achilles last
A massy spear amid the circle placed,
And ample charger of unsullied frame,
With flowers high wrought, not blacken'd
   yet by flame.
For these he bids the heroes prove their
   art,
Whose dext'rous skill directs the flying
   dart.

Here too great Merion hopes the noble
prize; 1050
Nor here disdain'd the King of Men to rise.
With joy Pelides saw the honour paid,
Rose to the Monarch, and respectful said:
' Thee first in virtue, as in power supreme,
O King of Nations! all thy Greeks proclaim;
In ev'ry martial game thy worth attest,
And know thee both their greatest and
their best;
Take then the prize, but let brave Merion
bear
This beamy jav'lin in thy brother's war.'
Pleas'd from the hero's lips his praise to
hear, 1060
The King to Merion gives the brazen spear;
But, set apart for sacred use, commands
The glitt'ring charger to Talthybius' hands.

BOOK XXIV

THE REDEMPTION OF THE BODY OF HECTOR

THE ARGUMENT

The Gods deliberate about the redemption of
Hector's body. Jupiter sends Thetis to
Achilles to dispose him for the restoring it,
and Iris to Priam, to encourage him to go in
person, and treat for it. The old King, notwithstanding the remonstrances of his Queen,
makes ready for the journey, to which he is
encouraged by an omen from Jupiter. He
sets forth in his chariot, with a wagon loaded
with presents, under the charge of Idæus the
herald. Mercury descends in the shape of a
young man, and conducts him to the pavilion
of Achilles. Their conversation on the way.
Priam finds Achilles at his table, casts himself at his feet, and begs for the body of his
son : Achilles, moved with compassion,
grants his request, detains him one night in
his tent, and the next morning sends him
home with the body: the Trojans run out to
meet him. The lamentation of Andromache,
Hecuba, and Helen, with the solemnities of
the funeral.
The time of twelve days is employed in this
book, while the body of Hector lies in the
tent of Achilles. And as many more are
spent in the truce allowed for his interment.
The scene is partly in Achilles's camp, and
partly in Troy.

Now from the finish'd games the Grecian band
Seek their black ships, and clear the
crowded strand:

All stretch'd at ease the genial banquet
share,
And pleasing slumbers quiet all their care.
Not so Achilles: he, to grief resign'd,
His friend's dear image present to his
mind,
Takes his sad couch, more unobserv'd to
weep,
Nor tastes the gifts of all-composing sleep;
Restless he roll'd around his weary bed,
And all his soul on his Patroclus fed: 10
The form so pleasing, and the heart so
kind,
That youthful vigour, and that manly
mind,
What toils they shared, what martial works
they wrought,
What seas they measured, and what fields
they fought;
All pass'd before him in remembrance
dear,
Thought follows thought, and tear succeeds
to tear.
And now supine, now prone, the hero lay,
Now shifts his side, impatient for the day:
Then starting up, disconsolate he goes 19
Wide on the lonely beach to vent his woes.
There as the solitary mourner raves,
The ruddy morning rises o'er the waves:
Soon as it rose, his furious steeds he join'd;
The chariot flies, and Hector trails behind.
And thrice, Patroclus! round thy monu-
ment
Was Hector dragg'd, then hurried to the
tent.
There sleep at last o'ercomes the hero's
eyes;
While foul in dust th' unhonour'd carcass
lies,
But not deserted by the pitying skies. 29
For Phœbus watch'd it with superior care,
Preserv'd from gaping wounds, and taint-
ing air;
And, ignominious as it swept the field,
Spread o'er the sacred corse his golden
shield.
All Heav'n was mov'd, and Hermes will'd
to go
By stealth to snatch him from th' insulting
foe:
But Neptune this, and Pallas this denies,
And th' unrelenting Empress of the Skies:
E'er since that day implacable to Troy,
What time young Paris, simple shepherd
boy, 39

Won by destructive lust (reward obscene)
Their charms rejected for the Cyprian
Queen.
But when the tenth celestial morning broke,
To Heav'n assembled, thus Apollo spoke:
  'Unpitying Powers! how oft each holy
    fane
Has Hector tinged with blood of victims
    slain?
And can ye still his cold remains pursue?
Still grudge his body to the Trojans' view?
Deny to consort, mother, son, and sire,
The last sad honours of a funeral fire?
Is then the dire Achilles all your care? 50
That iron heart, inflexibly severe;
A lion, not a man, who slaughters wide
In strength of rage and impotence of pride,
Who hastes to murder with a savage joy,
Invades around, and breathes but to de-
    stroy.
Shame is not of his soul; nor understood,
The greatest evil and the greatest good.
Still for one loss he rages unresign'd,
Repugnant to the lot of all mankind;
To lose a friend, a brother, or a son,   60
Heav'n dooms each mortal, and its will is
    done:
Awhile they sorrow, then dismiss their care;
Fate gives the wound, and man is born to
    bear.
But this insatiate the commission giv'n
By Fate, exceeds; and tempts the wrath of
    Heav'n:
Lo how his rage dishonest drags along
Hector's dead earth, insensible of wrong!
Brave tho' he be, yet by no reason awed,
He violates the laws of man and God!'
  'If equal honours by the partial skies 70
Are doom'd both heroes' (Juno thus re-
    plies),
'If Thetis' son must no distinction know,
Then hear, ye Gods! the Patron of the
    Bow.
But Hector only boasts a mortal claim,
His birth deriving from a mortal dame:
Achilles of your own ethereal race
Springs from a Goddess, by a man's em-
    brace
(A Goddess by ourself to Peleus giv'n,
A man divine, and chosen friend of
    Heav'n):
To grace those nuptials, from the bright
    abode   80
Yourselves were present; where this Min-
    strel God

(Well-pleas'd to share the feast) amid the
    quire
Stood proud to hymn, and tune his youth-
    ful lyre.'
  Then thus the Thund'rer checks th'
    Imperial Dame:
'Let not thy wrath the Court of Heav'n
    inflame;
Their merits, nor their honours, are the
    same.
But mine, and ev'ry God's peculiar grace
Hector deserves, of all the Trojan race:
Still on our shrines his grateful off'rings
    lay
(The only honours men to Gods can pay), 90
Nor ever from our smoking altar ceas'd
The pure libation, and the holy feast.
Howe'er, by stealth to snatch the corse
    away,
We will not: Thetis guards it night and day.
But haste, and summon to our courts above
The azure Queen: let her persuasion move
Her furious son from Priam to receive
The proffer'd ransom, and the corse to
    leave.'
  He added not: and Iris from the skies,
Swift as a whirlwind, on the message
    flies;   100
Meteorous the face of ocean sweeps,
Refulgent gliding o'er the sable deeps.
Between where Samos wide his forests
    spreads,
And rocky Imbrus lifts its pointed heads,
Down plunged the Maid (the parted waves
    resound);
She plunged, and instant shot the dark pro-
    found.
As, bearing death in the fallacious bait,
From the bent angle sinks the leaden
    weight;
So pass'd the Goddess thro' the closing
    wave,   109
Where Thetis sorrow'd in her secret cave:
There placed amidst her melancholy train
(The blue-hair'd Sisters of the Sacred
    Main)
Pensive she sat, revolving fates to come,
And wept her godlike son's approaching
    doom.
  Then thus the Goddess of the Painted
    Bow:
'Arise, O Thetis! from thy seats below;
'T is Jove that calls.' 'And why' (the
    Dame replies)
'Calls Jove his Thetis to the hated skies?

Sad object as I am for heav'nly sight!
Ah! may my sorrows ever shun the
  light!   120
Howe'er, be Heav'n's almighty Sire obey'd.'
She spake, and veil'd her head in sable
  shade,
Which, flowing long, her graceful person
  clad;
And forth she paced majestically sad.
  Then thro' the world of waters they re-
  pair
(The way fair Iris led) to upper air.
The deeps dividing, o'er the coast they
  rise,
And touch with momentary flight the skies.
There in the lightning's blaze the sire they
  found,   129
And all the Gods in shining synod round.
Thetis approach'd with anguish in her face
(Minerva rising gave the mourner place),
Ev'n Juno sought her sorrows to console,
And offer'd from her hand the nectar bowl:
She tasted, and resign'd it: then began
The sacred Sire of Gods and mortal Man:
  'Thou com'st, fair Thetis, but with grief
  o'ercast,
Maternal sorrows, long, ah long to last!
Suffice, we know, and we partake, thy
  cares:
But yield to Fate, and hear what Jove de-
  clares.   140
Nine days are past, since all the court
  above
In Hector's cause have mov'd the ear of
  Jove;
'T was voted, Hermes from his godlike
  foe
By stealth should bear him, but we will'd
  not so:
We will, thy son himself the corse re-
  store,
And to his conquest add this glory more.
Then hie thee to him, and our mandate
  bear;
Tell him he tempts the wrath of Heav'n
  too far:
Nor let him more (our anger if he dread)
Vent his mad vengeance on the sacred
  dead: 150
But yield to ransom and the father's
  prayer.
The mournful father Iris shall prepare,
With gifts to sue; and offer to his hands
Whate'er his honour asks or heart de-
  mands.'

  His word the Silver-footed Queen at-
  tends,
And from Olympus' snowy tops descends.
Arrived, she heard the voice of loud la-
  ment,
And echoing groans that shook the lofty
  tent.
His friends prepare the victim, and dis-
  pose
Repast unheeded, while he vents his
  woes.   160
The Goddess seats her by her pensive
  son;
She press'd his hand, and tender thus be-
  gun:
  'How long, unhappy! shall thy sorrows
  flow?
And thy heart waste with life-consuming
  woe?
Mindless of food, or love, whose pleasing
  reign
Soothes weary life, and softens human
  pain.
O snatch the moments yet within thy
  power;
Not long to live, indulge the am'rous hour!
Lo! Jove himself (for Jove's command I
  bear),
Forbids to tempt the wrath of Heav'n too
  far.   170
No longer then (his fury if thou dread)
Detain the relics of great Hector dead;
Nor vent on senseless earth thy vengeance
  vain,
But yield to ransom, and restore the
  slain.'
  To whom Achilles: 'Be the ransom
  giv'n,
And we submit, since such the will of
  Heav'n.'
  While thus they communed, from th'
  Olympian bowers
Jove orders Iris to the Trojan towers:
'Haste, winged Goddess, to the sacred
  town,
And urge her Monarch to redeem his
  son;   180
Alone, the Ilian ramparts let him leave,
And bear what stern Achilles may re-
  ceive:
Alone, for so we will: no Trojan near;
Except, to place the dead with decent care,
Some aged herald, who, with gentle hand.
May the slow mules and funeral car com-
  mand.

Nor let him death, nor let him danger
    dread,
Safe thro' the foe by our protection led:
Him Hermes to Achilles shall convey, 189
Guard of his life, and partner of his way.
Fierce as he is, Achilles' self shall spare
His age, nor touch one venerable hair:
Some thought there must be in a soul so
    brave,
Some sense of duty, some desire to save.'
  Then down her bow the winged Iris
    drives,
And swift at Priam's mournful court ar-
    rives:
Where the sad sons beside their father's
    throne
Sat bathed in tears, and answer'd groan
    with groan.
And all amidst them lay the hoary sire
(Sad scene of woe), his face, his wrapp'd
    attire 200
Conceal'd from sight; with frantic hands
    he spread
A shower of ashes o'er his neck and head.
From room to room his pensive daughters
    roam:
Whose shrieks and clamours fill the vaulted
    dome;
Mindful of those, who, late their pride and
    joy,
Lie pale and breathless round the fields of
    Troy!
Before the King Jove's messenger ap-
    pears,
And thus in whispers greets his trembling
    ears:
  'Fear not, oh Father! no ill news I bear;
From Jove I come, Jove makes thee still
    his care; 210
For Hector's sake these walls he bids thee
    leave,
And bear what stern Achilles may receive:
Alone, for so he wills: no Trojan near,
Except, to place the dead with decent care,
Some aged herald, who, with gentle hand,
May the slow mules and funeral car com-
    mand.
Nor shalt thou death, nor shalt thou dan-
    ger dread;
Safe thro' the foe by his protection led:
Thee Hermes to Pelides shall convey,
Guard of thy life, and partner of thy
    way; 220
Fierce as he is, Achilles' self shall spare
Thy age, nor touch one venerable hair:

Some thought there must be in a soul so
    brave,
Some sense of duty, some desire to save.'
  She spoke, and vanish'd. Priam bids
    prepare
His gentle mules, and harness to the car;
There, for the gifts, a polish'd casket lay:
His pious sons the King's commands
    obey.
Then pass'd the Monarch to his bridal-
    room,
Where cedar-beams the lofty roofs per-
    fume, 230
And where the treasures of his empire
    lay;
Then call'd his Queen, and thus began to
    say:
  'Unhappy consort of a King distress'd!
Partake the troubles of thy husband's
    breast:
I saw descend the messenger of Jove,
Who bids me try Achilles' mind to move,
Forsake these ramparts, and with gifts ob-
    tain
The corse of Hector, at yon navy slain.
Tell me thy thought: my heart impels to
    go
Thro' hostile camps, and bears me to the
    foe.' 240
  The hoary Monarch thus: her piercing
    cries
Sad Hecuba renews, and then replies:
  'Ah! whither wanders thy distemper'd
    mind;
And where the prudence now that awed
    mankind,
Thro' Phrygia once, and foreign regions
    known?
Now all confused, distracted, overthrown!
Singly to pass thro' hosts of foes! to face
(Oh heart of steel!) the murd'rer of thy
    race!
To view that deathful eye, and wander
    o'er
Those hands, yet red with Hector's noble
    gore! 250
Alas! my lord! he knows not how to spare,
And what his mercy, thy slain sons de-
    clare;
So brave! so many fall'n! to calm his
    rage
Vain were thy dignity, and vain thy age.
No — pent in this sad palace, let us give
To grief the wretched days we have to
    live.

Still, still, for Hector let our sorrows
   flow,
Born to his own, and to his parents' woe!
Doom'd from the hour his luckless life be-
   gun,   259
To dogs, to vultures, and to Peleus' son!
Oh! in his dearest blood might I allay
My rage, and these barbarities repay!
For ah! could Hector merit thus ? whose
   breath
Expired not meanly, in inactive death:
He pour'd his latest blood in manly fight,
And fell a hero in his country's right.'
   'Seek not to stay me, nor my soul af-
   fright
With words of omen, like a bird of night '
(Replied unmov'd the venerable man):
' 'T is Heav'n commands me, and you urge
   in vain.   270
Had any mortal voice th' injunction laid,
Nor Augur, Priest, nor Seer had been
   obey'd.
A present Goddess brought the high com-
   mand:
I saw, I heard her, and the word shall
   stand.
I go, ye Gods ! obedient to your call:
If in yon camp your powers have doom'd
   my fall,
Content: by the same hand let me expire !
Add to the slaughter'd son the wretched
   sire !
One cold embrace at least may be allow'd,
And my last tears flow mingled with his
   blood !'   280
   Forth from his open'd stores, this said,
   he drew
Twelve costly carpets of refulgent hue;
As many vests, as many mantles told,
And twelve fair veils, and garments stiff
   with gold;
Two tripods next, and twice two chargers
   shine,
With ten pure talents from the richest
   mine;
And last a large, well-labour'd bowl had
   place
(The pledge of treaties once with friendly
   Thrace);
Seem'd all too mean the stores he could
   employ,   289
For one last look to buy him back to
   Troy !
   Lo ! the sad father, frantic with his pain,
Around him furious drives his menial train:

In vain each slave with duteous care at-
   tends,
Each office hurts him, and each face
   offends.
'What make ye here, officious crowds !'
   (he cries)
'Hence, nor obtrude your anguish on my
   eyes.
Have ye no griefs at home, to fix ye there ?
Am I the only object of despair ?
Am I become my people's common show,
Set up by Jove your spectacle of woe ?   300
No, you must feel him too: yourselves
   must fall;
The same stern God to ruin gives you all:
Nor is great Hector lost by me alone:
Your sole defence, your guardian power, is
   gone !
I see your blood the fields of Phrygia
   drown;
I see the ruins of your smoking town !
Oh send me, Gods, ere that sad day shall
   come,
A willing ghost to Pluto's dreary dome !'
   He said, and feebly drives his friends
   away:
The sorr'wing friends his frantic rage
   obey.   310
Next on his sons his erring fury falls,
Polites, Paris, Agathon, he calls;
His threats Deïphobus and Dius hear,
Hippothoüs, Pammon, Helenus the seer,
And gen'rous Antiphon; for yet these nine
Survived, sad relics of his numerous line:
' Inglorious sons of an unhappy sire !
Why did not all in Hector's cause expire ?
Wretch that I am ! my bravest offspring
   slain,
You, the disgrace of Priam's house, re-
   main !   320
Mestor the brave, renown'd in ranks of
   war,
With Troilus, dreadful on his rushing car,
And last great Hector, more than man
   divine,
For sure he seem'd not of terrestrial line !
All those relentless Mars untimely slew,
And left me these, a soft and servile crew,
Whose days the feast and wanton dance
   employ,
Gluttons and flatt'rers, the contempt of
   Troy !
Why teach ye not my rapid wheels to run,
And speed my journey to redeem my
   son ?'   330

The sons their father's wretched age
   revere,
Forgive his anger, and produce the car.
High on the seat the cabinet they bind:
The new-made car with solid beauty shined:
Box was the yoke, emboss'd with costly
   pains,
And hung with ringlets to receive the reins:
Nine cubits long, the traces swept the
   ground;
These to the chariot's polish'd pole they
   bound,
Then fix'd a ring the running reins to
   guide,
And, close beneath, the gather'd ends were
   tied.   340
Next with the gifts (the price of Hector
   slain)
The sad attendants load the groaning wain:
Last to the yoke the well-match'd mules
   they bring
(The gift of Mysia to the Trojan King).
But the fair horses, long his darling care,
Himself receiv'd, and harness'd to his car:
Griev'd as he was, he not this task denied;
The hoary herald help'd him at his side.
While careful these the gentle coursers
   join'd,   349
Sad Hecuba approach'd with anxious mind;
A golden bowl, that foam'd with fragrant
   wine
(Libation destin'd to the Power divine),
Held in her right, before the steeds she
   stands,
And thus consigns it to the Monarch's
   hands:
'Take this, and pour to Jove; that, safe
   from harms,
His grace restore thee to our roof and
   arms.
Since, victor of thy fears, and slighting
   mine,
Heav'n, or thy soul, inspire this bold de-
   sign,
Pray to that God, who, high on Ida's brow
Surveys thy desolated realms below,   360
His winged messenger to send from high,
And lead the way with heav'nly augury:
Let the strong Sov'reign of the plumy race
Tower on the right of yon ethereal space.
That sign beheld, and strengthen'd from
   above,
Boldly pursue the journey mark'd by Jove;
But if the God his augury denies,
Suppress thy impulse, nor reject advice.'

''T is just' (said Priam) 'to the Sire
   above
To raise our hands; for who so good as
   Jove?'   370
He spoke, and bade th' attendant hand-
   maid bring
The purest water of the living spring
(Her ready hands the ewer and basin held);
Then took the golden cup his Queen had
   fill'd;
On the mid pavement pours the rosy wine,
Uplifts his eyes, and calls the Power divine:
'Oh First and Greatest! Heav'n's im-
   perial Lord!
On lofty Ida's holy hill ador'd!
To stern Achilles now direct my ways,   379
And teach him mercy when a father prays.
If such thy will, despatch from yonder sky
Thy sacred bird, celestial augury!
Let the strong sov'reign of the plumy race
Tower on the right of yon ethereal space:
So shall thy suppliant, strengthen'd from
   above,
Fearless pursue the journey mark'd by
   Jove.'
Jove heard his prayer, and from the
   throne on high
Despatch'd his bird, celestial augury!
The swift-wing'd chaser of the feather'd
   game,
And known to Gods by Percnos' lofty
   name.   390
Wide as appears some palace-gate dis-
   play'd,
So broad his pinions stretch'd their ample
   shade,
As, stooping dexter with resounding wings,
Th' imperial bird descends in airy rings.
A dawn of joy in ev'ry face appears;
The mourning matron dries her tim'rous
   tears.
Swift on his car th' impatient Monarch
   sprung;
The brazen portal in his passage rung.
The mules preceding draw the loaded wain,
Charged with the gifts; Idæus holds the
   rein: 400
The King himself his gentle steeds con-
   trols,
And thro' surrounding friends the chariot
   rolls;
On his slow wheels the foll'wing people
   wait,
Mourn at each step, and give him up to
   Fate;

With hands uplifted, eye him as he pass'd,
And gaze upon him as they gazed their last.
  Now forward fares the father on his way,
Thro' the lone fields, and back to Ilion
    they.
Great Jove beheld him as he cross'd the
    plain,
And felt the woes of miserable man.   410
Then thus to Hermes: 'Thou, whose con-
    stant cares
Still succour mortals, and attend their
    prayers!
Behold an object to thy charge consign'd;
If ever pity touch'd thee for mankind,
Go, guard the sire; th' observing foe pre-
    vent,
And safe conduct him to Achilles' tent.'
  The God obeys, his golden pinions binds,
And mounts incumbent on the wings of
    winds,
That high thro' fields of air his flight sus-
    tain,
O'er the wide earth, and o'er the boundless
    main: 420
Then grasps the wand that causes sleep to
    fly,
Or in soft slumbers seals the wakeful eye:
Thus arm'd, swift Hermes steers his airy
    way,
And stoops on Hellespont's resounding sea.
A beauteous youth, majestic and divine,
He seem'd; fair offspring of some princely
    line!
Now Twilight veil'd the glaring face of Day,
And clad the dusky fields in sober gray;
What time the herald and the hoary King,
Their chariot stopping at the silver spring,
That circling Ilus' ancient marble flows, 431
Allow'd their mules and steeds a short
    repose.
Thro' the dim shade the herald first espies
A man's approach, and thus to Priam cries:
'I mark some foe's advance: O King!
    beware;
This hard adventure claims thy utmost
    care;
For much I fear destruction hovers nigh:
Our state asks counsel. Is it best to fly?
Or, old and helpless, at his feet to fall
(Two wretched suppliants), and for mercy
    call?'   440
  Th' afflicted Monarch shiver'd with de-
    pair;
Pale grew his face, and upright stood his
    hair;

Sunk was his heart; his colour went and
    came;
A sudden trembling shook his aged frame:
When Hermes, greeting, touch'd his royal
    hand,
And, gentle, thus accosts with kind de-
    mand:
  'Say whither, Father! when each mortal
    sight
Is seal'd in sleep, thou wander'st thro'
    the night?
Why roam thy mules and steeds the plains
    along,
Thro' Grecian foes, so numerous and so
    strong?   450
What couldst thou hope, shouldst these
    thy treasures view:
These, who with endless hate thy race
    pursue?
For what defence, alas! couldst thou pro-
    vide?
Thyself not young, a weak old man thy
    guide.
Yet suffer not thy soul to sink with
    dread;
From me no harm shall touch thy rev'rend
    head:
From Greece I'll guard thee too; for in
    those lines
The living image of my father shines.'
  'Thy words, that speak benevolence of
    mind,
Are true, my son!' (the godlike Sire re-
    join'd)   460
'Great are my hazards; but the Gods sur-
    vey
My steps and send thee, guardian of my
    way.
Hail! and be blest; for scarce of mortal
    kind
Appear thy form, thy feature, and thy
    mind.'
  'Nor true are all thy words, nor erring
    wide'
(The sacred Messenger of Heav'n replied);
'But say, convey'st thou thro' the lonely
    plains
What yet most precious of thy store re-
    mains,
To lodge in safety with some friendly
    hand?
Prepared perchance to leave thy native
    land?   470
Or fly'st thou now? What hopes can Troy
    retain,

Thy matchless son, her guard and glory,
  slain ? '
 The King, alarm'd: 'Say what, and
  whence thou art,
Who search the sorrows of a parent's
  heart,
And know so well how godlike Hector
  died ? '
Thus Priam spoke, and Hermes thus re-
  plied:
 'You tempt me, Father, and with pity
  touch:
On this sad subject you inquire too much.
Oft have these eyes the godlike Hector
  view'd
In glorious fight, with Grecian blood im-
  brued: 480
I saw him, when, like Jove, his flames he
  toss'd
On thousand ships, and wither'd half a
  host:
I saw, but help'd not, stern Achilles' ire
Forbade assistance, and enjoy'd the fire.
For him I serve, of Myrmidonian race;
One ship convey'd us from our native
  place;
Polyctor is my sire, an honour'd name,
Old, like thyself, and not unknown to
  fame;
Of sev'n his sons, by whom the lot was cast
To serve our Prince, it fell on me the
  last.   490
To watch this quarter my adventure falls;
For with the morn the Greeks attack your
  walls;
Sleepless they sit, impatient to engage,
And scarce their rulers check their mar-
  tial rage.'
 'If then thou art of stern Pelides' train,'
('The mournful Monarch thus rejoin'd
  again),
' Ah, tell me truly, where, oh ! where are
  laid
My son's dear relics ? what befalls him
  dead ?
Have dogs dismember'd on the naked
  plains,   499
Or yet unmangled rest, his cold remains ? '
 'O Favour'd of the Skies ! ' (thus an-
  swer'd then
The Power that mediates between Gods and
  men)
' Nor dogs, nor vultures, have thy Hector
  rent,
But whole he lies, neglected in the tent:

This the twelfth ev'ning since he rested
  there,
Untouch'd by worms, untainted by the
  air.
Still as Aurora's ruddy beam is spread,
Round his friend's tomb Achilles drags the
  dead;
Yet undisfigured, or in limb or face,
All fresh he lies, with every living
  grace,   510
Majestical in death ! No stains are found
O'er all the corse, and closed is ev'ry
  wound;
Tho' many a wound they gave. Some
  heav'nly care,
Some hand divine, preserves him ever
  fair:
Or all the Host of Heav'n, to whom he
  led
A life so grateful, still regard him dead.'
 Thus spoke to Priam the celestial Guide,
And joyful thus the royal Sire replied:
Bless'd is the man who pays the Gods
  above   519
The constant tribute of respect and love !
Those who inhabit the Olympian bower
My son forgot not, in exalted power;
And Heav'n, that ev'ry virtue bears in
  mind,
Ev'n to the ashes of the just is kind.
But thou, oh gen'rous youth ! this goblet
  take,
A pledge of gratitude for Hector's sake;
And while the fav'ring Gods our steps
  survey,
Safe to Pelides' tent conduct my way.'
 To whom the latent God: 'O King, for-
  bear
To tempt my youth, for apt is youth to
  err: 530
But can I, absent from my Prince's sight,
Take gifts in secret, that must shun the
  light ?
What from our master's interest thus we
  draw,
Is but a licens'd theft that 'scapes the
  law.
Respecting him, my soul abjures th' of-
  fence;
And, as the crime, I dread the conse-
  quence.
Thee, far as Argos, pleas'd I could con-
  vey;
Guard of thy life, and partner of thy
  way:

On thee attend, thy safety to maintain,
O'er pathless forests, or the roaring
   main.'   540
He said, then took the chariot at a bound,
And snatch'd the reins, and whirl'd the lash
   around:
Before th' inspiring God that urged them
   on
The coursers fly, with spirit not their own.
And now they reach'd the naval walls, and
   found
The guards repasting, while the bowls go
   round:
On these the virtue of his wand he tries,
And pours deep slumber on their watchful
   eyes:
Then heav'd the massy gates, remov'd the
   bars,   549
And o'er the trenches led the rolling cars.
Unseen, thro' all the hostile camp they
   went,
And now approach'd Pelides' lofty tent.
Of fir the roof was rais'd, and cover'd o'er
With reeds collected from the marshy
   shore;
And, fenc'd with palisades, a hall of state
(The work of soldiers), where the hero sat.
Large was the door, whose well-compacted
   strength
A solid pine-tree barr'd of wondrous length;
Scarce three strong Greeks could lift its
   mighty weight,
But great Achilles singly closed the gate. 560
This Hermes (such the power of Gods) set
   wide;
Then swift alighted the celestial guide,
And thus, reveal'd: 'Hear, Prince! and
   understand
Thou ow'st thy guidance to no mortal hand;
Hermes I am, descended from above,
The King of Arts, the Messenger of Jove.
Farewell: to shun Achilles' sight I fly; ⎱
Uncommon are such favours of the sky, ⎰
Nor stand confess'd to frail mortality.
Now fearless enter, and prefer thy
   prayers;   570
Adjure him by his father's silver hairs,
His son, his mother! urge him to bestow
Whatever pity that stern heart can know.'
   Thus having said, he vanish'd from his
   eyes,
And in a moment shot into the skies:
The King, confirm'd from Heav'n, alighted
   there,
And left his aged herald on the car.

With solemn pace thro' various rooms he
   went,
And found Achilles in his inner tent: 579
There sat the hero; Alcimus the brave,
And great Automedon, attendance gave;
These serv'd his person at the royal feast;
Around, at awful distance, stood the rest.
   Unseen by these, the King his entry
   made;
And, prostrate now before Achilles laid,
Sudden (a venerable sight!) appears;
Embraced his knees, and bathed his hands
   in tears;
Those direful hands his kisses press'd, im-
   brued
Ev'n with the best, the dearest of his
   blood!
   As when a wretch (who, conscious of his
   crime,   590
Pursued for murder, flies his native clime)
Just gains some frontier, breathless, pale,
   amazed!
All gaze, all wonder: thus Achilles gazed:
Thus stood th' attendants stupid with sur-
   prise:
All mute, yet seem'd to question with their
   eyes:
Each look'd on other, none the silence
   broke,
Till thus at last the kingly suppliant spoke:
'Ah think, thou favour'd of the Powers
   divine!
Think of thy father's age, and pity mine!
In me, that father's rev'rend image
   trace,   600
Those silver hairs, that venerable face;
His trembling limbs, his helpless person,
   see!
In all my equal, but in misery!
Yet now, perhaps, some turn of human
   Fate
Expels him helpless from his peaceful
   state;
Think, from some powerful foe thou see'st
   him fly,
And beg protection with a feeble cry.
Yet still one comfort in his soul may rise;
He hears his son still lives to glad his eyes;
And, hearing, still may hope a better
   day   610
May send him thee, to chase that foe
   away.
No comfort to my griefs, no hopes re-
   main,
The best, the bravest of my sons are slain!

Yet what a race! ere Greece to Ilion
    came,
The pledge of many a lov'd and loving
    dame!
Nineteen one mother bore — Dead, all are
    dead!
How oft, alas! has wretched Priam bled!
Still one was left, their loss to recom-
    pense;
His father's hope, his country's last de-
    fence.
Him too thy rage has slain! beneath thy
    steel,   620
Unhappy, in his country's cause, he fell!
For him, thro' hostile camps I bent my
    way,
For him thus prostrate at thy feet I lay;
Large gifts, proportion'd to thy wrath, I
    bear:
Oh, hear the wretched, and the Gods re-
    vere!
Think of thy father, and this face behold!
See him in me, as helpless and as old;
Tho' not so wretched: there he yields to
    me,
The first of men in sov'reign misery.
Thus forc'd to kneel, thus grov'ling to
    embrace   630
  The scourge and ruin of my realm and
    race:
Suppliant my children's murd'rer to im-
    plore,
And kiss those hands yet reeking with their
    gore!'
  These words soft pity in the Chief in-
    spire,
Touch'd with the dear remembrance of his
    sire.
Then with his hand (as prostrate still he
    lay)
The old man's cheek he gently turn'd
    away.
Now each by turns indulged the gush of
    woe;
And now the mingled tides together flow:
This low on earth, that gently bending
    o'er,   640
A father one, and one a son deplore:
But great Achilles diff'rent passions rend,
And now his Sire he mourns, and now his
    Friend.
Th' infectious softness thro' the heroes
    ran;
One universal solemn shower began;
They bore as heroes, but they felt as man.

Satiate at length with unavailing woes,
From the high throne divine Achilles rose;
The rev'rend Monarch by the hand he
    rais'd;
On his white beard and form majestic
    gazed,   650
Not unrelenting: then serene began
With words to soothe the miserable man:
  ' Alas! what weight of anguish hast thou
    known,
Unhappy Prince! thus guardless and alone
To pass thro' foes, and thus undaunted face
The man whose fury has destroy'd thy
    race!
Heav'n sure has arm'd thee with a heart of
    steel,
A strength proportion'd to the woes you
    feel.
Rise then: let reason mitigate our care:
To mourn avails not: man is born to bear.
Such is, alas! the Gods' severe decree; 661
They, only they, are blest, and only free.
Two urns by Jove's high throne have ever
    stood,
The source of evil one, and one of good;
From thence the cup of mortal man he
    fills,
Blessings to these, to those distributes ills;
To most he mingles both: the wretch de-
    creed
To taste the bad, unmix'd, is curs'd in-
    deed:
Pursued by wrongs, by meagre famine
    driv'n,
He wanders, outcast both of earth and
    Heav'n.   670
The happiest taste not Happiness sincere,
But find the cordial draught is dash'd with
    Care.
Who more than Peleus shone in wealth
    and power?
What stars concurring bless'd his natal
    hour!
A realm, a Goddess, to his wishes giv'n,
Graced by the Gods with all the gifts of
    Heav'n!
One evil, yet, o'ertakes his latest day;
No race succeeding to imperial sway:
An only son! and he (alas!) ordain'd
To fall untimely in a foreign land!   680
See him, in Troy, the pious care decline
Of his weak age, to live the curse of thine!
Thou too, old man, hast happier days be-
    held;
In riches once, in children once excell'd;

Extended Phrygia own'd thy ample reign,⎫
And all fair Lesbos' blissful seats contain,⎬
And all wide Hellespont's unmeasured⎪
   main.⎭
But since the God his hand has pleas'd to
   turn,
And fill thy measure from his bitter urn,
What sees the sun, but hapless heroes' falls?
War, and the blood of men, surround thy
   walls!   691
What must be, must be.   Bear thy lot,
   nor shed
These unavailing sorrows o'er the dead;
Thou canst not call him from the Stygian
   shore,
But thou, alas! may'st live to suffer more!'
  To whom the King: 'O favour'd of the⎫
   skies!⎪
Here let me grow to earth! since Hector⎬
   lies⎪
On the bare beach, deprived of obsequies.⎭
O give me Hector: to my eyes restore
His corse, and take the gifts: I ask no
   more!   700
Thou, as thou may'st, these boundless stores
   enjoy;
Safe may'st thou sail, and turn thy wrath
   from Troy;
So shall thy pity and forbearance give
A weak old man to see the light, and live!'
  'Move me no more' (Achilles thus re-
   plies,
While kindling anger sparkled in his eyes),
'Nor seek by tears my steady soul to bend;
To yield thy Hector I myself intend:
For know, from Jove my Goddess-mother
   came   709
(Old Ocean's daughter, Silver-footed
   Dame);
Nor com'st thou but by Heav'n; nor com'st
   alone;
Some God impels with courage not thy
   own:
No human hand the weighty gate un-⎫
   barr'd,⎪
Nor could the boldest of our youth have⎬
   dared⎪
To pass our out-works, or elude the guard.⎭
Cease; lest, neglectful of high Jove's com-
   mand,
I shew thee, King! thou tread'st on hostile
   land;
Release my knees, thy suppliant arts give
   o'er,
And shake the purpose of my soul no more.'

The Sire obey'd him, trembling and o'er-
   awed.   720
Achilles, like a lion, rush'd abroad;
Automedon and Alcimus attend,
Whom most he honour'd, since he lost his
   friend;
These to unyoke the mules and horses went,
And led the hoary herald to the tent:
Next, heap'd on high, the numerous pre-
   sents bear
(Great Hector's ransom) from the polish'd
   car.
Two splendid mantles, and a carpet spread,
They leave, to cover and enwrap the dead:
Then call the handmaids, with assistant
   toil   730
To wash the body, and anoint with oil,
Apart from Priam; lest th' unhappy sire,
Provok'd to passion, once more rouse to
   ire
The stern Pelides; and nor sacred age,
Nor Jove's command, should check the ris-
   ing rage.
This done, the garments o'er the corse they
   spread;
Achilles lifts it to the funeral bed:
Then, while the body on the car they laid,
He groans, and calls on lov'd Patroclus'
   shade:
'If, in that gloom which never light must
   know,   740
The deeds of mortals touch the ghosts
   below;
O Friend! forgive me, that I thus fulfil
(Restoring Hector) Heav'n's unquestion'd
   will.
The gifts the Father gave, be ever thine,
To grace thy manes, and adorn thy shrine.'
  He said, and, ent'ring, took his seat of
   state,
Where full before him rev'rend Priam sate:
To whom, composed, the godlike Chief be-
   gun:
'Lo! to thy prayer restor'd, thy breathless
   son;
Extended on the funeral couch he lies; 750⎫
And, soon as morning paints the eastern⎬
   skies,⎪
The sight is granted to thy longing eyes.⎭
But now the peaceful hours of sacred
   night
Demand refection, and to rest invite:
Nor thou, O Father! thus consumed with
   woe,
The common cares that nourish life forego.

Not thus did Niobe, of form divine,
A parent once, whose sorrows equall'd
thine:
Six youthful sons, as many blooming
maids,   759
In one sad day beheld the Stygian shades:
Those by Apollo's silver bow were slain,
These, Cynthia's arrows stretch'd upon
the plain.
So was her pride chastised by wrath divine,
Who match'd her own with bright La-
tona's line;
But two the Goddess, twelve the Queen
enjoy'd;
Those boasted twelve th' avenging two
destroy'd.
Steep'd in their blood, and in the dust out-
spread,
Nine days, neglected, lay exposed the
dead;
None by to weep them, to inhume them
none
(For Jove had turn'd the nation all to
stone);   770
The Gods themselves, at length, relent-
ing, gave
Th' unhappy race the honours of a grave.
Herself a rock (for such was Heav'n's
high will)
Thro' deserts wild now pours a weeping
rill;
Where round the bed whence Acheloüs
springs,
The wat'ry fairies dance in mazy rings:
There, high on Sipylus's shady brow, ⎫
She stands, her own sad monument of ⎪
woe: ⎬
The rock for ever lasts, the tears for ever ⎪
flow.   ⎭
Such griefs, O King! have other parents
known: 780
Remember theirs, and mitigate thy own.
The care of Heav'n thy Hector has ap-
pear'd;
Nor shall he lie unwept, and uninterr'd;
Soon may thy aged cheeks in tears be
drown'd,
And all the eyes of Ilion stream around.'
He said, and, rising, chose the victim ewe
With silver fleece, which his attendants
slew.
The limbs they sever from the reeking
hide,
With skill prepare them, and in parts di-
vide: 789

Each on the coals the sep'rate morsels lays,
And hasty snatches from the rising blaze.
With bread the glitt'ring canisters they
load,
Which round the board Automedon be-
stow'd:
The chief himself to each his portion placed,
And each indulging shared in sweet re-
past.
When now the rage of hunger was re-
press'd,
The wond'ring Hero eyes his royal Guest;
No less the royal Guest the Hero eyes,
His godlike aspect, and majestic size;
Here, youthful grace and noble fire en-
gage,   800
And there, the mild benevolence of age.
Thus gazing long, the silence neither broke
(A solemn scene); at length the father
spoke:
'Permit me now, belov'd of Jove, to
steep
My careful temples in the dew of sleep:
For since the day that number'd with the
dead
My hapless son, the dust has been my bed,
Soft sleep a stranger to my weeping eyes,
My only food, my sorrows and my sighs!
Till now, encouraged by the grace you
give,   810
I share thy banquet, and consent to live.'
With that, Achilles bade prepare the bed,
With purple soft, and shaggy carpets
spread;
Forth, by the flaming lights, they bend their
way,
And place the couches, and the cov'rings
lay.
Then he: 'Now, Father, sleep, but sleep
not here,
Consult thy safety, and forgive my fear,
Lest any Argive (at this hour awake,
To ask our counsel, or our orders take),
Approaching sudden to our open tent,   820
Perchance behold thee, and our grace pre-
vent.
Should such report thy honour'd person
here,
The King of Men the ransom might defer,
But say with speed, if aught of thy desire
Remains unask'd, what time the rites re-
quire
T' inter thy Hector? For, so long we stay
Our slaught'ring arm, and bid the hosts
obey.'

'If then thy will permit' (the Monarch
   said),
'To finish all due honours to the dead,
This, of thy grace, accord: to thee are
   known   830
The fears of Ilion, closed within her town;
And at what distance from our walls as-
   pire
The hills of Ide, and forests for the fire.
Nine days to vent our sorrows I request,
The tenth shall see the funeral and the
   feast;
The next, to raise his monument be giv'n;
The twelfth we war, if war be doom'd by
   Heav'n !'
'This thy request' (replied the Chief)
   'enjoy:
Till then, our arms suspend the fall of
   Troy.'
   Then gave his hand at parting, to pre-
   vent   840
The old man's fears, and turn'd within the
   tent
Where fair Briseïs, bright in blooming
   charms,
Expects her hero with desiring arms.
But in the porch the King and Herald
   rest,
Sad dreams of care yet wand'ring in their
   breast.
   Now Gods and men the gifts of sleep
   partake;
Industrious Hermes only was awake,
The King's return revolving in his mind,
To pass the ramparts, and the watch to
   blind.
The Power descending hover'd o'er his
   head,   850
And, 'Sleep'st thou, Father?' (thus the
   vision said):
'Now dost thou sleep, when Hector is re-
   stor'd ?
Nor fear the Grecian foes, or Grecian lord ?
Thy presence here should stern Atrides
   see,
Thy still-surviving sons may sue for thee;
May offer all thy treasures yet contain,
To spare thy age; and offer all in vain.'
   Waked with the word, the trembling Sire
   arose,
And rais'd his friend: the God before him
   goes:
He joins the mules, directs them with his
   hand,   860
And moves in silence thro' the hostile land.

When now to Xanthus' yellow stream they
   drove
(Xanthus, immortal progeny of Jove),
The winged Deity forsook their view,
And in a moment to Olympus flew.
   Now shed Aurora round her saffron ray,
Sprung thro' the gates of light, and gave
   the day.
Charged with their mournful load to Ilion
   go
The Sage and King, majestically slow.
Cassandra first beholds, from Ilion's spire,
The sad procession of her hoary sire; 871
Then, as the pensive pomp advanc'd more
   near
(Her breathless brother stretch'd upon the
   bier),
A shower of tears o'erflows her beauteous
   eyes,
Alarming thus all Ilion with her cries:
'Turn here your steps, and here your eyes
   employ,
Ye wretched daughters, and ye sons of
   Troy !
If e'er ye rush'd in crowds, with vast de-
   light,
To hail your hero glorious from the fight;
Now meet him dead, and let your sorrows
   flow !   880
Your common triumph, and your common
   woe.'
   In thronging crowds they issue to the
   plains,
Nor man, nor woman, in the walls remains:
In ev'ry face the self-same grief is shewn,
And Troy sends forth one universal groan.
At Scæa's gates, they meet the mourning
   wain,
Hang on the wheels, and grovel round the
   slain.
The wife and mother, frantic with despair,
Kiss his pale cheek, and rend their scatter'd
   hair;   889
Thus wildly wailing, at the gates they
   lay;
And there had sigh'd and sorrow'd out the
   day;
But godlike Priam from the chariot rose,
'Forbear' (he cried) 'this violence of woes;
First to the palace let the car proceed,
Then pour your boundless sorrows o'er the
   dead.'
   The waves of people at his word divide;
Slow rolls the chariot thro' the foll'wing
   tide:

Ev'n to the palace the sad pomp they wait:
They weep, and place him on the bed of
  state.
A melancholy choir attend around,   900
With plaintive sighs and music's solemn
  sound:
Alternately they sing, alternate flow
Th' obedient tears, melodious in their woe;
While deeper sorrows groan from each full
  heart,
And Nature speaks at ev'ry pause of Art.
  First to the corse the weeping consort
    flew;
Around his neck her milk-white arms she
  threw:
And, 'Oh my Hector! oh my lord!' she
  cries,
'Snatch'd in thy bloom from these desiring
  eyes!
Thou to the dismal realms for ever gone!
And I abandon'd, desolate, alone!   911
An only son, once comfort of our pains,
Sad product now of hapless love, remains!
Never to manly age that son shall rise,
Or with increasing graces glad my eyes;
For Ilion now (her great defender slain)
Shall sink a smoking ruin on the plain.
Who now protects her wives with guardian
  care?
Who saves her infants from the rage of
  war?
Now hostile fleets must waft those infants
  o'er   920
(Those wives must wait them) to a foreign
  shore!
Thou too, my son! to barb'rous climes
  shalt go,
The sad companion of thy mother's woe;
Driv'n hence a slave before the victor's
  sword,
Condemn'd to toil for some inhuman lord:
Or else some Greek, whose father press'd
  the plain,
Or son, or brother, by great Hector slain,
In Hector's blood his vengeance shall enjoy,
And hurl thee headlong from the towers
  of Troy.
For thy stern father never spared a foe: 930
Thence all these tears, and all this scene of
  woe!
Thence, many evils his sad parents bore,
His parents many, but his consort more.
Why gavest thou not to me thy dying
  hand?
And why receiv'd not I thy last command?

Some word thou would'st have spoke,
  which, sadly dear,
My soul might keep, or utter with a tear;
Which never, never could be lost in air,
Fix'd in my heart, and oft repeated
  there!'
Thus to her weeping maids she makes
  her moan: 940
Her weeping handmaids echo groan for
  groan.
  The mournful mother next sustains her
    part:
'O thou, the best, the dearest to my heart!
Of all my race thou most by Heav'n ap-
  prov'd,
And by th' immortals ev'n in death be-
  lov'd!
While all my other sons in barb'rous bands
Achilles bound, and sold to foreign lands,
This felt no chains, but went, a glorious
  ghost,
Free, and a hero, to the Stygian coast. 949
Sentenc'd, 't is true, by his inhuman doom,
Thy noble corse was dragg'd around the
  tomb
(The tomb of him thy warlike arm had
  slain);
Ungen'rous insult, impotent and vain!
Yet glow'st thou fresh with ev'ry living
  grace,
No mark of pain, or violence of face;
Rosy and fair! as Phœbus' silver bow
Dismiss'd thee gently to the shades be-
  low!'
  Thus spoke the Dame, and melted into
    tears.
Sad Helen next in pomp of grief appears:
Fast from the shining sluices of her eyes 96o
Fall the round crystal drops, while thus she
  cries:
'Ah, dearest friend! in whom the Gods had
  join'd
The mildest manners with the bravest
  mind!
Now twice ten years (unhappy years) are
  o'er
Since Paris brought me to the Trojan
  shore
(Oh had I perish'd, ere that form divine
Seduced this soft, this easy heart of mine!)
Yet was it ne'er my fate from thee to find
A deed ungentle, or a word unkind:
When others curs'd the authoress of their
  woe,   970
Thy pity check'd my sorrows in their flow:

If some proud brother eyed me with dis-
    dain,
Or scornful sister with her sweeping
    train,
Thy gentle accents soften'd all my pain.
For thee I mourn; and mourn myself in
    thee,
The wretched source of all this misery !
The fate I caus'd, for ever I bemoan;
Sad Helen has no friend, now thou art
    gone !
Thro' Troy's wide streets abandon'd shall I
    roam,   979
In Troy deserted, as abhorr'd at home !'
  So spoke the Fair, with sorrow-streaming
    eye:
Distressful beauty melts each stander-by;
On all around th' infectious sorrow grows;
But Priam check'd the torrent as it rose:
'Perform, ye Trojans ! what the rites re-
    quire,
And fell the forests for a funeral pyre !
Twelve days nor foes nor secret ambush
    dread;
Achilles grants these honours to the dead.'
  He spoke; and at his word the Trojan
    train   989
Their mules and oxen harness to the wain,
Pour thro' the gates, and, fell'd from Ida's
    crown,
Roll back the gather'd forests to the town.
These toils continue nine succeeding days,
And high in air a sylvan structure raise.
But when the tenth fair morn began to
    shine,
Forth to the pile was borne the man di-
    vine,
And placed aloft: while all, with streaming
    eyes,
Beheld the flames and rolling smokes
    arise.
Soon as Aurora, Daughter of the Dawn,
With rosy lustre streak'd the dewy
    lawn,   1000
Again the mournful crowds surround the
    pyre,
And quench with wine the yet-remaining
    fire.
The snowy bones his friends and brothers
    place
(With tears collected) in a golden vase;
The golden vase in purple palls they
    roll'd,
Of softest texture, and inwrought with
    gold.

Last, o'er the urn the sacred earth they
    spread,
And rais'd the tomb, memorial of the
    dead
(Strong guards and spies, till all the rites
    were done,
Watch'd from the rising to the setting
    sun).   1010
All Troy then moves to Priam's court
    again,
A solemn, silent, melancholy train:
Assembled there, from pious toil they rest,
And sadly shared the last sepulchral feast.
  Such honours Ilion to her hero paid,
And peaceful slept the mighty Hector's
    shade.

POPE'S CONCLUDING NOTE.

WE have now passed through the Iliad, and
seen the anger of Achilles, and the terrible
effects of it, at an end: as that only was the
subject of the poem, and the nature of epic
poetry would not permit our author to proceed
to the event of the war, it may perhaps be acceptable to the common reader to give a short
account of what happened to Troy and the
chief actors in this poem, after the conclusion
of it.

I need not mention that Troy was taken soon
after the death of Hector, by the stratagem of
the wooden horse, the particulars of which are
described by Virgil in the second book of the
Æneis.

Achilles fell before Troy, by the hand of
Paris, by the shot of an arrow in his heel, as
Hector had prophesied at his death, book xxii.

The unfortunate Priam was killed by Pyr-
rhus, the son of Achilles.

Ajax, after the death of Achilles, had a contest with Ulysses for the armour of Vulcan,
but being defeated in his aim, he slew himself
through indignation.

Helen, after the death of Paris, married
Deïphobus his brother, and at the taking of
Troy betrayed him, in order to reconcile herself to Menelaus, her first husband, who received her again into favour.

Agamemnon at his return was barbarously
murdered by Ægisthus, at the instigation of
Clytæmnestra, his wife, who in his absence had
dishonoured his bed with Ægisthus.

Diomed, after the fall of Troy, was expelled
his own country, and scarce escaped with
life from his adulterous wife Ægiale; but at
last was received by Daunus in Apulia, and
shared his kingdom; it is uncertain how he
died.

Nestor lived in peace, with his children, in Pylos, his native country.

Ulysses also, after innumerable troubles by sea and land, at last returned in safety to Ithaca, which is the subject of Homer's Odyssey.

I must end these notes by discharging my duty to two of my friends, which is the more an indispensable piece of justice, as the one of them is since dead. The merit of their kindness to me will appear infinitely the greater, as the task they undertook was, in its own nature, of much more labour, than either pleasure or reputation. The larger part of the extracts from Eustathius, together with several excellent observations, were sent me by Mr. Broome: and the whole Essay upon Homer was written, upon such memoirs as I had collected, by the late Dr. Parnell, Archdeacon of Clogher in Ireland. How very much that gentleman's friendship prevailed over his genius, in detaining a writer of his spirit in the drudgery of removing the rubbish of past pedants, will soon appear to the world, when they shall see those

beautiful pieces of poetry, the publication of which he left to my charge, almost with his dying breath.

For what remains, I beg to be excused from the ceremonies of taking leave at the end of my work; and from embarrassing myself, or others, with any defences or apologies about it. But instead of endeavouring to raise a vain monument to myself, of the merits or difficulties of it (which must be left to the world, to truth, and to posterity), let me leave behind me a memorial of my friendship with one of the most valuable men, as well as finest writers, of my age and country; one who has tried, and knows by his own experience how hard an undertaking it is, to do justice to Homer; and one who (I am sure) sincerely rejoices with me at the period of my labours. To him, therefore, having brought this long work to a conclusion, I desire to *dedicate* it; and to have the honour and satisfaction of placing together, in this manner, the names of Mr. CONGREVE, and of

A. POPE.

March 25, 1720.

THE ODYSSEY

THE remarkable success which met the translation of *The Iliad*, encouraged Pope to attempt *The Odyssey*. He had already made some experiment at translating certain fragments, which had been published in one of Lintot's *Miscellanies* in 1714. His experience with *The Iliad* had, however, left him no strong inclination for the drudgery of translation. He therefore enlisted the services of two friends, Fenton and Broome. Eventually he himself translated only the third, fifth, seventh, ninth, thirteenth, fourteenth, seventeenth, twenty-first, twenty-second, and twenty-fourth books, and most of the tenth and the fifteenth. Pope

was slow in admitting publicly the extent of his indebtedness to his collaborators, but it has long been known that Fenton translated the first, fourth, nineteenth, and twentieth books, and Broome the rest. Fenton's manuscript has been preserved in the British Museum and shows few alterations in Pope's hand. Broome's work is said to have needed much more careful revision, but there is no direct evidence in the matter. Broome supplied all the notes. With the exception of the hardly distinguishable portions of the tenth and fifteenth books which he accredited to his helpers, only Pope's own work is included here.

BOOK III

THE INTERVIEW OF TELEMACHUS AND NESTOR

THE ARGUMENT

Telemachus, guided by Pallas in the shape of Mentor, arrives in the morning at Pylos, where Nestor and his sons are sacrificing on the sea-shore to Neptune. Telemachus declares the occasion of his coming, and Nestor relates what passed in their return from Troy, how their fleets were separated, and he never since heard of Ulysses. They discourse concerning the death of Agamemnon, the revenge of Orestes, and the injuries of the

suitors. Nestor advises him to go to Sparta, and inquire further of Menelaus. The sacrifice ending with the night, Minerva vanishes from them in the form of an eagle: Telemachus is lodged in the palace. The next morning they sacrifice a bullock to Minerva; and Telemachus proceeds on his journey to Sparta, attended by Pisistratus.

The scene lies on the sea-shore of Pylos.

THE sacred Sun, above the waters rais'd,
Thro' Heav'n's eternal brazen portals blazed;
And wide o'er earth diffused his cheering ray,
To Gods and men to give the golden day.

Now on the coast of Pyle the vessel falls,
Before old Neleus' venerable walls.
There, suppliant to the Monarch of the
    Flood,
At nine green theatres the Pylians stood.
Each held five hundred (a deputed train),
At each, nine oxen on the sand lay slain. 10
They taste the entrails, and the altars load
With smoking thighs, an off'ring to the
    God.
Full for the port the Ithacensians stand,
And furl their sails, and issue on the land.
Telemachus already press'd the shore;
Not first; the Power of Wisdom march'd
    before,
And, ere the sacrificing throng he join'd,
Admonish'd thus his well-attending mind:
   ' Proceed, my son ! this youthful shame
     expel;
An honest business never blush to tell. 20
To learn what Fates thy wretched sire de-
    tain,
We pass'd the wide immeasurable main.
Meet then the senior far renown'd for
    sense,
With rev'rend awe, but decent confidence:
Urge him with truth to frame his fair re-
    plies;
And sure he will: for Wisdom never lies.'
   ' O tell me, Mentor ! tell me, faithful
     guide '
(The youth with prudent modesty replied),
' How shall I meet, or how accost the sage,
Unskill'd in speech, nor yet mature of
    age. 30
Awful th' approach, and hard the task ap-
    pears,
To question wisely men of riper years.'
   To whom the martial Goddess thus re-
    join'd:
' Search, for some thoughts, thy own sug-
    gesting mind;
And others, dictated by heav'nly Power,
Shall rise spontaneous in the needful hour.
For nought unprosperous shall thy ways
    attend,
Born with good omens, and with Heav'n
    thy friend.'
   She spoke, and led the way with swiftest
    speed:
As swift, the youth pursued the way she
    led; 40
And join'd the band before the sacred fire,
Where sate encompass'd with his sons, the
    sire.

The youth of Pylos, some on pointed wood
Transfix'd the fragments, some prepared
    the food:
In friendly throngs they gather to embrace
Their unknown guests, and at the banquet
    place.
Pisistratus was first to grasp their hands,
And spread soft hides upon the yellow
    sands;
Along the shore th' illustrious pair he led,
Where Nestor sate with youthful Thrasy-
    med. 50
To each a portion of the feast he bore,
And held the golden goblet foaming o'er;
Then first approaching to the elder guest,
The latent Goddess in these words ad-
    dress'd:
   ' Whoe'er thou art, whom Fortune brings
     to keep
These rites of Neptune, Monarch of the
    Deep,
Thee first it fits, O Stranger ! to prepare
The due libation and the solemn prayer:
Then give thy friend to shed the sacred
    wine,
Tho' much thy younger, and his years
    like mine, 60
He too, I deem, implores the Powers
    divine:
For all mankind alike require their grace,
All born to want; a miserable race ! '
   He spake, and to her hand preferr'd the
    bowl:
A secret pleasure touch'd Athena's soul,
To see the pref'rence due to sacred age
Regarded ever by the just and sage.
Of Ocean's King she then implores the
    grace:
' O thou ! whose arms this ample globe
    embrace,
Fulfil our wish, and let thy glory shine 70
On Nestor first, and Nestor's royal line;
Next grant the Pylian states their just
    desires,
Pleas'd with their hecatomb's ascending
    fires;
Last, deign Telemachus and me to bless,
And crown our voyage with desired suc-
    cess.'
   Thus she: and, having paid the rite
    divine,
Gave to Ulysses' son the rosy wine.
Suppliant he pray'd. And now, the victims
    dress'd,
They draw, divide, and celebrate the feast.

The banquet done, the narrative old man, 80
Thus mild, the pleasing conference began:
'Now, gentle guests ! the genial banquet
    o'er,
It fits to ask ye, what your native shore,
And whence your race ? on what adventure,
    say,
Thus far you wander thro' the wat'ry way ?
Relate, if business, or the thirst of gain,
Engage your journey o'er the pathless
    main:
Where savage pirates seek thro' seas un-
    known
The lives of others, venturous of their
    own.'
    Urged by the precepts by the Goddess
        giv'n,   90
And fill'd with confidence infused from
    Heav'n,
The youth, whom Pallas destin'd to be wise
And famed among the sons of men, re-
    plies:
'Inquirest thou, father ! from what coast we
    came ?
(Oh grace and glory of the Grecian name!)
From where high Ithaca o'erlooks the floods,
Brown with o'er-arching shades and pen-
    dent woods,
Us to these shores our filial duty draws,
A private sorrow, not a public cause.   99
My sire I seek, where'er the voice of Fame
Has told the glories of his noble name,
The great Ulysses; famed from shore to
    shore
For valour much, for hardy suff'ring more.
Long time with thee before proud Ilion's
    wall
In arms he fought: with thee beheld her
    fall.
Of all the Chiefs, this hero's fate alone
Has Jove reserv'd, unheard of, and un-
    known;
Whether in fields by hostile fury slain,
Or sunk by tempests in the gulfy main,
Of this to learn, oppress'd with tender
    fears,   110
Lo, at thy knee his suppliant son appears.
If or thy certain eye, or curious ear,
Have learn'd his fate, the whole dark story
    clear:
And, oh ! whate'er Heav'n destin'd to be-
    tide,
Let neither flatt'ry smooth, nor pity hide.
Prepared I stand: he was but born to try
The lot of man; to suffer, and to die.

Oh then, if ever thro' the ten years' war
The wise, the good Ulysses claim'd thy
    care;   119
If e'er he join'd thy council, or thy sword,
True in his deed, and constant to his word;
Far as thy mind thro' backward time can ⎤
    see,   ⎟
Search all thy stores of faithful memory: ⎬
'T is sacred truth I ask, and ask of thee.' ⎦
    To him experienc'd Nestor thus rejoin'd:
'O friend ! what sorrows dost thou bring to
    mind !
Shall I the long, laborious scene review,
And open all the wounds of Greece anew ?
What toils by sea ! where dark in quest of
    prey   129
Dauntless we roved; Achilles led the way:
What toils by land ! where, mix'd in fatal
    fight,
Such numbers fell, such heroes sunk to
    night:
There Ajax great, Achilles there the brave:
There wise Patroclus, fill an early grave:
There, too, my son — ah ! once my best
    delight,
Once swift of foot, and terrible in fight;
In whom stern courage with soft virtue
    join'd,
A faultless body and a blameless mind:
Antilochus — what more can I relate ?
How trace the tedious series of our Fate? 140
Not added years on years my task could
    close,
The long historian of my country's woes:
Back to thy native islands might'st thou
    sail,
And leave half-heard the melancholy tale.
Nine painful years on that detested shore,
What stratagems we form'd, what toils we
    bore !
Still lab'ring on, till scarce at last we
    found
Great Jove propitious, and our conquest
    crown'd.
Far o'er the rest thy mighty father shin'd,
In wit, in prudence, and in force of mind. 150
Art thou the son of that illustrious sire ?
With joy I grasp thee, and with love ad-
    mire.
So like your voices, and your words so
    wise.
Who finds thee younger must consult his
    eyes.
Thy sire and I were one; nor varied aught
In public sentence or in private thought;

Alike to council or th' assembly came,
With equal souls, and sentiments the same.
But when (by wisdom won) proud Ilion
　　burn'd,
And in their ships the conquering Greeks
　　return'd,　　　　　　　　　　160
'T was God's high will the victors to divide,
And turn th' event, confounding human
　　pride:
Some he destroy'd, some scatter'd as the
　　dust
(Not all were prudent, and not all were
　　just).
Then Discord, sent by Pallas from above,
Stern daughter of the great avenger Jove,
The Brother-Kings inspired with fell de-
　　bate;
Who call'd to council all th' Achaian state,
But call'd untimely (not the sacred rite　169
Observ'd, nor heedful of the setting light,
Nor herald sworn the session to proclaim);
Sour with debauch, a reeling tribe they
　　came.
To these the cause of meeting they explain,
And Menelaüs moves to cross the main;
Not so the King of Men: he will'd to stay,
The sacred rites and hecatombs to pay,
And calm Minerva's wrath.　Oh blind to
　　Fate !
The Gods not lightly change their love, or
　　hate.
With ireful taunts each other they oppose,
Till in loud tumult all the Greeks arose. 180
Now diff'rent counsels ev'ry breast divide,
Each burns with rancour to the adverse
　　side:
Th' unquiet night strange projects enter-
　　tain'd
(So Jove, that urged us to our fate, or-
　　dain'd).
We with the rising morn our ships un-
　　moor'd,
And brought our captives and our stores
　　aboard;
But half the people with respect obey'd
The King of Men, and at his bidding stay'd.
Now on the wings of winds our course we
　　keep
(For God had smooth'd the waters of the
　　deep);　　　　　　　　　　　190
For Tenedos we spread our eager oars,
There land, and pay due victims to the
　　powers:
To bless our safe return, we join in prayer;
But angry Jove dispers'd our vows in air,

And rais'd new discord.　Then (so Heav'n
　　decreed)
Ulysses first and Nestor disagreed:
Wise as he was, by various counsels
　　sway'd,
He there, tho' late, to please the Monarch,
　　stay'd.
But I, determin'd, stem the foamy floods,
Warn'd of the coming fury of the Gods.
With us Tydides fear'd, and urged his
　　haste:　　　　　　　　　　201
And Menelaüs came, but came the last:
He join'd our vessels in the Lesbian bay,
While yet we doubted of our wat'ry way;
If to the right to urge the pilot's toil
(The safer road) beside the Psyrian isle;
Or the straight course to rocky Chios
　　plough,
And anchor under Mimas' shaggy brow ?
We sought direction of the Power divine:
The God propitious gave the guiding
　　sign;　　　　　　　　　　210
Thro' the mid seas he bid our navy steer
And in Eubœa shun the woes we fear.
The whistling winds already waked the
　　sky;
Before the whistling winds the vessels fly;
With rapid swiftness cut the liquid way,
And reach Gerestus at the point of day.
There hecatombs of bulls, to Neptune
　　slain,
High - flaming please the Monarch of the
　　Main.
The fourth day shone, when, all their la-
　　bours o'er,
Tydides' vessels touch'd the wish'd - for
　　shore.　　　　　　　　　　220
But I to Pylos scud before the gales,
The God still breathing on my swelling
　　sails;
Sep'rate from all I safely landed here;
Their fates or fortunes never reach'd my
　　ear.
Yet what I learn'd, attend; as here I sate, ⎫
And ask'd each voyager each hero's fate; ⎬
Curious to know, and willing to relate. ⎭
　'Safe reach'd the Myrmidons their native
　　land,
Beneath Achilles' warlike son's command.
Those, whom the heir of great Apollo's
　　art,　　　　　　　　　　230
Brave Philoctetes, taught to wing the dart;
And those whom Idomen from Ilion's plain
Had led, securely cross'd the dreadful
　　main.

How Agamemnon touch'd his Argive coast,
And how his life by fraud and force he
　lost,
And how the murd'rer paid his forfeit
　breath;
What lands so distant from that scene of
　death
But trembling heard the fame ? and heard,
　admire
How well the son appeas'd his slaughter'd
　sire !　　　　　　　　　　　　　239
Ev'n to th' unhappy, that unjustly bleed,
Heav'n gives posterity t' avenge the deed.
So fell Ægisthus : and mayst thou, my
　friend
(On whom the virtues of thy sire de-
　scend),
Make future times thy equal act adore,
And be what brave Orestes was before !'
　The prudent youth replied: ' O thou the
　grace
And lasting glory of the Grecian race !
Just was the vengeance, and to latest
　days
Shall long posterity resound the praise.
Some God this arm with equal prowess
　bless !　　　　　　　　　　　　250
And the proud suitors shall its force con-
　fess;
Injurious men! who, while my soul is sore
Of fresh affronts, are meditating more.
But Heav'n denies this honour to my hand,
Nor shall my father repossess the land:
The father's fortune never to return,
And the sad son's to suffer and to mourn!'
　Thus he; and Nestor took the word: 'My
　son,
Is it then true, as distant rumours run,
That crowds of rivals for thy mother's
　charms　　　　　　　　　　　260
Thy palace fill with insults and alarms?
Say, is the fault, thro' tame submission, ⎫
　thine? 　　　　　　　　　　　　 ⎪
Or, leagued against thee, do thy people ⎬
　join, 　　　　　　　　　　　　　 ⎪
Mov'd by some oracle, or voice divine ? ⎭
And yet who knows but ripening lies in
　Fate
An hour of vengeance for th' afflicted
　state;
When great Ulysses shall suppress these
　harms,
Ulysses singly, or all Greece in arms.
But if Athena, War's triumphant Maid,
The happy son will, as the father, aid　270

(Whose fame and safety was her constant
　care
In ev'ry danger and in ev'ry war :
Never on man did heav'nly favour shine
With rays so strong, distinguish'd, and di-
　vine,
As those with which Minerva mark'd thy
　sire;
So might she love thee, so thy soul in-
　spire !),
Soon should their hopes in humble dust be
　laid,
And long oblivion of the bridal bed.'
　' Ah ! no such hope ' (the Prince with
　sighs replies)
' Can touch my breast; that blessing Heav'n
　denies.　　　　　　　　　　　280
Ev'n by celestial favour were it giv'n,
Fortune or Fate would cross the will of
　Heav'n.'
　' What words are these, and what impru-
　dence thine ? '
(Thus interposed the Martial Maid divine)
' Forgetful youth ! but know, the Power
　above,
With ease can save each object of his love;
Wide as his will extends his boundless
　grace;
Nor lost in time, nor circumscribed by
　place.
Happier his lot, who, many sorrows pass'd,
Long lab'ring gains his natal shore at
　last,　　　　　　　　　　　　290
Than who, too speedy, hastes to end his
　life
By some stern ruffian, or adult'rous wife.
Death only is the lot which none can miss,
And all is possible to Heav'n but this.
The best, the dearest fav'rite of the sky
Must taste that cup, for man is born to
　die.'
　Thus check'd, replied Ulysses' prudent
　heir:
' Mentor, no more — the mournful thought
　forbear;
For he no more must draw his country's
　breath,
Already snatch'd by Fate, and the black
　doom of Death !　　　　　　　300
Pass we to other subjects; and engage
On themes remote the venerable sage
(Who thrice has seen the perishable kind ⎫
Of men decay, and thro' three ages shin'd ⎪
Like Gods majestic, and like Gods in ⎬
　mind) ;　　　　　　　　　　　 ⎭

For much he knows, and just conclusions
   draws,
From various precedents and various laws.
O son of Neleus! awful Nestor, tell
How he, the mighty Agamemnon, fell;
By what strange fraud Ægisthus wrought,
   relate   310
(By force he could not), such a hero's fate?
Liv'd Menelaüs not in Greece? or where
Was then the martial brother's pious care?
Condemn'd perhaps some foreign shore to
   tread;
Or sure Ægisthus had not dared the deed.'
   To whom the full of days: 'Illustrious
   youth,
Attend (tho' partly thou hast guess'd) the
   truth.
For had the martial Menelaüs found
The ruffian breathing yet on Argive ground,
Nor earth had hid his carcass from the
   skies,   320
Nor Grecian virgin shriek'd his obsequies,
But fowls obscene dismember'd his remains,
And dogs had torn him on the naked
   plains.
While us the works of bloody Mars em-
   ploy'd,
The wanton youth inglorious peace enjoy'd;
He, stretch'd at ease in Argos' calm recess
(Whose stately steeds luxuriant pastures
   bless),
With Flattery's insinuating art
Sooth'd the frail Queen, and poison'd all
   her heart.
At first, with worthy shame and decent
   pride,   330
The royal dame his lawless suit denied.
For virtue's image yet possess'd her mind,
Taught by a master of the tuneful kind:
Atrides, parting for the Trojan war,
Consign'd the youthful consort to his care.
True to his charge, the bard preserv'd her
   long
In honour's limits; such the power of song.
But when the Gods these objects of their
   hate
Dragg'd to destruction by the links of
   Fate,
The bard they banish'd from his native
   soil,   340
And left all helpless in a desert isle:
There he, the sweetest of the sacred train,
Sung dying to the rocks, but sung in vain.
Then Virtue was no more; her guard away,
She fell, to lust a voluntary prey.

Ev'n to the temple stalk'd th' adult'rous
   spouse,
With impious thanks, and mockery of
   vows,
With images, with garments, and with
   gold;
And od'rous fumes from loaded altars
   roll'd.
   'Meantime from flaming Troy we cut the
   way,   350
With Menelaüs, thro' the curling sea.
But when to Sunium's sacred point we
   came,
Crown'd with the temple of th' Athenian
   Dame;
Atrides' pilot, Phrontes, there expired
(Phrontes, of all the sons of men admired,
To steer the bounding bark with steady
   toil,
When the storm thickens, and the billows
   boil);
While yet he exercised the steersman's art,
Apollo touch'd him with his gentle dart;
Ev'n with the rudder in his hand, he
   fell.   360
To pay whose honours to the shades of
   Hell,
We check'd our haste, by pious office
   bound,
And laid our old companion in the ground.
And now, the rites discharged, our course
   we keep
Far on the gloomy bosom of the deep:
Soon as Malæa's misty tops arise,
Sudden the Thund'rer blackens all the
   skies,
And the winds whistle, and the surges roll
Mountains on mountains, and obscure the
   pole.   369
The tempest scatters, and divides our fleet;
Part, the storm urges on the coast of
   Crete,
Where, winding round the rich Cydonian
   plain,
The streams of Jardan issue to the main.
There stands a rock, high eminent and
   steep,
Whose shaggy brow o'erhangs the shady
   deep,
And views Gortyna on the western side;
On this rough Auster drove th' impetuous
   tide:
With broken force the billows roll'd away,
And heav'd the fleet into the neighb'ring
   bay.

Thus saved from death, they gain'd the
   Phæstan shores,   380
With shatter'd vessels and disabled oars:
But five tall barks the winds and waters
   toss'd,
Far from their fellows, on th' Ægyptian
   coast.
There wander'd Menelaüs thro' foreign
   shores,
Amassing gold, and gath'ring naval stores;
While curs'd Ægisthus the detested deed
By fraud fulfill'd, and his great brother bled.
Sev'n years, the traitor rich Mycenæ
   sway'd,
And his stern rule the groaning land
   obey'd;
The eighth, from Athens to his realm re-
   stor'd,   390
Orestes brandish'd the revenging sword,
Slew the dire pair, and gave to funeral
   flame
The vile assassin, and adult'rous dame.
That day, ere yet the bloody triumphs
   cease,
Return'd Atrides to the coast of Greece,
And safe to Argos' port his navy brought,
With gifts of price and pond'rous treasure
   fraught.
Hence warn'd, my son, beware ! nor idly
   stand
Too long a stranger to thy native land;
Lest heedless absence wear thy wealth
   away,   400
While lawless feasters in thy palace sway;
Perhaps may seize thy realm, and share ⎤
   the spoil;   ⎟
And thou return, with disappointed toil, ⎟
From thy vain journey, to a rifled isle. ⎦
Howe'er, my friend, indulge one labour
   more,
And seek Atrides on the Spartan shore.
He, wand'ring long, a wider circle made,
And many-languaged nations has survey'd;
And measured tracks unknown to other
   ships   409
Amid the monstrous wonders of the deeps
(A length of ocean and unbounded sky,
Which scarce the sea-fowl in a year o'er-
   fly):
Go then; to Sparta take the wat'ry way,
Thy ship and sailors but for orders stay;
Or if by land thou choose thy course to
   bend,
My steeds, my chariots, and my sons at-
   tend:

Thee to Atrides they shall safe convey,
Guides of thy road, companions of thy way.
Urge him with truth to frame his free re-
   plies,   419
And sure he will: for Menelaüs is wise.'
   Thus while he speaks, the ruddy sun de-
   scends,
And twilight gray her ev'ning shade ex-
   tends.
Then thus the Blue-eyed Maid: 'O Full
   of Days !
Wise are thy words, and just are all thy
   ways.
Now immolate the tongues, and mix the
   wine,
Sacred to Neptune and the Powers divine.
The lamp of day is quench'd beneath the
   deep,
And soft approach the balmy hours of
   sleep:
Nor fits it to prolong the heav'nly feast,
Timeless, indecent, but retire to rest.'   430
   So spake Jove's daughter, the celestial
   Maid.
The sober train attended and obey'd.
The sacred heralds on their hands around
Pour'd the full urns; the youths the gob-
   lets crown'd:
From bowl to bowl the holy bev'rage flows;
While to the final sacrifice they rose.
The tongues they cast upon the fragrant
   flame,
And pour, above, the consecrated stream.
And now, their thirst by copious draughts
   allay'd,   439
The youthful hero and th' Athenian maid
Propose departure from the finish'd rite,
And in their hollow bark to pass the
   night.
But this the hospitable sage denied:
'Forbid it, Jove! and all the Gods !' he
   cried,
'Thus from my walls the much-lov'd son to
   send
Of such a Hero, and of such a Friend !
Me, as some needy peasant, would ye
   leave,
Whom Heav'n denies the blessing to re-
   lieve ?
Me would ye leave, who boast imperial
   sway,
When beds of royal state invite your
   stay ?   450
No — long as life this mortal shall inspire,
Or as my children imitate their sire,

Here shall the wand'ring stranger find his
    home,
And hospitable rites adorn the dome.'
   'Well hast thou spoke' (the Blue-eyed
    Maid replies),
'Belov'd old man! benevolent as wise.
Be the kind dictates of thy heart obey'd,
And let thy words Telemachus persuade:
He to thy palace shall thy steps pursue;
I to the ship, to give the orders due,   460
Prescribe directions, and confirm the
    crew.
For I alone sustain their naval cares,
Who boast experience from these silver
    hairs;
All youths the rest, whom to this journey
    move
Like years, like tempers, and their Prince's
    love.
There in the vessel shall I pass the night;
And soon as morning paints the fields of
    light,
I go to challenge from the Caucons bold
A debt, contracted in the days of old.
But this thy guest, receiv'd with friendly
    care,   470
Let thy strong coursers swift to Sparta
    bear;
Prepare thy chariot at the dawn of day,
And be thy son companion of his way.'
   Then, turning with the word, Minerva
    flies,
And soars an eagle thro' the liquid skies.
Vision divine! the throng'd spectators gaze
In holy wonder fix'd, and still amaze.
But chief the rev'rend sage admired; he
    took
The hand of young Telemachus, and spoke:
   'Oh, happy Youth! and favour'd of the
    skies,   480
Distinguish'd care of guardian Deities!
Whose early years for future worth en-
    gage,
No vulgar manhood, no ignoble age.
For lo! none other of the court above
Than she, the daughter of Almighty Jove,
Pallas herself, the war-triumphant Maid,
Confess'd is thine, as once thy father's aid.
So guide me, Goddess! so propitious shine
On me, my consort, and my royal line!   489
A yearling bullock to thy name shall smoke,
Untamed, unconscious of the galling yoke,
With ample forehead, and yet tender horns,
Whose budding honours ductile gold
    adorns.'

   Submissive thus the hoary sire preferr'd
His holy vow: the fav'ring Goddess heard.
Then, slowly rising, o'er the sandy space
Precedes the father, follow'd by his race
(A long procession), timely marching home
In comely order to the regal dome.
There when arrived, on thrones around him
    placed,   500
His sons and grandsons the wide circle
    graced.
To these the hospitable sage, in sign
Of social welcome, mix'd the racy wine
(Late from the mell'wing cask restor'd to
    light,
By ten long years refin'd, and rosy bright).
To Pallas high the foaming bowl he
    crown'd,
And sprinkled large libations on the
    ground.
Each drinks a full oblivion of his cares,
And to the gifts of balmy sleep repairs.
Deep in a rich alcove the Prince was
    laid,   510
And slept beneath the pompous colonnade:
Fast by his side Pisistratus lay spread
(In age his equal), on a splendid bed:
But in an inner court, securely closed,
The rev'rend Nestor and his Queen re-
    posed.
   When now Aurora, Daughter of the
    Dawn,
With rosy lustre purpled o'er the lawn;
The old man early rose, walk'd forth, and
    sate
On polish'd stone before his palace-gate:
With unguents smooth the lucid marble
    shone,   520
Where ancient Neleus sate, a rustic throne;
But he descending to th' infernal shade,
Sage Nestor fill'd it, and the sceptre sway'd.
His sons around him mild obeisance pay,
And duteous take the orders of the day.
First Echephron and Stratius quit their
    bed;
Then Perseus, Aretus, and Thrasymed;
The last Pisistratus arose from rest:
They came, and near him place the stranger-
    guest.
To these the senior thus declared his will: 530
   'My sons! the dictates of your sire fulfil.
To Pallas, first of Gods, prepare the feast,
Who graced our rites, a more than mortal
    guest.
Let one, despatchful, bid some swain to lead
A well-fed bullock from the grassy mead;

One seek the harbour where the vessels
moor,
And bring thy friends, Telemachus! ashore
(Leave only two the galley to attend);
Another to Learceus must we send,
Artist divine, whose skilful hands infold 540
The victim's horn with circumfusile gold.
The rest may here the pious duty share,
And bid the handmaids for the feast pre-
pare,
The seats to range, the fragrant wood to
bring,
And limpid waters from the living spring.'
  He said, and busy each his care bestow'd;
Already at the gates the bullock low'd,
Already came the Ithacensian crew,
The dext'rous smith the tools already drew:
His pond'rous hammer, and his anvil
sound, 550
And the strong tongs to turn the metal
round.
Nor was Minerva absent from the rite;
She view'd her honours, and enjoy'd the
sight.
With rev'rent hand the King presents the
gold,
Which round th' intorted horns the gilder
roll'd,
So wrought, as Pallas might with pride
behold.
Young Aretus from forth his bridal bower
Brought the full laver, o'er their hands
to pour,
And canisters of consecrated flour.
Stratius and Echephron the victim led; 560
The axe was held by warlike Thrasymed,
In act to strike: before him Perseus stood,
The vase extending to receive the blood,
The King himself initiates to the Power;
Scatters with quiv'ring hand the sacred
flour,
And the stream sprinkles: from the curling
brows
The hair collected in the fire he throws.
Soon as due vows on every part were paid,
And sacred wheat upon the victim laid,
Strong Thrasymed discharged the speeding
blow 570
Full on his neck, and cut the nerves in two.
Down sunk the heavy beast: the females
round,
Maids, wives, and matrons, mix a shrilling
sound,
Nor scorn'd the Queen the holy choir to join.
(The first-born she, of old Clymenus' line;

In youth by Nestor lov'd, of spotless fame,
And lov'd in age, Eurydice her name.)
From earth they rear him, struggling now
with death;
And Nestor's youngest stops the vents of
breath.
The soul for ever flies: on all sides round 580
Streams the black blood, and smokes upon
the ground.
The beast they then divide, and disunite
The ribs and limbs, observant of the rite:
On these, in double cauls involv'd with
art,
The choicest morsels lay from ev'ry part.
The sacred sage before his altar stands,
Turns the burnt-off'ring with his holy
hands,
And pours the wine, and bids the flames
aspire:
The youth with instruments surround the
fire.
The thighs now sacrificed, and entrails
dress'd, 590
Th' assistants part, transfix, and broil the
rest.
While these officious tend the rites divine,
The last fair branch of the Nestorean line,
Sweet Polycaste, took the pleasing toil
To bathe the Prince, and pour the fragrant
oil.
O'er his fair limbs a flowery vest he
threw,
And issued, like a God, to mortal view.
His former seat beside the King he found
(His people's father with his peers around);
All placed at ease the holy banquet join, 600
And in the dazzling goblet laughs the wine.
  The rage of thirst and hunger now sup-
press'd,
The Monarch turns him to his royal guest;
And for the promis'd journey bids prepare
The smooth-hair'd horses, and the rapid
car.
Observant of his word, the word scarce
spoke,
The sons obey, and join them to the yoke.
Then bread and wine a ready handmaid
brings,
And presents, such as suit the state of
kings ;
The glitt'ring seat Telemachus ascends; 610
His faithful guide Pisistratus attends;
With hasty hand the ruling reins he drew:
He lash'd the coursers, and the coursers
flew.

Beneath the bounding yoke alike they held
Their equal pace, and smoked along the
　field.
The towers of Pylos sink, its views decay,
Fields after fields fly back, till close of
　day:
Then sunk the sun, and darken'd all the
　way.
　To Pheræ now, Diocleus' stately seat
(Of Alpheus' race), the weary youths re-
　treat. 620
His house affords the hospitable rite,
And pleas'd they sleep, the blessing of the
　night.
But when Aurora, Daughter of the Dawn,
With rosy lustre purpled o'er the lawn,
Again they mount, their journey to renew,
And from the sounding portico they flew.
Along the waving fields their way they hold,
The fields receding as their chariot roll'd:
Then slowly sunk the ruddy globe of light,
And o'er the shaded landscape rush'd the
　night. 630

BOOK V

THE DEPARTURE OF ULYSSES FROM CALYPSO

THE ARGUMENT

Pallas in a council of the Gods complains of the
detention of Ulysses in the island of Calypso;
whereupon Mercury is sent to command his
removal. The seat of Calypso described.
She consents with much difficulty; and
Ulysses builds a vessel with his own hands,
on which he embarks. Neptune overtakes
him with a terrible tempest, in which he is
shipwrecked, and in the last danger of death;
till Leucothea, a sea-goddess, assists him, and,
after innumerable perils, he gets ashore on
Phæacia.

THE saffron Morn, with early blushes
　spread,
Now rose refulgent from Tithonus' bed;
With new-born Day to gladden mortal
　sight,
And gild the courts of Heav'n with sacred
　light.
Then met th' eternal Synod of the Sky,
Before the God, who thunders from on
　high,
Supreme in might, sublime in majesty.
Pallas, to these, deplores th' unequal Fates
Of wise Ulysses, and his toils relates:
Her hero's danger touch'd the pitying
　Power, 10

The nymph's seducements, and the magic
　bower.
Thus she began her plaint. 'Immortal
　Jove!
And you who fill the blissful seats above!
Let Kings no more with gentle mercy
　sway,
Or bless a people willing to obey,
But crush the nations with an iron rod,
And ev'ry Monarch be the scourge of God;
If from your thoughts Ulysses you remove,
Who ruled his subjects with a father's love.
Sole in an isle, encircled by the main, 20
Abandon'd, banish'd from his native reign,
Unbless'd he sighs, detain'd by lawless
　charms,
And press'd unwilling in Calypso's arms.
Nor friends are there, nor vessels to con-
　vey,
Nor oars to cut th' immeasurable way.
And now fierce traitors, studious to de-
　stroy
His only son, their ambush'd fraud em-
　ploy;
Who, pious, foll'wing his great father's
　fame,
To sacred Pylos and to Sparta came.'
　'What words are these?' (replied the
　Power who forms 30
The clouds of night, and darkens Heav'n
　with storms);
'Is not already in thy soul decreed,
The Chief's return shall make the guilty
　bleed?
What cannot Wisdom do? Thou may'st
　restore
The son in safety to his native shore;
While the fell foes, who late in ambush lay,
With fraud defeated measure back their
　way.'
　Then thus to Hermes the command was
　giv'n.
'Hermes, thou chosen messenger of Heav'n!
Go, to the Nymph be these our orders
　borne: 40
'T is Jove's decree, Ulysses shall return:
The patient man shall view his old abodes,
Nor help'd by mortal hand, nor guiding
　Gods:
In twice ten days shall fertile Scheria find,
Alone, and floating to the wave and wind.
The bold Phæacians there, whose haughty
　line
Is mix'd with Gods, half human, half di-
　vine,

The Chief shall honour as some heav'nly
  guest,
And swift transport him to his place of
  rest.   49
His vessels loaded with a plenteous store
Of brass, of vestures, and resplendent ore
(A richer prize than if his joyful isle
Receiv'd him charged with Ilion's noble
  spoil),
His friends, his country, he shall see, tho'
  late;
Such is our sov'reign will, and such is
  Fate.'
  He spoke. The God who mounts the
  winged winds
Fast to his feet the golden pinions binds,
That high thro' fields of air his flight sus-
  tain
O'er the wide earth, and o'er the boundless
  main.
He grasps the wand that causes sleep to
  fly,   60
Or in soft slumber seals the wakeful eye:
Then shoots from Heav'n to high Pieria's
  steep,
And stoops incumbent on the rolling deep.
So wat'ry fowl, that seek their fishy food,
With wings expanded o'er the foaming
  flood,
Now sailing smooth the level surface sweep,
Now dip their pinions in the briny deep.
Thus o'er the world of waters Hermes
  flew,
Till now the distant island rose in view:
Then, swift ascending from the azure
  wave,   70
He took the path that winded to the cave.
Large was the grot, in which the Nymph he
  found
(The fair-hair'd Nymph with ev'ry beauty
  crown'd);
She sate and sung; the rocks resound her
  lays;
The cave was brighten'd with a rising
  blaze;
Cedar and frankincense, an od'rous pile,
Flamed on the hearth and wide perfumed
  the isle;
While she with work and song the time
  divides,
And thro' the loom the golden shuttle
  guides.
Without the grot a various sylvan scene 80
Appear'd around, and groves of living
  green;

Poplars and alders ever quiv'ring play'd,
And nodding cypress form'd a fragrant
  shade;
On whose high branches, waving with the
  storm,
The birds of broadest wing their mansions
  form,
The chough, the sea-mew, the loquacious
  crow,
And scream aloft, and skim the deeps be-
  low.
Depending vines the shelving cavern
  screen,
With purple clusters blushing thro' the
  green.
Four limpid fountains from the clefts
  distil;   90
And ev'ry fountain pours a sev'ral rill,
In mazy windings wand'ring down the hill;
Where bloomy meads with vivid greens
  were crown'd,
And glowing violets threw odours round.
A scene, where if a God should cast his
  sight,
A God might gaze, and wander with de-
  light !
Joy touch'd the Messenger of Heav'n: he
  stay'd
Entranc'd, and all the blissful haunts sur-
  vey'd.
Him, ent'ring in the cave, Calypso knew;
For Powers celestial to each other's
  view   100
Stand still confess'd, tho' distant far they
  lie
To habitants of earth, or sea, or sky.
But sad Ulysses, by himself apart,
Pour'd the big sorrows of his swelling
  heart;
All on the lonely shore he sate to weep,
And roll'd his eyes around the restless
  deep;
Toward his lov'd coast he roll'd his eyes in
  vain,
Till, dimm'd with rising grief, they
  stream'd again.
  Now graceful seated on her shining
  throne,
To Hermes thus the Nymph divine be-
  gun: 110
'God of the Golden Wand ! on what be-
  hest
Arrivest thou here, an unexpected guest ?
Lov'd as thou art, thy free injunctions lay:
'T is mine with joy and duty to obey.

Till now a stranger, in a happy hour
Approach, and taste the dainties of my
    bower.'
Thus having spoke, the Nymph the table
    spread
(Ambrosial cates, with nectar rosy-red);
Hermes the hospitable rite partook,   119
Divine refection! then, recruited, spoke:
'What mov'd this journey from my
    native sky,
A Goddess asks, nor can a God deny:
Hear then the truth. By mighty Jove's
    command
Unwilling have I trod this pleasing land;
For who, self-mov'd, with weary wing
    would sweep
Such length of ocean and unmeasured deep:
A world of waters! far from all the ways
Where men frequent, or sacred altars
    blaze?
But to Jove's will submission we must
    pay;   129
What Power so great to dare to disobey?
A man, he says, a man resides with thee,
Of all his kind most worn with misery;
The Greeks (whose arms for nine long
    years employ'd
Their force on Ilion, in the tenth de-
    stroy'd),
At length embarking in a luckless hour,
With conquest proud, incens'd Minerva's
    power:
Hence on the guilty race her vengeance
    hurl'd
With storms pursued them thro' the liquid
    world.
There all his vessels sunk beneath the wave!
There all his dear companions found their
    grave!   140
Saved from the jaws of death by Heav'n's
    decree,
The tempest drove him to these shores and
    thee.
Him, Jove now orders to his native lands
Straight to dismiss: so destiny commands:
Impatient Fate his near return attends,
And calls him to his country, and his
    friends.'
Ev'n to her inmost soul the Goddess
    shook;
Then thus her anguish and her passion
    broke:
'Ungracious Gods! with spite and envy
    curs'd!   149
Still to your own ethereal race the worst!

Ye envy mortal and immortal joy,
And love, the only sweet of life, destroy.
Did ever Goddess by her charms engage
A favour'd mortal, and not feel your rage?
So when Aurora sought Orion's love,
Her joys disturb'd your blissful hours
    above,
Till, in Ortygia, Dian's winged dart
Had pierc'd the hapless hunter to the
    heart.
So when the covert of the thrice-ear'd field
Saw stately Ceres to her passion yield,   160
Scarce could Iasion taste her heav'nly
    charms,
But Jove's swift lightning scorch'd him in
    her arms.
'And is it now my turn, ye mighty
    Powers!
Am I the envy of your blissful bowers?
A man, an outcast to the storm and wave,
It was my crime to pity and to save;
When he who thunders rent his bark in
    twain,
And sunk his brave companions in the
    main.
Alone, abandon'd, in mid-ocean toss'd,
The sport of winds, and driv'n from ev'ry
    coast,   170
Hither this man of miseries I led,
Receiv'd the friendless, and the hungry
    fed;
Nay, promis'd (vainly promis'd!) to be-
    stow
Immortal life, exempt from age and woe.
'T is past — and Jove decrees he shall re-
    move:
Gods as we are, we are but slaves to Jove.
Go then he may (he must, if he ordain,
Try all those dangers, all those deeps,
    again);
But never, never shall Calypso send
To toils like these her husband and her
    friend.   180
What ships have I, what sailors to convey,
What oars to cut the long laborious way?
Yet I 'll direct the safest means to go;
That last advice is all I can bestow.'
To her the Power who bears the Charm-
    ing Rod:
'Dismiss the man, nor irritate the God;
Prevent the rage of him who reigns above,
For what so dreadful as the wrath of
    Jove?'
Thus having said, he cut the cleaving sky,
And in a moment vanish'd from her eye.   190

The Nymph, obedient to divine command,
To seek Ulysses paced along the sand,
Him pensive on the lonely beach she found,
With streaming eyes in briny torrents
drown'd,
And inly pining for his native shore;
For now the soft enchantress pleas'd no
more:
For now, reluctant, and constrain'd by
charms,
Absent he lay in her desiring arms:
In slumber wore the heavy night away,
On rocks and shores consumed the tedious
day; 200
There sate all desolate, and sigh'd alone,
With echoing sorrows made the mountains
groan,
And roll'd his eyes o'er all the restless
main,
Till, dimm'd with rising grief, they stream'd
again.
　Here, on his musing mood the Goddess
press'd
Approaching soft; and thus the Chief ad-
dress'd:
　'Unhappy man! to wasting woes a prey,
No more in sorrows languish life away:
Free as the winds I give thee now to rove —
Go, fell the timber of yon lofty grove, 210
And form a raft, and build the rising ship,
Sublime to bear thee o'er the gloomy deep.
To store the vessel let the care be mine,
With water from the rock, and rosy wine,
And life-sustaining bread, and fair array,
And prosp'rous gales to waft thee on the
way.
These, if the Gods with my desire comply
(The Gods, alas, more mighty far than I,
And better skill'd in dark events to come),
In peace shall land thee at thy native
home.' 220
　With sighs Ulysses heard the words she
spoke,
Then thus his melancholy silence broke:
'Some other motive, Goddess! sways thy
mind
(Some close design, or turn of womankind),
Nor my return the end, nor this the way,
On a slight raft to pass the swelling sea,
Huge, horrid, vast! where scarce in safety
sails
The best-built ship, tho' Jove inspire the
gales.
The bold proposal how shall I fulfil,
Dark as I am, unconscious of thy will? 230

Swear, then, thou mean'st not what my
soul forebodes;
Swear by the solemn oath that binds the
Gods.'
　Him, while he spoke, with smiles Calypso
eyed,
And gently grasp'd his hand, and thus re-
plied:
'This shows thee, friend, by old experi-
ence taught,
And learn'd in all the wiles of human
thought,
How prone to doubt, how cautious are the
wise!
But hear, O earth, and hear, ye sacred
skies!
And thou, O Styx! whose formidable
floods
Glide thro' the shades, and bind th' attest-
ing Gods! 240
No form'd design, no meditated end,
Lurks in the council of thy faithful friend;
Kind the persuasion, and sincere my aim;
The same my practice, were my fate the
same.
Heav'n has not curs'd me with a heart of
steel,
But given the sense to pity and to feel.'
　Thus having said, the Goddess march'd
before:
He trod her footsteps in the sandy shore.
At the cool cave arrived, they took their
state;
He fill'd the throne where Mercury had
sate. 250
For him the Nymph a rich repast ordains,
Such as the mortal life of man sustains;
Before herself were placed the cates divine,
Ambrosial banquet, and celestial wine.
Their hunger satiate, and their thirst re-
press'd,
Thus spoke Calypso to her godlike guest:
'Ulysses!' (with a sigh she thus began)
'O sprung from Gods! in wisdom more
than man!
Is then thy home the passion of thy heart?
Thus wilt thou leave me, are we thus to
part? 260
Farewell! and ever joyful may'st thou be,
Nor break the transport with one thought
of me.
But, ah, Ulysses! wert thou giv'n to know
What Fate yet dooms thee, yet, to undergo;
Thy heart might settle in this scene of
ease,

And ev'n these slighted charms might learn
  to please.
A willing Goddess, and immortal life,
Might banish from thy mind an absent wife.
Am I inferior to a mortal dame ?
Less soft my feature, lest august my
  frame ?   270
Or shall the daughters of mankind compare
Their earth-born beauties with the heav'nly
  fair ? '
  'Alas ! for this ' (the prudent man replies)
' Against Ulysses shall thy anger rise ?
Lov'd and ador'd, O Goddess, as thou art,
Forgive the weakness of a human heart.
Tho' well I see thy graces far above
The dear, tho' mortal, object of my love,
Of youth eternal well the diff'rence know,
And the short date of fading charms be-
  low;   280
Yet ev'ry day, while absent thus I roam,
I languish to return and die at home.
Whate'er the Gods shall destine me to bear
In the black ocean, or the wat'ry war,
'T is mine to master with a constant mind;
Inured to perils, to the worst resign'd.
By seas, by wars, so many dangers run;
Still I can suffer: their high will be done ! '
  Thus while he spoke, the beamy sun de-
  scends,
And rising night her friendly shade ex-
  tends.   290
To the close grot the lonely pair remove,
And slept delighted with the gifts of love.
When rosy morning call'd them from their
  rest,
Ulysses robed him in the cloak and vest.
The Nymph's fair head a veil transparent
  graced,
Her swelling loins a radiant zone embraced
With flowers of gold: an under robe, un-
  bound,
In snowy waves flow'd glitt'ring on the
  ground.
Forth issuing thus, she gave him first to
  wield
A weighty axe, with truest temper steel'd,
And double-edg'd; the handle smooth and
  plain,   301
Wrought of the clouded olive's easy grain;
And next, a wedge to drive with sweepy
  sway:
Then to the neighb'ring forest led the way.
On the lone island's utmost verge there
  stood
Of poplars, pines, and firs, a lofty wood,

Whose leafless summits to the skies aspire,
Scorch'd by the sun, or sear'd by heav'nly
  fire
(Already dried). These pointing out to
  view,
The Nymph just show'd him, and with
  tears withdrew.   310
  Now toils the hero: trees on trees o'er-
  thrown
Fall crackling round him, and the forests
  groan:
Sudden, full twenty on the plain are
  strow'd,
And lopp'd and lighten'd of their branchy
  load.
At equal angles these disposed to join,
He smoothed and squared them by the rule
  and line
(The wimbles for the work Calypso found).
With those he pierc'd them, and with
  clinchers bound.
Long and capacious as a shipwright forms
Some bark's broad bottom to out-ride the
  storms,   320
So large he built the raft; then ribb'd it
  strong
From space to space, and nail'd the planks
  along;
These form'd the sides: the deck he fash-
  ion'd last;
Then o'er the vessel rais'd the taper mast,
With crossing sail-yards dancing in the
  wind;
And to the helm the guiding rudder join'd
(With yielding osiers fenc'd, to break the
  force
Of surging waves, and steer the steady
  course).
Thy loom, Calypso! for the future sails 329
Supplied the cloth, capacious of the gales.
With stays and cordage last he rigg'd the
  ship,
And, roll'd on levers, launch'd her in the
  deep.
  Four days were past, and now, the work
  complete,
Shone the fifth morn, when from her sacred
  seat
The Nymph dismiss'd him (od'rous gar-
  ments giv'n,
And bathed in fragrant oils that breathed
  of Heav'n):
Then fill'd two goat-skins with her hands
  divine,
With water one, and one with sable wine:

Of ev'ry kind provisions heav'd aboard;
And the full decks with copious viands
 stor'd.   340
The Goddess, last, a gentle breeze supplies,
To curl old Ocean, and to warm the skies.
 And now, rejoicing in the prosp'rous
 gales,
With beating heart Ulysses spreads his
 sails:
Placed at the helm he sate, and mark'd the
 skies,
Nor closed in sleep his ever-watchful eyes.
There view'd the Pleiads, and the Northern
 Team,
And great Orion's more refulgent beam,
To which, around the axle of the sky, 349
The Bear, revolving, points his golden eye:
Who shines exalted on th' ethereal plain,
Nor bathes his blazing forehead in the
 main.
Far on the left those radiant fires to keep
The Nymph directed, as he sail'd the deep.
Full sev'nteen nights he cut the foamy
 way;
The distant land appear'd the foll'wing day:
Then swell'd to sight Phæacia's dusky coast,
And woody mountains, half in vapours lost;
That lay before him indistinct and vast, 359
Like a broad shield amid the wat'ry waste.
 But him, thus voyaging the deeps below,
From far, on Solyme's aërial brow,
The King of Ocean saw, and seeing burn'd
(From Æthiopia's happy climes return'd);
The raging Monarch shook his azure head,
And thus in secret to his soul he said:
 ' Heav'ns ! how uncertain are the Powers
 on high !
Is then revers'd the sentence of the sky,
In one man's favour: while a distant guest
I shared secure the Æthiopian feast ? 370
Behold how near Phæacia's land he draws !
The land affix'd by Fate's eternal laws
To end his toils. Is then our anger vain ?
No; if this sceptre yet commands the main.'
 He spoke, and high the forky trident
 hurl'd,
Rolls clouds on clouds, and stirs the wat'ry
 world,
At once the face of earth and sea deforms,
Swells all the winds, and rouses all the
 storms.
Down rush'd the night: east, west, together
 roar;
And south and north roll mountains to the
 shore: 380

Then shook the hero, to despair resign'd,
And question'd thus his yet unconquer'd
 mind :
 ' Wretch that I am ! what farther Fates
 attend
This life of toils, and what my destin'd
 end ?
Too well, alas ! the island Goddess knew
On the black sea what perils should ensue.
New horrors now this destin'd head en-
 close;
Unfill'd as yet the measure of my woes:
With what a cloud the brows of Heav'n are
 crown'd !
What raging winds ! what roaring waters
 round !   390
'T is Jove himself the swelling tempest
 rears;
Death, present death, on ev'ry side ap-
 pears.
Happy ! thrice happy ! who, in battle slain,
Press'd, in Atrides' cause, the Trojan plain!
Oh ! had I died before that well-fought
 wall;
Had some distinguish'd day renown'd my
 fall
(Such as was that when showers of jav'lins
 fled
From conquering Troy around Achilles
 dead);
All Greece had paid me solemn funerals
 then,   399
And spread my glory with the sons of men.
A shameful fate now hides my hapless
 head,
Unwept, unnoted, and for ever dead ! '
 A mighty wave rush'd o'er him as he
 spoke,
The raft it cover'd, and the mast it broke:
Swept from the deck, and from the rudder
 torn,
Far on the swelling surge the Chief was
 borne;
While by the howling tempest rent in
 twain
Flew sail and sail-yards rattling o'er the
 main.
Long-press'd, he heav'd beneath the weighty
 wave,
Clogg'd by the cumb'rous vest Calypso
 gave: 410
At length emerging, from his nostrils wide
And gushing mouth effused the briny tide;
Ev'n then, not mindless of his last retreat,
He seiz'd the raft, and leap'd into his seat.

Strong with the fear of death. The rolling
    flood
Now here, now there, impell'd the floating
    wood.
As when a heap of gather'd thorns is cast
Now to, now fro, before th' autumnal blast;
Together clung, it rolls around the field;
So roll'd the float, and so its texture held:
And now the south, and now the north,
    bear sway,   421
And now the east the foamy floods obey,
And now the west wind whirls it o'er the
    sea.
    The wand'ring Chief, with toils on toils
      oppress'd,
Leucothea saw, and pity touch'd her breast
(Herself a mortal once, of Cadmus' strain,
But now an azure sister of the main).
Swift as a sea-mew springing from the
    flood,
All radiant on the raft the Goddess stood:
Then thus address'd him: 'Thou whom
    Heav'n decrees   430
To Neptune's wrath, stern Tyrant of the
    Seas
(Unequal contest)! not his rage and power,
Great as he is, such virtue shall devour.
What I suggest, thy wisdom will perform :
Forsake thy float, and leave it to the storm:
Strip off thy garments; Neptune's fury
    brave
With naked strength, and plunge into the
    wave.
To reach Phæacia all thy nerves extend,
There Fate decrees thy miseries shall end.
This heav'nly scarf beneath thy bosom
    bind,   440
And live; give all thy terrors to the wind.
Soon as thy arms the happy shore shall
    gain,
Return the gift, and cast it in the main;
Observe my orders, and with heed obey,
Cast it far off, and turn thy eyes away.'
    With that, her hand the sacred veil be-
      stows,
Then down the deeps she dived from whence
    she rose;
A moment snatch'd the shining form away,
And all was cover'd with the curling sea.
    Struck with amaze, yet still to doubt in-
      inclin'd,   450
He stands suspended, and explores his mind.
'What shall I do? unhappy me! who
    knows
But other Gods intend me other woes?

Whoe'er thou art, I shall not blindly join
Thy pleaded reason, but consult with mine:
For scarce in ken appears that distant isle
Thy voice foretells me shall conclude my
    toil.
Thus then I judge: while yet the planks
    sustain
The wild waves' fury, here I fix'd remain:
But when their texture to the tempest
    yields,   460
I launch adventurous on the liquid fields,
Join to the help of Gods the strength of
    man,
And take this method, since the best I
    can.'
    While thus his thoughts an anxious coun-
      cil hold,
The raging God a wat'ry mountain roll'd;
Like a black sheet the whelming billows
    spread,
Burst o'er the float, and thunder'd on his
    head.
Planks, beams, disparted fly; the scatter'd
    wood
Rolls diverse, and in fragments strews the
    flood
So the rude Boreas, o'er the field new-
    shorn,   470
Tosses and drives the scatter'd heaps of
    corn.
And now a single beam the chief bestrides:
There, pois'd awhile above the bounding
    tides,
His limbs discumbers of the clinging vest,
And binds the sacred cincture round his
    breast;
Then, prone on ocean in a moment flung,
Stretch'd wide his eager arms, and shot the
    seas along.
All naked now, on heaving billows laid,
Stern Neptune eyed him, and contemptu-
    ous said:
    'Go, learn'd in woes, and other foes
      essay!   480
Go, wander helpless on the wat'ry way:
Thus, thus find out the destin'd shore, and
    then
(If Jove ordains it) mix with happier
    men:
Whate'er thy fate, the ills our wrath could
    raise
Shall last remember'd in thy best of days.'
    This said, his sea-green steeds divide the
    foam,
And reach high Ægæ and the tow'ry dome.

Now, scarce withdrawn the fierce earth-
shaking Power,
Jove's daughter Pallas watch'd the fav'ring
hour;
Back to their caves she bade the winds to
fly, 490
And hush'd the blust'ring Brethren of the
Sky.
The drier blasts alone of Boreas sway,
And bear him soft on broken waves away;
With gentle force impelling to that shore,
Where Fate has destin'd he shall toil no
more.
And now two nights and now two days were
past,
Since wide he wander'd on the wat'ry
waste;
Heav'd on the surge with intermitting
breath,
And hourly panting in the arms of Death.
The third fair morn now blazed upon the
main; 500
Then glassy smooth lay all the liquid plain;
The winds were hush'd, the billows scarcely
curl'd,
And a dead silence still'd the wat'ry world,
When, lifted on a ridgy wave, he spies
The land at distance, and with sharpen'd
eyes.
As pious children joy with vast delight
When a lov'd sire revives before their
sight
(Who, ling'ring long, has call'd on death in
vain, 508
Fix'd by some demon to his bed of pain,
Till Heav'n by miracle his life restore);
So joys Ulysses at th' appearing shore;
And sees (and labours onward as he sees)
The rising forests, and the tufted trees.
And now, as near approaching as the sound
Of human voice the list'ning ear may
wound,
Amidst the rocks he hears a hollow roar
Of murm'ring surges breaking on the
shore:
Nor peaceful port was there, nor winding
bay,
To shield the vessel from the rolling sea,
But cliffs, and shaggy shores, a dreadful
sight! 520
All rough with rocks, with foamy billows
white.
Fear seiz'd his slacken'd limbs and beating
heart,
And thus he communed with his soul apart:

'Ah me! when o'er a length of waters
toss'd,
These eyes at last behold th' unhoped-for
coast,
No port receives me from the angry main,
But the loud deeps demand me back
again.
Above sharp rocks forbid access; around
Roar the wild waves; beneath is sea pro-
found! 529
No footing sure affords the faithless sand,
To stem too rapid, and too deep to stand.
If here I enter, my efforts are vain,
Dash'd on the cliffs or heav'd into the
main:
Or round the island if my course I bend,
Where the ports open, or the shores de-
scend,
Back to the seas the rolling surge may
sweep,
And bury all my hopes beneath the deep.
Or some enormous whale the God may
send
(For many such on Amphitrite attend);
Too well the turns of mortal chance I
know, 540
And hate relentless of my heav'nly foe.'
While thus he thought, a monstrous wave
upbore
The Chief, and dash'd him on the craggy
shore;
Torn was his skin, nor had the ribs been
whole,
But instant Pallas enter'd in his soul.
Close to the cliff with both his hands he
clung,
And stuck adherent, and suspended hung;
Till the huge surge roll'd off: then, back-
ward sweep
The refluent tides, and plunge him in the
deep. 549
As when the polypus, from forth his cave
Torn with full force, reluctant beats the
wave;
His ragged claws are stuck with stones and
sands;
So the rough rock had shagg'd Ulysses'
hands.
And now had perish'd, whelm'd beneath
the main,
Th' unhappy man; ev'n Fate had been in
vain;
But all-subduing Pallas lent her power,
And prudence saved him in the needful
hour.

Beyond the beating surge his course he
　　bore
(A wider circle, but in sight of shore),
With longing eyes, observing, to survey 560
Some smooth ascent, or safe sequester'd
　　bay.
Between the parting rocks at length he
　　spied
A falling stream with gentler waters glide;
Where to the seas the shelving shore de-
　　clin'd,
And form'd a bay impervious to the wind.
To this calm port the glad Ulysses press'd,
And hail'd the river, and its God address'd:
' Whoe'er thou art, before whose stream
　　unknown
I bend, a suppliant at thy wat'ry throne,
Hear, azure King! nor let me fly in
　　vain　　　　　　　　　　　　　 570
To thee from Neptune and the raging
　　main.
Heav'n hears and pities hapless men like
　　me,
For sacred ev'n to Gods is misery:
Let then thy waters give the weary rest,
And save a suppliant, and a man dis-
　　tress'd.'
　　He pray'd, and straight the gentle stream
　　subsides,
Detains the rushing current of his tides,
Before the wand'rer smooths the wat'ry
　　way,
And soft receives him from the rolling sea.
That moment, fainting as he touch'd the
　　shore,　　　　　　　　　　　　 580
He dropp'd his sinewy arms; his knees no
　　more
Perform'd their office, or his weight up-
　　held;
His swoln heart heav'd; his bloated body
　　swell'd;
From mouth and nose the briny torrent
　　ran;
And lost in lassitude lay all the man,
Deprived of voice, of motion, and of breath;
The soul scarce waking in the arms of
　　death.
Soon as warm life its wonted office found,
The mindful chief Leucothea's scarf un-
　　bound;
Observant of her word, he turn'd aside 590
His head, and cast it on the rolling tide.
Behind him far, upon the purple waves
The waters waft it, and the nymph re-
　　ceives.

Now parting from the stream, Ulysses
　　found
A mossy bank with pliant rushes crown'd;
The bank he press'd, and gently kiss'd the
　　ground;
Where on the flow'ry herb as soft he lay,
Thus to his soul the sage began to say:
　' What will ye next ordain, ye Powers on
　　high!
And yet, ah yet, what fates are we to
　　try?　　　　　　　　　　　　　 600
Here by the stream, if I the night out-
　　wear,
Thus spent already, how shall nature bear
The dews descending, and nocturnal air?
Or chilly vapours breathing from the flood
When morning rises? — If I take the
　　wood,
And in thick shelter of innumerous boughs
Enjoy the comfort gentle sleep allows;
Tho' fenc'd from cold, and tho' my toil be
　　past,
What savage beasts may wander in the
　　waste!
Perhaps I yet may fall a bloody prey 610
To prowling bears, or lions in the way.'
　　Thus long debating in himself he stood:
At length he took the passage to the wood,
Whose shady horrors on a rising brow
Waved high, and frown'd upon the stream
　　below.
There grew two olives, closest of the grove,
With roots entwin'd, and branches inter-
　　wove;
Alike their leaves, but not alike they smil'd
With sister-fruits; one fertile, one was
　　wild.
Nor here the sun's meridian rays had
　　power,　　　　　　　　　　　　 620
Nor wind sharp-piercing, nor the rushing
　　shower;
The verdant arch so close its texture kept:
Beneath this covert great Ulysses crept.
Of gather'd leaves an ample bed he made
(Thick strewn by tempest thro' the bow'ry
　　shade);
Where three at least might winter's cold
　　defy,
Tho' Boreas raged along th' inclement
　　sky.
This store with joy the patient hero found,
And, sunk amidst them, heap'd the leaves
　　around.
As some poor peasant, fated to reside 630
Remote from neighbours in a forest wide.

Studious to save what human wants require,
In embers heap'd, preserves the seeds of
  fire:
Hid in dry foliage thus Ulysses lies,
Till Pallas pour'd soft slumbers on his
  eyes:
And golden dreams (the gift of sweet re-
  pose)
Lull'd all his cares, and banish'd all his
  woes.

BOOK VII

THE COURT OF ALCINOÜS

ARGUMENT

The princess Nausicaa returns to the city, and
Ulysses soon after follows thither. He is
met by Pallas in the form of a young virgin,
who guides him to the palace, and directs
him in what manner to address the queen
Areté. She then involves him in a mist,
which causes him to pass invisible. The
palace and gardens of Alcinoüs described.
Ulysses falling at the feet of the Queen, the
mist disperses, the Phæacians admire, and
receive him with respect. The Queen inquiring by what means he had the garments
he then wore, he relates to her and Alcinoüs
his departure from Calypso, and his arrival
on their dominions.
The same day continues, and the book ends
with the night.

THE patient heav'nly man thus suppliant
  pray'd;
While the slow mules draw on th' imperial
  maid:
Thro' the proud street she moves, the pub-
  lic gaze;
The turning wheel before the palace stays.
With ready love her brothers gath'ring
  round,
Receiv'd the vestures, and the mules un-
  bound.
She seeks the bridal bower: a matron there
The rising fire supplies with busy care,
Whose charms in youth her father's heart
  inflamed,
Now worn with age, Eurymedusa named: 10
The captive dame Phæacian rovers bore,
Snatch'd from Epirus, her sweet native
  shore
(A grateful prize), and in her bloom be-
  stow'd
On good Alcinoüs, honour'd as a God;

Nurse of Nausicaa from her infant years,
And tender second to a mother's cares.
  Now from the sacred thicket, where he
    lay,
To town Ulysses took the winding way.
Propitious Pallas, to secure her care,   19
Around him spread a veil of thicken'd air;
To shun th' encounter of the vulgar crowd,
Insulting still, inquisitive and loud.
When near the famed Phæacian walls he
  drew,
The beauteous city opening to his view,
His step a virgin met, and stood before:
A polish'd urn the seeming virgin bore,
And youthful smil'd; but in the low dis-
  guise
Lay hid the Goddess with the Azure Eyes.
  'Show me, fair daughter' (thus the
    Chief demands),
'The house of him who rules these happy
  lands;   30
Thro' many woes and wand'rings, lo ! I
  come
To good Alcinoüs' hospitable dome.
Far from my native coast, I rove alone,
A wretched stranger, and of all unknown !'
  The Goddess answer'd: 'Father, I obey,
And point the wand'ring traveller his way:
Well known to me the palace you inquire,
For fast beside it dwells my honour'd sire:
But silent march, nor greet the common
  train
With question needless, or inquiry vain: 40
A race of rugged mariners are these:
Unpolish'd men, and boist'rous as their
  seas:
The native islanders alone their care,
And hateful he who breathes a foreign air.
These did the ruler of the deep ordain
To build proud navies, and command the
  main;
On canvas wings to cut the wat'ry way;
No bird so light, no thought so swift as
  they.'
  Thus having spoke, th' unknown Celestial
    leads:
The footsteps of the deity he treads,   50
And secret moves along the crowded space,
Unseen of all the rude Phæacian race
(So Pallas order'd. Pallas to their eyes
The mist objected, and condens'd the skies).
The Chief with wonder sees th' extended
  streets,
The spreading harbours, and the riding
  fleets;

He next their Princes' lofty domes ad-
   mires,
In sep'rate islands, crown'd with rising
   spires;
And deep intrenchments, and high walls of
   stone,
That gird the city like a marble zone.   60
At length the kingly palace gates he
   view'd;
There stopp'd the Goddess, and her speech
   renew'd.
  ' My task is done; the mansion you in-
   quire
Appears before you: enter, and admire.
High-throned, and feasting, there thou
   shalt behold
The sceptred rulers.   Fear not, but be
   bold:
A decent boldness ever meets with friends,
Succeeds, and ev'n a stranger recommends.
First to the Queen prefer a suppliant's ⎤
   claim,   ⎥
Alcinoüs' Queen, Aretè is her name,   70 ⎬
The same her parents, and her power the ⎥
   same.   ⎦
For know, from Ocean's God Nausithoüs
   sprung,
And Peribœa, beautiful and young;
(Eurymedon's last hope, who ruled of old
The race of giants, impious, proud, and
   bold;
Perish'd the nation in unrighteous war,
Perish'd the Prince, and left this only
   heir);
Who now, by Neptune's am'rous power
   compress'd,
Produced a Monarch that his people bless'd,
Father and Prince of the Phæacian name; 80
From him Rhexenor and Alcinoüs came.
The first by Phœbus' burning arrows fired,
New from his nuptials, hapless youth ! ex-
   pired.
No son survived: Aretè heir'd his state,
And her Alcinoüs chose his royal mate.
With honours yet to womankind unknown
This Queen he graces, and divides the
   throne;
In equal tenderness her sons conspire,
And all the children emulate their sire.
When thro' the street she gracious deigns
   to move   90
(The public wonder and the public love),
The tongues of all with transport sound
   her praise,
The eyes of all, as on a Goddess, gaze.

She feels the triumph of a gen'rous ⎤
   breast;   ⎥
To heal divisions, to relieve th' oppress'd; ⎬
In virtue rich; in blessing others, bless'd. ⎦
Go then secure, thy humble suit prefer,
And owe thy country and thy friends to
   her.'
  With that the Goddess deign'd no longer
   stay,
But o'er the world of waters wing'd her
   way: 100
Forsaking Scheria's ever-pleasing shore,
The winds to Marathon the virgin bore:
Thence, where proud Athens rears her
   tow'ry head,
With opening streets and shining struc-
   tures spread,
She pass'd, delighted with the well-known
   seats;
And to Erectheus' sacred dome retreats.
  Meanwhile Ulysses at the palace waits, ⎤
There stops, and anxious with his soul ⎬
   debates,   ⎥
Fix'd in amaze before the royal gates. ⎦
The front appear'd with radiant splendours
   gay,   110
Bright as the lamp of night, or orb of day.
The walls were massy brass : the cornice
   high
Blue metals crown'd in colours of the sky;
Rich plates of gold the folding doors in-
   case;
The pillars silver, on a brazen base,
Silver the lintels deep-projecting o'er,
And gold the ringlets that command the
   door.
Two rows of stately dogs on either hand,
In sculptured gold and labour'd silver
   stand.
These Vulcan form'd with art divine, to
   wait   120
Immortal guardians at Alcinoüs' gate;
Alive each animated frame appears,
And still to live beyond the power of
   years.
Fair thrones within from space to space
   were rais'd,
Where various carpets with embroid'ry
   blazed,
The work of matrons: these the Princes
   press'd,
Day foll'wing day, a long continued feast.
Refulgent pedestals the walls surround,
Which boys of gold with flaming torches
   crown'd:

The polish'd ore, reflecting every ray, 130
Blazed on the banquets with a double day.
Full fifty handmaids form'd the household
  train;
Some turn the mill, or sift the golden
  grain;
Some ply the loom; their busy fingers
  move
Like poplar-leaves when Zephyr fans the
  grove.
Not more renown'd the men of Scheria's
  isle,
For sailing arts and all the naval toil,
Than works of female skill their women's
  pride,
The flying shuttle thro' the threads to
  guide:
Pallas to these her double gifts imparts, 140
Inventive genius, and industrious arts.
  Close to the gates a spacious garden
  lies,
From storms defended and inclement
  skies.
Four acres was th' allotted space of
  ground,
Fenc'd with a green enclosure all around.
Tall thriving trees confess'd the fruitful
  mould;
The redd'ning apple ripens here to gold.
Here the blue fig with luscious juice o'er-
  flows,
With deeper red the full pomegranate
  glows;
The branch here bends beneath the weighty
  pear, 150
And verdant olives flourish round the year.
The balmy spirit of the western gale
Eternal breathes on fruits, untaught to
  fail;
Each dropping pear a foll'wing pear sup-
  plies,
On apples apples, figs on figs arise:
The same mild season gives the blooms to
  blow,
The buds to harden, and the fruits to
  grow.
  Here order'd vines in equal ranks ap-
  pear,
With all th' united labours of the year;
Some to unload the fertile branches run, 160
Some dry the black'ning clusters in the
  sun;
Others to tread the liquid harvest join,
The groaning presses foam with floods of
  wine,

Here are the vines in early flower de-
  scried,
Here grapes discolour'd on the sunny
  side,
And there in Autumn's richest purple
  dyed.
Beds of all various herbs, for ever
  green,
In beauteous order terminate the scene.
  Two plenteous fountains the whole pro-
  spect crown'd:
This thro' the gardens leads its streams
  around, 170
Visits each plant, and waters all the
  ground;
While that in pipes beneath the palace
  flows,
And thence its current on the town be-
  stows:
To various use their various streams they
  bring,
The people one, and one supplies the King.
  Such were the glories which the Gods
  ordain'd,
To grace Alcinoüs, and his happy land.
Ev'n from the Chief whom men and na-
  tions knew,
Th' unwonted scene surprise and rapture
  drew;
In pleasing thought he ran the prospect
  o'er, 180
Then hasty enter'd at the lofty door.
Night now approaching, in the palace
  stand,
With goblets crown'd, the rulers of the
  land;
Prepared for rest, and off'ring to the God
Who bears the virtue of the sleepy rod.
Unseen he glided thro' the joyous crowd,
With darkness circled, and an ambient
  cloud,
Direct to great Alcinoüs' throne he came,
And prostrate fell before th' imperial
  dame.
Then from around him dropp'd the veil of
  night; 190
Sudden he shines, and manifest to sight.
The nobles gaze, with awful fear op-
  press'd;
Silent they gaze, and eye the godlike
  guest.
  'Daughter of great Rhexenor!' (thus
  began,
Low at her knees, the much-enduring
  man),

'To thee, thy consort, and this royal
    train,
To all that share the blessings of your
    reign,
A suppliant bends: oh pity human woe!
'T is what the happy to th' unhappy owe.
A wretched exile to his country send,   200
Long worn with griefs, and long without a
    friend.
So may the Gods your better days in-
    crease,
And all your joys descend on all your
    race:
So reign for ever on your country's breast,
Your people blessing, by your people
    bless'd!'
    Then to the genial hearth he bow'd his
        face,
And humbled in the ashes took his place.
Silence ensued. The eldest first began,
Echeneus sage, a venerable man!
Whose well-taught mind the present age
    surpass'd,   210
And join'd to that th' experience of the
    last.
Fit words attended on his weighty sense,
And mild persuasion flow'd in eloquence.
' Oh sight ' (he cried) ' dishonest and un-
    just !
A guest, a stranger, seated in the dust !
To raise the lowly suppliant from the
    ground
Befits a Monarch. Lo ! the peers around
But wait thy word, the gentle guest to
    grace,
And seat him fair in some distinguish'd
    place.
Let first the herald due libation pay   220
To Jove, who guides the wand'rer on his
    way;
Then set the genial banquet in his view,
And give the stranger-guest a stranger's
    due.'
    His sage advice the list'ning King obeys;
He stretch'd his hand the prudent Chief to
    raise,
And from his seat Laodamas remov'd
(The Monarch's offspring, and his best-be-
    lov'd);
There next his side the godlike Hero sate;
With stars of silver shone the bed of state.
The golden ewer a beauteous handmaid
    brings,   230
Replenish'd from the cool translucent
    springs,

Whose polish'd vase with copious streams
    supplies
A silver laver of capacious size.
The table next in regal order spread,
The glitt'ring canisters are heap'd with
    bread :
Viands of various kinds invite the taste,
Of choicest sort and savour, rich repast !
Thus feasting high, Alcinoüs gave the sign,
And bade the Herald pour the rosy wine.
' Let all around the due libation pay   240
To Jove, who guides the wand'rer on his
    way.'
    He said. Pontonoüs heard the King's
        command;
The circling goblet moves from hand to
    hand;
Each drinks the juice that glads the heart
    of man.
Alcinoüs then, with aspect mild, began :
    ' Princes and Peers, attend ; while we
        impart
To you the thoughts of no inhuman heart.
Now pleas'd and satiate from the social
    rite
Repair we to the blessings of the night;
But with the rising day, assembled here, 250
Let all the elders of the land appear,
Pious observe our hospitable laws,
And Heav'n propitiate in the stranger's
    cause;
Then join'd in council, proper means ex-
    plore
Safe to transport him to the wished-for
    shore
(How distant that, imports not us to know,
Nor weigh the labour, but relieve the woe).
Meantime, nor harm nor anguish let him
    bear :
This interval, Heav'n trusts him to our
    care;   259
But to his native land our charge resign'd,
Heav'n's is his life to come, and all the woes
    behind.
Then must he suffer what the Fates ordain;
For Fate has wove the thread of life with
    pain !
And twins ev'n from the birth are Misery
    and Man !
But if, descended from th' Olympian bower,
Gracious approach us some immortal Power;
If in that form thou com'st a guest divine ;
Some high event the conscious Gods design.
As yet, unbid they never graced our feast,
The solemn sacrifice call'd down the guest;

Then manifest of Heav'n the vision stood, 271
And to our eyes familiar was the God.
Oft with some favour'd traveller they
    stray,
And shine before him all the desert way;
With social intercourse, and face to face,
The friends and guardians of our pious
    race.
So near approach we their celestial kind,
By justice, truth, and probity of mind;
As our dire neighbours of Cyclopean birth
Match in fierce wrong the giant - sons of
    earth.'   280
    'Let no such thought' (with modest
    grace rejoin'd
The prudent Greek) 'possess the royal
    mind.
Alas! a mortal, like thyself, am I;
No glorious native of yon azure sky:
In form, ah how unlike their heav'nly kind!
How more inferior in the gifts of mind!
Alas, a mortal! most oppress'd of those
Whom Fate has loaded with a weight of
    woes;
By a sad train of miseries alone   289
Distinguish'd long, and second now to none!
By Heav'n's high will compell'd from shore
    to shore,
With Heav'n's high will prepared to suffer
    more.
What histories of toil could I declare!
But still long-wearied nature wants repair;
Spent with fatigue, and shrunk with pining
    fast,
My craving bowels still require repast.
Howe'er the noble, suff'ring mind may grieve
Its load of anguish, and disdain to live,
Necessity demands our daily bread;
Hunger is insolent, and will be fed.   300
But finish, O ye Peers! what you propose,
And let the morrow's dawn conclude my
    woes.
Pleas'd will I suffer all the Gods ordain,
To see my soil, my son, my friends again.
That view vouchsafed, let instant death
    surprise
With ever-during shade these happy eyes!'
    Th' assembled Peers with gen'ral praise
    approv'd
His pleaded reason, and the suit he mov'd.
Each drinks a full oblivion of his cares,
And to the gifts of balmy sleep repairs. 310
Ulysses in the regal walls alone ⎤
Remain'd: beside him, on a splendid throne ⎬
Divine Aretè and Alcinoüs shone. ⎦

The Queen, on nearer view, the guest sur-
    vey'd,
Robed in the garments her own hands had
    made,
Not without wonder seen. Then thus be-
    gan,
Her words addressing to the godlike man:
    'Camest thou not hither, wondrous stran-
    ger! say,
From lands remote, and o'er a length of
    sea?
Tell then whence art thou? whence that
    princely air?   320
And robes like these, so recent and so
    fair?'
    'Hard is the task, O Princess! you im-
    pose'
(Thus sighing spoke the man of many
    woes),
'The long, the mournful series to relate
Of all my sorrows sent by Heav'n and
    Fate!
Yet what you ask, attend. An island lies
Beyond these tracts, and under other skies,
Ogygia named, in Ocean's wat'ry arms;
Where dwells Calypso, dreadful in her
    charms!
Remote from Gods or men she holds her
    reign,   330
Amid the terrors of the rolling main.
Me, only me, the hand of Fortune bore,
Unblest! to tread that interdicted shore:
When Jove tremendous in the sable deeps
Launch'd his red lightning at our scatter'd
    ships,
Then, all my fleet, and all my foll'wers
    lost,
Sole on a plank, on boiling surges toss'd,
Heav'n drove my wreck th' Ogygian isle to
    find,
Full nine days floating to the wave and
    wind.   339
Met by the Goddess there with open arms,
She bribed my stay with more than human
    charms;
Nay, promis'd, vainly promis'd, to bestow
Immortal life, exempt from age and woe;
But all her blandishments successless prove,
To banish from my breast my country's
    love.
I stay reluctant sev'n continued years,
And water her ambrosial couch with tears;
The eighth she voluntary moves to part,
Or urged by Jove, or her own changeful
    heart.

A raft was form'd to cross the surging
   sea;   350
Herself supplied the stores and rich array,
And gave the gales to waft me on the way.
In sev'nteen days appear'd your pleasing
   coast,
And woody mountains half in vapours lost.
Joy touch'd my soul: my soul was joy'd in
   vain,
For angry Neptune rous'd the raging main;
The wild winds whistle, and the billows
   roar;
The splitting raft the furious tempest tore;
And storms vindictive intercept the shore.
Soon as their rage subsides, the seas I
   brave   360
With naked force, and shoot along the
   wave,
To reach this isle; but there my hopes were
   lost;
The surge impell'd me on a craggy coast.
I chose the safer sea, and chanced to find
A river's mouth impervious to the wind,
And clear of rocks. I fainted by the flood;
Then took the shelter of the neighb'ring
   wood.
'T was night, and cover'd in the foliage
   deep,
Jove plunged my senses in the death of
   sleep.
All night I slept, oblivious of my pain: 370
Aurora dawn'd, and Phœbus shined in vain,
Nor, till oblique he sloped his ev'ning ray,
Had Somnus dried the balmy dews away.
Then female voices from the shore I heard:
A maid amidst them, goddess-like, ap-
   pear'd;
To her I sued, she pitied my distress;
Like thee in beauty, nor in virtue less.
Who from such youth could hope con-
   sid'rate care?
In youth and beauty wisdom is but rare!
She gave me life, reliev'd with just sup-
   plies   380
My wants, and lent these robes that strike
   your eyes.
This is the truth: and oh, ye Powers on high!
Forbid that want should sink me to a lie.'
   To this the King: 'Our daughter but
   express'd
Her cares imperfect to her godlike guest.
Suppliant to her since first he chose to pray,
Why not herself did she conduct the way,
And with her handmaids to our court
   convey?'

'Hero and King' (Ulysses thus replied),
'Nor blame her faultless, nor suspect of
   pride: 390
She bade me follow in th' attendant train;
But fear and rev'rence did my steps detain,
Lest rash suspicion might alarm thy mind:
Man 's of a jealous and mistaking kind.'
   'Far from my soul' (he cried) 'the Gods
   efface
All wrath ill-grounded, and suspicion base!
Whate'er is honest, stranger, I approve,
And would to Phœbus, Pallas, and to Jove,
Such as thou art, thy thought and mine
   were one,
Nor thou unwilling to be call'd my son. 400
In such alliance could'st thou wish to join,
A palace stor'd with treasures should be
   thine.
But if reluctant, who shall force thy stay?
Jove bids to set the stranger on his way,
And ships shall wait thee with the morn-
   ing ray.
Till then, let slumber cross thy careful
   eyes;
The wakeful mariners shall watch the
   skies,
And seize the moment when the breezes
   rise,
Then gently waft thee to the pleasing shore,
Where thy soul rests, and labour is no
   more.   410
Far as Eubœa tho' thy country lay,
Our ships with ease transport thee in a
   day.
Thither of old, earth's giant son to view,
On wings of winds with Rhadamanth they
   flew;
This land, from whence their morning
   course begun,
Saw them returning with the setting sun.
Your eyes shall witness and confirm my
   tale,
Our youth how dext'rous and how fleet our
   sail,
When justly timed with equal sweep they
   row,   419
And ocean whitens in long tracks below.'
   Thus he. No word the experienc'd man
   replies,
But thus to Heav'n (and Heav'nward lifts
   his eyes):
'O Jove! O Father! what the King ac-
   cords
Do thou make perfect! sacred be his
   words!

Wide o'er the world Alcinoüs' glory shine!
Let fame be his, and ah! my country
  mine!'
Meantime Aretè, for the hour of rest,
Ordains the fleecy couch, and cov'ring vest;
Bids her fair train the purple quilts pre-
  pare,
And the thick carpets spread with busy
  care.   430
With torches blazing in their hands they
  pass'd,
And finish'd all their Queen's command
  with haste:
Then gave the signal to the willing guest:
He rose with pleasure, and retired to rest.
There soft-extended, to the murm'ring
  sound
Of the high porch, Ulysses sleeps pro-
  found!
Within, releas'd from cares Alcinoüs lies;
And fast beside were closed Aretè's eyes.

BOOK IX

THE ADVENTURES OF THE CICONS, LOTO-
PHAGI, AND CYCLOPS

ARGUMENT

Ulysses begins the relation of his adventures;
how, after the destruction of Troy, he with
his companions made an incursion on the
Cicons, by whom they were repulsed; and
meeting with a storm, were driven to the
coast of the Lotophagi. From thence they
sailed to the land of the Cyclops, whose
manners and situation are particularly characterized. The giant Polyphemus and his
cave described; the usage Ulysses and his
companions met with there; and lastly, the
method and artifice by which he escaped.

THEN thus Ulysses: 'Thou whom first
  in sway,
As first in virtue, these thy realms obey;
How sweet the products of a peaceful reign!
The Heav'n-taught poet, and enchanting
  strain,
The well-fill'd palace, the perpetual feast,
A land rejoicing, and a people bless'd:
How goodly seems it ever to employ
Man's social days in union and in joy;
The plenteous board high-heap'd with cates
  divine,
And o'er the foaming bowl the laughing
  wine!   10

'Amid these joys, why seeks thy mind to
  know
Th' unhappy series of a wand'rer's woe?
Remembrance sad, whose image to review,
Alas! must open all my wounds anew!
And oh, what first, what last shall I relate,
Of woes unnumber'd sent by Heav'n and
  Fate?
'Know first the man (tho' now a wretch
  distress'd)
Who hopes thee, Monarch, for his future
  guest:
Behold Ulysses! no ignoble name,
Earth sounds my wisdom, and high Heav'n
  my fame.   20
'My native soil is Ithaca the fair,
Where high Neritus waves his woods in air;
Dulichium, Samè, and Zacynthus crown'd
With shady mountains, spread their isles
  around
(These to the north and night's dark re-
  gions run,
Those to Aurora and the rising sun);
Low lies our isle, yet bless'd in fruitful
  stores;
Strong are her sons, tho' rocky are her
  shores;
And none, ah none, so lovely to my sight,
Of all the lands that Heav'n o'erspreads
  with light!   30
In vain Calypso long constrain'd my stay,
With sweet, reluctant, amorous delay;
With all her charms as vainly Circe strove,
And added magic to secure my love.
In pomps or joys, the palace or the grot,
My country's image never was forgot,
My absent parents rose before my sight,
And distant lay contentment and delight.
'Hear, then, the woes which mighty Jove
  ordain'd   39
To wait my passage from the Trojan land.
The winds from Ilion to the Cicons' shore,
Beneath cold Ismarus, our vessels bore.
We boldly landed on the hostile place,
And sack'd the city, and destroy'd the race,
Their wives made captive, their possessions
  shared,
And ev'ry soldier found a like reward.
I then advised to fly; not so the rest,
Who stay'd to revel, and prolong the feast:
The fatted sheep and sable bulls they slay,
And bowls flow round, and riot wastes the
  day.   50
Meantime the Cicons, to their holds retired
Call on the Cicons, with new fury fired;

With early morn the gather'd country
  swarms
And all the continent is bright with arms;
Thick as the budding leaves or rising flowers
O'erspread the land, when spring descends
  in showers:
All expert soldiers, skill'd on foot to dare,
Or from the bounding courser urge the war.
Now fortune changes (so the Fates or-
  dain);
Our hour was come to taste our share of
  pain. 60
Close at the ships the bloody fight began,
Wounded they wound, and man expires on
  man.
Long as the morning sun increasing bright
O'er Heav'n's pure azure spread the grow-
  ing light,
Promiscuous death the form of war con-
  founds,
Each adverse battle gor'd with equal
  wounds;
But when his ev'ning wheels o'erhung the
  main,
Then conquest crown'd the fierce Ciconian
  train.
Six brave companions from each ship we
  lost,
The rest escape in haste, and quit the
  coast. 70
With sails outspread we fly th' unequal
  strife,
Sad for their loss, but joyful of our life.
Yet as we fled, our fellows' rites we paid,
And thrice we call'd on each unhappy
  shade.
  'Meanwhile the God, whose hand the
  thunder forms,
Drives clouds on clouds, and blackens
  Heav'n with storms,
Wide o'er the waste the rage of Boreas
  sweeps,
And night rush'd headlong on the shaded
  deeps.
Now here, now there, the giddy ships are
  borne,
And all the rattling shrouds in fragments
  torn. 80
We furl'd the sail, we plied the lab'ring
  oar,
Took down our masts, and row'd our ships
  to shore.
Two tedious days, and two long nights we
  lay,
O'erwatch'd and batter'd in the naked bay.

But the third morning when Aurora brings,
We rear the masts, we spread the canvas
  wings;
Refresh'd and careless on the deck reclin'd,
We sit, and trust the pilot and the wind.
Then to my native country had I sail'd:
But, the cape doubled, adverse winds pre-
  vail'd. 90
Strong was the tide, which, by the north-
  ern blast
Impell'd, our vessels on Cythera cast.
Nine days our fleet th' uncertain tempest
  bore
Far in wide ocean, and from sight of shore:
The tenth we touch'd, by various errors
  toss'd,
The land of Lotus, and the flow'ry coast.
We climb'd the beach, and springs of
  water found,
Then spread our hasty banquet on the
  ground.
Three men were sent, deputed from the
  crew 99
(A herald one) the dubious coast to view,
And learn what habitants possess'd the
  place.
They went, and found a hospitable race:
Not prone to ill, nor strange to foreign
  guest,
They eat, they drink, and Nature gives the
  feast:
The trees around them all their food pro-
  duce;
Lotus the name: divine, nectareous juice
(Thence called Lotophagi); which whoso
  tastes,
Insatiate riots in the sweet repasts,
Nor other home nor other care intends,
But quits his house, his country, and his
  friends. 110
The three we sent, from off th' enchanting
  ground
We dragged reluctant, and by force we
  bound:
The rest in haste forsook the pleasing
  shore,
Or, the charm tasted, had return'd no
  more.
Now placed in order on their banks, they
  sweep
The sea's smooth face, and cleave the hoary
  deep;
With heavy hearts we labour thro' the
  tide,
To coasts unknown, and oceans yet untried.

'The land of Cyclops first, a savage kind,
Nor tamed by manners, nor by laws con-
  fin'd: 120
Untaught to plant, to turn the glebe and
  sow,
They all their products to free Nature owe.
The soil untill'd a ready harvest yields,
With wheat and barley wave the golden
  fields;
Spontaneous wines from weighty clusters
  pour,
And Jove descends in each prolific shower.
By these no statutes and no rights are
  known,
No Council held, no Monarch fills the
  throne,
But high on hills, or airy cliffs, they dwell,
Or deep in caves whose entrance leads to
  Hell.   130
Each rules his race, his neighbour not his
  care,
Heedless of others, to his own severe.
  'Opposed to the Cyclopean coasts, there
  lay
An isle, whose hills their subject fields
  survey;
Its name Lachæa, crown'd with many a
  grove,
Where savage goats thro' pathless thickets
  rove:
No needy mortals here, with hunger bold,
Or wretched hunters thro' the wintry cold
Pursue their flight; but leave them safe to
  bound
From hill to hill, o'er all the desert
  ground.   140
Nor knows the soil to feed the fleecy care,
Or feels the labours of the crooked share;
But uninhabited, untill'd, unsown
It lies, and breeds the bleating goat alone.
For there no vessel with vermilion prore,
Or bark of traffic, glides from shore to
  shore;
The rugged race of savages, unskill'd
The seas to traverse, or the ships to build,
Gaze on the coast, nor cultivate the soil,
Unlearn'd in all th' industrious arts of
  toil.   150
Yet here all products and all plants
  abound,
Sprung from the fruitful genius of the
  ground;
Fields waving high with heavy crops are
  seen,
And vines that flourish in eternal green,

Refreshing meads along the murm'ring
  main,
And fountains streaming down the fruitful
  plain.
  'A port there is, inclosed on either side,
Where ships may rest, unanchor'd and un-
  tied;
Till the glad mariners incline to sail,   159
And the sea whitens with the rising gale.
High at the head from out the cavern'd
  rock,
In living rills a gushing fountain broke:
Around it, and above, for ever green,
The bushy alders form'd a shady scene.
Hither some fav'ring God, beyond our
  thought,
Thro' all-surrounding shade our navy
  brought;
For gloomy night descended on the main,
Nor glimmer'd Phœbe in th' ethereal
  plain:
But all unseen the clouded island lay,
And all unseen the surge and rolling
  sea,   170
Till safe we anchor'd in the shelter'd bay:
Our sails we gather'd, cast our cables o'er,
And slept secure along the sandy shore.
Soon as again the rosy morning shone,
Reveal'd the landscape and the scene un-
  known,
With wonder seiz'd, we view the pleasing
  ground,
And walk delighted, and expatiate round.
Rous'd by the woodland nymphs at early
  dawn,
The mountain goats came bounding o'er
  the lawn:
In haste our fellows to the ships repair, 180
For arms and weapons of the sylvan war;
Straight in three squadrons all our crew
  we part,
And bend the bow, or wing the missile
  dart;
The bounteous Gods afford a copious prey,
And nine fat goats each vessel bears away:
The royal bark had ten. Our ships com-
  plete
We thus supplied (for twelve were all the
  fleet).
  'Here, till the setting sun roll'd down
  the light,
We sat indulging in the genial rite:
Nor wines were wanting; those from am-
  ple jars   190
We drain'd, the prize of our Ciconian wars.

The land of Cyclops lay in prospect near;
The voice of goats and bleating flocks we
  hear,
And from their mountains rising smokes
  appear.
Now sunk the sun, and darkness cover'd
  o'er
The face of things: along the sea-beat
  shore
Satiate we slept; but when the sacred
  dawn
Arising glitter'd o'er the dewy lawn,
I call'd my fellows, and these words ad-
  dress'd:
" My dear associates, here indulge your
  rest: 200
While, with my single ship, adventurous I
Go forth, the manners of yon men to try;
Whether a race unjust, of barb'rous might,
Rude, and unconscious of a stranger's
  right,
Or such who harbour pity in their breast,
Revere the Gods, and succour the dis-
  tress'd."
  ' This said, I climb'd my vessel's lofty
  side;
My train obey'd me, and the ship untied.
In order seated on their banks, they sweep
Neptune's smooth face, and cleave the
  yielding deep.   210
When to the nearest verge of land we
  drew,
Fast by the sea a lonely cave we view,
High, and with dark'ning laurels cover'd
  o'er;
Where sheep and goats lay slumb'ring
  round the shore.
Near this, a fence of marble from the
  rock,
Brown with o'erarching pine and spreading
  oak:
A giant shepherd here his flock maintains
Far from the rest, and solitary reigns,
In shelter thick of horrid shade reclin'd;
And gloomy mischiefs labour in his
  mind.   220
A form enormous ! far unlike the race
Of human birth, in stature, or in face;
As some lone mountain's monstrous growth
  he stood,
Crown'd with rough thickets, and a nod-
  ding wood.
I left my vessel at the point of land,
And close to guard it gave our crew com-
  mand:

With only twelve, the boldest and the
  best,
I seek th' adventure, and forsake the
  rest.
Then took a goatskin, fill'd with precious
  wine,
The gift of Maron of Evantheus' line 230
(The priest of Phœbus at th' Ismarian
  shrine).
In sacred shade his honour'd mansion stood
Amidst Apollo's consecrated wood;
Him, and his house, Heav'n mov'd my mind
  to save,
And costly presents in return he gave;
Sev'n golden talents to perfection wrought,
A silver bowl that held a copious draught,
And twelve large vessels of unmingled
  wine,
Mellifluous, undecaying, and divine !
Which now, some ages from his race con-
  ceal'd,   240
The hoary sire in gratitude reveal'd.
Such was the wine: to quench whose fer-
  vent steam
Scarce twenty measures from the living
  stream
To cool one cup sufficed: the goblet crown'd
Breathed aromatic fragrances around.
Of this an ample vase we heav'd aboard,
And brought another with provisions stor'd.
My soul foreboded I should find the bower
Of some fell monster, fierce with barb'rous
  power;
Some rustic wretch, who liv'd in Heav'n's
  despite,   250
Contemning laws, and trampling on the
  right.
The cave we found, but vacant all within
(His flock the giant tended on the green):
But round the grot we gaze; and all we
  view,
In order ranged, our admiration drew:
The bending shelves with loads of cheeses
  press'd,
The folded flocks each sep'rate from the
  rest
(The larger here, and there the lesser
  lambs,
The new-fall'n young here bleating for
  their dams;
The kid distinguish'd from the lambkin
  lies):   260
The cavern echoes with responsive cries.
Capacious chargers all around were laid,
Full pails, and vessels of the milking trade.

With fresh provisions hence our fleet to
    store
My friends advise me, and to quit the
    shore;
Or drive a flock of sheep and goats away,
Consult our safety, and put off to sea.
The wholesome counsel rashly I declin'd,
Curious to view the man of monstrous
    kind,   269
And try what social rites a savage lends :
Dire rites, alas ! and fatal to my friends!
    ' Then first a fire we kindle, and prepare !
For his return with sacrifice and prayer.
The laden shelves afford us full repast;
We sit expecting. Lo! he comes at last.
Near half a forest on his back he bore,
And cast the pond'rous burden at the
    door.
It thunder'd as it fell. We trembled then,
And sought the deep recesses of the den.
Now, driv'n before him thro' the arching
    rock,   280
Came tumbling, heaps on heaps, th' un-
    number'd flock :
Big-udder'd ewes, and goats of female
    kind
(The males were penn'd in outward courts
    behind);
Then, heav'd on high, a rock's enormous
    weight
To the cave's mouth he roll'd, and closed
    the gate
(Scarce twenty four-wheel'd cars, compact
    and strong,
The massy load could bear, or roll along).
He next betakes him to his evening cares,
And, sitting down, to milk his flocks pre-
    pares;   289
Of half their udders eases first the dams,
Then to the mothers' teats submits the
    lambs.
Half the white stream to hard'ning cheese
    he press'd,
And high in wicker-baskets heap'd: the
    rest,
Reserv'd in bowls, supplied his nightly
    feast.
His labour done, he fired the pile, that gave
A sudden blaze, and lighted all the cave.
We stand discover'd by the rising fires ;
Askance the giant glares, and thus in-
    quires:
    ' " What are ye, guests ? on what adven-
    ture, say,   299
Thus far ye wander thro' the wat'ry way ?

Pirates perhaps, who seek thro' seas un-
    known
The lives of others, and expose your own ? "
    ' His voice like thunder thro' the cavern
    sounds :
My bold companions thrilling fear con-
    founds,
Appall'd at sight of more than mortal man!
At length, with heart recover'd, I began:
    ' " From Troy's famed fields, sad wand'-
    rers o'er the main,
Behold the relics of the Grecian train !
Thro' various seas, by various perils, toss'd,
And forc'd by storms, unwilling, on your
    coast;   310
Far from our destin'd course and native
    land,
Such was our fate, and such high Jove's
    command !
Nor what we are befits us to disclaim,
Atrides' friends (in arms a mighty name),
Who taught proud Troy and all her sons to
    bow:
Victors of late, but humble suppliants
    now !
Low at thy knee thy succour we implore;
Respect us, human, and relieve us, poor.
At least, some hospitable gift bestow;   319
'T is what the happy to th' unhappy owe :
'T is what the Gods require: those Gods
    revere;
The poor and stranger are their constant
    care;
To Jove their cause, and their revenge be-
    longs,
He wanders with them, and he feels their
    wrongs."
    ' " Fools that ye are " (the savage thus
    replies,
His inward fury blazing at his eyes),
" Or strangers, distant far from our abodes,
To bid me rev'rence or regard the Gods,
Know then, we Cyclops are a race above
Those air-bred people, and their goat-nurs'd
    Jove;   330
And learn, our power proceeds with thee
    and thine,
Not as he wills, but as ourselves incline.
But answer, the good ship that brought ye
    o'er,
Where lies she anchor'd ? near or off the
    shore ? "
    ' Thus he. His meditated fraud I find
(Vers'd in the turns of various human-
    kind),

And, cautious, thus: "Against a dreadful
   rock,
Fast by your shore, the gallant vessel broke.
Scarce with these few I 'scaped, of all my ⎫
   train :   ⎪
Whom angry Neptune whelm'd beneath ⎪
   the main :   340 ⎬
The scatter'd wreck the winds blew back ⎪
   again."   ⎭
   ' He answer'd with his deed : his bloody
   hand
Snatch'd two, unhappy! of my martial band;
And dash'd like dogs against the stony
   floor:
The pavement swims with brains and min-
   gled gore.
Torn limb from limb, he spreads his horrid
   feast,
And fierce devours it like a mountain
   beast:
He sucks the marrow, and the blood he
   drains,
Nor entrails, flesh, nor solid bone remains.
We see the death from which we cannot
   move,   350
And humbled groan beneath the hand of
   Jove.
His ample maw with human carnage fill'd,
A milky deluge next the giant swill'd;
Then, stretch'd in length o'er half the cav-
   ern'd rock,
Lay senseless, and supine, amidst the flock.
To seize the time, and with a sudden wound
To fix the slumb'ring monster to the ground,
My soul impels me! and in act I stand
To draw the sword; but wisdom held my
   hand.
A deed so rash had finish'd all our fate, 360
No mortal forces from the lofty gate
Could roll the rock. In hopeless grief we
   lay,
And sigh, expecting the return of day.
   ' Now did the Rosy-finger'd Morn arise,
And shed her sacred light along the skies.
He wakes, he lights the fires, he milks the
   dams,
And to the mothers' teats submits the
   lambs.
The task thus finish'd of his morning hours,
Two more he snatches, murders and de-
   vours.
Then pleas'd, and whistling, drives his flock
   before,   370
Removes the rocky mountain from the
   door,

And shuts again: with equal ease disposed
As a light quiver's lid is oped and closed.
His giant voice the echoing region fills :
His flocks, obedient, spread o'er all the
   hills.
   'Thus left behind, ev'n in the last de-
   spair
I thought, devised, and Pallas heard my
   prayer.
Revenge, and doubt, and caution, work'd
   my breast;
But this of many counsels seem'd the
   best :
The monster's club within the cave I
   spied,   380
A tree of stateliest growth, and yet un-
   dried,
Green from the wood: of height and bulk
   so vast,
The largest ship might claim it for a mast.
This shorten'd of its top, I gave my train
A fathom's length, to shape it and to
   plane:
The narrower end I sharpen'd to a spire;
Whose point we harden'd with the force of
   fire,
And hid it in the dust that strew'd the
   cave.
Then to my few companions, bold and
   brave,
Proposed, who first the venturous deed
   should try,   390
In the broad orbit of his monstrous eye
To plunge the brand, and twirl the pointed
   wood,
When slumber next should tame the man
   of blood.
Just as I wish'd, the lots were cast on
   four:
Myself the fifth. We stand and wait the
   hour.
He comes with ev'ning : all his fleecy
   flock
Before him march, and pour into the rock:
Not one, or male or female, stay'd be-
   hind
(So fortune chanc'd, or so some God de-
   sign'd);
Then heaving high the stone's unwieldy
   weight,   400
He roll'd it on the cave, and closed the
   gate.
First down he sits, to milk the woolly
   dams,
And then permits their udders to the lambs.

Next seiz'd two wretches more, and head-
  long cast,
Brain'd on the rock ; his second dire re-
  past.
I then approach'd him reeking with their
  gore,
And held the brimming goblet foaming
  o'er:
"Cyclop! since human flesh has been thy
  feast,
Now drain this goblet, potent to digest;
Know hence what treasures in our ship we
  lost,   410
And what rich liquors other climates boast.
We to thy shore the precious freight shall
  bear,
If home thou send us, and vouchsafe to
  spare.
But oh ! thus furious, thirsting thus for
  gore,
The sons of men shall ne'er approach thy
  shore,
And never shalt thou taste this nectar
  more."
  ' He heard, he took, and, pouring down
  his throat,
Delighted, swill'd the large luxurious
  draught.
"More! give me more " (he cried), " the
  boon be thine,
Whoe'er thou art that bear'st celestial
  wine!   420
Declare thy name: not mortal is this juice,
Such as th' unbless'd Cyclopean climes pro-
  duce
(Tho' sure our vine the largest cluster
  yields,
And Jove's scorn'd thunder serves to drench
  our fields);
But this descended from the bless'd abodes,
A rill of nectar, streaming from the Gods."
  ' He said, and greedy grasp'd the heady
  bowl,
Thrice drain'd, and pour'd the deluge on
  his soul.
His sense lay cover'd with the dozy fume;
While thus my fraudful speech I reas-
  sume.   430
"Thy promised boon, O Cyclop ! now I
  claim,
And plead my title; Noman is my name.
By that distinguish'd from my tender
  years,
'T is what my parents call me, and my
  peers."

' The giant then: " Our promised grace
  receive,
The hospitable boon we mean to give :
When all thy wretched crew have felt my
  power,
Noman shall be the last I will devour."
  ' He said: then, nodding with the fumes
  of wine,
Dropp'd his huge head, and snoring lay
  supine.   440
His neck obliquely o'er his shoulders hung,
Press'd with the weight of sleep, that tames
  the strong:
There belch'd the mingled streams of wine
  and blood,
And human flesh, his indigested food.
Sudden I stir the embers, and inspire
With animating breath the seeds of fire;
Each drooping spirit with bold words re-
  pair,
And urge my train the dreadful deed to
  dare:
The stake now glow'd beneath the burning
  bed
(Green as it was) and sparkled fiery red. 450
Then forth the vengeful instrument I bring;
With beating hearts my fellows form a ring.
Urged by some present God, they swift let
  fall
The pointed torment on his visual ball.
Myself above them from a rising ground
Guide the sharp stake, and twirl it round
  and round.
As when a shipwright stands his workmen
  o'er,
Who ply the wimble, some huge beam to
  bore;
Urged on all hands, it nimbly spins about,
The grain deep-piercing till it scoops it
  out: 460
In his broad eye so whirls the fiery wood;
From the pierc'd pupil spouts the boiling
  blood;
Singed are his brows ; the scorching lids
  grow black;
The jelly bubbles, and the fibres crack.
And as when arm'rers temper in the ford
The keen-edg'd pole-axe, or the shining
  sword,
The red-hot metal hisses in the lake,
Thus in his eye-ball hiss'd the plunging
  stake.
He sends a dreadful groan, the rocks around
Thro' all their inmost winding caves re-
  sound.   470

Scared we receded. Forth with frantic
    hand,
He tore, and dash'd on earth the gory
    brand:
Then calls the Cyclops, all that round him
    dwell,
With voice like thunder, and a direful yell.
From all their dens the one-eyed race re-
    pair,
From rifted rocks, and mountains bleak in
    air.
All haste, assembled at his well-known
    roar,
Inquire the cause, and crowd the cavern
    door.
    ' " What hurts thee, Polypheme ? what
    strange affright
Thus breaks our slumbers, and disturbs the
    night ?   480
Does any mortal, in th' unguarded hour
Of sleep, oppress thee, or by fraud or
    power ?
Or thieves insidious thy fair flock sur-
    prise ? "
Thus they : the Cyclop from his den re-
    plies:
    ' " Friends, Noman kills me; Noman, in
    the hour
Of sleep, oppresses me with fraudful
    power."
" If no man hurt thee, but the hand divine
Inflict disease, it fits thee to resign:
To Jove or to thy father Neptune pray! "
The brethren cried, and instant strode
    away.   490
    ' Joy touch'd my secret soul and con-
    scious heart,
Pleas'd with th' effect of conduct and of
    art.
Meantime the Cyclop, raging with his
    wound,
Spreads his wide arms, and searches round
    and round:
At last, the stone removing from the gate,
With hands extended in the midst he sate:
And search'd each passing sheep, and felt
    it o'er,
Secure to seize us ere we reach'd the door
(Such as his shallow wit he deem'd was
    mine);
But secret I revolv'd the deep design: 500
'T was for our lives my lab'ring bosom
    wrought;
Each scheme I turn'd, and sharpen'd ev'ry
    thought;

This way and that I cast to save my friends,
Till one resolve my varying counsel ends.
    ' Strong were the rams, with native pur-
    ple fair,
Well fed, and largest of the fleecy care.
These, three and three, with osier bands
    we tied
(The twining bands the Cyclop's bed sup-
    plied);
The midmost bore a man, the outward two
Secured each side : so bound we all the
    crew.   510
One ram remain'd, the leader of the flock;
In his deep fleece my grasping hands I
    lock,
And fast beneath, in woolly curls inwove,
There cling implicit, and confide in Jove.
When rosy morning glimmer'd o'er the
    dales,
He drove to pasture all the lusty males:
The ewes still folded, with distended thighs
Unmilk'd, lay bleating in distressful cries.
But heedless of those cares, with anguish
    stung,
He felt their fleeces as they pass'd along, 520
(Fool that he was), and let them safely
    go,
All unsuspecting of their freight below.
    ' The master ram at last approach'd the
    gate,
Charged with his wool, and with Ulysses'
    fate.
Him, while he pass'd, the monster blind be-
    spoke:
" What makes my ram the lag of all the
    flock ?
First thou wert wont to crop the flow'ry
    mead,
First to the field and river's bank to lead;
And first with stately step at ev'ning hour
Thy fleecy fellows usher to their bower. 530
Now far the last, with pensive pace and
    slow
Thou mov'st, as conscious of thy master's
    woe !
Seest thou these lids that now unfold in
    vain ?
(The deed of Noman and his wicked train!)
Oh! didst thou feel for thy afflicted lord,
And would but Fate the power of speech
    afford,
Soon might'st thou tell me, where in secret
    here
The dastard lurks, all trembling with his
    fear:

Swung round and round, and dash'd from
rock to rock,
His batter'd brains should on the pavement
smoke. 540
No ease, no pleasure my sad heart receives,
While such a monster as vile Noman
lives."
'The giant spoke, and thro' the hollow
rock
Dismiss'd the ram, the father of the flock.
No sooner freed, and thro' th' inclosure
pass'd,
First I release myself, my fellows last:
Fat sheep and goats in throngs we drive
before,
And reach our vessel on the winding shore.
With joy the sailors view their friends re-
turn'd,
And hail us living, whom as dead they
mourn'd. 550
Big tears of transport stand in ev'ry eye:
I check their fondness, and command to fly.
Aboard in haste they heave the wealthy
sheep,
And snatch their oars, and rush into the
deep.
'Now off at sea, and from the shallows
clear,
As far as human voice could reach the ear,
With taunts the distant giant I accost:
"Hear me, O Cyclop! hear, ungracious
host!
'T was on no coward, no ignoble slave,
Thou meditat'dst thy meal in yonder cave;
But one the vengeance fated from above 561
Doom'd to inflict; the instrument of Jove.
Thy barb'rous breach of hospitable bands
The God, the God revenges by my hands."
'These words the Cyclop's burning rage
provoke;
From the tall hill he rends a pointed rock;
High o'er the billows flew the massy load,
And near the ship came thund'ring on the
flood.
It almost brush'd the helm, and fell before:
The whole sea shook, and refluent beat the
shore. 570
The strong concussion on the heaving tide
Roll'd back the vessel to the island's side:
Again I shov'd her off; our fate to fly,
Each nerve we stretch, and ev'ry oar we ply.
Just 'scaped impending death, when now
again
We twice as far had furrow'd back the
main,

Once more I raise my voice; my friends,
afraid,
With mild entreaties my design dissuade:
"What boots the godless giant to provoke,
Whose arm may sink us at a single
stroke? 580
Already, when the dreadful rock he threw,
Old Ocean shook, and back his surges
flew.
The sounding voice directs his aim again;
The rock o'erwhelms us, and we 'scaped in
vain."
'But I, of mind elate, and scorning fear,
Thus with new taunts insult the monster's
ear:
"Cyclop! if any, pitying thy disgrace,
Ask who disfigured thus that eyeless face?
Say 't was Ulysses; 't was his deed, de-
clare,
Laërtes' son, of Ithaca the fair; 590
Ulysses, far in fighting fields renown'd,
Before whose arm Troy tumbled to the
ground."
'Th' astonish'd savage with a roar re-
plies:
"Oh Heav'ns! oh faith of ancient pro-
phecies!
This Telemus Eurymedes foretold
(The mighty seer who on these hills grew
old;
Skill'd the dark fates of mortals to de-
clare,
And learn'd in all wing'd omens of the
air);
Long since he menaced, such was Fate's
command; 599
And named Ulysses' as the destin'd hand.
I deem'd some godlike giant to behold,
Or lofty hero, haughty, brave, and bold;
Not this weak pigmy-wretch, of mean
design,
Who not by strength subdued me, but by
wine.
But come, accept our gifts, and join to pray
Great Neptune's blessing on the wat'ry
way;
For his I am, and I the lineage own;
Th' immortal father no less boasts the son.
His power can heal me, and re-light my
eye;
And only his, of all the Gods on high." 610
'"Oh! could this arm" (I thus aloud
rejoin'd)
"From that vast bulk dislodge thy bloody
mind,

And send thee howling to the realms of
night,
As sure as Neptune cannot give thee
sight!"
'Thus I; while raging he repeats his cries,
With hands uplifted to the starry skies:
"Hear me, O Neptune; thou whose arms
are hurl'd
From shore to shore, and gird the solid
world.
If thine I am, nor thou my birth disown,
And if th' unhappy Cyclop be thy son, 620
Let not Ulysses breathe his native air,
Laërtes' son, of Ithaca the fair!
If to review his country be his fate,
Be it thro' toils and suff'rings, long and late;
His lost companions let him first deplore;
Some vessel, not his own, transport him
o'er;
And when at home from foreign suff'rings
freed,
More near and deep, domestic woes suc-
ceed!"
'With imprecations thus he fill'd the air,
And angry Neptune heard th' unrighteous
prayer. 630
A larger rock then heaving from the plain,
He whirl'd it round; it sung across the
main;
It fell, and brush'd the stern: the billows
roar,
Shake at the weight, and refluent beat the
shore.
'With all our force we kept aloof to sea,
And gain'd the island where our vessels
lay.
Our sight the whole collected navy cheer'd,
Who, waiting long, by turns had hoped and
fear'd.
There, disembarking on the green sea side,
We land our cattle, and the spoil divide: 640
Of these due shares to ev'ry sailor fall;
The master ram was voted mine by all:
And him (the guardian of Ulysses' fate)
With pious mind to Heav'n I consecrate.
But the great God, whose thunder rends
the skies,
Averse, beholds the smoking sacrifice;
And sees me wand'ring still from coast to
coast:
And all my vessels, all my people, lost!
While thoughtless we indulge the genial
rite,
As plenteous cates and flowing bowls in-
vite; 650

Till ev'ning Phœbus roll'd away the light:
Stretch'd on the shores in careless ease we
rest,
Till ruddy morning purpled o'er the east;
Then from their anchors all our ships un-
bind,
And mount the decks, and call the willing
wind.
Now ranged in order on our banks, we
sweep
With hasty strokes the hoarse resounding
deep;
Blind to the future, pensive with our fears,
Glad for the living, for the dead in tears.'

BOOK X

ADVENTURES WITH ÆOLUS, THE LÆSTRY-
GONS, AND CIRCE

ARGUMENT

Ulysses arrives at the island of Æolus, who
gives him prosperous winds, and incloses the
adverse ones in a bag, which his companions
untying, they are driven back again, and rejected. Then they sail to the Læstrygons,
where they lose eleven ships, and, with one
only remaining, proceed to the island of
Circe. Eurylochus is sent first with some
companions, all which, except Eurylochus,
are transformed into swine. Ulysses then
undertakes the adventure, and by the help
of Mercury, who gives him the herb Moly,
overcomes the enchantress, and procures the
restoration of his men. After a year's stay
with her, he prepares, at her instigation, for
his voyage to the infernal shades.

'AT length we reach'd Æolia's sea-girt
shore,
Where great Hippotades the sceptre bore,
A floating isle! High rais'd by toil divine,
Strong walls of brass the rocky coast con-
fine.
Six blooming youths, in private grandeur
bred,
And six fair daughters, graced the royal
bed:
These sons their sisters wed, and all re-
main
Their parents' pride, and pleasure of their
reign.
All day they feast, all day the bowls flow
round,
And joy and music thro' the isle resound: 10

At night each pair on splendid carpets
lay,
And crown'd with love the pleasures of the
day.
'This happy port affords our wand'ring
fleet
A month's reception, and a safe retreat.
Full oft the Monarch urged me to relate
The fall of Ilion, and the Grecian Fate;
Full oft I told ; at length for parting
mov'd;
The King with mighty gifts my suit ap-
prov'd.
The adverse winds in leathern bags he
braced,
Compress'd their force, and lock'd each
struggling blast: 20
For him the mighty Sire of Gods assign'd
The tempest's lord, the Tyrant of the
Wind:
His word alone the list'ning storms obey,
To smooth the deep, or swell the foamy
sea.
These in my hollow ship the Monarch hung,
Securely fetter'd by a silver thong:
But Zephyrus exempt, with friendly ⎫
gales   ⎪
He charged to fill and guide the swelling ⎬
sails: ⎪
Rare gift! but O, what gift to fools avails ? ⎭
'Nine prosp'rous days we plied the la-
b'ring oar;   30
The tenth presents our welcome native
shore:
The hills display the beacon's friendly
light,
And rising mountains gain upon our sight.
Then first my eyes, by watchful toils op-
press'd,
Complied to take the balmy gifts of rest:
Then first my hands did from the rudder
part
(So much the love of home possess'd my
heart):
When lo! on board a fond debate arose,
What rare device those vessels might in-
close ?
What sum, what prize from Æolus I
brought ?   40
Whilst to his neighbour each express'd his
thought:
' " Say, whence, ye Gods, contending na-
tions strive
Who most shall please, who most our hero
give ?

Long have his coffers groan'd with Trojan
spoils;
Whilst we, the wretched partners of his
toils,
Reproach'd by want, our fruitless labours
mourn,
And only rich in barren fame return.
Now Æolus, ye see, augments his store:
But come, my friends, these mystic gifts
explore."
They said: and (oh curs'd Fate!) the thongs
unbound;   50
The gushing tempest sweeps the ocean
round;
Snatch'd in the whirl, the hurried navy
flew,
The ocean widen'd, and the shores with-
drew.
Rous'd from my fatal sleep, I long de-
bate
If still to live, or desp'rate plunge to
fate;
Thus doubting, prostrate on the deck I
lay,
Till all the coward thoughts of death gave
way.
'Meanwhile our vessels plough the ⎫
liquid plain,   ⎪
And soon the known Æolian coast regain; ⎬
Our groans the rocks remurmur'd to the ⎪
main.   60 ⎭
We leap'd on shore, and with a scanty
feast
Our thirst and hunger hastily repress'd;
That done, two chosen heralds straight at-
tend
Our second progress to my royal friend:
And him amidst his jovial sons we found;
The banquet steaming, and the goblets
crown'd:
There humbly stopp'd with conscious shame
and awe,
Nor nearer than the gate presumed to
draw.
But soon his sons their well-known guest
descried,
And, starting from their couches, loudly
cried,   70
" Ulysses here ! what dæmon couldst thou
meet
To thwart thy passage, and repel thy fleet ?
Wast thou not furnish'd by our choicest
care
For Greece, for home, and all thy soul held
dear ? "

Thus they ; in silence long my fate I
   mourn'd,
At length these words with accent low
   return'd:
" Me, lock'd in sleep, my faithless crew
   bereft
Of all the blessings of your godlike gift!
But grant, oh grant our loss we may re-
   trieve;
A favour you, and you alone can give." 80
   ' Thus I with art to move their pity
     tried,
And touch'd the youths ; but their stern
   Sire replied:
" Vile wretch, begone! this instant I com-
   mand
Thy fleet accurs'd to leave our hallow'd
   land.
His baneful suit pollutes these bless'd
   abodes,
Whose Fate proclaims him hateful to the
   Gods."
   ' Thus fierce he said: we sighing went
     our way,
And with desponding hearts put off to
   sea.
The sailors spent with toils their folly
   mourn,   89
But mourn in vain; no prospect of return.
Six days and nights a doubtful course we ⎫
   steer;   ⎪
The next proud Lamos' stately towers ⎬
   appear,   ⎪
And Læstrygonia's gates arise distinct in ⎪
   air.   ⎭
The shepherd, quitting here at night the
   plain,
Calls, to succeed his cares, the watchful
   swain;
But he that scorns the chains of sleep to
   wear,
And adds the herdsman's to the shepherd's
   care,
So near the pastures, and so short the ⎫
   way,   ⎪
His double toils may claim a double pay, ⎬
And join the labours of the night and ⎪
   day.   100 ⎭
   ' Within a long recess a bay there lies,
Edg'd round with cliffs high pointing to
   the skies;
The jutting shores that swell on either
   side
Contract its mouth, and break the rushing
   tide.

Our eager sailors seize the fair retreat,
And bound within the port their crowded
   fleet;
For here retired the sinking billows sleep,
And smiling calmness silver'd o'er the
   deep.
I only in the bay refused to moor,   109
And fix'd, without, my halsers to the shore.
   ' From thence we climb'd a point, whose
     airy brow
Commands the prospect of the plains be-
   low:
No tracks of beasts, or signs of men, we
   found,
But smoky volumes rolling from the ground.
Two with our herald thither we command,
With speed to learn what men possess'd the
   land.
They went, and kept the wheel's smooth
   beaten road
Which to the city drew the mountain
   wood;
When lo! they met, beside a crystal spring,
The daughter of Antiphates the king;   120
She to Artacia's silver streams came down
(Artacia's streams alone supply the town);
The damsel they approach, and ask'd what
   race
The people were ? who Monarch of the
   place ?
With joy the maid th' unwary strangers
   heard,
And show'd them where the royal dome
   appear'd.
They went; but, as they ent'ring saw the
   Queen
Of size enormous, and terrific mien
(Not yielding to some bulky mountain's
   height),   129
A sudden horror struck their aching sight.
Swift at her call her husband scour'd
   away
To wreak his hunger on the destin'd
   prey;
One for his food the raging glutton slew,
But two rush'd out, and to the navy flew.
   ' Balk'd of his prey, the yelling monster
     flies,
And fills the city with his hideous cries:
A ghastly band of giants hear the roar,
And, pouring down the mountains, crowd
   the shore.
Fragments they rend from off the craggy
   brow,
And dash the ruins on the ships below: 140

The crackling vessels burst; hoarse groans
    arise,
And mingled horrors echo to the skies:
The men, like fish, they stuck upon the flood,
And cramm'd their filthy throats with hu-
    man food.
Whilst thus their fury rages at the bay,
My sword our cables cut, I call'd to weigh;
And charged my men, as they from Fate
    would fly,
Each nerve to strain, each bending oar to
    ply.
The sailors catch the word, their oars they
    seize,
And sweep with equal strokes the smoky
    seas.   150
Clear of the rocks th' impatient vessel flies;
Whilst in the port each wretch encumber'd
    dies.
With earnest haste my frighted sailors
    press,
While kindling transports glow'd at our
    success;
But the sad fate that did our friends de-
    stroy,
Cool'd every breast, and damp'd the rising
    joy.
' Now dropp'd our anchors in the Ææan
    bay,
Where Circe dwelt, the Daughter of the
    Day!
Her mother Persè, of old Ocean's strain,
Thus from the Sun descended, and the
    Main   160
(From the same lineage stern Æætes came,
The far-famed brother of th' enchantress
    dame):
Goddess, and Queen, to whom the powers
    belong
Of dreadful magic, and commanding song.
Some God directing, to this peaceful bay
Silent we came, and melancholy lay,
Spent and o'erwatch'd.   Two days and
    nights roll'd on,
And now the third succeeding morning
    shone.
I climb'd a cliff, with spear and sword in
    hand,
Whose ridge o'erlook'd a shady length of
    land;   170
To learn if aught of mortal works appear,
Or cheerful voice of mortal strike the ear ?
From the high point I mark'd, in distant
    view,
A stream of curling smoke ascending blue,

And spiry tops, the tufted trees above,
Of Circe's palace bosom'd in the grove.
  ' Thither to haste, the region to explore,
Was first my thought: but, speeding back
    to shore,
I deem'd it best to visit first my crew,
And send out spies the dubious coast to
    view.   180
As down the hill I solitary go,
Some Power divine, who pities human woe,
Sent a tall stag, descending from the
    wood,
To cool his fervour in the crystal flood;
Luxuriant on the wave-worn bank he lay,
Stretch'd forth and panting in the sunny
    ray.
I launch'd my spear, and with a sudden
    wound
Transpierc'd his back, and fix'd him to the
    ground.
He falls, and mourns his fate with human
    cries:
Thro' the wide wound the vital spirit
    flies.   190
I drew, and casting on the river's side ⎤
The bloody spear, his gather'd feet I tied ⎟
With twining osiers which the bank sup- ⎟
    plied.   ⎦
An ell in length the pliant wisp I weav'd,
And the huge body on my shoulders
    heav'd:
Then, leaning on my spear with both my
    hands,
Upbore my load, and press'd the sinking
    sands
With weighty steps, till at the ship I
    threw
The welcome burden, and bespoke my
    crew:
  ' " Cheer up, my friends ! it is not yet
    our fate   200
To glide with ghosts thro' Pluto's gloomy
    gate.
Food in the desert land, behold ! is giv'n;
Live, and enjoy the providence of Heav'n."
  ' The joyful crew survey his mighty
    size,
And on the future banquet feast their
    eyes,
As huge in length extended lay the beast;
Then wash their hands, and hasten to the
    feast.
There, till the setting sun roll'd down the
    light,
They sate indulging in the genial rite.

When ev'ning rose, and darkness cover'd
   o'er   210
The face of things, we slept along the
   shore.
But when the rosy morning warm'd the
   east,
My men I summon'd, and these words ad-
   dress'd:
' " Foll'wers and Friends ! attend what I
   propose,
Ye sad companions of Ulysses' woes !
We know not here what land before us
   lies,
Or to what quarter now we turn our
   eyes,
Or where the sun shall set, or where
   shall rise.
Here let us think (if thinking be not vain)
If any counsel, any hope remain.   220
Alas ! from yonder promontory's brow
I view'd the coast, a region flat and low;
An isle encircled with the boundless flood;
A length of thickets, and entangled wood.
Some smoke I saw amidst the forest rise,
And all around it only seas and skies ! "
' With broken hearts my sad com-
   panions stood,
Mindful of Cyclops and his human food,
And horrid Læstrygons, the men of blood.
Presaging tears apace began to rain: 230
But tears in mortal miseries are vain.
In equal parts I straight divide my band,
And name a chief each party to command;
I led the one, and of the other side
Appointed brave Eurylochus the guide.
Then in the brazen helm the lots we
   throw,
And Fortune casts Eurylochus to go:
He march'd with twice eleven in his train;
Pensive they march, and pensive we re-
   main.
' The palace in a woody vale they found, 240
High rais'd of stone; a shaded space
   around;
Where mountain wolves and brindled lions
   roam
(By magic tamed), familiar to the dome.
With gentle blandishment our men they
   meet,
And wag their tails, and fawning lick their
   feet.
As from some feast a man returning late,
His faithful dogs all meet him at the gate,
Rejoicing round, some morsel to receive
(Such as the good man ever used to give),

Domestic thus the grisly beasts drew
   near;   250
They gaze with wonder not unmix'd with
   fear.
Now on the threshold of the dome they
   stood,
And heard a voice resounding thro' the
   wood:
Placed at her loom within, the Goddess
   sung;
The vaulted roofs and solid pavement
   rung.
O'er the fair web the rising figures shine,
Immortal labour ! worthy hands divine.
Polites to the rest the question mov'd
(A gallant leader, and a man I lov'd):
' " What voice celestial, chanting to the
   loom   260
(Or Nymph, or Goddess), echoes from the
   room ?
Say, shall we seek access ? " With that
   they call;
And wide unfold the portals of the hall.
' The Goddess, rising, asks her guests to
   stay,
Who blindly follow where she leads the
   way.
Eurylochus alone of all the band,
Suspecting fraud, more prudently remain'd.
On thrones around with downy cov'rings
   graced,
With semblance fair, th' unhappy men she
   placed.
Milk newly press'd, the sacred flour of
   wheat,   270
And honey fresh, and Pramnian wines the
   treat:
But venom'd was the bread, and mix'd the
   bowl,
With drugs of force to darken all the
   soul:
Soon in the luscious feast themselves they
   lost,
And drank oblivion of their native coast.
Instant her circling wand the Goddess
   waves,
To hogs transforms them, and the sty re-
   ceives.
No more was seen the human form divine;
Head, face, and members, bristle into
   swine:
Still curs'd with sense, their minds remain
   alone,   280
And their own voice affrights them when
   they groan.

Meanwhile the Goddess in disdain bestows
The mast and acorn, brutal food! and
strows
The fruits and cornel, as their feast,
around;
Now prone and grov'ling on unsav'ry
ground.
'Eurylochus, with pensive steps and slow,
Aghast returns; the messenger of woe,
And bitter fate. To speak he made es-
say;
In vain essay'd, nor would his tongue
obey.
His swelling heart denied the words
their way: 290
But speaking tears the want of words
supply,
And the full soul burst copious from his
eye.
Affrighted, anxious for our fellows' fates,
We press to hear what sadly he relates:
'"We went, Ulysses (such was thy
command),
Thro' the lone thicket and the desert land.
A palace in a woody vale we found,
Brown with dark forests, and with shades
around.
A voice celestial echoed thro' the dome,
Or Nymph or Goddess, chanting to the
loom. 300
Access we sought, nor was access denied:
Radiant she came; the portals open'd
wide:
The Goddess mild invites the guests to
stay:
They blindly follow where she leads the
way.
I only wait behind of all the train:
I waited long, and eyed the doors in vain:
The rest are vanish'd, none repass'd the
gate;
And not a man appears to tell their fate."
'I heard, and instant o'er my shoulder
flung
The belt in which my weighty faulchion
hung 310
(A beamy blade): then seiz'd the bended
bow,
And bade him guide the way, resolv'd to go.
He, prostrate falling, with both hands em-
braced
My knees, and weeping thus his suit ad-
dress'd:
'"O King, belov'd of Jove, thy servant
spare,

And ah, thyself the rash attempt forbear!
Never, alas! thou never shalt return,
Or see the wretched, for whose loss we
mourn.
With what remains from certain ruin fly,
And save the few not fated yet to die."
'I answer'd stern: "Inglorious then re-
main, 321
Here feast and loiter, and desert thy train.
Alone, unfriended, will I tempt my way;
The laws of Fate compel, and I obey."
'This said, and scornful turning from the
shore
My haughty step, I stalk'd the valley o'er.
Till now, approaching nigh the magic
bower,
Where dwelt th' enchantress skill'd in herbs
of power,
A form divine forth issued from the wood
(Immortal Hermes with the golden rod), 330
In human semblance. On his bloomy face
Youth smiled celestial, with each opening
grace.
He seiz'd my hand, and gracious thus be-
gan:
'"Ah whither roam'st thou, much-endur-
ing man?
O blind to Fate! what led thy steps to rove
The horrid mazes of this magic grove?
Each friend you seek in yon enclosure lies,
All lost their form, and habitants of sties.
Think'st thou by wit to model their escape?
Sooner shalt thou, a stranger to thy shape,
Fall prone their equal: first thy danger
know, 341
Then take the antidote the Gods bestow.
The plant I give thro' all the direful bower
Shall guard thee, and avert the evil hour.
Now hear her wicked arts. Before thy eyes
The bowl shall sparkle, and the banquet
rise;
Take this, nor from the faithless feast ab-
stain,
For temper'd drugs and poison shall be
vain.
Soon as she strikes her wand, and gives the
word,
Draw forth and brandish thy refulgent
sword, 350
And menace death: those menaces shall
move
Her alter'd mind to blandishment and love.
Nor shun the blessing proffer'd to thy
arms.
Ascend her bed, and taste celestial charms:

So shall thy tedious toils a respite find,
And thy lost friends return to human-kind.
But swear her first by those dread oaths
   that tie
The powers below, the blessed in the sky;
Lest to thee naked secret fraud be meant,
Or magic bind thee cold and impotent." 360
  'Thus while he spoke, the sov'reign
   plant he drew,
Where on th' all-bearing earth unmark'd
  it grew,
And show'd its nature and its wondrous
  power:
Black was the root, but milky white the
  flower;
Moly the name, to mortals hard to find,
But all is easy to th' ethereal kind.
This Hermes gave, then, gliding off the
  glade,
Shot to Olympus from the woodland shade.
While, full of thought, revolving fates to
  come, 369
I speed my passage to th' enchanted dome.
Arrived, before the lofty gates I stay'd;
The lofty gates the Goddess wide display'd:
She leads before, and to the feast invites;
I follow sadly to the magic rites.
Radiant with starry studs, a silver seat
Receiv'd my limbs: a footstool eas'd my
  feet.
She mix'd the potion, fraudulent of soul;
The poison mantled in the golden bowl.
I took, and quaff'd it, confident in Heav'n:
Then waved the wand, and then the word
  was giv'n. 380
"Hence to thy fellows!" (dreadful she
  began)
"Go, be a beast!"—I heard, and yet was
  man.
  'Then sudden whirling, like a waving
  flame,
My beamy faulchion, I assault the dame.
Struck with unusual fear, she trembling
  cries,
She faints, she falls; she lifts her weeping
  eyes.
  '"What art thou? say! from whence,
  from whom you came?
O more than human! tell thy race, thy
  name.
Amazing strength, these poisons to sustain!
Not mortal thou, nor mortal is thy brain. 390
Or art thou he, the man to come (foretold
By Hermes, powerful with the wand of
  gold),

The man from Troy, who wander'd ocean
  round;
The man for wisdom's various arts re-
  nown'd,
Ulysses? Oh! thy threat'ning fury cease,
Sheathe thy bright sword, and join our
  hands in peace!
Let mutual joys our mutual trust combine,
And love, and love-born confidence be
  thine."
  '"And how, dread Circe!" (furious I
  rejoin)
"Can love, and love-born confidence, be
  mine, 400
Beneath thy charms when my companions
  groan,
Transform'd to beasts, with accents not
  their own?
O thou of fraudful heart, shall I be led
To share thy feast-rites, or ascend thy bed;
That, all unarm'd, thy vengeance may have
  vent,
And magic bind me cold and impotent?
Celestial as thou art, yet stand denied;
Or swear that oath by which the Gods are
  tied,
Swear, in thy soul no latent frauds remain,
Swear by the vow which never can be
  vain." 410
  'The Goddess swore: then seiz'd my
  hand and led
To the sweet transports of the genial bed.
Ministrant to the Queen, with busy care
Four faithful handmaids the soft rites pre-
  pare;
Nymphs sprung from fountains, or from
  shady woods,
Or the fair offspring of the sacred floods.
One o'er the couches painted carpets threw,
Whose purple lustre glow'd against the
  view:
White linen lay beneath. Another placed
The silver stands, with golden flaskets
  graced: 420
With dulcet bev'rage this the beaker crown'd
Fair in the midst, with gilded cups around;
That in the tripod o'er the kindled pile
The water pours; the bubbling waters boil;
An ample vase receives the smoking wave;
And, in the bath prepared, my limbs I lave:
Reviving sweets repair the mind's decay,
And take the painful sense of toil away.
A vest and tunic o'er me next she threw,
Fresh from the bath, and dropping balmy
  dew. 430

Then led and placed me on the sov'reign
  seat,
With carpets spread; a footstool at my
  feet.
The golden ewer a nymph obsequious
  brings,
Replenish'd from the cool translucent
  springs;
With copious water the bright vase sup-
  plies
A silver laver of capacious size.
I wash'd. The table in fair order spread,
They heap the glitt'ring canisters with
  bread;
Viands of various kinds allure the taste,
Of choicest sort and savour, rich repast ! 440
Circe in vain invites the feast to share;
Absent I ponder, and absorb'd in care:
While scenes of woe rose anxious in my
  breast,
The Queen beheld me, and these words
  address'd:
' " Why sits Ulysses silent and apart,
Some hoard of grief close harbour'd at his
  heart ?
Untouch'd before thee stand the cates
  divine,
And unregarded laughs the rosy wine.
Can yet a doubt or any dread remain,
When sworn that oath which never can be
  vain ? "   450
' I answered: " Goddess ! human is my
  breast,
By justice sway'd, by tender pity press'd:
Ill fits it me, whose friends are sunk to
  beasts,
To quaff thy bowls, or riot in thy feasts.
Me would'st thou please ? for them thy
  cares employ,
And them to me restore, and me to joy."
  ' With that she parted : in her potent
  hand
She bore the virtue of the magic wand.
Then, hast'ning to the sties, set wide the
  door,
Urged forth, and drove the bristly herd
  before;   460
Unwieldy, out they rush'd with gen'ral
  cry,
Enormous beasts dishonest to the eye.
Now, touch'd by counter-charms, they
  change again,
And stand majestic, and recall'd to men.
Those hairs of late that bristled ev'ry part,
Fall off, miraculous effect of art !

Till all the form in full proportion rise,
More young, more large, more graceful to
  my eyes.
They saw, they knew me, and with eager
  pace   469
Clung to their master in a long embrace :
Sad, pleasing sight ! with tears each eye
  ran o'er,
And sobs of joy re-echoed thro' the bower ;
Ev'n Circe wept, her adamantine heart
Felt pity enter, and sustain'd her part.
  ' " Son of Laërtes ! " (then the Queen be-
  gan)
" Oh much-enduring, much-experienc'd man !
Haste to thy vessel on the sea-beat shore,
Unload thy treasures, and the galley moor;
Then bring thy friends, secure from future
  harms,
And in our grottoes stow thy spoils and
  arms."   480
  ' She said. Obedient to her high com-
  mand
I quit the place, and hasten to the strand.
My sad companions on the beach I found,
Their wistful eyes in floods of sorrow
  drown'd.
As from fresh pastures and the dewy field
(When loaded cribs their ev'ning banquet
  yield),
The lowing herds return; around them
  throng
With leaps and bounds their late impris-
  on'd young,
Rush to their mothers with unruly joy,
And echoing hills return the tender cry: 490
So round me press'd, exulting at my sight,
With cries and agonies of wild delight,
The weeping sailors; nor less fierce their
  joy
Than if return'd to Ithaca from Troy.
" Ah master ! ever honour'd, ever dear ! "
(These tender words on ev'ry side I hear)
" What other joy can equal thy return ?
Not that lov'd country for whose sight we
  mourn,
The soil that nurs'd us, and that gave us
  breath :   499
But ah ! relate our lost companions' death."
  ' I answer'd cheerful: " Haste, your gal-
  ley moor
And bring our treasures and our arms
  ashore:
Those in yon hollow caverns let us lay;
Then rise, and follow where I lead the
  way.

Your fellows live; believe your eyes, and
come
To taste the joys of Circe's sacred dome."
'With ready speed the joyful crew obey;
Alone Eurylochus persuades their stay.
'"Whither" (he cried), "ah whither will
ye run?
Seek ye to meet those evils ye should
shun? 510
Will you the terrors of the dome explore,
In swine to grovel, or in lions roar,
Or wolf-like howl away the midnight hour
In dreadful watch around the magic
bower?
Remember Cyclops, and his bloody deed;
The leader's rashness made the soldiers
bleed."
'I heard incens'd, and first resolv'd to
speed
My flying faulchion at the rebel's head.
Dear as he was, by ties of kindred bound,
This hand had stretch'd him breathless on
the ground; 520
But all at once my interposing train
For mercy pleaded, nor could plead in vain:
"Leave here the man who dares his Prince
desert,
Leave to repentance and his own sad heart,
To guard the ship. Seek we the sacred
shades
Of Circe's palace, where Ulysses leads."
'This with one voice declared, the rising
train
Left the black vessel by the murm'ring
main.
Shame touch'd Eurylochus's alter'd breast;
He fear'd my threats, and follow'd with
the rest. 530
'Meanwhile the Goddess, with indulgent
cares
And social joys, the late transform'd re-
pairs;
The bath, the feast, their fainting soul re-
news;
Rich in refulgent robes, and dropping
balmy dews:
Bright'ning with joy their eager eyes be-
hold
Each other's face, and each his story told;
Then gushing tears the narrative confound,
And with their sobs the vaulted roofs re-
sound.
When hush'd their passion, thus the God-
dess cries:
"Ulysses, taught by labours to be wise, 540

Let this short memory of grief suffice.
To me are known the various woes ye bore,
In storms by sea, in perils on the shore;
Forget whatever was in Fortune's power,
And share the pleasures of this genial hour.
Such be your minds as ere ye left the coast,
Or learn'd to sorrow for a country lost.
Exiles and wand'rers now, where'er ye go,
Too faithful memory renews your woe: 549
The cause remov'd, habitual griefs remain,
And the soul saddens by the use of pain."
'Her kind entreaty mov'd the gen'ral
breast;
Tired with long toil, we willing sunk to
rest.
We plied the banquet, and the bowl we
crown'd,
Till the full circle of the year came round.
But when the seasons, foll'wing in their
train,
Brought back the months, the days, and
hours again,
As from a lethargy at once they rise,
And urge their chief with animating cries:
'"Is this, Ulysses, our inglorious lot? 560
And is the name of Ithaca forgot?
Shall never the dear land in prospect rise,
Or the lov'd palace glitter in our eyes?"
'Melting I heard: yet till the sun's de-
cline
Prolong'd the feast, and quaff'd the rosy
wine:
But when the shades came on at ev'ning
hour,
And all lay slumb'ring in the dusky bower,
I came a suppliant to fair Circe's bed,
The tender moment seiz'd, and thus I said:
"Be mindful, Goddess! of thy promise
made; 570
Must sad Ulysses ever be delay'd?
Around their lord my sad companions
mourn,
Each breast beats homeward, anxious to
return:
If but a moment parted from thy eyes,
Their tears flow round me, and my heart
complies."
'"Go then" (she cried), "ah go! yet
think not I,
Not Circe, but the Fates, your wish deny.
Ah hope not yet to breathe thy native air!
Far other journey first demands thy care;
To tread th' uncomfortable paths beneath,
And view the realms of darkness and of
death. 581

There seek the Theban bard, deprived of
  sight;
Within, irradiate with prophetic light;
To whom Persephonè, entire and whole,
Gave to retain th' unseparated soul:
The rest are forms, of empty ether made;
Impassive semblance, and a flitting shade."
  'Struck at the word, my very heart was
  dead:
Pensive I sate: my tears bedew'd the bed:
To hate the light and life my soul begun,
And saw that all was grief beneath the
  sun.   591
Composed at length, the gushing tears sup-
  press'd,
And my toss'd limbs now wearied into
  rest,
"How shall I tread" (I cried), "ah, Circe!
  say,
The dark descent, and who shall guide the
  way ?
Can living eyes behold the realms below ?
What bark to waft me, and what wind to
  blow ? "
  '"Thy fated road" (the magic Power
  replied),
"Divine Ulysses! asks no mortal guide.
Rear but the mast, the spacious sail dis-
  play,   600
The northern winds shall wing thee on thy
  way.
Soon shalt thou reach old Ocean's utmost
  ends,
Where to the main the shelving shore de-
  scends :
The barren trees of Proserpine's black
  woods,
Poplars and willows trembling o'er the
  floods;
There fix thy vessel in the lonely bay,
And enter there the kingdoms void of day :
Where Phlegethon's loud torrents, rushing
  down,
Hiss in the flaming gulf of Acheron;
And where, slow-rolling from the Stygian
  bed,   610
Cocytus' lamentable waters spread:
Where the dark rock o'erhangs th' infernal
  lake,
And mingling streams eternal murmurs
  make.
First draw thy faulchion, and on ev'ry
  side
Trench the black earth a cubit long and
  wide:

To all the shades around libations pour,
And o'er th' ingredients strew the hallow'd
  flour:
New wine and milk, with honey temper'd
  bring,
And living water from the crystal spring.
Then the wan shades and feeble ghosts
  implore,   620
With promis'd off'rings on thy native
  shore:
A barren cow, the stateliest of the isle,
And, heap'd with various wealth, a blazing
  pile:
These to the rest; but to the seer must
  bleed
A sable ram, the pride of all thy breed.
These solemn vows, and holy off'rings,
  paid
To all the phantom nations of the dead,
Be next thy care the sable sheep to place
Full o'er the pit, and hellward turn their
  face;
But from th' infernal rite thine eye with-
  draw,   630
And back to Ocean glance with rev'rent
  awe.
Sudden shall skim along the dusky glades
Thin airy shoals, and visionary shades.
Then give command the sacrifice to haste,
Let the flay'd victims in the flame be cast,
And sacred vows and mystic song applied
To grisly Pluto and his gloomy bride.
Wide o'er the pool thy faulchion waved
  around
Shall drive the spectres from forbidden
  ground:
The sacred draught shall all the dead for-
  bear,   640
Till awful from the shades arise the seer.
Let him, oraculous, the end, the way,
The turns of all thy future fate display,
Thy pilgrimage to come, and remnant of
  thy day."
  'So speaking, from the ruddy orient
  shone
The Morn, conspicuous on her golden
  throne.
The Goddess with a radiant tunic dress'd
My limbs, and o'er me cast a silken vest.
Long flowing robes, of purest white, ar-
  ray   649
The Nymph, that added lustre to the day:
A tiar wreath'd her head with many a
  fold;
Her waist was circled with a zone of gold.

Forth issuing then, from place to place I
  flew;
Rouse man by man, and animate my crew.
" Rise, rise, my mates! 't is Circe gives com-
  mand:
Our journey calls us: haste, and quit the
  land."
All rise and follow, yet depart not all,
For Fate decreed one wretched man to fall.
'A youth there was, Elpenor was he
  named,
Not much for sense, nor much for courage
  famed: 660
The youngest of our band, a vulgar soul,
Born but to banquet, and to drain the
  bowl.
He, hot and careless, on a turret's height
With sleep repair'd the long debauch of
  night:
The sudden tumult stirr'd him where he
  lay,
And down he hasten'd, but forgot the way;
Full headlong from the roof the sleeper
  fell,
And snapp'd the spinal joint, and waked in
  Hell.
'The rest crowd round me with an eager
  look;
I met them with a sigh, and thus be-
  spoke: 670
" Already, friends! ye think your toils are
  o'er,
Your hopes already touch your native shore:
Alas! far otherwise the Nymph declares,
Far other journey first demands our cares:
To tread th' uncomfortable paths beneath,
The dreary realms of darkness and of
  death;
To seek Tiresias' awful shade below,
And thence our fortunes and our fates to
  know."
'My sad companions heard in deep de-
  spair;
Frantic they tore their manly growth of
  hair;   680
To earth they fell; the tears began to rain;
But tears in mortal miseries are vain.
Sadly they fared along the sea-beat shore:
Still heav'd their hearts, and still their eyes
  ran o'er.
The ready victims at our bark we found,
The sable ewe and ram, together bound.
For, swift as thought, the Goddess had been
  there,
And thence had glided viewless as the air:

The paths of Gods what mortal can survey?
Who eyes their motion? who shall trace
  their way?'   690

BOOK XIII

THE ARRIVAL OF ULYSSES IN ITHACA

THE ARGUMENT

Ulysses takes his leave of Alcinoüs and Aretè,
and embarks in the evening. Next morning
the ship arrives at Ithaca; where the sailors,
as Ulysses is yet sleeping, lay him on the
shore with all his treasures. On their return, Neptune changes their ship into a rock.
In the mean time, Ulysses awaking, knows
not his native Ithaca, by reason of a mist
which Pallas had cast round him. He breaks
into loud lamentations; till the Goddess appearing to him in the form of a shepherd,
discovers the country to him, and points out
the particular places. He then tells a feigned
story of his adventures, upon which she
manifests herself, and they consult together
on the measures to be taken to destroy the
suitors. To conceal his return, and disguise
his person the more effectually, she changes
him into the figure of an old beggar.

HE ceas'd; but left so pleasing on their
  ear
His voice, that list'ning still they seem'd
  to hear.
A pause of silence hush'd the shady rooms:
The grateful conf'rence then the King re-
  sumes:
'Whatever toils the great Ulysses pass'd,
Beneath this happy roof they end at last;
No longer now from shore to shore to
  roam,
Smooth seas and gentle winds invite him
  home.
But hear me, Princes! whom these walls
  enclose,
For whom my chanter sings, and goblet
  flows   10
With wine unmix'd (an honour due to age,
To cheer the grave, and warm the poet's
  rage),
Tho' labour'd gold, and many a dazzling
  vest
Lie heap'd already for our godlike guest:
Without new treasures let him not re-
  move,
Large, and expressive of the public love:

Each Peer a tripod, each a vase bestow,
A gen'ral tribute, which the state shall owe.'
  This sentence pleas'd: then all their steps
    address'd
To sep'rate mansions, and retired to rest. 20
  Now did the Rosy-finger'd Morn arise,
And shed her sacred light along the skies.
Down to the haven and the ships in haste
They bore the treasures, and in safety
    placed.
The King himself the vases ranged with
    care;
Then bade his foll'wers to the feast repair.
A victim ox beneath the sacred hand
Of great Alcinoüs falls, and stains the
    sand.
To Jove th' Eternal (Power above all
    Powers!
Who wings the winds, and darkens Heav'n
    with showers),   30
The flames ascend: till ev'ning they pro-
    long
The rites, more sacred made by heav'nly
    song:
For in the midst with public honours
    graced,
Thy lyre, divine Demodocus! was placed.
All, but Ulysses, heard with fix'd delight:
He sate, and eyed the sun, and wish'd the
    night:
Slow seem'd the sun to move, the hours to
    roll,
His native home deep-imaged in his soul.
As the tired ploughman spent with stub-
    born toil,
Whose oxen long have torn the furrow'd
    soil,   40
Sees with delight the sun's declining ray,
When home with feeble knees he bends his
    way
To late repast (the day's hard labour
    done),
So to Ulysses welcome set the sun;
Then instant to Alcinoüs and the rest
(The Scherian states) he turn'd, and thus
    address'd.
  'O thou, the first in merit and com-
    mand !
And you the Peers and Princes of the land!
May ev'ry joy be yours ! nor this the ⎤
    least, |
When due libation shall have crown'd ⎬
    the feast,   50 |
Safe to my home to send your happy |
    guest.   ⎦

Complete are now the bounties you have
    giv'n,
Be all those bounties but confirm'd by
    Heav'n !
So may I find, when all my wand'rings
    cease,
My consort blameless, and my friends in
    peace.
On you be ev'ry bliss; and ev'ry day,
In home-felt joys, delighted roll away:
Yourselves, your wives, your long-descend-
    ing race,
May ev'ry God enrich with ev'ry grace !
Sure fix'd on virtue may your nation
    stand,   60
And public evil never touch the land ! '
  His words well weigh'd, the gen'ral
    voice approv'd
Benign, and instant his dismission mov'd.
The Monarch to Pontonoüs gave the sign,
To fill the goblet high with rosy wine:
'Great Jove the Father first ' (he cried)
    'implore;
Then send the stranger to his native shore.'
  The luscious wine th' obedient herald
    brought;
Around the mansion flow'd the purple
    draught;
Each from his seat to each immortal
    pours,   70
Whom glory circles in th' Olympian
    bowers.
Ulysses sole with air majestic stands,
The bowl presenting to Aretè's hands;
Then thus: 'O Queen, farewell ! be still
    possess'd
Of dear remembrance, blessing still and
    bless'd !
Till age and death shall gently call thee
    hence
(Sure fate of ev'ry mortal excellence).
Farewell ! and joys successive ever spring
To thee, to thine, the people and the
    King ! '
  Thus he: then parting prints the sandy
    shore   80
To the fair port: a herald march'd before,
Sent by Alcinoüs; of Aretè's train
Three chosen maids attend him to the
    main:
This does a tunic and white vest convey,
A various casket that, of rich inlay,
And bread and wine the third. The cheer-
    ful mates
Safe in the hollow poop dispose the cates:

Upon the deck soft painted robes they
    spread,
With linen cover'd, for the hero's bed.
He climb'd the lofty stern; then gently
    press'd   90
The swelling couch, and lay composed to
    rest.
Now placed in order, the Phæacian train
Their cables loose, and launch into the
    main:
At once they bend, and strike their equal
    oars,
And leave the sinking hills and less'ning
    shores.
While on the deck the Chief in silence
    lies,
And pleasing slumbers steal upon his eyes.
As fiery coursers in the rapid race
Urged by fierce drivers thro' the dusty
    space,
Toss their high heads, and scour along the
    plain;   100
So mounts the bounding vessel o'er the
    main.
Back to the stern the parted billows flow,
And the black ocean foams and roars be-
    low.
    Thus with spread sails the winged galley
    flies;
Less swift an eagle cuts the liquid skies;
Divine Ulysses was her sacred load,
A man in wisdom equal to a God !
Much danger, long and mighty toils he
    bore,
In storms by sea, and combats on the
    shore:
All which soft sleep now banish'd from his
    breast,   110
Wrapp'd in a pleasing, deep, and death-
    like rest.
    But when the morning-star with early
    ray
Flamed in the front of Heav'n, and prom-
    is'd day,
Like distant clouds the mariner descries
Fair Ithaca's emerging hills arise.
Far from the town a spacious port appears,
Sacred to Phorcys' power, whose name it
    bears:
Two craggy rocks, projecting to the main,
The roaring wind's tempestuous rage re-
    strain;   119
Within, the waves in softer murmurs glide,
And ships secure without their halsers
    ride.

High at the head a branching olive grows,
And crowns the pointed cliffs with shady
    boughs.
Beneath, a gloomy grotto's cool recess
Delights the Nereids of the neighb'ring
    seas,
Where bowls and urns were form'd of liv-
    ing stone,
And massy beams in native marble shone:
On which the labours of the Nymphs were
    roll'd,
Their webs divine of purple mix'd with
    gold.
Within the cave the clust'ring bees at-
    tend   130
Their waxen works, or from the roof de-
    pend.
Perpetual waters o'er the pavement glide;
Two marble doors unfold on either side;
Sacred the south, by which the Gods de-
    scend;
But mortals enter at the northern end.
    Thither they bent, and haul'd their ship
    to land
(The crooked keel divides the yellow
    sand)
Ulysses sleeping on his couch they bore,
And gently placed him on the rocky shore.
His treasures next, Alcinoüs' gifts, they
    laid   140
In the wild olive's unfrequented shade,
Secure from theft; then launch'd the bark
    again,
Resumed their oars, and measured back
    the main.
    Nor yet forgot old Ocean's dread Su-
    preme
The vengeance vow'd for eyeless Poly-
    pheme.
Before the throne of mighty Jove he
    stood;
And sought the secret counsels of the God.
' Shall then no more, O Sire of Gods ! be
    mine
The rights and honours of a power divine ?
Scorn'd ev'n by man, and (oh severe dis-
    grace !)   150
By soft Phæacians, my degen'rate race !
Against yon destin'd head in vain I swore,
And menaced vengeance, ere he reach'd
    his shore;
To reach his natal shore was thy decree;
Mild I obey'd, for who shall war with thee ?
Behold him landed, careless and asleep,
From all th' eluded dangers of the deep;

Lo where he lies, amidst a shining store
Of brass, rich garments, and refulgent
    ore;
And bears triumphant to his native isle 160
A prize more worth than Ilion's noble
    spoil.'
    To whom the Father of th' immortal
        Powers,
Who swells the clouds, and gladdens earth
    with showers:
'Can mighty Neptune thus of man com-
    plain?
Neptune, tremendous o'er the boundless
    main!
Revered and awful ev'n in Heav'n's
    abodes,
Ancient and great! a God above the
    Gods!
If that low race offend thy power divine,
(Weak, daring creatures!) is not ven-
    geance thine?   169
Go then, the guilty at thy will chastise.'
He said. The Shaker of the Earth replies:
'This then I doom: to fix the gallant
    ship
A mark of vengeance on the sable deep;
To warn the thoughtless self-confiding
    train,
No more unlicens'd thus to brave the
    main.
Full in their port a shady hill shall rise,
If such thy will.' — 'We will it,' Jove re-
    plies.
'Ev'n when with transport, black'ning all
    the strand,
The swarming people hail their ship to
    land,
Fix her for ever, a memorial stone: 180
Still let her seem to sail, and seem alone.
The trembling crowds shall see the sud-
    den shade
Of whelming mountains overhang their
    head!'
    With that the God whose earthquakes
        rock the ground
Fierce to Phæacia cross'd the vast pro-
    found.
Swift as a swallow sweeps the liquid way,
The winged pinnace shot along the sea.
The God arrests her with a sudden stroke,
And roots her down an everlasting rock.
Aghast the Scherians stand in deep sur-
    prise;   190
All press to speak, all question with their
    eyes.

'What hands unseen the rapid bark re-
    strain?
And yet it swims, or seems to swim, the
    main!'
Thus they, unconscious of the deed divine:
Till great Alcinoüs, rising, own'd the sign.
'Behold the long-predestin'd day!' (he
    cries);
'O certain faith of ancient prophecies!
These ears have heard my royal sire dis-
    close
A dreadful story, big with future woes:
How, mov'd with wrath, that careless we
    convey   200
Promiscuous ev'ry guest to ev'ry bay,
Stern Neptune raged; and how by his
    command
Firm rooted in the surge a ship should
    stand
(A monument of wrath); and mound on
    mound
Should hide our walls, or whelm beneath
    the ground.
'The Fates have follow'd as declared the
    seer:
Be humbled, nations! and your Monarch
    hear.
No more unlicens'd brave the deeps, no
    more
With ev'ry stranger pass from shore to
    shore:
On angry Neptune now for mercy call; 210
To his high name let twelve black oxen
    fall.
So may the God reverse his purpos'd will,
Nor o'er our city hang the dreadful hill.'
    The Monarch spoke: they trembled and
        obey'd,
Forth on the sands the victim oxen led:
The gather'd tribes before the altars stand,
And Chiefs and rulers, a majestic band.
The King of Ocean all the tribes implore;
The blazing altars redden all the shore.
    Meanwhile Ulysses in his country lay,
Releas'd from sleep. and round him
    might survey   221
The solitary shore and rolling sea.
Yet had his mind thro' tedious absence
    lost
The dear resemblance of his native coast;
Besides, Minerva, to secure her care
Diffused around a veil of thicken'd air:
For so the Gods ordain'd, to keep unseen
His royal person from his friends and
    Queen:

Till the proud suitors for their crimes af-
    ford   229
An ample vengeance to their injured lord.
Now all the land another prospect bore,
Another port appear'd, another shore.
And long-continued ways, and winding
    floods,
And unknown mountains, crown'd with un-
    known woods.
Pensive and slow, with sudden grief op-
    press'd,
The King arose, and beat his careful breast,
Cast a long look o'er all the coast and main,
And sought, around, his native realm in
    vain:
Then with erected eyes stood fix'd in woe,
And, as he spoke, the tears began to flow:
    ' Ye Gods ' (he cried), ' upon what barren
    coast,   241
In what new region, is Ulysses toss'd ?
Possess'd by wild barbarians, fierce in arms?
Or men whose bosom tender pity warms ?
Where shall this treasure now in safety
    lie ?
And whither, whither its sad owner fly ?
Ah why did I Alcinoüs' grace implore ?
Ah why forsake Phæacia's happy shore ?
Some juster Prince perhaps had entertain'd,
And safe restor'd me to my native land. 250
Is this the promis'd, long-expected coast,
And this the faith Phæacia's rulers boast ?
O righteous Gods ! of all the great, how
    few
Are just to Heav'n, and to their promise
    true !
But he, the Power to whose all-seeing eyes
The deeds of men appear without disguise,
'T is his alone t' avenge the wrongs I bear:
For still th' oppress'd are his peculiar care.
To count these presents, and from thence
    to prove
Their faith, is mine: the rest belongs to
    Jove.'   260
    Then on the sands he ranged his wealthy
    store,
The gold, the vests, the tripods number'd
    o'er:
All these he found; but still, in error lost,
Disconsolate he wanders on the coast,
Sighs for his country, and laments again
To the deaf rocks, and hoarse resounding
    main.
When lo ! the guardian Goddess of the
    Wise,
Celestial Pallas, stood before his eyes;

In show a youthful swain, of form divine,
Who seem'd descended from some princely
    line.   270
A graceful robe her slender body dress'd;
Around her shoulders flew the waving vest;
Her decent hand a shining jav'lin bore,
And painted sandals on her feet she wore.
To whom the King: ' Whoe'er of human
    race
Thou art, that wander'st in this desert
    place,
With joy to thee, as to some God, I bend,
To thee my treasures and myself commend.
O tell a wretch in exile doom'd to stray,
What air I breathe, what country I sur-
    vey ?   280
The fruitful continent's extremest bound,
Or some fair isle which Neptune's arms
    surround ? '
    ' From what far clime ' (said she), ' re-
    mote from Fame,
Arrivest thou here, a stranger to our name ?
Thou seest an island, not to those unknown
Whose hills are brighten'd by the rising sun,
Nor those that placed beneath his utmost
    reign
Behold him sinking in the western main.
The rugged soil allows no level space
For flying chariots, or the rapid race;   290
Yet, not ungrateful to the peasant's pain,
Suffices fulness to the swelling grain:
The loaded trees their various fruits pro-
    duce,
And clust'ring grapes afford a gen'rous
    juice;
Woods crown our mountains, and in ev'ry
    grove
The bounding goats and frisking heifers
    rove:
Soft rains and kindly dews refresh the field,
And rising springs eternal verdure yield:
Ev'n to those shores is Ithaca renown'd,
Where Troy's majestic ruins strew the
    ground.'   300
    At this, the Chief with transport was
    possess'd;
His panting heart exulted in his breast:
Yet, well dissembling his untimely joys,
And veiling truth in plausible disguise,
Thus, with an air sincere, in fiction bold,
His ready tale th' inventive hero told:
    ' Oft have I heard in Crete this island's
    name;
For 't was from Crete, my native soil, I
    came,

Self-banish'd thence. I sail'd before the
    wind,
And left my children and my friends be-
    hind.   310
From fierce Idomeneus' revenge I flew,
Whose son, the swift Orsilochus, I slew
(With brutal force he seiz'd my Trojan
    prey,
Due to the toils of many a bloody day).
Unseen I 'scaped, and, favour'd by the
    night,
In a Phœnician vessel took my flight,
For Pyle or Elis bound: but tempests
    toss'd
And raging billows drove us on your coast.
In dead of night an unknown port we
    gain'd,
Spent with fatigue, and slept secure on
    land.   320
But ere the rosy morn renew'd the day,
While in th' embrace of pleasing sleep I
    lay,
Sudden, invited by auspicious gales,
They land my goods, and hoist their flying
    sails.
Abandon'd here, my fortune I deplore,
A hapless exile on a foreign shore.'
    Thus while he spoke, the Blue-eyed Maid
    began
With pleasing smiles to view the godlike
    man :
Then changed her form: and now, divinely
    bright,
Jove's heav'nly daughter stood confess'd to
    sight :   330
Like a fair virgin in her beauty's bloom,
Skill'd in th' illustrious labours of the
    loom.
  'O still the same Ulysses !' (she re-
    join'd)
' In useful craft successfully refin'd !
Artful in speech, in action, and in mind !
Sufficed it not, that, thy long labours pass'd,
Secure thou seest thy native shores at last?
But this to me ? who, like thyself, excel
In arts of counsel, and dissembling well;
To me ? whose wit exceeds the Powers di-
    vine,   340
No less than mortals are surpass'd by thine.
Know'st thou not me ? who made thy life
    my care,
Thro' ten years' wand'ring, and thro' ten
    years' war,
Who taught thee arts, Alcinoüs to per-
    suade,

To raise his wonder, and engage his aid;
And now appear, thy treasures to protect,
Conceal thy person, thy designs direct,
And tell what more thou must from Fate
    expect;
Domestic woes far heavier to be borne !
The pride of fools, and slaves' insulting
    scorn !   350
But thou be silent, nor reveal thy state;
Yield to the force of unresisted Fate,
And bear unmov'd the wrongs of base man-
    kind,
The last, and hardest, conquest of the
    mind.'
'Goddess of Wisdom !' (Ithacus re-
    plies)
' He who discerns thee must be truly wise,
So seldom view'd, and ever in disguise !
When the bold Argives led their warring
    powers
Against proud Ilion's well-defended tow-
    ers,
Ulysses was thy care, celestial Maid !   360
Graced with thy sight, and favour'd with
    thy aid.
But when the Trojan piles in ashes lay,
And bound for Greece we plough'd the
    wat'ry way,
Our fleet dispers'd and driven from coast
    to coast,
Thy sacred presence from that hour I
    lost;
Till I beheld thy radiant form once more,
And heard thy counsels on Phæacia's
    shore.
But, by th' Almighty Author of thy race,
Tell me, oh tell, is this my native place ?
For much I fear, long tracts of land and
    sea   370
Divide this coast from distant Ithaca;
The sweet delusion kindly you impose,
To soothe my hopes, and mitigate my
    woes.'
  Thus he. The Blue-eyed Goddess thus
    replies :
' How prone to doubt, how cautious are the
    wise !
Who, vers'd in fortune, fear the flatt'ring
    show,
And taste not half the bliss the Gods be-
    stow.
The more shall Pallas aid thy just de-
    sires,
And guard the wisdom which herself in-
    spires.

Others, long absent from their native
  place,   380
Straight seek their home, and fly with
  eager pace
To their wives' arms, and children's dear
  embrace.
Not thus Ulysses : he decrees to prove
His subjects' faith, and Queen's suspected
  love;
Who mourn'd her lord twice ten revolving
  years,
And wastes the days in grief, the nights in
  tears.
But Pallas knew (thy friends and navy
  lost)
Once more 't was given thee to behold thy
  coast :
Yet how could I with adverse Fate engage,
And mighty Neptune's unrelenting rage? 390
Now lift thy longing eyes, while I restore
The pleasing prospect of thy native shore.
Behold the port of Phorcys! fenc'd around
With rocky mountains, and with olives
  crown'd.
Behold the gloomy grot! whose cool re-
  cess
Delights the Nereids of the neighb'ring
  seas :
Whose now neglected altars, in thy reign,
Blush'd with the blood of sheep and oxen
  slain.
Behold! where Neritus the clouds divides,
And shakes the waving forests on his
  sides.'   400
  So spake the Goddess, and the prospect
  clear'd;
The mists dispers'd, and all the coast ap-
  pear'd.
The King with joy confess'd his place of
  birth,
And on his knees salutes his Mother Earth:
Then, with his suppliant hands upheld in
  air,
Thus to the sea-green Sisters sends his
  prayer :
'All hail! ye virgin Daughters of the
  Main!
Ye streams, beyond my hopes beheld again!
To you once more your own Ulysses bows;
Attend his transports, and receive his
  vows!   410
If Jove prolong my days, and Pallas crown
The growing virtues of my youthful son,
To you shall rites divine be ever paid,
And grateful off'rings on your altars laid.'

Thus then Minerva : 'From that anxious
  breast
Dismiss those cares, and leave to Heav'n
  the rest.
Our task be now thy treasured stores to
  save,
Deep in the close recesses of the cave :
Then future means consult.' She spoke,
  and trod
The shady grot, that brighten'd with the
  God.   420
The closest caverns of the grot she sought ;
The gold, the brass, the robes, Ulysses
  brought;
These in the secret gloom the Chief disposed;
The entrance with a rock the Goddess
  closed.
  Now, seated in the olive's sacred shade,
Confer the Hero and the Martial Maid.
The Goddess of the Azure Eyes began :
'Son of Laërtes! much-experienc'd man!
The suitor-train thy earliest care demand,
Of that luxurious race to rid the land: 430
Three years thy house their lawless rule has
  seen,
And proud addresses to the matchless
  Queen.
But she thy absence mourns from day to
  day,
And inly bleeds, and silent wastes away :
Elusive of the bridal hour, she gives
Fond hopes to all, and all with hopes de-
  ceives.'
  To this Ulysses : 'O celestial Maid!
Prais'd be thy counsel, and thy timely
  aid :
Else had I seen my native walls in vain,
Like great Atrides, just restor'd and slain.
Vouchsafe the means of vengeance to de-
  bate,   441
And plan with all thy arts the scene of
  fate.
Then, then be present, and my soul inspire,
As when we wrapp'd Troy's Heav'n-built
  walls in fire.
Though leagued against me hundred heroes
  stand,
Hundreds shall fall, if Pallas aid my hand.'
  She answer'd : 'In the dreadful day of
  fight
Know I am with thee, strong in all my
  might.
If thou but equal to thyself be found,
What gasping numbers then shall press the
  ground!   450

What human victims stain the feastful
  floor !
How wide the pavements float with guilty
  gore !
It fits thee now to wear a dark disguise,
And secret walk unknown to mortal eyes.
For this, my hand shall wither ev'ry grace,
And ev'ry elegance of form and face;
O'er thy smooth skin a bark of wrinkles
  spread,
Turn hoar the auburn honours of thy head;
Disfigure every limb with coarse attire,
And in thy eyes extinguish all the fire; 460
Add all the wants and the decays of life;
Estrange thee from thy own; thy son, thy
  wife :
From the loathed object ev'ry eye shall
  turn,
And the blind suitors their destruction
  scorn.
'Go first the master of thy herds to find,
True to his charge, a loyal swain and kind:
For thee he sighs; and to the royal heir
And chaste Penelope extends his care.
At the Coracian rock he now resides,
Where Arethusa's sable water glides; 470
The sable water and the copious mast
Swell the fat herd ; luxuriant, large re-
  past!
With him rest peaceful in the rural cell,
And all you ask his faithful tongue shall
  tell.
Me into other realms my cares convey,
To Sparta, still with female beauty gay:
For know, to Sparta thy lov'd offspring
  came,
To learn thy fortunes from the voice of
  Fame.'
At this the father, with a father's care: ⎫
' Must he too suffer ? he, O Goddess! bear ⎪
Of wand'rings and of woes a wretched ⎬
  share ? 481 ⎭
Thro' the wild ocean plough the dangerous
  way,
And leave his fortunes and his house a
  prey ?
Why would'st not thou, O all-enlighten'd
  Mind!
Inform him certain, and protect him,
  kind ? '
  To whom Minerva: ' Be thy soul at rest:
And know, whatever Heav'n ordains is
  best.
To fame I sent him, to acquire renown;
To other regions is his virtue known:

Secure he sits, near great Atrides placed: 490
With friendships strengthen'd, and with
  honours graced.
But lo! an ambush waits his passage o'er;
Fierce foes insidious intercept the shore:
In vain; far sooner all the murd'rous brood
This injured land shall fatten with their
  blood.'
  She spake, then touch'd him with her
  powerful wand:
The skin shrunk up, and wither'd at her
  hand:
A swift old age o'er all his members
  spread;
A sudden frost was sprinkled on his head;
Nor longer in the heavy eye-ball shined 500
The glance divine, forth-beaming from the
  mind.
His robe, which spots indelible besmear,
In rags dishonest flutters with the air:
A stag's torn hide is lapp'd around his
  reins;
A rugged staff his trembling hand sustains;
And at his side a wretched scrip was hung,
Wide-patch'd, and knotted to a twisted
  thong.
So look'd the chief, so mov'd; to mortal
  eyes
Object uncouth! a man of miseries!
While Pallas, cleaving the wide fields of
  air, 510
To Sparta flies, Telemachus her care.

BOOK XIV

THE CONVERSATION WITH EUMÆUS

THE ARGUMENT

Ulysses arrives in disguise at the house of
Eumæus, where he is received, entertained,
and lodged with the utmost hospitality. The
several discourses of that faithful old servant,
with the feigned story told by Ulysses to
conceal himself, and other conversations on
various subjects, take up this entire book.

BUT he, deep-musing, o'er the mountains
  stray'd
Thro' mazy thickets of the woodland
  shade,
And cavern'd ways, the shaggy coast
  along,
With cliffs and nodding forests overhung.
Eumæus at his sylvan lodge he sought,
A faithful servant, and without a fault.

Ulysses found him busied, as he sate
Before the threshold of his rustic gate:
Around, the mansion in a circle shone,
A rural portico of rugged stone   10
(In absence of his lord, with honest toil
His own industrious hands had rais'd the
    pile);
The wall was stone from neighb'ring quar-
    ries borne,
Encircled with a fence of native thorn,
And strong with pales, by many a weary
    stroke
Of stubborn labour hewn from heart of
    oak;
Frequent and thick. Within the space
    were rear'd
Twelve ample cells, the lodgments of his
    herd.
Full fifty pregnant females each contain'd:
The males without (a smaller race) re-
    main'd;   20
Doom'd to supply the suitors' wasteful
    feast,
A stock by daily luxury decreas'd;
Now scarce four hundred left. These to
    defend,
Four savage dogs, a watchful guard, attend.
Here sat Eumæus, and his cares applied
To form strong buskins of well-season'd
    hide.
Of four assistants who his labour share,
Three now were absent on the rural care:
The fourth drove victims to the suitor
    train:
But he, of ancient faith, a simple swain, 30
Sigh'd, while he furnish'd the luxurious
    board,
And wearied Heav'n with wishes for his
    lord.
  Soon as Ulysses near th' inclosure drew,
With open mouths the furious mastiffs
    flew:
Down sate the sage, and, cautious to with-
    stand,
Let fall th' offensive truncheon from his
    hand.
Sudden, the master runs: aloud he calls;
And from his hasty hand the leather falls;
With showers of stones he drives them far
    away;
The scatt'ring dogs around at distance
    bay.   40
  'Unhappy stranger' (thus the faithful
    swain
Began with accent gracious and humane),

'What sorrow had been mine, if at my
    gate
Thy rev'rend age had met a shameful
    fate!
Enough of woes already have I known:
Enough my master's sorrows and my own.
While here (ungrateful task!) his herds I
    feed,
Ordain'd for lawless rioters to bleed!
Perhaps, supported at another's board,
Far from his country roams my hapless
    lord!   50
Or sigh'd in exile forth his latest breath,
Now cover'd with th' eternal shade of
    death!
  'But enter this my homely roof, and see
Our woods not void of hospitality.
Then tell me whence thou art, and what the
    share
Of woes and wand'rings thou wert born to
    bear.'
  He said, and, seconding the kind re-
    quest,
With friendly step precedes his unknown
    guest.
A shaggy goat's soft hide beneath him
    spread,
And with fresh rushes heap'd an ample
    bed: 60
Joy touch'd the Hero's tender soul, to find
So just reception from a heart so kind;
And 'Oh, ye Gods! with all your blessings
    grace'
(He thus broke forth) 'this friend of hu-
    man race!'
  The swain replied: 'It never was our
    guise
To slight the poor, or aught humane de-
    spise:
For Jove unfolds our hospitable door,
'T is Jove that sends the stranger and the
    poor.
Little, alas! is all the good I can;
A man oppress'd, dependent, yet a man: 70
Accept such treatment as a swain affords,
Slave to the insolence of youthful lords!
Far hence is by unequal Gods remov'd
That man of bounties, loving and belov'd!
To whom whate'er his slave enjoys is ow'd,
And more, had Fate allow'd, had been be-
    stow'd.
But Fate comdemn'd him to a foreign
    shore;
Much have I sorrow'd, but my master
    more.

Now cold he lies, to Death's embrace re-
    sign'd:
Ah, perish Helen! perish all her kind!   80
For whose curs'd cause, in Agamemnon's
    name,
He trod so fatally the paths of Fame.'
    His vest succinct then girding round his
    waist,
Forth rush'd the swain with hospitable
    haste;
Straight to the lodgments of his herd he
    run,
Where the fat porkers slept beneath the
    sun;
Of two, his cutlass launch'd the spouting
    blood;
These, quarter'd, singed, and fix'd on forks
    of wood,
All hasty on the hissing coals he threw;
And, smoking, back the tasteful viands
    drew,   90
Broachers and all; then on the board dis-
    play'd
The ready meal, before Ulysses laid
With flour imbrown'd; next mingled wine
    yet new,
And luscious as the bees' nectareous dew:
Then sate, companion of the friendly feast,
With open look; and thus bespoke his
    guest:
    'Take with free welcome what our hands
    prepare,
Such food as falls to simple servants'
    share;
The best our lords consume; those thought-
    less peers,   99
Rich without bounty, guilty without fears.
Yet sure the Gods their impious acts de-
    test,
And honour justice and the righteous
    breast.
Pirates and conquerors of harden'd mind,
The foes of peace, and scourges of man-
    kind,
To whom offending men are made a prey
When Jove in vengeance gives a land
    away;
Ev'n these, when of their ill-got spoils pos-
    sess'd,
Find sure tormentors in the guilty breast:
Some voice of God close whisp'ring from
    within,   109
" Wretch! this is villany, and this is sin."
But these, no doubt, some oracle explore,
That tells, the great Ulysses is no more。

Hence springs their confidence, and from
    our sighs
Their rapine strengthens, and their riots
    rise:
Constant as Jove the night and day be-
    stows,
Bleeds a whole hecatomb, a vintage flows.
None match'd this hero's wealth, of all who
    reign
O'er the fair islands of the neighb'ring
    main.
Nor all the Monarchs whose far-dreaded
    sway
The wide-extended continents obey: 120
First, on the mainland, of Ulysses' breed
Twelve herds, twelve flocks, on ocean's
    margin feed;
As many stalls for shaggy goats are rear'd;
As many lodgments for the tusky herd;
Those, foreign keepers guard: and here are
    seen
Twelve herds of goats that graze our ut-
    most green;
To native pastors is their charge assign'd,
And mine the care to feed the bristly kind:
Each day the fattest bleeds of either herd,
All to the suitors' wasteful board pre-
    ferr'd.'   130
    Thus he, benevolent: his unknown guest
With hunger keen devours the sav'ry
    feast;
While schemes of vengeance ripen in his
    breast.
Silent and thoughtful while the board he
    eyed,
Eumæus pours on high the purple tide;
The King with smiling looks his joy ex-
    press'd,
And thus the kind inviting host address'd:
    'Say, now, what man is he, the man de-
    plor'd,
So rich, so potent, whom you style your
    lord?
Late with such affluence and possessions
    bless'd,   140
And now in honour's glorious bed at rest.
Whoever was the warrior, he must be
To Fame no stranger, nor perhaps to me;
Who (so the Gods and so the Fates or-
    dain'd)
Have wander'd many a sea and many a
    land.'
    'Small is the faith the Prince and Queen
    ascribe'
(Replied Eumæus) 'to the wand'ring tribe.

For needy strangers still to flatt'ry fly,
And want too oft betrays the tongue to
　　lie. 149
Each vagrant traveller, that touches here,
Deludes with fallacies the royal ear,
To dear remembrance makes his image
　　rise,
And calls the springing sorrows from her
　　eyes.
Such thou may'st be. But he whose name
　　you crave
Moulders in earth, or welters on the wave,
Or food for fish or dogs his relics lie,
Or torn by birds are scatter'd thro' the
　　sky.
So perish'd he: and left (for ever lost)
Much woe to all, but sure to me the most.
So mild a master never shall I find; 160 ⎤
Less dear the parents whom I left behind, ⎬
Less soft my mother, less my father kind. ⎦
Not with such transport would my eyes run
　　o'er,
Again to hail them in their native shore,
As lov'd Ulysses once more to embrace,
Restor'd and breathing in his natal place.
That name for ever dread, yet ever dear,
Ev'n in his absence I pronounce with
　　fear:
In my respect, he bears a Prince's part;
But lives a very brother in my heart.' 170
　Thus spoke the faithful swain, and thus
　　rejoin'd
The master of his grief, the man of patient
　　mind:
'Ulysses' friend shall view his old abodes
(Distrustful as thou art), nor doubt the
　　Gods.
Nor speak I rashly, but with faith averr'd,
And what I speak attesting Heav'n has
　　heard.
If so, a cloak and vesture be my meed; ⎤
Till his return, no title shall I plead, ⎪
Tho' certain be my news, and great my ⎬
　　need; ⎦
Whom want itself can force untruths to
　　tell, 180
My soul detests him as the gates of Hell.
　'Thou first be witness, hospitable Jove !
And ev'ry God inspiring social love !
And witness ev'ry household Power that
　　waits,
Guard of these fires, and angel of these
　　gates !
Ere the next moon increase, or this decay,
His ancient realms Ulysses shall survey,

In blood and dust each proud oppressor
　　mourn,
And the lost glories of his house return.'
　'Nor shall that meed be thine, nor ever
　　more 190
Shall lov'd Ulysses hail this happy shore'
(Replied Eumæus): 'to the present hour
Now turn thy thought, and joys within our
　　power.
From sad reflection let my soul repose;
The name of him awakes a thousand
　　woes.
But guard him, Gods ! and to these arms
　　restore !
Not his true consort can desire him more;
Not old Laërtes, broken with despair;
Not young Telemachus, his blooming heir.
Alas, Telemachus ! my sorrows flow 200
Afresh for thee, my second cause of woe !
Like some fair plant set by a heav'nly
　　hand,
He grew, he flourish'd, and he bless'd the
　　land;
In all the youth his father's image shined,
Bright in his person, brighter in his mind.
What man, or God, deceiv'd his better
　　sense,
Far on the swelling seas to wander hence ?
To distant Pylos hapless is he gone,
To seek his father's fate, and find his
　　own !
For traitors wait his way, with dire de-
　　sign 210
To end at once the great Arcesian line.
But let us leave him to their wills above;
The fates of men are in the hand of Jove.
And now, my venerable Guest ! declare
Your name, your parents, and your native
　　air:
Sincere from whence begun your course re-
　　late,
And to what ship I owe the friendly
　　freight ? '
　Thus he: and thus (with prompt inven-
　　tion bold)
The cautious Chief his ready story told:
　'On dark reserve what better can pre-
　　vail, 220
Or from the fluent tongue produce the
　　tale,
Than when two friends, alone, in peace- ⎤
　　ful place ⎪
Confer, and wines and cates the table ⎬
　　grace; ⎦
But most, the kind inviter's cheerful face? ⎦

Thus might we sit, with social goblets
crown'd,
Till the whole circle of the year goes
round;
Not the whole circle of the year would
close
My long narration of a life of woes.
But such was Heav'n's high will! Know
then, I came
From sacred Crete, and from a sire of
fame: 230
Castor Hylacides (that name he bore),
Belov'd and honour'd in his native shore;
Bless'd in his riches, in his children more.
Sprung of a handmaid, from a bought em-
brace,
I shared his kindness with his lawful race:
But when that Fate, which all must un-
dergo,
From earth remov'd him to the shades
below,
The large domain his greedy sons divide,
And each was portion'd as the lots decide.
Little, alas! was left my wretched
share, 240
Except a house, a covert from the air:
But what by niggard Fortune was denied,
A willing widow's copious wealth supplied.
My valour was my plea, a gallant mind
That, true to honour, never lagg'd behind
(The sex is ever to a soldier kind).
Now wasting years my former strength
confound,
And added woes have bow'd me to the
ground;
Yet by the stubble you may guess the
grain,
And mark the ruins of no vulgar man. 250
Me Pallas gave to lead the martial storm,
And the fair ranks of battle to deform;
Me Mars inspired to turn the foe to
flight,
And tempt the secret ambush of the
night.
Let ghastly Death in all his forms ap-
pear,
I saw him not, it was not mine to fear.
Before the rest I rais'd my ready steel;
The first I met, he yielded, or he fell.
But works of peace my soul disdain'd to
bear,
The rural labour, or domestic care. 260
To raise the mast, the missile dart to wing,
And send swift arrows from the bounding
string,

Were arts the Gods made grateful to my
mind;
Those Gods, who turn (to various ends
design'd)
The various thoughts and talents of man-
kind.
Before the Grecians touch'd the Trojan
plain,
Nine times commander or by land or main,
In foreign fields I spread my glory far,
Great in the praise, rich in the spoils of
war:
Thence, charged with riches, as increas'd
in fame, 270
To Crete return'd, an honourable name.
But when great Jove that direful war de-
creed,
Which rous'd all Greece, and made the
mighty bleed;
Our states myself and Idomen employ
To lead their fleets, and carry death to Troy.
Nine years we warr'd; the tenth saw Ilion
fall;
Homeward we sail'd, but Heav'n dispers'd
us all.
One only month my wife enjoy'd my stay;
So will'd the God who gives and takes
away.
Nine ships I mann'd, equipp'd with ready
stores, 280
Intent to voyage to th' Ægyptian shores;
In feast and sacrifice my chosen train
Six days consumed; the sev'nth we plough'd
the main.
Crete's ample fields diminish to our eye;
Before the Boreal blast the vessels fly;
Safe thro' the level seas we sweep our
way;
The steersman governs, and the ships obey.
The fifth fair morn we stem th' Ægyptian
tide,
And tilting o'er the bay the vessels ride:
To anchor there my fellows I command, 290
And spies commission to explore the land.
But, sway'd by lust of gain, and headlong
will,
The coasts they ravage, and the natives
kill.
The spreading clamour to their city flies,
And horse and foot in mingled tumult
rise.
The redd'ning dawn reveals the circling
fields,
Horrid with bristly spears, and glancing
shields.

Jove thunder'd on their side. Our guilty
head
We turn'd to flight; the gath'ring ven-
geance spread
On all parts round, and heaps on heaps
lie dead. 300
I then explor'd my thought, what course to
prove
(And sure the thought was dictated by
Jove);
Oh, had he left me to that happier doom,
And saved a life of miseries to come !
The radiant helmet from my brows un-
laced,
And low on earth my shield and jav'lin
cast,
I meet the Monarch with a suppliant's
face,
Approach his chariot, and his knees em-
brace.
He heard, he saved, he placed me at his
side;
My state he pitied, and my tears he
dried, 310
Restrain'd the rage the vengeful foe ex-
press'd,
And turn'd the deadly weapons from my
breast.
Pious ! to guard the hospitable rite,
And fearing Jove, whom mercy's works de-
light.
'In Ægypt thus with peace and plenty
bless'd,
I liv'd (and happy still had liv'd) a guest.
On sev'n bright years successive blessings
wait;
The next changed all the colour of my fate.
A false Phœnician, of insidious mind, 319
Vers'd in vile arts, and foe to humankind,
With semblance fair invites me to his
home.
I seiz'd the proffer (ever fond to roam):
Domestic in his faithless roof I stay'd,
Till the swift sun his annual circle made.
To Libya then he meditates the way;
With guileful art a stranger to betray,
And sell to bondage in a foreign land:
Much doubting, yet compell'd, I quit the
strand.
Thro' the mid seas the nimble pinnace
sails,
Aloof from Crete, before the northern
gales: 330
But when remote her chalky cliffs we lost,
And far from ken of any other coast,

When all was wild expanse of sea and air,
Then doom'd high Jove due vengeance to
prepare.
He hung a night of horrors o'er their head
(The shaded ocean blacken'd as it spread);
He launch'd the fiery bolt; from pole to
pole
Broad burst the lightnings, deep the thun-
ders roll;
In giddy rounds the whirling ship is toss'd,
And all in clouds of smoth'ring sulphur
lost. 340
As from a hanging rock's tremendous
height,
The sable crows with intercepted flight
Drop endlong; scarr'd and black with sul-
phurous hue,
So from the deck are hurl'd the ghastly
crew.
Such end the wicked found ! but Jove's
intent
Was yet to save th' oppress'd and innocent.
Placed on the mast (the last resource of
life),
With winds and waves I held unequal
strife;
For nine long days the billows tilting o'er,
The tenth soft wafts me to Thesprotia's
shore. 350
The Monarch's son a shipwreck'd wretch
reliev'd,
The Sire with hospitable rites receiv'd,
And in his palace like a brother placed,
With gifts of price and gorgeous garments
graced.
While here I sojourn'd, oft I heard the
fame
How late Ulysses to the country came,
How lov'd, how honour'd, in this court he
stay'd,
And here his whole collected treasure
laid;
I saw myself the vast unnumber'd store
Of steel elab'rate, and refulgent ore, 360
And brass high heap'd amidst the regal
dome;
Immense supplies for ages yet to come !
Meantime he voyaged to explore the will
Of Jove, on high Dodona's holy hill,
What means might best his safe return
avail,
To come in pomp, or bear a secret sail ?
Full oft has Phidon, whilst he pour'd the
wine,
Attesting solemn all the Powers divine,

That soon Ulysses would return, declared,
The sailors waiting, and the ships pre-
pared. 370
But first the King dismiss'd me from his
shores,
For fair Dulichium crown'd with fruitful
stores;
To good Acastus' friendly care consign'd:
But other counsels pleas'd the sailors' mind:
New frauds were plotted by the faithless
train,
And misery demands me once again.
Soon as remote from shore they plough the
wave,
With ready hands they rush to seize their
slave;
Then with these tatter'd rags they wrapp'd
me round
(Stripp'd of my own), and to the vessel
bound. 380
At eve, at Ithaca's delightful land
The ship arrived: forth issuing on the sand,
They sought repast: while, to th' unhappy
kind,
The pitying Gods themselves my chains un-
bind.
Soft I descended, to the sea applied
My naked breast, and shot along the tide.
Soon pass'd beyond their sight, I left the
flood,
And took the spreading shelter of the wood.
Their prize escaped the faithless pirates
mourn'd;
But deem'd inquiry vain, and to their ships
return'd. 390
Screen'd by protecting Gods from hostile
eyes,
They led me to a good man and a wise,
To live beneath thy hospitable care,
And wait the woes Heav'n dooms me yet
to bear.'
'Unhappy Guest! whose sorrows touch
my mind'
(Thus good Eumæus with a sigh rejoin'd),
'For real suff'rings since I grieve sincere,
Check not with fallacies the springing tear:
Nor turn the passion into groundless joy
For him whom Heav'n has destin'd to de-
stroy. 400
Oh! had he perish'd on some well-fought
day,
Or in his friends' embraces died away!
That grateful Greece with streaming eyes
might raise
Historic marbles to record his praise;

His praise, eternal on the faithful stone,
Had with transmissive honours graced his
son.
Now, snatch'd by Harpies to the dreary
coast,
Sunk is the hero, and his glory lost!
While pensive in this solitary den, 409
Far from gay cities and the ways of men,
I linger life; nor to the Court repair,
But when my constant Queen commands
my care;
Or when, to taste her hospitable board,
Some guest arrives, with rumours of her
lord;
And these indulge their want, and those
their woe,
And here the tears, and there the goblets
flow.
By many such have I been warn'd; but
chief
By one Ætolian robb'd of all belief,
Whose hap it was to this our roof to roam,
For murder banish'd from his native home
He swore, Ulysses on the coast of Crete 421
Stay'd but a season to refit his fleet;
A few revolving months should waft him
o'er,
Fraught with bold warriors, and a bound-
less store.
O thou! whom age has taught to under-
stand,
And Heav'n has guided with a fav'ring
hand!
On God or mortal to obtrude a lie
Forbear, and dread to flatter, as to die.
Not for such ends my house and heart are
free,
But dear respect to Jove, and charity.' 430
' And why, O swain of unbelieving mind!'
(Thus quick replied the wisest of man-
kind),
'Doubt you my oath? yet more my faith ⎫
to try, ⎪
A solemn compact let us ratify, ⎬
And witness ev'ry Power that rules the ⎪
sky! ⎭
If here Ulysses from his labours rest,
Be then my prize a tunic and a vest;
And, where my hopes invite me, straight
transport
In safety to Dulichium's friendly court.
But if he greets not thy desiring eye, 440 ⎫
Hurl me from yon dread precipice on ⎬
high; ⎪
The due reward of fraud and perjury.' ⎭

'Doubtless, O Guest! great laud and
    praise were mine'
(Replied the swain), 'for spotless faith
    divine,
If, after social rites and gifts bestow'd,
I stain'd my hospitable hearth with blood.
How would the Gods my righteous toils
    succeed,
And bless the hand that made a stranger
    bleed?
No more — th' approaching hours of silent
    night
First claim refection, then to rest invite; 450
Beneath our humble cottage let us haste,
And here, unenvied, rural dainties taste.'
    Thus communed these; while to their
        lowly dome
The full-fed swine return'd with ev'ning
    home:
Compell'd, reluctant, to their sev'ral sties,
With din obstrep'rous, and ungrateful cries.
Then to the slaves: 'Now from the herd
    the best
Select, in honour of our foreign guest:
With him let us the genial banquet share,
For great and many are the griefs we bear;
While those who from our labours heap
    their board   461
Blaspheme their feeder, and forget their
    lord.'
    Thus speaking, with despatchful hand
        he took
A weighty axe, and cleft the solid oak;
This on the earth he piled; a boar full fed,
Of five years' age, before the pile was led:
The swain, whom acts of piety delight,
Observant of the Gods, begins the rite;
First shears the forehead of the bristly ⎱
    boar,   ⎰
And suppliant stands, invoking ev'ry ⎱
    Power   470 ⎰
To speed Ulysses to his native shore. ⎰
A knotty stake then aiming at his head,
Down dropp'd he groaning, and the spirit
    fled.
The scorching flames climb round on ev'ry
    side:
Then the singed members they with skill
    divide;
On these, in rolls of fat involv'd with art,
The choicest morsels lay from ev'ry part.
Some in the flames bestrew'd with flour
    they threw;
Some cut in fragments from the forks they
    drew :   479

These, while on sev'ral tables they dispose,
A priest himself, the blameless rustic rose;
Expert the destin'd victim to dispart
In sev'n just portions, pure of hand and
    heart.
One sacred to the Nymphs apart they lay;
Another to the winged son of May:
The rural tribe in common share the rest,
The King, the chine, the honour of the
    feast;
Who sate delighted at his servant's board;
The faithful servant joy'd his unknown
    lord.   489
'O be thou dear' (Ulysses cried) 'to Jove,
As well thou claim'st a grateful stranger's
    love!'
    'Be then thy thanks' (the bounteous
        swain replied)
'Enjoyment of the good the Gods provide.
From God's own hand descend our joys and
    woes;
These he decrees, and he but suffers those:
All power is his, and whatsoe'er he wills,
The will itself, omnipotent, fulfils.'
This said, the first-fruits to the Gods he
    gave;
Then pour'd of offer'd wine the sable wave:
In great Ulysses' hand he placed the bowl;
He sate, and sweet refection cheer'd his
    soul.   501
The bread from canisters Mesaulius gave
(Eumæus' proper treasure bought this slave,
And led from Taphos, to attend his board,
A servant added to his absent lord);
His task it was the wheaten loaves to lay,
And from the banquet take the bowls
    away.
And now the rage of hunger was repress'd,
And each betakes him to his couch to rest.
    Now came the night, and darkness
        cover'd o'er   510
The face of things; the winds began to
    roar;
The driving storm the wat'ry west-wind
    pours,
And Jove descends in deluges of showers.
Studious of rest and warmth, Ulysses lies,
Foreseeing from the first the storm would
    rise;
In mere necessity of coat and cloak,
With artful preface to his host he spoke:
'Hear me, my friends, who this good ban-
    quet grace;
'Tis sweet to play the fool in time and
    place,

And wine can of their wits the wise be-
　　guile,　　　　　　　　　　　　520
Make the sage frolic, and the serious smile,
The grave in merry measures frisk about,
And many a long repented word bring
　　out.
Since to be talkative I now commence,
Let Wit cast off the sullen yoke of Sense.
Once I was strong (would Heav'n restore
　　those days !)
And with my betters claim'd a share of
　　praise.
Ulysses, Menelaüs, led forth a band,
And join'd me with them ('t was their own
　　command);
A deathful ambush for the foe to lay,　530
Beneath Troy walls by night we took our
　　way;
There, clad in arms, along the marshes
　　spread,
We made the ozier-fringed bank our bed.
Full soon th' inclemency of Heav'n I feel,
Nor had these shoulders cov'ring, but of
　　steel.
Sharp blew the north; snow whitening all
　　the fields
Froze with the blast, and, gath'ring, glazed
　　our shields.
There all but I, well-fenc'd with cloak and
　　vest,　　　　　　　　　　　　538
Lay cover'd by their ample shields at rest.
Fool that I was ! I left behind my own,
The skill of weather and of winds un-
　　known,
And trusted to my coat and shield alone !
When now was wasted more than half the
　　night,
And the stars faded at approaching light,
Sudden I jogg'd Ulysses, who was laid
Fast by my side, and shiv'ring thus I said:
'"Here longer in this field I cannot lie;
The winter pinches, and with cold I die;
And die ashamed (O wisest of mankind !),
The only fool who left his cloak behind." 550
　'He thought and answer'd; hardly wak-
　　ing yet,
Sprung in his mind the momentary wit
(That wit which, or in council or in fight,
Still met th' emergence, and determin'd
　　right).
"Hush thee " (he cried, soft whisp'ring in
　　my ear),
"Speak not a word, lest any Greek may
　　hear " —
And then (supporting on his arm his head),

"Hear me, Companions ! " (thus aloud he
　　said):
"Methinks too distant from the fleet we
　　lie:
Ev'n now a vision stood before my eye, 560
And sure the warning vision was from
　　high :
Let from among us some swift courier rise,
Haste to the Gen'ral, and demand supplies."
　'Up started Thoas straight, Andræmon's
　　son,
Nimbly he rose, and cast his garment down;
Instant, the racer vanish'd off the ground;
That instant in his cloak I wrapp'd me
　　round;
And safe I slept, till, brightly dawning,
　　shone
The Morn conspicuous on her golden
　　throne.
　'Oh were my strength as then, as then
　　my age !　　　　　　　　　　　570
Some friend would fence me from the
　　winter's rage.
Yet, tatter'd as I look, I challenged then
The honours and the offices of men:
Some master, or some servant would allow
A cloak and vest — but I am nothing now !'
　'Well hast thou spoke ' (rejoin'd th' at-
　　tentive swain);
'Thy lips let fall no idle word or vain !
Nor garment shalt thou want, nor aught
　　beside,
Meet for the wand'ring suppliant to pro-
　　vide.　　　　　　　　　　　　579
But in the morning take thy clothes again,
For here one vest suffices ev'ry swain;
No change of garments to our hinds is
　　known;
But when return'd, the good Ulysses' son
With better hand shall grace with fit at-
　　tires
His guest, and send thee where thy soul
　　desires.'
　The honest herdsman rose, as this he said,
And drew before the hearth the stranger's
　　bed;
The fleecy spoils of sheep, a goat's rough
　　hide
He spreads: and adds a mantle thick and
　　wide:　　　　　　　　　　　　589
With store to heap above him, and below,
And guard each quarter as the tempests
　　blow.
There lay the King, and all the rest supine;
All, but the careful master of the swine:

Forth hasted he to tend his bristly care;
W ll arm'd, and fenc'd against nocturnal
   air:
His weighty faulchion o'er his shoulder
   tied;
His shaggy cloak a mountain goat sup-
   plied:
With his broad spear, the dread of dogs
   and men,
He seeks his lodging in the rocky den. 599
There to the tusky herd he bends his way,
Where, screen'd from Boreas, high o'er-
   arch'd they lay.

BOOK XV

THE RETURN OF TELEMACHUS

ARGUMENT

The Goddess Minerva commands Telemachus
in a vision to return to Ithaca. Pisistratus
and he take leave of Menelaüs, and arrive at
Pylos, where they part; Telemachus sets
sail, after having received on board Theoclymenus the soothsayer. The scene then
changes to the cottage of Eumæus, who entertains Ulysses with a recital of his adventures. In the meantime Telemachus arrives
on the coast, and, sending the vessel to the
town, proceeds by himself to the lodge of Eumæus.

Now had Minerva reach'd those ample
   plains,
Famed for the dance, where Menelaüs
   reigns;
Anxious she flies to great Ulysses' heir,
His instant voyage challenged all her care.
Beneath the royal portico display'd,
With Nestor's son Telemachus was laid;
In sleep profound the son of Nestor lies;
Not thine, Ulysses! Care unseal'd his eyes:
Restless he griev'd, with various fears op-
   press'd,
And all thy fortunes roll'd within his
   breast. 10
When 'O Telemachus!' (the Goddess said)
'Too long in vain, too widely hast thou
   stray'd,
Thus leaving careless thy paternal right
The robbers' prize, the prey to lawless
   might.
On fond pursuits neglectful while you roam,
Ev'n now the hand of rapine sacks the
   dome.

Hence to Atrides; and his leave implore
To launch thy vessel for thy natal shore:
Fly, whilst thy mother virtuous yet with-
   stands
Her kindred's wishes, and her sire's com-
   mands; 20
Thro' both, Eurymachus pursues the dame,
And with the noblest gifts asserts his claim.
Hence therefore, while thy stores thy own
   remain;
Thou know'st the practice of the female
   train;
Lost in the children of the present spouse,
They slight the pledges of their former
   vows;
Their love is always with the lover past;
Still the succeeding flame expels the last.
Let o'er thy house some chosen maid pre-
   side, 29
Till Heav'n decrees to bless thee in a bride.
But now thy more attentive ears incline,
Observe the warnings of a Power divine;
For thee their snares the suitor lords shall
   lay
In Samos' sands, or straits of Ithaca;
To seize thy life shall lurk the murd'rous
   band,
Ere yet thy footsteps press thy native land.
No — sooner far their riot and their lust
All-cov'ring earth shall bury deep in dust.
Then distant from the scatter'd islands
   steer,
Nor let the night retard thy full career; 40
Thy heav'nly guardian shall instruct the
   gales
To smooth thy passage and supply thy
   sails :
And when at Ithaca thy labour ends,
Send to the town the vessel with thy
   friends;
But seek thou first the master of the swine,
(For still to thee his loyal thoughts in-
   cline);
There pass the night; while he his course
   pursues
To bring Penelope the wish'd-for news,
That thou, safe sailing from the Pylian
   strand,
Art come to bless her in thy native land.' 50
  Thus spoke the Goddess, and resumed
   her flight
To the pure regions of eternal light.
Meanwhile Pisistratus he gently shakes,
And with these words the slumb'ring youth
   awakes :

'Rise, son of Nestor; for the road pre-
pare,
And join the harness'd coursers to the car.'
'What cause,' he cried, 'can justify our
flight
To tempt the dangers of forbidding night?
Here wait we rather, till approaching day
Shall prompt our speed, and point the ready
way.   60
Nor think of flight before the Spartan
King
Shall bid farewell, and bounteous presents
bring;
Gifts, which to distant ages safely stor'd,
The sacred act of friendship shall record.'
  Thus he.   But when the dawn bestreak'd
the east,
The King from Helen rose, and sought his
guest.
As soon as his approach the Hero knew,
The splendid mantle round him first he
threw,
Then o'er his ample shoulders whirl'd the
cloak,   69
Respectful met the Monarch, and bespoke:
'Hail, great Atrides, favour'd of high
Jove!
Let not thy friends in vain for license
move.
Swift let us measure back the wat'ry way,
Nor check our speed, impatient of delay.'
  'If with desire so strong thy bosom
glows,
Ill,' said the King, 'should I thy wish op-
pose:
For oft in others freely I reprove
The ill-timed efforts of officious love;
Who love too much, hate in the like ex-
treme,   79
And both the golden mean alike condemn.
Alike he thwarts the hospitable end,
Who drives the free, or stays the hasty
friend:
True friendship's laws are by this rule ex-
press'd,
Welcome the coming, speed the parting
guest.
Yet stay, my friends, and in your chariot
take
The noblest presents that our love can
make;
Meantime commit we to our women's care
Some choice domestic viands to prepare;
The trav'ler, rising from the banquet gay,
Eludes the labours of the tedious way.   90

Then if a wider course shall rather please,
Thro' spacious Argos and the realms of
Greece,
Atrides in his chariot shall attend;
Himself thy convoy to each royal friend.
No Prince will let Ulysses' heir remove
Without some pledge, some monument of
love:
These will the cauldron, these the tripod ⎫
give;   ⎪
From those the well-pair'd mules we shall ⎬
receive,   ⎪
Or bowl emboss'd whose golden figures   ⎭
live.'
  To whom the youth, for prudence famed,
replied: 100
'O Monarch, Care of Heav'n! thy people's
pride!
No friend in Ithaca my place supplies,
No powerful hands are there, no watchful
eyes:
My stores exposed and fenceless house de-
mand
The speediest succour from my guardian
hand;
Lest, in a search too anxious and too vain
Of one lost joy, I lose what yet remain.'
  His purpose when the gen'rous Warrior
heard,
He charged the household cates to be pre-
pared.
Now with the dawn, from his adjoining
home,   110
Was Bœthœdes Eteoneus come;
Swift at the word he forms the rising
blaze,
And o'er the coals the smoking fragments
lays.
  Meantime the King, his son, and Helen
went
Where the rich wardrobe breathed a costly
scent.
The King selected from the glitt'ring
rows
A bowl; the Prince a silver beaker chose.
The beauteous Queen revolv'd with careful
eyes
Her various textures of unnumber'd dyes,
And chose the largest; with no vulgar
art   120
Her own fair hands embroider'd every
part:
Beneath the rest it lay divinely bright,
Like radiant Hesper o'er the gems of
night.

Then with each gift they hasten'd to their
   guest,
And thus the King Ulysses' heir address'd:
'Since fix'd are thy resolves, may thun-
   d'ring Jove
With happiest omens thy desires approve!
This silver bowl, whose costly margins
   shine
Enchased with gold, this valued gift be
   thine;
To me this present, of Vulcanian frame, 130
From Sidon's hospitable Monarch came;
To thee we now consign the precious load,
The pride of Kings, and labour of a God.'
   Then gave the cup, while Megapenthe
   brought
The silver vase with living sculpture
   wrought.
The beauteous Queen, advancing next, dis-
   play'd
The shining veil, and thus endearing said:
'Accept, dear youth, this monument of
   love,
Long since, in better days, by Helen wove:
Safe in thy mother's care the vesture
   lay, 140
To deck thy bride, and grace thy nuptial
   day.
Meantime may'st thou with happiest speed
   regain
Thy stately palace, and thy wide domain.'
   She said, and gave the veil; with grate-
   ful look
The Prince the variegated present took.
And now, when thro' the royal dome they
   pass'd,
High on a throne the King each stranger
   placed.
A golden ewer th' attendant damsel brings,
Replete with water from the crystal
   springs;
With copious streams the shining vase sup-
   plies 150
A silver laver of capacious size.
They wash. The tables in fair order
   spread,
The glitt'ring canisters are crown'd with
   bread;
Viands of various kinds allure the taste,
Of choicest sort and savour; rich repast!
Whilst Eteoneus portions out the shares,
Atrides' son the purple draught prepares.
And now (each sated with the genial feast,
And the short rage of thirst and hunger
   ceas'd),

Ulysses' son, with his illustrious friend, 160
The horses join, the polish'd car ascend.
Along the court the fiery steeds rebound,
And the wide portal echoes to the sound.
The King precedes; a bowl with fragrant
   wine
(Libation destin'd to the Powers divine)
His right hand held: before the steeds he
   stands,
Then, mix'd with prayers, he utters these
   commands:
'Farewell, and prosper, Youths! let Nes-
   tor know
What grateful thoughts still in this bosom
   glow,
For all the proofs of his paternal care, 170
Thro' the long dangers of the ten years'
   war.'
   'Ah! doubt not our report' (the Prince
   rejoin'd)
'Of all the virtues of thy gen'rous mind.
And oh! return'd might we Ulysses meet!
To him thy presents show, thy words re-
   peat:
How will each speech his grateful wonder
   raise!
How will each gift indulge us in thy
   praise!'
   Scarce ended thus the Prince, when on
   the right
Advanc'd the bird of Jove: auspicious
   sight!
A milk-white fowl his clinching talons
   bore, 180
With care domestic pamper'd at the floor.
Peasants in vain with threat'ning cries
   pursue,
In solemn speed the bird majestic flew
Full dexter to the car: the prosp'rous sight
Fill'd ev'ry breast with wonder and de-
   light.
   But Nestor's son the cheerful silence
   broke,
And in these words the Spartan Chief be-
   spoke:
'Say if to us the Gods these omens send,
Or fates peculiar to thyself portend?'
   Whilst yet the Monarch paus'd, with
   doubts oppress'd, 190
The beauteous Queen reliev'd his lab'ring
   breast:
'Hear me' (she cried), 'to whom the Gods
   have given
To read this sign, and mystic sense of
   Heav'n.

As thus the plumy sov'reign of the air
Left on the mountain's brow his callow care,
And wander'd thro' the wide ethereal way
To pour his wrath on you luxurious prey;
So shall thy godlike father, toss'd in vain
Thro' all the dangers of the boundless main,
Arrive (or is perchance already come), 200
From slaughter'd gluttons to release the dome.'
  'Oh! if this promis'd bliss by thund'ring Jove'
(The Prince replied) 'stand fix'd in Fate above;
To thee, as to some God, I'll temples raise,
And crown thy altars with the costly blaze.'
  He said; and, bending o'er his chariot, flung
Athwart the fiery steeds the smarting thong;
The bounding shafts upon the harness play,
Till night descending intercepts the way.
To Diocles at Pheræ they repair, 210
Whose boasted sire was sacred Alpheus' heir;
With him all night the youthful strangers stay'd,
Nor found the hospitable rites unpaid.
But soon as Morning from her orient bed
Had tinged the mountains with her earliest red,
They join'd the steeds, and on the chariot sprung;
The brazen portals in their passage rung.
  To Pylos soon they came; when thus begun
To Nestor's heir Ulysses' godlike son: 219
'Let not Pisistratus in vain be press'd,
Nor unconsenting hear his friend's request;
His friend by long hereditary claim,
In toils his equal, and in years the same.
No farther from our vessel, I implore,
The coursers drive; but lash them to the shore.
Too long thy father would his friend detain;
I dread his proffer'd kindness urged in vain.'
  The Hero paus'd, and ponder'd this request,
While love and duty warr'd within his breast.

At length resolv'd, he turn'd his ready hand, 230
And lash'd his panting coursers to the strand.
There, while within the poop with care he stor'd
The regal presents of the Spartan lord,
'With speed begone' (said he); 'call every mate,
Ere yet to Nestor I the tale relate:
'T is true, the fervour of his gen'rous heart
Brooks no repulse, nor couldst thou soon depart:
Himself will seek thee here, nor wilt thou find,
In words alone, the Pylian Monarch kind.
But when, arrived, he thy return shall know, 240
How will his breast with honest fury glow!'
This said, the sounding strokes his horses fire,
And soon he reach'd the palace of his sire.
  'Now' (cried Telemachus) 'with speedy care
Hoist ev'ry sail, and ev'ry oar prepare!'
Swift as the word his willing mates obey,
And seize their seats, impatient for the sea.
  Meantime the Prince with sacrifice adores
Minerva, and her guardian aid implores;
When lo! a wretch ran breathless to the shore, 250
New from his crime; and reeking yet with gore.
A seer he was, from great Melampus sprung,
Melampus, who in Pylos flourish'd long,
Till, urged by wrongs, a foreign realm he chose,
Far from the hateful cause of all his woes.
Neleus his treasures one long year detains:
As long he groan'd in Phylacus's chains:
Meantime, what anguish and what rage combin'd,
For lovely Pero rack'd his lab'ring mind!
Yet 'scaped he death: and, vengeful of his wrong, 260
To Pylos drove the lowing herds along:
Then (Neleus vanquish'd, and consign'd the fair
To Bias' arms) he sought a foreign air;

Argos the rich for his retreat he chose;
There form'd his empire: there his palace
   rose.
From him Antiphates and Mantius came;
The first begot Oïcleus great in fame,
And he Amphiaraüs, immortal name!
The people's saviour, and divinely wise,
Belov'd by Jove, and him who gilds the
   skies;   270
Yet short his date of life! by female
   pride he dies.
From Mantius Clitus, whom Aurora's
   love
Snatch'd for his beauty to the thrones
   above;
And Polyphides, on whom Phœbus shone
With fullest rays, Amphiaraüs now gone;
In Hyperesia's groves he made abode,
And taught mankind the counsels of the
   God.
From him sprung Theoclymenus, who
   found
(The sacred wine yet foaming on the
   ground)
Telemachus: whom, as to Heav'n he
   press'd   280
His ardent vows, the stranger thus ad-
   dress'd:
'O thou! that dost thy happy course pre-
   pare
With pure libations and with solemn
   prayer;
By that dread Power to whom thy vows are
   paid;
By all the lives of these; thy own dear
   head,
Declare sincerely to no foe's demand
Thy name, thy lineage, and paternal land.'
'Prepare, then,' said Telemachus, 'to
   know
A tale from falsehood free, not free from
   woe.
From Ithaca, of royal birth I came,   290
And great Ulysses (ever-honour'd name!)
Once was my sire, tho' now for ever lost,
In Stygian gloom he glides a pensive ghost!
Whose fate inquiring thro' the world we
   rove:
The last, the wretched proof of filial love.'
  The stranger then: 'Nor shall I aught
   conceal,
But the dire secret of my fate reveal.
Of my own tribe an Argive wretch I slew;
Whose powerful friends the luckless deed
   pursue

With unrelenting rage, and force from
   home   300
The blood-stain'd exile, ever doom'd to
   roam.
But bear, oh bear me o'er yon azure flood;
Receive the suppliant! spare my destin'd
   blood!'
  'Stranger' (replied the Prince), 'se-
   curely rest
Affianc'd in our faith, henceforth our
   guest.'
Thus affable, Ulysses' godlike heir
Takes from the stranger's hand the glit-
   t'ring spear:
He climbs the ship, ascends the stern with
   haste,
And by his side the guest accepted placed.
The Chief his order gives: th' obedient
   band   310
With due observance wait the Chief's com-
   mand.
With speed the mast they rear, with speed
   unbind
The spacious sheet, and stretch it to the
   wind.
Minerva calls; the ready gales obey
With rapid speed to whirl them o'er the
   sea.
Crunus they pass'd, next Chalcis roll'd
   away,
When thick'ning darkness closed the doubt-
   ful day;
The silver Phæa's glitt'ring rills they lost,
And skimm'd along by Elis' sacred coast.
Then cautious thro' the rocky reaches
   wind,   320
And, turning sudden, shun the death de-
   sign'd.
  Meantime, the King, Eumæus, and the
   rest,
Sate in the cottage, at their rural feast:
The banquet pass'd, and satiate ev'ry man,
To try his host, Ulysses thus began:
  'Yet one night more, my friends, indulge
   your guest;
The last I purpose in your walls to rest;
To-morrow for myself I must provide,
And only ask your counsel, and a guide;
Patient to roam the street, by hunger led,
And bless the friendly hand that gives me
   bread.   331
There in Ulysses' roof I may relate
Ulysses' wand'rings to his royal mate;
Or, mingling with the suitors' haughty train,
Not undeserving some support obtain.

Hermes to me his various gifts imparts,
Patron of industry and manual arts:
Few can with me in dext'rous works con-
tend,
The pyre to build, the stubborn oak to
rend;
To turn the tasteful viand o'er the flame; 340
Or foam the goblet with a purple stream.
Such are the tasks of men of mean estate,
Whom fortune dooms to serve the rich and
great.'
'Alas!' (Eumæus with a sigh rejoin'd)
'How sprung a thought so monstrous in thy
mind?
If on that godless race thou would'st at-
tend,
Fate owes thee sure a miserable end!
Their wrongs and blasphemies ascend the
sky,
And pull descending vengeance from on
high.
Not such, my friend, the servants of their
feast; 350
A blooming train in rich embroid'ry dress'd!
With earth's whole tribute the bright table
bends,
And smiling round celestial youth attends.
Stay, then; no eye askance beholds thee
here;
Sweet is thy converse to each social ear:
Well pleas'd, and pleasing, in our cottage
rest,
Till good Telemachus accepts his guest
With genial gifts, and change of fair at-
tires,
And safe conveys thee where thy soul de-
sires.'
To him the man of woes: 'O gracious
Jove 360
Reward this stranger's hospitable love!
Who knows the son of sorrow to relieve,
Cheers the sad heart, nor lets affliction
grieve.
Of all the ills unhappy mortals know,
A life of wand'rings is the greatest woe:
On all their weary ways wait Care and
Pain,
And Pine and Penury, a meagre train.
To such a man since harbour you afford,
Relate the farther fortunes of your lord;
What cares his mother's tender breast en-
gage, 370
And sire forsaken on the verge of age;
Beneath the sun prolong they yet their
breath,

Or range the house of darkness and of
death?'
To whom the swain: 'Attend what you
inquire;
Laërtes lives, the miserable sire;
Lives, but implores of ev'ry Power to lay
The burden down, and wishes for the day.
Torn from his offspring in the eve of life,
Torn from th' embraces of his tender wife,
Sole, and all comfortless, he wastes away
Old age, untimely posting ere his day. 381
She too, sad mother! for Ulysses lost
Pined out her bloom, and vanish'd to a ghost
(So dire a fate, ye righteous Gods! avert
From ev'ry friendly, ev'ry feeling heart);
While yet she was, tho' clouded o'er with
grief,
Her pleasing converse minister'd relief:
With Ctimene, her youngest daughter, bred,
One roof contain'd us, and one table fed.
But when the softly-stealing pace of time
Crept on from childhood into youthful
prime, 391
To Samos isle she sent the wedded fair;
Me to the fields, to tend the rural care;
Array'd in garments her own hands had
wove,
Nor less the darling object of her love.
Her hapless death my brighter days o'er-
cast,
Yet Providence deserts me not at last:
My present labours food and drink procure,
And more, the pleasure to relieve the poor.
Small is the comfort from the Queen to
hear 400
Unwelcome news, or vex the royal ear;
Blank and discountenanc'd the servants
stand,
Nor dare to question where the proud com-
mand:
No profit springs beneath usurping powers;
Want feeds not there, where Luxury de-
vours,
Nor harbours charity where riot reigns:
Proud are the Lords, and wretched are the
Swains.'
The suff'ring Chief at this began to melt;
And, 'O Eumæus! thou' (he cries) 'hast
felt
The spite of Fortune too! her cruel hand 410
Snatch'd thee an infant from thy native
land!
Snatch'd from thy parents' arms, thy par-
ents' eyes,
To early wants! a man of miseries!

The whole sad story, from its first, declare:
Sunk the fair city by the rage of war,
Where once thy parents dwelt ? or did
   they keep,
In humbler life, the lowing herds and
   sheep ?
So left perhaps to tend the fleecy train,
Rude pirates seiz'd, and shipp'd thee o'er
   the main ?
Doom'd a fair prize to grace some Prince's
   board,   420
The worthy purchase of a foreign Lord.'
  'If then my fortunes can delight my
   friend,
A story fruitful of events attend:
Another's sorrow may thy ear enjoy,
And wine the lengthen'd intervals employ.
Long nights the now declining year be-
   stows;
A part we consecrate to soft repose,
A part in pleasing talk we entertain;
For too much rest itself becomes a pain.
Let those, whom sleep invites, the call
   obey,   430
Their cares resuming with the dawning
   day:
Here let us feast, and to the feast be join'd
Discourse, the sweeter banquet of the
   mind;
Review the series of our lives, and taste
The melancholy joy of evils pass'd:
For he who much has suffer'd, much will
   know,
And pleas'd remembrance builds delight
   on woe.
  ' Above Ortygia lies an isle of fame,
Far hence remote, and Syria is the name
(There curious eyes inscribed with wonder
   trace   440
The sun's diurnal, and his annual race);
Not large, but fruitful; stored with grass,
   to keep
The bell'wing oxen and the bleating sheep;
Her sloping hills the mantling vines adorn,
And her rich valleys wave with golden corn.
No want, no famine, the glad natives know,
Nor sink by sickness to the shades below;
But when a length of years unnerves the
   strong,   448
Apollo comes, and Cynthia comes along.
They bend the silver bow with tender skill,
And, void of pain, the silent arrows kill.
Two equal tribes this fertile land divide,
Where two fair cities rise with equal pride,
But both in constant peace one Prince obey,

And Ctesius there, my father, holds the
   sway.
Freighted, it seems, with toys of ev'ry sort,
A ship of Sidon anchor'd in our port;
What time it chanc'd the palace enter-
   tain'd,
Skill'd in rich works, a woman of their
   land:
This nymph, where anchor'd the Phœnician
   train,   460
To wash her robes descending to the main,
A smooth-tongued sailor won her to his
   mind
(For love deceives the best of womankind).
A sudden trust from sudden liking grew;
She told her name, her race, and all she
   knew.
"I too" (she cried) "from glorious Sidon
   came.
My father Arybas, of wealthy fame;
But, snatch'd by pirates from my native
   place,
The Taphians sold me to this man's em-
   brace."
  '"Haste then" (the false designing youth
   replied),   470
"Haste to thy country; love shall be thy
   guide;
Haste to thy father's house, thy father's
   breast,
For still he lives, and lives with riches
   blest."
  '"Swear first" (she cried), "ye Sail-⎫
   ors ! to restore   ⎪
A wretch in safety to her native shore."   ⎬
Swift as she ask'd, the ready sailors   ⎪
   swore.   ⎭
She then proceeds: "Now let our compact
   made
Be nor by signal nor by word betray'd,
Nor near me any of your crew descried,
By road frequented, or by fountain side: 480
Be silence still our guard.   The Monarch's
   spies
(For watchful age is ready to surmise)
Are still at hand; and this reveal'd, must
   be
Death to yourselves, eternal chains to me.
Your vessel loaded, and your traffic pass'd,
Despatch a wary messenger with haste;
Then gold and costly treasures will I bring,
And more, the infant-offspring of the King.
Him, childlike wand'ring forth, I'll lead
   away
(A noble prize !) and to your ship convey."

'Thus spoke the dame, and homeward
   took the road. 491
A year they traffic, and their vessel load.
Their stores complete, and ready now to
   weigh,
A spy was sent their summons to convey:
An artist to my father's palace came,
With gold and amber chains, elab'rate
   frame:
Each female eye the glitt'ring links em-
   ploy;
They turn, review, and cheapen ev'ry toy.
He took th' occasion, as they stood intent,
Gave her the sign, and to his vessel went.
She straight pursued, and seiz'd my willing
   arm; 501
I follow'd smiling, innocent of harm.
Three golden goblets in the porch she
   found
(The guests not enter'd, but the table
   crown'd);
Hid in her fraudful bosom these she bore:
Now set the sun, and darken'd all the
   shore.
Arriving then, where, tilting on the tides,
Prepared to launch the freighted vessel
   rides,
Aboard they heave us, mount their decks,
   and sweep
With level oar along the glassy deep. 510
Six calmy days and six smooth nights we
   sail,
And constant Jove supplied the gentle
   gale.
The sev'nth, the fraudful wretch (no cause
   descried),
Touch'd by Diana's vengeful arrow, died.
Down dropp'd the caitiff-corse, a worth-
   less load,
Down to the deep; there roll'd, the future
   food
Of fierce sea-wolves, and monsters of the
   flood.
A helpless infant I remain'd behind;
Thence borne to Ithaca by wave and wind;
Sold to Laërtes by divine command, 520
And now adopted to a foreign land.'
   To him the King: 'Reciting thus thy
   cares,
My secret soul in all thy sorrow shares;
But one choice blessing (such is Jove's
   high will)
Has sweeten'd all thy bitter draught of ill:
Torn from thy country to no hapless end,
The Gods have, in a master, giv'n a friend.

Whatever frugal nature needs is thine
(For she needs little), daily bread and
   wine.
While I, so many wand'rings past and
   woes, 530
Live but on what thy poverty bestows.'
   So pass'd in pleasing dialogue away
The night; then down to short repose
   they lay;
Till radiant rose the messenger of day.
While in the port of Ithaca, the band
Of young Telemachus approach'd the land;
Their sails they loos'd, they lash'd the
   mast aside,
And cast their anchors, and the cables
   tied:
Then on the breezy shore, descending, join
In grateful banquet o'er the rosy wine. 540
When thus the Prince: 'Now each his
   course pursue:
I to the fields, and to the city you.
Long absent hence, I dedicate this day
My swains to visit, and the works survey.
Expect me with the morn, to pay the skies
Our debt of safe return in feast and sacri-
   fice.'
   Then Theoclymenus: 'But who shall lend,
Meantime, protection to thy stranger
   friend?
Straight to the Queen and Palace shall I
   fly, 549
Or, yet more distant, to some Lord apply?'
   The Prince return'd: 'Renown'd in days
   of yore
Has stood our father's hospitable door;
No other roof a stranger should receive,
No other hands than ours the welcome
   give.
But in my absence riot fills the place,
Nor bears the modest Queen a stranger's
   face;
From noiseful revel far remote she flies,
But rarely seen, or seen with weeping eyes.
No — let Eurymachus receive my guest,
Of nature courteous, and by far the best;
He woos the Queen with more respectful
   flame, 561
And emulates her former husband's fame:
With what success, 't is Jove's alone to
   know,
And the hoped nuptials turn to joy or woe.'
   Thus speaking, on the right up-soar'd in
   air
The hawk, Apollo's swift-wing'd messen-
   ger:

His deathful pounces tore a trembling
       dove;
The clotted feathers, scatter'd from above,
Between the hero and the vessel pour
Thick plumage, mingled with a sanguine
       shower.   570
  Th' observing augur took the Prince
       aside,
Seiz'd by the hand, and thus prophetic
       cried:
'Yon bird, that dexter cuts th' aërial road,
Rose ominous, nor flies without a God:
No race but thine shall Ithaca obey;
To thine, for ages, Heav'n decrees the
       sway.'
  'Succeed the omens, Gods!' (the youth
       rejoin'd)
'Soon shall my bounties speak a grateful
       mind,
And soon each envied happiness attend 579
The man who calls Telemachus his friend.'
Then to Peiræus: 'Thou whom time has
       prov'd
A faithful servant, by thy Prince belov'd!
Till we returning shall our guest demand,
Accept this charge with honour, at our
       hand.'
  To this Peiræus: 'Joyful I obey,
Well pleas'd the hospitable rites to pay.
The presence of thy guest shall best re-
       ward
(If long thy stay) the absence of my lord.'
  With that, their anchors he commands to
       weigh,
Mount the tall bark, and launch into the
       sea.   590
All with obedient haste forsake the shores,
And, placed in order, spread their equal
       oars.
Then from the deck the Prince his sandals
       takes;
Pois'd in his hand the pointed jav'lin shakes.
They part; while, less'ning from the hero's
       view,
Swift to the town the well-row'd galley flew:
The hero trod the margin of the main,
And reach'd the mansion of his faithful
       swain.

                    BOOK XVII

                     ARGUMENT

Telemachus, returning to the city, relates to
  Penelope the sum of his travels. Ulysses is

conducted by Eumæus to the palace, where
his old dog Argus acknowledges his master,
after an absence of twenty years, and dies
with joy. Eumæus returns into the country,
and Ulysses remains among the Suitors,
whose behaviour is described.

  Soon as Aurora, Daughter of the Dawn,
Sprinkled with roseate light the dewy
       lawn,
In haste the Prince arose, prepared to part;
His hand impatient grasps the pointed
       dart;
Fair on his feet the polish'd sandals shine,
And thus he greets the master of the
       swine:
  'My friend, adieu! let this short stay ⎤
       suffice; |
I haste to meet my mother's longing eyes, ⎬
And end her tears, her sorrows, and her |
       sighs,   ⎦
But thou, attentive, what we order heed: 10
This hapless stranger to the city lead:
By public bounty let him there be fed,
And bless the hand that stretches forth the
       bread;
To wipe the tears from all afflicted eyes,
My will may covet, but my power denies.
If this raise anger in the stranger's
       thought,
The pain of anger punishes the fault:
The very truth I undisguised declare;
For what so easy as to be sincere?'
  To this Ulysses: 'What the Prince re-
       quires   20
Of swift removal, seconds my desires.
To want like mine the peopled town can
       yield
More hopes of comfort than the lonely
       field:
Nor fits my age to till the labour'd lands,
Or stoop to tasks a rural lord demands.
Adieu! but since this ragged garb can
       bear
So ill th' inclemencies of morning air,
A few hours' space permit me here to ⎤
       stay: |
My steps Eumæus shall to town convey,   ⎬
With riper beams when Phœbus warms |
       the day.'   30 ⎦
  Thus he; nor aught Telemachus replied,
But left the mansion with a lofty stride:
Schemes of revenge his pond'ring breast
       elate,
Revolving deep the suitors' sudden fate.

Arriving now before th' imperial hall,
He props his spear against the pillar'd
   wall;
Then like a lion o'er the threshold bounds;
The marble pavement with his step re-
   sounds;
His eye first glanc'd where Euryclea
   spreads
With furry spoils of beasts the splendid
   beds: 40
She saw, she wept, she ran with eager
   pace,
And reach'd her master with a long em-
   brace.
All crowded round the family appears
With wild entrancement, and ecstatic
   tears.
Swift from above descends the royal Fair ⎫
(Her beauteous cheeks the blush of Venus ⎟
   wear,   ⎬
Chasten'd with coy Diana's pensive air); ⎭
Hangs o'er her son, in his embraces dies;
Rains kisses on his neck, his face, his eyes:
Few words she spoke, tho' much she had to
   say: 50
And scarce those few, for tears, could force
   their way.
  ' Light of my eyes ! he comes ! unhoped-
   for joy !
Has Heav'n from Pylos brought my lovely
   boy ?
So snatch'd from all our cares ! — Tell,
   hast thou known
Thy father's fate, and tell me all thy own.'
  ' Oh dearest ! most revered of woman-
   kind !
Cease with those tears to melt a manly
   mind '
(Replied the Prince); ' nor be our fates
   deplor'd,
From death and treason to thy arms re-
   stor'd.
Go, bathe, and robed in white ascend the
   towers;   60
With all thy handmaids thank th' immor-
   tal Powers:
To ev'ry God vow hecatombs to bleed,
And call Jove's vengeance on the guilty
   deed.
While to th' assembled council I repair;
A stranger sent by Heav'n attends me
   there;
My new accepted guest I haste to find,
Now to Peiræus' honour'd charge con-
   sign'd.'

  The matron heard, nor was his word in
   vain.
She bathed; and, robed in white, with all
   her train,
To ev'ry God vow'd hecatombs to bleed, 70
And call'd Jove's vengeance on the guilty
   deed.
Arm'd with his lance, the Prince then pass'd
   the gate;
Two dogs behind, a faithful guard, await;
Pallas his form with grace divine im-
   proves:
The gazing crowd admires him as he
   moves:
Him, gath'ring round, the haughty suitors
   greet
With semblance fair, but inward deep de-
   ceit.
Their false addresses gen'rous he denied,
Pass'd on, and sate by faithful Mentor's
   side;
With Antiphus, and Halitherses sage,   80
His father's counsellors, revered for age.
Of his own fortunes, and Ulysses' fame,
Much ask'd the seniors; till Peiræus came.
The stranger-guest pursued him close be-
   hind;
Whom when Telemachus beheld, he join'd.
He (when Peiræus ask'd for slaves to bring
The gifts and treasures of the Spartan
   King)
Thus thoughtful answer'd: ' Those we shall
   not move,
Dark and unconscious of the will of Jove:
We know not yet the full event of all;   90
Stabb'd in his palace if your Prince must
   fall.
Us, and our house, if treason must o'er-
   throw,
Better a friend possess them than a foe;
If death to these, and vengeance, Heav'n
   decree,
Riches are welcome then, not else, to me.
Till then retain the gifts.' — The hero said,
And in his hand the willing stranger led.
Then, disarray'd, the shining bath they
   sought
(With unguents smooth) of polish'd marble
   wrought;
Obedient handmaids with assistant toil   100
Supply the limpid wave, and fragrant oil;
Then o'er their limbs refulgent robes they
   threw,
And fresh from bathing to their seats with-
   drew.

The golden ewer a nymph attendant brings,
Replenish'd from the pure translucent springs:
With copious streams that golden ewer supplies
A silver laver of capacious size.
They wash: the table, in fair order spread,
Is piled with viands and the strength of bread.
Full opposite, before the folding gate, 110
The pensive mother sits in humble state;
Lowly she sate, and with dejected view
The fleecy threads her iv'ry fingers drew.
The Prince and stranger shared the genial feast,
Till now the rage of thirst and hunger ceas'd.
When thus the Queen: 'My son! my only friend!
Say, to my mournful couch shall I ascend
(The couch deserted now a length of years;
The couch for ever water'd with my tears)?
Say, wilt thou not (ere yet the suitor crew
Return, and riot shakes our walls anew), 121
Say, wilt thou not the least account afford?
The least glad tidings of my absent lord?'
To her the youth: 'We reach'd the Pylian plains,
Where Nestor, shepherd of his people, reigns.
All arts of tenderness to him are known,
Kind to Ulysses' race as to his own:
No father with a fonder grasp of joy
Strains to his bosom his long-absent boy.
But all unknown, if yet Ulysses breathe, 130
Or glide a spectre in the realms beneath:
For farther search, his rapid steeds transport
My lengthen'd journey to the Spartan court.
There Argive Helen I beheld, whose charms
(So Heav'n decreed) engaged the great in arms.
My cause of coming told, he thus rejoin'd;
And still his words live perfect in my mind:
'"Heav'ns! would a soft, inglorious, dastard train
An absent hero's nuptial joys profane!
So with her young, amid the woodland shades, 140
A tim'rous hind the lion's court invades,

Leaves in that fatal lair her tender fawns.
And climbs the cliffs, or feeds along the lawns;
Meantime returning, with remorseless sway
The monarch savage rends the panting prey:
With equal fury, and with equal fame,
Shall great Ulysses reassert his claim.
O Jove! Supreme! whom men and Gods revere;
And thou, whose lustre gilds the rolling sphere!
With power congenial join'd, propitious aid 150
The Chief adopted by the Martial Maid!
Such to our wish the warrior soon restore,
As when, contending on the Lesbian shore,
His prowess Philomelides confess'd,
And loud acclaiming Greeks the victor bless'd:
Then soon th' invaders of his bed and throne,
Their love presumptuous shall by death atone.
Now what you question of my ancient friend,
With truth I answer; thou the truth attend.
Learn what I heard the sea-born seer relate, 160
Whose eye can pierce the dark recess of fate.
Sole in an isle, imprison'd by the main,
The sad survivor of his numerous train,
Ulysses lies; detain'd by magic charms,
And press'd unwilling in Calypso's arms.
No sailors there, no vessels to convey,
No oars to cut th' immeasurable way."
This told Atrides, and he told no more.
Then safe I voyaged to my native shore.'
He ceas'd; nor made the pensive Queen reply, 170
But droop'd her head, and drew a secret sigh.
When Theoclymenus the seer began:
'O suff'ring consort of the suff'ring man!
What human knowledge could, those Kings might tell,
But I the secrets of high Heav'n reveal.
Before the first of Gods be this declared,
Before the board whose blessings we have shared;
Witness the genial rites, and witness all
This house holds sacred in her ample wall!

Ev'n now, this instant, great Ulysses,
   laid   180
At rest, or wand'ring in his country's shade,
Their guilty deeds, in hearing, and in view,
Secret revolves; and plans the vengeance
   due.
Of this sure auguries the Gods bestow'd,
When first our vessel anchor'd in your
   road.'
  'Succeed those omens, Heav'n!' (the
   Queen rejoin'd)
'So shall our bounties speak a grateful
   mind :
And every envied happiness attend
The man who calls Penelope his friend.'
  Thus communed they: while in the mar-
   ble court   190
(Scene of their insolence) the lords resort;
Athwart the spacious square each tries his
   art,
To whirl the disk, or aim the missile dart.
  Now did the hour of sweet repast arrive,
And from the field the victim flocks they
   drive :
Medon the Herald (one who pleas'd them
   best,
And honour'd with a portion of their feast),
To bid the banquet, interrupts their play :
Swift to the hall they haste; aside they
   lay
Their garments, and succinct the victims
   slay.   200
Then sheep, and goats, and bristly porkers
   bled,
And the proud steer was o'er the marble
   spread.
  While thus the copious banquet they
   provide,
Along the road, conversing side by side,
Proceed Ulysses and the faithful swain:
When thus Eumæus, gen'rous and humane:
  'To town, observant of our lord's behest,
Now let us speed: my friend, no more my
   guest !
Yet like myself I wish thee here preferr'd,
Guard of the flock, or keeper of the herd. 210
But much to raise my master's wrath I
   fear;
The wrath of Princes ever is severe.
Then heed his will, and be our journey
   made
While the broad beams of Phœbus are
   display'd,
Or ere brown ev'ning spreads her chilly
   shade.'

  'Just thy advice' (the prudent Chief re-
   join'd),
'And such as suits the dictate of my mind.
Lead on: but help me to some staff to stay
My feeble step, since rugged is the way.'
  Across his shoulders then the scrip he
   flung,   220
Wide-patch'd, and fasten'd by a twisted
   thong.
A staff Eumæus gave. Along the way
Cheerly they fare : behind, the keepers
   stay;
These with their watchful dogs (a constant
   guard)
Supply his absence, and attend the herd.
And now his city strikes the Monarch's eyes,
Alas! how changed! a man of miseries;
Propp'd on a staff, a beggar old and bare,
In rags dishonest flutt'ring with the air !
Now, pass'd the rugged road, they journey
   down   230
The cavern'd way descending to the town,
Where, from the rock, with liquid drops
   distils
A limpid fount, that, spread in parting
   rills,
Its current thence to serve the city brings ;
A useful work, adorn'd by ancient kings.
Neritus, Ithacus, Polyctor, there,
In sculptured stone immortalized their
   care ;
In marble urns receiv'd it from above,
And shaded with a green surrounding
   grove;   239
Where silver alders, in high arches twin'd,
Drink the cool stream, and tremble to the
   wind.
Beneath, sequester'd to the nymphs, is seen
A mossy altar, deep embower'd in green ;
Where constant vows by travellers are paid,
And holy horrors solemnize the shade.
  Here, with his goats (not vow'd to sacred
   flame,
But pamper'd luxury), Melanthius came:
Two grooms attend him. With an envious
   look
He eyed the stranger, and imperious spoke:
  'The good old proverb how this pair
   fulfil !   250
One rogue is usher to another still.
Heav'n with a secret principle endued
Mankind, to seek their own similitude.
Where goes the swineherd with that ill-
   look'd guest ?
That giant glutton, dreadful at a feast!

Full many a post have those broad shoul-
  ders worn,
From ev'ry great man's gate repuls'd with
  scorn:
To no brave prize aspired the worthless
  swain,
'T was but for scraps he ask'd, and ask'd in
  vain.   259
To beg, than work, he better understands;
Or we perhaps might take him off thy
  hands.
For any office could the slave be good,
To cleanse the fold, or help the kids to
  food,
If any labour those big joints could learn,
Some whey, to wash his bowels, he might
  earn.
To cringe, to whine, his idle hands to
  spread,
Is all by which that graceless maw is fed.
Yet hear me! if thy impudence but dare
Approach yon walls, I prophesy thy fare:
Dearly, full dearly, shalt thou buy thy
  bread   270
With many a footstool thund'ring at thy
  head.'
  He thus: nor insolent of word alone,
Spurn'd with his rustic heel his King un-
  known;
Spurn'd, but not mov'd: he like a pillar
  stood,
Nor stirr'd an inch, contemptuous, from the
  road:
Doubtful, or with his staff to strike him
  dead,
Or greet the pavement with his worthless
  head.
Short was that doubt; to quell his rage
  inured,
The hero stood self-conquer'd, and en-
  dured.   279
But hateful of the wretch, Eumæus heav'd
His hands obtesting, and this prayer con-
  ceiv'd:
'Daughters of Jove! who from th' ethereal
  bowers
Descend to swell the springs, and feed the
  flowers!
Nymphs of this fountain! to whose sacred
  names
Our rural victims mount in blazing flames!
To whom Ulysses' piety preferr'd
The yearly firstlings of his flock, and herd;
Succeed my wish, your votary restore:
Oh, be some God his convoy to our shore!

Due pains shall punish then this slave's
  offence,   290
And humble all his airs of insolence,
Who, proudly stalking, leaves the herds at
  large,
Commences courtier, and neglects his
  charge.'
  'What mutters he?' (Melanthius sharp
  rejoins)
'This crafty miscreant big with dark de-
  signs?
The day shall come; nay, 't is already
  near,
When, slave! to sell thee at a price too
  dear
Must be my care; and hence transport thee
  o'er,
A load and scandal to this happy shore.
Oh that as surely great Apollo's dart,   300
Or some brave suitor's sword, might pierce
  the heart
Of the proud son, as that we stand this hour
In lasting safety from the father's power!'
  So spoke the wretch, but, shunning
  farther fray,
Turn'd his proud step, and left them on
  their way.
Straight to the feastful palace he repair'd,
Familiar enter'd, and the banquet shared;
Beneath Eurymachus, his patron lord,
He took his place, and plenty heap'd the
  board.
  Meantime they heard, soft-circling in the
  sky,   310
Sweet airs ascend, and heav'nly minstrelsy
(For Phemius to the lyre attuned the
  strain):
Ulysses hearken'd, then address'd the
  swain:
  'Well may this palace admiration claim,
Great, and respondent to the master's
  fame!
Stage above stage th' imperial structure
  stands,
Holds the chief honours, and the town com-
  mands:
High walls and battlements the courts in-
  close,
And the strong gates defy a host of foes.
Far other cares its dwellers now employ; 320
The throng'd assembly and the feast of
  joy:
I see the smokes of sacrifice aspire,
And hear (what graces ev'ry feast) the
  lyre.'

Then thus Eumæus : 'Judge we which
  were best:
Amidst yon revellers a sudden guest
Choose you to mingle, while behind I
  stay ?
Or I first ent'ring introduce the way ?
Wait for a space without, but wait not
  long;
This is the house of violence and wrong:
Some rude insult thy rev'rend age may
  bear; 330
For like their lawless lords the servants
  are.'
  'Just is, O Friend ! thy caution, and
  address'd '
(Replied the Chief) 'to no unheedful breast:
The wrongs and injuries of base mankind
Fresh to my sense, and always in my mind.
The bravely-patient to no fortune yields:
On rolling oceans, and in fighting fields,
Storms have I pass'd, and many a stern
  debate;
And now in humbler scene submit to Fate.
What cannot Want ? The best she will
  expose, 340
And I am learn'd in all her train of woes;
She fills with navies, hosts, and loud alarms
The sea, the land, and shakes the world
  with arms!'
  Thus near the gates conferring as they
  drew,
Argus, the dog, his ancient master knew;
He, not unconscious of the voice and tread,
Lifts to the sound his ear, and rears his
  head;
Bred by Ulysses, nourish'd at his board,
But ah! not fated long to please his lord!
To him, his swiftness and his strength
  were vain; 350
The voice of glory call'd him o'er the main.
Till then in ev'ry sylvan chase renown'd,
With Argus, Argus, rung the woods
  around:
With him the youth pursued the goat or
  fawn,
Or traced the mazy lev'ret o'er the lawn.
Now left to man's ingratitude he lay,
Unhous'd, neglected in the public way;
And where on heaps the rich manure was
  spread,
Obscene with reptiles, took his sordid bed.
  He knew his lord; he knew, and strove
  to meet; 360
In vain he strove to crawl and kiss his
  feet;

Yet (all he could) his tail, his ears, his
  eyes
Salute his master, and confess his joys.
Soft pity touch'd the mighty master's soul;
Adown his cheek a tear unbidden stole,
Stole unperceiv'd; he turn'd his head and
  dried
The drop humane; then thus impassion'd
  cried:
  'What noble beast in this abandon'd
  state
Lies here all helpless at Ulysses' gate ?
His bulk and beauty speak no vulgar
  praise: 370
If, as he seems, he was in better days,
Some care his age deserves; or was he
  prized
For worthless beauty ? therefore now de-
  spised:
Such dogs and men there are, mere things
  of state:
And always cherish'd by their friends, the
  great.'
  'Not Argus so ' (Eumæus thus rejoin'd),
' But serv'd a master of a nobler kind,
Who never, never shall behold him more!
Long, long since perish'd on a distant
  shore!
Oh had you seen him, vig'rous, bold, and
  young, 380
Swift as a stag, and as a lion strong:
Him no fell savage on the plain withstood,
None 'scaped him bosom'd in the gloomy
  wood:
His eye how piercing, and his scent how
  true,
To wind the vapour in the tainted dew !
Such, when Ulysses left his natal coast;
Now years unnerve him, and his lord is
  lost!
The women keep the gen'rous creature
  bare,
A sleek and idle race is all their care:
The master gone, the servants what re-
  strains ? 390
Or dwells humanity where riot reigns ?
Jove fix'd it certain, that whatever day
Makes man a slave, takes half his worth
  away.'
  This said, the honest herdsman strode
  before:
The musing Monarch pauses at the door:
The dog, whom Fate had granted to behold
His lord, when twenty tedious years had
  roll'd,

Takes a last look, and, having seen him, dies:
So closed for ever faithful Argus' eyes!
　And now Telemachus, the first of all, 400
Observ'd Eumæus ent'ring in the hall;
Distant he saw, across the shady dome;
Then gave a sign, and beckon'd him to
　come.
There stood an empty seat, where late was
　placed,
In order due, the steward of the feast
(Who now was busied carving round the
　board);
Eumæus took, and placed it near his lord.
Before him instant was the banquet spread,
And the bright basket piled with loaves of
　bread;
　Next came Ulysses lowly at the door, 410
A figure despicable, old, and poor,
In squalid vests, with many a gaping rent,
Propp'd on a staff, and trembling as he went.
Then resting on the threshold of the gate,
Against a cypress pillar lean'd his weight
(Smooth'd by the workman to a polish'd
　plane);
The thoughtful son beheld, and call'd his
　swain:
' These viands, and this bread, Eumæus !
　bear,
And let yon mendicant our plenty share :
Then let him circle round the suitors'
　board, 420
And try the bounty of each gracious lord.
Bold let him ask, encouraged thus by me;
How ill, alas ! do want and shame agree !'
　His lord's command the faithful servant
　bears:
The seeming beggar answers with his
　prayers:
' Bless'd be Telemachus ! in ev'ry deed
Inspire him, Jove ! in ev'ry wish succeed!'
This said, the portion from his son convey'd
With smiles receiving on his scrip he laid.
Long as the minstrel swept the sounding
　wire, 430
He fed, and ceas'd when silence held the
　lyre.
Soon as the suitors from the banquet rose,
Minerva prompts the man of mighty woes
To tempt their bounties with a suppliant's
　art,
And learn the gen'rous from th' ignoble
　heart
(Not but his soul, resentful as humane,
Dooms to full vengeance all th' offending
　train);

With speaking eyes, and voice of plaintive
　sound,
Humble he moves, imploring all around.
The proud feel pity, and relief bestow, 440
With such an image touch'd of human
　woe;
Inquiring all, their wonder they confess,
And eye the man, majestic in distress.
　While thus they gaze and question with
　their eyes,
The bold Melanthius to their thought re-
　plies:
' My lords ! this stranger of gigantic port
The good Eumæus usher'd to your court.
Full well I mark'd the features of his face,
Tho' all unknown his clime, or noble race.'
　' And is this present, swineherd ! of thy
　hand ? 450
Bring'st thou these vagrants to infest the
　land ? '
(Returns Antinoüs with retorted eye)
' Objects uncouth, to check the genial joy ?
Enough of these our court already grace,
Of giant stomach, and of famish'd face.
Such guests Eumæus to his country brings,
To share our feast, and lead the life of
　Kings.'
　To whom the hospitable swain rejoin'd:
' Thy passion, Prince, belies thy knowing
　mind. 459
Who calls, from distant nations to his own,
The poor, distinguish'd by their wants
　alone ?
Round the wide world are sought those
　men divine
Who public structures raise, or who de-
　sign;
Those to whose eyes the Gods their ways
　reveal,
Or bless with salutary arts to heal;
But chief to poets such respect belongs,
By rival nations courted for their songs:
These states invite, and mighty Kings ad-
　mire,
Wide as the sun displays his vital fire. 469
It is not so with want ! how few that feed
A wretch unhappy, merely for his need !
Unjust to me, and all that serve the state,
To love Ulysses is to raise thy hate.
For me, suffice the approbation won
Of my great mistress, and her godlike son.'
　To him Telemachus: ' No more incense
The man by nature prone to insolence;
Injurious minds just answers but provoke:'
Then, turning to Antinoüs, thus he spoke:

'Thanks to thy care! whose absolute com-
mand 480
Thus drives the stranger from our court
and land.
Heav'n bless its owner with a better mind!
From envy free, to charity inclin'd.
This both Penelope and I afford:
Then, Prince! be bounteous of Ulysses'
board.
To give another's is thy hand so slow?
So much more sweet to spoil than to be-
stow?'
'Whence, great Telemachus! this lofty
strain?'
(Antinoüs cries with insolent disdain)
'Portions like mine if ev'ry suitor gave, 490
Our walls this twelvemonth should not see
the slave.'
He spoke, and lifting high above the
board
His pond'rous footstool, shook it at his
lord.
The rest with equal hand conferr'd the ⎫
bread; ⎪
He fill'd his scrip, and to the threshold ⎬
sped; ⎪
But first before Antinoüs stopp'd, and said: ⎭
'Bestow, my Friend! thou dost not seem
the worst
Of all the Greeks, but prince-like and the
first;
Then, as in dignity, be first in worth,
And I shall praise thee thro' the boundless
earth. 500
Once I enjoy'd in luxury of state
Whate'er gives man the envied name of
great;
Wealth, servants, friends, were mine in
better days;
And hospitality was then my praise;
In ev'ry sorrowing soul I pour'd delight,
And Poverty stood smiling in my sight.
But Jove, all-governing, whose only will
Determines Fate, and mingles good with
ill,
Sent me (to punish my pursuit of gain) 509
With roving pirates o'er th' Ægyptian
main:
By Ægypt's silver flood our ships we moor;
Our spies commission'd straight the coast
explore;
But, impotent of mind, with lawless will
The country ravage and the natives kill.
The spreading clamour to their city flies,
And horse and foot in mingled tumult rise:

The redd'ning dawn reveals the hostile
fields
Horrid with bristly spears, and gleaming
shields:
Jove thunder'd on their side: our guilty ⎫
head ⎪
We turn'd to flight; the gath'ring ven- ⎪
geance spread 520 ⎬
On all parts round, and heaps on heaps ⎪
lay dead. ⎭
Some few the foe in servitude detain;
Death ill-exchanged for bondage and for
pain!
Unhappy me a Cyprian took aboard,
And gave to Dmetor, Cyprus' haughty
lord:
Hither, to 'scape his chains, my course I
steer,
Still curs'd by fortune, and insulted here!'
To whom Antinoüs thus his rage ex-
press'd:
'What God has plagued us with this gor-
mand guest?
Unless at distance, Wretch! thou keep ⎫
behind, 530 ⎪
Another isle, than Cyprus more unkind, ⎬
Another Ægypt, shalt thou quickly find. ⎭
From all thou begg'st, a bold audacious
slave;
Nor all can give so much as thou canst
crave.
Nor wonder I at such profusion shown;
Shameless they give, who give what's not
their own.'
The Chief, retiring, 'Souls, like that in
thee,
Ill suit such forms of grace and dignity. 538
Nor will that hand to utmost need afford
The smallest portion of a wasteful board,
Whose luxury whole patrimonies sweeps,
Yet starving want, amidst the riot, weeps.'
The haughty suitor with resentment burns,
And, sourly smiling, this reply returns:
'Take that, ere yet thou quit this princely ⎫
throng; ⎪
And dumb for ever be thy sland'rous ⎬
tongue!' ⎪
He said, and high the whirling tripod ⎪
flung. ⎭
His shoulder-blade receiv'd th' ungentle
shock:
He stood, and moved not, like a marble rock;
But shook his thoughtful head, nor more
complain'd, 550
Sedate of soul, his character sustain'd,

And inly form'd revenge: then back with-
    drew:
Before his feet the well-fill'd scrip he
    threw,
And thus with semblance mild address'd
    the crew:
    'May what I speak your princely minds
    approve,
Ye Peers and Rivals in this noble love !
Not for the hurt I grieve, but for the cause.
If, when the sword our country's quarrel
    draws,
Or if, defending what is justly dear,
From Mars impartial some broad wound
    we bear,   560
The gen'rous motive dignifies the scar.
But for mere want, how hard to suffer
    wrong !
Want brings enough of other ills along !
Yet, if unjustice never be secure,
If fiends revenge, and Gods assert the
    poor,
Death shall lay low the proud aggressor's
    head,
And make the dust Antinous' bridal bed.'
    'Peace, wretch ! and eat thy bread with-
    out offence'
(The suitor cried), 'or force shall drag thee
    hence,
Scourge thro' the public street, and cast
    thee there,   570
A mangled carcass for the hounds to tear.'
    His furious deed the gen'ral anger
    mov'd;
All, ev'n the worst, condemn'd: and some
    reprov'd.
'Was ever Chief for wars like these re-
    nown'd ?
Ill fits the stranger and the poor to wound.
Unbless'd thy hand, if, in this low dis-
    guise,
Wander, perhaps, some inmate of the
    skies:
They (curious oft of mortal actions) deign
In forms like these to round the earth and
    main,
Just and unjust recording in their mind, 580
And with sure eyes inspecting all man-
    kind.'
    Telemachus, absorb'd in thought severe,
Nourish'd deep anguish, tho' he shed no
    tear;
But the dark brow of silent sorrow shook:
While thus his mother to her virgins
    spoke:

'On him and his may the bright God of
    Day
That base inhospitable blow repay !'
The nurse replies: 'If Jove receives my
    prayer,
Not one survives to breathe to-morrow's
    air.'
'All, all are foes, and mischief is their
    end;   590
Antinous most to gloomy death a friend'
(Replies the Queen): 'the stranger begg'd
    their grace,
And melting pity soften'd ev'ry face;
From ev'ry other hand redress he found,
But fell Antinous answer'd with a wound.'
Amidst her maids thus spoke the prudent
    Queen,
Then bade Eumæus call the pilgrim in.
'Much of th' experienc'd man I long to
    hear,
If or his certain eye, or list'ning ear,
Have learn'd the fortunes of my wand'ring
    lord ?'   600
Thus she, and good Eumæus took the
    word:
'A private audience if thy grace im-
    part,
The stranger's words may ease the royal
    heart.
His sacred eloquence in balm distils,
And the soothed heart with secret pleasure
    fills.
Three days have spent their beams, three
    nights have run
Their silent journey since his tale begun,
Unfinish'd yet; and yet I thirst to hear !
As when some Heav'n-taught poet charms
    the ear
(Suspending sorrow with celestial strain 610
Breathed from the Gods to soften human
    pain),
Time steals away with unregarded wing,
And the soul hears him, tho' he cease to
    sing.
'Ulysses late he saw, on Cretan ground
(His father's guest), for Minos' birth re-
    nown'd.
He now but waits the wind, to waft him
    o'er,
With boundless treasure, from Thesprotia's
    shore.'
    To this the Queen: 'The wand'rer let
    me hear,
While yon luxurious race indulge their
    cheer,   619

Devour the grazing ox, and browsing
    goat,
And turn my gen'rous vintage down their
    throat.
For where 's an arm, like thine, Ulysses !
    strong,
To curb wild riot, and to punish wrong ? '
    She spoke.   Telemachus then sneez'd
    aloud;
Constrain'd, his nostril echoed thro' the
    crowd.
The smiling Queen the happy omen bless'd:
    ' So may these impious fall, by Fate op-
    press'd ! '
Then to Eumæus: ' Bring the stranger,
    fly !
And if my questions meet a true reply,
Graced with a decent robe he shall re-
    tire,   630
A gift in season which his wants require.'
    Thus spoke Penelope.   Eumæus flies
In duteous haste, and to Ulysses cries:
' The Queen invites thee, venerable Guest!
A secret instinct moves her troubled
    breast,
Of her long absent lord from thee to
    gain
Some light, and soothe her soul's eternal
    pain.
If true, if faithful thou, her grateful mind
Of decent robes a present has design'd:
So finding favour in the royal eye,   640
Thy other wants her subjects shall supply.'
    ' Fair truth alone ' (the patient man re-
    plied)
' My words shall dictate, and my lips shall
    guide.
To him, to me, one common lot was giv'n,
In equal woes, alas ! involv'd by Heav'n.
Much of his fates I know: but check'd by
    fear
I stand; the hand of violence is here:
Here boundless wrongs the starry skies in-
    vade,
And injured suppliants seek in vain for
    aid.
Let for a space the pensive Queen at-
    tend,   650
Nor claim my story till the sun descend;
Then in such robes as suppliants may re-
    quire,
Composed and cheerful by the genial fire,
When loud uproar and lawless riot cease,
Shall her pleas'd ear receive my words in
    peace.'

Swift to the Queen returns the gentle
    swain:
' And say ' (she cries), ' does fear, or shame,
    detain
The cautious stranger ?   With the begging
    kind
Shame suits but ill.'   Eumæus thus re-
    join'd: 659
' He only asks a more propitious hour,
And shuns (who would not ?) wicked men
    in power;
At ev'ning mild (meet season to confer),
By turns to question, and by turns to
    hear.'
    ' Whoe'er this guest ' (the prudent
    Queen replies),
' His ev'ry step and ev'ry thought is wise.
For men like these on earth he shall not
    find
In all the miscreant race of human kind.'
    Thus she.   Eumæus all her words at-
    tends,
And, parting, to the suitor powers de-
    scends;   669
There seeks Telemachus, and thus apart
In whispers breathes the fondness of his
    heart:
    ' The time, my lord, invites me to re-
    pair
Hence to the lodge; my charge demands
    my care.
These sons of murder thirst thy life to
    take;
O guard it, guard it, for thy servants'
    sake ! '
    ' Thanks to my friend ' (he cries); ' but
    now the hour
Of night draws on; go seek the rural
    bower:
But first refresh; and at the dawn of
    day
Hither a victim to the Gods convey.
Our life to Heav'n's immortal Powers we
    trust,   680
Safe in their care, for Heav'n protects the
    just.'
    Observant of his voice, Eumæus sate,
And fed recumbent on a chair of state.
Then instant rose, and, as he mov'd along, ⎫
'T was riot all amid the suitor throng: ⎬
They feast, they dance, and raise the   ⎭
    mirthful song.
Till now, declining toward the close of
    day,
The sun obliquely shot his dewy ray.

BOOK XXI

THE BENDING OF ULYSSES' BOW

ARGUMENT

Penelope, to put an end to the solicitations of the suitors, proposes to marry the person who shall first bend the bow of Ulysses, and shoot through the ringlets. After their attempts have proved ineffectual, Ulysses, taking Eumæus and Philætius apart, discovers himself to them; then returning, desires leave to try his strength at the bow, which, though refused with indignation by the suitors, Penelope and Telemachus cause to be delivered to his hands. He bends it immediately, and shoots through all the rings. Jupiter at the same instant thunders from heaven; Ulysses accepts the omen, and gives a sign to Telemachus, who stands ready armed at his side.

AND Pallas now, to raise the rivals' fires,
With her own art Penelope inspires:
Who now can bend Ulysses' bow, and wing
The well-aim'd arrow thro' the distant ring,
Shall end the strife, and win th' imperial
 dame ;
But discord and black death await the
 game !
The prudent Queen the lofty stair ascends;
At distance due a virgin-train attends :
A brazen key she held, the handle turn'd,
With steel and polish'd elephant adorn'd: 10
Swift to the inmost room she bent her way,
Where, safe reposed, the royal treasures lay;
There shone high heap'd the labour'd brass
 and ore,
And there the bow which great Ulysses
 bore;
And there the quiver, where now guiltless
 slept
Those winged deaths that many a matron
 wept.
This gift, long since when Sparta's shores
 he trod,
On young Ulysses Iphitus bestow'd :
Beneath Orsilochus's roof they met;
One loss was private, one a public debt; 20
Messena's state from Ithaca detains
Three hundred sheep, and all the shepherd
 swains ;
And to the youthful Prince to urge the
 laws,
The King and elders trust their common
 cause.

But Iphitus, employ'd on other cares,
Search'd the wide country for his wand'ring
 mares,
And mules, the strongest of the lab'ring
 kind;
Hapless to search! more hapless still to find!
For journeying on to Hercules, at length
That lawless wretch, that man of brutal
 strength,   30
Deaf to Heav'n's voice, the social rite transgress'd;
And for the beauteous mares destroy'd his
 guest.
He gave the bow; and on Ulysses' part
Receiv'd a pointed sword, and missile dart:
Of luckless friendship on a foreign shore
Their first, last pledges ! for they met no
 more.
The bow, bequeath'd by this unhappy
 hand,
Ulysses bore not from his native land;
Nor in the front of battle taught to bend,
But kept in dear memorial of his friend. 40
 Now, gently winding up the far ascent,
By many an easy step, the matron went;
Then o'er the pavement glides with grace
 divine
(With polish'd oak the level pavements
 shine);
The folding gates a dazzling light display'd,
With pomp of various architrave o'erlaid.
The bolt, obedient to the silken string,
Forsakes the staple as she pulls the ring;
The wards respondent to the key turn
 round;
The bars fall back; the flying valves resound;   50
Loud as a bull makes hill and valley ring,
So roar'd the lock when it releas'd the
 spring.
She moves majestic thro' the wealthy room,
Where treasured garments cast a rich perfume;
There from the column, where aloft it
 hung,
Reach'd, in its splendid case, the bow unstrung;
Across her knees she laid the well-known
 bow,
And pensive sate, and tears began to flow.
To full satiety of grief she mourns,
Then silent to the joyous hall returns;   60
To the proud suitors bears in pensive state
Th' unbended bow, and arrows wing'd with
 fate.

Behind, her train the polish'd coffer
  brings,
Which held th' alternate brass and silver
  rings.
Full in the portal the chaste Queen ap-
  pears,
And with her veil conceals the coming
  tears :
On either side awaits a virgin fair;
While thus the matron, with majestic air :
' Say you, whom these forbidden walls
  inclose,
For whom my victims bleed, my vintage
  flows,   70
If these neglected, faded charms can
  move ?
Or is it but a vain pretence you love ?
If I the prize, if me you seek to wife,
Hear the conditions, and commence the
  strife.
Who first Ulysses' wondrous bow shall
  bend,
And thro' twelve ringlets the fleet arrow
  send,
Him will I follow, and forsake my home,
For him forsake this lov'd, this wealthy
  dome,
Long, long the scene of all my past delight,
And still to last the vision of my night!' 80
  Graceful she said, and bade Eumæus
  show
The rival Peers the ringlets and the bow.
From his full eyes the tears unbidden
  spring,
Touch'd at the dear memorials of his King.
Philætius too relents, but secret shed
The tender drops. Antinoüs saw, and
  said :
' Hence to your fields, ye Rustics ! hence
  away,
Nor stain with grief the pleasures of the
  day :
Nor to the royal heart recall in vain
The sad remembrance of a perish'd man. 90
Enough her precious tears already flow: ⎫
Or share the feast with due respect, or go ⎬
To weep abroad, and leave to us the bow: ⎭
No vulgar task! Ill suits this courtly crew
That stubborn horn which brave Ulysses
  drew.
I well remember (for I gazed him o'er
While yet a child), what majesty he bore!
And still (all infant as I was) retain
The port, the strength, the grandeur of the
  man.'   99

He said, but in his soul fond joys arise,
And his proud hopes already win the prize
To speed the flying shaft thro' ev'ry ⎫
  ring,   ⎪
Wretch ! is not thine : the arrows of the ⎬
  King   ⎪
Shall end those hopes, and fate is on the ⎪
  wing !   ⎭
  Then thus Telemachus : ' Some God I
  find
With pleasing frenzy has possess'd my
  mind;
When a lov'd mother threatens to depart,
Why with this ill-timed gladness leaps my
  heart ?
Come then, ye suitors ! and dispute a
  prize
Richer than all th' Achaian state sup-
  plies,   110
Than all proud Argos or Mycæne knows,
Than all our isles or continents inclose:
A woman matchless, and almost divine,
Fit for the praise of ev'ry tongue but mine.
No more excuses then, no more delay;
Haste to the trial — Lo ! I lead the way.
' I too may try, and if this arm can wing
The feather'd arrow thro' the destin'd
  ring,
Then, if no happier knight the conquest
  boast,
I shall not sorrow for a mother lost;   120
But, bless'd in her, possess these arms
  alone,
Heir of my father's strength, as well as
  throne.'
  He spoke; then, rising, his broad sword
  unbound,
And cast his purple garment on the ground.
A trench he open'd; in a line he placed
The level axes, and the points made fast.
(His perfect skill the wond'ring gazers
  eyed,
The game as yet unseen, as yet untried.)
Then, with a manly pace, he took his stand,
And grasp'd the bow, and twang'd it in his
  hand.   130
Three times, with beating heart, he made
  essay;
Three times, unequal to the task, gave way;
A modest boldness on his cheek appear'd;
And thrice he hoped, and thrice again he
  fear'd.
The fourth had drawn it. The great Sire
  with joy
Beheld, but with a sign forbade the boy.

His ardour straight th' obedient Prince
  suppress'd,
And, artful, thus the suitor-train address'd:
' O lay the cause on youth yet immature
(For Heav'n forbid such weakness should
  endure) !   140
How shall this arm, unequal to the bow,
Retort an insult, or repel a foe ?
But you ! whom Heav'n with better nerves
  has bless'd,
Accept the trial, and the prize contest.'
He cast the bow before him, and apart
Against the polish'd quiver propp'd the
  dart.
Resuming then his seat, Eupithes' son,
The bold Antinoüs, to the rest begun:
' From where the goblet first begins to flow,
From right to left in order take the bow;
And prove your sev'ral strengths.' — The
  Princes heard,   151
And first Leiodes, blameless priest, ap-
  pear'd:
The eldest born of Œnops' noble race,
Who next the goblet held his holy place;
He, only he, of all the suitor throng,
Their deeds detested, and abjured the
  wrong.
With tender hands the stubborn horn he
  strains,
The stubborn horn resisted all his pains !
Already in despair he gives it o'er:
' Take it who will ' (he cries), ' I strive no
  more.   160
What numerous deaths attend this fatal
  bow !
What souls and spirits shall it send below !
Better, indeed, to die, and fairly give
Nature her debt, than disappointed live,
With each new sun to some new hope a
  prey,
Yet still to-morrow falser than to-day.
How long in vain Penelope we sought !
This bow shall ease us of that idle thought,
And send us with some humbler wife to
  live,
Whom gold shall gain, or destiny shall
  give.'   170
Thus speaking, on the floor the bow he
  placed
(With rich inlay the various floor was
  graced);
At distance far the feather'd shaft he
  throws,
And to the seat returns from whence he
  rose.

To him Antinoüs thus with fury said:
' What words ill-omen'd from thy lips have
  fled ?
Thy coward-function ever is in fear;
Those arms are dreadful which thou canst
  not bear.
Why should this bow be fatal to the brave,
Because the priest is born a peaceful
  slave ?   180
Mark then what others can.' He ended
  there,
And bade Melanthius a vast pile prepare;
He gives it instant flame, then fast beside
Spreads o'er an ample board a bullock's
  hide.
With melted lard they soak the weapon
  o'er,
Chafe ev'ry knot, and supple ev'ry pore.
Vain all their art, and all their strength as
  vain:
The bow inflexible resists their pain.
The force of great Eurymachus alone,   189
And bold Antinoüs, yet untried, unknown,
Those only now remain'd; but those con-
  fess'd
Of all the train the mightiest and the best.
Then from the hall, and from the noisy
  crew,
The masters of the herd and flock with-
  drew.
The King observes them; he the hall for-
  sakes,
And past the limits of the court o'ertakes.
Then thus with accent mild Ulysses spoke:
' Ye faithful guardians of the herd and
  flock !
Shall I the secret of my breast conceal,   199
Or (as my soul now dictates) shall I tell ?
Say, should some fav'ring God restore
  again
The lost Ulysses to his native reign,
How beat your hearts ? what aid would
  you afford
To the proud suitors, or your ancient
  lord ? '
Philætius thus: ' O were thy word not
  vain !
Would mighty Jove restore that man
  again !
These aged sinews, with new vigour strung,
In his blest cause should emulate the
  young.'
With equal vows Eumæus too implor'd
Each power above, with wishes for his
  lord.   210

He saw their secret souls, and thus be-
  gan:
'Those vows the Gods accord; behold the
  man!
Your own Ulysses! twice ten years de-
  tain'd
By woes and wand'rings from this hapless
  land:
At length he comes; but comes despised,
  unknown,
And finding faithful you, and you alone.
All else have cast him from their very
  thought,
Ev'n in their wishes and their prayers for-
  got!
Hear then, my friends: If Jove this arm
  succeed,
And give yon impious revellers to bleed, 220
My care shall be to bless your future lives
With large possessions and with faithful
  wives:
Fast by my palace shall your domes as-
  cend,
And each on young Telemachus attend,
And each be call'd his brother and my
  friend.
To give you firmer faith, now trust your
  eye;
Lo! the broad scar indented on my thigh,
When with Autolycus's sons, of yore,
On Parnass' top I chased the tusky boar.'
His ragged vest then drawn aside, dis-
  closed 230
The sign conspicuous, and the scar exposed;
Eager they view'd; with joy they stood
  amazed;
With tearful eyes o'er all their master
  gazed:
Around his neck their longing arms they
  cast,
His head, his shoulders, and his knees em-
  braced;
Tears follow'd tears; no word was in their
  power;
In solemn silence fell the kindly shower.
The King too weeps, the King too grasps
  their hands,
And moveless, as a marble fountain, stands.
  Thus had their joy wept down the set-
    ting sun, 240
But first the wise man ceas'd, and thus be-
  gun:
'Enough — on other cares your thought
  employ,
For danger waits on all untimely joy.

Full many foes, and fierce, observe us near;
Some may betray, and yonder walls may
  hear.
Re-enter then, not all at once, but stay
Some moments you, and let me lead the way.
To me, neglected as I am, I know
The haughty suitors will deny the bow;
But thou, Eumæus, as 't is borne away, 250
Thy master's weapon to his hand convey.
At ev'ry portal let some matron wait,
And each lock fast the well-compacted
  gate:
Close let them keep, whate'er invades their
  ear;
Tho' arms, or shouts, or dying groans they
  hear.
To thy strict charge, Philætius, we consign
The court's main gate; to guard that pass
  be thine.'
  This said, he first return'd; the faithful
    swains
At distance follow, as their King ordains.
Before the flame Eurymachus now stands,
And turns the bow, and chafes it with his
  hands; 261
Still the tough bow unmov'd. The lofty
  man
Sigh'd from his mighty soul, and thus be-
  gan:
  'I mourn the common cause: for, oh my
    friends!
On me, on all, what grief, what shame at-
  tends!
Not the lost nuptials can affect me more
(For Greece has beauteous dames on ev'ry
  shore),
But baffled thus! confess'd so far below
Ulysses' strength, as not to bend his bow!
How shall all ages our attempt deride! 270
Our weakness scorn!' Antinoüs thus re-
  plied:
  'Not so, Eurymachus: that no man draws
The wondrous bow, attend another cause.
Sacred to Phœbus is the solemn day,
Which thoughtless we in games would
  waste away;
Till the next dawn this ill-timed strife
  forego,
And here leave fix'd the ringlets in a row.
Now bid the sewer approach, then let us
  join
In due libations, and in rites divine;
So end our night; before the day shall
  spring, 280
The choicest off'rings let Melanthius bring;

Let then to Phœbus' name the fatted thighs
Feed the rich smokes, high curling to the
  skies.
So shall the patron of these arts bestow
(For his the gift) the skill to bend the
  bow.'
  They heard well pleas'd ; the ready
    heralds bring
The cleansing waters from the limpid
  spring;
The goblet high with rosy wine they
  crown'd,
In order circling to the peers around.
That rite complete, uprose the thoughtful
  man,   290
And thus his meditated scheme began;
' If what I ask your noble minds approve,
Ye Peers and Rivals in the royal love!
Chief, if it hurt not great Antinoüs' ear
(Whose sage decision I with wonder hear),
And if Eurymachus the motion please,
Give Heav'n this day, and rest the bow in
  peace.
To-morrow let your arms dispute the prize,
And take it he, the favour'd of the skies!
But, since till then this trial you delay, 300
Trust it one moment to my hands to-day:
Fain would I prove, before your judging
  eyes,
What once I was, whom wretched you de-
  spise;
If yet this arm its ancient force retain;   ⎫
Or if my woes (a long-continued train)   ⎬
And wants and insults, make me less   ⎭
  than man.'
  Rage flash'd in lightning from the suitors'
    eyes,
Yet mix'd with terror at the bold emprise.
Antinoüs then: ' O miserable guest!
Is common sense quite banish'd from thy
  breast ?   310
Sufficed it not, within the palace placed,
To sit distinguish'd, with our presence
  graced,
Admitted here with Princes to confer,
A man unknown, a needy wanderer ?
To copious wine this insolence we owe,
And much thy betters wine can overthrow:
The great Eurytion when this frenzy
  stung,
Pirithoüs' roofs with frantic riot rung;
Boundless the Centaur raged; till one and
  all
The heroes rose, and dragg'd him from the
  hall: 320

His nose they shorten'd, and his ears they
  slit,
And sent him sober'd home, with better
  wit.
Hence with long war the double race was
  curs'd
Fatal to all, but to th' aggressor first.
Such fate I prophesy our guest attends,
If here this interdicted bow he bends:
Nor shall these walls such insolence con-
  tain;
The first fair wind transports him o'er the
  main;
Where Echetus to death the guilty brings
(The worst of mortals, ev'n the worst of
  Kings).   330
Better than that, if thou approve our
  cheer,
Cease the mad strife, and share our bounty
  here.'
  To this the Queen her just dislike ex-
    press'd:
' 'T is impious, Prince, to harm the stranger-
  guest;
Base to insult who bears a suppliant's
  name,
And some respect Telemachus may claim.
What if th' Immortals on the man bestow
Sufficient strength to draw the mighty
  bow ?
Shall I, a Queen, by rival chiefs ador'd,
Accept a wand'ring stranger for my
  lord ?   340
A hope so idle never touch'd his brain:
Then ease your bosom of a fear so vain.
Far be he banish'd from this stately scene
Who wrongs his Princess with a thought
  so mean.'
  ' O Fair! and wisest of so fair a kind ! '
(Respectful thus Eurymachus rejoin'd)
' Mov'd by no weak surmise, but sense of
  shame,
We dread the all-arraigning voice of
  Fame:
We dread the censure of the meanest
  slave,
The weakest woman: all can wrong the
  brave.   350
" Behold what wretches to the bed pre-
  tend
Of that brave Chief, whose bow they could
  not bend!
In came a beggar of the strolling crew,
And did what all those Princes could not
  do."

Thus will the common voice our deed de-
  fame,
And thus posterity upbraid our name.'
To whom the Queen: 'If Fame engage
  your views,
Forbear those acts which Infamy pursues;
Wrong and oppression no renown can
  raise;
Know, Friend! that virtue is the path to
  praise.   360
The stature of our guest, his port, his face,
Speak him descended from no vulgar
  race.
To him the bow, as he desires, convey;
And to his hand if Phœbus give the day,
Hence, to reward his merit, he shall bear
A two-edg'd faulchion and a shining spear,
Embroider'd sandals, a rich cloak and
  vest,
And safe conveyance to his port of rest.'
  'O royal Mother! ever-honour'd name!
Permit me ' (cries Telemachus) 'to claim
A son's just right. No Grecian Prince
  but I   371
Has power this bow to grant, or to deny!
Of all that Ithaca's rough hills contain,
And all wide Elis' courser-breeding plain,
To me alone my father's arms descend;
And mine alone they are, to give or lend.
Retire, O Queen! thy household task re-
  sume,
Tend, with thy maids, the labours of thy
  loom;
The bow, the darts, and arms of chivalry,
These cares to man belong, and most to
  me.'   380
  Mature beyond his years, the Queen ad-
  mired
His sage reply, and with her train retired;
There in her chamber as she sate apart,
Revolv'd his words, and placed them in her
  heart.
On her Ulysses then she fix'd her soul;
Down her fair cheek the tears abundant
  roll,
Till gentle Pallas, piteous of her cries,
In slumber closed her silver-streaming
  eyes.
  Now thro' the press the bow Eumæus
  bore,
And all was riot, noise, and wild uproar. 390
'Hold! lawless rustic! whither wilt thou
  go?
To whom, insensate, dost thou bear the
  bow?

Exil'd for this to some sequester'd den,
Far from the sweet society of men,
To thy own dogs a prey thou shalt be
  made;
If Heav'n and Phœbus lend the suitors
  aid.'
Thus they. Aghast he laid the weapon
  down,
But bold Telemachus thus urged him on:
' Proceed, false slave, and slight their empty
  words;
What! hopes the fool to please so many
  lords?   400
Young as I am, thy Prince's vengeful hand
Stretch'd forth in wrath shall drive thee
  from the land.
Oh! could the vigour of this arm as well
Th' oppressive suitors from my walls
  expel!
Then what a shoal of lawless men should
  go
To fill with tumult the dark courts be-
  low!'
  The suitors with a scornful smile survey
The youth, indulging in the genial day.
Eumæus, thus encouraged, hastes to bring
The strifeful bow, and gives it to the
  King.   410
Old Euryclea calling then aside,
' Hear what Telemachus enjoins' (he
  cried):
' At ev'ry portal let some matron wait,
And each lock fast the well-compacted
  gate;
And if unusual sounds invade their ear,
If arms, or shouts, or dying groans they
  hear,
Let none to call or issue forth presume,
But close attend the labours of the loom.'
  Her prompt obedience on his order
  waits;   419
Closed in an instant were the palace
  gates.
In the same moment forth Philætius flies,
Secures the court, and with a cable ties
The utmost gate (the cable strongly
  wrought
Of Byblos' reed, a ship from Egypt
  brought);
Then unperceiv'd and silent at the board
His seat he takes, his eyes upon his lord.
  And now his well-known bow the Master
  bore,
Turn'd on all sides, and view'd it o'er and
  o'er;

Lest time or worms had done the weapon
 wrong,
Its owner absent, and untried so long. 430
While some deriding : 'How he turns the
 bow !
Some other like it sure the man must
 know,
Or else would copy; or in bows he deals;
Perhaps he makes them, or perhaps he
 steals.' —
'Heav'n to this wretch' (another cried) ⎤
 'be kind ! |
And bless, in all to which he stands in- ⎬
 clin'd, |
With such good fortune as he now shall |
 find.'   ⎦
 Heedless he heard them: but disdain'd
  reply,
The bow perusing with exactest eye.
Then, as some heav'nly minstrel, taught to
 sing 440
High notes responsive to the trembling
 string,
To some new strain when he adapts the
 lyre,
Or the dumb lute refits with vocal wire,
Relaxes, strains, and draws them to and
 fro;
So the great master drew the mighty bow:
And drew with ease. One hand aloft dis-
 play'd
The bending horns, and one the string es-
 say'd.
From his essaying hand the string let fly
Twang'd short and sharp like the shrill
 swallow's cry.
A gen'ral horror ran thro' all the race, 450
Sunk was each heart, and pale was ev'ry
 face.
Signs from above ensued: th' unfolding sky
In lightning burst; Jove thunder'd from on
 high.
Fired at the call of Heav'n's almighty
 Lord,
He snatch'd the shaft that glitter'd on the
 board
(Fast by, the rest lay sleeping in the sheath,
But soon to fly, the messengers of Death).
 Now, sitting as he was, the cord he drew,
Thro' every ringlet levelling his view;
Then notch'd the shaft, releas'd, and ⎤
 gave it wing; 460 |
The whizzing arrow vanish'd from the ⎬
 string, |
Sung on direct, and threaded ev'ry ring. ⎦

The solid gate its fury scarcely bounds;
Pierc'd thro' and thro', the solid gate re-
 sounds.
Then to the Prince: 'Nor have I wrought
 thee shame;
Nor err'd this hand unfaithful to its aim;
Nor prov'd the toil too hard; nor have
 I lost
That ancient vigour once my pride and
 boast.
Ill I deserv'd these haughty Peers' disdain;
Now let them comfort their dejected
 train, 470
In sweet repast their present hour employ
Nor wait till ev'ning for the genial joy:
Then to the lute's soft voice prolong the
 night;
Music, the banquet's most refin'd delight.'
 He said, then gave a nod; and at the
 word
Telemachus girds on his shining sword.
Fast by his father's side he takes his
 stand:
The beamy jav'lin lightens in his hand.

BOOK XXII

THE DEATH OF THE SUITORS

ARGUMENT

Ulysses begins the slaughter of the suitors by
the death of Antinoüs. He declares himself, and lets fly his arrows at the rest. Telemachus assists, and brings arms for his
father, himself, Eumæus, and Philætius.
Melanthius does the same for the wooers.
Minerva encourages Ulysses in the shape of
Mentor. The suitors are all slain, only Medon and Phemius are spared. Melanthius
and the unfaithful servants are executed.
The rest acknowledge their master with all
demonstrations of joy.

THEN fierce the Hero o'er the threshold
 strode;
Stripp'd of his rags, he blazed out like a
 God.
Full in their face the lifted bow he bore,
And quiver'd deaths, a formidable store;
Before his feet the rattling shower he
 threw,
And thus, terrific, to the suitor-crew·
 'One venturous game this hand hath
 won to-day,
Another, Princes ! yet remains to play;

Another mark our arrow must attain.
Phœbus, assist ! nor be the labour vain.' 10
Swift as the word the parting arrow sings,
And bears thy fate, Antinoüs, on its
   wings:
Wretch that he was, of unprophetic soul !
High in his hands he rear'd the golden
   bowl !
Ev'n then to drain it lengthen'd out his
   breath;
Changed to the deep, the bitter draught of
   death:
For Fate who fear'd amidst a feastful
   band ?
And Fate to numbers, by a single hand ?
Full thro' his throat Ulysses' weapon
   pass'd,
And pierc'd his neck. He falls, and
   breathes his last. 20
The tumbling goblet the wide floor o'er-
   flows,
A stream of gore burst spouting from his
   nose;
Grim in convulsive agonies he sprawls:
Before him spurn'd the loaded table falls,
And spreads the pavement with a mingled
   flood
Of floating meats, and wine, and human
   blood.
Amazed, confounded, as they saw him fall,
Up rose the throngs tumultuous round the
   hall:
O'er all the dome they cast a haggard eye,
Each look'd for arms: in vain; no arms
   were nigh: 30
'Aim'st thou at Princes ? ' (all amazed
   they said)
'Thy last of games unhappy hast thou
   play'd;
Thy erring shaft has made our bravest
   bleed,
And Death, unlucky guest, attends thy
   deed.
Vultures shall tear thee.' Thus incens'd
   they spoke,
While each to chance ascribed the won-
   drous stroke,
Blind as they were; for Death even now
   invades
His destin'd prey, and wraps them all in
   shades.
Then, grimly frowning, with a dreadful
   look,
That wither'd all their hearts, Ulysses
   spoke: 40

' Dogs, ye have had your day ! ye fear'd
   no more
Ulysses vengeful from the Trojan shore;
While, to your lust and spoil a guardless
   prey,
Our house, our wealth, our helpless hand-
   maids lay:
Not so content, with bolder frenzy fired,
Ev'n to our bed presumptuous you aspired:
Laws or divine or human fail'd to move,
Or shame of men, or dread of Gods above;
Heedless alike of infamy or praise,
Or Fame's eternal voice in future days, 50
The hour of vengeance, wretches, now is
   come;
Impending fate is yours, and instant
   doom.'
   Thus dreadful he. Confused the suitors
   stood;
From their pale cheeks recedes the flying
   blood:
Trembling they sought their guilty heads
   to hide;
Alone the bold Eurymachus replied:
   'If, as thy words import ' (he thus
   began),
'Ulysses lives, and thou the mighty man,
Great are thy wrongs, and much hast thou
   sustain'd 59
In thy spoil'd palace, and exhausted land;
The cause and author of those guilty
   deeds,
Lo ! at thy feet unjust Antinoüs bleeds.
Not love, but wild ambition was his guide;
To slay thy son, thy kingdoms to divide,
These were his aims; but juster Jove
   denied.
Since cold in death th' offender lies, oh
   spare
Thy suppliant people, and receive their
   prayer !
Brass, gold, and treasures, shall the spoil
   defray,
Two hundred oxen ev'ry Prince shall pay
The waste of years refunded in a day. 70
Till then thy wrath is just.' Ulysses
   burn'd
With high disdain, and sternly thus re-
   turn'd:
   'All, all the treasures that enrich'd our
   throne
Before your rapines, join'd with all your
   own,
If offer'd, vainly should for mercy call;
'T is you that offer, and I scorn them all:

Your blood is my demand, your lives the prize,
Till pale as yonder wretch each suitor lies.
Hence with those coward terms; or fight or fly;
This choice is left you to resist or die;   80
And die I trust ye shall.' He sternly spoke:
With guilty fears the pale assembly shook.
Alone Eurymachus exhorts the train:
'Yon archer, comrades, will not shoot in vain;
But from the threshold shall his darts be sped
(Whoe'er he be), till ev'ry Prince lie dead ?
Be mindful of yourselves, draw forth your swords,
And to his shafts obtend these ample boards
(So need compels). Then, all united, strive
The bold invader from his post to drive; 90
The city rous'd shall to our rescue haste,
And this mad archer soon have shot his last.'
    Swift as he spoke, he drew his traitor sword,
And like a lion rush'd against his lord:
The wary Chief the rushing foe repress'd,
Who met the point and forc'd it in his breast:
His falling hand deserts the lifted sword,
And prone he falls extended o'er the board!
Before him wide, in mix'd effusion, roll
Th' untasted viands, and the jovial bowl. 100
Full thro' his liver pass'd the mortal wound,
With dying rage his forehead beats the ground;
He spurn'd the seat with fury as he fell,
And the fierce soul to darkness dived, and Hell.
Next bold Amphinomus his arms extends
To force the pass; the godlike man defends.
Thy spear, Telemachus, prevents th' attack;
The brazen weapon, driving thro' his back,
Thence thro' his breast its bloody passage tore;   109
Flat falls he thund'ring on the marble floor,
And his crush'd forehead marks the stone with gore.

He left his jav'lin in the dead, for fear
The long encumbrance of the weighty spear
To the fierce foe advantage might afford,
To rush between, and use the shorten'd sword.
With speedy ardour to his sire he flies,
And, 'Arm, great Father! arm' (in haste he cries):
'Lo ! hence I run for other arms to wield,
For missive jav'lins, and for helm and shield;   119
Fast by our side, let either faithful swain
In arms attend us, and their part sustain.'
    'Haste, and return' (Ulysses made reply),
'While yet th' auxiliar shafts this hand supply;
Lest thou alone, encounter'd by an host,
Driv'n from the gate, th' important pass be lost.'
    With speed Telemachus obeys, and flies
Where piled in heaps the royal armour lies;
Four brazen helmets, eight refulgent spears,
And four broad bucklers to his sire he bears:
At once in brazen panoply they shone,   130
At once each servant braced his armour on;
Around their King a faithful guard they stand,
While yet each shaft flew deathful from his hand:
Chief after chief expired at ev'ry wound,
And swell'd the bleeding mountain on the ground.
Soon as his store of flying fates was spent,
Against the wall he set the bow unbent;
And now his shoulders bear the massy shield,
And now his hands two beamy jav'lins wield:
He frowns beneath his nodding plume, that play'd   140
O'er the high crest, and cast a dreadful shade.
    There stood a window near, whence, looking down
From o'er the porch, appear'd the subject town.
A double strength of valves secured the place,
A high and narrow, but the only pass:
The cautious King, with all preventing care,
To guard that outlet, placed Eumæus there:

When Agelaüs thus: 'Has none the sense
To mount yon window, and alarm from
  thence
The neighbour-town? the town shall force
  the door,   150
And this bold archer soon shall shoot no
  more.'
  Melanthius then: 'That outlet to the
  gate
So near adjoins that one may guard the
  strait.
But other methods of defence remain;
Myself with arms can furnish all the
  train;
Stores from the royal magazine I bring,
And their own darts shall pierce the Prince
  and King.'
  He said: and mounting up the lofty
  stairs,
Twelve shields, twelve lances, and twelve
  helmets bears:
All arm, and sudden round the hall ap-
  pears   160
A blaze of bucklers, and a wood of spears.
  The Hero stands oppress'd with mighty
  woe,
On ev'ry side he sees the labour grow:
'Oh curs'd event! and oh unlook'd-for
  aid!
Melanthius or the women have betray'd—
Oh my dear son!'—The father with a
  sigh
Then ceas'd; the filial virtue made reply:
'Falsehood is folly, and 't is just to own
The fault committed: this was mine alone;
My haste neglected yonder door to bar, 170
And hence the villain has supplied their
  war.
Run, good Eumæus, then, and (what be-
  fore
I thoughtless err'd in) well secure that
  door:
Learn, if by female fraud this deed were
  done,
Or (as my thought misgives) by Dolius'
  son.'
  While yet they spoke, in quest of arms
  again
To the high chamber stole the faithless
  swain,
Not unobserv'd. Eumæus watchful eyed,
And thus address'd Ulysses near his side:
'The miscreant we suspected takes that
  way,   180
Him, if this arm be powerful, shall I slay?

Or drive him hither, to receive the meed
From thy own hand, of this detested
  deed?'
'Not so' (replied Ulysses); 'leave him
  there,
For us sufficient is another care:
Within the structure of this palace wall
To keep enclosed his masters till they fall.
Go you, and seize the felon; backward
  bind
His arms and legs, and fix a plank behind;
On this his body by strong cords ex-
  tend,   190
And on a column near the roof suspend:
So studied tortures his vile days shall
  end.'
  The ready swains obey'd with joyful
  haste;
Behind the felon unperceiv'd they pass'd,
As round the room in quest of arms he
  goes
(The half-shut door conceals his lurking
  foes)
One hand sustain'd a helm, and one the
  shield
Which old Laërtes wont in youth to wield,
Cover'd with dust, with dryness chapp'd
  and worn,   199
The brass corroded, and the leather torn.
Thus laden, o'er the threshold as he stepp'd,
Fierce on the villain from each side they
  leap'd,
Back by the hair the trembling dastard
  drew
And down reluctant on the pavement threw.
Active and pleas'd the zealous swains ful-
  fil
At every point their master's rigid will:
First, fast behind, his hands and feet they
  bound,
Then straiten'd cords involv'd his body
  round;
So drawn aloft, athwart the column tied,
The howling felon swung from side to
  side.   210
  Eumæus scoffing then with keen disdain:
'There pass thy pleasing night, O gentle
  swain!
On that soft pillow, from that envied
  height,
First may'st thou see the springing dawn of
  light;
So timely rise when morning streaks the
  east,
To drive thy victims to the suitors' feast.'

This said, they left him, tortured as he
lay,
Secured the door, and hasty strode away:
Each, breathing death, resumed his dan-
gerous post   219
Near great Ulysses; four against an host.
When lo! descending to her hero's aid,
Jove's daughter Pallas, War's triumphant
Maid;
In Mentor's friendly form she join'd his
side:
Ulysses saw, and thus with transport cried:
'Come, ever welcome, and thy succour
lend;
O ev'ry sacred name in one! my Friend!
Early we lov'd, and long our loves have
grown;
Whate'er thro' life's whole series I have
done,
Or good, or grateful, now to mind recall,
And, aiding this one hour, repay it all.' 230
Thus he ; but pleasing hopes his bosom
warm
Of Pallas latent in the friendly form.
The adverse host the phantom-warrior ey'd,
And first, loud-threat'ning, Agelaüs cried:
'Mentor, beware, nor let that tongue per-
suade
Thy frantic arm to lend Ulysses aid;
Our force successful shall our threat make
good,
And with the sire and son's commix thy
blood.
What hopest thou here ?   Thee first the
sword shall slay,
Then lop thy whole posterity away;   240
Far hence thy banish'd consort shall we
send;
With his thy forfeit lands and treasures
blend;
Thus, and thus only, shalt thou join thy
friend.'
His barb'rous insult ev'n the Goddess fires,
Who thus the warrior to revenge inspires:
'Art thou Ulysses ? where then shall we
find
The patient body and the constant mind ?
That courage, once the Trojans' daily
dread,
Known nine long years, and felt by heroes
dead ?
And where that conduct, which revenged
the lust   250
Of Priam's race, and laid proud Troy in
dust ?

If this, when Helen was the cause, were
done;
What for thy country now, thy Queen, thy
son ?
Rise then in combat, at my side attend; ⎤
Observe what vigour gratitude can lend, ⎬
And foes how weak, opposed against a ⎥
friend !'   ⎦
She spoke; but willing longer to survey
The sire and son's great acts, withheld the
day;
By farther toils decreed the brave to try,
And level pois'd the wings of victory;   260
Then with a change of form eludes their ⎤
sight,   ⎥
Perch'd like a swallow on a rafter's ⎬
height,   ⎥
And unperceiv'd enjoys the rising fight. ⎦
Damastor's son, bold Agelaüs, leads
The guilty war, Eurynomus succeeds;
With these Pisander, great Polyctor's son,
Sage Polybus, and stern Amphimedon,
With Demoptolemus: these six survive;
The best of all the shafts had left alive.
Amidst the carnage, desp'rate as they
stand,   270
Thus Agelaüs rous'd the lagging band:
'The hour is come, when yon fierce man
no more
With bleeding Princes shall bestrew the
floor;
Lo ! Mentor leaves him with an empty
boast;
The four remain, but four against an host.
Let each at once discharge the deadly
dart,
One sure of six shall reach Ulysses' heart;
Thus shall one stroke the glory lost regain:
The rest must perish, their great leader
slain.'
Then all at once their mingled lances
threw,   280
And thirsty all of one man's blood they
flew;
In vain ! Minerva turn'd them with her
breath,
And scatter'd short, or wide, the points of
death !
With deaden'd sound one on the threshold
falls,
One strikes the gate, one rings against the
walls:
The storm pass'd innocent.   The godlike
man
Now loftier trod, and dreadful thus began:

' 'T is now (brave friends) our turn, at once
    to throw
(So speed them Heav'n) our jav'lins at the
    foe.
That impious race to all their past mis-
    deeds   290
Would add our blood. Injustice still pro-
    ceeds.'
  He spoke: at once their fiery lances flew:
Great Demoptolemus Ulysses slew;
Euryades receiv'd the Prince's dart;
The goatherd's quiver'd in Pisander's
    heart;
Fierce Elatus, by thine, Eumæus, falls;
Their fall in thunder echoes round the
    walls.
The rest retreat: the victors now advance,
Each from the dead resumes his bloody
    lance.   299
Again the foe discharge the steely shower;
Again made frustrate by the Virgin-Power.
Some, turn'd by Pallas, on the threshold
    fall,
Some wound the gate, some ring against
    the wall;
Some weak, or pond'rous with the brazen
    head,
Drop harmless, on the pavement sounding
    dead.
  Then bold Amphimedon his jav'lin cast;
Thy hand, Telemachus, it lightly razed:
And from Ctesippus' arm the spear elanc'd
On good Eumæus' shield and shoulder
    glanc'd:
Not lessen'd of their force (so slight the
    wound)   310
Each sung along, and dropp'd upon the
    ground.
Fate doom'd thee next, Eurydamas, to bear
Thy death, ennobled by Ulysses' spear.
By the bold son Amphimedon was slain,
And Polybus renown'd, the faithful swain.
Pierc'd thro' the breast the rude Ctesippus
    bled,
And thus Philætius gloried o'er the dead:
  ' There end thy pompous vaunts, and high
    disdain;
O sharp in scandal, voluble, and vain !
How weak is mortal pride ! To Heav'n
    alone   320
Th' event of actions and our fates are
    known:
Scoffer, behold what gratitude we bear:
The victim's heel is answer'd with this
    spear.'

  Ulysses brandish'd high his vengeful
    steel,
And Damastorides that instant fell;
Fast by, Leocritus expiring lay;
The Prince's jav'lin tore its bloody way
Thro' all his bowels: down he tumbles
    prone,
His batter'd front and brains besmear the
    stone.
  Now Pallas shines confess'd; aloft she
    spreads   330
The arm of vengeance o'er their guilty
    heads;
The dreadful ægis blazes in their eye:
Amazed they see, they tremble, and they
    fly:
Confused, distracted, thro' the rooms
    they fling:
Like oxen madden'd by the breeze's sting,
When sultry days, and long, succeed the
    gentle spring.
Not half so keen fierce vultures of the
    chase
Stoop from the mountains on the feather'd
    race,
When the wide field extended snares beset;
With conscious dread they shun the quiv-
    'ring net: 340
No help, no flight; but, wounded ev'ry way,
Headlong they drop; the fowlers seize the
    prey.
On all sides thus they double wound on
    wound,
In prostrate heaps the wretches beat the
    ground,
Unmanly shrieks precede each dying groan,
And a red deluge floats the reeking stone.
  Leiodes first before the victor falls:
The wretched augur thus for mercy calls:
' Oh Gracious ! hear, nor let thy suppliant
    bleed:
Still undishonour'd, or by word or deed, 350
Thy house, for me, remains; by me re-
    press'd
Full oft was check'd th' injustice of the
    rest:
Averse they heard me when I counsell'd
    well,
Their hearts were harden'd, and they justly
    fell.
Oh, spare an augur's consecrated head,
Nor add the blameless to the guilty dead.'
  ' Priest as thou art ! for that detested
    band
Thy lying prophecies deceiv'd the land:

Against Ulysses have thy vows been made;
For them thy daily orisons were paid: 360
Yet more, even to our bed thy pride as-
    pires:
One common crime one common fate re-
    quires.'
    Thus speaking, from the ground the
        sword he took
Which Agelaüs' dying hand forsook:
Full thro' his neck the weighty falchion
    sped:
Along the pavement roll'd the mutt'ring
    head.
    Phemius alone the hand of vengeance
        spared,
Phemius the sweet, the Heav'n-instructed
    bard.
Beside the gate the rev'rend minstrel
    stands;
The lyre, now silent, trembling in his
    hands; 370
Dubious to supplicate the Chief, or fly
To Jove's inviolable altar nigh,
Where oft Laërtes holy vows had paid,
And oft Ulysses smoking victims laid.
His honour'd harp with care he first set
    down,
Between the laver and the silver throne;
Then, prostrate stretch'd before the dread-
    ful man,
Persuasive thus, with accent soft began:
    'O King! to mercy be thy soul inclin'd,
And spare the poet's ever-gentle kind. 380
A deed like this thy future fame would
    wrong,
For dear to Gods and man is sacred song.
Self-taught I sing; by Heav'n, and Heav'n
    alone,
The genuine seeds of poesy are sown:
And (what the Gods bestow) the lofty lay
To Gods alone and godlike worth we pay.
Save then the poet, and thyself reward;
'T is thine to merit, mine is to record.
That here I sung, was force, and not de-
    sire:
This hand reluctant touch'd the warbling
    wire; 390
And, let thy son attest, nor sordid pay,
Nor servile flattery, stain'd the moral lay.'
    The moving words Telemachus attends,
His sire approaches, and the bard de-
    fends.
    'O mix not, Father, with those impious
        dead
The man divine; forbear that sacred head;

Medon, the herald, too, our arms may
    spare,
Medon, who made my infancy his care;
If yet he breathes, permit thy son to
    give 399
Thus much to gratitude, and bid him
    live.'
    Beneath a table, trembling with dismay,
Couch'd close to earth, unhappy Medon
    lay,
Wrapp'd in a new-slain ox's ample hide;
Swift at the word he cast his screen aside,
Sprung to the Prince, embraced his knee
    with tears,
And thus with grateful voice address'd his
    ears:
    'O Prince! O Friend! lo! here thy Me-
        don stands:
Ah! stop the hero's unresisted hands,
Incens'd too justly by that impious brood,
Whose guilty glories now are set in
    blood.' 410
    To whom Ulysses with a pleasing eye:
'Be bold, on friendship and my son rely;
Live, an example for the world to read,
How much more safe the good than evil
    deed:
Thou, with the Heav'n-taught bard, in
    peace resort
From blood and carnage to yon open
    court:
Me other work requires.' — With tim'rous
    awe
From the dire scene th' exempted two
    withdraw,
Scarce sure of life, look round, and trem-
    bling move 419
To the bright altars of Protector Jove.
    Meanwhile Ulysses search'd the dome, to
        find
If yet there live of all th' offending kind.
Not one! complete the bloody tale he
    found,
All steep'd in blood, all gasping on the
    ground.
So, when by hollow shores the fisher-train ⎞
Sweep with their arching nets the hoary |
    main,   ⎬
And scarce the meshy toils the copious |
    draught contain,   ⎠
All naked of their element, and bare,
The fishes pant, and gasp in thinner air;
Wide o'er the sands are spread the stiff'n-
    ing prey, 430
Till the warm sun exhales their soul away.

And now the King commands his son to
    call
Old Euryclea to the deathful hall:
The son observant not a moment stays;
The aged governess with speed obeys;
The sounding portals instant they display;
The matron moves, the Prince directs the
    way.
On heaps of death the stern Ulysses stood,
All black with dust, and cover'd thick with
    blood.   439
So the grim lion from the slaughter comes,
Dreadful he glares, and terribly he foams,
His breast with marks of carnage painted
    o'er,
His jaws all dropping with the bull's black
    gore.
    Soon as her eyes the welcome object
    met,
The guilty fall'n, the mighty deed com-
    plete,
A scream of joy her feeble voice essay'd:
The hero check'd her, and composedly
    said:
'Woman, experienc'd as thou art, con-
    trol
Indecent joy, and feast thy secret soul.
T' insult the dead is cruel and unjust;   450
Fate and their crime have sunk them to
    the dust.
Nor heeded these the censure of mankind,
The good and bad were equal in their
    mind.
Justly the price of worthlessness they
    paid,
And each now wails an unlamented shade.
But thou sincere, O Euryclea, say,
What maids dishonour us, and what obey?'
    Then she: 'In these thy kingly walls
    remain
(My son) full fifty of the handmaid train,
Taught, by my care, to cull the fleece or
    weave,   460
And servitude with pleasing tasks deceive;
Of these, twice six pursue their wicked
    way,
Nor me, nor chaste Penelope obey;
Nor fits it that Telemachus command
(Young as he is) his mother's female band.
Hence to the upper chambers let me fly,
Where slumbers soft now close the royal
    eye;
There wake her with the news'—the ma-
    tron cried.
'Not so' (Ulysses, more sedate, replied),

'Bring first the crew who wrought these
    guilty deeds.'   470
In haste the matron parts; the King pro-
    ceeds:
    'Now to dispose the dead, the care re-
    mains
To you, my son, and you, my faithful
    swains;
Th' offending females to that task we
    doom,
To wash, to scent, and purify the room:
These (ev'ry table cleans'd, and ev'ry
    throne,
And all the melancholy labour done),
Drive to yon court, without the palace-
    wall.
There the revenging sword shall smite
    them all;   479
So with the suitors let them mix in dust,
Stretch'd in a long oblivion of their lust.'
    He said: the lamentable train appear,
Each vents a groan, and drops a tender
    tear:
Each heav'd her mournful burden, and be-
    neath
The porch deposed the ghastly heap of
    death.
The Chief severe, compelling each to move,
Urged the dire task imperious from above:
With thirsty sponge they rub the tables
    o'er
(The swains unite their toil); the walls,
    the floor
Wash'd with th' effusive wave, are
    purged of gore.   490
Once more the palace set in fair array,
To the base court the females take their
    way:
There compass'd close between the dome
    and wall
(Their life's last scene), they trembling
    wait their fall.
    Then thus the Prince: 'To these shall
    we afford
A fate so pure, as by the martial sword?
To these, the nightly prostitutes to shame,
And base revilers of our house and
    name?'
    Thus speaking, on the circling wall he
    strung   49
A ship's tough cable, from a column hung
Near the high top he strain'd it strongly
    round,
Whence no contending foot could reach the
    ground.

Their heads above connected in a row,
They beat the air with quiv'ring feet be-
low:
Thus on some tree hung struggling in the
snare,
The doves or thrushes flap their wings in
air.
Soon fled the soul impure, and left behind
The empty corse to waver with the wind.
  Then forth they led Melanthius, and be-
gan
Their bloody work; they lopp'd away the
man,   510
Morsel for dogs ! then trimm'd with brazen
shears
The wretch, and shorten'd of his nose and
ears;
His hands and feet last felt the cruel
steel:
He roar'd, and torments gave his soul to
Hell.
They wash, and to Ulysses take their
way,
So ends the bloody business of the day.
  To Euryclea then address'd the King:
' Bring hither fire, and hither sulphur bring,
To purge the palace: then the Queen at-
tend,
And let her with her matron-train de-
scend;   520
The matron-train, with all the virgin-
band,
Assemble here, to learn their lord's com-
mand.'
  Then Euryclea: ' Joyful I obey,
But cast those mean dishonest rags away;
Permit me first the royal robes to bring:
Ill suits this garb the shoulders of a King.'
  ' Bring sulphur straight, and fire ' (the
Monarch cries).
She hears, and at the word obedient flies.
With fire and sulphur, cure of noxious
fumes,
He purged the walls, and blood-polluted
rooms.   530
Again the matron springs with eager pace,
And spreads her lord's return from place
to place.
They hear, rush forth, and instant round
him stand,
A gazing throng, a torch in every hand.
They saw, they knew him, and with fond
embrace
Each humbly kiss'd his knee, or hand, or
face:

He knows them all; in all such truth appears,
Ev'n he indulges the sweet joy of tears.

BOOK XXIV

ARGUMENT

The souls of the suitors are conducted by Mercury to the infernal shades. Ulysses in the
country goes to the retirement of his father
Laërtes ; he finds him busied in his garden
all alone : the manner of his discovery to him
is beautifully described. They return together to his lodge, and the king is acknowledged by Dolius and the servants. The
Ithacensians, led by Eupithes, the father of
Antinoüs, rise against Ulysses, who gives
them battle, in which Eupithes is killed by
Laërtes: and the goddess Pallas makes a
lasting peace between Ulysses and his subjects, which concludes the Odyssey.

CYLLENIUS now to Pluto's dreary reign
Conveys the dead, a lamentable train !
The golden wand, that causes sleep to
fly,
Or in soft slumber seals the wakeful eye,
That drives the ghosts to realms of night
or day,
Points out the long uncomfortable way.
Trembling the spectres glide, and plaintive
vent
Thin hollow screams, along the deep de-
scent.
As in the cavern of some rifted den,
Where flock nocturnal bats, and birds ob-
scene;   10
Cluster'd they hang, till, at some sudden
shock,
They move, and murmurs run thro' all the
rock !
So cow'ring fled the sable heaps of ghosts,
And such a scream fill'd all the dismal
coasts.
And now they reach'd the earth's remotest
ends,
And now the gates where ev'ning Sol de-
scends,
And Leucas' rock, and Ocean's utmost
streams,
And now pervade the dusky land of dreams,
And rest at last, where souls unbodied dwell
In ever-flow'ring meads of asphodel.   20
The empty forms of men inhabit there.
Impassive semblance, images of air !

Not else are all that shined on earth be-
fore:
Ajax and great Achilles are no more!
Yet still a master-ghost, the rest he aw'd,
The rest ador'd him, tow'ring as he trod;
Still at his side is Nestor's son survey'd,
And loved Patroclus still attends his shade.
  New as they were to that infernal shore,
The suitors stopp'd, and gazed the hero
    o'er. 30
When, moving slow, the regal form they
    view'd
Of great Atrides: him in pomp pursued
And solemn sadness thro' the gloom of
    Hell,
The train of those who by Ægisthus fell:
  'O mighty Chief!' (Pelides thus began)
'Honour'd by Jove above the lot of man!
King of a hundred Kings! to whom re-
    sign'd
The strongest, bravest, greatest of man-
    kind,
Com'st thou the first, to view this dreary
    state?
And was the noblest the first mark of
    Fate, 40
Condemn'd to pay the great arrear so soon
The lot, which all lament, and none can
    shun!
Oh! better had'st thou sunk in Trojan
    ground,
With all thy full-blown honours cover'd
    round;
Then grateful Greece with streaming eyes
    might raise
Historic marbles to record thy praise:
Thy praise eternal on the faithful stone
Had with transmissive glories graced thy
    son.
But heavier fates were destin'd to attend:
What man is happy, till he knows the
    end?' 50
  'O son of Peleus! greater than mankind!'
(Thus Agamemnon's kingly shade rejoin'd)
'Thrice happy thou, to press the martial
    plain
'Midst heaps of heroes in thy quarrel slain:
In clouds of smoke rais'd by the noble ⎤
    fray, ⎟
Great and terrific ev'n in death you lay, ⎬
And deluges of blood flow'd round you ⎟
    ev'ry way. ⎦
Nor ceas'd the strife till Jove himself op-
    posed,
And all in tempests the dire ev'ning closed.

Then to the fleet we bore thy honour'd
    load, 60
And decent on the funeral bed bestow'd:
Then unguents sweet, and tepid streams ⎤
    we shed; ⎟
Tears flow'd from ev'ry eye, and o'er the ⎬
    dead ⎟
Each clipp'd the curling honour of his ⎦
    head.
Struck at the news, thy azure mother came;
The sea-green sisters waited on the dame:
A voice of loud lament thro' all the main
Was heard; and terror seiz'd the Grecian
    train:
Back to their ships the frighted host had
    fled; 69
But Nestor spoke, they listen'd and obey'd
(From old experience Nestor's counsel
    springs,
And long vicissitudes of human things).
  '"Forbear your flight: fair Thetis from
    the main
To mourn Achilles leads her azure train."
Around thee stand the daughters of the
    deep,
Robe thee in heav'nly vests, and round thee
    weep:
Round thee, the Muses, with alternate
    strain,
In ever-consecrating verse, complain.
Each warlike Greek the moving music
    hears,
And iron-hearted heroes melt in tears. 80
Till sev'nteen nights and sev'nteen days
    return'd,
All that was mortal or immortal mourn'd,
To flames we gave thee, the succeeding
    day,
And fatted sheep and sable oxen slay;
With oils and honey blaze th' augmented
    fires,
And, like a God adorn'd, thy earthly part
    expires.
Unnumber'd warriors round the burning
    pile
Urge the fleet courser's or the racer's toil;
Thick clouds of dust o'er all the circle
    rise,
And the mix'd clamour thunders in the
    skies. 90
Soon as absorb'd in all-embracing flame
Sunk what was mortal of thy mighty name,
We then collect thy snowy bones, and
    place
With wines and unguents in a golden vase

(The vase to Thetis Bacchus gave of old,
And Vulcan's art enrich'd the sculptured
    gold);
There we thy relics, great Achilles! blend
With dear Patroclus, thy departed friend:
In the same urn a sep'rate space contains
Thy next belov'd, Antilochus' remains.   100
Now all the sons of warlike Greece sur-
    round
Thy destin'd tomb, and cast a mighty
    mound:
High on the shore the growing hill we raise,
That wide th' extended Hellespont sur-
    veys:
Where all, from age to age, who pass the
    coast
May point Achilles' tomb, and hail the
    mighty ghost.
Thetis herself to all our Peers proclaims
Heroic prizes and exequial games;
The Gods assented; and around thee lay
Rich spoils and gifts that blazed against
    the day.   110
Oft have I seen with solemn funeral games
Heroes and Kings committed to the flames;
But strength of youth, or valour of the
    brave,
With nobler contest ne'er renown'd a grave.
Such were the games by azure Thetis giv'n,
And such the honours, O Belov'd of Heav'n!
Dear to mankind thy fame survives, nor
    fades
Its bloom eternal in the Stygian shades.
But what to me avail my honours gone,   119
Successful toils, and battles bravely won?
Doom'd by stern Jove at home to end my
    life,
By curs'd Ægisthus, and a faithless wife!'
    Thus they: while Hermes o'er the dreary
        plain
Led the sad numbers by Ulysses slain.
On each majestic form they cast a view,
And tim'rous pass'd, and awfully with-
    drew.
But Agamemnon, thro' the gloomy shade,
His ancient host Amphimedon survey'd:
'Son of Melanthius!' (he began) 'O say!
What cause compell'd so many, and so
    gay,   130
To tread the downward melancholy way?
Say, could one city yield a troop so fair?
Were all these partners of one native air?
Or did the rage of stormy Neptune sweep
Your lives at once, and whelm beneath the
    deep?

Did nightly thieves, or pirates' cruel bands,
Drench with your blood your pillaged coun-
    try's sands?
Or, well-defending some beleaguer'd wall,
Say, for the public did ye greatly fall?
Inform thy guest: for such I was of
    yore   140
When our triumphant navies touch'd your
    shore;
Forc'd a long month the wintry seas to
    bear,
To move the great Ulysses to the war.'
    'O King of Men! I faithful shall re-
        late'
(Replied Amphimedon) 'our hapless fate.
Ulysses absent, our ambitious aim
With rival loves pursued his royal dame;
Her coy reserve, and prudence mix'd with
    pride,
Our common suit nor granted, nor denied:
But close with inward hate our deaths de-
    sign'd;   150
Vers'd in all arts of wily womankind,
Her hand, laborious, in delusion spread
A spacious loom, and mix'd the various
    thread.
'"Ye Peers" (she cried), "who press to gain
    my heart,
Where dead Ulysses claims no more a
    part,
Yet a short space your rival suit suspend,
Till this funereal web my labours end:
Cease, till to good Laërtes I bequeath
A task of grief, his ornaments of death:
Lest, when the Fates his royal ashes claim,
The Grecian matrons taint my spotless
    fame;   161
Should he, long honour'd with supreme
    command,
Want the last duties of a daughter's hand."
'The fiction pleas'd: our gen'rous train
    complies,
Nor fraud distrusts in virtue's fair dis-
    guise.
The work she plied, but, studious of de-
    lay,
Each foll'wing night revers'd the toils of
    day.
Unheard, unseen, three years her arts pre-
    vail;
The fourth, her maid reveal'd th' amazing
    tale,
And show'd, as unperceiv'd we took our
    stand,   170
The backward labours of her faithless hand.

Forc'd, she completes it; and before us
    lay
The mingled web, whose gold and silver
    ray
Display'd the radiance of the night and
    day.
  ' Just as she finish'd her illustrious toil
Ill fortune led Ulysses to our isle.
Far in a lonely nook, beside the sea,
At an old swineherd's rural lodge he lay:
Thither his son from sandy Pyle repairs,
And speedy lands, and secretly confers. 180
They plan our future ruin, and resort
Confed'rate to the city and the court.
First came the son: the father next suc-
    ceeds,
Clad like a beggar, whom Eumæus leads;
Propp'd on a staff, deform'd with age and
    care,
And hung with rags that flutter'd in the
    air.
Who could Ulysses in that form behold ?
Scorn'd by the young, forgotten by the old,
Ill-used by all ! to ev'ry wrong resign'd,
Patient he suffer'd with a constant mind. 190
But when, arising in his wrath t' obey
The will of Jove, he gave the vengeance
    way:
The scatter'd arms that hung around the
    dome
Careful he treasured in a private room;
Then to her suitors bade his Queen propose
The archer's strife, the source of future
    woes,
And omen of our death ! In vain we drew
The twanging string, and tried the stub-
    born yew:
To none it yields but great Ulysses' hands;
In vain we threat; Telemachus commands:
The bow he snatch'd, and in an instant
    bent; 201
Thro' ev'ry ring the victor arrow went.
Fierce on the threshold then in arms he
    stood;
Pour'd forth the darts that thirsted for
    our blood,
And frown'd before us, dreadful as a
    God;
First bleeds Antinoüs: thick the shafts re-
    sound;
And heaps on heaps the wretches strew the
    ground:
This way and that we turn, we fly, we
    fall;
Some God assisted, and unmann'd us all:

Ignoble cries precede the dying groans; 210
And batter'd brains and blood besmear the
    stones.
  ' Thus, great Atrides ! thus Ulysses drove
The shades thou seest from yon fair realms
    above;
Our mangled bodies now, deform'd with
    gore,
Cold and neglected, spread the marble floor.
No friend to bathe our wounds, or tears to
    shed
O'er the pale corse the honours of the
    dead.'
  'Oh bless'd Ulysses !' (thus the King
    express'd
His sudden rapture) ' in thy consort
    bless'd !
Not more thy wisdom than her virtue
    shined; 220
Not more thy patience than her constant
    mind.
Icarius' daughter, glory of the past,
And model to the future age, shall last:
The Gods, to honour her fair fame, shall
    raise
(Their great reward) a Poet in her praise.
Not such, O Tyndarus ! thy daughter's
    deed,
By whose dire hand her King and Husband
    bled;
Her shall the Muse to infamy prolong,
Example dread, and theme of tragic song !
The gen'ral sex shall suffer in her shame,
And ev'n the best that bears a woman's
    name.' 231
  Thus in the regions of eternal shade
Conferr'd the mournful phantoms of the
    dead;
While from the town Ulysses and his band
Pass'd to Laërtes' cultivated land.
The ground himself had purchas'd with his
    pain,
And labour made the rugged soil a plain.
There stood his mansion of the rural sort,
With useful buildings round the lowly
    court;
Where the few servants that divide his
    care, 240
Took their laborious rest, and homely fare:
And one Sicilian matron, old and sage,
With constant duty tends his drooping age.
  Here now arriving, to his rustic band,
And martial son, Ulysses gave command.
' Enter the house, and of the bristly swine
Select the largest to the Powers divine.

Alone, and unattended, let me try
If yet I share the old man's memory:
If those dim eyes can yet Ulysses know 250
(Their light and dearest object long
  ago),
Now changed with time, with absence,
  and with woe.'
Then to his train he gives his spear and
  shield;
The house they enter: and he seeks the
  field
Thro' rows of shade, with various fruitage
  crown'd,
And labour'd scenes of richest verdure
  round.
Nor aged Dolius, nor his sons were there,
Nor servants, absent on another care;
To search the woods for sets of flow'ry
  thorn,
Their orchard bounds to strengthen and
  adorn.   260
  But all alone the hoary King he found;
His habit coarse, but warmly wrapp'd
  around;
His head, that bow'd with many a pensive
  care,
Fenc'd with a double cap of goatskin hair:
His buskins old, in former service torn,
But well repair'd; and gloves against the
  thorn.
In this array the kingly gard'ner stood,
And clear'd a plant, encumber'd with its
  wood.
  Beneath a neighb'ring tree, the Chief
  divine
Gazed o'er his sire, retracing ev'ry line, 270
The ruins of himself! now worn away
With age, yet still majestic in decay!
Sudden his eyes releas'd their wat'ry store;
The much-enduring man could bear no
  more.
Doubtful he stood, if instant to embrace
His aged limbs, to kiss his rev'rend face,
With eager transport to disclose the whole,
And pour at once the torrent of his soul. —
Not so: his judgment takes the winding
  way
Of question distant, and of soft essay; 280
More gentle methods on weak age em-
  ploys;
And moves the sorrows, to enhance the
  joys.
Then, to his sire with beating heart he
  moves
And with a tender pleasantry reproves:

Who, digging round the plant, still hangs
  his head,
Nor aught remits the work, while thus he
  said:
  'Great is thy skill, O Father! great thy
  toil,
Thy careful hand is stamp'd on all the
  soil;
Thy squadron'd vineyards well thy art
  declare,
The olive green, blue fig, and pendent
  pear;   290
And not one empty spot escapes thy care.
On ev'ry plant and tree thy cares are
  shown,
Nothing neglected, but thyself alone.
Forgive me, Father, if this fault I blame;
Age so advanc'd may some indulgence
  claim.
Not for thy sloth, I deem thy lord unkind:
Nor speaks thy form a mean or servile
  mind;
I read a Monarch in that princely air,
The same thy aspect, if the same thy care;
Soft sleep, fair garments, and the joys of
  wine,   300
These are the rights of age, and should be
  thine.
Who then thy master, say? and whose the
  land
So dress'd and managed by thy skilful
  hand?
But chief, oh tell me! (what I question
  most)
Is this the far-famed Ithacensian coast?
For so reported the first man I view'd
(Some surly islander, of manners rude),
Nor farther conference vouchsafed to stay,
Heedless he whistled, and pursued his way.
But thou, whom years have taught to un-
  derstand,   310
Humanely hear, and answer my demand:
A friend I seek, a wise one and a brave:
Say, lives he yet, or moulders in the grave?
Time was (my fortunes then were at the
  best),
When at my house I lodg'd this foreign
  guest;
He said, from Ithaca's fair isle he came,
And old Laërtes was his father's name.
To him, whatever to a guest is owed
I paid, and hospitable gifts bestow'd:
To him sev'n talents of pure ore I told, 320
Twelve cloaks, twelve vests, twelve tunics
  stiff with gold;

A bowl, that rich with polish'd silver
    flames,
And, skill'd in female works, four lovely
    dames.'
  At this the father, with a father's fears
(His venerable eyes bedimm'd with tears):
'This is the land ; but ah! thy gifts are
    lost,
For godless men, and rude, possess the
    coast:
Sunk is the glory of this once-famed shore!
Thy ancient friend, O Stranger, is no
    more!   329
Full recompense thy bounty else had borne;
For ev'ry good man yields a just return:
So civil rights demand; and who begins
The track of friendship, not pursuing, sins.
But tell me, stranger, be the truth con-
    fess'd,
What years have circled since thou saw'st
    that guest ?
That hapless guest, alas! for ever gone!
Wretch that he was! and that I am! my son!
If ever man to misery was born,
'T was his to suffer and 't is mine to mourn!
Far from his friends, and from his native
    reign,   340
He lies a prey to monsters of the main;
Or savage beasts his mangled relics tear,
Or screaming vultures scatter thro' the
    air:
Nor could his mother funeral unguents
    shed;
Nor wail'd his father o'er th' untimely
    dead:
Nor his sad consort, on the mournful bier,
Seal'd his cold eyes, or dropp'd a tender
    tear!
  ' But, tell me who thou art ? and what thy
    race ?
Thy town, thy parents, and thy native
    place ?
Or, if a merchant in pursuit of gain, 350
What port receiv'd thy vessel from the
    main ?
Or com'st thou single, or attend thy
    train ? '
  Then thus the son : ' From Alybas I
    came,
My palace there; Eperitus my name.
Not vulgar born; from Aphidas, the King
Of Polypemon's royal line, I spring.
Some adverse demon from Sicania bore
Our wand'ring course, and drove us on your
    shore;

Far from the town, an unfrequented bay
Reliev'd our wearied vessel from the sea.
Five years have circled since these eyes
    pursued   361
Ulysses parting thro' the sable flood;
Prosp'rous he sail'd, with dexter auguries,
And all the wing'd good omens of the skies.
Well hoped we then to meet on this fair
    shore,
Whom Heav'n, alas ! decreed to meet no
    more.'
  Quick thro' the father's heart these ac-
    cents ran;
Grief seiz'd at once, and wrapp'd up all the
    man:
Deep from his soul he sigh'd, and sorr'wing
    spread
A cloud of ashes on his hoary head.   370
Trembling with agonies of strong delight
Stood the great son, heart-wounded with
    the sight:
He ran, he seiz'd him with a strict em-
    brace,
With thousand kisses wander'd o'er his
    face:
' I, I am he; O Father, rise! behold
Thy son, with twenty winters now grown
    old;
Thy son, so long desired, so long detain'd,
Restor'd, and breathing in his native land:
These floods of sorrow, O my Sire, re-
    strain!
The vengeance is complete; the suitor
    train,   380
Stretch'd in our palace, by these hands
    lie slain.'
  Amazed, Laërtes: ' Give some certain
    sign '
(If such thou art) ' to manifest thee mine.'
  ' Lo here the wound ' (he cries) ' receiv'd
    of yore,
The scar indented by the tusky boar,
When, by thyself, and by Anticlea sent,
To old Autolycus's realms I went.
Yet by another sign thy offspring know;
The sev'ral trees you gave me long ago,
While, yet a child, these fields I lov'd to
    trace,   390
And trod thy footsteps with unequal pace ;
To ev'ry plant in order as we came,
Well-pleas'd, you told its nature and its
    name,
Whate'er my childish fancy ask'd, bestow'd:
Twelve pear-trees, bowing with their pen-
    dent load,

And ten, that red with blushing apples
    glow'd;
Full fifty purple figs; and many a row
Of various vines that then began to blow,
A future vintage! when the Hours pro-
    duce
Their latent buds, and Sol exalts the
    juice.'   400
Smit with the signs which all his doubts
    explain,
His heart within him melts; his knees sus-
    tain
Their feeble weight no more: his arms
    alone
Support him, round the lov'd Ulysses
    thrown;
He faints, he sinks, with mighty joys op-
    press'd:
Ulysses clasps him to his eager breast.
Soon as returning life regains its seat,
And his breath lengthens, and his pulses
    beat;
'Yes, I believe' (he cries) 'almighty Jove!
Heav'n rules us yet, and Gods there are
    above.   410
'T is so — the suitors for their wrongs have
    paid —
But what shall guard us, if the town in-
    vade?
If, while the news thro' ev'ry city flies,
All Ithaca and Cephalenia rise?'
    To this Ulysses: 'As the Gods shall
    please
Be all the rest; and set thy soul at ease.
Haste to the cottage by this orchard's
    side,
And take the banquet which our cares pro-
    vide:
There wait thy faithful band of rural
    friends,   419
And there the young Telemachus attends.'
    Thus having said, they traced the garden
    o'er,
And stooping enter'd at the lowly door.
The swains and young Telemachus they
    found,
The victim portion'd, and the goblet
    crown'd.
The hoary King his old Sicilian maid
Perfumed and wash'd, and gorgeously ar-
    ray'd.
Pallas attending gives his frame to shine
With awful port, and majesty divine;
His gazing son admires the godlike grace,
And air celestial dawning o'er his face.   430

'What God' (he cried) 'my father's form
    improves?
How high he treads, and how enlarged he
    moves!'
    'Oh! would to all the deathless Powers
    on high,
Pallas and Jove, and him who gilds the sky!
(Replied the King, elated with his praise)
My strength were still as once in better
    days:
When the bold Cephaleus the leaguer
    form'd,
And proud Nericus trembled as I storm'd.
Such were I now, not absent from your
    deed   439
When the last sun beheld the suitors bleed,
This arm had aided yours, this hand be-
    strown
Our shores with death, and push'd the
    slaughter on;
Nor had the sire been sep'rate from the
    son.'
    They communed thus; while homeward
    bent their way
The swains, fatigued with labours of the
    day:
Dolius the first, the venerable man;
And next his sons, a long succeeding train.
For due refection to the bower they came,
Call'd by the careful old Sicilian dame,
Who nurs'd the children, and now tends
    the sire;   450
They see their lord, they gaze, and they
    admire.
On chairs and beds in order seated round,
They share the gladsome board; the roofs
    resound.
While thus Ulysses to his ancient friend:
'Forbear your wonder, and the feast at-
    tend:
The rites have waited long.' The Chief
    commands
Their loves in vain; old Dolius spreads his
    hands,
Springs to his master with a warm embrace,
And fastens kisses on his hands and face;
Then thus broke out: 'O long, O daily
    mourn'd!   460
Beyond our hopes, and to our wish re-
    turn'd!
Conducted sure by Heav'n! for Heav'n
    alone
Could work this wonder: welcome to thy
    own!
And joys and happiness attend thy throne!

Who knows thy bless'd, thy wish'd re-
    turn ? oh say,
To the chaste Queen shall we the news
    convey ?
Or hears she, and with blessings loads
    the day ? '
' Dismiss that care, for to the royal bride
Already is it known,' the King replied,
And straight resumed his seat; while round
    him bows   470
Each faithful youth, and breathes out ar-
    dent vows:
Then all beneath their father take their
    place,
Rank'd by their ages, and the banquet
    grace.
  Now flying Fame the swift report had
    spread
Thro' all the city, of the suitors dead.
In throngs they rise, and to the palace
    crowd;
Their sighs were many, and the tumult
    loud.
Weeping they bear the mangled heaps
    of slain,
Inhume the natives in their native plain;
The rest in ships are wafted o'er the
    main.   480
Then sad in council all the seniors sate,
Frequent and full, assembled to debate:
Amid the circle first Eupithes rose,
Big was his eye with tears, his heart with
    woes:
The bold Antinoüs was his age's pride,
The first who by Ulysses' arrow died:
Down his wan cheek the trickling torrent
    ran,
As, mixing words with sighs, he thus be-
    gan:
' Great deeds, O Friends ! this wondrous
    man has wrought,
And mighty blessings to his country
    brought !   490
With ships he parted, and a numerous train;
Those, and their ships, he buried in the
    main.
Now he returns, and first essays his hand
In the best blood of all his native land.
Haste then, and ere to neighb'ring Pyle
    he flies,
Or sacred Elis, to procure supplies;
Arise (or ye for ever fall), arise !
Shame to this age, and all that shall suc-
    ceed !
If unrevenged your sons and brothers bleed.

Prove that we live, by vengeance on his
    head,   500
Or sink at once forgotten with the dead.'
  Here ceas'd he, but indignant tears let fall
Spoke when he ceas'd: dumb sorrow
    touch'd them all.
When from the palace to the wond'ring
    throng
Sage Medon came, and Phemius came
    along
(Restless and early sleep's soft bands they
    broke);
And Medon first th' assembled Chiefs be-
    spoke:
' Hear me, ye Peers and Elders of the
    land,
Who deem this act the work of mortal
    hand;   509
As o'er the heaps of death Ulysses strode,
These eyes, these eyes beheld a present
    God,
Who now before him, now beside him stood,
Fought as he fought, and mark'd his way
    with blood:
In vain old Mentor's form the God belied;
'T was Heav'n that struck, and Heav'n was
    on his side.'
  A sudden horror all th' assembly shook,
When, slowly rising, Halitherses spoke
(Rev'rend and wise, whose comprehensive
    view
At once the present and the future knew);
' Me too, ye Fathers, hear ! from you pro-
    ceed   520
The ills ye mourn; your own the guilty
    deed.
Ye gave your sons, your lawless sons, the
    rein
(Oft warn'd by Mentor and myself in
    vain);
An absent hero's bed they sought to soil,
An absent hero's wealth they made their
    spoil;
Immod'rate riot, and intemp'rate lust !
Th' offence was great, the punishment was
    just.
Weigh then my counsels in an equal scale,
Nor rush to ruin. Justice will prevail.'
  His mod'rate words some better minds
    persuade: 530
They part, and join him; but the number
    stay'd.
They storm, they shout, with hasty frenzy
    fired,
And second all Eupithes' rage inspired.

They case their limbs in brass; to arms
　　they run;
The broad effulgence blazes in the sun.
Before the city, and in ample plain,
They meet: Eupithes heads the frantic train.
Fierce for his son, he breathes his threats in
　　air;
Fate hears them not, and Death attends
　　him there.
　　This pass'd on earth, while in the realms
　　　　above　　　　　　　　　　　　　　540
Minerva thus to cloud-compelling Jove:
' May I presume to search thy secret soul ?
O Power Supreme, O Ruler of the Whole !
Say, hast thou doom'd to this divided⎤
　　state　　　　　　　　　　　　　　　⎟
Or peaceful amity, or stern debate ?　　⎬
Declare thy purpose, for thy will is Fate.'⎦
　　' Is not thy thought my own ? ' (the God
　　　　replies
Who rolls the thunder o'er the vaulted
　　skies)
' Hath not long since thy knowing soul⎤
　　decreed　　　　　　　　　　　　　　⎟
The Chief's return should make the⎬
　　guilty bleed ?　　　　　　　　　550⎟
'T is done, and at thy will the Fates suc-⎦
　　ceed.
Yet hear the issue; since Ulysses' hand
Has slain the suitors, Heav'n shall bless the
　　land.
None now the kindred of th' unjust shall
　　own;
Forgot the slaughter'd brother and the son:
Each future day increase of wealth shall
　　bring,
And o'er the past Oblivion stretch her wing.
Long shall Ulysses in his empire rest,
His people blessing, by his people bless'd.
Let all be peace.' — He said, and gave the
　　nod　　　　　　　　　　　　　　　560
That binds the Fates; the sanction of the
　　God:
And, prompt to execute th' eternal will,
Descended Pallas from th' Olympian hill.
　　Now sat Ulysses at the rural feast,
The rage of hunger and of thirst repress'd:
To watch the foe a trusty spy he sent:
A son of Dolius on the message went,
Stood in the way, and at a glance beheld
The foe approach, embattled on the field.
With backward step he hastens to the
　　bower,　　　　　　　　　　　　　570
And tells the news.　They arm with all
　　their power.

Four friends alone Ulysses' cause embrace,
And six were all the sons of Dolius' race:
Old Dolius too his rusted arms put on;
And, still more old, in arms Laërtes shone.
Trembling with warmth, the hoary heroes
　　stand,
And brazen panoply invests the band.
The opening gates at once their war dis-
　　play:
Fierce they rush forth: Ulysses leads the
　　way.　　　　　　　　　　　　　　579
That moment joins them with celestial aid,
In Mentor's form, the Jove-descended
　　Maid:
The suff'ring Hero felt his patient breast
Swell with new joy, and thus his son ad-
　　dress'd:
　　' Behold, Telemachus ! (nor fear the
　　　　sight)
The brave embattled, the grim front of
　　fight !
The valiant with the valiant must contend:
Shame not the line whence glorious you
　　descend;
Wide o'er the world their martial fame was
　　spread:
Regard thyself, the living, and the dead.'
　　' Thy eyes, great Father ! on this battle
　　　　cast,　　　　　　　　　　　　　590
Shall learn from me Penelope was chaste.'
　　So spoke Telemachus: the gallant boy
Good old Laërtes heard with panting joy;
And ' Bless'd ! thrice bless'd this happy
　　day !' (he cries)
' The day that shows me, ere I close my
　　eyes,
A son and grandson of th' Arcesian name
Strive for fair virtue, and contest for
　　fame !'
　　Then thus Minerva in Laërtes' ear:
' Son of Arcesius, rev'rend warrior, hear !
Jove and Jove's Daughter first implore in
　　prayer,　　　　　　　　　　　　　600
Then, whirling high, discharge thy lance
　　in air.'
She said, infusing courage with the word.
Jove and Jove's Daughter then the Chief
　　implor'd,
And, whirling high, dismiss'd the lance in
　　air.
Full at Eupithes drove the deathful spear:
The brass-cheek'd helmet opens to the
　　wound;
He falls, earth thunders, and his arms re-
　　sound.

Before the father and the conquering son
Heaps rush on heaps; they fight, they drop,
  they run.   609
Now by the sword, and now the jav'lin fall
The rebel race, and death had swallow'd all;
But from on high the blue-eyed Virgin cried
(Her awful voice detain'd the headlong tide):
'Forbear, ye Nations, your mad hands for-
  bear
From mutual slaughter; Peace descends
  to spare.'
Fear shook the Nations: at the voice divine
They drop their jav'lins, and their rage re-
  sign.
All scatter'd round their glitt'ring weapons
  lie;
Some fall to earth, and some confusedly
  fly.   619

With dreadful shouts Ulysses pour'd along,
Swift as an eagle, as an eagle strong.
But Jove's red arm the burning thunder
  aims:
Before Minerva shot the livid flames;
Blazing they fell, and at her feet expired;
Then stopped the Goddess, trembled, and
  retired.
'Descended from the Gods! Ulysses,
  cease;
Offend not Jove: obey, and give the peace.'
So Pallas spoke: the mandate from above
The King obey'd. The Virgin-seed of
  Jove,
In Mentor's form, confirm'd the full ac-
  cord,   630
And willing Nations knew their lawful
  lord.

POSTSCRIPT BY POPE

I CANNOT dismiss this work without a few observations on the true character and style of it. Whoever reads the Odyssey with an eye to the Iliad, expecting to find it of the same character, or of the same sort of spirit, will be grievously deceived, and err against the first principle of criticism, which is to consider the nature of the piece, and the intent of its author. The Odyssey is a moral and political work, instructive to all degrees of men and filled with images, examples, and precepts, of civil and domestic life. Homer is here a person

Qui didicit, patriæ quid debeat, et quid amicis,
Quo sit amore parens, quo frater amandus, et hospes:
Qui quid sit pulchrum, quid turpe, quid utile, quid non,
Plenius et melius Chrysippo et Crantore dicit.

The Odyssey is the reverse of the Iliad, in *moral, subject, manner*, and *style;* to which it has no sort of relation, but as the story happens to follow in order of time, and as some of the same persons are actors in it. Yet from this incidental connexion many have been misled to regard it as a continuation or second part, and thence to expect a parity of character inconsistent with its nature.

It is no wonder that the common reader should fall into this mistake, when so great a critic as Longinus seems not wholly free from it; although what he has said has been generally understood to import a severer censure of the Odyssey than it really does,

if we consider the occasion on which it is introduced, and the circumstances to which it is confined.

'The Odyssey,' says he, 'is an instance, how natural it is to a great genius, when it begins to grow old and decline, to delight itself in Narrations and Fables. For, that Homer composed the Odyssey after the Iliad, many proofs may be given, etc. From hence in my judgment it proceeds, that as the Iliad was written while his spirit was in its greatest vigour, the whole structure of that work is dramatic and full of action; whereas the greater part of the Odyssey is employed in narration, which is the taste of old age: so that in this latter piece we may compare him to the setting sun, which has still the same greatness, but not the same ardour or force. He speaks not in the same strain: we see no more that Sublime of the Iliad which marches on with a constant pace, without ever being stopped, or retarded: there appears no more that hurry and that strong tide of motions and passions, pouring one after another: there is no more the same fury, or the same volubility of diction, so suitable to action, and all along drawing in such innumerable images of Nature. But Homer, like the ocean, is always great, even when he ebbs and retires; even when he is lowest, and loses himself most in narrations and incredible fictions: as instances of this, we cannot forget the descriptions of tempests, the adventures of Ulysses with the Cyclops, and many others. But though all this be age, it is the age of Homer. — And it may be said for the credit of these fictions that they are beautiful dreams, or, if you will, the dreams of Jupiter himself. I spoke of the Odyssey only to show, that the greatest poets, when their genius wants strength and warmth for the pathetic, for the most part employ themselves in painting the manners. This Homer has done, in characterizing the suitors, and describing their way of life; which is properly a branch of comedy, whose peculiar business it is to represent the manners of men.'

We must first observe, it is the Sublime of which Longinus is writing: that, and not the nature of Homer's poem, is his subject. After having highly extolled the sublimity and fire of the Iliad, he justly observes the Odyssey to have less of those qualities, and to turn more on the side of moral, and reflections on human life. Nor is it his business here to determine, whether the *elevated spirit* of the one, or the *just moral* of the other, be the greater excellence in itself.

Secondly, that fire and fury of which he is speaking, cannot well be meant of the general spirit and inspiration which is to run through a whole epic poem, but of that particular warmth and impetuosity necessary in some parts, to image or represent actions or passions, of haste, tumult, and violence. It is on occasion of citing some such particular passages in Homer, that Longinus breaks into this reflection; which seems to determine his meaning chiefly to that sense.

Upon the whole, he affirms the Odyssey to have less sublimity and fire than the Iliad, but he does not say it wants the Sublime or wants fire. He affirms it to be narrative, but not that the narration is defective. He affirms it to abound in fictions, not that those fictions are ill invented, or ill executed. He affirms it to be nice and particular in painting the manners, but not that those manners are ill painted. If Homer has fully in these points accomplished his own design, and done all that the nature of his poem demanded or allowed, it still remains perfect in its kind, and as much a master-piece as the Iliad.

The amount of the passage is this; that in his own particular taste, and with respect to the Sublime, Longinus preferred the Iliad: and because the Odyssey was less active and lofty, he judged it the work of the old age of Homer.

If this opinion be true, it will only prove, that Homer's age might determine him in the choice of his subject, not that it affected him in the execution of it: and that which would be a very wrong instance to prove the decay of his imagination, is a very good one to evince the strength of his judgment. For had he, as Madam Dacier observes, composed the Odyssey in his youth, and the Iliad in his age, both must in reason have been exactly the same as they now stand. To blame Homer for his choice of such a subject, as did not admit the same incidents and the same pomp of style as his former, is to take offence at too much variety, and to imagine, that when a man has written one good thing, he must ever after only copy himself.

The Battle of Constantine, and the School of Athens, are both pieces of Raphael: shall we censure the School of Athens as faulty, because it has not the fury and fire of the other ? or shall we say, that Raphael was grown grave and old, because he chose to represent the manners of old men and philosophers ? There is all the silence, tranquillity, and composure in the one, and all the warmth, hurry, and tumult in the other, which the subject of either required: both of them had been imperfect, if they had not been as they are. And let the painter or poet be young or old, who designs and performs in this manner, it proves him to have made the piece at a time of life when he was master not only of his art, but of his discretion.

Aristotle makes no such distinction between the two poems: he constantly cites them with equal praise, and draws the rules and examples of epic writing equally from both. But it is rather to the Odyssey that Horace gives the preference, in the Epistle to Lollius, and in the Art of Poetry. It is remarkable how opposite his opinion is to that of Longinus; and that the particulars he chooses to extol, are those very *fictions* and *pictures of the manners*, which the other seems least to approve. Those fables and manners are of the very essence of the work: but even without that regard, the fables themselves have both more invention and more instruction, and the manners more moral and example, than those of the Iliad.

In some points (and those the most essential to the epic poem) the Odyssey is confessed to excel the Iliad; and principally in the great end of it, the *Moral*. The conduct, turn, and disposition of the *Fable* is also what the critics allow to be the better model for epic writers to follow: accordingly we find much more of the cast of this poem than of the other in the Æneid, and (what next to that is perhaps the greatest example) in the Telemachus. In the *Manners*, it is no way inferior: Longinus is so far from finding any defect in these, that he rather taxes Homer with painting them too minutely. As to the *Narrations*, although they are more numerous as the occasions are more frequent, yet they carry no more the marks of old age, and are neither more prolix nor more circumstantial, than the conversations and dialogues of the Iliad. Not to mention the length of those of Phœnix in the ninth book, and of Nestor in the eleventh (which may be thought in compliance to their characters), those of Glaucus in the sixth, of Æneas in the twentieth, and some others, must be allowed to exceed any in the whole Odyssey. And that the propriety of style, and the numbers, in the narrations of each are equal, will appear to any who compare them.

To form a right judgment, whether the genius of Homer had suffered any decay, we must consider, in both his poems, such parts as are of a similar nature, and will bear comparison. And it is certain we shall find in each the same vivacity and fecundity of invention, the same life and strength of imaging and colouring, the particular descriptions as highly painted, the figures as bold, the metaphors as animated, and the numbers as harmonious and as various.

The Odyssey is a perpetual source of poetry: the stream is not the less full for being gentle; though it is true (when we speak only with regard to the Sublime) that a river, foaming and thundering in cataracts from rocks and precipices, is what more strikes, amazes, and fills the mind, than the same body of water, flowing after-

wards through peaceful vales and agreeable scenes of pasturage.

The Odyssey (as I have before said) ought to be considered according to its own nature and design, not with an eye to the Iliad. To censure Homer because it is unlike what it was never meant to resemble, is, as if a gardener who had purposely cultivated two beautiful trees of contrary natures, as a specimen of his skill in the several kinds, should be blamed for not bringing them into pairs; when in root, stem, leaf, and flower, each was so entirely different, that one must have been spoiled in the endeavour to match the other.

Longinus, who saw this poem was "partly of the nature of comedy," ought not, for that very reason, to have considered it with a view to the Iliad. How little any such resemblance was the intention of Homer, may appear from hence, that although the character of Ulysses there was already drawn, yet here he purposely turns to another side of it, and shows him not in that full light of glory, but in the shade of common life, with a mixture of such qualities as are requisite to all the lowest accidents of it, struggling with misfortunes, and on a level with the meanest of mankind. As for the other persons, none of them are above what we call the higher comedy: Calypso, though a Goddess, is a character of intrigue; the suitors yet more approaching to it; the Phæacians are of the same cast; the Cyclops, Melanthius, and Irus, descend even to droll characters; and the scenes that appear throughout, are generally of the comic kind; banquets, revels, sports, loves, and the pursuit of a woman.

From the nature of the poem, we shall form an idea of the *Style*. The diction is to follow the images, and to take its colour from the complexion of the thoughts. Accordingly the Odyssey is not always clothed in the majesty of verse proper to tragedy, but sometimes descends into the plainer narrative, and sometimes even to that familiar dialogue essential to comedy. However, where it cannot support a sublimity, it always preserves a dignity, or at least a propriety. There is a real beauty in an easy, pure, perspicuous description even of a low action. There are numerous instances of this both in Homer and Virgil; and perhaps those natural passages are not the least pleasing of their works. It is often the same in history, where the representations of common, or even domestic things, in clear, plain, and natural words, are frequently found to make the liveliest impression on the reader.

The question is, how far a poet, in pursuing the description or image of an action, can attach himself to little circumstances, without vulgarity or trifling ? what particulars are proper, and enliven the image; or what are impertinent, and clog it ? In this matter painting is to be consulted, and the whole regard had to those circumstances which contribute to form a full, and yet not a confused, idea of a thing. *Epithets* are of vast service to this effect, and the right use of these is often the only expedient to render the narration poetical. The great point of judgment is to distinguish when to speak simply, and when figuratively: but whenever the poet is obliged by the nature of his subject to descend to the lower manner of writing, an elevated style would be affected, and therefore ridiculous; and the more he was forced upon figures and metaphors to avoid that lowness, the more the image would be broken, and consequently obscure. One may add, that the use of the grand style on little subjects, is not only ludicrous, but a sort of transgression against the rules of proportion and mechanics: it is using a vast force to lift a feather.

I believe, now I am upon this head, it will be found a just observation, that the low actions of life cannot be put into a figurative style without being ridiculous, but things natural can. Metaphors raise the latter into dignity, as we see in the Georgics; but throw the former into ridicule, as in the Lutrin. I think this may very well be accounted for: laughter implies censure; inanimate and irrational beings are not objects of censure: therefore these may be elevated as much as you please, and no ridicule follows: but when rational beings are represented above their real character, it becomes ridiculous in art, because it is vicious in morality. The bees in Virgil, were they rational beings, would be ridiculous by having their actions and manners represented on a level with creatures so superior as men; since it would imply folly or pride, which are the proper objects of ridicule.

The use of pompous expression for low actions or thoughts is the true Sublime of Don Quixote. How far unfit it is for epic poetry, appears in its being the perfection of the mock epic. It is so far from being the sublime of tragedy, that it is the cause of all bombast; when poets, instead of being, as they imagine, constantly lofty, only preserve throughout a painful equality of fustian; that continued swell of language, which runs indiscriminately even through their lowest characters, and rattles like some mightiness of meaning in the most indifferent subjects, is of a piece with that perpetual elevation of tone which the players have learned from it; and which is not speaking, but vociferating.

There is still more reason for a variation of Style in epic poetry than in tragic, to distinguish between that language of the Gods proper to the Muse who sings, and is inspired; and that of men who are introduced speaking only according to nature. Farther, there ought to be a difference of style observed in the speeches of human persons, and those of deities; and again, in those which may be called set harangues, or orations, and those which are only conversation or dialogue. Homer has more of the latter than any other poet: what Virgil does by two or three words of narration, Homer still performs by speeches: not only replies, but even rejoinders are frequent in him, a practice almost unknown to Virgil. This renders his poems more animated, but less grave and majestic; and consequently necessitates the frequent use of a lower style. The writers of tragedy lie under the same necessity, if they would copy nature: whereas that painted and poetical diction which they perpetually use, would be improper even in orations designed to move with all the arts of rhetoric; this is plain from the practice of Demosthenes and Cicero; and Virgil in those of Drances and Turnus gives an eminent example, how far removed the style of them ought to be from such an excess of figures and ornaments: which indeed fits only that language of the Gods we have been speaking of, or that of a muse under inspiration.

To read through a whole work in this strain, is like travelling all along on the ridge of a hill; which is not half so agreeable as sometimes gradually to rise, and sometimes gently to descend, as the way leads, and as the end of the journey directs. Indeed the true reason that so few poets have imitated Homer in these lower parts, has been the extreme difficulty of preserving that mixture of ease and dignity essential to them. For it is as hard for an epic poem to stoop to the narrative with success, as for a Prince to descend to be familiar, without diminution to his greatness.

The *sublime* style is more easily counterfeited than the *natural;* something that passes for it, or sounds like it, is common to all false writers: but nature, purity, perspicuity, and simplicity, never walk in the clouds; they are obvious to all capacities; and where they are not evident, they do not exist. The most plain narration not only admits of these, and of harmony (which are all the qualities of style) but it requires every one of them to render it pleasing. On the contrary, whatever pretends to a share of the sublime, may pass, notwithstanding any defects in the rest; nay sometimes without any of them, and gain the admiration of all ordinary readers.

Homer, in his lowest narrations or speeches, is ever easy, flowing, copious, clear, and harmonious. He shows not less *Invention*, in assembling the humbler, than the greater, thoughts and images; nor less *Judgment*, in proportioning the style and the versification to these, than to the other. Let it be remembered, that the same genius that soared the highest, and from whom the greatest models of the *Sublime* are derived, was also he who stooped the lowest, and gave to the simple Narrative its utmost perfection. Which of these was the harder task to Homer himself, I cannot pretend to determine; but to his translator I can affirm (however unequal all his imitations must be) that of the latter has been much more difficult.

Whoever expects here the same pomp of verse, and the same ornaments of diction, as in the Iliad, he will, and he ought to be, disappointed. Were the original otherwise, it had been an offence against Nature; and were the translation so, it were an offence against Homer, which is the same thing. It must be allowed that there is a majesty and harmony in the Greek language which greatly contribute to elevate and support the narration. But I must also observe that this is an advantage grown upon the language since Homer's time; for things are removed from vulgarity by being out of use: and if the words we could find in any present language were equally sonorous or musical in themselves, they would still appear less poetical and uncommon than those of a dead one, from this only circumstance, of being in every man's mouth. I may add to this another disadvantage to a translator, from a different cause: Homer seems to have taken upon him the character of an historian, antiquary, divine, and professor of arts and sciences, as well as a poet. In one or other of these characters he descends into many particulars, which as a poet only perhaps he would have avoided. All these ought to be preserved by a faithful translator, who in some measure takes the place of Homer; and all that can be expected from him is to make them as poetical as the subject will bear. Many arts, therefore, are requisite to supply these disadvantages, in order to dignify and solemnize these plainer parts, which hardly admit of any poetical ornaments.

Some use has been made to this end of the style of Milton. A just and moderate mixture of old words may have an effect like the working old abbey stones into a building, which I have sometimes seen to give a kind of venerable air, and yet not destroy the neatness, elegance, and equality requisite to a new work: I mean without rendering it too unfamiliar, or remote from the present purity of writing, or from that ease and smoothness which ought always to accompany narration or dialogue. In reading a style judiciously antiquated, one finds a pleasure not unlike that of travelling on an old Roman way: but then the road must be as good, as the way is ancient; the style must be such in which we may evenly proceed, without being put to short stops by sudden abruptness, or puzzled by frequent turnings and transpositions. No man delights in furrows and stumbling-blocks: and let our love to antiquity be ever so great, a fine ruin is one thing, and a heap of rubbish another. The imitators of Milton, like most other imitators, are not copies but caricatures of their original; they are a hundred times more obsolete and cramp than he, and equally so in all places: whereas it should have been observed of

Milton, that he is not lavish of his exotic words and phrases every where alike, but employs them much more where the subject is marvellous, vast, and strange, as in the scenes of Heaven, Hell, Chaos, &c., than where it is turned to the natural or agreeable, as in the pictures of paradise, the loves of our first parents, the entertainments of angels, and the like. In general, this unusual style better serves to awaken our ideas in the descriptions and in the imaging and picturesque parts, than it agrees with the lower sort of narrations, the character of which is simplicity and purity. Milton has several of the latter, where we find not an antiquated, affected, or uncouth word, for some hundred lines together; as in his fifth book, the latter part of the eighth, the former of the tenth and eleventh books, and in the narration of Michael in the twelfth. I wonder indeed that he, who ventured (contrary to the practice of all other Epic Poets) to imitate Homer's lownesses in the narrative, should not also have copied his plainness and perspicuity in the dramatic parts: since in his speeches (where clearness above all is necessary) there is frequently such transposition and forced construction, that the very sense is not to be discovered without a second or third reading: and in this certainly he ought to be no example.

To preserve the true character of Homer's style in the present translation, great pains have been taken to be easy and natural.

The chief merit I can pretend to, is, not to have been carried into a more plausible and figurative manner of writing, which would better have pleased all readers, but the judicious ones. My errors had been fewer, had each of those gentlemen who joined with me shown as much of the severity of a friend to me, as I did to them, in a strict animadversion and correction. What assistance I received from them, was made known in general to the public in the original proposals for this work, and the particulars are specified at the conclusion of it; to which I must add (to be punctually just) some part of the tenth and fifteenth books. The reader will now be too good a judge, how much the greater part of it, and consequently of its faults, is chargeable upon me alone. But this I can with integrity affirm, that I have bestowed as much time and pains upon the whole, as were consistent with the indispensable duties and cares of life, and with that wretched state of health which God has been pleased to make my portion. At the least, it is a pleasure to me to reflect, that I have introduced into our language this other work of the greatest and most ancient of poets, with some dignity; and I hope, with as little disadvantage as the Iliad. And if, after the unmerited success of that translation, any one will wonder why I would enterprise the Odyssey; I think it sufficient to say, that Homer himself did the same, or the world would never have seen it.

APPENDIX

APPENDIX

A. A GLOSSARY OF NAMES OF POPE'S CONTEMPORARIES MENTIONED IN THE POEMS.

This Glossary includes only such names as from their importance, from Pope's frequent mention of them, or for some other obvious reason, could not profitably be treated in the Notes.

Allen, Ralph. Friend and correspondent of Pope, and afterward patron of Fielding.

Anstis. Garter King at Arms.

Arbuthnot, John (1675-1735). Physician, mathematician, and classical scholar. A Tory in politics. Member of Scriblerus Club. Friend of Pope, Swift, and Gay, whom he rivalled in satire. Swift said, 'He has more wit than we all have, and more humanity than wit.'

Argyle, John, 2d Duke of (1678-1743). Statesman, soldier, and lover of letters; of a varied career both in war and in politics, but an honest man.

Arnall, William. Party-writer and journalist, of whom Pope complains that he admitted having 'received, in the space of four years, no less than £1997 6s. 8d. out of the Treasury.'

Atterbury, Francis, Bishop of Rochester. Friend of Pope and Swift. Banished as a plotting Jacobite in 1722, and thereafter influential at the court of the Pretender till his death in 1731.

Barnard, Sir John. Convert from Quakerism to the Church of England, member of Parliament for London City, and an authority upon questions of finance; Lord Mayor in 1738.

Bathurst, Allen Apsley, Lord, a Tory peer, was one of the most intimate of Pope's friends and associates. 'He united,' says Carruthers, 'a sort of French vivacity' ['Bathurst impetuous, whom you and I strive who shall love the most,' is the mention of him in Gay's catalogue of Pope's friends] 'to English principles, and mingled freely in society till past ninety, living to walk under the shade of lofty trees which Pope and he had planted, and to see his son Lord Chancellor of England.' He died in the year 1774, at the age of ninety-one. (Ward.)

Bentley, Richard. Master of Trinity College, Cambridge, and one of the great classical scholars of the time.

Berkeley, Dr., Bishop of Cloyne. Author of *Alciphron*, and a man of great learning and probity.

Bethel, Hugh. A Yorkshire gentleman with whom Pope was intimate, and frequently corresponded. He was a close friend of Pope's dear-

est friends, the Blounts of Mapledurham. He died in 1748. (Ward.)

Betterton, Thomas. Pope copied a portrait by Kneller of this famous actor, which is still extant. Betterton achieved success in all the major Shakespearean parts.

Blackmore, Sir Richard (1652-1729). Author of a philosophical poem called *The Creation*; and immortalized as the Quack Maurus of Dryden's prologue to *The Secular Masque*. 'His indefatigable muse,' says Pope, 'produced no less than six epic poems: *Prince and King Arthur*, twenty books; *Eliza*, ten; *Alfred*, twelve; *The Redeemer*, six; besides Job, in folio, the whole book of Psalms; *The Creation*, seven books; and many more. 'T is in this sense he is styled afterwards the *Everlasting Blackmore*.'

Bladen. Colonel Martin Bladen was a man of some literature and translated Cæsar's *Commentaries*. I never could learn that he had offended Pope. He was uncle to Wm. Collins, the poet, whom he left an estate. (Warton.)

Bland. Dr. Bland was Provost of Eton, and, according to Warton, 'a very bad writer.'

Blount, Martha. The woman for whom Pope seems to have cherished the feeling nearest akin to love. Indeed, it is supposed that if it had not been for the older sister Teresa, the attachment between Pope and Martha Blount might have come to marriage.

Blount, Teresa. See previous note, and Biographical Sketch.

Bolingbroke, Henry St. John, Lord (1678-1751). Tory and High Churchman, one of the great orators of the day, and member of several ministries. Friend of Prior and Swift, and later of Pope, much of whose later work was influenced by the shallow philosophy of Bolingbroke.

Booth, Barton. Actor, especially noted for his articulation; the original Cato in Addison's drama.

Boyle, Henry, Lord Carleton. Nephew of the famous Robert Boyle. Secretary of State under William III., and President of the Council under Queen Anne. (Pope.)

Boyle, Richard, Earl of Burlington (1695-1753). He took no prominent part in politics, although his high rank obtained for him a great post at court and the order of the Garter. But he obtained wide fame by his taste in architecture, inspired by a natural love of art and educated by studies in Italy. Horace Walpole says of him that he 'had every quality of genius and artist, except envy.' (Ward.)

Brydges, James, Duke of Chandos. Friend

of Pope and master of the Estate of Canons, which Pope was supposed to have satirized (*Moral Essays*, Epistle IV. 98-126). Paymaster of the Forces, under Godolphin.

Buckingham, Edmund, Duke of. Only son of John Sheffield, Duke of Buckinghamshire, by Katherine Darnley, natural daughter of James II. (Roscoe.)

Buckingham, more properly Buckinghamshire, John Sheffield, Duke of. See Sheffield.

Budgell, Eustace (1685-1737). Kinsman and friend of Addison. Accompanied Addison to Ireland as clerk, and became Under-Secretary of State. Wrote thirty-seven numbers of *The Spectator*. Was accused of forging a will in his own favor, fell into disgrace and debt, and committed suicide.

Burlington, Richard Boyle, Earl of. See Richard Boyle.

Campbell, John, 2d Duke of Argyle. See Argyle.

Carey, Henry. Author of *Sally in Our Alley;* and dramatist.

Carleton, Henry Boyle, Lord. See Henry Boyle.

Carteret, John, Earl Granville. Statesman, diplomat, and classical scholar. Political opponent of Walpole.

Caryll, John. Member of one of the Roman Catholic families living in the Leighborhood of Windsor Forest. *The Rape of the Lock* was due to his suggestion, and he remained a life-long friend of the poet.

Chandos, James Brydges, First Duke of. See Brydges.

Charteris, Francis. See Pope's note on *Moral Essays*, Epistle III., line 20.

Chesterfield, Philip Dormer Stanhope, Earl of. The most accomplished man of his time, wit, diplomatist, statesman, arbiter of manners; now mainly famous as the writer of the *Letters to his Son*.

Cibber, Colley (1671-1757). Actor, manager, and playwright; author of *The Careless Husband*. He incurred the enmity of Pope by burlesquing the farce, *Three Hours after Marriage*, and eventually displaced Theobald as hero of *The Dunciad*.

Cobham, Richard Temple, Lord. Sir Richard Temple, created Viscount Cobham by George I. in 1718, and made a Field Marshal in 1742, was on intimate terms with Pope during the latter part of the poet's life. Pope speaks, in his last letter to Swift, of 'generally rambling in the summer for a month to Lord Cobham's, the Bath, or elsewhere.' (Ward.)

Congreve, William (1669-1728), of good family, well educated. Studied law, gained fame by his plays. One tragedy, *The Mourning Bride*, and several licentious comedies are now associated with his name. He was one of those who encouraged Pope's earliest efforts. To him Pope dedicated the translation of *The Iliad*.

Cornbury, Lord. Afterwards Lord Hyde, 'a young Tory nobleman of literary tastes,' says

Ward, to whom Bolingboke addressed his *Letters on History*.

Cowper, William, First Earl. Lord Keeper, in 1705, and one of the Lords Justices on the death of Queen Anne.

Craggs, James. A man of low birth, who gained place and power. A friend of Pope's after 1711. Secretary of War in 1717, Secretary of State in 1720. His death in 1721 probably prevented his conviction of fraud in connection with the South Sea affair.

Curll, Edmund. A bookseller with whom Pope had for years a friendly connection, but who incurred Pope's resentment by publishing some of his private correspondence in 1727. The possible fact of his own complicity in the publication did not prevent Pope from placing Curll in the pillory of *The Dunciad*.

Dartineuf, Charles. A noted glutton.

Demoivre. A French mathematician especially famed for his skill in trigonometry.

Dennis, John (1657-1734). A forcible though unrefined critic, by no means the dunce Pope makes him out. His attack on Addison's *Cato*, and Addison's reception of Pope's unsolicited championship of the play, led to the estrangement between Pope and Addison. Dennis was not slow to retort upon Pope, who never forgave an injury to his self-esteem.

Digby, Robert. A frequent correspondent of Pope's during the years 1717 and 1724; died in 1726, and was lamented by Pope in a letter to his brother, Edward Digby, and in an epitaph.

Dodington, Bubb, afterwards Lord Melcombe, the author of a well-known diary, and the confidential adviser of Frederick, Prince of Wales. He is a character in many respects representative of his age; utterly unconscientious and cheerfully blind to his unconscientiousness; and a liberal rather than discriminating patron of literary men. He died in 1762. (Ward.)

Dorset, Charles Sackville, Earl of (1637-1706). Author of the ballad, 'To all you Ladies Now at Land,' some other songs, and a few satires. Belonged to the household of Charles II. and of William and Mary. He introduced *Hudibras* to notice, and was the friend and patron of Waller and Dryden.

Duck, Stephen. A modest and worthy man, who had the honour (which many, who thought themselves his betters in poetry, had not) of being esteemed by Mr. Pope. Queen Caroline chose this man for her favourite poet. (Warburton.)

Dunton, John. A broken bookseller and abusive scribbler; he writ *Neck or Nothing*, a violent satire on some ministers of state; a libel on the Duke of Devonshire and the Bishop of Peterborough. (Pope.)

Durfey or *D'Urfey*, Thomas. A scribbler and poetaster who would now be unknown if Pope had not named him so frequently.

Farquhar, George (1678-1707). An Irish actor and writer of comedies, whose work has a good deal of spirit. His two best-known plays are *The Recruiting Officer* and *The Beaux' Stratagem.*

Fenton, Elijah. A poet of no mean talent, and translator of four books of Pope's *Odyssey.*

Fleury, Cardinal. Prime minister of France from 1726 to his death, in 1743.

Fortescue, Hon. W. An intimate friend and a frequent associate and correspondent of the poet's, and a schoolfellow of Gay's. He afterwards became one of the Barons of the Exchequer, and ultimately Master of the Rolls. (Ward.)

Frowde, Philip. A dramatic writer and fine scholar, a friend of Addison's. (Carruthers.)

Garth, Sir Samuel. A physician, and author of the mock-heroic poem *The Dispensary.* He was one of the first to encourage the early efforts of Pope.

Gay, John (1638–1732). A close friend of Pope and Swift, a clever poet, and author of the famous *Beggars' Opera.*

Gildon, Charles (1665–1724) wrote a number of works, critical and dramatic. His plays were unsuccessful, but his *Complete Art of Poetry* (1718) is a work of considerable research and care. (Chambers.)

Godolphin, Lord. Lord Treasurer under Queen Anne. He was Addison's patron, but Macaulay says of him, ' Most of the time which he could save from public business was spent in racing, card-playing, and cock-fighting.'

Gonson, Sir John. A hanging judge said to have been particularly severe in his punishment of unfortunate women. His portrait is supposed to have been inserted by Hogarth in Plate III. of *The Harlot's Progress.*

Grafton, Charles, second Duke of.

Granville, George, afterward Lord Lansdowne (1667–1735). A poetical imitator of Waller; Secretary of War under Queen Anne, and raised to the peerage in 1717.

Grosvenor, Sir Thomas. A country baronet, member of Parliament. Remarkable for his obstinate independence.

Hale, Dr. Stephen. Not more estimable for his useful studies as a natural philosopher than for his exemplary life and pastoral charity as a parish priest. (Pope.)

Halifax, Charles Montagu, Earl of. A peer no less distinguished by his love of letters than his abilities in Parliament. He was disgraced in 1710, on the change of Queen Anne's ministry. (Pope.)

Hare, Francis, Bishop of Chichester. Tutor at Cambridge of (Sir) Robert Walpole.

Harley, Robert, Earl of Oxford and Earl Mortimer. Speaker of the House of Commons in 1701, Secretary of State in the Godolphin ministry. Subsequently created Earl of Oxford and appointed Lord Treasurer. A rival of Bolingbroke. Impeached for Jacobitism in 1716 and imprisoned in the Tower. Died in 1724. Subject of an epistle by Pope, p. 116, this edition.

Hearne, Thomas. Antiquary. He revenged himself, says Ward, for the sarcastic reference to him in *The Dunciad* by ill-natured reflections on Pope's education and parentage in his *Diary.*

Henley, John. A native of Leicestershire, had graduated at Cambridge; but set up a scheme of Universology on his own account, establishing his ' Oratory ' in a wooden booth in Newport market in 1726. Three years later he removed his pulpit to the corner of Lincoln's Inn Fields, and though subjected to a prosecution for profaning the clerical character, continued his exhibitions till the middle of the century. (Ward).

Hervey, John Lord. Author of *Memoirs of the Reign of George II.;* a courtier, Vice Chamberlain to George II., and later Lord Privy Seal. He married one of Pope's court friends, Miss Lepell (see *The Challenge).* The cause of Pope's enmity is unknown, but after the year 1727 Pope lost no opportunity to asperse the character of the peer, alluding to him as ' Lord Fanny,' ' Fannius,' and finally ' Sporus.' (*Epistle to Arbuthnot*, 305–333.)

Hopkins, ' Vulture.' See Pope's note on *Moral Essays*, III. 85.

Jacob Tonson. See Tonson.

Japhet Crook. A Londoner who amasses a large fortune by sharp practice. See Pope's note on *Moral Essays*, III. 86.

Jervas, Charles. See head-note to the *Epistle to Jervas*, p. 82.

Johnson, Charles. A second-rate dramatist. (Bowles.)

Kneller, Sir Godfrey (1648–1726). A German by birth, state painter to English royalty from Charles II. to George I.

Lansdowne, Lord. See George Granville.

Lintot, Bernard. A publisher pilloried with Curll in *The Dunciad ;* but he himself had published some of Pope's earlier work, to the advantage of the poet.

Marchmont, Earl of. A friend of Pope's, afterward one of his executors.

Mead, Dr. Physician to George II., and one of the eminent scientists of his day.

Mist, Nathaniel. Editor of a famous Tory journal. (Pope.)

Monroe, Dr. Physician to Bedlam Hospital. (Pope.)

Montagu, Lady Mary Wortley. One of the most interesting women of her day. A fair scholar and a clever versifier. Pope became acquainted with her in 1715, when she was already married to a dull man; and was for a time much attached to her. They quarrelled, and Pope thereafter lost no chance to insult her in prose and verse, commonly under the name of ' Sappho.'

Moore, James, afterward Moore-Smythe. A member of Pope's own circle, and a friend of Teresa Blount's, but the object of Pope's lasting rancour. The inoffensive author of many verses and a comedy, *The Rival Modes*, in which occurred certain lines which Pope accused him of having stolen from his lines to Martha Blount. Moore-Smythe retorted the charge.

Morris, Bezaleel. Author of some satires on the translators of Homer, with many other things printed in newspapers. (Pope.)

Murray, William, afterwards Lord Mansfield. A man of wit and cultivation, the incumbent of many high offices. He earned Pope's friendship by defending the *Essay on Man* from the attacks of various critics.

Oglethorpe, James Edward. Served under Prince Eugene, settled the colony of Georgia. 'Mr. Croker suggests,' says Ward, 'that to his supposed Jacobite leanings may be attributed much of the animosity displayed by the Whigs toward him, as well as of the friendliness existing between him and Pope and Johnson.'

Oldfield, Mrs. The most famous comédienne of the age.

Oldfield, Mr. This eminent glutton ran through a fortune of fifteen hundred pounds a year in the simple luxury of good eating. (Warburton.)

Onslow, Arthur. Sprung from a family members of which had already in two instances filled the chair, was elected Speaker in 1728, and occupied the post for thirty-three years, to the satisfaction of both parties in the House. (Ward.)

Osborne, Thomas. The bookseller who had the honour of a thrashing at the hands of Dr. Johnson; a tricky and unreliable man against whom Pope had more than one grievance.

Oxford, Robert Harley, Earl of. See Harley.

Ozell, John. A translator of French plays, whom Pope several times ridicules.

Page, Sir Francis. A justice popularly known as 'the hanging judge.'

Parnell, Thomas (1679–1717). Poet, and member of the Scriblerus Club. He wrote the life of Homer for Pope's *Iliad,* and after his death Pope brought out an edition of his poems.

Pelham, Henry. Became First Lord of the Treasury in 1743, through Walpole's influence; and died in 1754, the King exclaiming on his death: 'Now I shall have no more peace!' (Ward.)

Peter (Walter). See Walter.

Philips, Ambrose. Poet, Whig, and member of Addison's coterie. Author of the *Pastorals* with which Pope's were published, and frequent subject thereafter of Pope's satire.

Polwarth. The Hon. Hugh Hume, son of Alexander, Earl of Marchmont, grandson of Patrick, Earl of Marchmont, and distinguished, like them, in the cause of liberty. (Pope.) He was made one of Pope's executors.

Pulteney, William, afterward Earl of Bath. Orator and pamphleteer, and principal opponent to Sir Robert Walpole.

Queensbury, Duchess of. A leader of fashion and patron of letters; friend of Gay and Swift.

Ralph, James. A hack writer of American birth. Incurred Pope's anger by coming forward to defend Pope's victims in the first edition of *The Dunciad.*

Rich, John. Manager of the Theatre Royal in Covent Garden.

Rochester, Francis Atterbury, Bishop of. See Atterbury.

Rolli, Paolo Antonio. An Italian poet, and writer of many operas in that language, which, partly by the help of his genius, prevailed in England near twenty years. He taught Italian to some fine gentlemen, who affected to direct the operas. (Pope.)

Rowe, Nicholas (1673–1718). Friend of Addison, editor of Shakespeare, and writer of plays in blank verse, among the best known of which are *Jane Shore* and *The Fair Penitent.*

Rundel, Dr., Bishop of Derry. A friend of Pope and Swift, and frequently mentioned in their letters.

Sackville, Charles, Earl of Dorset. See Dorset.

Sandys, Samuel, First Baron. Opponent of Sir Robert Walpole. A man of steady industry rather than of talent.

Schutz, Augustus. Held, according to Carruthers, court offices near the person of George II., both before and after his accession to the throne.

Secker, Thomas (1693–1768). Bishop of Bristol, later of Oxford, and finally Archbishop of Canterbury. Noted for his piety and liberality.

Sheffield, John, Duke of Buckinghamshire (1649–1722). Author of an *Essay on Poetry,* which both Dryden and Pope praised, but which the modern critic finds of little value.

Shippen, William. A free-speaking Jacobite, who was sent to the Tower in 1718.

Shrewsbury, Charles Talbot, Duke of. Had been Secretary of State, Embassador in France, Lord Lieutenant of Ireland, Lord Chamberlain, and Lord Treasurer. He several times quitted his employments, and was often recalled. He died in 1718 (Pope).

Smythe, James Moore-. See Moore.

Somers, John Lord. He had been Lord Keeper in the reign of William III., who took from him the seals in 1700. The author had the honour of knowing him in 1706. A faithful, able, and incorrupt minister; who, to the qualities of a consummate statesman, added those of a man of learning and politeness. (Pope.)

Southern, Thomas (1660–1746). Author of *Oroonoko,* a play founded on Mrs. Behn's novel of the name, and very popular in its day.

Stanhope, James Earl. A nobleman of equal courage, spirit, and learning. General in Spain, and Secretary of State. (Pope.)

Talbot, Charles, Duke of Shrewsbury. See Shrewsbury.

Temple, Richard, Lord Cobham. See Cobham.

Theobald, Lewis. Usually called Tibbald by Pope. Author and translator. Editor of a respectable Shakespeare, and critic of Pope's edition of the dramatist: therefore made hero of *The Dunciad.*

Tibbald. See Theobald.

Tickell, Thomas. A member of Addison's coterie, and author of numerous papers in the *Spectator* and *Guardian;* notably the papers on English Pastoral which provoked Pope's enmity.

Tonson, Jacob. A leading bookseller in Pope's day, and publisher of much of his work.

Trumbull, or Trumbal, Sir William. See Biographical Sketch in this edition, p. xiii.

Vanbrugh, John, Sir (1666-1726). Architect and writer of comedies. Designer of Castle Howard and Blenheim, and author of *The Provoked Wife* and *The Relapse.*

Villiers, George, Duke of Buckingham. See Buckingham.

Walpole, Sir Robert. For twenty years Whig Prime Minister of England, and originator of the present Cabinet system of government.

Walter, Peter. A London capitalist whom Pope frequently mentions (under the name of Peter) as an example of extreme rapacity.

Warwick, Lord. Son of the Countess of Warwick, whom Addison married.

Wasse, Joseph. Fellow of Queen's College, Cambridge, and coeditor with Jebb of the *Bibliotheca Literaria.*

Welsted, Leonard. Journalist and Whig pamphleteer; author of some satirical verses on Pope.

Wharton, Philip, Duke of. Son of Addison's patron. A man of ability who died an exile, after a life of wild dissipation.

Withers, General Henry. A distinguished soldier. In his old age the friend of Pope and Gay.

Wortley, Lady Mary Wortley Montagu. See Montagu.

Wycherley, William (1640-1715). Dramatist and one of Pope's earliest friends.

Yonge, Sir William. A fop and small poet several times alluded to by Pope as 'Sir Will' and 'Sir Billy.'

B. NOTES AND ILLUSTRATIONS.

Page 2. To the Author of a Poem entitled Successio.

Lines 19, 20. Bavius, Mævius, Chærilus, Codrus. Minor Latin poets. See *The Dunciad*, Book III. 24; and note.

Page 2. The First Book of Statius's Thebais.

Line 24. The *mighty Cæsar* here referred to is Domitian, to whom Juvenal as well as Statius awarded divine honors.

Line 62. *The prophet.* Amphiaraus.

Line 65. *The youth.* Parthenopæus.

Line 399. *Such sons.* Eteocles and Polynices.

Line 470. *Scyron.* Pope evidently confounds the island of Scyros in the Ægean with the rocks between Megaris and Attica infested by the robber Sciron whom Theseus slew. See Ovid, *Metam.* vii. 444. (Ward.)

Page 15. Spenser: The Alley.

Stanza vi., line 5. *Jo—n.* Old Mr. Johnston, the retired Scotch Secretary of State, who lived at Twickenham. (Carruthers.)

Page 21. Spring: or, Damon.

Line 86. *A wondrous tree,* etc. An allusion to the Royal Oak, in which Charles II. had been hid from the pursuit after the battle of Worcester. (Pope.)

Line 90. *The thistle springs, to which the lily yields.* Alludes to the device of the Scots monarchs, the thistle worn by Queen Anne; and to the arms of France, the *fleur de lys.* (Pope.)

Page 24. Autumn; or, Hylas and Ægon.

Line 7. *Thou, whom the Nine,* etc. Mr. Wycherley, a famous author of comedies; of which the most celebrated were *The Plain-Dealer* and *The Country Wife.* He was a writer of infinite spirit, satire, and wit. The only objection made to him was that he had too much. However, he was followed, in the same way, by Mr. Congreve, though with a little more correctness. (Pope.)

Page 26. Winter; or, Daphne.

Mrs. Tempest. This lady was of an ancient family in Yorkshire, and particularly admired by the author's friend, Mr. Walsh, who, having celebrated her in a pastoral elegy, desired his friend to do the same, as appears from one of his letters, dated Sept. 9. 1706: 'Your last eclogue being on the same subject with mine on Mrs. Tempest's death, I should take it very kindly in you to give it a little turn as if it were to the memory of the same lady.' Her death having happened on the night of the great storm in 1703, gave a propriety to this eclogue, which in its general turn alludes to it. The scene of the pastoral lies in a grove, the time at midnight. (Pope.)

Lines 49, 50. *The balmy zephyrs,* etc. 'I wish,' said Johnson, 'that his fondness had not overlooked a line in which the zephyrs are made to lament in silence.'

Lines 89-92. These four last lines allude to the several subjects of the four pastorals, and to the several scenes of them, particularized before in each. (Pope.)

Page 28. Windsor Forest.

Line 65. *The fields are ravish'd,* etc. Alluding to the destruction made in the New Forest, and the tyrannies exercised there by William I. (Pope.)

Line 80. *Himself denied a grave.* The place of his interment at Caen in Normandy was claimed by a gentleman as his inheritance, the moment his servants were going to put him in his tomb; so that they were obliged to compound with the owner before they could perform the king's obsequies. (Warburton.)

Line 81. *His second hope.* Richard, Duke of Bernay, said to have been killed by a stag in the New Forest. (Ward.)

Line 207. The river Loddon.

Lines 211–216. These six lines were added after the first writing of this poem. (Pope.)

Line 355–368. The allusions are of course to the expected peace, for which the conferences were opened in 1711 at Utrecht; to the previous campaigns in Spain and Germany; to the war between Peter the Great and Charles XII.; and to the early difficulties of our East Indian settlements. (Ward.)

Line 398. *Unbounded Thames shall flow*, etc. A wish that London may be made a free port. (Pope.)

Page 52. THE TEMPLE OF FAME.

Line 1. *In that soft season*, etc. This poem is introduced in the manner of the Provençal poets, whose works were for the most part visions, or pieces of imagination, and constantly descriptive. From these, Petrarch and Chaucer frequently borrowed the idea of their poems. See the *Trionfi* of the former, and *Dream, Flower and the Leaf*, etc., of the latter. The author of this, therefore, chose the same sort of exordium. (Pope.)

Line 66. *Four faces had the dome*, etc. The Temple is described to be square, the four fronts with open gates facing the different quarters of the world, as an intimation that all nations of the earth may alike be received into it. The western front is of Grecian architecture; the Doric order was peculiarly sacred to Heroes and Worthies. Those whose statues are after mentioned were the first names of old Greece in arms and arts. (Pope.)

Line 81. *There great Alcides*, etc. This figure of Hercules is drawn with an eye to the position of the famous statue of Farnese. (Pope.)

Line 96. *And the great founder of the Persian name.* Cyrus was the beginning of the Persian, as Minas was of the Assyrian monarchy. The Magi and Chaldæans (the chief of whom was Zoroaster) employed their studies upon magic and astrology, which was in a manner almost the learning of the ancient Asian people. We have scarce any account of a moral philosopher except Confucius, the great law-giver of the Chinese, who lived about two thousand years ago. (Pope.)

Line 111. The learning of the old Egyptian priests consisted for the most part in geometry and astronomy; they also preserved the history of their nation. Their greatest hero upon record is Sesostris, whose actions and conquests may be seen at large in Diodorus, etc. (Pope.)

Line 152. *The youth that all things*, etc. Alexander the Great. The tiara was the crown peculiar to the Asian princes. His desire to be thought the son of Jupiter Ammon caused him to wear the horns of that God, and to represent the same upon his coins, which was continued by several of his successors. (Pope.)

Line 162. *Timoleon, glorious in his brother's blood.* Timoleon had saved the life of his brother Timophanes in the battle between the Argives and the Corinthians; but afterwards killed him when he affected the tyranny, preferring his duty to his country to all obligations of blood. (Pope.)

Line 172. *He whom ungrateful Athens*, etc. Aristides, who for his great integrity was distinguished by the appellation of *The Just*. When his countrymen would have banished him by the ostracism, where it was the custom for every man to sign the name of the person he voted to exile in an oyster-shell, a peasant, who could not write, came to Aristides to do it for him, who readily signed his own name. (Pope.)

Line 206. *Eliza.* El' sa (Dido).

Line 507. *While thus I stood*, etc. The hint is taken from a passage in another part of the third book, but here more naturally made the conclusion, with the addition of a moral to the whole. (Pope.)

Page 63. THE FABLE OF DRYOPE. Upon occasion of the death of Hercules, his mother Alcmena recounts her misfortunes to Iole, who answers with a relation of those of her own family, in particular the transformation of her sister Dryope, which is the subject of the ensuing Fable. (Pope.)

Page 67. AN ESSAY ON CRITICISM. *Part I.*

Line 15. *Let such teach others*, etc. 'Qui scribit artificiose, ab aliis commode scripta facile intelligere poterit.' *Cic. ad Herenn.* lib. iv. 'De pictore, sculptore, fictore, nisi artifex, judicare non potest.' *Pliny.* (Pope.)

Line 20. *Most have the seeds of judgment*, etc. 'Omnes tacito quodam sensu, sine ulla arte, aut ratione, quae sint in artibus ac rationibus recta et prava dijudicant.' *Cic. de Orat.* lib. iii. (Pope.)

Line 25. *So by false learning*, etc. 'Plus sine doctrina prudentia, quam sine prudentia valet doctrina.' *Quintilian.* (Pope.)

Line 98. *Just precepts*, etc. 'Nec enim artibus editis factum est ut argumenta inveniremus, sed dicta sunt omnia antequam praeciperentur; mox ea scriptoris observata et collecta ediderunt.' *Quintilian.* (Pope.)

Line 180. *Nor is it Homer nods*, etc. 'Modesto ac circumspecto judicio de tantis viris pronunciandum est, ne quod (quod plerisque accidit) damnent quod non intelligunt.' *Quintilian.* (Pope.)

Part II. Line 124. *Some by old words*, etc. 'Abolita et abrogata retinere, insolentiae cujusdam est, et frivolae in parvis jactantiae.' *Quintilian.* (Pope.)

Line 128. *Fungoso in the play.* In Ben Jonson's *Every Man out of his Humour.* (Pope.)

Lines 147, 148. *While expletives*, etc. 'He creeps along with ten little words in every line, and helps out his numbers with *for, to*, and *unto*, and all the pretty expletives he can find, while the sense is left half tired behind it.' Dryden, *Essay on Dramatic Poetry.*

Line 245. *Duck-lane.* A place where old and

second-hand books were sold formerly, near Smithfield. (Pope.)

Part III. Line 27. *And stares tremendous,* etc. This picture was taken to himself by John Dennis, a furious old critic by profession, who, upon no other provocation, wrote against this essay and its author, in a manner perfectly lunatic; for, as to the mention made of him in v. 270 (Part I.), he took it as a compliment, and said it was treacherously meant to cause him to overlook this abuse of his person. (Pope.) Dennis's unsuccessful play, *Appius and Virginia,* appeared in 1709. *Tremendous* was a favorite word of his.

Line 60. *Garth did not write,* etc. A common slander at that time in prejudice of that deserving author. Our poet did him this justice when that slander most prevailed, and it is now (perhaps the sooner for this very verse) dead and forgotten. (Pope.)

Line 64. *Paul's churchyard.* St. Paul's Churchyard was long the headquarters of the booksellers.

Line 157. *Roscommon.* Wentworth Dillon, Earl of Roscommon (1632–1684). A comparatively chaste poet of the Restoration, and projector of an English Academy of letters.

Page 82. EPISTLE TO MR. JERVAS.

Line 40. *This small well polish'd Gem, the work of years.* Fresnoy employed above twenty years in finishing his poem. (Pope.)

Line 60. *Worsley's eyes.* Frances, Lady Worsley. 'The name,' says Carruthers, ' originally stood Wortley, but the compliment was transferred from her [Lady Mary Wortley Montagu] after her quarrel with Pope, by the alteration of a single letter.'

Page 88. THE RAPE OF THE LOCK. *Canto I.*

Lines 1–4. Before Pope's successes in verse admitted him to the best society in England, he had moved in a small circle of Roman Catholic families in the immediate neighborhood of Windsor. To one of these families belonged Miss Arabella Fermor, the Belinda of *The Rape of the Lock;* to another, Lord Petre, called in the poem simply the Baron, the hero — or villain — of the story; and to a third belonged John Caryll. Lord Petre really stole a lock of Miss Fermor's hair, and some unpleasantness arose between the families in consequence. Caryll suggested to Pope that a humorous treatment of the incident in verse might help matters.

Line 23. *Birthnight Beau.* A fine gentleman such as might be seen at the state ball given on the anniversary of the royal birthday. (Hales.)

Line 44. *Box,* at the opera. *Ring,* a circus, or circular promenade, like that in Hyde Park, London.

Lines 54–56. *Succeeding vanities,* etc.

> ' Quae gratia currum
> Armorumque fuit vivis, quae cura nitentes
> Pascere equos, eadem sequitur tellure repostos.'
> *Æneid,* vi. (Pope.)

Line 108. *In the clear mirror,* etc. The language of the Platonists. (Pope.)

Canto II. Line 28. *And beauty draws us with a single hair.* In allusion to those lines of Hudibras, applied to the same purpose, —

> 'And tho' it be a two-foot trout,
> 'T is with a single hair pull'd out.'
> (Warburton.)

Line 38. *Twelve vast French romances.* Clélie, one of the popular French romances of the period, appeared in ten volumes of 800 pages each. (Hales.)

Line 45. *The Powers gave ear,* etc. See *Æneid,* xi. 794, 795. (Pope.)

Line 74. *Fays, Fairies, Genii,* etc. This line obviously echoes Satan's address to his followers: —

> ' Thrones, Dominations, Princedoms, Virtues, Powers ! '
> *Paradise Lost,* v. 601.

Line 106. *Or some frail China jar,* etc. Pope repeats this anti-climax in Canto iii. 159, below.

Canto III. Line 27. *Ombre* and *Piquet* were the fashionable card games of Queen Anne's day. Ombre was a game of Spanish origin. The three principal trumps were called Matadores; these are, in the order of their rank, Spadillio, the ace of spades; Manillio, the deuce of clubs when trumps are black, the seven when they are red; and Basto, the ace of clubs.

Line 61. *Mighty Pam.* Pam, the knave of clubs, is the highest card in the game of Loo.

Line 92. *Just in the jaws of ruin, and Codille.* Each has won four tricks. If the Baron, who is 'defending the pool,' takes more tricks than Belinda, who is ' defending the game,' he will ' win the Codille.'

Line 107. *Altars of Japan.* Small japanned tables.

Line 123. *Changed to a bird,* etc. See Ovid, *Metam.* viii. (Pope.)

Line 152. *But airy substance soon unites again.* Pope, in a note, refers us to the following passage : —

> ' But the ethereal substance closed,
> Not long divisible : and from the gash
> A stream of nectarous humor issuing flowed
> Sanguine, such as celestial spirits may bleed.'
> *Paradise Lost,* vi. 330–334.

Lines 163–170.

> ' Dum juga montis aper, fluvios dum piscis amabit,
> Semper honos nomenque tuum, laudesque manebunt.'
> Virgil, *Eclogues,* v. 76–77.

Line 165. Atalantis. *The new Atalantis,* by Mrs. Manley ; a book just then popular.

Lines 176, 177. *What wonder, then,* etc.

> 'Quid faciant crines, cum ferro talia cedant.'
> Catullus, *de Com. Berenice.* (Ward.)

Canto IV. Line 1. *But anxious cares,* etc.

> ' At regina gravi jamdudum saucia cura
> Vulnus alit venis, et caeco carpitur igni.'
> *Æneid,* iv. 1. (Pope.)

Line 24. *Megrim.* The ' megrims ' and ' the vapours ' were fashionable terms in Queen Anne's day for what we call ' the blues.'

Line 51. *Like Homer's tripod.* See *Iliad*, xviii. 372–381.

Line 52. *A Goose-pie talks.* Alludes to a real fact ; a lady of distinction imagined herself in this condition. (Pope.)

Line 69. *Citron-waters.* Spirits distilled from citron-rind.

Line 116. *The sound of Bow.* Within the sound of Bow-bells lay the least fashionable quarter, containing Grub Street, and other Bohemian haunts, as well as the dwellings of tradesmen.

Line 119. *Sir Plume.* Sir George Brown. He was the only one of the party who took the thing seriously. He was angry that the poet should make him talk nothing but nonsense. (Warburton.) *Thalestris* (line 87) was Mrs. Morley, Sir George's sister.

Canto V. Line 45. *So when bold Homer*, etc. See Homer, *Iliad*, xx. (Pope.)

Line 53. *Umbriel, on a sconce's height.* Minerva, in like manner, during the battle of Ulysses with the suitors, perches on a beam of the roof to behold it. (Pope.)

Line 65. *Thus on Mœander's flow'ry margin*, etc.

' Sic ubi fata vocant, udis abjectus in herbis,
    Ad vada Maeandri concinit albus color.'
        Ovid, *Epistle* vii. 2. (Pope.)

Line 71. *Now Jove suspends his golden scales in air.* See Homer, *Iliad*, viii., and Virgil, *Æneid*, xii. (Pope.)

Lines 89–96. *The same, his ancient personage to deck*, etc. In imitation of the progress of Agamemnon's sceptre in Homer, *Iliad*, ii. (Pope.)

Lines 137–138. *A hidden star*, etc.

' Flammiferumque trahens spatioso limite crinem
    Stella micat.'
        Ovid, *Metam.* xv. 849, 850. (Pope.)

Line 37. *Partridge.* John Partridge was a ridiculous star-gazer, who in his almanacks every year never failed to predict the downfall of the Pope and the King of France, then at war with the English. (Pope.) Partridge was the butt of Swift's famous hoax in 1707.

Page 102. MACER.

Line 8. *Crowne*, John, a dramatist and adapter of plays, died 1698.

Page 103. A FAREWELL TO LONDON.

Stanza ii. C—s is evidently Craggs ; and H—k, as Carruthers interprets the hiatus, Lord Hinchinbrook, a young nobleman of spirit and fashion. (Ward.)

Stanza viii., lines 3 and 4. Most likely Miss Younger and Mrs. Bicknell, sisters, both actresses. (Carruthers.)

Page 104. THE BASSET-TABLE.

Line 99. The Groom-Porter was an officer in the King's household, who, under a provision exempting royalty from the laws against gambling, was enabled to provide a resort for London gamesters.

Line 100. *Some dukes at Mary-bone.* The reference is supposed to have been to the Duke

of Buckinghamshire, who frequented a bowling-alley in Marylebone parish.

Page 106. EPIGRAM ON THE TOASTS OF THE KIT-CAT CLUB.

The Kit-cat Club, named for Christopher Katt, a pastry-cook, numbered among its members most of the town wits, including Steele and Addison.

Page 110. ELOISA TO ABELARD.

Line 24. *Forgot myself to stone.* ' Forget thyself to marble.' Milton, *Il Penseroso.* The expression ' caverns shagg'd with horrid thorn,' and the epithets ' pale-eyed,' ' twilight,' ' low-thoughted care,' and others, are first used in the smaller poems of Milton, which Pope seems to have been just reading. (Warton.)

Line 74. *Curse on all laws*, etc.

' And own no laws but those which love ordains.'
    Dryden, *Cinyras and Myrrha.* (Pope.)

Line 212. *Obedient slumbers*, etc. This line Pope confesses to having borrowed from Crashaw.

Line 342. *May one kind grave*, etc. Abelard and Eloisa were interred in the same grave, or in monuments adjoining, in the Monastery of the Paraclete ; he died in the year 1142, she in 1163. (Pope.)

Page 120. SANDYS' GHOST.

Stanza x. *Carey.* Probably John Carey.

Stanza xi. *Jacob.* Jacob Tonson. *Pembroke.* The Earl of Pembroke.

Stanza xii. *Tom Burnet.* Son of Bishop Burnet.

Stanza xiii. *Justice Philips.* Ambrose Philips.

Page 128. 1740 : A POEM.

These verses are supposed to be a fragment found by Lord Bolingbroke among Pope's papers. There is much doubt about many of the persons referred to ; the readings here suggested being merely a choice among many suggested by Bowles and Carruthers.

Page 137. AN ESSAY ON MAN. *Epistle I.*

Line 1. *St. John.* Henry St. John, afterwards Lord Bolingbroke, was the most intimate friend of Pope's later years. The themes treated in the *Essay on Man* had been much discussed between them ; it is, indeed, the shallow philosophy of Bolingbroke which supplies the substance of Pope's argument.

Line 6. *A mighty maze*, etc. The last verse, as it stood in the original editions, was —

' A mighty maze of walks without a plan;'

and perhaps this came nearer Pope's real opinion than the verse he substituted for it. (Lowell.)

Line 102. *The solar walk.* The sun's orbit. Pope cites in this connection ' the ancient opinion that the souls of the just went thither.'

Line 160. *Young Ammon.* Alexander the Great, who was saluted by the priests of the Libyan Jupiter Ammon as the son of their god.

Line 170. *And passions are the elements of life.* See this subject extended in Epistle II. from verse 100 to 122. (Pope.)

Line 213. *The headlong lioness.* 'The manner of the lion's hunting,' reads Pope's note,' is this : at their first going out in the night-time, they set up a loud roar, and then listen to the noise made by the beasts in their flight, pursuing them by the ear, and not by the nostril.'

Line 278. *The rapt Seraph.* Alluding to the name seraphim, signifying *burners.* (Warburton.)

Epistle II. Line 22. *Correct old Time,* etc. This alludes to Sir Isaac Newton's Grecian Chronology. (Warburton.)

Lines 71–74. *Self-love still stronger,* etc. Bowles quotes the following passage from Bacon : 'The affections carry ever an appetite to good, as reason doth. The difference is, that the affection holdeth merely the present ; reason beholdeth the future and sum of time.'

Epistle III. Line 68. *Favour'd man.* Several of the ancients, and many of the orientals since, esteemed those who were struck by lightning as favoured persons, and the particular favourites of Heaven. (Pope.)

Line 104. *Demoivre.* A noted French mathematician, and a friend of Sir Isaac Newton's.

Epistle IV. Line 74. *Mountains piled on mountains.* Alluding to the Titans' attempt to scale Olympus. (Ward.)

Line 99. Lucius Cary, Lord *Falkland* (1610–1643), a brilliant young statesman and versifier, was killed in the battle of Newburg, at the age of thirty-three.

Lines 100–101. Henry, Vicomte de *Turenne,* and Sir Philip *Sidney* both fell in battle before their extraordinary powers had reached full maturity.

Line 104. The Hon. Robert *Digby,* third son of Lord Digby, was a personal friend and correspondent of Pope's. He died in 1726.

Line 107. M. de Belsance was made bishop of Marseilles in 1709. In the plague of that city, in the year 1720, he distinguished himself by his zeal and activity, being the pastor, the physician, and the magistrate of his flock whilst that horrid calamity prevailed. (Warburton.)

Line 110. Pope's mother died in 1733, shortly before this epistle was written, at the age of ninety-one.

Line 123. *Shall burning Ætna,* etc. Alluding to the fate of those two great naturalists, Empedocles and Pliny, who both perished by too near an approach to Ætna and Vesuvius, while they were exploring the cause of their eruptions. (Warburton.)

Line 126. *Blameless Bethel.* Hugh Bethel, to whom the *Imitations of Horace* are addressed.

Line 220. *Macedonia's madman,* etc. An epigrammatic expression will also tempt him into saying something without basis in truth ; as where he ranks together 'Macedonia's madman and the Swede,' and says that neither of them 'looked forward farther than his nose,' a slang phrase which may apply well enough to Charles XII., but certainly not to the pupil of Aristotle, who showed himself capable of a large political forethought. So, too [line 236],

the rhyme, if correct, is sufficient apology for want of propriety in phrase, as where he makes Socrates ' bleed.' (Lowell.)

Line 278. *Lord Umbra.* Bubb Dodington, called Bubo in the Epistle to Arbuthnot (line 280), where Sir William Yonge's name is again coupled with his.

Lines 298–308. This passage evidently refers to the Duke of Marlborough.

Page 157. MORAL ESSAYS. *Epistle I.*

Line 57. *Manly.* The hero of Wycherley's *Plain-Dealer.* The name was commonly applied to Wycherley.

Line 58. *Umbra.* Bubb Dodington. See note on *Essay on Man,* IV. 278.

Line 61. *A Queen.* Queen Caroline, whom Swift, alluded to in the succeeding line, had satirized.

Line 77. *Catius.* Charles Dartineuf, according to Carruthers. See *Imitations of Horace,* Bk. II. Ep. ii. 87, note.

Line 81. *Patricio.* Conjectured by Warburton to be Lord Godolphin. See Glossary.

Line 89. *A perjur'd prince.* Louis XI. of France wore in his hat a leaden image of the Virgin Mary, which when he swore by he feared to break his oath. (Pope.)

Line 90. *A godless Regent tremble at a star.* Philip, Duke of Orleans, Regent of France in the minority of Louis XV., superstitious in judicial astrology, though an unbeliever in all religion. (Warburton.)

Line 91. *The throne,* etc. Philip V. of Spain, who, after renouncing the throne for religion, resumed it to gratify his queen ; and Victor Amadeus II., king of Sardinia, who resigned the crown, and trying to resume it, was imprisoned till his death. (Pope.)

Line 136. *A saint in crape.* That is, in the garb of the clergy.

Line 179. *Wharton.* Philip, Duke of Wharton. See Glossary.

Line 187. *Wilmot.* John Wilmot, Earl of Rochester, famous for his wit and extravagances in the time of Charles the Second. (Pope.)

Line 231. *Lanesb'row.* An ancient nobleman, who continued this practice long after his legs were disabled by the gout. (Pope.)

Line 247. *Were the last words,* etc. This story, like the others, is founded on fact, though the author had the goodness not to mention the names. Several attribute this in particular to a very celebrated actress who, in detestation of the thought of being buried in woollen, gave these her last orders with her dying breath. (Pope.) Warton says that the actress was Mrs. Oldfield.

Epistle II. Of this Epistle, which was published in 1735, parts had been long before written and even printed. As originally published, it wanted the portraits of Philomede, Chloë, and Atossa. According to Warburton's statement, Pope communicated the character of Atossa to the Duchess of Marlborough as intended for the Duchess of Buckingham ; according to Walpole he repeated the experiment *vice versa.* Immediately on the death of Pope, the Duchess of Marlborough applied to one of his executors, Lord Marchmont, with the view of ascertaining whether the poet had left behind him any satire on the Duke or herself. Marchmont consulted Bolingbroke; and it was found that in the edition of the *Moral Essays* prepared for the press by Pope just before his death, and printed off ready for publication, the character of Atossa was inserted. If Lord Marchmont made the statement attributed to him by the editor of his papers (Rose), Pope had received from the Duchess £1000, the acceptance of which implied forbearance towards the house of Marlborough. If this be so, it is probable that the motive which prompted Pope to the acceptance of this 'favor' was the desire to settle Martha Blount in independent circumstances for life. (Ward.)

Lines 7-14. *Arcadia's Countess — Pastora by a fountain — Leda with a swan — Magdalen — Cecilia.* Attitudes in which several ladies affected to be drawn, and sometimes one lady in them all. The poet's politeness and complaisance to the sex is observable in this instance, amongst others, that whereas in the *Characters of Men*, he has sometimes made use of real names, in the *Characters of Women* always fictitious. (Pope.)

Line 24. *Sappho.* A name for Lady Mary Wortley Montagu, first used by Pope in compliment, but later retained for purposes of abuse.

Line 53. *Narcissa.* Warton says that Narcissa stands for the Duchess of Hamilton. The lines were adopted from the earlier verses, which Pope had called *Sylvia, a Fragment.*

Line 83. *Philomede.* Henrietta, Duchess of Marlborough in her own right (daughter of Sarah), an admirer of Congreve. She married the second Earl of Godolphin.

Line 107. *Her Grace.* This refers, according to Warton, to the Duchess of Montagu, with whom Lady Mary Wortley Montagu was intimate.

Line 115. *Atossa.* Sarah, Duchess of Marlborough. In 1678 she was married to Colonel Churchill, and it was largely by her influence that he was made Duke of Marlborough.

Lines 139, 140. *The bust and temple rise.* This alludes to a temple she erected with a bust of Queen Anne in it, which mouldered away in a few years. (Wilkes.)

Line 157. *Chloë.* Lady Suffolk, mistress of George II., and friend of Pope, Swift, Gay, and Arbuthnot. See *On a Certain Lady*, etc., page 118.

Line 198. *Mah'met.* Servant to the late king (George I.), said to be the son of a Turkish Bassa, whom he took at the siege of Buda, and constantly kept about his person. (Pope.)

Hale. Dr. Stephen Hale, not more estimable for his useful discoveries as a natural philosopher than for his exemplary life and pastoral charity as a parish priest. (Pope.)

Line 251. *The Ring.* See note on *The Rape of the Lock*, Canto I. line 44.

Lines 253-256. Originally the last four lines of the short poem called *Erinna.*

Epistle III. This Epistle was written after a violent outcry against our author, on a supposition that he had ridiculed a worthy nobleman merely for his wrong taste. He justified himself upon that article in a letter to the Earl of Burlington; at the end of which are these words: 'I have learnt that there are some who would rather be wicked than ridiculous: and therefore it may be safer to attack vices than follies. I will therefore leave my betters in the quiet possession of their idols, their groves, and their high places; and change my subject from their pride to their meanness, from their vanities to their miseries; and as the only certain way to avoid misconstructions, to lessen offence, and not to multiply ill-natured applications, I may probably, in my next, make use of real names instead of fictitious ones.' (Pope.)

Line 20. John *Ward*, of Hackney, Esq.; Member of Parliament, being prosecuted by the Duchess of Buckingham, and convicted of forgery, was first expelled the House, and then stood in the pillory on the 17th of March, 1727. He was suspected of joining in a conveyance with Sir John Blunt, to secrete fifty thousand pounds of that Director's estate, forfeited to the South-Sea Company by Act of Parliament. The company recovered the fifty thousand pounds against Ward; but he set up prior conveyances of his real estate to his brother and son, and conceal'd all his personal, which was computed to be one hundred and fifty thousand pounds. These conveyances being also set aside by a bill in Chancery, Ward was imprisoned, and hazarded the forfeiture of his life, by not giving in his effects till the last day, which was that of his examination. During his confinement, his amusement was to give poison to dogs and cats, and to see them expire by slower or quicker torments. To sum up the *worth* of this gentleman, at the several æras of his life, At his standing in the Pillory he was *worth above two hundred thousand pounds;* at his commitment to Prison, he was *worth one hundred and fifty thousand;* but has been since so far diminished in his reputation, as to be thought a *worse man* by *fifty or sixty thousand.* (Pope.) From Pope's intimate acquaintance with Mr. Ward's career, it might almost be suspected that he is the same who is enumerated among Pope's friends in Gay's poem (Ward.)

Mr. *Waters*, the third of these worthies, was a man no way resembling the former in his military, but extremely so in his civil capacity; his great fortune having been rais'd by the like diligent attendance on the necessities of others. But this gentleman's history must be deferred till his death, when his *worth* may be known more certainly. (Pope.)

Fr. *Chartres*, a man infamous for all manner of vices. When he was an ensign in the army, he was drumm'd out of the regiment for a cheat; he was next banish'd Brussels, and drumm'd out of Ghent on the same account. After a hundred tricks at the gaming tables, he took to lending of money at exorbitant interest and on great penalties, accumulating premium, interest, and capital into a new capital, and seizing to a minute when the payments became due ; in a word, by a constant attention to the vices, wants, and follies of mankind, he acquired an immense fortune. His house was a perpetual bawdy-house. He was twice condemn'd for rapes, and pardoned : but the last time not without imprisonment in Newgate, and large confiscations. He died in Scotland in 1731, aged 62. The populace at his funeral rais'd a great riot, almost tore the body out of the coffin, and cast dead dogs, &c., into the grave along with it. The following Epitaph contains his character very justly drawn by Dr. Arbuthnot:

> HERE continueth to rot
> The Body of FRANCIS CHARTRES,
> Who with an INFLEXIBLE CONSTANCY,
> and INIMITABLE UNIFORMITY of Life,
> PERSISTED,
> In spite of AGE and INFIRMITIES,
> In the Practice of EVERY HUMAN VICE ;
> Excepting PRODIGALITY and HYPOCRISY :
> His insatiable AVARICE exempted him from the first,
> His matchless IMPUDENCE from the second.
> Nor was he more singular
> in the undeviating *Pravity* of his *Manners*
> Than successful
> in *Accumulating* WEALTH.
> For, without TRADE or PROFESSION,
> Without TRUST of PUBLIC MONEY,
> And without BRIBE-WORTHY Service,
> He acquired, or more properly created,
> A MINISTERIAL ESTATE.
> He was the only Person of his Time,
> Who could CHEAT without the Mask of HON-ESTY,
> Retain his Primeval MEANNESS
> When possess'd of TEN THOUSAND a YEAR,
> And having daily deserved the GIBBET for what he *did*,
> Was at last condemn'd to it for what he *could* not *do*.
> Oh Indignant Reader !
> Think not his Life useless to Mankind !
> PROVIDENCE conniv'd at his execrable Designs,
> To give to After-ages
> A conspicuous PROOF and EXAMPLE,
> Of how small Estimation is EXORBITANT WEALTH in the Sight of GOD,
> By his bestowing it on the most UNWORTHY of ALL MORTALS.

This Gentleman was *worth seven thousand pounds a year* estate in Land, and about *one hundred thousand* in Money. (Pope.)
And the Devil. Alluding to the vulgar opinion, that all mines of metal and subterraneous treasures are in the guard of the Devil : which seems to have taken its rise from the pagan fable of Plutus the God of Riches. (Warburton.)
Line 35. *Beneath the patriot's cloak.* This is a true story, which happened in the reign of William III., to an unsuspected old patriot, who coming out at the back-door from having been

closeted by the King, where he had received a large bag of guineas, the bursting of the bag discovered his business there. (Pope.)
Line 42. *Fetch or carry kings.* In our author's time, many Princes had been sent about the world, and great changes of kings projected in Europe. The partition-treaty had disposed of Spain ; France had set up a king for England, who was sent to Scotland and back again ; the Duke of Anjou was sent to Spain and Don Carlos to Italy. (Pope.)
Line 44. *Or ship off senates.* Alluding to several ministers, counsellors, and patriots banished in our times to Siberia, and to that more glorious fate of the Parliament of Paris, banished to Pontoise in the year 1720 (Pope.)
Line 62. *Worldly crying coals.* Some misers of great wealth, proprietors of the coal-mines, had entered at this time into an association to keep up coals to an extravagant price, whereby the poor were reduced almost to starve, till one of them, taking the advantage of underselling the rest, defeated the design. One of these misers was worth *ten thousand*, another *seven thousand* a year. (Pope.)
Line 65. *Colepepper.* Sir William Colepepper, Bart., a person of an ancient family and ample fortune, without one other quality of a gentleman, who, after ruining himself at the gaming-table, past the rest of his days in sitting there to see the ruin of others ; preferring to subsist upon borrowing and begging, rather than to enter into any reputable method of life, and refusing a post in the army which was offered him. (Pope.)
Line 67. *White's.* The most fashionable of London gambling resorts.
Line 82. *Turner.* A very wealthy miser.
Line 84. *Wharton.* Philip, Duke of Wharton.
Line 85. *Hopkins.* A citizen whose rapacity obtained him the name of Vulture Hopkins. He lived worthless, but died worth three hundred thousand pounds, which he would give to no person living, but left it so as not to be inherited till after the second generation. His counsel representing to him how many years it must be, before this could take effect, and that his money could only lie at interest all that time, he expressed great joy thereat, and said, ' They would then be as long in spending, as he had been in getting it.' But the Chancery afterwards set aside the will, and give it to the heir at law. (Pope.)
Line 86. *Japhet, nose and ears ?* Japhet Crook, alias Sir Peter Stranger, was punished with the loss of those parts, for having forged a conveyance of an Estate to himself, upon which he took up several thousand pounds. He was at the same time sued in Chancery for having fraudulently obtained a Will, by which he possessed another considerable Estate, in wrong of the brother of the deceased. By these means he was *worth* a great sum, which (in reward for the small loss of his ears) he enjoyed in prison till his death, and quietly left to his executor. (Pope.)

Line 96. *Die, and endow a College, or a Cat.* A famous Duchess of Richmond in her last will left considerable legacies and annuities to her Cats. (Pope.) [Warton more than vindicates the memory of this famous beauty of Charles II.'s court from Pope's taunt by stating that she left annuities to certain poor ladies of her acquaintance, with the burden of maintaining some of her cats ; this proviso being intended to disguise the charitable character of the bequests. (Ward.)

Line 99. *Bond damns the poor, &c.* This epistle was written in the year 1730, when a corporation was established to lend money to the poor upon pledges, by the name of the *Charitable Corporation;* but the whole was turned only to an iniquitous method of enriching particular people, to the ruin of such numbers, that it became a parliamentary concern to endeavour the relief of those unhappy sufferers, and three of the managers, who were members of the house, were expell'd. By the report of the committee, appointed to enquire into that iniquitous affair, it appears, that when it was objected to the intended removal of the office, that the Poor, for whose use it was erected, would be hurt by it, Bond, one of the Directors, replied, *Damn the poor.* That ' God hates the poor,' and, ' That every man in want is knave or fool,'' &c. were the genuine apothegms of some of the persons here mentioned. (Pope.) Dennis Bond, a member of Parliament, died in 1747. (Carruthers.)

Line 100. Sir Gilbert Heathcote, director of the Bank of England, and one of the richest men of his day. (Ward.)

Line 117. *South-Sea Year.* 1720. Pope was involved in the speculation, but is supposed to have escaped without loss.

Line 118. *To live on venison.* In the extravagance and luxury of the South-Sea year, the price of a haunch of venison was from three to five pounds.

Line 121. *Sappho.* This is a particularly gratuitous insult, as Lady Mary Wortley Montagu invested in South-Sea stock by Pope's advice and lost her money.

Line 123. *Wise Peter.* Peter Walter, a person not only eminent in the wisdom of his profession, as a dextrous attorney, but allowed to be a good, if not a safe conveyancer; extremely respected by the Nobility of this land, tho' free from all manner of luxury and ostentation : his Wealth was never seen, and his bounty never heard of, except to his own son, for whom he procured an employment of considerable profit, of which he gave him as much as was *necessary.* Therefore the taxing this gentleman with any Ambition, is certainly a great wrong to him. (Pope.)

Line 126. *Rome's great Didius.* A Roman Lawyer, so rich as to purchase the Empire when it was set to sale upon the death of Pertinax. (Pope.) Didius Julianus A. D. 193. The vendors were the Prætorian Guards. (Ward.)

Line 127. *The Crown of Poland, &c.* The two persons here mentioned were of Quality,

each of whom in the Mississippi despis'd to realize above *three hundred thousand pounds;* the Gentleman with a view to the purchase of the Crown of Poland, the Lady on a vision of the like royal nature. They since retired into Spain, where they are still in search of gold in the mines of the Asturies. (Pope.)

Line 128. A Mr. Gage, of the ancient Suffolk Catholic family of that name ; and Lady Mary Herbert, daughter of the Marquess of Powis and of a natural daughter of James II. : whence the phrase ' *hereditary* realm.' (Bowles.)

Line 133. *Much injur'd Blunt.* Sir John Blunt, originally a scrivener, was one of the first projectors of the South-Sea Company, and afterwards one of the directors and chief managers of the famous scheme in 1720. He was also one of those who suffer'd most severely by the bill of pains and penalties on the said directors. (Pope.)

Line 177. *Old Cotta.* Supposed to be the Duke of Newcastle, who died in 1711 ; and his son, the well-known peer of that name, who afterwards became prime minister. (Carruthers.)

Line 243. *Oxford's better part.* Edward Harley, Earl of Oxford. The son of Robert, created Earl of Oxford and Earl Mortimer by Queen Anne. This Nobleman died regretted by all men of letters, great numbers of whom had experienced his benefits. He left behind him one of the most noble Libraries in Europe. (Pope.)

Line 250. *The Man of Ross.* The person here celebrated, who with a small Estate actually performed all these good works, and whose true name was almost lost (partly by the title of the *Man of Ross* given him by way of eminence, and partly by being buried without so much as an inscription) was called Mr. John Kyrle. He died in the year 1724, aged 90, and lies interred in the chancel of the church of Ross in Herefordshire. (Pope.) We must understand what is here said, of *actually performing,* to mean by the contributions which the *Man of Ross,* by his assiduity and interest, collected in his neighbourhood. (Warburton.)

Line 296. *Eternal buckle,* etc. The poet ridicules the wretched taste of carving large periwigs on bustos, of which there are several vile examples at Westminster and elsewhere. (Pope.)

Line 305. *Great Villiers lies.* This Lord, yet more famous for his vices than his misfortunes, after having been possess'd of about £50,000 a year, and passed thro' many of the highest posts in the kingdom, died in the Year 1687, in a remote inn in Yorkshire, reduced to the utmost misery. (Pope.)

George Villiers, Duke of Buckingham, the son of the first Duke (the favourite and minister of James I. and Charles I.), was born in 1637. He lost his estates as a royalist, but recovered them by his marriage with the daughter of Lord Fairfax. He is the Zimri of the Absalom and Achitophel of Dryden, whom he had ridiculed as Bayes in the burlesque play of *The Rehearsal.* Thus we have portraits of this typical hero of the Restoration period by Dryden and Pope, as well as by Burnet and Butler, Count Grammont and Horace Walpole. The tenant's house at which he died (in 1687) was at Kirby Moor Side, near Helmsly in Yorkshire. (Ward.)

Line 307. *Cliveden.* A delightful palace, on the banks of the Thames, built by the D. of Buckingham. (Pope.)

Line 308. *Shrewsbury.* The Countess of Shrewsbury, a woman abandoned to gallantries. The Earl her husband was kill'd by the Duke of Buckingham in a duel ; and it has been said, that during the combat she held the Duke's horses in the habit of a page. (Pope.)

Line 315. Sir John Cutler, a wealthy citizen of the Restoration period, accused of rapacity on account of a large claim made by his execu-tors against the College of Physicians, which he had aided by a loan. (Carruthers.)

Line 339. *Where London's column,* etc. The monument on Fish Street Hill, built in memory of the fire of London of 1666, with an inscription importing that city to have been burnt by the Papists. (Pope.)

Epistle IV. Line 7. *Topham.* A gentleman famous for a judicious collection of drawings. (Pope.)

Line 8. *Pembroke.* Henry, Earl of Pembroke, a patron of the arts, and owner of many valua-ble paintings.

Line 10. *Mead — Sloane.* Two eminent phy-sicians ; the one had an excellent library, the other the finest collection in Europe of natural curiosities ; both men of great learning and humanity. (Pope.) Dr. Mead was physician to George II. ' He was, however,' says Ward, ' the reverse of a bookworm ; for Johnson says of him that " he lived more in the broad sunshine of life than almost any man." ' Sir John or Hans Sloane was a skilled botanist and physician. His natural history collection is now preserved in the British Museum.

Line 18. *Ripley.* This man was a carpenter, employed by a first Minister, who raised him to an Architect, without any genius in the art ; and after some wretched proofs of his insuffi-ciency in public buildings, made him Comptrol-ler of the Board of Works. (Pope.)

Line 20. *Bubo.* Bubb Dodington. See *Epistle to Arbuthnot,* line 280.

Line 23. *You show us Rome,* etc. The Earl of Burlington was then publishing the designs of Inigo Jones, and the *Antiquities of Rome* by Palladio. (Pope.)

Line 46. *Le Nôtre.* André Le Nôtre (1613–1700), landscape-gardener of Louis XIV.

Line 70. *Stowe.* The seat and gardens of the Lord Viscount Cobham in Buckinghamshire. (Pope.)

Line 78. *In a hermitage set Dr. Clarke.* Dr. L. Clarke's busto placed by the Queen in the Hermitage, while the doctor duly frequented the court. (Pope.) Dr. Clarke was one of Queen Caroline's chaplains.

Line 150. *Never mentions Hell,* etc. This is a

fact ; a reverend Dean preaching at court threatened the sinner with punishment in ' a place which he thought it not decent to name in so polite an assembly.' (Pope.)

Line 169. *Yet hence the poor,* etc. The Moral of the whole, where Providence is justified in giving wealth to those who squander it in this manner. A bad taste employs more hands, and diffuses expense more than a good one. (Pope.)

Line 173. *Another age,* etc. Had the poet lived but three years longer, he had seen this prophecy fulfilled. (Warburton.)

Lines 195–202. *Till Kings . . . Bid Harbours open,* etc. The poet after having touched upon the proper objects of Magnificence and Expense, in the private works of great men, comes to those great and public works which become a prince. This Poem was published in the year 1732, when some of the new-built Churches, by the act of Queen Anne, were ready to fall, being founded in boggy land (which is satirically alluded to in our author's imitation of Horace, Lib. ii. Sat. 2 : —

' Shall half the new-built Churches round thee fall ; '

others were vilely executed, thro' fraudulent cabals between undertakers, officers, &c. Da-genham-breach had done very great mischiefs ; many of the Highways throughout England were hardly passable ; and most of those which were repaired by Turnpikes were made jobs for private lucre, and infamously executed, even to the entrances of London itself : The proposal of building a Bridge at Westminster had been petition'd against and rejected ; but in two years after the publication of this poem, an Act for building a Bridge pass'd thro' both houses. After many debates in the committee, the exe-cution was left to the carpenter above-men-tioned, who would have made it a wooden one : to which our author alludes in these lines,

' Who builds a Bridge that never drove a pile ?
Should Ripley venture, all the world would smile.'

See the notes on that place. (Pope.)

Page 176. EPISTLE to DR. ARBUTHNOT. For John Arbuthnot see Glossary.

Advertisement. Lines 6, 7. Of these papers the former was said to be a joint production of Lady Mary Wortley Montagu and Lord Hervey; the latter was written by Hervey alone. See Carruthers' *Life of Pope,* ch. viii.

Line 1. John Searl, Pope's body-servant for many years.

Line 8. An artificial grotto, constructed under a road, was one of Pope's fanciful improvements of his little estate at Twickenham. Twitenham or Twit'nam (line 21) are forms of the name affected by Pope.

Line 13. *The Mint,* a place to which insolvent debtors retired, to enjoy an illegal protection, which they were there suffered to afford one another, from the persecution of their creditors. (Warburton.)

Line 23. *Arthur.* Arthur Moore, a prominent politician, father of the James Moore-Smythe whom Pope so often ridiculed.

Line 40. ' *Keep your piece nine years.*'

'Novemque prematur in annum.'
Horace, *De Arte Poetica*, 388.

Line 43. *Term.* The London ' season.'

Line 51. *Pitholeon*, the name taken from a foolish poet of Rhodes, who pretended much to Greek. (Pope.)

Line 53. Edmund Curll was a piratical bookseller who did Pope several ill turns, as in publishing some of his private letters (see 113 below), and printing in his name various sorts of rubbish (see 351 below, and Pope's note).

Line 54. The *London Journal* favored the Whigs. Pope was very little of a politician, but his leaning was toward the Tories.

Line 60. In the early editions the line read —

' Cibber and I are luckily no friends.'

Pope's one attempt at dramatic writing, *Three Hours after Marriage*, written in connection with Gay and Arbuthnot, was a flat failure. The legitimate fun made of it by Colley Cibber was the source of a feud between them, which ended only in Cibber's being made the main figure in *The Dunciad.*

Line 62. Bernard Lintot, after 1712, published much of Pope's work.

Line 72. *Some say his Queen.* The story is told by some of his Barber, but by Chaucer of his Queen. See *Wife of Bath's Tale.* (Pope.)

Line 88. Alluding to Horace, *Ode* iii. 3: —

' Si fractus illabatur orbis
Impavidum ferient ruinae.' (Pope.)

In translating this ode Addison had used the phrase ' the mighty crack ' (86 above), and Pope had ridiculed him for it.

Line 100. *Philips.* Ambrose Philips, of whom Bishop Bolter became patron.

Line 101. *Sappho.* Lady Mary Wortley Montagu.

Line 118. *You have an eye.* It is remarkable that, amongst these complaints on his infirmities and deformities, he mentions his eye, which was fine and piercing. (Warburton.)

Line 128. *I lisped in numbers.*

' Sponte sua carmen numeros veniebat ad aptos,
Et, quod tentabam dicere, versus erat.'
Ovid, *Tristia*, 4, x. 25, 26.

Line 135. *Granville.* George Granville, afterwards Lord Lansdown, known for his poems, most of which he composed very young. (Pope.)

Granville, Mr. Walsh, and Dr. Garth are mentioned in Pope's first note to the *Pastorals* as among those who encouraged him in his earliest efforts.

Line 139. *Talbot, Somers, Sheffield.* These are the persons to whose account the author charges the publication of his first pieces, persons with whom he was conversant (and he adds beloved) at sixteen or seventeen years of age, an early period for such acquaintance. The catalogue might have been made yet more illustrious had he not confined it to that time when

he writ the *Pastorals* and *Windsor Forest*, on which he passes a sort of censure in the lines following [147–150]. (Pope.)

Line 146. *Burnets*, etc. Authors of secret and scandalous history. (Pope.)

Line 149. *Fanny.* Lord Hervey, the Sporus of lines 305–333 below.

Line 151. *Gildon.* Charles Gildon, a critic who had abused Pope.

Line 153. *Dennis.* John Dennis, a free-lance in letters, and one of the favorite butts of Pope's satire. It was he who indirectly caused the difference between Pope and Addison. See Glossary.

Line 164. *Slashing Bentleys*, etc. Bentley's edition of *Paradise Lost*, which appeared in 1732, was at once the last and the least worthy effort of his critical prowess ; as to Theobald's Shakspere, it was an honest and not wholly unsuccessful piece of work, and a better edition than Pope's own. Bentley's Milton is better characterized in *Imitations of Horace*, i. Ep. of ii. Bk. vv. 103–4. (Ward.)

Line 179. *The bard whom pilfer'd pastorals renown.* Ambrose Philips. Charles Gildon ranked him with Theocritus and Virgil.

Line 190. *Tate.* Nahum Tate was then poet laureate, ' the author of the worst alterations of Shakespeare,' says Professor Craik, ' the worst version of the Psalms of David, and the worst continuation of a great poem [Dryden's *Absalom and Achitophel*] extant.'

Lines 193–214. The famous passage on Addison had been published twelve years before the *Epistle to Arbuthnot* was written. Addison's name appeared in the earlier version.

Line 218. *On wings of winds*, etc. Pope credits this line to Hopkins's paraphrase of Psalm civ.

Line 232. *Bufo* probably stands for Lord Halifax.

Line 236. *And a true Pindar stood without a head.* Ridicules the affectation of Antiquaries, who frequently exhibit the headless trunks and terms of statues, for Plato, Homer, Pindar, etc. (Pope.)

Line 248. *He help'd to bury*, etc. Mr. Dryden, after having lived in exigencies, had a magnificent funeral bestowed upon him by the contribution of several persons of quality. (Pope.)

Line 256. *Gay.* John Gay (1688–1732), author of the famous *Beggar's Opera*, and one of Pope's best friends. In his last years he was taken excellent care of by the Duke of Queensbury (260, below), and died by no means a pauper.

Line 280. *Sir Will or Bubo.* See *Essay on Man*, IV. 278 and note.

Line 299. *The Dean and Silver Bell.* Pope had been accused of ridiculing, in the *Essay on Taste*, the furniture and appointments of Canons, the seat of the Duke of Chandos, where Pope had been received. Pope's denial of the charge was accepted by the Duke.

Line 305. *Sporus* is John Lord Hervey, a well-known court favorite. He seems to have been at least harmless. Pope, for some unknown reason, conceived one of his violent antipathies for him ; and the following lines, hardly less celebrated than those on Addison, are the result.

Line 350. *The tale revived*, etc. As that he received subscriptions to *Shakespear*, that he set his name to Mr. Broome's verses, etc., which, though publicly disproved, were nevertheless repeated in the libels. (Pope.)

Line 351. *Th' imputed trash.* This imputed trash, such as profane psalms, court poems, and other scandalous things, printed in his name by Curll and others. (Pope.)

Line 365. *Knight of the post corrupt.* The so-called Knights of the Post stood about the sheriff's pillars near the courts, in readiness to swear anything for pay. (Ward.)

Line 371. *Friend to his distress.* In 1733 Pope wrote a prologue to a play given for the benefit of Dennis, who was then old, blind, and not far from death.

Line 374. *Ten years.* It was so long after many libels before the author of the *Dunciad* published that poem, till when he never writ a word in answer to the many scurrilities and falsehoods concerning him. (Pope.)

Line 375. *Welsted's lie.* This man had the impudence to tell in print that Mr. P. had occasioned a lady's death, and to name a person he never heard of. (Pope.)

Line 379. *Budgell* was charged with forging a will, with profit to himself.

Lines 382-387. Pope has a long note on this passage, in which he goes much into detail to prove the respectability of his parents.

Line 391. *Bestia.* L. Calpurnius Bestia, who here seems to signify the Duke of Marlborough, was a Roman proconsul, bribed by Jugurtha into a dishonorable peace. (Ward.)

Line 393. *Discord in a noble wife.* Dryden had married Lady Howard, and Addison the Countess of Warwick.

Line 397. He was a non-juror, and would not take the oath of allegiance or supremacy, or the oath against the Pope. (Bowles.)

Line 417. Dr. Arbuthnot had been the favorite physician of Queen Anne.

Page 182. SATIRES, EPISTLES AND ODES OF HORACE IMITATED. *First Satire, Second Book.*

Line 6. *Lord Fanny.* Lord Hervey.

Line 23. *Sir Richard.* Sir Richard Blackmore.

Lines 30, 31. *Carolina.* Queen Caroline. *Amelia.* Princess Amelia, second daughter of George II.

Line 34. *Their Laureate.* Colley Cibber.

Line 40. *Peter.* Peter Walter.

Line 46. *Scarsdale his bottle, Darty his hampie.* Lord Scarsdale and Charles Dartineuf, famous epicures.

Line 49. *Fox.* Probably Henry Fox, First Lord Holland. *Hockley-hole.* There was a noted bear-garden at Hockley-in-the-Hole. See the *Spectaor*, No 436.

Line 52. *Shippen.* William Shippen, an outspoken politician and a Jacobite, who was sent to the Tower in 1718. According to Coxe, he used to say of himself and Sir Robert Walpole,

'Robin and I are two honest men ; though he is for King George and I for King James.' (Ward.)

Line 81. *Slander or poison dread.* Alluding to a notorious rumor that a Miss Mackenzie had been poisoned by the Countess of Deloraine.

Line 82. *Page.* Judge Page. See *Epilogue to Satires*, II. 56.

Line 100. *Lee.* Nathaniel Lee (1657-1692), a tragic poet, author of *The Rival Queens.*

Line 129. *He whose lightning*, etc. Charles Mordaunt, Earl of Peterborough, who in the year 1705 took Barcelona, and in the winter following, with only 280 horse and 900 foot, enterprised and accomplished the conquest of Valencia. (Pope.)

Line 153. *Sir Robert.* Walpole.

Page 184. *Second Satire, Second Book.*

Mr. Bethel. Hugh Bethel.

Line 25. *Oldfield.* This eminent glutton ran through a fortune of fifteen hundred pounds a year in the simple luxury of good eating. (Warburton.)

Line 42. *Bedford-head.* A famous eating-house in Covent Garden.

Line 49. *Avidien.* Edward Wortley Montagu, the husband of Lady Mary. (Carruthers.)

Line 175. *Shades that to Bacon*, etc. Gorhambury, near St. Albans, the seat of Lord Bacon, was at the time of his disgrace conveyed by him to his quondam secretary, Sir J. Meantys, whose heir sold it to Sir Harbottle Grimston, whose grandson left it to his nephew (Wm. Lucklyn, who took the name of Grimston), whose second son was in 1719 created Viscount Grimston. This is the 'booby lord' to whom Pope refers. (Ward.)

Line 177. *Proud Buckingham's*, etc. Villiers, Duke of Buckingham. (Pope.) The estate of Helmsley was purchased by Sir Charles Duncombe, Lord Mayor in 1709, who changed its name to Duncombe Park. (Carruthers.)

Page 187. *First Epistle, First Book.*

Line 6. *Modest Cibber*, etc. Colley Cibber retired from the stage after a histrionic career of more than forty years in 1733 ; but returned in 1734 and did not make his 'positively last appearance' till 1745. (Ward.)

Line 16. *You limp, like Blackmore on a Lord Mayor's horse.* The fame of this heavy Poet, however problematical elsewhere, was universally received in the City of London. His versification is here exactly described: stiff and not strong; stately and yet dull, like the sober and slow-paced Animal generally employed to mount the Lord Mayor: and therefore here humorously opposed to Pegasus. (Pope.)

Line 51. *Cheselden.* In answer to Swift's inquiry who 'this Cheselden' was, Pope informed him that C. was 'the most noted and most deserving man in the whole profession of chirurgery, and had saved the lives of thousands' by his skill. There is an amusing letter from Pope to Cheselden in Roscoe's *Life ad ann.* 1737 ; speaking of the cataract to which v. 52 appears to allude. (Ward.)

Line 85. *Sir John Barnard.*

Line 89. *Bug and D*l*, etc. The meaning of this line has not been determined.

Line 112. Augustus *Schutz*. See Glossary.

Line 173. *Hale*. Dr. Hale of Lincoln's Inn Fields, a physician employed in cases of insanity. (Carruthers.)

Line 177. *Guide, Philosopher, and Friend*. Lord Bolingbroke. See *Essay on Man*, IV. 390.

Page 189. *Sixth Epistle, First Book*. The poem is dedicated to William Murray, afterwards Lord Mansfield. See Glossary.

Line 1. *Not to admire*, etc.

' Nil admirari prope res una, Numici,
Solaque, quae possit facere et servare beatum.'
Horace.

The translation is, as Pope admits, that of Richard Creech, translator of Homer and Lucretius.

Line 45. *Craggs's*. James Craggs's father had been in a low situation; but by industry and ability, got to be Postmaster-General and agent to the Duke of Marlborough. For James Craggs's own career, see Glossary.

Line 53. *Hyde*. Lord Clarendon, great-grandfather of the Lord *Cornbury* mentioned in line 61 below.

Line 64. *Tindal*. See Pope's note on *The Dunciad*, II. 399.

Line 82. *Anstis*, whom Pope often mentions, was Garter King of Arms. (Bowles.)

Line 87. *Or if three ladies like a luckless play*. The common reader, I am sensible, will be always more solicitous about the names of these *three Ladies*, the unlucky *Play*, and every other trifling circumstance that attended this piece of gallantry, than for the explanation of our Author's sense, or the illustration of his poetry; even where he is most moral and sublime. But had it been in Mr. Pope's purpose to indulge so impertinent a curiosity, he had sought elsewhere for a commentator on his writings. (Warburton.) Notwithstanding this remark of Dr. Warburton, I have taken some pains, though indeed in vain, to ascertain who these ladies were, and what the play they patronized. It was once said to be Young's *Busiris*. (Warton.)

Line 121. *Kinnoul's lewd cargo*, etc. Lords Kinnoul and Tyrawley, two ambassadors noted for wild immorality. (Carruthers.)

Line 126. *Wilmot*. John Wilmot, Earl of Rochester. See Glossary.

Page 191. *First Epistle, Second Book*.

Line 38. *Beastly Skelton*. Skelton, Poet Laureate to Henry VIII., a volume of whose verses has been lately reprinted, consisting almost wholly of ribaldry, obscenity, and scurrilous language. (Pope.) This judgment of Skelton is of course unfair.

Line 40. *Christ's Kirk o' the Green*. A ballad by James I. of Scotland.

Line 42. *The Devil*. The Devil Tavern, where Ben Jonson held his Poetical Club. (Pope.)

Line 66. *Look in Stowe*. Stowe's *Annals of England* appear to have been first published in 1580. (Ward.)

Line 91. *Gammer Gurton*. Gammer Gurton's Needle, according to Pope ' a piece of very low

humour, one of the first printed plays in English, and therefore much valued by some antiquaries.' The earliest extant edition bears the date 1575, but it was probably first printed at least thirteen years before this.

Line 92. *The Careless Husband*. By Colley Cibber.

Line 109. *Sprat, Carew, Sedley*. Thomas Sprat, Bishop of Rochester, Thomas Carew, and Sir Charles Sedley; all poets of the Restoration.

Line 142. A verse of the Lord Lansdown. (Pope.)

Lines 143–146. *In horsemanship — writ romance*. The Duke of Newcastle's book of Horsemanship; the romance of Parthenissa, by the Earl of Orrery; and most of the French romances translated by *persons of quality*. (Pope.)

Line 153. *On each enervate string*, etc. The *Siege of Rhodes* by Sir William Davenant, the first opera sung in England. (Pope.)

Line 182. *Ward*. A famous Empiric, whose Pill and Drop had several surprising effects, and were one of the principal subjects of writing and conversation at this time. (Pope.)

Line 197. *Peter*. Peter Walter.

Line 224. *The rights a Court attacked, a poet saved*. A reference to Swift's services as a pamphleteer, particularly as author of the *Drapier's Letters*.

Line 289. *Van*. John Vanbrugh. See Glossary.

Line 290. *Astræa*. Mrs. Aphra Behn.

Line 293. *Poor Pinky*. William Pinkethman, a low comedian.

Line 313. *From heads to ears, and now from ears to eyes*. From plays to operas, and from operas to pantomimes. (Warburton.)

Line 319. *Old Edward's armour*, etc. A spectacle presenting the Coronation of Henry VIII. and Anne Boleyn was produced in 1727 to celebrate the coronation of George II. and had a run of forty nights. ' The playhouses,' says Pope, ' vied with each other to represent all the pomp of a coronation. In this noble contention, the armour of one of the Kings of England was borrowed from the Tower, to dress the Champion.'

Line 331. *Quin — Oldfield*. James Quin and Mrs. Oldfield, the most popular comedians of their age.

Line 355. *Merlin's Cave*. A building in the Royal Gardens of Richmond, where is a small but choice collection of books. (Pope.)

Line 372. *Dubb'd historians*. ' The office of Historiographer Royal,' says Ward, ' was frequently united to that of Poet Laureate.'

Line 382. *Great Nassau*. William II.

Line 387. *Quarles*. Francis Quarles, author of the *Emblems*.

Line 413. This line, according to Carruthers, is quoted from an anonymous poem printed in Tonson's *Miscellany* in 1709.

Line 417. *Eusden, Philips, Settle*. Laurence Eusden, Ambrose Philips, and Elkanah Settle.

Page 197. *Second Epistle, Second Book.*
Line 1. *Colonel.* Colonel Cotterell of Rousham, near Oxford. (Warton.)
Line 4. *This lad, sir, is of Blois.* A town in Beauce, where the French tongue is spoken in great purity. (Warburton.) It will be recalled that it was to Blois that Addison went to learn French.
Line 24. *Sir Godfrey.* Sir Godfrey Kneller. (Warburton.)
Line 57. *Maudlin's learned grove.* Magdalen College, Oxford University.
Line 70. *Ten Monroes.* Dr. Monroe, physician to Bedlam Hospital. (Pope.)
Line 87. *Oldfield—Dartineuf.* Two noted gluttons. See Book II. Satire i. 46.
Line 113. *Tooting—Earl's-court.* Two villages within a few miles of London. (Pope.)
Lines 132-135. *Murray — Cowper — Talbot.* William Murray, afterward Lord Mansfield; William, first Earl Cowper; Charles Talbot, Duke of Shrewsbury.
Line 139. *Merlin's Cave.* See note on Book II. Epistle 1, 355.
Line 140. *Stephen.* Stephen Duck.
Line 218. *Golden angels.* A golden coin given as a fee by those who came to be touched by the royal hand for the Evil. (Warton.)
Line 220. *When servile Chaplains cry*, etc. The whole of this passage alludes to a dedication of Mr., afterwards Bishop, Kennet to the Duke of Devonshire, to whom he was chaplain. (Burnet.)
Line 240. *Heathcote.* Sir Gilbert Heathcote.
Line 273. *Townshend — Grosvenor.* Lord Townshend, Sir Thomas Grosvenor. Lord Townshend is said to have introduced the turnip into England from Germany.
Line 274. *Bubb.* Bubb Dodington.
Line 277. *Oglethorpe.* James Edward Oglethorpe.
Page 202. SATIRES OF DONNE VERSIFIED. *Satire II.* Line 6. *Sappho.* Lady Mary Wortley Montagu.
Line 36. *Sutton.* Sir Robert Sutton, expelled from the House of Commons on account of his share in the frauds of the company called the Charitable Corporation. (Carruthers.)
Line 80. *Paul Benfield*, a parliamentary financier, is suggested by Carruthers as the person here meant.
Page 204. *Satire IV.*
Line 30. *Sloane — Woodward.* Sir Hans Sloane, a natural historian; and John Woodward, founder of a chair of Geology in Cambridge University.
Line 73. *Hoadley.* Bishop Hoadley, here sarcastically referred to on account of his loyalty to the House of Hanover. (Ward.)
Line 95. *Aretine.* The Florentine poet who composed certain ill-favored sonnets to illustrate some designs of Giulio Romano.
Line 135. *Holinsheds, or Halls, or Stowes.* Tudor chroniclers.
Line 177. *Umbra.* Bubb Dodington.
Line 178. *Fannius.* Lord Hervey, whom Pope elsewhere calls ' Lord Fanny.'

Line 206. *Court in Wax.* A famous show of the Court of France, in wax-work. (Pope.)
Line 213. *At Fig's, at White's.* White's was a noted gaming-house; Fig's, a prizefighter's Academy, where the young nobility received instruction in those days. It was also customary for the nobility and gentry to visit the condemned criminals in Newgate. (Pope).
Line 274. *Hung with deadly sins.* The room hung with old tapestry, representing the seven deadly sins. (Pope.)
Page 208. EPILOGUE TO THE SATIRES. *Dialogue I.*
Lines 1-2. These two lines are from Horace; and the only two lines that are so in the whole poem; being meant to be a handle to that which follows in the character of an impertinent Censurer, *'T is all from Horace*, etc. (Pope.)
Line 13. *Sir Billy.* Sir William Yonge.
Line 14. *Huggins.* Formerly jailer of the Fleet prison; enriched himself by many exactions, for which he was tried and expelled. (Pope.)
Line 24. *Patriots.* This appellation was generally given to those in opposition to the court. Though some of them (which our author hints at) had views too mean and interested to deserve that name. (Pope.)
Line 26. *The great man.* A phrase by common use appropriated to the First Minister. (Pope.)
Line 39. *A Joke on Jekyl.* Sir Joseph Jekyl, Master of the Rolls, a true Whig in his principles, and a man of the utmost probity. He sometimes voted against the Court, which drew upon him the laugh here described of ONE who bestowed it equally upon Religion and Honesty. He died a few months after the publication of this poem. (Pope.)
Line 51. *Sejanus, Wolsey.* The one the wicked minister of Tiberius; the other, of Henry VIII. The writers against the Court usually bestowed these and other odious names on the Minister, without distinction, and in the most injurious manner. See *Dial. II.* v. 137. (Pope.)
Fleury. Cardinal: and Minister to Louis XV. It was a Patriot-fashion, at that time, to cry up his wisdom and honesty. (Pope.)
Line 66. *Henley — Osborne.* See them in their places in *The Dunciad.* (Pope.)
Line 68. Sir William Yonge, not, as Bowles conjectures to be possible, Dr. Edward Young, author of *The Night Thoughts*, although to the latter Dodington (Bubo) was a constant friend. (Ward.)
Line 69. *The gracious Dew.* Alludes to some court sermons, and florid panegyrical speeches; particularly one very full of puerilities and flatteries; which afterwards got into an address in the same pretty style; and was lastly served up in an Epitaph, between Latin and English, published by its author. (Pope.) An 'Epitaph' on Queen Caroline was written by Lord *Hervey*, and an address moved in the *House of*

Commons (the Senate) on the occasion by *H. Fox.* (Carruthers.)

Line 75. *Middleton and Bland.* Dr. Conyers Middleton, author of a *Life of Cicero.* Dr. Bland, of Eton, according to Burnet a very bad writer.

Line 78. *The 'Nation's Sense.'* Warburton says this was a cant phrase of the time.

Line 80. *Carolina.* Queen Caroline, died in 1737.

Line 92. *Selkirk — Delaware.* Pope's note would seem to apply to the names here suggested: 'A title [was] given *that* lord by King James II. He was of the Bedchamber to King William; he was so to George I.; he was so to George II. *This* lord was very skilful in all the forms of the House, in which he discharged himself with great gravity.'

Line 120. *Japhet.* Japhet Crook.

Line 121. *Peter.* Peter Walter.

Line 123. *If Blount.* Author of an impious and foolish book called *The Oracles of Reason,* who being in love with a near kinswoman of his, and rejected, gave himself a stab in the arm, as pretending to kill himself, of the consequence of which he really died. (Pope.)

Line 124. *Passeran!* Author of another book of the same stamp, called *A Philosophical Discourse on Death,* being a defence of suicide. He was a nobleman of Piedmont, banished from his country for his impieties, and lived in the utmost misery, yet feared to practise his own precepts; and at last died a penitent. (Warburton.)

Line 125. *But shall a Printer,* etc. A fact that happened in London a few years past. The unhappy man left behind him a paper justifying his action by the reasonings of some of these authors. (Pope.)

Line 129. *This calls the Church to deprecate our Sin.* Alluding to the *forms of prayer,* composed in the times of public calamity; where the fault is generally laid upon the *People.* (Warburton.)

Page 210. *Dialogue II.*

Line 11. *Ev'n Guthry.* The Ordinary of Newgate, who publishes the memoirs of the Malefactors, and is often prevailed upon to be so tender of their reputation, as to set down no more than the initials of their name. (Pope.)

Line 39. *Wretched Wild.* Jonathan Wild, a famous thief, and thief-impeacher, who was at last caught in his own train, and hanged. (Pope.)

Line 57. *Ev'n Peter trembles only for his ears.* Peter [Walter] had, the year before this, narrowly escaped the Pillory for forgery: and got off with a severe rebuke only from the bench. (Pope.)

Line 66. *Scarb'row.* Earl of, and Knight of the Garter, whose personal attachment to the king appeared from his steady adherence to the royal interest, after his resignation of his great employment of Master of the Horse; and whose known honour and virtue made him esteemed by all parties. (Pope.) He committed suicide in a fit of melancholy in 1740; and was mourned by Lord Chesterfield as 'the best man he ever

knew, and the dearest friend he ever had.' (Ward.)

Line 67. *Esher's peaceful Grove.* The house and gardens of Esher in Surrey, belonging to the Honourable Mr. Pelham, Brother of the Duke of Newcastle. The author could not have given a more amiable idea of his Character than in comparing him to Mr. Craggs. (Pope.)

Line 88. *Wyndham.* Sir William Wyndham.

Line 99. *The Man of Ross.* See *Moral Essays, Epistle III.* lines 240–290. *My Lord Mayor.* Sir John Barnard.

Line 132. *St. John.* Lord Bolingbroke.

Line 133. *Sir Roberts.* Sir Robert Walpole.

Line 158. *Sherlock,* Dr. William, Dean of St. Paul's, and the bête noire of the non-jurors in the reign of William III. (Ward.)

Line 160. *The bard.* Bubb Dodington, who wrote a poem to Sir Robert Walpole from which the following line is quoted.

Line 164. *The Priest,* etc. Pope disclaims any allusion to a particular priest, but the passage is understood to refer to Dr. Alured Clarke, who wrote a fulsome panegyric to Queen Caroline.

Line 166. *The florid youth.* Lord Hervey. Alluding to his painting himself. (Bowles.)

Lines 185–186. *Japhet — Chartres.* See the epistle to Lord Bathurst. (Pope.)

Line 222. *Cobwebs.* Weak and light sophistry against virtue and honour. Thin colours over vice, as unable to hide the light of truth, as cobwebs to shade the sun. (Pope.)

Line 228. *When black Ambition,* etc. The course of Cromwell in the civil war of England; (line 229), of Louis XIV. in his conquest of the Low Countries. (Pope.)

Line 231. *Nor Boileau turn the feather to a star.* See his *Ode on Namur;* where (to use his own words) 'il a fait un Astre de la Plume blanche que le Roy porte ordinairement à son chapeau, et qui est en effet une espèce de Comète, fatale à nos ennemis.' (Pope.)

Line 236. *Anstis.* The chief Herald at Arms. It is the custom, at the funeral of great peers, to cast into the grave the broken staves and ensigns of honour. (Pope.)

Line 238. *Stair.* John Dalrymple, Earl of Stair, Knight of the Thistle; served in all the wars under the Duke of Marlborough; and afterwards as Ambassador in France. (Pope.) Bennet, who supplies the blanks in v. 239 by the names of Kent and Grafton, has 'some notion that Lord Mordington kept a gaming-house.' (Ward.)

Lines 240, 241. *Hough — Digby.* Dr. John Hough, Bishop of Worcester, and the Lord Digby. The one an assertor of the Church of England in opposition to the false measures of King James II. The other as firmly attached to the cause of that King. Both acting out of principle, and equally men of honour and virtue. (Pope.)

Line 255. *Ver.* 255 in the MS.

'Quit, quit these themes, and write Essays on Man.'

This was the last poem of the kind printed by

our author, with a resolution to publish no more ; but to enter thus, in the most plain and solemn manner he could, a sort of PROTEST against that insuperable corruption and depravity of manners, which he had been so unhappy as to live to see. Could he have hoped to have amended any, he had continued those attacks ; but bad men were grown so shameless and so powerful, that Ridicule was become as unsafe as it was ineffectual. The Poem raised him, as he knew it would, some enemies ; but he had reason to be satisfied with the approbation of good men, and the testimony of his own conscience. (Pope.)

Page 214. BOOK SECOND, SIXTH SATIRE. IMITATED AFTER SWIFT.

Line 84. *October next it will be four.* Swift is recalling the length of his service of the Tory Party.

Line 85. *Harley.* Earl of Oxford.

Line 125. At this point Pope's part in the imitation begins.

Page 216. THE SEVENTH EPISTLE OF THE FIRST BOOK OF HORACE.

Line 67. *Child.* Sir Francis Child, the banker. (Bowles.)

Page 217. THE FIRST ODE OF THE FOURTH BOOK OF HORACE.

Line 8. *Number five.* The number of Murray's lodgings in King's Bench Walk.

Page 225. THE DUNCIAD. *Book I.*

Line 1. *The Mighty Mother,* etc., in the first Edd. it was thus : —

'Books and the Man I sing, the first who brings
The Smithfield Muses to the ear of Kings,' etc.
(Pope.)

Line 2. *The Smithfield Muses. Smithfield* is the place where Bartholomew Fair was kept, whose shows, machines, and dramatical entertainments, formerly agreeable only to the taste of the Rabble, were, by the Hero of this poem and others of equal genius, brought to the Theatres of Covent-garden, Lincolns-inn-fields, and the Haymarket, to be the reigning pleasures of the Court and Town. This happened in the reigns of King George I. and II. See Book III. (Pope.)

Line 30. *Monroe.* Physician to Bedlam Hospital.

Line 31. *His famed father.* Caius Cassius Cibber, father of Colley Cibber ; a sculptor in a small way. 'The two statues of the lunatics over the gate of Bedlam Hospital were done by him,' says Pope, 'and (as the son justly says of them) are no ill monuments of his fame as an artist.'

Line 40. *Lintot's rubric post.* Lintot, according to Pope, 'usually adorned his shop with titles in red letters.'

Line 41. *Hence hymning Tyburn's elegiac lines.* It is an ancient English custom for the Malefactors to sing a Psalm at their execution at Tyburn ; and no less customary to print Elegies on their deaths, at the same time, or before. (Pope.)

Line 42. *Magazines.* The common name of those upstart collections in prose and verse, in which, at some times, —

'New born nonsense first is taught to cry ; '

at others, dead-born Scandal has its monthly funeral, where Dulness assumes all the various shapes of Folly to draw in and cajole the Rabble. The eruption of every miserable Scribbler ; the scum of every dirty News-paper ; or Fragments of Fragments, picked up from every Dunghill, under the title of *Papers, Essays, Reflections, Confutations, Queries, Verses, Songs, Epigrams, Riddles,* etc., equally the disgrace of human Wit, Morality, Decency, and Common Sense. (Pope and Warburton.)

Line 44. *New-year Odes.* Made by the Poet Laureate for the time being, to be sung at Court on every New-year's day, the words of which are happily drowned in the voices and instruments. (Pope.)

Line 57. *Jacob.* Jacob Tonson.

Line 63. *Clenches.* Puns. Pope has a long note citing a punning passage from Dennis aimed at himself.

Line 86. In the former Editions, —

' 'T was on the day when Thorold, rich and grave.'

Sir George Thorold, Lord Mayor of London in the year 1720. The Procession of a Lord Mayor is made partly by land, and partly by water. — Cimon, the famous Athenian General, obtained a victory by sea, and another by land, on the same day, over the Persians and Barbarians. (Pope.)

Line 98. *Heywood.* John Heywood, whose interludes were printed in the time of Henry VIII. (Pope.)

Line 103. *Prynne,* William, sentenced in 1633 to a fine, the pillory, and imprisonment for his *Histriomastix.* Defoe was similarly punished for his *Shortest Way with the Dissenters.*

Line 103. *Daniel.* Daniel Defoe.

Line 104. *Eusden.* Laurence Eusden, Poet Laureate before Cibber.

Line 108. *Bayes's.* The name of Theobald (Tibbald) stood here originally. This of course stands for Cibber.

Line 126. *Sooterkins.* False births. (Ward.)

Line 134. *Hapless Shakespear,* etc. It is not to be doubted but Bays was a subscriber to Tibbald's Shakespear. He was frequently liberal this way ; and, as he tells us, 'subscribed to Mr. Pope's Homer, out of pure Generosity and Civility ; but when Mr. Pope did so to his Nonjuror, he concluded it could be nothing but a joke.' Letter to Mr. P., p. 24.

This Tibbald, or Theobald, published an edition of Shakespear, of which he was so proud himself as to say, in one of Mist's Journals, June 8, 'That to expose any Errors in it was impracticable.' And in another, April 27, 'That whatever care might for the future be taken by any other Editor, he would still give above five hundred emendations, that *shall* escape them all.' (Pope.)

Line 141. *Ogilby.* Originally dancing master,

then poet and printer. Author of a great many books which Pope ridicules in a note.

Line 142. *Newcastle.* The Duchess of Newcastle, one of the most copious of seventeenth-century writers.

Line 146. *Worthy Settle, Banks, and Broome.* The Poet has mentioned these three authors in particular, as they are parallel to our Hero in three capacities: 1. Settle was his brother Laureate; only indeed upon half-pay, for the City instead of the Court; but equally famous for unintelligible flights in his poems on public occasions, such as Shows, Birth-days, etc. 2. Banks was his Rival in *Tragedy* (tho' more successful) in one of his Tragedies, the *Earl of Essex*, which is yet alive: *Anna Boleyn*, the *Queen of Scots*, and *Cyrus the Great* are dead and gone. These he drest in a sort of *Beggar's Velvet*, or a happy Mixture of the thick Fustian and thin Prosaic; exactly imitated in *Perolla and Isidora, Cæsar in Egypt*, and the *Heroic Daughter*. 3. Broome was a serving-man of Ben Jonson, who once picked up a *Comedy* from his Betters, or from some cast scenes of his Master, not entirely contemptible. (Pope.)

Line 153. *De Lyra.* Or Harpsfield, a very voluminous commentator, whose works, in five vast folios, were printed in 1472. (Pope.)

Line 154. *Philemon.* Philemon Holland, Doctor in Physic. 'He translated so many books that a man would think he had done nothing else.' *Winstanley.* (Pope.)

Lines 180, 181. *As, forced from wind-guns*, etc. Adapted from lines 17, 18 of the early verses, *To the Author of Successio.*

Line 207. *Ridpath — Mist.* George Ridpath, author of a Whig paper, called the Flying-post; Nathaniel Mist, of a famous Tory Journal. (Pope.)

Line 214. *Gazetteers.* A band of ministerial writers, hired at the price mentioned in the note on Book II. ver. 316, who, on the very day their patron quitted his post, laid down their paper, and declared they would never more meddle in Politics. (Pope.)

Line 215. *Ralph.* James Ralph. See III. 163 below.

Line 221. *Hockley-hole.* See *Imitations of Horace*, Book III. Sat. i. 49, and note.

Line 232. *Ward.* Edward Ward.

Lines 249–255. The works referred to here are Colley Cibber's.

Line 257. *Thulé.* A fragmentary poem by Ambrose Philips.

Line 289. *A heideggre.* A strange bird from Switzerland, and not (as some have supposed) the name of an eminent person. (Pope.) The allusion is of course to the 'eminent person,' the German Heidegger, who managed English opera.

Line 296. *Withers.* 'George Withers was a great pretender to poetical zeal against the vices of the times, and abused the greatest personages in power, which brought upon him *frequent correction*. The Marshalsea and Newgate were no strangers to him.' *Winstanley.* (Pope.)

Gildon. Charles Gildon, a writer of criticisms and libels of the last age, bred at St. Omer's with the Jesuits; but renouncing popery, he published Blount's books against the divinity of Christ, the Oracles of Reason, etc. He signalized himself as a critic, having written some very bad Plays; abused Mr. P. very scandalously in an anonymous pamphlet of the Life of Mr. Wycherley, printed by Curll; in another called the New Rehearsal, printed in 1714; in a third, entitled the Complete Art of English Poetry, in two volumes; and others. (Pope.) See note to *Epistle to Arbuthnot*, line 151.

Line 297. *Howard.* Hon. Edward Howard, author of the British Princes, and a great number of wonderful pieces, celebrated by the late Earls of Dorset and Rochester, Duke of Buckingham, Mr. Waller, etc. (Pope.)

Line 300. *Under Archer's Wing.* Under cover of a special license given to a member of the king's household, a gambling establishment was conducted in the royal palace.

Line 323. *Needham.* Mother Needham, a notorious procuress.

Line 325. *The Devil.* The Devil Tavern in Fleet Street, where these Odes are usually rehearsed before they are performed at court.

Page 230. *Book II.*

Line 2. *Henley's gilt tub.* The pulpit of a Dissenter is usually called a Tub; but that of Mr. Orator Henley was covered with velvet, and adorned with gold. He had also a fair altar, and over it this extraordinary inscription, *The Primitive Eucharist.* See the history of this person, Book III. ver. 199. (Pope.)

Or Fleckno's Irish throne. Richard Fleckno was an Irish priest, but had laid aside (as himself expressed it) the mechanic part of priesthood. He printed some plays, poems, letters, and travels. I doubt not our Author took occasion to mention him in respect to the poem of Mr. Dryden, to which this bears some resemblance, though of a character more different from it than that of the Æneid from the Iliad, or the *Lutrin* of Boileau from the *Défait de Bouts Rimées* of Sarazin. (Pope.)

Line 3. *Or that whereon her Curlls*, etc. An allusion to an experience of Edmund Curll's in the pillory.

Line 15. *Querno.* Camillo Querno, a would-be poet of Apulia, introduced as a buffoon to Leo X. and given in return for his verses a mock coronation.

Line 68. *Jacob.* Jacob Lintot.

Line 70. *Corinna.* Supposed to refer to Mrs. Elizabeth Thomas, whom Pope accuses of having sold some private correspondence of his to Curll.

Line 82. The Bible, Curll's sign; the cross-keys, Lintot's. (Pope.)

Line 93. *Cloacina.* The Roman Goddess of the sewers. (Pope.)

Line 125. *Mears, Warner, Wilkins.* Booksellers, and printers of much anonymous stuff. (Pope.)

Line 126. *Breval, Bond, Bezaleel* [Bezaleel Morris]. Three small authors of the day.

Line 138. *Cook shall be Prior.* The man here specified writ a thing called The Battle of Poets, in which Philips and Welsted were the Heroes, and Swift and Pope utterly routed. He also published some malevolent things in the British, London, and Daily Journals; and at the same time wrote letters to Mr. Pope, protesting his innocence. His chief work was a translation of Hesiod, to which Theobald writ notes and half notes, which he carefully owned. (Pope.)
Concanen. See note to line 299 below.
Lines 149, 150. *Tutchin — Ridpath, Roper.* London editors of *The Observator, The Flying Post,* and *The Post-boy,* whom Pope, in long notes, accuses of scandalous practices.
Line 157. *Eliza.* Eliza Hagwood, authoress of those most scandalous books called *The Court of Carimania,* and *The New Utopia.* (Pope.)
Line 160. *Kirkall.* The name of an Engraver. Some of this lady's works were printed . . . with her picture thus dressed up before them. (Pope.)
Line 205. *Bentley his mouth,* etc. Not spoken of the famous Dr. Richard Bentley, but of one Tho. Bentley, a small critic, who aped his uncle in a *little Horace.* (Pope.)
Line 226. *Thunder rumbling from the mustard bowl.* The old way of making Thunder and Mustard were the same; but since, it is more advantageously performed by troughs of wood with stops in them. (Pope.)
Line 270. (*As morning prayer and flagellation end.*) It is between eleven and twelve in the morning, after church service, that the criminals are whipt in Bridewell. — This is to mark punctually the *time* of the day: Homer does it by the circumstance of the Judges rising from court, or of the Labourer's dinner; our author by one very proper both to the *Persons* and the *Scene* of his poem, which we may remember commenced in the evening of the Lord-mayor's day: The first book passed in that *night;* the next *morning* the games begin in the Strand, thence along Fleet-street (places inhabited by Booksellers); then they proceed by Bridewell toward Fleet-ditch, and lastly thro' Ludgate to the City and the Temple of the Goddess. (Pope.)
Line 291. *Smedley.* Jonathan, editor of the *Whitehall Journal,* and author of an attack on Pope and Swift called *Gulliveriana* and *Alexandriana.*
Line 299. *Concanen.* Matthew Concanen, an Irishman, bred to the law. He was author of several dull and dead scurrilities in the British and London Journals, and in a paper called the Speculatist. In a pamphlet, called a Supplement to the Profund, he dealt very unfairly with our Poet, not only frequently imputing to him Mr. Broome's verses (for which he might indeed seem in some degree accountable, having corrected what that gentleman did) but those of the duke of Buckingham and others. To this rare piece somebody humorously caused him to take for his motto, *De profundis clamavi.* He was since a hired scribbler in the Daily

Courant, where he poured forth much Billingsgate against the lord Bolingbroke, and others; after which this man was surprisingly promoted to administer Justice and Law in Jamaica. (Pope.)
Line 400. '*Christ's no kingdom here.*' This alludes to a series of sermons preached by Bishop Hoadley before George I.
Line 411. *Centlivre.* Mrs. Susanna Centlivre, wife to Mr. Centlivre, Yeoman of the Mouth to his Majesty. She writ many Plays, and a Song (says Mr. Jacob) before she was seven years old. She also writ a Ballad against Mr. Pope's Homer before he began it. (Pope.)
Line 412. *Motteux.* Peter Anthony Motteux, the excellent translator of Don Quixote, and author of a number of forgotten dramatic pieces. Dryden addressed a complimentary Epistle to him. He died in 1718. (Carruthers.)
Line 413. *Boyer the State, and Law the Stage gave o'er.* A. Boyer, a voluminous compiler of Annals, Political Collections, &c. — William Law, A. M. wrote with great zeal against the Stage; Mr. Dennis answered with as great. Their books were printed in 1726. (Pope.)
Line 414. *Morgan.* A man of some learning, and uncommon acuteness, with a strong disposition to Satire, which very often degenerated into scurrility. His most celebrated work is the *Moral Philosopher,* first published in the year 1737. (Bowles.)
Mandeville. Bernard de Mandeville was born in Holland, in 1670, and after residing in England during the latter half of his life, died in 1733. (Ward.)
Line 415. *Norton, from Daniel,* etc. Norton De Foe.
Page 236. *Book III.*
Line 19. *Taylor.* John Taylor, a Thames waterman and poet under Charles I. and James I.
Line 21. *Benlowes.* A country gentleman, famous for his own bad poetry, and for patronizing bad poets, as may be seen from many Dedications of Quarles and others to him. Some of these anagram'd his name, *Benlowes* into *Benevolus:* to verify which he spent his whole estate upon them. (Pope.)
Line 22. *Shadwell nods, the poppy,* etc. Shadwell [hero of MacFlecknoe] took opium for many years, and died of too large a dose, in the year 1692. (Pope.)
Line 24. Mr. Dennis warmly contends, that Bavius was no inconsiderable author; nay, that 'He and Mævius had (even in Augustus's days) a very formidable party at Rome, who thought them much superior to Virgil and Horace: for (saith he) I cannot believe they would have fixed that eternal brand upon them, if they had not been coxcombs in more than ordinary credit.' Rem. on Pr. Arthur, part II. c. 1. An argument which, if this poem should last, will conduce to the honour of the gentlemen of *The Dunciad.* (Pope.)
Line 28. *Browne and Mears.* Booksellers, and printers for anybody. (Pope.)
Line 34. *Ward in pillory.* John Ward of

Hackney, Esq., member of Parliament, being convicted of forgery, was first expelled the House, and then sentenced to the pillory on the 17th of February, 1727. (Pope.)

Line 96. *The soil that arts and infant letters bore.* Phœnicia, Syria, etc., where letters are said to have been invented. In these countries Mahomet began his conquests. (Pope.)

Line 104. *Bacon.* Roger Bacon.

Line 150. *Jacob, the scourge of grammar.* Giles Jacob, author of a *Lives of the Poets,* in which sufficiently obscure book he had abused Gay.

Lines 152, 153. *Popple, Horneck, and Roome.* London journalists and pamphleteers who had offended Pope.

Line 154. *Goode.* An ill-natured critic, who writ a satire on our author, called *The Mock Æsop,* and many anonymous libels in newspapers for hire. (Pope.)

Line 165. *Ralph.* James Ralph.

Line 168. *Morris.* Bezaleel Morris. See Book II. 126.

199. *Henley stands,* etc. J. Henley the Orator; he preached on the Sundays upon Theological matters, and on the Wednesdays upon all other sciences. Each auditor paid one shilling. He declaimed some years against the greatest persons, and occasionally did our Author that honour. After having stood some Prosecutions, he turned his rhetoric to buffoonery upon all publick and private occurrences. This man had an hundred pounds a year given him for the secret service of a weekly paper of unintelligible nonsense, called the Hyp-Doctor. (Pope.)

Line 204. *Sherlock, Hare, and Gibson.* Bishops of Salisbury, Chichester, and London; whose sermons and pastoral letters did honour to their country as well as stations. (Pope.)

Line 212. *Woolston.* Thomas. An impious madman, who wrote in a most insolent style against the miracles of the Gospel. (Pope.)

Line 232. *When Goodman prophesied.* One Goodman had prophesied that Cibber would be a good actor, and Cibber had boasted of it.

Line 233. *A sable sorcerer.* Dr. Faustus.

Line 248. *One vast egg.* Pope says that in one of the absurd farces of the period, Harlequin is hatched upon the stage out of a large egg.

Line 282. *Annual trophies,* on the Lord Mayor's day; *monthly wars,* in the artillery ground. (Pope.)

Line 305. *Polypheme.* A translation of the Italian opera *Polifemo.*

Lines 308, 309. *Faustus — Pluto.* Names of miserable farces which it was the custom to act at the end of the best tragedies, to spoil the digestion of the audience. (Pope.)

Line 310. *The Mourning Bride.* By Congreve.

Line 312. *Insure it but from fire.* In Tibbald's farce of Proserpine, a corn-field was set on fire: whereupon the other play-house had a barn burnt down for the recreation of the spectators. They also rivalled each other in sharing the burnings of hell-fire, in Dr. Faustus. (Pope.)

Line 313. *Another Æschylus appears.* It is

reported of Æschylus that when his Tragedy of the *Furies* was acted, the audience were so terrified that the children fell into fits. (Pope.)

Line 315. *Like Semele's.* See Ovid, *Met.* iii. (Pope.)

Line 325. *On poets' tombs see Benson's titles writ!* W—m Benson (Surveyor of the Buildings to his Majesty King George I.) gave in a report to the Lords, that their House and the Painted-chamber adjoining were in immediate danger of falling. Whereupon the Lords met in a committee to appoint some other place to sit in, while the House should be taken down. But it being proposed to cause some other builders first to inspect it, they found it in very good condition. In favour of this man, the famous Sir Christopher Wren, who had been Architect to the Crown for above fifty years, who built most of the churches in London, laid the first stone of St. Paul's, and lived to finish it, had been displaced from his employment at the age of near ninety years. (Pope.)

Line 328. *While Jones' and Boyle's united labours fall.* At the time when this poem was written, the banqueting-house at Whitehall, the church and piazza of Covent-garden, and the palace and chapel of Somerset-house, the works of the famous Inigo Jones, had been for many years so neglected, as to be in danger of ruin. The portico of Covent-garden church had been just then restored and beautified at the expense of the earl of Burlington and [Richard Boyle]; who, at the same time, by his publication of the designs of that great Master and Palladio, as well as by many noble buildings of his own, revived the true taste of Architecture in this kingdom. (Pope.)

Page 242. *Book IV.* This Book may properly be distinguished from the former, by the name of the GREATER DUNCIAD, not so indeed in size, but in subject; and so far contrary to the distinction anciently made of the *Greater* and *Lesser Iliad.* But much are they mistaken who imagine this work in any wise inferior to the former, or of any other hand than of our Poet; of which I am much more certain than that the *Iliad* itself was the work of *Solomon,* or the *Batrachomuomachia* of *Homer,* as *Barnes* hath affirmed. ' BENTLEY.' (Pope.)

Line 15. *A new world.* In allusion to the Epicurean opinion, that from the Dissolution of the natural World into Night and Chaos a new one should arise; this the Poet alluding to, in the Production of a new moral World, makes it partake of its original Principles. (Pope and Warburton.)

Line 21. *Beneath her footstool,* etc. We are next presented with the pictures of those whom the Goddess leads in captivity. *Science* is only depressed and confined so as to be rendered useless; but *Wit* or *Genius,* as a more dangerous and active enemy, punished, or driven away: *Dulness* being often reconciled in some degree with learning, but never upon any terms with wit. And accordingly it will be seen that she admits something *like* each Science, as Casuistry, Sophistry, etc., but nothing like Wit, *Opera* alone supplying its place. (Pope and Warburton.)

Line 30. *Gives her Page the word.* There was a Judge of this name, always ready to hang any Man that came before him, of which he was suffered to give a hundred miserable examples during a long life, even to his dotage. (Pope and Warburton.)

Line 31. *Mad Mathesis.* Alluding to the strange Conclusions some Mathematicians have deduced from their principles, concerning the *real Quantity of Matter,* the *Reality of Space,* etc. (Pope and Warburton.)

Line 36. *Watch'd both by envy's and by flatt'ry's eye.* One of the misfortunes falling on Authors from the act for subjecting plays to the power of a *Licenser,* being the false representations to which they were exposed, from such as either gratify'd their envy to merit, or made their court to greatness, by perverting general reflections against Vice into libels on particular Persons. (Pope and Warburton.)

Line 45. *A harlot form.* Italian Opera.

Line 110. *Benson.* See Book III. 325 *ante,* and note. Benson published several editions of Arthur Johnston's version of the *Psalms.*

Line 113. *The decent knight.* Sir Thomas Hanmer, who in 1744 published an edition of Shakespeare.

Line 131. *An alderman shall sit.* Alluding to the monument erected for Butler by Alderman Barber.

Line 144. *Winton.* Winchester.

Line 151. *The Samian letter.* The letter Y, used by Pythagoras as an emblem of the different words of Virtue and Vice : ' Et tibi quae Samios diduxit litera ramos.' *Persius.* (Pope and Warburton.)

Line 166. *Yonder house or hall.* Westminster Hall and the House of Commons. (Pope.)

Line 174. *That masterpiece of man.* Viz., an *epigram.* The famous Dr. South declared a perfect epigram to be as difficult a performance as an Epic poem. And the critics say, ' An Epic poem is the greatest work human nature is capable of.' (Pope and Warburton.)

Line 194. *Tho' Christ Church,* etc. Warburton gives a note for which Pope is doubtless responsible, accounting for the bracketing of this line on the score of its probable spuriousness, and signing the name ' Bentley.'

Line 196. *Still expelling Locke.* In the year 1703 there was a meeting of the heads of the University of Oxford to censure Mr. Locke's *Essay on Human Understanding,* and to forbid the reading it. See his Letters in the last Edit. (Pope.) But he was never expelled, only deprived of his studentship at Christ-Church ; and this on the ground of political suspicions, *before* he had written his great *Essay.* (Ward.)

Line 198. *Crousaz — Burgersdyck.* According to Dugald Stewart, Pope was in error in placing Crousaz, whose philosophy was founded upon the method of Locke, with Burgersdyck, an Aristotelian.

Line 199. *The streams.* The river Cam, running by the walls of these Colleges, which are

particularly famous for their skill in Disputation. (Pope and Warburton.)

Line 202. *Sleeps in port.* Viz. ' now retired into harbour, after the tempests that had long agitated his society.' So SCRIBLERUS. But the learned *Scipio Maffei* understands it of a certain wine called *Port,* from *Oporto,* a city of Portugal, of which this Professor invited him to drink abundantly. SCIP. MAFF. *De Compotationibus Academicis.* (Pope and Warburton.)

Line 206. *Walker.* John Walker, Vice-Master of Trinity College, Cambridge, while Bentley was Master. (Carruthers.)

Line 212. This refers to Bentley's editions of *Horace* and *Paradise Lost.*

Line 218. *Stands our Digamma.* Alludes to the boasted restoration of the Æolic Digamma, in his [Bentley's] long projected edition of Homer.

Line 220. *Me or te.* Whether at the end of the first Ode of Horace, the reading would be, *Me doctarum hederae,* or *Te doctarum hederae.*

Line 223. *Friend — Alsop.* Dr. Robert Friend, master of Westminster School ; Dr. Anthony Alsop, a happy imitator of the Horatian style. (Pope and Warburton.)

Line 237. *Kuster, Burman, Wasse.* Three contemporary German scholars and editors of merit.

Lines 245–246. *Barrow — Atterbury.* Isaac Barrow, Master of Trinity ; Francis Atterbury, Dean of Christ Church, both great geniuses and eloquent preachers. (Pope and Warburton.)

Line 326. *Jansen, Fleetwood, Cibber.* Three very eminent persons, all Managers of *Plays ;* who, tho' not Governors by profession, had, each in his way, concerned themselves in the education of youth : and regulated their wits, their morals, or their finances, at that period of their age which is the most important, their entrance into the polite world. Of the last of these, and his Talents for this end, see Book I. ver. 199, &c. (Pope and Warburton.) Fleetwood was patentee of Drury-Lane Theatre from 1734 to 1745 ; it was the attempted secession of his actors in 1743 which gave rise to the famous quarrel of Macklin with Garrick. (Ward.)

Line 371. *Mummius.* This name is not merely an allusion to the Mummies he was so fond of, but probably referred to the Roman General of that name, who burned Corinth, and committed the curious Statues to the captain of a ship, assuring him, ' that if any were lost or broken, he should procure others to be made in their stead : ' by which it should seem (whatever may be pretended) that Mummius was no Virtuoso. (Pope and Warburton.)

Line 394. *Douglas.* A Physician of great Learning and no less Taste ; above all curious in what related to *Horace,* of whom he collected every edition, translation, and comment, to the number of several hundred volumes. (Pope and Warburton.)

Line 492. *Silenus.* By Silenus, says Warton, Pope means ' Thomas Gordon, the translator of Tacitus, who published the *Independent Whig,* and obtained a place under government.'

Line 511. *K[ent] and B***. K* probably stands for the Duke of Kent ; but the next name is doubtful from the wide choice possible.

Line 512. *Wharton.* Philip, Duke of Wharton.

Line 545. Considerable doubt attaches to the names here hinted at ; though four of them may be Carteret, Hervey, Pulteney, and King.

Line 556. *Sève* and *verdeur*. French terms relating to wines, which signify their flavour and poignancy (Pope.)

Line 560. *Bladen — Hays.* Names of Gamesters. Bladen is a black man. Robert Knight, Cashier of the South-Sea Company, who fled from England in 1720 (afterwards pardoned in 1742). These lived with the utmost magnificence at Paris, and kept open Tables frequented by persons of the first Quality of England, and even by Princes of the Blood of France. (Pope and Warburton.)

Line 576. *A Gregorian, one a Gormogon.* A sort of Lay-brothers, *Slips* from the Root of the Free-Masons. (Pope and Warburton.) 'Gregorians' are mentioned as 'a convivial sect,' and 'a kind of Masons, but without their sign,' in Crabbe's *Borough*, Letter x. (Ward.)

Line 578. Pope refused this degree when offered to him on a visit undertaken to Oxford with Warburton, because the University would not confer the degree of D. D. upon Warburton, to whom some of its members had proposed it. (Roscoe.)

Line 608. *Gilbert.* Archbishop of York.

Line 629. *She comes! she comes!* etc. Here the Muse, like Jove's Eagle, after a sudden stoop at ignoble game, soareth again to the skies. As Prophecy hath ever been one of the chief provinces of Poesy, our Poet here foretells from what we feel, what we are to fear ; and, in the style of other prophets, hath used the future tense for the preterite : since what he says shall be, is already to be seen, in the writings of some even of our most adored authors, in Divinity, Philosophy, Physics, Metaphysics, &c. who are too good indeed to be named in such company. (Pope.)

BIBLIOGRAPHICAL NOTE

Mention is made in this list merely of the collected editions of Pope's poems which were published during his life, and of the best editions which have been published since.

1. *The Works of Mr. Alexander Pope.* London : Printed by W. Bowyer for Bernard Lintot, between the Temple Gates, 1717. Quarto and folio. (Containing all the acknowledged poems which Pope had hitherto published, and some new ones.)

2. Same title. *Vol. II.* London : Printed by J. Wright for Lawton Gilliver, at Homer's Head in Fleet Street, 1735. Quarto and folio. (Containing poems published by Pope after 1717.)

3. *The Works of Mr. Alexander Pope in Prose.* Letters of Mr. Alexander Pope and Several of his Friends. London : Knapton, Gilliver, Brindley and Dodsley, 1737. (The first avowed edition of his letters.)

4. Same title. *Vol. II.* London : Dodsley, 1741. (Containing correspondence with Swift, *Memoirs of Scriblerus*, papers from *The Guardian*, etc.)

5. *The Works of Alexander Pope,* Esq. In Nine Volumes complete. With his last corrections, additions, and improvements, as they were delivered to the editor a little before his death ; together with the Commentaries and Notes of Mr. Warburton. London : Knapton, Lintot, Tonson, and Draper, 1751. Octavo.

6. *The Works of Alexander Pope,* Esq., in Nine Volumes Complete, with a Memoir of the Author, and with Notes and Illustrations by Joseph Warton, D.D., and others. London : 1797.

7. *The Works of Alexander Pope, Esq. in Prose and Verse,* containing the principal Notes of Drs. Warburton and Warton, Illustrations and Critical and Explanatory Remarks by Johnson, Wakefield, A. Chalmers, and others. To which are added, now first published, some original Letters, additional Observations, and Memoirs of the Life of the Author, by the Rev. William Lisle Bowles. London : 1806. Octavo, 10 vols. (This edition led to some controversy between Bowles and Lord Byron.)

8. *The Works of Alexander Pope,* Esq. With Notes and Illustrations by himself and others : to which are added a New Life of the Author, an Estimate of his poetical Character and Writings, and occasional Remarks. By William Roscoe. London : 1824. Octavo, 10 vols.

9. *Poetical Works.* With extracts from his Correspondence, and Memoir by Robert Carruthers. London : 1858. Octavo, 2 vols.

10. *The Works of Alexander Pope.* New Edition. Including unpublished letters, and other new materials. Collected in part by J. W. Croker. With Introduction and Notes by Whitwell Elwin, and by W. J. Courthope. London : Murray, 1871–1889. Octavo, 10 vols. (This is now the standard edition of Pope.)

INDEX OF FIRST LINES

In these gay thoughts the Loves and Graces shine, 80.
In vain you boast poetic names of yore, 83.

Jonathan Swift, 130

Kneller, by Heav'n, and not a master, taught, 134.
Know then thyself, presume not God to scan, 142.

Learn then what morals Critics ought to show, 75.
Lest you should think that verse shall die, 217.

Muse, 't is enough, at length thy labour ends, 103.
My Lord complains that Pope, stark mad with gardens, 128.

Nature and Nature's laws lay hid in Night, 135.
No pleasing sleep had seal'd each mortal eye, 272.
Not to admire, is all the art I know, 189.
Not twice a twelvemonth you appear in print, 208.
Not with more glories, in th' ethereal plain, 90.
Nothing so true as what you once let fall, 161.
Now Europe balanced, neither side prevails, 79.
Now from the finish'd games the Grecian band, 520.
Now had Minerva reach'd those ample plains, 594.
Now Heav'n forsakes the fight ; th' immortals yield, 322.
Now in swift flight they pass the trench profound, 421.

O Happiness ! our being's end and aim ! 150.
O wretched B[ritain], jealous now of all, 128.
Of all the causes which conspire to blind, 70.
Of gentle Philips will I ever sing, 121.
Of Manners gentle, of Affections mild, 135.
Oh, be thou blest with all that Heav'n can send, 118.
On the cold earth divine Patroclus spread, 449.
Once in his life M[oo]re judges right, 132.
Once (says an author, where I need not say), 130.
Ozell, at Sanger's call, invoked his Muse, 80.

Pallas grew vapourish once and odd, 121.
Parson, these things in thy possessing, 18.
Peace, flatt'ring Bishop ! lying Dean ! 131.
Phryne had talents for mankind, 18.
Prodigious this ! the Frail-one of our play, 100.

Resign'd to live, prepared to die, 128.

St. John, whose love indulged my labours past, 187.
Say, lovely Youth, that dost my heart command, 60.
See, Sir, here 's the grand approach, 101.

See the wild waste of all-devouring years ! 174.
She said, and for her lost Galanthis sighs, 63.
She said : the pitying audience melt in tears, 79.
Should D(enni)s print, how once you robb'd your brother, 132.
'Shut, shut the door, good John ! ' fatigued, I said, 176.
Silence ! coeval with Eternity, 17.
Since my old friend has grown so great, 115.
So bright is thy beauty, so charming thy song, 80.
So spoke the Guardian of the Trojan state, 332.
So warr'd both armies on th' ensanguin'd shore, 433.
Soon as Aurora, Daughter of the Dawn, 602.
Soon as Aurora heav'd her orient head, 471.
Soon as Glumdalclitch miss'd her pleasing care, 122.
Speak, Gracious Lord, oh, speak ; thy servant hears, 1.
Statesman, yet Friend to Truth ! of Soul sincere, 134.
Such were the notes thy once-lov'd Poet sung, 116.

Tell, if you can, which did the worse, 132.
The Basset-Table spread, the Tallier come, 105.
The fair Pomona flourish'd in his reign, 65.
The Mighty Mother, and her son who brings, 226.
The patient heav'nly man thus suppliant pray'd, 553.
The playful smiles around the dimpled mouth, 109.
The sacred Sun above the waters rais'd, 535.
The saffron Morn, with early blushes spread, 374.
Then fierce the Hero o'er the threshold strode, 618.
Then thus Ulysses : ' Thou whom first in sway, 559.
There are (I scarce can think it, but am told), 182.
There liv'd in Lombardy, as authors write, 35.
This modest stone, what few vain marbles can, 135.
This verse be thine, my friend, nor thou refuse, 82.
Tho' Artemisia talks by fits, 18.
Tho' sprightly Sappho force our love and praise, 130.
Thou who shalt stop where Thames' translucent wave, 127.
Thus by their leader's care each martial band, 287.
Thus humbled in the dust the pensive train, 505.
Thus joyful Troy maintain'd the watch of night, 352.
Thus like the rage of fire the combat burns, 461.
Thus round Pelides breathing war and blood, 477.
Thus to their bulwarks, smit with panic fear, 496.
Thy forest, Windsor ! and thy green retreats, 28.

INDEX OF TITLES

[The titles of major works and general divisions are set in SMALL CAPITALS.]